EQUITY AND THE LAW OF T

CASES AND M

AUSTRALIA

LBC Information Services
Sydney

CANADA and USA

Carswell

NEW ZEALAND

Brookers
Wellington

SINGAPORE AND MALAYSIA

Thomson Information (S.E. Asia)
Singapore

EQUITY AND THE
LAW OF TRUSTS IN IRELAND:
CASES AND MATERIALS

HILARY DELANY

B.A.(Mod.), M.Litt., Ph.D., Barrister-at-Law
Fellow of Trinity College, Dublin
Senior Lecturer in Law, Trinity College, Dublin

DUBLIN
ROUND HALL SWEET & MAXWELL
2002

Published in 2002 by
Round Hall Ltd
43 Fitzwilliam Place
Dublin 2

Typeset by
Gough Typesetting Services
Dublin

Printed by
Colour Books, Dublin

ISBN 1-85800-274-5

A catalogue record for this book
is available from the British Library.

Preface

This book is aimed as a companion volume to *Equity and the Law of Trusts in Ireland*. For this reason its structure mirrors that adopted in the latter text and it is intended that the two should be used in conjunction with one another. The commentary included is designed to provide a guide to the general principles applicable in a given area, and illustrate the relevance of the cases from which extracts are set out. The majority of the extracts are from cases decided in this jurisdiction, although there are a number from Northern Ireland and a significant quantity of decisions handed down by the courts in England are also included. Particularly in areas such as constructive trusts and strangers, where authorities from this jurisdiction are thin on the ground, it is likely that our courts will take their lead from decisions handed down in England, and for this reason I have tried to include non-Irish authorities which may be of interest. Where relevant, extracts from statutes and statutory instruments and Law Reform Commission reports have also been included. A survey of this material quickly reveals how out of date our legislation in this area of the law is and it is to be hoped that it may receive attention in future legislative programmes.

I should point out that this casebook started out considerably more comprehensive in nature in terms of its content and numerous cuts had to be made in order to comply with the publishers' requirements. However, I hope that it contains a representative collection of the most important judgments and statutory provisions in this area.

I would like to express my appreciation to Rory O'Malley and Jason Stewart who proofread the text and to Patricia Brazil who did an excellent job compiling the tables. I would also like to thank Gilbert Gough who typeset the text, which included the unenviable job of scanning the material – as ever I am very grateful to him. Finally I would like to record my thanks to Patricia Baker who compiled the index and to the staff at Round Hall Ltd, in particular Thèrése Carrick, for their practical assistance.

Hilary Delany
31 January 2002

Acknowledgements

I wish to thank the following for allowing me to reproduce copyright material: The Incorporated Council of Law Reporting for Ireland for the *Irish Reports*; Round Hall Ltd for the *Irish Law Reports Monthly*; The Law Reform Commission for the Bill on Variation of Trusts (2000); The Courts Service for Unreported Judgments; The Stationery Office for Legislation and Statutory Instruments; The Incorporated Council of Law Reporting for England and Wales for the *Law Reports* and the *Weekly Law Reports*; and Butterworths for the *All England Reports* and the *Northern Ireland Law Reports*.

Contents

Table of Contents

CHAPTER 5 — SECRET TRUSTS

CHAPTER 6 — CONSTITUTION OF TRUSTS

CHAPTER 7 — RESULTING TRUSTS

Chapter 8 — Constructive Trusts

Chapter 9 — Purpose Trusts

CHAPTER 14 — SPECIFIC PERFORMANCE

CHAPTER 15 — RECTIFICATION

CHAPTER 16 — RESCISSION

Table of Cases

Table of Statutes

Other Tables

CONSTITUTION

EUROPEAN COMMUNITY DIRECTIVES

EUROPEAN COMMUNITY TREATY

EUROPEAN CONVENTION FOR THE PROTECTION OF HUMAN RIGHTS

STATUTORY INSTRUMENTS

CHAPTER 1

Introduction

FUSION OF LAW AND EQUITY – A PROCEDURAL FUSION ONLY

The enactment of the Supreme Court of Judicature (Ireland) Act 1877 effected a fusion of the administration of the common law and equity and led to the creation of one system from a procedural perspective. However, the accepted view at the time was that the Judicature Act did not effect fusion of the substantive principles inherent in the two systems, and that their distinct origins and principles could still be clearly discerned. Despite suggestions to the contrary by the House of Lords in *United Scientific Holdings Ltd v. Burnley Borough Council*[1] and by the Supreme Court in *Hynes Ltd v. Independent Newspapers Ltd*[2] the consensus today remains that no substantive fusion has occurred and that courts have continued to recognise the distinct features of the jurisdictions.[3]

Hynes Ltd v. Independent Newspapers Ltd
[1980] IR 204

The plaintiff sought a declaration that notice served by the defendant of a rent review, six weeks after the date stipulated in the lease, was ineffective to invoke the rent review clause. The essential question which the court had to consider was whether time was of the essence with regard to the rent review provision. In dismissing the plaintiff's claim, the Supreme Court stated that if the time stipulation would not have been deemed to be of the essence of the contract in a court of equity prior to the enactment of the Judicature Act then it would still receive the same construction. It concluded that in the absence of an express term to that effect or other special circumstances, the time stipulation in the lease would not have been deemed to be of the essence.

O'HIGGINS CJ stated at pp.209–217: "This is an appeal by the plaintiffs against the judgment and order of Mr. Justice McWilliam in the High Court dismissing their claim for a declaration that a rent review notice served by the defendants was ineffective as being out of time. The action was heard by Mr.

---

[1] [1978] AC 904.

[2] [1980] IR 204.

[3] See e.g. the decisions of the House of Lords in *Lord Napier and Ettrick v. Hunter* [1993] AC 713 and *Tinlsey v. Milligan* [1994] 1 AC 340.

Justice McWilliam, without oral evidence, but having regard to the provisions of a lease dated the 29th March, 1972, and made between Sisk Properties Ltd. of the one part and the plaintiffs of the other part under which the plaintiffs hold certain premises in Galway from the defendants (the successors of Sisk Properties Ltd.), and having regard to certain facts which were urged in the pleadings and were admitted. These facts can be set out shortly and succinctly but the issue which arises thereon cannot be disposed of so easily.

On the 29th March, 1972, Sisk Properties Ltd. demised to the plaintiffs certain premises in St. Augustine Street and Merchant's Road, Galway, for a term of 99 years commencing on the 1st January, 1972. The rent reserved was the yearly rent of £42,000 but provision was made for a rent review in the seventh year and at seven-year intervals thereafter. The lease went on to provide that, if the lessee wished to dispute the amount of the proposed new rent, he should within six weeks of the service upon him of the revised rent notice serve upon the lessor a notice of dispute and that, thereupon, the amount of the new rent would be determined by arbitration in the manner provided.

It was further provided as follows:– "But if no such Notice of Dispute is so served by the Lessee then the sums specified by the Lessor in such Revised Rent Notice shall become and be the yearly rent payable hereunder as from the seventh anniversary of the commencement of the term hereby created and for the residue then unexpired of the term hereby granted until varied by virtue of any further Revised Rent Notice that may be served by the Lessor pursuant to the provisions hereinbefore contained." The reddendum in the lease had earlier provided in the following terms:– "Yielding and Paying therefor during the said term unto the Lessor the yearly rent of £42,000 and such increased rent as may from time to time be payable hereunder as hereinafter provided …"

On the 17th November, 1978, the defendants (as lessors) served on the plaintiffs a revised rent notice claiming an increased or new rent of £160,000 p.a. While this notice was served in the seventh year of the term created by the lease, it was so served some six weeks later than the date specified in paragraph D.3 of the lease, namely, the 1st October. By letter dated the 14th December, 1978, the plaintiffs' solicitors indicated on behalf of the plaintiffs that the notice was out of time and ineffective and also, as a precaution, they gave notice of dispute. The plaintiffs then commenced these proceedings in which they claim a declaration that the defendants' notice was ineffective to require a rent review. Having lost in the High Court, the plaintiffs have brought this appeal to this Court.

The plaintiffs' claim raises the question whether, in relation to the effectiveness of the rent review notice, observance by the defendants of the time limited for such service was or was not essential. In holding in the High Court that such observance was not essential, Mr. Justice McWilliam was guided by his view that, since there was no express stipulation making time of the essence, neither the nature of the subject matter of the contract nor the surrounding circumstances showed that time should be of the essence. In applying this test he followed the recent decision of the House of Lords in *United Scientific Holdings v. Burnley Borough Council* [1978] AC 904 and *Cheapside Land Development Co. v. Messels Service Co.* [1978] AC 904 (together referred to as the *Burnley* case). The burden of the plaintiffs' appeal to this Court is that Mr. Justice McWilliam was wrong in so doing and that the decision of the House of Lords in the *Burnley* case ought not to be followed in our courts.

As this matter is of considerable importance both to practitioners and to those involved in the property market, it is necessary to make a few general observations about rent review clauses. Having done so, I propose to examine the manner in which the observance of time in such clauses was regarded, certainly in the English courts, prior to the decision in the *Burnley* case. Then I propose to consider the reasoning behind the *Burnley* case, and whether it is appropriate that that decision be followed in our courts.

Over the past two decades, in both the United Kingdom and Ireland, the prevalence of inflation in the property market has led to the introduction of some provision for rent review if the term being negotiated is for any significant number of years. Lessors, faced with constantly changing money and property values, have not been prepared to lease their property for a long period without providing for a periodic revision or adjustment of rent. Such rent review clauses vary in form and content. In some cases the rent review may be initiated only by the lessor, in others it may be initiated by either the lessor or the lessee. In some cases a rent review clause may be associated with a "break clause" which entitles a lessee to surrender the demised premises if he is unwilling or unable to pay the increased rent. In other cases the lease clearly contemplates periodic revisions of the rent and the lessee undertakes to pay the original rent and also any revised rent coming into operation during the term. Whatever form such clauses take, in general they specify a procedure for the determination of the revised rent and a timetable for the taking of the necessary steps in that procedure which, when followed, leads to the declaration of the new rent not later than the review date.

The question which has arisen in this case is whether the failure to observe the stipulated timetable has deprived the defendants of the review they seek; that question has not previously arisen in our courts. However, as indicated, it has arisen in a number of reported cases in England, the latest of these is the decision of the House of Lords in the *Burnley* case. In order to consider whether that decision ought to be followed, I find it necessary not only to examine the reasoning which led to it but also the basis upon which the earlier decisions (many of which it expressly overruled) were decided. Therefore, it seems convenient to consider the earlier decisions first.

In *Samuel Properties Ltd. v. Hayek* [1972] 1 WLR 1296 the Court of Appeal in England held that, where the words of the rent review clause import an option or privilege for the lessor to increase the rent which would otherwise be payable, any conditions as to time must be strictly observed and that, accordingly, the time specified for the exercise of the option must be treated as inflexible and mandatory. In that case particular attention was paid to the reddendum in the lease and in the course of his judgment Russell L.J. said at p. 1301 of the report:- "The language of the reddendum indicates that the basic rent is to remain unchanged throughout the term unless it be increased by compliance with those provisions. Clause 1 of the fourth schedule in terms confers an option on the lessor to require rent review in the manner thereafter provided. The process thereafter laid down in clause 2 uses the language of a condition precedent in requiring a notice in writing with an express time requirement." Having considered *Eaton v. Lyon* (1798) 3 Ves 690, *Harries v. Bryant* (1827) 4 Russ 89, *Reid v. Blagrave* (1831) 9 LJOS (Ch) 245 and *Barrow v. Isaacs & Son* [1891] 1 QB 417 (and particular passages from the judgments therein) on the question of equitable relief where the time requirement for the exercise of the option was not observed, Russell L.J. said at p. 1305 of the report:– "I am not prepared to extend those comments to a case such as the present. They are relevant to a case where a failure to comply with a covenanted obligation has exposed a person to the danger of forfeiture of a lease or other estate. I decline to extend them to a case such as the present, in which the party is given an option to improve his financial position if he chooses to take particular steps laid down."

Edmund Davies L.J. in his judgment in *Samuel Properties Ltd. v. Hayek*, drew a similar distinction about equitable relief against forfeiture; at p. 1307 of the report he said:– "The circumstances in which relief against forfeiture is granted are widely different from those under present consideration. In the former, a right of forfeiture is expressly reserved or implied by law in order to ensure the performance by the lessee of his obligations, and the court will grant relief if terms can be imposed which will ensure due protection for the lessor. But the power of a lessor on due notice to increase rent involves, in effect, the making of a new contract between the parties, subject in the present case to compliance by the lessor with a condition precedent. It resembles options and these are undoubtedly required to be exercised in strict conformity with the terms by which they were created: see *Hinds v. Randall* (1961) 177 EG 733 and *Peeling v. Guidice* (1963) 186 EG 113. If this is not done, relief will in general be granted only where, by unconscionable conduct by the proposed recipient of the notice to exercise the option, the other party has been led to believe that strict adherence to its terms will not be insisted upon."

A similar conclusion had been reached earlier by Goulding J. in *C. Richards & Son Ltd. v. Karenita Ltd* (1972) 221 EG 25. In both those cases the significant feature was that there was a fixed rent throughout the whole term with a provision granting an option or saying that the rent should be subject to increase or should be increased if the landlord took certain steps in accordance with the timetable laid down. However, where the terms of the lease were such as to express or imply on the part of the lessee an obligation to pay not only the original rent but also a revised rent, and the actual review provisions were merely machinery provisions for implementing the agreement, failure on the part of the lessor to act in time was not regarded as fatal to a review sought by him. This distinction was established in *Kenilworth Sites Ltd. v. Little & Co.* [1975] 1 WLR 143 and *Accuba Ltd. v. Allied Shoe Repairs* [1975] 1 WLR 1559. The result was that until the *Burnley* case the courts in England, in deciding in relation to such review clauses whether time was or was not of the essence, looked to see whether what the lessor sought to do was in purported exercise of an "option" or "privilege" or whether it was being done pursuant to an obligation already accepted by the lessee and as part of the machinery for implementing what was already agreed. In the former case time was presumed to be of the essence, while in the latter the presumption was to the contrary. This dichotomy between "option" on the one hand and "obligation" or "machinery" on the other continued until the leases involved in the *Burnley* case became the subject of litigation.

In the *Burnley* case proper a Court of Appeal (Buckley, Roskill and Browne L.JJ.) discarded the distinction between "option" clauses and "obligation" or "machinery" clauses. A different and new test was applied. The court held that the commercial character of the contract contained in a lease incorporating a rent review clause raised the presumption that the parties intended time to be of the essence of the contract in respect of each step to be taken by the lessor in order to obtain a determination of any increased rent under a rent review clause. In *Cheapside Land Development Co. v. Messels Service Co.* another Court of Appeal (Stamp, Scarman and Goff L.JJ.) also discarded the "option" or "machinery" test. The court concluded that time was of the essence, prima facie, in all rent review clauses. Its view was not based on the presumed intentions of the parties arising from the suggested commercial nature of the transaction, but upon the ground that in its legal nature a rent review clause is a grant of a unilateral right to the lessor and that equity would not have granted relief to the grantee of such a right for failure to perform any of the conditions of the grant timeously.

Appeals were taken against both decisions and the appeals were heard together by the House of Lords. As already indicated, I have referred to both decisions as the *Burnley* case. The issue which arose for decision was stated thus by Lord Diplock in his speech at pp. 923-4 of the report:

> "What the Court of Appeal have decided is that the commercial nature of the contract and/or the legal nature of the right granted to the landlord by a rent review clause raises a presumption that time specified in such a clause for anything that needs to be done by him is of the essence; and that this presumption will prevail unless there are strong contra-indications in the actual wording of the clause ... My Lords, the reason why these two appeals have been heard together in the House although the two rent review clauses that are in question differ widely in their wording, is to obtain a ruling whether the presumption as to the construction and effect of rent review clauses is as the Court of Appeal

> held it to be, or whether it is the contrary presumption, viz. that time is not of the essence."

In considering this issue the Law Lords were concerned with the application of equitable principles. This arose initially because of the provisions of s. 25(7) of the Supreme Court of Judicature Act, 1873, to the effect that stipulations in contracts as to time which would not before the passing of that Act have been deemed to be, or to have become, of the essence in a court of equity should receive in all courts the same construction as they would have theretofore received in equity. There was also the general provision in that Act that in case of conflict between the rules of equity and the rules of common law, the rules of equity should prevail.

I think it is clear from the report that, in considering the application of equitable principles or rules, the general view of the House of Lords was that neither the Act of 1873 nor the later and similar provisions of s. 41 of the Law of Property Act, 1925, placed any ban upon further development of equitable rules by judicial decision: see *per* Lord Diplock at p. 926 and Lord Fraser at p. 957 of the report.

It is not necessary to examine in any detail the careful, long and detailed speeches of the Law Lords who participated in the *Burnley* case. It is sufficient to say that, with one reservation, they were prepared to regard the inclusion in a lease of a rent review clause as an acceptance by the tenant of an obligation to pay to the landlord a rent so determined and, further, that this acceptance was an inseverable part of the whole consideration for the landlord's grant of the terms of years for the length agreed. The majority view was to this effect even when the right to initiate or to "trigger" the rent review was exclusively that of the landlord. It was recognised that there could be exceptions as where a break-clause was included in the lease entitling the tenant to surrender if the rent were increased.

Viewed in this light, the timetable for the review or determination of the new rent was regarded by the court as subsidiary to an obligation already accepted by the tenant and as mere machinery for carrying into effect the real intention of the parties that periodic increases of rent should take place. In particular, the majority view was that the unilateral right of the landlord to initiate or to commence a rent review was not a right to create a new relationship or contract between landlord and tenant but was merely a power or right to determine the amount of a new rent already agreed to. It merely altered a term in a continuing contract. In this respect it differed from an option under which one party was empowered to create a new and binding contract with the other. Accordingly, the House of Lords adopted and applied to such rent review clauses, when considered in relation to the observance of time limits, the following rule which appears in Halsbury's *Laws of England* (4th ed., vol. 9, para. 481):

> "Time will not be considered to be of the essence unless: (1) the parties expressly

stipulate that conditions as to time must be strictly complied with; or (2) the nature of the subject matter of the contract or the surrounding circumstances show that time should be considered to be of the essence . . ."

The result was that, in the absence of any contra indication in the lease itself, the House of Lords in the *Burnley* case ruled that there is a presumption (stemming from the application of equitable principles) that in all rent review clauses time should not be regarded as essential to the initiation or operation of the rent review, even if the right to review is unilateral.

I have considered very carefully the reasoning which led to the decision in the *Burnley* case. It is based on the assertion that such leases for long terms would not be granted or concluded without acceptance by the tenant of rent reviews and that, as a consequence, it would be unfair and inequitable that such a tenant should be allowed to repudiate an obligation he had accepted merely because, in carrying out what was agreed, a time clause was not observed. I find this reasoning compelling. I accept that there may be circumstances in which delay has been extreme or where, because of it, other factors have arisen which alter the equities. However, in the ordinary case where the payment of an increased rent is expressly envisaged and accepted, and where the failure to observe the requirements of a time clause is due to mere inadvertence and is not prolonged and in no way alters obligations already undertaken, I see no reason for saying that the equitable rule as to time in contracts should not apply. This is not to say that failure by the landlord to act in time may not be a breach of contract for which he may be liable in damages, if damage is caused. However, his failure in this respect should not be regarded as such a breach as would entitle the tenant to repudiate obligations which under the contract he has already accepted.

In Ireland the fusion of common-law and equitable rules was initiated by the Supreme Court of Judicature Act (Ireland), 1877, which contains similar provisions in s. 28(7) to those already noted in the English Acts, and was completed by the Courts of Justice Act, 1924, and the Courts (Establishment and Constitution) Act, 1961.

In the circumstances existing in this appeal, it seems to me that the reasoning in the *Burnley* case applies. The wording of the reddendum indicates that the plaintiffs accepted an obligation to pay not only the initial rent but also "such increased rent as may from time to time be payable hereunder." The lease contains no break clause or anything which would distinguish it from a lease under which the lessee accepts the normal obligation of periodic reviews of rent. It appears to me that the rent review clause amounts to machinery for the implementation of what was accepted from the commencement of the lease, that is to say, a review of the rent at the stipulated periods. In these circumstances, I am of the view that observance by the defendants of the time prescribed for the implementation of the agreed rent review was not of the essence and that, accordingly, the decision of the High Court judge to this effect was correct. Therefore, I would dismiss this appeal."

CHAPTER 2

Maxims of Equity

INTRODUCTION

The maxims of equity constitute the general principles developed by the Court of Chancery over the years and while they should not always be literally applied, they do reflect general trends in the manner in which equitable jurisdiction has been exercised. It should be pointed out that some of these maxims overlap or may even contradict each other and they should be treated with a certain degree of caution.

EQUITY FOLLOWS THE LAW

This maxim should not be interpreted too literally and it would be more accurate to say that equity will restrict or modify common law principles where the interests of fairness require it[1] but will otherwise follow the law. A good illustration of this maxim is that equity follows the law in requiring the necessary words of limitation to effect a conveyance of freehold land in respect of an executed trust.[2]

Jameson v. McGovern
[1934] IR 758

By virtue of a marriage settlement freehold premises had been conveyed to a husband for life, to his wife for life, then to any children, or if there were none, to those appointed by the husband and in default of appointment, for the survivor of the husband and wife absolutely. The parties had no children and no appointment was made by the husband. After his death, the question of the extent of the wife's interest under the settlement arose. The Supreme Court found that, in the absence of the necessary words of limitation, the wife only derived a life interest from it, although the court went on to hold that she had an equity independent of the settlement sufficient to give her an equitable fee simple in the property.

---

[1] E.g. in relation to the principle that equity will not allow a statute to be used as an instrument of fraud, *McCormick v. Grogan* (1869) LR 4 HL 82, 97.

[2] *Jameson v. McGovern* [1934] IR 758.

MURNAGHAN J stated at pp. 770–778: "This appeal raises in this Court the question upon which there has been a wide diversity of judicial opinion, viz., whether, in an executed declaration of trust, words and terms known to the common law must be given the same effect in equity, or whether the construction of the trust can be gathered from the intention of the settlor.

In Ireland in the case of *Meyler v. Meyler* (1883) 11 LR Ir 522 the Vice-Chancellor, in interpreting the equitable limitations in a marriage settlement, held that children could not take more than life estates in the absence of words of inheritance. He said (at pp. 529, 530): "But I have arrived at the conclusion that I am precluded by the authorities upon the subject from going into the question of intention, to be ascertained, as it must be in all cases where the technical rules applicable to deeds do not stand in the way, from a careful perusal of the whole instrument. It is admitted that if this were not the case of a trust estate, as it is, but of a legal estate, with uses executed, there could be no question as to the estates given to the children, who, for want of words of inheritance, could take no greater estates than for their respective lives. It was contended for the defendants that the technical rule on this subject does not apply to declarations of trusts where the whole legal fee is in the trustees, and that in such cases the Court is authorised to act upon the intention ascertained from the whole of the deed. For this contention there is certainly a great weight of opinion of eminent text-writers on the subject. But it appears to me that a series of cases, commencing with *Holliday v. Overton* (1852) 14 Beav 467, settles the rule, so far at least as Courts of first instance are concerned, that even in trust estates it is not a question of intention but a technical rule in all cases of deeds executed prior to the Conveyancing and Law of Property Act, 1881, and of all subsequent deeds, save so far as the 51st section of that Act alters that rule." Chatterton V.C., in thus following the cases of *Holliday v. Overton, Lucas v. Brandreth* (1860) 28 Beav 274 and *Tatham v. Vernon* (1861) 29 Beav 604, all decided by Sir John Romilly M.R., supported this position by citations from *Lewin on Trusts*, and he also directed attention to the 51st section of the Conveyancing Act which applies to future deeds of conveyance, whether of legal or equitable estates, and he observed that this Act "stopped very far short of enacting that an intention deduced from the context or the actual limitation itself should be sufficient to pass by deed an estate of inheritance without technical words." It is right to point out that *dicta* of Deasy L.J. in *Lysaght v. McGrath* (1882) 11 LR Ir 142 in support of the contrary view were cited to the Vice-Chancellor during the argument.

The cases of *Holliday v. Overton* and *Meyler v. Meyler* (1883) 11 LR Ir 522 appear to have been uniformly followed as, e.g., by Chitty J. in *In re Whiston's Settlement* [1894] 1 Ch 66, until in *In re Tringham's Trusts* [1904] 2 Ch 487 Joyce J., founding his judgment upon the opinions of earlier conveyancers and some remarks in *Pugh v. Drew* 17 WR 988, held that, where the intention was clear, an equitable estate could pass in a trust exceuted without words of inheritance. This decision of Joyce J. [1904] 2 Ch 487, has since, I think, been followed consistently in this country in preference to the ruling given by Chatterton V.C. in *Meyler v. Meyler*, as witness *In re Houston, Rogers v. Houston* [1909] 1 IR 319 decided by Wylie J.; *In re Stinson's Estate* [1910] 1 IR 47 decided by Ross J.; *In re Cross's Trusts* [1915] 1 IR 304 decided by O'Connor M.R.; and *In re Murphy and Griffin's Contract* [1919] 1 IR 187 decided by Powell J. In England the decision of Joyce J. in *In re Tringham's Trusts*, although followed in several cases, was not accepted in many reported decisions, and finally the point came before the Court of Appeal in England in *In re Bostock's Settlement, Norrish v. Bostock* [1921] 2 Ch 469 in which case the decision of Joyce J. was overruled. In the case of *The Land Purchase Trustee, Northern Ireland v. Beers* [1925] NI 191 the Court of Appeal in Northern Ireland considered the point subsequently to the decision given in *In re Bostock's Settlement*, but the case was determined without the necessity of making a ruling upon the correctness of the Irish decisions given since the case of *In re Tringham's Trusts*.

It is desirable at this stage to state briefly the facts upon which the question before the Court has arisen.

Certain premises in the town of Manorhamilton, held under a fee-farm grant made in pursuance of the Renewable Leasehold Conversion Act, were agreed to be sold to the tenant in occupation, and in the making of title a marriage settlement, dated 26th December, 1881, was relied upon as vesting the property in fee in Emily Robinson. By this settlement William Henry Robinson conveyed to a trustee and his heirs the said premises, and the intended wife assigned to the trustee her reversionary interest in certain moneys, and trusts were declared to pay the income " of all and singular the trust premises hereinbefore expressed to be hereby granted and assigned respectively." The first trust was to pay the income under a protected life estate for the husband, followed by a life estate with restraint upon anticipation in favour of the wife during her life, and thereafter a trust for the issue subject to appointment and in default of appointment "in trust for all the children or any the child [*sic*] of the said intended marriage who, being sons or a son, shall attain the age of 21 years, or, being daughters or a daughter, shall attain that age or marry, and if more than one in equal shares." The settlement went on to provide that in default or failure of children (which event happened) "the said trustees or trustee shall hold the trust premises hereinbefore brought into settlement by the said William Henry Robinson and the annual income thereof or so much thereof respectively as shall not have been applied under any of the trusts or powers herein contained in trust for such person or persons and for such estates and interests as the said William Henry Robinson shall by deed or will appoint and in default of such appointment and so far as no such appointment shall extend then for the survivor of them, the said William Henry Robinson and Emily Abbey, absolutely." Emily Abbey, otherwise Emily Robinson, was the survivor, and, as the estate given was an equitable estate, the point to be determined is whether, in the absence of words of inheritance, Emily Robinson became entitled to the equitable fee.

When the system of trusts came to be moulded after the Statute of Uses, the Court of Chancery had to lay down rules for the construction of gifts of these new equitable interests. In 1693 Lord Keeper Sommers in the case of *Sheldon v. Dormer* (1693) 2 Vern 310 stated the rule as follows:– "We are here upon a construction of a trust, where the intent of the party is to govern; and Courts of Equity have always in cases of trusts taken the same rule of expounding trusts, and of pursuing the intention of the parties therein, as in cases of wills; and that even in point of limitations of estates where the letter is to be as strictly pursued, as in any case." Lord Hardwicke also sought to construe all trusts according to the intention of the parties and even went so far in *Bagshaw v. Spencer* (1748) 1 Ves Sen 142 to deny the distinction between executory trusts and trusts executed. The principles of the Court of Chancery were, however, moulded gradually, and in the time of Lord Northington a definite ruling was made and the distinction between executory trusts and trusts executed became firmly established: *Wright v. Pearson* (1758) 1 Eden 119. In *Austen v. Taylor* (1759) 1 Eden p. 361 Lord Northington said: "But where the trusts and limitations are already expressly declared, the Court has no authority to interfere, and make them different from what they would be at law." Again, in *White v. Carter* (1766) 2 Eden p. 366 Lord Northington said: "For though the Court has no power, where the limitations are expressly declared, to give the words a different sense from what they would bear at law, yet, where its assistance is required to direct the conveyance, it will give that direction according to the intent of the testator apparent upon the face of the will, if that intent is not contrary to any rule of law." The distinction taken by Lord Northington became firmly established. I have only to refer to Lord Eldon's decision in *Jervoise v. Duke of Northumberland* (1821) 1 J & W 559. Lord Eldon decided this case in 1820 after a long judicial career in which he systematized the doctrines of equity; and, speaking of executed trusts, he said, at p. 571: "But these are cases where the testator has clearly decided what the trust is to be; and as equity follows the law, where the testator has left nothing to be done, but has himself expressed it, there the effect must be the same, whether the estate is equitable or legal."

It is to be remarked that these citations deal with the construction placed by the Court of Chancery upon executed declarations of trust and are independent of other heads in equity, such as, for example, to what extent equity will aid a purchaser for value who has obtained a transfer of an equitable estate without words of limitation. It is remarkable that the opinion which is said to be supported by the eminent conveyancers in the past is dependent upon their textbooks and is not supported by any citation of decisions in the Court of Chancery. It is, however, desirable to examine them in detail.

In Cruise's "Digest of the Law of Real Property," Title XI, "Use," Chap. 2, sect. 32, is found a passage which has been relied upon: "In the alienation of uses none of those technical words which the law requires in the limitation of particular estates were deemed necessary. Thus, a use might be limited in fee simple without the word heirs; for if a sufficient consideration was given, the Court of Chancery would decree the absolute property of the use to be well vested in the purchaser. And as a use was a thing which consisted merely in confidence and privity, and was not held by any tenure, the rules of the common law were not violated." This citation deals in terms with uses before the Statute of Uses, and I do not think the author meant it to apply to trusts. Certainly, in the 4th edition of this work published in 1835 the editor did not so understand it. For, in Title XII, " Trust," chap. 1, two sections appear to have been added by the editor which sum up in precise language the effect of the decisions which I have dealt with:

> "Sect. 87. [Notwithstanding the *dictum* of Lord Hardwicke in the case of *Bagshaw v. Spencer* (1748) 2 Atk 246 that all trusts were in notion of law executory (and which has been controverted by Fearne with his usual ability) the distinction is now well established between trusts executed and trusts executory, marriage articles and wills.

> "Sect. 88. Where the devise or trust is directly and wholly declared by the testator or settler, so as to attach on the lands immediately, under the deed or will itself, it is a trust executed and complete; and must be construed strictly according to its legal import, and in analogy to corresponding limitations of legal estates: but where the devise, trust, or agreement is directory or incomplete, describing the intended limitation of some future conveyance or settlement directed to be made for effectuating it, there the trust is executory; and the Court of Chancery will not construe the devise or articles strictly, but will endeavour to discover the intention, and execute the trust, according to that intention.]"

The next passage relied upon is Butler's note to Coke upon Littleton, 290 b (Note 249), XIV. The passage occurs in what Butler describes as an "Elementary outline of some leading points in the doctrine of trusts affecting real property." The passage, as cited, is given in some places as:- "A mere declaration of trust in favour of another has been held sufficient to transfer to him the equitable fee." So stated, the passage is cited as laying down a rule for the proper construction of executed trusts. But read in its context, Butler states:- "An equitable estate is by its nature incapable of livery of seizin, and of every form of conveyance which operates by the Statutes of Uses. In the transfer, therefore, of equitable estates these forms of conveyance have been dispensed with and a mere declaration of trust in favour of another has been held sufficient to transfer to him the equitable fee." It seems to me that Butler is contrasting the modes of conveyance at common law with a simple declaration of trust, but that he is not at all stating what form a declaration of trust must take.

The next citation relied upon is from Mr. Preston, in Vol. II of his "Elementary Treatise on Estates," p. 64. He writes:– "The general rule is that limitations of trust are to be construed in like manner and by the like rules as limitations of a legal estate; and therefore in deeds the fee cannot pass by grant or transfer *inter vivos* without appropriate words of inheritance. But in contracts to convey, and in trusts declared in a conveyance, the fee may pass, notwithstanding the omission of a limitation to the heirs. Therefore articles to convey to A. B. in fee; or a conveyance to A. B. and his heirs, in trust, to convey to C. D. in fee simple, would confer a right in equity to call for a conveyance of the inheritance. So a conveyance to A. and his heirs in trust, *totidem verbis*, for B. in fee, would pass a fee." As I understand this passage the first portion states the rule of construction applicable to trusts executed in very distinct terms, while the latter portion mentions certain exceptions which are either contracts executory or conveyances for value where equity will assist in the case of a defective conveyance. Unless by the last example Mr. Preston was stating the rule of equity as to conveyances for value, he states two contradictory propositions.

The last citation is the opinion of Mr. Hayes in his "Introduction to Conveyancing", 5th edit., Vol. I, p. 91, published in 1840. He says: "Trusts like uses before the Statute pursued the course of succession appointed for legal interests of a corresponding description. They were expounded to, by analogy to the rules of legal construction. But these rules did not always govern in equity with absolute sway. The rule, for example, which required the word *heirs* to pass the fee in a conveyance at common law, although it was extended to uses within the Statute, was not rigidly applied to trusts. If land was limited in trust for A. without more, equity, in conformity to the rule of law gave to A. the beneficial interest for life only; but it could be collected from the instrument that A. was meant to have the absolute interest, equity, esteeming the intention more than the rule, gave him the beneficial fee without the aid of the word heirs." Mr. Hayes in this passage was either speaking of a conveyance for value made in the form of conveyance with declaration of trust, which is, I think, more likely, or he was following the opinion of Lord Hardwicke without adverting to the fact that his opinion had been dissented from for over a century.

In his judgment in *In re Tringham's Trusts* [1904] 2 Ch 487 Mr. Justice Joyce relied upon these passages above examined, and these and several others were relied upon in *Lysaght v. McGrath* (1882) 11 LR Ir 142 where the limitations in a voluntary deed were ultimately to named children " absolutely." In reference to these citations May C.J. in *Lysaght v. McGrath* says at page 156: "Practically, however, I apprehend that conveyancers deal with executed trusts just as they would with legal estates." Deasy L.J. did not decide that the fee passed, although he thought the citations from text-writers might lead to that conclusion. FitzGibbon L.J. appears to have held that the fee did not pass, as he said the plaintiffs were not entitled at law and had no equity upon which to found a claim. Mr. Justice Joyce also relied in his judgment on *Pugh v. Drew* 17 WR 988. The deed to be construed was one settling freeholds upon such and the same trusts as were declared and contained in a settlement of leaseholds made by another deed. Under the settlement of the leaseholds, they were held in the events which happened for A. and B. in equal shares, share and share alike. The objection was taken that there was no mention of the heirs of A. and B. James V.C. overruled this objection, saying that the absence of words of limitation was not absolutely fatal under all circumstances. I regard the case of *Pugh v. Drew* 17 WR 988 as a clear case of a referential trust declared by reference to another deed and in its nature executory, where the intention of the settlor can be sought out by the Court.

In the Court of Appeal in England Lord Sterndale M.R. in *In re Bostock's Settlement* [1921] 2 Ch 469 at p. 480 did not deal with the authorities in detail, but stated his conclusions in the words used in Lewin on Trusts, 12th ed., p. 125: "'But though technical terms be not absolutely necessary, yet where technical terms are employed they shall be taken in their legal and technical sense. Lord Hardwicke, indeed, once added the qualification: "unless the intention of the testator or author of the trust plainly appeared to the contrary." But this position has since been repeatedly and expressly overruled, and at the present day it must be considered a clear and settled canon that a limitation in a trust, perfected and declared by the settlor, must have the same construction as in the case of a legal estate executed.'" Warrington L.J. and Younger L.J. agreed, and it is noticeable that Younger L.J. did not find any such difference of view in the view of older text-writers and conveyancers as has been suggested.

I have dealt at perhaps too great length with the decided cases and the opinions of conveyancers, because I find in so many recent Irish cases a welcome adhesion to the views put forward by Joyce J. in *In re Tringham's Trusts* [1904] 2 Ch 487. It may be that Lord Hardwicke was wiser than his successors and that equitable interests would have better flourished if they had not been measured so strictly by analogy to the rules of law. But my reading of the cases and authorities is that the stricter rule has prevailed for almost two centuries, and in my opinion the grounds put forward for departing from the rule were not justified by any authority. I agree with the decision of the Court of Appeal in England in *In re Bostock's Settlement*, and am of opinion that so many of the Irish authorities as are based on the authority of *In re Tringham's Trusts* must be overruled.

There is, however, on the facts of the present case a special feature which requires consideration. The settlement was made before marriage and the agreement was to settle the husband's lands on the wife absolutely if she survived him. Every provision with regard to her falls directly within the consideration: *Nairn v. Prowse* (1802) 6 Ves 752. In my opinion in this case the wife has an equity independent of the declaration of trust made by the settlor and this equity is sufficient to construe the settlement as giving her the equitable fee which it was contracted that she should have in the events which have happened. *Holliday v. Overton* (1852) 15 Beav 480 before Sir John Romilly M.R. was the case of a post-nuptial settlement by a widow, and the Master of the Rolls took the distinction, saying that the children were not purchasers of the fee or of any estate of inheritance under the contract.

But as the case was argued solely upon the point which we have decided in favour of the appellant, and as the respondents do not ask us to make a decree upon the terms as to costs which we would be obliged to order in ease of the appellant, in the circumstances the appeal must be allowed.

The same order will be made in the appeal conversant with the promissory note, both appeals being treated as one appeal."

HE WHO SEEKS EQUITY MUST DO EQUITY

Equity will only grant relief on terms which ensure that a defendant is treated fairly and to obtain equitable relief, a plaintiff must be prepared to act in an honourable manner. This maxim reflects the fact that equitable remedies are discretionary in nature and focuses on the likely future conduct of the party seeking equitable relief.

Chappell v. Times Newspapers Ltd
[1975] 1 WLR 482

The plaintiffs sought an interim injunction to restrain their employers from terminating their contracts of employment, although they refused to give the undertakings sought by the employers not to engage in disruptive behaviour. Although the plaintiffs themselves had not previously been directly involved in these activities, the Court of Appeal (Denning MR, Stephenson and Geoffrey Lane LJJ) refused to grant the relief sought. Lord Denning MR relied on the fact that the plaintiffs had failed to establish that they intended to act equitably by abiding by the terms of their contracts of employment.

LORD DENNING MR stated at pp. 501-503: "Long ago it was said that "No man can serve two masters." So here these men cannot serve both the union and the employers. When their duties conflict, they must choose between them. If they hold to the union, they may find themselves in breach of contract with their employers.

In passing, may I say that the conduct of the union in all this, in complaining, of the telegram of the N.P.A., reminds me of the complaint made in the old French proverb: "Cet animal est tres mechant: quand on l'attaque, il se defend.'" Put into English: "This animal is very wicked: when he is attacked, he defends himself."

So it seems to me there is ground for the publishers to submit that their telegram was justifiable. But I would not like to say more at this stage, because it is only an interlocutory application. Suffice it that it is at the least arguable.

Assume, however, that the publishers were in the wrong, and that they ought not to have said that they would regard the men as having terminated their own engagements, nevertheless the question arises whether an injunction should be granted restraining the publishers from terminating the agreements.

The general rule is that the courts will not order specific performance of contracts of employment. If there is a wrongful termination by one side, the remedy of the other party is in damages only. That has been the law for a very long time. It is reinforced by section 16 of the Trade Union and Labour Relations Act 1974, which says:

> "No court shall, whether by way of – (a) an order for specific performance or specific implement of a contract of employment, or (b) an injunction or interdict restraining a breach or threatened breach of a contract, compel an employee to do any work or attend at any place for the doing of any work."

An exception was created in this court in *Hill v. C.A. Parsons & Co. Ltd.* [1972] Ch 305, which was considered recently by Sir John Donaldson in *Sanders v. Ernest A. Neale Ltd.* [1974] ICR 565. *Hill v. Parsons* was exceptional, in that both employers and Mr. Hill had complete confidence in one another. Yet the employers – against their own wishes – gave Mr. Hill notice of the termination of his employment. It was given under pressure from a trade union. The notice was invalid. By granting an injunction the law was vindicated and justice was done. I would not detract from anything that was said in that case; but this case is very different. If an injunction were granted here, no one could have any confidence that the employment would continue peaceably. The N.G.A. have destroyed any expectation of peace by saying that they are going to resume industrial action. No employers can be expected to continue to employ a body of men – or any of them – who assert through their union that they intend to disrupt the business and bring losses on their employers. It may be that only a small group of the union will actually take industrial action. But that does not mean that the others (who are not actually taking the industrial action) can get an injunction. It would be quite unacceptable for the court to put such compulsion on the employers – so as to make them keep many men on at the place of work and to pay them wages – for doing nothing – while industrial action was being pursued by a small group.

There is another point which seems to me decisive. These men are saying that the publishers are about to break the contract of employment. But it is plain that they are not ready, and willing to perform their own side of it. It has long been settled both at common law and in equity that in a contract where each has to do his part concurrently with the other, then if one party seeks relief, he must be ready and willing to do his part in it. You will find the common law so stated in Smith's Leading Cases, 13th ed. (1929) vol. 2, p. 10: notes to *Cutter v. Powell* (1795) 6 Term 320. You will find the equity in *Measures Brothers Ltd. v. Measures* [1910] 2 Ch 248 where Sir H.H. Cozens-Hardy M.R. said, at p. 254:

> "I prefer to base my judgment upon the ground that the plaintiffs, who are seeking equitable relief by way of injunction, cannot obtain such relief unless they allege and prove that they have performed their part of the bargain hitherto and are ready and able also to perform their part in the future."

The principle was stated by Lord Radcliffe more recently in *Australian Hardwoods Pty. Ltd. v. Commissioner for Railways* [1961] 1 WLR 425, 432-433:

> ". . . where the agreement is one which involves continuing or future acts to be performed by the plaintiff, he must fail unless he can show that he is ready and willing on his part to carry out those obligations which are, in fact, part of the consideration for the undertaking of the defendant that the plaintiff seeks to have enforced."

In this case it seems to me impossible for any of the plaintiffs to say that he is ready and willing to perform his part of the contract when on the statement of his union, the National Graphical Association (which he has never disavowed) he may be called upon, or other members of his union may be called upon, to take industrial action so as to bring great losses to their employers. Not being ready to do their part, they cannot call on the employers to continue to employ them. They are seeking equity when they are not ready to do it themselves.

This is enough to decide the case. But 1 would mention one other point. Mr. Pain rather suggested that when men go out on strike or take industrial action, they are not repudiating their contracts of employment. They are only seeking better terms. I can see there is something to be said for that argument. But I should have thought it plain that they would be breaking their contracts of employment. I would refer to what I said when the railwaymen worked to rule. It was in *Secretary of State for Employment v. ASLEF (No. 2)* [1972] 2 QB 455, 492. I took the case:

> "when [a man] is employed, as one of many, to work in an undertaking which needs the service of all. If he with the others, takes steps wilfully to disrupt the undertaking, to produce chaos so that it will not run as it should, then each one who is a party to those steps is guilty of a breach of his contract . . . it is the wilful disruption which is the breach. It means that the work of each man goes for naught. It is made of no effect. I ask: Is a man to be entitled to wages for his work when he, with others, is doing his best to make it useless? Surely not. Wages are to be paid for services rendered, not for producing deliberate chaos."

So I would say if the members of the N.G.A. – or some of them – take industrial action wilfully to disrupt the employers' undertaking, they are certainly in breach of their contracts. So also are those who are party to them.

I return to the decisive point. These men are seeking equity but are not ready to do it themselves. No injunction will be granted on their behalf. I would dismiss the appeal."

Cheese v. Thomas
[1994] 1 WLR 129

An elderly plaintiff gave the defendant, his great-nephew, approximately half the purchase price of a house on the understanding that he could live there until he died. When the defendant failed to pay the mortgage instalments and the house had to be sold at a considerable loss, the plaintiff sought to have the transaction set aside on the grounds of undue influence. The Court of Appeal (Nicholls VC, Butler-Sloss and Peter Gibson LJJ) ordered that the property should be sold and that both parties should bear the loss on the sale in the same proportions as they had contributed to the purchase price on the basis that the court was concerned to achieve practical justice for both parties and not for the plaintiff alone.

NICHOLLS VC stated at pp.132-138: "This is a most unfortunate case. It arises out of the all too familiar situation where different generations of a family join to provide the older member with a home. Both sides have the best of intentions, but the arrangement breaks down. Difficulties then arise in unravelling what has been done. Here, two members of a family have become involved in proceedings which ought never to have seen the door of a court. Costs have been incurred over several full-day hearings in the county court, followed by an appeal to the Court of Appeal. On top of this the house suffered a steep decline in value. It was bought in June 1990 at a cost of £83,000 and sold in 1993 at a net price of about £55,400, a loss of over £27,500. The combined result of all this has been a financial disaster for one or other, or both, of the parties.

The plaintiff, Mr. Cheese, is 88 years of age. In 1990 he was living in a flat at Peacehaven, Sussex. After the death of his brother Joe, he arranged to move back to Hayes, Middlesex, where he had lived and where his wife and daughter were buried. In May 1990 he paid £43,000 to the defendant, Mr. Aubrey Thomas, in connection with the purchase of a house, 4, Jonson Close, Hayes. Mr. Thomas is aged 36 and is Mr. Cheese's great-nephew. He owns a freight consultancy business. The house was bought in his sole name. To cover the rest of the price and the expenses, Mr. Thomas borrowed £40,000 from the Halifax Building Society on the security of a mortgage over the house. In June 1990 Mr. Cheese moved in and lived there. Mr. Thomas continued to live in his own house at Bedfont. Over the next three or four months Mr. Thomas failed to pay the mortgage instalments. Mr. Cheese found out about this, and he felt his security threatened. He decided he wanted to withdraw, and he sought repayment of his £43,000. These proceedings ensued.

The case was tried by Judge Michael Oppenheimer sitting in the Uxbridge County Court. Both counsel paid tribute to the care and thoroughness with which the judge conducted the trial. On this appeal neither party has challenged the judge's findings of primary fact. In the proceedings Mr. Cheese claimed that he and Mr. Thomas had agreed that the house should be jointly owned. The judge rejected this. He accepted the nephew's case that Mr. Cheese knew and agreed that the house would be in Mr. Thomas's name. Mr. Cheese agreed that on his death the house would belong to Mr. Thomas. In return Mr. Cheese was to be entitled to live in the house for the rest of his life. However, the judge accepted Mr. Cheese's alternative case, that the transaction should be set aside on the ground of undue influence. It was common ground that the relationship between the two of them was of a fiduciary character: they were close, Mr. Thomas was considerably younger, and he had business experience and a degree of actual influence over Mr. Cheese. Undue influence was therefore to be presumed. The judge held the transaction was manifestly disadvantageous to Mr. Cheese, who did not enter into the transaction after full, free and informed thought about it. He had insufficient advice and understanding to make a proper judgment. Against that decision Mr. Thomas has appealed.

Manifest disadvantage
The necessity for a plaintiff to prove that the transaction was manifestly disadvantageous to him before he can succeed in a claim to set it aside for undue influence finds recent expression in *National Westminster Bank Plc. v. Morgan* [1985] AC 686 and *Bank of Credit and Commerce International S.A. v. Aboody* [1990] 1 QB 923. Here, Mr. Cheese paid £43,000, and in return he had the right to live rent-free for the rest of his life in a house approved by him, and which he himself could not afford to buy, in an area where he wished to live. But there were drawbacks in the transaction so far as he was concerned.

The principal drawbacks were threefold. First, he paid over all his capital. The £43,000 represented the major part of the proceeds of his flat at Peacehaven. He had no other money of his own. Second, if in future he needed or wished to live elsewhere, there was no way he could compel Mr. Thomas to sell the house or return his money or even some of it. At the time Mr. Cheese was 85 years old. He might become less robust and need to live in sheltered accommodation. He had moved house in 1985 and in 1986, and in 1990 he had in mind that he might wish to move again and not be confined to Jonson Close for the rest of his days. Third, and importantly, Mr. Cheese would be in jeopardy if Mr. Thomas failed to keep up the mortgage payments to the building society. When the house was acquired both Mr. Thomas and his company were financially embarrassed. If Mr. Thomas defaulted, Mr. Cheese had no money of his own with which to keep up the mortgage payments. If Mr. Cheese were evicted by the building society, he would have a claim against Mr. Thomas for damages for breach of contract. But that, for what it might be worth, would be poor consolation for all the upset and worry and possible loss involved. Indeed, these proceedings were prompted by Mr. Cheese's concern when he opened a letter from the building society in October 1990 and learned that Mr. Thomas was four months in arrears with the mortgage payments. He became fearful and anxious and disillusioned.

I agree with the judge that the transaction is properly to be described as manifestly, that is, clearly and obviously, disadvantageous to Mr. Cheese. He used all his money, and it was not an insignificant amount, in buying a right which was seriously insecure and which tied him to this particular house.

I add two points. First, their Lordships in the House of Lords are currently considering their judgments on two appeals where one of the issues is whether manifest disadvantage is an essential ingredient of an undue influence claim. Having regard to the view I have reached, it is not necessary to postpone giving judgment on this appeal until the outcome in those two cases is known (Reporter's note: see now *Barclays Bank v. O'Brien* [1993] 3 WLR 786 and *C.I.B.C. Mortgages Plc. v. Pitt* [1993] 3 WLR 802). Mr. Cheese has established manifest disadvantage whether or not, as remains to be seen, this is a necessary prerequisite to success on this claim. Second, a feature of importance is that before the trial judge Mr. Thomas conceded that the presumption of undue influence applied on the facts of this case. Mr. Thomas did not seek to rebut the application of the presumption, for instance, by showing that Mr. Cheese received independent advice. So the only issue the judge was called upon to decide on this part of the claim was whether or not the transaction was clearly disadvantageous to Mr. Cheese. I mention this in fairness to Mr. Thomas. Otherwise one might think Mr. Thomas had behaved improperly, and sought to trick or take advantage of his aged uncle. No conduct of this sort occurred. This point is also relevant on the next issue.

Setting aside the transaction

If, then, the transaction is to be set aside, the next step is the restoration of the parties to their original positions. Achieving this would mean sale of the house and repayment of what each had paid over. Mr. Cheese should get back his £43,000, and Mr. Thomas should get back and repay to the building society the money he borrowed for the purchase.

The house has now been sold. Unhappily, as already mentioned, although £83,000 was spent in buying the house, only £55,400 came from the sale. By the time of the sale the amount outstanding on the mortgage was about £37,700. On the sale the building society had to be repaid first. It had a mortgage over the house. The effect of paying back the building society was, in substance, to restore Mr. Thomas to his original position, although he had paid some mortgage instalments. The net balance remaining from the sale proceeds was only £17,667. Clearly, this sum has to be paid to Mr. Cheese, but that will still leave him more than £25,000 out of pocket. The shortfall represents, in round figures, the amount by which the house declined in value after its purchase in June 1990.

The question therefore arises: on whom should this loss fall? Mr. Cheese contends he is entitled to look to Mr. Thomas personally to make good the whole of the shortfall. He paid £43,000 to Mr. Thomas, and on the transaction being set aside he can look to Mr. Thomas for repayment of a like sum. The judge did not accept this. He held that the loss brought about by the fall in the market value of the house should be shared between the two of them in the same proportions (43:40) as they had contributed to the price. He said that the parties went into a joint venture, investing approximately similar sums in it: they should bear the loss equally. In short, this would mean that Mr. Cheese could look to Mr. Thomas for a further £11,000. Mr. Cheese would then recover altogether about £28,700, leaving him £14,300 out of pocket compared with his original contribution of £43,000. For his part Mr. Thomas would be out of pocket by a similar but proportionately smaller amount. He would be out of pocket to the extent of £13,300, made up of the £11,000 he would have to pay Mr. Cheese and £2,300 he had paid to the building society, before the sale, in reduction of the principal owing on the mortgage. From that decision Mr. Cheese has appealed.

Restoring the parties to their original positions
I can summarise the thrust of Mr. Hamer's argument as follows. When the court sets aside the transaction between Mr. Cheese and Mr. Thomas, the inflexible rule of equity which comes into play is that Mr. Cheese is entitled to have restored to him the benefits he passed to Mr. Thomas under the impugned transaction. It matters not if, for reasons unconnected with Mr. Cheese, the property being returned to the defendant has declined in value: that is irrelevant.

I approach the matter in this way. Restitution has to be made, not damages paid. Damages look at the plaintiff's loss, whereas restitution is concerned with the recovery back from the defendant of what he received under the transaction. If the transaction is set aside, the plaintiff also must return what he received. Each party must hand back what he obtained under the contract. There has to be a giving back and a taking back on both sides, as Bowen L.J. observed in *Newbigging v. Adam* (1886) 34 Ch D 582, 595. If, for this purpose, the transaction in this case is analysed simply as a payment of £43,000 by Mr. Cheese to Mr. Thomas in return for the right to live in Mr. Thomas's house, there is a strong case for ordering repayment of £43,000, the benefit received by Mr. Thomas, regardless of the subsequent fall in the value of the house. In the ordinary way, if a plaintiff is able to return to the defendant the property received from him under the impugned transaction, it matters not that the property has meanwhile fallen in value. This is not surprising. A defendant cannot be heard to protest that such an outcome is unfair when he is receiving back the very thing he persuaded the plaintiff, by undue influence or misrepresentation, to buy from him.

In my view the present case stands differently. Mr. Cheese paid Mr. Thomas £43,000, not outright, but as part of the purchase price of a house in which both would have rights: Mr. Cheese was to have sole use of the house for his life, and then the house would be Mr. Thomas's. Mr. Thomas was not free to dispose of the house, or use it, until then. In fact the money was handed over by Mr. Cheese in the form of a bankers' draft, made payable to the solicitors acting for Mr. Thomas in the purchase of 4, Jonson Close. For his part Mr. Thomas also contributed to the purchase of the house. He contributed £40,000, by obtaining a building society loan of this amount. In other words, the transaction was that each would contribute a sum of money to buying a house in which each was to have an interest. This is the transaction which has to be reversed. Doing so requires, first, that the house should be sold and, second, that each party should receive back his contribution to the price. There is no difficulty over the first requirement. Mr. Cheese sought an order for sale, the judge so directed, and the sale has taken place. The second requirement is more difficult. Indeed, it cannot be achieved, because under the transaction the money each contributed was spent in buying a house which then lost one third of its value.

This difficulty, rightly in my view, has not been allowed to stand in the way of setting aside the transaction. It is well established that a court of equity grants this type of relief even when it cannot restore the parties precisely to the state they were in before the contract. The court will grant relief whenever, by directing accounts and making allowances, it can do what is practically just: see *Erlanger v. New Sombrero Phosphate Co.* (1878) 3 App Cas 1218, 1278-1279, *per* Lord Blackburn. Here justice requires that each party should be returned as near to his original position as is now possible. Each should get back a proportionate share of the net proceeds of the house, before deducting the amount paid to the building society. Thus the £55,400 should be divided between Mr. Cheese and Mr. Thomas in the proportions of 43:40. Mr. Cheese should receive about £28,700 and Mr. Thomas £26,700. To achieve this result Mr. Thomas should pay £11,033 on top of the net proceeds, of £17,667, remaining after discharging the mortgage. This was the view of the judge, and I see no occasion to disturb his conclusion. On the contrary, I agree with him. It is interesting to note that this result accords with the primary relief sought by Mr. Cheese in the action. His primary claim was that the house belonged to them both in the proportions of 43:40. Had the claim succeeded, Mr. Cheese would have borne a proportionate share of the loss on the sale of the house.

Restitution for both parties
We were much pressed with an argument that there is no decided case in which a court has ever directed a sharing of the loss in this way. This is a principle unknown to English law. The court has no discretion in this regard. I have two observations on this argument.

First, when considering what was the original position of the parties it is important to identify, and properly characterise, the transaction being set aside. In a simple case of a purchase of property there is no difficulty. Before the transaction the plaintiff had a sum of money and the defendant owned the property. By the transaction the money passed to the defendant, and the property was transferred to the plaintiff. That is the transaction which has to be reversed.

Likewise there is no difficulty with a simple case of a gift. The present case, as already noted, is not so straightforward. Here the transaction involved both parties making a financial contribution to the acquisition of a new asset from which both were intended to benefit. This was so even though Mr. Cheese's only interest in the house was as a contractual licensee, and even though Mr. Thomas regarded the house as an investment. It is axiomatic that, when reversing this transaction, the court is concerned to achieve practical justice for both parties, not the plaintiff alone. The plaintiff is seeking the assistance of a court of equity, and he who seeks equity must do equity. Under the transaction Mr. Thomas parted with money, albeit borrowed, as well as Mr. Cheese.

This situation is to be contrasted with the facts in *Newbigging v. Adam* (1886) 34 Ch D 582. There the plaintiff was induced to enter into a partnership with the defendant by misrepresentations about the state of the business. The business foundered. On having the transaction set aside, the court held the plaintiff was entitled to the return of the capital introduced by him and to an indemnity against the liabilities he had assumed as a partner. In that case the transaction was akin to a sale of property, there a share in a partnership. The defendant had to return the capital sum introduced and reassume the burden of partnership debts which under the contract the plaintiff had taken upon himself.

My second observation is this. The basic objective of the court is to restore the parties to their original positions, as nearly as may be, consequent upon cancelling a transaction which the law will not permit to stand. That is the basic objective. Achieving a practically just outcome in that regard requires the court to look at all the circumstances, while keeping the basic objective firmly in mind. In carrying out this exercise the court is, of necessity, exercising a measure of discretion in the sense that it is determining what are the requirements of practical justice in the particular case. It is important not to lose sight of the very foundation of the jurisdiction being invoked. As Lord Scarman observed in the *Morgan* case [1985] AC 686, a court in the exercise of this jurisdiction is a court of conscience. He noted, at p. 709:

> "There is no precisely defined law setting limits to the equitable jurisdiction of a court to relieve against undue influence. . . . Definition is a poor instrument when used to determine whether a transaction is or is not unconscionable: this is a question which depends upon the particular facts of the case."

As with the jurisdiction to grant relief, so with the precise form of the relief to be granted, equity as a court of conscience will look at all the circumstances and do what fairness requires. Lord Wright adverted to this in *Spence v. Crawford* [1939] 3 All ER 271, which was a misrepresentation case. He said regarding rescission and restitution, at p. 288:

> "The remedy is equitable. Its application is discretionary, and, where the remedy is applied, it must be moulded in accordance with the exigencies of the particular case."

The law reports are replete with examples of the way courts have applied this principle. These, and the reasoning underlying them, afford valuable guidance when fairly comparable situations arise in the future. They are not immutable rules of law which must be applied irrespective of whether in the particular case they will assist in achieving an outcome which is practically just. A few examples will suffice. If the defendant has improved the property he is ordered to return, the plaintiff may be required to compensate him. On the other hand, if the plaintiff has improved the property he seeks to return, he will not necessarily be entitled to a further payment from the defendant; it may not be just to require the defendant to pay for improvements he does not want. If the plaintiff has permitted the property to deteriorate, he may be required to make an allowance to the defendant for this when seeking an order compelling him to retake the property. If a joint business venture is involved, such as an agreement between a pop star and a manager, and the agreement is set aside and an account directed of the profits received by the defendant under the agreement, the court in its discretion may permit the defendant to retain some profits, if it would be inequitable for the plaintiff to take the profits without paying for the expertise and work which produced them. In *O'Sullivan v. Management Agency and Music Ltd.* [1985] QB 428, 468, Fox L.J. observed it was clearly necessary that the court should have power to make an allowance to a fiduciary. He continued:

> "Substantial injustice may result without it. A hard and fast rule that the beneficiary can demand the whole profit without an allowance for the work without which it could not have been created is unduly severe. Nor do I think that the principle is only applicable in cases where the personal conduct of the fiduciary cannot be criticised. I think that the justice of the individual case must be considered on the facts of that case. Accordingly, where there has been dishonesty or surreptitious dealing or other improper conduct then, as indicated by Lord Denning M.R., it might be appropriate to refuse relief; but that will depend upon the circumstances."

What is true of profits must also be true of losses. In the ordinary way, when a sum of money is paid to a defendant under a transaction which is set aside, the defendant will be required to repay the whole sum. There may be exceptional cases where that would be unjust. This may the more readily be so where the personal conduct of the defendant was not open to criticism. Here, having heard the parties give evidence, the judge acquitted Mr. Thomas of acting in a morally reprehensible way towards Mr. Cheese. He described Mr. Thomas as an innocent fiduciary. Here also, and I return to this feature because on any view it was an integral element of the transaction, each party applied money in buying the house. In all the circumstances, to require Mr. Thomas to shoulder the whole of the loss flowing from the problems which have beset the residential property market for the last year or two would be harsh. That is not an outcome a court of conscience should countenance.

Interest

The judge declined to order Mr. Cheese to account for an occupation rent or to order Mr. Thomas to pay interest on the sum being repaid to Mr. Cheese. There is obvious good sense in letting these matters offset each other. On appeal Mr. Cheese has taken the point that he was not in occupation after 20 May 1992. He became ill on that day, and went to stay with his son-in-law. He has continued to live there. I am not impressed with this point. The period involved is about six months, until the judge gave judgment on 4 December 1992. The house remained available for Mr. Cheese, and was not used by Mr. Thomas. The sensible, practically just outcome is not to treat this period differently from the earlier period of two years when Mr. Cheese lived in the house.

I would dismiss Mr. Cheese's appeal and Mr. Thomas's cross-appeal."

HE WHO COMES TO EQUITY MUST COME WITH CLEAN HANDS

This maxim also reflects the discretionary nature of equity and requires that a person seeking equitable relief must refrain from fraud, misrepresentation or any other form of dishonest or disreputable conduct if he wishes to be granted a remedy. However unlike the maxim just considered, it refers principally to the past conduct of the plaintiff. While it is not necessary that the inequitable conduct has directly prejudiced the defendant[3] there must be a sufficient connection between it and the subject-matter of the dispute.[4] Further examples of the operation of this maxim are considered below in Chapter 13 on Injunctions (*Curust Financial Services Ltd v. Loewe-Lack-Werk Otto Loewe Gmbh & Co. KG*[5]) and Chapter 14 on Specific Performance (*Smelter Coporation v. O'Driscoll*[6]).

Parkes v. Parkes
[1980] ILRM 137

A husband bought land and the conveyance was taken in his wife's name to obviate the need for Land Commission consent. After the parties divorced, the husband registered an inhibition on the land and the wife instituted proceedings claiming that it had been wrongly registered. The husband counter-claimed that he was entitled to the beneficial ownership in the property. It was claimed on behalf of the wife that the husband should not be able to obtain relief in

---

[3] *Parkes v. Parkes* [1980] ILRM 137.
[4] *Moody v. Cox* [1917] 2 Ch 71, 87-88 and *Argyll v. Argyll* [1967] Ch 302.
[5] [1994] 1 IR 450.
[6] [1977] IR 305.

equity 'by setting up his own illegality or fraud'. Costello J concluded that the court should not grant relief to a purchaser who has placed property in his wife's name dishonestly and by means of an illegal act performed for the purpose of evading the law relating to the transfer of land.

COSTELLO J stated at pp. 142–145: "There are, it seems to me, four general principles of law which are relevant to the facts which I have just outlined. The first is that where a person buys property and pays the purchase money but takes the purchase in the name of another, who is neither his child, adopted child or his wife, there is *prima facie* no gift, but a resulting trust in favour of the person paying the money. The second principle is that where a person in whose name a purchase is taken is the wife, child, or adopted child of the person paying the purchase money there is a presumption that a gift was intended. Thirdly, however, the presumption in favour of a wife, child or adopted child may be rebutted by evidence which establishes that a gift was not intended. The defendant relies on these principles and claims that as his intention was that no gift was to be effected the plaintiff holds the lands as trustee for him. But the plaintiff's counsel ripostes with a fourth principle which it is claimed a court applying equitable principles should apply in this case. Put shortly, it is that a purchaser will not obtain relief in equity by setting up his own illegality or fraud. This is the crucial point of law in this case, and I will now consider the cases which it is claimed illustrate and justify its application to the facts I am now considering.

The first case to which I was referred by the plaintiff's counsel was that of *Gascoigne v Gascoigne* [1918] 1 KB 223. This was a case in which a husband took a lease of land in his wife's name and built a house on it with his own money. He used his wife's name with her knowledge and connivance because he was in debt and wished to protect the property from his creditors. He brought proceedings against his wife in which he sought a declaration that she held the property as trustee for him. His claim failed. In the course of the court's judgment reference was made to the findings of fact in the lower court and then went on (p.226)—

> These findings of fact must be taken to mean that the plaintiff, with his wife's knowledge and connivance, concocted the scheme of putting his property in her name, while retaining the beneficial interest, for the purpose of misleading, defeating and delaying present or future creditors. This was the whole basis of the plaintiff's case, and it could not be put in any other way consistently with his claim to the owner of the property. It was the reason he himself gave for his conduct. Now, assuming that there was evidence to support the finding that the defendant was a party to the scheme which the plaintiff admitted, but without deciding it, what the learned Judge has done is this: he has permitted the plaintiff to rebut the presumption which the law raises by setting up his own illegality and fraud, and to obtain relief in equity because he has succeeded in proving it. The plaintiff cannot do this: and whether the point was taken or not in the County

Court this Court cannot allow judgment to stand which has given relief under such circumstances as that.

The principle in *Gascoigne* was applied in somewhat different circumstances *In re Emery's Investment Trusts* [1959] 1 Ch 410. In that case the plaintiff (who was a British subject) was married to an American citizen. American savings bonds were purchased with the plaintiff's money (the defendant's husband) and were registered in the name of the wife with the husband expressly named as a beneficiary with her. Later the bonds were changed for common stock in American securities. These were registered in the name of the wife but with the intention that the beneficial interest in the securities should be as to one half in the wife and one half in the husband. But in order to avoid the payment of American withholding tax to which as an alien the plaintiff was liable under American Federal Law, no mention was made of his beneficial interest. After the wife had sold the securities the husband applied to the Courts in England for a declaration that at the date of the removal and sale of the securities his wife held them as to one half for him. His claim failed. Wynn-Parry J pointed out that had the tax involved in the case been United Kingdom tax the case would have been covered by *Gascoigne's* case and would have been concluded against the plaintiff. Having considered the facts of *Gascoigne's* case and the decision in it he went on as follows (p.419):

> In the analysis it will be found that there were two relevant intentions in *Gascoigne v Gascoigne*. The first was the intention of the husband that the house and land should, so far as the beneficial interest was concerned, be and remain his. The second intention was that he put the land and house into his wife's name with a view to protecting it from his creditors in case he should get into financial difficulties. In this case the first intention, corresponding to that in *Gascoigne v Gascoigne*, is the intention that the husband had throughout that the beneficial interest in the security should be shared between himself and his wife. The second intention, which corresponds with the second in *Gascoigne v Gascoigne* is the intention which the husband had in putting the securities in his wife's name, without any reference being made to the retention by him of any beneficial interest, namely to avoid payment of withholding tax on his beneficial interest.

The court held that it should apply the principle in *Gascoigne's* case even though the tax involved in the transaction was an American tax. The judge pointed out that there was a clear breach of the federal law in the way the transactions were carried out by the husband's non-disclosure of his beneficial interest in the security and he concluded that the plaintiff could not seek the aid of equity in such circumstances.

More recently the principle to which I have referred was considered in the Court of Appeal in England in *Tinker v Tinker* [1970] P 136. This was a case in which a husband intended to buy a house in his own name but was advised by his solicitors that if the new business venture he was then undertaking failed the house could be taken by his creditors as part of his business assets and his solicitors recommended that it should be put in his wife's name. This was done and the house was conveyed to her. The marriage broke down and the wife claimed the house as her own. It was held that on the evidence the husband had an honest intention at the time of the conveyance that the house would belong to his wife and accordingly the wife's claim to the property succeeded. In the course of his judgment Salmon LJ, said:

> It is trite law that anyone coming to equity to be relieved against his own act must come with clean hands. If, in a case such as the present, he were to put forward, as a reason for being relieved against his own act, a dishonest plot on his part, for example, to defraud his creditors, the court would refuse him relief and must say: let the estate lie where it falls. But, of course, this is not this case . . . (p.143).

Finally, I was referred to a decision of the Court of Appeal in Northern Ireland (*McEvoy v Belfast Banking Co. Ltd* [1934] NI 67; [1935] AC 24) in which the principle in *Gascoigne's* case was applied in relation to a deposit of £10,000 made by a father in the joint names of himself and his son. It was established that the object of the deposit was to avoid death duties. Although there was no intention on the father's part to benefit his son the Court took the view that it could not have regard to the evidence which established this fact 'because of its illegal taint' (see p.99).

In my opinion the fourth principle to which I have referred and which is illustrated in the cases quoted above should be applied in this case. Just as the courts will not grant relief to a person who has allowed property to be placed in a wife's or son's name for the fraudulent purpose of defeating creditors (*Gascoigne*) or for the illegal purpose of evading liability to tax (*Emery* and *McEvoy*) so it seems to me the courts should not grant relief to a purchaser who has placed property in his wife's name dishonestly and by means of an illegal act perfomed for the purpose of evading the law relating to the transfer of land. This is what the defendant has done in this case. The defendant claimed that he acted on his solicitor's advice – but I am sure that his solicitor did not advise him to commit a criminal offence and by suggesting that the property could be taken in his wife's name he did not advise him to produce a false certificate in the deed of transfer. The defendant said that he thought the certificate was a mere formality – but he is an experienced man of affairs and no neophyte in the business of buying and selling land and he knew he was asking his wife to execute a transfer which contained a certificate which was false. I am not obliged to reach a conclusion as to whether or not Mr Parkes committed a criminal offence under the section. It suffices in this case that he knowingly authorised the commission of an act which was prohibited by the section for the purpose of evading the statute. As a result the whole transaction is tainted with illegality. Mr Parkes is in the same inescapable dilemma in which the plaintiff in *Tinker's* case found himself: if he acted honestly, and the certificate was a true one, then the property belongs to his wife; if he acted dishonestly, and certificate was a false one, the courts will not allow him to take advantage of his own dishonesty. What the defendant asks is that the court should apply its equitable principles and hold that a resulting trust exists and that the plaintiff holds the land in trust for him. But the very equitable principles which the defendant calls in aid prevent the court making a declaration in his favour. The estate must lie where it falls; the plaintiff's claim succeeds; the defendant's counterclaim fails.

In conclusion, I should add that my decision has been based on the equitable principles applicable when a husband purchases land and transfers it into his wife's name. The result would have been the same had I applied another well known principle which seems to me to be relevant to the facts of this case, *ex dolo malo non oritur actio*, and which was applied in a case where it was established that a purchaser had practised a deceit on the public administration: see *Chettiar v Chettiar* [1962] AC 294."

DELAY DEFEATS EQUITY

It is well-established that delay is a discretionary factor which may influence a court's decision to grant or withhold relief. As a general principle, equitable considerations will have no application to cases to which the Statute of Limitations 1957 applies, although they may come into play where there has been inordinate and inexcusable delay in bringing proceedings which may give rise to a breach of implied constitutional principles of basic fairness of procedures.[7] The equitable concepts of laches and acquiescence may operate to bar a claim in equity where statutory limitation periods do not apply. Laches applies where there has been unreasonable delay in bringing proceedings coupled with factors which would render it unjust to grant relief.[8] Acquiescence describes a situation where a plaintiff either expressly or impliedly represents that he does not intend to enforce a claim and, as a result of this representation, it becomes unjust in all the circumstances to grant the remedy sought. It should be noted that there has been a tendency in a number of recent English decisions to treat laches and acquiescence as a single defence.[9]

J.H. v. W.J.H.
High Court (Keane J) 20 December 1979

The plaintiff signed a document in which she agreed to compromise her rights under the Succession Act 1965 to her late husband's farm in favour of her son.

---

[7] *O Domhnaill v. Merrick* [1984] IR 151 and *Toal v. Duignan (No.2)* [1991] ILRM 140.

[8] See e.g. *J.H. v. W.J.H.* High Court (Keane J) 20 December 1979.

[9] *Nelson v. Rye* [1996] 2 All ER 186 and *Gafford v. Graham* The Times, 1 May 1998.

While Keane J accepted that the transaction was an improvident one which the courts would in the normal course of events have set aside, he refused to grant her relief in the circumstances. Keane J referred to the delay by the plaintiff for a period of four years in seeking to assert her claim and the time and money invested in the running of the farm by the defendant on the basis that she had abandoned her rights, and concluded that lapse of time coupled with circumstances which made it inequitable to enforce the claim was sufficient to bar the plaintiff's action.

KEANE J stated at pp.33–38: "In this case, the plaintiff, on her own admission, became aware of her rights under the Succession Act, within a few months of the testator's death, although she claims that she was not so aware prior to the execution of the agreement of 27th January, 1969. In November, 1973, she was not merely aware of those rights, but had gone to a solicitor, obtained independent advice and threatened proceedings. She nonetheless delayed until the 23rd November 1977 before issuing the present proceedings. She accordingly allowed a period of nearly eight years to elapse before she sought to set aside the agreement and for at least half that time she was fully aware of her rights and was being independently advised in relation to them.

In these circumstances, the defendant says that the claim is barred by laches. It is clear that section 11 of the Statute of Limitations, 1957, which fixes a period of limitation in respect of actions in contract and tort has no application, as subsection (9)(c) provides that:

> This section shall not apply to any claim for specific performance of a contract or for an injunction or for other equitable relief.

The circumstances in which laches will normally constitute a defence to a claim of this nature are thus defined in Snell's *Principles of Equity* (27th edition) at p.35:

> Laches essentially consists of a substantial lapse of time coupled with the existence of circumstances which make it inequitable to enforce a claim. Delay will accordingly be fatal to a claim for equitable relief if it is evidence of an agreement by the plaintiff to abandon or release his right, or if it has resulted in the destruction or loss of evidence by which the claim might have been rebutted, or if the claim is to a business (for the plaintiff should not be allowed to wait and see if it prospers) or if the plaintiff has so acted as to induce the defendant to the reasonable faith that the claim has been released or abandoned.

I have no doubt that the interval of time which elapsed before the proceedings were issued in the present case could properly be described as substantial. That, however, is not sufficient; it is clear from the passage cited, which is amply supported by authority, that there must also be circumstances which would render it inequitable to enforce the claim after, such a lapse of time. I must accordingly consider the circumstances in which the defendant will now find himself if the plaintiff's claim is allowed, as contrasted with the circumstances in which he would have found himself if the plaintiff had successfully prosecuted proceedings in 1973 or earlier.

If the plaintiff succeeds in her present claim, it will mean that the defendant will either have to sell the farm or raise the necessary money by way of a loan. The evidence as to the value of the farm is unsatisfactory but using one's common sense it seems not improbable that the defendant, in order to pay the plaintiff's one-third, would have to try to raise a sum well in excess of £50,000. I cannot say what the value of the farm was in 1973 or in 1969 when the agreement was signed; and while it would be admittedly somewhat ingenuous to suppose that its value then was necessarily correctly reflected by the Inland Revenue Affidavit, again using one's common sense, it is obvious that the land must have shared in the enormous increase in the value of agricultural land which has taken place within recent years. During the period which has elapsed since the agreement was signed, there has, moreover, been a steady increase in interest rates. I accept the defendant's evidence that he was unable in 1969 to raise the sum of £1,000; and it may be that he would not have succeeded in raising the necessary money to pay the plaintiff at that stage. But if the plaintiff has instituted the necessary proceedings when she first became aware some months later of her rights under the Succession Act, 1965, or, at the very least, in November, 1973, I think the probabilities are that the financial burden which would have resulted to the defendant would have been significantly less.

Even if I were wrong in that conclusion, however, there is a further fact which I feel would render it unjust and inequitable to enforce the plaintiff's claim against the defendant at this late stage. It is not in dispute that since the testator's death, the defendant has worked this farm to the best of his ability. He has, in effect, invested ten years of his life's work in it. If the plaintiff's claim succeeds, he will be faced with the alternative of either selling the farm in which he has invested those ten years of work or of incurring a very substantial financial liability indeed. In a very real sense, I think that he can be said to have altered his position in the reasonable belief that the plaintiff was not making any claim of the nature now asserted. The plaintiff, for her part, would obtain a significant financial windfall as a result of her dilatoriness in prosecuting her claim. I fully appreciate that, in unfortunate family disputes of this nature, persons are sometimes more reluctant to prosecute their claims in the form of litigation than in ordinary commercial circumstances. I also appreciate that the plaintiff was prepared to acquiesce in the situation because she thought that her son would make whatever provision was proper for her. But these circumstances, in my view, are not sufficient to outweigh the injustice and inequity which would follow from the granting of the relief to which the plaintiff claims to be entitled at so late a stage: *vigilantibus non dormientibus jura subveniunt.*

It follows that the plaintiff's claim must be dismissed."

EQUALITY IS EQUITY

In circumstances where more than one person is entitled to property, equity has traditionally favoured a principle of equal division. The most common illustration of the maxim in practice is equity's tendency to lean in favour of a tenancy in common, where the interest of each tenant devolves upon his personal representatives on his death, as a method of holding property rather than joint tenancy under which the survivor may be entitled to the entire estate.

The maxim that 'equality is equity' is generally applied to the distribution of surplus funds on the dissolution of an unincorporated association.[10] However, it has not been employed as a means of dividing up family property and the Supreme Court has held that it should not necessarily apply where an application is brought pursuant to section 117 of the Succession Act by a child claiming that a parent has failed to make proper provision for him in accordance with his means.[11]

Feeney v. MacManus
[1937] IR 23

A club, known as the General Post Office (Dublin) Dining Club, which provided subsidized refreshments to certain classes of post office officials, ceased to function following the destruction of the GPO in 1916. When the building was reopened, a new club was formed with similar objectives and membership. The plaintiffs, who were the secretary and treasurer of the original club, sought directions from the court in relation to the distribution of its remaining property. It was held by Johnston J that the entire fund must be distributed in equal shares amongst the individuals who were members of the club at the time of its dissolution and the personal representatives of those who had died since that date.

JOHNSTON J stated at pp.30–33: "Previously to April, 1916, there was in the General Post Office in Dublin a social club called "The General Post Office Dining Club." The membership consisted of certain employees and assistants in the post office and the object was the provision of "refreshment for the members at reasonable prices." The members paid a small fee for membership, and assistance and facilities were received from the Postmaster-General in the shape of the provision of furniture and equipment and an annual grant. The club was undoubtedly a solvent and a flourishing concern, and at Easter, 1916, it—or rather its members—were in possession of funds amounting to some hundreds of pounds, arising, I suppose, from accumulated subscriptions and

---

[10] *Feeney v. MacManus* [1937] IR 23.
[11] *E.B. v. S.S.* [1998] 2 ILRM 141.

profits upon the sale of food and drink. It was, I think, a wise and prudent thing in every respect for the committee and office-bearers of the club to have maintained a small reserve of this kind, and I have no doubt that it was kept in hand with the full knowledge and consent of all the members.

One of the results of the destruction of the Post Office in April, 1916, was the break-up of the club as a going concern, the destruction of the property of the members— furniture, equipment and the like—and the release of the reserve fund which the office-bearers had in their hands.

When the Compensation Committee was set up to deal with the claims for compensation in respect of property destroyed at that unfortunate period, an application was made on behalf of the club in respect of the destruction of their property, and a substantial amount was awarded by the Committee and was duly paid by the Government of the day to the two gentlemen—the plaintiffs—who had been the honorary treasurer and the honorary secretary of the club at the time of its dissolution. Mr. Feeney, the secretary of the old club, says that he gave what he calls an undertaking that any grant which was made would be used to assist the members of a new club which was about to be formed, or which had been formed, on the lines of the old club.

I am now called upon to pronounce a decision as to the ownership of these two funds—the cash reserve fund and the amount of the grant made by the British Government—in an action in which the plaintiffs are the gentlemen who were the secretary and treasurer of the club at the time of its dissolution and the defendants are gentlemen who were members of the club at that time and who represent the general membership.

When the action came before me in the first instance, it occurred to me that the Attorney-General should receive notice of the proceedings, and I adjourned the hearing of the action for the purpose of enabling that to be done. The Attorney-General now appears by his counsel, and I have the advantage of having heard what his views are.

Three suggestions have been made as to the disposal of this fund.

The first is that it goes to the State as *bona vacantia*—that is, as personal property of which no owner can be found. The question of *bona vacantia* in the case of an owner dying intestate has been put on a statutory basis in England (Administration of Estates Act, 1925, sect. 46); in the Irish Free State it is yet a matter of prerogative. In Dr. Berridale Keith's recent text-book ("The King and the Imperial Crown" (1936), at p. 389) he says: "Prior to the measure [the Act of 1925] the Crown took land by escheat and personal property as *bona vacantia*; and it takes still by that title the personal property of a dissolved corporation, such as the assets of Russian companies destroyed by the operation of Soviet law, and any other property to which no person can establish a claim." In the present case counsel for the Attorney-General disclaims entirely any interest whatever in the fund with which I am dealing and makes no claim to it on behalf of the State.

The second suggestion is that the fund, or, at any rate, that portion of it which consists of the State grant, should be handed over to the members of the new dining club which has been formed in the restored General Post Office and which is being carried on for purposes similar to those of the old club. I shall say something as to that suggestion in a moment.

The third suggestion is that the money is the property of the persons who formed the membership of the old club at the time at what I may call its dissolution, and it seems to me that this is the proposition that contains the solution of the difficulty. A club is the most anomalous group of human beings that is known to the law. It is a union of persons for social intercourse or for the promotion of certain pursuits, which are closely allied to social intercourse, and the members usually regulate their conduct in accordance with bye-laws or regulations to which they subscribe. A club has no existence apart from its members. It differs from a corporation in that respect. It differs from those statutory bodies like Friendly Societies which have a sort of pseudo-corporate existence by virtue of the statute-law which regulates their activities, and even a trading partnership, regulated by the code of 1890, has a position and an existence which is superior to those of a club. In this connection I might refer to the valuable judgment of Lord St. Leonards in the case of *In re St. James's Club* (1852) 2 De GM & G 383.

It was decided by Jessel M.R. in the case of *Brown v. Dale* (1878) 9 Ch D 78, that when, in the case of a body of persons who are associated together by the club tie and who possess property, it becomes necessary to distribute that property, the only persons who can be regarded as its owners for the purpose of such distribution are the persons forming the entire membership of the club when the necessity for distribution arises. The principle of this decision was adopted and applied by the Master of the Rolls (Mr. Charles O'Connor) in a comparatively recent Irish case—*Tierney v. Tough* [1914] 1 IR 142. In that case the learned Judge says that "the Society is a voluntary one, and has not been registered or incorporated under any Act." He rejected the suggestion that the funds could be regarded as *bona vacantia* or that anything in the nature of a charitable trust had attached to them. "The Society," he said, "though it has ceased business, is not defunct in the sense that it has no members. There are many members in existence, and they constitute the Society, to whom the unexpended fund belongs."

I must now refer to the suggestion of Mr. Lavery, who appeared for the plaintiffs, that in view of Mr. Feeney's "undertaking" the portion of the fund which consists of the *ex gratia* grant ought to go to the new club or its members. I find it entirely impossible to adopt that suggestion. I think that the members of the new club neither have nor could have any shadow of claim to the money, and it is of some importance that counsel for the Attorney-General makes no such suggestion. I have not been referred to, and I have not myself been able to discover, the statutory authority existing in 1916 or 1917 for the expenditure of public money in the making of such grants; but I must presume that it was legally and properly done. I must assume also that the claim was made by or on behalf of the members of the club as a whole, and that it was made in respect of the destruction of their property. The only place where information is to be had as to the Compensation Committee that was set up by the Government and as to the details of their work is in an exceedingly useful publication, published by the "Weekly Irish Times," entitled "Sinn Féin Rebellion Handbook," and at pages 249 and 250 the persons who were entitled to compensation are described as "sufferers," including both insured and uninsured persons. There is no evidence before me that Mr. Feeney had any authority to give an undertaking which would be binding upon the members of the club as to the disposition of the grant, nor is there any evidence that the Committee attempted to attach any condition whatever as to the disposal of the money. On the whole I am satisfied that Mr. Feeney's "undertaking" was merely an amiable gesture made under a misconception as to the legal position.

Under the circumstances the whole of this fund must be distributed amongst the persons who were the members of the club at the time of its dissolution and the legal personal representatives of those members who have died since that time. It would be an impossible task to ascertain the proportion in which each of the members had subscribed to the funds or had participated in the purchase of the furniture, and accordingly the distribution will be on an equal basis.

I shall direct an inquiry to ascertain who were the members of the club on April 26th, 1916—the date when the fire first broke out in the Post Office—and who are the personal representatives of those members who have died since, and the Examiner will have power to insert such advertisements in the Dublin newspapers as he may direct.

I do not think that the fifteenth day of December, 1916, can be accepted as the day when the club ceased to exist. A meeting of an irregular character was held on that date when, it appears, persons who were not members of the club at all were present, and no club business was transacted.

The plaintiffs, of course, will lodge in Court the whole of the funds in their hands, whether invested or not, and all the parties will be declared entitled to their costs."

E.B. v. S.S.
[1998] 2 ILRM 141

The plaintiff instituted proceedings under section 117 of the Succession Act 1965 seeking a declaration that his mother had failed in her moral duty to make proper provision for him and an order making such provision as seemed to the court to be just. The testatrix had indicated that she wished to treat all her children equally and she purported to do this by dividing shares in a company equally between her three children during her lifetime. By the time she died, the plaintiff had dissipated all the money which his shares had realised but he did not receive any further benefit under his mother's will. Lavan J concluded that the plaintiff had not established that the testatrix had failed in her moral duty to make proper provision for him and dismissed the claim under section 117. The plaintiff's appeal to the Supreme Court (Keane, Lynch and Barron JJ) was dismissed.

KEANE J (Lynch J concurring) stated at pp. 148–152:

"The applicable law
S. 117 of the 1965 Act provides *inter alia* as follows:

> (1) Where, on application by or on behalf of a child of a testator, the court is of opinion that the testator has failed in his moral duty to make proper provision for the child in accordance with his means, whether by his will or otherwise, the court may order that such provision shall be made for the child out of the estate as the court thinks just.

> (2) The court shall consider the application from the point of view of a prudent and just parent, taking into account the position of each of the children of the testator and any circumstances which the court may consider of assistance in arriving at a decision that will be as fair as possible to the child to whom the application relates and to the other children.

The policy underlying these provisions is clear. Until its enactment, it was possible for a testator to dispose entirely of his or her property without any regard to the needs of his or her spouse or children. The Oireachtas in dealing with this possible social evil chose, in the case of the children, to adopt a scheme similar to those in other common law countries which allowed a degree of flexibility to the court in determining whether provision should be made for them.

In a frequently cited passage in *In re G.M.: F.M. v. T.M.* (1972) 106 ILTR 82, Kenny J, sitting as a High Court judge, said:

> It seems to me that the existence of a moral duty to make proper provision by will for a child must be judged by the facts existing at the date of death and must depend upon:
>
> (a) the amount left to the surviving spouse or the value of the legal right if the survivor elects to take this,
> (b) the number of the testator's children, their ages and their positions in life at the date of the testator's death,
> (c) the means of the testator,
> (d) the age of the child whose case is being considered and his or her financial position and prospects in life,
> (e) whether the testator has already in his lifetime made proper provision for the child.
>
> The existence of the duty must be decided by objective considerations. The court must decide whether the duty exists and the view of the testator that he did not owe any is not decisive.

That statement of the law was approved by Finlay CJ speaking for this Court in *C.C. v. W.C.* [1990] 2 IR 149, subject to one qualification which he expressed as follows:

> I am satisfied the phrase contained in s. 117(1), 'failed in his moral duty to make proper provision for the child in accordance with his means' places a relatively high onus of proof on an applicant for relief under the section. It is not apparently sufficient from these terms in the section to establish that the provision made for a child was not as great as it might have been, or that compared with generous bequests to other children or beneficiaries in the will, it appears ungenerous. The court should not, I consider, make an order under the section merely because it would on the facts proved have formed different testamentary dispositions.
>
> A positive failure in moral duty must be established.

The circumstances of the present case are somewhat unusual. Typically in applications under s. 117, the applicant child contends that there has been a failure of moral duty in relation to him or her, having regard to the provision made either by will or during the lifetime of the testator for other members of the family. Here the plaintiff has no complaint as to the division of the shares between him and his three sisters in the *inter vivos* transaction in 1987. His claim is that, having regard to his circumstances at the date of the death of the testatrix, she should have made provision for him at the expense of the other beneficiaries, *i.e.* the charities.

It is also clear that the court in the present case was not entitled to take into account, in considering whether the testatrix had failed in her moral duty within the terms of s. 117(1), the fact that the plaintiff, since his discharge from Cluain Mhuire in 1993, had not taken alcohol or drugs. Since his recovery from his addiction for that period was subsequent to the death of the testatrix, it was not relevant to the discharge or otherwise of her moral duty to him. It could only become relevant if the court were of the view that she had failed in her moral duty and was going on to consider, under subs. (2), the extent of the provision that should be made for him.

It is also obvious that it is not necessarily an answer to an application under s. 117 that the testator has simply treated all his or her children equally. The maxim 'equality is equity' can have no application where the testator has, by dividing his estate in that manner, disregarded the special needs (arising, for example, from physical or mental disability) of one of the children to such an extent that he could be said to have failed in his moral duty to that child. At the same time, the proper and understandable anxiety of parents to avoid any friction among their children by effecting, so far as possible, an equal distribution of their property among them must also be recognised. Thus, the clearly expressed wish of the testatrix in this case to treat all her children equally, although not a decisive factor, is not entirely irrelevant.

Conclusions
Ultimately, the issue which the High Court had to resolve was reasonably straightforward. It is beyond argument that the testatrix had made adequate, and indeed generous provision, for the plaintiff during her lifetime. His father had done everything in his power to give him the best start in life possible, including financing his returning to university when he was in his thirties and providing him with a house. In addition to that, he was given by the testatrix £275,000 which, properly managed, should have afforded him a degree of financial security for the rest of his life. Towards the end of her own life, she might have concluded that, rather than give the entire of her remaining wealth to the five charities of her choice, she should make at least some provision for him in the hope that this time he would use it to good effect. The alternative was to do what she did and make no further provision for him.

As has already been pointed out, the test to be applied is not which of these alternative courses the court itself would have adopted if confronted with the situation. It is whether the decision by the testatrix to opt for the second course of leaving unaltered the bequest to the charities, of itself and without more constituted a breach of her moral duty to the plaintiff. I am satisfied that it did not.

The court, in applications of this nature, cannot disregard the fact that parents must be presumed to know their children better than anyone else. In many cases that obvious fact would be of little weight where it is established that a child has been treated in a manner which points clearly to a failure of moral duty on the part of the testator. It is of considerable significance, however, in a case such as the present, where, even on the most favourable view of the plaintiff's case, it cannot be suggested that he was treated with anything other than generosity and support by both his parents up to the time that the shares in BMB Ltd were transferred to him. Against that background, the decision of the testatrix not to make further provision for him in her will may well have been prompted, not merely by a concern that her money should go where she could be sure that it could do most good, but also by a belief that, since the provision of significant financial assistance to the plaintiff had not in the past produced the best results, it might not have been in his own interest to provide him with further funds, even through the mechanism of a trust. It is, however, sufficient to say that this was clearly a view which a responsible and concerned parent could take and that it follows inevitably that the learned High Court judge was correct in concluding that the plaintiff had failed to establish that the testatrix had failed in her moral duty to him.

In the judgment which he is about to deliver, Barron J considers the obligation, if any, on the deceased, in a case such as the present, to have regard to the plaintiff's responsibilities to his children. A person in her position might be regarded as being under a moral duty to make some provision for the children of the plaintiff. That, however, is not the issue with which the High Court or this Court is concerned: we are solely concerned with the legal obligations of the deceased. In the case of her children, the Oireachtas has transposed the moral obligation which she, in common with all parents, owed to her children into a legal duty enforceable in the terms laid down in s. 117. The social policy underlying that provision – and which was, of course, exclusively a matter for the Oireachtas – was, it is reasonable to assume, primarily directed to protecting those children, who were still of an age and situation in life where they might reasonably expect support from their parents, against the failure of parents who were unmindful of their duties in that area. However, since the legislature, no doubt for good reasons, declined to impose any age ceilings which would preclude middle aged or even elderly offspring from obtaining relief, the courts must give effect to the provision, irrespective of the age which the child has attained. But to extend in effect the extremely ample protection which the Oireachtas has thus afforded to children, even in the middle aged and elderly category, to grandchildren seems to me to bring within the scheme of the Act a category of claimants the protection of whom was not envisaged by the legislature. I am accordingly satisfied that the apparent needs of the plaintiff's children are not a factor which would justify the court in the present case in setting aside the findings of the learned High Court judge.

There is one other matter, to which I drew attention at the hearing, and to which I would like to return. In the present case, the interests of the five charities benefited by the will could have been materially affected by the outcome of the present proceedings. It is surprising that at no stage was the Attorney General given notice, as the protector of charities, of the existence of the proceedings. Charities enjoy a special position in our law because they are established for the public benefit and the Attorney General has also a special role as their guardian. If he had been given notice of these proceedings, he might well have decided that, having regard to the attitude of the executrices, it would have been adding unnecessarily to the costs for him to be joined as a party. It is, however, in my view desirable (and it may be essential) in every case, whether it arises by way of a construction summons or an application under s. 117, where the interests of charities may be materially affected, that the Attorney General be given notice of the proceedings.

I would dismiss the appeal."

EQUITY LOOKS ON THAT AS DONE WHICH OUGHT TO HAVE BEEN DONE

Where a specifically enforceable obligation exists, equity regards the parties as being in the position in which they would have been had the obligation been performed, and their legal rights and duties are assessed by reference to this position. The maxim underlies the doctrine of conversion which operates by regarding one form of property as being another where there is an obligation to convert it.[12] Another common application of this principle is that, in equity,

---

[12] See *infra* Chapter 19.

a specifically enforceable contract for a lease is treated as being equivalent to a lease and the rights and duties of the parties are regarded as being the same as if the lease had actually been executed.[13] Similarly, a specifically enforceable contract for the sale of land transfers the equitable interest to the purchaser, although only to the extent to which the purchase price is paid, and the vendor holds the legal title on a constructive trust until completion.[14]

Traditionally, it has been accepted that the maxim cannot be relied on in this context by a volunteer and equity will regard the obligation as carried out only in favour of persons who are entitled to specifically enforce the contract. However, this requirement was not insisted upon by Carroll J in *Shanahan v. Redmond* in which the maxim was applied in favour of a volunteer.

Shanahan v. Redmond
High Court (Carroll J) 21 June 1994

The deceased named his cousin as sole beneficiary of a trust, the assets of which comprised a life insurance policy. The parties fell out and the deceased attempted unsuccessfully to exercise a power of appointment over the trust funds in his own favour. Subsequently he instructed the insurance company to cancel the policy and to replace it with a similar one under which he would be the sole beneficiary. Although this direction had not been carried out when the testator died, Carroll J applied the maxim that equity looks on that as done which ought to have been done and held that the existing policy should be treated as if it were a substitute policy in which the deceased was named as sole beneficiary.

CARROLL J stated at pp.1–11: "Martin Redmond died a bachelor without issue on the 17th of August, 1993 having by his Will dated the 1st of July, 1993 appointed Michael Shanahan, the Plaintiff herein, to be Executor thereof. Probate has not yet issued due to difficulties in completing the Inland Revenue Affidavit. Mary Sluds, who was added as a Notice Party, was appointed Residuary Legatee under the Will.

During his lifetime, Martin Redmond took out an I.B.I. Lifetime Policy No. 20263104 worth £139,397.87 at the date of his death. When he took it out, he named his cousin Joseph Redmond, the First named Defendant, as sole beneficiary on his death in default of appointment of another or other beneficiaries. The trust was declared in the Supplement to the application form which provided for a class of beneficiaries comprising any spouse, children or step-children and respective issue (born before the maturity of the policy) parents, brothers and sisters and their issue (born before the maturity of the

---

[13] *Walsh v. Lonsdale* (1882) 21 Ch D 9.
[14] *Tempany v. Hynes* [1976] IR 101, 114 *per* Kenny J.

policy) and "the additional beneficiary or beneficiaries (if any) named in Clause 3 hereof".

Clause 3 provided:

"The policy of assurance hereby applied for subject to its privileges and conditions is to be granted to and all payments thereunder are to be made to the Applicant and Investment Bank of Ireland Limited of 26 Fitzwilliam Place, Dublin 2 (hereinafter together called the "Trustees" which expression where the context so admits shall include the Trustee or Trustees for the time being hereof) and the Trustees shall hold the said policy and all monies which have become payable thereunder and all assets which may from time to time represent the same and all income derived therefrom (hereinafter called the "Trust Fund") for the benefit of and in trust for all such one or more exclusive of the other or others of the Beneficiaries in such shares and for such limited or other interests and with such powers of maintenance, education and advancement and in such manner as I shall from time to time or at any time before the maturity of the policy by deed or deeds revocable or irrevocable or by will or codicil without infringing the rule against perpetuities appoint and in default of such appointment or so far as no such appointment shall extend then the Trust Fund is to be held for the absolute benefit of Joseph Redmond, Ballyredmond, Clonegal, Enniscorthy, Co. Wexford as to 100%.

PROVIDED THAT
    (a) If any of the Beneficiaries named in this Clause shall die before the maturity of the policy, then his or her share in default of and subject to any appointment as aforesaid shall accrue to and enlarge the share or shares of the other or others of them and if more than one in proportions determined by the formula $A/B \times 100$ where A is the share of a surviving Beneficiary and B is the sum of the shares of each surviving Beneficiary but if the Beneficiary or (if more than one) all of the Beneficiaries named in this Clause shall die before the maturity of the policy then in default of and subject to any appointment as aforesaid the Trust Fund shall be held in trust for the benefit of myself absolutely.
    (b) I may at any time or from time to time before the maturity of the policy direct the Trustees in writing to surrender the policy or any part or parts thereof for cash (subject to the terms of the policy) and the Trustees shall pay the net proceeds of any such surrender or surrenders to myself for my own use and benefit and free from the trust powers and provisions contained in this Supplement."

Martin Redmond had a falling out with Joseph Redmond. He made contact with Mr. Joe Murphy, Manager of the Investment Division of the Investment Bank of Ireland Limited ("I.B.I."), the Third Defendant. Mr. Murphy wrote to Lifetime Assurance Company Limited ("Lifetime Assurance"), the Second Defendant, on the 26th of March, 1990 stating:

"The above policy document is written under Supplementary Trust whereby the beneficiary for 100% to the fund is Mr. Joseph Redmond.

Mr. Martin Redmond, the life assured, has requested that Joseph Redmond be deleted as beneficiary from this investment.

For the moment Martin has not decided who to replace Joseph with and has decided instead that he himself will be the 100% beneficiary until he makes up his mind.

In the circumstances I enclose herewith a Deed of Appointment to beneficiaries for a single life trust duly signed which I trust is now in order and I look forward to confirmation that this deletion has taken place."

The Deed of Appointment is dated the 16th of March, 1990. It recites the power of appointment in Clause 3. It further states that the settlor is desirous of revoking every previous appointment (if any) relating to the Trust Fund and of appointing the Trust Fund in manner thereinafter appearing.

The operative part of the deed provides:

"The settlor in exercise of the power conferred on him by the declaration of trust and of every other power enabling him in this behalf HEREBY REVOKES and makes void all the trust and interests appointed by every previous Deed of Appointment in relation to all or any part or parts of the Trust Fund and in lieu thereof and in exercise of the power conferred on him by the declaration of trust and of every other power enabling him in this behalf HEREBY APPOINTS that the Trust Fund shall be held by the Trustee or Trustees for the time being of the declaration of trust for the absolute benefit of Martin Redmond as to 100%."

Around this time Lifetime Assurance were in correspondence with the Revenue Commissioners.

In a letter dated the 27th of March, 1990 from Thomas Boland, Assistant Principal in the Capital Branch of the office of the Revenue Commissioners to Lifetime Assurance, Mr. Boland refers to an earlier letter and discussions concerning difficulties encountered with regard to trust forms and policies of assurance in that the trust form previously used excluded the Applicant from the list of beneficiaries and that the problem could only be rectified by setting up a new policy to replace the old one. He confirmed that stamp duty paid in respect of an earlier inadequate policy could be used as a credit against the duty payable when a replacement was executed. In a handwritten addition (probably by Sheila Dawson of Lifetime Assurance) at the bottom of the letter there is a note dated 2nd May, 1990 about confirmation that stamp duty included all duties payable. There is a further note at the bottom of that letter in the following terms:

"Phoned J. Murphy 2/5/1990. Advised we must have written confirmation for client to CFI old policy with trust and reset up without trust. He will call to Mr. Redmond to collection (SIC.) confirmation."

I am told that C.F.I. means "cancelled from inception".

Mr. Joe Murphy wrote on the 15th of May, 1990 to Sheila Dawson of Lifetime Assurance as follows:

"I refer to our recent telephone conversation in relation to my letter of the 26th of March, 1990.

To refresh your memory, Martin Redmond appointed his nephew Joseph Redmond as a 100% beneficiary. He has now had an argument with Joseph and he wants to delete him from this policy.

He has not made up his mind who he wants to replace Joseph with and for the moment, he requested that he himself be appointed as the beneficiary.

I understand from you that there were technical problems in the formation of the original trust documentation form and on your instruction, I called down to Martin again and got him to sign the enclosed letters.

I have got him to sign both letters and I trust you will use whichever letter is appropriate.

The main underlying point to understand is that Martin Redmond wants his nephew replaced, and does not want to incur any costs whatsoever in the event that we have to cash in the fund and replace it with a new policy. Please ensure that the new policy and all correspondence is directed initially to me here and after the policy document has been issued, all future correspondence c/o Bank of Ireland, Bunclody."

Endorsed on that letter in handwriting is a note (presumably by Sheila Dawson) as follows:

"Phoned R. Buckley 24/6/90 and he advised that it was in order to CFI old plan and reset up with no trust. No implications at a later date."

At the top of the letter there is a handwritten note "requested policy document from Joe Murphy".

The two letters from Martin Redmond addressed to the Secretary, Lifetime Assurance Company Limited referred to in Mr. Murphy's letter are both dated the 2nd of May, 1990 and read as follows:

"I wish to formally request that the above policy no. is to be replaced by a similar policy no., this time not written in trust for the moment. I understand from both you and the Investment Bank of Ireland that my original instructions to have my nephew, Joseph Redmond deleted as a beneficiary on the original policy cannot be done and I therefore request that the original policy be replaced by this new one."

The other letter read:

"I now request you to replace the above policy with a similar policy, this time not written in trust. Please note, it will be my intention to form a supplementary trust on this investment and I will let you have the details in due course."

Martin Redmond also instituted proceedings in the Circuit Court on the 16th of December, 1992 to set aside a deed of transfer dated the 18th of August, 1989 between himself and Joseph Redmond whereby approximately 61 acres was transferred for voluntary consideration to Joseph Redmond. These proceedings are still in being.

In practically identical Affidavits sworn respectively on behalf of Lifetime Assurance and I.B.I. by the Company Secretary and an associate Director, the Deponents say that they have obtained legal advice to the effect that the documentation completed by the deceased, Martin Redmond, is incomplete and that in those circumstances it is inappropriate to release the funds standing to the credit of the policy pending an Order of the Court. They each referred to the supplement to the application form, the Deed of Appointment and the two letters from Martin Redmond dated the 2nd of May, 1990. They then baldly state that there was no further correspondence between Martin Redmond and the I.B.I. on the one hand and between Martin Redmond and Lifetime Assurance on the other. There is no Affidavit from Joe Murphy on behalf of I.B.I. or from Sheila Dawson on behalf of Lifetime Assurance to explain why nothing happened following the instructions from Martin Redmond in May, 1990 or even to explain why they are unable to give evidence. It is further averred on behalf of both these Defendants that Martin Redmond did not comply with the strict wording of the policy and the proviso to Clause 3 concerning the surrender of the policy, but nowhere is it specified in what way he failed to comply.

When an express trust has been completely constituted, generally speaking it is irrevocable, whether it was for valuable consideration or not, unless a power of revocation has been expressly reserved. If such a power has been reserved it must be exercised in the manner provided in order to effect a valid revocation.

In this case the trust was completely constituted. There was a power of revocation implied in the power of appointment to a class of beneficiaries which could defeat the interest given to Joseph Redmond. His interest is expressed to exist "in default of such appointment or so far as such appointment shall not extend." Martin Redmond attempted to exercise the power of appointment in his own favour but this was ineffective because he did not belong to the class of beneficiaries who were the object of the power. In my opinion, in the absence of a valid appointment, the words of the trust must be given effect and therefore the trust in favour of Joseph Redmond remained. The power of revocation was not independent of the power of appointment, as was submitted on behalf of Mary Sluds.

I have no doubt as to what the intention of the deceased was. It was to remove Joseph Redmond as the named beneficiary and to get the benefit of the policy back in his own name. His first attempt to achieve this by the Deed of Appointment having failed, he gave the clearest instructions to Lifetime Assurance via the I.B.I. to cancel the policy and replace it with a similar one under which he would be the beneficiary. These instructions were never carried out. That he did not change his attitude to Joseph Redmond is evidenced by the fact that he instituted proceedings to get his lands back on the 16th of December, 1992.

There was a clause in the application form containing the declaration of trust which provided that the Applicant (i.e., Martin Redmond) could at any time or from time to time before the maturity of the policy direct the Trustees in writing to surrender the policy for cash. The policy itself provides that the policy could be surrendered at any time upon written notice being received by the Company (i.e., Lifetime Assurance) for cash.

Martin Redmond gave clear written instructions forwarded by I.B.I. who were co-Trustees with himself, to cancel the policy and issue another.

As I said before, while I.B.I. and Lifetime Assurance averred that the documentation completed by Martin Redmond was incomplete and that he did not comply with the strict wording of the policy and the proviso to Clause 3 concerning surrender, they did not specify how. According to the evidence before me, all that the declaration of trust and the policy required was that written notice be given and received and this was done.

While both the declaration of trust and the policy say the surrender should be for cash, that does not, in my opinion, make any significant difference. Martin Redmond was asking for the equivalent of cash i.e., another policy. In the absence of any further correspondence he could not have known or been under any apprehension that his directions had not been carried out.

In my opinion his estate is entitled to the application of the equitable principle "Equity looks on that as done which ought to have been done". The contractual obligation on Lifetime Assurance under the policy following the written notice, ought to be treated as if it had been performed.

The existing policy therefore must be treated as if it were a substitute policy in which Martin Redmond was named as the sole beneficiary.

The answer to the questions in the Summons are:

A. (i) Yes.
   (ii) No.
   (iii) Yes.
   (iv) Yes.
   (v) This was not argued.
   (vi) This was not argued.
   (vii) No.
   (viii) This was not argued".

EQUITY ACTS IN PERSONAM

Traditionally, it was one of the most fundamental principles of equity that equitable jurisdiction was exercised against the person of the defendant rather than against his property. The maxim has relevance to disputes relating to property outside the jurisdiction and it is immaterial that the property in question is not within a court's jurisdiction provided that the defendant himself is within its jurisdiction or can be served outside the jurisdiction.[15]

---

[15] *Penn v. Lord Baltimore* (1750) 1 Ves Sen 444.

Lett v. Lett
[1906] 1 IR 618

An injunction was sought by the plaintiff to restrain proceedings taken in an Argentine court which amounted to a repudiation of a settlement of divorce proceedings by virtue of which his wife, the defendant, had undertaken not to pursue any further claim against him. The Irish Court of Appeal (Sir Samuel Walker C and Fitzgibbon LJ, Holmes LJ dissenting) granted the injunction sought.

SIR SAMUEL WALKER C stated at pp.632–635: "In this case the Master of the Rolls has granted an injunction restraining the defendant, who is the wife of the plaintiff, from instituting or continuing any proceedings in the Court of the Argentine Republic, or elsewhere, against the plaintiff, or his property, for the purposes of claiming alimony, or separation of goods, or any payment, from the plaintiff, or out of his property, for her support, maintenance, debts, or otherwise.

The plaintiff and defendant were married on the 3rd April, 1874, in the Anglican Church, Buenos Aires, in the Argentine Republic. The plaintiff had an Irish domicile. They lived at Buenos Aires for some time, and the plaintiff had a school there. He appears to have formed an adulterous intercourse with a woman in his service, and in 1888 they were both in Ireland. He had become the owner of a farm and residence called Woodville, in Wexford. The adultery naturally led to unpleasantness, and on the 22nd September, 1888, the defendant presented a petition in the Irish Court for divorce *a mensa et thoro* on account of his adultery, which he answered. The Irish domicile of each was admitted in that suit, and a decree was pronounced in it by Judge Warren on the 17th December, 1888. In such a suit alimony *pendente lite,* and permanent alimony, subsequent to the decree are, of course, obtainable, and the obtaining of them was part of the object of that suit.

According to the Argentine law a woman becomes entitled to certain rights in her husband's property in the nature of a partnership, and it appears that all property acquired by them during the marriage belongs to both – everything except legacies or inheritances. The partnership is called "Sociedad conjugale." This is the statement given by the plaintiff, and is the only evidence given here of Argentine law. The husband is the administrator of it, and managing partner, and that partnership remains until it is dissolved by the decree of a competent Court on divorce, or by death; and on a divorce the wife can claim a separation of goods.

There was a petition for alimony *pendente lite,* in which the defendant set forth, according to her estimate, all the property to which her husband was entitled, both in Ireland and the Argentine Republic, and she included Woodville, and an estate or cattle-run in the Argentine Republic, and other property. The husband filed his answer on the 22nd November, 1888, in which he dealt with the various items in the petition; and as regards the Argentine property, alleged it had been realized, and that all from this source was represented by a sum of £2,000 in cash. No alimony was in fact awarded. The suit came on for hearing; the adultery was admitted, and a decree was made for divorce on the 17th December, 1888, and on the same day a consent was entered into and made a rule of Court to settle the suit, and all relief under it, and all claims for alimony, whether *pendente lite* or permanent.

This consent provided that the plaintiff should pay her a sum of £480 net, and should also pay her solicitor's costs, and execute a deed assigning to her the premises of Woodville, and furniture and chattels therein, and that she should execute a deed releasing him from all claims in respect of relief in the suit and costs, and alimony, *pendente lite* and permanent, and all debts to be incurred by her, and all claims whatsoever, by or on account of the said Charlotte Lett, and indemnifying the said Richard Lett against the same. Two deeds were accordingly executed, each bearing date the 3rd January, 1889, by one of which he assigned to her the premises of Woodville, and the furniture and chattels therein. The lands have since had a judicial rent fixed in respect of them, and it appears to be a valuable interest, and the moneys stipulated for were paid; and, by the other deed of the same date, she released the plaintiff from all claims for alimony, *pendente lite* and permanent, in the terms of the consent, " and from all claims whatsoever by or on account of the said Charlotte Lett against the said Richard Lett, or his estate or property, real or personal, movable or immovable, now in possession, or hereafter to be acquired by him, and from all rights and interests, claims, and demands which the said Charlotte Lett has, or may have, in, to, or upon the same, or any part thereof."

Such were the contracts contained in the consent and deeds. Was she competent to enter into them? I consider it to be settled law that a married woman suing her husband in the Matrimonial Court is at arm's length: and, in the absence of fraud, free to enter into a contract with him for the settlement of the litigation. *Besant v. Wood* (1878) 12 Ch D 605 is one of many cases establishing this. The compromise of litigation would itself furnish an ample consideration; but she also obtained the assignment of Woodville and furniture, of which she went into possession.

Next, what is the construction of the contract? Was she left free to assert a claim in the Argentine Republic against the property he might acquire there, seeking a division of property under the Argentine law? This is a question of construction, for I do not think it is open to serious argument that she could not bind herself not to enforce a claim in any Court – domestic or foreign – or a claim of any nature, whether under Argentine law or English law, against his property, whether it be in the nature of alimony, or of any other kind: and the claim for division of property is of the character of alimony, which she had specifically contracted not to claim. In 1895 she went over to Buenos Aries, and preferred a claim on account of her poverty, by reason of which he agreed by deed to give her an allowance of £100 per annum in addition to what she got under the deed of 1889. As this deed of 1895 is not relied on in the pleadings, or at the bar, I do not rest anything upon it.

Well, in 1903, she commenced proceedings in the Argentine Court, in which she claimed a divorce (though it had been already granted), and it is stated the divorce in that republic can only have the same efficacy as a divorce in Ireland, and as consequential to this divorce she claimed a separation of goods – in other words, claimed to be maintained out of the property he had acquired in the Republic, subsequent to the divorce and deeds in Ireland. He has defended that suit, and relies upon the contracts and transactions and deeds of 1889 as a defence, and also on the deed of 1895; and these proceedings are still pending, and the Argentine Court is, I assume, competent to pronounce on them.

It is not disputed that in the interval since the Irish proceedings he had acquired very considerable property, and was comparatively a wealthy man, and, therefore, she was interested in trying to get out of her contract of 1889, and get further maintenance; but whether she can do so or not depends, I think, on the contract she made. It is not suggested that it was obtained by, or can be avoided for, fraud, and the suggestion in the defence that it could be reformed was not argued.

Does it make any difference that the proceeding sought to be restrained is a proceeding in a foreign Court? I think not, because the equity against her is founded not upon the tribunal to which she has resorted, but upon the personal contract binding her conscience. The jurisdiction asserted is not against the foreign tribunal, but against the person within the jurisdiction, who has made a contract not to resort to proceedings; and whether such proceedings are in a foreign Court or not, is immaterial for the purposes of the equity on which the jurisdiction rests – an equity *in personam*.

The rule is clearly laid down in *The Carron Iron Co. Case* (1855) 6 HLC 416, and numerous other cases. I was for a time inclined to think that ascertainment of the Argentine law as to this division of property, and its limitations, and the circumstances under which it would arise, was material to the relief, and should be before the Court before we interfered; but, on further consideration, I do not think this is so. It is a claim against the husband's property covered by her contract; and if that be so, she is bound not to put it forward in any Court – just as she would be restrained according to the decision in *Gandy v. Gandy* (1882) 7 PD 168 from prosecuting a claim for further alimony in the Irish Court. The plaintiff has, no doubt, allowed three years to go by before instituting this suit on the 3rd March, 1906. He never could get an interlocutory injunction; but if he has the right under the covenant, the delay does not deprive him of the only remedy he has for its assertion.

I am of opinion that the decision of the Master of the Rolls should be affirmed, and the appeal dismissed; but having regard to the delay which has taken place, and the time he allowed the Argentine proceedings to continue before he resorted to his rights under the contract of 1889, and also to the relations between the parties, I think there should be no costs awarded against the defendant in the Court below or here."

WHERE THE EQUITIES ARE EQUAL, THE FIRST IN TIME PREVAILS, WHERE THE EQUITIES ARE EQUAL, THE LAW PREVAILS

These two related maxims are relevant to the question of priorities as between competing interests in land. However, they cannot be looked at in isolation; it is necessary to examine the distinction between equitable interests as opposed to mere equities and the effect of the doctrine of notice on the operation of the maxims. Finally, it is also necessary to consider the impact which registration has had on the question of priorities between competing interests in land.

Equitable Interests and Mere Equities

Equitable interests can be categorised as actual rights in property and include interests arising under a trust, equitable mortgages, equities of redemption, restrictive covenants and contracts to convey or create a legal estate in land. On the other hand, mere equities are better described as rights of a procedural nature which are ancillary to a property right and include e.g. the right to have a transaction set aside for fraud or undue influence or a right to have a document rectified for mistake. The most practical significance of the distinction between mere equities and equitable estates can be seen where a question of priorities arises. As the maxim makes clear, where the equities are equal, the first in time prevails, but where one equity is superior to another, the time of their creation cannot govern priority.

While a *bona fide* purchaser of a legal estate for value and without notice of an earlier equitable interest may take the property free of that interest, a *bona fide* purchaser of an equitable interest without notice of an earlier equitable interest will take subject to it on the basis of the maxim that where the equities are equal the first in time prevails. However, while such a purchaser does not take free of prior equitable interests, he will take free of any prior mere equities on the basis that the 'equities' are not equal.[16]

---

[16] See *Allied Irish Banks Ltd v. Glynn* [1973] IR 188.

Allied Irish Banks Ltd v. Glynn
[1973] IR 188

The first named defendant conveyed land to his son, the second named defendant, subject to the former's right to remain in residence in a house on the lands. The son deposited the land certificate with the plaintiff bank as security for monies advanced to him by the bank. As a result of proceedings brought by the father, the conveyance was set aside on the grounds of undue influence. The plaintiff bank which was not aware of these proceedings, then brought a claim to enforce the equitable mortgage. Kenny J held in giving priority to the bank that the equitable mortgage took precedence over the prior right of the father to have the deed set aside which was described as a chose in action rather than an equitable interest.

KENNY J stated at pp.190–194: "On the 3rd November, 1960, the first defendant was registered as full owner of the lands comprised in Folio 33488 of the register of freeholders for County Roscommon. On the 9th April, 1963, he transferred the lands to his son Michael, the second defendant, subject to his right to reside in the dwellinghouse on the lands and to be suitably supported and maintained there; but there was no covenant in connection with this. On the 17th June, 1963, the second defendant was registered as full owner and the right of the first defendant to reside in the dwellinghouse and to be supported and maintained was entered as a burden on the folio.

In October, 1964, the second defendant applied to the plaintiffs for an advance to be secured by a deposit of the land certificate relating to the folio. The land certificate was issued by the Land Registry to the second defendant's solicitor on the 19th November, 1964. On the 5th December, 1964, the second defendant deposited the land certificate with the plaintiffs as security for advances to be made to him; he now owes £893 for principal to the plaintiffs.

In June, 1967, the first defendant issued a civil bill in the Circuit Court against the second defendant claiming to have the deed of transfer of the 9th April, 1963, set aside because when the first defendant signed it he was entirely under the influence of the second defendant and had no independent advice, and because it was obtained by fraud and undue influence. The order made by the Circuit Court on the 6th March, 1968, recited that the second defendant's solicitor had entered an appearance and defence in that action but that he had not received any instructions for the hearing; and the order declared that the transfer deed was void, that the second defendant was to hand it up to the first defendant for the purpose of being cancelled (though it is not easy to understand how he could do this when it had been lodged in the Land Registry) and "that the land registry [*sic*] be rectified by deletion of the registration of the defendant as full owner on the said Folio 33488 of the Register of County Roscommon and the entry of the plaintiff as full owner thereof on the said Register." No enquiry seems to have been made by the Circuit Court about the custody of the land certificate although the folio showed that it had been issued, and the plaintiffs in this action had no notice of the proceedings in the Circuit Court and did not know anything about them until the Land Registry requested them to lodge the land certificate so that the first defendant could be registered as owner. The plaintiffs refused to do this but, despite this, the first defendant was registered as full owner on the 3rd July, 1968, and the burden in his favour was deleted. I think that a court should not order that a folio in the Land Registry should be rectified by deleting the name of one person as full owner and substituting someone else without requiring the land certificate to be produced when the folio shows that it has been issued. Such an order offends against elementary principle.

The plaintiffs have now sued the defendants for a declaration that they are entitled to a charge on the lands arising out of the deposit of the land certificate with them, and for a sale of the lands. At the time when the deposit was made, the Registration of Title (Ireland) Act, 1891, was in force and s. 81, sub-s. 5, of that Act provided that, subject to any registered rights, the deposit of a land certificate or certificate of charge should, for the purpose of creating a lien on the land or charge to which the certificate related, have the same effect as the deposit of the title deeds of land or of a charge thereon had theretofore: see now s. 105 of the Registration of Title Act, 1964.

The deposit, as security, of documents of title to land which is not registered gives the person with whom it is made an equitable estate in the lands until the money secured by it is repaid: the remedy for securing payment is to apply to the court for a declaration that the deposit has given a charge on the lands. The right created by the deposit is not limited to keeping the deeds until the money has been paid but gives an equitable estate in the lands. The plaintiffs' contention is that they took the deposit without notice of the first defendant's claim and that, although they got an equitable interest only, it ranks before the first defendant's equity. The terms "equity" and "equitable estate" and "equitable interest" have been used in different senses in Acts of Parliament, in decided cases and in text books; the difference between them is not capable of complete definition. The main difference is, I think, that " an equity" does not create or give any estate in the land: it is a right against persons and is enforceable against those who were parties to the transaction which created it.

In *National Provincial Bank Ltd. v. Ainsworth* [1966] AC 1175 Lord Upjohn emphasised that "an equity" does not create an estate or right in land. At pp. 1237-8 of the report he said: "So in principle, in my opinion, to create a right over the land of another that right must in contemplation of law be such that it creates a legal or equitable estate or interest in that land and notice of some-thing though relating to land which falls short of an estate or interest is insuf-ficient. There are no doubt many cases where judges have said the purchaser 'takes subject to all equities' but they meant 'equitable interests' . . . An equity to which a subsequent purchaser is subject must create an interest in the land."

When Parliament provided in s. 29, sub-s. 3, of the Act of 1891 that registration of a person as owner could be made subject to any rights or equities arising from the interest vested in him being deemed to be a graft upon his previous interest in the land, it meant that estates or interests existing at the time of registration were enforceable against the registered owner. The rights saved by the note as to equities in the Act of 1891 were equitable estates or interests and not equities. Parliament, like judges, sometimes uses imprecise language.

But what was the first defendant's interest in the lands when the deposit with the plaintiffs was made? It cannot be classified accurately as having been "an equity" only for, if the deed was procured by fraud or undue influence, the first defendant would acquire an estate in the lands when he succeeded in setting it aside. What he had was a *chose in action* which could become an estate if he brought proceedings and if they were successful. Lord Upjohn was dealing with the equity of a deserted wife to retain possession against a mortgagee from her husband who gave the security after he had left her: her claim could never become an estate and so the passage I have quoted does not assist the plaintiffs.

The plaintiffs' main argument is that they took the deposit in good faith without notice of the first defendant's claim and so have a valid security against both defendants; in my view that submission is correct. They had no notice of the facts giving rise to the claim to set the deed aside and there is persuasive authority that a purchaser or mortgagee of an equitable interest who takes in good faith without notice of a claim or the facts giving rise to it is not bound by it. Lord Westbury said in *Phillips v. Phillips* (1861) 4 De GF & J 208 that this was the law and Mr. Justice Fry expressed the same view in *Bainbrigge v. Browne* (1881) 18 Ch D 188.

The land certificate deposited with the plaintiffs showed them that the deed of 1963 was a transfer between father and son because of the similarity of the surnames and the addresses, and the burden entered was appropriate for such a transaction. But knowledge that the transfer was between father and son was not notice that it had been procured by fraud or undue influence and there was nothing to suggest that it would be set aside subsequently.

The plaintiffs argued that, if their main contention failed, they were entitled to a charge on the lands against the first defendant, the registered owner, because their interest, though later in time, was superior in equity to his and so should be preferred. Mr. Matheson relied on the much-discussed decision of the Irish Court of Appeal (*In re Ffrench's Estate* (1887) 21 LR Ir 288) to support this but, as the plaintiffs succeed on their main contention, it is not necessary to deal with this difficult and controversial problem on which the Irish Court of Appeal have expressed one view and the House of Lords another.

The next issue is whether the plaintiffs' interest is subject to any claim of the first defendant to reside on the lands and to be supported and maintained there. When the plaintiffs took the deposit of the land certificate, they got notice that these rights existed. If the first defendant had not brought the proceedings in the Circuit Court, his rights under the deed of 1963 would rank before those of the plaintiffs. The plaintiffs submitted that the first defendant cannot approbate and reprobate and that, as he brought successful proceedings to have the deed of 1963 set aside, he cannot now invoke the rights which it created. As the deed has been declared void, the rights which it created do not now exist. They have been deleted from the folio and the first defendant cannot revive them as an answer to the plaintiffs' claim. This has the unintended consequence that the plaintiffs' security has been improved in value by what the first defendant did but this is the result of his action, not of theirs.

Therefore, there will be a declaration that the sum secured by the equitable mortgage by deposit of the land certificate relating to the lands comprised in the folio is well charged on the interest of the first and second defendants in the lands."

There has been some dispute about the status of a beneficiary's equitable right to trace trust property into the hands of third parties and specifically as to whether it can be categorised as an equitable interest or as a mere equity. The position in England is that such a right is recognised as an equitable interest[17] although a different conclusion was reached by the Irish Court of Appeal in *Re Ffrench's Estate*.[18] Porter MR was the only member of the Irish Court of Appeal who decided the case on the basis that a right to trace was a mere equity, and while this view has been applied in several decisions in this jurisdiction,[19] it has nevertheless been the subject of academic criticism.[20]

Re Ffrench's Estate
(1887) 21 LR Ir 283

Trust funds were mixed by an equitable tenant for life with his own funds and used to buy property. A question of priorities arose between the right of beneficiaries to trace the trust funds and a bank in whose favour an equitable mortgage had been created, which had no knowledge of the fact that the trust funds had been converted. It was held by the Irish Court of Appeal (Porter MR, Fitzgibbon and Barry LLJ) that the rights of the equitable mortgagee must prevail over the rights of the beneficiaries.

PORTER MR stated at pp.304–315: "Now, assuming for the present that there is sufficient evidence of the fact that the trust funds of 1825 were used

---

[17] *Cave v. Cave* (1880) 15 Ch D 639.

[18] (1887) 21 LR Ir 283.

[19] *Scott v. Scott* [1924] 1 IR 141.

[20] Wylie in *Irish Land Law* (3rd ed., 1997) pp.129-130 has questioned its soundness on the basis that it seems to involve an 'unjustifiable limitation' of the beneficiaries' interests.

by Martin Ffrench in part payment of the purchase-money of Ballinamore, how are the priorities. At first Mr. Cheevers boldly claimed priority over the £15,000 mortgage of 1856, and indeed on the schedule as ruled before it came under the notice of the learned Judge it was so placed; but, that is given up. Of course, in the absence of notice, the legal estate shields a purchaser for value, and the attempt to prove constructive notice through the person of Mr. Blaquiere wholly failed. But as against the second mortgage, being the first vested in Tyrrell's representative, it is said the case of *Cave v. Cave* (1880) 15 Ch D 639 really decides the question. That case was as follows: [His Lordship stated the facts.] Lord Justice Fry, after discussing, in the first instance, the question of imputation of notice through the action of a common solicitor who was implicated in the fraud of the whole transaction, goes on to say: [His Lordship read from the judgment of Fry J., beginning at "The next question," p. 646, down to "*qui prior est tempore potior est jure*," p.648.] Kindersley V.C., in *Rice v. Rice* (1853) 2 Drew 73, there referred to, decided against the priority of the vendor's lien, on the ground of his having given a receipt for the purchase-money. Mr. Justice Fry thus concludes his judgment:

> "In my judgment the right of the vendor for the unpaid purchase-money is an equitable lien, and the right of the *cestuis que trustent*, whose money has been invested in the lands, is also an equitable lien. I do not think I can really distinguish this equity from such an equitable lien as the Vice-Chancellor held to be in that case an equitable estate or interest of the same description as the equity of an equitable mortgagee. Therefore I shall conclude that, within the case of *Phillips v. Phillips* (1861) 1 De GF & J 208, the interest of the plaintiff in this case is an equitable interest, and not merely an equity like the equity to set aside a deed, and therefore it must take its priority according to the priority of date."

In many of its leading features the case is strikingly like the present; and, in my opinion, Mr. Justice Monroe was bound to follow it, so far as it applied to the present case, leaving it to this Court or to the House of Lords to overrule it, if wrongly decided or (as he suggests) to the Legislature to alter the law, if not. There are points of distinction, however; but before noticing them, I think it may be taken as clear law that the Irish Registry Acts have no direct bearing upon this case. The right of the *cestuis que trustent*, under the settlement of 1825, to follow their funds into the lands of Ballinamore was a right incapable of registration; because the Statute of Anne only applies where there is an instrument in writing to be registered. Where there is none, and where, consequently, there can be no conflict between different deeds, the law is unaffected by the statute. Thus it is not easy to see how there can be any real difference in the rule applicable to this case in Ireland from that which would be applied in England, save to this extent, that the fact of registering a conveyance here is evidence of having taken an additional precaution, and in so far helps to negative any idea of laches.

In re Burke's Estate (1882) 9 LR Ir 24 has an important bearing on this branch of the case. There the Lord Chancellor emphatically condemned the idea that as between a title incapable of registration and a registered deed there is any superior equity arising from the fact of the registration of the latter, though Judge Flanagan had held that such superiority of equity existed. The passage I refer to is at page 35:

> "The case, indeed, was not argued here on the ground taken by the learned Judge as the basis of his judgmeat. The respondent's counsel were wholly silent as to the supposed 'superior equity' of a purchaser under a registered conveyance over one taking by a title incapable of registration, and contended that this decision should be affirmed on the ground that the case was within the Registry Acts, though the Judge held the contrary."

It is more important to observe, however, in reference to the present case, that *Burke's Estate* (1882) 9 LR Ir 24 was the case of an equitable mortgage by deposit of deeds, unaccompanied by writing, as to which Sir Edward Sullivan says (page 42):

> The law allows of the security, and there is no means of placing it on the registry: the provisions of the Act do not reach the case, and we here cannot make them do so. It is too much, however, in my view, to suggest, as has been done, that a deposit of deeds is entirely a secret dispositon. Deeds are, at all events, a strong symbol of ownership; and if a person subsequently dealing with an owner without deeds, makes no inquiry after them and utterly neglects to ascertain how they are circumstanced, he must only take the consequences."

As to the supposed registration equity, he says, agreeing with the Lord Chancellor:

> "Now, Judge Flanagan, in the case before us, held that Judge Lynch's ultimate view was wrong; and notwithstanding the decision in *Re M'Kinny's Estate* (1872) IR 6 Eq 445, he came to the conclusion that the Registry Act did not affect a title acquired by simple deposit; and in that I think he was entirely right. But he then went on to decide in favour of the registered deed against the deposit, upon a ground which, I think, cannot be sustained, viz. that there was some equity capable of being raised against the person taking a mere deposit, by reason of its being left open to another person to take a subsequent security which would be, and was, registered. In my opinion, that view rests upon a fallacy."

Now, as to *Cave v. Cave* (1880) 15 Ch D 639, I lay no stress upon the circumstances that there the whole purchase-money was produced by the breach of trust, while here only a part of it was.To that part the same principle would apply as to the whole, though it might be said that if a mortgagee was bound in 1863 to inquire where Ffrench got the money in 1832, he might be fairly satisfied if shown, after so long a time, that a substantial part of it was his own. I believe, however, no such inquiry was ever made, and no human being ever thought of making it.

Another distinction which is relied on is that the mortgage of 1856 was to the trustees of Tyrrell's marriage settlement, who under it were trustees presumably for Tyrrell for life at least, and that he was cognizant of it and aware that the title had been investigated when it was taken, and that the title-deeds were accounted for and went with it. It is argued on his behalf that he is entitled to tack his own mortgages to it. Tacking in any ordinary sense is out of the question. I cannot understand what is meant by speaking of tacking in the case of two securities immediately connected in point of time, as against an equitable lien prior in date to both. It may be another question whether Tyrrell could have claimed the aid of the legal estate as a shield against the alleged lien. My belief is he could not. The trustees got the legal estate with their mortgage and for it. The trusts of the mortgage money are not for Tyrrell alone. It is only an accident that he is (if he be) a *cestui que trust* at all. Had he desired the benefit of the legal estate (of which in truth he never thought as important in any way, knowing how it was situated), the only way in which he could have got it in would have been by getting the mortgagees to join, which of course they would not have done. My impression is that his representatives can only rely on the mortgage of 1856 as being a transaction of which he was aware, and therefore as completely exonerating him from all charge of negligence in not getting in the legal estate, and in not procuring title-deeds which he believed to be out of his reach and in the proper custody. I am unable to find any important distinction between the case before us and *Cave v. Cave*, except the time at which, and the circumstances under which, the claim is here made, (as to which I have something to say), if it be not the fact that there is either no breach of trust at all in this case or one differing widely from that which existed in *Cave v. Cave*.

Is *Cave v. Cave*, then, well decided? It was cited in *Harpham v. Shacklock* (1881) 19 Ch D 207 both in the Court below and in the Court of Appeal, but it was not noticed in the judgments; and *Harpham v. Shacklock* differs so completely in its facts from the present case as to afford no light in deciding it – [His Lordship shortly stated the facts in *Harpham v. Shacklock*] – The real question as to *Cave v. Cave* is whether Fry J., is right in holding that the right to follow a trust fund into land in which it has been improperly invested is an equitable estate, as distinguished from an equity, and if so, whether the equities are in all other respects equal. The case of a vendor's lien for unpaid purchase-money is obviously of a different character. There the estate is his at law till he conveys; and till he receives payment, he has his lien and right to come back upon the land for his money. This latter right he loses even though unpaid, by any negligence, such as giving a receipt for his purchase-money, whereby a third person may be misled and deceived. But everyone knows that this lien exists in case of sales, and that it is one of the ordinary risks to be guarded against by a subsequent purchase; and it is the business of a person dealing with one whose title depends upon a conveyance on sale to see not alone that the conveyance is executed, but that the purchase-money is paid; and this he can adequately do by taking care that a proper receipt by the vendor is produced for it.

The law is thus stated by Gifford, V.-C., in *Thorpe v. Holdsworh* (1868) LR 7 Eq 139 (p. 146):

> "From the case of *Brace v. Duchess of Marlborough* (1728) 2 P Wms 491 down to *Finch v. Shaw* (1854) 19 Beav 500, and *Rooper v. Harrison* (1855) 2 K & J 86, the rule has always been that which was laid down by Lord Justice Wood in the last of these cases, and in *Stackhouse v. Countess of Jersey* (1861) 1 J & H 731, namely, that, as between equitable incumbrancers, relief will be given to the incumbrancer prior in point of date, unless he has lost his priority by some act or neglect of his; and that relief will not be refused to him, as against a subsequent incumbrancer, on the sole ground of the latter being a purchaser for value without notice, unless he has the legal estate, *or the best right to call for it.*"

Now as to *Phillips v. Phillips* (1861) 4 De GF & J 208, which played such an important part in *Cave v. Cave*, it has to be observed that the prior equity there was of the clearest possible character. It was a case as between two purchasers for value; and as both of them had merely equitable rights, it could not be contended that either had a preference apart from time over the other. From the beginning to the end of his judgment the Lord Chancellor (Lord Westbury) does not throw any doubt upon the principle that underlies the decision in *Rice v. Rice* (1853) 2 Drew 73, viz. that a *better* equity is not afforded by a mere priority of time.

In *Rice v. Rice* the case arose as between an unpaid vendor and a subsequent mortgagee by equitable deposit. – [His Lordship stated the facts of that case.] – Kindersley, V.-C., there considers the proper mode of stating "the rule of a Court of Equity for determining the preference as between persons having adverse equitable interests", and he says it should be stated in some such form as this (p. 78):– "between persons having only equitable interests, *if their equities are in all other respect equal*, priority of time gives the better equity; or, *qui prior est tempore potior est jure.*" He added (p. 84) that in that particular case the mortgagee "was perfectly justified in trusting to the security of the equitable mortgage by deposit of the deeds, without the slightest obligation to go and inquire of the vendors whether they had received all their purchase-money, when they had already given their solemn assurance in writing that they had received every shilling of it, and had conveyed the estate and delivered over the deeds."

In *Lewis v. Madocks* (1810) 17 Ves 48 a husband was bound to settle all the personal property he should acquire during the joint lives of his wife and of himself for their benefit and that of the survivor. He purchased an estate with money partly his own and partly borrowed on his personal security and since paid off by him, and it was held after his death not to belong to the trust, but to the heir, charged for the benefit of the trust with the money that was his own, the debts paid on account of the purchase, and expenditure in repairs and improvements. The question arose there as between the widow and the heir whether her rights under her husband's bond extended to making her owner of the estate.

Lord Eldon says (p. 57): – "I still consider the declaration that the personal estate of which the husband was possessed during the coverture is liable to this bond, right; but the direction for inquiries is short in one respect, it ought to have gone further: by what funds, and how acquired, he paid off these sums? One great question is, whether this estate belongs to the heir or the wife? The claim of the wife is put in this way: that personal property bound by the trust or obligation, whatever it is called, of this bond, is traced into the purchaser of a real estate, which estate must therefore be hers; but I do not know any case in its circumstances sufficiently like this to authorize me to hold that doctrine. I am prepared to say that the personal estate bound by this obligation, and which has been laid out in this real estate; is personal property that may be demanded out of the real estate, that the estate is chargeable with it; but it was not so purchased with it as that the estate should belong not to the heir but to the wife."

It is to be observed that that was a case where there was no question of a subsequent purchase for value; so neither was there in *Hopper v. Conyers* (1866) LR 2 Eq 549 nor in *Scales v. Baker* (1859) 28 Beav 91.

In re Morgan, Pillgrem v. Pilllgrem (1881) 18 Ch D 93 was a case of purchaser for value, without notice, who did not get in the legal estate. It is a strong case as establishing the equitable right as against such a purchaser. He had been permitted to deal with the estate as his own, although he was only an executor; and having surrendered a lease of the premises in which his testator carried on business, he took a new lease in his own name of these and other premises. The new lease, which did not recite the surrender of the old one, was deposited with an equitable mortgagee, who thought the executor was beneficial owner; but the lease was afterwards held to belong to the *cestuis que trustent*, as against the mortgagee, who had dealt with a lender, having the legal estate and the poessession of the title-deeds. Without intimating any doubt as to the soundness of the decision, it was a case in which the equitable mortgagee had not done everything he might have done to make his title complete, since he could have got a legal mortgage instead of an equitable.

Taking all these cases together, therefore, as expounding and illustrating the law, it is impossible to avoid the conclusion that the equity which is prior in time is to be here preferred, unless there is in the present case something which makes the equity of those claiming through Tyrrell "a better equity," within the meaning of *Rice v. Rice*, than that of the respondents.

I am of opinion there is. For the present, even supposing that the right to follow a trust fund into an improper investment in land confers a lien upon and an interest in the land as distinguished from a mere equity or right of suit, yet it is plainly a lien which ought to be asserted without delay. It is a right hardly distinguishable from a right to sue, and that only. To allow the tenant for life to remain in possession of the estate and legal title, and to deal with it at his pleasure for upwards of thirty years (as was here done), was, in my opinion, to give him the power of committing a fraud upon Tyrrell. And, on any principle of equity, as between two persons otherwise innocent, the loss in such cases must fall on him by whose default it has been rendered possible. The trustees of 1825 could not have set up this alleged right against Tyrrell, and, as they advanced the money, they would have been necessary parties, plaintiff or defendant, to any proceeding to enforce it. They are not before us, nor are their representatives. In my opinion, in a case like the present, the delay or neglect of the trustees in not taking steps to enforce their rights against the lands must be held to bind their *cestuis que trustent*, whose remedy, if any, would be against the trustees and, their estates. Even as regards the *cestuis que trustent*, there is nothing before us to show that they, one and all, have not lain by with full knowledge of their rights, and allowed the lands to be dealt with by Mr. Ffrench. Mr. Cheevers has of course done so in a way rendering it impossible for him at least to assert priority over Tyrrell's representatives in respect of his £2,000 mortgage, or, indeed I am strongly inclined to think in respect of the £3,000 appointed to Miss Ffrench; and from the fact that the marriage of Mr. Ffrench was in 1825, I have little doubt that the other two appointees of the trust funds were of age long before the mortgages were effected. It is a mistake to suppose (as was contended) that their right to come to the Court would only arise when the title to payment accrued by the death of Mr. Ffrench.They had a right to come, and ought, under the peculiar circumstances of this case, to have come at the earliest moment, to trace out the trust fund, and see that it was brought back and properly invested, or get a conveyance of the lands, even though their own estate was then only in remainder.

But, apart from laches, in my opinion the equity of the appellants here is a superior equity to that of the respondents. The right to follow trust funds is a right to do something – to take steps to alter the existing, open, notorious enjoyment of property. The primary right of the *cestui que trust* is against his own trustees, whom he can compel to restore the funds out of their own estates. The right to trace the fund into its improper investment is ancillary to this, or in substitution for it. As against the trustees, it is as complete an equity as may be; but as against innocent purchasers, permitted to deal with the apparent owner of the property as if no such right existed, I cannot think that it ought to prevail – that is, when the purchaser has done all that is in his power to complete his title.The one man does everything that law and usage require to guard his rights; the other takes no step. With every respect for the high authority on which the apparently contrary opinion rests, I am unable to regard these equities as equal. So far as the trustees are concerned, and anyone dealing with them for the trust property, without notice, the equity is effective. But as against the purchased property, the right is, in my opinion, incomplete till steps are taken to assert it; and in the meantime, I regard the right as rather in the nature of a chose in action than an estate – an equity as distinguished from an equitable interest – and therefore inferior to that of Tyrrell's representatives.

For these reasons, I am of opinion, first, that the title of the mortgagee is a better one in equity than that of the respondents, by reason of the neglect of their trustees, or themselves, or both, and that therefore *Cave v. Cave* (1880) 15 Ch D 639 does not govern the case; and, second, than even if laches be out of the case, the equity itself is inherently a lower one than that of the equitable mortgagee.

But in this I have gone on the assumption that there is nothing in the document of 1838 to affect rights in the case. In my opinion it is of great moment.

It is relied on by the respondents as being a signed writing, containing an admission against interest by Martin Ffrench, viz. that he had got the £9,199 19*s.* 11*d.* from the trustees; and as if it could be looked at for that purpose only. The learned Judge describes it as an "escrow", of course not using that word in its technical sense (for of its being legally an escrow there is no suggestion), but probably meaning to indicate that it is not shown to be a real deed at all.

If it was not a perfect deed, what was it?

Of its being an admission against interest I have some doubt. It is settled that for such a purpose the whole context of the entry may be read; and I confess this document looks to me very like an "admission" by Mr. Ffrench in favour of himself and his family, to be used in his and their interest against his creditors when the occasion should arise: in other words, an "admission" that he and his children had an estate by virtue of a hidden equity. Be this as it may, in my opinion this document is a deed or nothing. That it was signed, sealed, and delivered by Mr. Ffrench there is no doubt. The attestation is complete. The receipt of the nominal consideration is also attested. The evidence in favour of the delivery is exactly the same as that of the signing and sealing by Mr. Ffrench. Nothing is wanting to its complete effectiveness if it be legally proved, and it is legally proved, if it came out of proper custody. It is a mistake to suppose that a deed uncommunicated to the grantee is not a deed, good as against the maker of it. The grantor may retain it, and even destroy it; but if it can be shown that he executed it as a deed; it is a deed, and will bind him. Now, did this deed come out of the proper custody?

No doubt the trustees would be the best custody. But a custody not the best, may yet be proper, within the role of law, as to proof of documents thirty years old. And in a case not cited in the argument, but singularly resembling the present in some of its features, the custody of one who occupied the identical position of Mr. Ffrench was held "proper" custody within the rule: *Doe d. Neale v. Samples* (1838) 8 A & E 151; see also *Croughton v. Blake* (1843) 12 M & W 203, and *Reg. v. Mytton* (1860) 2 E & E 537.

It was the duty of Mr. Ffrench to do what he purported to do by this deed of 1838, that is, having wrongfully obtained the trust funds, it was his duty to repair his breach of trust by repayment, or by conveying to the trustees property of adequate amount to represent it. The trustees had power to invest in land. It was the duty of the trustees to get him to execute such a deed.

The only evidence which traces the trust fund to his hands prior in time to the mortgages at all is this instrument itself, which cured the breach of trust, and did what he was legally and morally bound to do. Did Mr. Ffrench sign, seal, and deliver it? If he did, it was his deed; and he did this, if the attestation is not wholly untrue.

Every presumption is in favour of it; and if Martin Ffrench with or without the knowledge of his trustees, afterwards kept it concealed as a pocket instrument, to be used if and when convenient, it is none the less his deed, and put the legal estate out of him, and conveyed the property in accordance with the right and honesty of the transaction.

That this deed was afterwards suppressed, and fraudulently suppressed, by Mr. Ffrench there can be no doubt; but for present purpose that is not material. The moment the seal was put to it, the lien, or equity to follow the trust fund, or right of suit, or equitable estate, or whatever it was, was gone. The fund was followed, pursued, and captured; and had the deed been registered, the advances by Tyrrell would never have been made, and this case would never have arisen.

In this aspect it is then the case of a conflict between two instruments, the later of which is registered and the earlier not; and the statute settles the priority. It is in this view a curious case, and shows us again the engineer "hoist with his own petard." The very deed which was designed to shield the trustees against creditors is itself the means, or *a* means, of defeating the design.

Whether, after so many years, he forgot it (as he well may), or whether he was advised that it was better to rely on the equity which was susceptible of registration, I cannot say. To recite the deed of 1838, in the appointments of 1865, may have been avoided because it would look *too* fraudulent, in face of all the mortgages which intervened. Possibly this explains why it was unnoticed from the day it was executed till lately exhumed. As it is, I should be of opinion, if it were necessary to rest the case on it, that on that ground alone the appeal must succeed. But I prefer deciding the case for myself upon the other and broader ground.

I think the appeal must succeed, with costs."

Priorities and the Doctrine of Notice

As we have seen, estates and interests rank in priority according to the order of their creation where they are otherwise equal. The other important factor which affects the question of priorities is the doctrine of notice, which has in turn been affected and to some extent displaced by the modern systems of registration. As regards notice, the rule developed by equity was that a *bona fide* purchaser for value without notice of a legal estate or interest in land would take free of an equitable interest of which he had no notice. Similarly, a *bona fide* purchaser for value of an equitable interest without notice will take free of a mere equity. In addition, a purchaser for value of registered land will not be affected by an unregistered equitable claim even if he has notice of it.

It is generally accepted that there are three forms of notice, actual, constructive and imputed which can be identified in s.3(1) of the Conveyancing Act 1882. A person will be considered to have actual notice where he discovers information himself, so a subjective standard is imposed. A person will be deemed to have constructive notice where he fails to make the inquiries and inspections which he ought reasonably to have made, judged by reference to standard conveyancing procedures.[21] In addition, all knowledge acquired in the same transaction, of which an agent of a purchaser is actually aware or of which he would have been aware if he had made the inquiries and inspections which he ought reasonably to have made, will be attributed or 'imputed' to the purchaser. Finally, it should be noted that the onus of proving that a person had no notice of a prior interest lies on the party claiming that he took without notice.[22]

Northern Bank Ltd v. Henry
[1981] IR 1

The second named defendant purchased the leasehold interest in a house with money which belonged to the first named defendant, his wife, but the assignment of the interest was made to him alone. The wife sought a declaration that she was entitled in equity to the leasehold interest. On the same day the husband mortgaged the house to the plaintiff bank, which apart from making a search in the Registry of Deeds, made no investigation of the husband's title. The wife succeeded in obtaining a declaration that her husband held the leasehold interest in trust for her. The plaintiff subsequently sought a declaration that its estate in the property was superior to the interests of the husband and wife and the wife contended that her interest in the house prevailed. The plaintiff's claim was dismissed by the High Court and the Supreme Court. The Supreme Court (Henchy, Kenny and Parke JJ) held that the wife's claim to be entitled to an equitable estate in the house would have come to the knowledge of the plaintiff's agents if such inquiries and inspections had been made as ought reasonably to have been made and that at the date of the mortgage, the plaintiff was deemed to have had constructive notice of the wife's claim.

HENCHY J stated at pp. 7–12: "The contest in this case is between the plaintiff bank and the wife of one of its customers. The wife is the first defendant. The husband, who was the customer, is the second defendant; in 1969 he granted a legal mortgage of the family home to the third defendant.

In 1974 the husband's account with the plaintiff bank was heavily overdrawn

---

[21] See *Somers v. W.* [1979] IR 94, 108 and *Northern Bank Ltd v. Henry* [1981] IR 1, 9.

[22] *Heneghan v. Davitt* [1933] IR 375.

and his finances were in disarray generally. It was a source of urgent worry to the plaintiffs, who badly needed a collateral security for their debt. The plaintiffs needed that security quickly, for there were other creditors of the husband and cheques drawn by him in favour of some of those creditors had been dishonoured by the plaintiffs. The only substantial item of property that he appeared to have was the family home, and it was mortgaged to the third defendant. However, as a security it was better than nothing in the eyes of the plaintiffs; they required the husband to give a second mortgage on it and he agreed to do so.

The plaintiffs doubtless felt that they had to carry through the transaction swiftly. Advised by their legal department in Belfast, the plaintiffs took up the documents of title and saw the investigation of title that had been carried out when the mortgage to the third defendant was executed in 1969; the plaintiffs made no further investigation of the title, other than to get a Dublin firm of solicitors to have a negative search carried out in the Registry of Deeds. Having thereby established that no dealing with the property had been registered since 1969, the plaintiffs did not investigate the title further, although they knew that the property was the family home and that the husband had ceased to use it as his address in his correspondence with them. A competent solicitor, acting for a normal purchaser of the property, would not have been content to take the title on such a cursory investigation. But all the plaintiffs wanted was a second mortgage, and their advisers probably felt that if they took time to investigate the title fully they might lose priority to another creditor. For that reason I do not wish to criticise them for telescoping the investigation in the interests of business expediency. So, with the title thus looked at summarily, the plaintiffs got the second mortgage executed.

As was later proved, the husband had no title whatsoever to the property. If the plaintiffs had pursued the matter by means of appropriate requisitions on title, they would have discovered not only that it was the wife who was in occupation of the house but that she was in the process of formulating against the husband a claim that she was beneficially entitled to it. The High Court has made a declaration to that effect and that decision stands unchallenged. What the plaintiffs seek primarily to establish in these proceedings is that, as purchasers for value without notice of the wife's title, they should have priority over her.

Section 3, sub-s. 1, of the Conveyancing Act, 1882, deprives the plaintiffs of that priority if the wife's entitlement "would have come to [*the plaintiffs'*] knowledge if such inquiries and inspections had been made as ought reasonably to have been made . . ." Counsel for the wife argues that the plaintiffs ought reasonably to have inquired as to who was in occupation and as to whether there was any litigation threatened or pending affecting the property and that, if they had done so, they would have learned of the wife's claim. Accordingly, the argument goes, the plaintiffs should not be allowed to dislodge the wife from the property (which she admittedly owned at the time the plaintiffs got the second mortgage of it) because their abstention from making the suggested inquiries fixed them with constructive notice of the wife's claim. The answer depends on the scope or meaning that should be given to the expression "such inquiries and inspections . . . as ought reasonably to have been made" in s. 3, sub.-s. 1, of the Act of 1882.

In my judgment, the test of what inquiries and inspections ought reasonably to have been made by the plaintiffs is an objective test which depends not on what the particular purchaser thought proper to do in the particular circum-stances but on what a purchaser of the particular property ought reasonably to have done in order to acquire title to it. The words "purchaser" and "purchase" in this context have the meanings ascribed to them by s. 1 of the Act of 1882 and thus include "mortgagee" and "mortgage." In a particular case a purchaser, looking only at his own interests, may justifiably and reasonably consider that in the circumstances some of the normal inquiries and inspections may or should be dispensed with. The special circumstances, thus narrowly viewed, may justify the shortcut taken, or the purchaser may consider that they do so. In either event, such a purchaser is not the purchaser envisaged by s. 3, sub-s. 1, of the Act of 1882. That provision, because it is laying down the circumstances in which a purchaser is not to be prejudicially affected by notice of any instrument, fact or thing, is setting as a standard of conduct that which is to be expected from a reasonable purchaser. Reasonableness in this context must be judged by reference to what should be done to acquire the estate or interest being purchased, rather than by the motive for or the purpose of the particular purchase.

A purchaser cannot be held to be empowered to set his own standard of reasonableness for the purpose of the sub-section. He must expect to be judged by what an ordinary purchaser, advised by a competent lawyer, would reasonably inquire about or inspect for the purpose of getting a good title. If his personal preference, or the exigencies of the situation, impel him to lower the level of investigation of title below that standard, he is entitled to do so; but, if he does so, he cannot claim the immunity which s. 3, sub-s. 1, reserves for a reasonable purchaser. A reasonable purchaser is one who not only consults his own needs or preferences but also has regard to whether the purchase may affect, prejudicially and unfairly, the rights of third parties in the property. In particular, a reasonable purchaser would be expected to make such inquiries and inspections as would normally disclose whether the purchase will trench, fraudulently or unconscionably, on the rights of such third parties in the property.

In this case, the plaintiffs made no inquiry as to who was in occupation of the property. I consider that a reasonable purchaser would have done so. A minimum requirement for the proper investigation of a title is to see that the purchaser will either get vacant possession on completion or, if the contract or the needs of the purchaser do not so permit or require, get evidence of any estate or interest that will stand between him and vacant possession. Considering the many ways, both at common law and under statute, in which a person in occupation may have an estate or interest adverse to that of a vendor, and which would not appear on an investigation of the vendor's paper title, I consider that the plaintiffs, as purchasers, ought reasonably to have investigated this aspect of the title. Had the plaintiffs done so, the fact of the wife's possession of the property would have come to light, as well as her well-founded claim to the beneficial ownership of it.

Nor did the plaintiffs make any inquiry as to whether any litigation was threatened or pending in respect of the property. I consider that this also was an inquiry which a purchaser ought reasonably to have made. The plaintiffs knew that this was a "purchase" from the husband of the family home. Even if it had not been a family home, it was foolhardy for a purchaser not to inquire about pending or threatened litigation, particularly litigation stemming from statutory notices served under statutes such as the Housing Acts or the Planning Acts, which might fatally flaw the title. This property was known to the plaintiffs to be the family home. Notwithstanding that this purchase took place before the passing of the Family Home Protection Act, 1976 (which makes a transaction of this kind void for want of the prior written consent of the wife), the plaintiffs, as purchasers, ought reasonably to have adverted to the fact that there were decisions showing that a wife who had made payments towards the acquisition of the home, or towards the payment of the mortgage instalments on it, acquired a corresponding share in the beneficial ownership. As a matter of ordinary care, therefore, an inquiry as to threatened or pending claims was called for. In fact there was such an impending claim by the wife. By not inquiring about its existence the plaintiffs became an unwitting party to an unconscionable, if not an actually fraudulent, effort by the husband to mortgage the family home behind his wife's back at a time when he had no beneficial title to it. The plaintiffs, by not making the normal inquiry as to threatened or impending litigation affecting the property (indeed, by making no requisitions on title whatsoever), facilitated the husband in nefariously concealing his wife's well-founded claim to the ownership of the property. Because of that, the plaintiffs cannot be said to have shown the care to be expected from a reasonable purchaser. It must be held, therefore, that knowledge of the wife's claim would have been acquired by the plaintiffs if they had made the inquiries that ought reasonably to have been made.

The interpretation given in this judgment to s. 3, sub-s. 1, of the Act of 1882 does not amount to the imposition of any novel or unfair duty of investigation of title on purchasers. Well before the enactment of the Act of 1882, which aimed at setting statutory bounds to the existing doctrine of constructive notice, the Chancery judges had evolved this same test for determining whether a purchaser or mortgagee should have constructive notice attributed to him. Sir Edward Sugden (later Lord St. Leonards), in his Law of Vendors and Purchasers (14th ed. 1862), summed up the pre-1882 approach of the Chancery judges to the question of constructive notice as follows, at p. 755:—

"The question upon constructive notice is not whether the purchaser had the means of obtaining, and might, by prudent caution, have obtained the knowledge in question, but whether the not obtaining it was an act of gross or culpable negligence."

Nineteenth century judges were prone to stigmatising actionable negligence as "gross" or "culpable." Indeed, Rolfe B. at pp. 115-6 of the report of *Wilson v. Brett* (1843) 11 M & W 113 said that he "could see no difference between *negligence* and *gross* negligence—that it was the same thing, with the addition of a vituperative epithet;" this incisive view was approved by Willes J. in *Grill v. General Iron Screw Collier Co.* (1866) LR 1 CP 600. When, therefore, the pre-1882 Chancery judges applied the test of negligence to determine whether a purchaser should be fixed with constructive notice, they were doing no more than asking whether the purchaser's lack of knowledge was consistent with the conduct to be expected from a reasonable man in the circumstances.

Section 3, sub-s. 1, of the Act of 1882, in providing that a purchaser is not to be prejudicially affected by notice of any instrument, fact, or thing unless "it is within his own knowledge, or would have come to his knowledge if such inquiries and inspections had been made as ought reasonably to have been made by him," gave statutory stress to the existing judicial insistence that constructive notice could be found only when the lack of knowledge was due to such careless inactivity as would not be expected in the circumstances from a reasonable man. The default of a reasonable man is to be distinguished from the default of a prudent man. The prudence of the worldly wise may justifiably persuade a purchaser that it would be unbusinesslike to stop and look more deeply into certain aspects of the title. But the reasonable man, in the eyes of the law, will be expected to look beyond the impact of his decisions on his own affairs, and to consider whether they may unfairly and prejudicially affect his "neighbour," in the sense in which that word has been given juristic currency by Lord Atkin in *Donoghue v. Stevenson* [1932] AC 562.

In the present case, the plaintiffs may have been justified as a matter of business prudence in taking the second mortgage from the husband, hurriedly and without any proper investigation of the title. But it would be impossible to hold that a purchaser in this situation, given competent legal advice and having due regard to the prejudicial consequences to persons in proximity to him (such as the wife) that could result from a skimped investigation of the title, would have acted reasonably in thus taking a conveyance of the family home. The test for constructive notice is legal reasonableness, not business prudence.

I would reject this appeal by the plaintiffs, thus affirming the decision of Mr. Justice McWilliam which dismissed, on the ground of their constructive notice of the wife's title, the plaintiffs' claim to be given priority over her."

Heneghan v. Davitt
[1933] IR 375

The plaintiff entered into an agreement for the purchase of lands and while the agreement was awaiting completion the vendors entered into a further agreement for sale with another person which was carried into effect by a conveyance. The plaintiff brought a claim for specific performance. In the Circuit Court, the third party's plea of purchaser for value without notice was upheld but in the High Court it was held that it had been incorrect to impose the onus of proving that the other person had been a *bona fide* purchaser without notice on the plaintiff. The onus rested instead on the defendant and since he had not discharged this onus, the plaintiff was granted specific performance of the agreement.

O'BYRNE J stated at pp.378–382: "The question for determination on this appeal is whether the Circuit Judge was right in holding that the respondent Rowley was a purchaser for value without notice, and that accordingly the appellant was not entitled, as against him, to a decree for specific performance.

On the 30th December, 1931, the appellant entered into an agreement in writing for the purchase of the lands in question from the then owners, John and Patrick Davitt, for the sum of £350, and he thereupon paid over to the auctioneers, through whom the sale was negotiated, the sum of £70 by way of deposit and the sum of £17 10*s*. auctioneers' fees. While this agreement was in full force and awaiting completion, the Davitts entered into an arrangement for the sale of the same lands to Rowley for the sum of £380 and this arrangement was carried into effect by a deed of conveyance bearing date the 1st day of April, 1932. Shortly afterwards the appellant instituted proceedings for specific performance of the agreement of the 30th December, 1931, and named, as defendants, the Davitts and Rowley. The Davitts did not appear, and Rowley pleaded that he was a purchaser for value without notice of the prior agreement. The Circuit Judge gave judgment for damages as against the Davitts but upheld Rowley's plea. From this decision the plaintiff has appealed.

Various legal considerations and principles apply in the determination of the question whether a purchaser of lands had notice of a prior agreement or incumbrance affecting the lands, but nevertheless the question remains substantially a question of fact, and, accordingly, I would be very slow to interfere with the decision of the trial Judge if I were satisfied that, in the determination of the question submitted to him, he applied the correct legal principles.

In the present case I am satisfied, from the judgment of the learned Judge, that he misdirected himself in point of law, and dealt with the case in a manner contrary to well established principles of law. In the course of his judgment he says:– "I may have a good deal of suspicion about the Rowleys and their evidence, but I rather feel the burden of proof is on the plaintiff, who must satisfy me beyond all reasonable doubt that the true inference to draw from all the facts is that they had notice." It is clear from this that the learned Judge considered that the onus of proving that Rowley was not a purchaser for value without notice rested upon the appellant and dealt with the case upon this basis. Apart from this, and even if he were right as to where the onus of proof lay, he seems to me to have placed a very heavy burden upon the appellant when he required him to prove this matter *beyond all reasonable doubt*.

In the case of *Attorney-General v. Bisphosphated Guano Co.* (1879) 11 Ch D 327, Thesiger L.J, says at p. 337:– "The defence of a purchase without notice is one which ought to be specifically alleged as well as proved by those who rely upon it," and in the case of *Nisbet and Potts' Contract* [1905] 1 Ch 391, Farwell J. says at p. 402:– "The plea of purchaser for value without notice is a single plea, to be proved by the person pleading it; it is not to be regarded as a plea of purchaser for value, to be met by a reply of notice." In my opinion these are correct statements of the law, and accordingly the trial Judge should have dealt with the case upon the basis that the onus of proof rested upon Rowley and not upon the appellant.

There is one other matter to which I desire to refer before considering the evidence in the cases. In order to defeat a plea of purchaser for value without notice, it is not, in my opinion, necessary that the purchaser should have actual notice. If he has sufficient notice or knowledge to put him upon enquiry, and if he deliberately refrains from making such enquiry, he is thereupon deemed to have constructive notice of such facts as would have come to his knowledge if he had made proper enquiry; and such constructive notice is, in my opinion, sufficient to defeat the plea. Bearing these facts in mind, I, approach the evidence in this case.

As already stated, the agreement for the sale of the land to the appellant was entered into on the 30th day of December, 1931. On the 31st day of December, 1931, Rowley and his wife called at the office of Mr. Patrick O'Connor, solicitor, who was acting on behalf of the appellant, and had an interview with his assistant, Miss Frances Kelly. The accounts of that interview as given by Miss Kelly on the one hand, and by Mr. and Mrs. Rowley on the other hand, do not agree; and, in so far as they disagreed, the trial Judge accepted the evidence of Miss Kelly and rejected that of Mr. and Mrs. Rowley. Accordingly, I accept the evidence of Miss Kelly, particularly as it was fortified by a note of the interview taken down by Miss Kelly at the time. It will be noted that this interview took place the very day after the appellant entered into his agreement.

I take the following extracts from the evidence of Miss Kelly:

Q. 40. "What occurred there when you met Rowley?" "Himself and Mrs. Rowley called – Mrs. Rowley stated they wanted to see Mr. O'Connor to take instructions. She said that John Heneghan of Carrowbeg was intending to buy a holding of land from the Davitts for £350, that this land was adjoining hers and was a co-holding, and she was willing to give the same price, and she wished Mr. O'Connor to write to the Land Commission to sell her the land."

Q. 41. His Lordship: – "Did she say that John Heneghan was going to buy it or had bought it for £350?" "She said it was being sold to a man called John Heneghan."

Q. 42. His Lordship: – "You took her instructions?" "Yes."

Q. 43. His Lordship: – "And then you saw Mr. O'Connor?" "Yes."

Cross-examined by Mr. Conroy:–

Q. 44. " Mrs. Rowley seems to think that what she said was that John Heneghan had made a bid. Are you reading from your instructions now that she said a man named Heneghan was buying, or that it was being sold to a man called Heneghan?" "My own recollection is that *it was being sold.*"

Q. 45. " What does your note say?" "The note says 'being sold'."

Q. 46. Mr. Conroy: – "Had you any other conversation?" "No, except when I came back from Mr. O'Connor and told her that he couldn't act for her as he was acting for for John Heneghan, the purchaser."

Mr. and Mrs. Rowley both gave evidence, and the gist of that evidence is that they knew at the time that Heneghan had made a bid for the place but they deny any knowledge of his having entered into an agreement for purchase. It appears that after they left Mr. O'Connor's office they wrote, the same day, to the Land Commission and afterwards to the Davitts. They both deny that Miss Kelly made use of the expression that Mr. O'Connor was acting for the purchaser. Mrs. Rowley was asked in cross-examination: –

Q. 117. "Did you think, if you got the consent of the Land Commission before Heneghan got it, that you would get it, even if he had already bought the place ?" and, her answer was: – "I didn't know he had bought it. I knew he had bid for it. That is all."

Q. 119. "If you didn't know that Heneghan had bought the land, why were you so quiet about it; did you tell anybody you were writing to the Land Commission?" "I didn't know."

I extract the following from the evidence of James Rowley:–

Q. 138. "When did you pay the purchase money?" "The 23rd of March, I think."

Q. 137. "Did you know that Heneghan had agreed to buy that land?" "I heard common talk that he was buying it." .

Q. 138. "Did you think he had bought it?" "No, sir."

Q. 139. "Were you not told in Mr. O'Connor's office why Mr. O'Connor would not act for you?" "No."

Q. 142. "The typist told you, and you heard her say here to-day that she told you why Mr. O'Connor wouldn't act for you?" "No, she didn't."

After dealing at length with the evidence regarding the foregoing conversation the learned Judge says: – "I come to the conclusion with some hesitation, that that in itself cannot be held to saddle the Rowleys with notice of a prior agreement." This, of course, proceeds upon the basis that the onus of proving actual notice rested upon the appellant.

It is clear from the judgment of the learned Judge that he regarded the Rowleys and their evidence with grave suspicion, and that he rejected some of their evidence – at any rate such portions of it as conflicted with the evidence of Miss Kelly. He dismissed the action as against Rowley but without costs. The reason for refusing him his costs I give in the Judge's own words: – "The reason I do that is because I think, if the Rowleys had made the inquiries they should have made, they could very easily have ascertained what the true state of affairs was about this contract."

In all these circumstances should the plea of purchaser for value without notice be allowed to prevail? The actions and the evidence of the Rowleys seem to me, as they seemed to the trial Judge, to be open to grave suspicion. In so far as that evidence conflicted with the evidence of Miss Kelly, the trial Judge rejected it. He obviously did not regard them as trustworthy witnesses on whose evidence implicit reliance could be placed. Having regard to his view as to the evidence of these witnesses I am driven to the conclusion that, if he had considered that the onus of proving the plea of purchaser for value without notice rested upon Rowley, he would have held that the latter had not discharged the onus. Taking the evidence as a whole and considering it with the assistance of the trial Judge's estimate as to the trust to be imposed on the evidence of the various material witnesses, I am of opinion that the onus of proof was not discharged.

I am, therefore, of opinion that this appeal should be allowed and an order for specific performance granted."

CHAPTER 3

Trusts – An Introduction

TRUSTS DISTINGUISHED FROM OTHER FORMS OF LEGAL INSTITUTION

Trusts and Contract

Contracts and trusts are distinct concepts and the most far reaching consequence of the distinction is that beneficiaries can enforce a trust even though not party to its creation whereas only the actual parties to a contract can enforce it. There have been examples of the courts employing the concept of a constructive trust to provide a third party with a remedy by finding that one of the parties to a contract entered into it as a trustee with the intention of benefiting the third party.[1] However, in general terms the courts have shown a marked reluctance to infer the existence of a trust in these circumstances, unless it is clear both from the language used in creating the arrangement and from the surrounding circumstances that this was the clear intention of the parties.[2]

Drimmie v. Davies
[1899] 1 IR 176

By virtue of a deed a dentist and his son agreed to become partners for five years. In the event of a dissolution the son was to have the right to purchase the property and, in the event of his father's death, was to pay certain annuities to his brothers and sisters. The father died and his executors and the brothers and sisters brought an action to enforce payment of the annuities on the ground that the son was bound by the obligation to his father which was now being enforced by his executors. Chatterton VC held that the plaintiffs were entitled to maintain the action, a finding upheld by the Irish Court of Appeal (Fitzgibbon, Walker and Holmes LJJ).

CHATTERTON VC stated at pp.180–186: "The questions to be decided arise upon the clauses of the deed of partnership between F. Davies the elder, and his son F. Davies the younger, dated the 26th June, 1895, on the faith of which the father took the son into partnership with him in the business of surgeon dentist, which the father had carried on for several years previously. The deed

---

[1] *Drimmie v. Davies* [1899] 1 IR 176.
[2] *Cadbury Ireland Ltd v. Kerry Co-operative Creamery Ltd* [1982] ILRM 77 and *Inspector of Taxes Association v. Minister for the Public Service* High Court (Murphy J) 24 March 1983.

was an agreement under seal between the father of the one part, and the son of the other part, no other party being named as such, nor executing the deed. By it the father and son agreed to become partners on the terms and conditions therein stated from the 1st April, 1895, for a period of five years from that date. It provided that the profits should be divided into thirds, two-thirds to go to the father, and one-third to the son, the father to draw £20, and the son £10 monthly. It further contained a clause, No. 15, on which the plaintiffs' rights depend, which is as follows. [His Lordship read this clause.]

The agreement thereby created was of necessity between the father and the son, there being no other party to the deed, and the son thereby contracted with his father for the payments therein provided for his sisters and brothers, and this formed part of the consideration for the agreement on his part, and on the faith of it he was admitted to the partnership. F. Davies, sen., died in May, 1897, whereupon the partnership became dissolved, and F. Davies, jun., the defendant, has carried on the business since. The defendant refuses to pay the annual sums mentioned in the partnership agreement to his sisters and brothers, and denies his liability to pay them, first, on the ground of there having been no consideration for his agreement; secondly, on the ground that the provisions contained in the agreement whereby, in the event of the death of F. Davies, sen., while the partnership continued, he agreed to pay to his sisters and brothers the sums mentioned therein, are not enforceable against him, and do not give any right to the plaintiffs to sue for or in respect of such annuities, those of the plaintiffs who are children of F. Davies, sen., not being parties to said indenture or otherwise concerned therein, and the other plaintiffs who are the executors of F. Davies, sen., not being interested as such executors or otherwise in the payment of the said annuities. Thus, having derived all the benefits conferred upon him by the agreement, he seeks to repudiate his liability to any one on foot of his side of the contract. He introduces this contention in his defence by the averment that there are not, and never were, any assets of the partnership out of which to discharge the annuities. Assuming that this averment is true, it seems to me to be of no importance, as the claim of the plaintiffs is not upon the partnership assets, nor upon the defendant, in respect of any such assets, but personally on his covenant. I think it would not be possible to hold on the true construction of the agreement that the plaintiffs have any other claim, and that the case must be treated as one of personal covenant only.

As for the defence that there was no consideration to the defendant for such a covenant, it is unfounded in fact, for he was admitted a partner, which was a valuable consideration, if any were necessary, and it was one of the terms and conditions stated in the agreement upon which he and his father became partners. The agreement in clause 16 provides a corresponding liability for F. Davies, sen., in case he should survive the defendant, to pay £75 a year for seven years to the widow and children of the defendant.

The case therefore comes to this, whether any action can be brought by any one against the defendant for his breach of his contract. I say "by any one," because both the daughters and sons of F. Davies, sen., as the beneficiaries, and his acting executors are joined as co-plaintiffs, the latter of course suing only for the benefit of the former.

The defendant's contention is based on the common law rule that in the case of contracts under seal no one can sue who is not a party to the deed. That rule is fully stated in the case of *Tweddle v. Atkinson* (1861) 1 B & S 393, namely, that a stranger to the contract, that is to say, a person who is not a party to the contract, and from whom no consideration moved, cannot sue upon it. The test seems to be whether such a person could be sued upon the contract. Now here the daughters and son were not parties to the contract, nor did any consideration move from them, nor could they be sued upon the contract. But this rule did not prevail in equity, and since the Judicature Act the rules in equity are to prevail in cases where such a conflict exists. The equitable rule was that the party to whose use or for whose benefit the contract had been entered into has a remedy in equity against the person with whom it was expressed to be made. The Court deems the latter a trustee for the former, and would compel him to execute his trust according to the apparent intention of the contracting parties. In the case of *Page v. Cox* (1852) 10 Hare 163, which has much resemblance to the present case, an agreement was held to amount to a trust which, as stated by Wood, V.-C., may well be created, though there may be an absence of any expression in terms importing confidence, and a trust cannot be the less capable of being enforced, because it is founded on contract. It was sought to distinguish that case on the ground that there a trust was imposed to pay out of specific property, which, as I have stated, did not exist here, but it seems to me that as the contract here was such that, if the executors of the deceased partner had a right to sue on it, any money recovered by them must have been held by them in trust for the daughters and sons, there is sufficient to create an equity in favour of the beneficiaries. The case chiefly relied on by the defendant was that of the *Empress Engineering Company* (1880) 16 Ch D 125, where it was held that a contract made by the promoters of the Company with third parties for payment of a sum of money, and which was in itself null and void, could not be made the subject of a claim against the Company when formed by reason of its having been mentioned in the purchase deed as a charge subject to which the business was purchased by the Company. The case was decided principally on the ground that the agreement with the third parties being in itself null and void was not capable of ratification, but certainly the learned Judges who decided the appeal drew a distinction between cases where there was intended to be a charge in favour of the third party on specific property, and cases where there was a mere agreement to pay a sum of money to a third party. Jessel, M.R., guards his decision by the observation that he was far from saying that there might not be agreements which may make the third party a *cestui que trust*.

In the case of *Lloyd's v. Harper* (1880) 16 Ch D 290 a question bearing on the principle applicable to such transactions was considered first by Fry, J., and afterwards by the Court of Appeal, namely, whether a guarantee given by a father to Lloyd's Association on the admission of his son as an underwriter could be sued on by persons who had been underwritten by the son. "Lloyd's" were co-plaintiffs in the action with outside persons, not members of Lloyd's, who had been underwritten by the son. One of the questions raised was that Lloyd's not having sustained any damage, could only recover nominal damages for themselves, and could not recover for the losses sustained by third parties by reason of the default of the son as an underwriter. This contention was disallowed. As to it, Lush, L.J. (p. 321), says, "To my mind it is a startling and an alarming doctrine, and a novelty, because I consider it to be an established rule of law that where a contract is made with *A.* for the benefit of *B.*, *A.* can sue on the contract for the benefit of *B.*, and recover all that *B.* could have recovered if the contract had been made with *B.* himself." This principle shows that if the executors of F. Davies the elder, who are co-plaintiffs in this action, had sued alone, they could recover all that the defendant agreed with his father to pay, and of any sums so recovered they would of course be trustees for the daughters and sons.

In the case of *Murray v. Flavell* (1883) 25 Ch D 89, before North, J., and afterwards on appeal, in which the decision in *Lloyd's v. Harper* was referred to, the question arose as to the effect of partnership articles, in which it was provided that from the determination of the partnership the retiring partner or his widow should be entitled to receive out of the profits for a stated period an annuity; and it was contended that this was a mere bargain between the partners, and that no trust was created for the widow, and that she could not enforce an agreement to which she was not a party, and which was not communicated to her. The cases of *Gregory v. Williams* (1817) 3 Mer 582; *In re Empress Engineering Co.* (1880) 16 Ch D 125; and *Lloyd's v. Harper* (1880) 16 Ch D 290 were considered, and it was held both by North, J., and the Court of Appeal that a valid trust for the widow was created by the articles.

The last case referred to, *Gandy v. Gandy* (1885) 30 Ch D 57, is probably the most important. The action there was brought upon a deed of separation containing a covenant by the husband with trustees to maintain the children. The husband afterwards refused to maintain one of the children, and she sued the husband and the trustees to carry out the trusts of the deed. The husband raised an objection that the plaintiff was not competent to sue upon the deed, and that the only proper parties to sue were the trustees; and it was contended that the children were not parties to the deed, and that the consideration did not move from them. Bacon, V.-C., held that there was a relation of trustee and *cestui que trust* existing, and that as the trustees refused to sue, the *cestui que trust* could sue. From this the husband appealed, and the judgment of the Vice-Chancellor was reversed. Cotton, L.J., stated the rule of law to be as follows:– "As a general rule, a contract cannot be enforced except by a party to the contract; and either of two persons contracting together can sue the other, if the other is guilty of a breach of or does not perform the obligations of that contract. But a third person – a person who is not a party to the contract – cannot do so. That rule, however, is subject to this exception: if the contract, although in form it is with *A.*, is intended to secure a benefit to *B.*, so that *B.* is entitled to say he has a beneficial right as *cestui que trust* under that contract; then *B.* would, in a Court of Equity, be allowed to insist upon and enforce the contract." He considered the objection to the plaintiff suing as fatal to the action in its present form, but he allowed the case to stand over to see whether the plaintiff could induce the trustees to sue. Bowen, L.J., concurred, and said that whatever may have been the common law doctrine, if the true intent and effect of the deed were to give to the children a beneficial right under it, that is to say, to give them a right to have the covenants performed, and to call upon the trustees to protect their rights and interests under it, then the children would be outside the common law doctrine, and would in a Court of Equity be allowed to enforce their rights under the deed, but that the whole application of that doctrine depends upon its being made out that upon the true construction of the deed, it was a deed which gave the children such a beneficial right.

The case was allowed to stand over. The trustees refused to become plaintiffs. The statement of claim was amended by making the wife and her two eldest daughters co-plaintiffs, and the case came on again for hearing; and it was held that the wife was entitled to sue, for that the agreement was really one between the husband and wife, and the trustees were introduced merely to obviate the objection to the wife suing her husband, and that the case came within the authorities referred to, that where a covenant is entered into with one person for the benefit of another, then if the covenantee will not sue, the person beneficially interested may sue in equity. The case was accordingly heard on the merits and disposed of.

The difficulties raised in these cases do not arise here. In *Gandy v. Gandy* (1885) 30 Ch D 57 it was not disputed that the trustees could sue, and again that the wife could sue, these being parties to the contract. Here we have the personal representatives of F. Davies, senior, who was a party to the contract, and the persons beneficially interested joined as co-plaintiffs suing the defendant. He it was who expressly bound himself to pay these annual sums, and his obligation was to his father, who is now represented by his executors. The defendant having got the full benefit of that contract, now inequitably declines to perform his part of it. Consequently it is not necessary to decide the question whether a fiduciary relation exists between the executors and the beneficiaries for the purpose of enabling the suit to be maintained by the latter. The executors of course admit that any moneys recovered by them from the defendant will be held by them for the benefit of the daughters and sons as provided by the deed.

There must be judgment for payment by the defendant to the executors of the sums due on foot of the arrears of the annuities, and for payment of the accruing gales to be applied by them in accordance with the terms of the 15th clause of the deed.

The defendant must pay the costs of the action".

Trusts and Powers

There is a fundamental distinction between trusts and powers; while trusts are of an imperative nature, powers are discretionary. A trustee must carry out his functions according to the terms of a trust whereas the donee of a power has considerable discretion as to the manner in which he exercises the power, if indeed he exercises it at all. The most usual type of power is a power of appointment, which authorizes the creation or grant of beneficial interests in property and which gives authority to the donee to nominate objects of the power who will generally be chosen from a defined class.

A trust may also confer a measure of discretion on a trustee e.g. he may be given a discretion to select beneficiaries from a specified class or to decide the proportions in accordance with which the trust property is to be divided, and this is known as a discretionary trust. There is also a concept known as a power in the nature of a trust or a 'trust power' which arises where a court implies the existence of a trust in default of any appointment being made by the donee of a power. The manner in which a court should determine whether a mere power or a trust power exists in circumstances where there has been a failure to exercise a power of appointment involves seeking to ascertain the intention or presumed intention of the testator from the instrument. As Lord Cottenham stated in *Burrough v. Philcox*:[3] 'When there appears a general intention in favour of a class, and a particular intention in favour of individuals of a class to be selected by another person, and the particular intention fails, from that selection not being made, the court will carry into effect the general intention in favour of the class.' So, where a court concludes that a testator would have intended such a result, it will construe a power of appointment as a power in the nature of a trust.[4] However, there must be 'something in the instrument creating the power from which the intention that the objects shall take in default of appointment can be gathered' and where no such intention can be gleaned from the will there can be no gift by implication to these objects.[5]

Re Kieran: Matthews v. Kieran
[1916] 1 IR 289

A testator devised and bequeathed his farm and the rest of his property to his brother on trust for the latter's eldest son and, if this son should die before attaining the age of 21, to such of his other sons as his brother should appoint.

---

[3] (1840) 5 My & Cr 72, 92.
[4] *Re Kieran* [1916] 1 IR 289.
[5] *Clibborn v. Horan* [1921] 1 IR 93, 97.

The testator's brother's eldest son died before he reached the age of 21 and his brother died without making any appointment amongst his three surviving sons. Pim J held that in the circumstances these three surviving sons were entitled to the farm in equal shares as tenants in common.

PIM J stated at pp.294–298: "Christopher Kieran, of Tenure, in the County of Louth, farmer, by his will dated the 23rd day of March, 1876, made the following devise and bequest:–

> "I give devise and bequeath my farm of land in Tenure and all my estate and interest therein, and all my cattle farming stock and implements of husbandry and all other property whatsoever of which I may die seized or possessed unto my brother Owen Kieran of Kieran's Cross, upon trust for his son John Kieran until he shall attain his full age of twenty-one years, when I will and direct said farm of land, cattle, farming stock &c. to be given over to my said nephew John Kieran provided his father the said Owen Kieran shall consider his conduct deserving the same, but in the event of the death of my said nephew John Kieran before he shall attain his age of twenty-one years, or of his father deeming him undeserving of said bequest, then I direct my said trustee to hold said farm of land and all other goods and chattels of every kind whatsoever upon trust for such other son of my said brother Owen Kieran as my said brother shall appoint."

Christopher Kieran died on the 11th December, 1883, without having altered his said will.

John Kieran, the *cestui que trust* named in the will, died on the 29th day of April, 1889, without having attained the age of twenty-one years.

Owen Kieran, the brother of the testator, and the donee of the power, died on the 26th May, 1915, without having exercised the said power, leaving him surviving three sons, viz., the defendants, Michael Joseph Kieran, James Kieran, and Patrick Kieran.

The question now arises, whether the three sons of Owen Kieran take the estate of the deceased testator Christopher Kieran in equal shares as tenants in common, or whether there is a failure of the trust contained in the will, in which event the next-of-kin of Christopher Kieran would take the said estate.

There is no decision in the books which answers the question raised. There are several cases which give some assistance in arriving at a conclusion, but the point, as now raised, has not as yet been decided. It is true that there are two old cases which are not unlike this case. There is the case of *Moseley v. Moseley* Rep *temp* Finch, 53, in which a somewhat similar trust came before Lord Nottingham, and in which he seems to have decided that if the donee of a power failed to exercise a discretion similar to the discretion in this case, the Court would exercise it for him. That case is interesting historically, but is otherwise of very little value, for the Court of Chancery has now for a very long period of years uniformly refused to do what Lord Nottingham seems to have done, namely, to exercise a discretion in cases of this kind.

There is another case of *Richardson v. Chapman* (1760) 7 Bro PC 318 in which, under very special circumstances, the House of Lords nominated a person to take under a trust. This decision, however, depended entirely on the peculiar circumstances of the case as presented to the House, and is of little value in deciding the point now at issue.

Mr. Poole, in his argument on behalf of the plaintiffs, cited the well-known case of *Brown v. Higgs* (1799) 4 Ves 708; (1800) 5 Ves 495. In that case an estate was devised to "one of the sons of my nephew Samuel Brown as the said John Brown shall direct by a conveyance in his lifetime, or by his last will and testament," and John Brown, not having exercised the power, Lord Alvanley, then Sir Richard Pepper Arden, was inclined to think, though he would not decide the point, that the children of Samuel Brown could not establish a claim. He seemed to consider that the power was a mere power, and that no trust could be implied therefrom. It is not easy to ascertain what Lord Eldon's opinion was, when the case came before him on appeal from Lord Alvanley (8 Ves 561, 574), and all that can be said is that he upheld the Court below. Lord St. Leonards, in his book on Powers (8th ed., p. 593), in discussing this case, says that in his opinion the power was clearly a simple power, and he further says that a power to appoint to such one of a class as a person shall name, authorizes the gift to one only of the class; no larger number, much less the whole class, can be made objects of the power. He adds:– "If, therefore, the power is in the nature of a trust, or there is a gift in the power itself by implication, it can only be commensurate with the power, and therefore for only one of the objects," and he ends with this question, "Which one would be the proper *cestui que trust*, or the person in whose favour the implied gift was made?" Lord St. Leonards, with great discretion, left the question unanswered, but it has been assumed by text-writers since that time that the Lord Chancellor meant to convey that if any gift could be implied in default of appointment, it ought to be to one person only of the class, and as no gift can be implied to one more than to another, that none of the class can take by implication.

Now, it is quite clear that a trust implied through and by reason of a power cannot be greater than the power itself. It is commensurate with it; and there is a great deal to be said for the meaning taken by text-writers from Lord St. Leonards' words in the case of a power, and a trust to be implied from such power; but whether such writers are right or wrong in their interpretation of Lord St. Leonards' words, the point with which the Lord Chancellor dealt is not the same point that is raised in this case, and I think I may say that the exact question that is now before the Court has, since the time of Lord Nottingham, not only not been answered, but has probably never been put to any Court.

In this case it is not a question of a power coupled with an implied trust at all. It is a trust with a power engrafted on it. The trust created by the will in Owen Kieran is a trust, first for a named person, and, in case of his death under twenty-one, a trust (I assume this for the moment) for a successor as yet unascertained, but to be ascertained by the said Owen Kieran. The power given to the said Owen Kieran is a limited power. It enables him to choose the successor, but the trust still remains a trust pointing to a class with a limited power of appointment in the donee.

Now, before discussing the exact effect of this, I desire to say that the particular words used, viz.: "for such other son as my said brother shall appoint," do not seem to me to be as strong as Mr. Poole argued. If the words had been " for one only of the other sons of my said brother," it would be clear that the power could be exercised only by giving the estate to one of the sons; but the words "such other son" seem to me to be possibly wide enough to enable the Court to bring it within the doctrine laid down in *Sinnott v. Walsh* (1879) 3 LR Ir 12; 5 IR Ir 27. The words there were " whatever existing member of my family he may be disposed to will it to," and I am disposed to think that the reasoning of Lord Chancellor Ball in that case might be sufficient to rule this case also. But as Mr. Poole has argued this case on the supposition that the words could not be held to point to more than one of the sons, and do not point to a class, I desire to decide the case on that assumption.

Now, it is the recognized duty of every Court to carry out a trust if it is possible to do so, and, if it is possible, a Court will avoid a construction which must result in an intestacy, and in the carrying of the property, possibly wholly, probably largely, to persons whom the testator never meant to get it.

What is the position of the three surviving sons of Owen Kieran? The testator has clearly expressed his intention that one of them at least should get the property. Each of them has a kind of contingent estate in the assets. If any two of them died, the Court could not refuse to give it to the survivor. If any two of them renounced, the Court could not refuse to give the property to the third. They all possess a similar and equal contingent estate, and a similar *spes successionis*. To hold that this trust has utterly failed would be manifestly doing violence to the testator's wishes, and in connexion with this it is important to recollect that there is no gift over. To hold that the three sons took equally would be, at all events, carrying out to a certain extent his declared desire. It might be argued that this would amount to an extension of the doctrine of *cy près* to trusts, but I do not so regard it. I am inclined to think that the Court, without doing any violence to the canons of interpretation, may infer from the words used that the desire of the testator was that the three sons should take equally if for any reason the power were not exercised.

There is a case of *Longmore v. Broom* (1802) 7 Ves 124, in which a testator bequeathed property to his two brothers and his sister or their children in such shares as the trustees should think proper. The trustees failed to exercise any discretion, and the matter came before the Court to say what should be done. It was argued that the word "or" indicated that the property was to be given to the brothers and sister on the one hand, or their children on the other hand; and the Court was pressed to read the word "or" as "and." The Master of the Rolls (Sir William Grant) refused to do this, and he said as follows (p. 128):–

"A bequest to *A*. or *B*. is void; but a bequest to *A*. or *B*. at the discretion of *C*. is good; for he may divide it between them."

Now, what is this case but a bequest to *A*. or *B*. or *C*. at the discretion of the trustee? If this is the way in which it should be read, then the trustee has a power of dividing the property between them.

On every ground, whether the gift is to be regarded as a gift to a class, or is to be regarded as a gift to one of a class, if the donee of the power should exercise his discretion, I am of opinion that in default of the exercise of the power the class must take, and I so decide.

Question (1) will be answered "Yes"."

Clibborn v. Horan
[1921] 1 IR 93

A testator made a devise of lands to a named individual for life with a power of appointment to this person amongst her children. It was held by O'Connor MR that this individual took a life estate coupled with a power of appointment but that no intention that there should be a trust in favour of the objects of the power was expressed or could be gleaned from the will and in the circumstances there could be no gift by implication to these objects.

O'CONNOR MR stated at pp.96–101: "This was certainly a most curious piece of conveyancing. The draftsman evidently thought that he was giving an indefeasible title to the appointees, but he failed to see that if the appointment was bad, and if no subsequent appointment was made by will, the property would pass to the testator's heir-at-law as undisposed of realty, unless, indeed, the will could be construed as giving Louisa Hamilton's children an estate in default of appointment. This, however, is not so, as I shall show hereafter.

The infirmity of the titles of John Butler Hamilton and Charles James Hamilton under the appointment by deed, and the attempted confirmation of it seems to have occurred at a later date to the mind of Louisa Hamilton, because by her will dated the 24th December, 1898, she re-appointed the property in the same way as she had previously done by deed.

She died on the 17th December, 1902, and her will was proved on the 22nd October, 1903. Unfortunately her son, John Butler Hamilton, died a very short time before her, viz., on the 26th October, 1902, with the result that, so far as the appointment in his favour by the will was concerned, it failed. His title, however, was treated as valid, and the trustees of his will, who are the vendors in the present case, went into, and are still in receipt of, the fee-farm rent. The abstract of title as originally furnished was not complete. It was supplemented by giving the purchaser's solicitor a copy of the deed of appointment, and then the objection was taken that it was altogether inoperative. That was met by furnishing the deed of confirmation, dated the 9th March,

1898, but on perusing it the purchaser's solicitor wrote saying that his counsel, having carefully considered the matter, could not advise his client to accept the title, and he called for a return of his deposit. The vendor's solicitor then wrote asking what the objection to the title was. There was no immediate reply to this inquiry. Apparently the purchaser's solicitor thought that he had already stated his objection, and that he had rescinded the contract by asking for a return of his deposit. I think that this was a reasonable view to take, because he had previously objected to the appointment by deed, and that objection was met by the production of the deed of confirmation, which really had not the intended effect. Later on the purchaser's solicitor wrote saying that he was instructed to issue a writ for the return of the deposit. This was met by a declaration of the vendor's intention to issue a writ against the purchaser for specific performance. The present summons was taken out in lieu of the threatened action.

Now, it is perfectly clear that if the title as exhibited was defective, and the purchaser's objection was good, and remained unanswered for a reasonable time, he had a right to rescind. I think that it is equally clear that he did in fact rescind. He refused to complete the purchase, and demanded a return of the deposit. The question, therefore, is: was the title as exhibited bad? It was clearly bad unless there was an implied gift by the will of Bernard Butler to the children of Louisa Hamilton in default of appointment, which is the contention of the vendors.

Mr. Walker, for the vendors, relied on the general proposition that where there is a power to appoint among certain objects, and no gift in default of appointment, as is the case here, the Court will imply a gift to the objects. In my opinion the proposition thus stated is too wide. There must be something in the instrument creating the power from which the intention that the objects shall take in default of appointment can be gathered. This is the result of the authorities.

Healy v. Donnery (1853) 3 ICLR 213 is the leading Irish authority. There a testator by his will devised property to his daughter for life, with power to her by deed or will to dispose, devise, or bequeath it to and among her children in such shares and proportions as she should think fit and proper. It was held that the power was a naked one, not coupled with a trust, and that no estate was given to the children by implication. Pennefather B. stated the law in language which has received approval. He said: "It is argued that the power to appoint among the children is tantamount to a trust created for them. I have always considered that there was a distinction between a mere power and one coupled with a trust; and though I called on counsel for an authority to the contrary, no such case has been cited. But particular cases have been cited in which Courts have thought that they collected from the peculiar words of the power an intention of the testator to give to children in default of appointment." To the same effect is *In re Weekes' Settlement* [1897] 1 Ch D 289, where the gift was by a testatrix to her husband for life, with a power to the husband to appoint among the children of the husband and wife. It was held that this did not imply a gift to the members of the class in default of appointment. Romer J. said: "The authorities do not show, in my opinion, that there is a hard-and-fast rule that a gift to A for life, with a power to A to appoint among a class and nothing more, must, if there is no gift over in the will, be held a gift by implication to the class in default of the power being exercised. In my opinion, the cases show (though there may be found here and there certain remarks of a few learned Judges which, if not interpreted by the facts of the particular case before them, might seem to have a more extended operation) that you must find in the will an indication that the testatrix did intend the class or some of the class to take – intended, in fact, that this power should be regarded in the nature of a trust, only a power of selection being given, as, for example, a gift to A for life, with a gift over to such of a class as A shall appoint." Romer J. then goes on to deal with the authorities, and he cites *Healy v. Donnery*, quoting from the judgment of Pennefather B. the passage I have read, which, he said, contained a correct statement of the law.

He then deals with *Brown v. Higgs* (1799) 4 Ves 708, *Burrough v. Philcox* (1840) 5 My & Cr 72, and other cases, including *Re White's Trusts* (1860) Johnson 656, and *In re Caplin's Will* (1865) 2 Dr & Sm 527. He shows that in all these cases there were certain features which either indicate a trust in favour of the objects of the power, or which contained a gift to the objects with a mere power of selection to the appointee. Mr. Walker relied on *White's Trusts*, and the judgment therein of Woods V.-C., in which occurs the following passage:– "It is settled by *Brown v. Higgs* and *Borrough v. Philcox* that where there is a power to appoint among certain objects and no gift in default of appointment, the Court will imply a gift to the objects of the power equally." Romer J. comments on that in this way:– "I have pointed out that these two cases do not decide that. I have no doubt Woods V.-C. in making that statement meant it to be considered with reference to cases where the facts were similar or somewhat similar to those in *Brown v. Higgs* and *Burrough v. Philcox*, that is to say, cases where you can gather from the will that the class are intended to take, and a selection only is given to the person having the power of appointment, as was shown by the observation in *Burrough v. Philcox*, to which I have already referred."

On these authorities I am bound to hold that there was no implied gift to the children of Louisa Hamilton; that the will of Bernard Butler gave her a mere life estate, coupled with a power which she was free to exercise or not as she thought fit, and that there was no trust for the children. Possibly the testator intended that the children should take the estate, even though the power should not be exercised, but there is no such intention expressed or to be gathered from the will, and I am bound by the will. The title, as exhibited, was therefore bad, and the purchaser was entitled to rescind it, and did in fact rescind it.

In this state of affairs the summons was taken out, and the vendors now offer to make title in a different way – under the Statute of Limitations. Mr.

Murnaghan, for the purchaser, meets that offer by the reply that it is too late, as the contract was rescinded before the case came into Court, and that he is not now under any obligation to complete it. He relies upon the very case cited by Mr. Walker in support of the proposition, that a possessory title may be forced upon a purchaser if it appears, on the hearing of a vendor and purchaser summons or an action for specific performance, that title may be made in this way, although the abstract offered only a documentary title. This was *Atkinson and Horsell's Contract* [1912] 1 Ch 2; [1912] 2 Ch 1, in which a summons was taken out by a purchaser for a declaration that the vendor had not shown good title, and for a return of the deposit. The vendor showed that he was in a position to make title under the statute. The purchaser objected, 1, that he was not bound to take a possessory title under the contract; and, 2, that he had repudiated the contract, as he was entitled to do, because a good title had not been shown. This last point was held to be untenable in the circumstances, because the summons was taken out by the purchaser asking for rescission, and not for a declaration that the contract had been rescinded. He had treated the contract as a subsisting one. This is the judgment of Cozens-Hardy M.R. on the point:– "The purchaser takes out a summons, and asks for rescission, treating the contract as still subsisting, and does not raise the point either in the form of the summons or upon affidavit that the contract was well repudiated before the summons was taken out, and he is content to rely on that repudiation apart from anything else. On that ground I think that that particular objection is not open to him, and that if he succeeds at all in this appeal it cannot be on that ground." Fletcher-Moulton L.J. and Buckley L.J. concurred on this point. But the present summons has been taken out by the vendor, and the purchaser comes into Court and says he has rescinded the contract. That is an entirely different case, and I must hold that the purchaser is right on this point, and entitled to have the summons dismissed and to have his deposit returned.

This is an end of the matter, and I do not think that I ought to go into the question whether, if the rescission point had not been open, the purchaser would be bound to accept a possessory title in this case. It has been laid down in *Atkinson and Horsell's Contract*, as a general proposition, that a vendor is entitled to force a possessory title on a purchaser, notwithstanding that the contract was for a documentary title, and I would be bound by that decision; but I think that the question is still open whether – although it must be accepted as a general rule that a possessory title can be substituted for a documentary title – this is a proposition of universal application, no matter what the nature of the estate the subject of the contract. In *Ashe and Hogan's Contract* [1920] 1 IR 159 I discussed this question, and I pointed out the difficulty in applying it to leasehold estates, having regard to the quality of the title acquired by possession, as decided in *Tichbourne v. Weir* (1892) 67 LT 735.

The point may come up at a future time. Perhaps, too, the weighty reasons given by Fletcher-Moulton L.J. for not forcing a possessory title on a purchaser who had contracted for a title to be exhibited in the ordinary way will yet come up for consideration by the House of Lords."

CHAPTER 4

Trusts – Formalities and Essential Elements

FORMALITIES

Creation of Trusts *Inter Vivos* – Statute Not to be Used as an Instrument of Fraud

Primarily in order to prevent fraud, certain formalities must be observed in the creation of specified types of express trusts. Section 4 of the Statute of Frauds (Ireland) 1695 provides that to create an enforceable trust of land, whether freehold or leasehold, the trust must be evidenced in writing and signed by a person able to declare the trust, or by his will. However, the courts will not always insist on strict compliance with the such provisions where it would lead to the statute being used as an instrument of fraud. This principle can be clearly seen in the following *dicta* of Lord Westbury in *McCormick v. Grogan*:[1]

> The Court of Equity has, from a very early period, decided that even an Act of Parliament shall not be used as an instrument of fraud; and if in the machinery of perpetrating a fraud an Act of Parliament intervenes, the Court of Equity, it is true, does not set aside the Act of Parliament, but it fastens on the individual who gets a title under that Act, and imposes upon him a personal obligation, because he applies the Act as an instrument for accomplishing a fraud.

So, the court will not permit a beneficiary to be deprived of an interest in land under a trust in the absence of written evidence of the trust if such a result would amount to a fraud providing that there is some other evidence to establish the existence and nature of the trust.[2]

McGillycuddy v. Joy
[1959] IR 189

The plaintiff and the defendants agreed to purchase a farm jointly and the contract was signed by one of the defendants. The plaintiff paid one third of the purchase price and the defendants then reneged on the agreement. The plaintiff sought a declaration that the defendant, who had signed the agreement held the benefit of the contract in trust for him. Budd J held the defendant had

---

[1] (1869) LR 4 HL 82, 97.

[2] *Rochefoucauld v. Boustead* [1897] 1 Ch 196, *McGillycuddy v. Joy* [1959] IR 189 and *Gilmurray v. Corr* [1978] NI 99.

purchased that part of the lands previously agreed between them in trust for the plaintiff and that the former's repudiation of that trust constituted a fraud against which the court would grant relief.

BUDD J stated at pp. 210–214: "With regard to the agreement and the alleged repudiation of it, I accept the plaintiff's evidence that an arrangement was made with both the Joys to buy "Breen's farm"; that the price was to be divided between the Joys and the plaintiff in the proportion two-thirds to the Joys and one-third to the plaintiff; that "The Inches" – including in that expression the two fields I have already mentioned was to become the property of the plaintiff and the remainder of the land above the waist was to become the property of the defendants; and that the fishing appurtenant to "The Inches" was to go to the plaintiff and the fishing appurtenant to the rest of the land was to go to the defendants. The fact that such an agreement was come to is confirmed by the evidence of Mr. Downing and was recognised by David Joy in his conversations with Mr. Downing and the plaintiff after the sale. I am satisfied, as I have already indicated, that it was agreed between the parties that the fishing alongside "Breen's" portion of the land was to be sold or leased to the plaintiff and that in the event of disagreement as to the price or the length of the term of the lease or the amount of the rent or any other matter in connection with the terms of the lease, such matter was to be referred to an independent arbitrator. Accordingly, in my view, the terms of the agreement come to between the parties were certain; there was consideration for the agreement and the agreement, in my view, amounted to a binding agreement in law between the parties. There is, of course, no question but that the agreement was repudiated when David Joy announced to Mr. Downing on the 7th December, 1957, that he was keeping the whole place for himself and that he did not intend to implement the arrangement with the plaintiff.

The plaintiff relies on the letter of the 28th April, 1957 as constituting a sufficient memorandum within the Statute of Frauds. Mr. Micks says that the subject-matter of the agreement, "Breen's farm," was mentioned in that letter, so were the parties, namely, the plaintiff and David Joy, and that the proportions in which the purchase moneys were to be divided are, also, stated there. However, to my mind there is this also to be said on that memorandum: that William, whom I have already found to be a party to the agreement, is not stated as a party in the memorandum; that "The Inches," the portion to go to the plaintiff, was not mentioned in the memorandum as being his share; and that the method of determining the rent and terms of the lease is not mentioned in the memorandum. I am far from saying that the memorandum is not a sufficient memorandum within the Statute of Frauds – it may be good – but, for my part, I prefer to proceed in this case on the basis that there is no sufficient memorandum to satisfy the Statute. That being so, the plaintiff relies on the principle of law stated in *Rochefoucauld v. Boustead* [1897] 1 Ch 196.

The facts of the case were these: the plaintiff was the owner of certain estates in Ceylon. She was divorced from her husband who had acquired an interest in the lands under the order of the Divorce Court. The estates were subject to a mortgage for £25,000 which became vested in a Dutch company. The Dutch company wished to call in the mortgage. The plaintiff could not herself raise the necessary money and feared that the husband might obtain a transfer and foreclose. She therefore entered into an arrangement with the defendant for him to take a transfer of the mortgage, he being anxious to help her. It was arranged that the Dutch company should sell the estates by auction and that the defendant should buy at a price sufficient to cover the mortgage. He duly purchased under the arrangement. In the result, the position was this: Boustead had purchased, and, on the face of it, the estate was conveyed to him absolutely. He proceeded to manage the estates and later actually used them for security for certain advances which were made to him from certain bankers. He also remitted substantial sums to the plaintiff out of the property. He got into difficulties and became bankrupt and, then, this suit was brought by the plaintiff, who claimed that, though the purchase was absolute in form, Boustead had purchased in such circumstances that he held the estates as a trustee for her subject to a charge in his favour for all advances made by him and such moneys as he had expended in working the estates. There was no memorandum sufficient to satisfy the Statute of Frauds. The correspondence which passed between the parties was only relevant in so far as it showed that the circumstances gave rise to the implication of a trust. The defences relied on were, first, that the conveyance was to the defendant as beneficial owner, and, secondly, that the trusts alleged were not evidenced in writing, so that the Statute of Frauds applied. There were other defences not relevant to consider, such as the Statute of Limitations and laches. Lindley L.J., in the course of his judgment, at p. 205, having dealt with the circumstances of the case, laid down a general proposition of law which the plaintiff asks me to apply in this case. "This conclusion," he said, "renders it necessary to consider whether the Statute of Frauds affords a defence to the plaintiff's claim. The section relied upon is s. 7, which has been judicially interpreted in *Forster v. Hale* (1798) 3 Ves 696 and *Smith v. Matthews* (1861) 3 De GF & J 139. According to these authorities, it is necessary to prove by some writing or writings signed by the defendant, not only that the conveyance to him was subject to some trust, but also what that trust was. But it is not necessary that the trust should have been declared by such a writing in the first instance; it is sufficient if the trust can be proved by some writing signed by the defendant, and the date of the writing is immaterial. It is further established by a series of cases, the propriety of which cannot now be questioned, that the Statute of Frauds does not prevent the proof of a fraud; and that it is a fraud on the part of a person to whom land is conveyed as a trustee, and who knows it was so conveyed, to deny the trust and claim the land himself. Consequently, notwithstanding the statute, it is competent for a person claiming land conveyed to another to prove by parol evidence that it was so conveyed upon trust for the claimant, and that the grantee, knowing the facts, is denying the trust and relying upon the form of conveyance and the statute, in order to keep the land himself."

Mr. Liston, in the course of his argument, agreed that there was no distinction in principle between a case where a conveyance of land has been executed and a case where the proceedings had only reached a stage where a contract had been entered into between the vendor and purchaser and where the purchaser repudiates an agreement giving rise to a trust and denies the existence of a trust. It seems to me that the statement of Lindley L.J. covers the present case in principle and that his statement can be read with very little change of language to cover the facts of this case. If in the relevant portion of the quotation we substitute for the words, "conveyed," "grantee" and "form of conveyance," the words, "agreed to be conveyed," "purchaser" and "form of agreement," then it will be seen that what I say is correct. The relevant portion of the quotation thus reads:– "Consequently, notwithstanding the statute, it is competent for a person claiming land agreed to be conveyed to another to prove by parol evidence that it was so agreed to be conveyed upon trust for the claimant, and that the purchaser, knowing the facts, is denying the trust and relying upon the form of the agreement and the statute, in order to keep the land for himself." Mr. Liston submitted that the principle as stated by Lindley L.J., only applies to cases where the plaintiff in the proceedings is deprived by the repudiation of trust of some property which was formerly his, as distinct from being deprived of the benefit of a bargain. It seems to me that the case of *Chattock v. Muller* (1878) 8 Ch D 177 is an answer to this. That decision shows that the proposition of law enunciated by Lindley L.J. equally well applies to the case of a purchase, where the arrangement was that the purchaser was to cede portion of the property purchased, which the plaintiff had no previous interest in, and that in such case the purchaser takes as a trustee the part to be ceded, and, further, that an assumption of ownership of the whole will be regarded as fraud. While these two cases are English cases and are not binding upon me, with respect I see no reason whatsoever to differ from the principles enunciated and, it seems to me, these principles apply to a case such as the present. However, if there is any doubt about it, such doubts must be dispelled by reference to the case of *Devine v. Fields* (1920) 54 ILTR 101 to which I have already referred, where the principles laid down and applied in these two cases were applied in Ireland by the Master of the Rolls. The facts in *Devine's Case* are not very dissimilar to the present case. The parties there each wanted portion of a property which was going to be sold and agreed, as the Master of the Rolls found, that the plaintiff should bid for the property on behalf of both. He did so, he secured the property and then repudiated his arrangement to divide the property. On the basis that the plaintiff had agreed to cede portion of the property to the defendant and had lulled the defendant into not making an offer, the Master of the Rolls held that the plaintiff had purchased as a trustee as to part of the property. The parties, incidentally, had not agreed on any apportionment of the annuity, but the Master of the Rolls suggested that the Land Commission should apportion the annuity and said that if it did not do so there was no reason why it could not be done by the Court. Presumably, the Land Commission will do the same in this case if it agrees to the sub-division.

I am satisfied that the defendants here lulled the plaintiff into not bidding for the farm or making an offer for it. I am satisfied the plaintiff was ready to buy the whole farm himself, if necessary. I am satisfied that the evidence shows that the plaintiff and David Joy mutually agreed that the plaintiff should not bid or negotiate; that it was an arrangement for their mutual benefit in that they both thought the price would be put up if the plaintiff did bid. I am satisfied that the evidence shows that the plaintiff was lulled into trusting the defendants to make an arrangement on his behalf when he might have negotiated the purchase on his own. Therefore, in my view, the plaintiff has made out his case, he has shown that an agreement was come to as he has alleged. I take the view that, although the memorandum relied on may be insufficient to satisfy the Statute of Frauds, the principle laid down in *Rochefoucauld v. Boustead* applies and that the defendant, David Joy, purchased part of the lands as trustee for the plaintiff and that his repudiation of that trust constitutes a fraud. Accordingly, I propose to make a declaration in favour of the plaintiff in the terms of paragraph 1 of the prayer in the statement of claim to the effect that the defendant, David Joy, holds the benefit of the contract for the purchase of this farm in trust for the plaintiff as to that portion of the same known as "The Inches," including the two fields previously referred to, together with the fishing rights attached thereto. I shall also make such declaration as is appropriate, having regard to what I have already said, with regard to the sale or lease of the fishing rights, the precise form of which can be settled, I have no doubt, by agreement between counsel."

Creation of Trusts by Will

Where a trust is created by will, the testator must comply with the statutory requirements laid down by s.78 of the Succession Act 1965 in relation to the making of statutory dispositions, i.e. that the will be in writing, signed at the foot thereof by the testator or by some other person in his presence and at his direction and the testator's signature must be made or acknowledged in the presence of two or more witnesses present at the same time, each of whom must attest that signature by his own signature.

However, as with trusts created *inter vivos*, equity will not always strictly enforce the statutory formalities required where the statute is being used as an instrument of fraud and it was in obedience to this principle that so called 'secret trusts', which will be considered in Chapter 5, came to be recognised.

ESSENTIAL ELEMENTS

Essential Elements of a Trust

Apart from ensuring compliance with the formalities outlined above, no technical or precise language is necessary to create a valid express trust. However, certain essential elements which have come to be known as 'the three certainties' must be present if such a trust is to be created. These three conditions of substance are as follows; certainty of intention or words, certainty of subject matter and certainty of objects. These requirements were laid down by O'Byrne J in the decision of *Chambers v. Fahy*.[3]

Chambers v. Fahy
[1931] IR 17

The testator left all his property to his brother 'with full power to dispose of it as he thinks fit for the use and benefit of my wife and children'. It was held by the High Court (O'Sullivan P and O'Byrne J) that the brother did not take the property beneficially but as a trustee for the testator's wife and children with a power of appointment among them.

O'SULLIVAN P stated at pp.19–21: "The will of Patrick Fahy, father of the plaintiff, Margaret Chambers, reads as follows:–

> "I leave and bequeath to my brother, Rev. J. Fahy, 8 George's Quay, Cork, my two farms, the insurance on my life, and the insurance on the joint lives of myself and my wife, with all the property which I shall die possessed of or entitled to. He is to pay all my just debts and funeral expenses. After my debts are paid, I leave absolutely all my property to my brother, Rev. J. Fahy, with full power to dispose of it as he thinks fit for the use and benefit of my wife and children."

The plaintiff claims that under that will Father Fahy took the property not beneficially, but as a trustee for the testator's wife and children, as joint tenants or as tenants in common, and that he had not any power of appointment. For the defendants, Mr. Ryan submitted that Father Fahy took the property beneficially; and Mr. Hungerford and Mr. Walker contended that he took as a trustee, with wide powers of appointment among the beneficiaries.

In the course of the argument our attention was directed to *M'Cabe v. Campbell* [1918] 1 IR 429, and to earlier cases, in which wills in somewhat similar terms to the present will were considered and construed. There is, however, no contest here as to the general principles applicable in such cases.

---

[3] [1931] IR 17, 21. See also *Knight v. Knight* (1840) 3 Beav 148, 173 *per* Lord Langdale MR.

I am of opinion, notwithstanding the argument of Mr. Ryan, that the Rev. J. Fahy did not take for his own use. Mr. Ryan relies upon the words: "I leave absolutely all my property to my brother, Rev. J. Fahy." I do not think we can stop at that point and disregard what follows, namely, the words: "with full power to dispose of it as he thinks fit for the use and benefit of my wife and children." We must read the will as a whole; and, so doing, I am satisfied that the testator did not intend that his brother should hold the property beneficially. Accordingly, in my opinion, the Rev. J. Fahy held the property as a trustee.

The next question is whether the trustee had any power of appointment among the beneficiaries. I was influenced at first by Mr. M'Carthy's argument that "dispose" means to "realise," to "sell," but during the course of the argument I altered my opinion. I think that construction of the words "dispose . . . as he thinks fit," is unnecessarily narrow, and that the words confer a power to appoint among the wife and children in such shares as the trustee thinks proper. If that construction of the will be correct, there only remains for determination one question of fact. In the course of his administration of the trust Father Fahy did apportion the property in different shares among the children. Mrs. Chambers thinks she did not get a fair share, but that was a matter to be determined by the trustee. It was, however, suggested on her behalf that the trustee did not distribute among the *cestuis qui trustent* the entire trust property, and that he disposed of a part of it for which he did not account. It lay upon the plaintiff to adduce some evidence to support that suggestion, and to show that part of the trust property remained unadministered by Father Fahy. She stated in the course of her evidence that part of her father's farm was given by Father Fahy to Denis Duggan, the executor of her father's will. That was denied by Denis Duggan, and there the matter rested. The Circuit Judge accepted Denis Duggan's evidence, and was satisfied that Father Fahy had fully administered the trust created by the will. On the evidence, as it appears in the transcript before us, it would be difficult for us to differ from the Circuit Judge, but we have had the advantage of seeing the schedule of assets and the deed of assignment by Father Fahy to Denis Duggan of the land which it was alleged formed part of the testator's assets. These documents were not in evidence in the Circuit Court, and it was suggested that if they were produced they would support the case made by the plaintiff. These documents do not assist the plaintiff; on the contrary, they go to show that the land assigned to Duggan formed no part of the testator's estate.

The decision of the Circuit Judge was right, and this appeal must be dismissed. Mr. Ryan's client must bear his own costs. The other defendants will get their costs out of the estate."

O'BYRNE J stated at pp.21–23: "I agree with the decision of the President, and with the reasons expressed by him. I desire, however, to say a few words in regard to the construction of this will.

It is argued by Mr. Ryan that, on the true construction of the will, Rev.

Father Fahy took the entire residuary estate beneficially, unencumbered by any trust. The other parties in this suit contend that he took as a trustee. A considerable number of authorities have been cited before us, and I do not intend to go through them, or attempt to reconcile them. These authorities establish certain general principles which must be applied in this as in every other case, for the purpose of gathering, as best one can, the intention of the testator in the particular case.

It has been established that, in order that a trust may be created, the subject-matter must be certain, the objects of the trust must be certain, and the words relied upon as creating the trust must have been used in an imperative sense, so as to show that the testator intended to create an obligation. Now, as far as the first two matters are concerned, there is no difficulty. The subject-matter is certain: it consists of the entire estate after the testator's debts and funeral expenses were paid. The objects of the trust are certain: they are stated in the will to be the testator's wife and children. It only remains to be considered whether the words used by the testator were used in an imperative sense, so as to create an obligation upon Rev. Father Fahy to apply the property for the purpose stated by the testator in the will. The words relied upon are:– "I leave absolutely all my property to my brother, Rev. J. Fahy, with full power to dispose of it as he thinks fit for the use and benefit of my wife and children." That clause, Mr. Ryan contends, was merely intended to express the reason for the testator's gift of the property to Father Fahy – to express, perhaps, a pious hope that he might possibly dispose of the property in favour of some of the children. If that were the object of the testator, I must say that the words used were singularly inapt and inappropriate for that purpose.

The will is a very short one. After the appointment of executors, it consists of three sentences. In construing the will, we are entitled to have regard to all the circumstances in which the will was made. This will was made five days before the testator's death. He had at that time a wife and five young children, the youngest being aged eleven years. He had a brother who was a clergyman: a clergyman, as we gather from the evidence, who was well provided for; a gentleman who, out of his own private means, was able to supply very considerable sums of money for the benefit of this family. I take it he was quite independent; and it strikes one as being very strange that a testator with a wife and five young children should pass them over, and dispose of his entire property in favour of a reverend gentleman, who was obviously in no need of it. But it was competent for him to do so, and such a bequest, if clearly expressed by the testator, must be upheld by this Court. Now, the first sentence relied upon is: "I leave and bequeath to my brother, Rev. J. Fahy, 8 George's Quay, Cork, my two farms, the insurance on my life, and the insurance on the joint lives of myself and my wife, with all the property that I shall die possessed of or entitled to." This sentence is relied on by Mr. Ryan as showing that Father Fahy was not a trustee. He says that, in the first instance, the testator made a clear, absolute bequest to Father Fahy. In these circumstances, Mr.

Ryan contends that the gift is not to be cut down or controlled by any trust unless such was clearly intended. I think Mr. Ryan is right in that contention; but I think the subsequent words do clearly show that the testator intended that the gift was to be cut down and controlled by the following provisions. The next sentence is to the following effect:– "He is to pay all my just debts and funeral expenses." It is fairly clear that the testator did not know that the executors are bound to pay the testator's debts and funeral expenses. That consideration is of no importance; the important consideration is what effect was intended by the testator to be given to these words. They seem to me in the clearest manner to have been intended to create a legal obligation upon Rev. Father Fahy; an obligation binding upon this property. In other words, Father Fahy took this property upon trust, in the first instance, to apply it for the purposes named, namely, to pay the debts and funeral expenses. I now come to the next and final sentence: "After my debts are paid I leave absolutely all my property to my brother, Rev. J. Fahy, with full power to dispose of it as he thinks fit for the use and benefit of my wife and children." The first sentence (with reference to the debts and funeral expenses) clearly controlled the disposal of the property: I am of opinion that the succeeding sentence has a similar object. I think I am entitled to approach the construction of this sentence in the same manner as Holmes L.J. approached the construction of a similar clause in the case of *Hickey v. Hickey* [1913] 1 IR 390. Approaching it in this way, I leave out the words "with full power to dispose of it as he thinks fit." The clause now reads: "After my debts are paid I leave absolutely all my property to my brother, Rev. J. Fahy, for the use and benefit of my wife and children." If the clause were in that form it seems to me unarguable that a trust was not intended. Can it be suggested that the insertion of the words, "with full power to dispose of it as he thinks fit," so alters that construction as to give Father Fahy a beneficial interest? I consider that it would be impossible to give such a construction to these words. They were inserted for a definite purpose; they were not intended to give Father Fahy a beneficial interest, or to cut down the clear meaning of the trust. It seems to me that the object of the words was to give Father Fahy wide discretionary powers in connection with the execution of the trust, and not to give him a beneficial interest in the property.

As to the alleged power of appointment, I am of opinion that Father Fahy had full power to appoint among the children; and I agree with the President that to give the words the meaning contended for by Mr. M'Carthy would involve giving them an unnecessarily narrow construction.

It seems to me to be clear that the words, "with full power to dispose as he thinks fit for the use and benefit of my wife and children" were intended by the testator to confer upon Father Fahy rather wide discretionary powers. The words seem to me to confer a power to dispose of the property in favour of any of the persons named in the trust. I think he would be equally disposing of it for the benefit of the wife and children if he alienated it for their benefit, or distributed it amongst them. Accordingly, I am of opinion that Father Fahy was entitled to dispose of the property by appointing it amongst the objects of the trust.

I do not think it necessary to comment upon any of the questions of fact which have been dealt with by the President."

Certainty of Intention or Words

The requirement that the words used to create a trust be imperative does not mean that any precise form of wording must be used and the courts will examine the substance and effect of the words used in order to ascertain the actual intention of the settlor or testator. The prevailing view today is that so called 'precatory words', which express a hope, wish, expectation or desire that the donee would deal with the property in a particular manner, are usually insufficient to create a trust.[4] However, despite this general trend, precatory words may be sufficient to create a trust if it is clear from the language used in the will as a whole that this was the testator's intention.[5] So, it would be incorrect to assume that an analysis of the particular form of words used would of itself be sufficient to determine whether a trust had been created[6] and the view has been expressed that the courts will be guided by the testator's intentions apparent from the will rather than by the particular words used.[7]

Re Humphrey's Estate
[1916] 1 IR 21

A testator devised and bequeathed all his property, real and personal to his wife and added that he wished that she should leave by will or transfer during her lifetime a house and demense to his son and that the remainder of his property should be left or transferred to his daughters in such way as his wife should think fit. Ross J held that in the circumstances, the wife took an absolute interest.

ROSS J stated at pp.23–26: "The earlier words in the will confer an absolute interest on the wife. The question is whether the later clauses cut down this interest to an estate for life. In the latter event the daughter, who was born after the date of the will is altogether excluded from participation. To the ordinary man of intelligence, uninstructed in the doctrine of what are called precatory trusts, it would, no doubt, cause astonishment that there could be any doubt about the true meaning of this will.

---

[4] *Re Humphrey's Estate* [1916] 1 IR 21 and *Re Sweeney* [1976-77] ILRM 88.
[5] *Comiskey v. Bowring-Hanbury* [1905] AC 84.
[6] *Re Hamilton* [1895] 2 Ch 370, 373 and *Re McIntosh* [1933] IR 69, 71.
[7] *Re Williams* [1897] 2 Ch 12, 14 and *Re Coulson* (1953) 87 ILTR 93, 94.

The testator in clear words gives all his property to his wife, and appoints her executrix. He then expresses a wish that she should dispose of it for the benefit of his children in a certain way. I am sure the testator himself would have been amazed if the mere expression of his wish for the guidance of his wife should have the effect of creating a legal obligation of the strictest character, tying up all the property and preventing her from providing for any children that might be born after the making of the will. After a devise and bequest in clear and explicit terms, if a trust is intended to be created one would expect that this would be done in terms equally clear and explicit. When we come to consider the innumerable decisions in which the Courts of equity have displayed their benevolent astuteness in imposing an obligatory meaning upon words merely expressive of desire, the mind is reduced to a condition of perplexity and confusion. Trusts have been held to be created by the following expressions:— "I desire him to give," "I advise him to settle," "It is my dying request," "It is my will and desire," "I recommend," "Well knowing," and such like. All these one would think impose at most a moral obligation. On the other hand, an expression of hope that the devisee would continue the estate in the family has been held to create no trust. I think it is quite impossible to reconcile the cases. However that may be, there is no doubt that the tide has turned and is running strong against precatory trusts.

In *Lambe v. Eames* (1871) 6 Ch App 597, at p. 599, Lord Justice James said:— "In hearing case after case cited, I could not help feeling that the officious kindness of the Court of Chancery, in interposing trusts where in many cases the father of the family never meant to create trusts, must have been a very cruel kindness indeed." These words are approved of by Lopes L.J. in *Hill v. Hill* [1897] 1 QB 483, at p. 488, who further says: "It is inconceivable to me that a testator who really meant his hope, recommendation, confidence, or request to be imperative should not express his intention in a mandatory form. I agree with Mr. Farwell in his book on Powers, when he says at p. 480, 'It would not be a very strained inference to regard all such expressions as stating the motive that induced the absolute gift rather than as a fetter imposed upon it.'" He adds, " It is in every case a question of intention, and the whole document with the surrorunding circumstances must be considered."

Lord Lindley says in *In re Hamilton* [1895] 2 Ch 370, at p. 373:— "You must take the will which you have to construe and see what it means, and if you come to the conclusion that no trust was intended, you say so, although previous judges have said the contrary on some wills more or less similar to the one which you have to construe."

Lord St. Leonards, in his work on the Law of Property, published in 1849, wrote as follows (p. 375):— "The law as to the operation of words of recommendation, confidence, request, or the like, attached to an absolute gift, has in late times varied from the earlier authorities. In nearly every recent case the gift has been held to be uncontrolled by the request or recommendation made or confidence expressed. This undoubtedly simplifies the law, and it is not an unwholesome rule that, if a testator really mean his recommendation to be imperative, he should express his intention in a mandatory form; but this conclusion was not arrived at without a considerable struggle."

Lord Lindley approves of these words in *In re Williams* [1897] 2 Ch 12, and calls it a sensible rule. In the same case he puts the matter thus (at p. 18):— "There can be no doubt that equitable obligations, whether trusts or conditions, can be imposed by any language which is clear enough to show an intention to impose an obligation, and is definite enough to enable the Court to ascertain what the precise obligation is, and in whose favour it is to be performed. There is also abundant authority for saying that, if property is left to a person in confidence that he will dispose of it in a particular way as to which there is no ambiguity, such words are amply sufficient to impose an obligation. . . . Unless it appears from the whole will that an obligation was intended to be imposed, no obligation will be held to exist; yet, moreover, in some of the older cases obligations were inferred from language which in modern times would be thought insufficient to justify such an inference."

In *In re Hamilton* a testatrix left legacies to her two nieces, and added, "I wish them to bequeath the same equally between the families of O. and P." The English Court of Appeal held that these words merely amounted to an expression of the wish of the testatrix, and created no trust in favour of the families indicated.

In *In re Diggles* (1888) 39 Ch 253 the Court held that in considering whether on the whole will the testator's intention was to create a trust, regard may be had to any embarrassment and difficulty which would arise from a trust. Applying this to the case before me, surely the possibility that children might be born to the testator after making his will, for whom his wife could not provide, is such an embarrassment and difficulty.

In *Wright v. Atkyns* (1823) Turn & R 143, which was much relied on in the contention in favour of a trust, it was laid down (at p. 157) that three things are required to create such a trust:— "(1) the word must be imperative; (2) the subject must be certain; (3) the object must be certain. Assuming certainty in the subject and object indicated in this will, am I obliged to hold the words used imperative? I think not.

The outcome of these cases is simply this, that the words are to be interpreted in their ordinary sense, unless there is something in the terms of the will operating upon the property disposed of, from which a Court ought to infer that a trust is intended or a condition imposed. In this will there is not a trust, in language, from the beginning to the end of it, or anything in the will from which a trust can be legitimately inferred.

I therefore hold that Elinor Mary Augusta Longfield took the property absolutely uncontrolled by any legal obligation, and I make a declaration accordingly in respect of the £900 now in Court."

Re Sweeney: Hillary v. Sweeney
[1976-77] ILRM 88

The testator devised and bequeathed all his assets to his wife, the first named defendant, for her own absolute use and benefit 'subject to the express wish' that she make provision for the payment of certain legacies after her death to the other defendants. The question arose whether the words of the gift to the wife of all the testator's assets could be cut down by these subsequent words. Hamilton J concluded that it was the testator's intention that his wife should enjoy the assets for her own absolute use. He held that the words were not intended to create any trust in favour of the other defendants but were merely the expression of his wish for the guidance of his wife as to the manner in which she should dispose of her assets after her death.

HAMILTON J stated at pp.89–92: "By his last will and testament dated 9 August 1974 James A. Sweeney (hereinafter referred to as 'the testator') appointed the plaintiffs herein to be the executors of the said last will and testament.

The testator died on 22 November 1972 and probate of his said last will and testament issued forth of the principal probate registry on 14 August 1973 to the executors named therein, the plaintiffs herein.

The plaintiffs, as such executors, have sought the determination by the court of certain questions as set out in their special endorsement of claim on the special summons herein arising upon the construction of the said last will and testament.

By his said last will and testament, the testator after appointing the plaintiffs executors of his said last will and testament, gave, devised and bequeathed all his assets of every nature and description to his wife Margaret Madeline Bernadette Sweeney, the first named defendant herein, for her own absolute use and benefit subject to the express wish that she make provision for payment of the following legacies after her death:

> £6,000 to Master Owen Hillary, the second-named defendant herein.
> £6,000 to James Sweeney, son of Dr Michael Sweeney, the fourth-named defendant herein and
> £2,000 to Mrs Brigid Hillary, the third-named defendant herein.

The testator died leaving him surviving the first-named defendant as his lawful spouse and no children. The first-named defendant as the lawful spouse of the testator was entitled in accordance with the provisions of s. 3(1) of the Succession Act 1965 to a right to one half of the estate.

In accordance with the provision of s.115(1)(a) the said defendant did on 25 June 1975 elect to take the share to which she was entitled as a legal right in the estate of the said testator.

This exercise by her of her legal right does not, in my opinion, affect the determination by me of the questions which have been submitted to the court for determination.

The important question for determination by me is question 1 on the special endorsement of claim because the other questions depend upon my answer to that question.

This question reads as follows:

> Whether the provision in the said will as follows:
>
> 'I give and devise and bequeath all my assets of every nature and description to my wife Margaret Madeline Bernadette for her own absolute use and benefit subject to the express wish that she makes provision for payment of the following legacies after her death: £6,000 to Master Owen Hillary; £6,000 to James Sweeney, son of Dr Michael Sweeney; £2,000 to Mrs Brigid Hillary' is an absolute devise and bequest of all the deceased's assets and not subject to any trust.

I consider it desirable to amend the said questions by the addition thereto after the word 'trust' of the words 'or condition' and will amend the special endorsement of claim accordingly.

I have received considerable assistance from the submissions of counsel on behalf of all parties and a consideration of the cases to which they have referred me. However my task is as stated by Lindley J in *Williams v Williams* [1897] 2 Ch 22: 'to construe the will before me and other cases are useless for that purpose except so far as they establish some principles of law'.

In the same case and on the same page of the official report Lindley J stated that:

> There is no principle except to ascertain the intention of the testator from the words he has used and to ascertain and give effect to the legal consequences of that intention when ascertained.

In *In re Coulson* (1953) 87 ILTR 93, Dixon J agreed that the determining factor was: 'What shall be gathered from the will as a whole'. He however did not dismiss other reported cases as being useless because he stated that:

> It is only if one could not get any clear idea that the reported cases became helpful.

In all the cases to which I have been referred the general intention of the testator as gleaned from the will as a whole was always treated as the matter to be ascertained. As stated by Rigby LJ in *Williams v Williams* [1897] 2 Ch 22 at 29:

> I find indeed repeated warnings that the intention having regard to the whole will must always prevail.

Consequently I have to decide from a consideration of the will as a whole whether it was the intention of the testator to create a trust in favour of the second, third or fourth named defendants, or whether the gift, devise and bequest to the first-named defendant was subject to the condition that she make provision for the payment of the following legacies after her death namely:

> £6,000 to Master Owen Hillary.
> £6,000 to James Sweeney,
> £2,000 to Mrs Brigid Hillary, the second and third-named defendants respectively.

The same doctrines have been laid down as to conditions and trusts. As stated by Rigby LJ in *Williams v Williams* at 28:

> No authoritative case ever laid it down that there could be any other ground for deducing a trust or condition than the intention of the testator as shown by the will taken as a whole.

In order to create a trust or make a gift or devise subject to a condition Lord Eldon stated in *Wright v Atkyns* (1823) Turn & R 143 that the words must be imperative, the subject must be certain and the object must be as certain as the subject.

As stated by Dixon J in *Coulson's* case the tendency is against construing expressions in a will as creating a trust or imposing an obligation unless the provisions were clear.

Bearing these principles in mind I must endeavour to ascertain the intention of the testator from the terms of the will. In his will the testator stated that:

> I give and devise and bequeath all my assets of every nature and description to my wife Margaret Madeline Bernadette for her own absolute use and benefit.

I stop here to consider the nature and effect of that gift, devise and bequest. It is a statement in clear, express and explicit terms of a gift, devise and bequest of all his assets of every nature and description to his wife and a clear statement that they were to be for her own absolute use and benefit. He went on however to say:

> Subject to the express wish that she makes provision for payment of the following legacies after her death namely £6,000 to Master Owen Hillary, £6,000 to James Sweeney, son of Dr Michael Sweeney and £2,000 to Mrs Brigid Hillary.

Can the clear words of the gift, devise and bequest of all his assets to his wife Margaret for her own absolute use and benefit be cut down by the subsequent words, words which may operate as an expression of a desire without disturbing in any way the previous gift, devise and bequest.

In *In re Humphrey's Estate* [1916] 1 IR 21, Ross J at p. 24 of his judgment stated that:

> After a devise and bequest in clear and express terms, if a trust is intended to be created one would expect that this would be done in terms equally clear and explicit.

This statement also applies to conditions. In these circumstances a trust can only be created or a condition imposed if the words used are imperative, the subject is certain and the object is as certain as the subject.

Are the words 'subject to the express wish' imperative? These words are certainly capable of being imperative but if I were to hold that they were imperative I would be cutting down considerably the clear words of the gift, devise and bequest of all the testator's assets of every nature and description to his wife Margaret 'for her own absolute use'.

The wish expressed by the testator was that his wife make provision for payment of the following legacies after her death:

£6,000 to Master Owen Hillary.
£6,000 to James Sweeney, son of Dr Michael Sweeney, and £2,000 to Brigid Hillary.

He does not state that such provision for payment should be made out of his assets, already bequeathed to her and consequently I do not consider that the second leg of the test is satisfied namely that the subject must be certain.

It was submitted by Mr Fahy and Mr Danaher that the will of the testator contained the bequest of legacies to Master Owen Hillary, James Sweeney and Mrs Brigid Hillary. I do not accept this submission because there is no gift or bequest of any legacies contained in the will to these alleged legatees.

On the contrary the will explicitly contains a gift, devise and bequest of all his assets to his wife Margaret Madeline for her own absolute use and benefit.

Having considered the terms of the will as a whole I am satisfied that it was the intention of the testator that his wife should enjoy the gift, devise and bequest of all his assets for her own absolute use and benefit and that the words contained in the will after the said gift, devise and bequest were not intended by him to create any trust in favour of the second, third and fourth-named defendant or to impose any legal obligation on the first-named defendant with regard thereto but merely the expression of his wish for the guidance of his wife as to the manner in which she should dispose of her assets after her death.

Having regard to the foregoing I answer the first question, yes, the third question, no, the fifth question, none.

Questions two, six and seven do not arise."

Certainty of Subject Matter

To ensure the creation of a valid express trust, the subject matter of the trust must be defined with sufficient certainty. So, the beneficial interests to be taken by the beneficiaries must be defined with sufficient clarity unless the trustees are given a discretion to decide what the extent of these beneficial interests should be.

Where an objective criterion which can be applied by the court is provided by a settlor or testator, a failure to quantify precisely the extent of the subject matter of a trust will not prove fatal to its validity.[8]

---

[8] *Re Golay's Will Trusts* [1965] 1 WLR 969.

Re Golay's Will Trusts
[1965] 1 WLR 969

By his will the testator directed that a named individual was to be allowed use a flat during her lifetime and 'to receive a reasonable income' from his other properties. Ungoed-Thomas J held that by the use of the words 'reasonable income' the testator had given a sufficient indication of his intention to provide an effective determinant of what he intended and that the direction was not defeated by uncertainty.

UNGOED-THOMAS J stated at pp.970–972: "Another question that arises is whether this gift of reasonable income fails for uncertainty.

There are two classes of case with which I am concerned in interpreting this particular provision in the will: the first is where a discretion is given to specified persons to quantify the amount; the other class of case is where no such discretion is expressly conferred upon any specified person.

It is common ground that in this case the trustees are not given a discretion so that if "reasonable income" does not fail for uncertainty then it would be open to a beneficiary to go to court to ascertain whether any amount quantified by the trustees was a "reasonable" amount in accordance with the provisions of the will.

Does this gift of a "reasonable income" without specifying any person to quantify it fail for uncertainty?

The principal case referred to on this question was *Jackson v. Hamilton* (1846) 3 J & Lat 702, an Irish case, where the testator "did devise, and by his will request that the said trustees should from time to time retain in their hands any reasonable sum or sums of money which should be sufficient to remunerate them for the trouble they should have in carrying the trusts of his will into execution." It seems from the report that no objection on the ground of uncertainty was taken against the quantum. It was also argued before me that in that case a discretion was in the first place given to the trustees to decide what the amount should be and that the master quantified the amount, so that the court would merely have been exercising the discretion which the will had given to the trustees and had been surrendered to the court. But the master, when the matter came before him, had no difficulty in quantifying what was "reasonable" remuneration and Sir Edward Burtenshaw Sugden L.C. confirmed the course which the master had taken. Indeed, it is conceded in this case – and I think rightly conceded – that the court would have no difficulty in quantifying "reasonable income."

It is, however, submitted that what the court is concerned with in the interpretation of this will is not to ascertain what is "reasonable income" in the opinion of the court but to ascertain the testator's intention, in using the words "reasonable income."

The question therefore comes to this: Whether the testator by the words "reasonable income" has given a sufficient indication of his intention to provide an effective determinant of what he intends so that the court in applying that determinant can give effect to the testator's intention.

Whether the yardstick of "reasonable income" were applied by trustees under a discretion given to them by a testator or applied by a court in course of interpreting and applying the words "reasonable income" in a will, the yardstick sought to be applied by the trustees in the one case and the court in the other case would be identical. The trustees might be other than the original trustees named by the testator and the trustees could even surrender their discretion to the court. It would seem to me to be drawing too fine a distinction to conclude that an objective yardstick which different persons sought to apply would be too uncertain, not because of uncertainty in the yardstick but as between those who seek to apply it.

In this case, however, the yardstick indicated by the testator is not what he or some other specified person subjectively considers to be reasonable but what he identifies objectively as "reasonable income." The court is constantly involved in making such objective assessments of what is reasonable and it is not to be deterred from doing so because subjective influences can never be wholly excluded. In my view the testator intended by "reasonable income" the yardstick which the court could and would apply in quantifying the amount so that the direction in the will is not in my view defeated by uncertainty."

Lack of certainty of subject matter will be an issue where a settlor seeks to create a trust of an unascertained portion of assets of a tangible nature e.g. cases of wine.[9] However, where the assets in question are of an intangible nature, e.g. money or shares in a company, all will be equally capable of satisfying the trust and it will be unnecessary to identify any particular sum or shares before determining that the subject matter requirement is satisfied.[10]

Hunter v. Moss
[1993] 1 WLR 934 (DC); [1994] 1 WLR 452 (CA)

The defendant, who was the registered holder of 950 shares in a company with an issued share capital of £1,000, made a declaration of trust purporting to constitute himself as trustee for the plaintiff of 5% of the company's issued share capital. It was held by Colin Rimmer QC, in a decision upheld by the Court of Appeal (Dillon, Mann and Hirst LJJ), that the purported declaration of trust was sufficiently certain as to subject matter since the shares were of such a nature as to be indistinguishable from one another and were therefore all equally capable of satisfying the trust.

---

[9] *Re London Wine Co. Ltd* [1986] PCC 121.
[10] *Hunter v. Moss* [1993] 1 WLR 934 (DC); [1994] 1 WLR 452 (CA).

COLIN RIMMER QC stated at pp.935–949: "The trial of this action took place before me between 2 and 7 October 1992. At the conclusion of the argument I reserved my judgment, which I then delivered on 16 October 1992. The outcome was that I ordered judgment to be entered for the plaintiff, Mr. Hunter, against the defendant, Mr. Moss, in the sum of £112,723.70, including interest, and I awarded Mr. Hunter his costs of the action. I directed a stay of execution pending any appeal, on terms which I need not specify, and I asked counsel to agree a minute and lodge it with the associate. Counsel lodged the minute on the same day. However, in circumstances whose details I do not know, the order was not drawn up by the court with the promptness which might have been expected and it remains unperfected to this day,

In the meantime the defendant sought advice on my judgment from different counsel, Mr. Michael Hartman, and one outcome of that was on 12 November 1992 Mr. Hartman made an application to me in which he argued that I should recall my still unperfected order and instead dismiss the action with costs. Notice of that application was given to the plaintiff and he was represented, as before, by Mr. Davidson, who opposed it.

It is unnecessary in order to understand the basis of Mr. Hartman's application to recite the background facts relating to these proceedings in any detail. They appear from my previous judgment to which this judgment can be regarded as an addendum. All that I need to say is that the principal issue in the action was whether or not during the course of 1986 the defendant had made a valid declaration of trust constituting himself a trustee for the plaintiff of five per cent of the issued share capital of Moss Electrical Co. Ltd. ("M.E.L."). I found as a fact that in the course of a conversation between the plaintiff and the defendant in early September 1986 the defendant did declare himself to be a trustee for the plaintiff of such a five per cent holding, and thereby established a trust under which the plaintiff became absolutely entitled beneficially to such holding. M.E.L.'s issued share capital consisted of 1,000 shares, of which at the material time the defendant was the registered holder of 950, and I therefore held that that trust applied to 50 of the 950 shares held by the defendant.

Mr. Gerard Clarke was counsel for the defendant at the trial. He argued against the existence of any trust having been established on the facts but accepted that, if I were to find that such a trust was made out, then the plaintiff was entitled to appropriate relief in the action. The basis of Mr. Hartman's application was that he wished to submit to me that even accepting, which at least for the purpose of the application he does, that I was correct to find that the defendant purported to declare himself to be a trustee for the plaintiff of 50 of his 950 M.E.L. shares, nevertheless that could not have constituted a valid trust because the 50 shares expressed to be subject to it were not at any stage ascertained, appropriated or otherwise identified. Thus, Mr. Hartman wanted to submit that the purported trust wholly failed for want of certainty as to its subject matter and that the plaintiff's action should also fail.

The point is one which was not argued or referred to by Mr. Clarke, nor is it one which I considered when preparing my earlier judgment. If it is well-founded then, as Mr. Davidson accepted, it would mean that I had wrongly decided the action in the plaintiff's favour. In those circumstances I took the view that justice demanded that I should hear Mr. Hartman's argument and, although Mr. Davidson did not positively assent to my taking that course, nor did he resist it with any apparent strenuousness. Accordingly, I did allow Mr. Hartman to argue the new point. I should perhaps mention that I raised with counsel whether, before hearing the argument, I ought formally first to recall my order. Both counsel agreed that that was unnecessary and that I should simply hear the application and then make such order as then appeared to be appropriate. That is the basis on which I did hear the application.

I turn therefore to its substance. Mr. Hartman's submission is that for an express trust to be validly created the trust must satisfy the so-called "three certainties:" see *Snell's Equity,* 29th ed. (1990), p. 113. One of these is the requirement that the property intended to be subject to the trust must be identified with certainty. Mr. Hartman submits that, where that property forms part of a fund or of a group of assets, it is essential for the validity of the trust that the purporting trustee should clearly identify which particular part of the fund, or which particular asset forming part of the larger group, is to be subject to the trust, if necessary by appropriating or segregating such part or asset from the remainder of the fund or group.

In elaboration, Mr. Hartman submitted that if A purports to declare himself a trustee for B of two out of a set of 10 dining chairs, but omits to identify which particular chairs, then the trust will fail. For the trust to be valid A must first specifically identify the two chairs. He submits that a like principle applies to intangible assets and argues that if A is a registered holder of 1,000 shares in a company he cannot declare himself a trustee for B of, say, 50 of them without identifying which particular 50 are to be subject to the trust. Mr. Hartman submits that this could be done by indicating on the share certificates that, for example, the trust is to apply to shares 1 to 50 or to shares 51 to 100. If, however, the shares are unnumbered it can only be done by the establishment of a separate holding of 50 shares which can then be regarded as indisputably referable to the trust.

Mr. Hartman submitted further that, in the present case, even if the trust which I found to have been declared by the defendant were to be regarded as a trust of the defendant's entire holding of 950 shares, held as to 900 for the defendant and as to 50 for the plaintiff, such a trust would similarly fail because neither beneficiary could identify which particular shares in the entire holding he was beneficially interested in. He said that the position would be different if, instead, the entire 950 shares could be regarded as held on trust for the defendant and the plaintiff as tenants in common with 94.74 per cent and 5.26 per cent interests respectively in the 950 shares. In that event he said that there would be no uncertainty either as to the trust fund or as to the two beneficiaries' respective interests in it. That, however, was not the nature of the trust which I had found was purportedly declared by the defendant.

Mr. Hartman adopted as part of his submissions a passage in *Underhill and Hayton, Law of Trusts and Trustees,* 14th ed. (1987), p. 105 by Professor Hayton:

> "No problems arise as to certainty of subject matter of a declaration of trust where the settlor's declaration relates to specific property e.g. 'my one and only Picasso painting, all my shares in ICI Plc., all my money currently in my Woolwich Building Society account.' However, if it relates to unascertained property no trust can arise till there has been a segregation or appropriation of specific property out of the larger mass of property, e.g. where it is intended to create a trust of 20 cases out of 80 cases of Chateau Latour 1982 in the settlor's cellar or of £1,000 out of £5,000 in the settlor's Woolwich Building Society account."

Underhill and Hayton refers to two authorities said to support the examples in that final sentence: *In re London Wine Co. (Shippers) Ltd.* [1986] PCC 121, which is cited as supporting the Chateau Latour example, and *In re Andrabell Ltd.* [1984] 3 All ER 407, which is cited as supporting the Woolwich Building Society example. Mr. Hartman submits that the principles reflected in those authorities apply by analogy to the present case as well.

In re London Wine Co. (Shippers) Ltd. [1986] PCC 121 was a 1975 decision of Oliver J. It concerned a contest between the purchasers of consignments of wine from a company whose business was one of dealers in wine and the claimants under a floating charge granted by the dealers. The problem was that, although the purchasers had paid for their consignments and although the dealers had in stock sufficient wine to answer the purchasers' respective purchases, the dealers had not segregated or identified specific cases as having been appropriated to the respective purchasers' various contracts. One of the arguments advanced by the purchasers was that the dealers had become trustees for them of consignments of wine sufficient to answer their various purchases, Oliver J. rejected this argument. He dealt with it as follows, at pp. 135–137:

> "As regards the creation of a trust, this is put in this way. On the assumption that no property passed in the goods at law – and it is not argued that this could possibly be the case in the third category represented by Mr. Bailey and by Mr. Stamler's client – there was, it is submitted, clearly an intention that the property should pass so far as the company had it in its power to make it do so. One has only to look at the terms of its circulars with their references to 'your wines,' to the purchaser being 'the beneficial owner' and to the company having a lien. This is reinforced when one looks at the terms of the letters of confirmation which list the quantities and types of wine and confirm that the purchaser is 'the sole beneficial owner of these wines,' and is indeed further reinforced in the case of Compass and Vinum when reference is made to the master agreements with Compass and the company where the company joins in to warrant title to the wine. By issuing these documents, the acknowledged purpose of which was to enable the purchasers to deal with their wines by sale or charge, the company,

it is said, evinced the clearest possible intention to declare itself a trustee and once you find such an intention, it matters not that the instrument expressing it fails to do so in unequivocal terms or, indeed, that there is no instrument at all. Reliance is placed upon the recent case of *In re Kayford Ltd.* [1975] 1 WLR 279, 282 where Megarry J. said: 'it is well settled that a trust can be created without using the words "trust" or "confidence" or the like: the question is whether in substance a sufficient intention to create a trust has been manifested.'

That, of course, is a proposition with which it is impossible to quarrel, but I do not find that case, where the evidence of intention to create a trust was exceptionally clear and where the trust property was from the outset specifically set aside and identified, one which assists me very much in ascertaining whether, in the very different circumstances of the instant case, a trust has been effectively declared. Mr. Wright, in his reply, put it rather differently. A trust, he said, may be constituted not merely by direct and express declaration but also by the consequences flowing from the acts of the persons themselves to which consequences the law attaches the label 'trust.' A trust, to put it another way, is the technical description of a legal situation; and where you find (i) an intention to create a beneficial interest in someone else, (ii) an acknowledgment of that intention and (iii) property in the ownership of the person making the acknowledgment which answers the description in the acknowledgment, then there is, at the date of the acknowledgment, an effective and completed trust of all the property of the acknowledger answering to that description. This is, I think, in essence the same submission as that made by Mr. Stamler – he submits that where one is dealing with a homogeneous mass there is no problem about certainty. So long as the mass can be identified and there is no uncertainty about the quantitative interest of the beneficiary, the court will find no difficulty in administering the trust if it once finds the necessary intention to create an equitable interest in property of the type comprised in the mass. I think, indeed, that if the case is to be made out at all, it must be put in this way, for the submission itself is based on the premise that there are no specific or ascertained goods in which the beneficiary is interested. Were it otherwise there would be no need to invoke the concept of trust for the title would have passed under the Sale of Goods Act (as, indeed, Mr. Wright submits in categories 1 and 2, it did). If trust there be, then it must be a trust of the homogeneous *whole* and the terms of the trust must be that the trustee is to hold that whole upon trust to give effect thereout to the proportionate interest of the beneficiary. Thus if we postulate the case of the company having in warehouse 1,000 cases of a particular wine and selling 100 cases to X the circumstances of this case indicate, it is submitted, that the company created an equitable tenancy in common between itself and X in the whole 1,000 cases in the proportions of nine-tenths and one-tenth.

It is with regret that I feel compelled to reject these submissions, for I feel great sympathy with those who paid for their wine and received an assurance that they had title to it. But I find it impossible to spell either out of the acknowledgments signed by the company or out of the circumstances any such trust as is now sought to be set up. Granted that the references to 'beneficial interest' are appropriate words for the creation of a trust; granted, even (although this I think is very difficult to spell out) that that was the company's intention, it seems to me that any such trust must fail on the ground of uncertainty of subject matter. I appreciate the point taken that subject matter is part of a homogeneous mass so that specific identity is of as little importance as it is, for instance, in the case of money. Nevertheless, as it seems to me, to create a trust it must be possible to ascertain with certainty not only what the interest of the beneficiary is to be but to what property it is to attach.

I cannot see how, for instance, a farmer who declares himself to be a trustee of two sheep (without identifying them) can be said to have created a perfect and complete trust whatever rights he may confer by such declaration as a matter of contract. And it would seem to me to be immaterial that at the time he has a flock of sheep out of which he could satisfy the interest. Of course, he could by appropriate words, declare himself to be a trustee of a specified proportion of his whole flock and thus create an equitable tenancy in common between himself and the named beneficiary, so that a proprietary interest would arise in the beneficiary in an undivided share of all the flock and its produce. But the *mere* declaration that a given number of animals would be held upon trust could not, I should have thought, without very clear words pointing to such an intention, result in the creation of an interest in common in the proportion which that number bears to the number of the whole at the time of the declaration. And where the mass from which the numerical interest is to take effect is not itself ascertainable at the date of the declaration such a conclusion becomes impossible."

I do not question the correctness of the reasoning in those passages from Oliver J.'s judgment, and I agree that they provide support for *Underhill and Hayton's* Chateau Latour example. I recognise also that, although the particular decision was concerned with an alleged trust in respect of chattels in the nature of cases of wine, certain of Oliver J.'s observations can be construed as reflecting principles applicable to trusts of all types of property and not just to trusts of chattels, For example, he said, at p. 137:

"I appreciate the point taken that the subject matter is part of a homogeneous mass so that specific identity is of as little importance as it is, for instance, in the case of money. Nevertheless, as it seems to me, to create a trust it must be possible to ascertain with certainty not only what the interest of the beneficiary is to be but to what property it is to attach."

Again I do not question the correctness of that particular statement, and to the extent that Oliver J. was treating the assets in question before him as a homogeneous mass whose component parts were as indistinguishable one from the other as, for example, those in a fund of money his decision enables Mr. Hartman to argue, as he does, that so too in the present case the trust which the defendant purported to declare would only have been a valid one if he in some manner identified the particular 50 shares in his holding to which he intended it to attach.

I see the force of the argument, but in my judgment Oliver J.'s decision cannot safely be regarded as demonstrating its correctness. The decision was concerned solely with an alleged declaration of trust in respect of tangible assets in the nature of cases of wine. Even tangible assets which are regarded as forming part of a homogeneous mass are physically separate, and so distinguishable, from other assets comprised within the same mass. Further, certain of the assets in a group of ostensibly similar or identical assets may in fact have characteristics which distinguish them from other assets in the class. Consignments of wine provide a good example. Some of the cases in it may contain wine that is corked, or may have been stored badly and have deteriorated or may have other inherent defects. Oliver J. held that, before any trust could be said to attach to any tangible assets comprised within a class of assets, the particular assets have to be identified. I do not, however, consider that the principle which he applied with regard to the certainties requisite for the purposes of a trust relating to tangible assets is one which is necessarily also applicable by analogy to trusts of intangible assets, for example, to a purported trust of a specific sum of money forming part of a larger credit balance in a particular bank account. The latter trust will of course only be valid if its subject matter is certain, But the determination of whether the requisite degree of certainty has been achieved is, in my judgment, not necessarily governed by principles analogous to those which apply in the case of tangible assets.

The other authority referred to by *Underhill and Hayton, Law of Trusts and Trustees*, p, 105, apparently in support of the Woolwich Building Society account example, is *In re Andrabell Ltd.* [1984] 3 All ER 407. That was a retention of title case in which the purchaser sold the goods which were subject to the retention of title clause and paid the proceeds into its general bank account. The unpaid vendor argued, inter alia, that the purchaser had held the sold goods as bailee for the vendor, that as such a bailee it owed the vendor fiduciary duties and that it was accountable to the vendor for the proceeds of sale it had mixed with the other moneys in its account. The argument was rejected by Peter Gibson J. Mr. Hartman submitted that the part of the judgment which supported the proposition for which *Underhill and Hayton* referred to it was the following one, at pp. 415-416:

> "These dissimilarities seem to me to distinguish the position of the parties in the present case from the position of the buyer and seller in the *Romalpa* case [1976] 1 WLR 676 and to point to the relationship between Airborne and Andrabell as being not a fiduciary one, but merely that of creditor and debtor.
>
> There are three other considerations which, to my mind, lead to the same conclusion. First, it was accepted by counsel for Airborne that there was no obligation on Andrabell to keep separate from its own moneys the moneys it received from the sales which it made of the bags supplied by Airborne. Counsel persisted in this concession even after I had referred him to the principle stated by Channell J. in *Henry v. Hammond* [1913] 2 KB 515, 521 (cited with approval by Slade J. in *In re Bond Worth Ltd.* [1980] Ch 228, 260-261): 'It is clear that if the terms upon which the person receives the money are that he is bound to keep it separate, either in a bank or elsewhere, and to hand that money to be so kept as a separate fund to the person entitled to it, then he is a trustee of that money and must hand it over to the person who is his cestui que trust. If, on the other hand, he is not bound to keep the money separate, but is entitled to mix it with his own

money and deal with it as he pleases, and when called upon to hand over an equivalent sum of money, then, in my opinion, he is not a trustee of the money, but merely a debtor.' Slade J.'s comment on this and three other authorities, *In re Nevill, Ex parte White* (1871) LR 6 Ch App 397 (affirmed in the House of Lords sub nom. *John Towle & Co. v. White* (1873) 29 LT 78), *Foley v. Hill* (1848) 2 HL Cas 28, and *South Australian Insurance Co. v. Randell* (1869) LR 3 PC 101, was that those authorities and *Henry v. Hammond* were – 'clear authority for the proposition that, where an alleged trustee has the right to mix tangible assets or moneys with his own other assets or moneys and to deal with them as he pleases, this is incompatible with the existence of a *presently* subsisting fiduciary relationship in regard to such particular assets or moneys.' (My emphasis.) (See [1980] Ch. 228, 261.) But counsel for Airborne, no doubt rightly, said that he would have difficulty in submitting that the parties had contemplated that Andrabell would be obliged to keep separate accounts of the proceeds of sale. Certainly, there is nothing in the express terms of the April letter to support the implication of a term to that effect. Further, the method of payment expressly contemplated, that is to say bills of exchange protected by guarantees, together with a deposit in a bank, to which Airborne could have recourse if Andrabell defaulted, significantly is wholly unrelated to the actual proceeds of sales of bags."

In my judgment that particular passage does not establish the proposition for which *Underhill and Hayton* appears to have cited the case. All that Peter Gibson J. was there saying is that the relationship between A and B, under which A is lawfully at liberty to mix moneys or other assets which he receives with moneys and assets of his own, and is not obliged to keep the moneys or assets so received in a separate account or fund, is a relationship which is inconsistent with A being a trustee for B in respect of the moneys or assets received by him. However, I find it impossible to extract from *In re Andrabell Ltd* [1984] All ER 407 the proposition that an express declaration by A that he holds on trust for B a specific sum of money forming part of a larger credit balance is a purported declaration of trust which wholly fails for uncertainty. Neither that point in particular nor the concept of uncertainty in general was an issue with which the *Andrabell* case was concerned.

Mr. Davidson did not question the correctness of the decision in *In re London Wine Co. (Shippers) Ltd.* [1986] PCC 121. However, he submitted, rightly in my judgment, that that case could not be regarded as providing any conclusive guidance as to whether, given the essentially different nature of the subject matter of the trust which I found the defendant to have declared, the defendant's purported declaration of trust identified its subject matter with sufficient certainty. He also submitted and, as I have indicated, again I agree, that *In re Andrabell Ltd* [1984] 3 All ER 407 did not support the statement in *Underhill and Hayton, Law of Trusts and Trustees,* at p. 105, for which it was apparently cited. He submitted that the statement in *Underhill and Hayton* to the effect that a valid trust cannot be declared in respect of £1,000 forming part of a larger credit balance in a particular account without first in some manner specifically segregating or otherwise identifying the £1,000 was supported neither by authority nor reason and was wrong, and that there could be no question of uncertainty with regard to the identification of the property the subject of any such purported declaration of trust. He further submitted that there can similarly be no question of uncertainty with regard to the trust of the 50 M.E.L. shares which I found to have been declared by the defendant.

Mr. Davidson referred me to *In re Clifford; Mallam v. McFie* [1912] 1 Ch 29. That was a case concerning a specific bequest of "twenty-three of the shares belonging to me in the London and County Banking Co, Ltd." At the date of the will the testator held 104 such shares, the shares being £80 shares. By the date of his death each share had been subdivided into four £20 shares and the testator held 416. The issues in the case were: (1) whether the bequest was to be construed as at the date of the will or of the death, and (2) if the former, whether the bequest had been adeemed by the subsequent subdivision. Swinfen Eady J. held that the gift had to be construed as at the date of the will and that it had not been adeemed but that it took effect as a legacy of 92 of the new shares.

Mr. Davidson referred me to the case, not because he claimed that it expressly established his submission on the question of certainty of subject matter, but to point out that it does not appear to have occurred either to counsel or the judge in that case that the gift of an unidentified holding of 23 shares comprised in a larger holding was or might be void for uncertainty. It is to be noted that the legacy in that case was regarded as being a specific legacy rather than a general one, yet no one appears to have questioned that it could properly be satisfied by the appropriation to the legatee of any 92 of the testator's 416 shares.

The decision in *In re Clifford* is not in my judgment in any way a remarkable one, and I should have been surprised if anyone had sought to raise an argument based on uncertainty. There are other similar cases in the reports concerning gifts of shares forming part of a holding, where again no one has sought to take the point that the gift is void for uncertainty unless the particular shares intended to be the subject of the gift had been specifically identified by the testator: see, for example, *In re Cheadle; Bishop v. Holt* [1900] 2 Ch 620.

However, as no question of uncertainty or otherwise formed the subject matter of the argument or decision in *In re Clifford* [1912] Ch 29 I do not regard it as an authority providing any direct guidance in the present case, although the silent assumption as to the essential validity of the bequest is a feature of the case which I consider renders it of at least some assistance to Mr. Davidson. It appears to me to be odd that a testamentary gift of the type which was in question in *In re Clifford* should be certain and valid, yet, if Mr. Hartman's submission is right, that the trust which I found the defendant to have declared should be uncertain and void.

Mr. Davidson also referred me to *In re Kayford Ltd.* [1975] 1 WLR 279. That case concerned a mail order company which received advance payments from customers for goods which they ordered. Concerned at the prospect of insolvency, the company was advised to open a separate customers' trust deposit account into which it would pay moneys paid by customers for goods not yet delivered. The idea was that moneys would be withdrawn from it for the company's general use as and when goods were delivered but that if the company went into liquidation the moneys would be returned in full to those who had respectively paid them. The company did not open a new deposit account, but instead simply paid the further moneys it received from customers into a dormant account which it had, in which there was already a balance of £47.80 standing to the company's credit. The company went into liquidation and the issue was whether the moneys in the account were held on a valid trust for the customers from whom the moneys derived or whether the moneys formed part of the general assets of the company. By the time of the issue of the originating summons some £37,872.45, together with accrued interest, stood to the credit of the account derived from a number of customers. Megarry J. held that a valid trust had been created. He said, at pp. 281-282:

"Now there are clearly some loose ends in the case. Mr. Kay, advised to establish a 'Customers' Trust Deposit Account,' seems to have thought that it did not matter what the account was called so long as there was a separate account; and so the dormant deposit account suggested by the bank manager was used. The bank statement for this account is before me, and on the first page, for which the title is simply 'Deposit account Kayford Ltd.,' nearly £26,000 is credited. The second and third pages have the words 'Customer Trust Deposit Account' added after the previous title of the account; and Mr. Joels' payment was made after these words had been added. Mr. Kay also left matters resting on a telephone conversation with the bank manager until he wrote his letter of December to the bank. That letter reads: 'We confirm our instructions regarding the opening of the deposit account for customer deposits for new orders;' and he then makes some mention of other accounts with the bank. The letter goes on: 'Please ensure the reopened deposit account is titled "Customer Trust Deposit Account."' Then he gives the reference number and asks for confirmation that this has been done. Nevertheless, despite the loose ends, when I take as a whole the affidavits of Mr. Wainwright, Mr. Kay and Mr. Hall (the bank manager) I feel no doubt that the intention was that there should be a trust. There are no formal difficulties. The property concerned is pure personalty, and so writing, though desirable, is not an essential. There is no doubt about the so-called 'three certainties' of a trust. The subject matter to be held on trust is clear, and so are the beneficial interests therein, as well as the beneficiaries. As for the requisite certainty of words, it is well settled that a trust can be created without using the words 'trust' or 'confidence' or the like: the question is whether in substance a sufficient intention to create a trust has been manifested. In *In re Nanwa Gold Mines Ltd.* [1955] 1 WLR 1080 the money was sent on the faith of a promise to keep it in a separate account, but there is nothing in that case or in any other authority that I know of to suggest that this is essential. I feel no doubt that here a trust was created. From the outset the advice (which was accepted) was to establish a trust account at the bank. The whole purpose of what was done was to ensure that the moneys remained in the beneficial ownership of those who sent them, and a trust is the obvious means of achieving this. No doubt the general rule is that if you send money to a company for goods which are not delivered, you are merely a creditor of the company unless a trust has been created. The sender may create a trust by using appropriate words when he sends the money (though I wonder how many do this, even if they are equity lawyers), or the company may do it by taking suitable steps on or before receiving the money. If either is done, the obligations in respect of the money are transformed from contract to property, from debt to trust. Payment into a separate bank account is a useful (though by no means conclusive) indication of an intention to create a trust, but of course there is nothing to prevent the company from binding itself by a trust even if there are no effective banking arrangements."

Mr. Davidson submitted that the statement in *Underhill and Hayton, Law of Trusts and Trustees*, at p. 105, to the effect that no trust can be created in respect of a specific sum of money forming part of a larger overall account was irreconcilable with this authority. The essence of the argument was that the trust in respect of each customer's payment was created only upon or after the payment of his moneys to the credit of the relevant account, or that it was only the payment into the account that provided the conclusive evidence that it was intended to create a trust in respect of the moneys so paid. If *Underhill and Hayton* is right that it is impossible to declare a valid trust in respect of £1,000 forming part of an overall credit balance of £2,000, then, so the argument proceeds, it would be odd that in *In re Kayford Ltd.* [1975] 1 WLR 279 it was only the mixing of specific moneys in a larger overall balance which was the event which either established, or at least conclusively proved, the intention to create a trust in respect of the particular moneys so mixed.

Mr. Hartman argued that this approach to *In re Kayford Ltd.* was quite wrong and that the correct explanation for Megarry J.'s decision that a valid trust was there established was that the relevant trust fund was the entirety of the moneys standing for the time being to the credit of the relevant account and that the true terms of the trust were that under it all the customers were between them entitled to the entirety of the moneys so standing, together with the interest accruing thereon, in the proportions they had respectively contributed to the account. Thus he said the case was not one in which each customer was interested merely in a particular balance of money standing to the credit of the account together with the interest earned by such balance. Each customer was interested in a proportion of the whole balance from time to time and of the whole of the interest earned by it.

That analysis receives at least some support from the fact that the originating summons asked, inter alia, whether the relevant moneys belonged to the persons who paid them in proportion to the amounts in the affirmative. However, at any rate so far as the principal amount due to each customer was concerned, the result under this formula would be just the same as if each beneficiary's respective interest were regarded simply as in a sum equal to the particular amount paid by him to the company. Further, so far as the crediting of any accrued interest is concerned, Mr. Hartman's theory appears to me to present difficulties. It would seem to me that the company could not fairly have accounted for interest to the various customers except by reference to the particular amount which they had respectively paid and when they had respectively paid it. The customer who paid £1,000 in month one ought to be entitled to receive more of the total interest credited in month four than the customer who paid his £1,000 in month two. However, if the scheme was that the company was to be so accountable for the interest earned, that would appear to me to point away from an analysis under which the beneficiaries simply had a proportionate interest in the entire fund from time to time based on the amount of their respective original payments. The report in *In re Kayford Ltd.* does not, however, make it clear precisely how interest was in fact dealt with.

Accordingly, the inference which I would prefer to draw is that the company in *In re Kayford Ltd.* probably had a no more sophisticated intention when it set up the trust than that the face amount of each payment made into the account belonged in equity to the particular customer from whom it was derived and that each customer was to be entitled to the interest respectively earned on the money which he so paid. If this analysis is right, then I would regard the case as casting doubt on the correctness of the Woolwich Building Society account example in *Underhill and Hayton, Law of Trusts and Trustees,* at p. 105.

However, whilst Megarry J. did in terms refer to the so-called "three certainties," he did not discuss the particular point which Mr. Hartman has argued. In these circumstances, and given what I regard as at least an element of uncertainty as to the correct analysis of the *Kayford* case, I do not think that I can safely regard the case as having been decided on the basis of a principle which is inconsistent with *Underhill and Hayton's* Woolwich Building Society account example.

The position in which I find myself is therefore that no English authority has been cited to me which appears in terms to decide the particular point which Mr. Hartman has argued. I shall refer later to the assistance to be derived from certain overseas authorities, but I propose first to answer it by reference to the application of general principle.

So approaching the matter, I accept of course that the trust which the defendant purported to declare had to satisfy the "three certainties," including certainty as to its subject matter. However, it appears to me that the question of whether in any particular case there is such certainty depends, or ought to depend, not on the application of any immutable principle based on the requirements of a need for segregation or appropriation, but rather on whether, immediately after the purported declaration of trust, the court could, if asked, make an order for the execution of the purported trust. In any particular case it could and will only do so if, inter alia, the subject matter of the trust is identified with sufficient certainty.

If A has two bank accounts, each with a credit balance of £1,000, Mr.

Hartman accepts that a declaration of trust with regard to the entire balance standing to the credit of one such account is valid. Further, if immediately after making the declaration of trust the trustee were to transfer the trust money to his other account, the court would have no difficulty in recognising that the trust money could be traced into the latter account and in making all necessary orders for the execution of the trust. If, however, A has only one account with a credit balance of £2,000, Mr. Hartman submits that a purported declaration of trust 'in respect of £1,000 standing to the credit of such account will only be valid if and when such sum is first withdrawn from the account and identified as a distinct fund and that the court would be impotent to enforce the purported trust before that had happened.

As to the latter example, I can see no reason in principle why this should be so. If, immediately after such a purported declaration of trust, and before the £1,000 had been segregated in any way, the intended beneficiary were to apply to the court for an order for the execution of the trust, what difficulty could there be in the way of the court simply making an order for the payment of £1,000 to the beneficiary? Questions of uncertainty just would not arise. The trustee did not either need or intend to identify any particular element of his credit balance as being intended to answer the trust because it would have been both irrelevant and impossible to identify any part of the credit balance in the bank account as representing the particular £1,000 which he had in mind. Put simply, his intention was to hold £1,000 of his money in a particular bank account on trust for the beneficiary. What does it matter, either to him or the beneficiary, which £1,000? What is there about the trust which is in any degree uncertain?

If my reaction to the bank balance example is right, then it appears to me that similar considerations apply to the present case. The defendant did not identify any particular 50 shares for the plaintiff because to do so was unnecessary and irrelevant. All 950 of his shares carried identical rights. It mattered neither to him nor to the plaintiff which particular 50 shares were to be regarded as held for the plaintiff. The shares were therefore in my judgment of such a nature that each of them could satisfy the trust just as well as any other of them. Why therefore should equity be concerned that 50 particular shares were not identified? The mere fact that they formed part of a larger holding belonging to the defendant beneficially appears to me to be no obstacle. Again, if immediately after the declaration of trust which the defendant made the plaintiff had applied to the court for its execution, there would not have been any difficulty in ordering the trust to be carried into execution. There could and would have been no uncertainty as to the subject matter of the trust. The court could simply have ordered the transfer to the plaintiff of 50 of the defendant's shares or else could have ordered the defendant to establish a separate holding of such 50 shares. Any suggested uncertainty as to subject matter appears to me to be theoretical and conceptual rather than real and practical. Mr. Hartman submitted that one element of uncertainty would or might lie in the fact that the trustee's subsequent dealings with part of the larger holding might leave it uncertain whether or not such dealings were with his own assets or with the trust assets. I recognise that as a possibility: but, if any such uncertainty were to arise, that would not be because the trust fund was uncertain as to subject matter, but rather because the trustee had failed to keep proper accounts showing how he had subsequently dealt with it.

Approaching the matter as one of principle, I therefore take the view that the subject matter of the trust which the defendant declared was sufficiently certain and that in consequence the trust was a valid one. Although I have been referred to no English authority dealing specifically with the point, it was, however, the subject of a decision of the Supreme Court of Missouri in *Rollestone v. National Bank of Commerce in St. Louis* (1923) 252 SW 394. In that case the court found that a Mr. Milliken had purported to declare himself trustee for the plaintiff, Mr. Rollestone, of 10,000 shares with a par value of $1 each in a mining company, such shares forming part of a larger holding held by Mr. Milliken. The 10,000 shares were not specifically identified. With regard to the argument that this rendered the trust void for uncertainty as to its subject matter Ragland J. said, at p. 398:

> "It is next contended that, as the evidence does not show that any particular portion of the stock was set apart for Rollestone and a certificate issued therefor, the alleged trust must fail for lack of a definitely ascertained subject. But it clearly appears from Milliken's statements that he was carrying Rollestone for 10,000 shares of the capital stock of the Golden Cycle Mining Company. Now Milliken at that time had more than 1,000,000 shares standing in his name on the corporation's books, all of which were exactly alike in kind and value. There was no earmark by which any one of them could be distinguished from the others, so as to give it additional value or importance. They were like grain of a uniform quality, where in one bushel is of the same kind and value as another. *Caswell v. Putnam*, 120 NY 153, 157, 24 NE 287. The words '10,000 shares of capital stock' embodied, therefore, an accurate description of definite property rights in the corporation. A certificate of the same number of shares would have evidenced nothing more. *Richardson v. Shaw*, 209 US 365, 28 Sup Ct 512, 52 L Ed 835, 14 Ann Case 981. Appellants' contention under this head is disallowed."

Save that, with respect, I do not wholly agree that it was appropriate to answer the question there in point by analogy with tangible assets such as bushels of grain, I find those observations persuasive and convincing, and I agree with them. They appear to me to be directly in point in the present case.

A similar point potentially arose for decision in the Californian District Court of Appeal in the later case of *Busch v. Truitt* (1945) 160 P 2d 925. In that case Mr. Busch sought to establish a trust of shares in the Dried Food Products Company on the basis of a letter from Mr. Truitt, the alleged trustee, stating that "My records now show that I owe you 1,380 shares of escrowed stock which is made up of advances to me from time to time as follows" and then referring to, inter alia, various payments made by Mr. Busch. Mr. Truitt held 17,145 shares in the company in his own name, but there was no evidence that his holding had increased in consequence of his various transactions with Mr. Busch. Moore J., with whose judgment Wood and McComb JJ. both concurred, held first that there was no express trust, saying, at p. 928:

> "It could not have been an express trust, for there is no evidence that decedent ever declared that he held any shares of stock belonging to respondent or that he held certain corporate stock in which Busch had an ownership to the extent of 1,380 shares or in any amount."

He also rejected the argument that there was a resulting trust and then went on to say, at p. 928:

> "Before one who claims to be the beneficiary of a trust can realise upon his claim, he must identify the specific property to which he has title or which was acquired with funds furnished by him. *Holland v. Bank of Italy,* 115 Cal App 472, 1 P 2d 1031; *Roncelli v. Fugazi,* 44 Cal App 249, 186 P 373; *Lathrop v. Bampton,* 31 Cal 17, 89 Am Dec 141; *Byrne v. Byrne,* 113 Cal 294, 45 P 536. He who claims to be the beneficiary of an alleged trust must be able to identify the trust fund or follow it through its mutations. Failing to do so, he is no more than a general creditor."

In the next case to which I will refer there was a suggestion that that statement is inconsistent with the view expressed in the earlier *Rollestone* case, 252 SW 394 which I have quoted above. I do not, for my part, accept that it is. The statement is a general one, with the essence of which I do not in any way disagree. In the context in which it appears in the judgment I do not, however, read it as also making the narrower point that a trust declared in respect of part of a larger holding of shares will only be valid if particular shares are identified as being subject to the trust. The various cases referred to are not authorities which purport to decide that particular point and they do not justify the passage being so interpreted. If, however, the statement is to be so regarded, then I prefer the different view expressed in the *Rollestone* case.

Finally, the point raised by Mr. Hartman was also referred to in the decision of Gummow J. in *Herdegen v. Federal Commissioner of Taxation* (1988) 84 ALR 271. The question there was whether or not Mr. and Mrs. Herdegen had validly constituted themselves trustees for themselves and others of shares forming parts of larger holdings which each of them held in a particular company, Mr. and Mrs. Herdegen being respectively the holders of 59 and 41 shares. Gummow J. found on the facts that no such trusts as were alleged were established. He then said, at p. 279:

> "I should add that with respect to the 38 shares allegedly held on trust by Mr. Herdegen, no attempt was made to indicate how they were selected from among the parcel of 59 shares numbered 1 to 10 and 52 to 100. The same is true of Mrs. Herdegen's shares. As to whether such specific identification was essential to establish certainty of subject matter, or whether the shares might be treated as fungible for this purpose, the authorities appear to be unsettled: *Rollestone v.*

National Bank of Commerce (1923) 252 SW 394, 398; *Busch v. Truitt* (1945) 160 P 2d 925, 928; affd, 163 P 2d 739,"

Gummow J. accordingly appears to have regarded the point as less than clearly established and, being able to decide the case on other grounds, he left the point open.

In this case I cannot leave the point open. In my judgment the decision in *Rollestone v. National Bank of Commerce in St. Louis*, 252 SW 394 reflected the correct principle and I approach the present case in the same way. In the result I conclude that the trust which I have found the defendant to have declared was not void for lack of certainty as to its subject matter, and I do not accept Mr. Hartman's submissions to the contrary.

Whilst therefore I will consider with counsel whether the passage of time since I made my order of 16 October 1992 has resulted in any need to vary any particular aspects of it (I have in mind in particular the terms of the stay which I then directed) I refuse Mr. Hartman's request that I should recall my order and I do not accept his submission that I ought instead to have decided the actions in favour of the defendant."

Certainty of Objects

The objects or beneficiaries of a trust must be defined with a sufficient degree of certainty to enable the trustees, or if necessary the court, to administer the trust according to the settlor or testator's intentions. The requirements which must be satisfied will depend on whether the instrument being construed is characterised as a trust or a power and in addition may vary according to the nature of the trust involved.

Test for Fixed Trusts

In relation to a fixed trust, the persons who are to benefit under a trust must be clearly identified or identifiable by the time it comes into operation so where the trust property is to be divided amongst the members of a class either in equal or other specified shares, this task cannot be carried out unless it is possible to draw up a complete list of the members of that class.[11]

Test for Powers of Appointment

The donee of a power of appointment is under no duty to exercise it in a particular manner, if indeed he exercises it at all but a donee can only make a distribution amongst the classes of individuals specified by the settlor. The test for certainty of objects in relation to powers of appointment was formulated

---

[11] *IRC v. Broadway Cottages Trust* [1955] Ch 20, 29.

by Lord Upjohn in the decision of the House of Lords in *Re Gulbenkian's Settlements*[12] in the following terms viz., that it is valid 'if you can with certainty say whether any given individual is or is not a member of the class; you do not have to be able to ascertain every member of the class'. A similar viewpoint was put forward by Murnaghan J in the Supreme Court decision in *Re Bayley*[13] where he stated that 'it is sufficient if the person chosen as an object comes properly within the description of the class amongst which an appointment may be made'.

Re Bayley: Brown v. Gregg
[1945] IR 224

The testator by his will devised and bequeathed all his property to his sister for life subject to her ensuring that his brother was properly provided for during his lifetime and then stated that 'subject thereto, I wish my sister to dispose of same to take effect after her decease to and amongst such of my Irish relatives as she shall see fit'. The Supreme Court (O'Sullivan CJ, Murnaghan, Geoghegan and O'Byrne JJ) held that the will conferred a valid power of appointment on the testator's sister.

MURNAGHAN J stated at pp. 228–230: "This appeal has been taken against an order of the High Court (Mr. Justice Overend), dated 27th January, 1944, whereby, in answer to a question submitted for the determination of the Court, *viz.*, Did the will of the said Charles Scot Bayley confer a valid power of appointment of his residuary real and personal estate upon the said Henrietta Seward Riddall, the Court declared that the power of appointment was void for uncertainty.

Charles Scot Bayley, described as of Rocklodge in the County of Cork, Gentleman, made his will on the 29th August, 1902. By it he gave, devised and bequeathed "unto my sister, Henrietta Seward Riddall, all my estate and effects whatsoever and wheresoever both real and personal whether in possession, reversion, remainder or expectancy for her life, subject to her taking care that my brother, Henry Osborne Bayley, is properly provided for during his life." This brother in fact predeceased the testator. The will continued:– "and subject thereto I wish my sister to dispose of same to take effect after her decease to and amongst such of my Irish relatives as she shall see fit."

The testator died on the 6th May, 1920, and Henrietta Seward Riddall died on the 10th February, 1935, having purported by her will and several codicils to exercise the power of appointment contained in the will of Charles Scot Bayley.

---

[12] [1970] AC 508, 521.
[13] [1945] IR 224, 229.

The only question before the Court on this appeal is whether a valid power of appointment was created, and we are not concerned with the validity of the several appointments made under it.

Where in a will there is a direct gift to the relatives of the testator, the Court, as a rule of convenience, will select the persons who are, under the Statutes of Distribution, the next-of-kin. It cannot, however, be disputed that by relatives we mean persons connected by descent from a common ancestor. Cases have been referred to in which Courts have recognised relationship in degrees beyond the fourth degree of kinship. I think it to be clear that by his will the testator gave to his sister a power of selection, and, if the power were to select such of the testator's relatives as she thought fit, the power would be a valid one.

In stating the reasons for holding the power to be void for uncertainty, Mr. Justice Overend says:– "I do not know, and cannot know, what the testator meant by the words 'Irish relatives.' Did he mean relatives who are of Irish parentage, or who are resident in Ireland, or domiciled in Ireland, or are of Irish descent for a long period?"

It is not, I think, necessary for the valid exercise of a power of appointment that the donee should be able to range in his mind every person capable of taking under the power. It is sufficient if the person chosen as an object comes properly within the description of the class amongst which an appointment may be made. On the mere question of construction of the power, it may, in some cases, be said that the appointee fulfils the qualifications requisite by any and every suggested meaning of the words creating the power. Although the Court is not now concerned with expressing a view upon any of the particular appointments purported to have been made, it has been urged with a great amount of probability, that several of the appointments, if not most of them, are to persons who can answer any suggested test of the meaning of "Irish relatives."

Ireland is a known geographical entity and Irish is the adjective descriptive of that entity. The exact meaning to be given to the word "Irish" will necessarily be affected by the context, and may be affected by the circumstances of the person using the word. The words of Lord Brougham, spoken in *Winter v. Perratt* (1843) 9 Cl & F 606 at p. 687 in reference to a devise, seem to me equally applicable to the construction of this power. They are:– "Another principle is equally clear: we ought not, without absolute necessity, to let ourselves embrace the alternative of holding a devise void for uncertainty. Where it is possible to give a meaning, we should give it, that the will of the testator may be operative; and where two or more meanings are presented for consideration, we must be well assured that there is no sort of argument in favour of one view rather than another, before we reject the whole."

There seems to have been considerable difficulty on the part of various appointees in securing legal proof of their relationship, and the learned Judge observes in his judgment that he had no facts before him with regard to the testator's family or surroundings. The parties, however, agreed to argue in the first instance whether the will created a valid power of appointment. For the reasons which I have given, it is impossible to hold that the power was void for uncertainty.

If, in the case of a particular appointee, there are conflicting considerations based either upon birth, descent, domicile or residence, it must be a matter for determination whether the particular case falls within what the testator meant by the words "Irish relatives."

In my opinion the appeal should be allowed and the answer to question 1 in the summons should be "Yes"."

Test for Discretionary Trusts

Some doubt still surrounds the question of the correct test in relation to certainty of objects to be applied to discretionary trusts in this jurisdiction. Traditionally the test was recognised as being that the trust was invalid unless the entire class of potential beneficiaries is ascertained or capable of ascertainment.[14] However, the House of Lords held in *McPhail v. Doulton*[15] that the test for discretionary trusts ought to be similar to that forumlated by the House of Lords in *Re Gulbenkian's Settlements* for powers, namely, that the trust is valid if it can be said with certainty that any given individual is or is not a member of the class. The most recent view expressd on this issue in this jurisdiction is that of Murphy J, albeit in an *obiter* context in *O'Byrne v. Davoren*[16] in which he preferred the traditional test and declined to follow the one set out in *McPhail*. However, it should be borne in mind that the nature of the discretionary trust may have a bearing on which test is more likely to be appropriate in the circusmtances and where the class of potential beneficiaries is large the test formulated in *McPhail* may be preferable.[17]

Re Parker: Kilroy v. Parker
[1966] IR 309

By his will, the testator devised and bequeathed his property to his executors on trust to divide the income amongst his 'necessitous nieces and nephews' and their children in such manner as his executors might think fit for a period of ten years. Budd J held that the trust was not void for uncertainty.

BUDD J stated at pp.316–318: "The main matter at issue is as to whether or

---

[14] *IRC v. Broadway Cottages Trust* [1955] Ch 20; *Re Parker* [1966] IR 308.
[15] [1971] AC 424.
[16] [1994] 3 IR 373.
[17] See further Delany, *Equity and the the Law of Trusts in Ireland* (2nd ed., 1999) p.90–91.

not the gifts in trust of income and capital contained in the will are void for uncertainty. The contention made on behalf of the defendant, Joseph E. Parker, is that the gift of income is void for uncertainty and that since the whole residuary clause should be read as one the whole gift of residue is void and falls to be dealt with as on intestacy. Alternatively, it is contended that the gift of income is void for uncertainty and that there is an intestacy in respect thereof. The basis of the contention is that the gift by way of trust to the necessitous nieces and nephews of the testator takes the form of an imperative trust and that being so the result, as a matter of law, is that the gift will be void for uncertainty unless the whole class of potential beneficiaries can be ascertained. This, it is submitted, is something which cannot be done because the class of potential beneficiaries is not stated with sufficient certainty to enable it to be determined who are the members of the class. It is not possible, it is said, in the first place to give a sufficiently precise meaning to the word "necessitous" so as to enable the trustees to know who are included in the class amongst whom the income is to be distributed. It cannot be said, for example, whether it means those who are poor in the abstract sense of the word or those who are necessitous because of their particular circumstances in life. Further, that on the wording of the will it is uncertain as to whether the class is confined to nieces and nephews who are alive and "necessitous" at the date of the testator's death or to those who are alive at the date of the testator's death *or* become necessitous at any time during the period of ten years thereafter. Moreover, it is said, it is not clear as to whether or not the intention of the testator was to benefit the children of "necessitous" nephews and nieces whether they themselves were necessitous or not.

The bequest in the testator's will in so far as income is concerned takes the form of a devise and bequest to the executors in trust of his residuary estate with a direction, after dealing with matters of retention of investments and re-investment, out of the income therefrom, after paying all legal and necessary expenses, to pay a sum of £3 per week to a niece, Miss Marie Parker, for a period of ten years after his death and to divide the balance of such income amongst such of his necessitous nieces and nephews alive at the date of his death and such of their children as his executors in their discretion may see fit. Before dealing with the legal nature of a bequest in this form there is a preliminary matter to be considered. The gift in trust to Miss Parker was revoked by the codicil but the will was thereby in all other respects confirmed. It was submitted that, since the testator must manifestly know that the elimination (by the codicil) of the weekly payment to be paid out of the income would involve the result that the balance of the income would then be such balance as remained after the payment of all legal and necessary expenses, the confirmation of the will in all other respects indicated that his true intention was that this larger balance was to be divided in the fashion indicated. I agree with this view as to the proper construction of the clause as affected by the codicil and consequently proceed to deal with the nature of the bequest in trust on that basis.

The clause I am dealing with contains a direction to the executors to divide the balance of the income of the residuary estate – in effect, the whole income, having regard to the result of the operation of the codicil – amongst the class but according to their discretion. By reason of contentions made during the hearing, a question arises as to whether the testator has by virtue of the words he has used created a discretionary power or a power in the nature of a trust. The importance of the distinction as bearing on the question of uncertainty is as stated by Mr. Justice Cross in his judgment in *Re Saxone Shoe Co. Ltd's Trust Deed* [1962] 2 All ER 904, at p. 910, is that "a mere power given to trustees to apply income or capital for the benefit of members of a class, all the members of which cannot be ascertained, with a trust in default of the exercise of the power, is valid, whereas an imperative trust for the division of income or capital between such members of a class as the trustees may select is invalid if the whole class of potential beneficiaries cannot be ascertained." He amplified this, at p. 911, by a reference to the views of Mr. Justice Harman expressed in *In re Gestetner Settlement, Barnett v. Blumka* [1953] 1 Ch 672 as to the nature of the distinction. "He" (that is, Harman J.) "pointed out that, though trustees could not release any such power given to them and were under a duty to consider from time to time whether they would exercise it, they were under no duty to exercise it, and that even if all the objects of the power were ascertainable and joined together in calling on the trustees to exercise it, they could not compel them to do so. This being the position Harman J. saw no reason why trustees before exercising a power should have to be able to survey the whole field of objects. On the other hand, he considered that if trustees had a duty to distribute the capital or income in question it was essential that they should know before they performed their duty who were the potential beneficiaries among whom they had a right of selection. This, he thought, was implicit in the judgment of Lord Tomlin in *Re Ogden, Brydon v. Samuel* [1933] 1 Ch 678. This view of the position was accepted by the Court of Appeal in the *Broadway Cottages Case* [1955] 1 Ch 20. Jenkins L.J. pointed out in that case that if the Court had itself to execute a trust of this character because of the failure of the trustees to do so, it could only execute it by way of implying a trust in default of selection among all the beneficiaries equally, and that such a trust must necessarily fail unless all the beneficiaries could be ascertained." Mr. Justice Cross himself proceeded on the basis of accepting this statement of the distinctions stated and the results flowing therefrom as correct.

From a perusal of this case and those referred to therein, I am satisfied they establish in cases of the type under review, on the one hand, that in cases where the trustees have a duty to distribute the income in question it is essential that they should know, before they perform their duty, who are the potential beneficiaries among whom they have the right of selection, and, on the other hand, in the case of a power with a gift over that there is no reason why trustees, before exercising the power, should have to be able to survey the whole field of objects. The practical result is that a mere power to apply income for the benefit of the members of a class, all of whom cannot be ascertained, with a gift over in default, is valid, and an appointment can validly be made to a person who can properly be said to be a member of the class. But an imperative trust for the division of income between such members of the class as the trustees may select is invalid unless the whole class of potential beneficiaries can be ascertained. It was not suggested, nor do I think it could be, that there is any distinction in principle between English and Irish law on these matters."

McPhail v. Doulton
[1971] AC 424

A deed executed by the settlor provided that a fund was to be held on certain trusts for the benefit of the staff of a company and their 'relatives and dependents'. The House of Lords held that the deed created a trust rather than a power and Lord Wilberforce stated that a trust is valid if it can be said with certainty that any given individual is or is not a member of the class. It was ordered that the case should be remitted for determination of the question of whether the trust was valid or void for uncertainty.[18]

LORD WILBERFORCE stated at pp.447–457: "My Lords, this appeal is concerned with the validity of a trust deed dated July 17, 1941, by which Mr. Bertram Baden established a fund for the benefit, broadly, of the staff of the respondent company, Matthew Hall & Co. Ltd. Mr. Baden died in 1960 and the appellants are the executors of his will. They claim that the trust deed is invalid and that the assets transferred to the trustees by their testator revert to his estate. The trusts established by the deed are of a general type which has recently become common, the beneficiaries including a wide class of persons among whom the trustees are given discretionary powers or duties of distribution. It is the width of the class which in this and in other cases before the courts has given rise to difficulty and to the contention that the trusts are too indefinite to be upheld.

The trust deed begins with a recital that the settlor desired to establish a fund for providing benefits for the staff of the company and their relatives or dependants. The critical clauses are as follows:

"9. (a) The trustees shall apply the net income of the fund in making at their absolute discretion grants to or for the benefit of any of the officers and employees or ex-officers or ex-employees of the company or to any relatives or dependants of any such person in such amounts at such times and on such conditions (if

---

[18] It was held by the Court of Appeal in *Re Baden's Deed Trusts (No.2)* [1973] Ch 9 that the test of certainty had been satisfied in the circumstances of the case and that the trust was valid.

any) as they think fit and any such grant may at their discretion be made by payment to the beneficiary or to any institution or person to be applied for his or her benefit and in the latter case the trustees shall be under no obligation to see to the application of the money.

(b) The trustees shall not be bound to exhaust the income of any year or other period in making such grants as aforesaid and any income not so applied shall be dealt with as provided by clause 6(a) hereof.

[Clause 6. (a) All moneys in the hands of the trustees and not required for the immediate service of the fund may be placed in a deposit or current account with any bank or banking house in the name of the trustees or may be invested as hereinafter provided.]

(c) The trustees may realise any investments representing accumulations of income and apply the proceeds as though the same were income of the fund and may also (but only with the consent of all the trustees) at any time prior to the liquidation of the fund realise any other part of the capital of the fund which in the opinion of the trustees it is desirable to realise in order to provide benefits for which the current income of the fund is insufficient.

10. All benefits being at the absolute discretion of the trustees, no person shall have any right title or interest in the fund otherwise than pursuant to the exercise of such discretion, and nothing herein contained shall prejudice the right of the company to determine the employment of any officer or employee."

Clause 11 defines a perpetuity period within which the trusts are, in any event, to come to an end and clause 12 provides for the termination of the fund. On this event the trustees are directed to apply the fund in their discretion in one or more of certain specified ways of which one is in making grants as if they were grants under clause 9(a). There are certain other provisions in the deed upon which arguments have been based, but these are of a subsidiary character and citation of them is unnecessary.

The present proceedings were started in 1963 by an originating summons taken out in the Chancery Division by the trustees of the deed seeking the decision of the court upon various questions, including that of the validity or otherwise of the trusts of the deed. It came before Goff J. in 1967. He first decided that the references in clauses 9 and 12 to employees of the company were not limited to the "staff" but comprised all the officers and employees of the company. There was no appeal against this.

On the main question of validity, the learned judge was, it seems, invited first to decide whether the provisions of clause 9(a) constitute a trust or a power. This was on the basis that certain decided cases (which I shall examine) established a different test of invalidity for trusts on the one hand and powers on the other. He decided in favour of a power, and further that on this footing clause 9(a) was valid. On appeal, the Court of Appeal by a majority upheld the decision in favour of a power, but held also that the learned judge had applied the wrong test for the validity of powers, the correct test being that stated (subsequent to the hearing before Goff J.) by this House in *In re Gulbenkian's Settlement (Whishaw v. Stephens)* [1970] AC 508. The Court of Appeal therefore remitted the case to the Chancery Division to reconsider the validity of clause 9(a) as a power.

In this House, the appellants contend, and this is the first question for consideration, that the provisions of clause 9(a) constitute a trust and not a power. If that is held to be the correct result, both sides agree that the case must return to the Chancery Division for consideration, on this footing, whether this trust is valid. But here comes a complication. In the present state of authority, the decision as to validity would turn on the question whether a complete list (or on another view a list complete for practical purposes) can be drawn up of all possible beneficiaries. This follows from the Court of Appeal's decision in *Inland Revenue Commissioners v. Broadway Cottages Trust* [1955] Ch 20 as applied in later cases by which, unless this House decides otherwise, the Court of Chancery would be bound. The respondents invite your Lordships to review this decision and challenge its correctness. So the second issue which arises, if clause 9(a) amounts to a trust, is whether the existing test for its validity is right in law and, if not, what the test ought to be.

Before dealing with these two questions some general observations, or reflections, may be permissible. It is striking how narrow and in a sense artificial is the distinction, in cases such as the present, between trusts or as the particular type of trust is called, trust powers, and powers. It is only necessary to read the learned judgments in the Court of Appeal to see that what to one mind may appear as a power of distribution coupled with a trust to dispose of the undistributed surplus, by accumulation or otherwise, may to another appear as a trust for distribution coupled with a power to withhold a portion and accumulate or otherwise dispose of it. A layman and, I suspect, also a logician would find it hard to understand what difference there is.

It does not seem satisfactory that the entire validity of a disposition should depend on such delicate shading. And if one considers how in practice reasonable and competent trustees would act, and ought to act, in the two cases, surely a matter very relevant to the question of validity, the distinction appears even less significant. To say that there is no obligation to exercise a mere power and that no court will intervene to compel it, whereas a trust is mandatory and its execution may be compelled, may be legally correct enough, but the proposition does not contain an exhaustive comparison of the duties of persons who are trustees in the two cases. A trustee of an employees' benefit fund, whether given a power or a trust power, is still a trustee and he would surely consider in either case that he has a fiduciary duty: he is most likely to have been selected as a suitable person to administer it from his knowledge and experience, and would consider he has a responsibility to do so according to its purpose. It would be a complete misdescription of his position to say that, if what he has is a power unaccompanied by an imperative trust to distribute, he cannot be controlled by the court unless he exercised it capriciously, or outside the field permitted by the trust (cf. *Farwell on Powers*, 3rd ed., p. 524). Any trustee would surely make it his duty to know what is the permissible area of selection and then consider responsibly, in individual cases, whether a contemplated beneficiary was within the power and whether, in relation to other possible claimants, a particular grant was appropriate.

Correspondingly a trustee with a duty to distribute, particularly among a potentially very large class, would surely never require the preparation of a complete list of names, which anyhow would tell him little that he needs to know. He would examine the field, by class and category; might indeed make diligent and careful inquiries, depending on how much money he had to give away and the means at his disposal, as to the composition and needs of particular categories and of individuals within them; decide upon certain priorities or proportions, and then select individuals according to their needs or qualifications. If he acts in this manner, can it really be said that he is not carrying out the trust?

Differences there certainly are between trust (trust powers) and powers, but as regards validity, should they be so great as that in one case complete, or practically complete, ascertainment is needed, but not in the other? Such distinction as there is would seem to lie in the extent of the survey which the trustee is required to carry out: if he has to distribute the whole of a fund's income he must necessarily make a wider and more systematic survey than if his duty is expressed in terms of a power to make grants. But just as, in the case of a power, it is possible to underestimate the fidiciary obligation of the trustee, to whom it is given, so, in the case of a trust (trust power), the danger lies in overstating what the trustee requires to know or to inquire into before he can properly execute his trust. The difference may be one of degree rather than of principle: in the well-known words of Sir George Farwell, *Farwell on Powers*, 3rd ed. (1916), p. 10, trusts and powers are often blended, and the mixture may vary in its ingredients.

With this background I now consider whether the provisions of clause 9(a) constitute a trust or a power. I do so briefly because this is not a matter on which I or, I understand, any of your Lordships, have any doubt. Indeed, a reading of the judgments of Goff J. and of the majority in the Court of Appeal leave the strong impression that, if it had not been for their leaning in favour of possible validity and the state of the authorities, these learned judges would have found in favour of a trust. Naturally read, the intention of the deed seems to me clear: clause 9(a), whose language is mandatory ("shall"), creates, together with a power of selection, a trust for distribution of the income, the strictness of which is qualified by clause 9(b), which allows the income of any year to be held up and (under clause 6 (a)) either placed, for the time, with a bank, or, if thought fit, invested. Whether there is, in any technical sense, an accumulation seems to me in the present context a jejune inquiry: what is relevant is that clause 9(c) marks the difference between "accumulations" of income and the capital of the fund: the former can be distributed by a majority of the trustees, the latter cannot. As to clause 10, I do not find in it any decisive indication. If anything, it seems to point in favour of a trust, but both this and other points of detail are insignificant in the face of the clearly expressed scheme of clause 9. I therefore agree with Russell LJ. and would to that extent allow the appeal, declare that the provisions of clause 9(a) constitute a trust and remit the case to the Chancery Division for determination whether on this basis clause 9 is (subject to the effects of section 164 of the Law of Property Act, 1925) valid or void for uncertainty.

This makes it necessary to consider whether, in so doing, the court should proceed on the basis that the relevant test is that laid down in *Inland Revenue Commissioners v. Broadway Cottages Trust* [1955] Ch 20 or some other test.

That decision gave the authority of the Court of Appeal to the distinction between cases where trustees are given a *power* of selection and those where they are bound by a trust for selection. In the former case the position, as decided by this House, is that the power is valid if it can be said with certainty whether any given individual is or is not a member of the class and does not fail simply because it is impossible to ascertain every member of the class (*In re Gulbenkian's Settlements* [1970] AC 508). But in the latter case it is said to be necessary; for the trust to be valid that the whole range of objects (I use the language of the Cout of Appeal) should be ascertained or capable of ascertainment.

The respondents invited your Lordships to assimilate the validity test for trusts to that which applies to powers. Alternatively they contended that in any event the test laid down in the *Broadway Cottages* case [1955] Ch 20 was too rigid, and that a trust should be upheld if there is sufficient practical certainty in its definition for it to be carried out, if necessary with the administrative assistance of the court, according to the expressed intention of the settlor. I would agree with this, but this does not dispense from examination of the wider argument. The basis for the *Broadway Cottages* principle is stated to be that a trust cannot be valid unless, if need be, it can be executed by the court, and (though it is not quite clear from the judgment where argument ends and decision begins) that the court can only execute it by ordering an equal distribution in which every beneficiary shares. So it is necessry to examine the authority and reason for this supposed rule as to the execution of trusts by the court.

Assuming, as I am prepared to do for present purposes, that the test of validity is whether the trust can be executed by the court, it does not follow that execution is impossible unless there can be equal division.

As a matter of reason, to hold that a principle of equal division applies to trusts such as the present is certainly paradoxical. Equal division is surely the last thing the settlor ever intended: equal division among all may, probably would, produce a result beneficial to none. Why suppose that the court would lend itself to a whimsical execution? And as regards authority, I do not find that the nature of the trust, and of the court's powers over trusts, calls for any such rigid rule. Equal division may be sensible and has been decreed, in cases of family trusts, for a limited class; here there is life in the maxim "equality is equity," but the cases provide numerous examples where this has not been so, and a different type of execution has been ordered, appropriate to the circumstances

Mosely v. Mosely (1673) Fin 53 is an early example, from the time of equity's architect, where the court assumed power (if the executors did not act) to nominate from the sons of a named person as it should think fit and most worthy and hopeful, the testator's intention being that the estate should not be divided. In *Clarke v. Turner* (1694) Free Ch 198, on a discretionary trust for relations, the court decreed conveyance to the heir-at-law judging it "most reputable for the family that the heir-at-law should have it." In *Warburton v. Warburton* (1702) 4 Bro PC 1, on a discretionary trust to distribute between a number of the testator's children, the House of Lords affirmed a decree of Lord Keeper Wright that the eldest son and heir, regarded as necessitous, should have a double share, the court exercising its own discretionary judgment against equal division.

These are examples of family trusts but in *Richardson v. Chapman* (1760) 7 Bro PC 318 the same principle is shown working in a different field. There was a discretionary trust of the testator's "options" (namely, rights of presentation to benefices or dignities in the Church) between a number of named or specified persons, including present and former chaplains and other domestics; also "my worthy friends and acquaintance, particularly the Reverend Dr. Richardson of Cambridge." The House of Lords (reversing Lord Keeper Henley) set aside a "corrupt" presentation and ordered the trustees to present Dr. Richardson as the most suitable person. The grounds of decision in this House, in accordance with the prevailing practice, were not reported, but it may be supposed that the reported argument was accepted that where the court sets aside the act of the trustee, it can at the same time decree the proper act to be done, not by referring the matter to the trustee's discretion, but by directing him to perform as a mere instrument the thing decreed (*ibid.*, 326, 327). This shows that the court can in a suitable case execute a discretionary trust according to the perceived intention of the truster. It is interesting also to see that it does not seem to have been contended that the trust was void because of the uncertainty of the words "my worthy friends and acquaintance." There was no doubt that Dr. Richardson came within the designation.

In the time of Lord Eldon, the Court of Chancery adopted a less flexible practice: in *Kemp v. Kemp* (1795) 5 Ves Jr 849 Sir Richard Arden M.R., commenting on *Warburton v. Warburton* (1702) 4 Bro PC 1 ("a very extraordinary" case), said that the court now disclaims the right to execute a power (i.e., a trust power) and gives the fund equally. But I do not think that this change of attitude, or practice, affects the principle that a discretionary trust, can, in a suitable case, be executed according to its merits and otherwise than by equal division. I prefer not to suppose that the great masters of equity, if faced with the modern trust for employees, would have failed to adapt their creation to its practical and commercial character. Lord Eldon himself, in *Morice v. Bishop of Durham* (1805) 10 Ves Jr 522, laid down clearly enough that a trust fails if the object is insufficiently described or if it cannot be carried out, but these principles may be fully applied to trust powers without requiring a complete ascertainment of all possible objects. His earlier judgment in the leading, and much litigated, case of *Brown v. Higgs* (1803) 8 Ves Jr 561 shows that he was far from fastening any rigid test of validity upon trust powers. After stating the distinction which has ever since been followed, between powers, which the court will not require the donee to execute, and powers in the nature of a trust, or trust powers, he says of the latter that if the trustee does not discharge it, the court will, *to a certain extent*, discharge the duty in his room and place. To support this, he cites *Harding v. Glynn* (1739) 1 Atk 469, an early case where the court executed a discretionary trust for "relations" by distributing to the next-of-kin.

I dwell for a moment upon this point because, not only was *Harding v. Glyn* described by Lord Eldon (8 Ves Jr 561, 570) as having been treated as a clear authority in his experience for a long period, but the principle of it was adopted in several nineteenth-century authorities. When the *Broadway Cottages Trust* case came to be decided in 1955, these cases were put aside as anomalous (see [1955] Ch at pp.33, 35), but I think they illustrate the flexible manner in which the court, if called on, executes trust powers for a class. At least they seem to prove that the supposed rule as to equal division does not rest on any principle inherent in the nature of a trust. They prompt me to ask why a practice, or rule which has been long followed and found useful in "relations" cases should not also serve in regard to "employees", or "employees and their relatives," and whether a decision which says the contrary is acceptable.

I now consider the modern English authorities, particularly those relied on to show that complete ascertainment of the class must be possible before it can be said that a discretionary trust is valid.

In re H.J. Ogden [1933] Ch 678 is not a case which I find of great assistance. The argument seems to have turned mainly on the question whether the trust was a purpose trust or a trust for ascertained objects. The latter was held to be the case and the court then held that all the objects of the discretionary gift could be ascertained. It is weak authority for the requirement of complete ascertainment.

The modern shape of the rule derives from *In re Gestetner Settlement* [1953] Ch 672, where the judgment of Harman J., to his later regret, established the distinction between discretionary powers and discretionary trusts. The focus of this case was upon powers. The judgment first establishes a distinction between, on the one hand, a power collateral, or appurtenant, or other powers "which do not impose a trust on the conscience of the donee" (at p. 684) and on the other hand a trust imposing a duty to distribute. As to the first, the learned judge said (*ibid.*): "I do not think it can be the law that it is necessary to know of all the objects in order to appoint to one of them." As to the latter he uses these words (at p. 685): "It seems to me there is much to be said for the view that he must be able to review the whole field in order to exercise his judgment properly." He then considers authority on the validity of powers, the main stumbling-block in the way of his own view being some words used by Fry J. in *Blight v. Hartnoll* (1881) 19 Ch D 294, 301, which had been adversely commented on in *Farwell on Powers* (3rd ed., at pp. 168, 169), and I think it worth while quoting the words of his conclusion. He says ([1953] Ch 672, 688, 689):

> "The settlor had good reason, I have no doubt, to trust the persons whom he appointed trustees; but I cannot see here that there is such a duty as makes it essential for these trustees, before parting with any income or capital, to survey the whole field, and to consider whether A is more deserving of bounty than B. That is a task which was and which must have been known to the settlor to be impossible, having regard to the ramifications of the persons who might become members of this class.
>
> "If, therefore, there be no duty to distribute, but only a duty to consider, it does not seem to me that there is any authority binding on me to say that this whole trust is bad. In fact, there is no difficulty, as has been admitted, in ascertaining whether any given postulant is a member of a specified class. Of course, if that could not be ascertained the matter would be quite different, but of John Doe or Richard Roe it can be postulated easily enough whether he is or is not eligible to receive the settlor's bounty. There being no uncertainty in that sense, I am reluctant to introduce a notion of uncertainty in the other sense, by saying that the trustees must worry their heads to survey the world from China to Peru, when there are perfectly good objects of the class in England."

Subject to one point which was cleared up in this House in *In re Gulbenkian's Settlements* [1970] AC 508, all of this, if I may say so, seems impeccably good sense, and I do not understand the learned judge to have later repented of it. If the judgment was in any way the cause of future difficulties, it was in the indication given – not by way of decision, for the point did not arise – there was a distinction between the kind of certainty required for powers and that required for trusts. There is a difference perhaps but the difference is a narrow one, and if one is looking to reality one could hardly find better words than those I have just quoted to describe what trustees, in either case, ought to know. A second look at this case, while fully justifying the decision, suggests to me that it does not encourage the application of a similar test for the validity of trusts.

So I come to *Inland Revenue Commissioners v. Broadway Cottages Trust* [1955] Ch 20. This was certainly a case of trust, and, it proceeded on the basis of an admission, in the words of the judgment, "that the class of 'beneficiaries' is incapable of ascertainment." In addition to the discretionary trust of income, there was a trust of capital for all the beneficiaries living or existing at the terminal date. This necessarily involved equal division and it seems to have been accepted that it was void for uncertainty since there cannot be equal division among a class unless all the members of the class are known. The Court of Appeal applied this proposition to the discretionary trust of income, on the basis that execution by the court was only possible on the same basis of equal division. They rejected the argument that the trust could be executed by changing the trusteeship, and found the relations cases of no assistance as being in a class by themselves. The court could not create an arbitrarily restricted trust to take effect in default of distribution by the trustees. Finally they rejected the submission that the trust could take effect as a power: a valid power could not be spelt out of an invalid trust.

My Lords, it will have become apparent that there is much in this which I find out of line with principle and authority but before I come to a conclusion on it, I must examine the decision of this House in *In re Gulbenkian's Settlements* [1970] AC 508 on which the appellants placed much reliance as amounting to an endorsement of the *Broadway Cottages* case [1955] Ch 20. But is this really so? That case was concerned with a power of appointment coupled with a gift over in default of appointment. The possible objects of the power were numerous and were defined in such wide terms that it could certainly be said that the class was unascertainable. The decision of this House was that the power was valid if it could be said with certainty whether any individual was or was not a member of the class, and did not fail simply because it was impossible to ascertain every member of the class. In so deciding, their Lordships rejected an alternative submission, to which countenance had been given in the Court of Appeal, that it was enough that one person should certainly be within the class. So, as a matter of decision the question now before us did not arise or nearly arise. However, the opinions given were relied on, and strongly, as amounting to an endorsement of the "complete ascertainment" test as laid down in the *Broadway Cottages* case.

My Lords, I comment on this submission with diffidence, because three of those who were party to the decision are present here today, and will express their own views. But with their assistance, and with respect, for their views, I must endeavour to appraise the appellants' argument. My noble and learned friend Lord Reid's opinion can hardly be read as an endorsement of the *Broadway Cottages* case. It is really the opinion of my noble and learned friend Lord Upjohn which has to be considered. Undoubtedly the main part of that opinion, as one would expect, was concerned to deal with the clause in question, which required careful construction, and with the law as to powers of appointment among a numerous and widely defined class. But having dealt with these matters the opinion continues with some general observations. I have considered these with great care and interest: I have also had the advantage of considering a detailed report of the argument of counsel on both sides who were eminent in this field. I do not find that it was contended on either side that the *Broadway Cottages Trust* case was open to criticism – neither had any need to do so. The only direct reliance upon it appears to have been to the extent of the fifth proposition appearing on p. 31 of the report, which was relevant as referring to powers, but does not touch this case. It is consequently not surprising that my noble and learned friend Lord Upjohn nowhere expresses his approval of this decision and indeed only cites it, in the earlier portion, in so far as it supports a proposition as to powers. Whatever dicta therefore the opinion was found to contain, I could not, in a case where a direct and fully argued attack has been made on the *Broadway Cottages* case, regard them as an endorsement of it and I am sure that, my noble and learned friend, had he been present here, would have regarded the case as at any rate open to review. In fact I doubt very much whether anything his Lordship said was really directed to the present problem. I read his remarks as dealing with the suggestion that trust powers ought to be entirely assimilated to conditions precedent and powers collateral. The key passage is where he says [1970] AC 508, 525:

> "Again the basic difference between a mere power and a trust power is that in the first case trustees owe no duty to exercise it and the relevant fund or income falls to be dealt with in accordance with the trusts in default of its exercise, whereas in the second case the trustees *must* exercise the power and in default the court will. It is briefly summarised in *Halsbury's Laws of England,* 3rd ed., Vol. 30 (1959), p. 241, para. 445:
>
> > '. . . the court will not exercise or compel trustees to exercise a purely discretionary power given to them; but the court will restrain the trustees from exercising the power improperly, and, if it is coupled with a duty, the court can compel the trustees to perform their duty.'
>
> It is a matter of construction whether the power is a mere power or a trust power and the use of inappropriate language is not decisive (*Wilson v. Turner* (1883) 22 Ch D 521,525).
>
> So, with all respect to the contrary view, I cannot myself see how, consistently with principle, it is possible to apply to the execution of a trust power the principles applicable to the permissible exercise by the donees (even if trustees) of mere powers; that would defeat the intention of donors completely.
>
> But with respect to mere powers, while the court cannot compel the trustees to exercise their powers, yet those entitled to the fund in default must clearly be entitled to restrain the trustees from exercising it save among those within the power. So the trustees or the court must be able to say with certainty who is within and who is without the power. It is for this reason that I find myself unable to accept the broader proposition advanced by Lord Denning M.R. and Winn L.J., mentioned earlier, and agree with the proposition as enunciated in *In re Gestetner Settlement* [1953] Ch 672 and the later cases."

The reference to "defeating the intention of donors completely" shows that what he is concerned with is to point to the contrast between powers and trusts which lies in the facultative nature of the one and the mandatory nature of the other, the conclusion being the rejection of the "broader" proposition as to powers accepted by two members of the Court of Appeal. With this in mind it becomes clear that the sentence so much relied on by the appellants will not sustain the weight they put on it. This is:

"The trustees have a duty to select the donees of the donor's bounty from among the class designated by the donor; he has not entrusted them with any power to select the donees merely from among known claimants who are within the class, for that is constituting a narrower class and the donor has given them no power to do this" ([1970] AC 508, 524),

What this does say, and I respectfully agree, is that, in this case of a trust, the trustees must select from the class. What it does not say, as I read it, or imply, is that in order to carry out their duty of selection they must have before them, or be able to get, a complete list of all possible objects.

So I think that we are free to review the *Broadway Cottages* case [1955] Ch 20. The conclusion which I would reach, implicit in the previous discussion, is that the wide distinction between the validity test for powers and that for trust powers is unfortunate and wrong, that the rule recently fastened upon the courts by *Inland Revenue Commissioners v. Broadway Cottages Trust* ought to be discarded, and that the test for the validity of trust powers ought to be similar to that accepted by this House in *In re Gulbenkian's Settlements* [1970] AC 508 for powers, namely, that the trust is valid if it can be said with certainty that any given individual is or is not a member of the class.

I am interested, and encouraged, to find that the conclusion I had reached by the end of the argument is supported by distinguished American authority. Professor Scott in his well-known book on trusts (*Scott on Trusts* (1939)) discusses the suggested distinction as regards validity between trusts and powers and expresses the opinion that this would be "highly technical" (s. 122, p. 613). Later in the second *Restatement of Trusts* (1959), s. 122 (which *Restatement* aims at stating the better modern view and which annotates the *Broadway Cottages* case), a common test of invalidity is taken, whether trustees are "authorised" or "directed": this is that the class must not be so indefinite that it cannot be ascertained whether any person falls within it. The reporter is Professor Austin Scott. In his abridgment, published in 1960 (*Scott's Abridgement of The Law of Trusts*, s. 122, p. 239), Professor Scott maintains the same position:

"It would seem that if a power of appointment among the members of an indefinite class is valid, the mere fact that the testator intended not merely to confer a power but to impose a duty to make such an appointment should not preclude the making of such an appointment. It would seem to be the height of technicality that if a testator *authorises* a legatee to divide the property among such of the testator's friends as he might select, he can properly do so, but that if he *directs* him to make such a selection, he will not be permitted to do so."

Assimilation of the validity test does not involve the complete assimilation of trust powers with powers. As to powers, I agree with my noble learned friend Lord Upjohn in *In re Gulbenkian's Settlements* that although the trustees may, and normally will, be under a fiduciary duty to consider whether or in what way they should exercise their powers, the court will not normally compel its exercise. It will intervene if the trustees exceed their powers, and possibly if they are proved to have exercised it capriciously. But in the case of a trust power, if the trustees do not exercise it, the court will: I respectfully adopt as to this the statement in Lord Upjohn's opinion (p. 525). I would venture to amplify this by saying that the court, if called upon to execute the trust power, will do so in the manner best calculated to give effect to the settlor's or testator's intentions. It may do so by appointing new trustees, or by authorising or directing representative persons of the classes of beneficiaries to prepare a scheme of distribution, or even, should the proper basis for distribution appear by itself directing the trustees so to distribute. The books give many instances where this has been done, and I see no reason in principle why they should not do so in the modern field of discretionary trusts (see *Brunsden v. Woolredge* (1765) 1 Amb 507, *Supple v. Lowson* (1773) 2 Amb 729, *Liley v. Hey* (1842) 1 Hare 580 and *Lewin on Trusts,* 16th ed. (1964), 630). Then, as to the trustees' duty of inquiry or ascertainment, in each case the trustees ought to make such a survey of the range of objects or possible beneficiaries as will enable them to carry out their fiduciary duty (cf. *Liley v. Hey*). A wider and more comprehensive range of inquiry is called for in the case of trust powers than in the case of powers.

Two final points: first, as to the question of certainty. I desire to emphasise the distinction clearly made and explained by Lord Upjohn ([1970] AC 508, 524) between linguistic or semantic uncertainty which, if unresolved by the court, renders the gift void, and the difficulty of ascertaining the existence or whereabouts of members of the class, a matter with which the court can appropriately deal on an application for directions. There may be a third case where the meaning of the words used is clear but the definition of beneficiaries is so hopelessly wide as not to form "anything like a class" so that the trust is administratively unworkable or in Lord Eldon's words one that cannot be executed (*Morice v. Bishop of Durham* (1805) 10 Ves Jr 522, 527). I hesitate to give examples for they may prejudice future cases, but perhaps "all the residents of Greater London" will serve. I do not think that a discretionary trust for "relatives" even of a living person falls within this category.

I would allow the appeal and make the order suggested earlier in this opinion. The costs of the appellants and of the respondents of this appeal taxed on a common fund basis should be paid out of so much of the trust fund subject to the trust deed of July 17, 1941, as was derived from Bertram Baden deceased."

O'Byrne v. Davoren
[1994] 3 IR 373

The testatrix's will provided that the residue of her estate should be held on trust for the post primary education of such members of a class consisting of the children, grandchildren and direct descendants of named persons whom the trustees in their discretion should decide would be most likely to benefit therefrom. Murphy J was satisfied that the gift was sufficiently certain but held that it was void as its terms offended the rule against trusts of perpetual duration.

MURPHY J stated at pp.375–383: "This is a claim by the above plaintiff as executor of the will dated the 13th May, 1967, of Mary Davoren deceased who died a spinster on the 8th December, 1990, for the determination of certain questions arising on the construction of the deceased's will.

The residuary bequest contained in the said will is expressed in the following terms:–

> "I give devise and bequeath all the rest, residue and remainder of my estate both real and personal unto my TRUSTEES UPON TRUST to sell call in and convert the same into money (with power in their discretion to postpone such sale, calling in and conversion as hereinafter set out) and after payment thereout of my debts, funeral and testamentary expenses to hold the residue UPON TRUST for the post-primary education of such of the under mentioned as my trustees as in their discretion shall decide will be likely to benefit most namely:–
>
> The grandchildren and direct descendants of James Nagle of Castletown, Carron,
>
> The children and direct descendants of Patrick (Burke) Davoren of Kilcorney and of his brother Austin Davoren, Whitemount, Corofin and also the children and direct descendants of Michael Davoren of Ballyaliban, Ballyvaughan and of his brother Martin Davoren of Cahirconnell and also the children and direct descendants of John Davoren of Ennistymon (born at Ballyconnoe) and of his brother who married Miss Rynne and who resides at Ballyconnoe in the County of Clare.
>
> AND I DECLARE that my said trustees may in their absolute discretion decide which of the aforesaid children may benefit and also decide on the secondary, technological or university colleges or professional institutions where the aforesaid children take their courses AND I DECLARE that it is my intention that the income of the trust should be applied in the first instance for payment of fees and provision of textbooks and secondly for the maintenance while attending such schools colleges or courses AND I DECLARE that my Executors may postpone the sale, calling in or conversion of any part of my real and personal estate for such period as they in their absolute discretion may deem fit notwithstanding that it may be of a wasting, speculative or reversionary nature."

The first defendant, Michael Davoren, is sued as representing those persons who are potential beneficiaries under the residuary clause and the second defendant, Anne Coughlan, who is a niece of the deceased, was joined as a defendant to represent those persons who would be entitled to benefit in the event of the residuary estate passing as on an intestacy.

In these circumstances three questions were canvassed, namely:–

(1) Whether the residuary bequest aforesaid constituted a valid charitable gift.

(2) Whether the bequest offended the rule against perpetuities.

(3) Whether the bequest failed for uncertainty.

Having regard to the decisions in *In re McEnery; O'Connell v. Attorney General* [1941] IR 323; *In re Compton* [1945] Ch 123 and *Oppenheim v. Tobacco Securities Trust Co. Ltd.* [1951] AC 297 it was conceded by all parties that the gift could not be sustained as a valid charitable bequest as it did not possess the requisite public character.

The first question to be addressed is the extent of the class from which the particular beneficiaries may be chosen. Is the class confined to the particular categories of relations of the identified persons living at the date of death of the deceased or could relations of the particular kinship born after that date benefit from the trust? If the class did not close as at the date of death of the deceased then the class would be susceptible of enormous variations either by expansion or contraction and this would raise questions as to whether the gift possessed the requisite degree of certainty either on the basis that it was a beneficial trust or what is described as "a purpose" trust. However, the answer to that question is even more important in the context of the rule against perpetuities. If the class did not close as of the date of death then there could be no doubt at all but that the rule was breached and the gift void *ab initio*.

The widest and remotest of the degrees of kinship referred to in the bequest are the "descendants". That word was defined in Halsbury's Laws of England (4th Edition) Volume 50 at para. 521 in the following terms:–

> "Whatever may have been its meaning in earlier times, 'descendants' now ordinarily refers to children, grandchildren and other issue of every degree of remoteness in descent. Although the word may be confined to mean children by a sufficiently strong context, the Court does not restrict the word to that sense merely because the testator speaks of the descendants taking their parent's share."

It would appear from the same textbook that such misgivings as may have existed about the meaning of the word "descendants" in earlier times concerned whether or not collaterals were included within its meaning. It does not ever appear to have been doubted that descendants included issue of every degree of remoteness in descent. That being so a gift to descendants if not otherwise qualified expressly or by implication would appear to include all children of children indefinitely and without limit. It was argued by counsel representing the potential beneficiaries under the will that the class should be treated as having closed at the date of death of the deceased on the basis of the rule in *Andrews v. Partington* (1791) 3 Bro CC 401. It cannot be doubted that the law favours an early as opposed to a later vesting of interests in property. Whilst this rule has been criticised many times it has endured for over two hundred years. Under the rule it is presumed that where there is an immediate gift to a class without any provision as to the time of this vesting then if any members of the class are born at the time of the testator's death they take to the exclusion of after born members. It is, however, accepted by counsel on behalf of the potential beneficiaries under the trust that this rule could not be applied directly to the facts of the present case as there is no gift to the members of the class but merely an obligation on the trustees to employ the trust funds for a purpose which would be of benefit to some members of that class. In the circumstances the argument under this heading can be put no further than saying that the rule in *Andrews v. Partington* might be applied by analogy.

In any event the identification of the class or more correctly the date as of which it is to be ascertained is essentially a matter for the construction of the will itself with the aid of the appropriate principles governing such construction.

Unlike the wills in *In re Compton* [1945] Ch 123 and *Kilroy v. Parker* [1966] IR 309, the residuary bequest in the present case gives no specific guidance as to when the relevant class is to be ascertained. In *In re Compton* there was a trust for education of descendants of three named persons and it was expressly provided that the trust was to be "forever". In *Kilroy v. Parker* where income from a fund was to be paid amongst the testator's necessitous nieces and nephews and their children, it was expressly provided that the nephews and nieces who might benefit were those "alive at the date of my death".

The researches carried out by the executors have established that the number of persons who would constitute the class of potential beneficiaries if it were to be established as of the date of death of the deceased would be in the order of sixty. Moreover, it would be possible to estimate with reasonable accuracy the capital and likely income of the trust fund. However, these are not factors which are of much assistance in ascertaining the wishes of the deceased. It seems to me that the only guidance to be obtained from the will of the late Mary Davoren is the express trust for the sale and conversion of her residuary estate and the payment thereout of her debts funeral and testamentary expenses and the additional and express declaration that the trustees might "postpone the sale calling in or conversion of any part of my real and personal estate for such period as they in their absolute discretion may deem fit, notwithstanding that it may be of a wasting speculative or reversionary nature". Whilst those provisions have some significance it is obvious that they represent standard machinery to facilitate the administration of the estate and the trust fund to be created thereout. In particular the express power to postpone the realisation of the estate – even estate of "a wasting speculative or reversionary nature" – is clearly a protection for the trustees who might otherwise be liable for a breach of their duty rather than an indication of some particular policy or intention on the part of the deceased. Apart from the purpose of the trust and the selection of the beneficiaries the only special if somewhat ambiguous provision of the residuary bequest is expressed in the following terms:–

> "And I declare that it is my intention that the income of the trust should be
> applied in the first instance for payment of fees and provision of text books and

secondly for maintenance while attending such schools, colleges or courses."

As it is clear that both the capital and income of the residuary estate are subject to the trusts declared by the deceased the question must be asked, why did the deceased focus attention in this very specific way upon the manner and order in which the income of the trust fund should be applied. It seems to me that at the very least the deceased intended that the capital of the fund should be conserved if not actually preserved. It would be meaningless to prescribe an order in which resort was to be had to income if the trustees had an unfettered discretion to resort to capital for any of the purposes identified in the foregoing declaration. Such an action would appear to frustrate the wishes of the testatrix without expressly defying them. By this special declaration it seems to me that the testatrix revealed an expectation and intention that recourse would be had primarily to the income of the fund with a view to conserving the capital as a fund for indefinite duration. Moreover, this has a certain logic. The testatrix would not wish her trustees to deplete excessively the trust fund at any one time when their task would involve a review of their duties and an exercise of their discretions over a long period of time. When one accepts the concept of preserving the capital of the trust fund over a lifetime or even the infancy of the youngest members of the class living at the date of death of the deceased, the question would then arise as to how or why the trust should be wound up and the balance of the capital and income distributed amongst a diminishing class. It seems to me that the logic of the situation as best it may be inferred from the very limited evidence available, is that the testatrix intended to create a fund which would be available indefinitely for the children, grandchildren and descendants whenever born of the persons named in her will, and such a gift is unfortunately invalid as contravening the ancient but still respected rule against perpetuities.

Whilst that conclusion disposes of the issue as to the validity of the bequest I think it may be helpful having regard to the arguments which were addressed to the court (and to the state of the law on the topic) to express my views on the other issues raised.

Prior to the decision of the House of Lords in *In re Baden's Deed Trusts* [1971] AC 424, it was generally accepted that the objects of a trust must be certain, that is to say, that the language employed must be certain and that the trustees must at any time be able to ascertain definintely the persons who would have a vested interest in the capital and income of the trust property. On the other hand where the trustees were not bound by a trust but merely a power or discretion whether to confer or withhold a benefit then the requirement of certainty was recognised as being far less stringent. These rules appeared clearly from the decisions in *Inland Revenue Commissioners v. Broadway Cottages Trust* [1955] Ch 20 and *In re Gulbenkian's Settlements* [1970] AC 508. As Lord Upjohn pointed out in the latter case (at p. 521) the then recent authorities were to the effect that:–

". . . the rule is, that provided there is a valid gift over or trust in default of appointment . . . a mere or bare power of appointment among a class is valid if you can with certainty say whether any given individual is or is not a member of the class; you do not have to be able to ascertain every member of the class."

In the comprehensive judgment of Budd J. in *Kilroy v. Parker* [1966] IR 309 he accepted and applied that principle (at p. 318) in the following terms:–

"From a perusal of this case and those referred to therein, I am satisfied they establish in cases of the type under review, on the one hand, that in cases where the trustees have a duty to distribute the income in question it is essential that they should know, before they perform their duty, who are the potential beneficiaries among whom they have the right of selection, and, on the other hand, in the case of a power with a gift over that there is no reason why trustees, before exercising the power, should have to be able to survey the whole field of objects. The practical result is that a mere power to apply income for the benefit of the members of a class, all of whom cannot be ascertained, with a gift over in default, is valid, and an appointment can validly be made to a person who can properly be said to be a member of the class. But an imperative trust for the division of income between such members of the class as the trustees may select is invalid unless the whole class of potential beneficiaries can be ascertained. It was not suggested, nor do I think that it could be, that there is any distinction in principle between English and Irish law on these matters."

The statement contained in the final sentence quoted above ceased to be true as and from the decision of the House of Lords in *In re Baden's Deed Trust* [1971] AC 424. In that case the House of Lords by a majority of three to two overruled the decision in *Inland Revenue Commissioners v. Broadway Cottages Trust* [1955] Ch 20 and held that the test was substantially the same as that applicable to discretionary trusts. That is to say, the trust was valid if it could be said with certainty that any given individual was or was not a member of the class designated as potential beneficiaries.

Not only is the judgment of the late Budd J. a precedent of greater authority for me than a judgment (particularly a majority judgment) of the House of Lords but I confess that I find the reasoning of the Irish judgment (and indeed the earlier English judgments) more convincing than that contained in what was admittedly a conscious effort at law reform made in the *McPhail* case.

In *Kilroy v. Parker* [1966] IR 309 the court had to consider whether a trust to distribute the income of a fund amongst the necessitous nieces and nephews of the deceased and such of their children as the executors might think fit. As I have already remarked the category of nieces and nephews were expressly identified in the will as those being alive at the date of the death of the testatrix. It was, however, an imperative trust though confined to the income of the fund accruing over a period of ten years from the date of death of the testator. In those circumstances no question arose with regard to the rule against perpetuities nor in the identification of the class of potential beneficiaries insofar as it consisted of nephews and nieces of the testator, living at his death and their children. The major problem related to identifying and perhaps reidentifying the "inner" class of "necessitous" nephews and nieces. What degree of poverty or hardship is involved in that adjective? Was the standard to be an objective one or in some way related to the standard of living of the testator? What was to happen if during the ten years during which the income of the trust fund was to be distributed the financial circumstances of particular nephews or nieces altered significantly? To my mind a significant feature of the judgment is the dedication and determination with which Budd J. addressed and resolved those and other difficult problems.

Having accepted the need for certainty in the creation of the trust Budd J. considered the principles upon which a court approaches the problem of having to decide whether or not a gift is to be held void for uncertainty. He pointed out (at p. 320) that:–

> "The difficulties in interpreting a disposition which is ambiguously expressed are not enough to render the disposition void for uncertainty. To be void for this reason it must be utterly impossible to put a meaning on it."

He went on (at p. 321) to quote a passage previously cited with approval by Murnaghan J. in the following terms:–

> "Another principle is equally clear: we ought not, without absolute necessity, to let ourselves embrace the alternative of holding a devise void for uncertainty. Where it is possible to give a meaning, we should give it, that the will of the testator may be operative; and where two or more meanings are presented for consideration, we must be well assured that there is no sort of argument in favour of one view rather than another, before we reject the whole."

He accepted, as all of the parties would, that the presumption is that "when a man makes his will he does not intend to die intestate as to any part of his property".

It was those principles which imposed on the learned judge the duty to seek a construction of the will and an approach to the problems canvassed in relation to the administration of the trust which would resolve ambiguities and uncertainties where this was compatible with the expressed or implied wishes of the testator. Whilst the particular facts of *Kilroy v. Parker* [1966] IR 309 are unique, the significance of the judgment of Budd J. thereon, as I see it, is the determination with which he sought to salvage the validity of the particular testamentary trust notwithstanding the difficulties created by the manner in which the testatrix had expressed her intentions. Again I could respectfully agree that the learned judge was entirely correct in that course and as far as possible I believe that a similar approach should be taken in the present matter. It is noticeable that Budd J. recognised that the class of potential beneficiaries might fluctuate from year to year as would happen in the present case depending upon the educational requirements of the relatives of the persons designated by the testatrix. It was of that problem that the learned judge said (at page 334):–

"The fact that the class in the present case may fluctuate does undoubtedly increase the difficulty of ascertaining the class, but difficulties and impracticabilities should not be allowed to stand in the way if by any possibility the trust can be executed."

It seems to me that the helpful decision of Budd J. in *Kilroy v. Parker* [1966] IR 309 would be of decisive importance in upholding the validity of the residuary bequest in the present case if, but only if, the class of relatives out of whom the beneficiaries were to be selected was limited to those living at the date of death of the deceased and as I have held that the contrary is – regrettably – the true construction of the will, my conclusion in this regard can be of no comfort to the designated class of beneficiaries.

In the circumstances it seems to me that the questions raised in the statement of claim herein should be answered as follows:–

(a) The trust purported to be created by the residuary clause does not constitute a trust of a charitable nature.

(b) The words creating the trust are sufficiently certain for that purpose.

(c) The terms of the trust do offend against the rule against trusts of perpetual duration.

However, I will hear the parties in relation to any matter of detail as to how the questions raised should be dealt with."

Conceptual Certainty, Administrative Workability and Capriciousness

Irrespective of the nature of the trust or power involved, the description used to define the class of potential beneficiaries must be conceptually certain. In addition, even where a class is defined with sufficient conceptual certainty, a trust may still fail on the basis that it is administratively unworkable 'where the definition of the beneficiaries is so hopelessly wide as not to form "anything like a class"'.[19] However, the weight of authority supports the view that while administrative unworkability can invalidate a discretionary trust, it will not affect the validity of a power of appointment.[20]

Another related concept which may form the basis for a finding of uncertainty is that of capriciousness which has been held to apply to powers as well as trusts.[21] So where a settlor seeks to benefit 'an accidental conglomeration of persons'[22] who have no discernible link with him, it may be unrealistic to seek to give effect to his intentions and the instrument, whether construed as a trust or a power, may be found to be invalid on the grounds of capriciousness.

---

[19] *McPhail v. Doulton* [1971] AC 424, 457. See also *R. v District Auditor, ex p. West Yorkshire Metropolitan County Council* (1986) 26 RVR 24.

[20] *Re Manisty's Settlement Trusts* [1974] Ch 17 and *Re Hay's Settlement Trusts* [1982] 1 WLR 202.

[21] *Re Manisty's Settlement Trusts* [1974] Ch 17.

[22] *Ibid.* at 27.

Re Manisty's Settlement
[1974] Ch 17

By virtue of a deed, a settlor conferred on his trustees power to apply funds for the benefit of a class of his relatives apart from those who were members of an 'excepted class'. In addition, the trustees had the power at their absolute discretion to declare that any person, corporation or charity, other than a member of the excepted class or a trustee, should be included in the class of beneficiaries. Templeman J held that the power to add to the class of beneficiaries was valid and not void for uncertainty.

TEMPLEMAN J stated at pp.20–29: "This summons challenges the validity of a power conferred on trustees to nominate and add to a class of beneficiaries.

By the settlement dated December 20, 1971, the settlor, who is the first defendant, appointed his brother Henry and a chartered accountant, who are the two plaintiffs to be the first trustees, and by clause 4, read with clause 15, conferred on the trustees for the time being, provided that they include at least one trustee who is not a beneficiary, power at their absolute discretion to pay, apply, appoint or settle the trust funds for the benefit of any of the beneficiaries. The power is exercisable during a perpetuity period, that is to say, until the closing date defined by clause 1 as the date of the expiry of the period of 79 years from the execution of the settlement, or such earlier date as the trustees declare. The original beneficiaries were defined by clause 1 as the two existing infant children of the settlor, the future children and remoter issue of the settlor born before the closing date, the settlor's two brothers, Michael and Henry, and their children and remoter issue born before the closing date. It was provided that "every person who is for the time being a member of the excepted class shall be excluded from the class of beneficiaries."

The original excepted class defined by clause 1 comprised the settlor, the wife for the time being of the settlor, any other person or corporation settling property on the trusts of the settlement and the spouse of any such settlor. Clause 4, as limited by clause 15, also authorised the trustees, if they include at least one trustee who is not a beneficiary, to delete any person or corporation from the beneficiaries, to add any person, corporation or class to the excepted class and at their absolute discretion to exercise the power which is now challenged, and which, comprising clause 4(a)(iii) as follows:

> "Power by any deed or deeds revocable or irrevocable to declare that any person or persons, corporation or corporations or charity or charities (other than a person or corporation who shall for the time being be a member of the excepted class or one of the trustees) shall thenceforth and for such period as shall be specified in such deed or deeds (not extending beyond the closing date) be included in the class of beneficiaries hereinbefore defined provided always that any such deed shall not take effect, unless and until the same (or a memorandum stating the effect thereof) has been endorsed on this settlement."

Subject to the powers of disposition conferred on the trustees, and to a trust for accumulation for 21 years, the trust funds, which in the first instance consisted of policies of assurance on the life of the settlor, were settled by clause 3(2) on such of the children of the existing children of the settlor as shall be living on the closing date, or shall previously attain the age of 21 years, or if there shall be no such grandchildren of the settlor by clause 3(3) on such of the existing children as attain 21.

By a deed of declaration dated December 8, 1972, a memorandum of which was endorsed on the settlement and dated December 11, 1972, the trustees, who included one person who was not a beneficiary, added to the beneficiaries the mother of the settlor and any person who shall for the time being be the widow of the settlor. The settlor's wife, who may become his widow, and the settlor's mother are the second and third defendants and appear by Mr. Cozens-Hardy Horne to uphold the validity of the power to add beneficiaries and the validity of the deed of declaration which exercised that power.

The settlor's two existing infant children are the fourth and fifth defendants and they appear by Mr. Bradburn to argue in the interests of all the original beneficiaries that the power to add further beneficiaries is invalid and the deed of declaration is ineffective. The sixth defendant is Michael, the brother of the settlor, and has taken no part in the argument.

The power to add beneficiaries and to benefit the persons so added is exercisable in favour of anyone in the world except the settlor, his wife, the other members of the excepted class for the time being and the trustees, other than the settlor's brother Henry who was one of the original beneficiaries. This is not a general power exercisable in favour of anyone, nor a special power exercisable in favour of a class, but an intermediate power exercisable in favour of anyone, with certain exceptions.

Mr. Bradburn submits that an intermediate power cannot be conferred on trustees because of principles of non-delegation and uncertainty. The argument based on the principle of non-delegation stems from the proposition that a testator must not delegate to other persons the right to make a will for him. It is however, established by authority that a testator, and a fortiori a settlor, may create powers of disposition exercisable by individuals or by trustees without thereby infringing any rule against delegation. If delegation is the vice then delegation to an individual is as bad as delegation to a trustee. But in *In re Park* [1932] 1 Ch 580, Clauson J. held valid an intermediate power conferred by a testator on an individual to appoint to anyone in the world, except the donee of the power. If delegation is the vice then delegation to trustees by means of a special power is as bad as delegation to trustees by means of an intermediate power. But in *In re Gulbenkian's Settlements* [1970] AC 508 the House of Lords held valid a special power conferred by a settlor on trustees to benefit the settlor's son and his associates. To make assurance double sure, in *In re Abrahams' Will Trusts* [1969] 1 Ch 463, 474–476, Cross J. held valid an intermediate power conferred by a testator on trustees to appoint to anyone in the world except the trustees, and he expressly rejected the argument based on the principle of non-delegation. I conclude that the settlor in the present case was not precluded by the doctrine of non-delegation from conferring an intermediate power on his trustees.

The argument based on uncertainty is that the trustees are under a duty to consider from time to time whether and how to exercise their powers, and that they cannot perform that duty, and a court cannot judge the performance of that duty if the power is too wide. An intermediate power, it is said, is wider than any special power and is pratically unlimited, and is therefore too wide, uncertain and invalid.

Invalidity, based on uncertainty, was the subject of *In re Gulbenkian's Settlements* [1970] AC 508 relating to special powers in favour of a class, and *In re Baden's Deed Trust* [1971] AC 424, known as *Baden (No. 1)*, relating to discretionary trusts in favour of a class. Those authorities establish that such a power or trust is valid if it can be said with certainty that any given individual is or is not a member of the class. The principle of the rule thus established does not strike down an intermediate power provided that, having regard to the definition of excepted persons, it can be said with certainty that any given individual is or is not an object of the power. The principle for which Mr. Horne contends may be adopted from the summary of the effect of *In re Gulbenkian's Settlements* to be found in the dissenting speech of Lord Guest in *Baden (No. 1)* [1971] AC 424 where he said, at p. 445: "In the case of a power it is only necessary for the trustees to know whether a particular individual does or does not come within the ambit of the power." Mr. Horne says applying that principle to the present case, the definition of excepted class being certain, it follows that there is no uncertainty about the power.

The cases of *Gulbenkian* and *Baden (No. 1)* also establish, or rather reiterate, the rule that trustees of a power must consider from time to time whether and how to exercise the power, for in the words of Lord Reid in *Gulbenkian* [1970] AC 508, 518,

> "A settlor or testator who entrusts a power to his trustees must be relying on them in their fiduciary capacity so they cannot simply push aside the power and refuse to consider whether it ought in their judgment to be exercised. And they cannot give money to a person who is not within the classes of persons designated by the settlor: the construction of the power is for the court."

In *Baden (No. 1)* [1971] AC 424, 449, Lord Wilberforce, referring to special powers, suggested that:

> "Any trustee would surely make it his duty to know what is the permissible area of selection and then consider responsibly, in individual cases, whether a contemplated beneficiary was within the power and whether, in relation to other possible claimants, a particular grant was appropriate."

He added, at p.457, referring to special powers and to discretionary trusts in favour of a class that "in each case the trustees ought to make such a survey of the range of objects or possible beneficiaries as will enable them to carry out their fidicuary duty."

It is said that if a power is too wide the trustees cannot perform the duty reiterated in *Gulbenkian* and *Baden (No. 1)* of considering from time to time whether and how to exercise the power and the court cannot determine whether or not the trustees are in breach of their duty. In my judgment, however, the mere width of a power cannot make it impossible for trustees to perform their duty nor prevent the court from determining whether the trustees are in breach.

In *In re Gestetner Settlement* [1953] Ch 672 the trustees were given the power set forth at p. 674, exercisable in favour of a class which excluded the settlor, his wife and the trustees and comprised four named individuals, the living, and future descendants of the settlor's father and of an uncle of the settlor, the spouses, widows and widowers of those individuals and descendants, five named charitable bodies, former employees of the settlor or his wife and the widows and widowers of former employees of the settlor or his wife and any person who was for the time being a director or employee or former director or employee or the wife or husband or widow or widower of a former director or employee of Gestetner Ltd. or of any company of which the directors for the time being included any one or more of the person who were for the time being directors of Gestetner Ltd. This was a special power exercisable over an enormous class, and the great majority of beneficiaries by number and category will never learn that they are objects of the power or fall to be considered by the trustees. If a director of Gestetner Ltd. became a director of Woolwich or Unilever there would be added to the class of beneficiaries shop assistants throughout England and workers throughout the world. *Gestetner* was approved in *Gulbenkian* and does not exhaust the ingenuity of settlors in creating classes and numbers of beneficiaries of immeasurable width.

The argument that a discretionary trust in favour of a recognised class can be too wide was considered in *In re Baden's Deed Trusts (No. 2)* [1972] Ch 607, a case known as *Baden (No. 2)*, and a decision which for present purposes must apply to special powers as well as to discretionary trusts. In *Baden (No. 2)* it was submitted that a discretionary trust exercisable in favour of employees and former employees of a company and their relatives and dependants was void for uncertainty because it did not satisfy the test suggested at p. 620 of the judgment of Brightman J., namely, that such a trust is

> "invalid if the class is so large or arbitrary that the trustees cannot reasonably estimate the membership, or know how to set about instituting inquiries which will reveal the membership, including the membership of its subclasses or categories, and if the trustees cannot therefore properly discharge their duty to consider how the fund should be divided between the subclasses or categories, and what further inquiries they should make."

The suggested test only serves to illustrate how impossible it is to define the circumstances in which a recognised class may be said to be too wide.

Brightman J. rejected the test and held that the discretionary trust was valid, applying only the test established in *Baden (No. 1)* that a trust in favour of a recognised class is valid if it can be said with certainty that any given individual is or is not a member of the class. The decision of Brightman J. in *Baden (No. 2)* was confirmed by the Court of Appeal [1973] Ch 9. I conclude from *Gestetner, Gulbenkian* and the two *Baden* cases that a power cannot be uncertain merely because it is wide in ambit.

An alternative argument against the invalidity of an intermediate power conferred on trustees is that a power which is not confined to individuals or to classes recognised by the court is too vague. An intermediate power which does not attempt to classify the beneficiaries but only specifies or classifies excepted persons is therefore, it is said, too vague. It is admitted that it may be difficult to define or describe those classes which would not be recognised by the court, and are therefore also too vague, but the example suggested by Lord Wilberforce in *Baden (No. 1)* [1971] AC 424, 457 of "all the residents of Greater London" is given as an instance of a class which would not be so recognised. The submission that an intermediate power is too vague because the benficiaries are not limited to specified individuals or recognised classes is in the final analysis based on the same reasoning as the attack on wide discretionary trusts which was rejected in *Baden (No. 2)* [1972] Ch 607. The argument is that an intermediate power where the beneficiaries are not limited to specified individuals or recognised classes precludes the trustees from considering in a sensible manner whether and how to exercise the power, and prevents the court from judging whether the trustees have surveyed the field of objects and have properly considered whether and how to exercise the power.

Implicit in this argument are two assertions, first, that the terms of a special power in favour of recognised classes necessarily provide some guidance to the trustees with regard to the proper mode of considering how to exercise the power, and secondly, that the terms of a special power in favour of recognised classes enable the court to judge whether the trustees are in breach of their duty. In my judgment neither assertion is well founded. Some powers may give an indication of the expectations of the settlor. In *Gulbenkian* [1970] AC 508 it was plain that the trustees were expected to have regard to the best interests of Mr. Nubar Gulbenkian. There are similar powers where all the beneficiaries are equal but some are more equal than others. But in *Gestetner* [1953] Ch 672 it was impossible to derive any assistance from the terms of the power, save that the trustees, it could be assumed, were expected to have regard to the considerations which might move the settlor to confer bounty on the beneficiaries. A similar expectation may be implied from an intermediate power, and in the present case, if the settlement is read as a whole, expectations of the settlor are not difficult to discern. In *Gestetner* the terms of the power did not in themselves indicate how employees were to be compared with relations, charities, individuals and other classes of beneficiaries. The terms of the power in themselves did not indicate whether and on what grounds one employee might be considered, whether by reference to services rendered to Gestetner Ltd. or to the settlor or by reference to age, health or any other criterion. The terms of the power did not in themselves indicate whether and on what grounds one relation out of many was to be considered, whether by reference to his proximity to the settlor, poverty, educational requirements or any other circumstances. The terms of a special power do not necessarily indicate in themselves how the trustees are to consider the exercise of the power. That consideration is confided to the absolute discretion of the trustees.

The court cannot insist on any particular consideration being given by the trustees to the exercise of the power. If a settlor creates a power exercisable in favour of his issue, his relations and the employees of his company, the trustees may in practice for many years hold regular meetings, study the terms of the the power and the other provisions of the settlement, examine the accounts and either decide not to exercise the power or to exercise it only in favour, for example, of the children of the settlor. During that period the existence of the power may not be disclosed to any relation or employee and the trustees may not seek or receive any information concerning the circumstance of any relation or employee. In my judgment it cannot be said that the trustees in those circumstances have committed a breach of trust and that they ought to have advertised the power or looked beyond the persons who are most likely to be the objects of the bounty of the settlor. The trustees are of course, at liberty to make further inquiries, but cannot be compelled to do so at the behest of any beneficiary. The court cannot judge the adequacy of the consideration given by the trustees to the exercise of the power, and it cannot insist on the trustees applying a particular principle or any principle in reaching a decision.

If a person within the ambit of the power is aware of its existence he can require the trustees to consider exercising the power and in particular to consider a request on his part for the power to be exercised in his favour. The trustees must consider this request, and if they decline to do so or can be proved to have omitted to do so, then the aggrieved person may apply to the court which may remove the trustees and appoint others in their place. This, as I understand it, is the only right and only remedy of any object of the power: see, for example, *In re Gestetner Settlement* [1953] Ch 672, where Harman J. said, at p. 688, that the trustees

> "are not entitled entirely to release the power. That means that they are bound, as I see it, to consider at all times during which the trust is to continue whether or no they are to distribute any and if so what part of the fund and, if so, to whom they should distribute it. To that extent, I have no doubt that there is a duty on these trustees: a member of the specified class might, if he could show that the trustees had deliberately refused to consider any question at all as to the want or suitability of any member of the class, procure their removal; . . . there is no obligation on the trustees to do more than consider – from time to time, I suppose – the merits of such persons of the specified class as are known to them and, if they think fit, to give them something. The settlor had good reason, I

have no doubt, to trust the persons whom he appointed trustees; but I cannot see here that there is such a duty as makes it essential for these trustees, before parting with any income or capital, to survey the whole field, and to consider whether A is more deserving of bounty than B. That is a task which was and which must have been known to the settlor to be impossible, having regard to the ramifications of the persons who might become members of the class."

Similarly, in the case of an intermediate power the settlor has no doubt good reason to trust the persons whom he appoints trustees. In my judgment the reasoning is parallel.

The court may also be persuaded to intervene if the trustees act "capriciously," that is to say, act for reasons which I apprehend could be said to be irrational, perverse or irrelevant to any sensible expectation of the settlor; for example, if they choose a beneficiary by height or complexion or by the irrelevant fact that he was a resident of Greater London. A special power does not show the trustees how to consider the exercise of the power in a sensible manner and does not by its terms enable the court to judge whether the power is being considered in a proper manner. The conduct and duties of trustees of an intermediate power, and the rights and remedies of any person who wishes the power to be exercised in his favour, are precisely similar to the conduct and duties of trustees of special powers and the rights and remedies of any person who wishes a special power to be exercised in his favour. In practice, the considerations which weigh with the trustees will be no different from the considerations which will weigh with the trustees of a wide special power. In both cases reasonable trustees will endeavour, no doubt, to give effect to the intention of the settlor in making the settlement and will derive that intention not from the terms of the power necessarily or exclusively, but from all the terms of the settlement, the surrounding circumstances and their individual knowledge acquired or inherited. In both cases the trustees have an absolute discretion and cannot be obliged to take any form of action, save to consider the exercise of the power and a request from a person who is within the ambit of the power. In practice, requests to trustees armed with an intermediate power are unlikely to come from anyone who has no claim on the bounty of the settlor. In practice, requests to trustees armed with a special power in favour, for example, of issue, relations and employees of a company are unlikely to come from anyone who has no claim on the bounty of the settlor, or has no plausible grounds for being given a benefit from property derived from the settlor. The only difference between an intermediate power and a special power for present purposes is that a settlor by means of a special power cannot be certain that he has armed his trustees against all developments and contingencies. A settlor who creates a special power exercisable in favour of issue, relations and employees may later regret that the trustees have no power to benefit adopted issue, widows and other persons outside the ambit of the power. Hence the recent popularity, as I am informed, of intermediate powers which arm the trustees with a weapon which will enable them to consider all developments, and all future mishaps and disasters.

Logically, in my judgment there is no reason to bless a special power which prescribes the ambit of the power by classifying beneficiaries and at the same time to outlaw an intermediate power which prescribes the ambit of the power by classifying excepted persons. It may well be that there are some classes of special power which will not be recognised by the court, but this possibility does not affect the validity of intermediate powers. The objection to the capricious exercise of a power may well extend to the creation of a capricious, power. A power to benefit "residents of Greater London" is capricious because the terms of the power negative any sensible intention on the part of the settlor. If the settlor intended and expected the trustees would have regard to persons with some claim on his bounty or some interest in an institution favoured by the settlor, or if the settlor had at any other sensible intention or expectation, he would not have required the trustees to consider only an accidental conglomeration of persons who have no discernible link with the settlor or with any institution. A capricious power negatives a sensible consideration by the trustees of the exercise of the power. But a wide power, be it special or intermediate, does not negative or prohibit a sensible approach by the trustees to the consideration and exercise of their powers.

If there is no logical objection to intermediate powers it remains to be considered whether the authorities for historical or other reasons, forbid the conferment of intermediate powers on trustees. In *Morice v. Bishop of Durham* (1805) 10 Ves Jun 522 a trust for "such objects of benevolence and liberality as the trustee in his own discretion shall most approve" was held to be invalid and Lord Eldon L.C. said, at p. 539:

> "As it is a maxim, that the execution of a trust shall be under the control of the court, it must be of such a nature, that it can be under that control; so that the administration of it can be reviewed by the court; or, if the trustee dies, the court itself can execute the trust: a trust therefore, which in case of mal-administration could be reformed; and a due administration directed; and then, unless the subject and the objects can be ascertained, upon principles, familiar in other cases, it must be decided, that the court can neither reform mal-administration, nor direct a due administration."

The decision in that case does not touch the present controversy. In a trust where the objects are described by vague adjectives such as "benevolent" and "liberal" the trust breaks the rule that the trustees and the court must be able to determine with certainty whether a particular individual or a particular object is within the ambit of the power. Nor does an intermediate power break the principles laid down by Lord Eldon L.C. in the passage which I have read because, in relation to a power exercisable by the trustees at their absolute discretion, the only "control" exercisable by the court is the removal of the trustees, and the only "due administration" which can be "directed" is an order requiring the trustees to consider the exercise of the power, and in particular a request from a person within the ambit of the power. This control and direction may be exercised by the court in relation to a power, whether special or intermediate.

In *In re Park* [1932] 1 Ch 580 Clauson J. held that an intermediate power exercisable by an individual was valid, but, he said, at p. 583:

> "It is clearly settled that if a testator creates a trust he must mark out the metes and bounds which are to fetter the trustees or, as has been said, the trust must not be too vague for the court to enforce, and that is why a gift to trustees for such purposes as they may in their discretion think fit is an invalid trust; there are no metes and bounds within which the trust can be defined, and unless the trust can be defined the court cannot enforce it."

If the object of metes and bounds is to enable the trustees and the court to determine whether an individual is or is not a beneficiary then an intermediate power satisfies that test. If the requirement of certainty is the same as that mentioned by Lord Eldon L.C. in *Morice v. Bishop of Durham* (1805) 10 Ves Jun 522, this passage from the judgement of Clauson J. does not affect powers, whether special or intermediate, where the only "enforcement" allowed to the court is enforcement of the right of any person within the ambit of the power to require the trustees to consider the exercise of the power and his request. If the passage means more than this, it nevertheless does not in terms apply to powers, and even in relation to trusts may be required to be reconsidered in the light of the consequences of the decision of the majority of the House of Lords in *Baden (No. 1)* [1971] AC 424.

In *In re Abrahams' Will Trusts* [1969] 1 Ch 463, 474, Cross J. considered *In re Park* [1932] 1 Ch 580 and decided that an intermediate power exercisable by trustees was valid. Mr Bradburn points out that *In re Abrahams' Will Trusts* was decided before the decision of the House of Lords in *In re Gulbenkian's Settlements* [1970] AC 508, but it is plain that the judgment of Cross J. is not consistent with *Gulbenkian* and he discussed the nature of a power and the duty of the trustees in words which anticipated both *Gulbenkian* and *Baden*. Cross J. said [1969] 1 Ch 463, 474:

> "It is not a trust imposed on them; it is a mere power. Of course it is a fiduciary power given to them in their capacity of trustees and they could not release it. They must retain it unless and until they exercise it, and consider from time to time whether they ought to exercise it."

The judge clearly did not envisage that the trustees' function, to which he alluded in terms anticipating *Gulbenkian* and *Baden* would be difficult or impossible for trustees to carry out in connection with an intermediate power, and clearly did not envisage that the court would find any difficulty in carrying out its limited function with regard to the exercise by the trustees of powers.

In *Baden (No. 1)* [1971] AC 424, Lord Wilberforce, at p. 457, referred first to "linguistic or semantic uncertainty which, if unresolved by the court, renders the gift void" and secondly to "the difficulty of ascertaining the existence or whereabouts of members of the class, a matter with which the court can appropriately deal on an application for directions." Then he said;

> "There may be a third case where the meaning of the words used is clear but the definition of beneficiaries is so hopelessly wide as not to form 'anything like a class' so that the trust is administratively unworkable or in Lord Eldon L.C.'s words, one that cannot be executed,"

and he cited *Morice v. Bishop of Durham* (1805) 10 Ves Jun 522, 527. He continued:

> "I hesitate to give examples for they may prejudice future cases, but perhaps, 'all the residents of Greater London' will serve. I do not think that a discretionary trust for 'relatives' even of a living person falls within this category."

In these guarded terms Lord Wilberforce appears to refer to trusts which may have to be executed and administered by the court and not to powers, where the court has a very much more limited function. Moreover, a capricious power exercisable in favour of "residents of Greater London" may, as I have already outlined, well be uncertain. The settlor neither gives the trustees an unlimited power which they can exercise sensibly, nor a power limited to what may be described a "sensible" class, but a power limited to a class, membership of which is accidental and irrelevant to any settled purpose or to any method of limiting or selecting beneficiaries.

Finally, in *Blausten v. Inland Revenue Commissioners* [1972] Ch 256 there are passages beginning at p. 271, which are admittedly obiter to the decision of Buckley L.J. in which the Lord Justice accepted the validity of an intermediate power exercisable by trustees with the consent of the settlor but was clearly not disposed to accept the validity of an intermediate power exercisable by trustees at their sole discretion. The full consequence and implications of *In re Gestetner Settlement* [1953] Ch 672, *In re Gulbenkian's Settlements* [1970] AC 508 and the two *Baden* cases [1971] AC 424, *(No. 2)* [1973] Ch 9 do not, however, appear to have been fully explored, for the assistance of Buckley L.J. and that is not surprising in view of the fact that the Court of Appeal reached its conclusions on grounds which did not involve a final pronouncement on the validity of intermediate powers.

In the result, I conclude that I am not constrained by authority to strike down a power, which a settlor, disposing of his own property under skilled advice, wishes to confer on his trustees."

CHAPTER 5

Secret Trusts

INTRODUCTION

Just as equity will not always insist on strict compliance with the statutory formalities required when this would result in a statute being used as an instrument of fraud, the formalities which must normally be complied with to create a valid testamentary trust may in some circumstances be waived to give effect to what has become known as a 'secret trust'.

SECRET TRUSTS INVOLVING JOINT TENANTS AND TENANTS IN COMMON

Where a testamentary gift is made to more than one person but the testator's intentions with regard to the creation of a trust are not communicated to all of these parties during his lifetime, the question of who will be bound by the trust arises. Traditionally, it has been accepted that in the case of tenants in common, only those to whom the testator's intentions were communicated during his lifetime will be bound and any other person will take free of the trust and will be entitled to his share beneficially. However, in the case of joint tenants, a distinction was drawn in the decision of *Re Stead*[1] between a situation where one or more of these joint tenants had accepted the trust prior to the execution of the will and where the acceptance did not take place until after this. In the former case, all the joint tenants were bound and in the latter case only those who had accepted the secret trust were affected by it. This distinction in the case of joint tenants can be criticised as somewhat arbitrary and a better approach might be to apply the 'inducement theory' developed by Perrins.[2] In his view the only issue to which the court must address itself in such circumstances is whether the gift to the legatee who was unaware of the testator's intention to create a secret trust was induced by the promise of the legatee who knew of his intentions in this regard to carry out his wishes. If this approach is accepted, issues such as whether the legatees take as joint tenants or tenants in common and whether the promise was made prior to or after the execution of the will are merely matters of evidence and will not of themselves determine the issue.

---

[1] [1900] 1 Ch 237.
[2] (1972) 82 LQR 225.

Re Stead: Witham v. Andrew
[1900] 1 Ch 237

The testatrix devised and bequeathed her property in trust for the plaintiff and the defendant as joint tenants. After her death, the plaintiff alleged that prior to the execution of her will the testatrix informed her that she intended the property to be held subject to a trust not disclosed on the face of the will and that the testatrix had executed her will on the faith of a promise made to her by the plaintiff to carry out that trust. Farwell J held that the plaintiff had not discharged the burden of proving that communication had been made to her by the testator with a view to creating a trust before the execution of the will. In these circumstances he concluded that the defendant was not bound by the trust.

FARWELL J stated at pp.239–242: "In this case the plaintiff asserts, and the defendant Mrs. Andrew denies, that there is a secret trust binding a gift of residue to them as joint tenants. The plaintiff is supported by the defendant J.W. Collett, the other defendant taking no part in the contest. [His Lordship having examined the evidence both documentary and oral, observing that no satisfactory reason had been suggested why the testatrix should not have given the residue direct to the defendant Collett had she been minded so to do, and that there was no evidence to fix the defendant, Mrs. Andrew, with notice before the date of the testatrix's death of any trust, continued:—]

I give the fullest credit to the plaintiff for desiring to speak the truth, and I do not forget that her evidence is entirely against her own pecuniary interest; but the defendant Mrs. Andrew is affected by no knowledge that would render it inequitable in her to adhere to the will, and the onus, therefore, is on the plaintiff to displace the clear words of gift in this will, and it is essential to her case, for the reasons I shall presently state, to prove that communication was made to the plaintiff by the testatrix with a view to creating a trust before the execution of the will. After considering the plaintiff's evidence carefully, I hold that she has not discharged the burden placed upon her. The plaintiff is, of course, bound by her own admissions, but I am not quite satisfied that the testatrix ever intended to create a secret trust at all. But, assuming that the trust was communicated to the plaintiff after the execution of the will, the facts stand thus: A gift by will to the plaintiff and the defendant Mrs. Andrew in joint tenancy; a trust affecting that gift communicated by the testatrix to and accepted by the plaintiff alone after the execution of the will; entire ignorance of this trust by the defendant Mrs. Andrew until after the testatrix's death. The authorities establish the following propositions: If A. induces B. either to make or to abstain from revoking a will leaving him property, by expressly promising or tacitly consenting to carry out B.'s wishes concerning it, the Court will hold this to be a trust, and will compel A. to execute it: see *McCormick v. Grogan* (1869) LR 4 HL 82, 89 where Lord Hatherley says: "But this doctrine evidently requires to be carefully restricted within proper limits. It is in itself a doctrine which involves a wide departure from the policy which induced the Legislature to pass the Statute of Frauds, and it is only in clear cases of fraud that this doctrine has been applied – cases in which the Court has been persuaded that there has been a fraudulent inducement held out on the part of the apparent beneficiary in order to lead the testator to confide to him the duty which he so undertook to peform." If A. induces B. either to make, or to leave unrevoked, a will leaving property to A. and C. as tenants in common, by expressly promising, or tacitly consenting, that he and C. will carry out the testator's wishes, and C. knows nothing of the matter until after his death, A. is bound, but C. is not bound: *Tee v. Ferris* (1856) 2 K & J 357; the reason stated (*ibid.* 368) being, that to hold otherwise would enable one beneficiary to deprive the rest of their benefits by setting up a secret trust. If, however, the gift were to A. and C. as joint tenants, the authorities have established a distinction between those cases in which the will is made on the faith of an antecedent promise by A. and those in which the will is left unrevoked on the faith of a subsequent promise. In the former case, the trust binds both A. and C.: *Russell v. Jackson* (1852) 10 Hare 204; *Jones v. Badley* (1868) LR 3 Ch 362, the reason stated being that no person can claim an interest under a fraud committed by another; in the latter case A. and not C. is bound: *Burney v. Macdonald* (1845) 15 Sim 6 and *Moss v. Cooper* (1861) 1 J & H 352, the reason stated (1 J & H 367) being that the gift is not tainted with any fraud in procuring the execution of the will. Personally I am unable to see any difference between a gift made on the faith of an antecdent promise and a gift left unrevoked on the faith of a subsequent promise to carry out the testator's wishes; but apparently a distinction has been made by the various judges who have had to consider the question. I am bound, therefore, to decide in accordance with these authorities, and accordingly I hold that the defendant Mrs. Andrew, is not bound by any trust.

With regard to the costs of the action, the plaintiff has done her duty, and must have her costs as between party and party out of the moiety of the residue, which she admits that she holds for the defendant Collett. The defendant Mrs. Andrew has successfully resisted the claim against her – a claim which has been actively supported by the defendant Collett – and her costs must be taxed as between party and party and must also be paid out of the defendant Collett's moiety. These two ladies are trustees and executors, and their costs and those of the defendant Marsh (including costs, charges, and expenses properly incurred) will be taxed as between solicitor and client; the whole of Mr. Marsh's costs, and the difference between the party and party and solicitor and client costs of the two ladies will be paid out of the whole residue. I make no order as to the defendant Collett's costs."

Geddis v. Semple
[1903] 1 IR 73

The testator devised certain houses and a pecuniary legacy charged on land to three individuals as tenants in common, although at the time the will was executed only one of these individuals was aware of the testator's intention to create a secret trust for a charitable purpose.[3] The Irish Court of Appeal (Fitzgibbon, Walker and Holmes LJJ) held that while the gift to the individual who knew of the testator's wishes must fail, the other tenants in common, who knew nothing of the intended trust until after the testator's death, became beneficially entitled to their shares.

FITZGIBBON LJ stated at p.80–83: "We do not require a reply. The appeal was opened by Mr. Andrews in a manner that left nothing to be desired. He referred to all the authorities, and we have fully heard Mr. Matheson on the other side, and the question is a difficult case with much to be said on each side.

The disposition of the property in dispute is not one single gift to three people; there are three distinct gifts of different shares of property, one to each of three devisees, tenants in common, no doubt made with the purpose and in the expectation, on the part of the testator, that the property given to each and all shall and will be applied to the same charitable object. As regards one of the three, the Rev. Mr. Semple, it has been proved that he was party to an arrangement, or understanding, with the testator, before the will was made, that the property should be so applied; and whether that arrangement or understanding was indicated by express language, or by silent acquiescence on Mr. Semple's part, makes no difference. His conscience was bound by a secret trust which, in the event which has happened, invalidates the devise to him. He knew beforehand that the gift to him was made in form absolute, but with the intention on his part, as well as on that of the testator, of evading the law, which would make it void, if given for the charitable purpose, if the testator should die within three months.

It is established law that a secret trust invalidates the gift when, if the property had been given upon an express trust to the same effect, the gift would have failed.

It is also established that, where property is given to several persons jointly on a secret trust which binds one of them, and fails, the infirmity affects the whole gift. But where property is given in separate shares to distinct people as

---

[3]   At the time when the testator executed his will the effect of s.16 of the Charitable Donations and Bequests (Ireland) Act 1844 (repealed by section 4 of the Charities Act 1961) was to render void gifts of land for charitable purposes, unless the testator's will had been executed at least three months prior to his death and in this case the testator sought to create the secret trust with the intention of avoiding this statutory restriction.

devisees in common, one being bound by a secret trust, and the others not, the only gift which can be affected is that which is taken by the secret trustee. Whether the intended purpose is identical as to each of the shares, or whether, as in the case referred to by Lord Hatherley (see *Tee v. Ferris* (1856) 2 K & J 365), one piece of property is given to A for one purpose, another to B for another purpose, and a third to C for a third purpose, the result must be the same; if two of the devisees are not affected by any trust, though the third is bound, the devises to the two who are entitled to take absolutely cannot be avoided by the trust which affects the gift to the third.

A distinction was sought to be made between the case where the charitable purpose is indicated *before the will* to one of several devisees, and is accepted by him as a secret trust; and the case where the gift in terms absolute is first made in joint tenancy and a statement of the charitable purpose is afterwards made to one or more of the devisees. But I think the distinction must depend upon whether the gift is one single joint gift of the whole property, or there are several gifts; and a gift in common is, in my opinion, to be regarded as so many separate gifts of distinct things to different people. If the man who was the *dux facti*, in accepting the trust, took the property jointly with others, knowing it to be intended for a charitable purpose, none of it could be taken absolutely; but if it, or any part of it, was given absolutely to a person who, when it was given, knew nothing of the intention to devote it to charity, that devisee could not be deprived of it by the fact that some one else knew of the intention.

The "O'Hagan Clause" has been recognised in Ireland as a valid mode of disposition, and under it an express trust for a charitable purpose is followed by an absolute gift, very often to the same devisee, which is to take effect in the event of the charitable trust becoming or proving void.

The law is settled that an absolute gift by will cannot be defeated by proof that it was made in the expectation that the devisee will apply, or will even hold himself bound in honour to apply, the property to a charitable purpose which would otherwise fail, provided always that the gift is absolute, and that the property is intended by the testator to reach the destination for which it is intended, through the voluntary exercise by the devisee of his own right of ownership, and not through any obligation of conscience, or of contract, or in pursuance of any previous arrangement or understanding, binding the conscience of the devisee, and so making him a secret trustee for a purpose which is illegal.

The circumstances show that there never was a disposition of property which more clearly originated with the testator himself, or which was more clearly intended to be in law and fact an absolute gift, though expected to benefit a charity, than the present one. He first made a will expressing the charitable trust. He had some misgiving as to its validity; and he asked the solicitor's clerk, who was taking his instructions, whether it would be good if he died within three months. The clerk, who seems to have been a prudent and intelligent man, consulted his principals, and they advised that the property must be given absolutely, in order to make the devise good; but that it might be so given to persons upon whom the testator could rely to carry out his wishes, if he should die within three months. The first devisee was the clergyman of the church for the benefit of which the gift was intended. He knew all about it before the absolute gift was made; he and the testator mutually understood from the beginning that the property was to be devoted to the charity, and it is conceded that the gift to him is bound by a secret trust, and fails.

The second devisee was the doctor who was attending the testator, but he knew nothing about the trust. The third was Mr. Shean, who was first mentioned by the clergyman, and was made a devisee by the testator on the very shadowy statement that he would carry out anything that the testator wished. Mr. Shean knew nothing about the will until after the testator's death, and then he proclaimed that, so far as he was concerned, he would not take the property for himself, and that he would not have anything to do with it. That being so, we have three distinct gifts, each of one-third of the property, and two of them were made without any element of duty or trust, but simply in reliance on the willingness, or on the honour, of the devisees, to devote the property to the purpose to which the testator desired to devote it, in the event of his dying within three months.

The vast number of cases in which testators with children have given their property absolutely to their wives are really cases depending on the same principle. There is an intention, in every such case, that the property shall not be retained by the wife as exclusively her own, but that she shall devote it to the children; but the testator leaves it to her to apply it for their benefit, in the exercise of the absolute ownership which he confers upon her. It would be as impossible, as it would be inexpedient, to attempt to affect such gifts by trusts.

It was suggested that because, after the testator's death, Mr Shean said that he was a trustee, and that he would only take the property as a trustee, he could not take or keep it. But in effect he said: " I will take the property only to do with it what the testator intended." That is not a declaration of trust, and it can not affect the right of the devisee to take the property. If he were a trustee he could not take it at all; but he has not disclaimed the devise, he has only stated that he will not apply it for his own benefit, and he, as absolute devisee, is at liberty to apply it to the object of the charity none the less because that object was in the testator's mind.

We must vary the order of the Vice-Chancellor by limiting the declaration of invalidity to the one-third of the property which was left to the Rev. Mr. Semple, and declare that the other two-thirds went absolutely to Dr. Steele and Mr. Shean as tenants in common. The plaintiff will be allowed her costs of suit up to and including the hearing before the Vice-Chancellor, to be paid out of the estate, as she represents all the legatees, and the case is one in which it was necessary to take the opinion of the Court of Chancery. The executors will have their costs in the same manner, Dr. Steele and Mr. Shean must be allowed their costs in the Court below, and of the appeal. These costs will be paid, in the first instance, so far as the amount will allow, out of the one third portion of the property which was devised to the Rev. Mr. Semple. He must abide his own costs."

WALKER LJ stated at pp.83–85: "Upon the facts in this case I do not think there was any inducement used by Mr. Semple, even as regards Mr. Shean, to attract the doctrine of *Huguenin v. Baseley* (1807) 14 Ves 273 and *Russell v. Jackson* (1852) 10 Hare 204 so far as it applies to that case.

The testator knew the law perfectly well, and knew that he must rely on the honour of the persons whom he would name as legatees, and accordingly by a will which has been proved in solemn form he gives the houses by separate gifts to those three gentlemen as independent gifts. Mr. Semple first suggested, in order to satisfy the object of the testator, the name of M'Millan; the testator would not accept him, and then Mr. Semple mentioned the name of Shean, whom the testator accepted, being satisfied, with full knowledge of the law and the effect of the gift, that he might rely on his honour. The testator was as much the person who selected Shean as Mr. Semple was. Each legatee gets a separate interest; and I cannot see how any inducement of Semple as regards himself can be extended to Shean, much less to Dr. Steele, whom he did not name.

Then Mr. Matheson, on the hypothesis that Mr. Semple has induced the gifts in the will, argues as matter of law that the gifts not only to Semple, but to Dr. Steele and Mr. Shean, as tenants in common, fail, though neither of them had any knowledge of the dispositions in the will, or the testator's wishes, till after the death of the testator. I suggested to him during the argument that this could have no application to the case of Dr. Steele, whom Mr. Semple did not name; but, apart from that, I do not agree that the authorities bear out Mr. Matheson's contention.

It is true that the cases have established that if a testator is induced by A, on the faith of a promise made by him, that he will carry out a trust communicated to him to make a gift in joint tenancy to him A and B, the trust binds both A and B ; but if the gift having been made in joint tenancy without any knowledge or promise of A, he (A) after the will makes a similar promise by reason of which the will is left unrevoked, the trust binds A only. I share the difficulty felt by Farwell, J., in *Witham v. Andrew* [1900] 1 Ch 237 of seeing the difference between the two cases, but it is not necessary in the present case to express any opinion on the point. In the case before us the gift is to Semple, Steele, and Shean as tenants in common – gifts quite as separate and independent as if a different house were left to each of them – and in such a case *Tee v. Ferris* (1856) 2 K & J 357 and *Witham v. Andrew* have established that a different rule applies from the case of a joint tenancy. Farwell, J., says – "If A induces B either to make or leave unrevoked a will leaving property to A and C as tenants in common by expressly promising or tacitly consenting that he and C will carry out the testator's wishes, and C knows nothing of the matter until after B's death, A is bound, but C is not bound." On the two grounds therefore that there was no inducement, even in the case of Mr. Shean, within the meaning of the authorities, and that the gift here was to the devisees as tenants in common, I am unable to concur in the argument for the respondents.

The last contention put forward, viz. that there was here a trust declared after the death, which the Court should carry out, seems to me quite untenable. It proceeds on the assumption that the legatees had an absolute interest unfettered by any trust, and what they, or one of them, said was attributable to that ownership – an expression of intention to do what they liked with their own – in other words that, quite irrespective of any trust, they would as a matter of honour, and by virtue of their ownership, do what they know now the testator would have wished. Mr. Shean's statement means – I will hold the property for the church, because I am owner, and by virtue of my absolute ownership.

I concur in the rule as to costs."

HOLMES LJ stated at pp. 85–87: "It often happens, when the doctrine of secret trust is sought to be applied, that there is a difficulty in ascertaining the facts. This does not exist in the present case, as the evidence shows clearly what happened. The testator desired to give three houses and £600 in trust for a charitable purpose, and he executed a will containing a gift of this property to his executors upon the trust intended. It then occurred to him that if he were to die (as he did) within three months, the trust, in so far as it related to real estate or chattels real, would fail; and, having consulted his lawyer, he was advised that the only way in which the suggested difficulty could be avoided would be to give the property to one or more persons absolutely, in the hope that when they would come to know the testator's wishes, he or they would carry them out. The testator accordingly had a new will prepared, by which he gave the houses and money to three persons, named Semple, Steele, and Shean, as tenants in common, without attaching any trust. It has been assumed by Mr. Matheson in his argument that there was some impropriety in this; and, on my asking him in what it consisted, he said that it was a fraud upon the statute. I have heard this expression before, but I do not understand it. There is no fraud in doing what the law permits ; and an absolute devise of lands, unfettered by a trust, is valid, even if the testator were to die the next day, and if the devise were made on the chance and in the hope that the devisee would apply it to some charitable purpose. In this case there is no doubt that if the three legatees had heard nothing about the gift to them until after the testator's death, the property would have belonged to them in equal shares, each being entitled to do what he liked with his own share. This happened in the case of two of them, Dr. Steele and Mr. Shean. The first knowledge they had of the contents of the will, or of the fact that they were named in it, was when it was read on the day of the funeral. Mr. Semple was present when the matter was discussed between the testator and his lawyer, and he knew that the property was given to the devisees in the hope that it would be applied by them to the charitable purpose. Mr. Matheson has spoken of Mr. Semple inducing the testator to make the gift and of his being an agent in bringing about a fraud, There is nothing to justify either allegation, The plan of making an absolute gift came from the solicitor, and was adopted by the testator, Mr. Semple's only interference being that he suggested the name of Mr. Shean. The reference to fraud arises from a confusion of ideas. When we speak of fraud in connexion with secret trusts, what is referred to is the fraud of a man allowing a testator to bequeath him property in the expectation that he will hold it in trust, and afterwards claiming it as his own. To prevent such a fraud as this, the law attaches the trust to the property; and as Mr. Semple was informed by the testator of the object of the gift, he must be held to have taken his third share in trust, with all the consequences flowing therefrom. But why should any trust be attached to the other two-thirds?

It is, I think, settled that where a gift is given to two persons as joint tenants, a secret trust imparted to one of them will affect the whole gift; but that this arises from the peculiar nature of a joint estate is shown by repeated decisions that this rule does not apply to tenants in common. It is submitted that if, after, he had made the will, the testator had informed Mr. Semple alone of what he had done and of his object, the shares of the others would not have been affected with the trust; but a distinction is sought to be drawn from the fact that the communication was made before the will. This would be a purely arbitrary and illogical distinction. There is no difference in principle betwen the gift of undivided shares to three persons in severalty and a gift of one of the houses and £200 to each of the legatees. I hold, therefore, that Steele and Shean became absolutely entitled to their shares; and although they may now say they will hold them for the charitable purpose intended by the testator, this is their own act, and, not being a trust imposed by the testator, is legal and valid."

FULLY SECRET AND HALF SECRET TRUSTS

A fully secret trust usually arises where a testator makes a gift of property to a named person in his will without expressly stating that the latter is to hold it on trust. If either before or after making his will, but during his lifetime, he informs the legatee that he wishes him to hold the property on trust for a third party or a particular purpose and the legatee either expressly or by his silence impliedly agrees to do so, he will be bound by the trust. A half secret trust on the other hand is said to exist where it is clear from the will that the legatee is to hold the property on trust but neither the terms of the trust nor the identity of the beneficiaries are disclosed in the will.

However, by manifesting his intention to create some form of trust in this way, the testator is also removing the historical justification for non-compliance with the statutory formalities required in the case of secret trusts, namely the prevention of fraud and, perhaps for this reason, the courts have tended to adopt a more stringent attitude towards the enforcement of half secret trusts. One question which has led to considerable controversy and to an apparent divergence in the law as it applies in England and Ireland is whether there can be effective communication and acceptance of a half secret trust after the execution of the testator's will. It seemed clear from the *obiter* comments of Chatterton VC in *Riordan v. Banon*[4] and of Monroe J in *Re King's Estate*[5] that subsequent communication was probably acceptable.[6] This view is borne out by the *dicta* of Barron J on this point in *Re Prendiville*,[7] a decision in which he suggested, *inter alia*, that the principles to be applied to fully and half secret trusts should be the same. It should be noted that some question surrounds the actual time of communication and acceptance of the trust in this case and there is therefore some residual doubt about whether Barron J's rejection of the need for prior communication forms part of the *ratio* of the case.

Riordan v. Banon
(1876) IR 10 Eq 469

The testator's will directed that a legacy be disposed by the legatee 'in a manner of which he alone shall be cognizant, and as contained in a memorandum which I shall leave with him'. Prior to executing his will the testator had verbally informed the legatee that he intended to leave the legacy for a named person whom he did not wish to identify in his will and it was accepted that the legatee had agreed to carry out this obligation. Chatterton VC held that a valid secret trust had been created.

CHATTERTON VC stated at pp.472–479: "The bequest which forms the subject of the contention argued upon this hearing is in these words: "I give and bequeath to John White £2,000, to be disposed of by him in a manner of which he alone shall be cognizant, and as contained in a memorandum which I shall leave with him." Its terms show that it was not a gift to Mr. White for his own absolute use, and he, by his answer, disclaims any beneficial interest in it. He states that the testator, before making his will, informed him of his wish to provide a sum of £2,000 for the lady whom he named; that he would not wish to mention her name in his will; and that he was anxious, if Mr.

---

[4] (1869) IR 10 Eq 469.
[5] (1888) 21 LR Ir 273.
[6] Although note that the courts in England have not accepted this proposition, see *Re Keen* [1937] Ch 236 and *Re Bateman's Will Trusts* [1970] 1 WLR 1463.
[7] [1995] 2 ILRM 578.

White did not object, to leave that sum to him, so that he might pay it to her after the testator's death. To this Mr. White assented, and promised to carry out the testator's wishes. The testator also told Mr. White that he would leave or write a letter or memorandum containing his directions to Mr. White upon the matter, but only as a precaution, lest Mr. White should die in the testator's lifetime. Mr. White further states that sometime afterwards, and in or about July, 1874, the testator brought his will and the letter he had mentioned to Mr. White's house, read to him the will, or part of it, and this letter; sealed both up, and left them with him; and that he, Mr. White, retained them till the testator's death. Under these circumstances the question arises, who is beneficially interested in this sum? It is conceded that Mr. White is a trustee of it; but the controversy is, whether he is to take it in trust for the lady or for the residuary legatees. For the latter, it is submitted that this was an endeavour on the part of the testator to evade the Wills Act, and to reserve to himself a power of future testamentary disposition by parol, or by an instrument which might not be, and in the event was not, executed as prescribed by that statute. The law on this subject is not in a very satisfactory state, as the cases appear in some respects to differ in principle. The decisions on the Statute of Frauds relating to wills are equally authorities upon this question, though it arises under the subsequent Act. There are two distinct classes of cases on the subject: one, where no trust is disclosed on the face of the will ; and the other, where a trust appears, but the will does not disclose what the intended trust is, or only does so imperfectly. In the former it was settled at an early period that if, by the admissions of the apparent devisee or legatee, or by other sufficient proof, it was established that the gift was made to him in trust, equity fastened on his conscience and compelled him to give effect to such trust, and that a statute which was made to prevent frauds should not itself be turned into an engine of fraud. Such trusts too were enforced, not for the benefit of the heir-at-law, next-of-kin, or residuary devisee or legatee, but for the persons for whose benefit the secret trust was intended – provided always that it was lawful.

But the difficulty arises when, as in the present case, the will does disclose an intended trust, but does not do so perfectly. In such cases, the same kind of fraud cannot operate, as the will itself shows that the legatee or devisee cannot claim for his own benefit. It becomes therefore necessary to consider whether he takes for the benefit of the intended *cestui que trust*, or for the residuary legatee or devisee, if any, and if not, for the next-of-kin, or heir. It is here that the cases appear to differ. So early as the year 1688, in the case of *Crook v. Brooking* (1689) 2 Vern 50 where there was a gift by will to two persons named, to be by them disposed of on such secret trust as the testator had privately revealed to one of them, and the trust was admitted in a letter from one of those persons to the other, it was held by Jefferies, L.C., that the trust was well and sufficiently declared by the letter, and the legacy was given to the *cestui que trusts* so appearing. In that case it appeared by the will that the trust, whatever it was, had been communicated to one of the trustees before the will.

The cause was reheard before the Lords Commissioners, and the trust again given effect to, though the decree was varied on another point.

In the case of *Pring v. Pring* (1689) 2 Vern 99, the gift was to the executors in trust, a legacy being also given to them not clothed with a trust; and the testator's widow filed her bill, alleging that the testator intended and had declared that she should have the benefit of his personal estate, and had made the defendants executors in trust for her. Two of the executors admitted this trust, but the third denied it. It was contended that though the will called them executors in trust, yet it was not said for whom the trust was, and that therefore it should be taken to be a trust for all who could come in under the Statute of Distributions; but the Court held that, as the will declared that the executors were only in trust, and not declaring for whom, the person might be averred, and decreed the trust for the plaintiff. There, it does not appear whether the trust had been communicated to the executors before or after the making of the will. In *Smith v. Attersoll* (1826) 1 Russ 266 before Lord Gifford, M.R., the testator left personal estate to his executors "in trust for certain purposes which have been fully explained to them." On the same day, the executors signed a paper stating what those purposes were, to which the testator afterwards added a further direction in his own handwriting, but not signed by either him or the executors. The bill was filed by one of the parties mentioned in the paper to carry out the trusts contained in it, and the executors admitted the trusts; but they contended at the hearing that the paper was testamentary, and that, as it had not been admitted to probate, regard could not be had to it. Lord Gifford held that the paper was not to be considered as testamentary, but might be received as evidence against the executors of the nature of the trusts on which the property was held by them. He relies on the fact that the paper was not signed by the testator, but by the executors; and he declined to consider whether the case of *Inchquin v. French* (1845) 1 Cox Eq 1, relied on for the plaintiff, could be carried so far as to hold that a paper, signed by the testator himself, explanatory of the trusts of a legacy, could be regarded as a declaration of trust, and not testamentary. He says, " If they (the executors) had not signed any such paper, and it had been put to their consciences whether the legacy was not given to them upon trust for these children, their declaration or admission of those trusts, upon oath in their answer, would have been evidence against them, and would have entitled the plaintiff to the assistance of this Court." He therefore held that the children were entitled to the shares in question, not as legatees but as *cestui que trusts*. The same question was reconsidered by him on further argument in reference to the effect of the lines added by the testator in his own writing, and, after reviewing the cases, and especially relying on the authority of *Crook v. Brooking*, he expressed the same opinion. In *Podmore v. Gunning* (1836) 7 Sim 644 the testator left his real and personal estate absolutely to his wife, adding these words: "having a perfect confidence that she will act up to those views which I have communicated to her in the ultimate disposal of my property after her decease."

Sir L. Shadwell, V.C., expressed his opinion that, if the plaintiffs had established in evidence the facts they relied on, namely, that the testator had, at the time of making his will, directed his wife to give the property after her death to the plaintiffs, and that she had promised to do so, they would have been entitled to a decree establishing the trust for them. The plaintiffs having failed in this proof, the question was not actually decided. These cases, therefore, decide that when the will discloses that a trust was intended by the testator to be attached to a devise or bequest, it is open to the parties intended to be benefited thereby to prove, either by the admission of the devisee, or legatee, named, or by parol evidence, that such trust was in fact disclosed by the testator to such devisee, or legatee, and accepted by him. I next come to consider the case of *Johnson v. Ball* (1851) 5 De G & Sm 85, which it is difficult to reconcile with the preceding. There, the testator, before making his will, informed two persons that he was about to make it, and that he intended to leave a certain policy of insurance upon trust for the plaintiff and her children, and asked them to act as trustees for the children, which they consented to do. Some time afterwards, the testator made his will, and left the policy to those persons, "to hold upon the uses appointed by letter signed by them and myself." No such letter appears to have been ever written, but the testator subsequently made a memorandum stating the way in which he wished the policy left to those persons to be divided. This memorandum he signed, and handed to one of the trustees to be signed by him and the other trustee, and retained by them. The trustees admitted the trust and supported the plaintiff's claim. Parker, V.C., decided against the trust. He held that it was impossible to give effect to the letter written after the will as a declaration by the testator of the trusts on which he had bequeathed the policy to his trustees. He proceeded as follows: [HIS LORDSHIP read passages from the judgment in that case]. When he says that the trustees had no interest in the policy which enabled them to admit a trust, for that, by reason of the supposed resulting trust for the residuary legatees, they could not create any other trust, he seems certainly to differ from the opinions of the Judges who decided the cases I have before mentioned. In *Pring v. Pring* the very contention was raised that the executors were trustees for the next-of-kin, and yet the admission of the executors was received and acted on. His Honor professed to distinguish the case before him from those I have referred to, on the ground that, in them, the will referred to a trust, created by the testator by communication with the legatee, antecedently to, or contemporaneously with, the will. But, even if the distinction be well founded, there was proof in the case before him that the testator had before the making of his will communicated to his intended legatees in trust that his intention was to leave the policy upon trust for Mrs. Johnson and her children. In *Moss v. Cooper* (1861) 1 J & H 352, Wood, V.C., takes a distinction which is very intelligible between the cases in which the testator's intention is communicated to the legatee, and those in which no such communication takes place. He says, p. 366, "I apprehend, that, to fasten any trust upon an absolute bequest of property, it is necessary to prove knowledge on the part of the legatee of the intended trust, and acquiescence, either by words of consent or by silence, when the intention is communicated to him. If you attempt to raise a trust out of some uncommunicated intention you contravene the express provisions of the statute by varying the dispositions of the will by parol evidence. I have held in two cases that you cannot by parol evidence deprive a legatee of a benefit given to him by a will where there is no obligation – expressly or impliedly – accepted by him, and no communication made to him; for, if you did, you might adduce parol evidence in any case that an estate given to A was really meant for B. Parol evidence therefore is not admissible unless communication of the testator's intention is established." He further held that it is altogether immaterial whether the promise of the legatee to perform the trust is made before or after the execution of the will, with one distinction which has no bearing on the present case. The trust in that case was altogether secret, the legacy being apparently absolute; but the principles there enunciated appear to me to apply to cases where the will shows that the legacy was to be in trust, without disclosing the trust.

The result of the cases appears to me to be that a testator cannot by his will reserve to himself the right of disposing subsequently of property by an instrument not executed as required by the statute, or by parol; but that when, at the time of making his will, he has formed the intention that a legacy thereby given shall be disposed of by the legatee in a particular manner, not thereby disclosed, but communicated to the legatee and assented to by him, at or before the making of the will, or probably, according to *Moss v. Cooper*, subsequently to the making of it, the Court will allow such trust to be proved by admission of the legatee, or other parol evidence, and will, if it be legal, give effect to it. The same principle which led this Court, whether wisely or not, to hold that the Statute of Frauds and the Statute of Wills were not to be used as instruments of fraud, appears to me to apply to cases where the will shows that some trust was intended, as well as to those where this does not appear upon it. The testator, at least when his purpose is communicated to and accepted by the proposed legatee, makes the disposition to him on the faith of his carrying out his promise, and it would be a fraud in him to refuse to perform that promise. No doubt the fraud would be of a different kind if he could by means of it retain the benefit of the legacy for himself; but it appears that it would also be a fraud though the result would be to defeat the expressed intention for the benefit of the heir, next-of-kin, or residuary donees.

To apply this to the present case, I must consider the facts proved by the admission and the evidence of Mr. White. He proves satisfactorily that, before the making of the will, the intended trust was communicated to him by the testator, and was accepted by him. The will was plainly made by the testator on the faith of Mr. White's promise to perform the trust. This was complete in itself, and would, on the principle which the cases appear to me to establish, constitute a valid trust for the lady. There was no reservation of a future disposition of a testamentary character, but a communication which, if accompanied by a transfer to Mr. White by act *inter vivos* of the subject of the gift, would have been a present perfect trust. There is therefore an element which would supply what Parker, V.C., seems to have considered wanting in *Johnson v. Ball*. The testator also informed Mr. White that he would leave with him a paper containing the same directions in writing; but he added that it would be only as a precaution against Mr. White's dying in his lifetime. He did leave with him such a paper, but it has not been admitted to probate, and cannot be looked at as a testamentary disposition. There is no proof that it existed before the making of the will. The will refers to such a paper, but in terms which leave it doubtful whether it was already written or was to be thereafter written. The words of futurity in the will, as to this paper, point not to the writing of the paper, but to the leaving it with Mr. White. The words, "in a manner of which he alone shall be cognizant," may fairly mean, "which I shall not communicate to any one else," and thus be consistent with the undoubted evidence of Mr. White, that the testator had previously made the communication to him. I am accordingly of opinion that this is a valid legacy to Mr. White in trust for the lady named by the testator."

Prendiville v. Prendiville
[1995] 2 ILRM 578

The testator left his estate to his wife for life 'to be used by her according to my wishes – as she has been advised'. Before he died the testator told one of his sons that he had written out his wishes as to the passing of his estate after his wife's death and showed him a document containing these instructions which included the provision that a named residence and lands were to be offered for sale to another son at a reasonable valuation. Following the testator's death, his wife made a statutory declaration acknowledging that her husband's instructions had been communicated to and accepted by her. After her death a dispute arose between the next-of-kin of the testator and the son in whose favour the option to purchase had been made as to whether an enforceable secret or half secret trust existed. Barron J held that a trust existed on the face of the will and found there was sufficient evidence that the terms of the trust in relation to the option to purchase the house had been communicated by the testator to his wife and accepted by her during his lifetime.

BARRON J stated at pp. 580–586: "Joseph Prendiville died on 21 June 1964 having made his last will dated 13 October 1961. By this will he left everything he possessed to his wife Mary Prendiville 'to be used by her according to my wishes – as she has been advised'. A grant of administration with the will annexed issued to Mary Prendiville on 10 March 1965. She died on 3 January 1986 without having fully administered the estate. On 5 October 1989 a grant of administration with the will annexed of the unadministered estate was issued to Brendan Prendiville, a son of the deceased.

Some time before he died, the deceased informed his son Brendan that he had written out his wishes as to the passing of his estate after his wife's death. He then showed him a document in his own handwriting setting out those wishes which was dated 7 May 1961. He did not see the document again during his father's lifetime. After his father's funeral, he asked his mother to show him the document. She did so and later in August 1964 gave it to him having retained a copy.

The document is as follows.

After my wife's death

Dividend

£1,000	4.5% Nat. Loan – interest to Thomas
£1,000	5% Nat. Savings Bonds – dividend to Eileen
~~£1,000~~	~~50% Nat. Savings Bonds – dividend to Kitty~~
£3,000	5% ESB Loan – dividend to Jackie
£1,500	5% Nat. Loan – dividend to Maurice
£1,000	5% Nat. Loan and 6% Nat. Loan to Jim
£3,000 —	to Brendan
£1,000 —	to ~~Kitty~~ Dodo
£1,000 —	to Billy
£500 —	Joseph Aloysius
1,000 —	Michael (George's Son)
	Aunty May wish re her own money
1,000	£500 to ~~Kitty~~, Eileen, Dodo, Jim, Jackie.
2,000	Maurice, J. Brendan
2,000	(250 each)
3,000	
1,000	£1,000 for masses to be divided between the religious orders; for the dead souls.
<u>3,000</u>	
12,000	

Monies to be divided after my wife's death.
My wife Mary is to get all my monies
property and debts due, during her lifetime

Billy to get preference of Cluincorrig house — on a reasonable valuation — if he lives or intends to live in Killorglin.

Signed: J. Prendiville M.B.

Killorglin

7 May 1961

The reference to Aunty May is to his wife being the name by which she was known in the family. On the reverse side of this document there is an apparent assessment of the total value of the testator's own estate and that of his wife, the value of his residence being apparently put at £6,000. There is, however, no obvious correlation between those figures and the details on the side of the document which he signed.

The deceased's widow made a statutory declaration dated 6 June 1967 for the purpose of acknowledging her acceptance of the terms of her husband's written instructions. This document is not helpful in resolving the uncertainties contained in those instructions. She declares that she was to be entitled for life and that after her death the residence and lands of Cluincorrig should, in the first instance, be offered for sale to Dr Billy Prendiville at the price of £6,000. She then indicated how the £6,000 was to be distributed if the option to purchase was exercised and that, if it was not exercised, the property was to be sold and the proceeds of sale to be distributed in the same way as the £6,000. No provision was made for any different price being obtained. The declaration also purports to distribute the other moneys in the estate in accordance with the instructions. However, the persons indicated as beneficiaries do not fully correspond with those referred to in the instructions.

On 29 September 1970 Mary Prendiville made a will. By this will she, *inter alia,* purported to leave her husband's estate in accordance with his written instructions. On this occasion there were some minor discrepancies between the will and statutory declaration, but again she purported to indicate that the option to purchase his father's residence was to be given to her son Billy at the sum of £6,000.

On 29 April 1980 Mary Prendiville revoked this will. On the same date, she made a further statutory declaration in which she again acknowledged that her husband's instructions were communicated by him to her and accepted by her, but declared that the sum of £6,000 had never been mentioned by her husband as the option price of his residence Cluincorrig house.

Following the grant of letters of administration to Brendan Prendiville, an application was made to have the instructions admitted as a testamentary document, but such application was unsuccessful.

The present proceedings have developed into a contest between Dr Billy Prendiville on the one hand and the next-of-kin of the deceased on the other as to whether or not there is an enforceable secret trust or an enforceable half-secret trust whereby Dr Billy Prendiville should have an option to purchase the residence and lands of Cluincorrig house at a reasonable valuation. The parties have accepted that the remainder of the written instructions are insufficiently precise to be enforceable on either basis.

In *In re Browne, Ward v. Lawler* [1944] IR 90, the testator by his will dated 17 October 1935 gave and bequeathed unto the person named as his executor 'all my real and personal property of what [sic] nature or kind soever. I relying on his carrying out the wishes that I have expressed to him and/or may do so hereafter'.

These wishes were set out in written instructions which though dated 23 November 1939 were not given to the person named in the will until 25 February 1942 being the day upon which the testator died. It was made clear to the testator however that his wishes would be carried out. The executor accepted that he was not entitled beneficially, but sought the opinion of the court as to whether the instructions were binding. It was argued on behalf of the next-of-kin that the executor took as trustee and that the instructions were not enforceable because the testator was not entitled to reserve to himself the right to make further dispositions of his property.

Overend J held that on the proper construction of the clause in the will the executor took beneficially and not as trustee. Accordingly, he found that by accepting the trust the elements of a secret trust had been established. He also found that if a gift had been properly construed as creating a trust the terms of which were not disclosed, it would not have made any difference. In this regard he cited with approval the following passage from the judgment of Monroe J in *In re King's Estate* (1888) 21 LR Ir 273 at p. 277 where the relevant rules relating to secret trusts were set out as follows:

> 1. A testator cannot reserve to himself the right of declaring trusts by an instrument informally executed subsequent to the execution of his will. This would be to repeal the Statute of Wills.
>
> 2. If a testator at or before the execution of his will communicate to a person to whom he proposes to give a legacy that the legacy is given upon trust to be applied in a particular way, and if the legatee expressly or tacitly consents to take the legacy on these terms, the Court of Chancery will not permit him to be guilty of a fraud, but will compel the execution of the trust so communicated.
>
> 3. This rule applies whether the existence of a trust be indicated on the face of the will, or the legacy by the terms of the instrument be given absolutely.
>
> 4. The rule applies when the communication is made subsequently to the execution of the will: *Moss v. Taylor* (1861) 1 J & H 352 at p. 367.
>
> 5. It is essential to the creation of a valid trust that the communication should be made to the legatee in the testator's lifetime, and that the legatee should not object to execute the trust.
>
> 6. If the bequest be to two or more legatees, a valid trust is created if the communication be made to any of them, before or at the time of the execution of the will. If the communication be made after the execution of the will, it must be made to all the legatees on whom the trust is sought to be imposed.
>
> 7. The terms on which the trust is expressed must not be vague or uncertain.

Overend J also referred to *Blackwell v. Blackwell* [1929] AC 318 with approval. In that case the question to be determined was whether or not a half-secret trust which had been communicated to five trustees named in the will, four of them prior to its execution, and accepted by all of them could be enforced. Two principles emerge from the judgments in this case: (1) the basis of enforceability is the communication of the wishes of the testator to the person named in the will and the acceptance of the latter communicated to the testator; and (2) it is immaterial that in the case of a half-secret trust that the acceptance is by the person named as trustee and not by the person who would otherwise be entitled beneficially. Lord Sumner expressed the first of these principles at p. 339 as follows:

> It is communication of the purpose to the legatee, coupled with acquiescence or promise on his part, that removes the matter from the provision of the Wills Act and brings it within the law of trusts, as applied in this instance to trustees, who happen also to be legatees.

Lord Warrington of Clyffe dealing with the same principle said at p. 342:

> It is the fact of the acceptance of the personal obligation which is the essential feature, and the rest of the evidence is merely for the purpose of ascertaining the nature of that obligation.

Lord Sumner dealing with the second principle said at p. 335 as follows:

> In both cases the testator's wishes are incompletely expressed in his will. Why should equity, over a mere matter of words, give effect to them in one case and frustrate them in the other?

Lord Warrington of Clyffe expresses the same principle at p. 342 as follows:

> It was contended for the appellants, who claim as residuary legatees to be entitled to the fund should the trust not be established, that the fraud for the avoidance of which the trust is enforced must be the personal fraud of the legatee, but I think the answer is that, if it would be a fraud on the part of the legatees to refuse to carry out the trust, the residuary legatees cannot take advantage of and thus make themselves parties to such fraud.

On that point he agreed with the view expressed by Wood VC in *Moss v. Cooper* being the case referred to by Monroe J as authority for his rule 4. Nevertheless, in *Blackwell v. Blackwell* limits were put upon the doctrine. A testator cannot by creating a trust without expressing the nature of the trust reserve to himself the right to express the trust later other than by a testamentary instrument. If the person named has not assented to a trust, there cannot be a secret trust. In such circumstances, if the terms of the trust cannot be admitted to probate, they fail. This principle was expressed by Viscount Sumner at p. 339 as follows:

> The limits, beyond which the rules as to unspecified trusts must not be carried, have often been discussed. A testator cannot reserve to himself a power of making

future unwitnessed dispositions by merely naming a trustee and leaving the
purposes of the trust to be supplied afterwards, nor can a legatee give testamentary
validity to an unexecuted codicil by accepting an indefinite trust, never
communicated to him in the testator's lifetime ....

In the present case, *In re Keen, Evershed v. Griffiths* [1937] Ch 236 was relied
upon as an authority for the proposition that a half-secret trust cannot be
established unless its terms are communicated prior to the execution of the
will. In that case the relevant clause in the will gave a sum of money to named
persons to be held upon trust and disposed of by them 'among such person,
persons or charities as may be notified by me to them or either of them during
my lifetime and in default of such notification and so far as such notification
shall not extend I declare that the said sum . . . as shall not be disposed of in
manner aforesaid shall fall into and form port of my residuary estate'. The
court construed the clause as a reservation by the testator of a power to make
future dispositions without a duly attested codicil simply by notifying his
trustees in his lifetime and was therefore invalid. Lord Wright MR held that
the principles laid down by Viscount Sumner in the passage from his judgment
in *Blackwell v. Blackwell* at p. 339 to which I have already referred were fatal
to a claim being made to establish the secret trust.

In my view the proposition for which *In re Keen* is put forward cannot be
taken from that case. It merely shows the limit of the doctrine of secret trusts
as indicated in the passage from the judgment of Lord Sumner in *Blackwell v.
Blackwell*. There is nothing in the judgment to suggest that an acceptance of
the terms of a secret trust cannot be effected if made after the execution of the
will. The case turns on the construction of the particular clause of the will. In
that case the terms were never communicated to the persons named in the
clause subsequent to the execution of the will nor obviously therefore accepted
by such persons. Had they been then *Blackwell v. Blackwell* would have been
applied.

In re Bateman's Will Trusts, Brierley v. Perry [1970] 3 All ER 817 was
also relied upon. Here also the will referred to instructions to be given by the
testator as to the manner in which his trustees should apply a particular fund.
These were to be given in a sealed letter in the testator's own handwriting
addressed to his trustees. Such a letter existed at the date of the testator's
death on which the trustees acted. It was held that the will could not be construed
as referring to a letter already so given, so the directions contained therein
were held to be invalid. In my view, this case establishes, if it were necessary
to do so, that where communication and acceptance of the testator's wishes
during his lifetime cannot be established, then such wishes can only be validly
indicated by a testamentary writing admitted to probate.

In my view the principles of law applicable to secret trusts and half-secret
trusts are the same. The rules to be applied are those set out by Monroe J in the
passage in his judgment in *In re King's estate* cited with approval by Overend
J in *In re Browne*. The only difference between a half-secret trust and a secret

trust is that the person named in the will is an express trustee in the first case and a beneficiary in the latter. A person who had on his own behalf agreed to hold an apparently beneficial gift on trust could not in conscience refuse to carry out such trust. That is the position in the case of a secret trust. Should it be the same in the case of a half-secret trust where the beneficiary had not made any such promise to the testator? The answer is, yes and for the reasons set out in the passages from the judgment of *Blackwell v. Blackwell* to which I have referred.

In the present case, there was a trust on the face of the will. There is, however, sufficient evidence from which I am satisfied that the terms of the trust in relation to Cluincorrig house were communicated by the testator to his wife and accepted by her during his lifetime. On the authorities, this assent by her is sufficient to validate the half-secret trust.

Evidence was adduced to show that by the expression Cluincorrig house, the testator intended his entire holding which included both the house and surrounding lands. I accept that Cluincorrig house was a term by which the testator would have referred to both house and land and that it was so understood by his wife."

CHAPTER 6
Constitution of Trusts

INTRODUCTION

A trust is said to be completely constituted when the trust property has been vested in the trustees for the benefit of the beneficiaries and it remains incompletely constituted until this is done. The practical importance of identifying when a trust has been completely constituted lies in the fact that equity will not enforce or perfect an incompletely constituted trust in favour of a volunteer.[1] However a completely constituted trust will be enforceable at the suit of the beneficiaries irrespective of whether or not they are mere volunteers.

COMPLETE CONSTITUTION OF A TRUST

An express trust may be completely constituted either by a transfer of property to trustees to be held on certain trusts or by a settlor declaring himself to be trustee of his own property for the benefit of specified beneficiaries. In order for a trust to be validly constituted by transfer of the trust property, it is necessary to comply with whatever formalities apply to the method of transfer employed and the settlor must have done everything in his power[2] which it is necessary to do to effect the transfer.[3] Where a settlor seeks to ensure that a trust is completely constituted by a declaration of trust, there must be 'a present irrevocable declaration of trust'.[4] This does not depend on the use of any particular form of words but may be indicated by the character and general effect of the instrument creating it.[5]

It should be noted that the recent decision of the Privy Council in *T. Choithram International SA v. Pagarani*[6] suggests that where the settlor is one of a number of co-trustees the trust may be completely constituted by a declaration of trust made by him even though the property has still to be vested in the co-trustees.

---

[1] *Re Wilson* [1933] IR 729.
[2] *Re Rose* [1952] Ch 499, *Mascall v. Mascall* (1984) 50 P & CR 119 and *Brown & Root Technology Ltd v. Sun Alliance and London Assurance Co.Ltd* [1996] Ch 51.
[3] *Milroy v. Lord* (1862) 4 De G F & J 264.
[4] *Re Cozens* [1913] 2 Ch 478, 486.
[5] *Miller v. Harrison* (1871) IR 5 Eq 324.
[6] [2001] 1 WLR 1.

Re Wilson: Grove-White v. Wilson
[1933] IR 729

The testator entered into a voluntary agreement with his son whereby he agreed to pay him an allowance and to transfer certain properties to him. It was held by Johnston J that as the agreement was voluntary and incomplete it was not capable of being enforced.

JOHNSTON J stated at pp.739–749: "The late Mr. W. H. Wilson of Carrickmines was very generous in his benefactions to his relatives, servants and friends. Most of his gifts were perfected by one or other of the methods by which a valid gift may be regularly and legally made – methods which are set out comprehensively by Turner L.J. in *Milroy v. Lord* (1862) 4 De G F & J 264; but in the case of two of these alleged gifts a certain amount of doubt has been suggested as to whether the deceased had, in the words of Turner L.J., "done everything which, according to the nature of the property comprised in the settlement, was necessary to be done in order to transfer the property and render the settlement binding upon him." A gift is a gift, and, of course, if a donor, while expressing an intention to give something and taking certain steps in the direction of giving it, has not gone the whole way, the expectant donee has no equity to compel the completion of the gift. This is good sense and good law. As Grant M.R. put it in *Antrobus v. Smith* (1806) 12 Ves 39, there is a *locus poenitentiae* as long as the gift is incomplete. Story (London Edit., 1892, p.176.) puts it in this way: "For, regularly, equity is remedial to those only who come in upon an actual consideration, and therefore there should be some consideration, equitable or otherwise, expressed or implied."

The first matter arises in regard to a transaction that took place in December, 1918, just after the termination of the late war. The deceased was at the time a member of the Dublin Stock Exchange in partnership with his nephew, Mr. Ion Grove-White, and he resided in Carrickmines. He had had three sons killed in the war and he was anxious (as I am informed through the affidavit of Mr. Gerald Grove-White, who, also, is a nephew of the deceased and one of the executors of his will) to provide a sum of £5,000 by way of gift for his only surviving son, Mr. John Hugh Wilson, who is one of the defendants. To effect this he is said to have credited his son's account in the clients' ledger of his firm with the sum of £5,000 and to have debited his own account in the private ledger of the partners with the same sum. This sum was balanced on the other side of the account by £10,000 Manilla Railway Company preference shares and £3,000 United Havana Railway Company ordinary stock. These securities were in the name of the Hibernian Bank (with other securities) as collateral security for the testator's loan account. I am informed also by Mr. Grove-White that from time to time these investments were changed and certain substituted investments were lodged as security with the bank, and "at the date of the testator's death the investments representing the original £5,000 were £500 Rhodesian Railway Company debentures (bonds), £3,500 Manilla Railway 5 per cent debentures (bonds) and £5,000 Manilla Railway preference shares which were in the name or custody of the said bank." Mr. Grove-White exhibits a letter, dated November 7th, 1924, in the handwriting of the testator, "which the said J. Hugh Wilson informs me was handed to him by the testator." This letter was in these terms: "To my Executors. The Manilla Railway securities (both bonds and shares) and £500 Rhodesian Railway 3 per cent bonds deposited by me with the Hibernian Bank as part of the securities in my loan account, are the property of my son John Hugh Wilson and do not form part of my assets. W.H. Wilson, 7th November, 1924." The testator did not inform the bank then or subsequently that he had made over these securities to his son, but he addressed a letter to the bank on November 25th, 1925, in these terms: "Please accept release orders for shares held on my behalf when signed by my son, Mr. J. Hugh Wilson"; and all the dividends paid on the original and the substituted securities were credited by the late Mr. W.H. Wilson's firm to the account of Mr. J.H. Wilson since December, 1919. Mr. Grove-White states further: "After the transaction referred to had been effected the testator informed me that as I was an executor of his will he thought I ought to know that he had made over the said bonds and preference shares to his son."

The testator died in London on February 10th, 1931, without having done anything further to perfect or complete the gift of these securities to his son, and there can scarcely be any doubt that if there was nothing more in the case, the gift, being incomplete, was not one that could have been enforced in equity. There was no assignment by deed or delivery to the donee, nor was there any transfer of the shares into his name. The case is not unlike that of *Lambert v. Overton* 11 LT Rep 503, a case in which it appeared that shares had been deposited in a bank as security for a debt owing by the donor, and it was held that a gift of the shares by the donor to his son was incomplete and that the shares (when the debt to the bank had been satisfied) formed part of the estate of the deceased on the donor's death. In the present case, the shares, to the day of the death of the testator, remained in the Hibernian Bank as security for the deceased's liabilities, and under the circumstances the intended benefaction would have fallen to the ground had it not been for the fact that the testator nominated Mr. J.H. Wilson as one of the executors of his will, and thereby gave validity to what would have been otherwise an imperfect and invalid gift, as decided in the case of *In re Stewart* [1908] 2 Ch 251. I do not agree with Mr. Lavery's critical attitude towards that case. It was referred to with approval – or at any rate, without disapproval – by Kennedy L.J. in the Court of Appeal four years later in *Pink v. Pink* [1912] 2 Ch 528, and has never been doubted in any case of which I am aware.

It was decided in *Hyslop v. Hyslop* [1894] 3 Ch 522 that the mere appointment of a debtor of a deceased person as the executor of the will of the deceased was not in itself sufficient to enable a debt owing by the executor to be discharged. North J. said in that case that in order that the principle established in *Strong v. Bird* (1874) LR 18 Eq 315 should be brought into operation there must be evidence of the creation of some equity in the debtor apart from his appointment as executor. Now, here there are, in the first place, the entries in the books of the firm of which the late Mr. Wilson was a partner. I must assume that these books were under his control, and although the entries are not in the handwriting of the alleged donor (as they were in the case of *Pink* v. *Pink* – a case which in all other respects resembles the present case) I am satisfied that they were made by Mr. Wilson's direction and that they undoubtedly represented his wishes. I think also that Mr. J.H. Wilson is entitled to rely upon the letter of directions "to my executors." A very similar document formed the subject-matter of a decision of North J. in *In re Hyslop, Hyslop v. Chamberlain* [1894] 3 Ch 522. He held that, the document in question – "general instructions" to an executor – having been found amongst the papers of the deceased and never having been communicated to the alleged donee, must be regarded as testamentary in its character and, not having been executed as a will, could not be looked at. The document in this case, however, would appear to have been handed by the late Mr. Wilson to his son, and that fact raises the very distinguishing feature that is referred to by North J. in his judgment. The other matters that are set out in Mr. Grove-White's affidavit, in my opinion, place this question beyond controversy. I may say in conclusion that I have carefully considered the case of *In re Innes* [1910] 1 Ch 188, which has been so strongly relied upon by Mr. Lavery, and in my opinion it has no application to this case. The answer to question one, therefore, will be: "Yes, subject to the limitation that the excess, if any, in the value of the said securities when realised, over the sum of £5,000, belongs to the executors as assets of the deceased."

The second matter is more difficult and calls for rather more consideration. Mr. W.H. Wilson retired from the partnership in 1924, and, with the marked consideration that he had always shown for his son, he introduced Hugh as a partner in his place. Then in 1926 came the next benefit which the son was to receive from the father. On August 3rd in that year, Marcella Wilson, the testator's second wife, died, and he decided to make over the Carrickmines house and property to Hugh absolutely. This gift was properly and regularly effected by three deeds, executed on December 4th, 1926, and the property conveyed consisted of two parcels of land held by the testator in fee and registered in the Registry of Titles and another parcel of land held by the testator under two leases, made in 1861, and a third, made in 1862, for long terms, subject to three rents of £30, £10 and £24. These conveyances by the testator purported to be "for the natural love and affection for his son, the said John Hugh Wilson" and "for other good causes and considerations," none of which are set out. In the assignment of the leasehold premises there is a covenant by the son to pay the rent reserved by, and to observe the covenants contained in, the original leases. Mr. Grove-White in his affidavit says that in 1926 the testator decided to give up Carrickmines House to his son, "he, the said John

Hugh Wilson, agreeing to keep up Carrickmines House and grounds and to receive the testator as a guest whenever the testator wished to come there, and keep the testator's motor-car and chauffeur, the testator estimating the period during which he would probably desire to reside as four months in the year." It is strange that there is no reference to this agreement in any of the three deeds, or in any letter, note, or memorandum, supplemental to them. One would have thought that a donor who was giving up his home absolutely and for ever to another, even though that other was his only surviving son, would, if he had intended to reserve to himself a right of residence therein as a legal and enforceable right, have seen to it that the agreement and its conditions and terms were dependent upon something more tangible than the recollection of the parties. But something more was left unexpressed. Mr. Grove-White adds that when the property was conveyed to Hugh in December, 1926, "the testator agreed to make up an allowance to the said John Hugh Wilson, with the said ground rents, of £600 per annum to help towards the maintenance and upkeep of the property." It was not until almost a year later – namely, on August 22nd, 1927 – when the testator was on the point of marrying the second defendant, who was then Miss Edna Gladys White, that the document upon which Hugh Wilson relies was drawn up, and as to it I wish to say generally that it differs very materially from the verbal agreement of December, 1926, which was made at the time when the property was legally transferred.

The document of August, 1927, is a most peculiar one. Instead of covenanting to pay to his son a certain sum per annum, or of charging specific property with the payment of that sum, or of assigning to him such stocks and shares or other property as would produce that sum, the late Mr. Wilson "agrees" "to give directions" to certain persons to pay certain moneys to Hugh Wilson, "which several sums together with certain rents reserved by leases and issuing out of the property transferred to the said John Hugh Wilson and out of the lands of Rampere would produce £600 per annum or thereabouts," a most unusual and most cautious way of securing an annuity. The persons who are to be given directions to pay these sums to the defendant are "the trustees of the will of C. H. Wilson, deceased," the trustees of the donor's own marriage settlement, and the Northern Nigeria (Bauchi) Tin Company (in which company the testator owned £1,000 preference shares). Down to this point the agreement was one to pay, or to secure the payment of, the sum of £600 annually to Hugh, or rather to secure the payment of £600 yearly less the amount of the rents payable out of the property which had already been conveyed to Hugh. The agreement then proceeds in these terms:—

> "For the purpose of securing said sum of £600 per annum after the death of the said William Henry Wilson, the said William Henry Wilson hereby agrees to transfer the said sum of £1,000 Preference Shares in the Northern Nigeria (Bauchi) Tin Company into the joint names of himself and the said John Hugh Wilson, also to transfer three Policies of Insurance – 2 with the Scottish Amicable Co. and 1 with the Commercial Union Insurance Co. for £500 each on the life of

Alfred T. Collins – to the said John Hugh Wilson, also to transfer to the said John Hugh Wilson the following Policy of Insurance on the life of the said William Henry Wilson with the Scottish Provident Institution, viz., Policy No. 72748, which last mentioned Policy is subject to a mortgage of £3,500 to the said Scottish Provident Institution, and also to convey the fee farm rent issuing out of the lands of Rampere or the Land Bonds representing the same. And the said William Henry Wilson agrees to execute formal transfers of the said several policies and property whenever called on so to do by the said John Hugh Wilson, or else to bequeath same to him by will."

Immediately after the making of this agreement – namely, on September 3rd, 1927 – the testator executed a marriage settlement on his marriage to Miss Edna White, by which a sum of £6,000 was to be provided, at the latest, six months after the death of Mr. Wilson, "to be a first charge on his estate after payment of his debts, funeral and testamentary expenses;" and the income of that sum is to be paid to Mrs. Wilson during her life. The marriage took place on September 16th, and the husband and wife went to the South of France where they lived for some time; and then a flat was taken in London. In the summer of 1928 they went to visit at Carrickmines where (as Mr. Wilson says in one of his letters) "Hugh was most courteous and kind"; but he adds that when they went back in the summer of 1929, "there was an air of hostility and a feeling that we weren't wanted there;" and they remained only three weeks. It is only fair to Mr. Hugh Wilson to say that he denies that there was any ground for his father's feeling in this matter. This unfortunate episode – it can scarcely be called a quarrel – left no bad effects, for we find the father making his will on September 16th, 1929, and making provision therein for the allowance that he had promised to his son. By this will the testator directed that the £6,000 that had been provided by the marriage settlement was to be "treated as a first charge on my estate, ranking equally with my debts, funeral and testamentary expenses." The wife was to get £200, "to be paid to her out of the first available moneys in my executor's hands," and she was given also the income for her life from a sum of £4,000. The testator then proceeded to carry out the promise he had made in the memorandum of agreement with Hugh in these terms:— "I leave to my son, John Hugh Wilson, certain policies on the life of A. T. Collins, also the balance of all moneys coming to me on foot of policy number 72748 on my own life with the Scottish Provident Institution. I also bequeath to him a holding in Land Bonds representing a fee-farm rent formerly paid out of the lands of Rampere (Raheen)"; and he appointed Hugh as his residuary devisee and legatee to the extent of one-third of any residue. There is no mention in the will of the Northern Nigeria (Bauchi) Tin Company preference shares (which had never been transferred out of the testator's own name), and that omission was not an accident. The testator had sold those shares on October 4th, 1929, retaining the proceeds of the sale for his own use. Further, the Policy of Insurance on his own life which is recited in the memorandum of agreement to have been mortgaged to secure a sum of

£3,500, was utilised by the testator to raise a further sum of £500. There was no difficulty in carrying out that transaction, as there had been no assignment or delivery of the Policy to Hugh and no notice of any right in Hugh had been given to the Insurance Company.

On that state of facts can it be held that the defendant, Mr. Hugh Wilson, has any legal or equitable right that can be enforced in this Court by virtue of the memorandum of agreement of August, 1927, or any subsequent agreement *inter vivos*, whether supplemental or substituted? I think that a good deal could be said for the view, though it was not relied upon very strongly by Mr. Lavery, that an entirely new arrangement was arrived at between the father and son in 1929, by which the former agreed to pay to the latter a sum of £400 a year during the life of the father and that this arrangement was in substitution for the former one. The testator on October 21st, 1929, wrote to Mr. Grove-White:–
"I won't allow him more than £400 a year, and if he doesn't accept it I will stop the whole £600, and let him do what he likes." On November 1st, he wrote:– "Don't worry me with any more letters until you have fixed up the £400 a year allowance."

On November 18th Mr. Grove-White, writing on behalf of Hugh, says:-
"Hugh does not wish to go further into the question of the Bauchi shares, Moore's wages, *or any other matters*. If you have decided to reduce his £600 to £400 a year, he accepts your decision." On the 28th the testator wrote:- "I send you the list with the dividends I propose to take over." And on December 20th, Mr. Grove-White writes to his uncle: "We went through your suggestions about making up the £400 a year," and a list of securities and properties is set out in this letter, the annual income from which is stated to be £413 10s. 0d. I have analysed all this correspondence very closely and for myself I cannot see, in the face of the new terms that seem to have been arrived at, how the defendant can allege that any potency remained in the document of August, 1927, or how any part of the arrangement of that date remained in force.

However, I am willing to consider the case from the point of view that is most favourable to Mr. Hugh Wilson, and, on the assumption that the new arrangement was merely supplemental to the old, how does the matter stand? The document provides for the payment of an allowance of £600 a year, reduced subsequently to £400, to Hugh Wilson during the lifetime of his father, and I assume that this payment was made and that there are no arrears. If there is some small amount of this allowance outstanding, I shall hear counsel later as to what ought to be done.

The second half of the document provides that "for the purpose of securing said sum of £600 per annum after the death of the said William Henry Wilson" the latter "hereby agrees to transfer" the Bauchi shares into the joint names of himself and his son and to transfer to the donee three policies of life insurance – one on his own life and two on the lives of another – and to convey to him a fee-farm rent issuing out of certain lands or land bonds (payable by the Land Commission) "representing the same." The operative part of this clause is contained in the last sentence: "And the said William Henry Wilson agrees to execute formal transfers of the said several policies and property whenever called on so to do by the said John Hugh Wilson or else to bequeath same to him by his will."

This document is alleged by the defendant to be an agreement for valuable consideration and enforceable as such. I do not think that it can possibly be so regarded. It is simply an agreement by a father, who, having made over certain property to his only surviving son "for natural love and affection," desired to make that son an allowance "to help towards the maintenance and upkeep of said property." The covenant entered into by Hugh, in one of the conveyances, to pay the rent and observe certain covenants cannot be regarded as valuable consideration for an agreement executed nearly nine months later for a collateral purpose that was not spoken of in the conveyance of the property; but even if the liability undertaken by Hugh in December, 1926, could by any process of implication be read into the memorandum executed in August, 1927, the rule established by the Court of Appeal in *Lee v. Mathews* (1880) 6 LR Ir 530 would prevent it having the potency that Hugh Wilson wishes to give it. The principle of that decision is to be found very clearly set out in the judgment of FitzGibbon L.J. He decided that when leasehold premises are assigned subject to onerous burdens, the question "whether the transaction was a bargain involving mutual considerations, or was a gift involving merely bounty from one party to the other," was a question of fact to be decided upon the evidence and not a question of abstract law. The law on this question in England as laid down in *Price v. Jenkins* (1877) 5 Ch D 619 and some subsequent cases seems to be different; but I think that the decision of the Irish Court of Appeal, given three years later, is more in accordance with sound principle than that in the English case and I shall follow it. In *Price v. Jenkins*, Hall V.C., a very distinguished equity Judge, was reversed by the Court of Appeal; but that decision has not passed unscathed in England during the fifty years of its life. Applying, then, the test supplied by FitzGibbon L.J., it seems to me that, in view of the relationship of the parties and the circumstances under which the memorandum was drawn up, it would be impossible to do otherwise than find that it represented the conferring of bounty by a father upon a son and not the making of a bargain involving mutual considerations. Any other conclusion would be contrary both to common sense and sound judgment.

Then it is argued that there was an agreement between father and son in effect that the former should have a right of residence in Carrickmines House, and that this was part of the bargain. I can find no evidence of any such legal obligation. If such a right had been reserved by the deceased it would have been set out in the conveyance of the property to Hugh Wilson, but nothing of the kind is to be found in the deed; nor is there any reference to it in the subsequent memorandum. In the lengthy correspondence that took place in 1928 the deceased says: "There was an understanding that my wife and I were to be always welcome to Carrickmines House"; and later he said: "If he [Hugh] cannot keep Carrickmines House, let him sell it, or let it for four or five years." The complaint that runs through the whole of this correspondence is a complaint of inhospitable conduct on the part of the son; there is no definite suggestion of any breach of contract.

The memorandum of August, 1927, then, was a voluntary agreement and not one for valuable consideration, and it was an imperfect or incomplete contract at that. Indeed, there is on the face of the document a statement which amounts to an admission by the parties that the contract was incomplete. It was a mere promise on the part of the alleged donor to make a certain provision for his son after the death of the donor. If Hugh Wilson had taken proceedings in his father's lifetime to compel him to make the transfers referred to in the document, he would, I think, have failed, because he had no legal title to the property and equity would not have assisted him to enforce a voluntary settlement which was incomplete. The rest of the promise was of a testamentary character and had all the defects of such, as decided in cases of the type of *Cross v. Cross* (1877) 1 LR Ir 389 and *Towers v. Hogan* (1899) 23 LR Ir 53. Nor can the alleged donee gain any assistance from the principle established in *Strong v. Bird* (1874) LR 18 Eq 315 for the reason which is given by Neville J. in *In re Stewart* [1908] 2 Ch 251. In the latter case the learned Judge decided that when a testator has expressed the intention of making a gift of personal estate to one who, upon his death, becomes his executor, the intention continuing unchanged, the executor is entitled to hold the property for his own benefit; but, adds Neville J., "the intention to give, however, must not be an intention of testamentary benefaction, although the intended donee is the executor; for, in that case, the rule cannot apply, the prescribed formalities for testamentary disposition not having been observed." The plain meaning of the document is that if the promise is not translated into an effective disposition by a legal transfer in the lifetime of the testator, then the donee must be satisfied with whatever testamentary provision the testator may make for him. The testator did make provision for his son by his will, and he must be satisfied with that provision."

Milroy v. Lord
(1862) 4 De G F & J 264

A settlor executed a voluntary deed purporting to transfer shares in a bank to be held on trust for the plaintiff. Such a transfer could only be properly effected by registration of the name of the transferee in the bank's records. While the trustee held a power of attorney to act on the settlor's behalf, he failed to register the transfer. The Court of Appeal (Knight Bruce and Turner LJJ) held that no enforceable trust in favour of the plaintiffs had been created.

TURNER LJ stated at pp. 274–278: "Under the circumstances of this case it would be difficult not to feel a strong disposition to give effect to this settlement to the fullest extent, and certainly I have spared no pains to find the means of doing so, consistently with what I apprehend to be the law of the Court; but, after full and anxious consideration, I find myself unable to do so. I take the law of this Court to be well settled, that in order to render a voluntary settlement valid and effectual, the settler must have done everything which, according to the nature of the property comprised in the settlement, was necessary to be done in order to transfer the property and render the settlement binding upon him. He may of course do this by actually transferring the property to the persons for whom he intends to provide, and the provision will then be effectual, and it will be equally effectual if he transfers the property to a trustee for the purposes of the settlement, or declares that he himself holds it in trust for those purposes; and if the property be personal, the trust may, as I apprehend, be declared either in writing or by parol; but, in order to render the settlement binding, one or other of these modes must, as I understand the law of this Court, be resorted to, for there is no equity in this Court to perfect an imperfect gift. The cases I think go further to this extent, that if the settlement is intended to be effectuated by one of the modes to which I have referred, the Court will not give effect to it by applying another of those modes. If it is intended to take effect by transfer, the Court will not hold the intended transfer to operate as a declaration of trust, for then every imperfect instrument would be made effectual by being converted into a perfect trust. These are the principles by which, as I conceive, this case must be tried.

Applying, then, these principles to the case, there is not here any transfer either of the one class of shares or of the other to the objects of the settlement, and the question therefore must be, whether a valid and effectual trust in favour of those objects was created in the Defendant Samuel Lord or in the settlor himself as to all or any of these shares. Now it is plain that it was not the purpose of this settlement or the intention of the settlor, to constitute himself a trustee of the bank shares. The intention was that the trust should be vested in the Defendant Samuel Lord and I think therefore that we should not be justified in holding that by the settlement, or by any parol declaration made by the settlor, he himself became a trustee of these shares for the purposes of the settlement. By doing so we should be converting the settlement or the parol declaration to a purpose wholly different from that which was intended to be effected by it, and, as I have said, creating a perfect trust out of an imperfect transaction.

His Honour the Vice-Chancellor seems to have considered that the case, *Ex parte Pye* (1811) 18 Ves 140 warranted the conclusion that the settlor himself, became a trustee by virtue of the power of attorney which he had given to the Defendant Samuel Lord; but in *Ex parte Pye*, the power of attorney was given by the settlor for the express purpose of enabling the annuity to be transferred to the object of the settlor's bounty. The settlor had, it appears, already directed the annuity to be purchased for the benefit of that object, and had even paid over the money for the purpose of its being applied to the purchase of the annuity; and then when the annuity was, from the necessity of the case, purchased in the settlor's name, all that possibly could be wanted was to shew that the original purpose was not changed, and, that the annuity, though purchased in the settlor's name was still intended for the benefit of the same object of the settlor's bounty, and the power of attorney proved beyond all doubt that this was the case. These facts appear to me wholly to distinguish this case from the case of *Ex parte Pye*. In my opinion, therefore, this decree cannot be supported upon the authority of *Ex parte Pye*; and there does not appear to me to be any sufficient ground to warrant us in holding that the settlor himself became a trustee of these bank shares for the purposes of this settlement.

The more difficult question is, whether the Defendant Samuel Lord did not become a trustee of these shares? Upon this question I have felt considerable doubt; but in the result, I have come to the conclusion that no perfect trust was ever created in him. The shares, it is clear, were never legally vested in him; and the only ground on which he can be held to have become a trustee of them is, that he held a power of attorney under which he might have transferred them into his own name; but he held that power of attorney as the agent of the settlor; and if he had been sued by the Plaintiffs as trustee of the settlement for an account under the trust, and to compel him to transfer the shares into his own name as trustee, I think he might well have said – These shares are not vested in me; I have no power over them except as the agent of the settlor, and without his express directions I cannot be justified in making the proposed transfer, in converting an intended into an actual settlement. A Court of Equity could not, I think, decree the agent of the settlor to make the transfer, unless it could decree the settlor himself to do so, and it is plain that no such decree could have been made against the settlor. In my opinion, therefore, this decree cannot be maintained as to the fifty Louisisna Bank shares.

As to the thirteen North American Fire Insurance shares, the case seems to me to stand upon a different footing. Although the Plaintiffs' case fails as to the capital of the bank shares, there can, I think, be no doubt that the settlor made a perfect gift to Mrs. Milroy, then Miss Dudgeon, of the dividends upon these shares, so far as they were handed over or treated by him as belonging to her, and these insurance shares were purchased with dividends which were so handed over or treated. It seems to me, upon the evidence, that these shares were purchased with the money of Mrs. Milroy, then Miss Dudgeon, and that the purchase having been made in Thos. Medley's name, there would be a resulting trust for Miss Dudgeon. I think, therefore, that as to these shares the decree is right, the value of the shares being, as I presume, under £200, so that the case does not fall within the ordinary rule of the Court as to the wife's equity for a settlement.

The case being thus disposed of as to the title to the shares, I see no ground for the claim to compensation raised by this bill. The certificates for the shares would follow the legal title, and as to the fifty bank shares would therefore belong to the Defendant J.A. Otto, and as to the thirteen insurance shares the Plaintiffs recovering those shares must recover the certificates also; but this not being provided for by the decree, a direction for the delivery of these certificates should, I think, be added.

Upon the hearing of this appeal it was contended for the Plaintiffs, that so far as they might fail in recovering any of the shares in question they were entitled to recover the value of them against the estate of Thos. Medley. I am not sure that this point can properly be considered to be open upon these pleadings, but whether it be so or not, I agree with my learned brother that the Plaintiffs' claim in this respect cannot be maintained. There is no express covenant in the settlement, and whatever might be done as to implying a covenant to do no act in derogation of the settlement, it would, I think, be going too far to imply a covenant to perfect it. If there be a breach of any implied covenant by the delivery of the certificates to the Defendant, J.A. Otto, the Plaintiffs' remedy sounds in damages, and they may pursue that remedy at law; for which purpose, if the Plaintiffs desire it, there may be inserted in the decree a direction that they be at liberty to use the name of the Defendant Lord, of course upon the usual terms of indemnifying him. I have not adverted to the point which was raised as to this case being governed by the Spanish law, for I think that if that law was more favourable to the Plaintiffs, the onus was upon them to allege and prove it. As to the costs of the suit, my learned brother being of opinion that they ought to be paid out of the settlor's estate, I do not dissent. The decree must be altered accordingly as to the several points to which I have referred."

McArdle v. O'Donohoe
High Court (O'Donovan J) 8 June 1999

The settlor purported to execute a deed of settlement to make provision for his adopted daughter and her children in which he named the first and second named plaintiffs as trustees. The settlor's intention was that £200,000 was to be invested in a bond which would form part of the trust fund but in fact this transfer did not take place and the bond remained in the name of the settlor. The issue which O'Donovan J had to decide was whether the sum of £200,000 invested in the bond constituted part of the trust fund as defined in the deed of settlement or whether it was the personal property of the defendant settlor. O'Donovan J concluded that in his view there was never an effective transfer of the title in the bond to the trustees nor did the settlor ever express an intention to constitute himself a trustee of the settlement created by the deed. He held that the trust created by the deed of settlement was not completely constituted as the settlor had never effectively transferred any monies or property to the trustees and that a court of equity would not compel the completion of an incompletely constituted trust in the absence of valuable consideration. O'Donovan J therefore concluded that the sum of £200,000 invested by the settlor in the bond did not constitute part of the trust fund as defined by the deed of settlement but remained his personal property.

O'DONOVAN J stated at pp.11–20: "The issue that I have to decide in this case is whether the sum of £200,000.00 invested in the said Norwich Union Bond (Number U7000456T) constitutes part of the trust fund as defined in the Deed of Settlement of the 29th of August, 1997 or whether the said sum is the personal property of the Defendant.

In the light of my conclusions on the facts of this case, I am satisfied that, at the time that he executed the said Deed of Settlement of the 28th of August 1997, it was the intention of the Settlor, that the £200,000 which he had invested in the said Norwich Union Bond was to be included in the trust fund created by the said deed and, as I have already indicated, I am equally satisfied that, by virtue of the advice with regard to the tax implications of the creation of that trust which he had received from a Mr. Healy, the Settlor also appreciated that the trust thereby created was to take effect during his lifetime and that it was irrevocable. I might add that despite his protestations in that regard, I am also satisfied that after he had executed the said Deed of Settlement, the Settlor was provided with a copy thereof although I accept that it may well be that, as he maintains, he did not read it. I am also satisfied that the said bond was never transferred into the names of the trustees; either to the intent that it was to be included in the trust fund created by the said Deed of Settlement, or at all and that neither did the Trustees ever receive from the Settlor any monies or property (including the sum of £100 which is expressed in the said Deed of Settlement to have been paid by the Settlor to the Trustees) with a direction that such monies or property be invested in the said trust fund. Indeed, as I have also already indicated, I am satisfied that Trustees did not even open an account in any financial institution to which monies received by them on behalf of the trust fund might be invested. Moreover, although I accept that when, in November 1998, Mr. McArdle learned that the Settlor had withdrawn a sum of £35,000 from the said bond, he expressed reservations about that fact, those reservations were not based on any argument that those monies formed part of the trust fund created by the said Deed of Settlement and were not, therefore, available to the Settlor and, far from protesting that the Settlor was not entitled to withdraw those monies because they formed part of the trust fund created by the said Deed of Settlement of the 27th of August 1997 Mr. Jackson acquiesced in the withdrawal of those monies, in that, he actually signed the application therefor which was submitted to the Norwich Union Insurance Company. In this regard, while, as I have already indicated, I have no doubt but that, when he executed the Deed of Settlement of the 27th of August 1997, it was the Settlor's intention that the said bond would be included in the trust fund thereby created although he understood that he would continue to be entitled to receive annual interest thereon, I am persuaded by the events which occurred during the months of October, November and December 1998 which are hereinbefore referred to that, in or about that time, the Settlor changed his mind and decided that he wanted to have access to the monies represented by that bond and I think it probable that, notwithstanding his execution of the said Deed of Settlement, he believed that, by reason of the fact that the said Bond had never been transferred into the names of the Trustees but remained in his name, he was entitled to draw on those monies. Whether or not that decision and that belief was influenced by a third party; in particular, by the Settlor's natural son Patrick O'Donohoe which, apparently appears to be the suspicion, is, in my view, a moot point and is not relevant to the issue which I have to decide in this case although I accept that, at the time that he executed the said Deed of Settlement, the Settlor was adamant that his son, Patrick O'Donohoe, had already been well provided for and, accordingly, was not to be included as a beneficiary under the trust created by that deed; an assertion which he repeated in the Will which he made on the same date and in the subsequent Wills which he made on the 9th day of April 1998 and the 4th day of June 1998. I might add that it does not appear to me that there was any consideration for the creation of the trust given by the beneficiaries therein named and, in that regard, even though the Settlor, himself, is named as a beneficiary under the Trust and even had he paid the sum of £100 to the trustees which is stated in the Deed of Settlement as having being paid to them (which, as I have already indicated, I do not believe that he did) I am not persuaded that such payment would amount to valuable consideration. However, for the purpose of deciding the issue which I have to decide in this case, it is not, I think necessary to decide that question.

On behalf of the Plaintiffs, Ms Egan submitted:–

1. That, even allowing that the Settlor never paid to the Trustees the sum of £100 which is expressed in the said Deed of Trust to have been paid to them by him by virtue of his execution of the said Deed of Trust, he surrendered rights and fettered his ability to deal with property which amounted to valuable consideration. Accordingly, she submitted that, as the Settlor, himself, is a beneficiary named in the Deed of Trust and even though the trust created by the deed may be incomplete, the Court should enforce it and in that event, the beneficiaries under the trust who are volunteers will be able to enforce their rights under the Deed. In support of that proposition, Ms Egan referred to volume 48 of the *Fourth Edition of Halsbury's Laws* of *England* at paragraph 561 and to paragraph 8.09 on page 97 of *Equity and the Law of Trusts in the Republic of Ireland* by Mr. Justice Ronan Keane.

2. In the circumstance that the said Deed of Settlement of the 27th day of August 1997 does not require particular words of limitation, all that is necessary to completely constitute the trust thereby created was that the settlor should hand over monies to the Trustees which he did when he gave

to Mr. Jackson the necessary authority to enable him to withdraw the sum of £200,000 from his bank account, for the purpose of investing it in the said Norwich Union Bond which, in turn, was to be vested in the trust fund created by the said deed. Accordingly, the maxim "omnia praesumunter rite ac solemnieter esse acta" applies, in that, the Settlor had done everything in his power to complete the trust created by the said Deed and it is clear that he, himself, recognised that fact when, in a letter dated the 3rd day of December 1998 addressed to Mr. McArdle he said:

> 'I hereby instruct you to dissolve the Trust known as the 'O'Donohoe Settlement'.'

Moreover, the Bond purchased by Mr. Jackson out of the monies provided by the Settlor was retained by Mr. Jackson in his capacity as one of the Trustees named in the Deed of Settlement. In support of that proposition, Ms Egan referred to paragraph 8.07 on page 95 of *Equity and the Law of Trusts in the Republic of Ireland* by Mr. Justice Keane.

On behalf of the Defendant, Mr. Brady submitted:

1. That the burden of proving that the sum of £200,000 invested by the said Settlor in the said Norwich Union Bond constitutes part of the trust fund created by the Deed of Settlement dated the 27th of August 1997 rested with the Trustees and that they must establish that fact on the balance of probability. To that end, the Trustees must prove that the Settlor had divested himself of the legal and equitable estate in the bond and had no longer any control or direct personal interest in the bond or the proceeds of any encashment thereof or any income generated thereby and that the mere proof of an intention to vest the bond in the Trustees of the settlement created by the said Deed of the 29th of August 1997 does not, *ipso facto*, establish the fact that the legal title had been so vested. In that regard Mr. Brady pointed to the fact that, apart from the sum of £100 which is expressed in the said Deed of Trust to have been paid by the Settlor to the Trustees, the Deed recites that the "Settlor *may* hereafter *pay* or *transfer* . . . into the names of or otherwise placed under the *control* of the Trustees . . . the sum of £200,000 . . . to the intent that the same may be held upon the trust thereof" and further provides that the trust funds shall include "all monies investments, and property (including freehold or leasehold land) paid or transferred to the Trustees or otherwise vested in the Trustees and accepted by the Trustees as additions to the trust fund" whereas the fact of the matter is that the Settlor never exercised the option of paying or transferring the said sum of £200,000 into the names or under the control of the Trustees and neither of the Trustees ever accepted the said sum of £200,000 as additions to the trust fund" in the sense that they never opened an account in the name of the trust to which those monies or the bond which was purchased therewith, could be lodged. On the contrary, although the Settlor provided the sum of £200,000 with which the said bond was purchased, the bond issued in the name of the Settlor and remains in his name and the Trustees, by implication, recognise that the said bond was never vested in them, in that, in a Notice of Motion dated the 16th day of December 1998 issued in these proceedings

on behalf of the Trustees an Order is sought requiring the Settlor to take all steps as are necessary to ensure that the said trust fund is vested in the Trustees. Moreover, neither the insurance broker, Mr. Shay Cribben, who was instrumental in purchasing the said bond, or the Norwich Union Insurance Company were ever told that the bond was to be held in trust nor did the Settlor ever execute a Declaration of Trust in respect thereof. Indeed, in November 1998, it was the Settlor, rather than the Trustees, who made the decision to withdraw the sum of £35,000 from the said Bond through encashment and although, subsequently, the Trustees expressed reservations with regard to that withdrawal it was not on the grounds that the Settlor was not entitled to withdraw it. In support of these propositions, Mr. Brady referred to the *Law of Trusts and Equitable Obligations* by Robert A Pierse and John Stevens at page 555, a judgment of the High Court given in the case of *In the Matter of the Estate of William Henry Wilson Deceased; Ion Grove-White and Gerard Edward Grove-White v John Hugh Wilson and Others* [1933] IR 729, a judgment of the Court of Appeal in Chancery given in a case of *Milroy v. Lord* [1861–73] All ER Rep 783 and the 1995 edition of *Equity and the Law of Trusts in Ireland* by Hilary Delany at page 100.

In my view, the trust created by the said Deed of Settlement of the 27th of August 1997 was not completely constituted, in that, the Settlor never effectively transferred any monies or any property which might be included in the "Trust Fund" as defined in the said Deed to the Trustees. While, as I have indicated, I am satisfied that, at the time that he executed the said Deed of Settlement, it was the intention of the Settlor that the sum of £100 therein expressed to have been paid by him to the Trustees would be paid to them for inclusion in the trust fund and that the Norwich Union Bond which had been purchased out of monies provided by him would equally, be included in the said Trust Fund, I am satisfied that, in fact, the said sum of £100 was never paid to the Trustees and neither did the Settlor ever effectively transfer his title to the said Bond to the said Trustees. In this regard, the mere fact that, following its purchase, one of the Trustees, Mr. Jackson retained possession of the bond does not, in my view, have the effect of transferring title in it to the Trustees. Accordingly, as I have indicated, I do not consider that the trust created by the said Deed of Settlement was completely constituted and, as I understand the legal principles in that regard, a Court of Equity may not compel the completion of an incompletely constituted trust in the absence of valuable consideration; c/f Volume 48 of the 4th Edition of *Halsbury's Laws of England* at paragraph 561. In this regard, Ms Egan has submitted that, whether or not the Settlor paid to the Trustees the sum of £100 which is expressed to have been paid to them by the said Deed of Settlement of the 27th of August 1997, by his execution of that Deed, in which he, himself, is named as a beneficiary, he has surrendered rights and fettered his ability to deal with property which amounts to valuable consideration. I do not think that this is so. Consideration in the context of an incompletely constituted trust means the conferring of some benefit by the Settlor or the undergoing of some detriment by the beneficiary (c/f paragraph 8.09 of *Equity and the Law of Trusts in the Republic of Ireland* by Mr. Justice A. Ronan Keane) and it seems to me that the failure of the Settlor to transfer any monies or property to the names of the Trustees, as was his intention at the time that he executed the said Deed of Settlement and as was provided for therein, negatives the existence of a trust fund whereby the trust thereby created was incompletely constituted and there was no consideration therefore. In particular, in the absence of a trust fund, the Settlor surrendered no rights and had not fettered his ability to deal with his property. In this regard, while I accept the validity of Ms Egan's proposition that, at the behest of a beneficiary, who is not a volunteer, the Court may enforce an incomplete trust so that the trust becomes completely constituted and that, in that event, a volunteer beneficiary will be able to enforce his or her rights under the incompletely constituted trust, the fact of the matter in this case is that none of the beneficiaries named in the said Deed of Settlement of the 27th of August 1997 have sought to enforce the trust thereby created and the only beneficiary by whom it is suggested that valuable consideration was given for the creation of the trust, namely, the Settlor, specifically does not seek to enforce it. That being so, and given, that, in any event, it is my opinion that there was, in fact, no consideration given for the creation of the trust, I am not satisfied to compel its completion.

Arising from the foregoing, while as I have indicated, I am satisfied, that, when he executed the said Deed of Settlement of the 27th of August 1997 it was the Settlor's intention to vest the said Bond in the Trustees, he never, in fact, gave effect to that intention, in that, he took no steps whatsoever to have the title to the bond which was in his name transferred into the names of the Trustees and, in that regard, I would adopt the statement of Mr. Justice Johnson given in the course of his judgment in the case of *In the Matter of the Estate* of *William Henry Wilson deceased,* hereinbefore referred to in which he said (c/f page 739 of the Report of the Judgment):

> "A gift is a gift and, of course if a donor, while expressing an intention to give something and taking certain steps in the direction of giving it, has not gone the whole way, the expectant donee has no equity to compel the completion of the gift. This is good sense and good law".

Moreover, by virtue of the decision of the Court of Appeal in Chancery given in a case of *Milroy v. Lloyd* [1861–73] All ER Rep 783 it would appear that, if it is the intention to create a trust by transfer of property then, in the absence of a stated intention by the Settlor to constitute himself a trustee of the trust property and in the absence of an effective transfer of the trust property to the trustees, equity will not construe the ineffective transfer as a declaration of trust by the Settlor. In my view, there was never an effective transfer of the title to the Norwich Union Bond to the Trustees and neither did the Settlor ever express an intention to constitute himself a Trustee of the settlement created by the Deed of the 27th of August 1997.

In conclusion, I reject the submission that the maxim *"omnia praesumunter rite solemnieter esse acta"* has any application in this case. While it may well be that, when he executed the Deed of Settlement of the 27th day of August 1997, the Settlor intended that the Norwich Union Bond would be included in the Trust Fund as defined in that Deed, in fact, the Deed did not require that the said Bond or, indeed, any particular monies or property be transferred to the Trustees for inclusion in the trust fund but rather gave the Settlor an option to pay or transfer sum of £200,000 together with further sums of money or securities or other property to the Trustees to the intent that the same be held upon the trusts thereby created whereas I am satisfied that the Settlor never, in fact, exercised that option.

Having regard to the foregoing, it is my opinion that the sum of £200,000 invested by the Settlor in Norwich Union Bond No. U7000456G does not constitute part of the Trust Fund as defined by the said Deed of Settlement but remains the personal property of the Defendant."

Miller v. Harrison
(1871) IR 5 Eq 324

A dispute arose about the distribution of the property of an intestate who had died in America a naturalized US citizen. One of the next-of-kin executed a deed in which he agreed to share the property equally with the other next-of-kin and in reliance on this deed, these other individuals allowed a decree in the former's favour to be given by an American court in proceedings to determine ownership of the property. The Court of Appeal (Lord O'Hagan LC and Christian LJ) held that a subsequent attempt by this person to revoke the deed was invalid as its execution in the first instance had constituted a declaration of trust.

LORD O'HAGAN LC stated at pp.343–346: "Did Thomas Harrison constitute himself a trustee?

We must remember two things in approaching this question. First, that the validity of the trust does not depend on the existence of any consideration; and, next, that the declaration of it "is not confined to any express form of words," but may be indicated by the character and general effect of the instrument creating it. The so-called power of attorney of May, 1864, must be judged of by itself; but we need not forget the position of the person who signed it, and the antecedent circumstances which induced its execution. And it seems to me that it does constitute a declaration of trust clear, complete, and final, which bound the maker of it, and bound him irrevocably.

He recites the pendency of proceedings, and the position of his family, and the appointment of William Harrison and William Boyd as his attorneys, to recover his share of the estate of his uncle; and contemplating the decision of the Court in favour of his claim to priority on the ground of his naturalization, he then and there, and by the instrument before him, declares, consents, and agrees that he will accept an equal division with his brothers and sisters, and declines to insist on his own superior legal right.

So far, this is no mere power of attorney, as the instrument has been improperly called at the Bar. It is an agreement, a consent, a declaration, as between him and his relatives, without the intervention of any third parties. It divests him of his exclusive property and vests proportions of it in those relatives, "in like manner as if they had been naturalized citizens of the States of America," But, inasmuch as the legal estate in the whole was his own, he, thereupon, at once made himself a trustee for them, as to all the shares of it, save that which he reserved to himself.

Now, there is here no imperfect assignment, requiring the aid of any individual, or any Court to carry it into full effect; the declaration is absolute and unconditional, and operates at once.

No future act is contemplated; no promise remains to be fulfilled; there is a gift, and not an engagement to give. The words of the donor denude him equitably of the shares which he bestows, save as a trustee for those so obtaining the beneficial interest, whilst the legal interest remains in himself; or, in the words of Lord Justice Knight Bruce, "this gift was a perfect act – a completed gift, resting neither in promise merely, nor merely in unfulfilled intention." And, therefore, it binds him, though it states no consideration, and uses no language expressly creating trusts, and would do so equally if we did not know that it was only the culmination of a series of transactions, in the course of which sufficient consideration, in my opinion, was supplied to sustain it, if consideration had been necessary, and if the facts had been, *eo intuitu*, spread upon the face of it.

The concluding portion of the instrument, constituting William Harrison and William Boyd, the attorneys under the power of 1863, attorneys, also, to give effect to this declaration and consent in the suit then pending, and to bind Thomas Harrison thereby in the events to happen, has been more or less relied on by the Appellant; but it seems to me strongly in favour of the Plaintiff's argument. It is, really, a power of attorney, superadded to the "declaration and consent," but distinct from them, for the purpose merely of carrying them into execution. They were sufficient and perfect in themselves, and only needed, for their practical application, the agency which this power of attorney supplied. The Appellant's counsel have ably contended, but, I think, unsuccessfully, that there was here no creation of any present effectual trust, but only a prospective arrangement on the contingency of a favourable issue of the pending cause, and that there are no words to make Thomas Harrison a trustee for his relatives. But it apears to me, as I have said, very clear taking the whole instrument together, that he declared the rights of those relatives to shares in the property, whatever it was, which was then actually his, as derived from his uncle, and that the future judicial recognition of his right, which was then vested in him, could not take from the force of that declaration; and further, that in consenting to accept "an equal division" of that, in the whole of which he continued to possess the legal estate, he, *ex necessitate*, made himself a trustee for those to whom he so disposed of a beneficial interest.

Many cases were relied on for the Appellant, but I think it necessary only to advert, in the briefest manner, to one of them, *Dipple v. Corles* (1853) 11 Hare 183 which at first struck me as favouring his contention. But there no writing existed; there was "doubt and difficulty" on the words which had been used, and the precise character of which we do not know, as the report does not set them forth; and Lord Hatherley there relied on Lord Eldon's asscription of importance in *Ex parte Pye* (1811) 18 Ves 140 to the fact that the declaration had been "committed to writing." "The question before me," Lord Hatherley says, "is whether the conversation which took place on the day of the funeral of the father amounts to a declaration by the Defendant of an intention to constitute himself a trustee of this estate, or of any specific part of it, for his brothers and sisters?" And he adds:— "It appears to me that a clear expression of intention should be found, before the Court, in a case like the present, can hold that a party intended to subject himself to all the consequences of the liability to account and inquiry, which is involved in the position of a trustee." Now, in the case before us, I think there was such an expression of clear and deliberate intention by a man, *sui juris*, understanding his position, and acting in pursuance of an honourable engagement with his family, by which he ought to have abided; and that expression was made, not in casual words spoken at a funeral, and difficult to be accurately remembered or reliably reported, but by a solemn instrument, prepared with care, and with the aid of professional persons, and leaving, in my mind, no reasonable doubt as to the purpose with which it was executed. I do not, therefore, think that *Dipple v. Corles* is an authority for the Appellant under the peculiar circumstances with which we have to deal.

Upon the whole I am of opinion that the decision of the Vice-Chancellor was right, and that his decree must be affirmed; and having reached this conclusion, which is founded in no degree on any reference to the agreement of February, 1865, the subject of such lengthened controversy in the Court below, it is, notwithstanding, satisfactory to me to know that, after the fullest inquiry, and a *viva voce* examination of witnesses before him, the learned Vice-Chancellor considered that agreement well sustained in evidence, and of great importance as corroborating and supporting the views on which he decided in favour of the Plaintiff.

The decree of the Vice-Chancellor must be affirmed, with costs."

T. Choithram International SA and v. Pagarani
[2001] 1 WLR 1

The donor executed a trust deed establishing a philanthropic foundation appointing himself one of the trustees and stated orally that he was giving all his wealth to the foundation. This property was expressed to include his deposit balances and shares in the first to fourth defendants and the donor told the accountant to those companies that he was to transfer the deposit balances and shares to the foundation although in some instances his shares in the companies had not been transferred before he died. Some of the other trustees signed the trust deed the day the declaration of trust was made and the others subsequently did so. The Court of Appeal of the British Virgin Islands held that the plaintiffs, who claimed to be entitled to the donor's estate on his intestacy, had succeeded in establishing that the donor had not made a valid gift of the deposit balances and shares to the foundation. The defendants' appeal to the Privy Council was allowed. Lord Browne-Wilkinson stated that it would be unconscionable to allow the donor to resile from his declaration that he was giving and had given property to the trust which he had established and of which he had appointed himself to be a trustee and such property was therefore vested in the donor as trustee of the foundation and the gift was completed.

LORD BROWNE-WILKINSON stated at pp. 8–13: "On the main issue the defendants advanced a number of arguments with a view to demonstrating that the gift to the foundation was an immediate perfected gift by TCP of all or some of TCP's wealth. Their primary argument was that TCP, having executed the foundation trust deed under which he was one of the trustees and made a gift of all his wealth to "the foundation", thereafter held all his assets (or at least his shares in and deposits with the British Virgin Island companies which are the first four defendants) as trustee on the trusts of the foundation trust deed. The defendants also had a number of alternative arguments. First they argued that the principle in *Strong v. Bird* (1874) LR 18 Eq 315 entitled them to succeed because a grant of letters of administration to the estate of TCP had been obtained by Lekhraj, one of the trustees of the foundation. Next they argued that, as to the sums deposited with the companies, those companies had attorned to the trustees of the foundation when Mr Param or Mr Tejwani made the changes to the companies' books. Next, they submitted that TCP's words and actions amounted to an equitable assignment of the deposits with the companies to the trustees of the foundation, or alternatively constituted a release by TCP to the companies in consideration of the companies' undertaking contractual obligations to pay the trustees of the foundation a similar sum. Finally, the defendants repeated their argument before the judge that the trustees were validly registered as shareholders in the company either because of certain provisions in the articles of the company or under section 30 of the International Business Companies Ordinance 1984. Their Lordships will deal first with the main argument since, in their view, that is sufficient to dispose of the appeal.

In order to have made an effective gift of his shares and deposit balances to the foundation TCP must have intended to make an immediate gift on 17 February. The judge found, and repeated his finding on a number of occasions throughout the judgment, that on that date TCP did make, or attempted to make, a present immediate and unconditional gift to the foundation which was intended to be complete. This finding, if it had stood alone, would have been fully sufficient to establish TCP's intention to make an outright gift. However, at a later stage in his judgment the judge made a further finding. At this stage in the judgment the judge was seeking to answer the second question of fact left to him by counsel for decision (*viz.* did TCP continue his intention of gift down to the date of death?), a question only relevant to the *Strong v. Bird* argument. The judge reviewed the evidence as to the events occurring after the oral declaration of trust on 17 February and was very impressed by two elements in the evidence: first, that despite Lekhraj's promptings TCP refused to sign the further documents put before him and, second, that by the draft will (which he never executed) TCP expressly excluded his Indian property (which had been the home of Lalibai) and also contained a gift of his estate to the foundation. He reached the conclusion that the gift was not intended by the deceased to be irrevocable.

Their Lordships do not feel able to accept the judge's inference that TCP intended the gift to be revocable. First the judge quotes a passage from the affidavit of Mr Lock of Clifford Chance saying that TCP was intending "to prepare the necessary assignments and transfers for the assets to be transferred to the Choithram International Foundation". Now Mr Lock and Clifford Chance were concerned, not with the setting up of the foundation, but only with TCP's will: the setting up of the foundation was being dealt with by different solicitors, Macfarlanes. The only evidence of the further documents which Macfarlanes envisaged were the draft documents which were sent to Lekhraj by fax from Macfarlanes on 12 February 1992. These documents were not share transfers or deeds of assignment: they were declarations of trust by TCP in favour of the trustees of the foundation and notices of addition to the funds settled by the trust deed to be executed by the trustees. Therefore, so far as the evidence extends, it was always the intention of TCP and his relevant legal advisers that the foundation should be constituted by the following steps. First, TCP would declare the foundation trust by a trust deed, he and others being the trustees; second, TCP would declare himself as holding his assets on the trusts of the foundation trust deed; third, the other trustees would accept the gift as an addition to the trust fund constituted by the trust deed. Thus the machinery actually adopted was the same as that proposed by Macfarlanes save that the written declaration of trust was replaced by an oral immediate gift not to a person but for an abstract purpose, ie for the purposes of the foundation. A gift for "the foundation" can only properly be construed as a gift to the purposes declared by the trust deed and administered by the trustees.

The judge's doubts were also raised by the fact that TCP, an experienced businessman, was acting in defiance of his lawyers' advice "with whom he had remained in close consultation". There is no evidence of recent direct communication between TCP and Macfarlanes: the only evidence is the fax of 12 February which was sent not to TCP but to Lekhraj. The fact is that TCP was in his last illness as a result of which he went into intensive care on 9 March and died 10 days thereafter. The judge also seemed far from clear as to the nature of the documents sent by Macfarlanes on 12 February which formed the basis of the documents the signature of which Lekhraj was seeking from TCP. The judge refers to TCP having "the continuing intention of transferring assets by way of instruments of transfer" and "the transfer of shares . . . [remaining] unsigned". The judge seemed to have thought that the documents would actually have vested the legal interest in the deposits and the shares in the trustees whereas the new documents, even if executed, were to have done no more than constitute TCP as trustee for the whole body of trustees of the foundation.

Finally on this aspect of the case their Lordships do not attach such importance to the will as did the judge. It is certainly true that if the gift of all his wealth was valid TCP by executing the will would not have provided for his widow and daughters in India by leaving them the land: this is a real factor to be taken into account. But their Lordships do not, as did the judge, attach importance to the draft will containing a residuary bequest to the foundation by reference to the trust deed dated 17 February. There is no evidence that TCP had anything to do with the instructions for this will (beyond refusing to sign it) and in any event it would have been common prudence for TCP to execute a will giving to the foundation anything which the inter vivos trusts had failed to attach: their Lordships do not consider the existence of the testamentary residuary gift to the foundation as in any way inconsistent with TCP having intended to make an absolute gift in his lifetime.

For these reasons their Lordships are of the view that the judge in reaching his inference that the "gift" to the foundation was revocable was labouring under important misapprehensions. Their Lordships consider that once it is understood that, in any event, the transaction was to be carried through by TCP declaring that he held assets already vested in him as a trustee for the foundation, there is no ground for inferring that the gift was intended by TCP to be revocable or conditional on the transfer of the specific assets. In the light of all the other evidence pointing (as the judge found) quite clearly to an intention to make an immediate, unconditional gift to the foundation, their Lordships are satisfied that that was TCP's intention. Perhaps the most telling evidence of all is the minutes of the companies' meetings on the evening of 17 February. The plaintiffs launched an attack on the genuineness of the minutes but they were upheld as genuine by the judge. They record that the directors of each of the four companies, who in each case included TCP, "acknowledge and confirm that the trustees of the [foundation] are henceforth the holders of the shares and assets in the company gifted to the [foundation] by Mr TC Pagarani". Those minutes were signed by TCP. It is hard to imagine a clearer statement of what TCP understood to be the position, ie that he had already given outright to the foundation all his interests in the company balances and the shares.

In fairness to the judge, it does not appear that his decision that there was here no complete gift was based on the fact that in his view the gift was revocable. He founded his decision on the ground that the requirements laid down in *Milroy v. Lord* (1862) 4 De GF & J 264 had not been satisfied. It may well be that an immediate declaration of trust even though expressly or impliedly made revocable is a valid complete gift. Many voluntary settlements are expressly made revocable yet no one suggests that they are incompletely constituted trusts. If and so long as the trusts remain unrevoked, the trust is enforceable against the trustees and the trust property. But it is unnecessary to decide that point.

Their Lordships then turn to the central and most important question: on the basis that TCP intended to make an immediate absolute gift "to the foundation" but had not vested the gifted property in all the trustees of the foundation, are the trusts of the foundation trust deed enforceable against the deposits and the shares or is this (as the judge and the Court of Appeal held) a case where there has been an imperfect gift which cannot be enforced against TCP's estate whatever TCP's intentions.

The judge and the Court of Appeal understandably took the view that a perfect gift could only be made in one of two ways, viz (a) by a transfer of the gifted asset to the donee, accompanied by an intention in the donor to make a gift; or (b) by the donor declaring himself to be a trustee of the gifted property for the donee. In case (a), the donor has to have done everything necessary to be done which is within his own power to do in order to transfer the gifted asset to the donee. If the donor has not done so, the gift is incomplete since the donee has no equity to perfect an imperfect gift: *Milroy v. Lord* (1862) 4 De GF & J 264; *Richards v. Delbridge* (1874) LR 18 Eq 11; *In re Rose; Midland Bank Executor and Trustee Co. Ltd v. Rose* [1949] Ch 78; *In re Rose; Rose v. Inland Revenue Comrs.* [1952] Ch 499. Moreover, the court will not give a benevolent construction so as to treat ineffective words of outright gift as taking effect as if the donor had declared himself a trustee for the donee: *Milroy v. Lord* (1862) 4 De GF & J 264. So, it is said, in this case TCP used words of gift to the foundation (not words declaring himself a trustee): unless he transferred the shares and deposits so as to vest title in all the trustees, he had not done all that he could in order to effect the gift. It therefore fails. Further it is said that it is not possible to treat TCP's words of gift as a declaration of trust because they make no reference to trusts. Therefore the case does not fall within either of the possible methods by which a complete gift can be made and the gift fails.

Though it is understandable that the courts below should have reached this conclusion since the case does not fall squarely within either of the methods normally stated as being the only possible ways of making a gift, their Lordships do not agree with that conclusion. The facts of this case are novel and raise a new point. It is necessary to make an analysis of the rules of equity as to complete gifts. Although equity will not aid a volunteer, it will not strive officiously to defeat a gift. This case falls between the two common form situations mentioned above. Although the words used by TCP are those normally appropriate to an outright gift — "I give to X" — in the present context there is no breach of the principle in *Milroy v. Lord* if the words of TCP's gift (ie to the foundation) are given their only possible meaning in this context. The foundation has no legal existence apart from the trust declared by the foundation trust deed. Therefore the words "I give to the foundation" can only mean "I give to the trustees of the foundation trust deed to be held by them on the trusts of foundation trust deed". Although the words are apparently words of outright gift they are essentially words of gift on trust.

But, it is said, TCP vested the properties not in all the trustees of the foundation but only in one, ie TCP. Since equity will not aid a volunteer, how can a court order be obtained vesting the gifted property in the whole body of trustees on the trusts of the foundation. Again, this represents an over-simplified view of the rules of equity. Until comparatively recently the great majority of trusts were voluntary settlements under which beneficiaries were volunteers having given no value. Yet beneficiaries under a trust, although volunteers, can enforce the trust against the trustees. Once a trust relationship is established between trustee and beneficiary, the fact that a beneficiary has given no value is irrelevant. It is for this reason that the type of perfected gift referred to in class (b) above is effective since the donor has constituted himself a trustee for the donee who can as a matter of trust law enforce that trust.

What then is the position here where the trust property is vested in one of the body of trustees, viz TCP? In their Lordships' view there should be no question. TCP has, in the most solemn circumstances, declared that he is giving (and later that he has given) property to a trust which he himself has established and of which he has appointed himself to be a trustee. All this occurs at one composite transaction taking place on 17 February. There can in principle be no distinction between the case where the donor declares himself to be sole trustee for a donee or a purpose and the case where he declares himself to be one of the trustees for that donee or purpose. In both cases his conscience is affected and it would be unconscionable and contrary to the principles of equity to allow such a donor to resile from his gift. Say, in the present case, that TCP had survived and tried to change his mind by denying the gift. In their Lordships' view it is impossible to believe that he could validly deny that he was a trustee for the purposes of the foundation in the light of all the steps that he had taken to assert that position and to assert his trusteeship. In their Lordships' judgment in the absence of special factors where one out of a larger body of trustees has the trust property vested in him he is bound by the trust and must give effect to it by transferring the trust property into the name of all the trustees.

The plaintiffs relied on the decision of Sir John Romilly MR in *Bridge v. Bridge* (1852) 16 Beav 315 as showing that the vesting of the trust property in one trustee, the donor, out of many is not sufficient to constitute the trust: see p 324. Their Lordships have some doubt whether that case was correctly decided on this point, the judge giving no reasons for his view. But in any event it is plainly distinguishable from the present case since the judge considered that the trust could not be fully constituted unless the legal estate in the gifted property was vested in the trustees and in that case the legal estate was vested neither in the donor nor in any of the other trustees.

Therefore in their Lordships' view the assets, if any, validly included in TCP's gift to the foundation are properly vested in the trustees and are held on the trusts of the foundation trust deed.

What then are the gifted assets? It will be recalled that TCP referred to the subject matter of the gift in a number of different ways: "all my wealth", "everything", "all my wealth, all my shares, to the trust", "all his balances . . . with the company . . . and his shares as well", "all my wealth with the companies". The judge found that TCP made a gift of all his wealth with the companies, ie the deposit balances and the shares in the four defendant companies which together constitutes his whole wealth in the British Virgin Islands and are the only assets at issue in these proceedings. It was submitted that a gift of "all my wealth" was void for uncertainty. Their Lordships express no view on that point since there can be no question but that the deposit balances and the shares in the four companies were identified by TCP as being included in the gift and the gift of them is *pro tanto* valid.

Their Lordships will therefore humbly advise Her Majesty that the appeal ought to be allowed and the action dismissed on the grounds that at TCP's death the deposit balances and the shares in the companies were held on the trusts of the foundation trust deed and the same are now validly vested in the trustees of the foundation."

Exceptions to the Principle that Equity will not Perfect an Incompletely Constituted Trust in Favour of a Volunteer

1. The Rule in Strong v. Bird

The effect of the rule in *Strong v. Bird*[7] is that where an incomplete gift is made during a donor's lifetime and the legal title to this property subsequently becomes vested in the donee, the donor's prior intention to make the gift is regarded as having been perfected provided that the intention has continued until the date of the donor's death. An intention to make a gift in the future or

---

[7] (1874) LR 18 Eq 315.

to make a future testamentary gift will not come within the scope of the rule. The distinction between a present intention to make an immediate gift of property and the intention to make a testamentary gift is well illustrated by the decision in *Re Wilson*[8] (see *supra*).

2. Donatio Mortis Causa

A *donatio mortis causa* is the delivery of property to a donee in contemplation of the donor's death which is conditional on this event occurring and the gift is not regarded as complete until the donor dies. The essential elements of a *donatio mortis causa* are as follows: there must have been a gift made in contemplation, though not necessarily in the expectation, of the donor's death,[9] the subject matter of the gift must have been delivered to the donee[10] and the gift must have been made on the basis that it becomes absolute only on the donor's death and therefore remains revocable during his lifetime. In addition, the property in question must have been capable of forming the subject matter of a *donatio mortis causa*.[11]

Re Mulroy: M'Andrew v. Mulroy
[1924] 1 IR 98

Shortly before his death, the deceased opened a cash box in the presence of the defendant and took out a deposit receipt and two 'stale' cheques and said to him: 'Here is all belonging to me . . . I am sorry I haven't more to give you; You were very good to me.' He then replaced the documents and locked the box, putting the key in his pocket. The deceased subsequently died intestate and the Irish Court of Appeal (Molony CJ, Ronan and O'Connor LJJ) held that there was no valid *donatio mortis causa* on the grounds that the deceased, by replacing the documents, had led the court to believe that he had never intended to part with them in such a manner as to lose dominion over them during his lifetime.

MOLONY CJ stated at p.103–105: "In this case the Master of the Rolls came to the conclusion that the evidence did not establish a good donatio mortis causa; and, after a careful examination of the evidence, I am not disposed to differ from him.

In order to establish an effective donatio mortis causa three things must combine, as was laid down in *Cain v. Moon* [1896] 2 QB 283, *per* Lord Russell

---

[8] [1933] IR 729.
[9] *Bentham v. Potterton* High Court (Barr J) 28 May 1998.
[10] *Re Mulroy* [1924] 1 IR 98.
[11] Note that the English Court of Appeal has held in *Sen v. Headley* [1991] Ch 425 that a gift of land by the delivery of deeds may be the subject of a *donatio mortis causa*.

C.J., p. 286: "First, the gift or donation must have been made in contemplation, though not necessarily in expectation, of death; secondly, there must have been delivery to the donee of the subject-matter of the gift; and thirdly, the gift must be made under such circumstances as show that the thing is to revert to the donor in case he should recover." As regards delivery, it was established in the *Union of London and Smith's Bank Ltd v. Wasserberg* [1915] 1 Ch 195, that an inchoate or imperfect delivery of chattels may be sufficient for effectuating a *donatio mortis causa*. In that case the testator, when about to undergo a serious operation, expressed in the clearest possible way a desire to give to his wife certain bonds to bearer, which he had in his locked box in the bank; and having discussed the matter with the assistant manager, he put his wife's name on the outside of the parcel containing the bonds, and locked it up in his locked box; and having done this in the presence of his wife, he left the locked box with the bank, and gave his wife a list of the bonds, telling her to keep it safely. After they had reached home, he gave his wife a bunch of keys containing the key of the locked box, and told her to lock them up with the list of the bonds, which she accordingly did, in a drawer in her own room, of which she had always kept the key. The same day the testator went into a nursing home, where he shortly afterwards died; and it was held by Sargent J. that the delivery of the key transferring to the wife a partial dominion over or part of the means of getting at the box, though not a sufficient delivery to support a gift inter vivos, was under the circumstances a sufficient delivery to effectuate a donatio mortis causa. Sargent J. observed in the course of his judgment, p. 202: "With regard to the incident at the bank, the case of *Cochrane v. Moore* (1890) 25 QBD 57 shows that mere words of gift are not in themselves sufficient, but there must be delivery. If the testator had actually given the parcel to his wife, and she had handed it back to him for the purpose of safe custody, that would probably have been enough; but the facts are, I think, that the testator did not at any time during that incident part with the custody of the bonds."

The question of the effect of a redelivery of bank notes for the purpose of safe custody was discussed this year in the case of *In re Hawkins, Watts v. Nash* [1924] WN 131. In that case the testator, on his death-bed, handed over to his niece bank notes for £5,000, and to her husband bank notes for £2,000, and clearly indicated that the money was to be theirs respectively after his death. The niece, after having got possession of the notes, asked the testator if she should put the envelope in his deed-box for safety against fire, and upon the testator assenting, she took the key from a nail in the wall facing the testator's bed, unlocked the box, placed the envelope in the box, which she replaced under his bed, and she hung the key up again on its nail. It was contended on behalf of the niece and her husband that there was such a complete delivery of the notes as was sufficient to constitute a valid donatio mortis causa to each donee, and that the redelivery of the notes to the testator for safe custody on behalf of the donees did not affect the previous gift. P.O. Lawrence J. said in delivering judgment: "The only difficulty lay in the question whether the placing of the notes in the deed-box of the testator for safe custody destroyed the effect of the previous delivery by restoring to the donor possession of the notes."

Dealing with certain cases, including the case of *In re Wasserberg* [1915] 1 Ch 195 and *Bunn v. Markham* (1816) 7 Taunt 224 he said: "In the present case the previous effectual delivery was unaffected by the subsequent part of the transaction, namely, the placing of the envelope, with the donor's assent, in the deed-box by the donees for safe custody. The testator therefore was, until his death, merely the custodian of the notes for the donees. There was nothing in *Bunn v. Markham* (1816) 7 Taunt 224 inconsistent with the proposition that when once the gifts (mortis causa) were complete, the subsequent agreement by the donor to take back the notes for safe custody did not affect the prior gifts."

In the case now before us the deceased man, who was a confirmed invalid, and died four days afterwards, on the 24th of March, asked his brother, the defendant, with whom he lived, to bring him down his cash-box; and it having been brought to him, he opened it with a key which was in his vest pocket, and the vest was at the foot of the bed, and having opened it and taken out the three documents – namely, deposit receipt and two cheques – he called the defendant to his side, and said: "Here, Jamesie, is all belonging to me, all my property; and I am sorry I haven't more to give you; you were very good to me." And he added: "You will do for me the same as you did for Kitty and Tom," which was understood by the parties to mean to provide money for Masses and a monument. Nothing else was said; but it does appear that the documents were put into the hands of the defendant. Had the defendant thenceforward retained possession of the documents, there would have been strong evidence in favour of a donatio, but it appears that after the defendant had got possession of the documents he put them back into the box, and that the deceased himself locked the box, and having locked it, put the key back into his own waistcoat pocket, and then the defendant put away the box, and restored the vest containing the key to the place where it had previously been, at the foot of the bed. All this happened within the space of a couple of minutes, and the effect of the transaction is that, notwithstanding the gift, the deceased man had exactly the same dominion over the property that he had before. If the defendant had asked to be allowed to put the documents back into the box for safe custody, and the deceased had assented to this, *Watts v. Nash* shows that this would not have destroyed the effect of the gift; but the unexplained replacing of the documents in the box immediately afterwards leads to the belief that the deceased never intended to part with the actual possession of the documents in such a way as to lose dominion and control over them during his life.

The case is one of some difficulty, and I hesitated in coming to a conclusion; but on the whole I cannot bring myself to differ from the Master of the Rolls in his conclusion, and consequently I think the appeal ought to be dismissed."

RONAN LJ at pp.105–106: "I have very great difficulty in this case. Donatio mortis causa depends on the intention with which certain acts are done, and the first matter we must try to ascertain is the intention with which the acts were done here. The testator was in bed; there was a box containing some documents belonging to him, and this box also contained documents belonging to the donee of the alleged donatio mortis causa.

The evidence of the defendant is that when he (the defendant) came into the kitchen, where Michael was in bed, he said to him, "Jamesie." I said, "What, Michael?" "He told me to bring him down the little cash-box." The deceased therefore started the transaction by asking James for the box. What did he want the box for? Was it to see if the things were in it or not, or was it to do something with them? The witness continues, in reply to the question, "Was it locked or open?": "It was locked." "Who opened it?" "Michael." "Where did he get the key?" "He asked me for his vest. I got the vest and gave it to him." "What did he do with it?" "I didn't see what he did. He called me again, 'Jamesie, come here.'" "Was the box open when you went there?" "It was." "What did he say after he said 'Come here'?" "He said, 'Here, Jamesie, here is all belonging to me, all of my property; and I am sorry I haven't more to give you; you were very good to me.'" He did not hand him the box with the documents in it. That is a very important distinction between this and other cases. He handed him the very documents themselves. Beyond all doubt, if the transaction ended there, there was on the evidence a good donatio mortis causa. But a donatio mortis causa can be revoked by the donor just as a legacy can; and the question in this case appears to me to be whether this complete donatio mortis causa was revoked. It could have been revoked by an act or statement of the donor showing that he intended to destroy the effect of what he had done, and to resume the entire control of the property himself. No further statement by him was proved. No further act by him was proved. Taking the evidence as a whole, I am not satisfied that there is anything-proved sufficient to show that the donor said or did anything to revoke the gift he had already made. However, my view is immaterial, the majority of the Court holding the other way."

O'CONNOR LJ at p.106: "I am of opinion that the appeal should be dismissed.

Counsel for the appellant asks us to split the transaction into two: the one a transfer of the possession of the documents to his client, and the other a retransfer of them from his client to Michael on the terms of Michael keeping them on trust for the appellant. If this were the effect of the transaction, the case would be within the authority of the case in the Weekly Notes, to which we have been referred. That, however, is not the view I take of the matter at all. The whole business took only a couple of minutes or so; when it was all over, the position of the documents and the indicium of the control over them were precisely where they always were; the documents were in the deceased's box, and the key of the box was in the deceased's pocket. The momentary tradition of the documents into the hands of James seems to me quite consistent with its being done for the purpose of showing to James the property the deceased intended to give him, and of enabling James afterwards to claim them. For, I think, there was an intention to benefit James; but that is a different thing from transferring the possession to James. The transfer of possession is the element necessary; it is, in my opinion, not alone not established by the evidence, but is negatived by the transaction, taken as a whole."

Bentham v. Potterton
High Court (Barr J) 28 May 1998

The deceased in her will bequeathed cash legacies varying in amount from £1,000 to £3,000 to nine beneficiaries, including the first and second named plaintiffs, her grandnieces, and a residuary clause provided for the division of the remainder of the estate equally between all but one of the named beneficiaries. The deceased was hospitalised two months before her death and it was discovered that she was suffering from inoperable cancer. The trial judge was satisfied that there was no evidence that that she had ever been told that her condition was terminal and it was not until a week before she died that she told her niece that she knew that she was in fact dying. Three and a half weeks before her death the deceased asked the first named plaintiff to retrieve bank books from her home and put them in a safe in the latter's house, which she did. The following day, the first named plaintiff informed her grand aunt that she had carried out her wishes and the former deposed that the deceased had then told her that if anything was to happen to her, she was 'to keep the contents of the books and give [her sister] a few bob out of it'. After the deceased's death, an issue arose about whether this transaction amounted to a valid *donatio mortis causa* made in favour of the plaintiffs. Barr J held that the facts fell short of establishing that the gift had been made by the donor in contemplation of her death and that the plaintiffs had not established the validity of the alleged gift on the balance of probabilities.

BARR J stated at pp.1–7: "The facts of this case have been clearly established in evidence. I have no doubt as to the honesty, truthfulness and reliability of what has been deposed to by the various witnesses called on each side of the case. In particular, I commend the first plaintiff and her mother, Mrs. Sheila Monaghan, on their honesty and fairness in describing what transpired regarding certain bank books which the first plaintiff received from her grandaunt, Mrs. Annie Monaghan, in Our Lady's Hospital, Navan three and a half weeks before she died on 3rd October, 1990 when she was 86 years of age. The deceased had been a widow for about 30 years and had no children. She lived alone in a small dwelling house on a farm of 21 acres at Bollivor, Co. Meath. The land had been let by her on con-acre and her income comprised annual rents of about £100 per acre, the non-contributory old aged pension and occasional earnings from baby-sitting for friends in the locality. Despite her great age, Mrs. Monaghan was an independent person who was well able to look after herself and to manage her affairs. She was known to be a person who understood the value of money. Her needs were modest and through careful management she was able to amass quite considerable savings over the years which were lodged in four different bank accounts and at the time of her death amounted to a total in excess of £14,000. She had deposit books relating to each of the accounts which she kept in a suitcase in her bedroom.

Mr. Peter Higgins, the second defendant, is a solicitor who acted for the deceased from 1984. The first occasion was in connection with a claim which the deceased wished to bring regarding alleged infringement of her rights in a section of bog land. The deceased insisted on the action being brought to trial where she was successful and recovered an amount of £1,500. This episode underlines her forceful nature in the matter of protecting her property rights. Mrs. Sheila Monaghan was a niece of the deceased. I am satisfied that there was a close connection between them and that she gave her aunt family support, comfort and assistance when needed. I am also satisfied that the first plaintiff had a particularly close relationship with her grandaunt up to the time when she married and left the area. Prior to that event, she worked in a factory in Bollivor close to Mrs. Monaghan's home and for many years it was her practice to visit her grandaunt nearly every day on her way home from work or school in earlier times. Even after her marriage, the first plaintiff continued to visit her grandaunt frequently when she returned for visits to her own home. The second plaintiff, who is now 20 years of age, is a daughter of Sheila Monaghan and sister of the first plaintiff. The deceased was her godmother.

A year or two before her death, the late Annie Monaghan developed abdominal pain which necessitated conservative treatment in hospital which was sufficiently successful to allow her resume her independent life at home. However, in August, 1990 she had a relapse and was admitted to hospital again on the 6th of that month. A few days later a laperotomy was performed and it was discovered that the deceased was suffering from excessive fluid caused by cancer of the ovary. The condition was inoperable but a loop of the small bowel was extracted from the abdomen to relieve the situation. This gave rise to further complications and it was necessary to reverse that situation. She was under the care of Mr. Francis Cunningham, general surgeon, who gave evidence. He described the deceased as being debilitated at the time and not eating enough to sustain her. He saw her on a daily basis. She was suffering considerable pain and general discomfort. Mr. Cunningham stated that he put the deceased on a course of oral morphine medication, the primary purpose of which was to relieve pain and discomfort. Dr. Liam O'Sheron, a consultant in palliative medicine, has treated over 1,000 terminally ill cancer patients in course of his practice at two leading Dublin hospitals. He was not involved in the treatment of the deceased and was brought into the case for the purpose of commenting on the medical and nursing notes at Our Lady's Hospital, Navan relating to the deceased. He gave evidence that he had reviewed all of the relevant records. He found no reference in the notes indicating that the patient was confused, restless or agitated. It was stated that from 4th to 7th September, 1990 she needed pain relief and was also treated for nausea. On 8th September there was a reference to drowsiness. The oral morphine medication referred to by Mr. Cunningham was commenced on that day. It involved a slow release of morphine every twelve hours. The dose was very small, i.e., 10 milligrams, until 24th September when it was doubled in strength, thus indicating that on 11th/12th September Mrs. Monaghan was probably tolerating pain quite well. It was recorded that on those dates "she settled and rested well". There was no mention of cognitive impairment. If that had been found the morphine dosage would have been withheld or reduced and this did not happen. The witness expressed the opinion that the effect of the morphine treatment on the crucial dates was likely to be that the patient would have felt much better than she had done previously. This might have encouraged her to believe or hope that she was making a recovery similar to that which had happened when in hospital two years earlier. There is no evidence that the deceased was ever told that her situation was terminal and it seems that her family were encouraging her to believe that she was getting better. The first time that the deceased indicated that she thought she was dying was when visited by her niece, Mrs. Sheila Monaghan, a week before she died when she said "Sheila, I'm dying. I'm on the way out. You know what to do. You have to go to Mr. Regan's office and they will tell you what to do". This was a reference to her solicitors.

In August, 1990 the first plaintiff was living in Dublin. She visited her grandaunt nearly every day and used to stay over with her mother at times. In the early stages she found the patient to be in good humour but in a lot of pain. She did not notice any particular change after the morphine treatment was commenced on 8th September. She described her grandaunt as being always good humoured. In course of a visit on 11th September Mrs. Monaghan asked her grandniece to go to her house where she would find a suitcase behind an old chair in her bedroom. She would find bank books in the suit case. She was to take them away and put them in a safe which the witness had at home in Dublin. The deceased knew about the safe as she had seen it at an earlier time when staying with her grandniece. Nothing more was said about the bank books by Mrs. Monaghan at that time. The first plaintiff obtained the keys of the deceased's house from her mother and duly found the suitcase in question where indicated. She found four bank books under clothes in the case and there was an elastic band around them. She brought them to her home and put them in the safe as instructed.

Mrs. Bentham returned to the hospital on the following day with the second plaintiff, her sister, Sarah and her mother. Mrs. Annie Monaghan was sitting up in bed and she enquired "Mary, did you do that for me? Did you put the bank books in a safe place?" Mrs. Bentham deposed that the deceased went on to say "If anything was to happen to her I was to keep the contents of the books and give Sarah a few bob out of it". Some weeks later after the death of the deceased the first plaintiff handed over the bank books to the solicitor, Mr. Higgins, the second defendant, and informed him of what had transpired between her and the deceased on 11th and 12th September.

The deceased made her last will with Mr. Higgins on 5th October, 1987. Having appointed the defendants as executors and trustees, she directed them to sell her lands at Shanco and Clowan, Bollivor, County Meath. Having provided for payment of her debts and funeral expenses she bequeathed nine cash legacies in various sums from £1,000 to £3,000. These included a bequest of £3,000 to Mrs. Sheila Monaghan; £1,000 to the first plaintiff and £2,000 to the second plaintiff to be invested by the trustees until such time as she attains the age of 21 years. The will contained a residuary clause providing for the division of the remainder of the estate equally between all of the named beneficiaries with the exception of one of them who was to receive only the £1,000 bequeathed to her in the will. In the event, the entire of the funds which the testatrix had on bank deposit has passed into residue.

The net issue on appeal is whether or not the transaction between the deceased and the first plaintiff regarding the four bank deposits amounted to a donatio mortis causa made by the deceased in favour of the plaintiffs. The total amount of the fund including interest presently exceeds £14,500.

There are three essentials for a gift of property to constitute a valid *donatio mortis causa*:

(i) It must be made in contemplation of the donor's death;

(ii) it must be made subject to the condition that it will only become indefeasible in the event of the donor's death; and

(iii) the property must be delivered to the donee. (See *Re Mulroy* [1924] 1 IR 98 per Moloney C.J. and *Equity & The Law of Trusts in the Republic of Ireland*, at pp. 368 et seq. 1st Edition, 1988 by Mr. Justice Ronan Keane).

The onus is on the party claiming the gift to satisfy the court that the foregoing requirements have been met.

Was the gift made by the donor in contemplation of her death? It seems to me that the facts fall short of establishing that proposition on the balance of probabilities. At the relevant time the donor was of great age and was terminally ill. However, I have substantial doubt as to whether she appreciated her situation on 11th/12th September, 1990 when the transaction took place. She had been grievously ill in hospital two years earlier but had made a substantial recovery. At the relevant time when the alleged gift was made, Annie Monaghan may have believed by reason of the morphine treatment which had commenced three days earlier that she was making a recovery. There is no doubt that she was concerned about the safety of her bank deposit books. She knew that her grandniece, the first plaintiff, had a wall safe in her home. It is evident she decided that the books should be secured there while she was in hospital. If it was her intention at that time to make a gift of the funds on deposit to the plaintiffs, it seems probable that either she would have made the gift to the first plaintiff on 11th September when she referred to the deposit books for the first time and asked her to put them in her safe at home. In fact on that occasion she did no more than arrange for the safe keeping of the books. It was not until the following day when the first plaintiff confirmed that she had carried out her greataunt's wishes that the latter said anything which might be construed as a *donatio mortis causa*. The alternative course which the deceased might have taken if she wished to make what amounted to a radical change as to the disposition of her property after death would have been to send for her solicitor and make an appropriate new will or codicil to give effect to her revised intentions. As a person who had always been careful about her affairs and who appears to have been compos mentis at the time, it seems improbable that she did not do so if that were her intention. It also seems strange that she should have decided to benefit the first plaintiff far out of proportion to all others, including her niece, Mrs. Sheila Monaghan, who it seems had been constantly devoted to her for very many years. Likewise, it is strange that her direction was that her godchild, the second plaintiff, should benefit to the extent of a nominal amount of the fund only.

All in all I am not satisfied that the deceased positively intended to make a radical change in the disposition of her property in contemplation of her death. Although that may have been her intention, the surrounding facts raise substantial doubt in that regard and in the circumstances I am obliged to hold that the plaintiffs have not established the validity of the alleged gift on the balance of probabilities."

Sen v. Headley
[1991] Ch 425

The deceased and the plaintiff lived together for ten years and remained on close terms thereafter. When the deceased was very ill he told the plaintiff that his house was hers and that the deeds to it were in a steel box to which she had the keys. He died intestate and the plaintiff claimed that he had made a valid gift to her in contemplation of death. The defendant, who was the deceased's nephew and the administrator of his estate, counterclaimed for the return of the deeds to the house. The Court of Appeal (Purchas, Nourse and Legatt LJJ) upheld the plaintiff's claim.

NOURSE LJ stated at pp. 431–441: "There have been several judicial statements of what, in general terms, is necessary to constitute a donatio mortis causa: *Cain v. Moon* [1896] 2 QB 283, 286 (Lord Russell of Killowen C.J.); *In* *re Craven's Estate* [1937] Ch 423, 426 (Farwell J.); and *Delgoffe v. Fader* [1939] Ch 922, 927 (Luxmoore L.J.). Regard must also be had to what was said by the court in *Birch v. Treasury Solicitor* [1951] Ch 298, the most authoritative of the modern decisions. If the question whether the subject matter is capable of passing by way of donatio mortis causa is put on one side, the three general requirements of such a gift may be stated very much as they are stated in *Snell's Equity*, 29th ed. (1990), pp. 380–383. First, the gift must be made in contemplation, although not necessarily in expectation, of impending death. Secondly, the gift must be made upon the condition that it is to be absolute and perfected only on the donor's death, being revocable until that event occurs and ineffective if it does not. Thirdly, there must be a delivery of the subject matter of the gift, or the essential indicia of title thereto, which amounts to a parting with dominion and not mere physical possession, over the subject matter of the gift.

The trial extended over three days in November 1989, with judgment being reserved. Mummery J. gave a very careful judgment. He found no difficulty in holding that the first and second requirements were satisfied on the evidence and that part of his decision has not been questioned. He said [1990] Ch 728, 736:

> "The real difficulty in this case is caused by the third requirement which raises acutely the question whether it can ever be complied with in the case of real property when all that has occurred is an informal delivery of title deeds, or the means of access to the title deeds, accompanied by oral words of gift."

It was largely because the judge, after a conscientious review of English and Commonwealth authorities and texts, was of the opinion that that difficulty had not been overcome that he dismissed the action. He also regarded it as an area where judicial caution and certainty of precedent were appropriate and as one where the policy of the law in regard to the formalities for the creation and transmission of interests in land should be upheld. Against the judge's decision Mrs. Sen has now appealed to this court.

Although donationes mortis causa were taken from the Roman law, it is only the first two requirements which now bear evidence of that ancestry. They are embodied in the definition given in the *Institutes of Justinian*, Book 11, Title VII: "Mortis causa donatio est, quae propter mortis fit suspicionem . . ." which was adopted by Lord Loughborough L.C. in *Tate v. Hilbert* (1793) 2 Ves Jun 111, 119. With regard to the third requirement, the judgment of Lord Hardwicke L.C. in the leading case of *Ward v. Turner* (1752) 2 Ves Sen 431 shows that the necessity for a delivery in every case and the acts sufficient for that purpose are developments of English law. Moreover, while Roman law allowed every form of property which could be bequeathed by will as a legacy to be the subject of a donatio mortis causa, including, it would seem, land whether free from mortgage or not (see the argument of Mr. Longley in *Duffield v. Elwes* (1827) 1 Bli (NS) 497, 514), Mr. Hodge, in his excellent argument on behalf of Mrs. Sen, correctly as we think, has not suggested that that is a reliable guide to the species of property which are capable of passing by way of such a gift in English law. We can therefore turn away from the Roman law and give our whole attention to the English authorities.

In *Snellgrove v. Baily* (1744) 3 Atk 213 a bond for £100 was given by one Spackman to Sarah Baily, who delivered it to the defendant, saying: "In case I die, it is yours, and then you have something." Sarah Baily having died, the administrator of her estate sued unsuccessfully to have the bond delivered up. Lord Hardwicke L.C. said, at p. 214:

> "I am satisfied upon the reason of the thing, and the cases which have been cited, that this is a sufficient donatio causa mortis to pass the equitable interest of this bond on the intestate's death. . . . You cannot sue at law without the bond; for though you may give evidence of a deed at law that is lost, yet you cannot of a bond, because you must make a profert of it."

In *Ward v. Turner* (1752) 2 Ves Sen 431, 442, Lord Hardwicke, in expressing the opinion that that decision was correct, enlarged on his reasoning in the case of a bond. He held, however, that there could not be a donatio mortis causa of South Sea annuities by delivery of receipts for the purchase money. There had to be a transfer "or something amounting to that." His decision was evidently influenced by the consideration that, had it been otherwise, "all the anxious provisions" of the Statute Of Frauds (sections 19 to 22 laying down strict formalities for a nuncupative will of personalty) "will signify nothing:" see p. 443.

In *Gardner v. Parker* (1818) 3 Madd 184 Leach V.-C. made a declaration that the donee of a bond by way of donatio mortis causa, on indemnifying the donor's executors, was at liberty to sue on the bond in their names. He said, at p. 185, that *Snellgrove v. Baily* had established "that there may be a donatio, mortis causa of a bond, though not of a simple contract debt, nor by the delivery of a mere symbol." Although it would have been more accurate to say that that proposition had been established by *Snellgrove v. Bailey* (1744) 3 Atk 213 and *Ward v. Turner* (1752) 2 Ves Sen 431 together, that was the state of the authorities on bonds when *Duffield v. Elwes* (1823) 1 Sim & St 239 came for decision at first instance, again before Leach V.-C.

In *Duffield v. Elwes* the donor was entitled to principal sums of £2,927 and £30,000 and interest thereon respectively, secured as to the first by a bond and a mortgage of freehold property and as to the second by a mortgage of freehold property alone. On the day before his death the donor, with the intention of giving the bond and the mortgages and the money secured by them to his only daughter, Mrs. Duffield, the other requirements for a donatio mortis causa being satisfied, delivered the bond and the mortgage deeds into her hands. Leach, V.-C., being of opinion that a mortgage security could not by law be given by way of donatio mortis causa, held that Mrs. Duffield was not entitled to the mortgage moneys, even in the case where the mortgage was accompanied by a bond. He considered the case of a bond to be an exception and not a rule.

Mrs. Duffield appealed to the House of Lords, 1 Bli (NS) 497. The argument was heard on 6 and 10 April and judgment was delivered on 29 June, by which time Lord Eldon had finally surrendered the great seal (1 May 1827). The judgment of the House was embodied in a single lenthy and at times repetitive speech of the Earl of Eldon. The appeal was allowed and the Vice-Chancellor's declaration discharged.

The speech of Lord Eldon must be examined with care. At p. 528 he referred to a conversation he had had with the Vice-Chancellor at the time of the hearing below, in which he had expressed very great doubt whether a mortgage could be made the subject of a donatio mortis causa. He then proceeded to criticise the premise of the Vice Chancellor's decision and stated what he thought was the question which had to be decided. This he did more than once and in somewhat differing terms. Thus he stated it to be, at p. 530:

> "whether after the death of the individual who made that gift, the executor is not to be considered a trustee for the donee, and whether on the other hand, if it be a gift affecting the real interest, – and I distinguish now between a security upon land and the land itself, – whether if it be a gift of such an interest in law, the heir-at-law of the testator is not by virtue of the operation of the trust, which is created not by indenture but a bequest arising from operation of law, a trustee for that donee."

Having referred to *Gardner v. Parker* (1818) 3 Madd 184 and *Snellgrove v. Baily* (1744) 3 Atk 213, Lord Eldon continued, 1 Bli (N.S.) 497, 535:

> "The real question in this case is not whether this was good as a donatio causa mortis, if the subject of delivery had been a bond alone, but whether the subject of delivery being mortgages, that is, estates in land in one sense of the word, such interests in land as those are can or cannot be made the subject of a donatio causa mortis?"

Between pp. 536 and 540 he considered two other decisions of Lord Hardwicke: *Richards v. Syms* (1740) Barn C 90 and *Hassell v. Tynte* (1756) Amb 318, in the first of which it had been held that if a mortgagee, with the intention of forgiving the mortgage debt, made a gift of the mortgage deed to the mortgagor there was a valid gift of the mortgage moneys which was not within the Statute of Frauds. A careful reading of the report suggests that although the mortgagee had died and the action for the recovery of the mortgage moneys was brought by his son and heir, it had in fact been a gift inter vivos. However, in *Hassell v. Tynte* Lord Hardwicke appears to have treated it as a donatio mortis causa, although he thought the case was "but a very slight precedent:" see Amb 318, 319-320. Lord Eldon the other hand, considered *Richards v. Syms* as a precedent of very considerable authority in a case such as *Duffield v. Elwes*: see 1 Bli (N.S.) 497, 538.

In *Richards v. Syms* (1740) Barn C 90, 92-93, Lord Hardwicke said:

"The Statute [of Frauds] indeed lays down a very strict but proper rule, relating to real estates, that no interest, any longer than for three years, shall pass in them without writing, nor any trust in them for a longer time, unless the trust arises by operation of law. The same rule, by that statute, relates to the devising of real estates. But in all these cases there is a difference, both in law and equity, between absolute estates in fee or for a term of years, and conditional estates for securing the payment of a sum of money. In the case of absolute estates it cannot be admitted of, that parol evidence of the gift of deeds shall convey the land itself. But where a mortgage is made of an estate, that is only considered as a security for money due, the land is the accident attending upon the other; and when the debt is discharged, the interest in the land follows of course. In law the interest in the land is thereby defeated and in equity a trust arises for the benefit of the mortgagor."

In *Duffield v. Elwes* (1827) 1 Bli (NS) 497, 539-540, this passage, other than the first two sentences, was cited by Lord Eldon, who interpolated that a trust of the land arose by operation of law when the debt was discharged and likewise when a deed was given.

Next Lord Eldon, at p. 541, cited with approval the judgment of Lord Mansfield C.J. in *Martin v. Mowlin* (1760) 2 Burr 969, where it was held that a specific legacy of a mortgage entitled the legatee both to the mortgage debt and to the mortgaged property. Lord Mansfield C.J. said, at p. 979:

"A mortgage is a charge upon the land: and whatever would give the money, will carry the estate in the land along with it, to every purpose. The estate in the land is the same thing as the money due upon it. It will be liable to debts: it will go to executors; it will pass by a will not made and executed with the solemnities required by the Statute of Frauds. The assignment of the debt, or forgiving it, will draw the land after it, as a consequence: nay, it would do it, though the debt were forgiven only by parol: for the right to the land would follow, notwithstanding the Statute of Frauds."

Finally, at 1 Bli (NS) 497, 542-543, Lord Eldon reverted to Lord Hardwicke's reasoning in the case of a bond. He observed that notwithstanding intermediate decisions which had brought about a change in the doctrine of profert, it was admitted that there could be a donatio mortis causa of the money secured by a bond by delivery of the bond. Having then said that in both cases, whether with or without the bond, the deeds had been delivered in such a way that the donor could never have got them back again, he concluded, at p. 543:

"Then the question is, whether, regard being had to what is the nature of a mortgage, contradistinguishing it from an estate in land, those circumstances do not as effectually give the property in the debt as if the debt was secured by a bond only? The opinion which I have formed is, that this is a good donatio mortis causa, raising by operation of law a trust; a trust which being raised by operation of law is not within the Statute of Frauds, but a trust which a court of equity will execute; and therefore, in my humble judgment, this declaration must be altered by stating that this lady, the daughter, is entitled to the benefit of these securities. . . ."

The essentials of Lord Eldon's reasoning in *Duffield v. Elwes* may be stated as follows. Accepting that money secured by a bond was capable of passing by way of a donatio mortis causa, he explained equity's insistence that the donor's executors should permit their names to be used by the donee in order to recover the money at law as a consequence of a trust to perfect the gift which arose by operation of law on the death of the donor. In reliance on *Richards v. Syms* (1760) Barn C 90 and *Martin v. Mowlin* (1760) 2 Burr 969, he extended that principle to a donatio mortis causa of money secured by a mortgage, holding that a like trust 'bound the mortgagee's conditional estate in the land in the hands of the heir at law, a trust which, because it arose by operation of law, was not within the Statute of Frauds. In reaching that position, he emphasised the ancillary status of the mortgagee's conditional estate, the mortgage being, in Lord Hardwicke's words, "only considered as a security for money due, the land is the accident attending upon the other," so that the discharge of the debt, in Lord Mansfield's words "will draw the land after it as a consequence."

Lord Eldon's emphasis of the distinction between the absolute estate of the mortgagor and the conditional estate of the mortgagee necessarily presupposed an opinion, in which the arguments of counsel for Mrs. Duffield had throughout concurred, that the absolute estate could not have passed by delivery of the title deeds. That opinion was based on the provisions of the Statute of Frauds, to which Lord Hardwicke had drawn attention in the clearest possible terms in *Richards v. Syms* (1740) 1 Barn C 90. But those provisions apart, it was not suggested that delivery of the title deeds would not have been a sufficient transfer of the underlying property, any the less than in the case of a bond or a mortgage.

Duffield v. Elwes (1827) 1 Bli (NS) 497 was followed without comment in *Wilkes v. Allington* [1931] 2 Ch 104. Although no other decision in England throws any real light on the question whether there can be a donatio mortis causa of land, there have been important develoments of the doctrine in regard to choses in action. Thus in *Moore v. Darton* (1851) 4 De G & Sm 517 Knight-Bruce V.-C., having expressed the opinion, never since doubted, that the Wills Act 1837 did not avoid such gifts, held that there had been a valid donatio mortis causa of a debt of £500 by delivery of a receipt signed by the debtor stating that the debt was to bear interest at a specified rate. A similar decision was given by this court in regard to a banker's deposit note in *In re Dillon* (1890) 44 Ch D 76, where the judgments of Cotton and Lindley L.JJ. contain useful statements of the effect of *Duffield v. Elwes*.

The sufficiency of delivery in the case of a chose in action was considered at length in the judgment of this court (Sir Raymond Evershed M.R., Asquith and Jenkins L.JJ.). in *Birch v. Treasury Solicitor* [1951] Ch 298, where it was held that there had been donationes mortis causa of the money standing in four accounts, by the delivery of a Post Office Savings Bank book and three other bank books of various descriptions. Three questions arose for decision, of which the first has no bearing on the present inquiry. The second, at pp.

304-306, was whether the delivery of the books had amounted to a parting with dominion over the money in the accounts. The third, at pp. 306-311, was whether the money in the accounts was capable of passing by way of a donatio mortis causa by delivery of the books.

The second question arose in this way. Three weeks after the delivery of the bank books and four days before her death the donor put her mark on a document requesting one of the banks to make a payment in settlement of an outstanding builder's bill, and to debit it to her deposit account with that bank. The arrangements for the transaction were made by one of the joint donees after the donor had said to her: "I would like you to pay this. . . ." The transaction was relied on as showing that the donor had not parted with dominion over the money in the accounts. But it was held that there had been no antecedent reservation by the donor of a right to deal with the money and that the precatory nature of the request which she had made to the joint donee to pay the bill was consistent with her having parted with dominion. At most there might have been a partial revocation, an effective donatio of the rest being either made or reaffirmed in an interview which took place later in the day on which the request for payment was signed.

The discussion of the third question was largely directed to dispelling the notion that it was necessary for the document delivered to express the terms on which the subject matter of the chose in action was held. This court held, following the opinion of Lord Hardwicke in *Ward v. Turner* (1752) 2 Ves Sen 431 that there had to be a transfer "or something amounting to that," that delivery must be made of "the essential indicia of title, possession or production of which entitles the possessor to the money or property purported to be given;" see [1951] Ch 298, 308 and 311.

It cannot be doubted that title deeds are the essential indicia of title to unregistered land. Moreover, on the facts found by the judge, there was here a constructive delivery of the title deeds of 56, Gordon Road equivalent to an actual handing of them by Mr. Hewett to Mrs. Sen. And it could not be suggested that Mr. Hewett did not part with dominion over *the deeds*. The two questions which remain to be decided are, first, whether Mr. Hewett parted with dominion over the house; secondly, if he did, whether land is capable of passing by way of a donatio mortis causa.

We have traced the need for there to be a parting with dominion over the subject matter of the gift, i.e. with the ability to control it, to the judgment of Lord Kenyon C.J. in *Hawkins v. Blewitt* (1798) 2 Esp 663, where he said:

> "In the case of a donatio mortis causa, possession must be immediately given. That has been done here; a delivery has taken place; but it is also necessary that by parting with the possession, the deceased should also part with the dominion over it. That has not been done here."

A similar view was taken in *Reddel v. Dobree* (1839) 10 Sim 244 and *In re Johnson* (1905) 92 LT 357. In each of those three cases the alleged donor delivered a locked box to the alleged donee and either retained or took back the key to it; in *Reddel v. Dobree* he also reserved and exercised a right to take back the box. In each of them it was held that the alleged donor had retained dominion over the box and that there been no donatio mortis causa.

It appears therefore that the need for there to be a parting with dominion was first identified in cases where the subject matter of the gift was a locked box and its contents. In *Birch v. Treasury Solicitor* [1951] Ch 298, as we have seen, a similar need was recognised where the subject matter of the gift was a chose in action. Without in any way questioning that need, we think it appropriate to observe that a parting with dominion over an intangible thing such as a chose in action is necessarily different from a parting with dominion over a tangible thing such as a locked box and its contents. We think that in the former case a parting with dominion over the essential indicia of title will *ex hypothesi* usually be enough.

Mummery J. found great difficulty in seeing how the delivery of the title deeds could ever amount to a parting with dominion over the land to the extent that the donor "has put it out of his power to alter the subject matter of the gift between the date of the gift and the date of his death." We respectfully think that that test, which was taken from the judgment of Farwell J. in *In re Craven's Estate* [1937] Ch 423, 427, was misunderstood by the judge. Having pointed out that Mr. Hewett retained until his death the entire legal and equitable interest in the house, he continued [1990] Ch 728, 742-743:

> "Without taking any action against Mrs. Sen to recover the title deeds from her, he was fully empowered as absolute owner to make a declaration of trust in respect of the house in favour of another person or to enter into a binding contract with another person for the sale of the house. The beneficiary under such a declaration of trust and the purchaser under such a contract would be entitled to an equitable interest in the house which would take priority over any claim that Mrs. Sen would have by way of donatio mortis causa on Mr. Hewett's death."

To that it must be answered that the same objection could be taken in the case of a chose in action. A donor of money secured by a bond or a mortgage who had delivered the bond or the mortgage deed to the donee could in like manner constitute himself a trustee of the benefit of his security for some third party or he could assign it for value. But it has never been suggested that the donor's continuing ability to take either of those steps amounts to a retention of dominion over the chose in action. We therefore respectfully disagree with the judge's view, if such it was, that a delivery of title deeds can never amount to a parting with dominion over the land. As appears from *Birch v. Treasury Solicitor* [1951] Ch 298, the question is one to be decided on the facts of the individual case.

We do not suggest that there might never be a state of facts where there was a parting with dominion over the essential indicia of title to a chose in action but nevertheless a retention of dominion over the chose itself. And it is just possible to conceive of someone, who in contemplation of impending death, had parted with dominion over the title deeds of his house to an alleged donee, nevertheless granting a tenancy of it to a third party; for which purpose proof of the title to the freehold by production of the deeds is not usually necessary. On facts such as those there might be a case for saying that the alleged donor had not parted with dominion over the house. But nothing comparable happened here. It is true that in the eyes of the law Mr. Hewett, by keeping his own set of keys to the house, retained possession of it. But the benefits which thereby accrued to him were wholly theoretical. He uttered the words of gift, without reservation, two days after his readmission to hospital, when he knew that he did not have long to live and when there could have been no practical possibility of his ever returning home. He had parted with dominion over the title deeds. Mrs. Sen had her own set of keys to the house and was in effective control of it. In all the circumstances of the case, we do not believe that the law requires us to hold that Mr. Hewett did not part with dominion over the house. We hold that he did.

Having now decided that the third of the general requirements for a donatio mortis causa was satisfied in this case, we come to the more general question whether land is capable of passing by way of such a gift. For this purpose we must return to *Duffield v. Elwes* (1827) 1 Bli (NS) 497. While that decision was supported by pronouncements from both Lord Hardwicke and Lord Mansfield, we believe that it was for its times creative, if not quite revolutionary. However much he might seek to depreciate the status of the mortgagee's conditional estate, Lord Eldon recognised that a decision in favour of Mrs. Duffield postulated its informal transmission from the heir at law, a transmission which could only be allowed if it gave no offence to the Statute of Frauds and one which he himself, so it seems, had started by thinking was on that ground impossible. The creativity consisted not so much in the articulation of the trust arising on the donor's death, a concept inherent in Lord Hardwicke's judgment in *Snellgrove v. Baily* (1744) 3 Atk 213, as in its designation as one arising by operation of law; an exception to the statute which was not as well developed then as it has since become. However hard it would have been for him to contemplate the prospect, Lord Eldon had pushed ajar a door which others at another time might open wider.

Section 7 of the Statute of Frauds 1677 provided that a declaration of trust of land should be void unless "manifested and proved by some writing signed by the party who is by law enabled to declare such trust or by his last will in writing . . ." Section 8 was in these terms:

"Provided always, that where any conveyance shall be made of any lands or tenements by which a trust or confidence shall or may arise or result by the implication or construction of law, or be transferred or extinguished by an act or operation of law, then and in every such case such trust or confidence shall be of the like force and effect as the same would have been if this statute had not been made; anything herein before contained to the contrary notwithstanding."

Lord Eldon referred to a donatio mortis causa "raising by operation of law a trust." If he had followed the particular wording of section 8, he would have described it as a trust arising by the implication or construction of law. Sections 7 and 8 were replaced by section 53(1)(b) and (2) respectively of the Law of Property Act 1925. Section 53(2) is in these terms: "This section does not affect the creation or operation of resulting, implied or constructive trusts."

We have said that the exception now embodied in section 53(2) was not as well developed in Lord Eldon's time as it has since become. Two particular developments may be mentioned. Mr. Hodge referred to the doctrine of proprietary estoppel, whose evolution in the form in which we now know it cannot be dated before *Dillwyn v. Llewelyn* (1862) 4 De GF & J 517. Where an application of that doctrine gives the promisee a right to call for a conveyance of the land no doubt it could be said, perhaps it has been said, that that right is the consequence of an implied or constructive trust which arises once all the requirements of the doctrine have been satisfied. Another modern development, one of much wider application, is the constructive trust which arises under the principles of *Gissing v. Gissing* [1971] AC 886. In general it may be said that the constructive trust has been a ready means of developing our property law in modern times and that the process is a continuing one.

Let it be agreed that the doctrine is anomalous. Anomalies do not justify anomalous exceptions. If due account is taken of the present state of the law in regard to mortgages and choses in action it is apparent that to make a distinction in the case of land would be to make just such an exception. A donatio mortis causa of land is neither more nor less anomalous than any other. Every such gift is a circumvention of the Wills Act 1837. Why should the additional statutory formalities for the creation and transmission of interests in land be regarded as some larger obstacle? The only step which has to be taken is to extend the application of the implied or constructive trust arising on the donor's death from the conditional to the absolute estate. Admittedly that is a step which the House of Lords would not have taken in *Duffield v. Elwes* (1827) 1 Bli (NS) 497, and, if the point had been a subject of decision, we would have loyally followed it in this court. But we cannot decide a case in 1991 as the House of Lords would have decided it, but did not decide it, in 1827. We must decide it according to the law as it stands today.

Has any sound reason been advanced for not making the necessary extension? Having carefully considered the reasons put forward by Mummery J. as elaborated in the argument of Mr. Leeming for the defendant, we do not think that there has. While we fully understand the judge's view that there was a special need for judicial caution at his level of decision, it is notable that the two previous authorities in this court, *In re Dillon* (1890) 44 Ch D 76 and *Birch v. Treasury Solicitor* [1951] Ch 298, have extended rather than restricted the application of the doctrine. Indeed we think that the latter decision may have put others of the earlier authorities on choses in action in some doubt. Moreover, certainty of precedent, while in general most desirable, is not of as great an importance in relation to a doctrine which is as infrequently invoked as this. Finally, while we certainly agree that the policy of the law in regard to the formalities for the creation and transmission of interests in land should be upheld; we have to acknowledge that that policy has been substantially modified by the developments to which we have referred.

Mummery J. also considered the Commonwealth authorities and the views expressed in the texts which have dealt with the question.We agree with him that the two Canadian cases do not really assist us. As for the two Australian decisions at first instance, *Watts v. Public Trustee* (1949) 50 SR (NSW) 130 and *Bayliss v. Public Trustee* (1988) 12 NSWLR 540, we observe that in neither of them does it appear that the arguments covered the full extent of the ground which has been covered in the present case. In particular, it seems that in neither was the inner significance of Lord Eldon's speech in *Duffield v. Elwes* (1827) 1 Bli (NS) 497 brought to the court's attention. Moreover, of the views expressed in the texts, none is based on anything more than the briefest discussion of the question. Most, although not quite all, subscribe to the assumption which has generally been made since Lord Eldon's time. There used to be, no doubt there still is, a maxim "communis error facit jus." But the error referred to is one of decision, not of assumption. Here we would say "communis sumptio non facit jus."

We hold that land is capable of passing by way of a donatio mortis causa and that the three general requirements for such a gift were satisfied in this case. We therefore allow Mrs. Sen's appeal."

3. Proprietary Estoppel

Where an imperfect gift has been made and the donor knowingly allows the donee to improve the property or act to his detriment in some manner, equity may compel the donor to perfect the gift even where the donee is a volunteer. This will be considered *infra* in Chapter 17.

THE POSITION OF A VOLUNTEER

As we have seen, once a trust is completely constituted it can be enforced by any beneficiary, even if he is a mere volunteer. However, where a trust is still incompletely constituted, it may be of crucial importance to determine whether the beneficiaries are volunteers or have given consideration. A beneficiary will be regarded as a volunteer unless he had provided valuable consideration in the sense recognised at common law or comes within the scope of a marriage consideration. What is referred to as 'good consideration' comprised of natural love and affection is not considered to be valuable consideration and will not suffice to make an incompletely constituted trust enforceable in equity. A settlement made before and in consideration of marriage is treated as being one for valuable consideration although a settlement made in consideration of a past marriage will not be so regarded.[12]

---

[12] *Re Greer* (1877) IR 11 Eq 502.

CHAPTER 7

Resulting Trusts

INTRODUCTION

Resulting trusts can be said to arise by implication and are traditionally described as being founded on the unexpressed but presumed intention of the settlor. Due to the informal manner in which they come into being, such trusts are exempt from the formalities required in relation to the creation of express trusts. Traditionally resulting trusts were classified into two categories, presumed and automatically resulting trusts, as outlined by Megarry J in *Re Vandervell's Trusts (No. 2)*[1] in the following terms:

(a) The first class of case is where the transfer to B is not made on any trust. If, of course, it appears from the transfer that B is intended to hold on certain trusts, that will be decisive, and the case is not within this category; and similarly if it appears that B is intended to take beneficially. But in other cases there is a rebuttable presumption that B holds on a resulting trust for A.... The presumption thus establishes both that B is to take on trust and also what that trust is. Such resulting trusts may be called 'presumed resulting trusts'.

(b) The second class of case is where the transfer to B is made on trusts which leave some or all of the beneficial interest undisposed of. Here B automatically holds on a resulting trust for A to the extent that the beneficial interest has not been carried to him or others. The resulting trust here does not depend on any intentions or presumptions, but is the automatic consequence of A's failure to dispose of what is vested in him.... Such resulting trusts may be called 'automatic resulting trusts'.

More recently the suggestion made by Megarry J that trusts in category (b) above, so called automatically resulting trusts, do not depend on any intention has been questioned,[2] and it has been suggested that all resulting trusts are based on the lack of intention to benefit the recipient.[3] In any event, it should be borne in mind that such trusts rarely reflect the actual intention of the transferor and may arise whether or not he intended to retain a beneficial interest.[4] While the classification suggested by Megarry J may have been

---

[1] [1974] Ch 269, 294.

[2] *Westdeutsche Landesbank Girozentrale v. Islington London Borough Council* [1996] AC 669, 708 *per* Lord Browne-Wilkinson.

[3] Chambers, *Resulting Trusts* (1997) p.3.

[4] *Air Jamaica v. Charlton* [1999] 1 WLR 1399, 1412 *per* Lord Millett.

questioned it still provides a useful vehicle for examining the various types of resulting trusts.

AUTOMATICALLY RESULTING TRUSTS

Failure of the Trust

Where an express trust fails completely for any reason, e.g. because it is void,[5] no beneficial interests have been declared[6] or due to a complete failure of beneficiaries, a resulting trust will arise in favour of the settlor or his estate.

Failure to Exhaust the Beneficial Interest

Similarly a resulting trust will arise where there has been an incomplete disposal of the beneficial interest. Where a trust is created in favour of a named individual to achieve a specific purpose e.g. for their education, the question arises whether he should be allowed to retain the remaining trust property once the stated purpose has been achieved or whether there should be a resulting trust in favour of the donor. It would appear from the case law that where the specified purposes can be regarded as merely constituting the testator's motive for making the gift, the donee will be permitted to retain the property, but this may be difficult to establish particularly where it is the donee's estate, rather than the donee personally, who stands to benefit.

Re Trusts of the Abbott Fund: Smith v. Abbott
[1900] 2 Ch 326

Contributions were made to a fund to be used for the maintenance of two distressed ladies, although no provision was made in relation to the disposal of the fund on the death of the survivor. Stirling J held that on her death the balance of the fund should be held on a resulting trust for the subscribers.

STIRLING J stated at pp.330–331: "The difficulty in this case arises from the fact that there is no declaration of trust. The case is one which not infrequently happens, as I have reason to believe. The late Dr. Fawcett, a gentleman well known in Cambridge, collected a sum of upwards of 248*l.* for the purpose of being applied for the relief of two ladies who were deaf and dumb. These two ladies had been provided by their father with ample means of livelihood, but had been deprived of it by the defalcations of a gentleman

---

[5] *Re Diplock* [1948] Ch 465; *Re Pugh's Will Trusts* [1967] 1 WLR 1262.
[6] *Vandervell v. IRC* [1967] 2 AC 291.

whom he had appointed a trustee. We have no information as to the terms on which this fund was handed over to Dr. Fawcett. After his death, which took place before 1891, the matter was taken up by a gentleman still living, the plaintiff Mr. Hamblin Smith. He issued a circular stating what had been done by Dr. Fawcett.

[His Lordship read the circular, and also the statement which had been made by Mr. Smith in answer to his Lordship's request for further information, and continued:–]

It seems to me, having regard to that statement, that I may treat the fund which was collected by Dr. Fawcett as really applicable to the same purposes, for that is the effect of it, as that which was subscribed in response to the circular issued by Mr. Smith. The ladies are both dead, and the question is whether, so far as this fund has not been applied for their benefit, there is a resulting trust of it for the subscribers. I cannot believe that it was ever intended to become the absolute property of the ladies so that they should be in a position to demand a transfer of it to themselves, or so that if they became bankrupt the trustee in the bankruptcy should be able to claim it. I believe it was intended that it should be administered by Mr. Smith, or the trustees who had been nominated in pursuance of the circular. I do not think the ladies ever became absolute owners of this fund. I think that the trustee or trustees were intended to have a wide discretion as to whether any, and if any what, part of the fund should be applied for the benefit of the ladies and how the application should be made. That view would not deprive them of all right in the fund, because if the trustees had not done their duty — if they either failed to exercise their discretion or exercised it improperly – the ladies might successfully have applied to the Court to have the fund administered according to the terms of the circular. In the result, therefore, there must be a declaration that there is a resulting trust of the moneys remaining unapplied for the benefit of the subscribers to the Abbott Fund."

Re Andrew's Trust: Carter v. Andrew
[1905] 2 Ch 48

A fund was subscribed to by the friends of a deceased clergyman for the education of his children. Kekewich J held that when their formal education was complete, no resulting trust of the remaining balance should arise and that it should instead be divided equally amongst the children.

KEKEWICH J stated at pp.50–54: "The Court is asked to determine how these shares and dividends ought to be dealt with, all the children being still alive and of full age. The summons is framed on the footing that the children are entitled to be recouped out of this fund the moneys spent on their maintenance and education out of what came to them under their father's will.

They were entitled to some fortune under that will, and apparently it was in part applied in their maintenance and education. If the proposed plan were adopted each child would take, not an equal share of the fund, but such a share as would represent the amount expended on his or her education out of the father's estate. If they are masters of the fund it can, of course, be done by agreement; but the Court is asked to decide whether that is right or not, and it is necessary that the point should be decided.

The proposed mode of division is supported by reference to the judgment of Page Wood V.-C. in *In re Sanderson's Trust* (1857) 3 K & J 497. There the property had been given by will to pay and apply the whole or any part of the rents, issues, and profits for and towards the maintenance, attendance, and comfort of John Sanderson, an imbecile, and as a matter of fact all that was necessary for his maintenance, attendance, and comfort was supplied out of the income of the trust property, so that no such question arose as is here suggested. But in the course of the argument the Vice-Chancellor inquired whether John Sanderson had been maintained in any way out of his own property, and in his judgment (3 K & J 508) he thus states his reason for his inquiry: "I think he had a clear right to have this fund applied for all purposes requisite for his maintenance, attendance, and comfort. If, therefore, he had been left to his own funds for his maintenance, attendance, and comfort, I apprehend there would have been a clear right on the part of his personal representatives to have that fund recouped. Part of the personal estate of the intestate, whom they represent, having been applied for his maintenance, attendance, and comfort, when another fund ought properly to have been applied for that purpose, they would have had a right to say, recoup the fund that has been so improperly applied out of the fund which was given for that specific purpose." I should certainly be disposed to follow without hesitation the dictum of the Vice-Chancellor if I saw my way to apply it; but I do not see my way, because the equity which is thus asserted could only arise as against a stranger, and unless I first decided that apart from such equity the fund belonged to other persons there would be no ground for it. Can the fund be said to belong to other persons? If there are any such they must be the original subscribers to the fund and their legal personal representatives. [His Lordship then referred to the evidence, and said that inasmuch as there was no satisfactory evidence that the defendant R. Barclay was a subscriber and he had not been appointed to represent the body of subscribers, he was unable to decide that the fund did or did not belong to them. His Lordship then continued:–]

I have been referred by counsel for the applicants to *In re Trusts of the Abbott Fund* [1900] 2 Ch 326, but it is absolutely different from the case now before the Court. There a fund had been raised for the maintenance and support of two distressed ladies, and on the death of the survivor there was still money in the hands of the trustees. Stirling J. held that there was a resulting trust of this balance for the subscribers. He did not think that the ladies ever became absolute owners of the fund, and probably no one reading the case is likely to differ from that conclusion. Here I am dealing with different facts, including the fact that the children are still alive, and I do not think myself much guided, and certainly not in the slightest degree bound, by the authority of that case.

It seems to me that the guiding principle is to be found in several authorities examined by Wood V.-C. in the case to which reference has already been made – *In re Sanderson's Trust* (1857) 3 K & J 497 – and the judgment of the Vice-Chancellor in that case. One passage may be usefully cited 3 K & J 503: "There are two classes of cases between which the general distinction is sufficiently clear, although the precise line of demarcation is occasionally somewhat difficult to ascertain. If a gross sum be given, or if the whole income of the property be given, and a special purpose be assigned for that gift, this Court always regards the gift as absolute, and the purpose merely as the motive of the gift, and therefore holds that the gift takes effect as to the whole sum or the whole income, as the case may be." Here the only specified object was the education of the children. But I deem myself entitled to construe "education" in the broadest possible sense, and not to consider the purpose exhausted because the children have attained such ages that education in the vulgar sense is no longer necessary. Even if it be construed in the narrower sense it is, in Wood V.-C.'s language, merely the motive of the gift, and the intention must be taken to have been to provide for the children in the manner (they all being then infants) most useful.

Therefore, subject to two remarks to be presently made, I am prepared to hold that the shares and accumulated dividends belong to the children, and the only remaining question is in what proportions do they take. The letter states that the fund was not subscribed for equal division, but was intended to defray the expenses of all as deemed necessary, and apparently the trustees of the fund exercised their discretion in dividing the money so far as it was divided at all. But there is no longer room for discretion, and I think the only safe course is to hold that the children are entitled to what remains in equal shares.

Subject again to two remarks, the costs must first be paid, and the residue will belong to the children equally.

[His Lordship then referred to the claim of the defendant Andrew to be recouped out of the moneys coming to the eldest son, and said that he was not in a position to decide upon the evidence as it then stood whether the claim was well founded. He also stated that he could not decide that there was no resulting trust for the subscribers of the moneys not hitherto applied for the benefit of the children without giving the subscribers an opportunity of arguing the point, and that for that purpose it was necessary that he should have one of the number before him, and that that one should be appointed to represent the class. He observed, further, that the presence of the trustee in bankruptcy of the child who had been adjudicated a bankrupt was necessary in order to enable him to decide what that child was entitled to. His Lordship, therefore, directed the summons to stand over in order that these matters might set right.]"

Re Osoba: Osoba v. Osoba
[1978] 1 WLR 791 (ChD) [1979] 1 WLR 247 (CA)

A testator left property to his widow on trust to be used for her maintenance and 'for the training of my daughter....up to university grade and for the maintenance of my aged mother'. The testator's mother predeceased him and his widow died some years later. When the daughter completed her university education the issue of whether the testator's children from a previous marriage could claim the residue on intestacy arose. Megarry VC held that the court would readily construe the expressions of purpose as merely indicating the motive for the gift and not as restricting the gift to those purposes and that the daughter and the personal representatives of the widow were beneficially entitled to the residue in equal shares. The Court of Appeal (Buckley, Goff and Eveleigh LJJ) agreed that the specified purposes should be merely regarded as an expression of the testator's motives but varied the order of Megarry VC to hold that the daughter was entitled to the whole of the residue as the only surviving joint tenant.

MEGARRY VC stated at pp.792–797: "This summons raises a number of questions on a short will. The testator made his will on June 24, 1960, and died on April 21, 1965. Apart from various visits abroad, and some five years from 1943 to 1948, when he was in Scotland training as an accountant, his whole life appears to have been spent in Nigeria; and on the evidence before me it seems reasonably clear that he died domiciled in Nigeria. He married twice. By his first wife he had a son and two daughters. That marriage ended in divorce in 1955, and he then married his second wife. She survived him, but died in 1970; and by her he had one child, a daughter. The plaintiff in the summons is the son of the first marriage. The first defendant, the testator's brother, is the sole surviving executor of the will. The second and third defendants are the personal representatives of the testator's widow. The fourth defendant is the testator's daughter by his second marriage. She is named Abiola. The first three defendants have been duly served but have taken no part in the proceedings. It proved impossible to serve the fourth defendant, and so the Official Solicitor was added as the fifth defendant, to represent her interests. Mr. Munby appeared on behalf of the Official Solicitor, and not only argued the case for the fourth defendant but also made helpful submissions on behalf of the other defendants who took no part in the case. Mr. Nock appeared for the plaintiff.

The will, though not a very skilful document, shows signs of having been professionally drafted. Clause 1 appoints executors, and clause 2 gives all the personal chattels to the widow. Omitting clauses 3 and 5 for the moment, clause 4 devises a house in Lagos to Abiola. Clause 6 reads as follows: "My wife to take care of my children by my first wife, namely, Patricia, Anthony and Elizabeth provided they are resident in Nigeria." That is all. It is in that setting that clauses 3 and 5 appear; and it is they that give rise to the difficulty. Clause 3 reads as follows:

> "I bequeath to my wife all rents from my leasehold properties known as nos. 7, 9 and 11 Custom Street, Lagos, for her maintenance and for the training of my daughter Abiola up to university grade and for the maintenance of my aged mother provided my wife is resident in Nigeria."

Then there is clause 5: "I bequeath and devise the residue of my personal and real property whatsoever and wheresoever to my wife upon trust to be used as in paragraph three above." The testator's mother, I should say, died in May 1963, and so predeceased the testator; and Abiola's university education came to an end in 1975. At his death the testator owned a house in London, 1, Avondale Avenue, Finchley, N.10. It was then worth some £5,500, but is now said to be worth between £15,000 and £20,000. It is that house which is the subject of the dispute before me. Mr. Nock contends that, subject to the three purposes imported into clause 5 from clause 3, the house is undisposed of and passes as on intestacy. If he is right on this, then there is a second question, namely whether under section 49 of the Administration of Estates Act 1925 the hotchpot ordained on a partial intestacy requires foreign assets to be brought into account, as Mr. Nock contends, or whether it is confined to English assets. On the other hand, Mr. Munby contends that clause 5 carried the English house as an absolute gift in equal shares between the widow and Abiola.

There is evidence of Nigerian law before me. It was common ground that the English house devolved according to English law, as being the lex situs and that in the construction of the will there was no material difference between English law and Nigerian law. It soon became plain that the only real contest was between a partial intestacy and equal division. A third possibility, based on *In re Foord* [1922] 2 Ch 519, was discussed in argument, but in the end was found impossible to sustain. That possibility was that clause 5 operated as a beneficial gift to the wife absolutely, with a limited trust to use part of the property for the specified purposes, and that, subject to that limited trust, the beneficial gift to the wife took effect. Mr. Munby strove manfully to put forward this contention for the benefit of the wife's personal representatives, but in the end he had to accept that he could not sustain it. In particular, the home-made will in *In re Foord* contained a gift to the testator's sister "absolutely . . . on trust" for certain purposes, whereas in the present case there is nothing to match the "absolutely," or to show in any way an initial beneficial gift to the wife. I therefore return to the two main contentions.

At the centre of the argument lay a well-known contrasting pair of cases, *In re Trusts of Abbott Fund* [1900] 2 Ch 326 (which I shall call "*In re Abbott*") and *In re Andrew's Trust* [1905] 2 Ch 48. Mr. Nock said that *In re Abbott* laid down the general rule and that *In re Andrew's Trust* stood on its own and was of limited application. Mr. Munby, on the other hand, said that *In re Andrew's Trust* was his sheet anchor, and that I should apply the principle contained in it. In *In re Abbott* a fund was raised for the maintenance and support of two deaf-and-dumb ladies; and Stirling J. held that the surplus left in the hands of the trustees after both ladies had died was held on a resulting trust for the subscribers, and did not belong to the estates of the two ladies. In *In re Andrew's Trust* a fund was subscribed for the infant children of a deceased clergyman. The only evidence of the objects of the fund was in a letter which showed that the money was collected "for or towards the education" of the children; and the letter also stated that the money was not intended for the exclusive use of any of the children, nor for equal division among them, but "as deemed necessary to defray the expenses of all, and that solely in the matter of education." After some but not all of the fund had been used for educating and maintaining the children, and after, it seems, their formal education had been completed, the ownership of the balance had to be decided. Kekewick J. distinguished *In re Abbott* and held that the children were entitled in equal shares. He treated the references to education as expressing merely the motive for the gift, as well as construing "education" in the "broadest possible sense" and as not being exhausted by the children reaching ages when "education in the vulgar sense is no longer necessary." Certainly no judge who daily listens to the submissions of counsel would regard his education as having ended. The case is a strong decision, in the sense that the children were held to be entitled despite the words in the letter which negatived any exclusive use or equal division and confined the use of the money solely to education.

With that, I return to the words of the will before me. I think that it is reasonably plain that clause 5 of the will imposed a trust on the wife. The words "upon trust " are clear, and the will is plainly drafted by someone who has some knowledge of law and of the meaning of legal expressions. I can see no reason for saying that these words do not mean what they say. The property to be held on trust is also plain enough: it is the whole of the testator's residue. I can see no grounds for cutting it down to only the income from the residue, as Mr. Nock contended at one stage. True, clause 3 deals only with income, and clause 5 incorporates at least part of clause 3; but that incorporation affects only the beneficial interest under the trust, and I can see no reason for letting it invade the delineation of the trust property and cut that down in any way.

The question, then, is that of the trusts on which the residue is to be held. The phrase "to be used as in paragraph 3 above" must define those trusts. I do not think that the first part of clause 3 is incorporated: that part merely states what property is to be used for the purposes stated. I think that Mr. Munby is right when he says that what is incorporated is the latter part of clause 3, beginning with the words "for her maintenance." The result is that the residue went to the testator's wife "upon trust to be used for her maintenance and for the training of my daughter Abiola up to university grade." I omit the concluding words relating to the maintenance of the testator's mother, since she predeceased the testator.

That, of course, leads to the central question, namely, the beneficial ownership of the residue today. The testator's wife is now dead, and Abiola's university education has finished. The residue can therefore no longer be used for any of the purposes specified in clause 5 by incorporation from clause 3. I have a formal, effective, will to construe, and not, as is *In re Abbott* and *In re Andrew's Trust*, a trust to be spelled out of informal documents. With the end of the specified purposes, ought I to hold that the residue of the beneficial interest remains undisposed of, and so passes as on intestacy, or ought I to hold that, despite the specifying of the purposes, and their determination, the widow and Abiola took the whole beneficial interest between them?

Now, there are plainly some relevant distinctions between the present case and *In re Abbott* and *In re Andrew's Trust*. First, the latter cases were both what I may call "subscription" cases. The money was suscribed by living well-wishers, and so at least some were likely to be still living and able to take when the trusts failed. Here, on the other hand, I have a residuary gift made by a testator, so that if the gift fails or there is a resulting trust, there is no question of anything reverting to the testator himself. I would not place any great weight on the so-called presumption against intestacy; but I would lean towards construing a testamentary gift of residue as being wholly effective and not as leaving some part of the property given to pass as on intestacy. Second, in *In re Abbott* and *In re Andrew's Trust*, as I have indicated, the terms on which the money had been subscribed were ill-defined, and had to be collected from informal documents. In such cases I think that the court has a somewhat greater liberty of action in producing a sensible result, in the sense that the court has greater room for drawing inferences in holding what the terms of the trust are. Where, as in the present case, the court has before it a formal and operative document such as a will, then the duty of the court is merely that of construing the words used, and there is less scope for drawing inferences.

On the contrast between the two authorities I should say this. In *In re Abbott* every possible purpose for which the trust existed was at an end. The trust was for the benefit of the two ladies, and once they were dead it became impossible to use the funds for their benefit. No subscriber, touched by their plight, could very well be expected to have intended any surplus to pass under the wills or intestacies of the ladies to people who might well be totally unknown to the subscribers. In *In re Andrew's Trust*, on the other hand, the objects of the benefaction were still living. The immediate need had been to provide for their education, and that is what had prompted the subscriptions. But quite apart from "education" having an extended meaning, it seems improbable that any subscriber would have recoiled from the thought of any of the money being used for the benefit of the children after their formal education had ceased. I think that you have to look at the persons intended to benefit, and be ready, if they still can benefit, to treat the stated method of benefit as merely indicating purpose, and, no doubt, as indicating the means of benefit which are to be in the forefront. In short, if a trust is constituted for the assistance of certain persons by certain stated means there is a sharp distinction between cases where the beneficiaries have died and cases where they are still living. If they are dead, the court is ready to hold that there is a resulting trust for the donors; for the major purpose of the trust, that of providing help and benefit for the beneficiaries, comes to an end when the beneficiaries are all dead and so are beyond earthly help, whether by the stated means or otherwise. But if the beneficiaries are still living, the major purpose of providing help and benefit for the beneficiaries can still be carried out even after the stated means have all been accomplished, and so the court will be ready to treat the stated means as being merely indicative and not restrictive.

That is the position where the court has to gather the terms of the trusts from informal documents. What I have to consider is whether the result is the same where the court has instead to construe a formal document such as the will in the present case. By a somewhat different process of reasoning I think that in essence the distinction is valid. The courts have long shown that they are ready in appropriate cases to construe a gift to a donee that is expressed to be for specified purposes as being an absolute gift, with the expression of purposes as a mere indication of motive, and not a restriction to those purposes. This approach may, I think, be detected at least as far back as the judgment of Lord Guilford L.K. in *Barlow v. Grant* (1684) 1 Vern 255; and it is expounded more explicitly by Page Wood V.-C. in *In re Sanderson's Trust* (1857) 3 K & J 497, 503-505. Both cases were decisions on wills. I merely add that I am speaking only of cases in which the stated purposes extend to the whole of the fund given. In cases where, for instance, the gift merely provides for part of the fund to be used for maintenance very different questions arise.

In the case before me the testator plainly intended to provide for his wife and daughter. The maintenance of his wife and the education of his daughter were obviously in the forefront of his mind; but plainly the overriding purpose was to provide for his immediate dependents. In those circumstances I should be reluctant to read his will as showing an intention that once his daughter's training up to university level was at an end she was to have nothing more, and there should be no further testamentary provision for her. I do not think that the words, relating to using the residue for Abiola's training and the maintenance of the widow show that any residue not required for these purposes was to be withheld from Abiola and the widow. If the trusts had been similar to those for the ladies in *In re Abbott*, I would not consider that the case was appropriate for treating the expression of purposes as a mere indication of motive. Inter vivos benevolence towards those in distress is very different from testamentary provision for one's immediate family.

It accordingly seems to me that the wife and daughter became entitled to the whole of the residue between them, and, to echo Kekewich J. in *In re Andrew's Trust* [1905] 2 Ch 48, 53, I think the only safe course is to hold that they became entitled in equal shares. It it true that the will does not treat them equally, to the extent that the maintenance of the wife might be expected to consume more of the residue than the training of Abiola would; but on the footing that these are more expressions of motive, I do not think that they can affect the quantum of interest taken. There does not have to be equality of motives for making equal gifts, and I can see no sufficient indication of any basis other than equality. I therefore hold that the second and third defendants, as personal representatives of the testator's second wife, are entitled to half the residue, and the fourth defendant, Abiola, to the other half.

That decision accordingly makes it unnecessary for me to decide the point on hotchpot on a partial intestacy. However, the point was argued, and I propose simply to say this. As at present advised I can see no rational ground upon which it could be said that under section 49 of the Administration of Estates Act 1925, as amended, only English property has to be brought into account. The wording of section 49(1) (aa) and (a) is in terms of "beneficial interests" and "property," and these expressions seem to me to be perfectly capable of embracing beneficial interests in property abroad as well as at home. Any other rule would also obviously be capable of producing most unfair results, whereas the object of the section is to produce fair results. In my judgment the hotchpot provision must apply wherever the property in question may be."

The Distribution of Surplus Funds on the Dissolution of Unincorporated Associations

Where surplus funds remain on the dissolution of an unincorporated association, some method of distributing these funds must be determined. The traditional solution was to find that a resulting trust arose in favour of those who had subscribed to the fund either amongst the surviving members in proportion to the amount contributed[7] or amongst all the members past and present in shares proportionate to their contributions.[8] More recent case law in England has tended to lay emphasis on the manner in which an association's assets are held prior to its dissolution. Where the funds are considered as being held on trust for the association's purposes and particularly where persons other than members have also contributed, this will usually give rise to a resulting trust in the event of dissolution,[9] or where the donor effectively disclaims it, the assets will go to the Crown as *bona vacantia.*[10]

The alternative solution is a contractual one which seems to have been favoured in this jurisdiction[11] and also to have been accepted in the majority

---

[7] *Re Printers and Transferrers Amalgamated Trades Protection Society* [1899] 2 Ch 184.
[8] *Re Trusts of Hobourn Aero Components Ltd's Air Raid Distress Fund* [1946] Ch 86.
[9] *West Sussex Constabulary's Widows Childrens & Benevolent (1930) Fund Trusts* [1971] Ch 1 in respect of the category of donations and legacies.
[10] *West Sussex Constabulary's Widows Childrens & Benevolent (1930) Fund Trusts* [1971] Ch 1 in respect of the category of the proceeds of raffles, sweepstakes and collection boxes.
[11] *Tierney v. Tough* [1914] 1 IR 142 and *Feeney v. MacManus* [1937] IR 23.

of more recent cases in England.[12] While it was held by O'Connor MR in *Tierney v. Tough*[13] that the remaining funds should be distributed amongst the members in proportion to the contributions they had made, the solution preferred by Johnston J in *Feeney v. MacManus*[14] was to distribute the fund in equal shares amongst the individuals who were members of the club at the time of its dissolution and the personal representatives of those who had died since that date. This principle of equal distribution seems to have also been generally accepted in England[15] and it is submitted that from a practical perspective, it is the preferred approach.

Tierney v. Tough
[1914] 1 IR 142

A society was established by a canal company for the benefit of its employees and both the employees, who were members of the society, and the company contributed to it. When it was resolved to wind up the society, it was held by O'Connor MR that there was no resulting trust in favour of the company and that the remaining funds should be divided amongst the existing members in proportion to the contributions which they had made.

O'CONNOR MR stated at pp. 150–157: "The plaintiffs in this action are members of a society which was instituted and maintained for the benefit of boatmen and workmen in the employment of the Grand Canal Company, and they are suing on behalf of themselves and all other members of the society. There are several defendants, the first six being private individuals who form the committee of the sooiety. There is also the Grand Canal Company, sued as a trustee for the society, and also the Attorney-General for Ireland.

The action has been occasioned by the suspension of the business of the society, which was brought about by the operation of the National Insurance Act, 1911. It has become necessary to wind up the affairs of the society, and to determine the claims which are now enforceable against the accumulated funds, which are claimed by the individual members, by the Attorney-General on behalf of the Crown, and, as to a certain proportion, by the Grand Canal Company.

---

[12] See e.g. *Re Bucks. Constabulary Widows' and Orphans' Fund Friendly Society (No. 2)* [1979] 1 WLR 936 and *Re GKN Bolts & Nuts Ltd (Automotive Division) Birmingham Works, Sports and Social Club* [1982] 1 WLR 774.

[13] [1914] 1 IR 142.

[14] [1937] IR 23.

[15] *Re Sick and Funeral Society of St John's Sunday School, Golcar* [1973] Ch 51, *Re Bucks. Constabulary Widows' and Orphans' Fund Friendly Society (No. 2)* [1979] 1 WLR 936 and *Re GKN Bolts & Nuts Ltd (Automotive Division) Birmingham Works, Sports and Social Club* [1982] 1 WLR 774.

The society is a voluntary one, and has not been registered or incorporated under any Act. It was brought into existence in the year 1878, under the auspices of the Grand Canal Company, whose directors were no doubt influenced by benevolence to their servants, as well as by the consideration that an insurance against sickness and death among their employees must redound to the benefit of employers.

A constitution was framed for the society at its foundation, but on the 19th January, 1891, the constitution was amended; and as the affairs of the society have since been carried on under this amended constitution, it will not be necessary, except in one respect, to go behind it.

The essential provisions of the constitution were as follows: – All boatmen and crews of steamers, and workmen under weekly wages at James's Street Harbour, were qualified as members. Each member was to pay 4*d*. per week, the Grand Canal Company contributing a weekly sum for each member. (Under the original constitution the company contributed a sum equal to the member's subscription, but this was altered.) Any member leaving the service of the company of his own accord, or dismissed from the employment of the company, or struck off the list by the committee as a defaulter, would have no claim on the society's fund on account of past contributions. Provisions were made for allowances during sickness according to a scale regulated by the period of sickness, and also for allowances called "mortality allowances," under which certain payments were to be made for the funeral expenses of a deceased member, or the wife or children of a member, or the father or mother of an unmarried member. There was also a provision for the payment of a gratuity to the widow, or mother, or caretaker of the children, of a deceased member. The management of the society was committed to a committee, three of whom were to be elected annually by the members of the society, and three of them to be officials of the company, and this committee was given the regulation of the affairs of the society, and the power to frame or amend the rules when requisite. It was further provided that the subscriptions to the fund should be lodged regularly to the credit of the society, and that the company were to be trustees for the society.

These were the main provisions, and there were none others which seem to me to require notice.

Now there are a few features of the constitution which call for observation, as bearing on the questions which are to be decided. In the first place, the members of the society were to be the boatmen, crews, and workmen at weekly wages, and none others. The Canal Company was not made a member. Its only office was to be that of a trustee; but it had three representatives on the committee. The contributions were to become the property of the society exclusively. This is shown by the description of the fund as "the fund of the society," and by the provision for the lodgment of the subscriptions to the credit of the society, that society being made up of certain individuals. Under the constitution which I have briefly sketched, the business of the society was carried on until the passing of the National Insurance Act, 1911. It is obvious that on the passing of that Act there was no purpose to be served by prolonging the existence of the society. The Act had made compulsory what had previously been done voluntarily by the members. If the voluntary payments were continued, both employers and employed would have been duplicating subscriptions for practically the same form of insurance.

It is not surprising then to learn that the members of the society determined not to continue their subscriptions, and in fact no subscriptions have been paid since the passing of the Act, and from that date all business has been suspended. This gave rise to several questions, which made the present action necessary. Are the several members of the society now entitled to have the funds of the society distributed among them, and, if so, in what proportions? Has the canal company any claim upon the funds? Has the title to the funds gone to the Crown as *bona vacantia*? Are the funds held upon trust for a charity, and is the trust to be administered *cy-pres*, the primary object of the charity having failed?

This is not the first case in which similar questions under somewhat similar circumstances have arisen.

Cunnack v. Edwards [1895] 1 Ch 489 was a case in which a society had been established to raise a fund by the subscriptions and forfeitures of its members to provide annuities for the widows of its deceased members. In 1848, E. became a member, and remained a member till 1879, when he died a widower. He was the last surviving member, and his personal representatives claimed to be entitled to the unexpended funds. This claim was disputed by the Attorney-General, who was a defendant in the action, and he claimed that a charitable trust affected the fund, and as the primary purpose failed, that the fund should be administered *cy-pres*, or, in the alternative, that the fund belonged to the Crown as *bona vacantia*. The personal representatives of one of the deceased members claimed on behalf of the class that there was a resulting trust in favour of all the members in proportion to their contributions and fines. The action was tried by Chitty, J., who decided that there was a resulting trust in favour of the members of the society from time to time, or their respective legal personal representatives, in shares in proportion to the amounts contributed by each member to the funds of the society. This decision was reversed by the Court of Appeal [1896] 2 Ch 679, which held that there was no resulting trust; that the society was not a charity; and therefore the unexpended fund was not applicable *cy-pres* to charitable purposes, and that the fund passed to the Crown as *bona vacantia*. The reason for the decision was that the entire beneficial interest of each contributor had been exhausted; that each man contributed a certain sum of money to a common fund upon a bargain that his widow, if he left one, was to receive a certain annuity, and beyond this he had no interest whatever in the fund. It was also held that there was no charitable trust, and that the only remaining alternative was that the funds were *bona vacantia*, and belonged to the Crown. I think that that case is very different from the present. Here the members of the society bargained for benefits for themselves, so that it cannot be said that they have no interest in the fund. The society, though it has ceased business, is not defunct in the sense that it has no members. There are many members in existence, and they constitute the society, to whom the unexpended fund belongs. It is, moreover, competent for the society, through its committee, to amend its constitution, and apply the funds in some way other than that which had been prescribed. If the constitution were now so altered by the committee as to provide for a division of the funds between the members, I do not see how anyone who is not a member, save possibly the Grand Canal Company, could interfere. I think that these considerations get rid of the claim of the Attorney-General on the fund as *bona vacantia*; and it is established that a society of the kind I am considering is not a charity. The remaining alternatives are that the fund belongs to the society, which is nothing more than an aggregation of individuals, or to them and to the Grand Canal Company. I will deal later on with the claim of the company.

The next case in the books is *In re Printers' and Transferrers' Amalgamated Trades Protection Society* [1899] 2 Ch 184. In that case the society was registered under the Trades Union Acts, 1871 and 1876, to raise funds by means of weekly contributions to defend and support its members in obtaining and maintaining reasonable remuneration for their labour – in other words, to provide for weekly payments during strikes or lock-outs. There was no provision made for the distribution of the funds on a dissolution of the society. The society was dissolved, and its unexpended funds amounted to £1,000. In this case the Attorney-General disclaimed all interest in the fund, and did not claim it as *bona vacantia*, and the mode of distribution was the only matter for settlement by the Court. Byrne, J., held that there was a resulting trust in favour of those who contributed to the fund, and that it was divisible among the members existing at the time of the dissolution. He distinguished the case from *Cunnack v. Edwards* [1899] 1 Ch 489 by the circumstances that there were there no existing members of the society, and that each contributor parted with his whole interest in his money in favour of a third party, retaining no interest for himself, whereas in the case before him each contributor paid his money for a contingent benefit for himself. That case is very like the present.

I confess, however, that though agreeing in the decision that the fund was divisible among the members of the society existing at the date of the dissolution, I do not think that it can be supported in its entirety by the reason given by the learned Judge, viz.: that there was a resulting trust. As I understand that doctrine, it applies only to a case where the trusts or purposes to which a fund or property is dedicated do not exhaust the whole interest, whereupon such part of the fund or property as is not required for carrying out the trusts or the purposes of the settlement results, or, in other words, goes back to the settlor. Now, this principle would give back to the existing members only so much of the fund as represented their own contributions to it. To this extent the property resulted to them in what I consider to be the proper meaning of the term. But the existing members got something more than what they themselves contributed. The accumulated fund represented more than their own contributions. It was made up in part of the contributions of past members, and, in so far as the existing members were declared entitled to such part, their title must have arisen in some other way than by the doctrine of resulting trust. A resulting trust would have given the fund, so far as subscribed by deceased members, to their personal representatives, and not to other parties. I say then, with great respect, I am not able to follow the reasoning of the learned Judge who decided the *Printers' and Transferrers' Case*. It is to be noted that in *Cunnack v. Edwards*, Chitty, J., who relied on the doctrine of resulting trust, 'held that the fund was divisible among the respective personal representatives of all the contributors. The conclusion which I have arrived at in the present case is, that the fund belongs to the existing members, and I think that the true reason is to be found in the fact that the accumulated fund is the property of the society, which is composed of individual members. The society is only the aggregation of those individuals, and the property of the former is the property of the latter. This is not a case in which all the members have disappeared, and their claims have been satisfied, or never arose, as in *Cunnack v. Edwards*. There are here existing members with unsatisfied claims against the fund. As I said before, and I think that this cannot be controverted, if the existing members, with the assent of their committee and their trustee, agreed to divide the fund among themselves, there is no person qualified to call them to account for so doing. The fund is a private one. On the authorities it is clear that there is no charitable trust attaching to it, and I think I have shown that the fund cannot be regarded as *bona vacantia*. The Attorney-General then has no claim.

The only other claim to be considered is that of the Grand Canal Company. They were contributors to the fund, and as such they contend that they are entitled to so much thereof as represents their contributions. The fact that they were contributors is not conclusive in their favour. The question is, did they contribute under such circumstances as to give them a legal interest in the fund, or were their contributions absolute gifts to the society? I think that all the facts point to absolute gifts. The company is not a member of the society. The fund was declared by the constitution, drawn up with the assent and approbation of the company, to be the property of the society. The company was also declared to be the trustee of the fund and, of course, a trustee for the sooiety. A trustee as such has no beneficial interest. There are only two circumstances which give the shadow of a claim for the company. One is that the maintenance of the society was for the benefit of the company, as well as for the workmen. In a sense, no doubt, it was, but only in the sense that the well-being of employees always redounds to the benefit of their employers. This is not a benefit in the legal sense.

The other circumstance is, that three of a committee of six, to whom the management of the fund was entrusted, should always be officials of the Canal Company. This, no doubt, gave the company an indirect control over the funds, but it was a control which should be exercised for the benefit of the society, for whom the Canal Company were trustees. It gave no beneficial interest to the trustees.

I am therefore of opinion that the fund is divisible amongst the members of the society who were in existence at the time when the business of the society ceased, and that the fund is divisible among such members and the personal representatives respectively of such of them as have since died; and, following the mode of distribution in the *Printers' and Transferrers' Case*, I will declare that the fund is distributable in proportion to the amounts contributed by the members aforesaid.

I will direct an inquiry who were the existing members at the time the business of the society ceased to be carried on, which, I think, it is convenient to fix as of the date of the passing of the insurance Act; who are the personal representatives (if any) of such of them as have since died; also an inquiry as to the respective amounts contributed by the members aforesaid, and, in case there should be any debts due by the society, an inquiry what claims (if any) there are against the funds by any persons other than members.

I will declare all parties entitled to their costs up to and including the trial, to be paid out of the fund, and reserve further costs."

Feeney v. MacManus
[1937] IR 23

See *supra* Chapter 2, p.32.

Re Bucks. Constabulary Widows' and Orphans' Fund Friendly Society (No. 2)
[1979] 1 WLR 936

A fund was established in a constabulary area to provide benefits to the widows and orphans of deceased police officers and for the relief of members of the force during sickness or ill-health. When this constabulary was amalgamated with others the members resolved to wind up the society and the issue of the proper distribution of its assets arose. Walton J held that the surplus funds should be distributed equally amongst the members of the association alive at the date of dissolution.

WALTON J stated at pp.943–953: "I turn now to the authorities. The first case is *Cunnack v. Edwards* [1895] 1 Ch 489, on appeal [1896] 2 Ch 679. It is I think necessary to deal with the facts and arguments put forward in that case with some little care. The association there in question was established in 1810 to raise a fund by the subscriptions, fines and forfeitures of its members to provide annuities for the widows of its deceased members. It was later registered under the Friendly Societies Act 1829. This Act was later repealed, but its material provisions remained in force with regard to societies registered thereunder. There was no provision in that Act corresponding to section 49(1) of the Act of 1896. Sections 3, 8 and 26 are material but I cannot improve on the summary thereof given by Rigby L.J. in the Court of Appeal, at pp. 687-689:

> "Section 3 makes it obligatory on every society established under the Act, before confirmation of the rules by justices as afterwards directed, to declare, by one or more of the rules to be confirmed, all and every the intents and purposes for which the society is intended to be established, and by such rules to direct all and every the uses and purposes to which the money which shall from time to time be subscribed, paid or given to or for the use or benefit of such society, or which shall arise therefrom, or in any wise shall belong to the society, shall be appropriated and applied, and in what circumstances any member of the society or other person shall become entitled to any part thereof. Section 8 provides for the rules, when confirmed, becoming binding on the members and officers of the society and the several contributories thereto. Section 26 provides for the dissolution of the society, and, among other things, that it shall not be lawful for the society, by any rule made on the dissolution or determination, to direct the division or distribution of any part of the stock or fund to or amongst the members, other than for carrying into effect the general intents and purposes of the society declared by them and confirmed by the justices. Section 39 provides that the Act is to extend to all friendly societies thereafter to be established, and also to societies already established as soon as they should think fit to conform to it."

The scheme of the Act of 1829 thus was that the rules must specify all the circumstances under which any member of the society might become entitled to any part of its assets and that on a dissolution the distribution of the assets had to conform to the general intents and purposes of the society. It is at once apparent why in that case an alteration of the rules was essential before any member could take any part of the assets, as, on their face, the rules were exclusively concerned with the provision of the relief of the widows of deceased members. There was no provision whatsoever relating to any members. In the course of time the society was reduced to two members, one an honorary member who was in fact the ultimate survivor but who had disclaimed any interest in the society's assets, the other an ordinary member who died and whose personal representative claimed the surplus of the assets of the society after provision had been made for the payment of the last annuity to the last widow. There was a claim that the society was a charity but with that claim we are not concerned. Now the argument for the personal representatives was first of all that the successive members of the society were entitled to its surplus assets and that the last survivor of the ordinary members was therefore entitled to them by survivorship. I have already noted that this argument is untenable because there is no idea in any such societies that they are simply tontines.

The next argument was that he could have held a meeting and voted the funds to himself. It was of course necessary to put the argument in this way because of the provisions of the Act of 1829 which I have read. It would not have been necessary in the case of an association which had not registered under the Act, but of course in any event the result would have been the same having regard to the tontine point. And finally as a last throw the argument was put forward that there was a resulting trust on the basis that every subscription made and fine paid by the deceased member was paid to create a trust in favour of the widows and to the extent to which this created a fund in excess of what was required the moneys resulted back to the members. In the court of first instance Chitty J. disposed of the first argument by taking the tontine point, of the second by saying that even if the last member could have held a meeting he never did, but he acceded to the third submission. He held that the members had in substance settled their subscriptions by way of trust. In my judgment the short answer to the contention put in this way ought to have been – as is pointed out in a later case – that the money was not paid to establish a trust but by way of contract so that no resulting trust came into the picture at all. In the Court of Appeal the only point argued apart from a question of charity was the third, the resulting trust point, and in my view Lord Halsbury L.C. did indeed decide against this point on the contractual basis, for he said, at p. 681:

> "Chitty J. has held that there is a resulting trust in favour of the personal representatives of those who contributed to the fund. I think we are all of opinion that that view cannot be maintained. The entire beneficial interest has been exhausted in respect of each contributor. It was, as I shall have to repeat in another view of the case, a perfectly businesslike arrangement: each man contributed a certain sum of money to a common fund upon the bargain that his widow was to receive, upon terms definitely settled, a certain annuity proportionate to the time during which the husband had contributed to the common fund. There never was and there never could be any interest remaining in the contributor other than the right that his wife, if she survived him, should become entitled to a widow's portion thus provided. This was the final and exhaustive destination of all the sums contributed to the common fund. Under these circumstances, I am at a loss to see what room there is for the contention that there is any resulting trust."

A.L. Smith L.J. took the same position. He said, at p. 683:

> "Each subscriber to this common fund (I am not now dealing with honorary members) did so upon the terms that if he left a widow the trustees of the society should out of that fund provide for her in the prescribed manner during her widowhood. If a member died leaving no widow, there was no resulting trust in favour of his personal representative upon his death; his subscriptions were not to be returned to them, but were to remain with the society and form part of its common fund. If a member left a widow she was to be provided for during her widowhood, and although the amount of subscriptions the member had paid might possibly not have been exhausted by making the contemplated provision

for his widow, nevertheless the surplus was not to be returned to his personal representatives when the widow died, but the whole beneficial interest in what was left also formed part of the common fund of the society. In neither case was there any resulting trust in favour of the representatives of the deceased member."

I think it is fair to say he also really took the contractual position and his last remark is of course completely justified having regard to the combination of the expressed objects of the society and section 26 of the Act. Rigby L.J. after, as I have already noticed, calling specific attention to the relevant provisions of the Act of 1829 concluded, at p. 689:

> "The members were not cestuis que trust of the funds or of any part thereof, but persons who, under contracts or quasi-contracts with the society, secured for valuable consideration certain contingent benefits for their widows which could be enforced by the widows in manner provided by the Acts. Any surplus would, according to the scheme of the rules, be properly used up (under appropriate amendments of the rules) either in payment of larger annuities or in reduction of contributions. It is true that no such alterations were made, and it is now too late so to distribute the funds; but I do not think that such omission can give to the contracting parties any benefit which they did not bargain for. The rules, which, according to the Act, are to state all the uses of the stock, contain no provision in favour of members. It is difficult to see why the personal representatives of deceased members should be entitled to any money produced by voluntary contributions, fines and forfeitures, but no doctrine of resulting trust would entitle them."

So a careful examination of that case reveals that the really crucial fact was that the rules were required to state all the uses applicable to the assets of the society and they stated none in favour of members. On dissolution section 26 governed, and, following on the absence of any provision in favour of members in the rules, the members were not entitled to any interest in the assets. Hence the inescapable conclusion that the surplus assets had no owner and must go to the Crown. At the risk of repetition, the combined effect of the rules and the Act of 1829 made it quite impossible for any argument to the effect that on dissolution the assets vested in the then members in some shares and proportions, which is the normal argument to be put forward in such a case. The case therefore did not decide that this was not the usual position in the case of an unincorporated association not then registered under the Friendly Societies Act 1829.

The next case to which I was referred was *In re Printers and Transferrers Amalgamated Trades Protection Society* [1899] 2 Ch 184. I am afraid that I get little assistance from that case. There, there was no claim by the Crown to the assets as bona vacantia, obviously correctly, but the distribution which was ordered was on the basis of a resulting trust apparently influenced by Chitty J.'s decision at first instance in the case just cited. With all respect to Byrne J, who decided that case, I do not think that the method of distribution employed could, in the light of the judgment in the Court of Appeal in *Cunnack v. Edwards* [1896] 2 Ch 679, ever have been correct.

The next case was *Braithwaite v. Attorney-General* [1909] 1 Ch 510. Although it is undeniably correct that no mention was made at any point in the case of the fact in express terms, the society there in question having been established as a friendly society in 1808 and actually registered under the Act of 1793, was, like the society in *Cunnack v. Edwards* [1896] 2 Ch 679, governed by the provisions of the Act of 1829. It is therefore hardly surprising that, after deciding the new point namely that the contributions of honorary members were absolute gifts to the society and could not be recovered, it was held that the benefited members, of whom there were just two surviving both drawing annuities, did not take the fund. This was a straight following of *Cunnack v. Edwards* on identical legislation. The rules made no further provision for benefited members and hence it is not to be wondered at that Swinfen Eady J. summed the matter up in three pithy paragraphs, at p. 520:

> "In the present case the two surviving benefited members are entitled to the annuities for which their contract of membership provides, but not to any other interest in the funds. The entire beneficial interest has been exhausted in respect of each deceased benefited member, and when the annuities to the two surviving members cease to be payable upon their respective deaths, they too will have exhausted all their beneficial interest in the funds. All possible claimants to the fund having now been disposed of, I decide that the surplus of the benefited members' fund and the children's fund belong to the Crown as bona vacantia."

The next case is one from Ireland, *Tierney v. Tough* [1914] 1 IR 142. O'Connor M.R. though concurring in the decision, criticised the reasoning in the *Printers'* case [1899] 2 Ch 184 along the lines which appeal to me and which I have already noted. It is true that he did not in any way allude to the statutory provisions which appear to me to have played so large a part in *Cunnack v. Edwards* [1896] 2 Ch 679, but the basis upon which he rested his decision is short, simple and wholly convincing. It must be borne in mind that this was simply the case of an unincorporated association. No question of the statutory provisions arose. O'Connor M.R. put it thus, at p. 155:

> "The conclusion which I have arrived at in the present case is, that the fund belongs to the existing members, and I think that the true reason is to be found in the fact that the accumulated fund is the property of the society, which is composed of individual members. The society is only the aggregation of those individuals, and the property of the former is the property of the latter. This is not a case in which all the members have disappeared, and their claims have been satisfied, or never arose, as in *Cunnack v. Edwards* [1896] 2 Ch 679. There are here existing members with unsatisfied claims against the fund. As I said before, and I think this cannot be controverted, if the existing members, with the assent of their committee and their trustee, agreed, to divide the fund among themselves, there is no person qualified to call them to account for so doing. The fund is a private one. On the authorities it is clear that there is no charitable trust attaching to it, and I think I have shown that the fund cannot be regarded as

bona vacantia. The Attorney-General then has no claim."

The next case was *In re Customs and Excise Officers' Mutual Guarantee Fund* [1917] 2 Ch 18. I do not consider that this case adds anything by way of theory to the matter. The fund there in question became wholly unnecessary as a result of changes in excise practice on December 31, 1914, when there were still members of the fund in existence and it was held to be distributable amongst the members then living accordingly. Although the decision in *In re St. Andrew's Allotment Association* [1969] 1 WLR 229 is fully in line with the analysis which I have made, I do not think it in fact adds anything thereto. In *In re William Denby & Sons Ltd. Sick and Benevolent Fund* [1971] 1 WLR 973, the main finding was that, as the substratum of the association had not gone, it continued, but Brightman J. said, at p: 978:

> "One matter is common ground. It is accepted by all counsel that a fund of this sort is founded in contract and not in trust. That is to say, the right of a member of the fund to receive benefits is a contractual right and the member ceases to have any interest in the fund if and when he has received the totality of the benefits to which he was contractually entitled. In other words, there is no possible claim by any member, founded on a resulting trust. I turn to the question whether the fund has already been dissolved or terminated so that its assets have already become distributable. If it has been dissolved or terminated, the members entitled to participate would prima facie be those persons who were members at the date of dissolution or termination . . ."

and he refers to the *Printers and Transferrers'* case [1899] 2 Ch 184; *In re Lead Co. Workmen's Fund Society* [1904] 2 Ch 196, 207 and *In re St. Andrew's Allotment Association* [1969] 1 WLR 229. Once again, this is fully in line with the principle of the cases as I see them.

Finally, although there is at any rate one later case, for the purpose of this review there comes a case which gives me great concern, *In re West Sussex Constabulary's Widows, Children and Benevolent (1930) Fund Trusts* [1971] Ch 1. The case is indeed easily distinguishable from the present case in that what was there under consideration was a simple unincorporated association and not a friendly society, so that the provisions of section 49(1) of the Act of 1896 do not apply. Otherwise the facts in that case present remarkable parallels to the facts in the present case. Goff J. decided that the surplus funds had become bona vacantia. The headnote of that case, so far as material, reads

> " Members of the West Sussex Constabulary subscribed to a fund for the purpose of granting allowances to widows and dependants of deceased members. Revenue was also derived from other sources including the proceeds of: (a) entertainments, raffles and sweepstakes; (b) collecting-boxes; (c) donations, including legacies. On January 1, 1968, the constabulary was amalgamated with other police forces. On June 7, 1968, a meeting of members resolved to amend the fund's rules enabling them to wind up the fund and distribute its assets under a scheme prescribed in the resolution. On a summons by the trustees for the court's approval

of the proposed method of dealing with the fund the court ruled that the meeting of June 7, 1968, was abortive for there were no members after December 31, 1967, capable of holding a meeting, amending the rules, or winding up the fund. On the question what in those circumstances was the destination of the fund:

Held, (1) that the fund could not, on the analogy of the members' club cases, belong to the members themselves since, as the rules stood, only third parties could benefit; that there could not be a resulting trust for members since their money had been put up on a contractual, and not a trust basis; that accordingly, their contributions, apart from any claim members might have in contract arising from frustration or total failure of consideration, were bona vacantia. *Cunnack v. Edwards* [1895] 1 Ch 489; [1896] 2 Ch 679, C.A. applied."

And the material parts of that judgment read, at pp. 8–10:

"First, it was submitted that the fund belongs exclusively and in equal shares to all those persons now living who were members on December 31, 1967, and the personal representatives of all the then members since deceased, to all of whom I will refer collectively as ' the surviving members.' That argument is based on the analogy of the members' club cases, and the decisions," in *In re Printers* [1899] 2 Ch 184, the *Lead Co.* case [1904] 2 Ch 196 and *Tierney v. Tough* [1914] 1 IR 142. "The ratio decidendi of the first two of those cases was that there was a resulting trust, but that would not give the whole fund to the surviving members, unless rule 10 of the fund's rules could somehow be made to carry to them the contributions of the former members despite the failure of the purposes of the fund (as was pointed out by O'Connor M.R. in *Tierney v. Tough,* at p. 155), and unless indeed the moneys raised from outside sources also could somehow be made to accrue to the surviving members. I agree with Ungoed-Thomas J. that the ratio decidendi of *Tierney v. Tough* [1914] 1 IR 142 is to be preferred: see *In re St. Andrew's Allotment Association* [1969] 1 WLR 229, 238. This brings one back to the principle of the members' clubs, and I cannot accept that as applicable for three reasons: First, it simply does not look like it; this was nothing but a pensions or dependent relatives' fund not at all akin to a club; secondly, in all the cases where the surviving members have taken, with the sole exception of *Tierney v. Tough,* the club society or organisation existed for the benefit of the members for the time being exclusively, whereas in the present case, as in *Cunnack v. Edwards* [1896] 2 Ch 679, only third parties could benefit. Moreover, in *Tierney v. Tough* [1914] 1 IR 142 the exception was minimal and discretionary and can, I think, fairly be disregarded. Finally, this very argument was advanced and rejected by Chitty J. in *Cunnack v. Edwards* at first instance [1895] 1 Ch 489, 496, and was abandoned on the hearing of the appeal. That judgment also disposes of the further argument that the surviving members of the fund had power to amend the rules under rule 14 and could therefore have reduced the fund into possession, and so ought to be treated as the owners of it or the persons for whose benefit it existed at the crucial moment. They had the power but they did not exercise it, and it is now too late. Then it was argued that there is a resulting trust, with several possible consequences. If this be the right view there must be a primary division of the fund into three parts, one representing contributions from former members, another contributions from the surviving members, and the third moneys raised from outside sources. The surviving members then take the second, and possibly by virtue of rule 10, the first also. That rule is as follows: ' Any member who voluntarily terminates his membership shall forfeit all claim against the fund, except in the case of a member transferring to a similar fund of another force, in which instance the contributions paid by the member to the West Sussex Constabulary's Widows, Children and Benevolent (1930) Fund may be paid into the fund of the force to which the member transfers.' Alternatively, the first part may belong to the past members on the footing that rule 10 is operative so long only as the fund is a going concern, or may be bona vacantia. The third is distributable in whole or in part between those who provided the money, or again in bona vacantia.

In my judgment the doctrine of resulting trust is clearly inapplicable to the contributions of both classes. Those persons who remained members until their deaths are in any event excluded because they have had all they contracted for, either because their widows and dependants have received or are in receipt of the prescribed benefits, or because they did not have a widow or dependants. In my view that is inherent in all the speeches in the Court of Appeal in *Cunnack v. Edwards* [1896] 2 Ch 679. Further, whatever the effect of the fund's rule 10 may be upon the contributions of those members who left prematurely, they and the surviving members alike are also in my judgment unable to claim under a resulting trust because they put up their money on a contractual basis and not one of trust: see *per* Harman J. in *In re Gillingham Bus Disaster Fund* [1958] Ch 300, 314. The only case which has given me difficulty on this aspect of the matter is *In re Hobourn Aero Components Ltd.'s Air Raid Distress Fund* [1946] Ch 86 where in somewhat similar circumstances it was held there was a resulting trust. The argument postulated, I think, the distinction between contract and trust but in another connection, namely, whether the fund was charitable: see pp. 89 and 90. There was in that case a resolution to wind up but that was not, at all events as expressed, the ratio decidendi: see *per* Cohen J. at p. 97, but, as Cohen J. observed, there was no argument for bona vacantia. Moreover, no rules or regulations were ever made and although in fact £1 per month was paid or saved for each member serving with the forces, there were no prescribed contractual benefits. In my judgment that case is therefore distinguishable.

Accordingly, in my judgment all the contributions of both classes are bona vacantia, but I must make a reservation. with respect to possible contractual rights. In *Cunnack v. Edwards* [1895] 1 Ch 489 and *Braithwaite v. Attorney-General* [1909] 1 Ch 510 all the members had received, or provision had been made for, all the contractual benefits. Here the matter has been cut short. Those persons who died whilst still in membership cannot, I conceive, have any rights because in their case the contract has been fully worked out, and on a contractual basis I would think that members who retired would be precluded from making any claim by rule 10, although that is perhaps more arguable. The surviving members, on the other hand, may well have a right in contract on the ground of frustration or total failure of consideration, and that right may embrace contributions made by past members, though I do not see how it could apply to moneys raised from outside sources. I have not, however, heard any argument based on contract and therefore the declarations I propose to make will be subject to the reservation which I will later formulate. This will not prevent those parts of the fund which are bona vacantia from being paid over to the Crown as it has offered to give a full indemnity to the trustees."

And Goff J. then turned to consider the destination of moneys from outside sources, with which of course I am not here concerned.

It will be observed that the first reason given by Goff J. for his decision is that he could not accept the principle of the members' clubs as applicable. This is a very interesting reason because it is flatly contrary to the successful argument of Mr. Ingle Joyce in the case Goff J. purported to follow, *Cunnack v. Edwards* [1895] 1 Ch 489, at p. 494 where he said

> "This society was nothing more than a club, in which the members had no transmissible interest: *In re James' Club* (1852) 2 DM & G 383, 387. Whatever the members, or even the surviving member, might have done while alive, when they died their interest in the assets of the club died with them."

And in the Court of Appeal [1896] 2 Ch 679 he used the arguments he had used below. If all that Goff J. meant was that the purposes of the fund before him were totally different from those of a members' club then of course one must agree, but if he meant to imply that there was some totally different principle of law applicable one must ask why that should be. His second reason is that in all the cases where the surviving members had taken, the organisation existed for the benefit of the members for the time being exclusively. This may be so, so far as actual decisions go, but what is the principle? Why are the members not in control, complete control, save as to any existing contractual rights, of the assets belonging to their organisation? One could understand the position being different if valid trusts had been declared of the assets in favour of third parties, for example charities, but that this was emphatically not the case was demonstrated by the fact that Goff J. recognised that the members could have altered the rules prior to dissolution and put the assets into their own pockets. If there was no obstacle to their doing this, it shows in my judgment quite clearly that the money was theirs all the time. Finally, he purports to follow *Cunnack v. Edwards* [1896] 2 Ch 679 and it will be seen from the analysis which I have already made of that case that it was extremely special in its facts, resting on a curious provision of the Act of 1829 which is no longer applicable. As I have already indicated, in the light of section 49(1) of the Act of 1896 the case before Goff J. is readily distinguishable, but I regret that, quite apart from that, I am wholly unable to square it with the relevant principles of law applicable.

The conclusion therefore is that, as on dissolution there were members of the society here in question in existence, its assets are held on trust for such members to the total exclusion of any claim on behalf of the Crown. The remaining question under this head which falls now to be argued is, of course, whether they are simply held per capita, or, as suggested in some of the cases, in proportion to the contributions made by each."

WALTON J: "The question has now arisen, consequent upon my previous decision that in fact the surplus funds of this friendly society belong to its members, first of all as to whether those surplus funds ought to be distributed basically between such members in equal shares, or, alternatively, in proportion to the subscriptions respectively paid by the persons who were the members of the friendly society at the date of the dissolution thereof.

I think that there is no doubt that, as a result of modern cases springing basically from the decision of O'Connor M.R. in *Tierney v. Tough* [1914] 1 IR 142 judicial opinion has been hardening and is now firmly set along the lines that the interests and rights of persons who are members of any type of unincorporated association are governed exclusively by contracts; that is to say the rights between themselves and their rights to any surplus assets. I say that to make it perfectly clear that I have not overlooked the fact that the assets of the society are usually vested in trustees on trust for the members. But that is quite a separate and distinct trust bearing no relation to the claims of the members inter se upon the surplus funds so held upon trust for their benefit.

That being the case, prima facie there can be no doubt at all but that the distribution is on the basis of equality, because, as between a number of people contractually interested in a fund, there is no other method of distribution if no other method is provided by the terms of the contract, and it is not for one moment suggested here that there is any other method of distribution provided by the contract. We are, of course, dealing here with a friendly society, but that really makes no difference to the principle. The friendly societies legislation does not incorporate the friendly society in any way and the only effect that it has is, as I pointed out in my previous judgment in this case, that there is a section which makes it crystal clear in the Friendly Societies Act 1896 that the assets are held upon trust for the members.

Now the fact that the prima facie rule is a matter of equality has been recently laid down, not of course for the first time, in two cases to which I need do no more than refer, *In re St. Andrew's Allotment Association* [1969] 1 WLR 229, a decision of Ungoed-Thomas J., and *In re Sick and Funeral Society of St. John's Sunday School, Golcar* [1973] Ch 51, a decision of Megarry J. Neither of those cases was, however, the case of a friendly society, and there are a number of previous decisions in connection with friendly societies, and, indeed, *Tierney v. Tough* [1914] 1 IR 142 itself is such a case, where the basis of distribution according to the subscriptions paid by the persons among whom the fund is to be distributed has been applied, and it has been suggested that perhaps those decisions are to be explained along the lines that a friendly society, or similar society, is thinking more of benefits to members, and that, thinking naturally of benefits to members, you think, on the other side of the coin, of subscriptions paid by members. But in my judgment that is not a satisfactory distinction of any description, because one is now dealing with what happens at the end of the life of the association; there are surplus funds, funds which have not been required to carry out the purposes of the association, and it does not seem to me it is a suitable method of distribution to say that one then looks to see what the purposes of the society were while the society was a going concern.

An ingenious argument has been put up by Mr. McCombe and Miss Jackson, who are ad idem on this particular point, which runs very simply as follows: the members of the society are entitled in equity to the surplus funds which are distributable among them, therefore they are to be distributed among them according to equitable principles and those principles should, like all equitable principles, be moulded to fit the circumstances of the case, and in one case it would therefore be equitable to distribute in equal shares, in another case it might be equitable to distribute in proportion to the subscriptions that they have paid, and I suppose that in another case it might be equitable to distribute according to the length of their respective feet, following a very well-known equitable precedent. Well, I completely deny the basic premise. The members are not entitled in equity to the fund, they are entitled at law. It is a matter, so far as the members are concerned, of pure contract, and, being a matter of pure contract, it is, in my judgment, as far as distribution is concerned, completely divorced from all questions of equitable doctrines. It is a matter of simple entitlement, and that entitlement, in my judgment, at this time of day must be, and can only be, in equal shares."

PRESUMED RESULTING TRUSTS

As a general principle, where the ownership of property is transferred to a grantee who gives no consideration, it is presumed that the grantee holds the property by way of a resulting trust for the grantor. However, this is only a presumption which can be rebutted by evidence that a contrary result was intended or by the presumption of advancement, which involves the inference being drawn that a gift of property was intended rather than that it should be held on a resulting trust because of the relationship between the parties.

Voluntary Conveyance or Transfer

Where the owner of property makes a voluntary transfer of it to another person, a presumption of a resulting trust arises unless there is sufficient evidence of a contrary intention to rebut the presumption or the presumption of advancement dictates otherwise. The presumption of a resulting trust in these circumstances applies both to voluntary conveyances and transfers of personal property.

Joint Deposit Accounts

One of the most common situations in which a transfer of property takes place into the joint names of the transferor and transferee is where a joint deposit account is opened. This is usually done in a manner which allows the transferor or depositor alone to retain dominion over the money in the account during his lifetime but in circumstances where it is his intention that the balance should go to the other party should he survive him. Where such an arrangement is put in place the question arises whether the money which remains in the account on the depositor's death should be subject to a resulting trust in favour of his estate or whether it can be paid over to the other party. It was held by the Supreme Court in *Owens v. Greene*[16] that the co-depositers had failed to rebut the presumption of a resulting trust in favour of the deceased's personal representatives. As a result of the reasoning employed, namely that a transaction of this nature should be regarded as an unsuccessful attempt to make a testamentary disposition otherwise than by will, the courts in this jurisdiction felt obliged to reach the same conclusion in such cases for many years. However, the alternative reasoning employed by the High Court of Australia in *Russell v. Scott*[17] which involved regarding both parties upon the opening of the account as being jointly entitled at common law to a chose in action consisting of their contractual right against the bank which would accrue to the survivor, avoided the difficulties inherent in regarding the transaction as a testamentary disposition, namely the need for compliance with the requisite statutory formalities. It became clear that the courts were increasingly reluctant to follow *Owens*[18] and finally in *Lynch v. Burke,*[19] the Supreme Court held that it had been wrongly decided and should be overruled.

Owens v. Greene
[1932] IR 225

The deceased kept sums of money on deposit in the joint names of himself and a nephew, and of himself and a distant relative. He retained control over these funds during his lifetime but made it clear that he wished the money to go to his co-depositors in the event of his death. Fitzgibbon J concluded that the plaintiffs had failed to establish any present intention on the part of the deceased to part with his property in, and absolute dominion over, the deposited money during his lifetime. The Supreme Court (Kennedy CJ, Fitzgibbon and Murnaghan JJ) held that these co-depositers, who were volunteers, had failed to rebut the presumption of a resulting trust in favour of the deceased's personal representatives.

---

[16] [1932] IR 225.

[17] (1936) 55 CLR 440.

[18] See e.g the decision of the High Court in *Lynch v. Burke* [1990] 1 IR 1 and *AIB Finance Ltd v. Sligo County Council* [1995] 1 ILRM 81.

[19] [1995] 2 IR 159.

KENNEDY CJ stated at pp.237–240: "The actions were tried by Mr. Justice Meredith who held that the plaintiffs had established their title to the respective sums in question and made declarations accordingly. The present appeals are taken by the defendant, the executor of Austin Freeley, against the judgment of Mr. Justice Meredith.

If, at the death of Austin Freeley, there were nothing more of information as to the several transactions than the records of the deposit accounts in the books of the Bank, a resulting trust would clearly arise by equitable presumption in favour of Austin Freeley and his legal personal representatives as to all the monies which were, on the 8th of September and the 15th of December, 1930, lodged to the deposit accounts in the names of Austin Freeley and Patrick Freeley and in the names of Austin Freeley and the Rev. M. J. Owens. There was no such relationship between Austin Freeley and Patrick Freeley or between Austin Freeley and the Rev. M.J. Owens as would raise a presumption of advancement to rebut the implication of a resulting trust. The onus of rebutting the implication of such a resulting trust by evidence rests upon the plaintiffs, Patrick Freeley and the Rev. M. J. Owens, who instituted these actions claiming to be beneficially entitled by survivorship to the monies standing to the accounts in which they were respectively named as joint creditors with Austin Freeley. They may discharge the onus which they have undertaken and rebut the presumption of a resulting trust by proving that it was the intention of Austin Freeley, when putting the monies to the deposit accounts in the Bank, to give to the plaintiffs respectively, then and there and by that act, a right, that is to say an immediate present right to take the monies with which he associated their respective names by survivorship (should they survive him), for their own respective use and benefit as surviving joint beneficial owners with him. It will not suffice to prove a merely testamentary intention on his part, for a testamentary disposition can be made only by will. It will not suffice to show an incomplete, or a conditional, or a postponed gift, nor can such an attempted gift be made good by means of a fictitious trust. But a gift completed by immediate transfer of legal ownership or by declaration of trust taking immediate effect will, if proved, support an intention to give a voluntary benefit and rebut the presumption of resulting trust. These principles (neatly summarised by FitzGibbon L.J. in *O'Flaherty v. Browne* [1907] 2 IR 416 at 434) are well established, and we have only to consider their application to the facts before us.

I should, however, say a word as to the form of the deposit receipts which is stated to be peculiar to Banks in Northern Ireland. The form of these receipts does not, in my opinion, determine the question under consideration. The intention of the depositor must still be ascertained. The use of the particular form may be part of a scheme of convenience in transacting the depositor's business, the other name in the receipt being that of an agent for the actual depositor, such an arrangement, for instance, as existed in the case of *Marshall v. Crutwell* (1875) LR 20 Eq 328. Again, it may be an attempt to give whatever may remain undrawn to credit of the account at the depositor's death as Gibson J. appears to have held in the Circuit case of *Diver v. McCrea* (1908) 42 ILTR 249. In such a case, however, the intention is not to make a joint deposit operating as a present gift. It is an attempt to make an ambulatory and postponed gift of such (if any) monies as shall remain undrawn from the account at the depositor's death, which, in my opinion, is contrary to the established principles inasmuch as it is really testamentary in character and intention, and for that reason I am unable to accept the decision in *Diver v. McCrea* which is, I think, erroneous. It was a Circuit case and the report shows that some of the authorities were not cited to the learned Judge (who, however, gave judgment in Dublin after consideration). Again, this form of deposit receipt may be used for the purpose of creating a machinery of revocation of the trusts of a gift on trust, continuing until revoked, as the late Master of the Rolls held in the case of *McDowell v. McNeilly* [1917] 1 IR 117, which, however, could not, in the nature of things, apply to the case of a gift immediately complete and absolute, but only to the case of a gift on a continuing trust.

Now, in the present case, we have it on the evidence of Mr. McNelis that it was on his advice that the particular form of deposit receipt was adopted by Austin Freeley as a form which would allow him personally, without the concurrence of the other persons named in the account, to get the interest on the deposits paid to him from time to time while leaving the capital untouched. When Austin Freeley made the lodgments to the joint account in March, 1927, he had not yet formed an intention of making a final settlement and there would have been a resulting trust in his favour. But if he had finally made up his mind, on the 8th of September, 1930, as to how he would dispose of his monies, it was, in my opinion, competent for him to have placed his monies on joint deposit accounts as he did, with the intention of making then and there immediate complete gifts in trust for himself and Patrick Freeley in the one case and in trust for himself and Father Owens in the other case, as joint tenants with right of survivorship as regards the capital sums only, the interest to be paid to him (Austin Freeley) during his life, such intention as regards the capital not to be capable of alteration. For effectuating such purpose, he might well have adopted the form of deposit receipt in question with the intention and for the purpose only of drawing the interest payable on the deposits and his use of the deposit receipts would be limited by that intention, notwithstanding their form ("accountable to them or either of them"), for it would follow from the complete gift of capital made that the other parties would have the right to intervene by proper proceedings to prevent him drawing, or at least appropriating to his own use, any part of the capital. Such, in my opinion, would be the only tenable basis upon which the plaintiffs could rest their claims in these actions. I suggested it to their counsel during the argument but, probably because of the concealment of the transactions by the old man from the plaintiffs, his close retention of the deposit receipts under his own sole dominion, certain weaknesses and uncertainties in the evidence of the Bank

Manager and of the plaintiffs themselves and no doubt for other good reasons in the case as they have it upon their instructions, the suggestion was not pursued, and the case of an immediate gift such as I have indicated as perhaps open to argument on the evidence was not put forward. On the contrary, counsel for the plaintiffs, who also definitely disclaimed any question of trust in the case, took their stand rather on the line of the judgment in *Diver v. McCrea*, and pressed the matter as one of a gift in each case of whatever, if anything, would remain to credit of the deposit accounts at the death of Austin Freeley, admitting that, in the meantime, by reason of the form of the deposit receipts, he might at any time withdraw all or any part of the capital monies for his own use or benefit. In my opinion, such a gift is an invalid gift as an attempt to make a testamentary disposition otherwise than by will.

Mr. Leonard relied on possession of the deposit receipts obtained after Austin Freeley's death, as making a complete legal title to the money. Even if the plaintiffs got the receipts properly (I question whether in the circumstances the receipts should not have been delivered to the executor of Austin Freeley at whose disposition they were held by the Bank Manager and whose voice directing that they be handed to the plaintiffs was silenced by death), the legal title cannot defeat the resulting trust in equity.

I am, therefore, of opinion that the plaintiffs have failed to rebut the resulting trusts and that the appeals must be allowed with costs to be paid by the plaintiffs. The declarations and judgments of Meredith J. in favour of the plaintiffs respectively must be set aside, and the actions dismissed and the defendant must have judgment on his counterclaim in each case with a declaration and consequential relief as prayed.

The defendant will have his costs of action as executor's costs out of the assets of Austin Freeley deceased. No order as to plaintiffs' costs of action."

Lynch v. Burke
[1995] 2 IR 159

The deceased opened a joint account in the names of herself and the first named defendant, her niece. The latter had travelled from Scotland at her aunt's request and both signed the necessary documentation for opening the account. All lodgments were made by the deceased and the account deposit book was endorsed payable to the deceased only or survivor. On the facts, O'Hanlon J held that the deceased had intended that the first named defendant would be entitled by right of survivorship to the beneficial interest in this money and the equitable presumption in favour of the deceased's estate was therefore rebutted. However, he felt obliged on the authority of the *Owens* decision to hold that the transaction was an invalid gift and an unsuccessful attempt to make a testamentary disposition otherwise than by will. The deceased had bequeathed all her property to the plaintiff and O'Hanlon J held that a resulting trust arose and that therefore the plaintiff was entitled to the money remaining in the joint account. The Supreme Court (Hamilton CJ, O'Flaherty, Egan, Blayney and Denham JJ) allowed the appeal of the first named defendant. O'Flaherty J considered that by her presence and signature, it was manifest that the first named defendant was a party to the contract from the outset and she must be entitled to claim as a party to the contract under its terms. He held that the defendant had a legal interest in the monies on deposit either by reason of the contractual relationship of the parties or in the alternative as a gift, which should be upheld as being a gift subject to a contingency namely, the donor's death.

O'FLAHERTY J stated at pp. 162–168: "This is an appeal brought by Moira Burke from the judgment and order of the High Court (O'Hanlon J.) of the 16th January, 1990 (See [1990] 1 IR 1) granting the plaintiff declarations in her favour in respect of monies held on a deposit account with AIB Bank plc in the joint names of Frances McFadden, deceased, and her niece, the first defendant, Moira Burke.

Frances McFadden, a widow, died on the 10th January, 1986. She had made her last will on the 20th July, 1983, whereby she gave all the property of which she died possessed or entitled to to her sister, Mary Lynch, the plaintiff; she also appointed her sole executrix.

Moira Burke had a sad life. She lost her father when young. Her mother re-married. She migrated to Glasgow in 1971 when she was 17 and stayed for about two years with her aunt, Frances McFadden. She married in 1975 but the marriage broke up in 1976. After the marriage break-up, the husband ceased to make maintenance payments after some short time and, during these hard times, it appears that Frances McFadden had been generous to her.

In September, 1983, Frances McFadden (who at that time had returned to live in County Donegal) visited Moira Burke in Glasgow and told her that she wanted to put her name into a joint account with a bank in Falcarragh, Co. Donegal. On the 28th September, 1983, a deposit account was opened with the Falcarragh branch of the AIB Bank in the joint names of Frances McFadden and Moira Burke. A sum of £29,401.72 was lodged to the credit of the account by Frances McFadden and, thereafter, there were further lodgments made from time to time by Frances McFadden. At the date of trial the amount standing to the credit of the account was £53,364. At the hearing of the appeal we were told that the amount had now risen to about £65,000, including accumulated interest.

The deposit book was endorsed by the bank official as follows: "Payable to Frances McFadden only or survivor". The word "only" was underlined. Moira Burke's address in Glasgow was inserted beneath Frances McFadden's name though, as already stated, Mrs. McFadden lived in Co. Donegal at this time.

The learned trial judge said that he was satisfied that Frances McFadden, when opening the account in the joint names, intended that her niece, Moira Burke, should be entitled to the beneficial interest in any monies standing to the credit of the account on Frances McFadden's death, should she pre-decease her niece. He was further satisfied that Frances McFadden intended to retain control over the account during her lifetime to the extent that no withdrawals could be made from it save only on her application.

The judge also attached some significance to the fact that Frances McFadden, two months before she opened the joint deposit account, had made her last will and he was of the opinion that the opening of the joint deposit account was intended to exclude any claim by the plaintiff to those monies remaining on deposit in the account at the time of her death.

Notwithstanding these findings, the judge felt constrained on the authority of the decision of the former Supreme Court in *Owens v. Greene and Freeley v. Greene* [1932] IR 225 to hold that Moira Burke was not entitled by survivorship to these monies.

The question for resolution on this appeal is whether that result can be upheld as one that is justified in law or equity?

The first inquiry to make is to find out the legal effect of the opening of the deposit account in the joint names. Thereby, the bank undoubtedly became a debtor to Frances McFadden in the amount lodged. The bank and Frances McFadden contracted that only Frances McFadden could make withdrawals from the account but that on her death Moira Burke would be entitled to the monies standing to the credit of the account on that date. By her presence (she had journeyed especially from Glasgow to Falcarragh for the occasion, at Mrs. McFadden's request) and signature it is manifest that Moira Burke was a party to this contract from the outset. It is agreed on all sides that if the bank had paid over the monies then in the account of Moira Burke on Frances McFadden's death, it could incur no liability to the estate of the deceased. However, it is contended for the plaintiff that in that situation Moira Burke would have to account to the estate for the monies so received. The monies on deposit with the bank represent a debt or chose in action. Since Frances McFadden and Moira Burke contracted jointly with the bank it would seem right that the bank should be liable to both – in accordance with the terms of the contract. There was sufficient mutuality of interest between Frances McFadden and Moira Burke to justify this assessment of the legal situation.

Mr. McCann's essential submission before us is to leave aside any question of contract. He instead submits that what we are concerned with is that this chose in action or debt could not be gifted to Moira Burke except by a declaration of trust, a completed gift or by will.

He says that there has been no declaration of trust and he says that what we have here is an imperfect or incomplete transaction. Equity, it has been said, will not come to the aid of a volunteer to perfect an imperfect gift.

In this regard, we do well to recall something that Barry L.J. said in *Gason v. Rich* (1887) 19 LR Ir 391 at p. 402, a case relied upon as one which, together with *O'Flaherty v. Browne* [1907] 2 IR 416, is said to provide a basis for the decision in *Owens v. Greene and Freeley v. Greene* [1932] IR 225:

> "This question as to what does, or does not, constitute a complete voluntary gift of property so as to be supported in a Court of Equity has been the subject of discussion over and over again almost for a century, and the decisions upon it are very numerous, and not very easy to reconcile with each other, and it is difficult to extract any principle from them. It is impossible not to feel that legal ingenuity is far oftener exercised in defeating the intention of parties than in supporting them."

Leaving aside for the moment the concept of a gift, I think that it is best to consider, in the first instance, the contractual aspects of the case to find whether that provides a solution. In my judgment, it does. I have outlined what I think was agreed between the parties and it amounts to this: Moira Burke must be regarded as entitled to claim as a party to the contract under the actual terms of the contract.

In *McEvoy v. The Belfast Banking Company* [1935] AC 24 the House of Lords was concerned with a case which had many similarities to the instant case. The ultimate decision turned on whether the donee could claim money that he had, after the donor's death, assisted in appropriating to a business that failed – that aspect of the case need not detain us. However, Lord Atkin had the following of interest to say in the course of his speech relating to the form of contract that emerges when a deposit account is opened in joint names. He said, at p. 43:

> "The suggestion is that where A deposits a sum of money with his bank in the names of A and B, payable to A or B, if B comes to the bank with the deposit receipt he has no right to demand the money from the bank or to sue them if his demand is refused. The bank is entitled to demand proof that the money was in fact partly B's, or possibly that A had acted with B's actual authority. For the contract, it is said, is between the bank and A alone. My Lords, to say this is to ignore the vital difference between a contract purporting to be made by A with the bank to pay A or B and a contract purporting to be made by A and B with the bank to pay A or B. In both cases of course payment to B would discharge the bank whether the bank contracted with A alone or with A and B. But the question is whether in the case put B has any rights against the bank if payment to him is refused. I have myself no doubt that in such a case B can sue the bank. The contract on the face of it purports to be made with A and B, and I think with them jointly and severally. A purports to make the contract on behalf of B as well as himself and the consideration supports such a contract. If A has actual authority from B to make such a contract, B is a party to the contract *ab initio*. If he has not actual authority then subject to the ordinary principles of ratification B can ratify the contract purporting to have been made on his behalf and his ratification relates back to the original formation of the contract. If no events had happened to preclude B from ratifying, then on compliance with the contract conditions, including notice and production of the deposit receipt, B would have the right to demand from the bank so much of the money as was due on the

deposit account."

In this case, as I have pointed out, Moira Burke was a party to the contract from the outset.

In *Russell v. Scott* (1936) 55 CLR 440, the High Court of Australia was called upon to deal with a problem that I think is almost identical to the one presented to us. The question posed in that case was as follows:-

". . . whether the survivor of two persons opening a joint bank account is beneficially entitled to the balance standing at credit when the other dies, if all the moneys paid in have been provided by the deceased acting with the intention of conferring a beneficial interest upon the survivor in the balance left at his or her death but not otherwise, and of retaining in the meantime the right to use in any manner the moneys deposited."

Dixon and Evatt JJ in the course of a joint judgment said the following by way of answer:

"The contract between the bank and the customers constituted them joint creditor. They had, of course, no right of property in any of the moneys deposited with the bank. The relation between the bank and its customers is that of debtor and creditor. The aunt and the nephew upon opening the joint account became jointly entitled at common law to a chose in action. The chose in action consisted in the contractual right against the bank, i.e., in a debt, but a debt fluctuating in amount as moneys might be deposited and withdrawn. At common law this chose in action passed or accrued to the survivor . . .

The right at law to the balance standing at the credit of the account on the death of the aunt was thus vested in the nephew. The claim that it forms part of her estate must depend upon equity. It must depend upon the existence of an equitable obligation making him a trustee for the estate. What makes him a trustee of the legal right which survives to him? It is true a presumption that he is a trustee is raised by the fact of his aunt's supplying the money that gave the legal right a value. As the relationship between them was not such as to raise a presumption of advancement, prima facie there is a resulting trust. But that is a mere question of onus of proof. The presumption of resulting trust does no more than call for proof of an intention to confer beneficial ownership; and in the present case satisfactory proof is forthcoming that one purpose of the transaction was to confer upon the nephew the beneficial ownership of the sum standing at the credit of the account when the aunt died. As a legal right exists in him to this sum of money, what equity is there defeating her intention that he should enjoy the legal right beneficially?"

The answer the court gave was that there was none and distinguished *Owens v. Greene and Freeley v. Greene* [1932] IR 225, and certain Canadian cases in reaching this conclusion.

The case as pleaded and apparently presented in the High Court on the plaintiff's behalf was to say that the monies on deposit were held on an implied or resulting trust by Moira Burke for the benefit of the estate of the deceased. As already pointed out, the learned trial judge felt that he was constrained by the decision in *Owens v. Greene and Freeley v. Greene* [1932] IR 225, to uphold this submission.

Since historically the concept of an implied or resulting trust was an invention of equity to defeat the misappropriation of property as a consequence of potentially fraudulent or improvident transactions, it would surely be paradoxical if the doctrine is allowed to be invoked to defeat the clear intention of the donor as found by the trial judge, an intention so clear, as the Chief Justice observed in the course of the debate before us, that he could not possibly have made any other finding as regards the donor's intention than the one that he did make. In this regard it is apposite to recall what Lindley L.J. said in *Standing v. Bowring* (1886) 31 Ch D 282 at 289:

> "Trusts are neither created nor implied by law to defeat the intentions of donors or settlors; they are created or implied or are held to result in favour of donors or settlors in order to carry out and give effect to their true intentions, expressed or implied. It appears to me there are no equitable as distinguished from legal grounds on which the plaintiff can obtain relief."

As to *Owens v. Greene and Freeley v. Greene* [1932] IR 225, the requirement that that case seems to lay down for a donee to benefit, is that the deposit receipt is a joint one and that it is payable to the parties or the survivor thus putting it out of the depositor's power to deal with the fund without the concurrence of his co-owner during his lifetime. This certainly appears from the judgment of Fitzgibbon J. at pp. 245 and 246 of the report. This concept appears to be implicit, also, in the judgment of Kennedy C.J. (the relevant passage is quoted at length by the learned trial judge); or, at the least, that the donee should be entitled equally with the donor to resort to the funds during the joint lives. The judgments were also concerned to emphasise the importance in the legal scheme of things that testamentary dispositions should be required to comply with the relevant statutory requirements. Of course, if one were dealing with a testamentary disposition there would have to be compliance with the relevant requirements of the legislation in question. But that is to beg the question; if the arrangement made was not testamentary (which in my judgment it was not) then the legislative provisions (see Part VIII of the Succession Act, 1965) have no application.

Towards the end of his submissions, Mr. McCann, no doubt in the light of the trial judge's finding about the donor's intentions, came to submit that his client's claim rested in law and to say that the case was not concerned with a trust, express or implied. He says the situation is simply that the monies on deposit belonged to the estate of the deceased. However, I believe that at law the niece had a legal interest in the monies on deposit either by reason of the contractual relationship of the parties or, in the alternative, as a gift which admittedly was not a completed gift in the conventional sense but is nonetheless one that should be upheld as being a gift subject to a contingency *viz.* that of the death of the donor which contingency does not disqualify it as being a proper gift.

It seems to me that *Owens v. Greene and Freeley v. Greene* [1932] IR 255, gives cause for unease on a number of grounds. In the first place, the judgments contain a number of severe criticisms of witnesses in the case which sound strange to us since we are accustomed to holding that matters of primary fact are exclusively for the trial judge and even in regard to inferences of fact respect must always be afforded to the trial judge's finding. (*Hay v. O'Grady* [1992] 1 IR 210). But since no report of the judgment of the trial judge (Meredith J.) is existant, we do not know what findings of fact he made. Further, criticisms are made in the course of the judgments concerning counsel's submissions which are difficult to square with the manner in which the case was pleaded and, indeed, the account of the argument put forward for the donees as it appears in the report. The case pleaded was that the deceased declared that the monies on deposit were to belong beneficially to the plaintiff in the event of the death of the deceased and would not in that event form any part of his estate. The argument apparently presented to the Court was that the sole question was whether the trial judge was justified in finding as a fact, as he did find, that the donor intended and expressed the intention that each (donee) should be entitled beneficially to the property of which he became the legal owner on the death of the donor, thus rebutting the presumption of a resulting trust.

As his last stand, Mr. McCann has urged that if it is thought that the concept of trust must be considered (and in my view because of the course that the case took in the High Court it is clear that we must deal with the relevance of the trust concept) that we should not overrule *Owens .v. Greene and Freeley v. Greene* [1932] IR 225 since it has stood for so long and, therefore, has been relied upon over the years by practitioners in advising clients. In the circumstances, since I believe – a view shared by all members of the Court – that the decision was wrongly decided it should be overruled. (*The Attorney General v. Ryan's Car Hire Ltd.* [1965] IR 642; *Mogul of Ireland v. Tipperary (N.R.) County Council* [1976] IR 260 and *Finucane v. McMahon* [1990] 1 IR 165).

This will introduce a measure of consistency in our jurisprudence: it restores equity to the high ground which it should properly occupy to ameliorate the harshness of common law rules on occasion rather than itself to be an instrument of injustice. Further, it brings us into line with other common law jurisdictions.

I would allow the appeal."

Purchase in the Name of Another

Where a person provides the purchase money for property, whether real or personal, which is conveyed or transferred to another person or to himself and the other person jointly, it is presumed that the latter holds the property on a resulting trust for the person who provided the purchase money.[20]

---

[20] *Dyer v. Dyer* (1788) 2 Cox Eq Cas 92, 93.

Re Slattery
[1917] 2 IR 278

A policy of insurance was taken out by Lawrence Slattery in the name and on the life of his brother. Lawrence Slattery paid the premiums on the policy and retained it in his possession and at no time did his brother have any interest in the policy or make any claim to it. When his brother died it was held by Pim J that a resulting trust arose and that Lawrence Slattery was entitled to the monies payable on the policy.

PIM J stated at pp.279–280: "This is a claim made by Lawrence Slattery against the estate of a deceased man, and in such cases the Court should require corroboration of the claim. This is a rule, not of law, but, as it has been called by Jessell M.R. in *Finch v. Finch* (1883) 23 Ch D 267, a rule of prudence; and I have to see what corroboration is offered by Lawrence Slattery of the claim he now makes. [His Lordship then discussed the evidence, and decided that there was sufficient corroboration of the claim, and, having found the facts as set out above, he proceeded.] The Attorney General in his argument referred me to the statement in the 17th volume of Lord Halsbury's Laws of England, paragraph 1126, page 562, wherein it is stated that, when an insurance has been effected by one party on the life of another, the latter has, apart from any contract express or implied, no interest in the policy. I do not think that that statement necessarily refers to circumstances such as the present. In the principal case quoted in the note of cases, namely, *Bruce v. Garden* (1869) 5 Ch App 32, it appears that what was referred to was the case of a person effecting, in his own name, a policy on the life of another. There does not seem to be any case in which the facts are the same as in this one, but the Attorney-General referred me to the case of *In re a Policy No. 6402 of the Scottish Equitable Life Assurance Society* [1902] 1 Ch 282, in which Joyce J. has practically decided the question now raised.

In that case a policy of insurance was taken out by A on his own life for the behoof of B, his wife's sister, and the policy provided that B, her executors, administrators, and assigns, should be entitled to receive the policy moneys on A's death. A survived B, retained the policy, and paid the premiums until his death. It was held that the legal personal representative of B were trustees of the policy moneys for the legal personal representatives of A. Joyce J. brought the case which he was deciding, and also such a case as the present one, under the principle which is stated in Lewin on Trusts, 12th ed., p. 184, as follows: – "Not only real estate, but personalty also is governed by these principles, as if a man take a bond or purchase an annuity, stock, or other chattel interest, the equitable ownership results to the person from whom the consideration moves." In summing up the learned judge said:– "Now in the present case a policy was taken out by Mr. Saunderson (A) a great many years ago, and the name of Miss Styles (B) appears in the policy as the person to whom the money was to be paid. The policy was never handed to her, and she is now dead, and the premiums were always paid and were paid for many years after her death by Sanderson. That really is a case of a man taking a policy out in the name of another, that other person being a sister of his wife, and, therefore, not standing in any relation to him 'that would meet the presumption,' as Lord Eldon expressed it. It comes really to this – a purchase by one in the name of another, with no other circumstances at all proved"; and he decided that, although the legal personal representatives of Miss Styles (that is, B) would be the persons entitled to receive the money at law, and to give a receipt for it, in equity the money belonged to the legal personal representatives of Mr. Sanderson (that is, A), who took out the policy. What could be more absolutely in point than the reasoning and decision of Joyce J. in the case quoted? I admit that I am not bound by the decision, but, even if I thought it doubtful in law, I should hesitate before I disregarded the opinion of Sir Matthew Joyce. I am, however, satisfied that the learned judge is right, and I can see no real distinction between the case which he decided and the case before me.

I must, therefore, hold that Lawrence Slattery is entitled to the sum which he claims, namely, the sum of £771 paid to the National Provincial Bank of England, and afterwards lodged in Court."

It must be stressed that the presumption which arises in the case of a voluntary conveyance or transfer or where a purchase is made in the name of another is liable to be rebutted, either by evidence that the purchaser intended to benefit the other party or because of the operation of the presumption of advancement.

Rebutting the Presumption of a Resulting Trust

Evidence of an Intention to Benefit

Where evidence establishes that the transferor or purchaser intended to benefit the donee, no resulting trust will arise.

Fowkes v. Pascoe
(1875) 10 Ch App 343

The testatrix made various purchases of stock in the joint names of herself and the son of her daughter-in-law. After her death, the Court of Appeal (Jessel MR, James and Mellish LJJ) upheld the latter's claim to be entitled to the stock on the basis that the purchase had been intended as a gift and the presumption of a resulting trust had therefore been rebutted.

MELLISH LJ stated at pp.352–354: "There can be no doubt that the question in this case is a question of fact. It cannot be decided simply on the ground of legal presumption, because whatever effect is given to the evidence of Mr.

Pascoe and his wife, their evidence is evidence to rebut the presumption, and therefore the Court must consider whether the presumption is rebutted or not.

Now, the Master of the Rolls appears to have thought that because the presumption that it was a trust and not a gift must prevail if there were no evidence to rebut the presumption, therefore when there was evidence to rebut the presumption he ought not to consider the probability or improbability of the circumstances of the case, and whether the presumption was really true or not, but ought to decide the case on the ground that the evidence of Pascoe and his wife taken alone was not satisfactory. But, in my opinion, when there is once evidence to rebut the presumption, the Court is put in the same position as a jury would be, and then we cannot give such influence to the presumption in point of law as to disregard the circumstances of the investment, and to say that neither the circumstances nor the evidence are sufficient to rebut the presumption.

Now, the presumption must, beyond all question, be of very different weight in different cases. In some cases it would be very strong indeed. If, for instance, a man invested a sum of stock in the name of himself and his solicitor, the inference would be very strong indeed that it was intended solely for the purpose of a trust, and the Court would require very strong evidence on the part of the solicitor to prove that it was intended as a gift; and certainly his own evidence would not be sufficient. On the other hand, a man may make an investment of stock in the name of himself and some person, although not a child or wife, yet in such a position to him as to make it extremely probable that the investment was intended as a gift. In such a case, although the rule of law, if there was no evidence at all, would compel the Court to say that the presumption of trust must prevail, even if the Court might not believe that the fact was in accordance with the presumption, yet, if there is evidence to rebut the presumption, then, in my opinion, the Court must go into the actual facts. And if we are to go into the actual facts, and look at the circumstances of this investment, it appears to me utterly impossible, as the Lord Justice has said, to come to any other conclusion than that the first investment was made for the purpose of gift and not for the purpose of trust. It was either for the purpose of trust or else for the purpose of gift; and therefore any evidence which shews it was not for the purpose of trust is evidence to shew that it was for the purpose of gift. We find a lady of considerable fortune, having no nearer connections than Mr. Pascoe, who was then a young man living in her house, and for whom she was providing. We find her, manifestly out of her savings, buying a sum of £250 stock in the joint names of herself and him, and at the same time buying another sum of £250 stock, on the very same day, in the joint names of herself and a lady who was living with her as a companion. Then, applying one's common sense to that transaction, what inference is it possible to draw, except that the purchases were intended for the purpose of gifts? If they were intended for the purpose of trusts, what possible reason was there why the two sums were not invested in the same names? Besides, at the very same time the lady had a large sum of stock in her own name, and could anything be more absurd than to suppose that a lady with £4000 or £5000 in her own name at that time in the same stock, and having a sum of £500 to invest out of her savings, should go and invest £250 in the name of herself and a young gentleman who was living in her house, and another £250 in the name of herself and her companion, and yet intend the whole to be for herself? I cannot come to any other conclusion than that it must have been intended by way of a present after her death.

Then, when we have once arrived at the conclusion that the first investment was intended as a gift (and the second was exactly similar), and when we find that the account was opened for the purpose of gift, those facts appear to me to rebut the presumption altogether, because when an account is once found to be opened for the purpose of gift there is very strong reason to suppose that everything added to that account was intended for the purpose of gift also. Assuming the testatrix to know that she had made a gift, and had invested a sum of money in stock in the joint names of herself and Pascoe for the purpose of making a present to him, it would certainly be a very extraordinary thing that she should go and add other large sums to that account, not for the purpose of making a present to him, but for the purpose of his being a trustee. I cannot help coming to the conclusion that, as a matter of fact, these investments were intended for the purpose of gift.

There were one or two facts relied on against this conclusion. It was said that Mr. Pascoe kept the matter secret for a great number of years, and never revealed it. I do not greatly rely on that. Every one who has experience knows that some persons are very reticent about their affairs, and some persons are always talking about them. You cannot form any inference as to that. If he really and *bona fide* believed, and had no doubt that it was intended for a gift, and for his use, I do not see that there was anything extraordinary in his not mentioning it to the persons who now say it was not mentioned to them. The only fact that in the least degree, in my opinion, went against him was his not accounting for the dividend which was due at the death of the testatrix. I think it is not at all impossible that he might have honestly believed that that was his, although I entirely agree that in point of law it was not so; therefore on the whole I come to the same conclusion as the Lord Justice."

Standing v. Bowring
(1885) 31 Ch D 282

The plaintiff widow transferred stock into the joint names of herself and her late husband's godson, the defendant, having been warned that if she made the transfer she could not revoke it. It was held that the plaintiff could not claim a re-transfer on equitable grounds because she had not intended to make the defendant a mere trustee except in relation to the dividends payable on the stock. The Court of Appeal (Lord Halsbury LC, Cotton and Lindley LJJ) held that there was ample evidence to suggest that at the time of the transfer she intended to benefit the defendant and the presumption of a resulting trust was therefore rebutted.

COTTON LJ stated at pp.287–288: "The Plaintiff Mrs. Standing commenced this action in order to have it declared that the Defendant Bowring was a trustee for her of a sum of £6,000 Consols.

The facts have been sufficiently stated by the Lord Chancellor. Though the Defendant was the nephew of the first husband of the Plaintiff, she was not *in loco parentis* to him, and the rule is well settled that where there is a transfer by a person into his own name jointly with that of a person who is not his child, or his adopted child, then there is *prima facie* a resulting trust for the transferor. But that is a presumption capable of being rebutted by showing that at the time the transferor intended a benefit to the transferee, and in the present case there is ample evidence that at the time of the transfer, and for some time previously, the Plaintiff intended to confer a benefit by this transfer on her late husband's godson. In fact, when she desired to get the stock back again, what she said showed that she had originally intended to confer a benefit on the Defendant Bowring, but that in consequence of something he had done which had displeased her, she desired, if possible, to take back that which she had intended to be a benefit to him. That being so, the presumption that there would be a resulting trust for her is entirely rebutted, and it must be taken here, that although she did not intend Bowring to have any right to the dividends during her lifetime, she intended to give him a beneficial interest in the stock, and that on her death, as he survived her, the legal right must prevail, and he must take the property for his own benefit.

Another question, which has been already referred to by the Lord Chancellor, was raised in this case, viz., whether anything vested in Bowring, because until he was informed that the Plaintiff, Mrs. Standing, desired to get back this stock, he never was informed of the transfer. Now the transfer of stock in the public funds is regulated by Act of Parliament, and the statutory mode of transfer is by an instrument in the books of the Bank of England to be signed by the transferor. That was done here, and although the National Debt Act, 1870, recognises an acceptance by the transferee, yet it does not make that acceptance necessary or essential, for sect. 22 provides that " the person to whom a transfer is so made may, if he thinks fit, underwrite his acceptance thereof." Now, I take the rule of law to be that where there is a transfer of property to a person, even although it carries with it some obligations which may be onerous, it vests in him at once before he knows of the transfer, subject to his right when informed of it to say, if he pleases, "I will not take it." When informed of it he may repudiate it, but it vests in him until he so repudiates it. *Siggers v. Evans* (1855) 5 E & B 367, referred to by the Lord Chancellor, is a late case to that effect, in which the earlier authorities are reviewed, and one very remarkable case, *Smith v. Wheeler* 1 Vent 128, is quoted at p. 382, and also at greater length in *Small v. Marwood* (1829) 9 B & C 300, 306, where the right of the Crown was defeated by an assignment made before that right accrued, but not communicated to the assignee until after that right had accrued. It was held that although the assignee knew nothing of the assignment, it became effectual at once; so as to defeat the title of the Crown, which accrued before the knowledge was communicated to the assignee, and therefore of course before acceptance by the assignee. In my opinion therefore the appeal fails."

Where Fraud or Illegality Exists

Where a trust is intentionally created for an illegal purpose, a resulting trust in favour of the settlor or testator will not arise unless there is a failure to carry out this illegal purpose,[21] or where the direct consequence of allowing the trust to proceed would lead to the perpetration of an unlawful object, the defeat of a legal prohibition, or the protection of a fraud.[22] However, it would appear that even where a transfer of property occurs for an illegal purpose, this will not prevent a resulting trust arising in favour of the transferee where the claim can be made without reliance on this unlawful purpose. This point is illustrated by the decision of the House of Lords in *Tinsley v. Milligan.*

Tinsley v. Milligan
[1994] 1 AC 340

Two women purchased a house in the plaintiff's sole name but on the understanding that they should be joint beneficial owners of the property in order to assist in the perpetration of a fraud on the Department of Social Security. When the parties quarrelled, the defendant disclosed the fraud to the department and the plaintiff moved out and brought proceedings against the defendant claiming possession and sole ownership of the property. The defendant counter-claimed and sought a declaration that the property was held on trust for the parties in equal shares. The majority of the House of Lords (Lord Jauncey, Lord Lowry and Lord Browne-Wilkinson) held that the defendant had established a presumption of a resulting trust by showing that she had contributed to the purchase price of the house and that there was a common understanding between the parties that they owned it jointly. There was no need for her to establish the reason why the house had been conveyed solely into the plaintiff's name and it was held that there was no evidence to rebut the presumption of a resulting trust.

LORD BROWNE-WILKINSON stated at pp.369–377: "My Lords I agree

---

[21] *Symes v. Hughes* (1870) LR 9 Eq 475.
[22] *Ayerst v. Jenkins* (1873) LR 16 Eq 275.

with the speech of my noble and learned friend, Lord Goff of Chieveley, that the consequences of being a party to an illegal transaction cannot depend, as the majority in the Court of Appeal held, on such an imponderable factor as the extent to which the public conscience would be affronted by recognising rights created by illegal transactions. However, I have the misfortune to disagree with him as to the correct principle to be applied in a case where equitable property rights are acquired as a result of an illegal transaction.

Neither at law nor in equity will the court enforce an illegal contract which has been partially, but not fully, performed. However, it does not follow that all acts done under a partially performed contract are of no effect. In particular it is now clearly established that at law (as opposed to in equity), property in goods or land can pass under, or pursuant to, such a contract. If so, the rights of the owner of the legal title thereby acquired will be enforced, provided that the plaintiff can establish such title without pleading or leading evidence of the illegality. It is said that the property lies where it falls, even though legal title to the property was acquired as a result of the property passing under the illegal contract itself. I will first consider the modern authorities laying down the circumstances under which a legal proprietary interest acquired under an illegal transaction will be enforced by the courts. I will then consider whether the courts adopt a different attitude to equitable proprietary interests so acquired.

The position at law is well illustrated by the decision in *Bowmakers Ltd. v. Barnet Instruments Ltd.* [1945] KB 65. In that case Barnet acquired three parcels of machine tools which had previously belonged to Smith. The transaction was carried through by three hire-purchase agreements under which Smith sold the goods to Bowmakers who then hired them to Barnet. All three agreements were unlawful as being in breach of Defence Regulations: it is important to note that in the case of at least two of the parcels the illegality lay in the contract under which Bowmakers acquired the machine tools from Smith: see p. 69. Bowmakers succeeded in an action for conversion against Barnet. Even though it appeared from the pleadings and the evidence that the contract under which Bowmakers acquired the goods was illegal, such contract was effective to pass the property in the goods to Bowmakers who could therefore found their claim on the property right so acquired.

The position at law is further illustrated by *Ferret v. Hill* (1854) 15 CB 207 where A, with intent to use premises as a brothel, took a lease from B. B, having discovered that the premises were being used as a brothel, ejected A. A was held entitled to maintain ejectment against B notwithstanding that A entered into the lease for an illegal purpose.

In *Taylor v. Chester* (1869) LR 4 QB 309 the plaintiff had deposited with the defendant half a £50 note as security for payment due under an illegal contract with the defendant. The plaintiff was held unable to recover the half note as a special property in it (i.e. the security interest) had passed to the defendant. In *Alexander v. Rayson* [1936] 1 KB 169 the plaintiff had leased a property to the defendant. For the purpose of defrauding the rating authorities, the plaintiff had carried through the transaction by two documents, one a lease which expressed a low rent the other a service agreement providing for additional payments sufficient to bring up the annual payment to the actual rent agreed. The plaintiff failed in an action to recover rent due under the agreements but the Court of Appeal, at p. 186, said that if the plaintiff had let the flat to be used for an illegal purpose, the leasehold interest in the flat would have vested in the defendant who would have been entitled to remain in possession of the flat until and unless the plaintiff could eject her without relying on the unlawful agreement.

From these authorities the following propositions emerge: (1) property in chattels and land can pass under a contract which is illegal and therefore would have been unenforceable as a contract; (2) a plaintiff can at law enforce property rights so acquired provided that he does not need to rely on the illegal contract for any purpose other than providing the basis of his claim to a property right; (3) it is irrelevant that the illegality of the underlying agreement was either pleaded or emerged in evidence: if the plaintiff has acquired legal title under the illegal contract that is enough.

I have stressed the common law rules as to the impact of illegality on the acquisition and enforcement of property rights because it is the appellant's contention that different principles apply in equity. In particular it is said that equity will not aid Miss Milligan to assert, establish or enforce an equitable, as opposed to a legal, proprietary interest since she was a party to the fraud on the D.S.S. The house was put in the name of Miss Tinsley alone (instead of joint names) to facilitate the fraud. Therefore, it is said, Miss Milligan does not come to equity with clean hands: consequently, equity will not aid her.

Most authorities to which we were referred deal with enforcing proprietary rights under a trust: I will deal with them in due course. But before turning to them, I must point out that if Miss Tinsley's argument is correct, the results would be far reaching and, I suggest, very surprising. There are many proprietary rights, apart from trusts, which are only enforceable in equity. For example, an agreement for a lease under which the tenant has entered is normally said to be as good as a lease, since under such an agreement equity treats the lease as having been granted and the "lessee" as having a proprietary interest enforceable against the whole world except the bona fide purchaser for value without notice. Would the result in *Ferret v. Hill* (1854) 15 CB 207 have been different if there had only been an agreement for a lease? Say that in *Taylor v. Chester* (1869) LR 4 QB 309 the plaintiff had deposited by way of security share certificates instead of half a bank note (thereby producing only an equitable security): would the outcome have been different? Similarly, if the plaintiff were relying on an assignment of a chose in action would he succeed if the assignment was a legal assignment but fail if it were equitable?

In my judgment to draw such distinctions between property rights enforceable at law and those which require the intervention of equity would be surprising. More than 100 years has elapsed since the administration of law and equity became fused. The reality of the matter is that, in 1993, English law has one single law of property made up of legal and equitable interests. Although for historical reasons legal estates and equitable estates have differing incidents, the person owning either type of estate has a right of property, a right in rem not merely a right in personam. If the law is that a party is entitled to enforce a property right acquired under an illegal transaction, in my judgment the same rule ought to apply to any property right so acquired, whether such right is legal or equitable.

In the present case, Miss Milligan claims under a resulting or implied trust. The court below have found, and it is not now disputed, that apart from the question of illegality Miss Milligan would have been entitled in equity to a half share in the house in accordance with the principles exemplified in *Gissing v. Gissing* [1971] AC 886; *Grant v. Edwards* [1986] Ch 638 and *Lloyds Bank Plc. v. Rosset* [1991] 1 AC 107. The creation of such an equitable interest does not depend upon a contractual obligation but on a common intention acted upon by the parties to their detriment. It is a development of the old law of resulting trust under which, where two parties have provided the purchase money to buy a property which is conveyed into the name of one of them alone, the latter is presumed to hold the property on a resulting trust for both parties in shares proportionate to their contributions to the purchase price. In arguments, no distinction was drawn between strict resulting trusts and a *Gissing v. Gissing* type of trust.

A presumption of resulting trust also arises in equity when A transfers personalty or money to B: see *Snell's Equity,* 29th ed. (1990), pp. 183-184; *Standing v. Bowring* (1885) 31 ChD 282, 287, *per* Cotton L.J. and *Dewar v. Dewar* [1975] 1 WLR 1532, 1537. Before 1925, there was also a presumption of resulting trust when land was voluntarily transferred by A to B: it is arguable, however, that the position has been altered by the 1925 property legislation: see *Snell's Equity*, p. 182. The presumption of a resulting trust is, in my view, crucial in considering the authorities. On that presumption (and on the contrary presumption of advancement) hinges the answer to the crucial question "does a plaintiff claiming under a resulting trust have to rely on the underlying illegality?" Where the presumption of resulting trust applies, the plaintiff does not have to rely on the illegality. If he proves that the property is vested in the defendant alone but that the plaintiff provided part of the purchase money, or voluntarily transferred the property to the defendant, the plaintiff establishes his claim under a resulting trust unless either the contrary presumption of advancement displaces the presumption of resulting trust or the defendant leads evidence to rebut the presumption of resulting trust. Therefore, in cases where the presumption of advancement does not apply, a plaintiff can establish his equitable interest in the property without relying in any way on the underlying illegal transaction. In this case Miss Milligan as defendant simply pleaded the common intention that the property should belong to both of them and that she contributed to the purchase price: she claimed that in consequence the property belonged to them equally. To the same effect was her evidence in chief. Therefore Miss Milligan was not forced to rely on the illegality to prove her equitable interest. Only in the reply and the course of Miss Milligan's cross-examination did such illegality emerge: it was Miss Tinsley who had to rely on that illegality.

Although the presumption of advancement does not directly arise for consideration in this case, it is important when considering the decided cases to understand its operation. On a transfer from a man to his wife, children or others to whom he stands in loco parentis, equity presumes an intention to make a gift. Therefore in such a case, unlike the case where the presumption of resulting trust applies, in order to establish any claim the plaintiff has himself to lead evidence sufficient to rebut the presumption of gift and in so doing will normally have to plead, and give evidence of, the underlying illegal purpose.

Against this background, I turn to consider the authorities dealing with the position in equity where A transferred property to B for an illegal purpose. The earlier authorities, primarily Lord Eldon, support the appellant's proposition that equity will not aid a plaintiff who has transferred property to another for an illegal purpose. In *Cottington v. Fletcher* (1740) 2 Atk 155 a Roman Catholic had assigned an advowson to the defendant for a term of 99 years for the purpose of avoiding a statutory prohibition. On subsequently becoming a Protestant, he sought to recover the advowson from the defendant. The defendant pleaded the Statute of Frauds but also admitted that the advowson was assigned to him as trustee. On what appears to have been an interlocutory hearing, Lord Hardwicke L.C. held that, in view of the admission of trust, the plea of the Statute of Frauds was bad. However he said, at p. 156, that as the assignment was done in fraud of statute "I doubt at the hearing whether the plaintiff could be relieved, such fraudulent conveyances being make absolute against the grantor."

In *Muckleston v. Brown* (1801) 6 Ves 52 (a case concerning secret trusts) Lord Eldon, at p. 69, cast doubt on Lord Hardwicke's view, possibly misunderstanding that Lord Hardwicke was dealing with the question whether the Statute of Frauds provided a defence and not directly with the question of illegality. Lord Eldon said, at pp. 68-69:

> "Lord Hardwicke means to say, that, if the defendant admits the trust, though against the policy of the law, he would relieve: but if he does not admit the trust, but demurs, he would do, what does not apply in the least to this case; the plaintiff stating, he had been guilty of a fraud upon the law, to evade, to disappoint, the provision of the Legislature, to which he is bound to submit, and coming to equity to be relieved against his own act, and the defence being dishonest, between the two species of dishonesty the court would not act; but would say, 'Let the estate lie, where it falls.'"

Those remarks were obiter. But in *Curtis v. Perry* (1802) 6 Ves 739 Lord Eldon founded his decision on the same principle. In that case Nantes and Chiswell (who was a Member of Parliament) were partners. Ships had been purchased by Nantes out of partnership assets but registered in the sole name of Nantes. When Chiswell discovered the position, the ships were shown in the partnership books as being partnership property. However with Chiswell's connivance the ships remained registered in the sole name of Nantes so as to evade a statutory prohibition against the ships being used for Government contracts if owned by a Member of Parliament. In a dispute between the partnership creditors and Nantes' separate creditors, Lord Eldon held in favour of the latter. He said, at p. 746a:

> "The moment the purpose to defeat the policy of the law by fraudulently concealing, that this was his property, is admitted, it is very clear, he ought not to be heard in this court to say, that it is his property. In the case of a bill filed to have a reconveyance of a qualification given by the plaintiff to his son to enable him to sit in Parliament, the purpose being answered, the bill was very properly dismissed by Lord Kenyon with costs."

See also *Ex parte Yallop* (1808) 15 Ves 60.

The same broad principle was applied by the Exchequer Chamber in Equity in *Groves v. Groves* (1829) 3 Y & J 163. In that case the plaintiff had purchased land in the name of his brother so as to give the brother a necessary qualification to vote. The plaintiff claimed to recover the land under a resulting trust. His claim was dismissed on the grounds, inter alia, at p. 172, "that the illegal purpose for which this conveyance was made bars that equity." There are many other cases in the first half of the 19th century where the same principle was applied.

However, in my view, the law was not so firmly established as at first sight it appears to have been. The law on the effect of illegality was developing throughout the 19th century. In particular, if Lord Eldon's principle were to apply in its full vigour it would apply as much to claims by a guilty party to enforce an *express* trust as to enforce an implied or resulting trust: equity would not aid the plaintiff to enforce equitable claims against the holder of the legal estate. Yet in *Ayerst v. Jenkins* (1873) LR 16 Eq 275 Lord Selborne L.C. apparently treated a party to the illegality as being entitled to enforce express trusts against trustees. In that case, the settlor transferred investments to trustees and executed a settlement for the sole benefit of the defendant with whom he was about to go through a ceremony of marriage which, to the knowledge of both, was illegal, i.e. the settlement was made in contemplation of unlawful cohabitation. After the death of the settlor, his personal representative sought to recover the investments from the trustees claiming that the express trusts were invalid and that there was therefore a resulting trust to the settlor. The claim failed, partly on the ground that there was no equity in the settlor to recover from the trustees in whom the legal title was vested, but also on the ground that there was a fully executed trust vesting in the defendant "the immediate and absolute beneficial interest:" see the explanation, at pp. 284–285, of *Rider v. Kidder* (1805) 10 Ves 360, 366. The whole case proceeded on the footing that the defendant, even if a party to the illegality, was entitled to enforce against the trustees her equitable rights as beneficiary under the express trusts against the trustees. This view would be quite inconsistent with a general rule such as that propounded by Lord Eldon that a court of equity will never enforce equitable proprietary interests at the suit of a party to an illegality.

The law was developing in another direction during the 19th century. There was originally a difference of view as to whether a transaction entered into for an illegal purpose would be enforced at law or in equity if the party had repented of his illegal purpose before it had been put into operation, i.e. the doctrine of locus poenitentiae. It was eventually recognised both at law and in equity that if the plaintiff had repented before the illegal purpose was carried through, he could recover his property: see *Taylor v. Bowers* (1876) 1 QBD 291; *Symes v. Hughes* (1870) LR 9 Eq 475. The principle of locus poenitentiae is in my judgment irreconcilable with any rule that where property is transferred for an illegal purpose no equitable proprietary right exists. The equitable right, if any, must arise at the time at which the property was voluntarily transferred to the third party or purchased in the name of the third party. The existence of the equitable interest cannot depend upon events occurring after that date. Therefore if, under the principle of locus poenitentiae, the courts recognise that an equitable interest did arise out of the underlying transaction, the same must be true where the illegal purpose was carried through. The carrying out of the illegal purpose cannot, by itself, destroy the pre-existing equitable interest. The doctrine of locus poenitentiae therefore demonstrates that the effect of illegality is not to prevent a proprietary interest in equity from arising or to produce a forfeiture of such right: the effect is to render the equitable interest unenforceable in certain circumstances. The effect of illegality is not substantive but procedural. The question therefore is, "In what circumstances will equity refuse to enforce equitable rights which undoubtedly exist."

It is against this background that one has to assess the more recent law. Although in the cases decided during the last 100 years there are frequent references to Lord Eldon's wide principle, with one exception (*Cantor v. Cox* 239 EG 121) none of the English decisions are decided by simply applying that principle. They are all cases where the unsuccessful party was held to be precluded from leading evidence of an illegal situation in order to rebut the presumption of advancement. Lord Eldon's rule would have provided a complete answer whether the transfer was made to a wife or child (where the presumption of advancement would apply) or to a stranger. Yet with one exception none of the cases in this century has been decided on that simple basis.

The majority of cases have been those in which the presumption of advancement applied: in those authorities the rule has been stated as being that a plaintiff cannot rely on evidence of his own illegality to rebut the presumption applicable in such cases that the plaintiff intended to make a gift of the property to the transferee. Thus in *Gascoigne v. Gascoigne* [1918] 1 KB

223; *McEvoy v. Belfast Banking Co. Ltd.* [1934] NI 67; *In re Emery's Investments Trusts* [1959] Ch 410; *Palaniappa Chettiar v. Arunasalam Chettiar* [1962] AC 294 and *Tinker v. Tinker* [1970] P 136, 141H, 142C the crucial point was said to be the inability of the plaintiff to lead evidence rebutting the presumption of advancement. In each case the plaintiff was claiming to recover property voluntarily transferred to, or purchased in the name of, a wife or child, for an illegal purpose. Although reference was made to Lord Eldon's principle, none of those cases was decided on the simple ground (if it were good law) that equity would not in any circumstances enforce a resulting trust in such circumstances. On the contrary in each case the rule was stated to be that the plaintiff could not recover because he had to rely on the illegality to rebut the presumption of advancement.

In my judgment, the explanation for this departure from Lord Eldon's absolute rule is that the fusion of law and equity has led the courts to adopt a single rule (applicable both at law and in equity) as to the circumstances in which the court will enforce property interests acquired in pursuance of an illegal transaction, viz., the *Bowmakers* rule [1945] KB 65. A party to an illegality can recover by virtue of a legal or equitable property interest if, but only if, he can establish his title without relying on his own illegality. In cases where the presumption of advancement applies, the plaintiff is faced with the presumption of gift and therefore cannot claim under a resulting trust unless and until he has rebutted that presumption of gift: for those purposes the plaintiff does have to rely on the underlying illegality and therefore fails.

The position is well illustrated by two decisions in the Privy Council. In the first, *Singh v. Ali* [1960] AC 167 a plaintiff who had acquired legal title to a lorry under an illegal transaction was held entitled to succeed against the other party to the illegality in detinue and trespass. The Board approved the *Bowmakers* test. Two years later in *Palaniappa Chettiar v. Arunasalam Chettiar* [1962] AC 294 the Board had to consider the case where a father, who had transferred land to his son for an illegal purpose, sought to recover it under a resulting trust. It was held that he could not, since he had to rely on his illegal purpose in order to rebut the presumption of advancement. The Board distinguished, at p. 301, the decision in *Haigh v. Kaye* (1872) LR 7 Ch App 469 on the following grounds:

"It appears to their Lordships, however, that there is a clear distinction between *Haigh v. Kaye* and the present case. In *Haigh v. Kaye* the plaintiff conveyed a freehold estate to the defendant. In the conveyance it was stated that a sum of £850 had been paid by the defendant for it. The plaintiff proved that no such sum was paid and claimed that the defendant was a trustee for him. Now in that case the plaintiff had no reason to disclose any illegality and did not do so. It was the defendant who suggested that the transaction was entered into for a fraudulent purpose. He sought to drag it in without pleading it distinctly and he was not allowed to do so. But in the present case the plaintiff had of necessity to disclose his own illegality to the court and for this reason: He had not only to get over the fact that the transfer stated that the son paid $7,000 for the land. He had also to get over the presumption of advancement, for, whenever a father transfers property to his son, there is a presumption that he intended it as a gift to his son; and if he wishes to rebut that presumption and to say that his son took as trustee for him, he must prove the trust clearly and distinctly, by evidence properly admissible for the purposes; and not leave it to be inferred from slight circumstances: see *Shephard v. Cartwright* [1955] AC 431, 445."

Further, the Board distinguished *Singh v. Ali* [1960] AC 167. It was pointed out that in *Singh v. Ali* the plaintiff founded his claim on a right of property in the lorry and his possession of it. The Board continued [1962] AC 294, 303:

"[The plaintiff] did not have to found his cause of action on an immoral or illegal act. He was held entitled to recover. But in the present case the father has of necessity to put forward, and indeed, assert, his own fraudulent purpose, which he has fully achieved. He is met therefore by the principle stated long ago by Lord Mansfield 'No court will lend its aid to a man who founds his cause of action upon an immoral or an illegal act,' see *Holman v. Johnson* (1775) 1 Cowp 341, 343."

In my judgment these two cases show that the Privy Council was applying exactly the same principle in both cases although in one case the plaintiff's claim rested on a legal title and in the other on an equitable title. The claim based on the equitable title did not fail simply because the plaintiff was a party to the illegal transaction; it only failed because the plaintiff was bound to disclose and rely upon his own illegal purpose in order to rebut the presumption of advancement. The Privy Council was plainly treating the principle applicable both at law and in equity as being that a man can recover property provided that he is not forced to rely on his own illegality.

I therefore reach the conclusion that, although there is no case overruling the wide principle stated by Lord Eldon, as the law has developed the equitable principle has become elided into the common law rule. In my judgment the time has come to decide clearly that the rule is the same whether a plaintiff founds himself on a legal or equitable title: he is entitled to recover if he is not forced to plead or rely on the illegality, even if it emerges that the title on which he relied was acquired in the course of carrying through an illegal transaction.

As applied in the present case, that principle would operate as follows. Miss Milligan established a resulting trust by showing that she had contributed to the purchase price of the house and that there was common understanding between her and Miss Tinsley that they owned the house equally. She had no need to allege or prove *why* the house was conveyed into the name of Miss Tinsley alone, since that fact was irrelevant to her claim: it was enough to show that the house was in fact vested in Miss Tinsley alone. The illegality only emerged at all because Miss Tinsley sought to raise it. Having proved these facts, Miss Milligan had raised a presumption of resulting trust. There was no evidence to rebut that presumption. Therefore Miss Milligan should succeed. This is exactly the process of reasoning adopted by the Ontario Court of Appeal in *Gorog v. Kiss* (1977) 78 DLR (3d) 690 which in my judgment was rightly decided.

Finally, I should mention a further point which was relied on by Miss Tinsley. It is said that once the illegality of the transaction emerges, the court must refuse to enforce the transaction and all claims under it whether pleaded or not: see *Scott v. Brown, Doering, McNab & Co.* [1892] 2 QB 724. Therefore, it is said, it does not matter whether a plaintiff relies on or gives evidence of the illegality: the court will not enforce the plaintiff's rights. In my judgment, this submission is plainly ill founded. There are many cases where a plaintiff has succeeded, notwithstanding that the illegality of the transaction under which she acquired the property has emerged: see, for example, *Bowmakers Ltd. v. Barnet Instruments Ltd.* [1945] KB 65 and *Singh v. Ali* [1960] AC 167. In my judgment the court is only entitled and bound to dismiss a claim on the basis that it is founded on an illegality in those cases where the illegality is of a kind which would have provided a good defence if raised by the defendant. In a case where the plaintiff is not seeking to enforce an unlawful contract but founds his case on collateral rights acquired under the contract (such as a right of property) the court is neither bound nor entitled to reject the claim unless the illegality of necessity forms part of the plaintiff's case.

I would therefore dismiss the appeal."

The Presumption of Advancement

The presumption of advancement arises where because of the relationship which exists between the parties, the donor or purchaser is under an obligation recognised in equity to provide for the person to whom the property is given. Just as the presumption of a resulting trust can be rebutted by evidence showing that a gift was intended, so the presumption of advancement can be rebutted by evidence which establishes that the donor did not intend to benefit or make provision for the donee.[23] The manner in which these presumptions operate is explained well by Viscount Simonds in *Shephard v. Cartwright*.[24]

> "I think that the law is clear that on the one hand where a man purchases shares and they are registered in the name of a stranger there is a resulting trust in favour of the purchaser; on the other hand, if they are registered in the name of a child or one to whom the purchaser then stood in loco parentis, there is no such resulting trust but a presumption of advancement. Equally it is clear that the presumption may be rebutted but should not, as Lord Eldon said, give way to slight circumstances."

---

[23] *R.F. v. M.F.* [1995] 2 ILRM 572, 577 *per* Henchy J.
[24] [1955] AC 431, 445.

Husband and Wife

The presumption of advancement arises where a husband transfers property to his wife or purchases it in her name. However, traditionally where a wife bought property and put it in her husband's name, this did not give rise to the presumption of advancement and instead a resulting trust was presumed. As the decision in *R.F. v. M.F.* makes clear, the presumption can readily be rebutted by evidence establishing a contrary intention.

R.F. v. M.F.
[1995] 2 ILRM 572

A husband purchased a house, with the aid of a bank loan, in the joint names of himself and his wife. The wife instituted proceedings claiming, *inter alia*, that she was beneficially entitled to a half share in the house. The Supreme Court (Finlay CJ, Henchy and Hederman JJ) held that the presumption of advancement had been rebutted in the circumstances and that the wife had not obtained any beneficial interest in the house by virtue of the conveyance.

HENCHY J stated at pp.574–578: "The husband and wife in this case were married in 1956. He was an agricultural instructor and she was a clerk. It did not turn out to be a happy marriage. Over the years it passed through a series of vicissitudes which I need not recount. It is sufficient to say that the marriage, of which there is no issue, is now irretrievably broken down for some years.

The present proceedings were commenced by the wife in the High Court in 1980, following on the breakdown of the marriage, and in them she sought a series of reliefs against the husband. When the proceedings came on for hearing before D'Arcy J in December 1982 he made an order dealing with the several issues raised in the pleadings. I need not go into the various matters that were in dispute, for this appeal, which has been taken by the wife against the order of D'Arcy J, is limited to two matters, namely, the findings made by the judge as to the ownership of a farm in north Co. Dublin, and of a house in M., Co. Dublin.

When the parties married in 1956 they first lived in S., Co. Dublin. In 1961 they decided to purchase the farm in north Co. Dublin. It was a farm of some 35 acres and the purchase price was £4,200. Between money given by an aunt and money lent to her by a bank, the wife put up £4,100 of the purchase money. The husband's contribution was £100. With the aid of an advance from the bank as a security for which the title deeds of the farm were lodged - they stocked the lands with cows and began dairy farming. The farm had been acquired in the wife's name.

Meanwhile, relations between the parties were steadily deteriorating. They intended to leave S. and go to live on the farm, but the wife refused to do so. She has complained of physical ill-treatment by him, due, according to the judge, to persistent nagging by her. Her nervous health deteriorated and she had to get psychiatric treatment. Because it was he who was effectually running the farm he felt that she should assign it to him. In April 1963 he had transferred the house in S. to her. The running of the farm was financed out of a joint bank account. When she froze that account, he pressed her to assign the farm to him. Eventually she did so, by a deed executed in May 1965.

D'Arcy J held that this deed was a valid transfer. The wife contests that finding and asks this Court to hold that the deed should be set aside on the ground that she executed it under undue influence by the husband. In my opinion, that contention is unsound.

In the first place, the deed was not a voluntary one. While the transfer is expressed in the deed to be in consideration of natural love and affection, the reality was, as the judge held, that she was to be repaid everything she had expended on the purchase of the land, and he was to take over her liability to the bank for the amount the bank had advanced in respect of the purchase and stocking of the land. It was, therefore, an assignment for valuable consideration. But even if it could be said that the consideration was inadequate or illusory, she had been independently advised as to her rights by two separate firms of solicitors. In the circumstances, there is no equitable principle on which she could claim that the transaction could be set aside. It was not an improvident transaction. As well as that, the fact that she allowed eight years to pass before making any complaint that her execution of the transfer was oppressive or unfair was, as the judge held, so tainted with delay as to be inconsistent with her claim that she had acted under undue influence when she executed the transfer. I entertain no doubt that the judge was correct in holding that the transfer is valid and is binding on the wife.

The second ground of appeal argued is concerned with a house at O., M., Co. Dublin. This was a house acquired in the joint names of the husband and wife. The judge held that the wife's interest thus acquired was acquired as trustee for the husband. Whether that finding is correct is the issue that has mainly exercised the court in this appeal.

It is common case that the wife made no contribution towards the cost of the purchase of the house at O. and that, although she had promised to do so, she never resided there. The matrimonial home was the house in S., but the marital relationship there was poor. In 1974 the husband bought another house, in M., in his own name and went to live there. The marriage had now virtually collapsed, but the parties kept up desultory contacts. He pressed her to go to live with him in his house in M. She at first agreed to do so, but then refused because that house was not in their joint names. Instead of living together there, she suggested that he sell that house and buy a new house at O. in their joint names. If he did so, she would go to live with him there. Being anxious to attempt to revive the marriage in a new matrimonial home, he agreed to do so.

The husband thereupon proceeded in 1976 to buy the then unbuilt house at O. for £26,750 and the conveyance was taken in their joint names. He then sold his other house in M. for £18,750. The financing of the purchase of the house at O. was arranged by the husband getting a bank loan.

When the house at O. was built, the husband moved in and asked the wife to join him there. Despite her earlier promise, she was reluctant to do so. As an added inducement to her to honour her agreement to live with him in that house, he bought her a motor car which cost £1,600. All to no avail. She continued to live in the original matrimonial home in S. Despite all entreaty by him, she resolutely refused to go and live with him at O. She has never gone to live there. Nevertheless, she claims that, because the conveyance was taken in their joint names, she is now beneficially entitled to a half share in that house. D'Arcy J rejected that claim and the wife's second argued ground of appeal is that the judge was wrong in so deciding.

The equitable doctrine of advancement, as applied to transactions between husband and wife, has the effect that when a husband (at least where the circumstances show that he is to be expected to provide for the wife) buys property and has it conveyed to his wife and himself jointly, there is a presumption that the wife's paper title gives her a beneficial estate or interest in the property. Unless the presumption is rebutted by evidence showing a contrary intention on the part of the husband at the time of the transaction, he will be deemed to have entered into the transaction for the purpose of conferring a beneficial estate or interest on the wife. That estate or interest is treated in law as an advancement, that is to say, a material benefit given in anticipation of the performance by the husband of his duty to provide for the wife.

The presumption of advancement in those circumstances is, of course, rebuttable. For a rebuttal to be made out, it is for the husband to show, by reference to acts or statements before or around the transaction, that a beneficial interest was not intended to be conveyed in the circumstances relied on. As to subsequent acts or statements, the authorities show that they are admissible in evidence against the party making them, but not in his or her favour. Thus, subsequent acts or statements on the part of the wife are admissible in evidence to rebut the presumption of advancement.

The essence of the transaction in regard to the house in O. was – and the judge has so held – that the husband was to buy that particular house and take the conveyance of it in the joint names of the wife and himself, provided the wife was prepared to live there with him. The latter condition, from his point of view, was paramount. He was anxious to revive the faltering marriage. He had asked her to leave S. and come to live with him in his other house in M. She had refused because that house was in his sole name. That was the sticking point. She countered by agreeing to a resumption of normal marital relations if he bought the O. house in their joint names. This condition emanated from her and he fell in with it. It was the cornerstone of the transaction as far as he was concerned. Nevertheless, she has repudiated it and contends that the presumption of advancement stands unrebutted.

In construing conduct alleged to amount to advancement, the court's task is essentially a fact-finding one. It has to ascertain, from the admissible matters relied on by the parties, the true intention behind the transaction which has given the wife a paper title. If the relevant circumstances show that the paper result produced by the conveyance conceals the real intention of the husband in entering into the transaction, so that the benefit contended for by the wife was not intended, the court will hold that the presumption of advancement has been rebutted.

In the present case, I am satisfied that the presumption of advancement, arising from the terms of conveyance, was clearly rebutted. It is plain that the husband would never have agreed to the transaction if the wife had not promised to live in the house. That promise was an integral part of the arrangement. The wife cannot cast aside that promise and take the benefit of the conveyance. It is a fundamental rule that a person who comes to court seeking the benefit of an equitable doctrine will be denied that benefit if the grant of it would amount to a reward for unfair, unconscionable or inequitable conduct. To hold in this case that the wife acquired the beneficial interest she claims would, apart from being based on a false interpretation of the arrangement made by the parties, allow the wife to profit by her bad faith. That is something the court should not do. The position would be less clear if it were a question as to whether the wife had in reality or in substance performed her part of the agreement. For example, if she had gone to live with the husband in the house for only a short or nominal period, it might be difficult for the husband to contend successfully that she had not complied with her promise that she would go to live with him in the house if he bought it. But that is not the case here. She has made no attempt to live there. What she wants is to be allowed to renounce totally her promise to live in the house and at the same time to be allowed to get a beneficial interest in the house, when it is plain that the passing of such an interest was made conditional on the performance by her of the promise. In such circumstances it must be held that the presumption of advancement has been rebutted and that she has not acquired under the deed any beneficial interest in the house.

Being of opinion that the two grounds of appeal argued have not been made out, I would dismiss this appeal."

Father and Child

Similarly, where a father purchases property in the name of his child or transfers it into the child's name, the presumption of advancement will apply.

O'Brien v. Sheil
(1873) IR 7 Eq 255

A father lodged securities in a bank in the joint names of himself and his daughter. After his death, it was held by O'Sullivan MR that this was an advancement in the daughter's favour, despite evidence which suggested that the father had subsequently intended the securities to be applied to different purposes. Sullivan MR concluded that declarations made by the father subsequent to the advancement could not constitute evidence to rebut the presumption.

O'SULLIVAN MR stated at pp.257–264: "The question which remains undisposed of in this case is an important one. It is simply this: – Whether a sum of £2000 in Russian 5 per cent bonds, and £200 in Victoria 6 per cent bonds, having regard to the mode in which those securities were dealt with by Sir Justin Sheil, constituted any portion of his assets.

The facts with regard to these securities are as follows: – It appears that Sir Justin Sheil in his lifetime, as it appears by the books of the Bank of England Western Branch, Burlington Gardens, London, deposited the securities which I have mentioned in the name of his wife, Mary Leonora, Lady Sheil, and left them so deposited until her death. After that event, about the 5th of January, 1870, he transferred these securities into the joint names of himself, Sir Justin Shiel, and his daughter Miss Frances Sheil, one of the Defendants in this suit, and no alteration was made in this lodgment during the life of Sir Justin Sheil.

The question raised is, whether these securities have become the property of Miss Frances Sheil, she having survived her father, or whether they still remain assets of Sir Justin Sheil. The only evidence relating to the lodgment of the securities is what I have mentioned. There is no evidence of any contemporaneous writing under the hand of Sir Justin Sheil, or of any contemporaneous declaration by him as to the object he had in view in making the lodgment of these securities in the manner I have described. The securities, according to the evidence before me, are represented by bonds or certificates which pass from hand to hand like a bank note; and the lodgment of the securities at the bank was made personally as if actual cash had been the subject-matter of it. After the death of Sir Justin Sheil there was found among his papers a memorandum in his handwriting, in the following words:–

"To Frances, Edward, Emily, Laura, Justin, Stephen, Richard, Honor, Denis, Grace. The money invested at the Bank of England, or branch, on a joint account (myself and Frances), amounting to £2000 in Russian 5 per cents, and £200 in Victoria 6 per cents, besides the balance in hands, was and is intended for the purchase of a trousseau, should any of the girls happen to be married. The expenses of my funeral should be paid out of this money; a portion of the expenses of probate and succession duties should be paid out of this money. Let the executors determine what portion.

JUSTIN SHEIL

April 7th, 1871.

Of course, I do not mean that the above sums are intended for the purchase of one trousseau. The trousseau is to be regulated by one's station in life.

JUSTIN SHEIL

April 7th, 1871."

The Frances mentioned in the above memorandum is the daughter of the late Sir Justin Sheil and the other persons named therein are her brothers and sisters. The lodgment in the Bank of England Branch was on the 5th of January, 1870, a year and three months before the date of the memorandum. Frances, the daughter, claims these two sums under the ordinary doctrine of this Court, as being a gift by way of advancement, she having survived her father. She says she does not mean to keep the money herself, but to carry out the intention of her father; with that intention of hers I have nothing to do. She is at liberty to do what she likes with this money if she is entitled to it. But the course she has resolved upon is such as one would expect from a lady in her position, who has got a child's portion by her father's will.

It is contended on behalf of some of the children that this document is admissible in evidence, as indicating what the intention of Sir Justin Sheil was at the time he lodged these securities in the Branch of the Bank of England; and it is said that this is the document which regulates the trust which is to be attached to these two sums, and that the trust being vague and uncertain it must fail, and that the subject of it became the property of Sir Justin Sheil, and forms a portion of his personal estate. Now, the first point is, whether this document can be looked at at all – having regard to its date – as any evidence to control the lodgment of the securities made on the 5th of January, 1870.

Beyond a doubt, what took place on that day, unexplained by any contemporaneous evidence, would, on the authorities, amount to a plain and manifest advancement for Frances, she having survived her father. That is, I think, the clear result of the authorities. Whatever may at one time have been thought (see *Pole v. Pole* (1748) 1 Ves Sen 76) of a lodgment in the name of a parent and child being a weaker case of advancement than a lodgment in the name of the child alone, it is now settled law that a lodgment by a father in the joint names of himself and his child is as powerful and strong an indication of advancement as a lodgment in the name of the child alone. Now, what is the effect of that doctrine of advancement attaching on a sum lodged in the joint names of father and child (the latter surviving), or in the name of a child alone, unexplained by any evidence? It is a gift of the property to the child in the one case immediately, and in the other if the child survives. It takes effect immediately in possession in the one case, the beneficial enjoyment being postponed in the other. Case after case establishes that proposition, and I need only refer to one of the most recent, *Hepworth v. Hepworth* (1870) LR 11 Eq 10, where the consequence of advancement as being a direct gift, making the property pass, is explained and illustrated. That being so, it is difficult to see how a declaration by the father at a subsequent period can alter the property in the gift which he has made. In my opinion, the authorities are clear that the declarations of the father, subsequent to the advancement, if they are not so connected with it as to be reasonably regarded as contemporaneous, cannot be evidence to rebut the presumption of advancement. There is a case in this country of great importance, which was not referred to, *Fox v. Fox* (1863) 15 Ir Ch R 89, heard before Lord Chancellor Brady, Lord Justice Blackburne, and Baron Deasy. That was the case of a lodgment of a sum of money by a father in the joint names of himself and his son, and having regard to the state of the family, an advancement operated very unequally. The hardship of the case influenced the Lord Chancellor's judgment when the case was heard before him, and he seems to have admitted subsequent declarations of the father, which affected his mind very much, and he held that there was no advancement. That decision undoubtedly interfered with the well-acknowledged rules of law respecting advancements. But on appeal he himself reversed his own decision, and there are some valuable observations in the judgments of the Lord Justice and Baron Deasy in relation to the entire want of value and weight to be attached to subsequent declarations. In my opinion, nothing is more dangerous than to allow the facts of a particular case to invade a rule of law to which, when once settled, ought to be invariably applied.

Perhaps one of the most important cases on the subject is the decision of Lord Langdale in *Sidmouth v. Sidmouth* (1840) 2 Beav 447, a well known case. It was stated in the argument before me, that Lord Langdale in that case weighed and considered the subsequent declarations made by Lord Stowell, as to his intention in making the lodgment which he had made. Lord Langdale did nothing of the sort. He had to deal with two sets of conversations, one set which was actually contemporaneous with the lodgment, and another set which was subsequent to the lodgment. He put aside altogether the latter, and entertained solely the conversations and declarations which were contemporaneous with the lodgment. And he has so expressed himself very plainly. He says, p. 455, "That contemporaneous acts, and even contem-poraneous declarations of the parent, may amount to such evidence, has often been decided. Subsequent acts and declarations of the parent are not evidence to support the trust, although subsequent acts and declarations of the child may be so; but generally speaking we are to look to what was said and done at the time."

Sidmouth v. Sidmouth is accordingly one of the ruling authorities that subsequent declarations of the parent are not admissible to alter the presumption raised by the advancement; and if I were to name any one principle of law as better settled than another, I should say that it is the rule that no declaration of the father, at a period subsequent to the advancement, is admissible to control the gift which the law implies as against him. I should not have considered it necessary to comment on these principles of law but for the character and length of the arguments which were addressed to me.

But it is also contended that, whatever may have been the role of law before, it has been altered by Vice-Chancellor Stuart's decision in *Devoy v. Devoy* (1857) 3 Sm & G 403, which it is said is an express authority to compel me to admit this document of April, 1871, in evidence, and the following passage in the judgment of Vice-Chancellor Stuart is referred to:– He says (3 Sm & G 406), "In support of that argument it has been said, that if the father had died before he gave evidence of the nature of the transaction, no record would have been preserved of the transaction, and the Court must then have given effect to it as an advancement to the child. The circumstance that if the father had died, the evidence would have been lost, cannot in the slightest degree affect the truth of the case, where the evidence is not lost." And then it is said, that the evidence here is not lost, and that we have it under the hand of the man himself that he made the lodgment for the purpose stated in the memorandum. It would appear to me, assuming *Devoy v. Devoy* to have been rightly decided, that there is a marked distinction between the evidence of a living man on his oath, and a scrap of paper written by him, and found among his papers after his death. In the former case you can probe his conscience, and examine him as to the truth and grounds of his statement. That case was followed in *Stone v. Stone* 3 Jur NS 708; and it came again before the same Judge in *Forrest v. Forrest* 13 WR 380. Now the last case was a very peculiar case. Two points arose in it; first, whether certain transactions of the testator in relation to certain shares, he standing *in loco parentis* at the time, were to be considered as amounting to an advancement. These the Vice-Chancellor considered did not amount to an advancement, and it is unnecessary that I should go into the grounds on which he so decided. But I feel bound to say, that it appears to me that the report can scarcely be accurate as to the grounds on which he rested that decision. Because the Vice-Chancellor is made to state that, in order to support the advancement, it should be shown that the purchase of the shares, when it was made by the testator in the Defendant's name, was *intended* by him as an advancement. This view would throw the *onus* of proof on the party claiming the advancement, which is at right angles with all the authorities. But another question arose in that case, viz., whether there had been a subsequent gift *inter vivos*; and on this part of the case a document was produced in which the testator called the shares his own property: and the question was, whether that document was admissible in evidence. This case of *Forrest v. Forrest* has been relied on before me as an authority, that in a case of advancement, such a subsequent document was admissible. It decided no such thing. The document was offered in relation to the gift *inter vivos*; and Vice-Chancellor Stuart, apparently with great doubt, admitted the document, but at a stage of the case when he had entirely disposed of the question of advancement. He is reported to have said, that "he had great difficulty in making up his mind, whether the paper in the handwriting of the testator giving an account of his property, was receivable in evidence or not." There was this entry in the paper, "South Wales Railway in C.B.T.'s (the Defendant's) hands belong to J.R.F." the testator. The Vice-Chancellor proceeds, "No doubt, if an advancement was once made, subsequent declarations by the person who made the advancement were immaterial, inasmuch as the property had already passed." It was another question, however, in a case of alleged gift, where the only evidence was that of the claimant. In the very valuable Treatise of Mr. Lewin on Trusts, p. 137 (4th ed.), is this passage– "Of course the father cannot defeat the advancement by any subsequent declaration of intention. But his evidence is admissible for the purpose of showing what was the intention at the time." The only authority for that latter proposition was a case of *Devoy v. Devoy.* That was a very difficult case. There the father was living, and he had admitted his evidence as to the nature of the transaction. He still thought that he was justified in admitting the evidence of the father in that case; but he was not sure that the case went quite so far as to support the proposition of Mr. Lewin. After those observations I do not think that *Devoy v. Devoy* can be fairly cited as an authority that declarations of the father subsequently to the advancement are admissible. I say nothing about the actual decision in *Devoy v. Devoy.* I have no such case before me here; but I must say that it is no authority whatever for the admission in evidence of mere declarations of the father subsequent to the advancement. Vice-Chancellor Stuart himself, in *Forrest v. Forrest,* as will be observed in the passage I have quoted from his judgment, states the role of law to be otherwise.

I think it right that I should call attention to the case of *Williams v. Williams* (1863) 32 Beav 370, before Lord Romilly, who had to consider the admissibility of the father's evidence even in his lifetime. That was the case of a purchase of real estate made by the father in the name of the son, who afterwards had died. But the father was a living man, and the question was, whether that purchase was intended for the son, or whether the son was a trustee for the father. The father himself had given evidence, and Lord Romilly at page 372 says, "This is solely a question of intention; it depends on what the intention of the Plaintiff was when he made this purchase and these advances on mortgage, not what his intention now is." He then went through the evidence, and says, page 274, "I think myself therefore bound to reject from my consideration all that portion of the evidence of the father now, as to what his intention was before." That was the way Lord Romilly dealt with the evidence. "The decided cases show that his present declaration to that effect could not have been regarded after his decease to create a trust in the son, and I consider myself equally bound to disregard them now, although he is alive. On such occasions, the declaration to that effect by the father must be contemporaneous with the event itself." I am of opinion, therefore, that this document is not admissible in evidence.

It was also contended that this document was receivable in evidence, on the ground that it was an admission by Sir Justin Sheil against his pecuniary interest. I do not at all comprehend such a view of the memorandum. I have examined the cases relied on; they seem to me to have no application whatever, and that ground for the admission of the memorandum also fails.

The document being inadmissible, it is altogether unnecessary to consider the question whether the trust declared by it is too vague.

I shall, therefore, declare that the £2000 Russian 5 per cent bonds, and £200 Victoria 6 per cent bonds, form no part of the assets of Sir Justin Sheil."

Persons in Loco Parentis to a Child

The presumption also applies where the donor or purchaser of property stands *in loco parentis* to the person in whose name this property is held or bought.[25]

Does the Presumption Apply in other Circumstances?

The position in relation to gifts made by a mother to her child is far from settled and there are conflicting authorities on the question in this jurisdiction. While there have been no recent decisions in this area which might clarify the position, it is likely particularly given the reasoning of the Supreme Court in *Re Tilson*,[26] which stressed the concept of joint parental responsibility towards children, that the conclusion reached by Johnston J in *Re Grimes*[27] would be preferred to that arrived at by the Supreme Court in *McCabe v. Ulster Bank Ltd.*[28]

Re Grimes: Gore Grimes v. Grimes
[1937] IR 470

A widowed mother purchased securities in the joint names of herself and her son. After her death it was held by Johnston J that the presumption of advancement applied to the securities purchased in the joint names. He held further that even if the presumption did not apply, the mother's intention to benefit her son in the circumstances of the case was sufficiently strong to rebut any presumption of a resulting trust.

JOHNSTON J stated at pp.472–478: "This case raises a nice point upon which conflicting views have been expressed by great equity Judges in England. I am not aware that the matter has ever come before the Irish Courts.

The question upon which I am called upon to decide is whether a purchase of a miscellaneous block of securities – ordinary shares, preference shares and

---

[25] *Bennet v. Bennet* (1879) 10 Ch D 474. See also *Shephard v. Cartwright* [1955] AC 431, 445.
[26] [1951] IR 1.
[27] [1937] IR 470.
[28] [1939] IR 1.

debentures issued by a number of trading concerns – by a widowed mother in the joint names of herself and her son (who was her only child) is sufficient to raise the doctrine of advancement in the same way as would the purchase of such securities by a father in the names of himself and a son.

It appears that a Mr. Christopher Grimes, who was engaged during his lifetime in a number of profitable undertakings, died in the year 1904, leaving a considerable amount of property behind him. He had been married twice, first to a Miss Hickey, by whom he had a number of children, and secondly to a Miss Rochford, by whom he had one son, Patrick by name. He made a will disposing of his property, by which he made a certain provision for the members of his first marriage, for his widow and for his son Patrick. The widow, Mrs. Elizabeth Grimes, seems to have been provided for in a generous way, and she lived during her widowhood in comfortable circumstances and her son Patrick resided with her until her death in 1930. He was born in 1891 and came of age on January 4th 1912. His father by his will had provided a sum of £100 yearly for his education, and had left him a certain amount of property which was worth anything from £50 to £100 yearly. He received an excellent secondary education at Castleknock College, and he entered the office of his half-brother, Mr. Christopher Gore-Grimes, who has an established and well-known business as a solicitor, as an apprentice, when he was about eighteen years of age. Subsequently he became an assistant solicitor in his half-brother's office, and in 1918 he became a partner. His widowed mother seems to have had a considerable amount of ready cash with which to amuse herself, and during the years from, I think, 1913 until nearly the date of her death (which took place on July 11th, 1930) she bought a considerable amount of securities in public companies. Some of these – I think the greater part of them both in number and value – were purchased in her own name and some in the joint names of herself and her son. The only other dates to which I need refer to are the dates of Patrick's marriage to Miss Moira Finn which took place on August 16th, 1933, and that of his death in March, 1934. There was no issue of the marriage, and by Patrick's will he left all his property to his wife.

Probate of Mrs. Elizabeth Grimes' will was taken out by Mr. Christopher Grimes and Dr. Michael Walsh on October 29th, 1930, and the terms of the will have already given rise to a considerable amount of litigation. A summons for the construction of the will and for general administration was heard by me in October, 1935, and ultimately upon June 29th, 1936, it was found to be necessary to make a general order for the carrying out of the trusts of the will. On an inquiry before the Examiner as to the assets of the deceased, it was ruled by him that the shares which stood in the joint names of the deceased and her son were not assets of the late Mrs. Elizabeth Grimes, and the Court is now called upon to re-consider that ruling.

In the case of *Sayre v. Hughes* (1868) LR 5 Eq 376 it was definitely decided by Sir John Stuart V.C. in 1868 that the doctrine of advancement applied in the case of a widowed mother and her daughter and that that doctrine was not confined to the case of a father and a child. That was no mere *obiter dictum*, but a binding decision upon facts that actually raised the point. If that decision stood alone the matter would have been removed from the region of doubt, but ten years later, in the case of *Bennet v. Bennet* (1879) 10 Ch D 474, the decision was dissented from by no less an authority than Jessel M.R., and *hanc illae lacrimae*. Now, I have the utmost diffidence in proceeding to appear to criticise anything that Jessel M.R. ever uttered, but I am bound to say that his reasoning in *Bennet v. Bennet* is singularly unconvincing. First of all, it was very largely based upon the case of *In re de Visme* (1863) 2 De GJ & S 17; but that was the case of a mother who was living apart from her husband, and a son, and the existence of a father at the time when the controversy arose suggests a distinction which would appear to make an essential difference. Further, the evidence in *Bennet's Case*, when it is closely examined, does not disclose a claim with which a Court of law or equity could have much sympathy; and, lastly, it is difficult to understand what this great equity Judge really intended to express when he used the expression: "In other words, the presumption of gift arises from the moral obligation to give." It has been argued in the present case that the "moral obligation," so far as it is to be observed in a Court of equity, might reasonably be regarded as resting upon the shoulders of a widowed mother as well as upon the shoulders of a father.

The decision of the Court of Appeal in *Batstone v. Salter* (1875) 10 Ch App 431, so far as it goes, is in accordance with the decision of Stuart V.C. At any rate, it is not inconsistent with it; and in *Hepworth v. Hepworth* (1870) LR 11 Eq 10, Sir Richard Malins V.C. seems to have accepted the Vice-Chancellor's decision as a correct statement of the law. At p. 14 he said: "The case of *Sayre v. Hughes* before Vice-Chancellor Stuart is a positive authority in favour of what I am deciding upon the general presumption arising from the relation of parent and child. It was there decided that there being a transfer of stocks to a child by the parent, without any evidence to rebut the presumption of an intended benefit, the child was entitled absolutely to the money so transferred." It is to be observed that in this passage Malins V.C. spoke of the relationship of "parent and child" and not of "father and child."

In a matter of this kind, where there is a conflict of judicial authority, it is of interest to consider what the text-book writers say. It is true that "Halsbury" (second ed., vol. 15, p. 717) takes sides with Jessel M.R.; but I observe that in other text-books the principle laid down by Stuart V.C. is adopted. These include White and Tudor's Leading Cases, Seton on Decrees, and a recent edition of Story's Equity Jurisprudence (Second English ed., pp. 830, 831; Thirteenth ed. p. 190). In Lewin on Trusts it is suggested that the provision of sect. 21 of the Married Women's Property Act, 1882, rendering married women having separate property liable for the maintenance of their children, "may be material." However, be that as it may, it seems to me that there was a presumption in this case that the son was intended to be advanced and that for that reason the ruling of the Examiner ought to be upheld.

If, however, I am wrong in arriving at that conclusion for the reasons that I have stated, there is another matter which I must carefully consider. In *Bennet's Case* (1879) 10 Ch D 474, Jessel M.R., while disapproving of the principle by which Stuart V.C. was guided, said that he would have had no hesitation in deciding in the same way as the Vice-Chancellor did, having regard to the evidence. He added these important words (which, I take leave to say, suggest to me a certain degree of misgiving in his mind as to the principle that he was purporting to lay down): "In the case of a mother – that is, the case of a widowed mother – it is easier to prove a gift than in the case of a stranger; in the case of a mother very little additional evidence beyond the relationship is wanted, there being very little additional motive required to induce a mother to make a gift to her child."

I have been assisted greatly by the powerful argument which has been addressed to me by Mr. Binchy, who contends that whatever presumption is raised by the facts of the case, the evidence and the inferences that I ought to draw therefrom are conclusive in favour of the executors. He bases his contention chiefly on the fact that Patrick Grimes acquired such a considerable proportion of his father's assets – first, under his father's will and then indirectly under his mother's will, and he contends that the question of "advancement" could not arise under such circumstances. At the time of the purchase of the shares in the joint names his education was complete; he had been given a profession; he had reached twenty-one years of age; and he had been "fully advanced." Consequently, if a presumption of advancement arises, it must be regarded as having been rebutted by these facts. If, on the contrary, there is a resulting trust, there is no evidence of a rebutting character to displace it. That, I think, is the gist of Mr. Binchy's argument. There was a time, of course, when Chancery Judges were disposed to weigh the question of what they called the "full advancement" and the "partial advancement" of children; but, for my part, I am not aware of any fixed standard by which such a matter should be determined apart from the wishes of the settlor. That seems to have been the view of Chief Baron Eyre, who, in the case of *Dyer v. Dyer* (1788) 2 Cox Eq Cas 92, referring to a decision of Lord Nottingham and one of Lord Hardwicke, said: "And yet the rule in a Court of equity, as recognised in other cases, is that the father is the only judge as to the *quantum* of a son's possession. That distinction, therefore of a son's being provided for or not, is not very solidly taken or uniformly adhered to." In the case of *Fox v. Fox* (1863) 15 Ir Ch R 89, in 1863, in which these matters were all discussed before a very strong Court of Appeal, Baron Deasy said: "It would be difficult to act on the distinction suggested between full and partial provision – a distinction which Chief Baron Eyre said was neither solidly taken nor uniformly adhered to."

I think that, even if the doctrine of advancement does not apply, there is very strong evidence in the case upon which I ought to act in favour of Mrs. Patrick Grimes's claim. I accept the evidence of old Mrs. Walsh as to the terms of intimacy and affection that existed between the late Mrs. Grimes and her

son. "He was the only son of his mother and she was a widow." He resided
with her until the day of her death, and he did not marry until after her death,
when he was 42 years of age. It is plain from all the evidence in the case that
the deceased was an excellent business woman and that she knew all that was
to be known as to the buying and selling of stocks and shares and as to the ups
and downs of the share market. She had a large number of securities which
stood in her own name. Why did she acquire other securities, purchasing them
in the joint names of herself and her son? What motive could she possibly
have had for adopting that course except parental affection and the desire to
benefit her son? Why did she purchase stocks, shares and securities in certain
public companies in her own sole name and other stocks, shares and securities
in the very same public companies in the joint names of herself and her son?
The transaction in regard to the issue of bonus shares by the Munster and
Leinster Bank has been closely examined by Mr. FitzGibbon and is certainly
of a very remarkable character, if Patrick's name was introduced as a trustee
only. What possible reason could there be for the appearance of the son's
name as a trustee in these transactions? The answer to these questions is to be
found in the evidence of Mrs. Walsh who tells me that in 1912 she actually
advised her friend to adopt this method of benefiting Patrick. If I accept Mrs.
Walsh's evidence as to this matter – and I see no reason for rejecting it – I must
come to the conclusion that no resulting trust was intended by the deceased.

I may say that eminent equity Judges seem to think that the fact that the
settlor was purchasing shares in his own name at a time when he was purchasing
shares in the joint names of himself and his child was a consideration which
was almost, if not quite, conclusive against the suggestion of a resulting trust.
In the case of *Fox v. Fox* Baron Deasy says: "Now, with respect to the funded
property, there is no evidence whatever of any contemporaneous act or
declaration of the father. All we know is that at and after the time of the joint
investments, he held stock in his own name, which would seem to indicate a
difference of intention with respect to the two classes of property which he
kept so differently invested." The present is even a stronger case in favour of
the doctrine of advancement than *Fox v. Fox*. In this case not only did the
deceased acquire and hold stocks and shares in her own name and in the joint
names of herself and her son, but actually some of the securities so acquired
and held were securities in the same public companies.

There is a valuable passage in the judgment of Sir Edward Sullivan M.R.
in the case of *Talbot v. Cody* (1874) IR 10 Eq 138, to which I ought to refer. It
is true that in that case the investment of the money was an investment by
means of deposit receipts in a bank, but that does not alter the principle. At p.
147, the Master of the Rolls said: "Here is a case where the testator for a great
number of years had been constantly taking out deposit receipts in his own
name alone and other deposit receipts in the joint names of himself and his
wife. The inference from that, surely, is that he conceived that the effect of a
deposit receipt in their joint names would be different from the effect of a

deposit receipt in his own name. Why should he put in his wife's name at all if he conceived that the consequences would be the same? Why did he not keep all the deposit receipts in his own name? His not doing so is almost conclusive to show that he had some reason for putting the money in his wife's name . . . The only motive that can be reasonably suggested, I think, is, that his wife should have it by survivorship."

I am satisfied that from 1912, when the buying of these securities began, Mrs. Grimes knew, or, at any rate, believed, that a purchase in the joint names would benefit her son, and, consequently, I see no reason whatever for disturbing the ruling of the Examiner."

McCabe v. Ulster Bank Ltd
[1939] IR 1

A widow lodged money in a deposit account in the names of herself and her three daughters. Her executor brought an application for a declaration that the sum remaining in the account at her death was part of her assets. The Supreme Court held, in granting the declaration, that the mother's intention to confer a benefit on her daughters was not sufficient to rebut the presumption of a resulting trust. Murnaghan J added that where there were no circumstances to go on save the mere relationship of mother and child, there was no ground for inferring a presumption which would rebut a resulting trust.

MURNAGHAN J stated at pp.9–15: "This appeal brings before this Court in a rather precise way the question whether a rule of equity jurisprudence, which has on several occasions been accepted, and yet has been denied by high authority, should now be adopted as valid.

This alleged rule sets up in the case of a purchase by a mother in the name of a child a presumption sufficient to rebut a resulting trust.

I shall first briefly state the facts which bring the question before the Court, and then proceed to examine the authorities and the principles upon which they are founded.

The plaintiff sues as executor of Mary Anne Lynch, deceased, for a declaration that the sum of £225 lodged with the Ulster Bank, Ltd., in the names of the deceased, Mrs. Mary Donohoe, Mrs. Bridget Devine and Mrs. Anne McGovern was assets of the said deceased. Mary Anne Lynch was a widow, who resided at Killycleggan, County Cavan. She had a small farm with some stock, and a sum of money, in respect of which the question arises. She died on 25th September, 1932, having made a specific bequest of her farm, and having bequeathed her residuary estate for charitable purposes. The evidence was very meagre, both as to the relationship of the deceased, and as to the facts of the deposit.

Three of the defendants were daughters of Mary Anne Lynch, and were all married and living in the United States of America. So far as the evidence shows, they might have been brought up by their father, and have emigrated while he was alive. The defendants were not represented at the hearing, and beyond a statement that the deceased had written asking some of them to come home, no facts are in evidence beyond the mere relationship. There are, therefore, in this case no grounds for the view that the deceased had placed herself *in loco parentis* to her children – meaning by this phrase that she had undertaken to bring them up and provide for them.

The deceased lodged £50 on deposit in her sole name in 1917, and gradually added to this amount sums from time to time. On 12th November, 1926, she lodged £265 in the names of herself and Father Brady. The deposit receipt was in the form that it was payable to either of the persons named, and accordingly as between herself and the Bank the depositor could, if she retained the deposit receipt, always withdraw the money. There was no evidence, besides, of any declaration of intention to benefit Father Brady, and, as he was a stranger, equity would raise the implication of a resulting trust if he were the survivor while the money remained in the Bank. After about 15 months, *i.e.*, in February, 1928, Mrs. Lynch drew out the money, then amounting to £250, and relodged it in her own name and that of her three daughters, the same form of receipt being adopted. Mr. F. C. Hartness, the Bank Manager, during this period, was examined at the trial, but he could give no account of the circumstances under which the change in the deposit was made. Between 10th February, 1928, and 6th September, 1932, the deceased withdrew and relodged varying sums, the amount last deposited being £225. All the lodgments were in the name of deceased and her three daughters and were in the same form – payable to any of them.

The learned Circuit Court Judge pointed out that the deposit receipt was in the same form as that in *Owens v. Greene and Freeley v. Greene* [1932] IR 225 in this Court; and he quoted from the judgment of Kennedy C.J. passages to show that either a relationship which would rebut the inference of a resulting trust or express declaration of present intention to benefit would affect the ownership of the depositors. He further said "in these circumstances the law is that I am bound to presume an intention to advance, which presumption may be rebutted by evidence to the contrary."

On appeal being taken to the High Court, the President referred to the decision in *In re Grimes* [1937] IR 470, where Johnston J. held that there was a presumption of advancement in the case of a purchase by a mother in the name of her child, but the learned President took the view that this presumption was rebutted by the form of the deposit receipt, and that Mrs. Lynch intended to retain full dominion during her lifetime and to pass what was left to her daughters as survivors – an intention which would be invalid as it would be testamentary in character. Mr. Justice O'Byrne held that the doctrine of advancement applied, and that the facts of the case were not sufficient to rebut this presumption.

On appeal to this Court Mr. McGonigal has very fully opened all the relevant authorities, and these have been examined with care in the absence of the defendants, who have not appeared. I shall therefore proceed to refer to these authorities in order to ascertain upon what principle they are founded.

The leading case on this subject is that of *Dyer v. Dyer* (1788) 2 Cox Eq Cas 92; White & Tudor's L. C. in Equity, 9th Ed., vol. 2, p. 749. The decision in that case is, however, largely based on Sir Heneage Finch's decision in *Grey v. Grey* (1677) 2 Swans 594. That was a purchase of fee simple estates by a father in the name of his son. In Finch's Chancery Cases, ed. of 1725, at p. 341, the reason is given why such a purchase is for the son's benefit: "Now, where there is no clear proof of any trust between the *father and son*, the law will never imply a trust, because the natural consideration of blood and the obligation which lies on the father in conscience to provide for his son are predominant, and must overrule all manner of implications." At this time (1678) the Chancellor sought to arrive at a determination by considering whether the son had been fully advanced, in which case there might be a resulting trust.

Dyer v. Dyer was a case of copyhold estate, determined in the Exchequer. Eyre L.C.B. delivered the judgment of the Court, and stated the rule of a Court of Equity in raising the implication of a resulting trust where a conveyance was taken in the name of one who did not provide the purchase money. He then said: "The cases go one step further, and prove that the circumstance of one or more of the nominees, being a child or children of the purchaser, is to operate by rebutting the resulting trust; and it has been determined in so many cases that the nominee being a child shall have such operation as a circumstance of evidence, that we should be disturbing landmarks if we suffered either of these propositions to be called in question." Later on in his judgment he pointed out "that distinction, therefore, of the son being provided for or not, is not very solidly taken or uniformly adhered to."

In the case of *Finch v. Finch* (1883) 15 Ves 43, before Lord Eldon L.C. *Dyer v. Dyer* was approved of. Lord Eldon said:– "Where the purchase is in the name of a son, that purchase is an advancement *prima facie*; and in this sense, that this principle of law and presumption is not to be frittered away by nice refinements."

I do not find, however, that Lord Eldon always stated the principle in precisely the same way, because in *Rider v. Kidder* (1805) 10 Ves 360, at p. 367, after referring to *Dyer v. Dyer*, he said:– "But the case of a child was distinguished from that of a stranger, in which there is not that natural affection which would beat down the presumption, arising from the advance of the money."

No case of a purchase by a mother in the name of a child appears in the reported cases until *In re De Visme* (1863) 2 De GJ & S 17 in the year 1863. A mother living apart from her husband had invested the savings out of her separate estate in the names of her son and daughter. After the mother's death the daughter, who was executrix, presented a petition by reason of her brother having become a lunatic, asking for a transfer to herself, as executrix of her mother, of the stock in the joint names. Counsel making the application submitted that there was no presumption that a purchase by a mother in the name of a child is intended as an advancement, and the Lords Justices made the order, but there was, I think, a stronger reason, as stated in the case, viz., that the mother's object in making the investments in the names of her son and daughter was alleged by the petitioner to be the securing the funds from the control of her husband.

Sayre v. Hughes (1868) LR 5 Eq 376, decided by Sir John Stuart V.C. in 1868 is the first reported decision that the doctrine of advancement applied in the case of a widowed mother and her daughter. The Vice-Chancellor seems to found his opinion on the use by Chief Baron Eyre in *Dyer v. Dyer* (1788) 2 Cox Eq Cas 92 of the terms "parent" and "child" instead of "father" and "son," and on the principle that natural affection is sufficient to rebut a resulting trust.

In *Hepworth v. Hepworth* (1870) LR 11 Eq 10, decided in 1870, a case of father and son, Sir John Malins V.C. referred to *Sayre v. Hughes* as an authority.

In the case of *Batstone v. Salter* (1875) LR 10 Ch App 431 where a widowed mother transferred stocks into the names of herself, her married daughter and her son-in-law, Lord Cairns used language which seems to imply that he allowed, as did counsel in arguing the case, the presumption in the case of a mother. For he said:- "Whatever presumption there is in favour of an unmarried daughter in the case of a transfer to her, the same presumption arises in this case where the transfer was to a married daughter and her husband."

Bennet v. Bennet (1879) LR 10 Ch D 474 was strictly not a case of rebuttal of a resulting trust, but was whether a sum of money raised by mortgage and paid over to a son was a gift or a loan. The case was, however, dealt with on the same principles. Jessel M.R. examined the authorities and criticised the decision in *Sayre v. Hughes*. He quotes Lord Eldon, in *Ex parte Pye* (1811) 18 Ves 140, that a person *in loco parentis* is a person "meaning to put himself *in loco parentis*: in the situation of the person described as the lawful father of the child," and, as explained by Lord Cottenham in *Powys v. Mansfield* (1837) 3 My & Cr 359, as "applicable to these parental offices and duties to which the subject in question has reference, namely, to the office and duty of the parent to make provision for the child." Jessel M.R. points out that in *Sayre* v. *Hughes* the presumption is supposed to be founded upon maternal affection as a motive of bounty, and his criticism is that, although this may arise from moral obligation, it is not a moral obligation which is enforced in a Court of Equity.

Although Jessel M.R. seems to me to push too far what was involved in the order made in *In re De Visme* when he says:– "All the Court of Appeal decided was that there was no such moral obligation in the case of a mother as the Court could take notice of as such," his criticism deserves very serious consideration. The issue really centres about the point whether the presumption is to be rebutted by a moral obligation arising through natural affection or other causes, or whether the obligation must be that of a father, or one who has undertaken the duties of a father, to provide for his child.

Where a husband makes a purchase in the name of his wife there is no resulting trust, but in the earliest cases this seems to have been arrived at from an artificial rule that a wife could not be trustee for her husband. Where a wife deposits her money in the name of herself and her husband there is no presumption in favour of the husband. In *Foley v. Foley* [1911] 1 IR 281, at p. 285, in the Court of Appeal, the Lord Chancellor said:– "It is, no doubt, settled law that the onus lies on the husband to establish, as a matter of evidence to the satisfaction of the Court, that his wife paid this money into their joint names in order that it should be their joint property and should belong to the survivor." Natural affection as a motive of bounty has not been regarded as sufficient to rebut a resulting trust where a wife places her money in the joint names of herself and her husband.

Soar v. Foster (1858) 4 K & J 152 was a case in which a man purchased stocks in his own name and that of his deceased wife's sister, with whom he had gone through a form of marriage after Lord Lyndhurst's Act (5 & 6 Wm. 4, c. 54) had made such a marriage null and void. Sir Page Wood V.C. recognised the moral obligation to provide, but held that it could not amount to a presumption sufficient to displace the resulting trust in Equity.

In the case of *In re Grimes deceased; Grimes v. Grimes* [1937] IR 470 Johnston J. held in favour of the presumption, but he noted the uncertainty prevailing in the minds of authoritative text writers, having regard to the conflicting decisions.

During the argument the inclination of my mind was to uphold as far as possible the presumption in the case of mother and child, but upon full examination of the cases I find it difficult to base the presumption upon any sound principle. Neither natural affection nor moral obligation has been consistently relied upon to found the presumption, and I have come to the conclusion that the presumption must be based upon the obligation to make provision which a Court of Equity recognises in the case of a father, or of one who has assumed his obligation in this respect.

In many cases of widowed mothers very slight circumstances may be sufficient to place the widow *in loco parentis, i.e.,* of having assumed the father's obligation to provide. In such cases there will be a basis for the presumption, but in a case such as the present, where there are no circumstances to go upon save the mere relationship of mother and child, there is, in my opinion, no ground for an equitable presumption which will rebut a resulting trust.

In my opinion the appeal should be allowed and a declaration made, but in the circumstances costs should not be given against the defendants, who have not appeared to contest the matter."

Rebutting the Presumption of Advancement

The presumption of advancement will be rebutted if evidence is adduced to show that no gift was intended by the donor or transferor.[29] However, it would appear that the presumption of advancement cannot be rebutted by evidence that the transfer was made for a fraudulent or illegal purpose where this purpose has been wholly or partly carried out.[30] So, where for example, a husband transfers land into his wife's name with a view to achieving an unlawful purpose, he cannot adduce evidence of the improper purpose to rebut the presumption of advancement.[31]

However, the effect of the decision of the English Court of Appeal in *Tribe v. Tribe*[32] is that evidence of an illegal purpose can be relied upon where this purpose has not been wholly or partly carried into effect.

Parkes v. Parkes
[1980] ILRM 137

See *supra* Chapter 2, p.25.

Tribe v. Tribe
[1996] Ch 107

The plaintiff had transferred shares in a family company to his son with a view to defrauding his creditors. The difficulties which might have led to claims being made against him were resolved and when the plaintiff sought to recover the shares from the defendant, the latter resisted his claim. The Court of Appeal held that the plaintiff transferor was entitled to adduce evidence of his intentions to rebut the presumption of advancement in favour of his son, which he successfully did.

MILLETT LJ stated at pp.122–135: "The plaintiff transferred his shareholding in his family company to his son, the defendant, for a pretended consideration which was not paid and was not intended to be paid. The transfer was, therefore, made for no consideration. If the transferee had been a nephew or a trusted stranger, the transaction would have given rise to a resulting trust. In such a

---

[29] *Per* Henchy J in *R.F. v. M.F.* [1995] 2 ILRM 572, 577.

[30] *Tribe v. Tribe* [1996] Ch 107. See also the *dicta* of Lord Denning MR in *Chettiar v. Chettiar* [1962] AC 294, 302. However, note that the High Court of Australia has recently rejected this principle in *Nelson v. Nelson* (1995) 132 ALR 133.

[31] *Parkes v. Parkes* [1980] ILRM 137.

[32] [1996] Ch 107, 124. This is one of the exceptions to the general rule against relying on one's own illegality and is known as the doctrine of *locus poenitentiae*.

case equity places the burden of proving that the transfer was intended to be by way of gift upon the transferee. If he cannot discharge that burden, he holds the shares as nominee and in trust for the transferor. The plaintiff, however, transferred the shares to his son, and accordingly the transaction gave rise to the presumption of advancement. In such a case the transfer is presumed to have been intended by way of gift. The burden of proving that it was not intended as a gift lies upon the transferor.

The judge found that the plaintiff did not intend to make a gift of the shares to his son. The company represented his life's work, and his shareholding in the company was his largest asset. He had other children besides the son to whom in the ordinary course of things he would wish to leave his property. But he faced substantial claims for dilapidations in respect of two leasehold properties which were occupied by the company but of which he was the tenant, and he was concerned that he could lose the shares. The judge accepted his evidence that he transferred the shares to his son as a nominee in order to conceal them from his creditors, and specifically from his two landlords, by creating the appearance that he no longer owned any shares in the company. That, of course, was an illegal purpose. Ordinarily a man who makes a gratuitous transfer of property to another for an illegal purpose is not allowed to rely on his purpose in making the transfer in order to rebut the presumption of advancement: see *Tinsley v. Milligan* [1994] 1 AC 340, 375, where Lord Browne-Wilkinson said:

> "In cases where the presumption of advancement applies, the plaintiff is faced with the presumption of gift and therefore cannot claim under a resulting trust unless and until he has rebutted that presumption of gift: for those purposes the plaintiff does have to rely on the underlying illegality and therefore fails."

The question in the present case is whether there is an exception to this principle where the transferor withdraws from the transaction before any part of the illegal purpose has been carried into effect. Unless that exception applies, the plaintiff's claim to recover his own shares from the son whom he trusted to hold them as his nominee must fail.

The judge held that there was such an exception and that it was applicable. The illegal purpose was never carried into effect. Neither of the landlords knew of the plaintiff's shareholding or was aware that he had disposed of it. Negotiations with the landlords were brought to a satisfactory conclusion without resorting to deception. It never became necessary.

The judge held that, because the illegal purpose had not been carried out, the plaintiff was entitled to withdraw from the transaction and to rely on his evidence of the reason why he transferred the shares to his son in order to rebut the presumption of advancement. According to the judge he had what is called a locus poenitentiae. It is submitted on behalf of the son that the judge was in error. First, it is said, the doctrine of the locus poenitentiae allows a party to an illegal contract to withdraw while the contract is still executory, but it has no application to a transfer of property; in such a case the illegal purpose is partly carried into effect as soon as the property is transferred. Secondly, and in the alternative, a transferor cannot rely on his illegal purpose to rebut the presumption of advancement, and it makes no difference that the illegal purpose has not been carried into effect. Thirdly, there was no true repentance in the present case. The plaintiff never abandoned his illegal purpose; he did not demand the return of his shares until the danger had passed and it was no longer necessary to conceal them from his creditors.

There are, in my opinion, two questions of some importance which fall for decision in the present case. The first is whether, once property has been transferred to a transferee for an illegal purpose in circumstances which give rise to the presumption of advancement, it is still open to the transferor to withdraw from the transaction before the purpose has been carried out and, having done so, give evidence of the illegal purpose in order to rebut the presumption of advancement. The second is whether, if so, it is sufficient for him to withdraw from the transaction because it is no longer necessary and without repenting of his illegal purpose. I shall deal with these two questions in turn.

The presumption of advancement and the locus poenitentiae
In *Tinsley v. Milligan* [1994] 1 AC 340, 370 Lord Browne-Wilkinson summarised the common law rules which govern the effect of illegality on the acquisition and enforcement of property rights in three propositions:

> "(1) property in chattels and land can pass under a contract which is illegal and would therefore have been unenforceable as a contract; (2) a plaintiff can at law enforce property rights so acquired provided that he does not need to rely on the illegal contract for any purpose other than providing the basis of his claim to a property right; and (3) it is irrelevant that the illegality of the underlying agreement was either pleaded or emerged in evidence: if the transferee has acquired legal title under the illegal contract that is enough."

The decision of the majority of their Lordships in that case was that the same principles applied in equity. It is, therefore, now settled that neither at law nor in equity may a party rely on his own fraud or illegality in order to found a claim or rebut a presumption, but that the common law and equity alike will assist him to protect and enforce his property rights if he can do so without relying on the fraud or illegality. This is the primary rule.

It is, however, also settled both at law and in equity that a person who has transferred property for an illegal purpose can nevertheless recover his property provided that he withdraws from the transaction before the illegal purpose has been wholly or partly performed. This is the doctrine of the locus poenitentiae and it applies in equity as well as at law: see *Symes v. Hughes* (1870) LR 9 Eq 475 for the former and *Taylor v. Bowers* (1876) 1 QBD 291 for the latter. The availability of the doctrine in a restitutionary context was expressly confirmed by Lord Browne-Wilkinson in *Tinsley v. Milligan* [1994] 1 AC 340, 374.

While both principles are well established, the nature of the relationship between them is unclear. Is the doctrine of the locus poenitentiae co-extensive with and by way of general exception to the primary rule? The question in the present case is whether a plaintiff who has made a gratuitous transfer of property to a person in whose favour the presumption of advancement arises can withdraw from the transaction before the illegal purpose has been carried into effect and then recover the property by leading evidence of his illegal purpose in order to rebut the presumption. Closely connected with this question is its converse: is a plaintiff who has made such a transfer in circumstances which give rise to a resulting trust so that he has no need to rely on the illegal purpose, as in *Tinsley v. Milligan* itself, barred from recovering if the illegal purpose has been carried out? If both questions are answered in the negative, then either the locus poenitentiae is a common law doctrine which has no counterpart in equity, or it is a contractual doctrine which has no place in the law of restitution.

It is convenient to consider first the position at common law. It is important to bear in mind that the common law starts from the opposite premise from that on which equity bases the presumption of resulting trust. In an action for money had and received, for example, whatever the relationship between the parties, the burden lies on the plaintiff to prove that the money was not paid by way of gift or pursuant to an enforceable contract. Absence of consideration is not of itself a ground of restitution: it is for the transferor to show that no gift was intended.

The leading case is *Taylor v. Bowers*. In order to prevent his creditors seizing his goods the plaintiff transferred all his stock-in-trade to one Alcock in exchange for fictitious bills of exchange. In the Divisional Court Cockburn CJ held, at p. 295:

> "where money has been paid, or goods delivered, under an unlawful agreement, but there has been no further performance of it, the party paying the money or delivering the goods may repudiate the transaction, and recover back his money or goods."

The decision was affirmed in the Court of Appeal. All four members of the court held that the plaintiff could prove his title without having to rely on the fraud. Significantly, however, Mellish LJ (with whom Baggallay JA agreed) laid stress on the fact that the illegal purpose had not been carried out and made it clear that, even though the plaintiff did not need to rely on the illegality in order to prove title, he could not have recovered the goods if the illegal purpose had been carried out.

The case is described as controversial and criticised in Goff and Jones, *Law of Restitution* (4th ed., 1993) p. 513 partly on the ground that the contract was not wholly executory because the goods had been handed over to Alcock. But the principle has been applied in subsequent cases and the case itself is cited without disapproval in *Tinsley v. Milligan* [1994] 1 AC 340, 374. It is too late now to hold that it was an illegitimate application of a contractual doctrine to a claim for restitution. But the proposition that the plaintiff did not need to rely on the illegality could not be supported today. It is explicable only on the basis that the rule that title can pass under an illegal contract had not yet been clearly established. Nowadays we would say that Alcock (or his successor in title) did not need to rely on the illegal nature of the contract pursuant to which the goods were delivered because the title passed to him despite the illegality and want of consideration; but the plaintiff did. In order to recover the goods as goods received and held to his own use he had to show that they had not been delivered by way of gift or pursuant to an enforceable contract. This required him to show that they had been delivered pursuant to an illegal contract which he had repudiated; and he could not repudiate the contract once the illegal purpose had been wholly or partly achieved.

In *Taylor v. Bowers* the goods were delivered for an illegal purpose but the delivery itself was not illegal. In *Bowmakers Ltd v. Barnet Instruments Ltd* [1945] KB 65 the transfers were assumed to be illegal and it was obviously too late for the transferor to invoke the locus poenitentiae. (In any case the transferor did not bring a claim in restitution but contented itself with pleading illegality as a defence to a claim in conversion.) In *Singh v. Ali* [1960] AC 167 Lord Denning, giving the opinion of the Board, confirmed the rule that title passes at law notwithstanding the illegal purpose for which the transfer was made. But he was clearly of the opinion that the transferor's claim to restitution was barred only where the illegal purpose had been carried out. He explained, at p. 176:

> "The reason is because the transferor, *having fully achieved his unworthy end,* cannot be allowed to turn round and repudiate the means by which he did it — he cannot throw over the transfer." (emphasis added.)

Lord Denning clearly intended it to be understood that the converse applies: the transferor is allowed to repudiate the transfer provided that the illegal purpose has not been achieved.

This has not been displaced by anything in *Tinsley v. Milligan*. Lord Browne-Wilkinson, at p. 374, expressly confirmed the existence of the doctrine of the locus poenitentiae and its application in a restitutionary context; indeed, he founded part of his reasoning upon it. Moreover, it is in accordance with ordinary restitutionary principles. The fact that title has passed is no bar to a claim for restitution; on the contrary, this is the normal case. But to succeed at law it is necessary for the transferor to repudiate the transaction which gave rise to its passing, and this is what the locus poenitentiae allows him to do.

The locus poenitentiae is not therefore an exclusively contractual doctrine with no place in the law of restitution. It follows that it cannot be excluded by the mere fact that the legal ownership of the property has become lawfully vested in the transferee. It would be unfortunate if the rule in equity were different. It would constitute a further obstacle to the development of a coherent and unified law of restitution. Most of the cases in equity have been concerned with gratuitous transfers made with the intention of defrauding creditors and often for a pretended consideration. It is not easy to discern any difference in principle between a transfer of property against fictitious bills of exchange and a transfer of shares for a stated consideration which it is not intended shall be paid.

The leading cases on illegality and resulting trusts prior to *Tinsley v. Milligan* are: *Curtis v. Perry* (1802) 6 Ves 739, *Ex parte Yallop* (1808) 15 Ves 60, *Groves v. Groves* (1829) 3 Y & J 163, *Coultwas v. Swan* (1871) 18 WR 746, *Symes v. Hughes* (1870) LR 9 Eq 475, *In re Great Berlin Steamboat Co.* (1884) 26 Ch D 616, *Chetty v. Servai* (1908) LR 35 Ind App 98 and *Rowan v. Dann* (1991) 64 P & CR 202.

In *Curtis v. Perry*, *Ex parte Yallop* and *Groves v. Groves* the claimant failed to recover. None of these cases is of assistance on the present question. In the first two it would have been unlawful for the claimant to have any beneficial interest in the property in dispute, and the claim to such an interest arising under an implied or resulting trust necessarily failed. *Groves v. Groves* cannot be regarded as a satisfactory case, since no consideration at all appears to have been given to the fact that the claimant did not need to rely on the illegal purpose of the transaction, and on this point the case must be taken to have been overruled by *Tinsley v. Milligan*. Moreover, a very narrow view was taken of the doctrine of the locus poenitentiae. But it is an early example of the refusal of the court to assist a transferor to recover his property where the illegal purpose has been carried out or where 'if the crime has not been completed, the merit is not his'. See 3 Y & J 163, 164.

In *Coultwas v. Swan*, *Symes v. Hughes* and *Rowan v. Dann* the property was transferred into the name of a nominee in order to put it beyond the reach of creditors (though in the first of these cases there was found to be no intent to defraud). In all three cases the transferor was permitted to recover. In none of them does it appear that any creditor was deceived. In *Symes v. Hughes* this appears to have been the principal ground of the decision; the case would have gone the other way if a creditor had been deceived. *Rowan v. Dann*, on the other hand, was decided at a time when *Tinsley v. Milligan* was under appeal to the House of Lords. Scott LJ contented himself by saying that every principle of law led to the conclusion that the transferor could recover: he could claim under a resulting trust and did not need to rely on his dishonest scheme; and he could withdraw from the scheme because the illegal purpose had not been carried out: see 64 P & CR 202, 209. The structure of the judgment of Scott LJ suggests that he regarded these as independent principles either one of which would have sufficed, but the court was not required to decide this and the case cannot be regarded as authority for the proposition. Woolf LJ did not refer to the fact that no creditor had been deceived.

In *In Re Great Berlin Steamboat Co.* the transferor was not allowed to recover because the illegal purpose had been partially carried out. In *Chetty v. Servai* the transferor was allowed to recover because the illegal purpose had not been carried out. That case concerned an Indian benami transaction in which the name of the apparent transferee is merely an alias for the transferor, but which bears obvious similarities to a nominee arrangement in English law. The opinion of Lord Atkinson contains a clear exposition of the law (at p. 102):

> "The fact that A has assumed the name of B in order to cheat X can be no reason whatever why a Court should assist or permit B to cheat A. But if A requires the help of the Court to get the estate back into his own possession, or to get the title into his own name, it may be very material to consider whether A has actually cheated X or not. If he has done so by means of his alias, then it has ceased to be a mere mask and has become a reality. It may then be very proper for a Court to say that it will not allow him to resume the individuality which he has once cast off in order to defraud others. If, however, he has not defrauded any one, there can be no reason why the Court should punish his intention by giving his estate away to B, whose roguery is even more complicated than his own. This appears to be the principle of the English decisions. For instance, persons have been allowed to recover property which they had assigned away . . . where they had intended to defraud creditors, who, in fact, were never injured . . . *But where the fraudulent or illegal purpose has actually been effected by means of the colourable grant, then the maxim applies, "In pari delicto potior est conditio possidentis". The Court will help neither party. "Let the estate lie where it falls."* " (emphasis added).

Prior to *Tinsley v. Milligan* no transferor had ever succeeded in recovering his property by enforcing a resulting trust where he had transferred the property for an illegal purpose and that purpose had been carried out. In *In Re Great Berlin Steamboat Co.* the transferor failed to recover for this very reason; in other cases where the transferor has succeeded he did so only because the illegal purpose had not been carried out.

In *Tinsley v. Milligan* the parties, who both contributed to the purchase of a house, arranged for the conveyance to be taken in the name of the appellant alone but on the understanding that it was to belong to them jointly. The purpose of this arrangement was to enable the respondent to perpetrate frauds on the Department of Social Security, and over a number of years the respondent, with the connivance of the appellant, made false claims for benefit. Despite this the respondent was allowed to recover.

In his dissenting speech Lord Goff refused to draw any distinction between cases where the presumption of advancement applied and cases in which the plaintiff could rely on a resulting trust. From the authorities he derived a single principle: that if one party puts property in the name of another for a fraudulent or illegal purpose neither law nor equity will allow him to recover the property. Even if he can establish a resulting trust in his favour he cannot enforce it. Given Lord Goff's opinion that there was but one principle in play, it was natural for him to describe the doctrine of the locus poenitentiae as an exception to that principle. Since the respondent could not bring herself within the exception, he would have allowed the appeal. This was not, however, the view of the majority. Lord Browne-Wilkinson expressly held at p. 371 that the rule was the same whether the plaintiff founded himself on a legal or an equitable title: he was entitled to succeed if he was not forced to rely on his own illegality, even if it emerged that the title on which he relied was acquired in the course of carrying through an illegal transaction. The respondent had established a resulting trust by showing that she had contributed to the purchase price and that there was a common understanding between her and the appellant that they should own the house equally. She had no need to allege or prove why she had allowed the house to be conveyed into the sole name of the appellant, since that fact was irrelevant to her claim.

The necessary consequence of this is that where he can rely on a resulting trust the transferor will normally be able to recover his property if the illegal purpose has not been carried out. In *Tinsley v. Milligan* she recovered even though the illegal purpose had been carried out. It does not, however, follow that the transferor will invariably succeed in such circumstances, so that the presence or absence of a locus poenitentiae is irrelevant where the transfer gives rise to a resulting trust. A resulting trust, like the presumption of advancement, rests on a presumption which is rebuttable by evidence (see *Standing v. Bowring* (1885) 31 Ch D 282, 287). The transferor does not need to allege or prove the purpose for which property was transferred into the name of the transferee; in equity he can rely on the presumption that no gift was intended. But the transferee cannot be prevented from rebutting the presumption by leading evidence of the transferor's subsequent conduct to show that it was inconsistent with any intention to retain a beneficial interest. Suppose, for example, that a man transfers property to his nephew in order to conceal it from his creditors, and suppose that he afterwards settles with his creditors on the footing that he has no interest in the property. Is it seriously suggested that he can recover the property? I think not. The transferor's own conduct would be inconsistent with the retention of any beneficial interest in the property. I can see no reason why the nephew should not give evidence of the transferor's dealings with his creditors to rebut the presumption of a resulting trust and show that a gift was intended. He would not be relying on any illegal arrangement but implicitly denying it. The transferor would have to give positive evidence of his intention to retain a beneficial interest and dishonestly conceal it from his creditors, evidence which he would not be allowed to give once the illegal purpose had been carried out.

This analysis is not, in my view, inconsistent with a passage in Lord Browne-Wilkinson's speech [1994] 1 AC 340, 374 where he said:

> "The equitable right, if any, must arise at the time at which the property was voluntarily transferred to the third party or purchased in the name of the third party. The existence of the equitable interest cannot depend upon events occurring

after that date. Therefore if, under the principle of locus poenitentiae, the courts recognise that an equitable interest did arise out of the underlying transaction, the same must be true where the illegal purpose was carried through. The carrying out of the illegal purpose cannot, by itself, destroy the pre-existing equitable interest."

But it does not follow that subsequent conduct is necessarily irrelevant. Where the existence of an equitable interest depends upon a rebuttable presumption or inference of the transferor's intention, evidence may be given of his subsequent conduct in order to rebut the presumption or inference which would otherwise be drawn.

Tinsley v. Milligan is, in my opinion, not authority for the proposition that a party who transfers property for an illegal purpose in circumstances which give rise to a resulting trust can invariably enforce the trust and recover the property even though the illegal purpose has been carried into effect. I do not accept the suggestion that cases such as *In re Great Berlin Steamboat Co.* have been impliedly overruled or that the dicta in the many cases, including *Taylor v. Bowers* and *Singh v. Ali*, indicating that the result would have been otherwise if the illegal purpose had or had not been carried out, must be taken to have been overruled.

The question in the present case is the converse: whether the transferor can rebut the presumption of advancement by giving evidence of his illegal purpose so long as the illegal purpose has not been carried into effect. The leading cases on illegality and the presumption of advancement are *Childers v. Childers* (1857) 3 K & J 310; *Crichton v. Crichton* [1896] 1 Ch 870; *Perpetual Executors and Trustees Association of Australia Ltd v. Wright* (1917) 23 CLR 185; *Gascoigne v. Gascoigne* [1918] 1 KB 223; *McEvoy v. Belfast Banking Co. Ltd* [1935] AC 24; *In re Emery's Investments' Trusts* [1959] Ch 410; *Chettiar v. Chettiar* [1962] AC 294 and *Tinker v. Tinker* [1970] P 136.

McEvoy v. Belfast Banking Co. Ltd and *In re Emery's Investments' Trusts* and the actual decision in *Chettiar v. Chettiar* can be put on one side, since in each of them the illegal purpose was carried out. In the latter case, however, Lord Denning repeated the view which he had expressed two years earlier in *Singh v. Ali*. He said [1962] AC 294, 302:

> "If the fraudulent purpose had not been carried out, there might well have been room for repentance and the father might have been allowed to have the land re-transferred to him, as in the cases to which counsel for the respondent referred, such as *Davies v. Otty* (1865) 35 Beav 208 and *Symes v. Hughes* (1870) LR 9 Eq 475, to which might be added *Petherpermal Chetty v. Muniandi Servai* (1908) LR 35 Ind App 98 where the subject was fully considered by their Lordships' Board. Where, however, the fraudulent purpose has actually been effected by means of the colourable transfer, there is no room for repentance."

This was plainly obiter, and the force of the passage is somewhat weakened by the fact that, of the three cases which Lord Denning cited in support, two were cases of resulting trust and the other was not a case of illegality at all. But it was undoubtedly his view that both at law and in equity property transferred for an illegal purpose was recoverable provided that the illegal purpose had not been carried out.

The other cases fall into two groups. *Childers v. Childers* and *Crichton v. Crichton* are examples of a number of cases, mostly in the first half of the nineteenth century, in which a father transferred property to his son in order to qualify him for office. In all the other cases the transferor put the property in the name of his wife or son in order to put it out of the reach of his creditors.

In *Childers v. Childers* the son died shortly afterwards without being aware of the transfer and without having been appointed to the office. Sir William Page Wood V-C held that the father could not recover the property, since he 'could not be heard to say' that he intended the transfer to take effect in fraud of the law. The Vice-Chancellor expressed some initial doubt whether the father might not have a locus poenitentiae where the object for which he had executed the deed altogether failed; but on consideration he came to the conclusion that earlier dicta to that effect could not stand. The same result was reached in *Crichton v. Crichton*, where it does not appear whether the son was appointed to the office or not. North J contented himself by remarking that the creation of a trust in favour of the father would have been in fraud of the law and that the father 'could not be heard to aver' its existence. This formulation is open to criticism since the case was not concerned with the creation of a trust. If the presumption of advancement was rebutted the father would never have parted with the beneficial interest at all; that is what is meant by saying that the property was held on a resulting trust for him. The real question was whether he 'could be heard to aver' his illegal purpose in order to rebut the presumption of advancement. But while the question was misstated the answer was clearly in the negative.

The remaining English cases are *Gascoigne v. Gascoigne* and *Tinker v. Tinker*. In each case a man put property into the name of his wife (so that the presumption of advancement applied) in order to protect it from his creditors, and then sought to recover the property from her when the marriage broke down. The two cases, however, were very different. In *Gascoigne v. Gascoigne* the husband was in financial difficulties and, in the words of Lush J (at p. 226) 'concocted the scheme of putting his property in her name, while retaining the beneficial interest, for the purpose of misleading, defeating, and delaying present or future creditors'. Furthermore his subsequent conduct was inconsistent with the retention of a beneficial interest: when called upon to pay taxes in respect of the property, he had refused, saying that it was his wife's property. The husband was trying to rebut the presumption of advancement which his own conduct confirmed by setting up his own dishonest intention after he had acted on it.

In *Tinker v. Tinker* the husband was an honest man who bought a house intending it to be the matrimonial home and put it into his wife's name in order to avoid any risk of its being taken by his creditors in case his business was not a success. The business was not in financial difficulty and was never in danger of becoming so. It is, of course, perfectly legitimate for a person who is solvent to make a gift of his property, particularly the matrimonial home, to his wife in order to protect her against the possibility of future business failure. It was not, therefore, a case of illegality at all. The husband intended to make a gift to his wife, and claimed to recover the subject matter of the gift only when his wife left him.

Accordingly, the question whether a transferor can repudiate his fraudulent scheme before it is carried into effect and then give evidence of his dishonest intention in order to rebut the presumption of advancement did not fall for consideration in either of those cases. It was not considered in *Gascoigne v. Gascoigne*, where it was arguably too late for him to do so; and it did not arise in *Tinker v. Tinker*, where he was found to have had no dishonest intention.

In *Perpetual Executors and Trustees Association of Australia Ltd v. Wright* (1917) 23 CLR 185 the High Court of Australia held that the fact that the purpose with which a man put property in his wife's name as trustee for him was to defraud his creditors does not prevent him from recovering the property from her provided that the illegal purpose has not been carried into effect. The facts of the case bear a superficial resemblance to those in *Tinker v. Tinker* with this difference, that the wife signed a letter declaring that she held the property in trust for her husband. As in *Tinker v. Tinker*, there was no evidence that the husband had any creditors at the time he put the property in his wife's name or afterwards during her life. This husband's intention, however, was dishonest. The letter which he procured his wife to sign was clear evidence that she held the property in trust for him. It was, however, part of the fraud, to be used or suppressed as circumstances required, for the husband testified that his purpose in transferring the property to his wife was to conceal his interest from his creditors. After the death of his wife he brought proceedings to recover the property and succeeded. Barton ACJ based his judgment on the fact that the husband did not need to set up his illegal purpose in order to recover the property. The fact that the wife was merely a trustee for her husband was sufficiently evidenced by the letter which contained her declaration of that fact. To this extent, therefore, his judgment was a straightforward application of the primary rule as confirmed in *Tinsley v. Milligan*. But he also laid stress on the fact that no creditor had been deceived. He cited from an earlier decision of the same court in *Payne v. McDonald* (1908) 6 CLR 208, 211, where Griffith CJ had said:

> "I doubt, indeed, very much whether the doctrine ex turpi causa non oritur actio applies at all to a case where the only illegality or impropriety alleged is an intent, not effectuated, to defeat creditors."

Barton ACJ expressly stated, 23 CLR 185, 193, that the case would probably have been different if any creditor had been deceived. The other three members of the court based their decision exclusively on the fact that the illegal intention had not been carried out. They said in a joint judgment at p. 196:

> "The test appears to be, not whether the plaintiff in such a case relies on the illegal agreement, because in one sense he always does so, but whether the illegal purpose from which the plaintiff insists on retiring still rests in intention only. If either he is seeking to carry out the illegal purpose, or has already carried it out in whole or in part, then he fails."

And at p. 198:

> "In this case no creditors have been defrauded, the illegal purpose has never in any respect been carried into effect, and therefore the [husband] was entitled to succeed."

There are obvious difficulties with this approach in the light of *Tinsley v. Milligan*. The opening lines of the first passage clearly no longer represent the law of this country. But there is nothing in my opinion in *Tinsley v. Milligan* which compels the conclusion that the second passage does not.

There is no modern case in which restitution has been denied in circumstances comparable to those of the present case where the illegal purpose has not been carried out. In *Tinsley v. Milligan* Lord Browne-Wilkinson expressly recognised the availability of the doctrine of the locus poenitentiae in a restitutionary context, and cited *Taylor v. Bowers* as well as *Symes v. Hughes* without disapproval. In my opinion the weight of the authorities supports the view that a person who seeks to recover property transferred by him for an illegal purpose can lead evidence of his dishonest intention whenever it is necessary for him to do so provided that he has withdrawn from the transaction before the illegal purpose has been carried out. It is not necessary if he can rely on an express or resulting trust in his favour; but it is necessary (i) if he brings an action at law and (ii) if he brings proceedings in equity and needs to rebut the presumption of advancement. The availability of the locus poenitentiae is well documented in the former case. I would not willingly adopt a rule which differentiated between the rule of the common law and that of equity in a restitutionary context. It is of course true that equity judges are fond of saying that a party 'cannot be heard to say' that his purpose was dishonest, and that this approach represents a mainspring of equitable jurisprudence. A man who puts himself in a position where his interest conflicts with his duty, for example, 'cannot be heard to say' that he acted in accordance with his interest; he is treated as having acted in accordance with his duty: see for example *In re Biss* [1903] 2 Ch 40 and *Attorney-General for Hong Kong v. Reid* [1994] 1 AC 324. But this is a substantive rule of equity, not a merely procedural rule as the primary rule appears to be, and it does not preclude the court from taking cognisance of an uneffectuated intention from which the party in question has resiled. I would hold that Page Wood V-C's first thoughts in *Childers v. Childers* are to be preferred to his second. I would also hold that there was no 'inescapable dilemma' in *Tinker v. Tinker*, where it was said by

Salmon L.J. in the course of the argument at p. 139 that the transferor was either an honest man, in which case the property belonged to his wife, or he would have to give evidence of his dishonesty, it being implicit that this was something which he could not do. Such statements are due to an instinctive feeling that a dishonest man should not succeed where an honest man would fail, but this is to misrepresent the effect of allowing a locus poenitentiae. The dishonest man is not treated more favourably than the honest man: provided that the illegal purpose has not been carried out they are treated in the same way. The outcome is different because their intentions were different. The honest man intended a gift; the dishonest man did not.

At heart the question for decision in the present case is one of legal policy. The primary rule which precludes the court from lending its assistance to a man who founds his cause of action on an illegal or immoral act often leads to a denial of justice. The justification for this is that the rule is not a principle of justice but a principle of policy: see the much-quoted statement of Lord Mansfield CJ in *Holman v. Johnson* (1775) 1 Cowp 341, 343. The doctrine of the locus poenitentiae is an exception which operates to mitigate the harshness of the primary rule. It enables the court to do justice between the parties even though, in order to do so, it must allow a plaintiff to give evidence of his own dishonest intent. But he must have withdrawn from the transaction while his dishonesty still lay in intention only. The law draws the line once the intention has been wholly or partly carried into effect.

Seen in this light the doctrine of the locus poenitentiae, although an exception to the primary rule, is not inconsistent with the policy which underlies it. It is, of course, artificial to think that anyone would be dissuaded by the primary rule from entering into a proposed fraud, if only because such a person would be unlikely to be a studious reader of the law reports or to seek advice from a lawyer whom he has taken fully into his confidence. But if the policy which underlies the primary rule is to discourage fraud, the policy which underlies the exception must be taken to be to encourage withdrawal from a proposed fraud before it is implemented, an end which is no less desirable. And if the former objective is of such overriding importance that the primary rule must be given effect even where it leads to a denial of justice, then in my opinion the latter objective justifies the adoption of the exception where this enables justice to be done.

To my mind these considerations are even more compelling since the decision in *Tinsley v. Milligan*. One might hesitate before allowing a novel exception to a rule of legal policy, particularly a rule based on moral principles. But the primary rule, as it has emerged from that decision, does not conform to any discernible moral principle. It is procedural in nature and depends on the adventitious location of the burden of proof in any given case. Had the plaintiff transferred the shares to a stranger or distant relative whom he trusted, albeit for the same dishonest purpose, it cannot be doubted that he would have succeeded in his claim. He would also have succeeded if he had given them to his son and procured him to sign a declaration of trust in his favour. But he chose to transfer them to a son whom he trusted to the extent of dispensing with the precaution of obtaining a declaration of trust. If that is fatal to his claim, then the greater the betrayal, the less the power of equity to give a remedy.

In my opinion the following propositions represent the present state of the law. (1) Title to property passes both at law and in equity even if the transfer is made for an illegal purpose. The fact that title has passed to the transferee does not preclude the transferor from bringing an action for restitution. (2) The transferor's action will fail if it would be illegal for him to retain any interest in the property. (3) Subject to (2) the transferor can recover the property if he can do so without relying on the illegal purpose. This will normally be the case where the property was transferred without consideration in circumstances where the transferor can rely on an express declaration of trust or a resulting trust in his favour. (4) It will almost invariably be so where the illegal purpose has not been carried out. It may be otherwise where the illegal purpose has been carried out and the transferee can rely on the transferor's conduct as inconsistent with his retention of a beneficial interest. (5) The transferor can lead evidence of the illegal purpose whenever it is necessary for him to do so provided that he has withdrawn from the transaction before the illegal purpose has been wholly or partly carried into effect. It will be necessary for him to do so (i) if he brings an action at law or (ii) if he brings proceedings in equity and needs to rebut the presumption of advancement. (6) The only way in which a man can protect his property from his creditors is by divesting himself of all beneficial interest in it. Evidence that he transferred the property in order to protect it from his creditors, therefore, does nothing by itself to rebut the presumption of advancement; it reinforces it. To rebut the presumption it is necessary to show that he intended to retain a beneficial interest and conceal it from his creditors. (7) The court should not conclude that this was his intention without compelling circumstantial evidence to this effect. The identity of the transferee and the circumstances in which the transfer was made would be highly relevant. It is unlikely that the court would reach such a conclusion where the transfer was made in the absence of an imminent and perceived threat from known creditors.

The doctrine of the locus poenitentiae

It is impossible to reconcile all the authorities on the circumstances in which a party to an illegal contract is permitted to withdraw from it. At one time he was allowed to withdraw so long as the contract had not been completely performed but later it was held that recovery was barred once it had been partly performed: see *Kearley v. Thompson* (1890) 24 QBD 742. It is clear that he must withdraw voluntarily, and that it is not sufficient that he is forced to do so because his plan has been discovered. In *Bigos v. Bousted* [1951] 1 All ER 92 this was (perhaps dubiously) extended to prevent withdrawal where the scheme has been frustrated by the refusal of the other party to carry out his part.

The Academic articles, Grodecki, 'In pari delicto potior est conditio defendentis' (1955) 71 LQR 254, Beatson, 'Repudiation of illegal purpose as a ground for restitution' (1975) 91 LQR 313 and Merkin 'Restitution by withdrawal from executory illegal contracts' (1981) 97 LQR 420, are required reading for anyone who attempts the difficult task of defining the precise limits of the doctrine. I would draw back from any such attempt. But I would hold that genuine repentance is not required. Justice is not a reward for merit; restitution should not be confined to the penitent. I would also hold that voluntary withdrawal from an illegal transaction when it has ceased to be needed is sufficient. It is true that this is not necessary to encourage withdrawal, but a rule to the opposite effect could lead to bizarre results. Suppose, for example, that in *Bigos v. Bousted* exchange control had been abolished before the foreign currency was made available: it is absurd to suppose that the plaintiff should have been denied restitution. I do not agree that it was correct in *Groves v. Groves* (1829) 3 Y & J 163, 174 and similar cases for the court to withhold its assistance from the plaintiff because 'if the crime has not been completed, the merit was not his'.

Conclusion
On the facts found by the judge the plaintiff was entitled to judgment. I would dismiss the appeal."

Trusts of the Family Home

As outlined above, a resulting trust may arise when property is purchased in another party's name. It is quite common for a house to be conveyed solely into a husband or male partner's name and a question which has often arisen in practice is whether the wife or female partner should have any beneficial interest in the property arising from her contributions. In circumstances where legislation does not govern the situation,[33] the court may rely on equitable principles, in particular the purchase money resulting trust, to resolve disputes concerning family property. However, there are fundamental theoretical difficulties in employing the traditional concept of the purchase money resulting trust in circumstances where property may have been bought with the aid of a mortgage.[34] The Irish courts have tended to deal with this difficulty by treating

---

[33] A scheme for making property adjustment orders in the context of separation proceedings is set out in the Judicial Separation and Family Law Reform Act 1989 and the Family Law Act 1995, and in the context of divorce proceedings, by the Family Law (Divorce) Act 1996.

[34] In theory the beneficial interests of the parties should be assessed at the time the purchase occurs but such an assessment could not accommodate the practical reality of the situation

mortgage repayments as the practical equivalent to paying the initial purchase price and as capable of giving rise to a proportionate beneficial interest under a resulting trust, or alternatively have treated the repayment of the mortgage as the buying back of the equity of redemption from the mortgagee.[35]

It has been clearly established that where property is purchased in one spouse or partner's name but the other party has made direct contributions to the purchase price or the payment of instalments on the mortgage, the property will be held on a resulting trust to the extent of these contributions.[36] In addition, the courts have held that a partner should be entitled to a beneficial interest in property to the extent of indirect financial contributions made in the absence of proof of an agreement to the contrary.[37] However, where a non-owning partner expends monies or carries out work in the improvement of a property, he or she will not be entitled to any beneficial interest in the absence of an express or readily implied agreement.[38]

Controversy has surrounded the effect of other forms of contribution by a non-owning partner. It was held by the Supreme Court in *L. v. L.*[39] that a contribution by working in the home, whether in performing housework or looking after children, may not give rise to a beneficial interest. Finlay CJ made it clear in his judgment that extending the circumstances in which a partner may claim a beneficial interest to a situation where she has made no direct or indirect financial contribution to the acquisition of the property or to a family fund but has performed the constitutionally preferred role of wife and mother in the home would not be to develop any principle known to the common law but rather would involve the creation of an entirely new right. However, in *N. v. N.*[40] the Supreme Court appeared to accept that unpaid work in the legal owner's business was a recognisable form of contribution as it was 'different from and not to be identified with the activities of a wife and mother in the home'.

While the tenor of the Supreme Court's judgment in *L. v. L.* would seem to rule out further judicial development of the concept of the resulting trust in this context, it should be noted that the potential of the constructive trust as a device which will provide a remedy in such circumstances where 'justice and good conscience demand it' has been explored by the High Court in *Murray v. Murray.*[41]

---

which may involve the repayment of a mortgage loan over a period of years subsequent to the actual purchase.

[35] *W. v. W.* [1981] ILRM 202, 204-205.

[36] *C. v. C.* [1976] IR 254, 258; *W. v. W* [1981] ILRM 202, 204.

[37] *W. v. W.* [1981] ILRM 202, 204; *McC. v. McC.* [1986] ILRM 1, 2.

[38] *N. v. N.* [1992] 2 IR 116, 122 *per* Finlay CJ. Note that in his earlier judgment in *W. v. W.* [1981] ILRM 202, Finlay P spoke about a partner's entitlement in such circumstances being confined to a right to recompense in monies only.

[39] [1992] 2 IR 77. See also *N. v. N.* [1992] 2 IR 116.

[40] [1992] 2 IR 116.

[41] [1996] 3 IR 251.

W. v. W.
[1981] ILRM 202

The plaintiff wife claimed to be entitled to a beneficial interest in a family farm which was registered in her husband's sole name. Finlay P suggested that by virtue of her contributions she was entitled to approximately 50% of the beneficial interest in the property although in so far as her claim derived from contributions to improvements it was not sustainable.

FINLAY P stated at pp.203–206: "This is an issue arising in certain proceedings brought by the plaintiff, who is the wife, against the defendant, who is the husband, pursuant to the provisions of the Guardianship of Infants Act, 1964, the Family Law (Maintenance of Spouses and Children) Act, 1976, and by order, the Married Women's Status Act, 1957.

The issue with which this judgment is concerned is solely confined to a claim made by the wife to be entitled to a beneficial interest in a farm of land registered on a folio in the name of the husband.

Upon this issue evidence was given by the wife and by an agricultural expert on her behalf but no evidence was given by or on behalf of the husband. [At this point the judge recited the facts of the case and then continued] . . . I am solely concerned with the claim of the wife for an interest in the main holdings of land.

This claim was presented to me by counsel on behalf of the wife in two alternative and in a sense concurrent forms. It is firstly submitted that insofar as the transfer of the lands originally made to the husband was subject to encumbrances that on the evidence I should hold that the wife had contributed over the years both by her industry, by the bringing into the farm of her own personal savings on marriage and her share in the monies received by way of gift on the wedding; by bringing in her original bloodstock and working with them thus making income for the farm and by her actual work at the ordinary dairy portion of the farm to the general farm income out of which I should assume on the evidence those encumbrances were discharged and that those facts gave her an interest arising from that transaction in the farm. A similar submission was made in regard to the evidence adduced by the wife that upon the building of the modern milk-parlour a further mortgage was raised on the farm and subsequently discharged and the sums of money brought in by her.

In addition and as I have said not only as an alternative but as a concurrent submission it is claimed on behalf of the wife that since she consistently worked on the farm both in relation to the dairying end of it and in relation to the bloodstock end of it that that work added to the general fund or income from the farm in each year and that insofar as that was used for the purpose of making improvements to the farm in particular represented by improvements in the buildings and yards etc., that that was a contribution by her towards the acquisition of the entity which now constitutes the farm as improved and that as such would give her a claim to an equitable interest in the farm.

In considering this claim on the facts as I have found them I have in particular been referred to and carefully considered the following decisions. *C. v. C.* [1976] IR 254; *Heavey v. Heavey* (1977) ILTR 1; *McGill v. S.* [1979] IR 238.

From these three decisions, the two former of which are decisions of Kenny J whilst a High Court judge and the third of which is a decision of Gannon J and from the judicial decisions quoted with approval in them, I am satisfied that the following broad propositions of law arise which are applicable to the facts of this case.

1. Where a wife contributes by money to the purchase of a property by her husband in his sole name in the absence of evidence of some inconsistent agreement or arrangement the court will decide that the wife is entitled to an equitable interest in that property approximately proportionate to the extent of her contribution as against the total value of the property at the time the contribution was made.

2. Where a husband makes a contribution to the purchase of property in his wife's sole name he will be presumed by a rebuttable presumption to have intended to advance his wife and will have no claim to an equitable estate in the property unless that presumption is rebutted. If it is, he would have a claim similar to that indicated in respect of the wife with which I have already dealt.

3. Where a wife contributes either directly towards the repayment of mortgage instalments or contributes to a general family fund thus releasing her husband from an obligation which he otherwise would have to discharge liabilities out of that fund and permitting him to repay mortgage instalments, she will in the absence of proof of an inconsistent agreement or arrangement be entitled to an equitable share in the property which had been mortgaged and in respect of which the mortgage was redeemed approximately proportionate to her contribution to the mortgage repayments: to the value of the mortgage thus redeemed and to the total value of the property at the relevant time. It is not expressly stated in the decisions to which I have referred but I assume that the fundamental principle underlying this rule of law is that the redemption of any form of charge or mortgage on property in truth consists of the acquisition by the owner or mortgagor of an estate in the property with which he had parted at the time of the creating of the mortgage or charge and that there can be no distinction in principle between a contribution made to the acquisition of that interest and a contribution made to the acquisition of an interest in property by an original purchase.

4. Where a husband contributes either directly or indirectly in the manner which I have already outlined to the repayment of mortgage charges on property which is in the legal ownership of his wife subject to the presumption of advancement and in the event of a rebuttal of that presumption he would have a like claim to an equitable estate in the property.

5. Where a wife expends monies or carries out work in the improvement of

a property which has been originally acquired by and the legal ownership in which is soley vested in her husband she will have no claim in respect of such contribution unless she established by evidence that from the circumstances surrounding the making of it she was led to believe (or of course that it was specifically agreed) that she would be recompensed for it. Even where such a right to recompense is established either by an expressed agreement or by circumstance in which the wife making the contribution was led to such belief it is a right to recompense in monies only and cannot and does not constitute a right to claim equitable share in the estate of the property concerned.

6. A husband making contributions in like manner to property originally acquired by and solely owned as to the legal estate by his wife may again subject to a rebuttal of a presumption of advancement which would arise have a like claim to compensation in similar circumstances but would not have a claim to any equitable estate in the property. Applying these principles of law which I believe to be the relevant principles to be derived from the decisions to which I have referred to the facts as so far found by me in this case I am satisfied that the following conclusions and consequences arise.

Whilst the evidence of the wife concerning the encumbrances affecting the property when it was first transferred to her husband, was explicably without detail, it has not been contradicted by any evidence adduced on behalf of her husband nor was she in fact cross-examined about it. I must therefore conclude that such encumbrances did exist and were discharged after the transfer of the farm to the husband. A precisely similar conclusion arises with regard to her evidence as to the raising of a charge and its subsequent redemption at the time of the construction of the modern milking-parlour.

I will therefore direct that a further issue be tried before me as to: (1) the extent of the encumbrances subject to which the lands were transferred to the husband and the time at which they were finally redeemed together with the value of the lands at the date of transfer and at the date of the eventual redemption of these charges; (2) the amount of the charges raised by way of mortgage on the lands at the time of the construction of the milking parlour the value of the lands at the time that mortgage was created; the date on which they were eventually redeemed and the method by which they were redeemed and the value of the lands at the date at which they were redeemed.

In this context I intend of course to deal not only with legal mortgages but with any form of charge raised on the land whether secured by the equitable deposit of title deeds or otherwise.

Since the husband did not give evidence before me on the issues so far tried and since he did not produce, at this or any other stage in the proceedings, any documentary evidence other than certain farm accounts which are irrelevant to this question I will direct that he make discovery of all documents relevant to the issue now still to be tried and I will give liberty to the wife if she is so advised to serve interrogatories on the husband concerning the transactions to which I have have referred.

I am needless to say, concerned with the cost of the proceedings which have already been maintained between the husband and wife in this case and with the thought of imposing upon the parties further expense and costs. It seems to me that both discovery and interrogatories should be capable of being properly achieved without formality and that it might be possible for the parties upon full examination of the documentary proofs available to reach agreement on the extent of the share to which as a consequence the wife is entitled in these lands. If such an agreement cannot be reached I will, of course, re-enter the matter for further hearing at a suitable time.

To assist the parties in reaching an agreement which might avoid expense I feel I should indicate that it would be my intention from the evidence I have already heard to hold that the contribution of the wife during the two relevant periods in which prima facie charges on these lands were being redeemed would be approximately 50% which takes into account both her work, the monies brought in by her and in particular the results of her dealing in bloodstock. The proportion or share to which she should be entitled to be declared an equitable owner in these lands would therefore be half of the proportion represented by the amount of the charge redeemed and the value of the lands at the relevant time which would in effect be a combination of the value of the lands at the time of the raising of a mortgage and the value of the lands at the time when it was finally redeemed. This statement of my intention on the evidence already heard by me may assist the parties to reach an agreement as to a share in respect of which the wife is entitled to claim in these lands. Insofar as the wife has claimed an equitable estate in these lands solely derived from her contribution to improvements I must on the authorities hold that it is not sustainable in law."

L. v. L.
[1992] 2 IR 77

The plaintiff wife sought an order, *inter alia*, declaring the respective beneficial interests of herself and her husband, the defendant, in the family home and farm. The plaintiff had made no direct or indirect financial contribution to the property although she played a crucial role in refurbishing and redecorating it and her role was that of full time homemaker and mother. In the High Court Barr J concluded that having regard to Article 41.2 of the Constitution, a woman who elected to adopt the full time role of wife and mother and was thus precluded from contributing directly or indirectly in money or money's worth from independent employment towards the acquisition by the husband of the family home and contents, should have her work in the home taken into account. In these circumstances Barr J held that the wife was entitled to a 50% beneficial interest in the family home and its contents. However, the Supreme Court allowed the defendant's appeal against that part of the High Court decision which awarded her such an interest.

FINLAY CJ stated at pp.102–109: "This is an appeal brought by the defendant who is the husband against so much of the order made by Barr J. in the High Court, on the hearing of a summons pursuant to the provisions of the Married Women's Status Act, 1957, as declared that the husband held a moiety of his beneficial interest in the family home, its curtilage and gardens, in trust for the wife.

The wife had instituted in the High Court two sets of proceedings, one being a petition for divorce *a mensa et thoro* and the other being the claim for declarations pursuant to the Married Women's Status Act, 1957.

The proceedings were heard in 1988, and judgment was delivered in both of them together by the learned trial judge on the 3rd October, 1988. Originally, the husband appealed against certain aspects of the order made in the proceedings for divorce *a mensa et thoro*, but that appeal was abandoned and the only issue which arose before us was the appeal against the finding of a trust in favour of the wife as to one half of the beneficial ownership in the family home.

No issue arose on the hearing of this appeal as to the correctness of the findings of fact made by the learned trial judge in the High Court. In so far as they are relevant to this aspect of the proceedings between the parties, they are as follows. The parties married in 1968 and originally resided in rented accommodation. In 1970 the husband purchased and had conveyed to him in his own name a family home and a substantial farm of land for the sum of £40,000. This purchase was funded by way of a gift of £30,000 from the husband's father and by way of a deferred payment of the balance of the purchase price by the vendor over a period of five years. The latter amount was discharged out of farming profits.

The family took up residence in the property in 1971, and the parties resided in the family home, with some interruptions, when one or other of them left it for a period, from that time up to 1988 when, as a result of differences between the parties and a threatened application by the wife for a barring order the husband voluntarily left the home. At the time of the trial in the High Court the wife was still residing in the family home and the husband was excluded from it. It would appear that at the time of the hearing in the High Court the family home was unencumbered by any mortgage or charge.

From the time of the marriage the wife did not earn in any outside employment or profession. Having reviewed these facts in considerable detail, and having reviewed the existing authorities with regard to the claim made by a spouse to an interest in the family home, arising from contributions towards its acquisition, the learned trial judge stated as follows:

> "Reviewed in the light of the formidable line of judicial authority on this topic since 1976, the conclusion is inescapable that the wife is not entitled to a

beneficial interest in the family home or farm because she has made no contribution in money or money's worth, directly or indirectly, towards the acquisition of either property. Her claim in that regard must fail unless she can rely upon other rights not previously considered by the courts."

The learned trial judge then went on to consider submissions which had been made to him on behalf of the wife, concerning the provisions of Article 41 of the Constitution and the jurisdiction which it was contended that those provisions gave to the courts with regard to a claim by a wife to a share in the beneficial ownership of the family home. That jurisdiction was to declare her entitled to a share in trust in such beneficial ownership arising not from any contribution by her, direct or indirect, to the acquisition of the home, but on the basis that the Constitution warrants the declaration of such a share as a method of endorsing the constitutionally preferred option that a wife who is also a mother should remain at home and devote herself entirely to the family after the marriage.

The portion of the judgment in which the learned trial Judge sets out this concept reads as follows (pp. 98 and 99, *ante*):-

"Article 41 contains two fundamental concepts which are interrelated. First, the family is recognised as the natural, primary and fundamental unit group of society which is the necessary basis of social order and it possesses inalienable rights that are superior to all positive law. Secondly, it is recognised that a woman's life within the home gives to the State a support without which the common good cannot be achieved. It seems to me that Article 41, in so far as it relates to woman, underscores the pivotal role which she has within the family, and recognises that in the day-to-day life of the unit group she plays a crucial part in weaving the fabric of the family and in sustaining the quality of its life. The strongest possible emphasis is placed on woman's role within the home. Having regard to the terms of s. 2, sub-s. 2, which casts a specific duty on the State to endeavour to ensure that mothers will not be obliged by economic necessity to engage in labour to the neglect of their duties in the home, it is evident that the Constitution envisages that, ideally, a mother should devote all her time and attention to her duties in the home and that it is desirable that she ought not to engage in gainful occupation elsewhere unless compelled to do so by economic necessity. It follows that, if the Article is to be given flesh and meaning in practical terms, a mother who adopts that concept and devotes herself entirely to the family after marriage, has a special place in society which should be buttressed and preserved by the State in its laws. In my view the judiciary has a positive obligation to interpret and develop the law in a way which is in harmony with the philosophy of Article 41 as to the status of woman in the home. It is also in harmony with that philosophy to regard marriage as an equal partnership in which a woman who elects to adopt the full-time role of wife and mother in the home may be obliged to make a sacrifice, both economic and emotional, in doing so. In return for that voluntary sacrifice which the Constitution recognises as being in the interest of the common good, she should receive some reasonable economic security within the marriage. That concept can be achieved, at least in part, by recognising that as her role as full-time wife and mother precludes her from contributing, directly or indirectly, in money or money's worth from independent employment or avocation towards the acquisition by the husband of the family home and contents, her work as home-maker and in caring for the family should be taken into account in calculating her contribution towards that acquisition – particularly, as such work is of real monetary value. In this regard I draw no distinction between the purchase of the family home entirely or substantially by the husband out of his independent assets and the more usual case where the home is acquired by him subject to a mortgage repayable over a term of years."

In brief, the husband's appeal against that finding consisted of an assertion that the remedy of granting to a wife and mother in the position of the plaintiff a share in the beneficial ownership of the family home, in addition to other rights she might have to maintenance or to her occupation of the family home, was unknown to the law and that it was not possible from the provisions of Article 41 of the Constitution to identify that particular remedy as a constitutional right which the courts could protect and grant to the wife.

The wife did not enter any cross-appeal or notice to vary, and does not contest the finding by the trial judge that on the authorities concerning the acquisition of a share in the family home by way of constructive or resulting trust arising from contributions, direct or indirect, towards that home by a spouse, that the plaintiff on the facts of the case cannot be entitled to a share.

Relevant constitutional provisions
The relevant constitutional provisions are Article 41, sections 1 and 2. They read as follows:-

> "*Article 41*
>
> 1. 1° The State recognises the Family as the natural primary and fundamental unit group of Society, and as a moral institution possessing inalienable and imprescriptible rights, antecedent and superior to all positive law.
>
>   2° The State, therefore, guarantees to protect the Family in its constitution and authority, as the necessary basis of social order and as indispensable to the welfare of the Nation and the State.
>
> 2. 1° In particular, the State recognises that by her life within the home, woman gives to the State a support without which the common good cannot be achieved.
>
>   2.2° The State shall, therefore, endeavour to ensure that mothers shall not be obliged by economic necessity to engage in labour to the neglect of their duties in the home."

The conclusion reached by Barr J. in this case, as set out in his judgment which I have quoted, receives support from a judgment which appears to be *ex tempore* and which was delivered on the 20th June, 1989, by Barrington J., but is not reported, in *H. v. H.* In the course of that judgment, though clearly *obiter* to the question which he had to decide, the learned judge stated as follows:

> "I am quite satisfied that this house was held by the husband in trust for himself and his wife, jointly in equal shares, if I may use that phrase, of a joint tenancy, and there is the additional factor, I think I feel entitled to add, that I can resolve the principal issue of the case on the basis of the traditional approach but it does appear to me that this is a classic example of the situation which Mr. Justice Barr had to deal with in *L. v. L.*, and it appears to me the issue in the case in relation to financial contribution of the wife, in relation to the purchase of the matrimonial home belongs to a legal approach which is quite foreign to the legal approach contained in Article 41 of our Constitution. They start from the wrong point in the law, equity, and the proper starting point is the one taken by Mr. Justice Barr, and on that interpretation it would appear that the courts should recognise the contribution the wife makes by her work as a carer and rearer of the family within the home, because it appears to be quite inconsistent with the values in Article 41 in the Constitution that the wife, who leaves the home and has an independent income and is therefore able to make a financial contribution towards the repayment of the family mortgage, might, at the end of the day, be in a very much better position than the wife who fulfils the constitutionally preferred role and remains at home to rear the children. That seems to me to be an inconsistent conclusion and inconsistent with the principles of Article 41. My judgment does not turn on that."

I would accept the inconsistency pointed out by Barrington J. in this extract from his judgment, and pointed out by Barr J. in the instant case, between the position of a wife who leaves the home for the purpose of carrying out remunerated work and contributes either directly to the repayment of a mortgage or, indirectly, to the repayment of the mortgage by a contribution to the family pool, and the less advantageous position with regard to ownership of an interest in the family home of the wife who appears to follow the preferred constitutional activity of staying at home to look after the family.

I would have little difficulty in appreciating the very significant social and other values which are attached to what experience would indicate is a very common modern habit, whereby the parties to a marriage and the parents of a family, by agreement between them, become joint owners of the family home. It is difficult to deny the fact that anything that would help to encourage that basis of full sharing in property values as well as in every other way between the partners of a marriage, must directly contribute to the stability of the marriage, the institution of the family, and the common good.

However, the problem which appears to me to arise is a simple question as to whether if this court were to follow the reasoning contained in the judgment of Barr J. it would in truth, as he suggests, and as the comments of Barrington J. suggest, be developing an existing law within the permissible limits of judicial interpretation, or whether in fact it would be legislating.

After careful consideration and with a reluctance arising from the desirable objective which the principle outlined in the judgment of Barr J. would achieve, I conclude that to identify this right in the circumstances set out in this case is not to develop any known principle of the common law, but is rather to identify a brand new right and to secure it to the plaintiff. Unless that is something clearly and unambiguously warranted by the Constitution or made necessary for the protection of either a specified or unspecified right under it, it must constitute legislation and be a usurpation by the courts of the function of the legislature.

The doctrine of a constructive or resulting trust applied towards the situation where a spouse makes contributions towards the acquisition of a family home, which was first elaborated by Kenny J. in the High Court in *C. v. C.* [1976] IR 254 which was eventually considered by this Court in the case of *McC. v. McC.* [1986] ILRM 1 had as its basic requirements a contribution of money towards the acquisition of a family home. To an extent the development of that doctrine in its application to the position of husband and wife, as distinct from the principles which would apply to persons jointly involved in the purchase of property who were not so related, has not been more extensive than this. In addition to the direct contribution towards purchase price, whether the cash price of an actual purchase of a home or the acquisition of the equity of redemption by contribution to the clearing off of a mortgage, a trust could, having regard to the particular features of dealings between husband and wife in a marriage which was amicable, arise from what are described as indirect contributions by the provision through earnings of monies into the family pool.

To extend or develop such a doctrine so as to provide that a person who did not make any monied contribution either towards the acquisition of a family home or towards the clearing off of a mortgage to it, whether of either a direct or indirect nature, but who by carrying out the constitutionally endorsed activities of a wife and mother within the home saved her husband from the possibility of having to hire outside help to carry out those functions or who, by the ordinary maintenance of a house, kept the house in good order, would be not to develop a doctrine, in my view, but to introduce a new one.

The provisions of Article 41 of the Constitution can, in my view, be separated in their purpose and object in two ways. Section 1, sub-ss. 1 and 2, clearly represent the recognition by the State of the existing fundamental rights of the family and the undertaking by the State to protect those rights. Neither sub-s. 1 nor sub-s. 2 of s. 1 of Article 41 purports to create any particular right within the family, or to grant to any individual member of the family rights, whether of property or otherwise, against other members of the family, but rather deals with the protection of the family from external forces.

With regard to Article 41, s. 2, on the other hand, the State by sub-s. 1 clearly recognises the value to the common good of the activities of the wife within the home, and by sub-s. 2 accepts an obligation to ensure that if the wife is a mother as well she shall not be obliged by economic necessity to engage in labour to the neglect of her duties in the home.

It is this last sub-section which was particularly relied upon by the plaintiff in this case, both in the High Court and in this Court. I accept the contention made that the judiciary is one of the organs of the State and that, therefore, the obligation taken by the State to endeavour to ensure that mothers shall not be obliged by economic necessity to engage in labour outside the home to the neglect of their duties is an obligation imposed on the judiciary as well as on the legislature and the executive.

There is, however, I am satisfied, no warrant for interpreting that duty on the judiciary as granting to it jurisdiction to award to a wife and mother any particular interest in the family home, where that would be unrelated to the question of her being obliged by economic necessity to engage in labour to the neglect of her duties. If a court is assessing the alimony or maintenance payable by a husband to a wife and mother, either pursuant to a petition for separation or to a claim under the Family Law (Maintenance of Spouses and Children) Act, 1976, it should, in my view, have regard to and exercise its duty under this sub-section of the Constitution in a case where the husband was capable of making proper provision for his wife within the home by refusing to have any regard to a capacity of the wife to earn herself, if she was a mother in addition to a wife and if the obligation so to earn could lead to the neglect of her duties in the home. In other words, maintenance or alimony could and must be set by a court so as to avoid forcing by an economic necessity the wife and mother to labour out of the home to the neglect of her duties in it. Beyond that capacity of the judiciary to take part in the endeavour to comply with the provisions of Article 41, s. 2, sub-s. 2 of the Constitution, I do not consider that the transfer of any particular property right could be a general jurisdiction capable of being exercised in pursuance of that sub-section of the Constitution.

It is, of course, clear that if the legislature decides, as in fact it has done, by virtue of the provisions of the Judicial Separation and Family Law Reform Act, 1989, to give to the courts powers to declare a right in a spouse to a beneficial interest in the family home as part of the general jurisdiction of the court upon the granting of a separation, to make monetary provisions arising from it, the court may exercise that expressed statutory power in obedience to and furtherance of the provisions of this sub-section of the Constitution.

For these reasons, I would allow this appeal."

N. v. N.
[1992] 2 IR 116

The plaintiff wife sought a declaration as to her entitlement to a beneficial interest in the family home against her deceased husband's insolvent estate. She based her claim on direct contributions from her earnings, indirect contributions to a family fund, her work managing flats into which the house had been converted and also on her work in the home as a wife and mother.

Barron J held that she was entitled to a one-fifteenth beneficial interest and on appeal the Supreme Court held that she was entitled to a half share in this interest.

FINLAY CJ stated at pp.118–124: "This is an appeal by the plaintiff against an order made in the High Court on the 27th June, 1989, by Barron J. in certain proceedings instituted by the plaintiff against the executors of her deceased husband in which she claimed a declaration that she was entitled to a fifty *per cent* beneficial interest in the property of the family home consisting of a house situate in the city of Dublin. The learned trial judge held that she was entitled to a one-fifteenth share only in the said premises.

The facts
The facts out of which the claim arose which were not in dispute, no evidence being adduced on behalf of the defendants, were as follows. The plaintiff married her late husband in 1964. At the time of the marriage he was a qualified architect carrying on practice in the city of Dublin, and she was a state registered nurse who was employed in the city of Dublin.

Upon marriage the plaintiff gave up her employment so as to be a full-time wife and three children were born of the marriage, a son in June, 1965, a daughter in May, 1967, and a second daughter in January, 1969. Except for extremely limited temporary employment the plaintiff did not work as a nurse after the marriage until the youngest of the children was quite grown up, and resumed employment again only in 1983. From then until 1987 she was full-time employed for a period and part-time employed for a further period as a nurse. In 1987 she ceased to be employed, apparently due to a disability.

Her husband died in April, 1988.

In January, 1966, the husband purchased the property concerned in this action for the sum of £5,000. That purchase money was provided from a bequest made to him by his late father and also by a further gift from his mother. He borrowed by way of mortgage on the house a further sum of £5,000 to renovate the house and convert it into apartments. The plaintiff and her husband and the one child who was then born then occupied one apartment, which the family did for the rest of the husband's lifetime, and the balance of the house was converted into bedsitter apartments. The title of the house was in the sole name of the husband. From the commencement of the occupation of the house after it had been renovated, the evidence, which was accepted by the learned trial judge, was to the effect that the plaintiff took over the entire management of the bedsitter apartments which originally numbered nine, but which in 1984, when the husband moved his office to the house, were reduced to five. Throughout the entire period up to the date of the death of the husband, the plaintiff had managed these apartments to the extent of making the lettings in them, dealing with complaints, collecting the rents and providing for and organising the maintenance of the apartments. At all stages the rents of the apartments would appear to have been devoted either directly or indirectly towards the payment of interest on the mortgage. In the first instance on the mortgage of £5,000, the entire of the sum went directly towards that purpose; later at periods it may have gone into a mixed family fund out of which mortgage repayments were made.

The evidence established that a total of five mortgages were raised on the premises during the lifetime of the husband, that four of them had been discharged in his lifetime and that the fifth was discharged because it was an insured endowment policy which was redeemed at his death. These mortgages were as follows:

1. To the Lombard & Ulster Bank on the 13th June, 1966, for £5,000. The purpose of this mortgage was, as has been indicated, the renovation and conversion of the house so as to create nine bedsitters and a garden flat.

2. To the Lombard & Ulster Bank in October, 1966, for an unascertained sum.

3. To Allied Irish Banks for a sum of £6,000, the date of which was not established.

4. To Lombard & Ulster Bank in 1975 for £5,000.

5. To the Irish Nationwide Building Society for £15,000 in 1977. With regard to this mortgage the evidence was that it was taken out largely for the purpose of adding a single storey extension to the house.

Evidence was given that due to difficulties in the husband's architectural practice the family's financial situation deteriorated significantly in the years prior to his death, having been quite comfortable previously. In particular, it would appear that arrears of income tax had built up with regard to the practice which left his estate at the date of his death apparently insolvent.

For that reason steps were being taken by the husband, shortly before his death, to try and ascertain whether he could give to his wife, in the event of his death, an interest in the house which, in a sense, would be protected against debts which he had incurred. Though he was willing to execute any necessary documents to grant to her a fifty per cent interest in the house, no transaction had actually taken place.

The judgment in the High Court

The claim for a declaration of a fifty per cent interest in the premises was substantially based in the High Court on a submission that on the facts of the case the learned trial judge should follow the decision of Barr J. in *L. v. L.* [1992] 2 IR 77, to the effect that where a wife and mother worked in the home and rendered services of substantial value in looking after the home, providing for the husband, housekeeping and looking after the children, instead of going out to work, that, having regard to the provisions of Article 41 of the

Constitution it was open to the courts in their discretion to declare such a wife entitled to an appropriate share, probably in most cases to be an equal share of fifty per cent, in the family home. The learned trial judge rejected that submission and stated that he was unable to follow the decision of Barr J. With regard to the alternative claims, the learned trial judge concluded, firstly, that he must reject any assertion that the plaintiff by reason of her work in the home as a mother and housekeeper was entitled to any share in the family home and, secondly, that he must reject any claim arising from the wife's activities in looking after the rented bedsitters, on the one hand, or her subsequent earnings from 1983 to 1988, on the other hand, except in so far as her original organisation and running of the rented bedsitter apartments contributed to the discharge of the interest and capital of the loan on the £5,000 mortgage which was obtained for the purpose of renovating and converting the house and except in so far as some contribution must be taken to have been made by her to the £15,000 mortgage taken out in 1977 which also yielded improvements to the house in the form of the extension. With regard to the latter contribution the learned trial judge concluded that they did no more than to keep alive a one-fifteenth interest which the original contributions, by way of management of the apartments, had made to the £5,000 mortgage which in turn had yielded an ascertained increase in the value of the premises of £3,000.

The decision

With regard to so much of the appeal as was based on an assertion that the learned trial judge erred in failing to follow the decision of Barr J. in *L. v. L.* [1992] 2 IR 77, I have just delivered judgment in the appeal which came before this court in *L. v. L.*, and have reached a conclusion, which is supported by the other members of the Court, to the effect that that decision cannot be upheld. For the reasons set out in my judgment in that case I would, therefore, reject this appeal in so far as it was based on an assertion that the decision should have been followed by Barron J.

With regard to the other submissions that have been made, I have come to the following conclusions.

The reasoning contained in my judgment in *L. v. L.* [1992] 2 IR 77 is based upon the fact that it does not appear to me that the Court has jurisdiction, by reason of the constitutional provisions contained in Article 41 of the Constitution, or by reason of any general principle to be derived from them, to make specific declarations concerning ownership of the property consisting of the family home which are derived from a principle of reward or implied benefit not known to the existing doctrines of resulting or constructive trust.

Having regard to that fact, I am satisfied that, no matter how desirable it may be that a wife who is also a mother should if at all possible work in the family home and carry out the duties involved, in particular, of rearing children there rather than be employed outside, if she does not wish so to be employed, I do not consider that it is possible from that constitutionally preferred course of conduct to construe any form of resulting or constructive trust, even on the basis, as was submitted in this case, that by so doing she made a saving to what otherwise would have been a probable expenditure from the husband's earnings for the housekeeper or nanny, and therefore enabled him with greater facility to discharge outgoings on the house, including the repayment of mortgages raised from time to time.

For the same reason, namely, the confining of the rights to interests in the family home to the broad concept of resulting and constructive trust which would arise between persons other than husband and wife, I do not consider as I indicated in my decision in *W. v. W.* [1981] ILRM 202, that a direct contribution, even in money's worth, to an improvement made on the family home by a wife, where the husband is the sole owner of it, can, in the absence of express or readily implied agreement, constitute a claim for a beneficial interest in it. To that extent it appears to me that the rejection by the learned trial judge in this case of a specific claim arising from the fact that the mortgage to which the plaintiff contributed, certainly, from 1983 onwards, by contributions to the family funds from her earnings as a nurse, which was used for the extension constituted an additional percentage interest in the beneficial ownership of the home, was correct.

Where, however, it seems to me the learned trial judge in this case has fallen into an error, is in his refusal to have regard to the mortgages which were raised and apparently repaid on the premises, between the initial mortgage of £5,000 in 1966 for the conversion into bedsitter apartments and the later mortgage in 1977 for the extension of the house.

In the course of my judgment in *W. v. W.* [1981] ILRM 202 dealing with the situation where a wife contributed either directly towards the repayment of a mortgage or to a general family fund, thus releasing her husband from obligations which facilitated his redeeming a mortgage, I stated as follows at p. 204:

> "It is not expressly stated in the decisions to which I have referred but I assume that the fundamental principle underlying this rule of law is that the redemption of any form of charge or mortgage on property in truth consists of the acquisition by the owner or mortgagor of an estate in the property with which he had parted at the time of the creating of the mortgage or charge and that there can be no distinction in principle between a contribution made to the acquisition of that interest and a contribution made to the acquisition of an interest in property by an original purchase."

I would adhere to that view and its application to this case means that throughout the period of the ownership by the wife and husband of this house between 1966 and 1988, the wife has made contributions to the discharge not only of the first and fifth mortgages, as was found in the High Court, but of all the five mortgages which were raised and which have been redeemed. Those contributions consist, firstly, of the contribution by the wife throughout the entire of that period, consisting of her total management of the bedsitter apartments, the organisation and collection of the rents payable in respect of them and their general maintenance and care. Such activities are different from and not to be identified with the activities of a wife and mother in the home. Secondly, from the year 1983 to 1987, when she was earning as a nurse, she made contributions into the family fund which indirectly contributed towards the repayment of the amounts due on mortgages. This was at a time when the family finances were not as good as they had been and constituted a very important contribution.

Having regard to my view of the extreme importance on the evidence accepted by the learned trial judge of the contribution made by the wife in this case in the entire management of the bedsitter units and the position that the rental from them took in the family finances, over all the years, and having regard to the fact that I am satisfied she is entitled to credit for contribution towards the redemption of all the mortgages, it follows that the share of one-fifteenth assessed by the learned trial judge in the value of this house as being the share of the wife, is quite inadequate.

Having regard to all the considerations which are appropriate, I take the view that the proper share to which she is entitled on the facts as established and accepted by the trial judge is one-half. I would allow the appeal and vary the order of the High Court accordingly."

Murray v. Murray
[1996] 3 IR 251

See *infra* Chapter 8, p.408.

CHAPTER 8

Constructive Trusts

INTRODUCTION

A constructive trust is one which arises by operation of law and which is generally regarded as coming into being as a result of conduct and irrespective of the intention of the parties. In general terms it can be described as a trust which is imposed by equity in order to satisfy the demands of 'justice and good conscience'[1] and is employed e.g. to prevent a person deriving profit from fraudulent conduct or taking unfair advantage of a fiduciary position.

In practice, there may be a degree of overlap between the circumstances in which resulting and constructive trusts can arise and from a practical perspective it makes little difference as the formalities which apply to express trusts do not need to be complied with in either case.

ADVANTAGES GAINED BY PERSONS IN FIDUCIARY POSITIONS

General Principles

It is a fundamental principle that a trustee or other party in a fiduciary position will not be permitted to take advantage of his position to make a personal profit and any profit which he makes in this manner will be held by him as a constructive trustee for the benefit of the persons equitably entitled to the property. This principle was laid down by Chatterton VC in *Gabbett v. Lawder*.

Gabbett v. Lawder
(1883) 11 LR Ir 295

The administrator of the estate of an intestate held lands under a lease as trustee. The fee simple reversion of the land became vested in the Church Temporalities Commissioners who were authorized to sell it but before doing so they were bound to offer it to the lessee at a price to be named by them. The reversion was offered to the lessee who declined to buy it on the ground that the price was too high but he then bought it for himself at a public auction for a lower sum. It was held by the Irish Court of Appeal that in the circumstances the

---

[1] *Hussey v. Palmer* [1972] 1 WLR 1286, 1290. See also *Kelly v. Cahill* [2001] 2 ILRM 205, 210.

administrator became a constructive trustee of the reversion for the persons beneficially entitled to the personal estate of the deceased although he was entitled to the costs incurred by him in purchasing the reversion.

CHATTERTON VC stated at pp.299–310: "The Plaintiff, as administratrix *de bonis non* of William Lawder, claims to have it declared that the estate in fee-simple conveyed by the Commissioners of Church Temporalities to Matthew Nesbitt Lawder, the first administrator of William Lawder, in certain lands mentioned in the statement of claim, is personal estate of the intestate. The intestate held those lands under an ecclesiastical lease for twenty-one years customarily renewable, the last renewal to him being a lease of the 1st of February, 1870, from the Church Temporalities Commissioners, for twenty-one years. After his death Matthew Nesbitt Lawder, as his administrator, obtained a further renewal from the Commissioners for twenty-one years, dated the 14th of September, 1876. Under the 34th section of the Irish Church Act the Commissioners, in whom the reversion in fee became by that Act vested, were authorised to sell it by public auction or private contract; but were bound before selling to the public to offer the purchase to Matthew Nesbitt Lawder as their immediate tenant, at a price to be named by them. They did so offer it, and he declined to buy at the price named. The reversion in fee was thereupon set up by the Commissioners for sale by auction; and Matthew Nesbitt Lawder bought it for a less price, paid for it, and took the conveyance of it from the Commissioners, which the Plaintiff as administratrix contends he took as a constructive trustee for the persons entitled to the personal estate of William Lawder.

The fundamental principle upon which the doctrine of constructive trusts proceeds is, that no person in a fiduciary capacity shall be allowed to retain any advantage gained by him in his character as trustee. His *cestuis que trusts* are entitled to the benefit of any advantage so gained by him, to any addition or accretion to the trust estate which he may have acquired, and to all profit which he may have made by any dealing with it. It has long been settled by a current of authorities that a trustee of a leasehold interest who obtains a renewal of the lease, whether by covenant or custom, or by the voluntary act of the reversioner, comes within this principle, and that he cannot hold the interest he so acquired for his own benefit, but as a constructive trustee of it for his *cestuis que trusts*. In such cases this Court will not allow the trustee to say that he did not obtain the additional interest as trustee, or that he procured it from personal favour to himself, or from the refusal of the landlord to deal with the *cestuis que trusts*, or for any similar reason. If his position could have caused or even contributed to his obtaining the advantage, it is in my opinion enough; and the Court will not undertake the difficult and often impossible task of investigating the motives of the parties to the transaction. If it results in either gain to the trustee, or loss to the *cestuis que trusts*, the trustee is liable to hand over to them the one, or to make good the other. This principle of course applies to executors and administrators who stand in fiduciary relation to those entitled to the personal estate of their testator or intestate equal to that of any express trustees to their *cestuis que trusts*, and are subject to the same equities. It was therefore necessarily admitted that the renewal of the 14th September, 1876, to Matthew Nesbitt Lawder was a graft on the previous term, and that he held it as trustee for the persons entitled to the personal estate of the intestate. It was however contended by the Defendant James Ormsby Lawder that the purchase of the reversion in fee by Matthew from the Commissioners does not come within the principle, and that he took it for his own personal benefit. This contention was based on the cases of *Hardman v. Johnson* (1815) 3 Mer 347, and *Randall v. Russell* (1817) 3 Mer 190, before Sir William Grant. These cases appear to have proceeded on the authority of the case of *Norris v. Le Neve* (1743) 3 Atk 26, before Lord Hardwicke, which upon a careful examination will be found not to have been a decision on this question. In that case the owner of a reversion in fee, after several prior limitations by his will, made in pursuance of a power in the settlement by which the estate was limited, appointed the settled lands to Norris for a term of ten years, which took priority of the previously existing limitations, upon trust to raise money for payment of debts and legacies; and he did not, either by the settlement or his will, dispose of his reversion in the lands. Norris, who was only a trustee of the term so created, purchased from the heir-at-law this ultimate reversion, which afterwards fell into possession by the failure of the prior limitations. A protracted litigation took place which it is unnecessary to go into; and at a very late stage of it the question was directly raised, whether Norris was not to be held to be a trustee of the reversion so purchased. Lord Hardwicke pointed out the difficulty in that case of saying for whom he was to be deemed a trustee; and while he stated his opinion that the *Rumford Market Case* and other cases of leases were different from that, he refused, on the ground of the lapse of time and transactions between the parties, to allow the matter to be discussed, and dismissed the petition for rehearing. The case of *Hardman v. Johnson* came before Sir William Grant before *Randall v. Russell*, though it appears later in the Reports. There a testator, seised and possessed of a leasehold for three lives and twenty-one years, devised it to one of his daughters, Betty, with a gift over to another daughter, Sarah, in case the former should die without issue living at her death, which event happened. Betty obtained a renewal of the lease and devised it to the defendant, who brought an ejectment and recovered possession, and while in possession purchased the reversion in fee. The plaintiff, the husband of Sarah and claiming in her right, brought his bill claiming to be entitled to the benefit of the purchase of the reversion, and insisting that Betty took the now lease obtained by her subject to the limitations in the will. Sir William Grant said that the question of the purchase of the reversion was a new one, but that he should hesitate a good deal before he refused to apply to it the principle which had been established as to the renewal of a lease, and that it would be dangerous to allow the trustee of a term to resort to the owner of the reversion to become a purchaser for his own benefit; for by that means he would debar his *cestuis que trust* of the fair chance of a renewal, getting into his own hands the power to grant a renewal or not at his option. He took time to consider, and held that the plaintiff was entitled to the benefit of the renewed lease, but not of the purchase of the reversion. It is to be observed that there was no fiduciary relation subsisting at the time of the purchase between the defendant who purchased the reversion and the plaintiff. The defendant insisted on his legal right as devisee of Betty Johnson in the new lease obtained by her, and claimed the interest for his own benefit adversely to the plaintiff. Sir William Grant gave no reason for not acting on the opinion he expressed at the hearing.

In *Randall v. Russell* (1817) 3 Mer 190 the bill prayed that a tenant for life of lands held by a testator, under St. John's College, Oxford, as yearly tenant after the expiration of a lease, which appears to have been customarily renewable, should be declared a trustee of a new lease obtained by her from the college, and also of the reversion in fee, which she purchased from a third person, in whom, by a private Act of Parliament sanctioning an exchange, it had after the granting of the new lease become vested. It was held that the renewed lease was subject to the trusts of the will which created the tenancy for life, but that the reversion in fee was not, and that the tenant for life was entitled to hold it for her own benefit. Sir William Grant said that the ground commonly stated on which a renewed lease becomes subject to the trusts of a will disposing of the original lease is that the one is merely an extension or continuation of the other, but that the fee is a totally different subject which the testator had it not in his contemplation to acquire or dispose of. He suggested that it might be different if the purchase had been from the college; for, if so, it might be said that the tenant for life intercepted and cut off the chance of future renewals, and consequently made use of her situation to prejudice the interests of those who stood behind her, and that there might be a sort of equity in their claim to have the reversion considered as a substitution for those interests, though he was not aware of any decision to that effect. He distinguished the case before him from those as to the renewal of leases, on the ground that by the act of the landlord, without any intervention of the tenant for life, the situation of the parties was altered, and the tenant-right of renewal with a public body was gone, a lease at a rack-rent being all that was to be expected from a private proprietor. He held that it was not enough to say that the situation of the tenant for life gave her the opportunity of making the purchase, and that the persons interested in the lease must go on and show what right of theirs she acquired or defeated by making the purchase.

As this case constitutes the main support to the argument of the Defendant James Ormsby Lawder, and as at first sight it appears to countenance his contention, it is necessary to consider carefully whether it is substantially distinguishable from the present. If it be not, I should certainly consider myself bound by it, though I should not follow it in a case like this without hesitation;

for I think that the rule supposed to be established by it would be a dangerous limitation of the application of the general principle. I first venture to say that Sir William Grant appears to me to have treated *Norris v. Le Neve* (1743) 3 Atk 26 as a decision of Lord Hardwicke on the point, which for the reasons already stated I do not think it is. I also think that there is a material difference between that case and the present, in this, that there, as in *Hardman v. Johnson* (1815) 3 Mer 347, the purchase of the reversion was made by a person who before and at the time of the purchase did not stand in relation to the persons who claimed to have the benefit of it. There is no such relation between successive remaindermen or persons entitled under successive limitations of any kind. It is the fact of a renewal being obtained by the possessor of an interest earlier in the series that creates *de novo* the fiduciary relation in the nature of a constructive trust. The position of a trustee or personal representative, who fills the fiduciary relation altogether independently of and prior to such a purchase, and therefore has duties to his *cestuis que trusts* to discharge in respect of property of which he is already the legal owner, seems to me to impose on him the disability to hold for his personal benefit any advantage he may obtain which is attributable, or possibly attributable, to that position. This distinction would accord with the views expressed by Sir William Grant in *Randall v. Russell* (1817) 3 Mer 190, which would otherwise appear opposed to the general rule. It would sustain his decision in the case of renewals by persons having limited interests, by placing such cases on what he states to be the common ground for holding them to be subject to a constructive trust, namely, that the new lease is deemed a continuation of the former, and therefore within the possible contemplation of the author of the limitations; and not upon the ground of any supposed pre-existing fiduciary relation which would impose on such persons the disability which attaches to trustees, and it would probably support the distinction he takes between such renewals and purchases of the reversion in fee. It would explain the reason assigned by him for this distinction, namely, that the testator may have had the former in his contemplation, but not the latter; for this reason could well apply to cases between persons taking under successive limitations, whereas it would be altogether inapplicable to cases of pre-existing fiduciary relations, which may have been created without either will or deed or other written instrument, as in that before me, where the relation flows from the office of administrator; cases in which the existence of the relation creates the disability, no matter what may be the subject of the trust. I cannot think that he intended to apply to cases of ordinary fiduciary relation the proposition that it is not enough to say that the situation of the person making the purchase gave him the opportunity of making it, but that the persons interested must go on and show what right of theirs he acquired or defeated by making the purchase. His language on this is in express terms applied by him to the case of a purchase by a tenant for life, and the rights arising therefrom to the other persons interested in the lease; and I must understand him as confining his argument to such cases. I do not think that his decision can affect a case like the present, where a leasehold interest with a statutory right of renewal is vested in an administrator as such; where he takes the legal estate with all its incidental rights, not for his own benefit, but merely as a trustee for the creditors and next-of-kin of the intestate. The law casts upon him the duty of protecting the interests of those entitled to the personal estate; and he is in duty bound to realise for them every right incidental to it. Even in the case of persons respectively entitled in succession, the principle upon which Sir William Grant appears to have proceeded was not confined to renewals strictly so called, but extended to acquisitions of higher interests.

In *Giddings v. Giddings* (1827) 3 Russ 241 the leasehold interest which was held in trust was an underlease of premises called the Byde Mill, for eighteen years, carved out of a superior lease for twenty-one years of these and other premises, which was again carved out of a lease made by the Bishop of Salisbury. The tenant for life of the underlease purchased the interest in the superior lease, and obtained renewals of it from time to time from the immediate tenant to the See, the last of which bore date in the year 1819; and on his death the person entitled in remainder under the will which created the trusts of the underlease filed his bill against the representative of the tenant for life, to have it declared that the new lease of 1819, which it will be remembered was a renewal of the superior lease, was held upon the trusts of the will. The defendant claimed to hold the renewal in his own right, and not as trustee; and his counsel relied on *Randall v. Russell* and *Hardman v. Johnson,* and contended that those cases proceeded not on any peculiarity in the nature of a reversion in fee, but on the ground that the purchase of the reversion was not an extension or continuation of the preceding lease, and did not defeat any right of the remainderman. Lord Lyndhurst, then Sir J. Copley, M.R., says:– "If an underlessee who has only a life estate in his lease, instead of taking a renewed lease, purchases the interest of an immediate lessor, and obtains from the superior lessor a renewal of the lease which he has so purchased, will he under such circumstances be entitled to the property absolutely? That state of things falls within the general rule; the mere circumstance of the lease being taken not from the immediate lessor but from a superior lessor cannot defeat the right of a remainderman; and the remainderman will still be entitled, on the principle that a lease obtained by a tenant for life enures for the benefit of all in remainder. What difference can it make in the application of that whether the lease be taken from the immediate lessor or from a superior lessor?" He stated that he did not think that the cases before Sir William Grant established a contrary principle, for they were cases where the reversion in fee was purchased, and there was no longer a leasehold interest existing. He deemed that the lease of 1819, so far as regards the Byde Mill and the premises held therewith, ought to be held upon the trusts of the will.

It will be observed that the Master of the Rolls did not declare that the original underlease was to be kept up out of the superior interest purchased by the tenant for life, but that the new lease of 1819, which was a renewal of the lease so purchased, was itself subject to the trusts of the will. Again, in *Buckley v. Lanauze* (1836) Ll & Gt Plunk 327 a tenant for life of a lease for lives without any covenant for renewal obtained from the landlord a new lease for three lives (one of whom was the surviving *cestui que vie* in the former lease), with covenant for perpetual renewal at a largely increased rent. He sold his newly-acquired interest for valuable consideration; but, as it was held, with notice, and though a similar argument based on *Randall v. Russell,* and also on *Norris v. Le Neve,* was put forward for the defendant the purchaser, Lord Plunket held that the new lease was a graft on the old one, and decreed accordingly. He no doubt, as well as Sir J. Copley, distinguished the case from those cited to him for the defendant, as not being a purchase of a reversion in fee, and also on some special circumstances; but he expressed doubt as to the effect of the decision in *Randall v. Russell,* and pointed out that in reality the question was not affected by *Norris v. Le Neve.*

The case of *Postlethwaite v. Lewthwaite* (1862) 2 J & H 237, before Sir W.P. Wood, was cited in argument, but has not much application to this case. It was a purchase of a reversion in fee from the Ecclesiastical Commissioners of England by an immediate lessee, and an underlessee with a *toties quoties* covenant for renewal claimed a declaration that the interest so purchased was subject to his underlease. The Vice-Chancellor considered that the relation of a *purchasing* lessee was very much that of a fiduciary or partner with respect to his subleases, and held that the equity of the latter was to call for a conveyance of the fee of the particular property comprised in his underlease, upon the terms of paying his share of the expenses of acquiring it. The question there was rather as to the terms on which the plaintiff was so entitled, and the construction was therefore different. In *Trumper v. Trumper* (1872) LR 14 Eq 295 the plaintiff sought to charge certain sums, which were originally charged upon an estate for lives renewable for ever, upon the reversion in fee which had been purchased by a tenant for life of the leasehold interest subsequently to the creation of the charges. The defendant, who was the devisee of the reversion so purchased, disputed this claim. Bacon, V.C., held that the plaintiff was entitled to the relief he sought, and that the charges should be raised out of the entire estate in the lands. He held that, upon the general principles applicable in a Court of Equity to the circumstances, there ought to be no doubt, and that there could be no danger in holding, that a trustee or person in any degree in a fiduciary position who had acquired the legal possession of and dominion over an estate subject to a covenant for perpetual renewal, and who should so deal with the property as to make the renewal impossible by his own act, and for his benefit, would be bound to give full effect to the charges on the trust estate, and to satisfy these charges out of the acquired estate so far as might be necessary. He referred to the cases of *Evans v. Walshe* (1805) 2 Sch & Lef 519, and *Randall v. Russell,* as confirming his view, and said that the dangers which would attend the exclusion of the principle were so numerous and so serious that they would go near to destroy the fixed rules by which the dealings of persons in a fiduciary position with respect to trust estates and interests are governed. This case is an important authority in favour of the Plaintiff here; and I fully concur, not only in the decision, but in Sir J. Bacon's statement of the equitable principle on which he placed it. His decision was affirmed by the Court of Appeal in Chancery ((1873) LR 8 Ch App 870). James, L.J., does not in terms apply to it the broad principle relied on by Sir J. Bacon, and in his judgment says that the right of the plaintiff would not be to claim the fee, but only a right to a leasehold interest subject to the life estate of the defendant, and with a right of renewal; and on that basis discusses the position of the tenant for life as paying off a charge on the entire leasehold interest – a question having no bearing on the case before me. His observations to which I refer would appear to be in accordance with those of Sir William Grant in *Randall v. Russell,* as to the extent of the right of a *quasi* remainderman of a leasehold interest to the benefit of a purchase of the fee by a prior tenant for life. It was not necessary for him to go farther than to hold that the charges on the original interest must under the circumstances of that case be let in on the fee; and he expressed no dissent from Sir James Bacon's statement and application of the general principle. The only relation between the parties in that case also was that of tenant for life and remainderman.

In none of the cases which have been cited in argument, or which I have found, is there any distinction taken as to the nature of the additional estate or interest acquired save in those between tenant for life and tenant *quasi* in remainder. I certainly am not disposed to extend this distinction to any other cases, and I am of opinion that it does not apply to cases like the present, where the relation is expressly fiduciary, and existed independently of the purchase. I think it would be impossible to hold that, if Matthew Lawder had accepted the offer of pre-emption given by the 34th section, he would be entitled to the reversion in fee so acquired, for his own benefit. It would have clearly been an estate acquired by him by virtue of his fiduciary position, which alone entitled him to the tenancy in possession to which the Act accords that right. It is, no doubt, true that the 34th section enacts that any person purchasing the reversion shall hold it subject to all tenants' rights of renewal to which the same was subject in the hands of the Commissioners at the time of the sale. That would not, however, be the measure of the right of the creditors or next-of-kin, for their trustee, *qua* trustee, would have gained an additional estate, presumably an advantageous one, but certainly one which they could claim as their own on recouping him what he had given for it. Surely the rule supposed to have been laid down by Sir William Grant could not have applied to such a case. I have no doubt that he never intended to express so wide a proposition.

I had occasion to apply this general rule to the acquisition by an administratrix of a new tenancy from year to year, in the case of *Kelly v. Kelly* (1874) IR 8 Eq 403, where the old tenancy had been determined by notice to quit, and a new letting made to the widow of the former tenant, who was also his administratrix; and though there were circumstances relied on as showing that the new letting was to her as the widow, not as the administratrix, I refused to entertain that question, and held her to be a constructive trustee. Again, in *M'Cracken v. M'Clelland* (1877) IR 11 Eq 172, I had to deal with a purchase by an executor of a farm subject to the Ulster tenant-right custom, which he paid for with his own money, and obtained a new letting of, according to the custom of the estate; and on the same principle I held him to be a trustee. In those cases I stated my views of the principle applicable to them; and I am of opinion that that principle applies with equal force to cases like the present.

It was urged here, as in those cases, that the circumstances of the purchase show that the administrator did not buy in his fiduciary capacity, but for his own personal benefit. It was contended that the statutory offer of pre-emption having been refused, he was at liberty to bid for the estate as any other member of the public could. If this were so, it would open a wide door to fraud, for a trustee, whose duty it is to secure for his *cestuis que trusts* every advantage incident to the trust property, would be at liberty for his own purposes to decline the offer of pre-emption, and thus secure the setting up of the estate by public auction, and then buy, as he did here, at a less price, and hold the property as his own. The fact of his being the possessor of the leasehold interest might, and probably would, be a reason for his getting it at a less price than a stranger. But into these probabilities this Court, in such cases, declines for wise reasons to enter, and holds that every advantage which may possibly arise from the fiduciary position shall enure to the benefit of the *cestuis que trusts*. If no statutory right of pre-emption had been conferred, and the reversion at once set up for public sale, a purchase by a trustee would, according to the opinion I have expressed, be held so to enure. It seems to me to make the case stronger against a trustee that he had previously been offered the purchase and declined it. I do not mean to say that Matthew N. Lawder declined the offer of the Commissioners fraudulently, with a view to a purchase by auction for his own use, and he possibly had no other reason for so doing, but that he thought the price too high. That consideration is, however, beside the question, for actual fraud is not necessary in cases between trustee and *cestui que trust*.

I am accordingly of opinion that Matthew N. Lawder became a constructive trustee of the reversion so purchased, for the persons entitled beneficially to the personal estate of Wm. Lawder, and that it forms part of such personal estate; the persons claiming the benefit of it, of course, paying the purchase-money and all expenses incurred by M.N. Lawder in the purchase."

The Fiduciary Position of Trustees

The 'fundamental position' referred to above by Chatterton VC in *Gabbett v. Lawder* applies strictly to trustees and personal representatives. In addition, these principles also apply to a varying degree to other categories of persons who act in a fiduciary capacity, an issue which will be examined in more detail below.

Renewal of a Lease

Where a trustee of leasehold property obtains a renewal of a lease in his own name, he will be regarded as holding it as a constructive trustee for the beneficiaries.[2] This principle also extends to administrators and executors,[3] although in order for the so-called doctrine of graft to apply there must be 'life in the old stock'.[4]

Kelly v. Kelly
(1874) IR 8 Eq 403

A widow and administratrix of her husband's estate continued in possession of land held on a tenancy from year to year. The landlord determined the tenancy by serving a notice to quit and the administratrix did not oppose this and was left in occupation at the same rent. It was held by Chatterton VC that while her conduct did not amount to fraud, the new tenancy was a graft on the old one and she was regarded as being in occupation of the premises as constructive trustee for the next of kin who would have been entitled to the original tenancy on her husband's death.

CHATTERTON VC stated at pp.404–406: "There is no controversy about the facts of this case, which lie in a narrow compass. It appears that a person of the name of Hugh Kelly was tenant of a farm at Cloughgor, in the county of Tyrone, containing about fifty acres, which he held, from year to year, under the Duke of Abercorn, at the annual rent of £51 9s. Hugh Kelly died intestate on the 25th of January, 1863, and, on 14th of March following, letters of administration of his personal estate and effects were granted to his widow, the Defendant, Sarah Kelly. He had no children, but left sisters, or nephews, and nieces – children of sisters – some of whom are Plaintiffs in the suit. After his death no change of tenancy took place, but the Defendant continued in possession until the month of January, 1865, when a civil bill ejectment was brought upon a notice to quit. This ejectment was not defended, and a decree having been obtained, the landlord took formal possession of the premises. It is quite evident that, notwithstanding these proceedings, the possession of the Defendant was not in fact disturbed, and it is not an unfair inference that they were merely friendly. It was insisted upon that the transaction was a collusive one, but the affidavit of the landlord's agent displaces this allegation. The tenant was put back again at the same rent precisely, and was continued in the occupation until the year 1872, when she agreed to sell her interest, and what

---

[2] *Keech v. Sanford* (1726) Sel Cas T King 61; *Gabbett v. Lawder* (1883) 11 LR Ir 295.
[3] *Kelly v. Kelly* (1874) IR 8 Eq 403; *M'Cracken v. M'Clelland* (1877) IR 11 Eq 172.
[4] *Dempsey v. Ward* [1899] 1 IR 463, 474.

certainly to one not acquainted with the value of such interests seems a very surprising price – namely, £1150 – was paid to her for it by one Robert Roulston, and an assignment having, with the consent of the landlord, been executed to him, he went into possession. I am of opinion that the case is to be dealt with entirely independently of the Ulster Tenant-right customs or the Land Act.

The Land Act in no way affects the present case, except that it happens to have increased the value of the land. The case is to be dealt with simply as an ordinary yearly tenancy, the property of an intestate whose estate is being administered in this Court. The fact of this being a yearly tenancy does not interfere with its being administered. The Court frequently directs a sale, for the purpose of administration of yearly tenancies, and I have often done so myself. Dealing with it, then, merely as the case of a yearly tenancy, the personal representative continued in possession, her only legal right being that of personal representative. In herself she had no legal right. If the suit had been instituted before any change in her tenancy had taken place, the proper course would have been to direct a sale of the early tenancy, and, if it happened to be subject to the Ulster Tenant-right Custom, such a circumstance would have in no way affected the rights of the parties except probably by rendering a sale more profitable. The Defendant relies on the transactions of 1865 as altering her position. She says that, having been put out of possession by legal process, and there having been a new letting, such letting was made to her not as personal representative but as the widow of the intestate in her individual capacity. The affidavit of the landlord's agent goes considerably in that direction. But suppose a letting made expressly in consideration of her – the administratrix – parting with the estate of the intestate, and for no other consideration, the effect of her fiduciary capacity would be that she could reap no benefit from such new letting. The principle involved is one of public policy, and think it would be a most mischievous restriction of that policy if I held that she should be entitled to benefit herself by such a transaction. If this had been the case of a lease made by a landlord, after ejectment and in consideration of non-resistance to the ejectment, to the personal representative of the old tenant, the case would not have been taken out of the operation of the principle, and she would have been bound as a trustee. It is quite clear that it makes no difference whether the tenancy is a yearly one or under a lease, nor is it necessary that there should have been fraud in the transaction. All these matters are entirely beside the question. The principle is a much broader one. It is the great principle that no person, in a fiduciary position aecepting any benefit attributable in any degree to that fiduciary position can be allowed to enjoy such benefit for himself. In every such case the person will be bound to account for what he has so acquired for the benefit of the persons for whom he happens to be a trustee. It does not affect the rights of the landlord to hold that it is a trust, for the landlord still may exercise all his rights, and a purchaser would take the tenancy with the liability of its being determined by a notice to quit. It is quite possible that, if proceedings had been taken to fix a graft upon this new yearly tenancy, before it was sold by the Defendant, the result might have been that it would, by action on the part of the landlord, have been rendered comparatively valueless; but the fact that it has been sold, and a large sum realised, does not affect the matter, and once it is fixed with the character of a graft it is the same as regards the Defendant, who will in the one case be liable for the price received by her, or the value at the option of the persons beneficially interested, and in the other will be obliged to convey to a purchaser under the decree of the Court. I shall, therefore, make a decree for the Plaintiff. The costs must come out of the personal estate in the administration proceedings, as, there being no fraud, I do not feel called upon to fix the Defendant with the Plaintiff's costs, and nothing has, in my opinion, occurred to disentitle her to obtain her costs as portion of her administration expenses."

M'Cracken v. M'Clelland
(1877) IR 11 Eq 172

An executor surrendered a holding which was subject to the Ulster Custom while the old tenancy was still in existence and, in compliance with the custom, was given a new tenancy on his own behalf. Chatterton VC concluded that the defendant held the new tenancy on a constructive trust for the persons entitled under the will.

CHATTERTON VC stated at pp.174–177: "In approaching the question which I have to decide, it seems to me desirable that I should state clearly what appears to me to be the due course of administration in cases like the present, which are now of rather frequent occurrence, where the assets of the party whose estate is being administered consist of or include tenancies subject to tenant-right. In such cases, the Court must treat the property exactly as it finds it, that is, as a yearly tenancy with the benefit of the tenant-right custom, whatever that may be, varying as it does on different estates, and even on different portions of the same estate. In dealing with such properties the Court has no power, nor have I any desire, to interfere in any way with the rights of the landlord. Nothing that I can do can give the tenant any additional right against the landlord, nor in any way fetter his powers nor deprive him of the free exercise of the rights which the law gives him modified as these rights have been by the Irish Land Act of 1870. It is possible that in some of these cases the custom may be such as will enable the landlord very materially to abridge the powers of the Court, or of the personal representatives of the tenant out of Court, in the disposal of the tenant's interest; for in such cases the Court or the personal representatives cannot sell or assign the deceased tenant's interest except on the same conditions that he could do if he were living. If a sale and assignment were to take place in violation of those conditions, the landlord would have the same right of evicting the assignee upon a notice to quit, whether the sale were by the tenant, the personal representatives, or the Court. But all this cannot alter the rules of this Court as to the administration of assets or the principles of equity as to purchases by persons in a fiduciary position.

Now in this case the question between the parties arises in respect of the farm held by the Defendants, on the estate of the Clothworkers' Company, to which a more or less extended tenant-right applied. With the extent of that custom I have nothing to do. The testator disposed of his farm; after his death his widow went into possession of the part of it left to her, and another person named M'Cracken into possession of the part given to him, the Defendants not having parted with control over the property, and certainly not having absolutely assented to these bequests. Circumstances occurred which rendered it undesirable that that state of things should continue, and accordingly those parties went to the agent of the Company, and made arrangements for the disposal of the farm according to the custom of the estate. The sale of the farm was carried out through the medium of the agent, and the result was that it was divided into three portions, and the first portion was given to Martin M'Cracken, the second, a small portion consisting of 8A. 3R. 32P. to one John Morrison, and the third, containing about 28A. 2R. 16P. was purchased by the Defendant William M'Clelland. Now William M'Clelland, when he made that purchase, was the executor of the testator; and the law of this Court, is that under no circumstances can an executor purchase and hold for his own benefit any part of the testator's assets. He was the party actively engaged in giving up possession of this farm to the landlord; he immediately got possession of the portion of it which he now holds; he paid the price of it, and is now in possession of it. As executor, I am at a loss to see how in this Court he can contend that he is entitled to retain it for his own benefit. It is said that the transaction did not in fact amount to such a purchase, but that it was a surrender out and out of the premises, and then that the landlord's agent disposed of them as he pleased, and that he chose to give the offer of this farm to the Defendant. I think it would be most dangerous to allow such an exception to be grafted on the doctrine that executors are liable to the persons entitled for the value of the property purchased by them. I am, therefore, of opinion that there was a purchase by the Defendant of part of the assets, and that he must be held accountable for it. It was argued that, at the time of this transaction, the executor had no legal estate to surrender, and that the surrender was not by the executor but by the tenant herself; but the answer of the Defendants is a conclusive reply to this, for they state in the sixth and eighteenth paragraphs that they, with the others, surrendered the premises to the landlord. They exercised control over them to the very last, they received money for them, and dealt with the money so received as assets; and it is idle to say that there had been an assent to the bequest of this farm, and a parting with all control over it, and a release to them from all liability as to it.

The Court in these cases cannot go into the motives of the executor; but I think that, in cases like the present, the arm of the Court would be very much shortened if it were to be held that the fact of a purchase like this having passed through the Estate Office would preclude the Court from comprising the transaction within the principles I have spoken of. How can the Court go into the reasons which may have existed in the minds of the parties for accepting this person as tenant? I must take it as a fact in this case, that the executor has bought the property of the testator, and he must therefore hold it as a trustee for the Plaintiffs. And I think it is clear that he purchased it at an undervalue, for it is proved – and even admitted by the Defendant M'Clelland himself, who declines to say what would be the worth of the farm if it were set up and sold – that the property is now of more intrinsic value than the price which was paid for it. Even if the custom prevents more than five years' purchase being given, that does not make this the less a purchase by an executor, whose bounden duty it was to set up such a property and get the best value he could for it. But I do not rest my decision upon the value; I rest it upon the general principle upon which I went in *Kelly v. Kelly* (1874) Ir R 8 Eq 403, 406, viz., that no person in a fiduciary position accepting any benefit, attributable in any degree to that fiduciary position, can be allowed to enjoy such benefit for himself.

I am of opinion that in taking the accounts in this case the executor will be entitled to credit for all sums paid out of his own money for this farm, with interest, and also for the value of all permanent improvements made by him."

Other Types of Fiduciary Relationships

Introduction

As a general principle, a person in a fiduciary position is not entitled to make a profit out of that position,[5] although in order to found liability it will be necessary to establish a connection between the fiduciary position and the profit made. It should also be borne in mind that there are various types of fiduciary relationships which may attract different kinds of fiduciary obligations[6] and while universal principles can be identified, the standards imposed may differ depending on the nature of the relationship.

The Liability of a Fiduciary to Account for Secret Commissions and Bribes

As a general principle, a fiduciary may not accept secret commissions or bribes arising out of a transaction in which he is acting on behalf of a principal without the knowledge and consent of his principal. It is now established that where a

---

[5] *Bray v. Ford* [1896] AC 44, 51 *per* Lord Herschell.
[6] *Attorney General v. Blake* [1998] 1 All ER 833, 842 *per* Woolf MR.

fiduciary receives a secret commission[7] or bribe[8] as a result of his position, he will be liable as a constructive trustee in relation to the monies received.

Attorney-General for Hong Kong v. Reid
[1994] 1 AC 324

While employed by the legal service of the government of Hong Kong, the first named respondent accepted bribes in breach of his fiduciary duty. He pleaded guilty to a number of bribery offences and was sentenced to eight years' imprisonment and ordered to pay a sum equivalent to the value of his assets which could only have been derived from bribes. These sums were not paid over and the Attorney-General for Hong Kong lodged caveats in New Zealand against the titles to properties in that jurisdiction which it was alleged had been purchased with monies received as bribes. The appeal of the Attorney-General for Hong Kong against a decision by the Court of Appeal of New Zealand to refuse to renew the caveats was allowed by the Privy Council. It held that when a bribe is accepted by a fiduciary in breach of his duty, he holds the bribe on a constructive trust for the person to whom that duty is owed and to the extent to which they represented bribes received by the first named respondent, the New Zealand properties were held in trust for the Crown.

LORD TEMPLEMAN stated at pp.330–339: "The first respondent Mr. Reid, a solicitor and New Zealand national, joined the legal service of the Government of Hong Kong and became successively Crown Counsel, Deputy Crown Prosecutor and ultimately Acting Director of Public Prosecutions. In the course of his career the first respondent, in breach of the fiduciary duty which he owed as a servant of the Crown, accepted bribes as an inducement to him to exploit his official position by obstructing the prosecution of certain criminals. The first respondent was arrested, pleaded guilty to offences under the Prevention of Bribery Ordinance and was sentenced on 6 July 1990 to eight years' imprisonment and ordered to pay the Crown the sum of H.K.$12.4m., equivalent to N.Z.$2.5m., being the value of assets then controlled by the first respondent which could only have been derived from bribes. No part of the sum of H.K.$12.4m. has been paid by the first respondent.

Among the first respondent's assets are three freehold properties in New Zealand. The trial judge's finding that the Attorney-General for Hong Kong had established an arguable case that each of the three properties was acquired

---

[7] *Williams v. Barton* [1927] 2 Ch 9.

[8] *Attorney-General for Hong Kong v. Reid* [1994] 1 AC 324. The Privy Council rejected the earlier decision of *Lister & Co. v. Stubbs* (1890) 45 Ch D 1 in which it had been held that where a fiduciary received a bribe from a third party, although he was liable to account, he was not regarded as a constructive trustee of this sum.

with moneys received by the first respondent as bribes has not been challenged. Two of the freehold properties were conveyed to the first respondent and his wife and one to the first respondent's solicitor, Mr. Molloy. The three New Zealand properties were purchased for approximately N.Z.$500,000. Their current value was not the subject of evidence before the New Zealand Court of Appeal. The total amount thought to have been received by the first respondent from bribes exceeds N.Z.$2.5m.

In the courts of New Zealand the first and second respondents argued that part of the costs of the three New Zealand properties might not be derived from bribes. If so, the courts have ample means of discovering by means of accounts and inquiries the amount (if any) of innocent money invested in the properties and the proportion of the present value of the properties attributable to innocent money. It was also argued that the second respondent might have a beneficial interest in the properties. This also could be investigated in due course but it does not appear that either the second respondent or the third respondent was a bona fide purchaser of a legal estate without notice. For present purposes this appeal proceeds on the assumption that the freehold New Zealand properties were purchased with bribes received by the first respondent and are held in trust for the first respondent subject to the claims of the Crown in these proceedings.

A bribe is a gift accepted by a fiduciary as an inducement to him to betray his trust. A secret benefit, which may or may not constitute a bribe, is a benefit which the fiduciary derives from trust property or obtains from knowledge which he acquires in the course of acting as a fiduciary. A fiduciary is not always accountable for a secret benefit but he is undoubtedly accountable for a secret benefit which consists of a bribe. In addition a person who provides the bribe and the fiduciary who accepts the bribe may each be guilty of a criminal offence. In the present case the first respondent was clearly guilty of a criminal offence.

Bribery is an evil practice which threatens the foundations of any civilised society. In particular bribery of policemen and prosecutors brings the administration of justice into disrepute. Where bribes are accepted by a trustee, servant, agent or other fiduciary, loss and damage are caused to the beneficiaries, master or principal whose interests have been betrayed. The amount of loss or damage resulting from the acceptance of a bribe may or may not be quantifiable. In the present case the amount of harm caused to the administration of justice in Hong Kong by the first respondent in return for bribes cannot be quantified.

When a bribe is offered and accepted in money or in kind, the money or property constituting the bribe belongs in law to the recipient. Money paid to the false fiduciary belongs to him. The legal estate in freehold property conveyed to the false fiduciary by way of bribe vests in him. Equity, however, which acts in personam, insists that it is unconscionable for a fiduciary to obtain and retain a benefit in breach of duty. The provider of a bribe cannot recover it because he committed a criminal offence when he paid the bribe.

The false fiduciary who received the bribe in breach of duty must pay and account for the bribe to the person to whom that duty was owed. In the present case, as soon as the first respondent received a bribe in breach of the duties he owed to the Government of Hong Kong, he became a debtor in equity to the Crown for the amount of that bribe. So much is admitted. But if the bribe consists of property which increases in value or if a cash bribe is invested advantageously, the false fiduciary will receive a benefit from his breach of duty unless he is accountable not only for the original amount or value of the bribe but also for the increased value of the property representing the bribe. As soon as the bribe was received it should have been paid or transferred instanter to the person who suffered from the breach of duty. Equity considers as done that which ought to have been done. As soon as the bribe was received, whether in cash or in kind, the false fiduciary held the bribe on a constructive trust for the person injured. Two objections have been raised to this analysis. First it is said that if the fiduciary is in equity a debtor to the person injured, he cannot also be a trustee of the bribe. But there is no reason why equity should not provide two remedies, so long as they do not result in double recovery. If the property representing the bribe exceeds the original bribe in value, the fiduciary cannot retain the benefit of the increase in value which he obtained solely as a result of his breach of duty. Secondly, it is said that if the false fiduciary holds property representing the bribe in trust for the person injured, and if the false fiduciary is or becomes insolvent, the unsecured creditors of the false fiduciary will be deprived of their right to share in the proceeds of that property. But the unsecured creditors cannot be in a better position than their debtor. The authorities show that property acquired by a trustee innocently but in breach of trust and the property from time to time representing the same belong in equity to the cestui que trust and not to the trustee personally whether he is solvent or insolvent. Property acquired by a trustee as a result of a criminal breach of trust and the property from time to time representing the same must also belong in equity to his cestui que trust and not to the trustee whether he is solvent or insolvent.

When a bribe is accepted by a fiduciary in breach of his duty then he holds that bribe in trust for the person to whom the duty was owed. If property representing the bribe decreases in value the fiduciary must pay the difference between that value and the initial amount of the bribe because he should not have accepted the bribe or incurred the risk of loss. If the property increases in value, the fiduciary is not entitled to any surplus in excess of the initial value of the bribe because he is not allowed by any means to make a profit out of a breach of duty.

The courts of New Zealand were constrained by a number of precedents of the New Zealand, English and other common law courts which established a settled principle of law inconsistent with the foregoing analysis. That settled principle is open to review by the Board in the light of the foregoing analysis of the consequences in equity of the receipt of a bribe by a fiduciary. In *Keech v. Sandford* (1726) Sel Cas Ch 61 a landlord refused to renew a lease to a trustee for the benefit of an infant. The trustee then took a new lease for his own benefit. The new lease had not formed part of the original trust property, the infant could not have acquired the new lease from the landlord and the trustee acted innocently, believing that he committed no breach of trust and that the new lease did not belong in equity to his cestui que trust. Lord King L.C. held nevertheless, at p. 62, that "the trustee is the only person of all mankind who might not have the lease;" the trustee was obliged to assign the new lease to the infant and account for the profits he had received. The rule must be that property which a trustee obtains by use of knowledge acquired as trustee becomes trust property. The rule must, a fortiori, apply to a bribe accepted by a trustee for a guilty criminal purpose which injures the cestui que trust. The trustee is only one example of a fiduciary and the same rule applies to all other fiduciaries who accept bribes.

In *Fawcett v. Whitehouse* (1829) 1 Russ & M 132 the defendant, Whitehouse, intending to enter into partnership with the plaintiffs, Shand and Fawcett, negotiated for the grant of a lease by a landlord to the partnership. The landlord paid Whitehouse £12,000 for persuading the partnership to accept the lease. Sir John Leach V.-C. said, at p. 149, that Whitehouse

> "was bound to obtain the best terms possible for the intended partnership . . . and that all he did obtain will be considered as if he had done his duty and had actually received the £12,000 for the new partnership, as upon every equitable principle he was bound to do. I am of opinion, therefore, that this is what must be called in a court of equity a fraud on the part of the defendant. It was in fact selling his intended partners for £12,000; . . ."

Sir John Leach V.-C. made a declaration, at p. 135, that Whitehouse

> "had received the £12,000 on behalf of himself and the plaintiffs Shand and Fawcett equally, and that he was a trustee, as to one third part of that sum, for Shand, and as to another third part . . . for the plaintiff Fawcett . . ."

An appeal to the Lord Chancellor was dismissed by Lord Lyndhurst L.C. Although in that case, there was no need to trace the sum of £12,000 into other assets, the bribe of £12,000 was plainly held to be trust property.

In *Sugden v. Crossland* (1856) 3 Sm & G 192 a trustee was paid £75 for agreeing to retire from the trust and to appoint in his place the person who had paid the £75. Sir John Stuart V.-C. said, at p. 194:

> "It has been further asked that the sum of £75 may be treated as a part of the trust fund, and as such may be directed to be paid by Horsfield to the trustee for the benefit of the cestui que trusts under the will. It is a well-settled principle that, if a trustee make a profit of his trusteeship, it shall enure to the benefit of his cestui que trusts. Though there is some peculiarity in the case, there does not seem to be any difference in principle whether the trustee derived the profit by means of the trust property, or from the office itself."

This case is of importance because it disposes succinctly of the argument which appears in later cases and which was put forward by counsel in the present case that there is a distinction between a profit which a trustee takes out of a trust and a profit such as a bribe which a trustee receives from a third party. If in law a trustee, who in breach of trust invests trust moneys in his own name, holds the investment as trust property, it is difficult to see why a trustee who in breach of trust receives and invests a bribe in his own name does not hold those investments also as trust property.

In *Tyrrell v. Bank of London* (1862) 10 HLC 26 a solicitor acting for a bank in negotiating the purchase by the bank of a building known as the Hall of Commerce acquired for himself an interest in a larger property which included the Hall of Commerce and then sold the Hall of Commerce to the bank at a profit. The House of Lords held that the solicitor was a trustee for the bank of his interests in the Hall of Commerce but was not a trustee for the bank of that part of the retained property which the bank never had any intention of acquiring. The solicitor was obliged to bring into account the value of the retained property in calculating the profit which the solicitor had made at the expense of the bank. No difficulty arises from the decision in this case but, at pp. 59-60, Lord Chelmsford said that if the solicitor had been paid a sum of £5,000 to induce the bank to purchase the Hall of Commerce at an excessive price, the bank could have recovered damages from the solicitor but could not have obtained the £5,000 on the grounds that it belonged to the bank. No reason was given and no authority cited for these observations which were unnecessary for the decision of the appeal before the House and which appear to be inconsistent with the authorities to which the Board have already referred.

In *In re Canadian Oil Works Corporation (Hay's Case)* (1875) LR 10 Ch App 593 the vendors of property to a company gave money forming part of the purchase price to a director of the company to enable him to subscribe for shares in the company. It was held that the money was the money of the company and that the shares registered in the name of the director were therefore unpaid. The judgment emphasised the rule that "no agent can in the course of his agency derive any benefit whatever without the sanction or knowledge of his principal," *per* James L.J., at p. 601.

In *In re Morvah Consols Tin Mining Co. (McKay's Case)* (1875) 2 Ch D 1, upon the application of the liquidator of an insolvent company a director was ordered to pay under section 165 of the Companies Act 1862 (25 & 26 Vict. c. 89) compensation for his misfeasance in accepting 600 paid-up shares in the company from the vendor of property to the company. Mellish L.J. said, at p. 5:

> "Either as a matter of bargain or as a present to the agent of the purchaser, it was in consideration of a benefit which the vendor had received from the company's agents. Now it is quite clear that, according to the principles of a Court of Equity, all the benefit which the agent of the purchaser receives under such circumstances from the vendor must be treated as received for the benefit of the purchaser."

A similar decision was reached in *In re Caerphilly Colliery Co. (Pearson's Case)* (1877) 5 Ch D 336 where a director received paid-up shares from the vendor of property to the company. Jessel M.R. referring to Sir Edwin Pearson the director in question said, at pp. 340-341:

> "That being the position of Sir Edwin Pearson, can he be allowed to say in a Court of Equity that he, having received a present of part of the purchase money, and being knowingly in the position of agent and trustee for the purchasers, can retain that present as against the actual purchasers? It appears to me that, upon the plainest principles of equity and good conscience, he cannot . . . . he cannot, in the fiduciary position he occupied, retain for himself any benefit or advantage that he obtained under such circumstances. He must be deemed to have obtained it under circumstances which made him liable, at the option of the cestui que trust, to account either for the value at the time of the present he was receiving, or to account for the thing itself and its proceeds if it had increased in value."

This is an emphatic pronouncement by the most distinguished equity judge of his generation that the recipient of a bribe holds the bribe and the property representing the bribe in trust for the injured person.

Different reasoning and a different result followed in *Metropolitan Bank v. Heiron* (1880) 5 Ex D 319. This was a decision of a distinguished Court of Appeal heard and determined on one day, 5 August 1880, perilously close to the long vacation without citation of any of the relevant authorities. An allegation of the receipt of a bribe by a director was considered in 1872 by the board of directors of the company and they decided to take no action. In 1879 the company sued to recover the bribe of £250 and it was held that the action was barred by the Statute of Limitations (3 & 4 Will. 4, c. 27). James L.J. said, at p. 323:

> "The ground of this suit is concealed fraud. If a man receives money by way of a bribe for misconduct against a company or cestui que trust, or any person or body towards whom he stands in a fiduciary position he is liable to have that money taken from him by his principal or cestui que trust. But it must be borne in mind that that liability is a debt only differing from ordinary debts in the fact that it is merely equitable, and in dealing with equitable debts of such a nature Courts of Equity have always followed by analogy the provisions of the Statute of Limitations, in cases in which there is the same reason for making the length of time a bar as in the case of ordinary legal demands."

This judgment denies that any proprietary interest exists in the bribe. Brett L.J. said, at p. 324:

> "It seems to me that the only action which could be maintained by the company or by the liquidator of the company against this defendant would be an action in equity founded upon the alleged fraud of the defendant. Neither at law nor in equity could this sum of £250 be treated as the money of the company, until the court, in an action by the company, had decreed it to belong to them on the ground that it had been received fraudulently as against them by the defendant."

This is a puzzling passage which appears to mean that a proprietary interest in the bribe arises as soon as a court has found that a bribe has been accepted. Cotton L.J. said, at p. 325:

> "Here the money sought to be recovered was in no sense the money of the company, unless it was made so by a decree founded on the act by which the trustee got the money into his hands. It is a suit founded on breach of duty or fraud by a person who was in the position of trustee, his position making the receipt of the money a breach of duty or fraud. It is very different from the case of a cestui que trust seeking to recover money which was his own before any act wrongfully done by the trustee."

This observation does draw a distinction between moneys which are held on trust and are taken out by the trustee and moneys which are not held on trust but which the trustee receives in circumstances which oblige him to pay the money into the trust. The distinction appears to be inconsistent with *Keech v. Sandford* (1726) Sel Cas Ch 61, and with those authorities which make the recipient of the bribe liable for any increase in value. The decision in *Metropolitan Bank v. Heiron* (1880) 5 Ex D 319, is understandable given the finding that the fraud was made known to the company more than six years before the action was instituted. But the same result could have been achieved by denying an equitable remedy on the grounds of delay or ratification.

It has always been assumed and asserted that the law on the subject of bribes was definitively settled by the decision of the Court of Appeal in *Lister & Co. v. Stubbs* (1890) 45 Ch D 1.

In that case the plaintiffs, Lister & Co., employed the defendant, Stubbs, as their servant to purchase goods for the firm. Stubbs, on behalf of the firm, bought goods from Varley & Co. and received from Varley & Co. bribes amounting to £5,541. The bribes were invested by Stubbs in freehold properties and investments. His masters, the firm Lister & Co., sought and failed to obtain an interlocutory injunction restraining Stubbs from disposing of these assets pending the trial of the action in which they sought, inter alia, £5,541 and damages. In the Court of Appeal the first judgment was given by Cotton L.J. who had been party to the decision in *Metropolitan Bank v. Heiron* (1880) 5 Ex D 319. He was powerfully supported by the judgment of Lindley L.J. and by the equally powerful concurrence of Bowen L.J. Cotton L.J. said, at p. 12, that the bribe could not be said to be the money of the plaintiffs. He seemed to be reluctant to grant an interlocutory judgment which would provide security for a debt before that debt had been established. Lindley L.J. said, at p. 15, that the relationship between the plaintiffs, Lister & Co., as masters and the defendant, Stubbs, as servant who had betrayed his trust and received a bribe:

> "is that of debtor and creditor; it is not that of trustee and cestui que trust. We are asked to hold that it is – which would involve consequences which, I confess, startle me. One consequence, of course, would be that, if Stubbs were to become bankrupt, this property acquired by him with the money paid to him by Messrs.

Varley would be withdrawn from the mass of his creditors and be handed over bodily to Lister & Co. Can that be right? Another consequence would be that, if the appellants are right, Lister & Co. could compel Stubbs to account to them, not only for the money with interest, but for all the profits which he might have made by embarking in trade with it. Can that be right?"

For the reasons which have already been advanced their Lordships would respectfully answer both these questions in the affirmative. If a trustee mistakenly invests moneys which he ought to pay over to his cestui que trust and then becomes bankrupt, the moneys together with any profit which has accrued from the investment are withdrawn from the unsecured creditors as soon as the mistake is discovered. A fortiori if a trustee commits a crime by accepting a bribe which he ought to pay over to his cestui que trust, the bribe and any profit made therefrom should be withdrawn from the unsecured creditors as soon as the crime is discovered.

The decision in *Lister & Co. v. Stubbs* is not consistent with the principles that a fiduciary must not be allowed to benefit from his own breach of duty, that the fiduciary should account for the bribe as soon as he receives it and that equity regards as done that which ought to be done. From these principles it would appear to follow that the bribe and the property from time to time representing the bribe are held on a constructive trust for the person injured. A fiduciary remains personally liable for the amount of the bribe if, in the event, the value of the property then recovered by the injured person proved to be less than that amount.

The decisions of the Court of Appeal in *Metropolitan Bank v. Heiron* (1880) 5 Ex D 319, and *Lister & Co. v. Stubbs* (1890) 45 ChD 1, are inconsistent with earlier authorities which were not cited. Although over 100 years has passed since *Lister & Co. v. Stubbs,* no one can be allowed to say that he has ordered his affairs in reliance on the two decisions of the Court of Appeal now in question. Thus no harm can result if those decisions are not followed.

The decision in *Lister & Co. v. Stubbs* was followed in *Powell & Thomas v. Evans Jones & Co.* [1905] 1 KB 11 and *Attorney-General v. Goddard* (1929) 98 LJKB 743. In *Regal (Hastings) Ltd. v. Gulliver (Note)* [1967] 2 AC 134 shares intended to be acquired by directors at par to avoid them giving a guarantee of the obligations under a lease were sold at a profit and the directors were held to be liable to the company for the proceeds of sale, applying *Keech v. Sandford* (1726) Sel Cas Ch 61.

In *Reading v. Attorney-General* [1951] AC 507, the Crown confiscated thousands of pounds paid to an army sergeant who had abused his official position to enable drugs to be imported. The Crown was allowed to keep the confiscated moneys to avoid circuity of action.

Finally in *Islamic Republic of Iran Shipping Lines v. Denby* [1987] 1 Lloyd's Rep 367 Leggatt J. followed *Lister & Co. v. Stubbs* (1890) 45 Ch D 1, as indeed he was bound to do.

The authorities which followed *Lister & Co. v. Stubbs* do not cast any new light on that decision. Their Lordships are more impressed with the decision of Lai Kew Chai J. in *Sumitomo Bank Ltd. v. Kartika Ratna Thahir* [1993] 1 SLR 735. In that case General Thahir who was at one time general assistant to the president director of the Indonesian state enterprise named Pertamina opened 17 bank accounts in Singapore and deposited DM.54m. in those accounts. The money was said to be bribes paid by two German contractors tendering for the construction of steel works in West Java. General Thahir having died, the moneys were claimed by his widow, by the estate of the deceased general and by Pertamina. After considering in detail all the relevant authorities Lai Kew Chai J. determined robustly, at p. 810, that *Lister & Co. v. Stubbs* (1890) 45 Ch D 1, was wrong and that its "undesirable and unjust consequences should not be imported and perpetuated as part of" the law of Singapore. Their Lordships are also much indebted for the fruits of research and the careful discussion of the present topic in the address entitled "Bribes and Secret Commissions" [1993] RLR 7 delivered by Sir Peter Millett to a meeting of the Society of Public Teachers of Law at Oxford in 1993. The following passage, at p. 20, elegantly sums up the views of Sir Peter Millett:

> "[The fiduciary] must not place himself in a position where his interest may conflict with his duty. If he has done so, equity insists on treating him as having acted in accordance with his duty; he will not be allowed to say that he preferred his own interest to that of his principal. He must not obtain a profit for himself out of his fiduciary position. If he has done so, equity insists on treating him as having obtained it for his principal; he will not be allowed to say that he obtained it for himself. He must not accept a bribe. If he has done so, equity insists on treating it as a legitimate payment intended for the benefit of the principal; he will not be allowed to say that it was a bribe."

The conclusions reached by Lai Kew Chai J. in *Sumitomo Bank Ltd. v. Kartika Ratna Thahir* [1993] 1 SLR 735 and the views expressed by Sir Peter Millett were influenced by the decision of the House of Lords in *Phipps v. Boardman* [1967] 2 AC 46 which demonstrates the strictness with which equity regards the conduct of a fiduciary and the extent to which equity is willing to impose a constructive trust on property obtained by a fiduciary by virtue of his office. In that case a solicitor acting for trustees rescued the interests of the trust in a private company by negotiating for a takeover bid in which he himself took an interest. He acted in good faith throughout and the information which the solicitor obtained about the company in the takeover bid could never have been used by the trustees. Nevertheless the solicitor was held to be a constructive trustee by a majority in the House of Lords because the solicitor obtained the information which satisfied him that the purchase of the shares in the takeover company would be a good investment and the opportunity of acquiring the shares as a result of acting for certain purposes on behalf of the trustees; see *per* Lord Cohen, at p. 103. If a fiduciary acting honestly and in good faith and making a profit which his principal could not make for himself becomes a constructive trustee of that profit then it seems to their Lordships that a fiduciary acting dishonestly and criminally who accepts a bribe and thereby causes loss and damage to his principal must also be a constructive trustee and must not be allowed by any means to make any profit from his wrongdoing.

The New Zealand Court of Appeal in the present case declined to enter into the merits of *Lister & Co. v. Stubbs* (1890) 45 Ch D 1, founding itself on a passage in the judgment of this Board delivered by Lord Scarman in *Tai Hing Cotton Mill Ltd. v. Liu Chong Hing Bank Ltd.* [1986] AC 80, 108, where his Lordship said the duty of the New Zealand Court of Appeal was not to depart from a settled principle of English law. While their Lordships regard the application of stare decisis in the New Zealand Court of Appeal as a matter for that court, they desire to make the following remarks, in case Lord Scarman's comments in *Tai Hing Cotton Mill Ltd. v. Liu Chong Hing Bank Ltd.* have in any way been misunderstood.

In the present case the Court of Appeal did not say and could not have meant that it was bound by a decision of the English Court of Appeal, since for many years the New Zealand courts have not regarded themselves as bound by decisions of the House of Lords, although of course continuing to pay great respect to them. The reasoning of the Court of Appeal, as their Lordships understand it, was rather that in the absence of differentiating local circumstances the court should follow a decision representing contemporary English law, leaving its correctness for consideration by this Board. Without in any way criticising that approach in the circumstances of this case, where the decision in question was of such long standing, their Lordships wish to add that nevertheless the New Zealand Court of Appeal must be free to review an English Court of Appeal authority on its merits and to depart from it if the authority is considered to be wrong. *Hart v. O'Connor* [1985] AC 1000 to which Lord Scarman referred in the passage mentioned by the Court of Appeal concerned the very different situation of the Court of Appeal wishing to apply English law but, in the judgment of this Board, misapprehending the state of the contemporary law. In any case where the New Zealand Court of Appeal has to decide whether to follow an English authority, its own views on the issue, untrammelled by authority, will always be of great assistance to the Board.

The Attorney-General for Hong Kong has registered caveats against the title of the three New Zealand properties. He seeks to renew the caveats to prevent any dealing with the property pending the hearing of proceedings which, their Lordships are informed, have been initiated for the purpose of claiming the properties on a constructive trust. The respondents oppose the renewal of the caveats on the grounds that the Crown had no equitable interest in the three New Zealand properties. For the reasons indicated their Lordships consider that the three properties so far as they represent bribes accepted by the first respondent are held in trust for the Crown.

Before parting with this appeal their Lordships wish to express their appreciation for the eloquent and well structured submissions made by Mr.

David Oliver on behalf of the Attorney-General for Hong Kong and by Mr. Antony White on behalf of the respondents.

Their Lordships will therefore humbly advise Her Majesty that this appeal should be allowed. Since an unfulfilled order has been made against the first respondent in the courts of Hong Kong to pay H.K.$12.4m., his only purpose in opposing the relief sought by the Crown in New Zealand must reflect that the properties, in the absence of a caveat, can be sold and the proceeds whisked away to some Shangri La which hides bribes and other corrupt moneys in numbered bank accounts. In these circumstances the first and second respondents must pay the costs of the Attorney-General before the Board and in the lower courts; as regards the third respondent the costs orders in his favour in the High Court and in the Court of Appeal should be set aside and the third respondent must repay any sums that have been paid to him. There will be no order against the third respondent for costs incurred by the Attorney-General before the Board."

The Position of Agents

Where an agent makes a profit out of his fiduciary position without the knowledge of his principal he will be liable to account for this, although where an agent makes full disclosure to the principal and the latter assents, he may retain the profit.[9] However, liability does not depend on any finding of fraud or of advantage having been taken and it is irrelevant that the principal has not suffered any loss.[10]

Sherrard v. Barron
[1923] 1 IR 21

The defendant house agents acted as agents for the plaintiff to collect rents and effect the necessary repairs to her property. When the defendants opened their own repairs yard they carried out the repairs themselves and charged the usual trade prices which included an element of profit. The plaintiff's claim to have the accounts between the parties reopened was dismissed on the grounds that the plaintiff knew and approved of the repair work being carried out by the defendants and that the defendants had made sufficient disclosure to the plaintiff that they were deriving a profit from the work.

MOORE LJ stated at pp.23–25: "This action was brought by the plaintiff, an owner of house property in Belfast, against the defendants, who are house

---

[9] *Sherrard v. Barron* [1923] 1 IR 21.
[10] *Boardman v. Phipps* [1967] 2 AC 46.

agents, for an account of their dealings with her as her agents over the property from 1908 to 1919.

As originally framed, the action charged that the accounts were not true or proper accounts, because (*a*) they included charges for repairs which in fact were not paid; (*b*) charges for repairs in fact not executed; (*c*) charges in respect of which the defendants made secret profits in the execution of repairs without disclosing to the plaintiff the nature or extent of their interest.

The first two heads involve clearly a charge of fraud, but these were abandoned at the trial before Mr. Justice Wilson; and in the arguments before us charges of fraud of any sort have been specifically disclaimed by Mr. Whitaker, appellant's counsel.

Mr. Justice Wilson had evidence on which he could find that the charges made were reasonable in the sense that they were at the rate which would have been charged by an ordinary contractor, and, as I understand the appellant's case, this finding is not contested, but it is alleged that it is irrelevant to the issue in the case. Certainly if it were shown that the charges were unreasonable or unfair, it would have a most important bearing on the case, because if this were once established, the Court would make it a ground for directing an account. In *Lambert v. Still* [1894] 1 Ch 73 at p. 80, A. L. Smith L.J. says: "An account settled and a release executed cannot be set aside for the asking. What is necessary in order to set aside a settled account or a release or both together when the release proceeds upon the footing of an account? It is essential to show that there has been some injustice done, some fraud, pressure, overcharge. Prove that and the release cannot stand." I use this because fraud and pressure have been abandoned by the plaintiff, and overcharge is negatived by the finding that the sums charged were the ordinary trade prices.

There is no dispute about the law, which is that an agent cannot without the knowledge of his principal make any profit for himself out of services rendered to his principal. Should he do so, he must account. It is equally settled law that it is the duty of the agent to make the fullest disclosure to his principal of all transactions in which the agent is making, directly or indirectly, a profit out of his principal. If this is done and if the principal, expressly or by course of conduct, impliedly assents, the agent can retain his profit. The plaintiff's case, if I understand it correctly, is now based on the breach of duty in this respect alleged against the defendants. The question, therefore, in the present action is one of fact: did or did not the plaintiff know that the defendants were charging profits like any ordinary contractor on the repairs to her property which she from time to time employed them to execute for her? If she did know, in the other circumstances of this case she cannot now reopen the accounts settled between them; if she did not know, the defendants cannot rely upon them.

The first account furnished by the defendants was to the trustees of the late Captain Downes (representing the plaintiff) in respect of the period from June 22nd, 1908, to 27th July, 1908, and, like all the subsequent accounts, bore upon the head of it the printed statement – "We are agents for several insurance companies, and get the usual commission. General Repairs. – Unless instructed to the contrary, we do all necessary repairs and charge the usual trade prices." I do not think that the defendants could have been more explicit as to their position in the form of accounts. The statement means we are your agents, of course, but we give you notice that if we do your business in insurance or in repairs we are to benefit in the usual way notwithstanding our relationship. As a matter of fact, the repairs from 1908 to 1911 were executed by outside contractors, and items of payment to them appear in the accounts which were regularly furnished to the plaintiff. In 1911 the defendants opened their own repairs yard, and from that time on executed the repairs themselves, and paid over moneys to themselves, and furnished the vouchers for such payment to the plaintiff, being invoices or receipts on printed bill-heads to themselves, with the added words, "Repair Department." But the matter did not stop there. The defendants wrote on September 9th, 1911, to inform the plaintiff that they were repairing some of the most urgent cases, and asking her to write to them on the question; and in reply, on 11th September, 1911, the plaintiff's husband wrote requesting them to "do what repairs you consider cannot stand over," until an intended visit of himself to the property. Plaintiff in her evidence says that in March, 1911, defendants introduced their repairs department, and did the repairs themselves. She was evidently dissatisfied, because she said, "I sent over my husband, and he saw the defendants; his visit did no good. By 1911 I came over myself. I wrote several letters to the defendants during these years complaining of the repairs."

The husband also describes his coming over in 1911 and inspecting the property with Barron. He found Barron's complaint about the state of the property exaggerated, and authorized Barron to do the repairs. The plaintiff herself said in her cross-examination that she had no objection to the defendants doing the repairs themselves. She also says she did not expect them to give her better value than strangers would.

I have gone through all the documents put in evidence, and there is no doubt of the following facts: – 1st, That the defendants were authorized by plaintiff to do the repairs; 2nd, that they did do them; 3rd, that there is no overcharge, and that the prices were ordinary trade prices; and 4th, that these matters were regularly brought to the plaintiff's knowledge at each settlement of account and never objected to.

In *Isaacs & Son v. Campion & Co.* (1901) 17 TLR 321 the following were the facts: Plaintiffs, fruit-brokers, who had acted as agents for the sale of defendants' fruit, rendered them accounts from time to time which showed deductions inter alia for wharfage, porterage, and warehouse rent. Defendants objected to these deductions on the ground that they were not disbursements but profit charges. It appeared that in accordance with the practice in the fruit trade, plaintiffs employed their own men at the wharf to handle the goods, and warehoused the goods in their own warehouse; that the charges made were the usual and customary charges made by fruit-brokers, and that defendants had been in the trade for many years, and were fully aware of the nature of the charges. The plaintiffs were held to be entitled to make the deductions on the ground of defendants' knowledge.

In my opinion there was no secret profit; the plaintiff and her husband were told everything that Barron was bound to tell them.

There is another element in the case which to some extent affects my judgment, that is, its triviality. Up to 1917 the evidence for the plaintiff, especially that of her husband, would go to show that they were fairly satisfied. I think this is a fair summary of the position. This means that the period attacked is from 1917 to 1919, when the agency terminated. The charge is made that the defendants charged in their ledgers against plaintiff sums generally in excess of the actual cost in their yard-book. But even assuming with the plaintiff that the defendants were not entitled to do this, there is evidence that the total amount of the overcharge during the seven years from 1912 – five years of which are not now attacked – is only £12 7s. 4d. I do not know how much of this is referable to the last two years, but I would be slow to put the parties to the cost of reopening the accounts where, on the uncontradicted evidence, there can only be such a small sum in dispute. To my mind it makes the action look vexatious.

On the whole case I have arrived at the conclusion that plaintiff is not entitled to have the accounts reopened, that the judgment of Mr. Justice Wilson was right, and that the appeal should be dismissed with costs."

Boardman v. Phipps
[1967] 2 AC 46

Assets were held on trust for the benefit of a testator's children, the trustees being his widow, who was senile, his daughter and an accountant. The trust had a sizable minority shareholding in a textile company and with the consent of the two active trustees, the appellants, who were the trustees' solicitor and one of the beneficiaries, set about acquiring a majority shareholding in the company in order to make it more profitable. By purporting to act on behalf of the trust they obtained detailed information about the company and succeeded in gaining control of it, making a considerable profit as a result. The majority of the House of Lords (Lord Cohen, Lord Hodson and Lord Guest) held that the trustees' solicitor and the beneficiary were liable to account to the trust for the profits which they had made, although it was held that they were entitled to payment for the work which they had carried out.

LORD HODSON stated at pp.105–112: "The proposition of law involved in this case is that no person standing in a fiduciary position, when a demand is made upon him by the person to whom he stands in the fiduciary relationship to account for profits acquired by him by reason of his fiduciary position and by reason of the opportunity and the knowledge, or either, resulting from it, is entitled to defeat the claim upon any ground save that he made profits with the knowledge and assent of the other person.

I take the above proposition from the opening words of the speech of Lord Wright in *Regal (Hastings) Ltd. v. Gulliver* where he states the proposition in the form of the question which he answered as had all the members of your Lordships' House in such a way as to affirm the proposition.

It is obviously of importance to maintain the proposition in all cases and to do nothing to whittle away its scope or the absolute responsibility which it imposes.

The persons concerned in this case, namely, Mr. Thomas Boardman and Mr. Tom Phipps, are not trustees in the strict sense but are said to be constructive trustees by reason of the fiduciary position in which they stood. As Lord Selborne pointed out in *Barnes v. Addy* (1874) 9 Ch App 244, 251, 252:

> "That responsibility" (viz., that of trustees) "may no doubt be extended in equity to others who are not properly trustees, if they are found either making themselves trustees de son tort, or actually participating in any fraudulent conduct of the trustee to the injury of the cestui que trust. But, on the other hand, strangers are not to be made constructive trustees merely because they act as the agents of trustees in transactions within their legal powers, transactions, perhaps, of which a Court of Equity may disapprove, unless those agents receive and become chargeable with some part of the trust property, or unless they assist with knowledge to a dishonest and fraudulent design on the part of the trustees."

There is no question of fraud in this case; it has never been suggested that the appellants acted in any other than an open and honourable manner.

If, however, they are in a fiduciary position they are as trustees bound by duty, succinctly stated by Lord Cranworth L.C. in *Aberdeen Railway Co. v. Blaikie Brothers* (1854) 1 Macq 461, 471, HL:

> "And it is a rule of universal application, that no one, having such duties to discharge, shall be allowed to enter into engagements in which he has, or can have, a personal interest conflicting, or which possibly may conflict, with the interests of those whom he is bound to protect."

So far as Mr. Tom Phipps is concerned, he was not placed in a fiduciary position by reason of his being a beneficiary under his father's will. He was acting as agent for the trustees with Mr. Boardman before any question of acting with him for his own benefit arose. He has not, however, sought to be treated in a different way from Mr. Boardman upon whom the conduct of the whole matter depended and with whom he has acted throughout as a co-adventurer; he does not claim that he should succeed in this appeal if Mr. Boardman fails.

Mr. Boardman's fiduciary position arose from the fact that he was at all material times solicitor to the trustees of the will of Mr. Phipps senior. This is admitted, although counsel for the appellants has argued, and argued correctly, that there is no such post as solicitor to trustees. The trustees either employ a solicitor or they do not in a particular case and there is no suggestion that they were under any contractual or other duty to employ Mr. Boardman or his firm. Nevertheless as a historical fact they did employ him and look to him for advice at all material times and this is admitted. It was as solicitor to the trustees that he obtained the information which is so clearly summarised in the judgment of Wilberforce J. [1964] 1 WLR 993, 1013 and repeated in the speech of my noble and learned friend Lord Upjohn. This information enabled him to acquire knowledge of a most extensive and valuable character, as the learned judge pointed out, which was the foundation upon which a decision could and was taken to buy the shares in Lester & Harris Ltd.

This information was obtained on behalf of the trustees, most of it at a time during the history of the negotiations when the proposition was to divide the assets of the company between two groups of shareholders. This object could not have been effected without a reconstruction of the company and Mr. Boardman used the strong minority shareholding which the trustees held, that is to say, 8,000 shares in the company, wielding this holding as a weapon to enable him to obtain the information of which he subsequently made use.

As to this it is said on behalf of the appellants that information as such is not necessarily property and it is only trust property which is relevant. I agree, but it is nothing to the point to say that in these times corporate trustees, e.g., the Public Trustee and others, necessarily acquire a mass of information in their capacity of trustees for a particular trust and cannot be held liable to account if knowledge so acquired enables them to operate to their own advantage, or to that of other trusts. Each case must depend on its own facts and I dissent from the view that information is of its nature something which is not properly to be described as property. We are aware that what is called "knowhow" in the commercial sense is property which may be very valuable as an asset. I agree with the learned judge and with the Court of Appeal that the confidential information acquired in this case which was capable of being and was turned to account can be properly regarded as the property of the trust. It was obtained by Mr. Boardman by reason of the opportunity which he was given as solicitor acting for the trustees in the negotiations with the chairman of the company, as the correspondence demonstrates. The end result was that out of the special position in which they were standing in the course of the negotiations the appellants got the opportunity to make a profit and the knowledge that it was there to be made.

The appellants argue that this is not enough, and in support of the contention rely on the authority of *Aas v. Benham* [1891] 2 Ch 244. This case was concerned with a partnership of ship-brokers, and the defendant carried on the business of ship builder, using knowledge acquired in the partnership business. A claim against him to account to the partnership for the profits of his business as ship builder failed. Lindley L.J. said at p. 256 that it is not the source of the information but the use to which it is put which is important—

"To hold that a partner" (or trustee) "can never derive any personal benefit from information which he obtains as a partner would be manifestly absurd."

It was held that the defendant was not liable to account because the profit was made outside the scope of the partnership and that in no sense was the defendant acting as the agent of the partners. Similarly the appellants contend that the purchase of the shares in question was outside the scope of the fiduciary relationship existing between them and the trustees.

The case of partnership is special in the sense that a partner is the principal as well as the agent of the other partners and works in a defined area of business so that it can normally be determined whether the particular transaction is within or without the scope of the partnership.

It is otherwise in the case of a general trusteeship or fiduciary position such as was occupied by Mr. Boardman, the limits of which are not readily defined, and I cannot find that the decision in the case of *Aas v. Benham* [1891] 2 Ch 244 assists the appellants, although the purchase of the shares was an independent purchase financed by themselves. *Aas v. Benham* was a case depending on the alleged relationship of principal and agent as it exists between one partner and another. There was no such relationship here but the position of an agent is relevant and the expression "self-appointed agent" used by the learned judge is a convenient way to describe someone who, assuming to act as agent for another, receives property belonging to that other so that the property is held by the self-constituted agent as trustee for such other. Such a case was *Lyell v. Kennedy* (1889) 14 App Cas 437, HL. Thus the learned judge found that the appellants were in the same position as if they had been agents for the trustees in the technical sense for the purpose of using the trust shareholding to extract knowledge of the affairs of the company and ultimately to improve the company's profit-earning capacity.

Keech v. Sandford (1726) Sel Cas Ch 61 was a case in which it was impossible for the cestui que trust to obtain the renewal of a lease, nevertheless the trustee was held accountable for renewal obtained by him. Similarly in *Regal (Hastings) Ltd. v. Gulliver* from which some of your Lordships have cited passages, the directors of Regal were held accountable to the company for the profit they made in acquiring shares when the opportunity fell to them as directors of the company, notwithstanding the fact that it was impossible for Regal to take the shares owing to lack of funds.

Regal (Hastings) Ltd. v. Gulliver differs from this case mainly in that the directors took up shares and made a profit thereby, it having been originally intended that the company should buy these shares. Here there was no such intention on the part of the trustees. There is no indication that they either had the money or would have been ready to apply to the court for sanction enabling them to do so. On the contrary, Mr. Fox, the active trustee and an accountant who concerned himself with the details of the trust proper, was not prepared to agree to the trustees buying the shares and encouraged the appellants to make the purchase. This does not affect the position. As *Keech v. Sandford* (1726)

Sel Cas Ch 61 shows, the inability of the trust to purchase makes no difference to the liability of the appellants, if liability otherwise exists. The distinction on the facts as to intention to purchase shares between this case and *Regal (Hastings) Ltd.* v. *Gulliver* is not relevant. The company (Regal) had not the money to apply for the shares upon which the profit was made. The directors took the opportunity which they had presented to them to buy the shares with their own money and were held accountable. Mr. Fox's refusal as one of the trustees to take any part in the matter on behalf of the trust, so far as he was concerned, can make no difference. Nothing short of fully informed consent which the learned judge found not to have been obtained could enable the appellants in the position which they occupied having taken the opportunity provided by that position to make a profit for themselves.

Likewise it is no answer to the respondent's claim that there was no contract of agency and that the appellants were at all times acting for themselves without concealment and indeed with the encouragement of one of the trustees, namely, Mr. Fox.

If they received confidential information from Lester & Harris in their capacity as representing the trustees it matters not whether or no there was a true agency. I refer again to the passage from Lord Wright's judgment in *Regal (Hastings) Ltd. v. Gulliver* when he speaks of "an agent, a director, a trustee or other person in an analogous fiduciary position" and, as an illustration, says that the most usual and typical case of this nature is that of principal and agent.

The relevant information is not any information but special information which I think must include that confidential information given to the appellants which is so fully detailed in the judgment of Wilberforce J. There is a passage in *Aas v. Benham* [1891] 2 Ch 244, 258 in the judgment of Bower L.J. which I think is of assistance, although the learned Lord Justice was dealing with partnership, not trusteeship: he was explaining some observations of Cotton L.J. in *Dean v. MacDowell* (1878) 8 Ch D 345, 354. These were:

> "Again, if he" (that is, a partner) "makes any profit by the use of any property of the partnership, including, I may say, information which the partnership is entitled to, there the profit is made out of the partnership property."

Bowen L.J. commented (at p. 258):

> "He is speaking of information which a partnership is entitled to in such a sense that it is information which is the property, or is to be included in the property of the partnership – that is to say, information the use of which is valuable to them as a partnership, and to the use of which they have a vested interest. But you cannot bring the information obtained in this case within that definition."

Aas v. Benham is an important case as showing that a partner may make a profit from information obtained in the course of the partnership business where he does so in another firm which is outside the scope of the partnership business. In that case the partnership business was ship-broking and the profit made was in a business which had no connection with that of the partnership. This shows the limitation which must be kept in mind in considering the sense in which each partner is the agent of the partnership, but does not assist the appellants. Mr. Boardman continued to be in a fiduciary position up to and including the time when the shares were purchased (March, 1959), and the scope of the trust concerning which his fiduciary relationship existed was not limited in the same way as a partnership carrying on a particular business.

It cannot, in my opinion, be said that the purchase of shares in Lester & Harris was outside the scope of the fiduciary relationship in which Mr. Boardman stood to the trust.

The confidential information which the appellants obtained at a time when Mr. Boardman was admittedly holding himself out as solicitor for the trustees was obtained by him as representing the trustees, the holders of 8,000 shares of Lester & Harris. As Russell L.J. put it [1965] Ch 992, 1031:

> "The substantial trust shareholding was an asset of which one aspect was its potential use as a means of acquiring knowledge of the company's affairs, or of negotiating allocations of the company's assets, or of inducing other shareholders to part with their shares."

Whether this aspect is properly to be regarded as part of the trust assets is, in my judgment, immaterial. The appellants obtained knowledge by reason of their fiduciary position and they cannot escape liability by saying that they were acting for themselves and not as agents of the trustees. Whether or not the trust or the beneficiaries in their stead, could have taken advantage of the information is immaterial, as the authorities clearly show. No doubt it was but a remote possibility that Mr. Boardman would ever be asked by the trustees to advise on the desirability of an application to the court in order that the trustees might avail themselves of the information obtained. Nevertheless, even if the possibility of conflict is present between personal interest and the fiduciary position the rule of equity must be applied. This appears from the observations of Lord Cranworth L.C. in *Aberdeen Railway Co. v. Blaikie* (1854) 1 Macq 461, 471.

In the later case of *Bray v. Ford* [1896] AC 44, 51, 52; 12 TLR 119, HL Lord Herschell stated the rule in a way which has peculiar application to the facts of this case, when he said:

> " It is an inflexible rule of a Court of Equity that a person in a fiduciary position, such as the respondent's is not, unless otherwise expressly provided, entitled to make a profit; he is not allowed to put himself in a position where his interest and duty conflict. It does not appear to me that this rule is, as has been said, founded upon principles of morality. I regard it rather as based on the consideration that human nature being what it is, there is danger, in such circumstances, of the person holding a fiduciary position being swayed by interest rather than by duty, and thus prejudicing those whom he was bound to protect. It has, therefore, been deemed expedient to lay down this positive rule. But I am

satisfied that it might be departed from in many cases, without any breach of morality, without any wrong being inflicted, and without any consciousness of wrong-doing. Indeed, it is obvious that it might sometimes be to the advantage of the beneficiaries that their trustee should act for them professionally rather than a stranger, even though the trustee were paid for his services."

It is said that the appellants never had the necessary facts pleaded against them to raise the question of conflict of interest so that they did not have the opportunity of dealing with allegations which would be relevant thereto: I cannot see what further facts were relevant to be raised other than those to which reference has been made in the judgments in the court below and in the speeches of your Lordships. The question whether or not there was a fiduciary relationship at the relevant time must be a question of law and the question of conflict of interest directly emerges from the facts pleaded, otherwise no question of entitlement to a profit would fall to be considered. No positive wrongdoing is proved or alleged against the appellants but they cannot escape from the consequences of their acts involving liability to the respondent unless they can prove consent. This they endeavoured without success to do for, although they gave the respondent some information, that which they gave was held by the learned judge to be insufficient and there is no appeal against his decision on this point.

I agree with the decision of the learned judge and with that of the Court of Appeal which, in my opinion, involves a finding that there was a potential conflict between Boardman's position as solicitor to the trustees and his own interest in applying for the shares. He was in a fiduciary position vis-à-vis the trustees and through them vis-à-vis the beneficiaries. For these reasons in my opinion the appeal should be dismissed; but I should add that I am in agreement with the learned judge that payment should be allowed on a liberal scale in respect of the work and skill employed in obtaining the shares and the profits therefrom."

The Position of Company Directors

Company directors are treated as being fiduciaries in so far as they owe a duty to their company and they will not be permitted to place themselves in a position where their duty to the company and their personal interests will conflict or to derive a profit from their fiduciary relationship. This principle has been applied in a rigourous manner and even where a director has acted in an honest and *bona fide* manner in what he believes are the best interests of the company, he will nevertheless be liable to account for any personal profit made as a result of his fiduciary relationship with the company.[11]

---

[11] *Regal (Hastings) Ltd v. Gulliver* [1967] 2 AC 134.

Regal (Hastings) Ltd v. Gulliver
[1967] 2 AC 134

A company which owned a cinema formed a subsidiary to take up the lease of two additional cinemas so that they might be all sold as a going concern. The landlord insisted on the subsidiary company having a paid up share capital of 5,000 ordinary £1 shares and as the parent company had insufficient resources to subscribe for more than 2,000, the directors of the company agreed to take up the remainder. When the business was transferred to new controllers the directors made a personal profit on the transaction. The House of Lords upheld the claim of the purchaser brought in the company's name to account for this profit on the grounds that the directors had derived such profit by virtue of their office.

LORD RUSSELL stated at pp.143–153: "I now proceed to consider whether the appellants are entitled to succeed against any and which of the respondents. The case has, I think, been complicated and obscured by the presentation of it before the trial judge. If a case of wilful misconduct or fraud on the part of the respondents had been made out, liability to make good to Regal any damage which it had thereby suffered could, no doubt, have been established; and efforts were apparently made at the trial, by cross-examination and otherwise, to found such a case. It is, however, due to the respondents to make it clear at the outset that this attempt failed. The case was not so presented to us here. We have to consider the question of the respondents' liability on the footing that, in taking up these shares in Amalgamated, they acted with bona fides, intending to act in the interest of Regal.

Nevertheless, they may be liable to account for the profits which they have made, if, while standing in a fiduciary relationship to Regal, they have by reason and in course of that fiduciary relationship made a profit. This aspect of the case was undoubtedly raised before the trial judge, but, in so far as he deals with it in his judgment, he deals with it on a wrong basis. Having stated at the outset quite truly that what he calls this stroke of fortune only came the way of the respondents because they were the directors and solicitor of the Regal, he continues thus:

> "But in order to succeed the plaintiff company must show that the defendants both ought to have caused and could have caused the plaintiff company to subscribe for these shares, and that the neglect to do so caused a loss to the plaintiff company. Short of this, if the plaintiffs can establish that, though no loss was made by the company, yet a profit was corruptly made by the directors and the solicitor, then the company can claim to have that profit handed over to the company, framing the action in such a case for money had and received by the defendants for the plaintiffs' use."

Other passages in his judgment indicate that, in addition to this "corrupt" action by the directors, or, perhaps, alternatively, the plaintiffs in order to succeed must prove that the defendants acted mala fide and not bona fide in the interests of the company, or that there was a plot or arrangement between them to divert from the company to themselves a valuable investment. However relevant such considerations may be, in regard to a claim for damages resulting from misconduct, they are irrelevant to a claim against a person occupying a fiduciary relationship towards the plaintiff for an account of the profits made by that person by reason and in course of that relationship.

In the Court of Appeal, upon this claim to profits, the view was taken that in order to succeed the plaintiff had to establish that there was a duty on the Regal directors to obtain the shares for Regal. Two extracts from the judgment of Lord Greene M.R., show this. After mentioning the claim for damages, he says:

> "The case is put on an alternative ground. It is said that, in the circumstances of the case, the directors must be taken to have been acting in the matter of their office when they took those shares; and that accordingly they are accountable for the profits which they have made . . . There is one matter which is common to both these claims which, unless it is established, appears to me to be fatal. It must be shown that in the circumstances of the case it was the duty of the directors to obtain these shares for their company."

Later in his judgment he uses this language:

> "But it is said that the profit realised by the directors on the sale of the shares must be accounted for by them. That proposition involves that on October 2, when it was decided to acquire these shares, and at the moment when they were acquired by the directors, the directors were taking to themselves something which properly belonged to their company."

Other portions of the judgment appear to indicate that upon this claim to profits, it is a good defence to show bona fides or absence of fraud on the part of the directors in the action which they took, or that their action was beneficial to the company, and the judgment ends thus:

> " That being so, the only way in which these directors could secure that benefit for their company was by putting up the money themselves. Once that decision is held to be a bona fide one, and fraud drops out of the case, it seems to me that there is only one conclusion, namely, that the appeal must be dismissed with costs."

My Lords, with all respect I think there is a misapprehension here. The rule of equity which insists on those, who by use of a fiduciary position make a profit, being liable to account for that profit, in no way depends on fraud, or absence of bona fides; or upon such questions or considerations as whether the profit would or should otherwise have gone to the plaintiff, or whether the profiteer was under a duty to obtain the source of the profit for the plaintiff, or whether he took a risk or acted as he did for the benefit of the plaintiff, or whether the plaintiff has in fact been damaged or benefited by his action. The liability arises from the mere fact of a profit having, in the stated circumstances, been made. The profiteer, however honest and well-intentioned, cannot escape the risk of being called upon to account.

The leading case of *Keech v. Sandford* (1726) Sel Cas Ch 61 is an illustration of the strictness of this rule of equity in this regard, and of how far the rule is independent of these outside considerations. A lease of the profits of a market had been devised to a trustee for the benefit of an infant. A renewal on behalf of the infant was refused. It was absolutely unobtainable. The trustee, finding that it was impossible to get a renewal for the benefit of the infant, took a lease for his own benefit. Though his duty to obtain it for the infant was incapable of performance, nevertheless he was ordered to assign the lease to the infant, upon the bare ground that, if a trustee on the refusal to renew might have a lease for himself, few renewals would be made for the benefit of cestuis que trust. Lord King L.C. said:

> "This may seem hard, that the trustee is the only person of all mankind who might not have the lease: but it is very proper that the rule should be strictly pursued, and not in the least relaxed. . . ."

One other case in equity may be referred to in this connection, viz., *Ex parte James* (1803) 8 Ves 337 decided by Lord Eldon L.C. That was a case of a purchase of a bankrupt's estate by the solicitor to the commission, and Lord Eldon L.C. refers to the doctrine thus:

> "This doctrine as to purchases by trustees, assignees, and persons having a confidential character, stands much more upon general principles than upon the circumstances of any individual case. It rests upon this: that the purchase is not permitted in any case however honest the circumstances; the general interests of justice requiring it to be destroyed in every instance; as no court is equal to the examination and ascertainment of the truth in much the greater number of cases."

Let me now consider whether the essential matters, which the plaintiff must prove, have been established in the present case. As to the profit being in fact made there can be no doubt. The shares were acquired at par and were sold three weeks later at a profit of £2 16s. 1d. per share. Did such of the first five respondents as acquired these very profitable shares acquire them by reason and in course of their office of directors of Regal? In my opinion, when the facts are examined and appreciated, the answer can only be that they did. The actual allotment no doubt had to be made by themselves and Garton (or some of them) in their capacity as directors of Amalgamated; but this was merely an executive act, necessitated by the alteration of the scheme for the acquisition of the lease of the two cinemas for the sole benefit of Regal and its shareholders through Regal's shareholding in Amalgamated. That scheme could only be altered by or with the consent of the Regal board. Consider what in fact took place on October 2, 1935. The position immediately before that day is stated in Carton's letter of September 26, 1935. The directors were willing to guarantee the rent until the subscribed capital of Amalgamated reached £5,000. Regal was to control Amalgamated and own the whole of its share capital, with the consequence that the Regal shareholders would receive their proportion of the sale price of the two new cinemas. The respondents then meet on October 2, 1935. They have before them an offer to purchase the Regal cinema for £77,500 and the lease of the two cinemas for £15,000. The offer is accepted. The draft lease is approved and a resolution for its sealing is passed in anticipation of completion in five days. Some of those present, however, shy at giving guarantees, and accordingly the scheme is changed by the Regal directors in a vital respect. It is agreed that a guarantee shall be avoided by the six respondents bringing the subscribed capital up to £5,100. I will consider the evidence and the minute in a moment. The result of this change of scheme which only the Regal directors could bring about may not have been appreciated by them at the time; but its effect upon their company and its shareholders was striking. In the first place, Regal would no longer control Amalgamated, or own the whole of its share capital. The action of its directors had deprived it (acting through its shareholders in general meeting) of the power to acquire the shares. In the second place, the Regal shareholders would only receive a large reduced proportion of the sale price of the two cinemas. The Regal directors and Garton would receive the moneys of which the Regal shareholders were thus deprived. This vital alteration was brought about in the following circumstances – I refer to the evidence of the respondent Garton. He was asked what was suggested when the guarantees were refused, and this is his answer:

> "Mr. Gulliver said 'We must find it somehow. I am willing to find £500. Are you willing,' turning to the other four directors of Regal, 'to do the same?' They expressed themselves as willing. He said, 'That makes £2,500 and he turned to me and said, Garton, you have been interested in Mr. Bentley's companies; will you come in to take £500?' I agreed to do so."

Although this matter is recorded in the Amalgamated minutes this was in fact a decision come to by the directors of Regal, and the subsequent allotment by the directors of Amalgamated was a mere carrying into effect of this decision of the Regal board. The resolution recorded in the Amalgamated minute runs thus:

> "After discussion it was resolved that the directors be invited to subscribe for 500 shares each, and that such shares be allotted accordingly."

As I read that resolution, and my reading agrees with Garton's evidence, the invitation is to the directors of Regal, and is made for the purpose of effectuating the decision which the five directors of Regal had made, that each should take up 500 shares in Amalgamated. The directors of Amalgamated were not conveying an " invitation" to themselves. That would be ridiculous. They were merely giving effect to the Regal directors' decision to provide £2,500 cash capital themselves, a decision which had been followed by a successful appeal by Gulliver to Garton to provide the balance.

My Lords, I have no hesitation in coming to the conclusion, upon the facts of this case, that these shares, when acquired by the directors, were acquired by reason, and only by reason of the fact that they were directors of Regal, and in the course of their execution of that office.

It now remains to consider whether in acting as directors of Regal they stood in a fiduciary relationship to that company. Directors of a limited company are the creatures of statute and occupy a position peculiar to themselves. In some respects they resemble trustees, in others they do not. In some respects they resemble agents, in others they do not. In some respects they resemble managing partners, in others they do not. In *In re Forest of Dean Coal Mining Co.* (1878) 10 Ch D 450 a director was held not liable for omitting to recover promotion money which had been improperly paid on the formation of the company. He knew of the improper payment, but he was not appointed a director until a later date. It was held that, although a trustee of settled property which included a debt would be liable for neglecting to sue for it, a director of a company was not a trustee of debts due to the company and was not liable. I cite two passages from the judgment of Sir George Jessel M.R. (at 451, 452):

> "Directors have sometimes been called trustees, or commercial trustees, and sometimes they have been called managing partners, it does not matter what you call them so long as you understand what their true position is, which is that they are really commercial men managing a trading concern for the benefit of themselves and all other shareholders in it."

Later, after pointing out that traders have a discretion whether they shall sue for a debt, which discretion is not vested in trustees of a debt under a settlement, he said at 453:

> "Again directors are called trustees. They are no doubt trustees of assets which have come to their hands, or which are under their control, but they are not trustees of a debt due to the company. . . . A director is the managing partner of the concern, and although a debt is due to the concern I do not think it right to call him a trustee of that debt which remains unpaid, though his liability in respect of it may in certain cases and in some respects be analogous to the liability of a trustee."

The position of directors was considered by Kay J., in *In re Faure Electric Accumulator Co.* (1888) 40 Ch D 141. That was a case where directors had applied the company's money in payment of an improper commission, and a claim was made for the loss thereby occasioned to the company. In referring to the liability of directors, the judge pointed out that directors were not trustees in the sense of trustees of a settlement, that the nearest analogy to their position would be that of a managing agent of a mercantile house with large powers, but that there was no analogy which was absolutely perfect; and he added:

> "However, it is quite obvious that to apply to directors the strict rules of the Court of Chancery with respect to ordinary trustees might fetter their action to

an extent which would be exceedingly disadvantageous to the companies they represent."

In addition a passage from the judgment of Bowen L.J. in *Imperial Hydropathic Hotel Co., Blackpool v. Hampson* (1882) 23 Ch D 1, 12 may be usefully recalled. He said:

> "I should wish . . . to begin by remarking this, that when persons who are directors of a company are from time to time spoken of by judges as agents, trustees, or managing partners of the company, it is essential to recollect that such expressions are not used as exhaustive of the powers and responsibilities of those persons but only as indicating useful points of view from which they may for the moment and for the particular purpose be considered – points of view at which for the moment they seem to be either cutting the circle, or falling within the category of the suggested kind. It is not meant that they belong to the category, but that it is useful for the purpose of the moment to observe that they fall pro tanto within the principles which govern that particular class."

These three cases, however, were not concerned with the question of directors making a profit; but that the equitable principle in this regard applies to directors is beyond doubt. In *Parker v. McKenna* (1874) 10 Ch App 96 a new issue of shares of a joint stock bank was offered to the existing shareholders at a premium. The directors arranged with one Stock to take, at a larger premium, the shares not taken up by the existing shareholders. Stock, being unable to fulfil his contract, requested the directors to relieve him of some. They did so, and made a profit. They were held accountable for the profit so made. Lord Cairns L.C. said:

> "The court will not enquire and is not in a position to ascertain, whether the bank has or has not lost by the acts of the directors. All the court has to do is to examine whether a profit has been made by an agent, without the knowledge of his principal, in the course and execution of his agency, and the court finds, in my opinion, that these agents in the course of their agency have made a profit, and for that profit they must, in my opinion, account to their principal."

In the same case James L.J. stated his view in the following terms:

> " . . . it appears to me very important that we should concur in laying down again and again the general principle that in this court no agent in the course of his agency, in the matter of his agency, can be allowed to make any profit without the knowledge of his principal; that the rule is an inflexible rule, and must be applied inexorably by this court, which is not entitled, in my judgment, to receive evidence, or suggestion, or argument, as to whether the principal did or did not suffer any injury in fact, by reason of the dealing of the agent; for the safety of mankind requires that no agent shall be able to put his principal to the danger of such an inquiry as that."

In *Imperial Mercantile Credit Association (Liquidators) v. Coleman* (1873) LR 6 HL 189 one Coleman, a stockbroker and a director of a financial company, had contracted to place a large amount of railway debentures for a commission of 5 per cent. He proposed that his company should undertake to place them for a commission of 1½ per cent. The 5 per cent commission was in due course paid to the director, who paid over the 1½ per cent to the company. He was held liable to account for the 3½ per cent, by Malins V.-C. (1870) 6 Ch App 563, who said:

> "It is of the highest importance that it should be distinctly understood that it is the duty of directors of companies to use their best exertions for the benefit of those whose interests are committed to their charge, and that they are bound to disregard their own private interests whenever a regard to them conflicts with the proper discharge of such duty."

His decree was reversed by Lord Hatherley (1871) 6 Ch App 558, 566 *et seq.* on the ground that the transaction was protected under the company's articles of association. Your Lordships' House, LR 6 HL 189, however, thought that in the circumstances of the case the articles of association gave no protection, and restored the decree with unimportant variations. The liability was based on the view, which was not disputed by Lord Hatherley, that the director stood in a fiduciary relationship to the company. That relationship being established, he could not keep the profit which had been earned by the funds of the company being employed in taking up the debentures. The courts in Scotland have treated directors as standing in a fiduciary relationship towards their company and, applying the equitable principle, have made them accountable for profits accruing to them in the course and by reason of their directorships. It will be sufficient to refer to *Huntington Copper Co. v. Henderson* (1877) 4 R 294, 308 in which the Lord President cites with approval the following passage from the judgment of the Lord Ordinary:

> "Whenever it can be shown that the trustee has so arranged matters as to obtain an advantage whether in money or money's worth to himself personally through the execution of his trust, he will not be permitted to retain, but be compelled to make it over to his constituent."

In the result, I am of opinion that the directors standing in a fiduciary relationship to Regal in regard to the exercise of their powers as directors, and having obtained these shares by reason and only by reason of the fact that they were directors of Regal and in the course of the execution of that office, are accountable for the profits which they have made out of them. The equitable rule laid down in *Keech v. Sandford* and *Ex parte James* (1803) 8 Ves 337 and similar authorities applies to them in full force. It was contended that these cases were distinguishable by reason of the fact that it was impossible for Regal to get the shares owing to lack of funds and that the directors in taking the shares were really acting as members of the public. I cannot accept this argument. It was impossible for the cestui que trust in *Keech v. Sandford* (1726) Sel Cas Ch 61 to obtain the lease, nevertheless the trustee was accountable. The suggestion that the directors were applying simply as members of the public is a travesty of the facts. They could, had they wished, have protected themselves by a resolution (either antecedent or subsequent) of the Regal shareholders in general meeting. In default of such approval, the liability to account must remain. The result is that, in my opinion, each of the respondents Bobby, Griffiths, Bassett and Bentley is liable to account for the profit which he made on the sale of his 500 shares in Amalgamated.

The case of the respondent Gulliver, however, requires some further consideration, for he has raised a separate and distinct answer to the claim. He says: "I never promised to subscribe for shares in Amalgamated. I never did so subscribe. I only promised to find others who would be willing to subscribe. I only found others who did subscribe. The shares were theirs. They were never mine. They received the profit. I received none of it." If these are the true facts, his answer seems complete. The evidence in my opinion establishes his contention. Throughout his evidence Gulliver insisted that he only promised to find £500, not to subscribe it himself. The £500 was paid by two cheques in favour of Amalgamated, one a cheque for £200 signed by Gulliver as director and on behalf of the Swiss company Seguliva, the other a cheque for £300 signed by Gulliver as managing director of South Downs Land Co., Ltd. They were enclosed in a letter of October 3, 1935, from Gulliver to Garton, in which Gulliver asks that the share certificates be issued as follows, 200 shares in the name of himself, Charles Gulliver, 200 shares in the name of South Downs Land Co., Ltd., and 100 shares in the name of Miss S. Geering. The money for Miss Geering's shares was apparently included in South Downs Land Co.'s cheque. The certificates were made out accordingly, the 200 shares in Gulliver's name being, he says, the shares subscribed for by the Swiss company.

When the sale and purchase of the Amalgamated shares was arranged, the agreement for the sale and purchase was signed on behalf of the vendor shareholders (other than the respondent Bentley) by Garton & Co.; and in a letter of October 17, 1935, Gulliver sent to Garton (who held the three certificates) three transfers, viz. (1) a transfer of 200 shares executed by South Downs Land Co. Ltd. (2) a transfer of 200 shares executed by himself, and (3) a transfer of 100 shares executed by Miss Geering. When the purchase money was paid cheques were drawn as follows: a cheque for £360 in favour of Miss Geering, a cheque for £720 in favour of South Downs Land Co. Ltd., and a cheque for the same amount in favour of Gulliver. By letter of October 24, 195 written by Gulliver to the National Provincial Bank, these cheques were paid into the respective accounts of Miss Geering, South Downs Land Co. Ltd., and Seguliva, A.G.

From the evidence of Gulliver it appeared that Miss Geering is a friend who from time to time makes investments on his advice; that the issued capital of South Downs and Co. Ltd., is £1,000 in £1 shares, held by some 11 or 12 shareholders, of whom Gulliver is one and holds 100 shares; and that in the Swiss company Gulliver holds 85 out of 500 shares.

It is of the first importance on this part of the case to bear in mind that these directors have been acquitted of all suggestion of mala fides in regard to the acquisition of these shares. They had no reason to believe that they could be called to account. Why then should Gulliver go to the elaborate pains of having the shares put into the names of South Downs Land Co. and Miss Geering and of having the proceeds of sale paid into the respective accounts before mentioned, if the shares and proceeds really belonged to him? Ex hypothesi he had no reason for concealment; and no question was raised against the transaction until months after the proceeds of sale had been paid into the banking accounts of those whom Gulliver asserts to have been the owners of the shares. I can see no reason for doubting that the shares never belonged to Gulliver, and that he made no profit on the sale thereof.

Counsel for the appellant, however, contended that the trial judge had found as a fact that Gulliver was the owner of the shares; and he relied on certain scattered passages in the judgment, the strongest of which seems to me to be the one in which the judge said:

> "I may say this with regard to Mr. Gulliver, that I have not been misled in any way or led to decide in his favour by the fact that he handed over his shares to his nominees but rather the reverse."

I cannot regard that as a finding by the judge that the shares were subscribed for by Gulliver under aliases, and that the shares and the proceeds of sale in fact belonged to him. It is equally susceptible of the meaning that he allowed others to subscribe for the shares which he could have obtained for himself had he so wished. If it be claimed as a finding of fact in the former sense, all I can say is that there is no evidence which in my opinion would justify such a finding.

It was further argued that, even if the shares and the proceeds of sale did not belong to Gulliver, he is nevertheless liable to account to Regal for the profit made by the owners of the shares and that upon the authority of *Imperial Mercantile Credit Association (Liquidators) v. Coleman* (1873) LR 6 HL 189, to which I have already referred. One of the contentions put forward there by Coleman was that his transaction was a transaction for the benefit of a partnership in the profits of which he was only interested to the extent of a half, and that accordingly he could only be made accountable to that extent. That contention was disposed of by Lord Cairns in the following terms:

> "My Lords, I think there is no foundation for this argument. The profit on the transaction was obtained by Mr. Coleman, and, in the view that I take, was obtained by him as a director of the association. Whether he desired or whether he determined to reserve it all to himself or to share it with his firm appears to me to be perfectly immaterial. The source from which the profit is derived is Mr. Coleman. It is only through him that his firm can claim. He is liable for the whole of the profits which were obtained; and it is not the course for a Court of Equity to enter into the consideration of what afterwards would have become of those profits."

I am unable to see how this authority helps Regal if it be assumed that neither the shares nor the profit ever belonged to Gulliver.

It was further said that Gulliver must account for whatever profits he may have made indirectly through his shareholding in the two companies, and that an inquiry should be directed for this purpose. As to this, it is sufficient to say that there is no evidence upon which to ground such an inquiry. Indeed, the evidence so far as it goes, shows that neither company has distributed any part of the profit. Finally, it was said that Gulliver must account for the profit on the 200 shares as to which the certificate was in his name. If in fact the shares belonged beneficially to the Swiss company (and that is the assumption for this purpose), the proceeds of sale did not belong to Gulliver, and were rightly paid into the Swiss company's banking account. Gulliver accordingly made no profit for which he is accountable. As regards Gulliver, this appeal should, in my opinion, be dismissed.

There remains to consider the case of Garton. He stands on a different footing from the other respondents in that he was not a director of Regal. He was Regal's legal adviser; but, in my opinion, he has a short but effective answer to the plaintiffs' claim. He was requested by the Regal directors to apply for 500 shares. They arranged that they themselves should each be responsible for £500 of the Amalgamated capital, and they appealed, by their chairman, to Garton to subscribe the balance of £500 which was required to make up the £3,000. In law his action, which has resulted in a profit, was taken at the request of Regal, and I know of no principle or authority which would justify a decision that a solicitor must account for profit resulting from a transaction which he has entered into on his own behalf, not merely with the consent, but at the request of his client.

My Lords, in my opinion the right way in which to deal with this appeal is (i) to dismiss the appeal as against the respondents Gulliver and Garton with costs, (ii) to allow it with costs as against the other four respondents, and (iii) to enter judgment as against each of these four respondents for a sum of £1,402 1s. 8d. with interest at 4 per cent from October 25, 1935, as to £1,300 part thereof and from December 5, 1935, as to the balance. As regards the liability of these four respondents for costs, I have read the shorthand notes of the evidence at the trial, and it is clear to me that the costs were substantially increased by the suggestions of mala fides and fraud with which the cross-examination abounds, and from which they have been exonerated. In my opinion a proper order to make would be to order these four respondents to pay only three-quarters of the appellants' taxed costs of the action. The taxed costs of the appellants in the the Court of Appeal and in this House they must pay in full.

One final observation I desire to make. In his judgment Lord Greene M.R. stated that a decision adverse to the directors in the present case involved the proposition that, if directors bona fide decide not to invest their company's funds in some proposed investment, a director who thereafter embarks his own money therein is accountable for any profits which he may derive therefrom. As to this, I can only say that to my mind the facts of this hypothetical case bear but little resemblance to the story with which we have had to deal."

THE LIABILITY OF STRANGERS AS CONSTRUCTIVE TRUSTEES

Introduction

Where a stranger to a trust takes it upon himself to act as a trustee and subsequently commits a breach of trust, he will be liable for such a breach.[12] In addition, a third party may incur liability where he dishonestly assists in a breach of trust[13] or where he receives or deals with trust property in circumstances where his degree of knowledge is sufficient to justify the imposition of liability.[14]

Assisting in the Misappropriation of Trust Property

It has been accepted by the Privy Council that 'a liability in equity to make good resulting loss attaches to a person who dishonestly procures or assists in a breach of trust or fiduciary obligation'.[15] While the courts in England have been far from consistent in their attitude towards the degree of knowledge or wrongdoing required to found liability under this heading, they appear to be focussing increasingly on the concept of dishonesty. Although it remains to be seen how the courts in this jurisdiction will address this question, it is likely that they too would favour such an approach.

Agip (Africa) Ltd v. Jackson
[1990] Ch 265

A senior officer in the plaintiff company fraudulently altered a payment order to a creditor by substituting the name of a company managed by the defendants which had been set up in order to launder the money. The money was credited to the company's bank account and following a series of transactions in which the money was transferred to various recipients, the company was wound up. The plaintiffs brought an action against the defendants to recover the money in which they claimed, *inter alia*, that the defendants were constructive trustees of the funds on the basis of knowing receipt and knowing assistance. Millett J held that none of the defendants could be held liable on the basis of knowingly receiving trust funds for their own benefit but that the defendants were liable

---

[12] *Mara v. Browne* [1896] 1 Ch 199.
[13] *Royal Brunei Airlines Sdn Bhd v. Tan* [1995] 2 AC 378.
[14] Considered in more detail *infra* pp. 381 *et seq.*
[15] *Royal Brunei Airlines Sdn Bhd v. Tan* [1995] 2 AC 378, 392.

under the heading of knowing assistance. On appeal, the Court of Appeal dismissed the defendants' appeal and affirmed the decision of Millett J.

Note that in his judgment in the Court of Appeal, Fox LJ appeared to accept that actual or constructive knowledge would suffice to ground liability. However, this reasoning has been criticised[16] and the approach adopted by Millett J at first instance is more in line with present thinking on this issue.

MILLETT J stated at pp.292–295: "A stranger to the trust will also be liable to account as a constructive trustee if he knowingly assists in the furtherance of a fraudulent and dishonest breach of trust. It is not necessary that the party sought to be made liable as a constructive trustee should have received any part of the trust property; but the breach of trust must have been fraudulent. The basis of the stranger's liability is not receipt of trust property but participation in a fraud: *Barnes v. Addy* (1874) 9 Ch App 244, and see the explanation of the distinction between the two categories of the case given by Jacobs P. in *D. P. C. Estates Pty. Ltd. v. Grey* [1974] 1 NSWLR 443.

The authorities at first instance are in some disarray on the question whether constructive notice is sufficient to sustain liability under this head. In the *Baden* case [1983] BCLC 325, Peter Gibson J. accepted a concession by counsel that constructive notice is sufficient and that on this point there is no distinction between cases of "knowing receipt" and "knowing assistance." This question was not argued before me but I am unable to agree. In my view the concession was wrong and should not have been made. The basis of liability in the two types of cases is quite different; there is no reason why the degree of knowledge required should be the same, and good reason why it should not. Tracing claims and cases of "knowing receipt" are both concerned with rights of priority in relation to property taken by a legal owner for his own benefit; cases of "knowing assistance" are concerned with the furtherance of fraud. In *Belmont Finance Corporation Ltd. v. Williams Furniture Ltd* [1979] Ch 250, the Court of Appeal insisted that to hold a stranger liable for "knowing assistance" the breach of trust in question must be a fraudulent and dishonest one. In my judgment it necessarily follows that constructive notice of the fraud is not enough to make him liable. There is no sense in requiring dishonesty on the part of the principal while accepting negligence as sufficient for his assistant. Dishonest furtherance of the dishonest scheme of another is an understandable basis for liability; negligent but honest failure to appreciate that someone else's scheme is dishonest is not.

In *In re Montagu's Settlement Trusts* [1987] Ch 264, 285, Sir Robert Megarry V.C. doubted whether constructive notice is sufficient even in cases of "knowing receipt." Whether the doubt is well founded or not (as to which I express no opinion), "knowing assistance" is an a fortiori case.

---

[16] See Harpum [1991] CLJ 409, 411.

Knowledge may be provided affirmatively or inferred from circumstances. The various mental states which may be involved were analysed by Peter Gibson J. in *Baden's* case [1983] BCLC 325 as comprising: (i) actual knowledge; (ii) wilfully shutting one's eyes to the obvious; (iii) wilfully and recklessly failing to make such inquiries as an honest and reasonable man would make; (iv) knowledge of circumstances which would indicate the facts to an honest and reasonable man; and (v) knowledge of circumstances which would put an honest and reasonable man on inquiry.

According to Peter Gibson J., a person in category (ii) or (iii) will be taken to have actual knowledge, while a person in categories (iv) or (v) has constructive notice only. I gratefully adopt the classification but would warn against over refinement or a too ready assumption that categories (iv) or (v) are necessarily cases of constructive notice only. The true distinction is between honesty and dishonesty. It is essentially a jury question. If a man does not draw the obvious inferences or make the obvious inquiries, the question is: why not? If it is because, however foolishly, he did not suspect wrongdoing or, having suspected it, had his suspicions allayed, however unreasonably, that is one thing. But if he did suspect wrongdoing yet failed to make inquiries because "he did not want to know" (category (ii)) or because he regarded it as "none of his business" (category (iii)), that is quite another. Such conduct is dishonest, and those who are guilty of it cannot complain if, for the purpose of civil liability, they are treated as if they had actual knowledge.

In the present case, Mr. Bowers did not participate in the furtherance of the fraud and he cannot be held directly liable on this ground. Mr. Jackson and Mr. Griffin, however, clearly did. Mr. Jackson set up the arrangements and employed Mr. Griffin to carry them out. The money was under their control from the time it was paid into Baker Oil's account until the time it left Jackson & Co.'s clients' account in the Isle of Man Bank. One or other of them gave the actual instructions to the banks which disposed of the money. They plainly assisted in the fraud. The sole remaining question is: did they do so with the requisite degree of knowledge?

The defendants' state of mind

Mr. Jackson and Mr. Griffin knew that the money was coming from the plaintiffs, an oil company with a branch in Tunis; that most of it was being paid to Kinz, which ran a jewellery business in France; that more than $10m. had been dealt with in this way in less than two years; and that their instructions came from the recipients and not from the plaintiffs. They knew of no connection or dealings between the plaintiffs and Kinz or of any commercial reason for the plaintiffs to make substantial payments to Kinz. They must have realised that the only function which the payee companies or Euro-Arabian performed was to act as "cut-outs" in order to conceal the true destination of the money from the plaintiffs. They must also have realised that the only purpose in having two "cut-outs" instead of one was to make it impossible for investigators to make any connection between the plaintiffs and Kinz without having recourse to Lloyds Bank's records; and their object in frequently replacing the payee company by another must have been to reduce the risk of discovery by the plaintiffs.

This is damning evidence; but it does not stop there. The letter dated 14 August 1984 from Knapp-Fishers shows that Mr. Jackson was concerned – whether for himself or his clients is immaterial – at the possibility that the plaintiffs might obtain disclosure of Lloyds Bank's records, discover what had happened to the money, and try to recover it.

Mr. Jackson and Mr. Griffin are professional men. They obviously knew that they were laundering money. They were consciously helping their clients to make arrangements designed for the purpose of concealment from, inter alios, the plaintiffs. It must have been obvious to them that their clients could not afford their activities to see the light of day. Secrecy is the badge of fraud. They must have realised at least that their clients might be involved in a fraud on the plaintiffs.

Can Mr. Jackson and Mr. Griffin possibly have believed that their arrangements had an honest purpose? They pleaded no such belief. They have given no evidence. On their behalf it was submitted that they were entitled to be reassured by the fact that they were taking over arrangements which had been established for some years; that they were introduced to them by a partner in a well known and reputable firm of chartered accountants; and that, if there was any wrongdoing, it would surely have come to light long before. Had Mr. Jackson and Mr. Griffin given evidence to this effect, I might or might not have believed it. But I will not assume it when they do not tell me so.

Reliance was also placed on Miss Freeman's assurance on 8 January that, so far as Lloyds Bank was concerned, the defendants were at liberty to dispose of the money. But this was not an assurance that they could do so as far as the plaintiffs were concerned. Just as Miss Freeman's first message about the recall was not an alert, so her second was not an all clear.

What did Mr. Jackson and Mr. Griffin think was going on? There is some evidence of this in the minutes of the first meeting of the directors of Keelward Ltd. on 22 March 1984, and it would be wrong of me to ignore it. It suggests that they thought that their clients were engaged in evading Tunisian exchange control, possibly with the connivance of the plaintiffs and on their behalf – though the minutes do not say so. In my judgment, however, it is no answer for a man charged with having knowingly assisted in a fraudulent and dishonest scheme to say that he thought that it was "only" a breach of exchange control or "only" a case of tax evasion. It is not necessary that he should have been aware of the precise nature of the fraud or even of the identity of its victim. A man who consciously assists others by making arrangements which he knows are calculated to conceal what is happening from a third party, takes the risk that they are part of a fraud practised on that party.

But it is not necessary to rest my decision on this ground. After Mr. Smyth's letter of 14 August 1984, the defendants cannot claim that the possibility of a fraud on the plaintiffs never crossed their minds; it was specifically drawn to their attention. Yet they never made any inquiries of the plaintiffs or took any steps to satisfy themselves that the arrangements had the plaintiffs' knowledge and approval. They comforted themselves with the fact that there was "no clear case of fraud under English law."

I am led to the conclusion that Mr. Jackson and Mr. Griffin were at best indifferent to the possibility of fraud. They made no inquiries of the plaintiffs because they thought that it was none of their business. That is not honest behaviour. The sooner that those who provide the services of nominee companies for the purpose of enabling their clients to keep their activities secret realise it, the better. In my judgment, it is quite enough to make them liable to account as constructive trustees."

Royal Brunei Airlines Sdn Bhd v. Tan
[1995] 2 AC 378

The plaintiff airline appointed a company of which the defendant was the managing director and principal shareholder as its agent for the sale of passenger and cargo transportation. With the knowledge and assistance of the defendant, the company paid money it received from sales into its current bank account instead of into a separate account in breach of trust and used these monies for its own purposes. The company became insolvent and the plaintiff brought proceedings against the defendant seeking to recover the money owed to it. The Court of Appeal of Brunei Darussalam held that the defendant was not liable as it had not been established that the company had been guilty of fraud or dishonesty in relation to the money it held on trust for the airline. The Privy Council reversed this decision and held the defendant liable on the basis of his conduct in dishonestly assisting in a breach of trust, concluding that there was no need to establish that the company as trustee had acted dishonestly or fraudulently.

LORD NICHOLLS stated at pp.381–393: "The proper role of equity in commercial transactions is a topical question. Increasingly plaintiffs have recourse to equity for an effective remedy when the person in default, typically a company, is insolvent. Plaintiffs seek to obtain relief from others who were involved in the transaction, such as directors of the company or its bankers or its legal or other advisers. They seek to fasten fiduciary obligations directly onto the company's officers or agents or advisers, or to have them held personally liable for assisting the company in breaches of trust or fiduciary obligations.

This is such a case. An insolvent travel agent company owed money to an airline. The airline seeks a remedy against the travel agent's principal director and shareholder. Its claim is based on the much-quoted dictum of Lord Selborne LC, sitting in the Court of Appeal in Chancery, in *Barnes v. Addy* (1874) LR 9 Ch App 244 at 251-252:

> "[The responsibility of a trustee] may no doubt be extended in equity to others who are not properly trustees, if they are found . . . actually participating in any fraudulent conduct of the trustee to the injury of the cestui que trust. But . . . strangers are not to be made constructive trustees merely because they act as the agents of trustees in transactions within their legal powers, transactions, perhaps of which a Court of Equity may disapprove, unless those agents receive and become chargeable with some part of the trust property, or unless they assist with knowledge in a dishonest and fraudulent design on the part of the trustees."

In the conventional shorthand the first of these two circumstances in which third parties (non-trustees) may become liable to account in equity is 'knowing receipt', as distinct from the second where liability arises from 'knowing assistance'. Stated even more shortly, the first limb of Lord Selborne LC's formulation is concerned with the liability of a person as a recipient of trust property or its traceable proceeds. The second limb is concerned with what, for want of a better compendious description, can be called the liability of an accessory to a trustee's breach of trust. Liability as an accessory is not dependent upon receipt of trust property. It arises even though no trust property has reached the hands of the accessory. It is a form of secondary liability in the sense that it only arises where there has been a breach of trust. In the present case the plaintiff relies on the accessory limb. The particular point in issue arises from the expression 'a dishonest and fraudulent design on the part of the trustees'.

The proceedings
The essential facts are these. In 1986 Royal Brunei Airlines Sdn Bhd (the airline) appointed Borneo Leisure Travel Sdn Bhd (BLT) to act, in various places in Sabah and Sarawak, as its general travel agent for the sale of passenger and cargo transportation. The terms of the appointment were set out in a written agreement of 1 April 1986. BLT was required to account to the airline for all amounts received from sales of tickets. For its services it was to be paid a sales commission. The agreement was expressed to be subject to the regulations of the International Air Transport Association, one of which provided:

> "All monies collected by the Agent for transportation and ancillary services sold under this Agreement, including applicable commissions which the Agent is entitled to claim thereunder, shall be the property of the Carrier and shall be held by the Agent in trust for the Carrier or on behalf of the Carrier until satisfactorily accounted for to the Carrier and settlement made . . . Unless otherwise instructed by the Carrier the Agent shall be entitled to deduct from remittances the applicable commission to which it is entitled hereunder."

It was common ground that the effect of this provision was to constitute BLT a trustee for the airline of the money it received from the sale of passenger and cargo transportation by the airline.

In practice what happened was that money received by BLT on behalf of the airline was not paid into a separate bank account. It was paid into BLT's ordinary current account with its bank. By a standing arrangement with the bank, any balance in its current account in excess of a stated amount was transferred to a fixed deposit account of BLT or, at times, of the defendant, Philip Tan Kok Ming. The defendant had founded BLT. He was managing director and principal shareholder. He was effectively in charge and control of BLT. The other director and shareholder was his wife. Nothing turns on these transfers of money to other accounts because, with one immaterial exception, all the transferred money eventually found its way back to BLT's current account.

BLT was required to pay the airline within 30 days, but at various times from 1988 onwards it was in arrears. In August 1992 the airline terminated the agreement. In January 1993 the airline commenced this action against the defendant in respect of the unpaid money. The defendant was not himself a party to the agency agreement, although he had signed it on behalf of BLT.

At the trial held in October 1993 Roberts CJ rejected a claim by the airline that the defendant had orally guaranteed payment of the money. Roberts CJ also rejected a claim that the defendant had diverted the money to his own use. He upheld a claim that the defendant was liable as a constructive trustee, under the accessory limb of Lord Selborne L.C.'s formulation in *Barnes v. Addy* (1874) LR 9 Ch App 244, 251–252. Although not particularised, this issue was pleaded explicitly and unequivocally. The defendant knew there was an express trust of the money. The money appeared to have been used by BLT for its ordinary business purposes, paying salaries, overheads and other expenses and keeping down its bank overdraft. It must be assumed that the defendant authorised the use of the money for these purposes. That was sufficient to make him liable. A fraudulent and dishonest design is not confined to personal gain. It is sufficient if the stranger knowingly assists in the use of trust property in a way which is not permitted by the trust. Judgment was entered for the airline for $B.335,160.

The Court of Appeal of Brunei Darussalam allowed the defendant's appeal. Counsel for the defendant conceded that a trust of the money had been created, and that there had been a breach of that trust in which the defendant had assisted with actual knowledge. The issue was whether a dishonest and fraudulent design on the part of BLT had been established. The court held that the evidence revealed a sorry tale of mismanagement and broken promises, but that it was not established that BLT was guilty of fraud or dishonesty in relation to the amounts it held in trust for the airline. Delivering the judgment of the court, Fuad P stated:

> "As long standing and high authority shows, conduct which may amount to a breach of trust, however morally reprehensible, will not render a person who has knowingly assisted in the breach of trust liable as a constructive trustee, if that conduct falls short of dishonesty."

This view of the state of the law has the support of the (English) Court of Appeal. In *Selangor United Rubber Estates Ltd v. Cradock (a bankrupt) (No. 3)* [1968] 1 WLR 1555, 1591 Ungoed-Thomas J held that the expression 'dishonest and fraudulent design' was to be understood according to the principles of a court of equity. That approach was emphatically rejected by the Court of Appeal in *Belmont Finance Corp Ltd v. Williams Furniture Ltd* [1979] Ch 250. Buckley LJ observed, at p. 267, that the rule as formulated by Lord Selborne LC had stood for more than 100 years, and that to depart from it would introduce an undesirable degree of uncertainty to the law over what degree of unethical conduct would suffice if dishonesty was not to be the criterion. Goff LJ, at p. 274, agreed that it would be dangerous and wrong to depart from 'the safe path of the principle as stated by Lord Selborne' to the 'uncharted sea of something not innocent . . . but still short of dishonesty'.

In short, the issue on this appeal is whether the breach of trust which is a prerequisite to accessory liability must itself be a dishonest and fraudulent breach of trust by the trustee.

The honest trustee and the dishonest third party

It must be noted at once that there is a difficulty with the approach adopted on this point in the *Belmont* case. Take the simple example of an honest trustee and a dishonest third party. Take a case where a dishonest solicitor persuades a trustee to apply trust property in a way the trustee honestly believes is permissible but which the solicitor knows full well is a clear breach of trust. The solicitor deliberately conceals this from the trustee. In consequence, the beneficiaries suffer a substantial loss. It cannot be right that in such a case the accessory liability principle would be inapplicable because of the innocence of the trustee. In ordinary parlance, the beneficiaries have been defrauded by the solicitor. If there is to be an accessory liability principle at all, whereby in appropriate circumstances beneficiaries may have direct recourse against a third party, the principle must surely be applicable in such a case, just as much as in a case where both the trustee and the third party have been dishonest. Indeed, if anything, the case for liability of the dishonest third party seems stronger where the trustee is innocent, because in such a case the third party alone was dishonest and that was the cause of the subsequent misapplication of the trust property.

The position would be the same if, instead of *procuring* the breach, the third party dishonestly *assisted* in the breach. Change the facts slightly. A trustee is proposing to make a payment out of the trust fund to a particular person. He honestly believes he is authorised to do so by the terms of the trust deed. He asks a solicitor to carry through the transaction. The solicitor well knows that the proposed payment would be a plain breach of trust. He also well knows that the trustee mistakenly believes otherwise. Dishonestly he leaves the trustee under his misapprehension and prepares the necessary documentation. Again, if the accessory principle is not to be artificially constricted, it ought to be applicable in such a case.

These examples suggest that what matters is the state of mind of the third party sought to be made liable, not the state of mind of the trustee. The trustee will be liable in any event for the breach of trust, even if he acted innocently, unless excused by an exemption clause in the trust instrument or relieved by the court. But *his* state of mind is essentially irrelevant to the question whether the *third party* should be made liable to the beneficiaries for the breach of trust. If the liability of the third party is fault-based, what matters is the nature of his fault, not that of the trustee. In this regard dishonesty on the part of the third party would seem to be a sufficient basis for his liability, irrespective of the state of mind of the trustee who is in breach of trust. It is difficult to see why, if the third party dishonestly assisted in a breach, there should be a further prerequisite to his liability, namely that the trustee also must have been acting dishonestly. The alternative view would mean that a dishonest third party is liable if the trustee is dishonest, but if the trustee did not act dishonestly that of itself would excuse a dishonest third party from liability. That would make no sense.

Earlier authority

The view that the accessory liability principle cannot be restricted to fraudulent breaches of trust is not to be approached with suspicion as a latter-day novelty. Before the accessory principle donned its *Barnes v. Addy* strait-jacket, judges seem not to have regarded the principle as confined in this way. In *Fyler v. Fyler* (1841) 3 Beav 550, 568, Lord Langdale MR expressed the view that if trustees invested in an unauthorised investment, solicitors who knowingly procured that to be done for their own benefit 'ought to be considered as partakers in the breach of trust' even though the trustees intended in good faith that the investment would be beneficial to the life tenant and not prejudicial to the beneficiaries with interests in capital. The same judge, in *A-G v. Leicester Corp* (1844) 7 Beav 176, 179 stated:

> "it cannot be disputed, that if the agent of a trustee, whether a corporate body or not, knowing that a breach of trust is being committed, interferes and assists in that breach of trust, he is personally answerable, although he may be employed as the agent of the person who directs him to commit that breach of trust."

In *Eaves v. Hickson* (1861) 30 Beav 136 trustees, acting in good faith, paid over a fund to William Knibb's adult children on the strength of a forged marriage certificate produced to them by William Knibb. Romilly MR held that William Knibb was liable to replace the fund, to the extent that it was not recovered from his children, and to do so in priority to the liability of the trustees. Far from this being a case of fraud by the trustees, Sir John Romilly MR, at p. 141, described it as a very hard case on the trustees, who were deceived by a forgery which would have deceived anyone who was not looking out for forgery or fraud.

This point did not arise in *Barnes v. Addy*. There the new sole trustee was engaged in a dishonest and fraudulent design. He intended to misapply the trust fund as soon as it reached his hands. The two solicitors were held not liable because there was no evidence that either of them had any knowledge or suspicion of this.

What has gone wrong? Their Lordships venture to think that the reason is that ever since the *Selangor* case highlighted the potential uses of equitable remedies in connection with misapplied company funds, there has been a tendency to cite, interpret and apply Lord Selborne LC's formulation as though it were a statute. This has particularly been so with the accessory limb of Lord Selborne's apothegm. This approach has been inimical to analysis of the underlying concept. Working within this constraint, the courts have found themselves wrestling with the interpretation of the individual ingredients, especially 'knowingly' but also 'dishonest and fraudulent design on the part of the trustees', without examining the underlying reason why a third party who has received no trust property is being made liable at all. One notable exception is the judgment of Thomas J in *Powell v. Thompson* [1991] 1 NZLR 597, 610-615. On this point he observed, at 613:

> "Once a breach of trust has been committed, the commission of which has involved a third party, the question which arises is one as between the beneficiary and that third party. If the third party's conduct has been unconscionable, then irrespective of the degree of impropriety in the trustee's conduct, the third party is liable to be held accountable to the beneficiary as if he or she were a trustee."

To resolve this issue it is necessary to take an overall look at the accessory liability principle. A conclusion cannot be reached on the nature of the breach of trust which may trigger accessory liability without at the same time considering the other ingredients including, in particular, the state of mind of the third party. It is not necessary, however, to look even more widely and consider the essential ingredients of recipient liability. The issue on this appeal concerns only the accessory liability principle. Different considerations apply to the two heads of liability. Recipient liability is restitution-based; accessory liability is not.

No liability

The starting point for any analysis must be to consider the extreme possibility: that a third party who does not receive trust property ought never to be liable directly to the beneficiaries merely because he assisted the trustee to commit a breach of trust or procured him to do so. This possibility can be dismissed summarily. On this the position which the law has long adopted is clear and makes good sense. Stated in the simplest terms, a trust is a relationship which exists when one person holds property on behalf of another. If, for his own purposes, a third party deliberately interferes in that relationship by assisting the trustee in depriving the beneficiary of the property held for him by the trustee, the beneficiary should be able to look for recompense to the third party as well as the trustee. Affording the beneficiary a remedy against the third party serves the dual purpose of making good the beneficiary's loss should the trustee lack financial means and imposing a liability which will discourage others from behaving in a similar fashion.

The rationale is not far to seek. Beneficiaries are entitled to expect that those who become trustees will fulfil their obligations. They are also entitled to expect, and this is only a short step further, that those who become trustees will be permitted to fulfil their obligations without deliberate intervention from third parties. They are entitled to expect that third parties will refrain from intentionally intruding in the trustee-beneficiary relationship and thereby hindering a beneficiary from receiving his entitlement in accordance with the terms of the trust instrument. There is here a close analogy with breach of contract. A person who knowingly procures a breach of contract, or knowingly interferes with the due performance of a contract, is liable to the innocent party. The underlying rationale is the same.

Strict liability

The other extreme possibility can also be rejected out of hand. This is the case where a third party deals with a trustee without knowing, or having any reason to suspect, that he is a trustee. Or the case where a third party is aware he is dealing with a trustee but has no reason to know or suspect that their transaction is inconsistent with the terms of the trust. The law has never gone so far as to give a beneficiary a remedy against a non-recipient third party in such circumstances. Within defined limits, proprietary rights, whether legal or equitable, endure against third parties who were unaware of their existence. But accessory liability is concerned with the liability of a person who has not received any property. His liability is not property-based. His only sin is that he interfered with the due performance by the trustee of the fiduciary obligations undertaken by the trustee. These are personal obligations. They are, in this respect, analogous to the personal obligations undertaken by the parties to a contract. But ordinary, everyday business would become impossible if third parties were to be held liable for unknowingly interfering in the due performance of such personal obligations. Beneficiaries could not reasonably expect that third parties should deal with trustees at their peril, to the extent that they should become liable to the beneficiaries even when they received no trust property and even when they were unaware and had no reason to suppose that they were dealing with trustees.

Fault-based liability

Given, then, that in some circumstances a third party may be liable directly to a beneficiary, but given also that the liability is not so strict that there would be liability even when the third party was wholly unaware of the existence of the trust, the next step is to seek to identify the touchstone of liability. By common accord dishonesty fulfils this role. Whether, in addition, negligence will suffice is an issue on which there has been a well-known difference of judicial opinion. The *Selangor* decision in 1968 was the first modern decision on this point. Ungoed-Thomas J, at p.1590, held that the touchstone was whether the third party had knowledge of circumstances which would indicate to 'an honest, reasonable man' that the breach in question was being committed or would put him on inquiry. Brightman J reached the same conclusion in *Karak Rubber Co. Ltd v. Burden (No. 2)* [1972] 1 WLR 602. So did Peter Gibson J in 1982 in *Baden v. Société Générale pour Favoriser le Developpement du Commerce et de l'Industrie en France SA* [1993] 1 WLR 509. In that case the judge accepted a five-point scale of knowledge which had been formulated by counsel.

Meanwhile doubts had been expressed about this test by Buckley and Goff LJJ in the *Belmont* case [1979] Ch 250 at 267, 275. Similar doubts were expressed in Australia by Jacobs P in *DPC Estates Pty Ltd v. Grey* [1974] 1 NSWLR 443, 459. When that decision reached the High Court of Australia the doubts were echoed by Barwick CJ, Gibbs and Stephen JJ: see *Consul Development Pty Ltd v. DPC Estates Pty Ltd* (1975) 132 CLR 373, 376, 398, 412.

Since then the tide in England has flowed strongly in favour of the test ·being one of dishonesty: see, for instance, *Re Montagu's Settlement Trusts* [1987] Ch 264, 285 per Megarry V-C and *Agip (Africa) Ltd v. Jackson* [1990] Ch 265, 293 *per* Millett J. In *Eagle Trust plc v. SBC Securities Ltd* [1993] 1 WLR 484, 495 Vinelott J stated that it could be taken as settled law that want of probity was a prerequisite to liability. This received the imprimatur of the Court of Appeal in *Polly Peck International Plc v. Nadir (No. 2)* [1992] 4 All ER 769, 777 *per* Scott LJ.

Judicial views have diverged also in New Zealand. In *Westpac Banking Corp v. Savin* [1985] 2 NZLR 41, 70, Sir Clifford Richmond preferred the approach in *Belmont Finance Corporation Ltd. v. Williams Furniture Ltd.* [1979] Ch 250, as did Tompkins J in *Marr v. Arabco Traders Ltd* (1987) 1 NZBLC 102, 732, 102, 762. In *Powell v. Thompson* [1991] 1 NZLR 597 at 612, 613, 615 Thomas J considered that the suggestion that negligence is not enough to found liability is to be resisted. The test is one of unconscionable behaviour. This, and knowledge to match, whether actual or constructive, will suffice to herald a visit from equity. In *Equiticorp Industries Group Ltd v. Hawkins* [1991] 3 NZLR 700, 728 Wylie J disagreed. He adhered to the concept of want of probity as the standard by which unconscionability was to be measured. In *Marshall Futures Ltd v. Marshall* [1992] 1 NZLR 316 at 325 Tipping J was concerned about the difficulty of identifying as unconscionable conduct which was less reprehensible than conduct which can be described as dishonest. He would, he said, prefer the herald of equity to be wearing more distinctive clothing than that suggested by Thomas J. In *Nimmo v. Westpac Banking Corp* [1993] 3 NZLR 218, 228 Blanchard J preferred a test of dishonesty. Most recently, in *Springfield Acres Ltd v. Abacus (Hong Kong) Ltd* [1994] 3 NZLR 502, 510 Henry J observed that the law in New Zealand could not be regarded as settled.

Most, but not all, commentators prefer the test of dishonesty: see, among others, Peter Birks 'Misdirected funds: restitution from the recipient' [1989] LMCLQ 296; M J Brindle and R J A Hooley 'Does constructive knowledge make a constructive trustee?' (1987) 61 ALJ 281; Charles Harpum 'The stranger as constructive trustee' (1986) 102 LQR 114, 267 and 'The basis of equitable liability' in Birks, *The Frontiers of Liability* (1994) vol. 1, p. 9; Patricia Loughlan 'Liability for assistance in a breach of fiduciary duty' (1989) 9 OJLS 260; Parker and Mellows, *The Modern Law of Trusts* (6th ed., 1994), p. 253; Pettit, *Equity and the Law of Trusts* (7th ed., 1993), p. 172; Philip Sales 'The tort of conspiracy and civil secondary liability' (1990) 49 CLJ 491; *Snell's Equity* (29th ed., 1990), p. 194; and *Underhill and Hayton Law Relating to Trusts and Trustees* (14th ed., 1987) p 355 and noter-up.

Dishonesty
Before considering this issue further it will be helpful to define the terms being used by looking more closely at what dishonesty means in this context. Whatever may be the position in some criminal or other contexts (see, for instance, *R. v. Ghosh* [1982] QB 1053), in the context of the accessory liability principle acting dishonestly, or with a lack of probity, which is synonymous, means simply not acting as an honest person would in the circumstances. This is an objective standard. At first sight this may seem surprising. Honesty has a connotation of subjectivity, as distinct from the objectivity of negligence. Honesty, indeed, does have a strong subjective element in that it is a description of a type of conduct assessed in the light of what a person actually knew at the time, as distinct from what a reasonable person would have known or appreciated. Further, honesty and its counterpart dishonesty are mostly concerned with advertent conduct, not inadvertent conduct. Carelessness is not dishonesty. Thus for the most part dishonesty is to be equated with conscious impropriety.

However, these subjective characteristics of honesty do not mean that individuals are free to set their own standards of honesty in particular circumstances. The standard of what constitutes honest conduct is not subjective. Honesty is not an optional scale, with higher or lower values according to the moral standards of each individual. If a person knowingly appropriates another's property, he will not escape a finding of dishonesty simply because he sees nothing wrong in such behaviour.

In most situations there is little difficulty in identifying how an honest person would behave. Honest people do not intentionally deceive others to their detriment. Honest people do not knowingly take others' property. Unless there is a very good and compelling reason, an honest person does not participate in a transaction if he knows it involves a misapplication of trust assets to the detriment of the beneficiaries. Nor does an honest person in such a case deliberately close his eyes and ears, or deliberately not ask questions, lest he learn something he would rather not know, and then proceed regardless. However, in the situations now under consideration the position is not always so straightforward. This can best be illustrated by considering one particular area: the taking of risks.

Taking risks

All investment involves risk. Imprudence is not dishonesty, although imprudence may be carried recklessly to lengths which call into question the honesty of the person making the decision. This is especially so if the transaction serves another purpose in which that person has an interest of his own.

This type of risk is to be sharply distinguished from the case where a trustee, with or without the benefit of advice, is aware that a particular investment or application of trust property is outside his powers, but nevertheless he decides to proceed in the belief or hope that this will be beneficial to the beneficiaries or, at least, not prejudicial to them. He takes a risk that a clearly unauthorised transaction will not cause loss. A risk of this nature is for the account of those who take it. If the risk materialises and causes loss, those who knowingly took the risk will be accountable accordingly. This is the type of risk being addressed by Peter Gibson J in the *Baden* case [1993] 1 WLR 509, 574, when he accepted that fraud includes taking 'a risk to the prejudice of another's rights, which risk is known to be one which there is no right to take' (quoting from the Court of Appeal judgment in *R. v. Sinclair* [1968] 1 WLR 1246, 1249).

This situation, in turn, is to be distinguished from the case where there is genuine doubt about whether a transaction is authorised or not. This may be because the trust instrument is worded obscurely, or because there are competing claims as in *Carl Zeiss Stiftung v. Herbert Smith & Co. (a firm) (No. 2)* [1969] 2 Ch 276, or for other reasons. The difficulty here is that frequently the situation is neither clearly white nor clearly black. The dividing edge between what is within the trustee's powers and what is not is often not clear cut. Instead there is a gradually darkening spectrum which can be described with labels such as clearly authorised, probably authorised, possibly authorised, wholly unclear, probably unauthorised and, finally, clearly unauthorised.

The difficulty here is that the differences are of degree rather than of kind. So far as the trustee himself is concerned the legal analysis is straightforward. Honesty or lack of honesty is not the test for his liability. He is obliged to comply with the terms of the trust. His liability is strict. If he departs from the trust terms he is liable unless excused by a provision in the trust instrument or relieved by the court. The analysis of the position of the accessory, such as the solicitor who carries through the transaction for him, does not lead to such a simple, clear cut answer in every case. He is required to act honestly, but what is required of an honest person in these circumstances? An honest person knows there is doubt. What does honesty require him to do?

The only answer to these questions lies in keeping in mind that honesty is an objective standard. The individual is expected to attain the standard which would be observed by an honest person placed in those circumstances. It is impossible to be more specific. Knox J captured the flavour of this, in a case with a commercial setting, when he referred to a person who is 'guilty of commercially unacceptable conduct in the particular context involved': see *Cowan de Groot Properties Ltd v. Eagle Trust Plc* [1992] 4 All ER 700, 761. Acting in reckless disregard of others' rights or possible rights can be a tell-tale sign of dishonesty. An honest person would have regard to the circumstances known to him, including the nature and importance of the proposed transaction, the nature and importance of his role, the ordinary course of business, the degree of doubt, the practicability of the trustee or the third party proceeding otherwise and the seriousness of the adverse consequences to the beneficiaries. The circumstances will dictate which one or more of the possible courses should be taken by an honest person. He might, for instance, flatly decline to become involved. He might ask further questions. He might seek advice, or insist on further advice being obtained. He might advise the trustee of the risks but then proceed with his role in the transaction. He might do many things. Ultimately, in most cases, an honest person should have little difficulty in knowing whether a proposed transaction, or his participation in it, would offend the normally accepted standards of honest conduct.

Likewise, when called upon to decide whether a person was acting honestly, a court will look at all the circumstances known to the third party at the time. The court will also have regard to personal attributes of the third party such as his experience and intelligence, and the reason why he acted as he did.

Before leaving cases where there is real doubt, one further point should be noted. To inquire, in such cases, whether a person dishonestly assisted in what is later held to be a breach of trust is to ask a meaningful question, which is capable of being given a meaningful answer. This is not always so if the question is posed in terms of 'knowingly' assisted. Framing the question in the latter form all too often leads one into tortuous convolutions about the 'sort' of knowledge required, when the truth is that 'knowingly' is inapt as a criterion when applied to the gradually darkening spectrum where the differences are of degree and not kind.

Negligence
It is against this background that the question of negligence is to be addressed. This question, it should be remembered, is directed at whether an honest third party who receives no trust property should be liable if he procures or assists in a breach of trust of which he would have become aware had he exercised reasonable diligence. Should he be liable to the beneficiaries for the loss they suffer from the breach of trust?

The majority of persons falling into this category will be the hosts of people who act for trustees in various ways: as advisers, consultants, bankers and agents of many kinds. This category also includes officers and employees of companies in respect of the application of company funds. All these people will be accountable to the trustees for their conduct. For the most part they will owe to the trustees a duty to exercise reasonable skill and care. When that is so, the rights flowing from that duty form part of the trust property. As such they can be enforced by the beneficiaries in a suitable case if the trustees are unable or unwilling to do so. That being so, it is difficult to identify a compelling reason why, in addition to the duty of skill and care vis-à-vis the trustees which the third parties have accepted, or which the law has imposed upon them, third parties should also owe a duty of care directly to the beneficiaries. They have undertaken work for the trustees. They must carry out that work properly. If they fail to do so, they will be liable to make good the loss suffered by the trustees in consequence. This will include, where appropriate, the loss suffered by the trustees being exposed to claims for breach of trust.

Outside this category of persons who owe duties of skill and care to the trustees, there are others who will deal with trustees. If they have not accepted, and the law has not imposed upon them, any such duties in favour of the trustees, it is difficult to discern a good reason why they should nevertheless owe such duties to the beneficiaries.

There remains to be considered the position where third parties are acting for, or dealing with, dishonest trustees. In such cases the trustees would have no claims against the third party. The trustees would suffer no loss by reason of the third party's failure to discover what was going on. The question is whether in this type of situation the third party owes a duty of care to the beneficiaries to, in effect, check that a trustee is not misbehaving. The third party must act honestly. The question is whether that is enough.

In agreement with the preponderant view, their Lordships consider that dishonesty is an essential ingredient here. There may be cases where, in the light of the particular facts, a third party will owe a duty of care to the beneficiaries. As a general proposition, however, beneficiaries cannot reasonably expect that all the world dealing with their trustees should owe them a duty to take care lest the trustees are behaving dishonestly.

Unconscionable conduct
Mention, finally, must be made of the suggestion that the test for liability is that of unconscionable conduct. Unconscionable is a word of immediate appeal to an equity lawyer. Equity is rooted historically in the concept of the Lord Chancellor, as the keeper of the royal conscience, concerning himself with conduct which was contrary to good conscience. It must be recognised, however, that unconscionable is not a word in everyday use by non-lawyers. If it is to be used in this context, and if it is to be the touchstone for liability as an accessory, it is essential to be clear on what, in this context, unconscionable means. If unconscionable means no more than dishonesty, then dishonesty is the preferable label. If unconscionable means something different, it must be said that it is not clear what that something different is. Either way, therefore, the term is better avoided in this context.

The accessory liability principle
Drawing the threads together, their Lordships' overall conclusion is that
dishonesty is a necessary ingredient of accessory liability. It is also a sufficient
ingredient. A liability in equity to make good resulting loss attaches to a person
who dishonestly procures or assists in a breach of trust or fiduciary obligation.
It is not necessary that, in addition, the trustee or fiduciary was acting
dishonestly, although this will usually be so where the third party who is
assisting him is acting dishonestly. 'Knowingly' is better avoided as a defining
ingredient of the principle, and in the context of this principle the *Baden* scale
of knowledge is best forgotten.

Conclusion
From this statement of the principle it follows that this appeal succeeds. The
money paid to BLT on the sale of tickets for Royal Brunei Airlines was held
by BLT upon trust for the airline. This trust, on its face, conferred no power on
BLT to use the money in the conduct of its business. The trust gave no authority
to BLT to relieve its cash flow problems by utilising for this purpose the rolling
30-day credit afforded by the airline. Thus BLT committed a breach of trust by
using the money instead of simply deducting its commission and holding the
money intact until it paid the airline. The defendant accepted that he knowingly
assisted in that breach of trust. In other words, he caused or permitted his
company to apply the money in a way he knew was not authorised by the trust
of which the company was trustee. Set out in these bald terms, the defendant's
conduct was dishonest. By the same token, and for good measure, BLT also
acted dishonestly. The defendant was the company and his state of mind is to
be imputed to the company.

   The Court of Appeal held that it was not established that BLT was guilty of
fraud or dishonesty in relation to the amounts it held for the airline. Their
Lordships understand that by this the Court of Appeal meant that it was not
established that the defendant intended to defraud the airline. The defendant
hoped, maybe expected, to be able to pay the airline, but the money was lost in
the ordinary course of a poorly run business with heavy overhead expenses.
These facts are beside the point. The defendant had no right to employ the
money in the business at all. That was the breach of trust. The company's
inability to pay the airline was the consequence of that breach of trust.

   The Court of Appeal observed that it would have been unrealistic to expect
BLT to keep the money in a separate bank account and not use any of the
money in the conduct of the business, particularly as BLT was also the ticketing
agent for a number of other airlines. Their Lordships express no view on this,
or on what the parties are to be taken to have intended would happen in practice
when the company's current bank account was overdrawn. It is possible that
in certain circumstances these points might sustain an argument that, although
there was a failure to pay, there was no breach of trust. They do not arise in

this case because of the defendant's acceptance that there was a breach of trust.

Their Lordships will report their advice to His Majesty The Sultan and Yang Di-Pertuan that this appeal should be allowed, the order of the Court of Appeal set aside and the order of Roberts CJ restored. The defendant must pay the appellant's costs before their Lordships' Board and before the Court of Appeal."

Knowing Receipt of and Inconsistent Dealing with Trust Property

A recipient of property which has been misappropriated in breach of trust may be liable as a constructive trustee of this property provided that he possesses the necessary degree of knowledge of the breach of trust. Similarly, where a recipient of trust property deals with it in a manner which he knows to be inconsistent with the terms of the trust, he will be regarded as a constructive trustee of the property. However, considerable controversy surrounds the question of the degree of knowledge required to found liability under this heading.

The courts in this jurisdiction have applied the approach adopted by Buckley LJ in *Belmont Finance Corporation v. Williams Furniture Ltd (No. 2),* [17] namely that where a stranger to a trust receives trust property with either actual or constructive knowledge of the breach of trust, he will be regarded as a constructive trustee of this property. [18] Subsequent decisions in England have variously favoured the imposition of liability where the recipient possesses actual knowledge [19] or either actual or constructive knowledge [20] of the breach of trust and have even sought to distinguish between the type of knowledge required to found liability in commercial and non-commercial transactions. [21] In the recent decision of *Bank of Credit and Commerce International (Overseas) Ltd v. Akindele* [22] Nourse LJ expressed doubts about the utility of the traditional categorisation of knowledge in cases of knowing receipt and suggested that all that is necessary is that the recipient's state of knowledge should be such as to make it unconscionable for him to retain the benefit of the receipt.

---

[17] [1980] 1 All ER 393.
[18] *Re Frederick Inns Ltd* [1994] 1 ILRM 387 and *Ulster Factors Ltd v. Entoglen Ltd* High Court (Laffoy J) 21 February 1997.
[19] *Re Montagu's Settlement Trusts* [1987] Ch 264.
[20] *Agip (Africa) Ltd v. Jackson* [1990] Ch 265.
[21] *Eagle Trust plc v. SBC Securities Ltd* [1993] 1 WLR 484.
[22] [2000] 3 WLR 1423.

Re Frederick Inns Ltd
[1994] 1 ILRM 387

Payments were made by a group of associated companies to the Revenue Commissioners in the six months immediately preceding the commencement of the winding up of four of these companies out of the proceeds of sale of various licensed premises which had belonged to the companies. This sum was appropriated by the commissioners in reduction of the tax liabilities of not only the four companies involved in the proceedings but also those of six other companies in the group. The liquidator challenged these payments as being *ultra vires* in so far as they had effected an alienation of the companies' assets when they were insolvent. The Supreme Court upheld the liquidator's claim on the basis that no clause in the memoranda of association of any of the companies, properly construed, gave them power to pay the debts of an associate company. Blayney J held that the *ultra vires* payments constituted a misapplication by the directors of company funds in breach of their fiduciary duties and that these monies had been received by the Revenue Commissioners with constructive knowledge of this breach as the memoranda of association of the four companies revealed the absence of capacity. So, apart from the monies which the Revenue Commissioners had originally appropriated towards the discharge of the respective tax liabilities of the four companies involved in the proceedings, the payments were held by them on a constructive trust and had to be repaid to the official liquidator.

BLAYNEY J stated at pp. 397–399: "I would accordingly uphold the finding of the learned trial judge that the payments made by the four companies in reduction of the amounts owing by the other six companies were *ultra vires* and therefore void.

That brings me to the second issue to which I referred earlier and which is whether the learned trial judge was correct in the order he made in regard to how the *ultra vires* payments should be dealt with. He directed the Revenue Commissioners to credit to each of the four companies the difference between the amount of its contribution to the £1.2 million and the amount originally appropriated to it in reduction of what it owed to the Revenue Commissioners. This resulted in the entire of the contributions made by Frederick Inns Ltd, The Rendezvous Ltd and The Graduate Ltd being credited to those companies respectively and to £95,058 being credited to Motels Ltd, this amount being sufficient to discharge the entire of that company's liability. The only sum which the learned trial judge directed to be repaid was the balance of Motels Ltd's contribution which came to £651,919.

In my opinion the learned trial judge was not correct in directing that the *ultra vires* payments should be dealt with in this way. I am satisfied that the entire of these payments are held by the Revenue Commissioners on a constructive trust for the four companies and accordingly that they must be repaid to the companies without any deduction being made from them. I would respectfully adopt and apply the principle set out in the judgment of Buckley LJ (with whom Goff and Waller LJJ agreed) in *Belmont Finance Corporation Ltd v. Williams Furniture Ltd (No. 2)* [1980] 1 All ER 393 at p. 405:

> "A limited company is of course not a trustee of its own funds: it is their beneficial owner; but in consequence of the fiduciary character of their duties the directors of a limited company are treated as if they were trustees of those funds of the company which are in their hands or under their control, and if they misapply them they commit a breach of trust *(In re Lands Allotment Co.* [1894] 1 Ch 616 at p. 638, *per* Lindley and Kay LJJ). So, if the directors of a company in breach of their fiduciary duties misapply the funds of their company so that they come into the hands of some stranger to the trust who receives them with knowledge (actual or constructive) of the breach, he cannot conscientiously retain those funds against the company unless he has some better equity. He becomes a constructive trustee for the company of the misapplied funds. This is stated very clearly by Jessel MR in *Russell v. Wakefield Waterworks Co.* (1875) LR 20 Eq 474 at p. 479 where he said:
>
> > In this Court the money of the company is a trust fund, because it is applicable only to the special purposes of the company in the hands of the agents of the company, and it is in that sense a trust fund applicable by them to those special purposes; and a person taking it from them with notice that it is being applied to other purposes cannot in this Court say that he is not a constructive trustee."

This passage was cited with approval by Slade LJ in *Rolled Steel Products (Holdings) Ltd v. British Steel Corporation* [1986] Ch 246 at p. 298, and he added this comment which is particularly relevant to the present appeal:

> "The *Belmont* principle thus provides a legal route by which a company may recover its assets in a case where its directors have abused their fiduciary duties and a person receiving assets as a result of such abuse is on notice that they have been misapplied. The principle is not linked in any way to the capacity of the company; it is capable of applying whether or not the company had the capacity to do the acts in question."

The *ultra vires* payments in the present case were made on the authority of the directors of the four companies and, being *ultra vires,* they constituted a misapplication by the directors of the companies' funds and were found as a fact by the learned trial judge to be such a misapplication. The misapplication was a breach by the directors of their fiduciary duties and the monies were received by the Revenue Commissioners with constructive knowledge of the breach since, if they had read the memoranda of association of the four companies, as they could have done since they are documents of public record, they would have seen that the companies had no power to make the payments. It follows in my opinion that the Revenue Commissioners are constructive trustees of the sums which were the subject of the *ultra vires* payments and must repay them to the official liquidator for each of the companies. The particular amounts to be repaid are as follows:

Frederick Inns Ltd	£172,000
The Rendezvous Ltd	£76,506
The Graduate Ltd	£68,517
Motels Ltd	£746,977
TOTAL:	£1,064,000

I would therefore allow this appeal and direct that these sums be repaid by the Revenue Commissioners to the respective companies together with interest thereon at the statutory rate from time to time payable on judgment debts from 8 December 1986, being the date of the payment of the final instalment making up the £1.2 million, to the date of repayment."

Bank of Credit and Commerce International (Overseas) Ltd v. Akindele
[2000] 3 WLR 1423

The claimants were the liquidators of two banking companies, the employees of one of which had fraudulently procured the other to enter into an artificial but legally binding agreement with the defendant for the purpose of giving the false impression that certain dummy loans were performing normally. The claimants contended that the defendant was liable to account to them as a constructive trustee on the basis that he had knowingly assisted in a breach of trust or had received trust monies with knowledge of the breaches. Carnwath J dismissed the claim on the grounds that dishonesty by the defendant was the essential foundation of claimants' case whether under the head of knowing assistance or knowing receipt and this had not been established by the claimants. The claimants' appeal to the Court of Appeal (Nourse, Ward and Sedley LJJ) was dismissed on the basis that on his primary findings of fact, Carnwath J had been entitled to conclude that the defendant had acted honestly. However, Nourse LJ held that dishonesty was not a prerequisite to liability under the heading of knowing receipt and concluded that this assumption, on which the trial judge had proceeded, was incorrect in law.

NOURSE LJ stated at pp. 1430–1442:

"Dishonesty: the judge's findings
The judge stated his conclusions on the question of dishonesty, at p. 682:

> "In the end it does not seem to me to matter very much who negotiated the 1985 agreement. Whoever was actually dealing with the defendant, it would no doubt have been clear that the offer was being made with the authority of the senior management of BCCI. On the other hand, whoever it was, there is no basis for suggesting guilt by association. There is no evidence that anyone outside BCCI

had reason to doubt the integrity of the BCCI management at that time."

I interpose to make a point which, in the light of the arguments presented to us in this court, has assumed a great importance in the case. It is clear both from that passage and from the tenor of his judgment as a whole, in particular from the three concluding paragraphs quoted below, that the judge was of the view that the defendant had no knowledge of the underlying frauds within the BCCI group either in general or in relation to the 1985 and divestiture agreements in particular.

The judge then considered the defendant's credibility, saying that on the whole he found him to be a credible witness on most points, though on one issue, his interest in BCCI shares, he thought his answers at his oral examination were more reliable. He said that against that background the essential question he had to decide was a very narrow one. Was the defendant's involvement in the 1985 agreement dishonest, in the sense explained in the cases to which he had referred? He said at p. 682:

> "I am satisfied that he did not himself see it as a dishonest transaction. He saw it simply as an arm's-length business transaction with a major bank, for whom he was one of a select group of 'high net worth' customers, and was tying up US$10m for two years."

Accordingly, the judge said that the question was whether the defendant was dishonest by the objective standard explained by the Privy Council in *Royal Brunei Airlines Sdn Bhd v. Tan* [1995] 2 AC 378. He continued:

> "The plaintiffs' case depends on the high rate of interest and the artificial nature of the agreement. Were these two factors sufficient to put an honest person in the defendant's position on notice that some fraud or breach of trust was being perpetrated, even if he did not know its precise nature or purpose? I am not prepared to draw that conclusion. As I have said, in 1985 BCCI were regarded as a reputable international bank. The defendant would have had no reason to question the form of the transaction. It did not concern him, so long as his investment was guaranteed. Even though he was an experienced businessman, he had no duty to the bank or to its regulators which made it dishonest for him to do other than look after his own interests. If he had seen anything suspicious in it, I do not think he would have wanted to be involved. That would have been a matter of self-interest, just as it was when he decided to disassociate himself from BCCI in 1988. The form of the agreement was undoubtedly artificial, but there was nothing obviously illegal about it. The interest was very high, but he was entitled to assume that the bank were offering it in good faith and for proper reasons.
>
> The same considerations apply to the 1988 agreement. Although by that time the defendant did have suspicions as to the conduct of BCCI's affairs, he was entitled to take steps to protect his own interest. There was nothing dishonest in his seeking to enforce the 1985 agreement. As I have said, there is no suggestion that he was directly involved in the internal mechanics within BCCI, designed to avoid the scrutiny of the auditors.

> Dishonesty in one form or another is the essential foundation of the plaintiffs' case. They have not established it, and accordingly the claim must be dismissed."

The claimants' case in this court

The judge [1999] BCC 669, 675–676 identified the two main issues arising on the pleadings as being, first, was the defendant liable for dishonestly assisting or participating in breaches of trust by Messrs Naqvi, Hafeez and Kazmi (knowing assistance) and, secondly, was the defendant liable for receiving the divestiture payment with knowledge of the breaches of trust (knowing receipt). In this court the claimants' case has been maintained under both heads. In regard to knowing assistance, while accepting the judge's findings of primary fact, Mr Sheldon submitted that he was wrong not to infer from them that the defendant had acted dishonestly. I cannot accept that submission. Having seen and heard the defendant give evidence and found him to be a credible witness on most points, and after a conscientious consideration of the evidence as a whole, the judge was entitled to find that he had acted honestly. It cannot be said either that there was no evidence to support that finding or that it was against the weight of the evidence as a whole. The defendant not having acted dishonestly, the case in knowing assistance is bound to fail. If the claim is to succeed at all, it can only be in knowing receipt.

Knowing receipt

The essential requirements of knowing receipt were stated by Hoffmann LJ in *El Ajou v. Dollar Land Holdings Plc* [1994] 2 All ER 685, 700:

> "For this purpose the plaintiff must show, first, a disposal of his assets in breach of fiduciary duty; secondly, the beneficial receipt by the defendant of assets which are traceable as representing the assets of the plaintiff; and thirdly, knowledge on the part of the defendant that the assets he received are traceable to a breach of fiduciary duty."

In the present case the first two requirements were satisfied in relation to the defendant's receipt of the $16.679m paid to him pursuant to the divestiture agreement. But the satisfaction of the third requirement, knowledge on the part of the defendant that the sum received by him was traceable to a breach or breaches of fiduciary duty by Mr. Naqvi, Mr. Hafeez and Mr. Kazmi, is problematical.

So far as the law is concerned, the comprehensive arguments of Mr Sheldon and Mr Moss have demonstrated that there are two questions which, though closely related, are distinct: first, what, in this context, is meant by knowledge; second, is it necessary for the recipient to act dishonestly? Because the answer to it is the simpler, the convenient course is to deal with the second of those questions first.

Knowing receipt — dishonesty

As appears from the penultimate sentence of his judgment, Carnwath J proceeded on an assumption that dishonesty in one form or another was the essential foundation of the claimants' case, whether in knowing assistance or knowing receipt. That was no doubt caused by the acceptance before him (though not at any higher level) by Mr Sheldon, recorded at p. 677F, that the thrust of the recent authorities at first instance was that the recipient's state of knowledge must fall into one of the first three categories listed by Peter Gibson J in *Baden v. Société Générale pour Favoriser le Developpement du Commerce et de l'Industrie en France SA* [1993] 1 WLR 509, 575–576, on which basis, said Carnwath J, it was doubtful whether the test differed materially in practice from that for knowing assistance. However, the assumption on which the judge proceeded, derived as I believe from an omission to distinguish between the questions of knowledge and dishonesty, was incorrect in law. While a knowing recipient will often be found to have acted dishonestly, it has never been a prerequisite of the liability that he should.

An authoritative decision on this question, the complexity of whose subject transactions has sometimes caused it to be overlooked in this particular context, is *Belmont Finance Corp v. Williams Furniture Ltd (No. 2)* [1980] 1 All ER 393, where the plaintiff (Belmont) was the wholly-owned subsidiary of the second defendant (City), which in turn was the wholly-owned subsidiary of the first defendant (Williams). The chairman of all three companies and the sole effective force in the management of their affairs was Mr John James. Reduced to its essentials, what had happened there was that the shareholders of a fourth company (Maximum) had agreed to sell its shares to Belmont for £500,000 and to buy the share capital of Belmont from City for £489,000, a transaction which, as carried out, constituted a contravention of section 54 of the Companies Act 1948 (prohibition of provision of financial assistance by a company for the purchase of its own shares) and was thus a misapplication of Belmont's funds.

Belmont having subsequently become insolvent, its receiver obtained an independent valuation of the shares in Maximum as at the date of the transaction which suggested that, instead of being worth £500,000, they were only worth some £60,000. The receiver brought an action in Belmont's name principally against Williams, City and the shareholders of Maximum, claiming that they were liable to Belmont, first, for damages for conspiracy and, secondly, as constructive trustees on the grounds of both knowing assistance and knowing receipt. At the trial, Foster J found that Mr James genuinely believed that to buy the capital of Maximum for £500,000 was a good commercial proposition for Belmont. He held that there had been no contravention of section 54 and dismissed the action.

On Belmont's successful appeal to this court Buckley LJ is recorded, at p. 403, as having pointed out that Mr James had genuinely believed that the transaction was a good commercial proposition for Belmont without having any good grounds for that belief. He continued:

> "After careful consideration I do not feel that we should be justified in disturbing the judge's finding that Mr James genuinely believed that the agreement was a good commercial proposition for Belmont. It was a belief which, on his view of the commercial aspects of the case, Mr James could have sincerely held."

Having observed, at p. 404ᴇ, that Mr James, as a director of both Williams and City knew perfectly well what the objects of the transaction were, that other officers of City had the same knowledge and that their knowledge must be 'imputed' to the respective companies, and having referred, at p. 405ᴄ, to the judgment of Lord Selborne LC in *Barnes v. Addy* (1874) LR 9 Ch App 244 at 251-252, Buckley LJ dealt with the claim in constructive trust [1980] 1 All ER 393, 405:

> "In the present case, the payment of the £500,000 by Belmont to [the shareholders of Maximum], being an unlawful contravention of section 54, was a misapplication of Belmont's money and was in breach of the duties of the directors of Belmont. £489,000 of the £500,000 so misapplied found their way into the hands of City with City's knowledge of the whole circumstances of the transaction. It must follow, in my opinion, that City is accountable to Belmont as a constructive trustee of the £489,000 under the first of Lord Selborne LC's two heads. There remains the question whether City is chargeable as a constructive trustee under Lord Selborne LC's second head on the ground that Belmont's directors were guilty of dishonesty in buying the shares of Maximum and that City with knowledge of the facts assisted them in that dishonest design. As I understand Lord Selborne LC's second head, a stranger to a trust notwithstanding that he may not have received any of the trust fund which has been misapplied will be treated as accountable as a constructive trustee if he has knowingly participated in a dishonest design on the part of the trustees to misapply the fund; he must himself have been in some way a party to the dishonesty of the trustees. It follows from what I have already held that the directors of Belmont were guilty of misfeasance but not that they acted dishonestly."

Goff LJ also held that City was liable in knowing receipt (see at 410-412). Waller LJ did not add anything of his own on the question of constructive trust.

Accordingly, though the claim in knowing assistance failed because the directors of Belmont did not act dishonestly, the claim in knowing receipt succeeded. I will return to that decision when dealing with the question of knowledge.

The decision in *Belmont (No. 2)* is clear authority for the proposition that dishonesty is not a necessary ingredient of liability in knowing receipt. There have been other, more recent, judicial pronouncements to the same effect. Thus in *Polly Peck International Plc v. Nadir (No. 2)* [1992] 4 All ER 769, 777ᴅ, Scott LJ said that liability in a knowing receipt case did not require that the misapplication of the trust funds should be fraudulent. While in theory it is possible for a misapplication not to be fraudulent and the recipient to be dishonest, in practice such a combination must be rare. Similarly, in *Agip (Africa) Ltd v. Jackson* [1990] Ch 265, 292, Millett J said that in knowing receipt it was immaterial whether the breach of trust was fraudulent or not. The point was made most clearly by Vinelott J in *Eagle Trust plc v. SBC Securities Ltd* [1993] 1 WLR 484, 497:

> "What the decision in *Belmont (No. 2)* shows is that in a 'knowing receipt' case it is only necessary to show that the defendant knew that the moneys paid to him were trust moneys and of circumstances which made the payment a misapplication of them. Unlike a 'knowing assistance' case it is not necessary, and never has been necessary, to show that the defendant was in any sense a participator in a fraud."

Knowing receipt — the authorities on knowledge
With the proliferation in the last 20 years or so of cases in which the misapplied assets of companies have come into the hands of third parties, there has been a sustained judicial and extra-judicial debate as to the knowledge on the part of the recipient which is required in order to found liability in knowing receipt. Expressed in its simplest terms, the question is whether the recipient must have actual knowledge (or the equivalent) that the assets received are traceable to a breach of trust or whether constructive knowledge is enough. The instinctive approach of most equity judges, especially in this court, has been to assume that constructive knowledge is enough. But there is now a series of decisions of eminent first instance judges who, after considering the question in greater depth, have come to the contrary conclusion, at all events when commercial transactions are in point. In the Commonwealth, on the other hand, the preponderance of authority has been in favour of the view that constructive knowledge is enough.

In *Karak Rubber Co Ltd v. Burden (No. 2)* [1972] 1 WLR 602, 632, Brightman J referred to a person:

> "who is a constructive trustee because (though not nominated as a trustee) he has received trust property with actual or constructive notice that it is trust property transferred in breach of trust . . ."

In *Belmont (No. 2)* [1980] 1 All ER 393, 405 Buckley LJ referred to the principle, established by the decision of this court in *In re Lands Allotment Co.* [1894] 1 Ch 616, that the directors of a company are treated as if they were actual trustees of the assets of the company which are in their hands or under their control. He continued:

> "So, if the directors of a company in breach of their fiduciary duties misapply the funds of their company so that they come into the hands of some stranger to the trust who receives them with knowledge (actual or constructive) of the breach, he cannot conscientiously retain those funds against the company unless he has some better equity. He becomes a constructive trustee for the company of the misapplied funds."

Goff LJ [1980] 1 All ER 393, 410 said that what Belmont had to show, amongst other things, was that City received all or part of the £500,000 'knowing, or in circumstances in which it ought to know, that it was a breach of trust'. He answered that question saying at p. 412:

> "In my judgment the answer to that question must plainly be Yes, for they are fixed with all the knowledge that Mr James had. Now, he had actual knowledge of all the facts which made the agreement illegal and his belief that the agreement was a good commercial proposition for Belmont can be no more a defence to City's liability as constructive trustees than in conspiracy. Apart from this, clearly, in my judgment, Mr James knew or ought to have known all the facts that I have rehearsed, showing that there was in any event a misfeasance apart from illegality."

Similarly, in *Rolled Steel Products (Holdings) Ltd v. British Steel Corp* [1986] Ch 246, 306-307, Browne-Wilkinson LJ said:

> "A third party, who has notice – actual or constructive – that a transaction, although intra vires the company, was entered into in excess or abuse of the powers of the company, cannot enforce such transaction against the company and will be accountable as constructive trustee for any money or property of the company received by [him]."

In *Agip (Africa) Ltd v. Jackson* [1990] Ch 265, 291, Millett J, in reference to a person who receives for his own benefit trust property transferred to him in breach of trust, said:

> "He is liable as a constructive trustee if he received it with notice, actual or constructive, that it was trust property and that the transfer to him was a breach of trust . . ."

In *Houghton v. Fayers* [2000] 1 BCLC 511, 516, I myself said that it was enough for the claimant company to establish that the second defendant 'knew or ought to have known that the money had been paid to him in breach of [the first defendant's] fiduciary duty to [the claimant]'.

Collectively, those observations might be thought to provide strong support for the view that constructive knowledge is enough. But it must at once be said that in each of the three cases in this court (including, despite some apparent uncertainty in the judgment of Goff LJ (at p. 412F) in *Belmont (No. 2)*), actual knowledge was found and, further, that the decisions in the *Karak* case and the *Agip* case were based on knowing assistance, not knowing receipt. Thus in none of the five cases was it necessary for the question to be examined in any depth and there appears to be no case in which such an examination has been conducted in this court. The groundwork has been done in other cases at first instance. I will refer to those of them in which the question has been considered in depth.

The seminal judgment, characteristically penetrative in its treatment of authority and, in the best sense, argumentative, is that of Megarry V-C in *Re*

Sir Robert Montagu's Settlement Trusts, Duke of Manchester v. National Westminster Bank Ltd (1985) [1987] Ch 264. It was he who first plumbed the distinction between notice and knowledge. It was he who, building on a passage in the judgment of this court in *In re Diplock* [1948] Ch 465, 478-479, first emphasised the fundamental difference between the questions which arise in respect of the doctrine of purchaser without notice on the one hand and the doctrine of constructive trusts on the other. Reading from his earlier judgment in the same case, he said [1987] Ch 264, 278:

> "The former is concerned with the question whether a person takes property subject to or free from some equity. The latter is concerned with whether or not a person is to have imposed upon him the personal burdens and obligations of trusteeship. I do not see why one of the touchstones for determining the burdens on property should be the same as that for deciding whether to impose a personal obligation on a [person]. The cold calculus of constructive and imputed notice does not seem to me to be an appropriate instrument for deciding whether a [person's] conscience is sufficiently affected for it to be right to bind him by the obligations of a constructive trustee."

He added that there is more to being made a trustee than merely taking property subject to an equity.

The practical importance of that distinction had been explained by Megarry V-C in his earlier judgment. The question in that case was whether the widow and executrix of the will of the tenth Duke of Manchester was liable to account to the eleventh Duke in respect of certain settled chattels or the proceeds of sale thereof. Having found that the tenth Duke had had no knowledge that the chattels received by him were still subject to any trust and that he believed that they had been lawfully and properly released to him by the trustees, Megarry V-C continued, at p. 272:

> "If liability as a constructive trustee depended on his knowledge, then he was not liable as a constructive trustee, and his estate is not liable for any chattels that have been disposed of, as distinct from any traceable proceeds of them. Even if he was not a constructive trustee and was a mere volunteer, his estate is liable to yield up any chattels that remain, or the traceable proceeds of any that have gone ... But, unless he was a constructive trustee, there appears to be no liability if the chattels have gone and there are no traceable proceeds."

Megarry V-C summarised his conclusions in eight subparagraphs, at p. 285. I read the first three:

> "(1) The equitable doctrine of tracing and the imposition of a constructive trust by reason of the knowing receipt of trust property are governed by different rules and must be kept distinct. Tracing is primarily a means of determining the rights of property, whereas the imposition of a constructive trust creates personal obligations that go beyond mere property rights. (2) In considering whether a constructive trust has arisen in a case of the knowing receipt of trust property, the basic question is whether the conscience of the recipient is sufficiently

affected to justify the imposition of such a trust. (3) Whether a constructive trust arises in such a case primarily depends on the knowledge of the recipient, and not on notice to him; and for clarity it is desirable to use the word 'knowledge' and avoid the word 'notice' in such cases."

The effect of Megarry V-C's decision, broadly stated, was that, in order to establish liability in knowing receipt, the recipient must have actual knowledge (or the equivalent) that the assets received are traceable to a breach of trust and that constructive knowledge is not enough.

In *Eagle Trust Plc v. SBC Securities Ltd* [1993] 1 WLR 484, 503E, Vinelott J did not think it would be right to found a decision that the statement of claim in that case disclosed no cause of action solely on the authority of *In re Montagu's Settlement Trusts*. However, on the ground that he (unlike Megarry V-C) was dealing with a commercial transaction, he arrived at the same conclusion and held that in such a transaction constructive knowledge is not enough. He cited [1993] 1 WLR 484, 504 a well-known passage in the judgment of Lindley LJ in *Manchester Trust v. Furness* [1895] 2 QB 539, 545, the latter part of which reads thus:

> "In dealing with estates in land title is everything, and it can be leisurely investigated; in commercial transactions possession is everything, and there is no time to investigate title; and if we were to extend the doctrine of constructive notice to commercial transactions we should be doing infinite mischief and paralyzing the trade of the country."

The decision of Vinelott J was followed by Knox J in *Cowan de Groot Properties Ltd v. Eagle Trust Plc* [1992] 4 All ER 700 (another case of a commercial transaction) and the decisions of both of them by Arden J at the trial of the action in *Eagle Trust Plc v. SBC Securities Ltd (No. 2)* [1996] 1 BCLC 121.

We were also referred to three decisions in New Zealand and one in Canada. In each of *Westpac Banking Corp v. Savin* [1985] 2 NZLR 41, *Equiticorp Industries Group Ltd v. Hawkins* [1991] 3 NZLR 700 and *Lankshear v. ANZ Banking Group (New Zealand) Ltd* [1993] 1 NZLR 481 the preferred view was that constructive knowledge was enough, although in the last-named case the point went by concession. All of them were cases of commercial transactions. In *Westpac Banking Corp v. Savin*, a decision of the Court of Appeal, Richardson J, having expressed a provisional preference for the view that constructive knowledge was enough, said, at p. 53:

> "Clearly courts would not readily import a duty to inquire in the case of commercial transactions where they must be conscious of the seriously inhibiting effects of a wide application of the doctrine. Nevertheless there must be cases where there is no justification on the known facts for allowing a commercial man who has received funds paid to him in breach of trust to plead the shelter of the exigencies of commercial life."

In *Citadel General Assurance Co v. Lloyds Bank Canada* (1997) 152 DLR (4th) 411, another case of a commercial transaction, the Supreme Court of Canada held, as a matter of decision, that constructive knowledge was enough.

The Baden case
It will have been observed that up to this stage I have made no more than a passing reference to the fivefold categorisation of knowledge accepted by Peter Gibson J in the *Baden* case [1993] 1 WLR 509, 575-576: (i) actual knowledge; (ii) wilfully shutting one's eyes to the obvious; (iii) wilfully and recklessly failing to make such inquiries as an honest and reasonable man would make; (iv) knowledge of circumstances which would indicate the facts to an honest and reasonable man; (v) knowledge of circumstances which will put an honest and reasonable man on inquiry. Reference to the categorisation has been made in most of the knowing receipt cases to which I have referred from *Re Montagu's Settlement Trusts* onwards. In many of them it has been influential in the decision. In general, the first three categories have been taken to constitute actual knowledge (or its equivalent) and the last two constructive knowledge.

Two important points must be made about the *Baden* categorisation. First, it appears to have been propounded by counsel for the plaintiffs, accepted by counsel for the defendant and then put to the judge on an agreed basis. Secondly, though both counsel accepted that all five categories of knowledge were relevant and neither sought to submit that there was any distinction for that purpose between knowing receipt and knowing assistance (a view with which the judge expressed his agreement (see [1993] 1 WLR 509, 582E-F), the claim in constructive trust was based squarely on knowing assistance and not on knowing receipt (see p. 572D). In the circumstances, whatever may have been agreed between counsel, it is natural to assume that the categorisation was not formulated with knowing receipt primarily in mind. This, I think, may be confirmed by the references to 'an honest and reasonable man' in categories (iv) and (v). Moreover, in the *Agip* case (at p. 293) Millett J warned against over refinement or a too ready assumption that categories (iv) and (v) are necessarily cases of constructive knowledge only, reservations which were shared by Knox J in the *Cowan de Groot* case [1992] 4 All ER 700, 761G.

Knowing receipt – the recipient's state of knowledge
In *Royal Brunei Airlines Sdn Bhd v. Tan*, which is now the leading authority on knowing assistance, Lord Nicholls of Birkenhead, in delivering the judgment of the Privy Council, said at p. 392G that 'knowingly' was better avoided as a defining ingredient of the liability, and that in that context the *Baden* categorisation was best forgotten. Although my own view is that the categorisation is often helpful in identifying different states of knowledge which may or may not result in a finding of dishonesty for the purposes of knowing assistance, I have grave doubts about its utility in cases of knowing receipt. Quite apart from its origins in a context of knowing assistance and the

reservations of Millett and Knox JJ, any categorisation is of little value unless the purpose it is to serve is adequately defined, whether it be fivefold, as in the *Baden* case, or twofold, as in the classical division between actual and constructive knowledge, a division which has itself become blurred in recent authorities.

What then, in the context of knowing receipt, is the purpose to be served by a categorisation of knowledge? It can only be to enable the court to determine whether, in the words of Buckley LJ in *Belmont (No. 2)* [1980] 1 All ER 393, 405, the recipient can 'conscientiously retain [the] funds against the company' or, in the words of Megarry V-C in *In re Montagu's Settlement Trusts*, '[the recipient's] conscience is sufficiently affected for it to be right to bind him by the obligations of a constructive trustee'. But if that is the purpose, there is no need for categorisation. All that is necessary is that the recipient's state of knowledge should be such as to make it unconscionable for him to retain the benefit of the receipt.

For these reasons I have come to the view that, just as there is now a single test of dishonesty for knowing assistance, so ought there to be a single test of knowledge for knowing receipt. The recipient's state of knowledge must be such as to make it unconscionable for him to retain the benefit of the receipt. A test in that form, though it cannot, any more than any other, avoid difficulties of application, ought to avoid those of definition and allocation to which the previous categorisations have led. Moreover, it should better enable the courts to give commonsense decisions in the commercial context in which claims in knowing receipt are now frequently made, paying equal regard to the wisdom of Lindley LJ on the one hand and of Richardson J on the other.

Knowing receipt – a footnote
We were referred in argument to 'Knowing Receipt: The Need for a New Landmark', an essay by Lord Nicholls in Cornish, Nolan, O'Sullivan and Virgo (eds), *Restitution Past, Present and Future: Essays in Honour of Gareth Jones* (1998), p. 231, a work of insight and scholarship taking forward the writings of academic authors, in particular those of Professors Birks, Burrows and Gareth Jones. It is impossible to do justice to such a work within the compass of a judgment such as this. Most pertinent for present purposes is the suggestion made by Lord Nicholls, at p. 238, in reference to the decision of the House of Lords in *Lipkin Gorman v. Karpnale Ltd* [1991] 2 AC 548:

> "In this respect equity should now follow the law. Restitutionary liability, applicable regardless of fault but subject to a defence of change of position, would be a better-tailored response to the underlying mischief of misapplied property than personal liability which is exclusively fault-based. Personal liability would flow from having received the property of another, from having been unjustly enriched at the expense of another. It would be triggered by the mere fact of receipt, thus recognising the endurance of property rights. But fairness would be ensured by the need to identify a gain, and by making change of position

available as a defence in suitable cases when, for instance, the recipient had changed his position in reliance on the receipt."

Lord Nicholls goes on to examine the Diplock principle, suggesting at p. 241 that it could be reshaped by being extended to all trusts but in a form modified to take proper account of the decision in *Lipkin Gorman v. Karpnale Ltd.*

No argument before us was based on the suggestions made in Lord Nicholls' essay. Indeed, at this level of decision, it would have been a fruitless exercise. We must continue to do our best with the accepted formulation of the liability in knowing receipt, seeking to simplify and improve it where we may. While in general it may be possible to sympathise with a tendency to subsume a further part of our law of restitution under the principles of unjust enrichment, I beg leave to doubt whether strict liability coupled with a change of position defence would be preferable to fault-based liability in many commercial transactions, for example where, as here, the receipt is of a company's funds which have been misapplied by its directors. Without having heard argument it is unwise to be dogmatic, but in such a case it would appear to be commercially unworkable and contrary to the spirit of the rule in *Royal British Bank v. Turquand* (1856) 6 E & B 327 that, simply on proof of an internal misapplication of the company's funds, the burden should shift to the recipient to defend the receipt either by a change of position or perhaps in some other way. Moreover, if the circumstances of the receipt are such as to make it unconscionable for the recipient to retain the benefit of it, there is an obvious difficulty in saying that it is equitable for a change of position to afford him a defence.

Knowing receipt – the facts of the present case
I return to the facts of the present case, in order to determine whether the defendant is liable in knowing receipt to repay (together with interest) $6.679m of the sum received by him pursuant to the divestiture agreement, being the excess over the $10m he paid to ICIC Overseas pursuant to the 1985 agreement. (By a decision whose forensic good sense dispensed with an analysis of its juristic foundation the claimants abandoned a claim for the full $16.679m.) The answer to that question depends on whether the judge's findings, though made in the course of an inquiry as to the defendant's honesty, are equally supportive of a conclusion that his state of knowledge was not such as to make it unconscionable for him to retain the benefit of the receipt.

I start with the defendant's state of knowledge at the date of the 1985 agreement. As to that, the judge found that there was no evidence that anyone outside BCCI had reason to doubt the integrity of its management at that time. More specifically, it is clear that the judge was of the view that the defendant had no knowledge of the underlying frauds within the BCCI group either in general or in relation to the 1985 agreement. He found that the defendant saw it simply as an arm's-length business transaction. Moreover, he was not prepared to draw the conclusion that the high rate of interest and the artificial nature of the agreement were sufficient to put an honest person in the defendant's position on notice that some fraud or breach of trust was being perpetrated. He said that the defendant would have had no reason to question the form of the transaction.

Those findings, expressed in language equally appropriate to an inquiry as to constructive notice, appear to me to be consistent only with the view that the defendant's state of knowledge at the date of the 1985 agreement was not such as to make it unconscionable for him to enter into it. However, that point, though of great importance, is not in itself decisive. We have also to consider the defendant's state of knowledge at the date of the divestiture agreement, by which time, as the judge said, he did have suspicions as to the conduct of BCCI's affairs.

In order to understand the judge's reference, it is necessary to go back to what he said [1999] BCC 669, 675:

> "Towards the end of 1988 the defendant decided to end his relationship with BCCI, and in particular to terminate the share agreement. A number of factors led to this decision. In late 1987 there had been rumours in the Nigerian press of irregularities involving BCCI. He had received warnings from senior business figures in Nigeria. One was Dr Onaolapo Soleye, a former Nigerian Minister of Finance, who has provided a witness statement. He says that he informed the defendant of "unorthodox and irregular banking practices around the world", and warned him of the effect a scandal relating to BCCI could have on his business image and that of BCCI Nigeria. The defendant also became aware later in 1988 that various BCCI officials had been arrested by US Customs in Tampa in connection with money laundering offences. He considered selling his shares in BCCI Nigeria, but was dissuaded from doing so by Dr Soleye and others, because of the tribal imbalance it would create within the bank. At this time the defendant was seeking to realise £20m of his own money, and to raise a further £40m, to finance a property investment venture in the UK. The major banks involved, including NM Rothschild in London and BNP, objected to him raising part of the finance from BCCI."

So in late 1987, more than two years after the 1985 agreement was entered into, there were press rumours of irregularities involving BCCI and warnings to the defendant from senior business figures in Nigeria of unorthodox and irregular banking practices around the world. Later in 1988 the defendant became aware that various BCCI officials had been arrested in connection with money laundering offences. He also knew that the major banks involved in financing his property investment venture in the United Kingdom objected to his raising part of the finance from BCCI.

There having been no evidence that the defendant was aware of the internal arrangements within BCCI which led to the payment to him of the $16.679m pursuant to the divestiture agreement, did the additional knowledge which he acquired between July 1985 and December 1988 make it unconscionable for him to retain the benefit of the receipt? In my judgment it did not. The additional knowledge went to the general reputation of the BCCI group from late 1987 onwards. It was not a sufficient reason for questioning the propriety of a particular transaction entered into more than two years earlier, at a time when no one outside BCCI had reason to doubt the integrity of its management and in a form which the defendant had no reason to question. The judge said that the defendant was entitled to take steps to protect his own interest, and that there was nothing dishonest in his seeking to enforce the 1985 agreement. Nor was there anything unconscionable in his seeking to do so. Equally, had I thought that that was still the appropriate test, I would have held that the defendant did not have actual or constructive knowledge that his receipt of the $6.79m was traceable to a breach or breaches of fiduciary duty by Messrs Naqvi, Hafeez and Kazmi.

Conclusion
For these reasons, though by a different route in relation to knowing receipt, I have come to the conclusion that Carnwath J's decision to dismiss the action was correct. I would affirm it and dismiss the claimants' appeal."

THE VENDOR AS CONSTRUCTIVE TRUSTEE

Where a vendor enters into a specifically enforceable contract for sale, equity regards him as a type of constructive trustee of the property which forms the subject matter of the contract until completion, but only to the extent to which the purchase price has been paid.[23] Once the beneficial interest passes, the vendor is treated as a constructive trustee[24] of the property in the sense that he is obliged to take reasonable care of it.[25] However, it is only where the vendor acts in breach of his trust obligations or fails to take reasonable care that he can be made liable and any damage to the property which occurs without any fault on the part of the vendor is the responsibility of the purchaser. Traditionally it was accepted that when a purchaser entered into a specifically enforceable contract for sale, the risk of accidental damage to the property passed to him and that he should insure against such risk.[26] However, this position has been criticised as being unfair to purchasers[27] and clause 43 of the Law Society

---

[23] *Tempany v. Hynes* [1976] IR 101, 114 *per* Kenny J. The minority view expressed by Henchy J (at p.109) was that the beneficial ownership is treated as having passed to the purchaser from the time the contract was entered into, irrespective of whether the purchase money has been paid. See also *Lysaght v. Edwards* (1876) 2 Ch D 499, 506.

[24] Although as Cotton LJ pointed out in *Rayner v. Preston* (1881) 18 Ch D 1, 6 a vendor is treated as a trustee 'in a qualified sense only'.

[25] *Clarke v. Ramuz* [1891] 2 QB 456.

[26] *Lysaght v. Edwards* (1876) 2 Ch D 499, 507.

[27] The Law Reform Commission (LRC 39 - 1991) recommended that the risk should instead

Standard Conditions of Sale provides that the risk shall remain with the vendor until completion.

Clarke v. Ramuz
[1891] 1 QB 456

While the vendor of land remained in possession, a trespasser removed all the surface soil. It was held by the Court of Appeal (Lord Coleridge CJ, Bowen and Kay LJJ) that the purchaser could maintain an action against the vendor for breach of trust by reason of the fact that he had taken no care to prevent the removal of the soil.

LORD COLERIDGE CJ stated at pp.459–461: "The contention is that such an action as this will not lie. It appears to be well established in equity that, in the case of a contract for the sale and purchase of land, although the legal property does not pass until the execution of the conveyance, during the interval prior to completion the vendor in possession is a trustee for the purchaser, and as such has duties to perform towards him, not exactly the same as in the case of other trustees, but certain duties, one of which is to use reasonable care to preserve the property in a reasonable state of preservation, and, so far as may be, as it was when the contract was made. Of course, where from any cause a long period of time elapses during which such possession of the vendor continues and deterioration of the property takes place, other considerations may come in; but in this case the injury complained of is the removal of a considerable portion of the soil for purposes for which the vendor had no right to allow such removal without the consent of the purchaser. The case of *Phillips v. Silvester* (1872) LR 8 Ch App 173 is stated by Mr. Dart to have been commented upon by Jessel, M.R.; but the doctrine that the vendor in possession is under such circumstances a trustee for the purchaser appears to have been entirely acquiesced in by him in the subsequent case of *Earl of Egmont v. Smith* (1877) 6 Ch D 469. *Phillips v. Silvester* is a decision with which we not only agree, but which is binding upon us. It lays down in clear terms under circumstances hardly distinguishable from those which exist in the present case, that there is such a duty as I have mentioned incumbent upon a vendor in possession after a contract for sale. If there is such a duty, it is clear in the present case that there has been a breach of it, because no care has been taken by the vendor to keep the property in the state in which it was when the contract was made. The counsel for the defendant were driven to contend that no care was under the circumstances reasonable care, a position which cannot possibly be supported. Then it was contended that by reason of the execution of the

---

pass to the purchaser 'in all situations where the purchaser goes into possession of the premises, or on completion of the purchase whichever is the earlier'.

conveyance there was an end of any remedy for the breach of trust which had taken place, and which had lessened the value of the land. I could understand that, where the purchaser knew what had happened, it might possibly be argued that, by reason of his taking a conveyance without making any claim in respect of the breach of trust, there was evidence of a waiver by him of his right; but, where, as in this case, neither party, at the time when the conveyance was executed, knew anything about what had happened, I cannot see any ground whatever for the suggestion that the execution of the conveyance had the effect contended for by the defendant. It appears to me clear on principle, and upon the authority of the decision in *Phillips v. Silvester*, followed, as it has been, by Jessel M.R., in *Earl of Egmont v. Smith* and by Kekewich J., in *Royal Bristol Permanent Building Society v. Bomash* (1887) 35 Ch D 390, that this action is maintainable; and that, therefore, this application must be dismissed."

MUTUAL WILLS

Where two people, usually although not necessarily husband and wife, make an arrangement concerning the disposal of their property and execute mutual wills which are intended to be irrevocable and the survivor subsequently alters his will, his estate will be held by his personal representatives on a constructive trust to give effect to the arrangement provided for in the mutual wills. However, there must be evidence of an agreement to make mutual wills in substantially similar form and not to revoke them. While the fact that the wills are made simultaneously and in substantially similar form is a relevant factor to be taken into account in determining whether such an agreement exists,[28] it is not of itself sufficient proof that the parties have entered into a legally binding agreement to make mutual wills and not to revoke them.[29]

Re Goodchild
[1997] 1 WLR 1216

The testator and his wife both executed wills in identical terms leaving their respective estates to each other and there was evidence that their intention was that after their deaths the first named plaintiff, their only son, should inherit their estates. After his wife's death, the testator married the defendant and six weeks after making a new will in which he left his entire estate to her, he died. The first named plaintiff brought an action seeking, *inter alia*, a declaration that after the death of his first wife, the testator held her estate on trust for the plaintiff, and that after the testator's death, the defendant held his estate

---

[28] *Re Cleaver* [1981] 1 WLR 939.
[29] *Re Oldham* [1925] Ch 75.

similarly. The Court of Appeal held that the wills were not mutually binding, although it concluded that Carnwath J had been correct to grant the first named plaintiff an order under section 2 of the Inheritance (Provision for Family and Dependants) Act 1975.

LEGATT LJ stated at pp. 1221–1226:

"Mutual Wills
Crucial to this topic is the evidence. The judge attached particular weight to that of three friends of the family, Mrs Fiddy, Mr Cutler and Laura White. Mrs Fiddy was a qualified accountant who acted as such for the business run by her husband and Dennis. The Fiddys had made wills in each other's favour, with the estate going to their son after they had both died. The Goodchilds later told her that they had done the same. But the Fiddys' wills were made at different times and were not expressed to be mutually binding. Mr Cutler similarly told Dennis that he and his wife had made mutually binding wills, and in 1988 Dennis told him that the Goodchilds had done the same. On another occasion Dennis told Mr Cutler that when he died Gary would inherit the whole estate. Mr Cutler understood that Joan and Dennis intended the wills to be mutually binding, with the result that money owed by Gary to his parents for his business would in effect be cancelled after the death of Dennis. But Mr Cutler's will stated that the survivor would be bound, and the wills of himself and his wife were in the same form and contained the words "mutually agreed". Laura White was the Goodchilds' housekeeper between 1986 and 1988. Joan told her that she and her husband had made mutually binding wills leaving everything to Gary, so that his business debts would die with them.

Against this evidence the judge had to set that of Mr George, the family solicitor. He had never advised a client to make a "mutually binding will", nor would he have done so. He would have advised a client either to leave the property to the other spouse with a provision for the estate to go to the heir in default of survivor, or to grant a life interest to the survivor. The judge said of Mr George, at p. 706, that:

> "He had no doubt that the Goodchilds wished to adopt the former course, because Dennis would not have favoured the limitations of a life interest."

The judge expressed his conclusion in the four passages that I must now set out. First, he said at p. 706:

> "Faced with this conflict of evidence, I have to bear in mind that the onus of proof lies on the plaintiffs, and that, as the cases show, there must be established evidence of a specific agreement outside the wills, not just some loose understanding or sense of moral obligation. I also bear in mind that this was part of a wider scheme under which the Goodchilds made arrangements for the disposal of their business to their son. Considerable care was taken to obtain legal and accountancy advice on these arrangements. This is a far cry from the

simple domestic arrangements made by Mr and Mrs Fiddy in the early 1950's. I also bear in mind that Dennis was an experienced businessman, who knew his own mind, and was likely to have made his wishes known to his solicitor. In those circumstances, the weight of the evidence of his family solicitor, with whom he had worked closely on a number of occasions is considerable."

Next he said at pp. 706–707:

"I am prepared to accept that Joan understood that her intentions would be binding upon her husband after her death, indeed that one of the reasons for making the will at that time in that form was to get that assurance. However, I would not have expected her to have taken much part in the conversation with Mr George on 13 January. Equally, I would accept that Dennis would at that stage have taken it for granted that the common intention would be put into effect. From what I have heard, he was a devoted husband and would have wanted to do everything he could to ease her suffering and put her mind at rest. However, he may not have thought it necessary to have any particular provisions in the will to force him to do what he would have envisaged himself doing in any event."

The judge then remarked, at p. 707:

"It is also important, as I have said, that this took place at the time when the future of the business was being provided for. If any of the parties, including Gary, had thought that some form of mutually binding agreement was to be made for the position after the parents' death, I am sure there would have been a specific record of its being mentioned in connection with the other formal arrangements being made for the transfer of the business."

Finally in relation to the argument that there was some form of binding agreement or estoppel outside the formal 1988 documents upon which Gary was entitled to rely the judge said, at pp. 708–709:

"The plaintiff needs to show that there was some agreement, or representation intended to have legal effect, to which the court should give effect. However, the evidence fails to convince me that there was anything, apart from the genuine understanding to which I have already referred. In particular, none of the witnesses who spoke of the payments under the legal charge ceasing on death, suggested there was a separate agreement distinct from the effect of what they thought to be mutually binding wills. Obviously, if Gary had inherited the whole estate, then there would have been no further payments under the charge, since he would have become the beneficiary. However, I have no evidence of any separate agreement to that effect, and, as I have already observed, the comprehensive and formal nature of the legal documents drawn up in September 1988 makes it difficult to infer any such collateral agreement or representation. I therefore reject this part of the claim."

Mr Gordon submitted that on the authorities, it is sufficient for Gary to show a common understanding between the two testators at the time of the wills. If neither testator has given notice to the other that they withdraw from the understanding, upon the death of the first testator the obligation becomes a legal one. He drew an analogy with secret trusts, where equity will not permit property transferred to another on the faith of an agreement or understanding to be dealt with differently from that understanding. For that principle he relied on *In re Cleaver dec'd* [1981] 1 WLR 939 in which, after citing extensively from the judgment of Dixon J. in *Birmingham v. Renfrew* (1937) 57 CLR 666, Nourse J. said at page 947:

> "It is also clear from *Birmingham v. Renfrew* . . . that these cases of mutual wills are only one example of a wider category of cases, for example secret trusts, in which a court of equity will intervene to impose a constructive trust. . . . The principle of all these cases is that a court of equity will not permit a person to whom property is transferred by way of gift, but on the faith of an agreement or clear understanding that it is to be dealt with in a particular way for the benefit of a third person, to deal with that property inconsistently with that agreement or understanding. . . . I would emphasise that the agreement or understanding must be such as to impose on the donee a legally binding obligation to deal with the property in the particular way and that the other two certainties, namely, those as to the subject matter of the trust and the persons intended to benefit under it, are as essential to this species of trust as they are to any other."

He added, at p. 947 that:

> ".... the principal difficulty is always whether there was a legally binding obligation or merely what Lord Loughborough L.C. in *Lord Walpole v. Lord Orford* (1797) 3 Ves 402, 419, described as an honourable engagement."

Nourse J. emphasised that "an enforceable agreement to dispose of property in pursuance of mutual wills can be established only by clear and satisfactory evidence." Mr Gordon referred to *Ottaway v. Norman* [1972] 1 Ch 698, which concerned a secret trust. Brightman J. said at p. 711:

> "It will be convenient to call the person upon whom such a trust is imposed the 'primary donee' and the beneficiary under that trust the 'secondary donee.' The essential elements which must be proved to exist are: (i) the intention of the testator to subject the primary donee to an obligation in favour of the secondary donee; (ii) communication of that intention to the primary donee; and (iii) the acceptance of that obligation by the primary donee either expressly or by acquiesence."

Mr Gordon contended that those three elements had been found by the judge in this case.

In support of his submission that the taking of benefit on the strength of a binding engagement suffices to create a constructive trust, Mr Gordon referred to *In re Dale decd.* [1994] Ch 31 for its extensive citations from the judgment of Lord Camden L.C. in *Dufour v. Pereira* (1769) 1 Dick 419. He referred also to *In re Gardner; Huey v. Cunnington* [1920] 2 Ch 523 and to *In re Hagger; Freeman v. Arscott* [1930] 2 Ch 190 for the proposition that a common intention of husband and wife and taking of benefit are sufficient to establish mutual wills.

In my judgment all Mr Gordon's submissions founder at the same point. As Morritt LJ put to him in argument, the reason why, if mutual wills are to take effect, an agreement is necessary, is that without it the property of the second testator is not bound, whereas a secret trust concerns only the property of a person in the position of the first testator.

If there were room for argument about this it is concluded by the language of Nourse J. himself in *In re Cleaver* [1981] 1 WLR 939, 945 after reviewing the cases:

> "It is therefore clear that there must be a definite agreement between the makers of the two wills; but that must be established by evidence; that the fact that there are mutual wills to the same effect is a relevant circumstance to be taken into account, although not enough of itself; and that the whole of the evidence must be looked at."

I am satisfied that for the doctrine to apply there must be a contract at law: see *per* Morritt J. in *In re Dale dec'd.* [1994] Ch 31, 38. In reaching this conclusion Morritt J. was guided, even if not in strictness bound, by the high authority of Lord Camden L.C. in *Dufour v. Pereira* (1769) 1 Dick 419 (as more fully set out in Hargrave, *Juridical Arguments and Collections* (1799) vol. 2), Lord Loughborough in *Walpole v. Orford* (1797) 3 Ves 402, the High Court of Australia in *Birmingham v. Renfrew*, and the Privy Council in *Gray v. Perpetual Trustee Co Ltd* [1928] AC 391. Delivering the opinion of the Board in the latter case Viscount Haldane said at p. 400:

> "The case before [their Lordships] is one in which the evidence of an agreement, apart from that of making the wills in question, is so lacking that they are unable to come to the conclusion that an agreement to constitute equitable interests has been shown to have been made. As they have already said, the mere fact of making wills mutually is not, at least by the law of England, evidence of such an agreement having been come to. And without such a definite agreement there can no more be a trust in equity than a right to damages at law."

These cases lead unequivocally to the judge's conclusion [1996] 1 WLR 694, 702 that:

> ". . . if a clear agreement can be found, in the wills or elsewhere, that they are to be mutually binding, whether or not that is expressed in language of revocation, the law will give effect to that intention by way of a 'floating trust', which becomes irrevocable following the death of the first testator and crystallises on the death of the second."

The distinction drawn by Nourse J. between a legally binding obligation and an 'honourable engagement', upon which Mr Gordon also relies, was not drawn in the context of declaring that, for purposes of mutual wills, either will do. I am not impressed by Mr Gordon's table comparing this case with *In re Cleaver*. I never heard of such a method of seeking to support a submission that essential facts in one case should be found in the same way as in another. The judgment of facts is not an exercise in counting similarities: it is the product of an evaluation and appraisal of the evidence. So here I see no reason to criticise Carnwath J's conclusion at p. 708:

> "It may be that *In re Cleaver* is an extreme example of the circumstances in which an agreement may be found on the basis of oral evidence. It does not provide any precedent for this case."

The crucial difference between the cases is that in *In re Cleaver* there was specific evidence as to the testators' mutual intentions at the time the wills were made, whereas here there was not. Even if a binding agreement were not required, it would still have to be proved that both testators intended not merely that Gary should be the ultimate beneficiary but that the survivor should not prevent that happening, if he or she thought fit.

Two wills may be in the same form as each other. Each testator may leave his or her estate to the other with a view to the survivor leaving both estates to their heir. But there is no presumption that a present plan will be immutable in future. A key feature of the concept of mutual wills is the irrevocability of the mutual intentions. Not only must they be binding when made, but the testators must have undertaken, and so must be bound, not to change their intentions after the death of the first testator. The test must always be, 'suppose that during the lifetime of the surviving testator the intended beneficiary did something which the survivor regarded as unpardonable, would he or she be free not to leave the combined estate to him?' The answer must be that the survivor is so entitled unless the testators agreed otherwise when they executed their wills. Hence the need for a clear agreement.

Dennis and Joy executed wills in the same terms save that each left his or her estate to the other. Thus the survivor was to have both estates. They wanted Gary to inherit the combined estates. But there was no express agreement not to revoke the wills. Nor could any such agreement be implied from the fact that the survivor was in a position to leave both estates to Gary. The fact that each expected that the other would leave them to him is not sufficient to impress the arrangement with a floating trust, binding in equity. A mutual desire that Gary should inherit could not of itself prevent the survivor from resiling from the arrangement. What is required is a mutual intention that both wills should remain unaltered and that the survivor should be bound to leave the combined estates to the son. That is what is missing here. The judge found that Joan regarded the arrangement as irrevocable, but that Dennis did not. No mutual intention was proven that the survivor should be bound to leave the joint estate to Gary. That is what they meant to achieve. It could not happen unless they first left their respective estates to the survivor of them. But the fact that each was able to leave the combined estate to Gary does not without more mean that both were bound to do so.

The judge declined to infer any agreement between Dennis and Joan that would prevent the survivor of them from interfering with the succession. That was a conclusion to which he was entitled to come on the evidence. Mr Gordon has helpfully marshalled the judge's references to what had to be shown to establish binding mutual wills. Though Joan believed that they mutually intended to leave their estates to Gary, Dennis was not shown to have shared it. So the intention was not in fact mutual. Hence the result that Dennis had no more than a moral obligation to give effect to Joan's belief at least in so far as it affected what had been her estate.

I would accordingly dismiss the appeal."

FUTURE DEVELOPMENT OF THE CONSTRUCTIVE TRUST

New Model Constructive Trusts

It has generally been acknowledged throughout the common law world that the concept of 'justice' is too uncertain a basis on which to found a constructive trust which will create proprietary rights which may operate in a wider context than anticipated or required. However, Lord Denning pioneered just such a development in the English Court of Appeal in the late 1960s and early 1970s and in *Hussey v. Palmer*[30] Denning MR stated that a constructive trust would be imposed 'whenever justice and good conscience require it'. While the influence of the so called 'new model constructive trust' has waned in England, Lord Denning's creation has met with a degree of approval here in a number of cases which illustrate well the diversity of situations in which it may be employed.

H.K.N. Invest Oy v. Incotrade Pvt Ltd
[1993] 3 IR 152

The plaintiffs had obtained judgment against the defendants, namely a company and the individuals responsible for conducting its affairs, and sought to be allowed to complete execution of this judgment. In relation to monies received by way of commission on pre-incorporation contracts, Costello J held that although the individual defendants concerned might not have been fiduciaries at the time they received this commission, these funds were held on trust for the company and could not be the subject of a garnishee order. In addition, Costello J held that the monies received after incorporation were held by the individual defendants as fiduciaries on a constructive trust for the company and he made an order declaring that the liquidator was beneficially entitled to the proceeds of both sets of contracts as the assets of the company.

---

[30] [1972] 1 WLR 1286, 1290.

COSTELLO J stated at pp.163–166:

"The law

(iii) *Equity*
It is to be borne in mind (a) that our first concerns are with pre-incorporation contracts by which the first defendant purportedly agreed to supply services in consideration for the payment of commission and to refund the commission if the agreed services were not provided, and (b) that payments of commission were made pursuant to these purported contracts. The issue in the case is not the enforceability of the pre-incorporation contracts but the beneficial ownership of money paid under them. Secondly, the beneficial ownership of monies paid after incorporation also falls for consideration. If it can be shown that the monies were received by the second and third defendants as constructive trustees of the first defendant then it would follow (a) that the first defendant has a proprietary remedy against them for the return of the monies, and (b) their creditors cannot levy execution against these sums (by garnishee proceedings or otherwise) to satisfy debts that they may personally owe. Alternatively, if it can be shown that a fiduciary relationship existed between them and the first defendant then they would hold the monies as constructive trustees for the first defendant.

I will consider firstly the position concerning monies received before incorporation by way of commission on pre-incorporation contracts. It seems to me that it would be straining past breaking point the concept of a fiduciary relationship to hold that such a relationship existed at a time prior to the incorporation of the first defendant. This was the view of Lindley L.J. in *Lydney and Wigpool Iron Ore Co. v. Bird* (1886) 33 Ch D 85. Dealing with a case in which the promoter of a company received a secret profit prior to incorporation the learned judge pointed out at p. 93 of the report:-

> "It is not correct to say that James Bird was the agent of the company when it did not exist, nor is it much less objectionable to talk of his being in a fiduciary relation to the company before the company had any existence."

But he went on to point out at p. 94 of the report:

> "[It] is perfectly well settled that a promoter of a company is accountable to it for all moneys secretly obtained by him from it just as if the relationship of principal and agent or trustee and *cestuis que trust* had really existed between them and the company when the money was so obtained."

Although, the second and third defendants may not have been fiduciaries at the time they received the pre-incorporation commission I think they received it as constructive trustees. A constructive trust will arise when the circumstances render it inequitable for the legal owner of property to deny the title of another to it. It is a trust which comes into existence irrespective of the will of the parties and arises by operation of law. The principle is that where a person who holds property in circumstances which in equity and good conscience should be held or enjoyed by another he will be compelled to hold the property in trust for another (Hanbury "Modern Equity" p. 218; *Hussey v. Palmer* [1972] 1 WLR 1286 at p. 1290 *per* Lord Denning M.R.).

It will help the analysis in this case, I think, if I first examine a situation in which no fraud is involved. Let me assume that a promoter who is to be a controlling shareholder in a company shortly to be incorporated purports to contract in the name of a company and receives advance commission for services which the company is to render. In such circumstances he has received the commission for the benefit of the company which is to be incorporated and not for his own benefit. If, before the company is incorporated and before it has either formally or informally had an opportunity to ratify the contract, he is adjudicated a bankrupt and ratification then takes place a question would arise as to whether the creditors in the bankruptcy of the promoter are entitled to the commission or whether it can be claimed by the company. It seems to me that as a matter of equity and good conscience the court should uphold the company's claim. The commission was never beneficially owned by the promoter - he held it in trust for the company which he was forming and which was to perform the services he had agreed would be performed. If this was not the case (a) considerable injustice could be suffered by the company, its shareholders or creditors who were deprived of the commission whilst (b) the creditors in the bankruptcy would obtain a greater interest in the property than the bankrupt himself enjoyed. It seems to me therefore that the court should hold that the promoter of a company who received payment on behalf of a company which he is incorporating and pursuant to a pre-incorporation contract which the company is empowered to ratify holds the commission as a constructive trustee for the company.

I think the same principle would apply even if the company did not formally ratify the contract because as a matter of law the payments made in the circumstances I have outlined would have been received by the promoter as a trustee for the company he was proposing to establish and did in fact establish. And I do not think that the fraud of the promoters can affect this position. The fact that the promoters did not pay the commission to the first defendant and that they had no intention of supplying the promised services when they received it and that they misapplied the funds they received does not, in my view, affect the trust which arose when they received the monies; what they did was to act in breach of trust, not disestablish the trust by their fraud.

It follows therefore that in so far as the monies in the two accounts I am considering represent the balance of commissions received prior to incorporation on the 13th August, 1991, this balance is held in trust for the first defendant and cannot be the subject of a garnishee order.

The monies in the accounts may represent in whole or in part commissions paid after incorporation in respect of pre-incorporation contracts or post-incorporation contracts and which should have been paid over to the first defendant but instead were retained by the second and third defendants for their own use. The position in such cases is clear. If they had been appointed directors of the first defendant (the evidence does not disclose whether formal appointments were ever made) they would have a fiduciary relationship with the first defendant. Even if they had not been formally appointed they would have received the commission as agents for the first defendant and a fiduciary relationship would also exist. As fiduciaries they would hold the commission on a constructive trust for the first defendant. It follows therefore that as all the monies in these accounts are trust monies to which the first defendant is beneficially entitled they cannot be the subject of execution by any of the creditors of the second or third defendants, including execution by means of garnishee proceedings. I will therefore refuse to make absolute the order of garnishee and discharge the conditional order. I think it would be appropriate also to make a declaratory order that the liquidator is entitled to the monies in these accounts as assets of the company.

With respect to the motion of the 26th February, 1992, this raised questions as to the ownership of the proceeds of sale of four motor cars and two motor cycles. It has been agreed that these issues can more appropriately be dealt with by an application by the liquidator in the winding-up of the first defendant and so no order is now required on this motion."

Murray v. Murray
[1996] 3 IR 251

The defendant was the legal owner of premises in respect of which he had paid the initial deposit; the remainder, approximately three quarters of the price, was paid by way of a mortgage. The plaintiff, his nephew, had lived in the premises with his aunt, the defendant's sister, for many years and it was accepted by Barron J that the defendant had intended to transfer the house to his sister. While she was alive she paid the mortgage instalments and most of the outgoings on the property, although there was evidence that she had at one point refused to accept a transfer of the property. After her death the plaintiff claimed a declaration that the entire beneficial ownership in the house was vested in his aunt at the date of her death and the defendant claimed the legal and beneficial ownership himself. Barron J concluded that in the case before him the equity to create a constructive trust arose from the payment of monies which had resulted in the property being freed from the mortgage and the owner being relieved of other outgoings. He held that the aunt was at the date of her death entitled to three quarters of the beneficial interest in the property so, the plaintiff, being her next of kin, was a tenant in common of the premises with the defendant.

BARRON J stated at pp. 253–256: "The defendant married in 1957. He and his wife decided to build their own home and together with three other couples they formed what was known as the Ashgrove Utility Society which built four houses, of which the premises involved in the present action, was one. At the date when it was built it was known as No. 6 Ashgrove, Kill Avenue, Dun Laoghaire, but is presently known as 35 Kill Avenue.

The defendant and his wife never went to live in the premises. An agreement was entered into on the 15th November, 1959, between the defendant and his parents whereby he became entitled to the premises known as "Prague" and his parents were to live in 35 Kill Avenue. On the day before, the 14th November, 1959, the defendant signed a document relinquishing all claims to No. 6 Ashgrove, Kill Avenue, in favour of his sister Elizabeth Murray. However, he says, and I accept, that this arrangement was superseded by the agreement of the 15th, the terms of which were subsequently acknowledged by his parents to have been fulfilled.

The financing of 35 Kill Avenue was as follows: The defendant paid the initial deposit of £200 to £300. There was an obligation under the lease to build a house of a value not less than £1,850. He borrowed the sum of £1,400 by way of a local authority loan from the Dun Laoghaire Corporation and would have paid all other costs and expenses.

The first person to reside at 35 Kill Avenue was his sister Lily. The plaintiff is the son of another sister of the defendant. His father died and his mother emigrated. At the age of two and a half he went to live with his grandparents. He lived with them from 1959 to 1962, when all three went to live in 35 Kill Avenue with Lily.

His grandfather died in 1967 and his grandmother died in 1972. During this period Lily married and her husband lived in the premises, 35 Kill Avenue, from 1965 to 1969. They separated in that year and thereafter Lily and the plaintiff remained on in the premises until her death on the 16th April, 1988.

During the period that Lily was resident in the premises she paid the rent, rates and the instalments due on foot of the mortgage. The defendant appears to have paid insurance. It is quite clear that the defendant at all times wished to benefit his sister and wished to transfer the premises to her. Solicitors prepared the necessary documentation in the year 1973, but notwithstanding this Lily never executed the documents which would have transferred the property to her. This beneficial intention continued up to very shortly before her death. There are letters showing that at the end of 1987 and the beginning of 1988, the defendant was prepared to transfer the property to his sister. There was a sum of £400 approximately owing on foot of the mortgage and he was agreeable to pay all the costs involved provided that his sister paid off the mortgage and some water charges amounting to some forty odd pounds. While these sums were paid, no transfer was ever executed and unfortunately Lily died before the arrangement could be completed. Of the several letters which have been put in evidence, the last in time is one dated the 6th April, 1988, written by the defendant's wife on his behalf to the plaintiff on behalf of his aunt as follows:–

"Dear Ian,

Our solicitor will be away until the end of April. Hopefully, we will be in hand with the deed by then, and we will contact you on his return with news of an appointment. In the meantime I trust all is in order by now from your end and that late April or early May should see a completion of our business.

Regards,
Rita."

Once his sister died it seems that the defendant did no more. The plaintiff was allowed to remain on in the premises. In January, 1992, the plaintiff became engaged and his fiancée came to live in the premises. The defendant was not told of this engagement. He arrived one day at the premises and unfortunately the plaintiff's fiancée, who did not know who he was, was not prepared to accept that he was entitled to come into the premises. She believed that the house belonged to her fiancée and had no idea that his uncle claimed to be the owner of the premises. From that time on there was a very definite dispute between the parties. Letters of administration to the estate of Lily were granted to the defendant on the 12th July, 1993.

These proceedings have been commenced by the plaintiff because in the Schedule of Assets the defendant made no mention of any interest of the deceased in the premises. These proceedings are brought for a declaration that the entire beneficial ownership in the premises was vested in the deceased at the date of her death. In turn, the defendant counterclaims for rent from the date of the death of his sister upon the basis that the entire legal and beneficial interest was at that date vested in him.

The claim as pleaded relies upon the acknowledgement dated the 15th November, 1959. This case was waived at the trial, the plaintiff relying upon a constructive trust arising by virtue of the payment of the mortgage instalments and other outgoings by the deceased. The plaintiff contends that the circumstances are such that it would be unconscionable for the defendant to rely upon his legal title. Particular reliance is placed upon *Hussey v. Palmer* [1972] 1 WLR 1286. In that case the plaintiff went to live with her daughter and son-in-law. She had sold her own house and lent her son-in-law the money necessary to build an addition to the house to accommodate her. This was done and she went to live with them. Unfortunately, things did not work out and in a relatively short time she left her daughter and son-in-law's home and went to live elsewhere. She sought to recover the money which she had lent to her son-in-law for the purposes of the improvement of his house. He refused to pay her back. She brought proceedings based on a contract of loan and withdrew them. She subsequently commenced proceedings claiming that the payment of the money created a constructive trust in her favour. She succeeded in this claim.

It is, I think, quite clear that the law will impose a constructive trust in all circumstances where it would be unjust and unconscionable not to do so. So far as *Hussey v. Palmer* [1972] 1 WLR 1286 is concerned, it seems to me that the court was satisfied that it would be a severe injustice if the plaintiff did not have some form of security for what was, in her own words, a loan. In my view, the case is an authority for the proposition that in certain circumstances where equity so requires, a debt may well be secured by the device of a constructive trust on the property created by the money involved.

In that case, the law was in effect returning what was hers to the lender. Here the equities to create a constructive trust arise from the payment of monies which have resulted in the property being freed from the mortgage and the owner relieved of other outgoings. The legal owner of the property wished to provide both for his parents and for his sister. He did this by allowing them to live in his property but at the same time requiring them to pay the majority of the overheads. He did this because he and his parents and sister were a close knit family and he had the financial resources which they did not. The situation factually is complicated because Lily apparently refused to accept a transfer of the property. After her death the necessary documents furnished to her in 1973, which she would have been required to execute, were found hidden away behind a cupboard and it is quite clear that she did not intend to take a transfer of the property nor apparently to let anybody know that she had the opportunity to do so.

What I have to consider is what is fair and whether it would be unconscionable to deny the deceased any part of the beneficial interest in the premises and, if so, what share therein. It is undoubtedly true that the defendant intended to benefit his sister and would have done so had she remained alive and had she signed the necessary documents. Equity cannot force him to perfect the gift which he intended to make now that his sister has died. So far as this gift is concerned, his sister would have been a volunteer. Although the promise to make the gift was dependent upon the payments to be made on her behalf, the claim is not made in contract, but upon the basis of trust. The question to be determined is the interest which she would have had in any event without the gift. Having regard to the amount of the loan from the local authority which amounts to approximately three-quarters of the purchase value of the house at the date of its construction, it seems to me that the appropriate share which would have passed to her by reason of her contributions would have been that proportion. Accordingly, I will hold that at the date of her death she was entitled to three-quarters of the beneficial interest in the property.

So far as the counterclaim is concerned, no effort was made by the defendant to seek any rent until the beginning of 1992. The plaintiff is by virtue of the declaration being made, and his position as a next-of-kin of the deceased, a tenant-in-common occupying the premises and as such would not have been required to pay any rent for such occupation. Nor in the particular circumstances of this case was there any obligation upon him to account to the defendant."

Kelly v. Cahill
[2001] 2 ILRM 205

The deceased informed his solicitor that he wanted to alter his will since he no longer wished to benefit his nephew, the second named defendant, but intended to leave all his property to his wife, the first named defendant. His solicitor advised him to execute a deed transferring his property into the joint names of himself and his wife to avoid a charge to probate tax subsequently arising and the parties believed that the deed executed included all of the lands owned by the deceased. However, through the inadvertence of the solicitor, the lands comprised in a numbered folio had not been transferred and would pass on the deceased's death to the first named defendant for life with remainder to the second named defendant, subject to her legal right to half of the lands concerned. Barr J concluded that it had been established that the deceased had expressed the necessary intention to his solicitor and that he had good reason for believing that the deed of transfer had achieved this intention. In these circumstances he held that 'justice and good conscience' required that the interest in remainder under the will should be deemed to be held by the second named defendant on a constructive trust for the first named defendant.

BARR J stated at pp. 207–211: "The facts relating to this matter are not in dispute and are as follows: The plaintiff is the sole surviving executor named in the last will and testament of Michael Cahill Senior (the deceased) made on 23 October 1969 who died on 20 March 1996 without having revoked or altered the will. The other executor appointed by the deceased predeceased him and was not replaced. The plaintiff applied for and obtained probate of the deceased's will on 22 January 1998 and pursuant thereto entered into the administration of the estate.

The first named defendant (the widow) is the widow of the deceased. The second named defendant is a nephew of the testator. The deceased was a farmer and the owner of substantial holdings of registered land. He died without issue. By his last will the deceased devised all of his property to his widow and his brother, Martin Cahill, as joint tenants for life with remainder to trustees in trust for his nephew, the second named defendant. Martin Cahill, the deceased's brother, died on 16 March 1998.

In course of administration of the deceased's estate certain facts have come to light relating to the ownership of part of the lands comprised in the estate which have caused the plaintiff as administrator to seek directions from the court, thus giving rise to this action. The matters raised by him include:

1. The answers [to] the following questions arising in relation to the administration of the estate of the said Michael Cahill Senior, deceased:

(a) Whether the lands contained in Folio GY043846F of the Register County of Galway pass under the terms of the will of Michael Cahill deceased dated 23 October 1969 to the first named defendant for life and thereafter in remainder to the second named defendant, subject to the widow's right to one half of the lands pursuant to the provisions of Part IX of the Succession Act 1965.

(b) Whether in the events which have happened, the second named defendant is a constructive trustee of the remainder interest in the lands comprised in Folio GY043846F for the benefit of the first named defendant.

2. Such directions as may appear to this Honourable Court to be proper on foot of the answers to the questions at paragraph 1(a) and 1(b) above.

3. In the event that the court holds that the second named defendant is a trustee of the lands comprised in Folio GY043846F as a constructive trustee for the first named defendant, an order directing the second named defendant to execute such assurance as may be necessary to vest the said lands in the first named defendant.

The facts which have posed the foregoing questions are deposed to by Mr Joseph O'Hara who was the deceased's solicitor at all material times and are summarised as follows: In or about the month of January 1994 Mr Michael Cahill, the testator since deceased, and his wife, the first named defendant, called upon Mr O'Hara and he obtained instructions from Mr Cahill that he wished to alter the will which he had made on 23 October 1969. He informed his solicitor that he no longer wished to benefit his nephew Michael Cahill Junior, the second named defendant, and that he wished to leave all of his property to his wife, the first named defendant. There is no doubt that the testator had at that time changed his mind regarding the disposition of his property and had decided that his entire estate should be inherited by his wife absolutely on his death without any remainder provision and that this should be achieved by way of a new or revised will. However, Mr O'Hara foresaw a likely disadvantage for the testator's wife if his revised testamentary intention was achieved in the way intended by him. The difficulty was that a 2% probate tax had been created by the Finance Act 1993 which the solicitor believed would be payable by the widow on the value of the estate inherited by her. At that time there were no exemptions in respect of such tax. In the light of this Mr O'Hara advised his client, the testator, that he could achieve the same result without liability for probate tax by transferring his lands into the joint names of himself and his wife, the effect of which would be that the property would then pass to his wife, as sole owner if she survived him. The testator agreed to that course of action. Mr O'Hara had also ascertained that all of the other assets of his client and his wife were in their joint names. A deed of transfer dated 14 January 1994 was duly drawn up by Mr O'Hara to give effect to the revised instructions which he had received. The deed provided that lands comprised in Folio 46909 of the Register County of Galway were transferred from the sole ownership of Michael Cahill into the joint names of the latter and his wife, Nellie Cahill. The deed was duly executed and at that time the joint owners and their solicitor believed that it included all of the lands then owned by Michael Cahill. In fact in drawing the deed the solicitor had made an error. He was not then aware that as noted thereon Folio 46909 had been prior to the date of execution of the deed closed to Folio GY043846F of the Register County of Galway (the second folio) of which Mr O'Hara had no knowledge at that time. The second folio comprised 17 entries of which Nos. 6 to 9 were the lands transferred from Folio 46909. The end result was that through the inadvertence of the solicitor and unknown to the testator and his wife the lands comprised in entries 1 to 5 and 10 to 17 in the second folio were not included in the deed of transfer contrary to the express intentions of the testator. No new will was made and the end result was that having regard to the terms of the original will and of the deed of transfer *per se* the lands which had not been transferred into the joint names of the deceased and his wife would on his death pass to her for life with remainder to the second named defendant, Michael Cahill Junior, but subject to the widow's legal right share under the Succession Act 1965 to one half of the lands concerned, should she elect to make such a claim. Mr O'Hara has deposed that he does not believe that that would accord with the stated intention of the deceased, which was that his nephew, Michael Cahill Junior, would not benefit from the estate and that his wife would be the sole beneficiary.

The law

The nett issue which I must address is whether in the light of Mr O'Hara's inadvertence regarding the folios in question which resulted in a failure to carry out his client's instructions to include all his lands in the deed of transfer made in January 1994, a constructive trust arises comprising the lands which were not transferred into joint ownership as intended by the testator. This raises the question as to whether in the circumstances under review it is established that a 'new model' constructive trust as Keane J described it in *Equity and the Law of Trusts in the Republic of Ireland* has been established and, if so, whether such a trust has a place in Irish law.

The concept of 'new model' constructive trusts is explained by Keane J (as he then was) in the following passage from his learned work at p. 186:

> In recent years, there has been much discussion in other jurisdictions as to whether a constructive trust can be said to arise in any circumstances where permitting the defendant to retain the property would result in his being 'unjustly enriched'. This, it has been said, effectively means treating the constructive trust as a form of remedy intended to restore property to a person to whom in justice it should belong rather than as an institution analogous to the express or resulting trust. The constructive trust, in its traditional form, arises because of equity's refusal to countenance any form of fraud: in this wider modern guise it is imposed by law 'whenever justice and good conscience require it'.

The latter is a quotation from the landmark judgment in this area of Lord Denning MR in *Hussey v. Palmer* [1972] 3 All ER 744 at p. 747. In that case, the plaintiff had been living with her daughter and son-in-law. She had paid £607.00 to a contractor to build on another room in the expectation that she could live there for the rest of her life. When disputes later arose and she left, she sought the return of the £607.00. Having regard to the informal nature of the arrangement, she was in obvious difficulty in establishing that it was a loan rather than a gift. However, Lord Denning did not consider that problem insuperable. Having observed that it did not matter whether one proceeded by way of a resulting trust or a constructive trust, he went on (at p. 747):

> By whatever means it is described, it is a trust imposed by law wherever justice and good conscience require it. It is a liberal process, founded upon large principles of equity to be applied in cases where a defendant cannot conscientiously keep the property for himself alone, but ought to allow another to have the property or a share of it. . . . It is an equitable remedy by which the court can enable an aggrieved party to obtain restitution.

The end result was that the plaintiff was entitled to a share in the house proportionate to her contribution.

Keane J commented (at p. 187) that:

> Broadly speaking, it may be said that the application of the principle of unjust enrichment requires the restoration by the defendant to the plaintiff of a benefit which it would be unjust for him to retain. Sometimes this can be done by a simple award of money, e.g., the refund of money paid under a mistake of fact. But sometimes the restoration of the benefit can only be achieved by giving the plaintiff an interest in property. Thus, the constructive trust is imposed by the court as an equitable remedy intended to restore to the plaintiff the benefit of which he has been deprived. In the words of Cardozo J 'a constructive trust is the formula through which the conscience of equity finds expression'. *Beatty v. Guggenheim Exploration Co.* 225 NY 380 at p. 386.

I adopt with respect the foregoing assessment of 'new model' constructive trusts by Keane J.

It seems to me that the kernel of the question I have to determine is whether the evidence establishes a clear, positive intention on the part of the testator that his wife should inherit all of his property on his death; that he took appropriate steps to bring that about and that he could not reasonably have known that through his solicitor's error the deed of transfer, which he and his wife duly executed, did not include all of his lands and that his stated intention to benefit his wife exclusively on his death was defeated in part. In the light of Mr O'Hara's and the first named defendant's affidavits, the accuracy of which is not in dispute it is established that the testator expressed such an intention to his solicitor in clear terms and that he had good reason for believing that the deed of transfer did in fact achieve his intention that his wife would acquire absolutely as surviving joint owner all of his lands on his death as Mr O'Hara had advised. In my view it is irrelevant that the second named defendant was neither aware of nor had any responsibility for the error which was made. The essential element is that the testator changed his mind regarding the disposition of his estate after death and that he took appropriate steps to give effect to his revised intention. That having been established, it follows that in the words of Lord Denning, 'justice and good conscience' require that the second named defendant should not be allowed to inherit the testator's property or any part of it on the death of his widow and that his interest in remainder under the will should be deemed to be a constructive trust in favour of the widow. In my opinion a 'new model' constructive trust of that nature the purpose of which is to prevent unjust enrichment is an equitable concept which deserves recognition in Irish law. In that regard I note also that it accords with the following observations of Costello J (as he then was) in *HKN Invest OY v. Incotrade PVT Ltd* [1993] 3 IR 152 at p. 162:

> A constructive trust will arise when the circumstances render it inequitable for the legal owner of property to deny the title of another to it. It is a trust which comes into existence irrespective of the will of the parties and arises by operation of law. The principle is that where a person who holds property in circumstances which in equity and good conscience should be held or enjoyed by another he will be compelled to hold the property in trust for another. . . .

And in that context that the learned judge referred with apparent approval to the judgment of Lord Denning MR in *Hussey v. Palmer supra.*

In the light of my findings the answers to the questions posed in paragraph 1 of the plaintiff's claims are:

(a) No.

(b) Yes.

I direct that the second named defendant shall execute such assurance as may be necessary to vest in the first named defendant all of the lands comprised in Folio GY043846 of the Register County of Galway."

CHAPTER 9

Purpose Trusts

INTRODUCTION

Trusts for non-charitable purposes will not generally be regarded as valid as they are considered to lack the human beneficiaries necessary to secure their enforcement, to be too uncertain in nature, and will often offend the rule against inalienability.

RATIONALE FOR POLICY OF NON-ENFORCEMENT OF PURPOSE TRUSTS

One of the principal objections to non-charitable purpose trusts is that there is no one who can ensure that the court will secure performance of the trust if this should become necessary.[1] A further objection is that purpose trusts are often not expressed in terms which are sufficiently clear and certain to enable a court to oversee their performance.[2]

Re Astor's Settlement Trusts: Asotr v. Scholfield
[1952] Ch 534

An *inter vivos* settlement provided that shares were to be held on trust for a specified period for non-charitable objects including 'the establishment, maintenance and improvement of good understanding, sympathy and co-operation between nations' and 'the preservation of the independence and integrity of newspapers'. Roxburgh J held that the trusts were invalid as they were for the benefit of non-charitable purposes which no one could enforce and because they included objects which were too uncertain in nature.

ROXBURGH J stated at pp.540–549: "The question upon which I am giving this reserved judgment is whether the non-charitable trusts of income during "the specified period" declared by clause 5 and the third schedule of the settlement of 1945 are void. Mr. Jennings and Mr. Buckley have submitted that they are void on two grounds: (1) that they are not trusts for the benefit of individuals; (2) that they are void for uncertainty.

---

[1] *Morice v. Bishop of Durham* (1804) 9 Ves 399. See also *Re Astor's Settlement Trusts* [1952] Ch 534.
[2] *Ibid.*

Lord Parker considered the first of these two questions in his speech in *Bowman v. Secular Society Ld.* [1917] AC 406 and I will cite two important passages. The first is: "The question whether a trust be legal or illegal or be in accordance with or contrary to the policy of the law, only arises when it has been determined that a trust has been created, and is then only part of the larger question whether the trust is enforceable. For, as will presently appear, trusts may be unenforceable and therefore void, not only because they are illegal or contrary to the policy of the law, but for other reasons." The second is: "A trust to be valid must be for the benefit of individuals, which this is certainly not, or must be in that class of gifts for the benefit of the public which the courts in this country recognize as charitable in the legal as opposed to the popular sense of that term."

Commenting on those passages Mr. Gray observed that *Bowman v. Secular Society Ld.* arose out of a will and he asked me to hold that Lord Parker intended them to be confined to cases arising under a will. But they were, I think, intended to be quite general in character. Further, Mr. Gray pointed out that Lord Parker made no mention of the exceptions or apparent exceptions which undoubtedly exist, and from this he asked me to infer that no such general principle can be laid down. The question is whether those cases are to be regarded as exceptional and anomalous or whether they are destructive of the supposed principle. I must later analyse them. But I will first consider whether Lord Parker's propositions can be attacked from a base of principle.

The typical case of a trust is one in which the legal owner of property is constrained by a court of equity so to deal with it as to give effect to the equitable rights of another. These equitable rights have been hammered out in the process of litigation in which a claimant on equitable grounds has successfully asserted rights against a legal owner or other person in control of property. Prima facie, therefore, a trustee would not be expected to be subject to an equitable obligation unless there was somebody who could enforce a correlative equitable right, and the nature and extent of that obligation would be worked out in proceedings for enforcement. This is what I understand by Lord Parker's first proposition. At an early stage, however, the courts were confronted with attempts to create trusts for charitable purposes which there was no equitable owner to enforce. Lord Eldon explained in *Attorney-General v. Brown* (1818) 1 Swans 265, 290 how this difficulty was dealt with: "It is the duty of a court of equity, a main part, originally almost the whole, of its jurisdiction, to administer trusts; to protect not the visible owner, who alone can proceed at law, but the individual equitably, though not legally, entitled. From this principle has arisen the practice of administering the trust of a public charity: persons possessed of funds appropriated to such purposes are within the general rule; but no one being entitled by an immediate and peculiar interest to prefer a complaint, who is to compel the performance of their obligations, and to enforce their responsibility? It is the duty of the King, as parens patriae, to protect property devoted to charitable uses; and that duty is executed by the officer who represents the Crown for all forensic purposes. On this foundation rests the right of the Attorney-General in such cases to obtain by information the interposition of a court of equity . . . . " But if the purposes are not charitable, great difficulties arise both in theory and in practice. In theory, because having regard to the historical origins of equity it is difficult to visualize the growth of equitable obligations which nobody can enforce, and in practice, because it is not possible to contemplate with equanimity the creation of large funds devoted to non-charitable purposes which no court and no department of state can control, or in the case of maladministration reform. Therefore, Lord Parker's second proposition would prima facie appear to be well founded. Moreover, it gains no little support from the practical considerations that no officer has ever been constituted to take, in the case of non-charitable purposes, the position held by the Attorney-General in connexion with charitable purposes, and no case has been found in the reports in which the court has even directly enforced a non-charitable purpose against a trustee. Indeed where, as in the present case, the only beneficiaries are purposes and an at present unascertainable person, it is difficult to see who could initiate such proceedings. If the purposes are valid trusts, the settlors have retained no beneficial interest and could not initiate them. It was suggested that the trustees might proceed ex parte to enforce the trusts against themselves. I doubt that, but at any rate nobody could enforce the trusts against them. This point, in my judgment, is of importance, because in most of the cases which are put forward to disprove Lord Parker's propositions the court had indirect means of enforcing the execution of the non-charitable purpose. These cases I must now consider. First of all, there is a group relating to horses, dogs, graves and monuments, among which I was referred to *Pettingall v. Pettingall* (1842) 11 LJ Ch 176; *Mitford v. Reynolds* (1848) 16 Sim 105; *In re Dean* (1889) 41 Ch D 552; *Pirbright v. Salwey* [1896] WN 86; and *In re Hooper* [1932] 1 Ch 38.

In *Pettingall v. Pettingall* (1842) 11 LJ Ch 176, 177 a testator made the following bequest by his will: "Having a favourite black mare, I hereby bequeath, that at my death, £50 per annum be paid for her keep in some park in England or Wales; her shoes to be taken off, and she never to be ridden or put in harness; and that my executor consider himself in honour bound to fulfil my wish, and see that she will be well provided for, and removable at his will. At her death all payment to cease.' It being admitted that a bequest in favour of an animal was valid, two questions were made: first, as to the form of the decree on this point; and secondly, as to the disposition of the surplus not required for the mare. Knight Bruce V.C. said, that so much of the £50 as would be required to keep the mare comfortably, should be applied by the executor, and that he was entitled to the surplus. He must give full information, whenever required, respecting the mare; and if the mare were not properly attended to, any of the parties interested in the residue might apply to the court. The decree on this point ought to be, that £50 a year should be paid to the executor during the life of the mare, or until further order; he undertaking

to maintain her comfortably; with liberty for all parties to apply." The points
which I wish to make are (1) that it was there admitted that a bequest in favour
of an animal was valid, and (2) that there were persons interested in residue
who having regard to the decree made would have had no difficulty in getting
the terms of the "bequest" enforced.

Mitford v. Reynolds (1842) 16 Sim 105 related to a sepulchral monument
and to horses, and there again there was a remainderman on behalf of charity
to see to the enforcement of the directions, and an administration action was
on foot.

In *In re Dean* (1889) 41 Ch D 552 a testator devised his freehold estates,
subject to and charged with an annuity of £750, and to a term of 50 years
granted to his trustees to the use of the plaintiff for life, with remainders over;
and he gave to his trustees his horses, ponies and hounds; and he charged his
said freehold estates with the payment to his trustees, for the term of 50 years,
if any of the said horses and hounds should so long live, of an annual sum of
£750. And he declared that his trustees should apply the said annual sum in
the maintenance of the horses and hounds for the time being living, and in
maintaining the stables, kennels and buildings inhabited by the said animals
in such condition of repair as his trustees might deem fit; and in consideration
of the maintenance of his horses, ponies, and hounds being a charge upon his
said estate as aforesaid, he gave all his personal estate not otherwise disposed
of to the plaintiff absolutely. North J. said (at p. 556): "Then it is said, that
there is no cestui que trust who can enforce the trust, and that the court will not
recognize a trust unless it is capable of being enforced by someone. I do not
assent to that view. There is not the least doubt that a man may if he pleases,
give a legacy to trustees, upon trust to apply it in erecting a monument to
himself, either in a church or in a churchyard, or even in unconsecrated ground,
and I am not aware that such a trust is in any way invalid, although it is difficult
to say who would be the cestui que trust of the monument. In the same way I
know of nothing to prevent a gift of a sum of money to trustees, upon trust to
apply it for the repair of such a monument. In my opinion such a trust would
be good, although the testator must be careful to limit the time for which it is
to last, because, as it is not a charitable trust, unless it is to come to an end
within the limits fixed by the rule against perpetuities, it would be illegal. But
a trust to lay out a certain sum in building a monument, and the gift of another
sum in trust to apply the same to keeping that monument in repair, say, for ten
years, is, in my opinion, a perfectly good trust, although I do not see who
could ask the court to enforce it. If persons beneficially interested in the estate
could do so, then the present plaintiff can do so; but, if such persons could not
enforce the trust, still it cannot be said that the trust must fail because there is
no one who can actively enforce it."

This is the best case in the series from Mr. Gray's point of view, because
North J. did undoubtedly uphold the particular directions, whether or not they
could be "actively enforced." But putting it at its highest, he merely held that

there were certain classes of trusts, of which this was one, in which that objection was not fatal. He did not suggest that it was not generally fatal outside the realms of charity.

In *Pirbright v. Salwey* [1896] WN 86 a testator, after expressing his wish to be buried in the inclosure in which his child lay in a certain churchyard, bequeathed to the rector and churchwardens of the parish church £800 Consols, the interest and dividends to be derived therefrom to be applied, so long as the law for the time being permitted, in keeping up the inclosure and decorating the same with flowers. It was held that the gift was valid for at least a period of 21 years from the testator's death, and *semble* that it was not charitable.

In *In re Hooper* [1932] 1 Ch 38, 39 a testator bequeathed to his executors and trustees money out of the income of which to provide, so far as they legally could do so, for the care and upkeep of certain graves, a vault and certain monuments. Maugham J. said: "This point is one to my mind of doubt, and I should have felt some difficulty in deciding it if it were not for *Pirbright v. Salwey* [1896] WN 86 . . . That was a decision arrived at by Stirling J., after argument by very eminent counsel. The case does not appear to have attracted much attention in textbooks, but it does not appear to have been commented upon adversely, and I shall follow it." In this case, and probably also in *Pirbright v. Salwey*, there was a residuary legatee to bring before the court any failure to comply with the directions. But I think that Maugham J. regarded them both as exceptions from general principle.

Last in this group is *In re Thompson* [1934] Ch 342. I have included it in this group because, although it relates to the furtherance of foxhunting and thus moves away from the subject-matter of the group and much nearer to the present case, it is expressly founded on *Pettingall v. Pettingall* (1842) 11 LJ Ch 176 and it is indeed a most instructive case. The testator bequeathed a legacy of £1,000 to a friend to be applied by him in such manner as he should think fit towards the promotion and furthering of foxhunting, and devised and bequeathed his residuary estate to Trinity Hall in the University of Cambridge. An originating summons was taken out by the executors to determine whether the legacy was valid or failed for want of a definite object or for uncertainty or on other grounds. When counsel, during the course of the argument, observed [1934] Ch 343, "True, there is no cestui que trust who can enforce the application of the legacy, but that is immaterial: *In re Dean* (1889) 41 Ch D 552. The object to which the legacy is to be applied is sufficiently defined to be enforced," Clauson J. interposed: "The college, as residuary legatees, seem to have an interest in the legacy, as, but for the trust for its application, they would be entitled to it. The procedure adopted by Knight Bruce V.-C. in *Pettingall v. Pettingall*, cited in Jarman on Wills, 7th ed., vol. 2, p. 877, might be followed in this case." And in his judgment he said: "In my judgment the object of the gift has been defined with sufficient clearness and is of a nature to which effect can be given. The proper way for me to deal with the matter will be, not to make, as it is asked by the summons, a general declaration, but following the example of Knight Bruce V.-C. in *Pettingall v. Pettingall*, to order that, upon the defendant Mr. Lloyd" [the friend] "giving an undertaking (which I understand he is willing to give) to apply the legacy when received by him towards the object expressed in the testator's will, the plaintiffs do pay to the defendant Mr. Lloyd the legacy of £1,000; and that, in case the legacy should be applied by him otherwise than towards the promotion and furthering of foxhunting, the residuary legatees are to be at liberty to apply." I understand Clauson J. to have held in effect that there was somebody who could enforce the purpose indicated because the college, as residuary legatees, would be entitled to the legacy but for the trust for its application and they could apply to the court to prevent any misapplication or breach of the undertaking given by Mr. Lloyd. I infer from what he said that he would not have upheld the validity of this non-charitable purpose if there had been no residuary legatee, and no possibility of making such an order as was made in *Pettingall v. Pettingall*.

Lastly, I was referred to *In re Price* [1943] Ch 422, where a testatrix by her will gave one-half of her residuary estate to the Anthroposophical Society in Great Britain "to be used at the discretion of the chairman and executive council of the society for carrying on the teachings of the founder, Dr. Rudolf Steiner." At first sight this case would appear to be a strong card in Mr. Gray's hand. The first part of the judgment proceeds upon the footing that the purposes were not charitable. The society was the residuary legatee and there was no room for such an order as was made in *In re Thompson* [1934] Ch 342. There was nobody who could have enforced the carrying out of the purposes. On closer inspection, however, it will be found that this point was not raised in argument or referred to in the judgment, and the decision was based upon *In re Drummond* [1914] 2 Ch 90, which is a different class of case. As the present case cannot, on any view, be assimilated to *In re Drummond*, I need not further consider *In re Price* [1943] Ch 422.

Let me then sum up the position so far. On the one side there are Lord Parker's two propositions with which I began. These were not new, but merely re-echoed what Sir William Grant had said as Master of the Rolls in *Morice v. The Bishop of Durham* (1804) 9 Ves 399, 405 as long ago as 1804: "There must be somebody, in whose favour the court can decree performance." The position was recently restated by Harman J. in *In re Wood* [1949] Ch 498, 501: "A gift on trust must have a cestui que trust," and this seems to be in accord with principle. On the other side is a group of cases relating to horses and dogs, graves and monuments – matters arising under wills and intimately connected with the deceased in which the courts have found means of escape from these general propositions and also *In re Thompson* and *In re Price* which I have endeavoured to explain. *In re Price* belongs to another field. The rest may, I think, properly be regarded as anomalous and exceptional and in no way destructive of the proposition which traces descent from or through Sir William Grant through Lord Parker to Harman J. Perhaps the late Sir Arthur

Underhill was right in suggesting that they may be concessions to human weakness or sentiment (see Law of Trusts, 8th ed., p. 79). They cannot, in my judgment, of themselves (and no other justification has been suggested to me) justify the conclusion that a Court of Equity will recognize as an equitable obligation affecting the income of large funds in the hands of trustees a direction to apply it in furtherance of enumerated non-charitable purposes in a manner which no court or department can control or enforce. I hold that the trusts here in question are void on the first of the grounds submitted by Mr. Jennings and Mr. Buckley.

The second ground upon which the relevant trusts are challenged is uncertainty. If (contrary to my view) an enumeration of purposes outside the realm of charities can take the place of an enumeration of beneficiaries, the purposes must, in my, judgment, be stated in phrases which embody definite concepts and the means by which the trustees are to try to attain them must also be prescribed with a sufficient degree of certainty. The test to be applied is stated by Lord Eldon in *Morice v. Bishop of Durham* (1805) 10 Ves 521 as follows: "As it is a maxim, that the execution of a trust shall be under the control of the court, it must be of such a nature, that it can be under that control; so that the administration of it can be reviewed by the court; or, if the trustee dies, the court itself can execute the trust: a trust therefore, which, in case of mal-administration could be reformed; and a due administration directed; and then, unless the subject and the objects can be ascertained, upon principles, familiar in other cases, it must be decided, that the court can neither reform mal-administration, nor direct a due administration." See also *In re Macduff* [1896] 2 Ch 451, 463.

Mr. Gray argued that this test was not properly applicable to trusts declared by deed, but I can see no distinction between a will and a deed in this respect.

Applying this test, I find many uncertain phrases in the enumeration of purposes, for example, " different sections of people in any nation or community" in paragraph 1 of the third schedule, "constructive policies" in paragraph 2, "integrity of the press" in paragraph 3, "combines" in paragraph 5, "the restoration . . . of the independence of . . . writers in newspapers" in paragraph 6, and "benevolent schemes" in paragraph 7. Mr. Gray suggested that in view of the unlimited discretion bestowed upon the trustees (subject only to directions from the settlors) the trustees would be justified in excluding from their purview purposes indicated by the settlors but insufficiently defined by them. But I cannot accept this argument. The purposes must be so defined that if the trustees surrendered their discretion, the court could carry out the purposes declared, not a selection of them arrived at by eliminating those which are too uncertain to be carried out. If, for example, I were to eliminate all the purposes except those declared in paragraph 4, but to decree that those declared in paragraph 4 ought to be performed, should I be executing the trusts of this settlement?

But how in any case could I decree in what manner the trusts applicable to income were to be performed? The settlement gives no guidance at all. Mr. Hunt suggested that the trustees might apply to the court ex parte for a scheme. It is not, I think, a mere coincidence that no case has been found outside the realm of charity in which the court has yet devised a scheme of ways and means for attaining enumerated trust purposes. If it were to assume this (as I think) novel jurisdiction over public but not charitable trusts it would, I believe, necessarily require the assistance of a custodian of the public interest analogous to the Attorney-General in charity cases, who would not only help to formulate schemes but could be charged with the duty of enforcing them and preventing maladministration. There is no such person. Accordingly, in my judgment, the trusts for the application of income during "the specified period" are also void for uncertainty.

But while I have reached my decision on two separate grounds, both, I think, have their origin in a single principle, namely, that a court of equity does not recognize as valid a trust which it cannot both enforce and control. This seems to me to be good equity and good sense.

I dealt at the hearing with the trusts for accumulation and the trusts to take effect at the end of "the specified period," and the order will be drawn up accordingly."

The Need for Compliance with the Rules against Perpetuities and Inalienability

A trust for non-charitable purposes will be rendered void if it comprises property which might remain inalienable beyond the perpetuity period.[3] It is interesting to note that the English Law Commission has commented that the 'rule against inalienability is in reality, just one of the devices that is employed to keep the development of such trusts in check.'[4]

EXCEPTIONAL CASES IN WHICH PURPOSE TRUSTS HAVE BEEN ENFORCED

Tombs, Graves and Monuments

At common law a trust for the erection of a tomb, grave or monument or other memorial to a deceased person was not regarded as being charitable in nature and while s.50 of the Charities Act 1961 has modified this position in a limited

---

[3] A life or lives in being plus 21 years. See *Re Fossitt's Estate* [1934] IR 504. Note that while the Law Reform Commission has recommended the statutory abolition of the rule against perpetuities in its *Report on the Rule Against Perpetuities and Cognate Rules* (LRC 62-2000 paragraph 4.32), it has not recommended the abolition of the rule against trusts of undue duration (paragraphs 5.08, 5.13).

[4] Law Com No. 251 (1998) *The Rules Against Perpetuities and Excessive Accumulations* paragraph 1.14.

way[5] many gifts of this nature will exceed the statutory limits. In these circumstances a bequest for such a purpose will have to come within the rather anomalous exception which has developed at common law, the effect of which is that gifts for the erection of a tomb or monument or for its maintenance will be upheld as valid purpose trusts provided that they do not offend the rule against inalienability.[6] In practice gifts for the maintenance of tombs, graves or monuments will generally be declared void for this reason.[7] The only alternative options in these circumstances are to limit gifts of this nature to such period as the law permits[8] or to make a gift to a cemetery company, where one exists, to be applied for the maintenance of a grave or tomb.[9]

S.50 of the Charities Act 1961:

> **50.**—(1) Every gift made after the commencement of this Act for the provision, maintenance or improvement of a tomb, vault or grave or of a tombstone or any other memorial to a deceased person or deceased persons which would not otherwise be charitable shall, to the extent provided by this section, be a charitable gift.
>
> (2) Such a gift shall be charitable so far as it does not exceed—
>
> > (a)   in the case of a gift of income only, sixty pounds a year,
> >
> > (b)   in any other case, one thousand pounds in amount or value.

Re Conner's Trusts: Provincial Bank of Ireland Ltd. v. General Cemetery Co. of Dublin
[1960] IR 67

The testatrix bequeathed a sum of £1,000 'to the General Cemetery Company of Dublin to be applied for the maintenance and care of the family vault at Mount Jerome'. Haugh J upheld the gift as an outright bequest to the cemetery company which did not infringe the rule against perpetuities or inalienability.

HAUGH J stated at pp.70–73: "The testatrix, Mary Leonora Conner, who died on the 2nd August, 1956, by her will, dated the 15th March, 1945, made the following bequest, among others:– "One thousand pounds to the General

---

5   Set out *infra*. Note that the Law Reform Commission has recommended (*Report on the Rule Against Perpetuities and Cognate Rules* LRC 62-2000 paragraph 5.15) that as there was no index-linking provision in the Act of 1961, the monetary limits set out in s.50 should be increased to £1,000 in the case of income and £16,000 in the case of capital as of the year 2000.

6   *Mussett v. Bingle* [1876] WN 170.

7   E.g. *Toole v. Hamilton* [1901] 1 IR 383.

8   E.g. *Re Hooper* [1932] 1 Ch 38.

9   *Re Conner's Trusts* [1960] IR 67.

Cemetery Company of Dublin to be applied for the maintenance and care of the family vault at Mount Jerome."

She appointed the plaintiffs her executors. Mr. Moloney appeared for the residuary legatee, Susan Bridget Lucas, and Mr. O'Shaughnessy for the Dublin Cemetery Company. The deceased's gross assets amounted to some £44,000.

Because of this bequest the plaintiffs have issued a summons in which two questions are asked and which in short are 1, whether this legacy of £1,000 is a valid charitable gift? and 2, if it is not a charitable gift, is it a valid non-charitable gift, or is it invalid or void as infringing the rule against perpetuities?

Counsel for all parties have agreed that the first question must be answered, "No."

Mr. Matheson, for the plaintiffs, did not seek any particular answer, but awaited the direction of the Court. He did, however, draw my attention to the fact that this particular bequest differed from the bequests in all the leading cases on the subject, in that no reference was made by the testatrix to investment or income.

Mr. Moloney, for the residuary legatee, contended that this bequest infringed the rule against perpetuities, in that £1,000 properly invested should yield an income of about £60 per annum and, in ordinary circumstances, the capital sum would not be required to be touched within twenty-one years. In support, he cited three Irish cases – *Toole v. Hamilton* [1901] 1 IR 383, *Roche v. M'Dermott* [1901] 1 IR 394, *Morris v. Larkin* [1902] 1 IR 103 – and a number of English cases.

One English case, referred to by counsel for both defendants, was *In re Chardon; Johnston v. Davies* [1928] 1 Ch 464, in which a testator gave £200 to his trustees upon trust to invest it and to pay the income thereof to a cemetery company "during such period as they shall continue to maintain and keep" two specified graves "in good order and condition with flowers and plants thereon as the same have hitherto been kept by me."

The decision of Romer J. was criticised in a later edition of Jarman on Wills, but, later again, was viewed with approval by the House of Lords.

At this stage I wish to make a brief digression. I can almost take judicial notice of the fact that the income on the sum of £1,000 would purchase about the same amount of flowers and plants in 1958 as the income on £500 would purchase in the year 1927. Yet the bequest in *Chardon's Case*, with its investment and income clause and with the restrictive use of the income to be spent on flowers and plants only, was held to be a valid bequest. In the case before me there is no restriction as to how the money is to be spent, provided it is devoted to the care and maintenance of this family grave.

It seems plain to me that care and maintenance can well include, not only flowers and plants, but painting, repairing, and works of major or minor reconstruction. It may well happen that a sum of £60 (a year's income) might not be sufficient to meet a demand for work of necessary repair or reconstruction, having regard to present-day prices.

Mr. O'Shaughnessy, on behalf of the Cemetery Company, began by stating that while he was instructed to seek only the order of the Court, he felt justified in making certain legal submissions, which can be summarised as follows:– That this was an outright bequest of the £1,000 to the defendants; there was no time limit and the sum vested on death. Therefore, the capital sum is not inalienable and if it can be resorted to, at any time, the bequest does not infringe the rule.

Mr. O'Shaughnessy pointed out that it was significant that, unlike all the authorities quoted, this clause in the testatrix's will makes no reference whatever to capital investments, dividends, or income. He has submitted that I am being asked to read into the plain terms of the will words that do not appear therein – words that she could have had written in, but did not: that if it was her intention that the £1,000 should be tied, and only income utilised, why did she not say so? Counsel further suggested that if his clients, during the next two years or twenty years, decided that some reconstruction was necessary to the vault and that an expenditure of £200 was thereby necessary, they would be entitled at any time to resort to the capital to discharge their obligations should the amount of accumulated income be below £200.

He asked that the will should be construed in the manner laid down in vol. 2 of Jarman on Wills, 6th ed., 1910, articles 8 and 16, at pp. 2209 and 2210 – words should be read in their ordinary sense, and the implication was that the testatrix and her legal advisers knew the law and appreciated that an express gift of income only might well be void and accordingly the bequest deliberately avoided any reference to income, inalienability or perpetuity, so as to ensure the validity of the bequest. That is a brief summary of Mr. O'Shaughnessy's submissions.

I was strongly impressed by Mr. O'Shaughnessy's submissions. I do not have to follow *Chardon's Case* – or any case opened to me – though I would follow *Chardon's Case* if necessary. They are all quite different. They all deal with investment and the application of income. The clause in this will clearly and expressly avoids any such reference. I have no doubt whatever as to the way this question should be answered. The testatrix clearly, and in the plainest possible terms, bequeathed this sum of £1,000 to the defendant Company with one limitation only, that is, that it, the sum of £1,000, should be spent by them in the care and maintenance of this family vault at Mount Jerome and I can see nothing whatever in law, in equity, or in fact, that prevents them from resorting to the capital if, and when, they think it proper in their discretion to do so for the purposes mentioned in the will.

Accordingly, I answer the second question (which cannot be answered by a mere "Yes" or "No" by reason of the way it is framed) as follows:–

"The gift is a valid non-charitable gift which does not offend against the rule against perpetuities or any other rule"."

Animals

Gifts to provide for the welfare of animals generally or for the care and maintenance of a class of animals are regarded as being charitable in law,[10] although gifts to provide for the care of specified animals are not. While gifts in the latter category would *prima facie* seem to fall foul of the beneficiary principle they have been upheld as coming within the limited class of exceptions to the principle that non-charitable purpose trusts will not be enforced provided that they are expressed with sufficient clarity and are limited to a period of 21 years or so long as the law allows.[11]

Re Kelly: Cleary v. Dillon
[1932] IR 255

A testator bequeathed a sum of money to be applied in the care and maintenance of his dogs with a gift over should any surplus remain on the death of the last dog. Meredith J upheld the gift as being valid for a period of 21 years following the testator's death, although it was technically void for remoteness thereafter and he further concluded that the gift over was void for remoteness.

MEREDITH J stated at pp.258–264: "The first clause in the testator's will that the Court is asked to construe does not present any great difficulty that I can see. The testator says: "I devise and bequeath all my stock (except those hereinbefore bequeathed to the said Catherine Duggan) and all my property in America, and the residue of my estate of every nature and kind wheresoever situated to my executors and trustees to be sold by them and converted into money." The testator had given a number of pecuniary legacies, and he had specifically devised and bequeathed his several farms in Ireland to several persons, and had also bequeathed the stock on these farms to Catherine Duggan. Accordingly, as he expressly mentions all his stock, he excepts the stock which he had specifically dealt with. Hence the expression "the residue of my estate of every nature and kind wheresoever situated" obviously includes what remained over and above what had just been mentioned in the same sentence and the stock specifically bequeathed to Catherine Duggan and the farms that had been specifically devised and bequeathed. Here "the residue of my estate" describes the rest of the property that is to come into the hands of the executors and trustees, to be converted by them into money. So coming into their hands, the proceeds of the conversion, which comprises the said residue, all stock not previously bequeathed to Catherine Duggan, and all the property in America, are clearly applicable to the payment of the pecuniary legacies. The testator

---

[10] *Swifte v. Attorney General* [1912] 1 IR 133. See *infra* Chapter 10, p. 545.
[11] *Re Kelly* [1932] IR 255.

then adds "with the directions that my said executors and trustees shall divide the residue of my estate in equal shares between my first cousin Mary Cleary (Mamie) and my first cousins James Cleary and Catherine Cleary of Urard aforesaid, Doctor Thomas Cleary and Laurence Cleary and Patrick Dunne." Here the testator is dealing with the beneficial interest, and "the residue of my estate" means the residue of what is converted into money remaining over after the payment of the debts, funeral and testamentary expenses and pecuniary legacies. As the testator is dealing with what has all been converted into money he appropriately leaves out the previous words "of every nature and kind." The testator then adds, "and I appoint my said first cousins residuary legatees and devisees of this my will as tenants in common." This addition is quite proper, and indicates the careful manner in which the will was drawn. The residue of what was contemplated as being converted into money might not be thought to include any of the farms specifically devised and bequeathed should any such devise or bequest fail. Consequently, to prevent any uncertainty, the cousins named are made residuary legatees and devisees. The expression, "the residue of my estate," is not used in two different senses in a will simply because in two different connections it may denote different residues. In each case the expression naturally means "that which remains after what has previously been given is withdrawn," *Greville v. Browne* (1857) 7 HLC 689, at p. 705. But in the case of the residue devised and bequeathed to the executors and trustees for the purposes of the will, the residue denotes what remains after the specific devises or bequests, whereas in the case of the residue given to the residuary legatees it means what remains after what the will had expressly or impliedly provided the executors and trustees should do with the residue of the estate coming into their hands. The present case is *a fortiori* to that of *Thorman v. Hilhouse* 5 Jur. (N.S.) 563, which was cited to the Court. Question 1 (*d*) must, therefore, be answered in the affirmative, and questions 1 (*a*), (*b*) and (*c*) and question 2 need not be answered as 1 (*d*) covers the only point that arises.

The remaining question concerns the validity of the following bequest: "I leave one hundred pounds sterling to my executors and trustees for the purpose of expending four pounds sterling on the support of each of my dogs per year, and I direct that my dogs be kept in the old house at Upper Tullaroan aforesaid. Should any balance remain in the hands of my trustees on the death of the last of my dogs I leave same to the Parish Priest for the time being of the Parish of Tullaroan for masses for the repose of my soul and the souls of my parents, brothers and stepfather."

Mr. Michael Comyn, for the plaintiff, contended that both the gift for the support of the dogs and the gift over, which is to take effect on the death of the last of the dogs, are void.

It will be more convenient to deal first with the gift of any possible surplus remaining over on the death of the last of the dogs. Here the question, so far as there can be any question, is strictly one of remoteness. If the lives of the dogs or other animals could be taken into account in reckoning the maximum period of "lives in being and twenty-one years afterwards" any contingent or executory interest might be properly limited, so as only to vest within the lives of specified carp, or tortoises, or other animals that might live for over a hundred years, and for twenty-one years afterwards, which, of course, is absurd. "Lives" means human lives. It was suggested that the last of the dogs could in fact not outlive the testator by more than twenty-one years. I know nothing of that. The Court does not enter into the question of a dog's expectation of life. In point of fact neighbour's dogs and cats are unpleasantly long-lived; but I have no knowledge of their precise expectation of life. Anyway the maximum period is exceeded by the lives even of specified butterflies and twenty-one years afterwards. And even, according to my decision – and, I confess, it displays this weakness on being pressed to a logical conclusion – the expiration of the life of a single butterfly, even without the twenty-one years, would be too remote, despite all the world of poetry that may be thereby destroyed. In *Robinson v. Hardcastle* (1786) 2 Bro CC 22, at p. 30, Lord Thurlow defined a perpetuity in these words: "What is a perpetuity, but the extending the estate beyond a life in being, and twenty-one years after?" Of course by "a life" he means lives; and there can be no doubt that "lives" means lives of human beings, not of animals or trees in California.

Mr. McGuckin, for the Attorney-General, contended that the rule does not apply in the case of charities, but *Chamberlayne v. Brockett* (1872) LR 8 Ch App 206, at p. 211, cited by Mr. Price, and *Kingham v. Kingham* [1897] 1 IR 170, dispose of that contention. For these reasons, I am clearly of opinion that the gift over of the unascertained surplus on the death of the last of the dogs is void for remoteness.

I come now to the question of the validity of the trust in favour of the testator's dogs. The point that in this case there is no *cestui que trust* – for certainly the Court cannot recognise a dog as a *cestui que trust* – was treated as disposed of by *In re Dean; Cooper-Dean v. Stevens* (1889) 41 Ch D 552, and was not relied on. The trustees are ready and willing to apply the £100 for the support of the dogs, as provided by the will, and counsel expressly confined themselves to the question as to whether or not the legacy is void as tending to a perpetuity. I have had the advantage of reading the learned discussions in Mr. Gray's valuable work on "Perpetuities" and in Jarman on "Wills," but it is quite competent to counsel to refrain from raising a point on which eminent authorities differ – and I think they are well advised in so doing where the amount in dispute is so small – and, consequently, I shall deal with the question solely in connection with the perpetuity point.

Now, to begin with, I must refuse to read into the will an implied limitation to a period of twenty-one years or "for so long as the law permits." It is well established that I must first construe the will independently of the rule, and, having so construed it, then determine if any of its provisions offend. But that does not prevent me, when I have impartially construed the terms of the will, from analysing a provision which is manifestly not good in its entirety, for the purpose of determining whether the entire provision does not include a severable part which does not offend. The provision may be for a single, entire and indivisible purpose, and be *ab initio* a provision for a perpetuity and nothing less. Or the provision may in essence be constituted by what, fully and explicitly stated, is a series of provisions each for a limited period, say a week, or a month, or a year, and the whole provision may only come to offend by reason of the series being carried on indefinitely or beyond the prescribed period, and not because the provision is *ab initio* a provision for the series as a whole and nothing less. The question is clearly one of construction of the precise terms of the will. No doubt the distinction may be a fine one, but it clearly exists and is a well recognised logical distinction, and, if the adoption of the distinction saves a provision for what is in itself quite lawful from total failure, it seems to me that the intentions of the testator are entitled to the benefit of the subtlety, and certainly the object of the rule is abundantly secure by the invalidation simply of so much of the total provision as offends. So far as a provision for expenditure in a particular way for a term of years is simply provision for expenditure in a particular way for a mere sum of years, I cannot see any reason why that sum should not be treated as a mere mathematical sum divisible in any required manner. Mathematically 50 years can be dealt with as 21 + 29 years, and a provision for 50 years as a series of provisions for 21 years with an additional provision for 29 years. Hence a provision for a term of years may always be split up into provisions for lesser terms, which are comprised in one sum total, unless the provision is qualitatively of such an integral character as to prevent a mere quantitative division. In the present case the trustees are given £100 for the purpose of expending the sum of £4 "per year" on the support of each of the testator's dogs. As he would appear to have had four dogs the £100 would be exhausted in a very few years by the annual expenditure of the £16 per annum. Consequently, if I am not to speculate on a dog's expectation of life, I am actually definitely precluded from regarding the provision as one for the support of the dogs for life, though I have no doubt the testator hoped that the £100 would be sufficient to make such a provision. But the dogs might all die before the £100 was fully expended, and accordingly the testator made provision for the application of the contingent residue. It was only in that connection that there was any reference to the lives of the dogs, and there was no reference to any definite term. The provision is simply one for an amount, depending upon the number of dogs continuing to live, per year. The provision seems to me to be essentially one for successive annual expenditures, to be accounted for by the trustees at the end of each year. Each of these successive expenditures is what it is, independently of whether sufficient of the capital sum of £100 remains to provide for the future, and independently of whether I hold that any provision for expenditure in the twenty-second and succeeding years is void. The dogs have to take their chance of expenditure year by year without the benefit of any policy of insurance.

Accordingly, unless coerced by authority, I shall hold that the provision for the expenditure on the support of the dogs per year is good for the twenty-one years succeeding the death of the testator, but that the possible provision for the twenty-second and succeeding years is void for remoteness. On this view the question of perpetuity in the primary sum does not arise. It is only certain possible future expenditures that are regarded as contravening the rule against perpetuity on the ground of remoteness.

In the majority of the cases of immediate interests which have been held void as tending to create a perpetuity the trust was for an integral purpose involving a perpetuity and for nothing less, and was therefore, *ab initio* for a perpetuity. The only authority in which the possibility of there being a complete trust for a limited period was considered is *Small v. Torley* (1890) 25 LR Ir 388. Referring to *Dillon v. Reilly* (1875) IR 10 Eq 152, Porter M.R. said: "It cannot be treated as a decision that in a case where words are used which purport to tie up property beyond legal limits the Court will from thence carve out a life estate, hold it good to that extent, and reject the rest." But in that case what it was suggested to carve out was a life estate, for which severance there was no justification on the words of the will. The learned Master of the Rolls makes it clear in his judgment that the possibility of a severance must turn on the precise words of the will. The trust provided for an annual sum for saying masses for a mere term of years, and the suggestion that there was a complete and severable trust for each succeeding year, and therefore for the first twenty-one years of the term, was not raised. The invalidation of the trust for the residue of the term would have in no way affected the trust for any of the preceding years. Some reason has yet to be suggested why what is compendiously described as a mere aggregate is not as divisible in law as it is in mathematics. Suppose the trust had been worded "for twenty-one years and for one additional year," could the words "and for one additional year" have made the trust void? The suggestion seems to me absurd. For these reasons I adhere to the view that in the present case there is a valid severable trust for twenty-one years succeeding the death of the testator, provided any of the dogs live so long."

Gifts to Unincorporated Associations

While a gift to a body corporate even for non-charitable purposes will be valid because such a body has a separate legal personality and therefore can enforce it, difficulties arise where it is sought to confer a gift of a non-charitable nature on an unincorporated association. An unincorporated association has no separate personality in law and gifts of this nature may fall foul of the beneficiary principle or may contravene the rule against inalienability. A number of different methods of conferring a benefit on unincorporated associations have been devised which have been recognised as essentially overcoming these potential problems.

A *Gift to the Members of the Association for the Time Being*

A gift to an unincorporated association may be enforced if it is recognised as a gift to the members of the association alive at the time of the disposition, or in the case of a will, at the date of the testator's death. The beneficiary principle is satisfied as it is possible to ascertain who these members are and the rule against inalienability will not be infringed provided that the members are free to dispose of the property, both income and capital, at any time.

This approach of construing a gift to an association as being for the benefit of the members for the time being was successfully employed on a number of occasions particularly in the context of gifts to associations of a religious nature which were not considered at the time to be charitable in law.[12]

Re Byrne: Shaw v. Attorney General
[1935] IR 782

A testator left his residuary estate for the use and benefit of the Jesuit Order in Ireland. The majority of the Supreme Court (Fitzgibbon and Murnaghan JJ; Kennedy CJ dissenting) held that the work of the order, while largely charitable in nature, was not exclusively so and that it did not qualify as a charitable gift. Murnaghan J instead upheld the bequest as a valid gift of a non-charitable nature for the benefit of an ascertainable class of persons.

MURNAGHAN J stated at pp.811–819: "Two appeals have been brought before the Court from determinations of Mr. Justice Johnston, made on the hearing of a Summary Summons.

This summons was taken out to obtain the opinion of the Court upon several questions of construction of the will of Daniel Byrne deceased. The deceased died on 12th May, 1934, within five days of the making of his will, having bequeathed certain legacies for charitable purposes. These legacies were pecuniary legacies of which the principal in amount was £1,000 to the Most Rev. Thomas Mulvany or other the Bishop for the time being of the Catholic Diocese of Meath for the new Cathedral Building Fund.

Sect. 16 of the Charitable Donations and Bequests Act, 1844, enacts "That after the commencement of this Act no donation, devise, or bequest for pious or charitable uses in Ireland shall be valid to create or convey any estate in lands, tenements, or hereditaments for such uses, unless the deed, will, or other instrument containing the same shall be duly executed three calendar

---

[12] Note that the decision of Gavan Duffy J in *Maguire v. Attorney General* [1943] IR 238 (see *infra* Chapter 10, p. 509) marked a change in judicial attitudes towards the question of the public benefit inherent in gifts of this nature and that the provisions of s.45 of the Charities Act 1961 now confirm that gifts to contemplative religious orders are valid charitable gifts. See further Chapter 10.

months at the least before the death of the person executing the same, and unless every such deed or instrument, not being a will, shall be duly registered in the office for registering deeds in the City of Dublin within three calendar months after the execution thereof."

This section does not apply to pecuniary legacies, but in the present case the testator, having appointed executors and declared that the same persons should be his trustees for the purposes of his will, and, after bequeathing legacies, charitable and non-charitable, continued:– "I devise unto and to the use of my said trustees all the real estate I die possessed of and I bequeath to them all the personal estate I may die possessed of, upon trust to sell and convert into money my said estates or such parts thereof as may be of a saleable or convertible nature and to get in the other parts thereof, and I empower my said trustees to suspend for such period as they shall think expedient the sale, conversion or getting in of my said estates and during the suspense of the sale, conversion or getting in to manage and order all the affairs thereof. And I declare that for the purposes of enjoyment and transmission under the trusts hereinafter contained my said estates shall be considered as money from the time of my death and the rents, dividends, interest, etc., respectively to accrue due after my death shall be deemed the actual income thereof applicable as such for the purposes of the said trusts until the actual sale or conversion of the said property. And as to the moneys to arise from the sale, conversion and getting in of my said estates and moneys I direct my trustees thereout in the first place to pay or retain all the expenses incident to the execution of the preceding trusts and powers and my debts, funeral and testamentary expenses and in the next place to pay the pecuniary legacies hereinbefore bequeathed and to invest the ultimate surplus with power from time to time in the discretion of my trustees to vary such investments."

Now, these provisions of the will made a blended or mixed fund – the proceeds of realty and personalty – casting upon the lands portion of the amounts bequeathed to charitable purposes. It has been held in *Sherlock v. Blake* 10 Ir Jur NS 350 as well as in *Beardwood v. Coates* 18 WR 1154 that, if lands are directed to be sold and the proceeds applied for charitable purposes, sect. 16 of the above mentioned Act applies as it applies to a direct bequest of the lands for charitable purposes. These decisions have never since been called in question, and they have been recognised in *Donnellan v. O'Neill and Others* (1870) IR 5 Eq 523; *Stewart v. Barton* (1872) IR 6 Eq 215; *Murland v. Perry* (1879) 3 LR Ir 135, and *M'Dermott v. Attorney-General* [1922] 1 IR 139. The principle was applied by Barton J. in *Leonard v. Dowling* [1916] 1 IR 359 and in a case like the present, where the legacies were paid out of a mixed fund, an order was made for payment *pro rata*, with the consequence that the portion to be borne out of the proceeds of land failed by reason of the statute.

For the Attorney-General it is now urged that the decision in *Sherlock v. Blake* was erroneous in principle and that the section was not intended by the Legislature to apply in cases where the land was directed to be sold. It will be observed that in the cases referred to various reasons have been put forward in support of the decisions, sometimes that notwithstanding the trust for conversion into money the charity might elect to take the lands *in specie* and accomplish what the statute was intended to prevent; sometimes the reason is stated more technically that the beneficial gift to the charity must be regarded as an equitable estate in the land. Mr. Gavan Duffy has sought to criticise such an exposition of the statute and argues that the object was to prevent land itself from being held in perpetuity, and that the section has no application when the land is directed to be sold.

Although land might not be held by corporate bodies without licence from the Crown, there does not appear to have been in Ireland any restriction prior to the passing of 7 & 8 Vict., c. 97, upon the holding of land by trustees for charitable purposes. In England since the passing of 9 Geo. 2, c. 36, gifts of land or money to be laid out in the purchase of land to be held for charitable uses were declared void unless made more than 12 months before the death of the donor. This statute commenced with a preamble or recital as follows:-"Whereas gifts or alienations of lands, tenements or hereditaments in mortmain are prohibited or restrained by Magna Charta and divers other wholesome laws as prejudicial to and against the common utility, nevertheless this publick mischief has of late greatly increased by many large and improvident alienations or dispositions made by languishing or dying persons or by other persons to uses called charitable uses to take place after their deaths to the disherison of their lawful heirs." Scotland was excepted from this Act and whatever may have been the causes which led to its adoption in England the scope of the Act was very wide. In more recent times the Legislature has made substituted provisions and instead of preventing "the disherison of heirs" has directed the land in many of the cases dealt with by the earlier statute to be sold and the money proceeds to be given to the charitable purpose: Mortmain and Charitable Uses Act, 1891 (54 & 55 Vict. c. 73). This latter statute did not, however, purport to deal with Ireland and we are left to deal with 7 & 8 Vict. c. 97, which has so far not been altered by the Legislature.

Mr. Gavan Duffy's argument is based upon the proposition that the Legislature in 1844 had no object in view save to prevent the dedication of land in perpetuity and he complains that the Judges of the day imported notions derived from the English Act of George 2 as to the gifts of "languishing or dying persons" and "the disherison of their lawful heirs." It is true, as he points out, that the section in question – sect. 16 – is interpolated in an Act which is for the maintenance of charities rather than their suppression. It follows sect. 15 which enables lands or goods to be given to the Commissioners of Charitable Donations and Bequests to be held for certain purposes in connection with the Roman Catholic religion, and an argument is based on the omission in sect. 16 of any reference to chattels. But if we take the simple case of a devise of land to A upon trust to sell and apply the proceeds to charitable purposes, the very words of the Act prevent any estate passing to the trustee, and the heir-at-law by force of the statute could recover in an ejectment. Further, where a devise is made to a trustee the equitable estate is to be regarded as well as the legal estate, and in my opinion the section by its terms destroys the equitable estate sought to be created in the circumstances dealt with by the statute. The statute did have an object in naming the period of three months before death, and it is not possible to harmonise Mr. Duffy's proposition as to the object of the statute with this provision. In my opinion there is no just ground to suppose that the rule laid down in *Sherlock v. Blake* 10 Ir Jur NS 350 is wider than the statute intended. It is for the Legislature to say whether any alteration such as was made in England in 1891 should now be made.

The other appeal is concerned with the construction of the final clause contained in the will of Daniel Byrne, deceased. It reads:– "And I further direct my trustees to stand possessed of the said trust moneys or the stocks, funds and securities whereon the same shall be invested as aforesaid upon trust to pay the annual income to my nephew Gerard Shaw and my niece Aileen Shaw in equal shares during the term of their respective lives and to the survivor during his or her life. And after the death of such survivor as to as well the capital as the income of the said trust moneys, stocks, funds or securities for the absolute use and benefit of the Jesuit Order in Ireland."

Both the persons entitled to the income are alive, but it has become necessary to determine whether the ultimate gift "for the absolute use and benefit of the Jesuit Order in Ireland" is valid or not. There is considerable property both real and personal subject to the trusts of the will and, if this ultimate gift is not valid, the heir-at-law and the next-of-kin will be entitled to this undisposed of property.

The Attorney-General contends that this ultimate gift is for the benefit of a charity, and in the circumstances of the case, if this view be the correct one, the gift would be good in so far as it is not derived out of land. Evidence has been given showing that many of the activities of the Jesuit Order are charitable in the legal sense as there is no doubt that much of these activities are either for the advancement of religion or for the advancement of education. Mr. Justice Johnston has, however, quoted from Jarman on Wills (Edit. of 1910), p. 474, the following passage, and there has been no real attempt to question or qualify the principles stated in the passage. It reads:– "Where property is given to trustees for purposes that are partly charitable and partly of an indefinite nature not charitable, so that the whole might be applied for either purpose, the gift is void." I do not think it necessary to go through the evidence in detail but I am satisfied that the work of the Jesuit body, although largely charitable in the legal sense, is not so exclusively charitable in this sense that a gift may be considered as a charitable gift, if given for the purposes of the Jesuit Order in Ireland. I think it right to point out that the testator has not himself used the word charitable in this connection and it would be an undue strain upon the usual meaning of the words employed by him to say that the money has been devoted by him to a charitable purpose. In my opinion this contention of the

Attorney-General cannot be accepted.

Mr. Justice Johnston has, however, held that this gift is void for uncertainty, and an appeal has been taken against this portion of the order by two named persons who have been appointed by the Court to represent the individual members of the Jesuit Order in Ireland. Evidence has been given by affidavit which shows that the Jesuit Order is world-wide and that the Order is organised into provinces – one being the Irish province. The material portions of this affidavit are quoted in the judgment of Mr. Justice Johnston as follows:– "The said Society is a religious body or association consisting of Catholic Priests, Scholastics (that is, those in course of training for the priesthood) and lay brothers and comprises about 447 members in Ireland. The members of the said Society are bound, or in the case of novices will be bound at the end of their novitiate, by the ordinary monastic and religious vows." The learned Judge comments on this affidavit as not making clear whether or not lay brothers are bound by these vows. The affidavit then states the objects of the Society in detail and adds: "The members of the said Society are frequently referred to and known as the Jesuit Fathers or the Jesuits and the Society itself as the Jesuit Order."

The learned Judge gives the reasons which led him to hold that the gift was void for uncertainty. After commenting upon the facts of the case of *Bradshaw v. Jackman* (1887) 21 LR Ir 12, he says:– "But this is a wholly different case. The gift is to the Jesuit Order in Ireland. The members of it reside both in Northern Ireland and in the Irish Free State. They have, so far as I know, no local habitation which is common to all and they consist of three different classes of persons – priests, novices and lay brothers – who, as I gather from Father Kieran's affidavit, have widely different rights, duties and ecclesiastical status. There is in the will no expression of intention as to when the class of those who it is said are to benefit from the gift are to be ascertained, whether at the death of the testator or at some future period. There is nothing to indicate whether it is a gift to 'members' in a complete sense – that is, professed members – or whether lay brothers and scholastics are to be included as beneficiaries. Nor, indeed, is there anything to suggest whether members of the Order temporarily in Ireland, at a particular time, are objects of the testator's bounty or not. The whole thing is so uncertain that I do not see how the Court could carry out the bequest."

Several of the matters thus referred to do not appear to me to lead to the kind of uncertainty which makes a gift void at law. It is, in my opinion, settled that where a gift is to a class subsequent to life interests, in the absence of any indication to the contrary, the members of the class to take are to be ascertained at the death of the tenants-for-life or the survivor of them. Again, the amount dealt with is close upon £20,000 and, even if the number amounts to 447 persons entitled to share, there would be no difficulty in ascertaining these individuals. A gift to the crew of a ship or to members of a regiment could not be said to be void for uncertainty merely on the ground of the large number entitled to share. There are undoubtedly difficulties of construction in the other points dealt with by the learned Judge, but the Court can give a ruling as to the meaning of the words used by the testator although there are several plausible alternatives. To hold that a gift is void for uncertainty means that it is impossible for the Court to ascertain what the testator did intend.

If, by a gift for the absolute use and benefit of the Jesuit Order in Ireland, the testator meant his gift to enure for a continuing body whose existence has not received legal recognition, the gift would fail. If, on the other hand, he meant to divide his money amongst the individuals forming a class, I can see no legal objection to the validity of such a gift.

Members of religious Orders were formerly subject to legal disabilities under 10 Geo. 4, c. 7, and 7 & 8 Vict. c. 97, sect. 15. But, as Mr. Justice Johnston pointed out, all such disabilities were swept away by the Government of Ireland Act, 1920, sect. 5, sub-sect. 2:– "Any existing enactment by which any penalty, disadvantage, or disability is imposed on account of religious belief or on a member of any religious Order as such shall, as from the appointed day, cease to have effect in Ireland." It is not necessary to discuss whether this Act of 1902 has been repealed or not, as in regard to the point before the Court any repeal would not revive those enactments which were themselves repealed by the Government of Ireland Act, 1920.

Many authorities were cited stating the principle that gifts to a convent or religious or other body may be construed as gifts to the individuals associated together to form the convent or religious or other body: *Cocks v. Manners* (1871) LR 12 Eq 574; *In re Clarke, Clarke v. Clarke* [1901] 2 Ch 110; *In re Smith, Johnson v. Bright-Smith* [1914] 1 Ch 937. In the last mentioned case Joyce J. (at p. 948) remarks:– "So, in my opinion, a bequest to any un-incorporated society or association not charitable is good because, and only because, it is treated as being and is a bequest to the several members of such society or association, who can spend the money as they please. If there should be any understanding, or even contract, between these persons as to how the moneys so derived, that is from legacies, are to be expended, that is something with which in the absence of any express trust or direction in the will the executors who pay the legacy have nothing whatever to do."

I may pass by another class of case where the language used allows the Court to gather that the gift is for a charitable purpose, *e.g.*, a gift for Masses in *Bourne v. Keane* [1919] AC 815. A number of authorities have also been cited, such as *Stewart v. Green* (1871) IR 5 Eq 470; *Morrow v. M'Conville* (1883) 11 LR Ir 236, where from the language used the Court has determined that the gift was not to individuals but for a *quasi*-continuing body not recognised by law. The language of the testator must in each case be the guide and even slight indications may lead to the real meaning of the testator. A recent case in England may illustrate the difficulties of ascertaining the testator's meaning. *In re Barclay, Stewart v. Barclay* [1929] 2 Ch 173 dealt with a bequest to the Superior of the Jesuit Fathers at Farm Street, London, in which it was held in the first instance that the gift was an absolute gift to the Superior, but in the Court of Appeal it was determined that the language used led to the conclusion that a charitable gift for the maintenance of Farm Street Church was intended.

The legal principles involved are thus well settled, but it is a question of nicety to say which principle is applicable to the facts of this case. There is no difficulty in the language used by the testator which prevents it from indicating a beneficial gift to the members of the class indicated. Can it be said that it is unlikely that the testator would make such a gift? The brother of the testator was a member of the Jesuit Order in Ireland and the testator knew the practice of individual members of the Order in reference to legacies. *In re Delany's Estate* (1882) 9 LR Ir 226 was a case determined by the Court of Appeal in Ireland and the gift in that case was "to the Sisters of Mercy at Bantry." But it seems to me that on the point now under consideration the words of FitzGibbon L.J. are very applicable. He said (at p. 245):– "I decline to impute to 'the Sisters of Mercy at Bantry' the attributes of a corporate body, which they do not legally possess, merely in order to destroy the gift to them. At the same time, I see no reason to suppose that the testator imputed those attributes to them in any sense by which his gift would have been invalidated if his meaning had been more fully expressed." If it be asked what is there in the will which indicates that the individual members of the community were not to take beneficially the suggested answer is based on the number of these individuals and the improbability that they would be given personal benefits. But the testator was making a disposition to take effect only upon the decease of his nephew and niece – a younger generation – and, if he wished to devote his money to the purposes of the Order, the end would be accomplished by a legal gift to all the members for their personal benefit in law.

In my opinion the ultimate gift is a valid gift of a non-charitable nature for the benefit of a class. It is premature to determine what members the class consists of, and we have not before us the persons interested under the possible alternatives suggested. In my opinion the appeal must be allowed so far as it deals with the answer to Question 9, to which the answer is that the bequest of the remainder is not void for uncertainty. In that view Question 10 does not call for any answer."

The only real theoretical difficulty with the approach as set out in *Re Byrne* is that any member who leaves the association can take his share with him unless he assigns it to the other members and a new member will have no share in the property. More recently in England an alternative theory has been developed which has found favour with the courts in that jurisdiction and which may well also prove to be the most suitable approach for the courts here to employ.

Property Held on Trust to be Applied in Accordance with the Contract Between the Members

This so called 'contract-holding theory' involves construing a gift as one to the members of an association beneficially as an accretion to their funds to be applied in accordance with the contract existing between the members contained in the rules of the association.[13] It will satisfy the requirements of the rule against inalienability provided that the members are entitled to wind up the association and divide its property between them at any time. One clear advantage of this approach is that compliance with the beneficiary principle is not an issue as the property is held subject to the terms of a contract rather than on trust. However it is important to emphasise that the rules of the association must provide the necessary contractual element to the relationship between the members and the members must have the requisite authority to divide the assets between themselves.

Re Lipinski's Will Trusts: Gosschalk v. Levy
[1976] Ch 235

A testator bequeathed half of his residuary estate to trustees to the 'Hull Judaeans (Maccabi) Association' in memory of his late wife to be used in the work of constructing new buildings for the association and/or improving them. Oliver J upheld the gift as valid an absolute gift to the members of the association beneficially as an accretion to its funds subject to the rules of the association.

OLIVER J stated at pp. 243–250: "I approach question 1 of the summons, therefore, on the footing that this is a gift to an unincorporated non-charitable association. Such a gift, if it is an absolute and beneficial one, is of course perfectly good: see, for instance, the gift to the Corps of Commissionaires in *In re Clarke* [1901] 2 Ch 110. What I have to consider, however, is the effect of the specification by the testator of the purposes for which the legacy was to be applied.

The principles applicable to this type of case were stated by Cross J. in *Neville Estates Ltd. v. Madden* [1962] Ch 832, 849, and they are conveniently summarised in Tudor, *Charities*, 6th ed. (1967) p. 150, where it is said:

> "In *Neville Estates Ltd. v. Madden* Cross J. expressed the opinion (which is respectfully accepted as correct) that every such gift might according to the actual words used, be construed in one of three quite different ways: (a) As a gift to the members of the association at the date of the gift as joint tenants so

---

[13] *Re Lipinski's Will Trusts* [1976] Ch 235. See also *Re Recher's Will Trusts* [1972] Ch 526.

that any member could sever his share and claim it whether or not he continued to be a member. (b) As a gift to the members of the association at the date of the gift not as joint tenants, but subject to their contractual rights and liabilities towards one another as members of the association. In such a case a member cannot sever his share. It will accrue to the other members on his death or resignation, even though such members include persons who become members after the gift took effect. If this is the gift, it will not be open to objection on the score of perpetuity or uncertainty unless there is something in its terms or circumstances or in the rules of the association which precludes the members at any given time from dividing the subject of the gift between them on the footing that they are solely entitled to it in equity. (c) The terms or circumstances of the gift or the rules of the association may show that the property in question – i.e., the subject of the gift – is not to be at the disposal of the members for the time being but is to be held in trust for or applied for the purposes of the association as a quasi-corporate entity. In this case the gift will fail unless the association is a charitable body."

That summary may require, I think, a certain amount of qualification in the light of subsequent authority, but for present purposes I can adopt it as a working guide. Mr. Blackburne, for the next-of-kin, argues that the gift in the present case clearly does not fall within the first category, and that the addition of the specific direction as to its employment by the association prevents it from falling into the second category. This is, therefore, he says, a purpose trust and fails both for that reason and because the purpose is perpetuitous. He relies upon this passage from the judgment of the Board in *Leahy v. Attorney-General for New South Wales* [1959] AC 457, 478:

"If the words 'for the general purposes of the association' were held to import a trust, the question would have to be asked, what is the trust and who are the beneficiaries? A gift can be made to persons (including a corporation) but it cannot be made to a purpose or to an object: so also, a trust may be created for the benefit of persons as cestuis que trust but not for a purpose or object unless the purpose or object be charitable. For a purpose or object cannot sue, but, if it be charitable, the Attorney-General can sue to enforce it."

Mr. Blackburne points out, first, that the gift is in memory of the teacher's late wife (which, he says, suggests an intention to create a permanent memorial or endowment); secondly, that the gift is *solely* for a particular purpose (which would militate strongly against any suggestion that the donees could wind up and pocket the money themselves, even though their constitution may enable them to do so); and, thirdly, that the gift contemplates expenditure on "improvements," which connotes a degree of continuity or permanence. All this, he says, shows that what the testator had in mind was a permanent endowment in memory of his late wife.

For my part, I think that very little turns upon the testator's having expressed the gift as being in memory of his late wife. I see nothing in this expression which suggests any intention to create a permanent endowment. It indicates merely, I think, a tribute which the testator wished to pay, and is not without significance that this self-same tribute appeared in the earlier will in which he made an absolute and outright gift to the association. The evidential value of this in the context of a construction summons may be open to doubt, and I place no reliance upon it. It does, however, seem to me that nothing is to be derived from these words beyond the fact that the testator wished the association to know that his bounty was a tribute to his late wife.

I accept, however, Mr. Blackburne's submission that the designation of the sole purpose of the gift makes it impossible to construe the gift as one falling into the first of Cross J.'s categories, even if that were otherwise possible. But I am not impressed by the argument that the gift shows an intention of continuity. Mr. Blackburne prays in aid *In re Macaulay's Estate* [1943] Ch 435 which is reported as a note to *In re Price* [1943] Ch 422, where the gift was for the "maintenance and improvement of the Theosophical Lodge at Folkestone." The House of Lords held that it failed for perpetuity, the donee being a non-charitable body. But it is clear from the speeches of both Lord Buckmaster and Lord Tomlin that their Lordships derived the intention of continuity from the reference to "maintenance." Here it is quite evident that the association was to be free to spend the capital of the legacy. As Lord Buckmaster said in *In re Macaulay's Estate*, at p. 436:

> "In the first place it is clear that the mere fact that the beneficiary is an unincorporated society in no way affects the validity of the gift . . . . The real question is what is the actual purpose for which the gift is made. There is no perpetuity if the gift were for the individual members for their own benefit, but that, I think, is clearly not the meaning of this gift. Nor again is there a perpetuity if the society is at liberty in accordance with the terms of the gift, to spend both capital and income as they think fit."

In re Price itself is authority for the proposition that a gift to an unincorporated non-charitable association for objects upon which the association is at liberty to spend both capital and income will not fail for perpetuity, although the actual conclusion in that case has been criticised – the point that the trust there (the carrying on of the teachings of Rudolf Steiner) was a purpose trust and thus unenforceable on that ground was not argued. It does not seem to me, therefore, that in the present case there is a valid ground for saying that the gift fails for perpetuity.

But that is not the end of the matter. If the gift were to the association simpliciter, it would, I think, clearly fall within the second category of Cross J.'s categories. At first sight, however, there appears to be a difficulty in arguing that the gift is to members of the association subject to their contractual rights inter se when there is a specific direction or limitation sought to be imposed upon those contractual rights as to the manner in which the subject matter of the gift is to be dealt with. This says Mr. Blackburne, is a pure "purpose trust" and is invalid on that ground, quite apart from any question of perpetuity. I am not sure, however, that it is sufficient merely to demonstrate that a trust is a "purpose" trust. With the greatest deference, I wonder whether the dichotomy postulated in the passage which I have referred to in the judgment of the Board in *Leahy's* case [1959] AC 457, 478 is not an over-simplification. Indeed, I am not convinced that it was intended as an exhaustive statement or to do more than indicate the broad division of trusts into those where there are ascertainable beneficiaries (whether for particular purposes or not) and trusts where there are none. Indeed, that this is the case, as it seems to me, is to be derived from a later passage on p. 484 of the report, which is in these terms:

> "At the risk of repetition their Lordships would point out that, if a gift is made to individuals, whether under their own names or in the name of their society, and the conclusion is reached that they are not intended to take beneficially, then they take as trustees. If so, it must be ascertained who are the beneficiaries. If at the death of the testator the class of beneficiaries is fixed and ascertained or ascertainable within the limit of the rule against perpetuities, all is well. If it is not so fixed and not so ascertainable the trust must fail. Of such a trust no better example could be found than a gift to an Order for the benefit of a community of nuns, once it is established that the community is not confined to living and ascertained persons. A wider question is opened if it appears that the trust is not for persons but for a non-charitable purpose. As has been pointed out no one can enforce such a trust. What follows? Ex hypothesi the trustees are not themselves the beneficiaries yet the trust fund is in their hands, and they may or may not think fit to carry out their testator's wishes. If so, it would seem that the testator has imperfectly exercised his testamentary power; he has delegated it, for disposal of his property lies with them, not with him. Accordingly, the subject matter of the gift will be undisposed of or fall into the residuary estate as the case may be."

There would seem to me to be, as a matter of common sense, a clear distinction between the case where a purpose is prescribed which is clearly intended for the benefit of ascertained or ascertainable beneficiaries particularly where those beneficiaries have the power to make the capital their own, and the case where no beneficiary at all is intended (for instance, a memorial to a favourite pet) or where the beneficiaries are unascertainable: as in the case, for instance, of *In re Price* [1943] Ch 422. If a valid gift may be made to an unincorporated body as a simple accretion to the funds which are the subject matter of the contract which the members have made inter se – and *Neville Estates Ltd. v. Madden* [1962] Ch 832, and *In re Recher's Will Trusts* [1972] Ch 526 show that it may – I do not really see why such a gift, which specifies a purpose which is within the powers of the association and of which the members of the association are the beneficiaries, should fail. Why are not the beneficiaries able to enforce the trust or, indeed, in the exercise of their contractual rights to terminate the trust for their own benefit? Where the donee association is itself the beneficiary of the prescribed purpose, there seems to me to be the strongest argument in common sense for saying that the gift should be construed as an absolute one within the second category – the more so where, if the purpose is carried out, the members can by appropriate action vest the resulting property in themselves, for here the trustees and the beneficiaries are the same persons.

Is such a distinction as I have suggested borne out by the authorities? The answer is, I think, "not in terms," until recently. But the cases appear to me to be at least consistent with this. For instance, *In re Clarke* [1901] 2 Ch 110 (the case of the Corps of Commissionaires); *In re Drummond* [1914] 2 Ch 90 (the case of the Old Bradfordians) and *In re Taylor* [1940] Ch 481 (the case of the Midland Bank Staff Association), in all of which the testator had prescribed purposes for which the gifts were to be used, and in all of which the gifts were upheld, were all cases where there were ascertainable beneficiaries; whereas in *In re Wood* [1949] Ch 498 and *Leahy's* case (where the gifts failed) there were none. *In re Price* is perhaps out of line, because there there was no ascertained beneficiary and yet Cohen J. was prepared to uphold the gift even on the supposition that (contrary to his own conclusion) the purpose was non-charitable. But, as I have mentioned, the point about the trust being a purpose trust was not argued before him.

A striking case which seems to be not far from the present is *In re Turkington* [1937] 4 All ER 501, where the gift was to a masonic lodge "as a fund to build a suitable temple in Stafford." The members of the lodge being both the trustees and the beneficiaries of the temple, Luxmoore J. construed the gift as an absolute one to the members of the lodge for the time being.

Directly in point is the more recent decision of Goff J. in *In re Denley's Trust Deed* [1969] 1 Ch 373 where the question arose as to the validity of a deed under which land was held by trustees as a sports ground:

> "primarily for the benefit of employees of [a particular company] and secondarily for the benefit of such other person or persons as the trustees may allow to use the same. . . ."

The latter provision was construed by Goff J. as a power and not a trust. The same deed conferred on the employees a right to use and enjoy the land subject to regulations made by the trustees. Goff J. held that the rule against enforceability of non-charitable "purpose or object" trusts, was confined to those which were abstract or impersonal in nature where there was no beneficiary or cestui que trust. A trust which, though expressed as a purpose, was directly or indirectly for the benefit of an individual or individuals was valid provided that those individuals were ascertainable at any one time and the trust was not otherwise void for uncertainty. Goff J. said, at p. 382:

> "I think there may be a purpose or object trust, the carrying out of which would benefit an individual or individuals, where that benefit is so indirect or intangible or which is otherwise so framed as not to give those persons any locus standi to apply to the court to enforce the trust, in which case the beneficiary principle would, as it seems to me, apply to invalidate the trust, quite apart from any question of uncertainty or perpetuity. Such cases can be considered if and when they arise. The present is not, in my judgment, of that character, and it will be seen that clause 2 (d) of the trust deed expressly states that, subject to any rules and regulations made by the trustees, the employees of the company shall be

entitled to the use and enjoyment of the land. Apart from this possible exception, in my judgment the beneficiary principle of *In re Astor's Settlement Trusts* [1952] Ch 534, which was approved in *In re Endacott, decd.* [1960] Ch 232 – see particularly by Harman L.J., at p. 250 – is confined to purpose or object trusts which are abstract or impersonal. The objection is not that the trust is for a purpose or object per se, but that there is no beneficiary or cestui que trust . . . Where, then, the trust, though expressed as a purpose, is directly or indirectly for the benefit of an individual or individuals, it seems to me that it is in general outside the mischief of the beneficiary principle."

I respectfully adopt this, as it seems to me to accord both with authority and with common sense.

If this is the right principle, then on which side of the line does the present case fall? Mr. Morritt has submitted in the course of his argument in favour of charity that the testator's express purpose "solely in the work of constructing the new buildings for the association" referred and could only refer to the youth centre project, which was the only project for the erection of buildings which was under consideration at the material time. If this is right, then the trust must, I think, fail, for it is quite clear that that project as ultimately conceived embraced not only the members of the association, but the whole Jewish community in Hull, and it would be difficult to argue that there was any ascertainable beneficiary. I do not, however, so construe the testator's intention. The evidence it that the testator knew the association's position and that he took a keen interest in it. I infer that he was kept informed of its current plans. The one thing that is quite clear from the minutes is that from 1965 right up to the testator's death there was great uncertainty about what was going to be done. There was a specific project for the purchase of a house in 1965. By early 1966 the youth centre was back in favour. By October 1966 it was being suggested that the association should stay where they were in their rented premises. The meeting of March 21 is, I think, very significant because it shows that they were again thinking in terms of their own exclusive building and that the patrons (of whom the testator was one) would donate the money when it was needed. At the date of the will, the association had rejected the youth centre plans and were contemplating again the purchase of premises of their own, and thereafter interest shifted to the community centre. I am unable to conclude that the testator had any specific building in mind; and, in my judgment, the reference to "the" buildings for the association means no more than whatever buildings the association may have or may choose to erect or acquire. The reference to improvements reflects, I think, the testator's contemplation that the association might purchase or might, at his death, already have purchased an existing structure which might require improvement or conversion, or even that they might, as had at one time been suggested, expend money in improving the premises which they rented from the Jewish Institute. The association was to have the legacy to spend in this way for the benefit of its members.

I have already said that, in my judgment, no question of perpetuity arises here, and accordingly the case appears to me to be one of the specification of a particular purpose for the benefit of ascertained beneficiaries, the members of the association for the time being. There is an additional factor. This is a case in which, under the constitution of the association, the members could, by the appropriate majority, alter their constitution so as to provide, if they wished, for the division of the association's assets among themselves. This has, I think, a significance. I have considered whether anything turns in this case upon the testator's direction that the legacy shall be used "solely" for one or other of the specified purposes. Mr. Rossdale has referred me to a number of cases where legacies have been bequeathed for particular purposes and in which the beneficiaries have been held entitled to override the purpose, even though expressed in mandatory terms.

Perhaps the most striking in the present context is *In re Bowes* [1896] 1 Ch 507, where money was directed to be laid out in the planting of trees on a settled estate. That was a "purpose" trust, but there were ascertainable beneficiaries, the owners for the time being of the estate; and North, J. held that the persons entitled to the settled estate were entitled to have the money whether or not it was laid out as directed by the testator. He says, at p. 510:

> "Then, the sole question is where this money is to go to. Of course, it is a perfectly good legacy. There is nothing illegal in the matter, and the direction to plant might easily be carried out; but it is not necessarily capable of being performed, because the owner of the estate might say he would not have any trees planted upon it at all. If that were the line he took, and he did not contend for anything more than that, the legacy would fail; but he says he does not refuse to have trees planted upon it; he is content that trees should be planted upon some part of it; but the legacy has not failed. If it were necessary to uphold it, the trees can be planted upon the whole of it until the fund is exhausted. Therefore, there is nothing illegal in the gift itself; but the owners of the estate now say: 'It is a very disadvantageous way of spending this money; the money is to be spent for our benefit, and that of no one else; it was not intended for any purpose other than our benefit and that of the estate. That is no reason why it should be thrown away by doing what is not for our benefit, instead of being given to us, who want to have the enjoyment of it.' I think their contention is right. I think the fund is devoted to improving the estate, and improving the estate for the benefit of the persons who are absolutely entitled to it."

I can see no reason why the same reasoning should not apply in the present case simply because the beneficiary is an unincorporated non-charitable association. I do not think the fact that the testator has directed the application "solely" for the specified purpose adds any legal force to the direction. The beneficiaries, the members of the association for the time being, are the persons who could enforce the purpose and they must, as it seems to me, be entitled not to enforce it or, indeed, to vary it.

Thus, it seems to me that whether one treats the gift as a "purpose" trust or as an absolute gift with a superadded direction or, on the analogy of *In re Turkington* [1937] 4 All ER 501 as a gift where the trustees and the beneficiaries are the same persons, all roads lead to the same conclusion.

In my judgment, the gift is a valid gift, and I will answer question 1 of the summons in sense (a).

The second question relates to clause 4 (c) of the will. I feel no real difficulty about this. The Board of Guardians is and was at the material time a charity. It had some buildings upon which money could be expended; so no question of practicability, in my judgment, arises. The attack on this clause has been on the basis that the reference to "the association" was a reference not to the Board of Guardians but to the association named in clause 4 (a). Having regard to the conclusion to which I have come on clause 4 (a), this would not, I think, even if correct, help the next-of-kin, but in fact the interpretation sought to be put upon the gift attributes to the testator a degree of eccentricity for which there is no warrant in the evidence before me, which gives no indication of any noticeable irrationality. I can think of no possible reason why a testator who desired to confer a benefit on the Hull Judeans should give two-thirds to the Judeans direct in memory of his wife and one-third via a charitable body which took no interest under the will and without any reference to his wife. "Association" is a perfectly apt description of the Board of Guardians, which is an unincorporated body, and I have no doubt at all that this body is what the testator referred to when he used the word in the designation of his purpose under clause 4 (c). I will accordingly answer question 2 likewise in sense (a).

I will appoint Mr. Shtein, the third-defendant, to represent the next-of-kin of the testator. I will order the costs of the plaintiffs to be taxed and the costs of all the other parties to be taxed on the common fund basis, and direct that the costs as so taxed be raised, retained or paid out the estate in the ordinary course of administration."

Conclusion

Trusts for the erection and maintenance of tombs, graves and monuments and for the care of animals seem to be accepted as enforceable provided that they do not offend the rule against inalienability. In addition, provided that the certainty requirement is met it would appear that trusts for unincorporated associations can be enforced if one of the constructions outlined above is applied. However, doubt remains about the validity of other forms of non-charitable purpose trusts and the warning given by Harman LJ in the decision of the Court of Appeal in *Re Endacott* [14] that the categories of these 'anomalous' cases should not be extended should be borne in mind.

---

[14] [1960] Ch 232.

Re Endacott: Corpe v. Endacott
[1960] Ch 232

The testator bequeathed his residuary estate to a specified parish council 'for the purpose of providing some useful memorial to myself'. The Court of Appeal (Lord Evershed MR, Sellers and Harman LJJ) held that the gift was void on the grounds that it did not fall within the 'anomalous' class of non-charitable purpose trusts which would be enforced and that it was of too wide and uncertain a nature to qualify as an enforceable trust.

HARMAN LJ stated at pp.250–251: "At first sight, my mind recoiled from the possibility of this gift being held valid, and I have not seen any cause in the course of the hearing to resile from that view. One must first construe the will; and my view of that is that this testator, as my Lord has said, intended by his will to provide himself with a memorial in his native town. He added that the memorial to himself should also be useful. In other words, it must not consist of a statue of the testator "in his habit as he lived" (Hamlet, Act III, Scene iv), unless that would serve some useful purpose; but it was not primarily of the benefit to the inhabitants of North Tawton that he thought, but of perpetuation of his own memory. So read, it seems to me apparent that the law cannot uphold the will, unless connected with the fabric of a church, without throwing over every kind of authority on this subject. A gift for public purposes in the parish of North Tawton, a gift for patriotic purposes, a gift for benevolent purposes, are all, as we all know, universally now held to be bad. How, then, shall it be held that a gift for useful purposes is good without upsetting the whole structure so elaborately built up and, one had hoped after *Diplock's* case [1941] Ch 253; [1944] AC 341; [1944] 2 All ER 60, so firmly established? I cannot think that charity has anything to do with this bequest. As for establishing it without the crutch of charity, I applaud the orthodox sentiments expressed by Roxburgh J. in the *Astor* case [1952] Ch 534 and I think, as I think he did, that though one knows there have been decisions at times which are not really to be satisfactorily classified, but are perhaps merely occasions when Homer has nodded, at any rate these cases stand by themselves and ought not to be increased in number, nor indeed followed, except where the one is exactly like another. Whether it would be better that some authority now should say those cases were wrong, this perhaps is not the moment to consider. At any rate, I cannot think a case of this kind, the case of providing outside a church an unspecified and unidentified memorial, is the kind of instance which should be allowed to add to those troublesome, anomalous and aberrant cases.

In my judgment, Danckwerts J. came to the right conclusion, and this appeal ought to be dismissed."

CHAPTER 10

Charitable Trusts

INTRODUCTION

Charitable trusts are an exception to the general principle that trusts for purposes rather than for the benefit of persons are invalid. They do not depend on the existence of human beneficiaries to enforce them for their validity and are considered to be of a public nature and as such are enforceable by the Attorney General. In addition, the rule against inalienability does not apply to them, although the initial vesting must take place within the relevant perpetuity period.

Definition of Charity

A list of charitable purposes was contained in the Preamble to the Irish Statute of Charitable Uses 1634[1] although this was intended merely to enumerate a variety of purposes recognised as being legally charitable. In addition, this list was never intended to be exhaustive and as Keane J has recently re-iterated in *Re Worth Library*,[2] a trust might be considered charitable if it fell within the 'spirit or intendment' of the statute. Now a claim to charitable status is generally determined by considering whether a particular purpose comes within one of the four broad categories identified by Lord Macnaghten in *Commissioners for Special Purposes of Income Tax v. Pemsel*,[3] which are as follows:

1. Trusts for the relief of poverty
2. Trusts for the advancement of education
3. Trusts for the advancement of religion
4. Trusts for other purposes beneficial to the community

What this classification fails to make clear explicitly is that for a trust to be regarded as legally charitable, it must not only contain some element of benefit, e.g. the relief of poverty, but also incorporate an element of *public* benefit. As explained below, this concept of public benefit varies considerably as between the different categories of charitable trusts. Many of these issues are considered by Keane J in his comprehensive judgment in *Re Worth Library*[4] which examines issues ranging from the definition of what is legally charitable to the

---

[1] Repealed by the Statute Law Revision Act (Ireland) 1878.
[2] [1995] 2 IR 301, 333.
[3] [1891] AC 531, 583.
[4] [1995] 2 IR 301.

circumstances in which *cy-près* jurisdiction may be exercised by the High Court.

Re Worth Library: Trinity College Dublin v. Attorney General
[1995] 2 IR 301

By his will drawn up in 1723, Dr Worth left a collection of books to trustees to be kept in a room in Dr Steevens' Hospital for the use and benefit of the physician, chaplain and surgeon for the time being of the hospital. When the hospital was closed in 1988, the trustees of the library decided to transfer it temporarily to Trinity College, Dublin for safekeeping and the college sought a *cy-près* order from the High Court to enable the books to be permanently transferred to their care. The second named defendant, the Eastern Health Board, which had purchased the hospital premises, opposed the application. Keane J concluded that the *cy-près* scheme to be framed by the court must provide for the retention of the books in their original setting and adjourned the matter to enable a draft scheme to this effect to be prepared.

KEANE J stated at pp.331–348:

"*V. Legal submissions of the parties*
At the outset of the legal arguments in the case, I indicated to counsel that I would require submissions to be made on the following matters:–

  (a) Whether the bequest by Dr. Worth of the Worth Library was in law a charitable bequest;
  (b) If it was a charitable bequest, the nature of the charity intended to be benefited by Dr. Worth;
  (c) If it was a charitable bequest, whether conditions had arisen for the exercise by the court of the *cy-près* jurisdiction;
  (d) If the answer to (c) was in the affirmative, whether the scheme proposed by the plaintiffs was one which should be ordered by the court to be carried into effect.

Counsel said they were in agreement that the bequest was a charitable bequest. However, I took the view that this was not a case in which the court was solely concerned with the resolution of issues between private parties, where the court might be unwilling to raise matters which the parties had agreed not to raise. This was a case in which the court was being invited to exercise its *cy-près* jurisdiction, a jurisdiction which can only be exercised in the case of charitable donations and bequests and no other bequests. Counsel for the plaintiffs and the Health Board were reluctant to advance any submissions to the effect that there was no charitable bequest, for obvious reasons: if the bequest was found to be non-charitable, it would clearly contravene the rule against perpetuities and there would be a resulting trust in favour of the descendants of Dr. Worth. If those descendants were not ascertainable, the library would presumably escheat to the State under the State Property Act, 1954. While the Attorney General had a contingent interest in the latter possibility, it was understandable that counsel on his behalf did not seek to argue that the bequest was not charitable, since he appeared in the case in his role as the protector of charities. In the result, there was no *legitimus contradictor* to contest the proposition that this was a charitable bequest. While this did not make the resolution of the matter any easier, I considered it essential, for the reasons already stated, to consider the issue as to whether the bequest was a charitable bequest.

Mr. Gordon on behalf of the plaintiffs submitted that the bequest was a charitable gift for the advancement of education or, in the alternative, the advancement of learning and in either case was for the benefit of the community. He submitted that since the intentions of Dr. Worth could no longer be carried out and the Governors, having considered the various possibilities, had decided to entrust the future custody of the books to Trinity College, the appropriate conditions had arisen for the framing of the *cy-près* scheme in the manner proposed by the plaintiffs. He said that preserving the library as an integral collection in a great centre of scholarship and learning such as Trinity College would be the most appropriate means of carrying into effect Dr. Worth's intentions in the greatly changed circumstances of today. He submitted that, apart from these considerations, Dr. Worth's own associations with Trinity College, of which he was graduate, and the long association of Trinity College with Dr. Steevens' Hospital, signified by the presence of the Provost as an *ex officio* Governor, also indicated that this would be an appropriate means of carrying into effect Dr. Worth's intentions. He also submitted that the maintenance by the Health Board of the library in their headquarters and the expenditure of funds to that end was *ultra vires* the powers of the Health Board under the Health Acts, 1947 to 1991.

Mr. Butler on behalf of the Attorney General submitted that the bequest was a charitable gift analogous to the bequest of money for the maintenance of a library for a regimental officers' mess found to be charitable by Farwell J. in *In re Good, Harrington v. Watts* [1905] 2 Ch 60. He said that it was the view of the Attorney General that it would be preferable to keep the books in the hospital where they were originally housed, provided the practical difficulties that had been discussed during the course of the hearing could be resolved to the satisfaction of the court.

Mr. Herbert on behalf of the Health Board submitted that the bequest was a charitable gift for the benefit of the hospital. He said the charitable nature of gifts to hospitals had been established beyond doubt by the decision of the former Supreme Court in *Barrington's Hospital v. Commissioner of Valuation* [1957] IR 299. He submitted that the whole tenor of the will reflected Dr. Worth's intention to benefit the hospital rather than any individuals and that the words in the will "for the use, benefit and behoof of the physician, chaplain and surgeon for the time being of the said hospital" and the directions as to the safe-keeping of the books should be regarded as imposing a precatory trust on the trustees with which they were not necessarily obliged to comply, citing in support the decision of Murray J. in the Northern Ireland case of *In re Steele, Northern Bank Executor and Trustees Ltd v. Linton and Others* [1976] NI 66. He submitted that, in the alternative, the gift could be regarded as one for educational purposes which was beneficial to the community and that the fact that it was for the benefit of a numerically insignificant group was not of importance. He submitted that, whether the gift was for the benefit of the hospital or for educational purposes, the library itself should be preserved in the building for which it had been originally intended by Dr. Worth and that the evidence before the court established that this could be done without endangering the books themselves or rendering them less accessible to scholars. He submitted that the views of the Attorney General as the protector of charities on a matter of this nature should carry particular weight with the court. He finally submitted that the Health Board clearly had power under the Health Acts to maintain the library and apply funds for that purpose, referring in particular to s. 78 of the Act of 1947, and s. 60, sub-s. 3 of the Act of 1970.

VI. The applicable law

Although the jurisdiction of the Court of Chancery to enforce charitable status is sometimes referred to as originating in the English and Irish Statutes of Charitable Uses (43 Eliz. 1, c. 4; 10 Car. 1, Sess. 3, c. 1) passed respectively in the reigns of Elizabeth I and Charles I, it is generally accepted that the jurisdiction dates from an earlier time. The significance of the two statutes (both long repealed) is that the preambles have, in numerous cases, been treated by judges as providing an "index" to charities recognised by the law. In addition, however, the law has identified new purposes as charitable as they arose for consideration. Thus, the list of charitable purposes in the relevant statute is not exhaustive and a trust may still be charitable if it is within "its spirit and intendment": *Morice v. Bishop of Durham* (1804) 9 Ves 399. Although the wording of the preambles is different, it has also been held that the Irish Act was an "exact pattern" of the English Act and intended to effect the same results: *Incorporated Society v. Richards* (1841) 1 Dr & War 258.

The charitable purposes set out in the Irish Statute are:

> "The erection, maintenance or support of any college, school, lecturer in divinity, or in any of the liberal arts or sciences, or for the relief of any manner of poor, succourless, distressed or impotent persons, or for the building, re-edifying or maintaining in repair of any Church, college, school or hospital, or for the maintenance of any minister or preacher of the Holy Word of God, or for the erection, building, maintenance or repair of any bridges, causeyes, cashes paces and highways within this realm, or for any other like lawful and charitable use and uses, warranted by the laws of this realm now established and in force . . ."

In the course of his argument in *Morice v. Bishop of Durham* (1804) 9 Ves 399, Sir Samuel Romilly said in a much cited passage at p. 532:–

"There are four objects, within one of which all Charity, to be administered in this Court, must fall: 1st, Relief of the indigent; in various ways: Money: Provisions: Education: Medical Assistance: etc. 2ndly, the Advancement of Learning: 3rdly, the Advancement of Religion and, 4thly, which is the most difficult, the advancement of objects of general public utility".

He also drew a distinction, which was repeatedly echoed in subsequent cases, between "charity" and what he called "liberality" (or "benevolence", to use the expression more popular in the later cases), which is not synonymous in law with "charity".

Romilly's classification of legal charities into four categories was adopted by Lord Macnaghten in his celebrated speech in *Commissioners of Income Tax v. Pemsel* [1891] AC 531 with one amendment, which is of some significance in the present context. The frequently cited passage, at p. 583, is as follows:-

"How far then, it may be asked, does the popular meaning of the word 'charity' correspond with its legal meaning? 'Charity' in its legal sense comprises four principal divisions: trusts for the relief of poverty; trusts for the advancement of education; trusts for the advancement of religion; and trusts for other purposes beneficial to the community, not falling under any of the preceding heads. The trusts last referred to are not the less charitable in the eye of the law, because incidentally they benefit the rich as well as the poor, as indeed every charity that deserves the name must do either directly or indirectly."

Lord Macnaghten's substitution of "education" for "learning" does not mean that gifts which can be regarded as for the advancement of learning but cannot be regarded as gifts for the advancement of education, as the latter expression has been construed by the courts, are not charitable. They may be charitable if they are for the benefit of the public. The distinction is material, since it has been held in England that gifts in the first three categories are presumed to be for the public benefit. In *National Anti-Vivisection Society v. Inland Revenue Commissioners* [1948] AC 31, at p. 65, Lord Simonds said:–

"If the purpose is within one of the heads of charity forming the first three classes in the classification which Lord Macnaghten borrowed from Sir Samuel Romilly's argument in *Morice v. Bishop of Durham*, the Court will easily conclude that it is a charitable purpose . . . When a purpose appears broadly to fall within one of the familiar categories of charity, the Court will assume it to be for the benefit of the community and, therefore, charitable, unless the contrary is shown, and . . . the Court will not be astute in such a case to defeat on doubtful evidence the avowed benevolent intention of a donor."

To that statement of the law, one rider is necessary in Ireland: in the case of gifts for the advancement of religion, the presumption that they are charitable is conclusive by virtue of s. 45 of the Charities Act, 1961.

There was some discussion in the arguments of counsel in the present case as to the divergence of views between Irish and English judges as to whether charitable trusts within the fourth category are to be examined by reference to a subjective or an objective test. That divergence of view also existed, in a far more acute form, in the case of trusts for the advancement of religion but is no longer relevant since the enactment of s. 45 of the Act of 1961 to which I have already referred. In the case of gifts in the fourth category, it is of less significance than is sometimes supposed, as a careful study of the judgment of FitzGibbon L.J. in *In re Cranston, Webb v. Oldfield* [1898] 1 IR 431 and the speech of Lord Simonds in *National Anti-Vivisection Society v. Inland Revenue Commissioners* [1948] AC 31 makes clear. In the present case I do not think that the distinction, to the extent that it can be said to exist, has any relevance. In every case, the intention of the testator is of paramount importance. If he intended to advance a charitable object recognised as such by the law, his gift will be a charitable gift. In the case of gifts which do not come within the first three categories, the fact that the testator's view as to the public utility of his favoured object – e.g. vegetarianism – is not shared by many people will not of itself prevent it from being, in the eyes of the law, a valid charitable object within the fourth category, provided it is not illegal, irrational or *contra bonos mores*. That, as I understand it, is the effect of the majority decision of the Irish Court of Appeal in *In re Cranston, Webb v. Oldfield* [1898] 1 IR 431. In the present case, the two possible charitable objects which came into the fourth category – the advancement of learning and of hospitals – would be considered as beneficial to the public by an appreciable number of people and are obviously not illegal, irrational or *contra bonos mores*. Consequently, the divergence of view sometimes thought to exist between the English and Irish courts is not material.

There is one other principle of general application to which I should refer. The court leans in favour of charities and, consequently, will prefer a construction which gives effect to the testator's desire to benefit a stated object rather than one which leads to a failure of the bequest.

I now turn to the specific forms of charitable bequests which arise for consideration in the present case. The first category - gifts for the advancement of education - would embrace, not merely gifts to schools and universities and the endowment of university chairs and scholarships: "education" has been given a broad meaning so as to encompass gifts for the establishment of theatres, art galleries and museums and the promotion of literature and music. In every case, however, the element of public benefit must be present and, if the benefit extends to a section of the community only, that section must not be numerically negligible. In *Re McEnery, O'Connell v. Attorney General* [1941] IR 323 at p. 327, Gavan Duffy J. laid particular stress on this last aspect of education charities. In that case, the bequest was of a trust fund for enabling the nephews and nieces of the testator and their male descendants to obtain professions. The learned judge pointed out that it was then over 200 years since Lord

Hardwicke L.C. in *Attorney-General v. Pearce* (1740) 2 Atk 87 declared that it was its extensiveness that constitutes a public charity. Gavan Duffy J. concluded that:–

> "The trust here is, in my opinion, too narrow to be charitable; the motive may have been charitable, but the intention was to benefit specific individuals, and the fact, though not conclusive, is worthy of note that, if the trust were good, each suitable beneficiary would appear to have an enforceable claim upon the trust . . ."

Even more strikingly, in *Oppenheim v. Tobacco Securities Trust Company Ltd* [1951] AC 297 a trust for the education of children of employees, or former employees, of a group of companies was held not charitable, although the number of employees exceeded 110,000. In each of these cases, the trust failed, of course, not simply because the numbers were insignificant (they could certainly not have been so described in the *Oppenheim* case): they also suffered from the generally fatal defect of a requirement that the beneficiaries be related to or connected with a named *propositus*.

In the present case, even if it would be said that the bequest was for educational purposes (and, given the insignificant proportion of the library devoted to medicine and surgery, that would involve some straining of the concept of "education" even beyond the liberal limits of the modern decisions), it would be impossible to hold that this was an educational charity for the benefit of the public. The books are given and bequeathed to the trustees "for the use, benefit and behoof of the physician, chaplain and surgeon for the time being of the said hospital . . .". The only form of educational charity (if such indeed this is) more limited than this which it is possible to envisage is one for the benefit of one or two named individuals or office holders. I have no hesitation in rejecting the submission that the bequest was a charitable gift for the advancement of education.

The next category to which it was submitted that the bequest belonged was that of a charitable gift for the advancement of learning. As I have already mentioned, under Lord Macnaghten's classification, this species of charitable gift, to the extent that it is recognised by the law, belongs to the fourth category of trusts for purposes beneficial to the community not coming within any of the other categories.

In *Re Shaw, Public Trustee v. Day* [1957] 1 WLR 729 at p. 737, Harman J. said:–

> ". . . If the objective [of the gift] be merely the increase of knowledge, that is not in itself a charitable object unless it be combined with teaching or education.
> . . ."

This view, which was based to some extent on the decision of the House of Lords in *Whicker v. Hume* (1858) 7 HLC 124, might not command universal acceptance today. Thus in *Re Hopkins' Will Trusts, Naish v. Francis Bacon Society Inc.* [1965] Ch 669, at p. 680, Wilberforce J., as he then was, when considering a gift establishing a fund "to be earmarked and applied towards finding the Bacon-Shakespeare Manuscripts", said that:-

> "I should be unwilling to treat [Harman J.'s words] as meaning that the promotion of academic research is not a charitable purpose unless the researcher were engaged in teaching or education in a conventional meaning; and I am encouraged in this view by some words of Lord Greene M.R. in *Re Compton* [1945] Ch 123."

It may well be that the words of Harman J., literally applied, would exclude from the legal definition of charity certain trusts for the advancement of knowledge, e.g. the encouragement of academic research, which might reasonably be regarded as for the public benefit. If that were so, I would prefer the view of Wilberforce J.

A gift of a library may be charitable as being for the public benefit. However, it is clear from the authorities that a gift of a library is not charitable *per se*: thus, gifts to private bodies for the purpose of establishing libraries for the benefit of persons paying subscriptions have been held not to be charitable in *Carne v. Long* (1860) 2 De GF & J 75 and *Re Prevost, Lloyds Bank Ltd. v. Barclays Bank* [1930] 2 Ch 383. But a gift of a library which is open to the public has been held, as one would expect, to be charitable: see *Re Scowcroft, Ormrod v. Wilkinson* [1898] 2 Ch 638, 642. So too have gifts of libraries where they can be reasonably described as being conducive to the attainment of a charitable object, such as the gift for the purchase of books for Trinity College, Oxford, in *Attorney General v. Marchant* (1866) LR 3 Eq 424, where it was held to be for the advancement of education and the gift in the decision cited by Mr. Butler of a fund to purchase a library for an officers' mess, where it was held to be conducive to increasing the efficiency of the British army, a recognised charitable purpose.

There is, in my view, no indication in the will of Dr. Worth that he intended the library to be for the benefit of any persons other than the named office holders. If he had wished his books to be available to scholars generally, he would have bequeathed them to the library of Trinity College or Marsh's Library, with both of which he was obviously well acquainted. Far from doing so, he was meticulous in ensuring that the books should only be available to the three designated office holders. They alone were to have keys to the library and under no circumstances were any of the books to be removed. He laid down a stringent procedure under which the Governors were to satisfy themselves at regular intervals that none of the said books were "wanting and defaced". I see no reason to attribute to Dr. Worth any motive or intention that does not appear plainly from his will. His wishes are in fact abundantly clear: to provide in the hospital, the establishment of which was so obviously so close to his heart, a fine library to be used by the physician, surgeon and chaplain, who alone would have access to the room in which the library was housed. The only argument put forward in support of the contention that Dr.

Worth intended his books to be generally available to scholars from everywhere is the direction that the books should be catalogued and copies of the catalogues placed in the library of Trinity College and Marsh's Library. I accept entirely the expert opinion of Dr. Donlon and Mrs. McCarthy that the catalogues prepared were in the form which would have been adopted by a learned bibliophile who wished scholars to have access to his library. But there was obviously another reason which might have promoted Dr. Worth to have two copies of the catalogue available in what he clearly considered responsible hands. Given his concern with the security of the books, it would have been a sensible precaution for him to have ensured that other copies of the catalogue were available, if the original was lost or mislaid or pages torn out of it by some person anxious to conceal a theft from the library. Happily, it is unnecessary to speculate on Dr. Worth's reasons for giving these directions: he, or the draftsman of the will on his instructions, has spelt out the reason with his usual meticulous clarity:–

> "*and to the end that they may be better preserved* I will and direct that three catalogues may be made of them . . ."

There was nothing to prevent Dr. Worth from directing copies of the catalogues to be made "to the end that scholars and others of learning and repute may peruse the said books" or words to that effect. He chose an entirely different formula and it is not for me to ascribe to him motives which nowhere appear in the will. I am satisfied, accordingly, that this was not a charitable gift for the advancement of learning within the fourth *Pemsel* classification.

The third category of charitable gifts within which it was sought to place this disposition was that of a gift for the benefit of a hospital. That such a gift is charitable is clear beyond doubt from the decision of the former Supreme Court in *Barrington's Hospital v. Commissioner of Valuation* [1957] IR 299. As Kingsmill Moore J. pointed out in that case, the wording of the preamble to the Irish Act points even more clearly to that conclusion than the wording employed in the preamble to the English Act, since it refers to: "the relief of any manner of poor, succourless, distressed or impotent persons . . ." The words in the English statute are: "the relief of aged, impotent and poor people . . ." The disjunctive "or" in the preamble to the Irish Act lent further support, in the learned judge's view, to the proposition that the relief of "impotent" persons was within the intendment of the statute. It was also clear from that decision that the fact that the hospital admitted fee paying patients in addition to those treated without charge (as Dr. Steevens' Hospital undoubtedly did) did not affect its charitable status.

The question arises, however, as to whether a gift of a library such as this for the benefit of the holders of particular offices within the hospital can properly be regarded as a gift for the benefit of the hospital itself and hence charitable. I cannot accept Mr. Herbert's submission for the Health Board that those parts of the will which follow the bequest to the trustees of the hospital and which make it clear that the gift is to be for the benefit of the office holders and imposed the conditions in relation to the security of the books are "precatory" in nature, *i.e.* imposing no more than a form of moral obligation on the trustees to comply with the testator's wishes but having no effect in law. Mr. Herbert relies in support of this submission on the absence of any gift over and also on the decision of Murray J. in *In re Steele, Northern Bank Executive and Trustees Ltd v. Linton & Others* [1976] NI 66. In that case, it was held that a condition attached to an admittedly charitable gift for the repair and upkeep of a parish church under which the testators' family burial plot was to be maintained was a precatory condition which did not affect the validity of the gift for the repair of the church. In the present case, however, the gift to the trustees "for the use, benefit and behoof of" the office holders is not in any sense a condition: it is quite clearly a bequest to trustees for the benefit of designated individuals. That of itself is fatal to Mr. Herbert's contention but, in any event, the language used in the conditions which follow is not consonant with their being treated as precatory only: they are plainly directions which the testator wished to be complied with to the letter.

I am, however, satisfied that the gift is one for the benefit of the hospital on the other grounds advanced by Mr. Herbert. That Dr. Worth intended to benefit Dr. Steevens' Hospital in his will is beyond question: he begins his will with a bequest of money for that purpose and it is noteworthy that it is to the trustees of the hospital that he gives his library for the benefit of the designated persons. It is, moreover, the holders of the offices, and not named individuals, who are to benefit. In addition, he was concerned that the hospital and its patients should not be at any loss as a result of the bequest.

While the relatively small number of medical and surgical books in the library would not have rendered it of much practical benefit to the physician and surgeon, and the vast number of books devoted to purely secular and profane topics would not have been of any great assistance to the chaplain in his studies of divinity, the library in its beautiful setting would have provided a haven of quiet intellectual relaxation for the beneficiaries. Doctors and surgeons, as we all know, develop a necessary professional detachment from the scenes of death and suffering which greet them every day in the course of their work. But it is equally obvious that they value the solace of a completely different environment from time to time and I think there can be no doubt that this is what Dr. Worth intended to provide. How much more necessary it was in the terrible conditions of the early eighteenth century, when the days of anaesthetics and modern drugs lay far in the future, need not be emphasised. A nurses' home was found to be charitable for not dissimilar reasons in *Re White's Will Trusts, Tindall v. Board of Governors of United Sheffield Hospitals* [1951] 1 All ER 528.

No case of the gift of a library for such a purpose appears to have come before the courts before, the nearest equivalent being the gift of the library to the officers' mess in *In re Good, Harrington v. Watts* [1905] 2 Ch 60. The view of Farwell J. that the purchase of books for the library would in some sense be conducive to the efficiency of the army seems, with respect, a little fanciful and this may have prompted the doubts expressed by Lord Normand as to the correctness of the decision in *Inland Revenue Commissioners v. City of Glasgow Police Athletic Association* [1953] AC 380, 391. But for the reasons I have already given, I do not think that there is any ground for scepticism in the present case as to the capacity of the gift to play a part in the advancement of the great charity represented by the hospital itself. I conclude, accordingly, that the bequest in the will was a valid charitable bequest for the benefit of Dr. Steevens' Hospital, falling within the fourth category of Lord Macnaghten's classification.

The next issue that has to be considered is as to whether circumstances have arisen which justify the invocation of the *cy-près* jurisdiction of the court. The circumstances in which that jurisdiction may be invoked were defined as follows by Budd J. in *In re Royal Kilmainham Hospital* [1966] IR 451 at p. 469:–

"The law requires that if a charity can be administered according to the directions of the founder, it should be so administered. When it is established that a gift has been made with a general intention of charity and a failure of purposes ensues, it is not allowed to fail but will be carried out *cy-près*. Likewise, where there is an absolute perpetual gift to a charity, even though the trusts be only for the accomplishment of a particular charitable purpose, the same results ensue. The principle is applied where the method indicated by the donor carrying out his charitable intention becomes impracticable, or his intentions cannot be executed literally, most frequently owing to altered circumstances . . .

However, the *cy-près* principle is confined to cases where property is given with a general intention to charity with this exception, that where property is given absolutely and perpetually to charity for a particular purpose and has vested in the charity the fund can be applied *cy-près* irrespective of the donor's particular intention. As to what is to be regarded as a general charitable intention, no hard and fast rule can be laid down."

The provisions of s. 47 of the Charities Act, 1961, must also be borne in mind. They provide *inter alia* that:–

"the circumstances in which the original purposes of a charitable gift may be altered to allow the property given or part of it to be applied *cy-près* shall be as follows:

(a) Where the original purposes, in whole or in part –
   (i) have been as far as may be fulfilled; or
   (ii) cannot be carried out, or cannot be carried out according to the directions given and to the spirit of the gift; . . .
(c) Where the property available by virtue of the gift and other property applicable for similar purposes can be more effectively used in conjunction, and to that end can suitably, regard being had to the spirit of the gift, be made applicable to common purposes; . . .

(e) Where the original purposes, in whole or in part, have, since they were laid
down – . . .
(iii) ceased . . . to provide a suitable and effective method of using the
property available by virtue of the gift, regard being had to the spirit
of the gift."

I do not think that any "general charitable intention", in the sense referred to
in the authorities, can be inferred in the case of this gift. It is quite clear from
the terms of the will that Dr. Worth intended to benefit Dr. Steevens' Hospital
and no other institution. It was, however, undoubtedly an absolute and perpetual
gift of the library for the benefit of Doctor Steevens' Hospital, which I have
already found to be a charitable purpose. It is also clear that, since the hospital
no longer exists, the original purposes of the charitable gift cannot be carried
out according to the directions given and to the spirit of the gift. It follows that
the original purposes should now be altered so as to allow the property to be
applied *cy-près*.

Before considering how the property should be applied *cy-près*, one further
legal matter remains to be considered. It was submitted on behalf of the plaintiffs
that it would be *ultra vires* the powers of the Health Board under the Health
Acts, 1947 to 1991, to undertake the custody and management of the library if
it were to be housed in the hospital building. This is clearly not a particularly
meritorious argument, since, even if it were technically correct both the plaintiffs
and the Health Board were in agreement that the books should be returned to
the hospital, there could be no legal objection to the ownership of the books
remaining vested in the plaintiffs as trustees while mere *de facto* possession
remained with the Health Board. However, I am also satisfied that it is without
legal substance.The Health Board is expressly empowered under s. 78 of the
Act of 1947 and s. 60, sub-s. 3 of the Act of 1970, to acquire for its statutory
purposes "any estate or interest in land". Like all other corporations, it also
enjoys, in addition to its express powers, an implied power to do any acts
which are incidental to or consequential upon its express objects: see *Attorney-
General v. Great Eastern Railway* (1880) 5 App Cas 483. If a health board is
in a position to acquire a property which is suitable for carrying out its statutory
objects - and it is not suggested that Doctor Steevens' Hospital was not such a
building - the vendors might very well stipulate that, as part of the sale, the
purchasers should pay for certain fixtures and fittings, e.g. carpets, etc. They
might also make such a stipulation in relation to pictures and furnishings. If
the Governors and the Health Board had agreed on the sale at a stage when the
Governors had not approached Trinity College with a view to transferring the
library into its custody and the Governors had satisfied themselves that the
Health Board would be a responsible custodian of the books, I do not think it
could be plausibly argued for a moment that the Health Board would be acting
ultra vires in agreeing to accept custody of the books. If acquiring a premises
suitable in every way for its statutory purposes involved taking on an additional
role as custodian of the books, I have not the slightest doubt that it could

reasonably be regarded as one of the incidental or consequential powers it enjoyed in addition to the express power of acquiring property conferred on it by the Acts. The situation cannot be altered by the fact that the books have been temporarily removed to the safe custody of another body pending a decision as to their future. If all the other requirements of both the law and expert opinion are satisfied and particularly if all the aesthetic considerations indicate that Dr. Steevens' Hospital is indeed the appropriate repository for these books, then I have no doubt that the Health Board should be regarded as having, in addition to its statutory powers to acquire and hold property, an implied power to become the custodian of the library.

VII. Application of the property cy-près
In considering how the property should be applied *cy-près* and, in particular, whether a scheme should be framed in the manner proposed by the plaintiffs, it is, of course, desirable that the original intentions of the testator should be adhered to so far as is possible. The difficulties, however, of both ascertaining those intentions and giving effect to them in the case of so venerable a bequest as this are obvious. As Meredith J. remarked in *Governors of Erasmus Smith Schools v. Attorney General and Others* (1932) 66 ILTR 57 at p. 61:–

> "To apply without modification a charitable intention that is only expressed in relation to assumed facts and under different conditions is obviously not to carry out the real intention at all. It is on this principle that courts of law adapt the statement of a charitable intention to suit altered circumstances and conditions with a view to giving effect to the real intention. Donors cannot be expected to provide expressly for more than the world and the times with which they are familiar. Accordingly, the perpetuity for which charities may endure throws upon the court the burden of providing for that which the donor did not foresee, in accordance with what it finds to be the underlying intention of the charity foundation."

Thus, in a case such as the present, it is a futile exercise to transport Dr. Worth in one's imagination in some form of time machine to Dublin in 1993. All that the court can do is to apply the gift as it might be applied by a late twentieth century equivalent of Dr. Worth. Our hypothetical benefactor should be a medically qualified person with a passionate interest in bibliophilia and of a charitable disposition. It is also reasonable to credit him with a desire to associate his charitable work with the building in which Dr. Steevens' Hospital was housed, since his eighteenth century equivalent wished the hospital to be the object of his benevolence in perpetuity. If this approach is adopted, I think that it brings one as close as is reasonably possible to what the draftsman of the Charities Act, 1961, has called "the spirit of the gift". Such a person would not seriously consider relocating the library in one of the modern Dublin hospitals. He would have in the forefront of any plan he might devise the paramount necessity of preserving the library in the custody of an appropriate and responsible body. He would recognise that the principal value of the library is not the provision of knowledge or intellectual stimulus or excitement to readers of the books: it is making available to scholars and others the books as books, considered both individually and as a collective library. The typography, paper and bindings, altogether apart from the contents, are of enormous interest to scholars and bibliophiles the world over. Hence, he would be concerned to ensure that such persons had reasonable but supervised access to the library and also the other scholarly tools necessary for making an informed study of the contents of the library, such as a modern computerised catalogue, suitable reference books and other comparable books. Finally, he would consider whether the broader aesthetic considerations to which I have referred in an earlier part of this judgment would point towards preserving the books in Dr. Steevens' Hospital or transferring them to Trinity College, the only other institution which has been suggested as a possible repository.

As to the Governors, they, it would seem, are still theoretically in existence as a corporate body, since the Act which incorporated them has not been repealed. They were satisfied to transfer custody of the library to Trinity College at a stage when there was no potential purchaser of the hospital building who might be prepared to act as its custodian and who might be regarded as a responsible guardian of the books. In those circumstances, it would not be proper to impute to them any views as to the merits of the present controversy, even if such views were relevant to its resolution.

If these are the criteria to be applied, it will be evident from my summary of the evidence in the case that either Doctor Steevens' Hospital or Trinity College would provide, in some respects at least, a suitable repository. In both buildings, it will be possible to preserve the books from the dangers of fire, accidental or intentional damage or loss and theft. To the extent that conditions in Doctor Steevens' Hospital fall short of the most rigorous standards in this area - and they are undoubtedly the standards which should be applied - there is no inherent difficulty, as the reports of the technical experts demonstrate, in remedying those deficiencies. Those reports, so far as the evidence goes, highlight two possible difficulties in the area of fire precautions. It was pointed out that the ceilings were not impervious to water and that there might be some hazard in a firefighting situation. It was not suggested, however, that this was an insuperable problem and it would be surprising if it were so. Secondly, it was said that because the interior of the library was listed for preservation in the development plan, it would not be possible to comply with the specification of Class O for interior surfaces in the Building Regulations, 1991. At worst, this means that the owners of the building are subjected to conflicting legal requirements. If responsible fire safety experts are satisfied that all reasonable precautions have been taken, then the Building Regulations - which were not opened in any detail - presumably cannot be enforced against the owners to require them to commit an illegal act by violating the planning code. Again, it was not suggested that this was in any sense an insuperable problem.

The advantage which Trinity College possesses is the ready availability of conservation techniques which are acknowledged to be by far the best available in the Republic of Ireland. I am satisfied, however, that while this is undoubtedly a factor to be weighed, it cannot be regarded as a conclusive factor. All the evidence indicates that a remarkable feature of the books comprising the library is the magnificent condition in which they have been preserved. It is not in any way to denigrate the skills of the conservators in Trinity College to say that this result was achieved without any assistance from modern technology: it was the result of the books being housed in the glass fronted bookcases in Doctor Steevens' Hospital for 260 years and of the relatively sparing use to which they were subjected during that period. Since any scheme approved of by the court for either institution would require the rigorous maintenance of an appropriate environment in terms of humidity, temperature and freedom from dust and other pollutants, it follows that the existence of the conservation facilities in Trinity College cannot be in any sense a decisive factor.

Trinity College is at most a fifteen minutes' car journey from Dr. Steevens' Hospital and it is implausible to suggest that, on the relatively rare occasions that it might be necessary to seek the assistance of the conservation facilities, the relevant books could not be transported in reasonable safety to the college. That, of course, presupposes the continued involvement of Trinity College in the administration of the charity: if their assistance were not available, it would be necessary to seek conservation facilities elsewhere. This would undoubtedly involve some additional expense if, for example, the relevant expert was to travel from the British Library or some equivalent institution in England with any necessary equipment. That would raise again the question of funding, but certainly does not constitute an insuperable obstacle.

So far as the existence of cataloguing, comparisons with other books and the availability of reference books is concerned, Trinity College undoubtedly possesses advantages which the hospital does not. I am satisfied, however, that there is no technical difficulty in providing the necessary computer equipment in the hospital which can be linked in turn to computer-based catalogues in other libraries. It is equally clear that, provided the necessary funds are forthcoming, the necessary reference library can also be provided in the hospital and the services of a professional librarian secured.

It is undoubtedly the case that comparisons with other books can be made by scholars if the books are housed in Trinity Library which cannot be made if they are to be returned to the hospital. But this is heavily outweighed by another consideration. If the books are not returned to the hospital, it will be impossible for scholars interested in the history of libraries, art historians and sociologists to study the contents, arrangements and fittings of an eighteenth century library, the manner in which the books were arranged on the shelves and how the library cases and presses were constructed to accommodate the different format of the books. They would have to examine the books in Trinity College, then go to the empty and deserted Worth Room in the hospital and attempt to construct a mental picture of how the library must originally have looked. Provided all the requirements I have mentioned of security and environmental control can be met, that is a result which should be avoided.

There is a general acceptance by those who gave evidence that the library will be of interest to a relatively limited number of scholars and that it would indeed be undesirable, not least for security reasons, for the public in general to be allowed unrestricted access to the books. I think it is most unlikely that scholars with a genuine interest in the library will be inhibited in gaining access to it by its being situated in the hospital building rather than in Trinity College.

There remains what I have referred to as the general aesthetic considerations. As to these, I have little doubt as to the direction in which our imaginary benefactor would lean. That Trinity College is a centre of living and vibrant scholarship is beyond question. That Dr. Steevens' Hospital is now the headquarters of what might be described without disrespect as a bureaucratic organisation is also true. I can only say that on a visit to the latter building and on entering the Worth Room for the first time, I was in no way conscious of the sense of "alienation" of which Dr. Donlon spoke. I bear in mind the dangers of converting oneself into a witness and the possibility that, on the day on which I paid my visit, conditions were unusually quiet: all I can say is that I found in the building an atmosphere of relative calm which provided a striking contrast to the necessarily intense bustle and activity of a modern acute hospital.

More decisively still, however, I think the considerations so eloquently advanced by Dr. Craig and Mr. Breugelmans must in the end prevail. In this context, I was much struck by the belief expressed by Dr. Donlon and Mrs. McCarthy and, I have no doubt whatever, genuinely held by these eminent experts, that returning the collection to Doctor Steevens' Hospital is "to seek to freeze the collection in time rather than as a vibrant and continuous legacy to a scholarly community" and that this is to be resisted. That preserving the Worth Library in its original home in Dr. Steeven's Hospital will be to "freeze it in time" is probably true. Many who have visited carefully preserved or restored buildings of historic, architectural or artistic interest in Ireland or abroad will have been conscious of precisely that feeling of moving into long vanished worlds. Far from it being a serious disadvantage, it seems to me, and ultimately I must make the decision, one of the chief glories of the treasures of which we are now the custodians. I see no reason why, under careful and responsible management subject to the ultimate control of the court, the Worth Library should not join them, preserving almost exactly as it existed 250 years ago in its original setting the private library of a man of taste and learning at the flood tide of the Enlightenment.

I am accordingly satisfied that any *cy-près* scheme framed by the court in this case must provide for the retention of the books and the portraits in their original setting in Doctor Steevens' Hospital. At the moment, the only scheme before the court is that set out in Appendix 1 providing for the retention of the books in their present temporary home in Trinity College. It will accordingly be necessary to adjourn the further hearing of the case in order to enable a new draft scheme to be prepared. It is obviously extremely desirable that the plaintiffs should remain as trustees, although it might be appropriate to join the Health Board as a new trustee. I think it is of importance that the various skills of Trinity College and the expertise of Dr. Donlon should continue to be available in the administration of the trust. It is, however, to be borne in mind that Trinity College only became involved in this matter originally at the request of the Governors and it may be that they will not wish to participate further in the administration of the trust. That is entirely a matter for them and neither they nor Dr. Donlon can or should be compelled by the court to continue their interest in the matter. It is also the case that the present proposals by the Health Board are somewhat vague in the area of funding and that the two questions of fire safety - and any others which I may have overlooked - will also have to be addressed. It is to be hoped that when the matter comes on after an interval there will be more concrete proposals before the court in relation to funding, specifying the actual costs of maintaining the library and the manner in which they will be met. I would naturally hope that, during the period of the adjournment, further discussions would take place between the plaintiffs and the Health Board as to the best method of re-establishing the Worth Library in Doctor Steevens' Hospital subject to all the necessary security and other arrangements. I will, however, hear counsel as to the form of order I should make, having regard to the findings in this judgment."

THE MACNAGHTEN CLASSIFICATION

Trusts for the Relief of Poverty

The term 'poverty' has been broadly interpreted for the purposes of determining what will qualify as legally charitable and it is not to be equated with destitution. As Evershed MR stated in *Re Coulthurst*[5] 'it may not unfairly be paraphrased for present purposes as meaning persons who have to "go short" in the ordinary acceptation of that term, due regard being had to their status in life and so forth'. It is important to distinguish a gift for the relief of poverty amongst a class of persons, which will be charitable in nature, from a gift to individuals albeit with the relief of poverty amongst those individuals as the motive for the gift, which will not be.[6] A likely basis for disqualification as a charitable gift will be that the restricted nature of the class leads to the conclusion that the gift is really one to the individual members of a class and it may be useful for a testator to leave the class open for a further period of years after his death

---

[5] [1951] Ch 661, 665. See also *Re Segelman deceased* [1996] Ch 171, 190.
[6] *Re Scarisbrick* [1951] Ch 622, 655 *per* Jenkins LJ. See also *Dingle v. Turner* [1972] AC 601, 617 and *Re Segelman deceased* [1996] Ch 171, 192.

on the basis that it will be impossible to attribute to him an intention to make a gift to after born issue as such.

It is fair to say that the public benefit test in the case of trusts for the relief of poverty has been 'reduced....almost to vanishing point'[7] and so called 'poor relations'[8] and 'poor employees'[9] trusts have been regarded as an exception to the general principle that 'a gift under which the beneficiaries are defined by reference to a purely personal relationship to a named *propositus*, cannot on principle be a valid charitable gift.'[10]

Re Scarisbrick: Cockshott v. Public Trustee
[1951] Ch 622

A testatrix directed her trustees after the death of her son and daughters to hold property on trust, *inter alia*, for 'such relations of my said son and daughters as in the opinion of the survivor of my said son and daughters shall be in needy circumstances'. The Court of Appeal upheld this as a valid charitable trust.

JENKINS LJ stated at pp.646–658: "It will be apparent from the foregoing narrative that questions of considerable difficulty arose with respect to the destination of the trust property on the death of Mrs. Kraemer, particularly in view of the inclusion amongst the objects of the unexecuted power of "such relations of my said son and daughters as in the opinion of the survivor of my said son and daughters shall be in needy circumstances". The remaining objects of the power are of course, by the express terms of the will exclusively charitable, and, if the power had been confined to these, it would only have been necessary to apply to the court for the settlement of a scheme with a view to the application of the trust property to charitable objects in Germany or in the United Kingdom selected with due regard to the preference expressed by the testatrix for charitable objects connected with the Roman Catholic Church and Faith. But is the trust charitable at all so far as it includes as objects of the power such relations of the three children of the testatrix as in the opinion of the survivor of them shall be in needy circumstances? If it is charitable quoad these objects, then no doubt the court can and should give effect to the charitable purpose of the testatrix by means of a scheme providing for the selection of the persons who are to take and the amounts they are to receive, and thus making good the failure of Mrs. Kraemer to exercise the power herself. If, on the other hand, the trust is not charitable quoad these objects, what effect (if

---

[7] Hanbury and Martin *Modern Equity* (16th ed., 2001) p. 428.

[8] *Re Scarisbrick* [1951] Ch 661 and *Re Segelman deceased* [1996] Ch 171.

[9] *Dingle v. Turner* [1972] AC 601.

[10] *Re Compton* [1945] Ch 123, 131 *per* Lord Greene MR.

any) can be given to this branch of it in default of appointment? Is there an intestacy on the ground of uncertainty or is there an implied trust in default of appointment in favour of some ascertainable class of "relations" of the three children, limited or not to such members of the class as can be shown to be in " needy circumstances"?

Apart from the agreement to which I am about to refer, that question would on the face of it give rise to two further questions, namely: If there is such an implied trust, to what proportion of the property does it extend; and if there is an intestacy is it limited to some proportion of the property or does the uncertainty to which it is due extend to and vitiate the entire disposition?

Before Roxburgh, J., the area of controversy was limited in the following respects:– (1) In the proceedings as then constituted the plaintiffs were Sir Everard Scarisbrick and Mr. George Cockshott as the present trustees of the will, and the only defendants were the Public Trustee (as representing the estate of Sir Tom, the heir-at-law) and the Attorney-General (as representing the claims of charity). In those circumstances (to quote the learned judge) [1950] Ch 226, 228: "It appeared early in the argument that there might be some conflict between the heir-at-law, who was represented by counsel, and other persons who were not represented, as to the destination of any part of the fund not effectually given to charity, and it was thereupon agreed that my decision should be confined to the question whether the whole, or, if not, how much of the fund was thus effectually given. The bequest plainly falls into two parts, and the second is admittedly charitable". (2) It was agreed before Roxburgh, J., between the Public Trustee and the Attorney General that half the property should in any event be considered as having been effectively devised for the admittedly and expressly charitable objects mentioned in the second branch of the trust.

In view of this agreement and the state of the case as regards parties the learned judge, in effect, confined himself to the question whether the remaining half of the trust property, that is to say, the half to which the trust for relations in needy circumstances (as distinct from the trust for charitable objects eo nomine) was in accordance with such agreement treated as confined, was effectively devoted to charity, and on grounds to which I will presently refer decided this question in the negative, declaring accordingly that one-half and no more of the trust property was effectively so devoted, and directing the settlement of a scheme for the regulation and management of such one-half.

When the case first came before this court it was adjourned with a view to amendment as regards parties, in order that we might deal with the destination of the half of the property not effectively devoted to charity according to Roxburgh, J.'s decision in the event of that decision being upheld. Accordingly, Sir Everard was struck out as a plaintiff and he and Frau von Schmieder were added as defendants.

Sir Everard's counsel argued for a trust in default of appointment in favour of the relations (limited on the principle stated in *Wilson v. Duguid* (1883) 24

Ch D 244, 251 to next of kin) of the testatrix's son and daughters. Frau von Schmieder's counsel argued for a trust in default of appointment in favour of such relations similarly limited, but with a further limitation to next of kin in needy circumstances. Sir Everard's counsel supported counsel for the Public Trustee in defending Roxburgh, J.'s decision, while opposing him in his claim that an intestacy resulted. Frau von Schmieder's counsel steered a somewhat complicated course, his primary claim being to the effect that his client being in needy circumstances should participate on the footing of a valid charitable trust, and the contention above indicated being in the nature of an alternative in the event of the trust being held not to be charitable.

It should be noted that the agreement between the Public Trustee and the Attorney-General by which the contest was limited to half the trust property was in this court adhered to by them and accepted by the other parties. But it does not follow that for the purpose of determining the primary question whether the trust is charitable so far as it includes relations in needy circumstances as objects of the power, cl. 11 should be construed as if it gave one-half of the property to such relations of the testatrix's three children as in the opinion of the survivor of them should be in needy circumstances for such interests, etc., as such survivor should appoint, and the other half to such charitable objects eo nomine for such interests, etc., as such survivor should appoint. Whatever the position in default of appointment may be, it is clear that under cl. 11 as a matter of construction Mrs. Kraemer, as the survivor of the three children of the testatrix, could have appointed the whole of the property to relations in her opinion in needy circumstances, to the exclusion of charitable objects eo nomine, or could have appointed the whole to charitable objects eo nomine to the exclusion of relations in needy circumstances, or could have appointed in any proportions she thought fit between or amongst any relations in needy circumstances and any charitable object or objects eo nomine.

As regards what I have termed the primary question, the following general propositions may be stated:– (i) It is a general rule that a trust or gift in order to be charitable in the legal sense must be for the benefit of the public or some section of the public: see *In re Compton* [1945] Ch 123, *In re Hobourn Aero Components Ld.'s Air Raid Distress Fund* [1946] Ch 194, and *Gilmour v. Coats* [1949] AC 426.

(ii) An aggregate of individuals ascertained by reference to some personal tie (e.g., of blood or contract), such as the relations of a particular individual, the members of a particular family, the employees of a particular firm, the members of a particular association, does not amount to the public or a section thereof for the purposes of the general rule: see *In re Drummond* [1914] 2 Ch 90, *In re Compton, In re Hobourn Aero Components Ld.'s Air Raid Distress Fund*, and *Oppenheim v. Tobacco Securities Trust Co. Ld.* [1951] AC 297.

(iii) It follows that according to the general rule above stated a trust or gift under which the beneficiaries or potential beneficiaries are confined to some aggregate of individuals ascertained as above is not legally charitable even though its purposes are such that it would have been legally charitable if the range of potential beneficiaries had extended to the public at large or a section thereof (e.g., an educational trust confined as *In re Compton*, to the lawful descendants of three named persons, or, as in *Oppenheim v. Tobacco Securities Trust Co. Ld.*, to the children of employees or, former employees of a particular company).

(iv) There is, however, an exception to the general rule, in that trusts or gifts for the relief of poverty have been held to be charitable even though they are limited in their application to some aggregate of individuals, and are therefore not trusts or gifts for the benefit of the public or a section thereof. This exception operates whether the personal tie is one of blood (as in the numerous so-called "poor relations" cases, to some of which I will presently refer) or of contract (e.g., the relief of poverty amongst the members of a particular society, as in *Spiller v. Maude* (1881) 32 Ch D 158, or amongst employees of a particular company or their dependants, as in *Gibson v. South American Stores (Gath & Chaves) Ld.* [1950] Ch 177).

(v) This exception cannot be accounted for by reference to any principle, but is established by a series of authorities of long standing, and must at the present date be accepted as valid, at all events as far as this court is concerned (see *In re Compton*) though doubtless open to review in the House of Lords (as appears from the observations of Lords Simonds and Morton of Henryton in *Oppenheim v. Tobacco Securities Trust Co. Ld.*).

Applying these general propositions to the present case, I ask myself whether the trust in cl. 11 for "such relations . . . as in the opinion of the survivor of" the testatrix's "son and daughters shall be in needy circumstances for such interests and in such proportions . . . as the survivor . . . shall by deed or will appoint" is a trust for the relief of poverty. If it is such a trust, then, as I understand the exception above referred to, it matters not that the potential objects of such trust are confined to relations of the son and daughters. If language means anything, a person in needy circumstances is a person who is poor and as such a proper object of charity, and no one can take under this trust who is not in needy circumstances. I do not think that the effect of the expression " in needy circumstances" is materially altered by the qualifying words "in the opinion of the survivor . . . ".

"Poverty" is necessarily to some extent a relative matter, a matter of opinion, and it is not to be assumed that the person made the judge of "needy circumstances" in the present case would have acted otherwise than in accordance with an opinion fairly and honestly formed as to the circumstances, needy or otherwise, of anyone coming into consideration as a potential object of the power. Under a similar trust which did not expressly make the appointor's opinion the test of eligibility, the appointor would in practice have to make the selection according to the best of his or her opinion or judgment. The express reference to the appointor's opinion merely serves to reduce the possibility of dispute as to the eligibility or otherwise of any particular individual on the score of needy circumstances. Accordingly, I dismiss the words "in the opinion of the survivor" as having no material bearing on the character of this trust. In so doing, I am fortified by the similar conclusion reached in this court as to the effect of the word "in the opinion of the London Board" in *Gibson v. South American Stores (Gath & Chaves) Ld.* [1950] Ch 177, 186.

It is no doubt true that a gift or trust is not necessarily charitable as being in relief of poverty because the object or objects of it in order to take must be poor. Such a gift or trust may be no more than an ordinary gift to some particular individual or individuals limited to the amount required to relieve his or their necessities if in necessitous circumstances. One can conceive of a testator making a limited provision of this character for a child or children whose conduct in his view had reduced their claims on his bounty to a minimum. A disposition of that sort would obviously not be for the relief of poverty in the charitable sense. The same must be said of gifts to named persons if in needy circumstances, or to a narrow class of near relatives, as for example to such of a testator's statutory next of kin as at his death shall be in needy circumstances.

It is difficult to draw any exact line, but I do not think the trust here in question can fairly be held disqualified as a trust for the relief of poverty in the charitable sense on grounds such as those illustrated above. The class of relations to whom the selective power of appointment here extends is not confined to relations of the testatrix herself but consists of relations of the testatrix's son and daughters. "Relations" in this context cannot, in my opinion, be construed as meaning only the statutory next of kin of the son and daughters. It is, I, think, well settled that a power of selection amongst the relations of a given person, as distinct from a plain gift to such relations, extends to relations in the full sense (i.e., all persons who can claim a common ancestor with the person in question) and is not confined to statutory next of kin as has been done in cases of plain gifts to "relations" to prevent complete failure of such gifts on the ground of uncertainty: see *Harding v. Glyn* (1739) 1 Atk 469 and *Mahon v. Savage* (1803) 1 Sch & Lef 111. Moreover, the language used points to a class of "relations" common to all three children of the testatrix, which is appropriate to "relations" in any degree, but hardly to statutory next of kin, as the statutory next of kin of each child would comprise a different class, and the trust is not expressed to be for the respective relations of the three children. The ambit of the trust thus extends to relations in every degree of the three children on both sides of the family. It should be added that the class of potential beneficiaries falls to be ascertained at the death of the survivor of the three children, not at the testatrix's own death. The power therefore extends to such of the relations in every degree of the three children on both sides of the family as might be in existence at the death of the survivor of the three children and should then in the opinion of such survivor be in needy circumstances. Thus the class of potential beneficiaries, so far from being confined to a limited number of individuals whom the testatrix might be taken to have regarded as having some personal claim on her bounty, at all events to the extent necessary to relieve them from want, is so extensive as to be incapable of being exhaustively ascertained and includes persons whom the testatrix may never have seen or heard of, and persons not even in existence at the time of her death.

Some gifts of the "poor relations" type may be found on their true construction to be gifts to the poorest of the class or to the class with a preference for the poorest, thus failing to satisfy the observation of Sir George Jessel, M.R., in *Attorney-General v. Duke of Northumberland* (1877) 7 Ch D 745, 749 that: "A gift which is not a gift to the poor, that is, the actually poor, is not a charity". That is not the case here. As pointed out above, no part of the property is appropriated to the exclusive purpose of appointment amongst the relations in needy circumstances. A person shown to be a relation and to be in needy circumstances would have become eligible as an object of the power, but neither any one relation individually nor even all the relations collectively (on the impossible supposition that they could be exhaustively ascertained) would have been entitled to claim that some part of the property must in any event come to him, or to them or some of them, inasmuch as the whole of the property could have been appointed to charitable objects eo nomine.

Accordingly, in the view I take, this is a trust for the relief of poverty in the charitable sense amongst the class of relations described, and, being a trust for the relief of poverty, is in view of the exception above stated, not disqualified from ranking as a legally charitable trust by the circumstance that its application is confined to a class of relations (albeit a wide class), with the result that its potential beneficiaries do not comprise the public or a section thereof under the decisions to which I have referred.

I am accordingly of opinion that as the law now stands the trust in question should be upheld as a valid charitable trust for the relief of poverty.

The judge took a different view. He founded himself, in effect, on the reluctance with which this court in *In re Compton* recognized the exception of gifts or trusts for the relief of poverty from the general rule, that all forms of charity to be legally such must be for the benefit of the public or a section thereof, as an exception of an anomalous character, which could not be assigned to any principle, but rested simply on the effect of a series of old decisions not now properly open to question in this court. The exception being of that nature, the learned judge reasoned, in effect, that where a gift ostensibly for the relief of poverty, but lacking the element of public benefit required under the general rule, is in question, it should, in accordance with the general rule, be held invalid as a charitable gift, unless it is in such terms as to fall unequivocally within the exception as established by the decided cases. Approaching the authorities from this point of view, the judge found that while gifts in perpetuity for poor relations had been uniformly held charitable, there was a conflict of authority as to the charitable status of gifts for immediate distribution amongst poor relations. He held that the trust in the present case was of the latter description, and accordingly that as the decided cases showed no more than that there was a conflict of authority on the question whether it was to be regarded as charitable or not, its claim to fall within the exception was not made out; with the result that the general rule must be applied, and that the trust in the present case did not qualify as a valid charitable trust, because it was not for the benefit of the public or a section thereof.

We were referred, as was the judge, to a large number of the so-called "poor relations" cases. In some of them gifts for immediate distribution amongst poor relations variously described have been held charitable : see, e.g., *Attorney-General v. Bucknall* (1741) 2 Atk 328, also referred to sub nom. *Attorney-General v. Buckland* 1 Amb 71; *Mahon v. Savage* (1803) 1 Sch & Lef 111. In others, gifts for immediate distribution amongst such persons have been held (like gifts to "relations" simpliciter) to be confined to the statutory next of kin of the propositus, the implication being that they were regarded as mere gifts to individuals not falling within the ambit of charity at all, which would accordingly fail for uncertainty unless so confined: see, e.g., *Edge v. Salisbury* 1 Amb 70; *Goodinge v. Goodinge* (1749) 1 Ves Sen 231; *Brunsden v. Woodredge* (1765) 1 Amb 507; *Widmore v. Woodroffe* (1766) 2 Amb 636.

On the other hand, gifts of a perpetual character for the benefit of poor relations variously described have uniformly been held charitable: see *Isaac v. Defriez* (1754) 2 Amb 595; *White v. White* (1802) 7 Ves 423; *Attorney-General v. Price* (1810) 17 Ves 371, 374; *Gillam v. Taylor* (1873) LR 16 Eq 581. It does not appear that in all the cases of this type the perpetual character of the gift was the ratio decidendi. Indeed, *White v. White* may be said to cut both ways, as while the record shows the trust for putting out apprentices to have extended to the children of two families and their descendants (which implies perpetuity) it also shows that the capital as well as the income was applicable for that purpose (which in practice would necessarily limit the duration of the trust by exhaustion of the fund).

But in *Attorney-General v. Price* (1810) 17 Ves 371 Sir William Grant, M.R., following *Isaac v. Defriez* (1754) 2 Amb 595, said: "This seems to be just as much in the nature of a charitable bequest as that. It is to have perpetual continuance, in favour of a particular description of poor; and it is not like an immediate bequest of a sum to be distributed among poor relations". It was, I think, upon this observation of Sir William Grant, M.R., that Roxburgh, J., largely founded himself in deciding as he did in the present case. In this connexion reference may also be made to the following passage from the judgment in *Gillam v. Taylor* (1873) LR 16 Eq 581, 584: "The words here seem to me to import, beyond all question, the creation of a perpetual fund or institution, in which no person or persons is or are to have a personal right, but which is to be given only to such as need in the opinion of the trustees, and to be given to them according to their necessities".

I should also refer to *Thomas v. Howell* (1874) LR 18 Eq 198, where a gift of 200*l.* each to ten poor clergymen to be selected by a specified person was held to be simply a gift to individuals, just as if they had been actually named in the will and therefore not a charitable gift, and not defeated by the Mortmain Act, 1736. *Liley v. Hey* (1842) 1 Hare 580, which also raised the question of mortmain, concerned a trust on the face of it unlimited in time to distribute the rents and profits of land annually amongst certain families according to their circumstances as in the opinion of the trustees they might need such assistance. This trust was held by Wigram, V.-C., not to involve a perpetuity and not to be avoided by the statute of Mortmain. But the decision, which has been doubted, seems to have turned on the construction which the Vice-Chancellor placed on the gift as being, in the first instance (in effect) no more than a discretionary trust for a number of persons during their respective lives, and therefore free from objection during that period.

I find myself unable to accept the judge's view as to the effect of the authorities. I think the true question in each case has really been whether the gift was for the relief of poverty amongst a class of persons, or rather, as Sir William Grant, M.R., put it, a particular description of poor, or was merely a gift to individuals, albeit with relief of poverty amongst those individuals as the motive of the gift, or with a selective preference for the poor or poorest amongst those individuals. If the gift is perpetual in character, that no doubt is an important circumstance as demonstrating that the intention cannot have been merely to benefit the statutory next of kin of the propositus or other particular individuals identified by the gift. Moreover, the gift, if perpetual, can only be supported on the footing that it is charitable – an illogical though in past practice probably a persuasive reason for holding it such.

But I see no sufficient ground in the authorities for holding that a gift for the benefit of poor relations qualifies as charitable only if it is perpetual in character. I do not think that the observation of Sir William Grant, M.R., above referred to goes by any means as far as that. It is fully satisfied if taken as meaning that an immediate bequest of a sum to be distributed among poor relations may on its true construction be no more than a gift to particular individuals (i.e., the next of kin of the propositus), whereas a gift having perpetual continuance cannot be so confined. If a gift or trust on its true construction does extend to those in need amongst relations in every degree, even though it provides for immediate distribution, then, inasmuch as the class of potential beneficiaries becomes so wide as to be incapable of exhaustive ascertainment, the impersonal quality, if I may so describe it, supplied in continuing gifts by the element of perpetuity, is equally present. To use the words of the passage quoted from *Gillam v. Taylor* (1873) LR 16 Eq 581, although no " permanent fund or institution" is set up, the fund in such a case is nevertheless one in which "no person or persons is to have a personal right, but which is to be given only to such as need in the opinion of the trustees". It may further be observed that, just as a gift in perpetuity can only be supported if it is charitable, so, too, a gift to relations in every degree – in the absence, or in default of any exercise of, some power of selection – must fail for uncertainty unless it is charitable; this indeed being the reason for the restriction of any implied trust in default of appointment in such cases to statutory next of kin: see *Wilson v. Duguid* (1883) 24 Ch D 244.

The exception of gifts or trusts in relief of poverty from the general rule under which an element of public benefit is essential to every other form of legal charity may be anomalous. But that cannot in my view justify the restriction of its effect by recourse to yet another anomaly, the result of which would be that gifts or trusts in relief of poverty, which alone among charitable dispositions require no element of public benefit to make them valid, must alone among charitable dispositions – unless indeed it so happens that they do possess the element of public benefit – be of perpetual duration in order to be legally charitable. A disposition obviously cannot be held charitable merely because it involves a perpetuity or conversely be held not charitable merely because it is to take immediate effect. In cases of the class here in question its presence may aid the inference of charitable intent, but where a charitable intent is otherwise to be inferred from the terms of the disposition, the absence of perpetuity is surely immaterial.

Perpetuity in the strict sense could, as it seems to me, be a very capricious test to apply. The judge does, however, appear to have taken this as the test, and to have held that no trust for poor relations could qualify as legally charitable unless liable to exceed in duration the limit of a life in being and twenty-one years thereafter allowed by the rule against perpetuities. On this footing, a trust to apply the income of a fund in perpetuity in the relief of poverty amongst the poor relations of "X" would be charitable, but a trust precisely similar in every respect, save that it was limited in its duration to the period of the life of the last survivor of the issue now in being of His late Majesty King Edward VII and twenty-one years thereafter – a period which might reasonably be estimated at ninety, and might perhaps extend to 100 years or so – would not be charitable. I find myself wholly unable to accept that position. This difficulty was raised in the course of the argument, and I understood Mr. Pennycuick, for the Public Trustee, to concede that perpetuity in the strict sense was not essential, and that some degree of continuity would suffice. But what degree of continuity? To that he could provide no satisfactory answer, save that the distribution must not be "immediate". But what amounts to "immediacy" in this context? On this basis, the test propounded leads to nothing but a morass of uncertainty. One might add that if "immediate distribution" is fatal on account of the personal quality it imports into the disposition, surely the relevant starting point from which to measure "immediacy" (in the case of a testamentary disposition) is the death of the testator, not the date on or from which distribution is to take place. In this case the date marked out for distribution and ascertainment of potential beneficiaries was the death of the survivor of the testatrix's three children – an event which did not in fact take place till some thirty-three years after her death.

For my part I am content to accept as correctly stating the law on this subject the final paragraph of the passage from *Tudor on Charities* (5th ed.),

p. 27, quoted by the judge: "The sounder view is thought to be that a gift for immediate distribution among poor relations, kindred, and so forth, is charitable, except in cases where the intention of the donor, derived from the construction of the documents, is to confine the benefit of the gift to statutory next of kin. Outside this limit no line can be drawn, and the objects ought not therefore to be treated as less extensive where the gift is for immediate distribution than where a perpetual trust is intended".

I should perhaps add that I do not think any assistance can be derived from *Thomas v. Howell* (1874) LR 18 Eq 198. It was not a " poor relations" case, and must, I think, be regarded as of at least doubtful authority. As it happened, it seems from the report that the person named to select the ten poor clergymen in fact survived to perform that function. Had he not done so, it seems that according to the terms of the will the power of selection would have devolved on the testator's executors. But if the power of selection had been confined to an individual who died without exercising it, I venture to suspect that (questions of mortmain apart) the court would have had no difficulty in making the selection itself on the ground that the gift was clearly charitable. But, the selector having survived, the gift could be carried out literally in accordance with its terms. Effect could be given to it without recourse to the special powers of the court in relation to charities, just as if it had been a simple gift of a pecuniary legacy to each of ten named persons. In these circumstances, the court found it possible, to hold that the gift was not charitable for the purposes of, and therefore not defeated by, the Mortmain Act, 1736. I therefore find nothing in that case to displace the conclusion to which I have come; and I would say the same of *Liley v. Hay* (1842) 1 Hare 580, having regard to the grounds on which that decision appears to have proceeded.

For the reasons which I have endeavoured to state I hold that this appeal should be allowed, and that in lieu of the order made by Roxburgh, J., there should be a declaration to the effect that the whole of the residuary estate is effectively devoted to charitable purposes with appropriate consequential directions as to the settlement of a scheme.

The view I have formed on the primary question makes it unnecessary for me to decide what the destination of the half of the property, to which by the agreement above mentioned the issue was confined, might have been on the basis of Roxburgh J.'s decision. Accordingly, notwithstanding the interesting arguments addressed to the court on this question, I refrain from expressing any opinion on it."

Dingle v. Turner
[1972] AC 601

A testator directed trustees to apply the income of a fund for the purpose of paying pensions to poor employees of a firm, which at the time of his death employed over 600 people, who were at least 60 years of age, or who were at least 45 years of age and incapacitated from earning a living. The House of Lords (Viscount Dilhorne, Lord MacDermott, Lord Hodson, Lord Simon and Lord Cross) held that this was a valid charitable trust.

LORD CROSS stated at pp.615–625: "My Lords, by his will dated January 10, Frank Hanscomb Dingle (whom I will call the testator) after appointing Lloyds Bank Ltd., his wife Annie Dingle and his solicitor Henry Elliot Turner to be his executors and trustees made the following – among other – dispositions. By clause 5 he gave to his trustees his ordinary and preference shares in E. Dingle & Co. Ltd. upon trust to pay the income arising therefrom to his wife for her life and after her death to hold the same in trust for such person or persons as she should by will or codicil appoint but without any trust in default of appointment. By clause 8 (a) he directed his trustees to pay the income of his residuary estate after payment thereout of his debts and funeral and testamentary expenses to his wife for her life. By clause 8 (b), (c), (d), (e) and (f) he directed his trustees to raise various sums out of his residuary estate after the death of his wife. Clause 8 (e) was in the following terms:

> "(e) To invest the sum of £10,000 in any of the investments for the time being authorised by law for the investment of trust funds in the names of three persons (hereinafter referred to as 'the pension fund trustees') to be nominated for the purpose by the persons who at the time at which my executors assent to this bequest are directors of E. Dingle & Co. Ltd. and the pension fund trustees shall hold the said sum and the investments for the time being representing the same (hereinafter referred to as 'the pensions fund') upon trust to apply the income thereof in paying pensions to poor employees of E. Dingle & Co. Ltd. or of any other company to which upon any reconstruction or amalgamation the goodwill and assets of E. Dingle & Co. Ltd. may be transferred who are of the age of 60 years at least or who being of the age of 45 years at least are incapacitated from earning their living by reason of some physical or mental infirmity provided always that if at any time the pension fund trustees shall for any reason be unable to apply the income of the pensions fund in paying such pensions to such employees as aforesaid the pension fund trustees shall hold the pensions fund and the income thereof upon trust for the aged poor in the parish of St. Andrew, Plymouth."

Finally by clause 8 (g) the testator directed his trustees to hold the ultimate residue of his estate on the trusts set out in clause 8 (e).

The testator died on January 10, 1950. His widow died on October 8, 1966, having previously released her testamentary power of appointment over her husband's shares in E. Dingle & Co. Ltd. which accordingly fell into the residuary estate. When these proceedings started in October 1970 the value of the fund held on the trusts declared by clause 8 (e) was about £320,000 producing a gross income of about £17,800 per annum.

E. Dingle & Co. Ltd. was incorporated as a private company on January

20, 1935. Its capital was owned by the testator and one John Russell Baker and it carried on the business of a departmental store. At the time of the testator's death the company employed over 600 persons and there was a substantial number of ex-employees. On October 23, 1950, the company became a public company. Since the testator's death its business has expanded and when these proceedings started it had 705 full time and 189 part-time employees and was paying pensions to 89 ex-employees.

The trustees took out an originating summons in the Chancery Division on July 30, 1970, asking the court to determine whether the trusts declared by clause 8 (e) were valid and if so to determine various subsidiary questions of construction – as, for example, whether part-time employees or employees of subsidiary companies were eligible to receive benefits under the trust. To this summons they made defendants (1) representatives of the various classes of employees or ex-employees, (2) those who would be interested on an intestacy if the trusts failed and (3) Her Majesty's Attorney-General. It has been common ground throughout that the trust at the end of clause 8 (e) for the aged poor in the parish of St. Andrew, Plymouth is dependent on the preceding trust for poor employees of the company so that although it will catch any surplus income which the trustees do not apply for the benefit of poor employees it can have no application if the preceding trust is itself void.

By his judgment given on April 2, 1971, Megarry J. held inter alia, following the decision of the Court of Appeal in *Gibson v. South American Stores (Gath & Chaves) Ltd.* [1950] Ch 177, that the trust declared by clause 8 (e) was a valid charitable trust but, on the application of the appellant Betty Mary Dingle, one of the persons interested under an intestacy, he granted a certificate under section 12 of the Administration of Justice Act 1969 enabling her to apply to this House directly for leave to appeal against that part of his judgment and on May 17, 1971, the House gave her leave to appeal.

Your Lordships, therefore, are now called upon to give to the old "poor relations" cases and the more modern "poor employees" cases that careful consideration which, in his speech in *Oppenheim v. Tobacco Securities Trust Co. Ltd.* [1951] AC 297, 313, Lord Morton of Henryton said that they might one day require.

The contentions of the appellant and the respondents may be stated broadly as follows. The appellant says that in the *Oppenheim* case this House decided that in principle a trust ought not to be regarded as charitable if the benefits under it are confined either to the descendants of a named individual or individuals or to the employees of a given individual or company and that though the "poor relations" cases may have to be left standing as an anomalous exception to the general rule because their validity has been recognised for so long the exception ought not to be extended to "poor employees" trusts which had not been recognised for long before their status as charitable trusts began to be called in question. The respondents, on the other hand, say, first, that the rule laid down in the *Oppenheim* case with regard to educational trusts ought not to be regarded as a rule applicable in principle to all kinds of charitable trust, and, secondly, that in any case it is impossible to draw any logical distinction between "poor relations" trusts and "poor employees" trusts, and that, as the former cannot be held invalid today after having been recognised as valid for so long, the latter must be regarded as valid also.

By a curious coincidence within a few months of the decision of this House in the *Oppenheim* case the cases on gifts to "poor relations" had to be considered by the Court of Appeal in *In re Scarisbrick's Will Trusts* [1951] Ch 622. Most of the cases on the subject were decided in the 18th or early 19th centuries and are very inadequately reported, but two things at least were clear. First, that it never occurred to the judges who decided them that in the field of "poverty" a trust could not be a charitable trust if the class of beneficiaries was defined by reference to descent from a common ancestor. Secondly, that the courts did not treat a gift or trust as necessarily charitable because the objects of it had to be poor in order to qualify, for in some of the cases the trust was treated as a private trust and not a charity. The problem in *In re Scarisbrick's Will Trusts* was to determine on what basis the distinction was drawn. Roxburgh J. [1950] Ch 226 – founding himself on some words attributed to Sir William Grant M.R. in *Attorney-General v. Price* (1810) 17 Ves Jun 371, 374 – had held that the distinction lay in whether the gift took the form of a trust under which capital was retained and the income only applied for the benefit of the objects, in which case the gift was charitable, or whether the gift was one under which the capital was immediately distributable among the objects, in which case the gift was not a charity. The Court of Appeal rejected this ground of distinction. They held that in this field the distinction between a public or charitable trust and a private trust depended on whether as a matter of construction the gift was for the relief of poverty amongst a particular description of poor people or was merely a gift to particular poor persons, the relief of poverty among them being the motive of the gift. The fact that the gift took the form of a perpetual trust would no doubt indicate that the intention of the donor could not have been to confer private benefits on particular people whose possible necessities he had in mind; but the fact that the capital of the gift was to be distributed at once did not necessarily show that the gift was a private trust. The appellant in the instant case, while of course submitting that the judges who decided the old cases were wrong in not appreciating that no gift for the relief of poverty among persons tracing descent from a common ancestor could ever have a sufficiently "public" quality to constitute a charity, did not dispute the correctness of the analysis of those cases made by the Court of Appeal in *In re Scarisbrick's Will Trusts* [1951] Ch 622.

Later in the 19th century came the friendly society cases – *Spiller v. Maude* decided in 1881 but reported in a note [to *Pease v. Pattinson* (1886) 32 Ch D 154] in 32 Ch D 158–160; *Pease v. Pattinson* (1886) 32 Ch D 154 and *In re Buck* [1896] 2 Ch 727. In all these cases the court had to consider whether funds held on trust for the relief of poverty among members of a voluntary association were held on charitable trusts – such funds being derived in each case in part from subscriptions made by the members and in part from donations or bequests by well-wishers. In each case the court held that the funds were held on a charitable trust but it does not appear to have been argued in any of them that the fact that the benefits were confined to persons who were linked by the common tie of membership of an association prevented the trusts from being charitable. The arguments against "charity" were either that the association in question was really no more than a private mutual insurance society or that at all events on a winding up so much of the funds as were derived from donations or bequests should he returned to the donors or the estates of the testators and not applied "cy-près."

The first of the "poor employees" cases was *In re Gosling* (1900) 48 WR 300. There the testator sought to establish a fund for "pensioning off" the old and worn-out clerks of a banking firm of which he had been a member. It was argued by those interested in contending that the gift was not charitable that there was no public element in it, and that a distinction should be drawn between the relief of poverty among employees of a firm and the relief of poverty among inhabitants of a geographical area. In rejecting that argument Byrne J. said, *inter alia*, that it was inconsistent with *Attorney-General v. Duke of Northumberland* (1877) 7 Ch D 745, which was one of the "poor relations" cases. His judgment continued as follows, at p. 301:

> "The fact that the section of the public is limited to persons born or residing in a particular parish, district, or county, or belonging to or connected with any special sect, denomination, guild, institution, firm, name, or family, does not itself render that which would be otherwise charitable void for lack of a sufficient or satisfactory description or take it out of the category of charitable gifts. I therefore hold it to be a good charitable gift."

It is to be observed that he does not confine what he says there to trusts for the relief of poverty as opposed to other forms of charitable trust.

In *In re Drummond* [1914] 2 Ch 90 the testator bequeathed some shares in a company of which he had been a director to trustees upon trust to pay the income to the directors of the company

> "for the purposes of contribution to the holiday expenses of the workpeople employed in the spinning department of the said company in such manner as a majority of the directors should in their absolute discretion think fit . . ."

There were some 500 employees in the department. It was first submitted that this was a trust for the relief of poverty. Eve J. rejected that submission but, in doing so, he did not suggest that if he could have held that the workpeople in question were "poor persons " within the meaning of the Statute of Elizabeth [Charitable Uses Act 1601] the gift would nevertheless have failed on the ground that it was confined to employees of a particular company. Next it was submitted that the gift fell under the last of the four heads of charity set out by Lord Macnaghten in *Income Tax Special Purposes Commissioners v. Pemsel*

[1891] AC 531, 583. It was a trust to secure a holiday for a substantial number of the inhabitants of Ilkley who though not poor might in many cases not otherwise to able to get a holiday. Such a trust – it was said – promoted the general well-being of the community; and the beneficiaries could well be considered as constituting a "section of the community" for the purpose of the law of charity. Eve J. – with some regret – rejected that contention saying, at p. 97:

> "This is not a trust for general public purposes; it is a trust for private individuals, a fluctuating body of private individuals it is true, but still private individuals..."

So Eve J., while not disagreeing with the decision in *In re Gosling* (1900) 48 WR 300, plainly thought that the words of Byrne J. which I have quoted though true of poverty cases were not of general application in the law of charity.

Next comes *In re Sir Robert Laidlaw*, a decision of the Court of Appeal given in 1935 but not reported and only brought to light in 1949 [see *Gibson v. South American Stores (Goth & Chaves) Ltd.* [1950] Ch 177, 195]. There the testator had bequeathed a legacy of £2,000 upon certain trusts for the relief of poor members or former members of the staff of Whiteaway, Laidlaw & Co. Ltd. The judge at first instance [Eve J.] having held that the gift failed as not being charitable the Court of Appeal reversed his decision and declared that it was a valid charitable legacy. Unfortunately neither the reasons given by the judge for holding that the gift failed nor those given by the Court of Appeal for holding that it was charitable have been recorded; but the decision of the Court of Appeal was plainly in line with *In re Gosling* (1900) 48 WR 300.

In *In re Compton* [1945] Ch 123 the Court of Appeal had to decide whether a trust for the education of the descendants of three named persons was a charitable trust. In a reserved judgment in which Finlay L.J, and Morton L.J. concurred Lord Greene M.R. began by stating that no trust can be charitable unless it is directed to the benefit of the community or a section of the community as opposed to the benefit of private individuals or a fluctuating class of private individuals. He went on to say that in his opinion no trust under the terms of which a claimant in order to establish his title as a potential beneficiary has to show that he is related to some individual or that he is or was employed by some person or company can ever be a charitable trust since in such cases a personal relationship to individuals or an individual which is in its essence non-public enters into the qualification. In this connection he expressly approved the decision of Eve J. in *In re Drummond* [1914] 2 Ch 90 that in the law of charity a class of employees – unlike the inhabitants of a geographical area – must be regarded as a fluctuating class of private individuals and not a section of the public. Next Lord Greene M.R. said that even if his view that the necessity of founding a claim upon the fact of kinship to an individual precluded the possibility of regarding a gift as charitable was too widely stated yet the sort of educational trust which the testator there had created must be regarded as a private family trust and not as one for the benefit of a section of the community on any fair view of what that phrase might mean. Finally he said of the "poor relations" cases that the decisions were given at a time when the public character of charitable gifts had not yet been clearly laid down, that if the validity of such gifts had first come before the courts in modern days they would very likely have been held to be invalid and that though as they had been accepted as valid for so long it was not possible now to overrule them they should be regarded as anomalous and not be extended by analogy to cover such a trust as that with which the court there was concerned.

Next year in *In re Hobourn Aero Components Ltd.'s Air Raid Distress Fund* [1946] Ch 194 the Court of Appeal consisting of Lord Greene M.R. and Morton L.J. and Somervell L.J. had to consider the character of a fund built up by agreed deductions from the wages of the employees of a company with factories at Coventry, Market Harborough and Kettering, the purpose of the fund being at the relevant time to relieve employees who had suffered damage and distress from air raids. It could not be suggested that the purpose of the trust was the relief of poverty but the Attorney-General argued that it was a charitable trust falling within Lord Macnaghten's fourth category. In rejecting that submission Lord Greene M.R. relied largely on the fact that the fund was a mutual insurance fund. In that connection he pointed out [at pp. 203-204] that the decisions in the friendly society cases to which I have already referred could only be justified – if at all – because "poverty" was a necessary qualification for the receipt of benefits. But both Lord Greene M.R. and Morton L.J. were also clearly of opinion that even if this fund had been provided by the employers or an outside donor it would not have been held on charitable trusts since, as Eve J. had held in *In re Drummond* [1914] 2 Ch 90 and the Court of Appeal had held in *In re Compton* [1945] Ch 123, the employees of a company were not a section of the public for the purpose of the law of charity.

The facts in *Gibson v. South American Stores (Gath & Chaves) Ltd* [1950] Ch 177 – the case followed by Megarry J. in this case – were that a company had vested in trustees a fund derived solely from its profits to be applied at the discretion of the directors in granting gratuities, pensions or allowances to persons

> "who are or shall be necessitous and deserving and who for the time being are or have been in the company's employ . . . and the wives, widows, husbands, widowers, children, parents and other dependants of any person who for the time being is or would, if living have been himself or herself a member of the class of beneficiaries."

The Court of Appeal held that this trust was a valid charitable trust but it did so without expressing a view of its own on the question of principle involved, because *In re Sir Robert Laidlaw* (unreported), January 11, 1935, which was unearthed in the course of the hearing, showed that the Court of Appeal had already accepted the decision in *In re Gosling* (1900) 48 WR 300 as correct.

In *Oppenheim v. Tobacco Securities Trust Co. Ltd.* [1951] AC 297 this House had to consider the principle laid down by the Court of Appeal in *In re Compton* [1945] Ch 123. The trustees of a fund worth over £125,000 were directed to apply its income and also if they thought fit all or any part of the capital

> "in providing for or assisting in providing for the education of children of employees or former employees of British-American Tobacco Co. Ltd . . . or any of its subsidiary or allied companies . . ."

There were over 110,000 such employees. The majority of your Lordships – namely Lord Simonds (in whose opinion Lord Oaksey concurred), Lord Normand and Lord Morton of Henryton – in holding that the trust was not a valid charitable trust gave unqualified approval to the *Compton* principle. They held, that is to say, that although the "poverty" cases might afford an anomalous exception to the rule it was otherwise a general rule applicable to all charitable trusts that no class of beneficiaries can constitute a "section of the public" for the purpose of the law of charity if the distinguishing quality which links them together is relationship to a particular individual either through common descent or through common employment. My noble and learned friend, Lord MacDermott, on the other hand, in his dissenting speech, while not challenging the correctness of the decisions in *In re Compton* or in the *Hobourn Aero* case [1946] Ch 194, said that he could not regard the principle stated by Lord Greene M.R. as a criterion of general applicability and conclusiveness. He said, at p. 317:

> "I see much difficulty in dividing the qualities or attributes, which may serve to bind human beings into classes, into two mutually exclusive groups, the one involving individual status and purely personal, the other, disregarding such status and quite impersonal. As a task this seems to me no less baffling and elusive than the problem to which it is directed, namely, the determination of what is and what is not a section of the public for the purposes of this branch of the law."

He thought that the question whether any given trust was a public or a private trust was a question of degree to be decided in the light of the facts of the particular case and that viewed in that light the trust in *Oppenheim* was a valid charitable trust.

In *In re Cox* [1955] AC 627 a Canadian testator directed his trustees to hold the balance of his residuary estate upon trust to pay its income in perpetuity for charitable purposes only, the persons to benefit directly in pursuance of such charitable purposes being such as were or had been employees of a certain company and/or the dependants of such employees. This disposition raised, of course, a question of construction namely whether "charitable purposes" was simply a compendious mode of referring to any purposes a trust to promote which would be charitable provided that the beneficiaries were the public or a section of the public or whether the words meant such purposes only as having regard to the class of beneficiaries named could be the subject of a valid charitable trust. It was only on the latter construction that the question whether *Gibson v. South American Stores (Gath & Chaves) Ltd.* [1950] Ch 177 was rightly decided would arise and in fact both the courts below and the Privy Council held that the former construction was the right one. It is, however, to be observed that the Court of Appeal for Ontario [1951] OR 205 unanimously held that even if the second construction was right the trust would still fail for want of any possible purposes since the "poor relations" cases formed a class apart and the "poor employees" cases could not stand with the decision in *Oppenheim* [1951] AC 297. The Privy Council expressly refrained from expressing any opinion on this point.

In *In re Young, decd.* [1955] 1 WLR 1269 Danckwerts J. held that a gift by a testator of his residuary estate to the trustees of the benevolent fund of the Savage Club to be used by them as they should think fit for the assistance of any of his fellow members as might fall on evil days created a valid charitable trust. In so deciding he referred to *Gibson's* case [1950] Ch 177 and said that he could see no distinction in principle between the employees of a limited company and the members of a club.

Finally, we were referred to the Privy Council case of *Davies v. Perpetual Trustee Co. Ltd.* [1959] AC 439. There a testator who died on January 21, 1897, after giving successive life interests in certain property in Sydney to several life tenants, the last of whom died in 1957, gave the property

> "to the Presbyterians the descendants of those settled in the colony hailing from or born in the North of Ireland to be held in trust for the purpose of establishing a college for the education and tuition of their youth in the standards of the Westminster Divines as taught in the Holy Scriptures."

On an originating summons issued in 1918 by the then sole trustee for the determination of certain questions it was held (inter alia) by the trial judge and on appeal by the Supreme Court of New South Wales that this device created a valid charitable trust; but after the death of the last life tenant special leave was given to a representative of the next of kin to appeal to the Privy Council which held the trust to be invalid. The Board held as a matter of construction that a child would only be eligible to be educated at the college if (i) he was descended from a Presbyterian living on January 21, 1897; (ii) that Presbyterian was himself descended from a Presbyterian who had settled in the colony and (iii) that settler either hailed from or was born in Northern Ireland. After quoting passages from the opinions of Lord Simonds and Lord Normand in *Oppenheim v. Tobacco Securities Trust Co. Ltd.* [1951] AC 297 the Board held that this class of beneficiaries the nexus between whom was simply their personal relationship to several propositi was not a section of the public but merely a fluctuating class of private individuals and that though the purposes of the trust – being for the advancement of religion and education – were prima facie charitable the trust did not possess the necessary public quality and was invalid.

After this long – but I hope not unduly long – recital of the decided cases I turn to consider the arguments advanced by the appellant in support of the appeal. For this purpose I will assume that the appellant is right in saying that the *Compton* rule [1945] Ch 123 ought in principle to apply to all charitable trusts and that the "poor relations" cases, the "poor members" cases and the "poor employees" cases are all anomalous – in the sense that if such cases had come before the courts for the first time after the decision in *In re Compton* [1945] Ch 123 the trusts in question would have been held invalid as "private" trusts.

Even on that assumption – as it seems to me – the appeal must fail. The status of some of the "poor relations" trusts as valid charitable trusts was recognised more than 200 years ago and a few of those then recognised are still being administered as charities today. In *In re Compton* Lord Greene MR said, at p. 139, that it was "quite impossible" for the Court of Appeal to overrule such old decisions and in *Oppenheim* [1951] AC 297 Lord Simonds in speaking of them remarked, at p. 309, on the unwisdom of casting doubt on "decisions of respectable antiquity in order to introduce a greater harmony into the law of charity as a whole." Indeed, counsel for the appellant hardly ventured to suggest that we should overrule the "poor relations" cases. His submission was that which was accepted by the Court of Appeal for Ontario in *In re Cox* [1951] OR 205 – namely that while the "poor relations" cases might have to be left as long-standing anomalies there was no good reason for sparing the "poor employees" cases which only date from *In re Gosling* (1900) 48 WR 300 and which have been under suspicion ever since the decision in *In re Compton* [1945] Ch 123. But the "poor members" and the "poor employees" decisions were a natural development of the "poor relations" decisions and to draw a distinction between different sorts of "poverty" trusts would be quite illogical and could certainly not be said to be introducing "greater harmony" into the law of charity. Moreover, though not as old as the "poor relations" trusts "poor employees" trusts have been recognised as charities for many years; there are now a large number of such trusts in existence; and assuming, as one must, that they are properly administered in the sense that benefits under them are only given to people who can fairly be said to be, according to current standards, "poor persons," to treat such trusts as charities is not open to any practical objection. So as it seems to me it must be accepted that wherever else it may hold sway the *Compton* rule has no application in the field of trusts for the relief of poverty and that there the dividing line between a charitable trust and a private trust lies where the Court of Appeal drew it in *In re Scarisbrick's Will Trusts* [1951] Ch 622.

Oppenheim [1951] AC 297 was a case of an educational trust and though the majority evidently agreed with the view expressed by the Court of Appeal in the *Hobourn Aero* case [1946] Ch 194 that the *Compton* rule [1945] Ch 123 was of universal application outside the field of poverty it would no doubt be open to this House without overruling *Oppenheim* to hold that the scope of the rule was more limited. If ever I should be called upon to pronounce on this question – which does not arise in this appeal – I would as at present advised be inclined to draw a distinction between the practical merits of the *Compton* rule and the reasoning by which Lord Greene M.R. sought to justify it. That reasoning – based on the distinction between personal and impersonal relationships – has never seemed to me very satisfactory and I have always – if I may say so – felt the force of the criticism to which my noble and learned friend Lord MacDermott subjected it in his dissenting speech in *Oppenheim*. For my part I would prefer to approach the problem on far broader lines. The phrase a "section of the public" is in truth a vague phrase which may mean different things to different people. In the law of charity judges have sought to elucidate its meaning by contrasting it with another phrase: "a fluctuating body of private individuals." But I get little help from the supposed contrast for as I see it one and the same aggregate of persons may well be describable both as a section of the public and as a fluctuating body of private individuals. The ratepayers of the Royal Borough of Kensington and Chelsea, for example, certainly constitute a section of the public; but would it be a misuse of language to describe them as a "fluctuating body of private individuals"? After all, every part of the public is composed of individuals and being susceptible of increase or decrease is fluctuating. So at the end of the day one is left where one started with the bare contrast between "public" and "private." No doubt some classes are more naturally describable as sections of the public than as private classes while other classes are more naturally describable as private classes than as sections of the public. The blind, for example, can naturally be described as a section of the public; but what they have in common – their blindness – does not join them together in such a way that they could be called a private class. On the other hand, the descendants of Mr. Gladstone might more reasonably be described as a "private class" than as a section of the public, and in the field of common employment the same might well be said of the employees in some fairly small firm. But if one turns to large companies employing many thousands of men and women most of whom are quite unknown to one another and to the directors the answer is by no means so clear. One might say that in such a case the distinction between a section of the public and a private class is not applicable at all or even that the employees in such concerns as I.C.I. or G.E.C. are just as much "sections of the public" as the residents in some geographical area. In truth the question whether or not the potential beneficiaries of a trust can fairly be said to constitute a section of the public is a question of degree and cannot be by itself decisive of the question whether the trust is a charity. Much must depend on the purpose of the trust. It may well be that, on the one hand, a trust to promote some purpose, prima facie charitable, will constitute a charity even though the class of potential beneficiaries might fairly be called a private class and that, on the other hand, a trust to promote another purpose, also prima facie charitable, will not constitute a charity even though the class of potential beneficiaries might seem to some people fairly describable as a section of the public. In answering the question whether any given trust is a charitable trust the courts – as I see it – cannot avoid having regard to the fiscal privileges accorded to charities. As counsel for the Attorney-General remarked in the course of the argument the law of charity is bedevilled by the fact that charitable trusts enjoy two quite different sorts of privilege. On the one hand, they enjoy immunity from the rules against perpetuity and uncertainty and though individual potential beneficiaries cannot sue to enforce them the public interest arising under them is protected by the Attorney-General. If this was all there would be no reason for the courts not to look favourably on the claim of any "purpose" trust to be considered as a charity if it seemed calculated to confer some real benefit on those intended to benefit by it whoever they might be and if it would fail if not held to be a charity. But that is not all. Charities automatically enjoy fiscal privileges which with the increased burden of taxation have become more and more important and in deciding that such and such a trust is a charitable trust the court is endowing it with a substantial annual subsidy at the expense of the taxpayer. Indeed, claims of trusts to rank as charities are just as often challenged by the revenue as by those who would take the fund if the trust was invalid. It is, of course, unfortunate that the recognition of any trust as a valid charitable trust should automatically attract fiscal privileges, for the question whether a trust to further some purpose is so little likely to benefit the public that it ought to be declared invalid and the question whether it is likely to confer such great benefits on the public that it should enjoy fiscal immunity are really two quite different questions. The logical solution would be to separate them and to say – as the Radcliffe Commission proposed – that only some charities should enjoy fiscal privileges. But, as things are, validity and fiscal immunity march hand in hand and the decisions in the *Compton* [1949] Ch 123 and *Oppenheim* [1951] AC 297 cases were pretty obviously influenced by the consideration that if such trusts as were there in question were held valid they would enjoy an undeserved fiscal immunity. To establish a trust for the education of the children of employees in a company in which you are interested is no doubt a meritorious act; but however numerous the employees may be the purpose which you are seeking to achieve is not a public purpose. It is a company purpose and there is no reason why your fellow taxpayers should contribute to a scheme which by providing "fringe benefits" for your employees will benefit the company by making their conditions of employment more attractive. The temptation to enlist the assistance of the law of charity in private endeavours of this sort is considerable – witness the recent case of the Metal Box scholarships – *Inland Revenue Commissioners v. Educational Grants Association Ltd.* [1967] Ch 993 – and the courts must do what they can to discourage such attempts. In the field of poverty the danger is not so great as in the field of education – for while people are keenly alive to the need to give their children a good education and to the expense of doing so they are generally optimistic enough not to entertain serious fears of falling on evil days much before they fall on them. Consequently the existence of company "benevolent funds" the income of which is free of tax does not constitute a very attractive "fringe benefit." This is a practical justification – though not, of course, the historical explanation – for the special treatment accorded to poverty trusts in charity law. For the same sort of reason a trust to promote some religion among the employees of a company might perhaps safely be held to be charitable provided that it was clear that the benefits were to be purely spiritual. On the other hand, many "purpose" trusts falling under Lord Macnaghten's fourth head [*Income Tax Special Purposes Commissioners v. Pemsel* [1891] AC 531, 583] if confined to a class of employees would clearly be open to the same sort of objection as educational trusts. As I see it, it is on these broad lines rather than for the reasons actually given by Lord Greene M.R. that the *Compton* rule [1945] Ch 123 can best be justified.

My Lords, for the reasons given earlier in this speech I would dismiss this appeal; but as the view was expressed in the *Oppenheim* case [1951] AC 297 that the question of the validity of trusts for poor relations and poor employees ought some day to be considered by this House and as the fund in dispute in this case is substantial your Lordships may perhaps think it proper to direct that the costs of all parties to the appeal be paid out of it."

Re Segelman deceased
[1996] Ch 171

The testator directed that his residuary estate should be held on trust for the poor and needy members of a class of the testator's relatives which was not to close until 21 years after his death. Chadwick J held that this should not be disqualified from being a valid charitable gift by virtue of the restrictive nature of the class.

CHADWICK J stated at pp.187–194: "The second main question raised by the construction summons — question 1(B) — is whether clause 11(a) of the will creates a valid charitable gift. This question must, I think, be answered in conjunction with question 1(H)(1) of the summons: whether the gift in clause 11(b) of the will in favour of 'the poor and needy of the persons set out in the Second Schedule then living in such proportions as my Trustees may then in their uncontrolled discretion determine' creates a valid charitable gift. Further, it is convenient to determine in this context the true meaning and effect of the words in clause 11(b) 'and in the event of there being no such persons eligible to benefit', which precede the gift over in favour of charitable institutions and charitable purposes. Accordingly, I address these three questions together.

Prima facie, a gift for the benefit of poor and needy persons is a gift for the relief of poverty, and so falls squarely within the first of the four divisions of charity identified by Lord Macnaghten in *Income Tax Special Purposes Comrs v. Pemsel* [1891] AC 531, 583. Further, a gift for the relief of poverty is no less charitable because those whose poverty is to be relieved are confined to a particular class limited by ties of blood or employment: see *In re Scarisbrick* [1951] Ch 622, 648-649 and *Dingle v. Turner* [1972] AC 601, 622-623. In the latter case, Lord Cross — with whom each of the other members of the House of Lords agreed on this point — referred to the position that had been established in *In re Scarisbrick* in these terms at pp. 616–617:

> ". . . the cases on gifts to "poor relations" had to be considered by the Court of Appeal in *In re Scarisbrick* [1951] Ch 622. Most of the cases on this subject were decided in the 18th or early 19th centuries and are very inadequately reported but two things at least were clear. First, that it never occurred to the judges who decided them that in the field of "poverty" a trust could not be a charitable trust if the class of beneficiaries was defined by reference to descent from a common ancestor. Secondly, that the courts did not treat a gift or trust as necessarily charitable because the objects of it had to be poor in order to qualify, for in some of the cases the trust was treated as a private trust and not a charity. The problem in *In re Scarisbrick* was to determine on what basis the distinction was drawn. Roxburgh J — founding himself on some words attributed to Sir William Grant MR in *A-G v. Price* (1810) 17 Ves 371, 374 — had held that the distinction lay in whether the gift took the form of a trust under which capital was retained and the income only applied for the benefit of the objects, in which case the gift was charitable, or whether the gift was one under which the capital was immediately distributable among the objects, in which case the gift was not a charity. The Court of Appeal rejected this ground of distinction. They held that in this field the distinction between a public or charitable trust and a private trust depended on whether as a matter of construction the gift was for the relief of poverty amongst a particular description of poor people or was merely a gift to particular poor persons, the relief of poverty among them being the motive of the gift. The fact that the gift took the form of a perpetual trust would no doubt indicate that the intention of the donor could not have been to confer private benefits on particular people whose possible necessities he had in mind; but the fact that the capital of the gift was to be distributed at once did not necessarily show that the gift was a private trust."

Lord Cross then analysed the numerous cases in which courts had had to consider gifts for the benefit of poor employees. He referred also to the 'education' cases and, in particular, to *In re Compton; Powell v. Compton* [1945] Ch 123 in which Lord Greene MR had emphasised the distinction between benefit to the community and benefit to a fluctuating class of private individuals. He went on to say [1972] AC 601, 622:

> "I will assume that the appellant is right in saying that the *Compton* rule ought in principle to apply to all charitable trusts and that the 'poor relations' cases, the 'poor members' cases and the 'poor employees' cases are all anomalous — in the sense that if such cases had come before the courts for the first time after the decision in *In re Compton* the trusts in question would have been held invalid as 'private' trusts."

Nevertheless, even on that assumption, Lord Cross held that the appeal in *Dingle v. Turner* must fail. It was too late to overrule the 'poor relations' cases on the grounds of anomaly; and there was no sensible distinction to be drawn between the 'poor relations' cases and the 'poor members' and 'poor employees' cases. Lord Cross expressed his conclusion in the following words at p. 623:

> "So as it seems to me it must be accepted that wherever else it may hold sway the *Compton* rule has no application in the field of trusts for the relief of poverty and that there the dividing line between a charitable trust and a private trust lies where the Court of Appeal drew it in *In re Scarisbrick*."

The position is, therefore, that the court must decide, as a matter of construction, whether the gift is (a) for the relief of poverty amongst poor people of the particular description, or (b) a gift to particular poor persons, the relief of poverty among them being the motive of the gift.

The structure of the will, which provides the textual context within which clause 11 must be construed, may be summarised as follows. By clause 2 the testator appointed executors. By clause 3 he gave pecuniary legacies to a number of named individuals, including certain of his relatives. By clause 4 he gave legacies of £2,000 each to nine named charitable institutions. By clause 5 he directed that his trustees should pay to Miss Farnsworth all rent, rates and service charges relating to Flat 14, 22 Park Crescent, London W1 for a period of ten years from the date of his death or until her death, whichever should be the shorter period; and he confirmed that all the contents of the flat were her absolute property. Clause 6 contained a definition of his estate in the widest terms. Clause 7 contained a direction that his executors should hold his estate upon trust for sale, but with power to postpone sale and with power to invest. Clause 8 contained definitions of 'the Trust Fund', 'the Trustees' and 'the Trust Period'. Clause 9 contained a direction that, after payment of debts, funeral, testamentary and administration expenses and legacies, the executors were to transfer the trust fund to the trustees to be held upon the trust's powers and provisions following. Clause 10 gave power to the trustees at any time during the trust period to accept such additional money, investments or other property as might be transferred to them by other persons upon the trusts of the will. Clause 11 was in the terms which I have already set out. Clause 12 of the will conferred on the trustees and executors the administrative powers set out in the first schedule thereto.

In order further to set in context the provisions of the clause which I have to construe it is necessary to describe the testator's family in some detail. (a) The testator was one of seven children of Max and Florence Segelman. (b) The testator's elder brother, Sydney, survived him but has since died. He was neither a pecuniary legatee nor a person named in the second schedule. Sydney had two children: Leonard, who is a pecuniary legatee and a person named in the second schedule, and Stanley, who predeceased the testator. Stanley left a daughter and two grandchildren. They are not named as beneficiaries in the will. (c) Leonard Segelman has two children, David and Barry. Barry is not a pecuniary legatee, but, as one of the issue of Leonard Segelman, is a person within the class constituted by the second schedule. He has been joined as a defendant to the construction summons in order to represent issue alive at, or born within 21 years of, the testator's death who are not otherwise parties. David, the son of Leonard, may or may not be the pecuniary legatee named in clause 3(e); but he is in any event within the second schedule class either in his own name or as issue of his father. This David Segelman has 10 children, all below the age of 21 years. Leonard Segelman and his issue comprise at present 13 individuals. (d) The testator's brother Jack predeceased him, leaving two children, Philip and Naomi. Naomi is neither a pecuniary legatee nor a person within the second schedule class. Philip is both a pecuniary legatee and a person named in the second schedule. (e) Philip Segelman has six children, of whom one is his son, David Segelman, a great nephew of the testator. This David Segelman may or may not be the pecuniary legatee named in clause 3(e) but he, also, is within the second schedule class either in his own name or as issue of his father. Philip Segelman and his issue comprise at present seven individuals. (f) The testator's brother Oscar predeceased him, leaving two children, Shirley and Lorna. They are both named as pecuniary legatees in clause 3 of the will but neither is within the second schedule class. (g) The testator's sister, Sarah Cohen, also predeceased him, leaving four children. Two of those children, Maurice (referred to in the will as 'my nephew Morris Cohen') and David, are named as pecuniary legatees in clause 3. The other two children, Barry and Harry, are not pecuniary legatees. Maurice and his issue are within the second schedule class. He has one child, and so at present his stirps comprises two individuals. The remaining children of Sarah Cohen and their issue are not within the second schedule class. Harry Cohen has been joined as a defendant to represent those who would be entitled to benefit upon an intestacy and who are not otherwise parties. (h) The testator's sister, Rebecca Lee, predeceased him leaving one child, Brian. He is named as pecuniary legatee in clause 3, but he is not a member of the second schedule class. (i) The testator's youngest sister, Gertrude Sissling, is both a pecuniary legatee and a member of the second schedule class. So also is her only child, Lawrence Sissling. Lawrence has at present two children. Gertrude Sissling, her son Lawrence and his issue comprise four individuals.

The position, therefore, is that there are at present 26 members of the second schedule class. Of those, 11 are in the third generation of descent from the testator's parents and 10 are in the fourth generation. Their ages are such that it is reasonable to assume that, by the end of the period of 21 years from the testator's death — when the dispositions in clause 11(b) take effect — the second schedule class will be substantially larger.

On the other hand, there are at present at least ten living descendants of the testator's parents who are not members of the second schedule class. It is clear that the testator has made a considered selection of the members of the class from amongst the descendants of his parents. He has not included all those descendants; nor all the descendants in any particular line of descent (other than the stirps of which his sister Gertrude is the head); nor all those descendants who have been named as pecuniary legatees.

It is clear, also, that the testator has not selected the members of the second schedule class on the basis that they are all poor. The evidence which has been filed on the construction summons by or on behalf of members of that class does not suggest uniform poverty. Rather, it suggests that most members of the class are comfortably off — in the sense that they are able to meet their day-to-day expenses out of income — but not affluent. Like many others in similar circumstances, they need a helping hand from time to time in order to overcome an unforeseen crisis: the failure of a business venture, urgent repairs to a dwelling house or expenses brought on by reason of failing health. Further, the second schedule class includes the issue of named individuals, many of whom are still minors. It is impossible to conclude that the minors have been selected because they are, or are likely to be, poor. No doubt, in common with most of their contemporaries, they will experience relative poverty as students. There will be periods when their income from grants or parental resources fails to cover expenditure on their actual or perceived needs. But they are not as a class 'poor persons' within any ordinarily accepted meaning of that expression.

The conclusion that I draw from the evidence is that the testator selected the members of the second schedule class on the basis that they were persons who might need financial help from time to time in the future — as had been the case (at least in relation to some of those named) in the past — and that they were persons who, by reasons of ties of blood or affection, he would wish to help after his death, as he had done from time to time during his lifetime.

In *In re Scarisbrick* the Court of Appeal had to consider a testamentary gift in the following terms:

> ". . . for such relations of my said son and daughters as in the opinion of the survivor of my said son and daughters shall be in needy circumstances and for such charitable objects either in Germany or in the United Kingdom of Great Britain ... for such interests and in such proportions . . . as the survivor of my said son and daughters shall by deed or will appoint."

Jenkins LJ, at p. 650 dismissed the suggestion that the words 'in the opinion of the survivor of my said son and daughters' had any material bearing on the character of that trust. He treated the gift as being in effect a trust for such relations as 'shall be in needy circumstances'. He went on to say at pp. 650-652:

> "It is, no doubt, true that a gift or trust is not necessarily charitable as being in relief of poverty because the object or objects of it in order to take must be poor. Such a gift or trust may be no more than an ordinary gift to some particular

individual or individuals limited to the amount required to relieve his or their necessities if in necessitous circumstances. One can conceive of a testator making a limited provision of this character for a child or children whose conduct, in his view, had reduced their claims on his bounty to a minimum. A disposition of that sort would obviously not be for the relief of poverty in the charitable sense. The same must be said of gifts to named persons if in needy circumstances, or to a narrow class of near relatives, as, for example, to such of a testator's statutory next of kin as at his death shall be in needy circumstances. It is difficult to draw any exact line, but I do not think the trust here in question can fairly be held disqualified as a trust for the relief of poverty in the charitable sense on grounds such as those illustrated above. The class of relations to whom the selective power of appointment here extends is not confined to relations of the testatrix herself but consists of relations of the testatrix's son and daughters . . . The ambit of the trust thus extends to relations in every degree of the three children on both sides of the family. It should be added that the class of potential beneficiaries falls to be ascertained at the death of the survivor of the three children, not at the testatrixs' own death. The power, therefore, extends to such of the relations in every degree of the three children on both sides of the family as might be in existence at the death of the survivor of the three children, and should then, in the opinion of such survivor, be in needy circumstances. Thus the class of potential beneficiaries, so far from being confined to a limited number of individuals whom the testatrix might be taken to have regarded as having some personal claim on her bounty, at all events to the extent necessary to relieve them from want, is so extensive as to be incapable of being exhaustively ascertained, and includes persons whom the testatrix may never have seen or heard of, and persons not even in existence at the time of her death."

Jenkins LJ held that the gift was a trust for the relief of poverty in the charitable sense amongst the class of relations described and that, being a trust for the relief of poverty, it was not disqualified from ranking as a legally charitable trust by the circumstances that it was confined to a class of relations. He went on, at p. 655, to formulate the following test, which was later approved by the House of Lords in *Dingle v. Turner* [1972] AC 601 at 622-623:

"... the true question in each case has really been whether the gift was for the relief of poverty among a class of persons, or rather . . . was merely a gift to individuals, albeit with relief of poverty amongst those individuals as the motive of the gift."

As Jenkins LJ observed, at p. 651, it is difficult to draw any exact line. Wherever the line is to be drawn, it is clear that the present gift is nearer to it than that which the Court of Appeal had to consider in *In re Scarisbrick*. The second schedule class is narrower than a class of relations of every degree on both sides of the family. The question is whether the class is so narrow that the gift must be disqualified as a trust for the relief of poverty in the charitable sense on grounds such as those illustrated by Jenkins LJ in the examples set out at the beginning of the passage to which I have referred. Is this properly to be regarded as a gift to such of a narrow class of near relatives as at the testator's death shall be in needy circumstances?

The basis for disqualification as a charitable gift must be that the restricted nature of the class leads to the conclusion that the gift is really a gift to the individual members of the class. In my view, the gift in clause 11 of the will is not of that character. The gift with which I am concerned has, in common with the gift which the Court of Appeal had to consider in *In re Scarisbrick*, the feature that the class of those eligible to benefit was not closed upon the testator's death. It remained open for a further period of 21 years. During that period issue of the named individuals born after the death of the testator will become members of the class. It is, in my view, impossible to attribute to the testator an intention to make a gift to those after-born issue as such. His intention must be taken to have been the relief of poverty amongst the class of which they would become members.

It follows that I am satisfied that the gift to the poor and needy of the class of persons set out in the second schedule to the will falls on the charitable side of the line, wherever that line has to be drawn. I hold that the gift in clause 11(a) of the will for the assistance of poor and needy of the class during the period of 21 years from the death of the testator is a gift for charitable purposes; and that the gift for distribution among the poor and needy of the class upon the expiration of that 21-year period is also a gift for charitable purposes.

The size of the testator's estate is such that it is probable that the relief of poverty amongst the poor and needy of the second schedule class during and at the end of the 21-year period will not exhaust the fund. The question which arises is whether, in that event, the gift over 'for such charitable institutions or societies established in the United Kingdom of Great Britain and Northern Ireland or for such charitable purposes ... as my Trustees in their absolute discretion think fit' can take effect.

The gift over is introduced by the words 'in the event of there being no such persons eligible to benefit'. It has been submitted on behalf of the Inland Revenue that if there is any person within the class defined by the second schedule living at the expiration of 21 years from the death of the testator, that person is eligible to benefit and the condition precedent to the gift over cannot be satisfied. In that event, so it is submitted, the gift over in favour of charitable institutions and charitable purposes cannot take effect; the surplus remaining after the relief of poverty amongst the second schedule class is not disposed of by the gift over and must fall into intestacy. It would follow, of course, that the dispositions in clause 11 of the will are not for purposes which are exclusively charitable, and accordingly that those dispositions do not constitute an exempt transfer for the purposes of s 23(1) of the Inheritance Tax Act 1984.

The Revenue's contention — which is supported by those who would be entitled under an intestacy — is based on the premise that the words 'in the event of there being no such persons eligible to benefit' mean either (i) that there should be no person living at the end of the 21-year period who is a member of the second schedule class or (ii) that there should be no such person who is then poor and needy.

I reject the first alternative. To hold that the words 'no such persons eligible to benefit' mean 'no person living at the end of the 21-year period who is a member of the second schedule class' is to give no weight to the phrase 'eligible to benefit'. A person is not eligible to benefit merely because he or she is a member of the second schedule class. To be eligible to benefit the member of the class must be poor and needy. If eligible to benefit, the member of the class becomes entitled to receive so much by way of distribution '... as my Trustees may then in their uncontrolled discretion determine.' The real question, therefore, is whether the words 'no such persons eligible to benefit' mean 'no member of the second schedule class living at the end of the 21-year period who is poor and needy'.

Five observations may be made. First, that given the size and composition of the second schedule class, it must have been clear to the testator at the time he made his will that the overwhelming probability was that there would be some members of that class living at the expiration of 21 years from his death. Secondly, that notwithstanding the gift for the relief of poverty during the 21-year period which is contained in clause 11(a) of the will the testator contemplated that there would or might be some members of the class who remained poor and needy — and so remained eligible to benefit — at the end of that period. Thirdly, that the existence of a single poor and needy member of the second schedule class living at the end of the 21-year period would require the trustees to distribute capital to him '... in such proportions as [they] may in their uncontrolled discretion determine.' Fourthly, that the obligation to distribute in such proportions as the trustees might determine must be construed within the context of a charitable gift; and so cannot authorise or require a distribution which goes beyond the relief of poverty and need. Fifthly, that the size of the trust fund was such that the testator must be taken to have appreciated that there would or might be a substantial surplus after the proper claims of the poor and needy members of the second schedule class had been satisfied.

In these circumstances, to hold that the testator had the intention that the existence of a single needy member of the class in existence at the end of the 21 years should defeat the charitable gift over would be to attribute to him an intention which is so bizarre that I reject it. I am satisfied that upon the true construction of clause 11(b) the intention of the testator was that the gift over in favour of charitable institutions and charitable purposes should take effect once the primary purpose — the relief of poverty among the poor and needy of the class of persons set out in the second schedule — had been fulfilled.

It follows that I hold that the dispositions of the residuary estate made by clause 11 of the will are for purposes which are exclusively charitable. Accordingly, those dispositions constitute an exempt transfer for the purposes of s 23(1) of the 1984 Act. I allow the appeal against the determination by the Commissioners of Inland Revenue that those dispositions are not so exempt."

Trusts for the Advancement of Education

The concept of what is 'educational' in the sense of what will be recognised as legally charitable has been broadened considerably by a process of judicial interpretation.[11] The judgment of Keane J in *Re Worth Library*[12] illustrates that he favoured such a broad interpretation and he stated that 'gifts for the advancement of education...would embrace, not merely gifts to schools and universities and the endowment of university chairs and scholarships' but would also encompass 'gifts for the establishment of theatres, art galleries and museums and the promotion of literature and music'. However, he stressed that in every case, the element of public benefit must be present and, if the benefit extends to a section of the community only, that section must not be numerically negligible.

The courts in this jurisdiction have emphasized the importance of conferring a benefit on the community, or a section of the community[13] and Lord Simonds in *Oppenheim v. Tobacco Securities Trust Co. Ltd*[14] suggested that the words 'section of the community' indicate that the possible beneficiaries must not be numerically negligible and that the quality which distinguishes them from other members of the community must be one which does not depend on their relationship to a particular individual. However, it should be noted that the view was subsequently expressed by Lord Cross in *Dingle v. Turner*[15] that the decision of the majority in *Oppenheim* seemed to have been 'pretty obviously influenced by considerations of a perceived undeserved fiscal immunity' and the speech of Lord Cross shows some element of empathy with the views expressed by Lord MacDermott in his dissent in *Oppenheim*.

Re Hopkins' Will Trusts
[1965] Ch 669

The testatrix left one third of her residuary estate to a society to be applied towards finding the 'Bacon-Shakespeare manuscripts'. Wilberforce J held that this bequest was of a charitable nature.

WILBERFORCE J stated at pp.678–682: "I come, then, to the only question of law: is the gift of a charitable character? The society has put its case in the alternative under the two headings of education and of general benefit to the community and has argued separately for each. This compartmentalisation is

---

[11] See *Re Hopkins' Will Trusts* [1965] Ch 669. Compare this with the earlier decision of Harman J in *Re Shaw* [1957] 1 WLR 729.
[12] [1995] 2 IR 301, 336.
[13] *Re McEnery's Estate* [1941] IR 323.
[14] [1951] AC 297.
[15] [1972] AC 601.

derived from the accepted classification into four groups of the miscellany found in the Statute of Elizabeth (43 Eliz. 1, c. 4). That statute, preserved as to the preamble only by the Mortmain and Charitable Uses Act, 1888, lost even that precarious hold on the Statute Book when the Act of 1888 was repealed by the Charities Act, 1960, but the somewhat ossificatory classification to which it gave rise survives in the decided cases. It is unsatisfactory because the frontiers of "educational purposes" (as of the other divisions) have been extended and are not easy to trace with precision, and because, under the fourth head, it has been held necessary for the court to find a benefit to the public within the spirit and intendment of the obsolete Elizabethan statute. The difficulty of achieving that, while at the same time keeping the law's view of what is charitable reasonably in line with modern requirements, explains what Lord Simonds accepted as the case-to-case approach of the courts: see *National Anti-Vivisection Society v. Inland Revenue Commissioners* [1948] AC 31; 63 TLR 424; [1947] 2 All ER 217, HL. There are, in fact, examples of accepted charities which do not decisively fit into one rather than the other category. Examples are institutes for scientific research (see the *National Anti-Vivisection* case [1948] AC 31, 42, *per* Lord Wright), museums (see *In re Pinion* [1963] 3 WLR 778, 783), the preservation of ancient cottages (*In re Cranstoun* [1932] 1 Ch 537; [1932] 48 TLR 226), and even the promotion of Shakespearian drama (*In re Shakespeare Memorial Theatre Trust* [1923] 2 Ch 398; 39 TLR 676). The present may be such a case.

Accepting, as I have the authority of Lord Simonds for so doing, that the court must decide each case as best it can, on the evidence available to it, as to benefit, and within the moving spirit of decided cases, it would seem to me that a bequest for the purpose of search, or research, for the original manuscripts of England's greatest dramatist (whoever he was) would be well within the law's conception of charitable purposes.The discovery of such manuscripts, or of one such manuscript, would be of the highest value to history and to literature. It is objected, against this, that as we already have the text of the plays, from an almost contemporary date, the discovery of a manuscript would add nothing worth while. This I utterly decline to accept. Without any undue exercise of the imagination, it would surely be a reasonable expectation that the revelation of a manuscript would contribute, probably decisively, to a solution of the authorship problem, and this alone is benefit enough. It might also lead to improvements in the text. It might lead to more accurate dating.

Is there any authority, then, which should lead me to hold that a bequest to achieve this objective is not charitable? By Mr. Fox, for the next-of-kin, much reliance was placed on the decision on Bernard Shaw's will, the *"British Alphabet"* case (*In re Shaw, decd.* [1957] 1 WLR 729). Harman J. held that the gift was not educational because it merely tended to the increase of knowledge and that it was not within the fourth charitable category because it was not in itself for a beneficial purpose but for the purpose of persuading the public by propaganda that it was beneficial. The gift was very different from the gift here. But the judge did say this: "if the object be merely the increase of knowledge, that is not in itself a charitable object unless it be combined with teaching or education" (*ibid.* 737); and he referred to the House of Lords decision, *Whicker v. Hume* (1858) 7 HLC 124, HL, where, in relation to a gift for advancement of education and learning, two of the Lords read "learning" as equivalent to "teaching," thereby in his view implying that learning, in its ordinary meaning, is not a charitable purpose.

This decision certainly seems to place some limits upon the extent to which a gift for research may be regarded as charitable. Those limits are that either it must be "combined with teaching or education," if it is to fall under the third head, or it must be beneficial to the community in a way regarded by the law as charitable, if it is to fall within the fourth category. The words "combined with teaching or education," though well explaining what the judge had in mind when he rejected the gift in *Shaw's* case [1957] 1 WLR 729, are not easy to interpret in relation to other facts. I should be unwilling to treat them as meaning that the promotion of academic research is not a charitable purpose unless the researcher were engaged in teaching or education in the conventional meaning; and I am encouraged in this view by some words of Lord Greene M.R. in *In re Compton* [1945] Ch 123, 127. The testatrix there had forbidden the income of the bequest to be used for research, and Lord Greene M.R. treated this as a negative definition of the education to be provided. It would, he said, exclude a grant to enable a beneficiary to conduct research on some point of history or science. This shows that Lord Greene M.R. considered that historic research might fall within the description of "education." I think therefore, that the word "education" as used by Harman J. in *In re Shaw, decd.; Public Trustee v. Day* [1957] 1 WLR 729, must be used in a wide sense, certainly extending beyond teaching, and that the requirement is that, in order to be charitable, research must either be of educational value to the researcher or must be so directed as to lead to something which will pass into the store of educational material, or so as to improve the sum of communicable knowledge in an area which education may cover – education in this last context extending to the formation of literary taste and appreciation (compare *Royal Choral Society v. Inland Revenue Commissioners* [1943] 2 All ER 101, CA). Whether or not the test is wider than this, it is, as I have stated it, amply wide enough to include the purposes of the gift in this case.

As regards the fourth category, Harman J. is evidently leaving it open to the court to hold, on the facts, that research of a particular kind may be beneficial to the community in a way which the law regards as charitable, "beneficial" here not being limited to the production of material benefit (as through medical or scientific research) but including at least benefit in the intellectual or artistic fields.

So I find nothing in this authority to prevent me from finding that the gift falls under either the third or fourth head of the classification of charitable purposes.

On the other side there is *In re British School of Egyptian Archaeology* [1954] 1 WLR 546, also a decision of Harman J., a case much closer to the present. The trusts there were to excavate, to discover antiquities, to hold exhibitions, to publish works and to promote the training and assistance of students – all in relation to Egypt. Harman J. held that the purposes were charitable, as being educational. The society was one for the diffusion of a certain branch of knowledge, namely, knowledge of the ancient past of Egypt; and it also had a direct educational purpose, namely, to train students. The conclusion reached that there was an educational charity was greatly helped by the reference to students, but it seems that Harman J. must have accepted that the other objects – those of archaeological research – were charitable, too. They were quite independent objects on which the whole of the society's funds could have been spent, and the language "the school has a direct educational purpose, namely, to train students" seems to show that the judge was independently upholding each set of objects.

Mr. Fox correctly pointed out that in that case there was a direct obligation to diffuse the results of the society's research and said that it was this that justified the finding that the archaeological purposes were charitable. I accept that research of a private character, for the benefit only of the members of a society, would not normally be educational – or otherwise charitable – as did Harman J., but I do not think that the research in the present case can be said to be of a private character, for it is inherently inevitable, and manifestly intended, that the result of any discovery should be published to the world. I think, therefore, that the *British School of Egyptian Archaeology* case supports the society's contentions.

A number of other authorities were referred to as illustrating the wide variety of objects which have been accepted as educational or as falling under the fourth category but, since none of them is close to the present, I shall not refer to them. They are well enough listed in the standard authorities.

One final reference is appropriate: to *In re Shakespeare Memorial Trust* [1923] 2 Ch 398. The scheme there was for a number of objects which included the performance of Shakespearian and other classical English plays, and stimulating the art of acting. I refer to it for two purposes, first as an example of a case where the court upheld the gift either as educational or as for purposes beneficial to the community – an approach which commends itself to me here – and secondly as illustrative of the educational and public benefit accepted by the court as flowing from a scheme designed to spread the influence of Shakespeare as the author of the plays. This gift is not that, but it lies in the same field, for the improving of our literary heritage, and my judgment is for upholding it. The answer to 1 (a) on the summons is "no," to 1 (b) is "yes," I make a declaration in the sense of 1 (b), and answer question 2 in the sense of (a)."

Re McEnery: O'Connell v. Attorney General
[1941] IR 323

A testator directed in his will that after the death of his wife moneys invested should be held on trust to enable 'the sons and daughters and male descendants of my brothers to obtain professions'. Gavan Duffy J held that the trust was not charitable in nature.

GAVAN DUFFY J stated at pp.326–330: "This is an interesting will, and I am called upon to decide whether or not the testator's bountiful provisions for the sons and daughters and male descendants of his brothers are valid, and, if not valid generally, whether or not they can be supported to a limited extent.

On the general question I shall assume, for the purposes of this case, that charitable purposes in law comprise those described, and those analogous to the purposes described, in the English Act of Elizabeth and the Act passed in the reign of Charles I for this country; both of those Acts have been repealed, though the Elizabethan classification has been kept alive by statute in England; I shall also assume, for the purposes of educational charity here, that there is, apart from certain religious questions, no substantial difference between the intent of the old English Act and that of the unintelligible Irish Act. The English Act speaks of the maintenance of schools of learning, free schools, and scholars in universities, and the Irish Act speaks of the erection, maintenance or support of any college, school, lecturer in divinity or in any of the liberal arts or sciences, and any other like lawful and charitable uses.

Observe the public character of all these purposes. No doubt the scope of statutes passed in another era has been expanded by judicial decisions, and the process has been marked by some inevitable inconsistencies, but Courts of Equity generally have been consistently insistent on the public character of legal charity, importing a benefit to the community, or a section of the community, in the eyes of the common law of the two countries, reproduced, we are told, in the statutes. The vagaries of the supposedly uniform law of charities may be illustrated by one extract from Serjeant Moor's "Learned Reading," appended to the edition of Duke's "Charitable Uses" published in London in 1676:– as to "Scholars in Universities," he says: "These general words must be restrained to the particular Universities of Oxford and Cambridge; and to such students that study divinity, physick or law, not students in arts only, nor to any students of divinity in popery, etc.," and he explains that "Schools of Learning" do not include schools for catechising, because religion is variable and not within the statute. I was not surprised that counsel, insisting that the law of charities for Ireland and England, as explained by the two statutes, is identical, refrained from drawing upon such authentic sources as Sir Francis Moor, who must have known more about the true purposes of the Act of Elizabeth than any of his contemporaries, if, as we are assured, he penned it. The fact is that we sadly need a modern, home-made statute for charitable trusts.

While some of the purposes associated with poverty in the Elizabethan Act seem to have a personal touch, perhaps the nearest approach to anything like an individual purpose in connection simply with education in either Act is in the maintenance of scholars in universities; I take that to have in view the foundation of scholarships, as "if one devise £10 a year for ever, out of his land, to maintain two scholars in Oxford and Cambridge," though by nuncupative will, this shall be good (Duke, cap. VI, case 29); but there is a wide gap between such an endowment at some university college and, for instance, a trust for the personal educational benefit, between the ages of 18 and 22, of the heir for the time being of a testator for ever, committed by the testator to his trustees; there is nothing public about that purpose and it would, in my view, be too narrow to be charitable; those prospective heirs would not constitute a section of the community for whom a charitable trust could be established.

In a search for precedent upon which, by Judge-made law, to establish the testator's bounty here as an educational charity, reliance was placed in particular upon such cases as *Spencer v. All Souls' College* (1762) Wilm 163, *Attorney-General v. Sidney Sussex College* (1869) LR 4 Ch App 722, and *In re Lavelle* [1914] 1 IR 194, decisions showing that the founder of a charity or a benefactor may lawfully associate his descendants with his bequest to a charitable institution and thus enable them to participate in his liberality; those cases find their prototype in *Griffith Flood's Case* (1724) Hob 136; Duke, cap VI, case 40, where it was laid down that the Act of Elizabeth, overriding the law of mortmain, allowed a man to make a devise to a college at Oxford, to find a scholar of his blood from time to time. But they do nothing to validate the very different provisions of our testator's will.

The trust here is, in my opinion, too narrow to be charitable; the motive may have been charitable, but the intention was to benefit specific individuals, and the fact, though not conclusive, is worthy of note that, if the trust were good, each suitable beneficiary would appear to have an enforceable claim upon the trust, unless the number of suitable beneficiaries were so great a tax on the income as to give the trustees the special discretion allowed to them in that event. I mean that each male descendant of a brother, as he grows to manhood, if he rejects trade as a career for the moment and makes up his mind to qualify himself for an eventual archbishopric or chief justiceship or presidency of the College of Surgeons, will be entitled, on signifying his election, to call for £100 a year during a reasonable time to enable him to become a priest or barrister or surgeon, provided he be a suitable student and that his competitors be not too many.

It is just 200 years since Lord Hardwicke L.C. in *Attorney-General v. Pearce* (1740) Atk 87 declared that it is its extensiveness that constitutes a public charity:– "a devise to the poor of a parish is charitable. Where testators have not any particular person in their contemplation, but leave it to the discretion of a trustee to chuse out the objects, though such person is private, and each particular object may be said to be private, yet in the extensiveness of the benefit accruing from them they may very properly be called publick charities. A sum to be disposed of by A. B. and his executors, among poor housekeepers, is of this kind."

And a further difficulty in the present case is that touched upon by Mr. Justice Barton in *Laverty v. Laverty* [1907] 1 IR 9, that the trust would allow the trustees to pay £100 a year to a delicate descendant, at least if he needed this pecuniary help, to enable him to have a private "coach" in his father's private house to steer him through the examinations for some specialised profession. I do not see my way to adopting Mr. Sweeney's ingenious suggestion that I should validate an invalid trust by reading it as requiring the trustees to establish a number of scholarships, either in some university or elsewhere; that would mean resorting to the *cy-près* doctrine in order to convert a non-charitable into a charitable trust, at the expense of the persons lawfully entitled. You cannot, under cover of *cy-près*, rob Peter to pay Paul.

As to *In re Rayner* (1920) 89 LJ Ch 369, also relied upon by Mr. Connolly, the gift to educate the children of Maple's numerous employees took in, no doubt, a field wide enough to cover a section of the community, who were, moreover, people "comparatively poor" within Lord Bramwell's definition of a charity in *Pemsel's Case* [1891] AC 531, 564.

I pass now to the argument in favour of a limited validity for the trust. It is urged that at least those sons and daughters and male descendants of brothers who were alive at the death of the testator are entitled to benefit. Unhappily the gifts to these beneficiaries, if severable, are subject to multiple contingencies; any beneficiary to enjoy the gift must:

(*a*) survive the testator's widow and tenant for life;

(*b*) by reason of the codicil, survive the time, at testator's death necessarily uncertain, when, after her death, the income of the trust fund shall have proved sufficient to pay legacies amounting to £620;

(*c*) and, at or after that time when the income has become available, be about to enter, as a suitable student, upon a profession and ask for the testator's annuity to enable him to obtain his profession – incidentally I do not think he will be qualified, if at that time in affluent circumstances, but my decision is given quite independently of this view, which turns on the word "enable"; and he must

(*d*) take his chance of selection by the trustees in case the legitimate competitors for an annuity shall be more numerous than the number of £100 units produced for the time being by the income of the fund, the single trust fund intended to produce all the annuities.

It is very difficult on the language of the will to discern more than one class here, the single, though composite, class for whom, as ascertained from time to time, the single trust fund is established. It is impossible to say with certainty in advance how many years may elapse before a potential beneficiary may wish to enter a profession, unless one has regard to the actual state of the families concerned at testator's death and that I cannot do – indeed, I could only find probabilities, if I did; the first beneficiary entitled to claim and receive an annuity may be a person unborn at the death of the testator; and participation by any beneficiary depends upon the amount of available income and the number of competitors and his selection, if they are too many, by the trustees, and that may first happen at too remote a time. On principle the case seems indistinguishable from *Moore v. Moore* 6 Jones, Eq 132, as summarised in par. 396 of Gray on Perpetuities (3rd Edn.), except that that case appears to have been concerned with payments out of capital; for a case of annuities out of income void under the rule against perpetuities, see *In re Gassiot* (1901) 70 LJ Ch 242; see also *In re Whiteford* [1915] 1 Ch 347, where the limit was cut down by a special power, but the same principle as to uncertainty applied.

The fifth rule in *Cattlin v. Brown* (1853) 11 Hare 372, 377, relied upon by Mr. McCarthy, has no application, because the annuity desired by a particular beneficiary may be, not merely diminished, but withheld in case of a deficiency of income to meet all the demands of the competing students; nor is the time fixed when distribution depending on a personal penchant for a profession of a suitable student, is to begin. And, as Mr. Ryan pointed out, the difficulty of escaping from the general rule under any exceptional sub-rule is greatly increased by the testator's restriction of his bounty to suitable students.

Accordingly, much as I should have liked to hold for a limited validity of the testator's gift, I cannot see my way to upholding it at all."

Oppenheim v. Tobacco Securities Trust Co. Ltd
[1951] AC 297

By a settlement trustees were directed to apply certain income for the education of the children of employees or former employees of a named company or any of its subsidiary or allied companies. The number of the employees of these companies exceeded 110,000. It was held by the majority of the House of Lords (Lord Simonds, Lord Normand, Lord Oaksey and Lord Morton; Lord MacDermott dissented) that the trust did not satisfy the test of public benefit required in order to establish it as charitable in nature.

LORD SIMONDS stated at pp.305–309: "My Lords, once more your Lordships have to consider the difficult subject of charitable trusts, and this time a question is asked to which no wholly satisfactory answer can be given.

Before I turn to the authorities I will make some preliminary observations. It is a clearly established principle of the law of charity that a trust is not charitable unless it is directed to the public benefit. This is sometimes stated in the proposition that it must benefit the community or a section of the community. Negatively it is said that a trust is not charitable if it confers only private benefits. In the recent case of *Gilmour v. Coats* [1949] AC 426 this principle was reasserted. It is easy to state and has been stated in a variety of ways, the earliest statement that I find being in *Jones v. Williams* (1767) 2 Amb 651, in which Lord Hardwicke, L.C., is briefly reported as follows: "Definition of charity: a gift to a general public use, which extends to the poor as well as to the rich . . . ". With a single exception, to which I shall refer, this applies to all charities. We are apt now to classify them by reference to Lord Macnaghten's division in *Income Tax Commissioners v. Pemsel* [1891] AC 581, 583, and, as I have elsewhere pointed out, it was at one time suggested that the element of public benefit was not essential except for charities falling within the fourth class "other purposes beneficial to the community". This is certainly wrong except in the anomalous case of trusts for the relief of poverty with which I must specifically deal. In the case of trustees for educational purposes the condition of public benefit must be satisfied. The difficulty lies in determining what is sufficient to satisfy the test, and there is little to help your Lordships to solve it.

If I may begin at the bottom of the scale, a trust established by a father for the education of his son is not a charity. The public element, as I will call it, is not supplied by the fact that from that son's education all may benefit. At the other end of the scale the establishment of a college or university is beyond doubt a charity. "Schools of learning and free schools and scholars of universities" are the very words of the preamble to the Statute of Elizabeth. So also the endowment of a college, university or school by the creation of scholarships or bursaries is a charity and none the less because competition may be limited to a particular class of persons. It is upon this ground, as Lord Greene, M.R., pointed out in *In re Compton* [1945] Ch 123, 136, that the so-called Founder's Kin cases can be rested. The difficulty arises where the trust is not for the benefit of any institution either then existing or by the terms of the trust to be brought into existence, but for the benefit of a mass of persons at large. Then the question is whether that class of persons can be regarded as such a "section of the community" as to satisfy the test of public benefit. These words "section of the community" have no special sanctity, but they conveniently indicate first, that the possible (I emphasize the word "possible") beneficiaries must not be numerically neglible, and secondly, that the quality which distinguishes them from other members of the community, so that they form by themselves a section of it, must be a quality which does not depend on their relationship to a particular individual. It is for this reason that a trust for the education of members of a family or, as in *In re Compton*, of a number of families cannot be regarded as charitable. A group of persons may be numerous but, if the nexus between them is their personal relationship to a single propositus or to several propositi, they are neither the community nor a section of the community for charitable purposes.

I come, then, to the present case where the class of beneficiaries is numerous but the difficulty arises in regard to their common and distinguishing quality.

That quality is being children or employees of one or other of a group of companies. I can make no distinction between children of employees and the employees themselves. In both cases the common quality is found in employment by particular employers. The latter of the two cases by which the Court of Appeal held itself to be bound, *In re Hobourn Aero Components Ld.'s Air Raid Distress Fund* [1946] Ch 194, is a direct authority for saying that such a common quality does not constitute its possessors a section of the public for charitable purposes. In the former case, *In re Compton*, Lord Greene, M.R., had by way of illustration placed members of a family and employees of a particular employer on the same footing, finding neither in common kinship nor in common employment the sort of nexus which is sufficient. My Lords, I am so fully in agreement with what was said by Lord Greene in both cases and by my noble and learned friend, then Morton, L.J., in the *Hobourn* case, that I am in danger of repeating without improving upon their words. No one who has been versed for many years in this difficult and very artificial branch of the law can be unaware of its illogicalities, but I join with my noble and learned friend in echoing the observations which he cited from the judgment of Russell, L.J., in *In re Grove-Grady* [1929] 1 Ch 557, 582, and I agree with him that the decision in *In re Drummond* [1914] 2 Ch 90 "imposed a very healthy check upon the extension of the legal definition of 'charity'". It appears to me that it would be an extension, for which there is no justification in principle or authority, to regard common employment as a quality which constitutes those employed a section of the community. It must not, I think, be forgotten that charitable institutions enjoy rare and increasing privileges, and that the claim to come within that privileged class should be clearly established. With the single exception *In re Rayner* (1920) 89 LJ (Ch) 369, which I must regard as of doubtful authority, no case has been brought to the notice of the House in which such a claim as this has been made, where there is no element of poverty in the beneficiaries, but just this and no more, that they are the children of those in a common employment.

Learned counsel for the appellant sought to fortify his case by pointing to the anomalies that would ensue from the rejection of his argument. For, he said, admittedly those who follow a profession or calling, clergymen, lawyers, colliers, tobacco workers and so on, are a section of the public; how strange then it would be if, as in the case of railwaymen, those who follow a particular calling are all employed by one employer. Would a trust for the education of railwaymen be charitable, but a trust for the education of men employed on the railways by the Transport Board not be charitable? And what of service of the Crown whether in the civil service or the armed forces? Is there a difference between soldiers and soldiers of the King? My Lords, I am not impressed by this sort of argument and will consider on its merits, if the occasion should arise, the case where the description of the occupation and the employment is in effect the same, where in a word, if you know what a man does, you know who employs him to do it. It is to me a far more cogent argument, as it was to my noble and learned friend in the *Hobourn* case, that if a section of the public is constituted by the personal relation of employment, it is impossible to say that it is not constituted by 1,000 as by 100,000 employees, and, if by 1,000, then by 100, and, if by 100, then by 10. I do not mean merely that there is a difficulty in drawing the line, though that too is significant: I have it also in mind that, though the actual number of employees at any one moment might be small, it might increase to any extent, just as, being large, it might decrease to any extent. If the number of employees is the test of validity, must the court take into account potential increase or decrease, and, if so, as at what date?

I would end, my Lords, where I began, by saying that I concur in the reasoning of the Court of Appeal in the *Hobourn* case, but there are certain points in the argument for the appellant about which I should say a few words. It was urged by counsel for the Attorney-General, who was allowed to address the House, that there was here a valid charitable trust created, since there was no private person who could sue to enforce the trust. I am not persuaded that this would be so, if the trust were otherwise enforceable. But in any case the test is not a valid one. If this trust is charitable, the Attorney-General can sue to enforce it: it does not follow that it is charitable because no one else can sue to enforce it. I would also, as I have previously indicated, say a word about the so-called "poor relations" cases. I do so only because they have once more been brought forward as an argument in favour of a more generous view of what may be charitable. It would not be right for me to affirm or justify these decisions: I am concerned only to say that the law of charity, so far as it relates to "the relief of aged, impotent and poor people" (I quote from the statute) and to poverty in general, has followed its own line, and that it is not useful to try to harmonize decisions on that branch of the law with the broad proposition on which the determination of this case must rest. It is not for me to say what fate might await those cases if in a poverty case this House had to consider them. But, as was observed by Lord Wright in *Admiralty Commissioners v. Valverda* [1938] AC 173, 194, while "this House has no doubt power to overrule even a long established course of decisions of the courts provided it has not itself determined the question", yet "in general this House will adopt this course only in plain cases where serious inconvenience or injustice would follow from perpetuating an erroneous construction or ruling of law". I quote with respect those observations to indicate how unwise it would be to cast any doubt upon decisions of respectable antiquity in order to introduce a greater harmony into the law of charity as a whole.

The appeal should in my opinion be dismissed with costs."

Trusts for the Advancement of Religion

Trusts purporting to fall into this category have always been numerous in this jurisdiction and legislative intervention has helped to clarify what has been a most complex and uncertain area of the law.

Gifts for the Celebration of Masses

The fact that a bequest for the saying of masses whether in private or in public was a good charitable gift was confirmed by the Irish Court of Appeal in *O'Hanlon v. Logue* despite considerable earlier uncertainty about this question. The issue was put beyond doubt by s.45(2) of the Charities Act 1961, which provides that gifts for the celebration of Masses, whether in public or private, are valid charitable gifts.

O'Hanlon v. Logue
[1906] 1 IR 247

A testatrix devised and bequeathed her property to trustees upon certain trusts and then directed that it should be sold and the proceeds invested to pay the income thereof from time to time to the Roman Catholic Primate of Ireland for the time being for the celebration of masses for the repose of the souls of her late husband, her children and herself, the will containing no direction that these masses be said in public. The Irish Court of Appeal (Walker C, Palles CB, Fitzgibbon and Holmes LJJ) upheld the charitable nature of the gift and made it clear that a bequest for the saying of masses whether in public or not, constituted a valid charitable gift.

PALLES CB stated at pp.274–276: "I am of opinion that the narrow view taken in *The Attorney-General v. Delaney* (1875) IR 10 CL 104, that the only element of public benefit in the celebration of the Mass is the instruction and edification of the congregation present, fails to appreciate it as a gift to God, as a gift made in the expectation that, because of it, the divine service of a Christian Church, a supreme act of divine worship, would be offered in the name of and by the authority of the whole Church, by ministers specially consecrated to represent her, as an act from which the Common Law knew previous to the Reformation, and therefore knows now, that benefits spiritual and temporal flow to the general body of the faithful – benefits which, even were they spiritual only, would render the service charitable within 10 Car. 1, sess. 3, c. 1. In my mind, if the object of the gift could be separated from its effect (which is impossible), either would render the gift charitable. This certainly is the effect of both combined.

This, then, is my first reason for holding that the decision in *The Attorney-General v. Delaney* was wrong, and that the present appeal should be allowed.

I now revert to the effects of the Reformation. It, as I have already said, altered the service; and without entering upon a consideration of the difference between the old and new services, the latter is identified, by the Act of Edw. 6, as being in law the divine service of the Mass, as altered. Each, the old and the new, is an act of divine worship of the Church, an offering of praise, adoration, and thanksgiving, involving a petition for benefit; temporal and spiritual, for all the faithful alive, whether present or absent. All will admit that the divine service of the Reformed Church was, by virtue of its spiritual efficacy, a charitable act, so long as it remained the established church; and if so, having regard to section 20 of the Church Act, which, subject to a power of change, continues all the "doctrines, rites, and ceremonies," notwithstanding disestablishment, so must it have continued thereafter.

Now knowing, as does the Common Law, that the old service contains in substance all of that which renders that new service charitable, together with something else, that old service, at least since 1869 (when the Roman Catholic and the Reformed Church became equal in the sight of the law), must, too, be charitable, unless those elements which it contains, and which are absent in the new service, prevent the legal result which otherwise would flow from that which is common to both. But such prevention could result only from illegality; and there is now no illegality in the essential differences between the two services. Therefore, because the new service is charitable, so also must be the old. This is my second reason for holding the gift charitable.

There is, however, a third reason, which is of wider application, and which it is therefore right that I should state. The existence of a divine service is essential to all religions; and equally essential is the existence of a privileged class, a priesthood or a class of ministers, by whom that divine service shall be celebrated, on behalf of the Church. The divine service of the particular religion must be defined by the doctrines of its own religion. Without those doctrines it cannot exist as a divine service. Without a knowledge of those doctrines, the spiritual effect of the service cannot be understood. Consequently, the effect of the divine service cannot be known, otherwise than from the doctrines of its religion, coupled with a hypothetical admission of their truth. But the advancement of *any* theistic religion is charitable, and each advancement may result from an increased number of the celebrations of its divine services. Therefore the charitable nature of a divine service must (when the religion is not an established one) depend upon the character of the act, not objectively, but according to the doctrines of the religion in question. The same proposition may be stated in different words. When, in a country like ours at present, where there is no established church, it is alleged that a religion (whose doctrines are not known to the law) is advanced by the performance of an act of divine service, the law, from the fact that it is a divine service, admits that which is involved in its being such an act, viz. that its celebration tends to the advancement of the religion, and, consequently, a gift to procure the performance of the act is charitable. Further, the knowledge that it is a divine service necessarily involves a knowledge of those doctrines but for which it would not exist as a divine service, and therefore renders admissible evidence of these doctrines. But when it knows those doctrines, although it knows that, according to them, such an act has the spiritual efficacy alleged, it cannot know it objectively and as a fact, unless it also knows that the doctrines in question are true. But it never can know that they are objectively true, unless it first determines that the religion in question is a true religion. This it cannot do. It not only has no means of doing so, but it is contrary to the principle that all religions are now equal in the law. It follows that there must be one of two results: either (1) the law must cease to admit that *any* divine worship can have spiritual efficacy to produce a public benefit; or (2) it must admit the sufficiency of spiritual efficacy, but ascertain it according to the doctrines of the religion whose act of worship it is.

The first alternative is an impossible one. The law, by rendering all religions equal in its sight, did not intend to deny that which is the basis of, at least, all Christian religions, that acts of divine worship have a spiritual efficacy. To do so would, virtually, be to refuse to recognize the essence of all religion. The other result must, therefore, necessarily ensue. It must ascertain the spiritual efficacy according to the doctrines of the religion in question; and if, according to those doctrines, that divine service does result in public benefit, either temporal or spiritual, the act must, in law, be deemed charitable.

These considerations have satisfied me that, in this respect also, the decision in *The Attorney-General v. Delaney* (1875) IR 10 CL 104 was erroneous, and that the celebration of the Mass, whether in private or in public, is charitable; and for this third reason, also, I am of opinion that this appeal should be allowed."

Gifts to Religious Orders

Gifts to contemplative religious orders were traditionally not regarded as charitable in nature as they did not fulfil the necessary public benefit requirement.[16] Such bequests would only be valid if they could be construed as a gift to the superior of the order for the time being for the benefit of its existing members.[17] However, the view that contemplative religious orders did not provide any benefit to the community began to be questioned[18] and in *Maguire v. Attorney General*[19] Gavan Duffy J upheld such a gift as charitable in nature. The issue of the public benefit requirement in relation to gifts for the purpose of the advancement of religion was further clarified by s.45(1) of the Charities Act 1961 which provides that in such cases it shall be conclusively presumed that the purpose includes and will occasion public benefit.

---

[16] *Cocks v. Manners* (1871) LR 12 Eq 574 and *Commissioners of Charitable Donations and Bequests v. McCartan* [1917] 1 IR 388.
[17] *Cocks v. Manners* (1871) LR 12 Eq 574 and *Re Wilkinson's Trusts* (1887) 19 LR IR 531.
[18] *Munster and Leinster Bank Ltd v. Attorney General* [1940] IR 19.
[19] [1943] IR 238.

Maguire v. Attorney General
[1943] IR 238

The testatrix directed in her will that a sum of money be spent founding a convent 'of perpetual adoration' in a specified place or elsewhere as the trustees might determine. Gavan Duffy J held that this was a valid charitable gift.

GAVAN DUFFY J stated at pp. 243–249 and 253–254: "The purpose of the testatrix was unquestionably to secure the perpetual adoration of the Blessed Sacrament; the Convent is the means to that end.

Lisnaskea is a little place in Fermanagh; its population is stated to be mainly Catholic. The testatrix was born there.

A bequest of £4,000 Consolidated Stock upon trust to apply the income for the exclusive benefit of the Dublin Home for Starving and Forsaken Cats was held by the Court of Appeal in Ireland thirty years ago to be a valid charitable gift, *Swifte v. Attorney-General* [1912] 1 IR 133 – because cats are useful to man. Since the legal concept of charity stretches so far, it is a shock to one's sense of propriety and a grave discredit to the law that there should, in this Catholic country, be any doubt about the validity of a trust to expend money in founding a convent for the perpetual adoration of the Blessed Sacrament; but the law of charitable donations has strayed far from reality and its perspective has grown hazy, and a gift for secluded devotion, as I must assume this gift to be, has been held by eminent Judges to be outside the purview of the charity recognisable in the Courts. A gift, now recognised as charitable, for the celebration of the Most Holy Sacrifice of the Mass, though to be said in private, may be thought to stand alone as a provision for the central act of the Catholic faith: *In re Caus; Lindeboom v. Camille* [1934] 1 Ch 162, and I must, therefore, look further into the authorities. The fundamental objection must be that this bequest cannot be charitable because no public benefit will necessarily result from it; unhappily the test is elusive, since men's notions of public benefit will vary with the outlook of their age. Of other possible objections, any difficulty as to the power of the Court to ensure the proper administration of the endowment seems to be fully met by the judgments in *Attorney-General v. Hall* [1897] 2 IR 426. As to remoteness, though an indefinite time must elapse before the executors can carry out this quite impersonal trust, the gift must be deemed immediate and free of the rule against perpetuities, provided I find an intention to make an unconditional gift to charity: Gray on Perpetuities, 4th ed., par. 607. The fundamental objection is therefore the only one that I need examine to determine whether this is a valid charitable bequest.

The recognition of religious purposes as charitable in law, because religious, is thoroughly well settled. In 1817 Lord Eldon held that a bequest to maintain and propagate the worship of God was charitable: *Attorney-General v. Pearson* (1817) 3 Mer 396, at p. 409. In 1824 Lord Manners in this country found a good charitable gift in a direction to the trustees of a will to lay out £2,000 at their discretion, until a boy came of age, "in the service of my Lord and Master, and I trust Redeemer": *Powerscourt v. Powerscourt* (1824) 1 Moll 616. Lindley L.J., speaking for an eminent Bench, in 1893 declared that a bequest to a religious institution, or for a religious purpose, is *prima facie* a bequest for a charitable purpose: *In re White; White v. White* [1893] 2 Ch 41, at p. 52. Contrast *Stewart v. Green* (1871) IR 5 Eq 470.

It has proved impracticable to define the test of public benefit. Very narrow sections of the community have answered the test for non-religious charity, a bequest to a man's poor relations: *Attorney-General v. Northumberland* (1877) 7 Ch D 745, for instance, and a gift to the incapacitated employees of a large emporium in London: *In re Rayner; Clontman v. Regnart* (1920) 89 LJ Ch 369, and for the education of the children of employees, and even a fund for a firm's old and worn-out clerks (with one candidate for relief): *In re Gosling; Gosling v. Smith* (1900) 48 WR 300; religion seldom fares so well, though Romilly M.R. upheld a testamentary annuity for three persons for ever to study the Bible and to say a prayer on his anniversary in praise of God: *In re Michel* (1860) 28 Beav 39, and actually held charitable a bequest to diffuse "the sacred writings" of a patently demented visionary, whose sectaries had practically disappeared after her death: *Thornton v. Howe* (1862) 31 Beav 14.

On the other hand, a gift by a Chinese testatrix for the erection of a house where rites should be performed to her late husband and herself was held non-charitable and void, because meant for an observance which could lead to no public advantage and would benefit or solace only the family: *Yeap Chea Neo v. Org Cheng Neo* (1875) LR 6 PC 381; and a legacy to a pretended Society for the Suppression of Cruelty to Animals by United Prayers failed, when Chitty J., finding the main intention to be the improvement of the supplicants by private prayer, and not the suppression of cruelty, held that there was no purpose of general utility to make the gift charitable "within the statute" of Elizabeth – a phrase to be noted. The piety of enclosed religious orders has been assigned to the same category, on the authority of an English case which has enjoyed a remarkable vogue since 1871; Sir John Wickens V.C. decided in *Cocks v. Manners* (1871) LR 12 Eq 574:

(*a*) that a non-charitable testamentary gift to a religious institution may, if involving no perpetuity, be sustainable as a personal gift to the members, provided they be free in law to spend the money as they please (and it is under this head that the case has often been called in aid by the Irish Courts);

(*b*) that a certain gift to a contemplative convent was not charitable in law; and

(*c*) that a gift for religious purposes, provided it be for religious services tending to edify the public, is charitable in law (and I regret any need that there may be to uphold a pious gift for its accidental effect and not for its intrinsic merit).

The word "services" must be construed broadly; it could not, on the authorities, have meant only rites and ceremonies.

Two convents were residuary legatees and either, if charitable, had, under an English Act, to forfeit part of the gift, payable out of leasehold land; one, a Dominican convent, presented as a body of celibates, associated for the purpose of sanctifying their souls by prayer and contemplation, was held to have none of the requisites of a charitable body, since it tended neither directly nor indirectly towards the instruction or edification of the public and the gift was "neither within the letter nor the spirit" of the Elizabethan statute; and the gift was held valid as an immediate bequest to the existing community; the other convent was a house of Sisters of Charity of St. Paul, who taught the poor and nursed the sick as a means to the personal sanctification, which was certified to the Judge after an inquiry to be their primary object; this body was held to be charitable by reason of its work and competent to share in the pure personalty only; the Vice-Chancellor trusted the Reverend Mother to apply the money properly; (that is the principle of *Walsh v. Gladstone* (1843) 1 Ph 290); but, in affirming the charity, he passed over both the primary object (which had made the other convent non-charitable) and the rule that a gift to be charitable in law, must be destined exclusively to purposes wholly charitable in law; the apparent inconsistency is critically examined by Mr. Justice Black in *Munster and Leinster Bank v. Attorney-General* [1940] IR 19, at pp. 37-38. A quarter of a century later Rigby L.J. in an illuminating comment, explained that the Dominican Convent, which abstained "even from good works as regards the outside public" could not be called a charity: *In re Macduff; Macduff v. Macduff* [1896] 2 Ch 451, at p. 474; and shortly afterwards Farwell J. declared unequivocally that there was no "charity" in attempting to save one's own soul, because charity, that is charity in law, was necessarily altruistic: *In re Delany; Conoley v. Quick* [1902] 2 Ch 642, at p. 648. Lord Macnaghten in *Dunne v. Byrne* [1912] AC 407, at p. 410 added his high authority to the view that the gift to the Dominicans was certainly not charitable.

It was, no doubt, hard for these Judges to apprehend the true *raison d'être* of a Catholic religious Order, but as recently as 1917 a distinguished Irish Catholic Judge went further than Wickens V.C. In *Commissioners of Charitable Donations and Bequests v. McCartan* [1917] 1 IR 388; 51 ILTR 197 observing that a monastery is not necessarily devoted to works of charity, such as education or the nursing of the sick poor, and that monasteries of men or women are often institutions whose members devote their lives exclusively to piety, and that *prima facie* a monastery, either for men or women, is not charitable, O'Connor M.R. plainly held a trust to establish a monastery not to be charitable; perhaps his reasons were not quite so plain as the conclusion; he did not use the non-edification argument, which would have sounded grotesque in Ireland, and he seems (particularly from the non-official report) to have proceeded on the assumption that a contemplative Order of monks or nuns is in law deemed to be of no benefit to the public and on the principle that without public benefit there can be no charity in law.

These several judgments seem to me to postulate egoism as the note of the monastic life. If an orthodox Catholic can be so strangely misled, perhaps it is hardly possible for any unbeliever to form a clear picture of the higher vocation without passing some days in a monastery, but it is necessary that Christian and pagan critics alike should understand what a monastery is and what it means, and the "egoists" are most willing to let outsiders into the secret.

A monastery of St. Benedict, to take an outstanding example, "has no function in the life of the Church save to provide an ordered way of life based on the teaching of the gospel, according to which its inmates may serve God and sanctify their souls apart from the life of the world . . . the evils of corporate selfishness are excluded by its *raison d'être*, which is the service of God in simplicity of life and without contact with the world."

I quote from the study of early Benedictine and other foundations in England by Dom David Knowles, O.S.B.,

> "The Monastic Order in England," pp. 4-5, 15 (Cambridge University Press, 1940), where a beautiful description will be found of the life of the "Black Monks" according to the Rule of St. Benedict; "through all vicissitudes the Rule has remained one of the great formative influences in the life of the Church, outlining in majestic simplicity the broad principles of monastic life and government."

The law laid down by Lord Eldon and Lord Manners seemed plain enough, but a strange effect upon their established principles has been attributed to *Cocks v. Manners*: a testamentary gift to maintain the worship of God or a gift to be applied in the service of the Redeemer remained charitable, unless the donor had been so maladroit as to express his bounty in the form of a gift to a society of cloistered men or women, wholly devoted to those charitable purposes, when the charity was submerged in the overwhelming egoism of the chosen instruments (who with sublime love of their Redeemer – I must not say "sublime charity" – had consecrated their lives to His worship in their monastery); but, if the donees were a pious community engaged in civic works of mercy, the ensuing public benefit somehow redeemed the inherent vice of the spiritual family, and charity triumphed.

It has been assumed that Sir John Wickens decided, as a matter of law, that a testamentary gift to a contemplative religious Order cannot be charitable on the ground that, in the eyes of the law, the public is neither instructed nor edified by the gift. I agree with the very different view, adumbrated by Mr. Ó Cuív on behalf of the Attorney-General. The decision on this point seems to me incontrovertibly to have been a judgment on fact, and the essential fact determined was the fact that the England of 1871 was not edified by sequestered piety, unaccompanied by civic works of mercy. Perhaps all cloistered cenobites were regarded as eccentrics in mid-Victorian England. Possibly they may be so regarded in England to-day. The law laid down was that religious purposes, to be charitable, required services tending to instruct or edify the public; the fact was assumed that the Dominicans did not pass that test. Taking that view of *Cocks v. Manners* (1871) LR 12 Eq 574 I hold that there is not now, and never has been, the flimsiest warrant for attributing the same outlook to public opinion here. I shall waste no time in establishing the proposition of fact that the cloister is a powerful source of general edification in this country. The finding, or assumption, in *Cocks v. Manners* that the convent of a contemplative community tended neither directly nor indirectly towards public edification has no scintilla of authority as a determinant of the actual position among us.

I have said so much about the judgment of Sir John Wickens because it loomed so large in argument here; I was earnestly invited to overrule *Cocks v. Manners* in order to validate the bequest before me; that prayer was made under the common misapprehension as to the true result of *Cocks v. Manners* on the material point. But I should be very sorry to appear to reduce the validity of this particular gift to the level of an appraisement of public opinion; moreover the convent here is only an instrument to achieve the desired end. I believe the gift to be valid, and, if it is valid, the Attorney-General and the executors are in my judgment entitled, under a Christian polity, to have its validity established upon a truer and a more substantial foundation."

. . . .

"The common law knew the Mass. The common law knew the Blessed Sacrament. The common law knew the adoration of the Blessed Sacrament. Therefore I know them judicially. The doctrine known to the common law is the doctrine of the Catholic Church. In my judgment, a testamentary gift to found a convent for the perpetual adoration of the Blessed Sacrament is, beyond all doubt, a gift charitable at common law, because it is a gift to God, a gift directly intended to perpetuate the worship of God.

And that conclusion is in harmony with the Constitution enacted by the Irish people "In the Name of the Most Holy Trinity . . . to Whom, as our final end, all actions both of men and States must be referred."

Palles C.B. and FitzGibbon L.J. justified their decision in *O'Hanlon v. Logue* [1906] 1 IR 247 on the dual grounds that the gift was charitable at common law and that it imported the element of public benefit necessary to bring a gift within the Statute of Pious Uses. But one ground would have sufficed, since the Act neither codified the law of charity nor superseded the common law of pious uses. I rest my judgment upon the common law. I have no occasion to look beyond it for the resultant good to the common weal. I question the relevance here of the public benefit "within the statute" and that public benefit has shown itself an importunate and unruly *amicus curiae* in an epoch addicted to disparaging the Kingdom of God. Now that I have found the purpose of the testamentary trust, the perpetual adoration of the Blessed Sacrament, to be a valid charitable purpose in law, no difficulty arises from the fact that the executants of the charity are to be the nuns of a convent, however strictly enclosed; see the judgments of Lord O'Hagan in *Stewart v. Green* (1871) IR 5 Eq 470, at p. 477 and of Sullivan M.R. in *Mahony v. Duggan* (1880) 11 LR Ir 260. From the very nature of the subject-matter, the greatness of the purpose must have placed it in the donor's mind on an immeasureably higher plane than her concern for the convent intended to secure that purpose.

I think the trustees are at liberty, in their discretion, to found the convent either at Lisnaskea or elsewhere in Ireland. I have read the judgments in *Revenue Commissioners v. Doorley* [1933] IR 750; I do not think that "elsewhere" extends in the particular context and circumstances beyond this country, but, if this view is not accepted, I shall defer my decision on the point for argument.

I must thank Mr. O'Reilly for acquainting me with the brilliant study of the decisions on religious bequests in the nineteenth century, contributed by the late Archbishop Walsh to the *Irish Ecclesiastical Record* for 1895 (vol. 26)."

S.45 of the Charities Act 1961:

> **45.**—(1) In determining whether or not a gift for the purpose of the advancement of religion is a valid charitable gift it shall be conclusively presumed that the purpose includes and will occasion public benefit.
>
> (2) For the avoidance of the difficulties which arise in giving effect to the intentions of donors of certain gifts for the purpose of the advancement of religion and in order not to frustrate those intentions and notwithstanding that certain gifts for the purpose aforesaid, including gifts for the celebration of Masses, whether in public or in private, are valid charitable gifts, it is hereby enacted that a valid charitable gift for the purpose of the advancement of religion shall have effect and, as respects its having effect, shall be construed in accordance with the laws, canons, ordinances and tenets of the religion concerned.

Trusts for Other Purposes Beneficial to the Community

The Public Benefit Requirement

This category embraces purposes which do not fall within any of the three categories already considered but which are nevertheless beneficial to the community in a way recognised by the law as charitable. The public benefit requirement has tended to be fairly strictly applied[20] and while a trust may appear to be one of general public utility, it may fail because its application is confined to too limited a group of persons. These issues are explored in the judgment of Carswell J in *Re Dunlop*,[21] although it should be noted that he appeared to hold that the bequest in question qualified as a charitable trust under Macnaghten's first category, interpreted as it has been in the UK, to include gifts for the relief of the aged.

---

[20] However, it should be noted that in *Re Worth Library* [1995] 2 IR 301 Keane J held that the bequest of the library, even though it was stated to be for the benefit of three named office holders, played a role in the advancement of the charity represented by the hospital and as such constituted a valid charitable bequest for the benefit of that institution within the fourth category.

[21] [1984] NI 408.

Re Dunlop
[1984] NI 408

The testator left his residuary estate on trust for his sisters during their lifetime and then directed his trustees to hold the remainder of the estate to found or assist in the founding of a home for 'Old Presbyterian Persons'. Carswell J held that the public benefit requirement had been satisfied and that the gift was a valid charitable one.

CARSWELL J stated at pp.414–427: "It seems to me that it is because of an implication of the kind I have mentioned that it has been held in a number of decided cases that provision for the aged, without specific reference to impotence or poverty, brings a gift within the intendment of the preamble to the Statute of Charitable Uses 1601, 43 Eliz. 1, c.4. For the purposes of this judgment I do not find it necessary to investigate the relationship between that statute and its Irish analogue of 1634, 10 Car.1 sess.3 cap.1, in which the wording of the preamble varies in a number of material respects, not least that concerning poverty. It seems to me that if there were any doubt remaining after the judgments of Sugden L.C. in *Incorporated Society v. Richards* (1841) 1 Dr & Warr 258, 320 *et seq*. and of Palles C.B. in *Attorney-General v. Delaney* (1876) IR 10 CL 114, 125, that has been dispelled by the authoritative decision of the House of Lords in *Commissioners for Special Purposes of Income Tax v. Pemsel* [1891] AC 531, in which Lord Macnaghten, just before propounding his celebrated definition of "charity", said at page 582:

> "In Ireland, though neither the statute of Elizabeth nor the so-called statute of Mortmain extended to that country, the legal and technical meaning of the term 'charity' is precisely the same as it is in England."

It is not without importance to remind oneself that the wording of the material part of the preamble to the Statute of Elizabeth is "the relief of the aged, impotent and poor people", and that the Irish statute refers to "the relief or maintenance of any manner of poor, succourless, distressed or impotent persons." I lay some stress upon the word "relief" because it seems to me of some significance in defining the limits of charitable purposes from which aged, impotent or poor people are to derive benefit. If it is to he held, as judges have by now decided in a material number of cases, that the words are to be read disjunctively, an approach which emphasises the concept of relief and its connotation of meeting a need is in my view preferable to one which would admit as beneficiaries any aged persons, whatever may be the amount of their resources and irrespective of their needs arising from their condition of advancing years.

    I am happy to find support for this approach in the recent judgment of Peter Gibson J. in *Joseph Rowntree Memorial Trust Housing Association Ltd. v. Attorney General* [1983] 1 All ER 288. In considering the charitable status of a number of slightly differing schemes for the erection of dwellings designed for the needs of the elderly and the letting of these dwellings to elderly tenants, on a contractual basis rather than their provision by way of bounty, the learned judge expressed his opinion on the charitable purpose of the relief of aged persons as follows at page 295:

> ". . . it is appropriate to consider the scope of the charitable purpose which the plaintiffs claim the scheme carries out, that is to say in the words of the preamble to the Statute of Elizabeth (43 Eliz 1 c.4, the Charitable Uses Act 1601) 'the relief of aged persons'. That purpose is indeed part of the very first set of charitable purposes contained in the preamble: 'the relief of aged, impotent and poor people.' Looking at those words without going to authority and attempting to give them their natural meaning, I would have thought that two inferences therefrom were tolerably clear. First, the words 'aged, impotent and poor, must be read disjunctively. It would be as absurd to require that the aged must be impotent or poor as it would be to require the impotent to be aged or poor', or the poor to be aged or impotent. There will no doubt be many cases where the objects of charity prove to have two or more of the three qualities at the same time. Second, essential to the charitable purpose is that it should relieve aged, impotent and poor people. The word 'relief' implies that the persons in question have a need attributable to their condition as aged, impotent or poor persons which requires alleviating, and which those persons could not alleviate, or would find difficulty in alleviating, themselves from their own resources. The word 'relief' is not synonymous with 'benefit'.
>
> Those inferences are in substance what both counsel submit are the true principles governing the charitable purpose of the relief of aged persons. Counsel for the plaintiffs stresses that any benefit provided must be related to the needs of the aged. Thus a gift of money to the aged millionaires of Mayfair would not relieve a need of theirs as aged persons. Counsel for the Attorney General similarly emphasises that to relieve a need of the aged attributable to their age would be charitable only if the means employed are appropriate to the need. He also points out that an element of public benefit must be found if the purpose is to be charitable. I turn then to authority to see if there is anything that compels a different conclusion."

The judge proceeded to examine the series of modern cases, from *In re Lucas* [1922] 2 Ch 52 to *Le Cras v. Perpetual Trustee Co. Ltd.* [1969] 1 AC 514, in which the disjunctive construction of the words in the preamble has been considered. It is unnecessary for me to set them out here in extenso, as they are conveniently summarised in his judgment at pages 296–297. He then expressed his conclusion in the following terms at page 297j:

> "These authorities convincingly confirm the correctness of the proposition that the relief of the aged does not have to be relief for the aged poor. In other words the phrase 'aged, impotent and poor people' in the preamble must be read disjunctively. The decisions in *Re Glyn Will Trusts, Re Bradbury, Re Robinson, Re Cottam's Will Trusts* and *Re Lewis* give support to the view that it is a sufficient charitable purpose to benefit the aged, or the impotent without more. But these

are all decisions at first instance and with great respect to the judges who decided them they appear to me to pay no regard to the word 'relief'. I have no hesitation in preferring the approach adopted in *Re Neal* and *Le Cras v. Perpetual Trustee Co. Ltd.* that there must be a need which is to be relieved by the charitable gift, such need being attributable to the aged or impotent condition of the person to he benefited. My attention was drawn to Picarda, *The Law and Practice Relating to Charities* (1977) p. 79, where a similar approach is adopted by the learned author."

I respectfully agree with the approach adopted by Peter Gibson J. in the *Rowntree Housing Association* case, which accords with my own construction of the import of the preamble. Its requirements are in my judgment satisfied in the present case, by reason of the implication which I have found of need for the accommodation on the part of those who were to be considered as residents of the home which the testator wished to found.

It is necessary that the prospective beneficiaries should be sufficiently identifiable to satisfy the requirements of certainty of objects. This point was taken up by Mr. Thompson for the representatives of the next-of-kin, after I had raised it in the course of argument. He submitted that it could not be said on the terms of the will that members of the Free Presbyterian Church or the Non-Subscribing Presbyterian Church are outside the category of potential beneficiaries. If the testator's intention extended to members of these churches, I should not necessarily consider that fatal to the gift as creating an element of uncertainty. It does appear to me to be sufficiently clear, however, that the testator had in mind the Presbyterian Church in Ireland and not any other denomination, since the gift was made to the Presbyterian Residential Trust which is a creation solely of that church. The difficulties encountered in *Attorney-General v. Bruce* (1867) LR 6 Eq 563 accordingly do not arise.

I do need to be satisfied that it is possible to define adequately who may he considered to be "Presbyterian persons". I regard it as possible for the persons who select the residents for accommodation to make their choice with sufficient certainty for present purposes. It may be observed that neither the members of the Presbyterian Church in Ireland as a body nor "Presbyterian persons", if that be a wider class, are as such the beneficiaries of the gift. The gift was made to found a home whose occupants have to be selected by the Presbyterian Residential Trust from persons qualified for their consideration. It is not necessary to define with precision how far the class of such candidates for selection extends, so long as it can be said at the time of selection that any given candidate comes within it. The candidates in this respect are ranked not as beneficiaries of a trust but members of a class for whose benefit a power may be exercised, be it a power simpliciter or a trust power, and the degree of certainty which I have set out will suffice: see *In re Gulbenkian's Settlements* [1970] AC 508; *McPhail v. Doulton; In re Baden's Deed Trust* [1971] AC 424. That degree of certainty may be found by having regard to the definitions in the Code of the Presbyterian Church in Ireland. By paragraph 15 all persons in full communion with a congregation of the Church are Church members. Paragraphs 153-154 make provision for keeping a roll of members of the congregation in full communion, correcting it and revising it and the removal of names from the roll. It is accordingly a matter of no great difficulty to ascertain whether a given candidate is a member of the Presbyterian Church in Ireland, and any such person will in my view certainly qualify as a "Presbyterian person".

These findings do not suffice to qualify the gift as being held upon a charitable trust, for the criterion of public benefit still has to be fulfilled. This was expressed, or re-affirmed, by Lord Simonds in *Oppenheim v. Tobacco Securities Trust Co. Ltd.* [1951] AC 297, 305 in the following terms:

> "It is a clearly established principle of the law of charity that a trust is not charitable unless it is directed to the public benefit. This is sometimes stated in the proposition that it must benefit the community or a section of the community. Negatively it is said that a trust is not charitable if it confers only private benefits .... With a single exception, to which I shall refer, this applies to all charities."

The principle is not a new one – Lord Simonds made reference to its expression by Lord Hardwicke L.C. in *Jones v. Williams* (1767) Amb 652, and it appears as an accepted tenet in the speech of Earl Cairns in *Goodman v. Mayor of Saltash* (1882) 7 App Cas 633, 650-651 – but the locus classicus in the modern law of the test for its application is to he found in the decision of the Judicial Committee of the Privy Council given by Lord Wrenbury in *Verge v. Somerville* [1924] AC 496, 499:

> "To ascertain whether a gift constitutes a valid charitable trust so as to escape being void on the ground of perpetuity, a first inquiry must be whether it is public – whether it is for the benefit of the community or of an appreciably important class of the community. The inhabitants of a parish or town, or any particular class of such inhabitants, may, for instance, be the objects of such a gift, but private individuals, or a fluctuating body of private individuals, cannot."

The principle in its application to the Presbyterian Church received direct consideration by the Northern Ireland Courts in *Trustees of the Londonderry Presbyterian Church House v. Commissioners or Inland Revenue* [1946] NI 178. A trust deed vested four properties in trustees

> "upon trust to permit the same or any part thereof to be used as a hall for meetings or for Social or Recreational purposes in connection with the various Presbyterian Churches in the City of Londonderry and the surrounding district or as a Hostel or Boarding House or as a Library or for such other purpose or purposes as the Board of Governors shall from time to time think fit, it being the true intention and meaning of these presents that said premises shall be used for the purposes of assisting and helping in the religious, moral, social and recreative life of those connected with the Presbyterian Church in the City of Londonderry and surrounding district in such manner as the said Board shall from time to time think right."

The trustees' claim for exemption from income tax was rejected by the Special Commissioners, who stated a case for the opinion of the High Court. In the King's Bench Division MacDermott J. held that the trust, although too wide to be a valid charitable trust for the advancement of religion, qualified as a charitable trust under Lord MacNaughten's fourth head as being for purposes beneficial to the community. It was an essential part or his reasoning that in order to give the trust the necessary public character it had to benefit a sufficient section of the public. In his decision, reported in 27 TC 431, he reached the conclusion that the beneficiaries constituted a sufficient section. He declined to accept the Revenue contention that to benefit, one had to be a Presbyterian; that this involved the personal faith and convictions of each member as an individual, which made the class one designated by reference to matters personal to the individuals composing it and therefore not a section of the public. After citing a number of decisions relied upon by the Revenue, MacDermott J. continued:

> "All these cases are, in my opinion, distinguishable on their facts. They undoubtedly go to show that, where admission to the class to benefit depends on certain personal qualifications or relationships, the requisite public character will be absent, the 'class' being then regarded as a number of private individuals or a fluctuating body of private individuals, and, therefore, non-public. But I do not read these authorities as laying down any principle to the effect that any class which is designated by reference to some quality or fact that is personal to each of its members must be reckoned as non-public in this sense. See *In re Tree* [1945] Ch 325. Poverty is personal. So is blindness. So are the afflictions of maimed soldiers. So is adherence to a particular faith. Possibly the personal element which suffices to negative a public character must be one which arises by reason of some definite bond or relationship to others. Membership of a club may depend on election though, in themselves, its objects may be charitable in nature. And the provision of facilities for healthy recreation, which would be a charitable activity on the part of a local authority, may be but a matter of private benevolence if made by employers for the benefit of their employees, no matter how numerous. But, however this may be, I do not think the bond of a common creed or religion has yet been held of such a character as of itself to render the class it creates non-public and I am unable to find any principle in the decisions relied upon by the Respondents (and in these I include *Keren's* case), which would warrant such a conclusion."

The Court of Appeal held, allowing the Revenue's appeal, that the trust did not constitute a valid charitable trust either as a trust for the advancement of religion or under the fourth head, because of the width of the purposes specified in the trust deed. It was accordingly not necessary for the court to decide the question whether the beneficiaries constituted a sufficient section of the public, and Black J. did not express an opinion upon it. The other members of the court, however, reached diametrically opposed conclusions on the question, and the conflict between them has not since been resolved. Since each has received support in the House of Lords, I approach that resolution with some diffidence.

In his judgment, Andrews L.C.J. stated it as his clear opinion that the case was essentially different from the case of a club membership, or an employees' voluntary association, no matter how benevolent or charitable their objects or purposes may be. After considering *In re Compton* [1945] Ch 123, where a trust for the education of the lawful descendants of three named persons was held not to be charitable because of its lack of public character, the Lord Chief Justice accepted the validity of the test propounded by Lord Greene M.R., that the beneficiaries should not enjoy the benefit by virtue of their character as individuals, but by virtue of their membership class, the common quality uniting potential beneficiaries into the class being essentially an impersonal one. He continued at page 190:

> "A 'section' is nothing but a portion or a division; and when that portion is ascertained or that division of the public is affected by reference to something such as religious belief, which is not personal in the sense in which that term is used in this connection, I think it may properly be described as a 'section of the public'. Indeed, are we not all very familiar with the use of the term 'sect' as referring to a body of men and women who are united in holding some particular religious belief? If the Presbyterians in Londonderry are not a 'section of the community' there, neither then, logically, can the whole Presbyterian body be such a 'section', though it constitutes the largest religious denomination in our Province. So to hold would in my opinion be an abuse of language, and accordingly unjustifiable. In truth, these Presbyterians in Londonderry constitute in my opinion a particular section of the public at large which is essentially different in character from a particular section of private individuals . . . . They are in my opinion sufficiently defined and identifiable by a common quality of a public nature . . . ."

Babington L.J. expressed a strong contrary opinion in his judgment, in the course of which he said in several places that the Presbyterian Church is not a section of the public, and its members are a fluctuating body of private individuals. He said at pages 197-198:

> "One distinction between a body such as the Presbyterian Church, or that part of it with which we are concerned, and a section of the public is taken in *In re Compton* in the judgment of Lord Greene M.R., namely, that the relationship between members of the class is a personal one and in no way dependent on their status or condition as members of the community.
>
> The trust here is not a trust for religious purposes but for a class of persons to be ascertained by reference to their connection with a named religious denomination. In determining whether or not this class is a section of the public no legal significance can be attached to its religious affiliations but it must be treated in the same way as any non-religious class such as the members of a club or of a trading concern.
>
> Looked at from this point of view the members of a religious denomination cannot be said to be a section of the public. Its members are associated voluntarily and their membership has nothing to say to their status or condition as members

of the public. Such associations may cease to exist at any time but their members will nevertheless continue to he members of the community, which will be neither greater nor less than before, and the fact that all the members of an association are members of the public does not make the association a section of the public."

In the course of his judgment, Babington J. drew a clear distinction between the requirements in relation to the public element in cases under the different categories in Lord Macnaghten's classification of charities. At page 196 he said:

> "Considerable confusion has, I think, arisen from a failure to distinguish between the public element in cases under the first three of Lord Macnaghten's categories and the fourth. Under the first three the charitable intention must be established, i.e., for the relief of poverty, the advancement of religion, or the advancement of education. The objects must be of a public nature, as Fitzgibbon L.J. says, but it is immaterial under these categories how the class is delineated, provided it is adequate in numbers or importance.
>
> In cases falling within category number four, however, there can be no charity until it is shown that the gift is to or for the benefit of the public or a section of the public and this is a primary test which must he satisfied before the gift can he held charitable."

He came back to the same point at page 199, where he said:

> "If this trust had been for the advancement of religion, the class would clearly be sufficient in numbers and importance to sustain it as a good charitable trust though it only benefits a particular faith, the members of which do not constitute a section of the public. But as the trust is not for the advancement of religion only, the public element which is essential to make it a good charitable trust is lacking."

As Lord Reid observed in *Inland Revenue Commissioners v. Baddeley* [1955] AC 572, 612, the reasoning in that passage has been affected by the decision of the House of Lords in *Oppenheim's* case. I shall return a little later in this judgment to the content of that criticism and the extent to which the foundation of Babington L.J.'s views can be accepted in the light of subsequent developments in the law.

In *Oppenheim v. Tobacco Securities Trust Co. Ltd.* [1951] AC 297, the House of Lords had to consider the status of an educational trust, founded to provide for the education of children of employees or former employees of British American Tobacco Co. Ltd., or any of its subsidiary or allied companies. The number of employees of BAT and its subsidiary and allied companies exceeded 110,000. Notwithstanding the numerical size of the class, the House held that it did not constitute a section of the public, but rather, because of the nexus between its members constituted by employment by particular employers, it was composed of private individuals. It dispatched the heresy that the element of public benefit was not essential except for charities falling within Lord Macnaghten's fourth class, with the exception of the anomalous case of trusts for the relief of poverty, which were left for future consideration. The burden of the speeches delivered by the majority was that the quality which distinguishes the beneficiaries from other members of the community, so that they form by themselves a section of it, must be a quality which does not depend upon their relationship to a particular individual. Common employment by one employer was not such a quality, in their Lordships' view. As Lord Simonds said at page 306:

> "A group of persons may be numerous but, if the nexus between them is their personal relationship to a single propositus or to several propositi, they are neither the community nor a section of the community for charitable purposes."

Lord Simonds was unable to accept that its sheer numerical size was of itself enough to make such a class a section of the community, if it was capable of decrease down to an insignificant number, which carried an echo of the ancient philosophical conundrum of the mare's tail.

Lord MacDermott dissented from the opinion of the majority, and attacked the use of the *Compton* test as a criterion of general applicability and conclusiveness. He said at page 317:

> "In the first place I see much difficulty in dividing the qualities or attributes, which may serve to bind human beings into classes, into two mutually exclusive groups, the one involving individual status and purely personal, the other disregarding such status and quite impersonal. As a task this seems to me no less baffling and elusive than the problem to which it is directed, namely, the determination of what is and what is not a section of the public for the purposes of this branch of the law. After all, what is more personal than poverty or blindness or ignorance? Yet none would deny that a gift for the education of the children of the poor or blind was charitable: and I doubt if there is any less certainty about the charitable nature of a gift for, say, the education of children who satisfy a specified examining body that they need and would benefit by a course of special instruction designed to remedy their educational defects."

Inland Revenue Commissioners v. Baddeley [1955] AC 572 concerned trusts under which a number of properties were to be used, in the one case "for the promotion of the religious, social, and physical well-being" of persons in a certain area and in the other "for promotion of the moral, social, and physical well-being" of persons in that area. In each case the benefits were restricted to persons who for the time being were in the opinion of the leaders of a Methodist Mission members or likely to become members of the Methodist Church. The House of Lords, by a majority, held that the trusts were not charitable, since they did not fall within the first three heads set out by Lord Macnaghten, and they were expressed in language so vague as to permit the property to be used for purposes which the law did not regard as charitable and which did not satisfy the necessary element of public benefit.

Viscount Simonds also turned his attention to the question whether the beneficiaries constituted a sufficient section of the community, when they were confined to members or potential members of a particular church within a limited geographical area. His main ground for holding against the trustees on this issue was the necessity that the benefit under a fourth class charity must be available to all, if it is to be of "general public utility". As he put it, at page 592:

> "For example, a bridge which is available for all the public may undoubtedly be a charity and it is indifferent how many people use it. But confine its use to a selected number of persons, however numerous and important: it is then clearly not a charity. It is not of general public utility: for it does not serve the public purpose which its nature qualifies it to serve."

As a secondary ground, Viscount Simonds expressed the view that he would also regard the class of beneficiaries as constituting private individuals rather than a section of the community, and said that he found himself in agreement with Babington L.J. in the *Londonderry Church House* case.

Lord Porter and Lord Tucker declined to express an opinion as to whether the beneficiaries constituted a sufficient class of the public, and Lord Somervell of Harrow did not come to a direct conclusion on the point. In the speech of Lord Reid, however, who dissented from the majority on the charitable nature of the purposes of the trust, there is a good deal of discussion on the sufficiency of the class of beneficiaries as a section of the public. After citing the tests adopted in *Verge v. Somerville* and *Oppenheim v. Tobacco Securities Trust Co. Ltd,* Lord Reid said at page 606:

> "If these are the criteria to be applied in this case, then it was not disputed that members of the Methodist Church are a section of the community and an appreciably important class of the community and are a particular class of the inhabitants of West Ham and Leyton. I would not embark on any theological inquiry, but it appears to me to be beyond doubt that membership of any branch of the Christian Church is a quality which does not depend on the members' relationship to any individual propositus. There may be small sects which are not sufficiently numerous to form an appreciably important class of a community, but no one would suggest that that is true of the Methodist Church."

Lord Reid pointed out that it was admitted by counsel for the Revenue that the beneficiaries would be a sufficient class to be proper objects for a charitable gift for educational or religious purposes or for the relief of any kind of disability or distress. He rejected the suggestion that it was necessary for a trust to qualify under the fourth head that the benefits must he open to the whole community or at least to all the inhabitants of an area. He said at page 612:

> "Poverty may be in a special position but otherwise I can see no justification in principle or authority for holding that when dealing with one deed for one charitable purpose, the members of the Methodist Church or any other church are a section of the community, but when dealing with another deed for a different charitable purpose, they are only a fluctuating body of private individuals."

Lord Reid's reasoning in *I.R.C. v. Baddeley* is accordingly founded upon the premise that the definition of the class of persons necessary to constitute a section of the community must be the same under each of Lord Macnaghten's four heads of charity. It is this premise which leads him to the conclusion that the class in that case was sufficient for the purposes of the fourth head, and forms the foundation of his criticism of Babington L.J.'s judgment in the *Londonderry Church House* case. Although I do not myself find it possible to agree with the views expressed by Babington L.J. about the sufficiency of the Presbyterian Church as a section of the community, even under the fourth head, I respectfully suggest that Lord Reid's premise may require re-consideration in the light of the speeches in *Dingle v. Turner* [1972] AC 601, to which I am about to refer. Moreover, although the House of Lords in *Oppenheim's* case held that the requirements under the first three heads were more stringent than Babington L.J. had supposed, it does not necessarily follow that his conclusion about the requirements under the fourth head is thereby invalidated. I shall venture to suggest in due course that that conclusion is not a correct one, but not altogether for the reasons given by Lord Reid in *I.R.C. v. Baddeley*.

I pass over the decision of the judicial Committee of the Privy Council in *Davies v. Perpetual Trustee Co.* [1959] AC 439, which is at most a negative authority, and proceed to consider the House of Lords' decision under the poverty category in *Dingle v. Turner*. In his speech in that case, Lord Cross of Chelsea, with the content of whose speech the other members very largely agreed, preferred to approach the problem on what he described as "far broader lines". I would respectfully adopt his approach as giving a means of determining the sufficiency of the public element under the different heads, which seems to me to provide a more satisfactory principle and to be more workable in practice. The decision itself dealt with the validity of the "poor relations" cases, which in *Oppenheim's* case had been left for future consideration, and how far that exception, if now upheld, could extend. The case concerned a trust to apply the income of the trust fund in paying pensions to poor employees of a company. The company had at the date of the testator's death over 600 employees, while at the date when the prior life interest terminated they numbered in all nearly 900, and the company was paying pensions to 89 ex-employees.

Lord Cross declined to overrule the "poor relations" cases, which were left intact as long standing anomalies. He also left standing the poor employees' trusts, which were exempted in the same manner from the *Compton* rule and held that that rule "has no application in the field of trusts for the relief of poverty". His decision in favour of the charity in the instant case constituted, however, a carefully defined circumscription of the exceptions and extended in terms only to poor relations and poor employees. Lord Cross said at page 623 that in the field of trusts for the relief of poverty, the dividing line between a charitable trust and a private trust lies where the Court of Appeal drew it in

In re Scarisbrick [1951] Ch 622. The discussion in *In re Scarisbrick* centred solely round trusts for the relief of poor persons, and there was no case cited in the judgments which concerned only aged or impotent persons without the added qualification of poverty. They were treated in those judgments very much as an anomaly, not to be accounted for by reference to any principle but established by a series of authorities of long standing: per Jenkins L.J. at page 649. The same can he said of the discussion of the poor relations cases in *In re Compton* [1945] Ch 123. In all of the cases in which gifts were left to aged persons – set out in the *Rowntree Housing Association* case, supra – or to impotent persons (*In re Lewis* [1955] Ch 104 and *In re Bradbury deceased* [1950] 2 All ER 1150n) there was a sufficient public element by reason of the width of the class from which potential beneficiaries were to be drawn. Although Lord Simonds said in *Oppenheim v. Tobacco Securities Trust Co. Ltd.* [1951] AC 297, 308, that the law of charity, so far as it relates to "the relief of aged, impotent and poor people", has followed its own line, which might indicate a willingness to regard the exception as applying to the whole of Lord Macnaghten's first head, I consider that the House of Lords in *Dingle v. Turner* intended to circumscribe it more closely and to confine it to cases concerning the relief of actual poverty.

After reaching that conclusion, Lord Cross turned his attention to the *Compton* rule and the definition of a sufficient section of the public. Three other members of the House dissociated themselves from the final section of his speech, in which he said that the courts cannot avoid having regard to the fiscal privileges accorded to charities in answering the question whether any given trust is a charitable trust. I do not understand them, however, to have extended that reservation to the passage in which Lord Cross dealt with the distinction between a section of the public and a fluctuating body of private individuals, even though it was not strictly necessary for the decision of the case, and indeed Lord MacDermott specifically welcomed his commentary on the difficulties of the phrase "a section of the public". That passage in Lord Cross's speech reads as follows:

> "*Oppenheim* [1951] AC 297 was a case of an educational trust and though the majority evidently agreed with the view expressed by the Court of Appeal in the *Hobourn Aero* case [1946] Ch 194 that the *Compton* rule [1945] Ch 123 was of universal application outside the field of poverty, it would no doubt be open to this House without overruling *Oppenheim* to hold that the scope of the rule was more limited. If ever I should be called upon to pronounce on this question – which does not arise in this appeal – I would, as at present advised, be inclined to draw a distinction between the practical merits of the *Compton* rule and the reasoning by which Lord Greene M.R. sought to justify it. That reasoning – based on the distinction between personal and impersonal relationships – has never seemed to me very satisfactory and I have always – if I may say so – felt the force of the criticism to which my noble and learned friend Lord MacDermott subjected it in his dissenting speech in *Oppenheim*. For my part I would prefer to approach the problem on far broader lines. The

phrase a 'section of the public' is in truth a vague phrase which may mean different things to different people. In the law of charity, judges have sought to elucidate its meaning by contrasting it with another phrase: 'a fluctuating body of private individuals'. But I get little help from the supposed contrast for as I see it, one and the same aggregate of persons may well be describable both as a section of the public and as a fluctuating body of private individuals. The ratepayers of the Royal Borough of Kensington and Chelsea, for example, certainly constitute a section of the public: but would it be a misuse of language to describe them as a 'fluctuating body of private individuals'? After all, every part of the public is composed of individuals and being susceptible of increase or decrease is fluctuating. So at the end of the day, one is left where one started with the bare contrast between 'public' and 'private'. No doubt some classes are more naturally describable as sections of the public than as private classes, while other classes are more naturally describable as private classes than as sections of the public. The blind, for example, can naturally be described as a section of the public: but what they have in common – their blindness – does not join them together in such a way that they could be called a private class. On the other hand, the descendants of Mr. Gladstone might more reasonably be described as a 'private class' than as a section of the public, and in the field of common employment the same might well be said of the employees in some fairly small firm. But if one turns to large companies employing many thousands of men and women, most of whom are quite unknown to one another and to the directors, the answer is by no means so clear. One might say that in such a case the distinction between a section of the public and a private class is not applicable at all or even that the employees in such concerns as I.C.I. or G.E.C. are just as much 'sections of the public' as the residents in some geographical area. In truth the question whether or not the potential beneficiaries of a trust can fairly be said to constitute a section of the public is a question of degree and cannot be, by itself, decisive of the question whether the trust is a charity. Much must depend on the purpose of the trust. It may well be that, on the one hand a trust to promote some purpose, prima facie charitable, will constitute a charity even though the class of potential beneficiaries might fairly be called a private class and that, on the other hand, a trust to promote another purpose also prima facie charitable, will not constitute a charity even though the class of potential beneficiaries might seem to some people fairly describable as a section of the public."

This approach, whereby a distinction is drawn between the different heads of charity when considering the public element, was not a new development of thought when Lord Cross articulated it *in extenso* in *Dingle v. Turner*. As I have said, Lord Reid opposed the idea in *I.R.C. v. Baddeley,* but Viscount Simonds appeared willing to recognise the possibility at page 590 of the report of his speech in that case, and Lord Somervell of Harrow at page 615 declined to accept the principle that a section of the public sufficient to support a valid trust in one category must, as a matter of law, be sufficient to support a trust in any other category.

Lord Cross's approach may furnish the means of determining the existence of the necessary public element in charitable trusts without the aridity of the test accepted in *In re Compton* and *Oppenheim's* case. If it is recognised that the way in which the essential benefit to the public is achieved varies between the different heads of charity, it becomes a more feasible task to determine its existence when dealing with any given trust, and the tests for qualification seem to be more comprehensible. Under the first head, the relief of poverty (including help for the aged and impotent) necessarily confers individual benefits upon the recipients of the donor's bounty. In order for it to constitute a public, as opposed to a merely private, benefaction it has to include a public element, so that it transcends the conferring of benefit upon individuals selected by the donor and serves the wider purpose of benefiting the public weal by the provision of material assistance to classes of persons who require it by reason of their particular disability. In the same way, a trust for the advancement of education confers the benefit of assistance with their educational careers upon the individual recipients (except where the gift is for the purpose of spreading education by training teachers), but in order to constitute a valid charity there must be a paramount public purpose on the same lines as under the first head.

The advancement of religion stands upon rather a different footing. It is not designed to confer benefit upon those who may receive it as an end in itself, but to advance the ultimate purpose of spreading the word of God and accomplishing the divine purpose by such means as the building of churches and the promotion of worship. Accordingly, a gift for a comparatively small group, such as a particular congregation, may not be ruled out from qualifying as one which conduces to the public benefit because of the limited number of people making up the immediate beneficiaries, since the ultimate purpose is to benefit the public as a whole by advancing religion and the purposes of God's kingdom upon earth.

At the other end of the scale stand trusts for purposes beneficial to the community under Lord Macnaghten's fourth head. The essence of the chartitable nature of such trusts is that the beneficiaries should not be a private class, nor should any limitations be placed upon the gift which would prevent the public as a whole from enjoying the advantage which the donor intends to provide for the benefit of all of the public. It would be quite consonant with this concept that it should be more difficult for a trust under the fourth head to satisfy the requirements of public benefit and that a bridge to be used only by Methodists should fail to qualify where a gift for the education of the children of members of that church might be a valid charity.

If I am entitled to avail myself of the approach adopted by Lord Cross, on the facts of the instant case, the answer seems to me to present itself fairly clearly. The testator's gift cannot, in my judgment, be regarded on any sensible meaning as being a private benefaction; it seems to be incapable of real dispute that it was designed to serve a wider purpose of benefiting the public by providing accommodation for the relief of a class of persons requiring it by reason of their age. On this approach, the fact that the persons selected to occupy the accommodation were to be Presbyterians rather than any other denomination does not, in my view, negative the paramountcy of the public purpose of assistance for the aged. This was, no doubt, the basis of the concession in *I.R.C. v. Baddeley* that the beneficiaries in that case would be a sufficient class to be proper objects for a charitable gift under the first head. If it is permissible to adopt this approach, then I have no hesitation in reaching the conclusion that the gift in question in this case is a valid charitable gift.

I am conscious, however, that it may not be open to me to adopt this approach to the law, since it is not in harmony with the ratio decidendi of the House of Lords in *Oppenheim v. Tobacco Securities Trust Co. Ltd.,* which still stands despite the doubts concerning its underlying reasoning expressed by Lord Cross and the concurrence with him of the other members of the House in *Dingle v. Turner.* If I am obliged to consider whether the Presbyterian Church in Ireland constitutes a section of the public, or a fluctuating body of individuals united only by a common personal bond of voluntary association, I must express my preference for the views which I have cited of MacDermott J. and Andrews L.C.J. in the *Londonderry Church House* case over those of Babington L.J. It does not appear to me to be inconsistent with any authority binding upon me to adopt these views, and I consider that they accord more closely with the law as it has developed since that decision, and that they correspond a great deal better with common sense and the ordinary person's perception of a large religious denomination. I respectfully agree with Andrews L.C.J.'s conclusion that the members of the Presbyterian Church are "sufficiently defined and identifiable by a common quality of a public nature" and Lord Reid's opinion that "membership to any branch of the Christian Church is a quality which does not depend on the member's relationship to any individual propositus". They accordingly constitute a particular section of the public at large, certainly for the purposes of a gift under Lord Macnaghten's first head. In my judgment, the trust to the present case for the provision of accommodation for "old Presbyterian persons" contains a sufficient public element and should be regarded as a valid charitable gift.

The conclusion which I have reached means that I need not examine the issue of validation of an imperfect trust under section 24 of the Charities Act (Northern Ireland) 1964, an issue which posed some difficult problems for the parties seeking to uphold the gift, and can pass directly to that of the destination of the trust property. It is common case that it is now impracticable to carry out the testator's intention in the manner set out in the will, but I have held that it would have been practicable at the date of his death. On the authority of the line of cases represented by *In re Wright* [1954] Ch 347 and *In re Tacon* [1958] Ch 477, that is sufficient to stamp the gift with an indefeasible charitable trust. The present case comes within section 22(1)(a)(ii) and section 22 (1)(e)(iii) of the Charities Act (Northern Ireland) 1964, and possibly also section 22(1)(c). I therefore direct the preparation of a scheme for the application cy-près of the trust property."

'For Other Purposes Beneficial to the Community' — *an Objective or Subjective Test?*

There has traditionally been a divergence in the position adopted by the judiciary in Ireland and England in relation to the test which should be applied by the courts in determining whether a purpose satisfies the requirement of being 'beneficial to the community' to the extent that it may be regarded as being charitable in law. The Irish authorities suggest that a subjective test should be applied and that due weight should be given to the donor's view of the charitable nature of his bequest provided that this purpose is not obviously illegal or immoral.[22] However, the accepted view now in England and Northern Ireland is to adopt an objective test and allow the court to form an opinion on the issue based upon the evidence before it. [23]

In *Re Worth Library*[24] Keane J stated that as the objects under consideration in the case before him were such that an appreciable number of reasonable people would consider them to be charitable, it was not necessary for him to express any firm view on the divergence of opinion referred to above, although his comments would support the view that the court should give due weight to a donor's intentions in these circumstances.

Re Cranston: Webb v. Oldfield
[1898] 1 IR 431

By her will the testatrix made a devise to the trustee or other proper officer from time to time of two named vegetarian societies in equal moieties. It was held by the majority of the Irish Court of Appeal (Lord Ashbourne C, Fitzgibbon and Walker LJJ; Holmes LJ dissenting) that they were valid charitable gifts.

LORD ASHBOURNE C stated at pp.442–445: "This is an appeal from the Master of the Rolls, and it turns upon the question whether certain gifts in a will can be regarded as charitable under the Irish Statute 10 Charles 1, which is analogous to the English Statute 43 Elizabeth. The gifts are to the officials of the London Vegetarian Society, and the English Vegetarian Society in Manchester. These societies have been formed to induce abstinence from all forms of the flesh of animals, and to encourage instead the use of all kinds of vegetable produce. They hold out not only that their teachings will improve health but encourage humaneness by tending to diminish the destruction of animal life.

Are these gifts charitable? They are certainly not so in the ordinary meaning

---

[22] *Re Cranston* [1898] 1 IR 431.
[23] *Re Hummeltenberg* [1923] 1 Ch 237 and *Re Grove-Grady* [1929] 1 Ch 557.
[24] [1995] 2 IR 301, 335.

of the word – in its popular sense. But the word "charity" under the statute has acquired a wide, elastic, meaning, which has been laid down or developed in numerous cases. Mr. Justice Chitty in the case of *Cross v. The London Anti-vivisection Society* [1893] 2 Ch 501, 504 has truly said:– "Charity in law is a highly technical term. The method employed by the Court is to consider the enumeration of charities in the statute, bearing in mind that the enumeration is not exhaustive. Institutions whose objects are analogous to those mentioned in the statute are admitted to be charities; and again, institutions which are analogous to those already admitted by reported decisions are held to be charities. The pursuit of these analogies obviously requires caution and circumspection. After all the best that can be done is to consider each case as it arises, upon its own special circumstances. To be a charity there must be some public purpose – something tending to the benefit of the community."

In seeking our analogies it is essential to note that the Irish Statute 10 Charles 1, after mentioning a variety of objects (even including the erection and maintaining of bridges), adds "or for any other like lawful or charitable use or uses warranted by the laws of this realm."

Therefore the question really is – having regard to the authorities, can these gifts to these two vegetarian societies be excluded from the very wide class, deemed to be charitable, according to the broad and gradually widening interpretation of Courts of law?

The gifts here are for rich and for poor, for general public use, not for any particular class or religion, They are for a public purpose – deemed by the testatrix beneficial to the community. Are they charitable within the meaning of the statute and the decided cases? The analogies provided by decided cases are very numerous and very various. Gifts to the British Museum, the Royal Society, for founding a Botanical Society for supporting lectures against cruelty to animals; to the Chancellor of the Exchequer for the benefit of Great Britain, for the repair of sea banks; for the relief of houses of correction; for keeping chimes in repair; for assisting a school for sons of the clergy, and many others, entirely outside the scope of the ordinary popular meaning of the word, have been held to be charitable.

Mr. Justice Romer in the case of *In re Lord Stratheden and Campbell* [1894] 3 Ch 265 was of opinion that a gift for the benefit of a volunteer corps was a charity.

The case of *Thornton v. Howe* (1862) 31 Beav 14 has naturally been keenly relied on because it decided that gifts to encourage the teachings of Joanna Southcote were charitable.

The case of the *Commissioners for Special Purposes of Income Tax v. Pemsel* [1891] AC 531 has been also much discussed before us. It was not suggested there by any of the noble and learned lords that cases coming under the statutes of Elizabeth or Charles should receive a less broad construction than had been theretofore usual: and Lord Macnaghten took the opportunity of laying down with precision that trusts for purposes beneficial to the community, not falling under the other heads of relief of poverty education or religion might equally be held to be charitable.

In *Armstrong v. Reeves* (1890) 25 LR Ir 325 the Vice-Chancellor held that gifts to an Antivivisection Society were charitable – a decision not now questioned and followed in England in a case I have already referred to.

The case of *In re Nottage* [1895] 2 Ch 649 is interesting as showing that a Court plainly felt some regret and hesitation in deciding that a gift for the sport of yacht racing was not a charity – holding that it was not for a public purpose, but for the amusement of individuals.

The cases to my mind all show a desire on the part of the Court to include every reasonable case in a liberal interpretation of the word charity. Can the gift in the present case be excluded? Here there is nothing private, individual or circumscribed in the gift. It is given freely in the hope that it would be widely availed of by all, earnestly aspiring to be a general public benefit. The advantage of all mankind is the object, the elevation of the world is sought by teaching, which the testatrix believed would improve the general health, and foster a general spirit of humaneness. It may be that this idea of vegetarianism has not as yet made its way in the world. It may be showing no growth. The vast majority may be opposed to it. It may be disapproved of by medical men. Possibly no member of the Bench may believe in it. But these considerations cannot be regarded as decisive to exclude it from the wide class of gifts regarded by the law as charitable. The gifts are given to societies which rightly or wrongly set a public purpose before them, and which have been founded and maintained in the belief that their teaching is for the benefit of the community. I do not feel at liberty to sit in judgment upon objects or purposes, or to measure the success they now have, or hereafter may attain to. In my opinion the judgment of the Master of the Rolls was right, and this appeal should be dismissed with costs."

FITZGIBBON LJ stated at pp.445–447: "I concur. We must define the sense in which the law uses the world "charity." In its popular sense, charity involves the idea of *misericordia*, or pity, and of aiding those who are in distress. Though the legal sense includes the popular one, it is far wider, and includes many objects to which the popular idea does not extend. The reason of the extension is material; it is because the legal notion is founded upon the analogy of the statute. When we find that the statute includes a number of objects to which the idea of *misericordia* or pity is wholly foreign, it follows that the idea which the law recognizes as essential to "charity" is something different.

Lord Macnaghten's attempt to divide charitable purposes into four categories fails to satisfy the requirements of a logical division, because, if adequate, it is not distinct. He has defined three classes, but he has put everything else, without any definition, into the fourth class. He has, in fact, divided charitable objects into – I., Relief of the poor; II., Religion; III., Education; IV., Et cetera. Such a division gives no help to determine the question which we have here, viz. whether a particular gift, not for poor-relief, religion, or education, is one which the law recognizes as charitable. The first category rests on the good old popular idea of charity. The second and third rest on the statute, because the advancement of religion and education are expressly mentioned therein. But "analogy" has immensely enlarged their application. For example, disseminating the works, and thereby propagating the opinions, of Joanna Southcote, has been held charitable, and under the heads of "religion" and "education," cases of gifts to further the tenets, or to advance the teaching, of very small and very peculiar classes in the community, have been established as charitable, even though, if at all beneficial, they were restricted to a very few, and even though the "benefits" conferred on these few were opposed in the strongest manner to the creeds, or to the judgments, or to the prejudices, of the vast majority, and were even regarded as heretical, or even mischievous, by that majority. The essential attributes of a legal charity are, in my opinion, that it shall be *unselfish – i.e.* for the benefit of other persons than the donor – that it shall be *public*, i.e. that those to be benefited shall form a class worthy, in numbers or importance, of consideration as a public object of generosity, and that it shall be *philanthropic or benevolent –* i.e. dictated by a desire to do good. We must remember, in cases of the fourth category, that these conditions have been held to be satisfied, in cases of the second and third, by gifts for the benefit of very small sects and sections. Under those circumstances, being bound to clear our minds of the idea of *misericordia*, I can not reconcile the cases by anything short of adopting the principle that any gift which proceeds from a philanthropic or benevolent motive, and which is intended to benefit an appreciably important class of our fellow-creatures (including, under decided cases, animals), and which will confer the supposed benefit without contravening law or morals, will be "charitable." Chitty, L.J., rightly points out that benevolence or philanthropy alone will not suffice, because there charity, like faith, is dead, being "without works," and there are plenty of philanthropic and benevolent people who stop at words, or at ideas, and to be "charitable" they must *do* something or *give* something for the benefit of others.

Having got thus far – What is the tribunal which is to decide whether the object is a beneficent one? It cannot be the individual mind of a Judge, for he may disagree, *toto caelo*, from the testator as to what is or is not beneficial. On the other hand, it cannot be the *vox populi*, for charities have been upheld for the benefit of insignificant sects, and of peculiar people. It occurs to me that the answer must be – that the benefit must be one which *the founder* believes to be of public advantage, and his belief must be at least rational, and not contrary either to the general law of the land, or to the principles of morality. A gift of such a character, dictated by benevolence, believed to be beneficent, devoted to an appreciably important object, and neither *contra bonos mores* nor *contra legem*, will, in my opinion, be charitable in the eye of the law, as settled by decisions which bind us. It is not for us to say that these have gone too far.

Addressing myself to the question of fact in the present case – whether we call it a fad or not, "Vegetarianism" is a fact. In various forms it has existed from ancient times; it has been the practice, and it is the creed of many, including the most numerous sect under the Queen's sway. The Vegetarian Society has existed for half a century, and its adherents are numerous and widespread. Its principles appeal to humanity, and tend to mercy and to morality, whether they are practical or visionary. Comfort and economy would be promoted by a vegetable diet, even though it might be in some respects injurious. It is hard to see why the promotion of total abstinence from flesh should not be a "charitable" object in the legal sense, if we are at liberty to recognize the promotion of total abstinence from intoxicants as charitable; moderation and temperance maybe carried to excess, and though the benefits and the drawbacks may differ in degree, they seem to be the same in kind. The motives of the promoters of teetotalism and of vegetarianism are equally unselfish, and equally benevolent, and the efforts of vegetarians, so far as I can form a judgment, seem less likely to do mischief than those of the anti-vivisectionists, or even than those of the promulgators of the works of Joanna Southcote.

For the reasons which I have summarized, I think that the case falls within the decisions which have established gifts to be charitable."

Specific Types of Trusts which may Qualify as being 'for Other Purposes Beneficial to the Community'

A wide variety of different types of trust may qualify under this heading and while it is not possible to classify them strictly into different classes, or to rule out the emergence of previously unrecognised heads of charity, generally the types of trusts which will be enforced fall into one of a number of categories which will be considered below.

Gifts for the Aged, the Disabled and the Sick

It is generally accepted that in order to qualify under this heading, the trust must be for the relief of a need attributable to the condition of the persons to be benefited, whether this be old age,[25] disability or ill health.[26] One of the most important authorities in this area is the judgment of Kingsmill Moore J in *Barrington's Hospital v. Commissioner of Valuation*[27] where he made it clear that a trust for the maintenance of a hospital, even one which admitted fee paying patients, is a charitable one.[28]

---

[25] *Re Dunlop* [1984] NI 408, 414. See also *Joseph Rowntree Memorial Trust Hospital Association Ltd v. Attorney General* [1983] Ch 159.

[26] *Barrington's Hospital v. Commissioner of Valuation* [1957] IR 299 and *Re McCarthy's Will Trusts* [1958] IR 311.

[27] [1957] IR 299.

[28] Note that this decision was made in the context of a challenge by the plaintiff to the

Barrington's Hospital v. Commissioner of Valuation
[1957] IR 299

Barrington's Hospital was originally entered in the valuation lists as being used exclusively for charitable purposes and therefore exempt from rating. Subsequently it was no longer distinguished as exempt and the committee of management appealed to the Circuit Court against this decision. The Circuit Court judge stated a case for the Supreme Court in relation to whether the premises were being used exclusively for charitable purposes. The Supreme Court (Maguire CJ, O'Byrne, Lavery, Kingsmill Moore and O'Daly JJ) in answering the questions posed concluded that the hospital was being used exclusively for charitable purposes and should be exempt from rates.

KINGSMILL MOORE J stated at pp.318–324 and 332–335: "Having regard, however, to the numerous and not always uniform decisions given upon the section as a whole, and the dicta contained in those decisions, it seems desirable to consider in more detail what is meant by "charitable purposes" in the section and what effect should be given to the use of the word, "exclusively." In so doing, it seems simplest to begin by ascertaininng the ordinary legal meaning of "charitable purposes," and then to see how far such meaning is narrowed by any express wording of the section or other provisions of the rating code.

I turn first to *Commissioners for Special Purposes of Income Tax v. Pemsel* [1891] AC 531.

That case was a decision on 5 & 6 Vict., c. 35, s. 61, No. VI, Schedule A, which gave allowances from income tax on the rents and profits of property belonging to any hospital, public school or almshouse or vested in trustees for charitable purposes so far as the same were applied to charitable purposes. It was held that the words, "charitable purposes" in the Act were not restricted to the meaning of relief from poverty, but must be construed according to the legal and technical meaning given to those words by English law and by legislation applicable to Scotland and Ireland as well as England. The decision is on a particular statute, but the legal meaning of "charitable purposes" in Ireland and England was minutely examined and the judgment of Lord Macnaghten has ever since been the *locus classicus* on the subject. I venture to quote once more the most famous passage, at p. 583:– "How far then, it may be asked, does the popular meaning of the word 'charity' correspond with its legal meaning? 'Charity' in its legal sense comprises four principal divisions: trusts for the relief of poverty; trusts for the advancement of

---

changing of its exemption from rating valuation on the basis that its purposes were exclusively charitable in nature within the meaning of s.63 of the Poor Relief (Ireland) Act 1838. While Kingsmill Moore J accepted that 'charitable purposes' within the meaning of the section has a less extensive meaning than that given to those words in *Pemsel's* case, his judgment nevertheless contains some important statements of general principle.

education; trusts for the advancement of religion; and trusts for other purposes beneficial to the community, not falling under any of the preceding heads. The trusts last referred to are not the less charitable in the eye of the law, because incidentally they benefit the rich as well as the poor, as indeed, every charity that deserves the name must do either directly or indirectly."

Lord Macnaghten's words were considered and developed in *Verge v. Somerville* [1924] AC 496 where Lord Wrenbury gave the opinion of the Privy Council. "His [Lord Macnaghten's] fourth head does not contain the word 'poor.' He does not say 'beneficial to the poorer members of the community'; he says, 'beneficial to the community.' Did he mean his words to be read 'as confined to the poor? Education and religion, two of the heads which he had just mentioned, do not require any qualification of poverty to be introduced to give them validity. If he was going by general words to add a fourth class in which poverty must be an ingredient, he would surely have said so. He goes on to say: 'The trusts last referred to' (i.e. the fourth class) 'are not the less charitable in the eye of the law because incidentally they benefit the rich as well as the poor.'

"Upon the word 'incidentally' might, perhaps, have been founded an argument that the trust is invalid as a charitable trust if it benefits the rich in any way other than indirectly – but for the fact that *Goodman v. Mayor of Saltash* (1882) 7 App Cas 633 had nine years before upheld as charitable a trust under which rich as well as poor could, not incidentally but directly, claim to share the benefit. Their Lordships understand Lord Macnaghten's words as meaning 'beneficial to the community' and not 'beneficial to the poor members of the community.'"

In *Webb v. Oldfield* [1898] 1 IR 431 Walker L.J. says, at p. 448: "As early as 1767 the Lord Chancellor gave a definition of charity under the statute [43 Eliz. 1, c. 4] as 'a gift to a general public use which extends to the poor as well as the rich.'"

It is well settled that the necessity of a gift being public in order to be charitable is satisfied if it benefits an appreciably important class of the community such as the inhabitants of a parish or town, or any particular class of such inhabitants: *Verge v. Somerville* [1924] AC 496, 500. The same case decides, at p. 501, that a trust is not the less charitable when the selection of the objects from an eligible class is in the hands of trustees, and that this is so where rich persons can be, and are, selected by the trustees. Thus neither the fact that the persons for whom Barrington's Hospital was intended, and is chiefly used, are the inhabitants of Limerick City, nor the fact that a recommendation from a governor is necessary for admission, deprive it of the public element which is always necessary for a charitable purpose. It remains to consider further whether the healing of the sick, as such, and independently of their poverty, can properly be regarded as a charitable purpose within Lord Macnaghten's fourth class as being beneficial to the commnmnity.

In *Webb v. Oldfield* [1898] 1 IR 431 the Lord Chancellor adopted the words of Mr. Justice Chitty in *Cross v. The London Anti-vivisection Society* [1895] 2 Ch 501, at p. 504:– "Charity in law is a highly technical term. The method employed by the Court is to consider the enumeration of charities in the statute, bearing in mind that the enumeration is not exhaustive. Institutions whose objects are analogous to those mentioned in the statute are admitted to be charities; and again, institutions which are analogous to those already admitted by reported decisions are held to be charities. The pursuit of these analogies obviously requires caution and circumspection. After all the best that can be done is to consider each case as it arises, upon its own special circumstances. To be a charity there must be some public purpose – something tending to the benefit of the community."

The English statute, 43 Eliz. 1, c. 4, includes among its charitable purposes the "relief of aged, impotent and poor people." It has been held in *In re Glynn, deceased* [1950] 2 TLR 510 and followed in *In re Bradbury deceased* [1951] 1 TLR 130 and in *In re Robinson, deceased* [1951] 1 TLR 132, that these words should be read disjunctively so that a trust for the refief of aged, or impotent, or poor people would be charitable. In the Irish statute, 10 Car. I, Sess. 3, c. 1, the words are "for the relief or maintenance of any manner of poor, succourless, distressed, or impotent persons" so that the words themselves are framed disjunctively and need no interpretation to give them a disjunctive meaning. What then is meant by "impotent"? Does it include sick and injured persons ? I think it does so, directly. "Impotence" – from the Latin, *"impotentia"* – had the primary meaning of powerless, but developed a secondary meaning of "feebleness in body through illness or old age": Oxford Dictionary. An exactly similar transition is to be found in the meaning of the words "infirm," from the Latin *"infirmus,"* and "invalid," from the Latin, *"invalidus."* In each case the original meaning was "lacking in strength" and the secondary meaning of "sick or ill" attached. The monk who looked after the sick in the mediaeval monastery was the "infirmarian" and the most usual name for a hospital in the eighteenth century was "infirmary." As for "invalid," the primary meaning has almost disappeared and it is used to describe those chronically ill. In England it has been held that the word, "impotent," covered a bequest for patients in named hospitals (*Re Roadley* [1930] 1 Ch 524); for the "sick and wounded" (*Re Hillier* [1944] 1 All ER 480); for a home of rest for persons in a condition of strain (*Re Chaplin* [1933] Ch 115); and for the maintenance of aged persons in a nursing home.

The Irish Act of Charles I goes on to mention specifically trusts "for the building, re-edifying, or maintaining in repair any church, college, school or hospital . . . or for any other like lawful and charitable use and uses." Even if the word, "impotent," could not be read as meaning "sick," it would be impossible to hold that, where a trust for repairing or building a hospital was charitable by the express words of the statute, a trust for the care and maintenance of the sick persons in that hospital was not, by analogy, equally charitable.

I am therefore of opinion that a trust for the care of the sick or the maintenance of a hospital is a charity in the legal meaning of that term: and I agree with Vaisey J. in *Re Hillier*, that it would equally fall within the meaning of charity in the sense in which that word is used by the ordinary man.

It was next submitted on behalf of the Commissioner that, even if a trust designed for the care of sick persons, irrespective of their means or want of means, could be considered a charitable purpose, yet when the care and treatment, were not entirely gratuitous, the purpose ceased to be charitable. In so far as this submission dealt with cases where patients, though paying a certain amount, did not pay the full amount of the cost of their care and treatment, I am unable to understand it. If I give a person, entirely gratuitously, care and treatment which costs two guineas, it is equivalent to making him a present of two guineas. If I give him care and treatment which costs four guineas and charge him two guineas, again it is equivalent to making him a present of two guineas.

If a hospital is being conducted exclusively for the well-to-do, it ceases to be charitable, as in the *Royal Victoria Hospital Case* (1939) 73 ILTR 236. "I am quite aware that a trust may be charitable though not confined to the poor; but I doubt very much whether a trust would be declared to be charitable which excluded the poor," said Lindley L.J. in *In re Macduff* [1896] 2 Ch 451, at p. 464. I have been unable to find any case where a trust for the care of the sick was held to lose its charitable quality because the patients contributed to the cost of their treatment and there are authorities to the contrary. In *Inland Revenue v. Peeblesshire Nursing Association* 1927 SC 215, the question was whether the income on investments and the annual value of a house owned by a nursing association should be exempted from income tax under s. 37, sub-s. 1 (b), of the Income Tax Act, 1918, on the grounds that the income was that of a "body of persons or trust established for charitable purpose only, or which, according to the rules or regulations are applicable *to charitable purposes only and so far as the same are applied to charitable purposes only*." Nursing facilities were provided for members of the association at rates varying with their means, the highest rate being reasonably equivalent to the cost. Similar facilities were granted to non-members at further increased rates. The Court of Session upheld the decision of the Special Commissioners granting exemption. In the course of his judgment the Lord President says (at p. 221):–
"There is nothing which is necessarily inconsistent with a purely charitable object in the inclusion in the organisation of the charitable association of some department intended to be run at a profit, and so to contribute to the accomplishment of the association's charitable purpose. A hospital, erected entirely for the benefit of the poor, *is none the less solely directed to that purpose* because in order to provide it with some nucleus of revenue apart from voluntary subscriptions, it runs a special ward for paying patients. I see nothing to entitle one to say that to provide cheap first class nursing for those who cannot afford it is any the less a purely charitable undertaking only because,

as an incident and adjunct of its operation, it also provides some services to persons who are perfectly well able to pay, and actually pay, a full price for them." *Cawse v. Committee of Nottingham Lunatic Hospital* [1891] 1 QB 585 is even stronger. Here exemption was claimed from landlord's property tax under s. 61, rule 6, of the Income Tax Act, 1842, and from inhabited house duty under 48 Geo. 3, c. 55, Schedule B, Case IV. To qualify for the exemption under the Income Tax Act it was necessary to show that the institution was a "hospital": to qualify for exemption from inhabited house duty it had to be a "hospital provided for the reception or relief of poor persons." The asylum received annual subscriptions and had an endowment fund, and the buildings had been provided from charity, but for the last three years the receipts from paying patients and sales of produce from a farm had been sufficient in themselves to pay all expenses, and leave an appreciable balance. It was held by the Divisional Court that the asylum was exempt under both statutes. Pollock B. considered that the institution had not ceased to bear an eleemosynary character because for a short time the fees exceeded the expenses, and he adopts the words of Denman J. in *Blake v. Mayor of London* (1886) 18 QBD 437, at p.445:– "The hospital would not be the less entitled to the exemption because certain fees were taken from rich persons who chose to take the benefit of the hospital." He continues, at p. 591:– "This hospital, at Nottingham, *quoad* the buildings in respect of which the assessment is made, has always been, and to my mind still is, a hospital provided for the reception or the relief of poor persons, and it is not the less so although considerable monies have been received by taking in persons who can pay, and whose payments have during two or three years led to an annual balance which the trustees are enabled to invest."

It may be noted that the words of Denman J. and their adoption by Pollock B. were cited with approval by Palles C.B. in *Clancy's Case* [1911] 2 IR 173, at p. 183.

Needham v. Bowers (1888) 21 QBD 436 indicates the limits which must not be exceeded if a hospital is to retain its right to exemption. Here there was a lunatic asylum which was unendowed and which received no appreciable subscriptions, but was maintained entirely out of fees received. Each year there was a surplus of receipts over expenditure but the surplus was applied in enlarging and improving the institution. The Court held that it was not entitled to exemption from tax or inhabited house duty.

From the authorities cited, the following conclusions emerge:

(1) The care of the sick of the community in general or of any limited portion of the community is a charitable purpose within the fourth class mentioned in *Pemsel's Case* [1891] AC 532.

(ii) It is no less a charitable purpose if the sick persons benefited are rich as well as poor.

(iii) It is no less a charitable purpose if the care is not given gratuitously, provided that the institution in or by which it is afforded is not so conducted as to show habitually a surplus of receipts over expenditure.

(iv) The mere fact that, some patients pay more than the cost of their treatment, or that portion of the institution is so run as to show a profit does not prevent the institution from being one which is solely devoted to charitable purposes if the profit is applied for the benefit of the poorer patients and the institution as a whole does not show a profit."

. . . .

"The correct interpretation of the word, "exclusively," is illustrated by the case of the *Good Shepherd Nuns* [1930] IR 646. The nuns maintained an asylum and a school, which were charitable, and a laundry which was not. The question arose in regard to the convent buildings where lived the nuns engaged in both the charitable and non-charitable undertakings. It was held that the residence was not used exclusively for charitable purposes. In *Doré v. Commissioner of Valuation* (1913) 50 ILTR 105 and *O'Connell's Case* [1906] 2 IR 479 the occupation of premises by persons who were not in themselves objects of charity involved a private profit or use directly derived therefrom which prevented the premises from qualifying for exemption.

Counsel for the Commissioner also relied on the small payments made to the doctors and other emoluments enjoyed by them as precluding exemption. It is sufficient to note that Palles C.B. in the *Waterford Case* [1896] 2 IR 538 expressly said that he did not regard the payments to the teachers as raising any difficulty, that the same view was taken in *University College Cork v. Commissioner of Valuation* [1911] 2 IR 593 and that in *McKenna v. Commissioner of Valuation* (1915) 49 ILTR 103 Madden J., with whom Kenny and Dodd JJ. concurred, held that the provision in a hospital of residental accommodation for surgeons, physicians and nurses did not affect the charitable nature of the institution.

Finally, counsel suggested that as doctors treated their private patients in the hospital it was not being used exclusively for charitable purposes but in order to provide fees for the doctors. Such a suggestion seems to me to misconceive the nature of the relation between doctor and patient. Whether the patient is treated at home, in a nursing home, or in a hospital rests on the choice of the patient, not of the doctor, though, no doubt, the patient is guided by his doctor's advice. If the patient is treated in his own home, could it be argued that the doctor is "using" the patient's home to provide fees for himself?

The following propositions would appear to be warranted by the Irish authorities and the wording of s. 63.

1. Apart from specific exceptions to be found in other statutes (such as Marsh's Library, Armagh Observatory, and buildings belonging to certain societies instituted for purposes of science, literature, or fine arts) the grounds for exemption from rates must be found in the proviso to s. 63 of the Act of 1838 (*McGahan and Ryan's Case* [1934] IR 736).

2. "Charitable purposes" in s. 63 has a meaning less extensive than the meaning given to those words in *Pemsel's Case*. How much less extensive has

never been decided, but at least there must be excluded from the denotation of "charitable purposes" in the section any charitable purpose which is mentioned expressly in the section (*O'Neill's Case* [1914] 2 IR 447 and *Scott's Case* [1892] 2 QB 152 as applied to s. 63).

3. Neither the wording of s. 63 nor any authority leads to the conclusion that "charitable purposes" means, or is confined to, "charitable purposes devoted exclusively to the benefit of the poor."

4. The word, " exclusively," in no way alters or modifies the meaning of "charitable purpose." It does ensure that, in order to qualify for exemption, a building must be used for charitable purposes only. Where a building is used for mixed purposes, some charitable, some non-charitable, it is not exempt, though if the purposes are carried on in different buildings or in different parts of the same building s. 2 of the Valuation Act, 1854, gives power to the Commissioner to distinguish as exempt the buildings or portions of buildings which are exclusively used for charitable purposes. (*O'Connell's Case* [1906] 2 IR 479, *Clancy's Case* [1911] 2 IR 173, case of the *Good Shephard Nuns* [1930] IR 646).

5. Although, where a building is used for education, in order to secure exemption, it must on the express wording of s. 63, be used "exclusively for the education of the poor," yet, even in the case of educational charities, the receipt of fees or income is not necessarily a bar to exemption if the fees are incidental to such user (Gibson J. in *O'Neill's Case*.) When the fees or income are subject to a trust which requires them to be applied for the charitable purpose their receipt does not make the user any the less "exclusively for charitable purposes." (Suggested by Palles C.B. in the *Waterford Case* adopted by all members of the Court in the *Pembroke Case* [1904] 2 IR 439 and two members of the Court in *University College Cork Case* and further endorsed by Palles C.B. in *Clancy's Case*.)

6. By parity of reasoning, *even if* the section required hospitals to be used exclusively for the treatment of the poor, the receipt of fees would not be a bar to exemption if such fees were subject to a trust to be applied to the use of the hospital and such hospital predominantly treated poor patients. As there is no such limitation to the treatment of poor patients in the section, the charging of fees in a hospital, where by the nature of the trust such fees must be applied to the use of the hospital, cannot affect the right to exemption.

7. Neither schools (*O'Neill's Case*) nor hospitals (*Royal Victoria Hospital Case*) are used for charitable purposes if they are carried on exclusively, or predominantly, for the well-to-do.

8. The payment of masters, or doctors to carry-on the charitable work does not prevent the building in which the work is carried on from being used exclusively for charitable purposes.

These propositions, if sound, as I believe them to be, are sufficient to show that Barrington's Hospital, in so far as its intern department is concerned, should be exempt from rates. I assume that, taking one year with another, the fees charged for the private wards do not bring in more than sufficient to cover the cost of food, treatment, nursing, medicines, and general maintenance of the private patients: but even if there were a small net profit from private patients yet, if such profit were subject to an obligation to apply it to the general purposes of the Hospital, this would not, in my opinion, prevent the Hospital from being used "exclusively for charitable purposes." It seems to me that any profits made are subject to such an obligation.

More difficult questions are raised by the "extern department," with its sub-division known as the "Specialist Department." The Case as stated finds that "a certain number of patients treated in the Specialist Department as extern patients, are able to pay and are charged the full cost of treatment, and this applies more particularly in the X-ray department and massage department where patients of ample means may attend and are charged at the rates current for such attendance in the district."

In a case where the hospital authorities carry on a separate business on commercial lines the building or portion of a building in which such business is carried on could not be distinguished as exempt even if the profits of such business were applied to the general purposes of the hospital. But the mere charging of fees at rates current in the district to a limited number of patients may be, in the words of Gibson J., at p. 485 of *O'Neill's Case*, only "incidental" or "accidental" in the general running of the hospital. Modern medicine requires much expensive apparatus and it may be that such apparatus cannot be provided and maintained for the benefit of the poor patients unless, when not immediately in use for such poor patients it is made available at such rates for those who are willing to pay for such facilities. I notice from the accounts that in one year the cost of X-ray films and renewals alone, without taking into account the cost of services and other incidental expenses, exceeded the whole takings of the X-ray department. It seems to me that the cases where "patients of ample means" are charged at rates current for such attendance in the district" represent such a small item in the activities of the external department and of the Hospital in general that they do not deprive the institution of its charitable character. If authority is needed for this conclusion it is to be found in the *Peeblesshire Nursing Association Case*."

Re McCarthy's Will Trusts: National Bank Ltd v. McQuaid
[1958] IR 311

A testatrix made a number of bequests in her will including for the travelling expenses and maintenance of invalids making pilgrimages to Lourdes, to a hospital at Lourdes, to a society who care for the sick making pilgrimages there and to a fund for the benefit of 'elderly and infirm nurses'.

BUDD J stated at pp.316–319: "I must now deal with the questions as to whether the other bequests referred to in the summons are valid charitable bequests.

The first is in the following terms:

> "To the Archbishop of Dublin for the time being the sum of Six hundred pounds upon trust to invest the same and invest the annual income arising therefrom in defraying wholly or partially the travelling expenses and maintenance of two or more invalid persons taking part in organised Religious Pilgrimages to the Grotto of Our Lady at Lourdes, such invalid persons to be chosen for the benefit of such income to be in equal numbers each year from the areas now represented by the Catholic Parishes of Dun Laoghaire and Glasthule."

Now the form of words used by the testatrix is significant. She refers to "organised Religious Pilgrimages" and I have evidence before me that such organised religious pilgrimages are only permitted with the sanction and approval of the ecclesiastical authorities, and are either organised by such ecclesiastical authorities or religious organisations that are approved of by them. I have before me an affidavit from Father Carroll, the Secretary of the Dublin Diocesan Pilgrimage to Lourdes, which deals with the nature of these pilgrimages. He says that pilgrimages are encouraged by the Catholic Church and are recognised by the Church as a public manifestation of religion. Pilgrimages, he says further, are regarded as a salutary mode of penance and a form of thanksgiving. He states that Lourdes is the most frequented place of pilgrimage in the Catholic world. One of the principal objects of the pilgrimage to Lourdes is to pray for the spiritual and temporal welfare of the invalids, and care is always taken to ensure that it maintains its religious character. Various religious exercises are also performed by the pilgrims at Lourdes.

Apart from what is stated in the affidavit, I think a pilgrimage has always been regarded as a religious act. It is something done in the public eye and is, therefore, a matter of public benefit and edification. Furthermore, I have had pointed out to me the definition of a pilgrimage in the Oxford Dictionary:– "A journey (usually of considerable duration) made to some sacred place as an act of religious devotion." This gift is to aid one or two of the sick people of the two parishes mentioned to take part in these organised religious pilgrimages, and having regard to the nature of these pilgrimages, it is clearly a gift for the advancement of religion and I hold that it is a valid charitable gift.

The second gift queried is in the following terms:

> "To the trustees for the time being of the Sisters of Charity of Nevers at the Asile Hospital, Lourdes, France, for the benefit of the sick in that hospital the sum of One Thousand Pounds."

The Bishop of Lourdes, in his affidavit states that the hospital referred to is Catholic Church property the ownership and control thereof being vested in the Bishop of Lourdes while the running of the hospital is entrusted by him to the Sisters of Charity of Nevers. The main objects of the Order are the sanctification of its members and the relief of the poor and sick. The finances of the hospital are in the hands of the Bishop and all the money received is devoted to the care of the sick and the improvement of the hospital. The very words used by the testatrix indicate that the gift is for the benefit of the sick and it seems to me to be clearly charitable. The point was made in argument that the beneficiaries were out of the jurisdiction and the administration of the fund could not be controlled by the Court. There is no substance in that point as there is no question of any fund being administered by the Court. It is an outright gift to the Bishop as trustee for an object chosen by the testatrix, and of course there has been no suggestion that the Bishop would use the money for any purpose other than that indicated by the testatrix.

The third bequest I have to deal with is in the following terms "To the Irish Society of Our Lady of Lourdes the sum of £500."

This organisation, to accord with international practice, has now changed its name to The Irish Hospitalité of Our Lady of Lourdes, but I am satisfied that it is the same organisation that the testatrix wished to benefit. Its principal object is the care of the sick poor and its members devote their care and attention, during a pilgrimage, to the sick poor, conveying them to Lourdes and providing them with care in the hospital. I am satisfied that the objects and activities of the Society are charitable – unless it can be said that the fact that they care for the rich sick as well as the poor makes it not so. But on this point the judgment of Kingsmill Moore J., concurred in by Maguire C.J. and Lavery J. in *The Governors of Barrington's Hospital v. The Commissioner of Valuation* [1957] IR 299 is decisive that this would not affect the issue, where he says:– "The care of the sick of the community in general or any limited portion of the community is an element of the purposes and is no less charitable if the rich benefit as well as the poor." This society is exclusively charitable in its objects and organisation and I hold this to be a good charitable gift.

The fourth gift in question is in the following terms:

> "To the Trustees for the time being of the Nurses Benevolent Fund attached to the Irish Nurses' Organisation having its office at 24 Nassau St., Dublin, the sum of Five Hundred Pounds for the benefit of elderly or infirm nurses."

The unincorporated body "The Irish Nurses' Organisation" which had its office at 24 Nassau St., Dublin, no longer exists, but I am satisfied from the evidence before me that its continuity both in membership and objects is preserved in the new incorporated body also known as "The Irish Nurses' Organisation" and that it was this body that the testatrix intended to be the object of her bounty.

The second question which I have to deal with in connection with this legacy is whether it is a valid charitable gift. In the first place I notice that the testatrix leaves the gift to the trustees of the "Benevolent Fund" of the Organisation. I emphasise the word "Benevolent" because it seems to me to indicate an intention to aid distress. Benevolent funds are generally formed to aid the needy. Secondly, it is a gift for the benefit of the "infirm or elderly" nurses of the Organisation and not for the general purposes of the Organisation. In my view, having regard to the cases cited, it is not necessary to find that the relief of poverty be expressed in a testator's will as the object of his gift before the gift can be held charitable; it is sufficient if the Court can find that the relief of poverty was intended by the testator. In the case of *In re Glyn, Deceased, Public Trustee v. Attorney-General* [1950] WN 373, it was held that a gift to endow cottages for old women of the working classes of the age of sixty years or upwards was a valid charitable gift. Danckwerts J. having referred to *In re Lucas* [1922] 2 Ch 52 said that a trust for the relief of aged persons would be charitable unless qualified in some way that would clearly make it not charitable. In that case, there was a sufficient context to show that the testatrix intended to benefit indigent persons, for the beneficiaries were to be women of sixty years of age or upwards who had had to work for their living and who by reason of their age were unlikely to be able to support themselves any longer. In *In re Bradbury, Needham v. Reekie* [1950] WN 558, a trust to maintain an aged or aged persons in a nun's home was held to be a good charitable gift by Vaisey J. and it is to be implied from what he said that his finding was based on his view that the intention of the donor was to aid the indigent. Likewise in the case of *In re Dudgeon, Truman v. Pope* (1896) 74 LT Rep 613, a gift for the benefit of "respectable single women of good character above the age of sixty years" was held to be a good charitable gift on the grounds that the intention of the gift was the relief of poverty. In the present case I think the testatrix had in mind the relieving of distress. The gift is for elderly or infirm nurses and it is clear that infirm people would be unable to carry on their work. I think that by implication this is a gift for the relief of poverty and that it is a good charitable bequest and I so hold."

Gifts for Sporting and Recreational Purposes and for the Benefit of a Locality

Trusts to make provision for recreational or leisure facilities will generally be upheld as charitable provided they benefit a sufficient section of the community although traditionally some doubt has surrounded the charitable nature of gifts to promote sporting activities *simpliciter* unless they will qualify as being for the advancement of education.[29]

Gifts for the Benefit of Animals

Gifts for the welfare of animals generally or for a particular type of animal are recognised as charitable in law. As noted above, gifts for the benefit of individual animals while they are not considered to be charitable, may be upheld

---

[29] E.g. *IRC v. McMullen* [1981] AC 1.

as an anomalous exception to the principle that purpose trusts will not be enforced provided they are limited to the perpetuity period.[30]

Swifte v. Attorney General
[1912] 1 IR 133

A testatrix bequeathed a sum to the Commissioners of Charitable Donations and Bequests on trust to apply the income for the maintenance of 'the Dublin Home for Starving and Forsaken Cats'. It was held by Barton J that this was a valid charitable gift.

BARTON J stated at pp,137–140: "The question for decision is, whether this bequest of £4000 Consols to the Commissioners of Charitable Donations and Bequests, upon trust to pay the income and dividends for the exclusive benefit of the Dublin Home for Starving and Forsaken Cats, is a valid charitable bequest. [His Lordship referred to the object of the institution and the circumstances connected with it, and proceeded]:–

The law applicable to this class of charitable gifts is tolerably well settled. The prevention of cruelty to animals is an object which the law recognizes as legally charitable. This is especially so in the case of animals useful to man. In *In re Douglas; Obert v. Barrow* (1887) 35 Ch D 472, 479 the principle was applied to a bequest to a "Home for Lost Dogs." The late Master of the Rolls has applied the principle to this very institution. In *Swifte v. Colam*, unreported, Feb. 16, 1909 he ordered the balance of a sum of £450, after payment of costs, "to be held by the Commissioners of Charitable Donations and Bequests, upon trust to invest the corpus, and to pay the interest as it accrues due, to the said Miss Alice May Swifte, or other the Hon. Treasurer for the time being of the institution known as the Home for Starving and Forsaken Cats." The bequest in that case was a simpler one than the present case; and the only question in the present case seems to be whether there is anything to distinguish it from *Swifte v. Colam.*

I now turn to the will. We have, in the first place, a bequest of £4000 Consols "to the Commissioners of Charitable Donations and Bequests, . . . upon trust to apply the income and dividends thereof for the exclusive maintenance of the Dublin Home for Starving and Forsaken Cats." That is a good charitable bequest, unless there is something in what follows to invalidate it. The next material sentence is as follows:– "Including the maintenance of the chloroform chamber now existing, or any other painless method of putting an end to cases of hopeless pain, and the maintenance of the boarding department." This sentence commences with the word "including", which in its ordinary and natural meaning means "comprehending *inter alia*." The

---

[30] *Re Kelly* [1932] IR 255. See *supra* Chapter 9, p. 428.

mention of the chloroform chamber, the use of which is limited to cases of hopeless pain, does not, in my opinion, affect the charitable character of the gift. The boarding department has been criticized because it appears to be self-supporting. That does not, in my opinion, affect the charitable character of the bequest. It appears to be a subordinate adjunct of the Home, and is intended to provide shelter and food for cats who otherwise would be forsaken by their owners when they leave town. The testatrix then uses the words "but for no other purpose." These words refer back, in my opinion, to the word *exclusive,* and mean "for the exclusive maintenance of the 'Cats' ' Home, and for no other purpose." She then proceeds to explain why she gives this bequest for the exclusive maintenance of the "Cats' " Home, and for no other purpose. The explanation is given in the sentence of the will commencing with the word "as." [His Lordship then referred to the deed of Feb. 27,1888, and to the lease of Nov. 28th, 1884, and proceeded]:

The contents of the deed and lease explain why the testatrix insisted that her bequest was to be for the exclusive maintenance of the Cats' Home, and for no other purpose. The reason was, that the general maintenance charges which were common to the Dogs' Home and to the Cats' Home were defrayed by the Society under the deed to which she refers, and by the lease of the common site of the Dogs' and Cats' Home. I need not refer to the gift over.

It seems to me that the construction which I have just put upon the language of the testatrix is the natural one, and that there is nothing to cut down or invalidate the original bequest, which in itself is merely a valid charitable gift.

I turn to the arguments which have been adduced *contra.* It was argued that the sentence commencing "as" is a condition precedent to the bequest, and that unless the Dublin Society for Prevention of Cruelty to Animals is under an enforceable legal obligation to pay the rent, taxes, repairs, and caretaker's wages, &c., of these premises, the gift fails. I assume, for the purpose of argument, that the Society is under no such obligation, but I can find no condition precedent. The word "as" is not conditional but explanatory.

It was argued, in the next place, that the word "including" is equivalent to "meaning," and was to be taken as introducing an exhaustive definition of the object of the gift; that the words "but for no other purpose" refer only to the two preceding departments of the Home, and that the bequest was, in fact, a bequest for the exclusive purpose of maintaining the chloroform chamber and the boarding department of the Home, which, by themselves, it is contended, could not constitute a legal charity.

I need not discuss the latter question, because I am of opinion that this would be a strained construction of the bequest. It would be cutting down the clear bequest to the Home by giving to the word "including" a secondary meaning, which it would require a strong context to support.

On the whole, I am of opinion that this is a good charitable gift. The parties are agreed that, in view of these and the other provisions of the will, the order should direct the settlement of a scheme for the regulation and management of the charity, and for the application of its present and future income."

Gifts for Political Purposes

A trust for the advancement of political purposes is not charitable[31] although where the predominant motive is educational rather than political, they may be upheld.[32] Often trusts for political purposes will involve advocating a change in the law and this is one of the primary reasons why trusts of this nature will not be regarded as charitable as the court has no means of judging whether a proposed change in the law will or will not be for the public benefit.[33]

McGovern v. Attorney General
[1982] Ch 321

Amnesty International executed a declaration of trust with the intention of hiving off into a trust some of its activities which it had been advised were charitable. These purposes included the relief of needy persons who were, had been or were likely to become prisoners of conscience and their families, attempting to secure the release of such prisoners, procuring the abolition of torture or inhuman or degrading treatment or punishment, the promotion of research into the maintenance and observance of human rights and the dissemination of the results of such research. The trustees sought a declaration that the trust ought to be regarded as a charity. It was held by Slade J that the trust was not a charitable one.

SLADE J stated at pp. 331–343 and 353–354:

"Relevant principles of the law of charities
With a view to making clear the reasons for my ultimate decision I think that, before turning to the particular provisions of the trust deed, I should attempt to state what I conceive to be a few of the relevant basic principles of the law of charities.

Trusts for charitable purposes in this country enjoy a number of privileges which are not enjoyed by trusts for purposes of a non-charitable nature. Thus, if a trust deed shows a clear intention to devote the trust assets to charity, the trust purposes will not fail for uncertainty merely because they are inadequately defined. Charitable trusts are in most respects exempt from the rule against perpetuities. They are capable of being varied by way of scheme. Finally, they are enforceable at the suit of the Crown: *Wallis v. Solicitor-General for New Zealand* [1903] AC 173, 181–182, *per* Lord Macnaghten:

> "It is the province of the Crown as parens patriae to enforce the execution of charitable trusts, and it has always been recognised as the duty of the law officers

---

[31] E.g. *Re Ni Brudair* High Court (Gannon J) 5 February 1979.
[32] *Re Trusts of the Arthur McDougall Fund* [1957] 1 WLR 81.
[33] *Bowman v. Secular Society Ltd* [1917] AC 406, 442 *per* Lord Parker.

of the Crown to intervene for the purpose of protecting charities and affording advice and assistance to the court in the administration of charitable trusts."

In the circumstances, it is not surprising that the law requires a number of conditions to be fulfilled before trusts can be accepted as being charitable. The general rule is that in order to achieve charitable status a trust, however philanthropic, must satisfy each of the following three requirements. (1) It must be of a charitable nature, within the spirit and intendment of the preamble to the Charitable Uses Act 1601 (43 Eliz. 1, c. 4), as interpreted by the courts and extended by statute. (2) It must promote a public benefit of a nature recognised by the courts as a public benefit. (3) The purposes of the trust must be wholly and exclusively charitable: see generally *Snell's Principles of Equity,* 27th ed. (1973), pp. 143 et seq. I will make some observations on each of these three requirements in turn.

The requirement of a charitable nature
A recent authoritative statement of the legal test to be applied in considering whether purposes are of a charitable nature is to be found in the speech of Lord Wilberforce in *Scottish Burial Reform and Cremation Society Ltd. v. Glasgow Corporation* [1968] AC 138, 154:

> "On this subject, the law of England, though no doubt not very satisfactory and in need of rationalisation, is tolerably clear. The purposes in question, to be charitable, must be shown to be for the benefit of the public, or the community, in a sense or manner within the intendment of the preamble to the statute 43 Eliz. I, c. 4. The latter requirement does not mean quite what it says; for it is now accepted that what must be regarded is not the wording of the preamble itself, but the effect of decisions given by the courts as to its scope, decisions which have endeavoured to keep the law as to charities moving according as new social needs arise or old ones become obsolete or satisfied."

The preamble to the Statute of Elizabeth contained the following list of charitable objects:

> " . . . the relief of aged, impotent and poor people . . . maintenance of sick and maimed soldiers and mariners, schools of learning, free schools, and scholars in universities . . . repair of bridges, ports, havens, causeways, churches, seabanks and highways . . . education and preferment of orphans . . . relief, stock or maintenance for houses of correction . . . marriages of poor maids . . . supportation, aid and help of young tradesmen, handicraftsmen and persons decayed . . . relief or redemption of prisoners or captives, and for aid or ease of any poor inhabitants concerning payments of fifteens, setting out of soldiers and other taxes."

It is at first sight difficult to detect any common thread running through this list of diverse objects. Lord Macnaghten, however, in *Income Tax Special Purposes Commissioners v. Pemsel* [1891] AC 531, 583 categorised charity in its legal sense as comprising four principal divisions, namely:

". . . trusts for the relief of poverty; trusts for the advancement of education; trusts for the advancement of religion; and trusts for other purposes beneficial to the community, not falling under any of the preceding heads."

This grouping of the heads of recognised charity has proved to be of great value, as is indicated by its frequent subsequent citation. Nevertheless, Lord Wilberforce in *Scottish Burial Reform and Cremation Society Ltd.v. Glasgow Corporation* [1968] AC 138, 154, gave three warnings in this context:

". . . first that, since it is a classification of convenience, there may well be purposes which do not fit neatly into one or other of the headings; secondly, that the words used must not be given the force of a statute to be construed; and thirdly, that the law of charity is a moving subject which may well have evolved even since 1891."

As Mr. Hoffmann pointed out on behalf of the trustees, a number of the specific objects mentioned in the preamble to the Statute of Elizabeth and recognised by decided cases as charitable do not fall neatly within any of the first three of the categories mentioned by Lord Macnaghten. Examples of such are the relief of aged and impotent people. The words "aged, impotent and poor people" fall to be read disjunctively: see *In re Robinson, decd* [1951] Ch 198 and *In re Lewis, decd.* [1955] Ch 104. Aged and impotent persons may thus qualify as objects of charity without necessarily being poor. A similar comment may be made in relation to some other objects referred to in the statute, such as the "education and preferment of orphans," "the supportation, aid and help of young tradesmen" and the "relief or redemption of prisoners or captives." Persons falling within any of the categories are not necessarily suffering from poverty. All persons included within any of these categories, however, have this much in common namely, that they are suffering from some form of human suffering or distress. Thus, Mr. Hoffmann submitted, it is possible to detect in the preamble to the statute a genus or division of charity not mentioned by Lord Macnaghten, of which poverty is merely a species; this genus includes the relief of human suffering and distress in all the various forms enumerated. In general terms I accept this analysis, which derives some support from what Lord Herschell said in *Pemsel's* case [1891] AC 531, 572:

"I think, then, that the popular conception of a charitable purpose covers the relief of any form of necessity, destitution, or helplessness which excites the compassion or sympathy of men, and so appeals to their benevolence for relief."

Adopting a similar approach, Lord Greene M.R. in *In re Hobourn Aero Components Ltd.'s Air Raid Distress Fund* [1946] Ch 194, 200-201, said:

"I am not concerned to dispute the proposition that a fund put up for air raid distress in Coventry generally would be a good charitable gift. I have very little doubt that it would be."

As a broad proposition, I would thus accept that a trust for the relief of human suffering and distress would prima facie be capable of being of a charitable nature, within the spirit and intendment of the preamble to the Statute of Elizabeth, as being what Mr. Hoffmann termed "a charity of compassion." It does not, however, follow that a trust established for good compassionate purposes will necessarily qualify as a charity according to English law, any more than it necessarily follows that such a qualification will attach to a trust for the relief of poverty or for the advancement of education or for the advancement of religion. There are other requirements which it must still satisfy if it is to enjoy charitable status. I now turn to the requirement of public benefit.

The requirement of public benefit

Save in the case of gifts to classes of persons, a trust must always be shown to promote a public benefit of a nature recognised by the courts as being such if it is to qualify as being charitable. The question whether a purpose will or may operate for the public benefit is to be answered by the court forming an opinion on the evidence before it: see *National Anti-Vivisection Society v. Inland Revenue Commissioners* [1948] AC 31, 44, *per* Lord Wright. No doubt in some cases a purpose may be so manifestly beneficial to the public that it would be absurd to call evidence on this point. In many other instances, however, the element of public benefit may be much more debatable. Indeed, in some cases the court will regard this element of being incapable of proof one way or the other and thus will inevitably decline to recognise the trust as being of a charitable nature.

Trusts to promote changes in the law of England are generally regarded as falling into the latter category and as being non-charitable for this reason. Thus Lord Parker of Waddington said in *Bowman v. Secular Society Ltd.* [1917] AC 406, 442:

> "The abolition of religious tests, the disestablishment of the Church, the secularisation of education, the alteration of the law touching religion or marriage, or the observation of the Sabbath, are purely political objects. Equity has always refused to recognise such objects as charitable. It is true that a gift to an association formed for their attainment may, if the association be unincorporated, be upheld as an absolute gift to its members, or, if the association be incorporated, as an absolute gift to the corporate body; but a trust for the attainment of political objects has always been held invalid, not because it is illegal, for everyone is at liberty to advocate or promote by any lawful means a change in the law, but because the court has no means of judging whether a proposed change in the law will or will not be for the public benefit, and therefore cannot say that a gift to secure the change is a charitable gift. The same considerations apply when there is a trust for the publication of a book. The court will examine the book, and if its objects be charitable in the legal sense it will give effect to the trust as a good charity: *Thornton v. Howe* (1862) 31 Beav 14; but if its objects be political it will refuse to enforce the trust: *De Themmines v. De Bonneval* (1828) 5 Russ 288."

In the latter case a gift of some stock in trust to apply the dividends in printing and promoting the circulation of a treatise written in French and Latin, which inculcated the doctrine of absolute supremacy of the Pope in ecclesiastical matters, was held void. As was said in the judgment in that case (1828) 5 Russ 288, 292:

> "It is against the policy of the country to encourage, by the establishment of a charity, the publication of any work which asserts the absolute supremacy of the Pope in ecclesiastical matters over the sovereignty of the state."

The passage from Lord Parker's speech in the *Bowman* case [1917] 1 AC 406 which I have read is often cited as authority for the broad proposition that trusts for "political objects" can never be supported as legal charities. However, before this proposition is accepted, it is necessary to consider what is meant by "political objects" in this context. It would appear that Lord Parker himself in using the phrase was referring primarily to objects which involved changes in the existing laws of England. The implementation of any item in the list of examples of political objects given by him, at p. 442, beginning with the words "The abolition of religious tests" would have involved changes in the law of this country. The object of the trust in *De Themmines v. De Bonneval* (1828) 5 Russ 288, would likewise have involved the advocacy of a change in English law, because this would have been the only means of giving the Pope the absolute supremacy in ecclesiastical matters over the sovereignty of the state which the donor desired to secure.

There is no doubt whatever that a trust of which a principal object is to alter the law of this country cannot be regarded as charitable. In *National Anti-Vivisection Society v. Inland Revenue Commissioners* [1948] AC 31, a society which had as its object the total suppression of vivisection was held not to be "a body of persons . . . established for charitable purpose only" within section 37(1)(b) of the Income Tax Act 1918, on two separate grounds. The first was that any assumed public benefit in the advancement of morals would be far outweighed by the detriment to medical science and research and consequently to public health. This was a finding on the evidence. The second ground was that a main object of the society was the promotion of legislation. As Lord Wright said, at pp. 49-50:

> "But there is another and essentially different ground on which in my opinion it must fail; that is, because its object is to secure legislation to give legal effect to it. It is, in my opinion, a political purpose within the meaning of Lord Parker's pronouncement in *Bowman v. Secular Society Ltd.*"

Similarly, Lord Simonds, in a very significant passage in his speech, said, at pp. 62-63:

> "My Lords, I see no reason for supposing that Lord Parker in the cited passage used the expression 'political objects' in any narrow sense or was confining it

to objects of acute political controversy. On the contrary he was, I think, propounding familiar doctrine, nowhere better stated than in a text-book, which has long been regarded as of high authority but appears not to have been cited for this purpose to the courts below (as it certainly was not to your Lordships), *Tyssen on Charitable Bequests,* 1st ed. (1888). The passage which is at p. 176, is worth repeating at length: 'It is a common practice for a number of individuals amongst us to form an association for the purpose of promoting some change in the law, and it is worth our while to consider the effect of a gift to such an association. It is clear that such an association is not of a charitable nature. However desirable the change may really be, the law could not stultify itself by holding that it was for the public benefit that the law itself should be changed. Each court in deciding on the validity of a gift must decide on the principle that the law is right as it stands. On the other hand, such a gift could not be held void for illegality.' Lord Parker uses slightly different language but means the same thing, when he says that the court has no means of judging whether a proposed change in the law will or will not be for the public benefit. It is not for the court to judge and the court has no means of judging. The same question may be looked at from a slightly different angle. One of the tests, and a crucial test, whether a trust is charitable, lies in the competence of the court to control and reform it. I would remind your Lordships that it is the King as parens patriae who is the guardian of charity and that it is the right and duty of his Attorney-General to intervene and inform the court, if the trustees of a charitable trust fall short of their duty. So too it is his duty to assist the court, if need be, in the formulation of a scheme for the execution of a charitable trust. But, my Lords, is it for a moment to be supposed that it is the function of the Attorney-General on behalf of the Crown to intervene and demand that a trust shall be established and administered by the court, the object of which is to alter the law in a manner highly prejudicial, as he and His Majesty's Government may think, to the welfare of the state? This very case would serve as an example, if upon the footing that it was a charitable trust it became the duty of the Attorney-General on account of its maladministration to intervene."

The House of Lords in *National Anti-Vivisection Society v. Inland Revenue Commissioners* [1948] AC 31, like Lord Parker of Waddington in *Bowman v. Secular Society Ltd.* [1917] AC 406, was directing its attention primarily, if not exclusively, to one particular form of political trust, namely, a trust of which it was a main object to obtain an alteration of the law of England. Lord Simonds and Lord Wright clearly felt some difficulty about the generality of the words which had been used by Lord Parker, in saying, at p. 442, that "the court has no means of judging whether a proposed change in the law will or will not be for the public benefit." In most cases the court would not have the means to judge this question. On the particular facts of *National Anti-Vivisection Society v. Inland Revenue Commissioners* [1948] AC 31, however, their Lordships clearly did regard themselves as having such means, because one ground of their decision was that the proposed change in the law would be detrimental to the public. The explanation and justification for Lord Parker's opinion was expressed by Lord Wright. After having referred to the passage from *Tyssen on Charitable Bequests,* 1st ed., cited by Lord Simonds, he said, at p. 50:

> "It is, I think, a very important contribution to this question. It appears to me to go to explain and justify Lord Parker's opinion. I refer especially to Tyssen's words: 'the law could not stultify itself by holding that it was for the public benefit that the law itself should be changed' and again: 'each court . . . must decide on the principle that the law is right as it stands.' I am reminded of the words of a great common law judge who warned the courts against usurping the functions of the legislature. I do not regard the statements of Lord Parker and Tyssen as inconsistent but as complementary."

From the passages from the speeches of Lord Parker, Lord Wright and Lord Simonds which I have read I extract the principle that the court will not regard as charitable a trust of which a main object is to procure an alteration of the law of the United Kingdom for one or both of two reasons: first, the court will ordinarily have no sufficient means of judging as a matter of evidence whether the proposed change will or will not be for the public benefit. Secondly, even if the evidence suffices to enable it to form a prima facie opinion that a change in the law is desirable, it must still decide the case on the principle that the law is right as it stands, since to do otherwise would usurp the functions of the legislature. I interpret the point made by Lord Simonds concerning the position of the Attorney-General as merely illustrating some of the anomalies and undesirable consequences that might ensue if the courts began to encroach on the functions of the legislature by ascribing charitable status to trusts of which a main object is to procure a change in the law of the United Kingdom, as being for the public benefit.

A further warning to the courts against usurping the functions of the legislature has recently been given by the House of Lords in *Duport Steels Ltd. v. Sirs* [1980] 1 WLR 142. Lord Diplock, at p. 157, pointed out that certain trade union legislation might in actual operation have turned out to have injurious consequences that Parliament had not anticipated at the time when the statutes were passed. However, he said, at p. 157: "But if this be the case it is for Parliament, not for the judiciary, to decide whether any changes should be made to the law as stated in the Acts." Later, at the same page, he referred to "public confidence in the political impartiality of the judiciary, which is essential to the continuance of the rule of law.

Thus far, the only types of political trust to which I have directed specific attention have been those of which a main object is to procure a change in the law of this country. The principles established by *Bowman's* case [1917] AC 406 and the *National Anti-Vivisection Society* case [1948] AC 31 will render such trusts non-charitable whether or not they are of a party-political nature. Conversely, however, several cases cited to me illustrate that trusts of which a main object is to promote the interests of a particular political party in this country fail to achieve charitable status, even though they are not directed towards any particular change in English law: see, for example, *Bonar Law*

Memorial Trust v. Inland Revenue Commissioners (1933) 17 TC 508, and *In re Hopkinson, decd.* [1949] 1 All ER 346. In my judgment any such trusts are plainly "political trusts" within the spirit, if not the letter, of Lord Parker of Waddington's pronouncement, and the same reasons for the court's refusing to enforce them would apply, but a fortiori. Since their nature would ex hypothesi be very controversial, the court could be faced with even greater difficulties in determining whether the objects of the trust would be for the public benefit; correspondingly, it would be at even greater risk of encroaching on the functions of the legislature and prejudicing its reputation for political impartiality, if it were to promote such objects by enforcing the trust.

I now turn to consider the status of a trust of which a main object is to secure the alteration of the laws of a foreign country. The mere fact that a trust was intended to be carried out abroad would not by itself necessarily deprive it of charitable status. A number of trusts to be executed outside this country have been upheld as charities, though the judgment of Sir Raymond Evershed M.R. in *Camille and Henry Dreyfus Foundation Inc. v. Inland Revenue Commissioners* [1954] Ch 672, 684–685 illustrates that certain types of trust – for example, trusts for the setting out of soldiers or the repair of bridges or causeways – might be acceptable as charities only if they were to be executed in the United Kingdom. The point with which I am at present concerned is whether a trust of which a direct and main object is to secure a change in the laws of a foreign country can *ever* be regarded as charitable under English law. Though I do not think that any authority cited to me precisely covers the point, I have come to the clear conclusion that it cannot.

I accept that the dangers of the court encroaching on the functions of the legislature or of subjecting its political impartiality to question would not be nearly so great as when similar trusts are to be executed in this country. I also accept that on occasions the court will examine and express an opinion upon the quality of a foreign law. Thus, for example, it has declined to enforce or recognise rights conferred or duties imposed by a foreign law, in certain cases where it has considered that, on the particular facts, enforcement or recognition would be contrary to justice or morality. I therefore accept that the particular point made by Mr. Tyssen (about the law stultifying itself) has no application in this context. There is no obligation on the court to decide on the principle that any foreign law is ex hypothesi right as it stands; it is not obliged for all purposes to blind itself to what it may regard as the injustice of a particular foreign law.

In my judgment, however, there remain overwhelming reasons why such a trust still cannot be regarded as charitable. All the reasoning of Lord Parker of Waddington in *Bowman v. Secular Society Ltd.* [1917] AC 406 seems to me to apply a fortiori in such a case. A fortiori the court will have no adequate means of judging whether a proposed change in the law of a foreign country will or will not be for the public benefit. Sir Raymond Evershed M.R. in *Camille and Henry Dreyfus Foundation Inc. v. Inland Revenue Commissioners* [1954] Ch

672, 684 expressed the prima facie view that the community which has to be considered in this context even in the case of a trust to be executed abroad is the community of the United Kingdom. Assuming that this is the right test, the court in applying it would still be bound to take account of the probable effects of attempts to procure the proposed legislation, or of its actual enactment, on the inhabitants of the country concerned, which would doubtless have a history and social structure quite different from that of the United Kingdom. Whatever might be its view as to the content of the relevant law from the standpoint of an English lawyer, it would, I think, have no satisfactory means of judging such probable effects upon the local community.

Furthermore, before ascribing charitable status to an English trust of which a main object was to secure the alteration of a foreign law, the court would also, I conceive, be bound to consider the consequences for this country as a matter of public policy. In a number of such cases there would arise a substantial prima facie risk that such a trust, enforced, could prejudice the relations of this country with the foreign country concerned: compare *Habershon v. Vardon* (1851) 4 De G & Sm 467. The court would have no satisfactory means of assessing the extent of such risk, which would not be capable of being readily dealt with by evidence and would be a matter more for political than for legal judgment. For all these reasons, I conclude that a trust of which a main purpose is to procure a change in the laws of a foreign country is a trust for the attainment of political objects within the spirit of Lord Parker of Waddington's pronouncement and, as such, is non-charitable.

Thus far, I have been considering trusts of which a main purpose is to achieve changes in the law itself or which are of a party-political nature. Under any legal system, however, the government and its various authorities, administrative and judicial, will have wide discretionary powers vested in them, within the framework of the existing law. If a principal purpose of a trust is to procure a reversal of government policy or of particular administrative decisions of governmental authorities, does it constitute a trust for policital purposes falling within the spirit of Lord Parker's pronouncement? In my judgment it does. If a trust of this nature is to be executed in England, the court will ordinarily have no sufficient means of determining whether the desired reversal would be beneficial to the public, and in any event could not properly encroach on the functions of the executive, acting intra vires, by holding that it should be acting in some other manner. If it is a trust which is to be executed abroad, the court will not have sufficient means of satisfactorily judging, as a matter of evidence, whether the proposed reversal would be beneficial to the community in the relevant sense, after all its consequences, local and international, had been taken into account. It may be added that Lord Normand, in the *National Anti-Vivisection Society* case [1948] AC 31, specifically equated legislative change and changes by way of government administration in the present context. As he said, at p. 77:

"The society seems to me to proclaim that its purpose is a legislative change of policy toward scientific experiments on animals, the consummation of which will be an Act prohibiting all such experiments. I regard it as clear that a society professing these purposes is a political association and not a charity. If for legislative changes a change by means of government administration was substituted the result would be the same."

If the crucial test whether a trust is charitable formulated by Lord Simonds in the same case, at p. 62 – namely, the competence of the court to control and reform it – is applied, I think one is again driven to the conclusion that trusts of the nature now under discussion, which are to be executed abroad, cannot qualify as charities any more than if they are to be executed in this country. The court, in considering whether particular methods of carrying out or reforming them would be for the public benefit, would be faced with an inescapable dilemma, of which a hypothetical example may be given. It appears from the Amnesty International Report 1978, p. 270, that Islamic law sanctions the death penalty for certain well-defined offences, namely, murder, adultery and brigandage. Let it be supposed that a trust were created of which the object was to secure the abolition of the death penalty for adultery in those countries where Islamic law applies, and to secure a reprieve for those persons who have been sentenced to death for this offence. The court, when invited to enforce or to reform such a trust, would either have to apply English standards as to public benefit, which would not necessarily be at all appropriate in the local conditions, or would have to attempt to apply local standards, of which it knew little or nothing. An English court would not, it seems to me, be competent either to control or reform a trust of this nature, and it would not be appropriate that it should attempt to do so.

Summary of conclusions relating to trusts for political purposes
    Founding them principally on the House of Lords decisions in the *Bowman* case [1917] AC 406 and the *National Anti-Vivisection Society* case [1948] AC 31, I therefore summarise my conclusions in relation to trusts for political purposes as follows. (1) Even if it otherwise appears to fall within the spirit and intendment of the preamble to the Statute of Elizabeth, a trust for political purposes falling within the spirit of Lord Parker's pronouncement in *Bowman's* case can never be regarded as being for the public benefit in the manner which the law regards as charitable. (2) Trusts for political purposes falling within the spirit of this pronouncement include, inter alia, trusts of which a direct and principal purpose is either (i) to further the interests of a particular political party; or (ii) to procure changes in the laws of this country; or (iii) to procure changes in the laws of a foreign country; or (iv) to procure a reversal of government policy or of particular decisions of governmental authorities in this country; or (v) to procure a reversal of government policy or of particular decisions of governmental authorities in a foreign country.
    This categorisation is not intended to be an exhaustive one, but I think it

will suffice for the purposes of this judgment; I would further emphasise that it is directed to trusts of which the *purposes* are political. As will appear later, the mere fact that trustees may be at liberty to employ political *means* in furthering the non- political purposes of a trust does not necessarily render it non-charitable.

The requirement that trust purposes must be wholly and exclusively charitable
The third requirement for a valid charitable trust is that each and every object or purpose designated must be of a charitable nature. Otherwise, there are no means of discriminating what part of the trust property is intended for charitable purposes and what part for non-charitable purposes, and the uncertainty in this respect invalidates the whole trust.

Nevertheless, in any case where it is asserted that a trust is non-charitable on the ground that it introduces non-charitable as well as charitable purposes, a distinction of critical importance has to be drawn between (a) the designated purposes of the trust; (b) the designated means of carrying out those purposes; and (c) the consequences of carrying them out. Trust purposes of an otherwise charitable nature do not lose it merely because, as an incidental consequence of the trustees' activities there may enure to private individuals benefits of a non-charitable nature. Thus, for example, in *Incorporated Council of Law Reporting for England and Wales v. Attorney-General* [1972] Ch 73 the Court of Appeal rejected contentions that the Council of Law Reporting was a non-charitable body merely because publication of The Law Reports supplied members of the legal profession with the tools of their trade: see at p. 87E, *per* Russell L.J.

Similarly, trust purposes of an otherwise charitable nature, do not lose it merely because the trustees, by way of furtherance of such purposes, have incidental powers to carry on activities which are not themselves charitable. In *In re Hood* [1931] 1 Ch 240, 241, a testator by his will, after certain recitals, directed that his residuary estate should be applied "in spreading the Christian principles before mentioned and in aiding all active steps to minimise and extinguish the drink traffic." If regard had been paid solely to the grammatical form of the gift, it might therefore have been held that the reference to minimising and extinguishing the drink traffic was an independent additional object in itself. Having regard to the recitals to the gift, however, the Court of Appeal found that, on its true construction, the main object of the bequest was the application of Christian principles to all human relationships, and thereby to spread such principles, and that the reference to the drink traffic was not an independent additional object but was merely introduced by the testator as pointing out one of the ways by which his main object could be obtained: see at p. 252, *per* Lawrence L.J, and at p. 253, *per* Romer L.J. On this basis, as one of the two alternative grounds for the decision, the court held that the main purpose was a valid charitable purpose. As Lawrence L.J. said, at p. 252:

"That main purpose being charitable, it seems to me that it is none the less good because the testator has pointed out one of the means by which in his opinion that main object could best be obtained, which in itself might not have been charitable if it had stood alone."

The distinction is thus one between (a) those non-charitable activities authorised by the trust instrument which are merely subsidiary or incidental to a charitable purpose, and (b) those non-charitable activities so authorised which in themselves form part of the trust purpose. In the latter but not the former case, the reference to non-charitable activities will deprive the trust of its charitable status. The distinction is perhaps easier to state than to apply in practice. It was actively canvassed in the *National Anti-Vivisection Society* case [1948] AC 31. The society's counsel submitted, at pp. 36-37:

"So far as the society is seeking to alter the law its object is to secure the abolition of vivisection; the ultimate object is charitable and the incidental political means to be adopted do not vitiate it."

The House of Lords seems to have accepted that the object of the society could have been a charitable one if, on a true analysis, this was to secure the abolition of vivisection and if legislation was merely to be regarded as ancillary to the attainment of this object: see, for example, at p. 61 *per* Lord Simonds and at p. 77 *per* Lord Normand.

The difference of opinion between the majority of the House and Lord Porter, who dissented, centred on the question whether an alteration in the law should itself be regarded as being a main object of the trust. Lord Porter thought it should not. He referred to the illustration given by Lord Parker in *Bowman's* case [1917] AC 406 of the political matters which he had in mind. Lord Porter continued 11948] AC 31, 54-55:

"The object in each case is to do away with a positive injunction to which an end can only be put by repealing the law; an Act of Parliament is required in order to do so. An example may be taken from the first illustration given by Lord Parker. No agreement come to by individuals or groups could dispense with the obligation of complying with the provisions of the Test Acts, whereas slavery or vivisection could be put an end to without disobedience to the law if all members of the community could be induced to desist from these practices. It is in the narrower sense in which I think the phrase 'purely political objects' is rightly used, i.e., as applicable to objects whose only means of attainment is a change in the law."

A little later Lord Porter said, at p. 55:

"Their primary object, as I see it, is to prevent animal suffering caused by vivisection, though a main method of effecting that end is to repeal the present Act and such repeal is in that sense a main object of the society."

The rest of their Lordships took a view different from that of Lord Porter, on this point. Lord Simonds dealt with it thus, at p. 61:

"... I cannot agree that in this case an alteration in the law is merely ancillary to the attainment of a good charitable object. In a sense no doubt, since legislation is not an end in itself, every law may be regarded as ancillary to the object which its provisions are intended to achieve. But that is not the sense in which it is said that a society has a political object. Here the finding of the commissioners is itself conclusive. 'We are satisfied,' they say, ' that the main object of the society is the total abolition of vivisection . . . and (for that purpose) the repeal of the Cruelty to Animals Act 1876, and the substitution of a new enactment prohibiting vivisection altogether.' This is a finding that the main purpose of the society is the abolition of vivisection by Act of Parliament. What else can it mean? And how else can it be supposed that vivisection is to be abolished? Abolition and suppression are words that connote some form of compulsion. It can only be by Act of Parliament that that element can be supplied."

Thus Lord Simonds reached the conclusion, at p. 62, that ". . . it is a main object, if not the main object, of the society, to obtain an alteration of the law." Lord Normand, at pp. 76-77, formulated the question:

"The problem is therefore to discover the general purposes of the society and whether they are in the main political or in the main charitable. It is a question of degree of a sort well known to the courts."

In *In re Bushnell, decd.* [1975] 1 WLR 1596, 1604, Goulding J. observed that a test propounded in such general terms is easier to state than to apply. Earlier in his judgment, at p. 1603, he had pointed out that the existence of some political motive is not necessarily fatal to a good charitable trust. In that case the trust in question was, in effect, one to further knowledge of the application of socialised medicine to public and personal health in a socialised state. Ultimately, applying Lord Normand's test, Goulding J., at p. 1605, concluded that its main or dominant or essential object was a political one and that it did not constitute a valid charitable trust.

From all these authorities, I think that two propositions follow in the present case. First, if any one of the main objects of the trusts declared by the trust deed is to be regarded as "political," in the relevant sense then, subject to the effect of the proviso to clause 2, the trusts of the trust deed cannot qualify as being charitable. Secondly, however, if all the main objects of the trust are exclusively charitable, the mere fact that the trustees may have incidental powers to employ political means for their furtherance will not deprive them of their charitable status."

. . . .

"Conclusion

In eloquent passages at the end of their addresses, Mr. Knox and Mr. Hoffmann made reference to the classic problem facing Antigone, who believed that there are certain laws of men which a higher law may require them to disregard. Mr. Hoffmann, by reference to the various international conventions, to which this country has been a party, submitted that it is committed to the elimination of unjust laws and action wherever these may exist or occur throughout the world.

Indisputably, laws do exist both in this country and in many foreign countries which many reasonable persons consider unjust. No less indisputably, laws themselves will from time to time be administered by governmental authorities in a manner which many reasonable persons consider unjust, inhuman or degrading. Amnesty International, striving to remedy what it considers to be such injustices, is performing a function which many will regard as being of great value to humanity. Fortunately, the laws of this country place very few restrictions on the rights of philanthropic organisations such as this, or of individuals, to strive for the remedy of what they regard as instances of injustice, whether occurring here or abroad. However, for reasons which I think adequately appear from Lord Parker of Waddington's pronouncement in *Bowman's* case [1917] AC 406, the elimination of injustice has not as such ever been held to be a trust purpose which qualifies for the privileges afforded to charities by English law. I cannot hold it to be a charitable purpose now.

For all these reasons, I must decline to make the declaration by the originating summons, namely, that the trust constituted by the trust deed ought to be registered as a charity."

CY-PRÈS JURISDICTION

Introduction

The *cy-près* doctrine allows for the making of a scheme for the application of property for other charitable purposes as near as possible to those intended by the donor in circumstances where it has become impossible or impracticable to give effect to the intentions of the donor in the precise terms which he intended. As a prerequisite to the exercise of *cy-près* jurisdiction, a court must satisfy itself that the purpose for which the bequest was originally made was charitable.[34]

In practice, a distinction must be drawn between circumstances where a gift fails *ab initio*, in which case the property can only be applied *cy-près* where the donor has manifested a general charitable intention, and cases of subsequent failure, where it is not necessary to show such an intention provided that the donor has made an absolute and perpetual gift to a particular charity. This distinction is usefully summarised by Murray J in *Re Dunwoodie*[35] in which he displayed a fairly flexible approach towards the concept of general

---

[34] *Re Worth Library* [1995] 2 IR 301. However, note that in *Representative Church Body v. Attorney General* [1988] IR 19, O'Hanlon J made a *cy-près* order in relation to a collection of books in a Cathedral Library without raising the question of the charitable nature of the bequest.

[35] [1977] NI 141.

charitable intention in contrast to the more restrictive attitude displayed by MacKenzie J in *Re Prescott.*[36] As the decisions in *Re Royal Hospital Kilmainham*[37] and *Re Worth Library*[38] confirm, in cases of subsequent failure it is not necessary to establish general charitable intention on the part of the donor provided there is evidence of an absolute and perpetual gift to charity.

Re Dunwoodie: Northern Bank Executor and Trustee Co. Ltd v. Moss
[1977] NI 141

The testatrix bequeathed the residue of her estate on trust for a particular Presbyterian Church with a direction that the bequest should be used for the installation of bells at that church. The committee of the church decided not to install the bells and the question arose whether the residuary bequest should devolve as on an intestacy or be applied *cy-près*. Murray J held that the testatrix had shown a general intention to further the general purposes of the particular church and that the property should be applied *cy-près*.

MURRAY J stated at pp. 144–148: "On the facts of the case it is now clear that the carrying out of the trust for the bells is impossible. The committee, in exercise of its undoubted powers over the fabric of McCracken Memorial Church, has firmly and finally resolved that bells are not to be installed in the church; and that decision has the backing of the majority of the congregation – albeit the narrowest possible one. In the very nature of things, therefore, there can be no question in this case of the Court appointing some other trustees to carry out the trust in place of the original trustees chosen by the testatrix. The decision of the committee not to have bells in the church has effectively put an end to the testatrix's plan for this.

As I read the minutes of the Congregation Meeting the main reason for the decision taken at the meeting was the view that, with all due respect to the wishes of the testatrix, the spending in this day and age of a sum of money running into thousands of pounds to put a carillon of bells into a Belfast church, when so many other and more deserving causes are crying out for financial support, is not an acceptable use of money. I see no reason whatever to doubt that this decision was the result of deep and conscientious consideration by those who attended the meeting and, in particular, by those who also served on the committee, and I fully accept that there is today among responsible people a division of opinion as to the ethics of putting charitably donated money into the building or adornment of churches in areas of this country already well served with churches. On one point, however, I feel that the decision taken is

---

[36] [1990] 2 IR 342.
[37] [1966] IR 451.
[38] [1995] 2 IR 301.

open to some question. Mr. Moss, in addressing the Congregation Meeting, appears to have assumed that it was necessary to spend £15,000 to carry out the wishes of the testatrix, but, as I have already pointed out, the will gave the committee a complete discretion as to the nature and size of the installation and I imagine that it would have been possible for the expert bell manufacturers (if asked to do so) to have devised a much smaller and less costly carillon than the 25-bell project apparently envisaged by Mr. Moss. However, the committee appears to have taken up its final stand in the matter and I must accept that it has set its fate resolutely against any re-opening of it. I must also, and do, respect their decision taken after long and deep consideration of the issues involved.

On the basis that the bells trust is now impossible of fulfilment the next question is what is to happen to the property bequeathed by the testatrix for the purposes of the trust. Does it, as part of a residuary gift which has failed, go to the next-of-kin as on intestacy, or should the Court decree its application cy-près?

There is an important difference between a charitable trust which is initially impossible or impracticable, i.e. impossible or impracticable as at the death of the testator, and a charitable trust which becomes impossible or impracticable after his death. As regards the former type, the property involved will not be applied cy-près unless the Court finds that the testator had a general charitable intention, but as regards the latter type – usually referred to as the case of supervening impossibility – the Court will direct a cy-près application whether or not a general charitable intention on the part of the testator can be found in the relevant will: *In re Lysaght deceased* [1966] 1 Ch 191. On the particular point I am now dealing with I refer to the following passage from the judgment of Buckley J. (as he then was) in that case:

> "Since *In re Robinson* [1923] 2 Ch 332, was decided it has been recognised that different considerations govern the application of the cy-près doctrine when impracticability supervenes after a charitable trust has once taken effect from those which apply in cases of initial impracticability. In cases of supervening impracticability it matters not whether the original donor had or had not a general charitable intention (see *In re Wright* [1954] Ch 347)" (p. 208).

The same principle is also discussed in *In re Wright* [1954] Ch 347 and in particular in the following words in the judgment of Romer L.J.:

> "Once money is effectually dedicated to charity, whether in pursuance of a general or a particular charitable intent, the testator's next of kin or residuary legatees are for ever excluded and no question of subsequent lapse, or of anything analogous to lapse, between the date of the testator's death and the time when the money becomes available for actual application to the testator's purpose can affect the matter so far as they are concerned " (pp. 362-363).

Is the present a case of initial or supervening impossibility? I think it is the former. So far as the trust for the bells is concerned it is clear that if the matter is looked at as at the death of the testatrix the trust would be practicable if, but only if, the committee agreed to the installation of the bells. They never agreed to such installation, and, after much delay, they finally said (as we now know) "No bells." Accordingly, the trust never was practicable and I hold this to be a case of initial impracticability or impossibility. In so holding I am in principle following a relevant part of the decision of Buckley J. (as he then was) in *In re Lysaght deceased* cited above. In that case the charitable gift was to establish certain medical studentships at the Royal College of Surgeons in London and it was clear that the trust would only be practicable if the College was willing to permit, and operate, the studentship scheme. The testator attached certain conditions to the scheme including a condition excluding from benefit a student who was a Jew or Roman Catholic. In correspondence following the notification of the gift for the studentships the proposed trustees' solicitors said that the College could not accept or operate the scheme with this condition attached since it was so invidious and alien to the College's work as to make the gift inoperable. In the result the learned judge struck out the offending condition, but for the purposes of this judgment the relevant fact is that he treated the case as one of initial, not supervening, impracticability. His actual words on the point are these:

> "In the present case, if the trust is impracticable, this is due to initial difficulty, not to any change of circumstances" (p. 208).

In this case therefore the crucial question is whether or not the testatrix in setting up the bells trust had a general charitable intention. There is a great deal of reading in the cases on this topic but I personally find the way it is explained by Parker J. in *In re Wilson* [1913] 1 Ch 314 the most helpful. The relevant passage is at the beginning of the judgment and is as follows:

> "For the purposes of this case I think the authorities must be divided into two classes. First of all, we have a class of cases where, in form, the gift is given for a particular charitable purpose, but it is possible, taking the will as a whole, to say that, notwithstanding the form of the gift, the paramount intention, according to the true construction of the will, is to give the property in the first instance for a general charitable purpose rather than a particular charitable purpose, and to graft on to the general gift a direction as to the desires or intentions of the testator as to the manner in which the general gift is to be carried into effect. In that case, though it is impossible to carry out the precise directions, on ordinary principles the gift for the general charitable purposes will remain and be perfectly good, and the Court, by virtue of its administrative jurisdiction, can direct a scheme as to how it is to be carried out. In fact the will will be read as though the particular direction had not been in the will at all, but there had been simply a general direction as to the application of the fund for the general charitable purpose in question.
>
> Then there is the second class of cases, where, on the true construction of the will, no such paramount general intention can be inferred, and where the gift, being in form a particular gift – a gift for a particular purpose – and it

being impossible to carry out that particular purpose, the whole gift is held to fail. In my opinion, the question whether a particular case falls within one of those classes of cases or within the other is simply a question of the construction of a particular instrument" (p. 320-1).

Looking at the bells trust in the light of Parker J.'s judgment I have no hesitation in saying that it falls within his first class. In the first place, the testatrix begins by making the Residuary Bequest to the plaintiffs upon a general trust for the committee. She then grafts on to this the bells trust: but she finally directs that any surplus of the Residuary Bequest not required for the bells trust is to be invested and the income applied to such general Church purposes as the Committee may in its absolute discretion think fit. I think it quite clear (a) that the testatrix had a general intention to further the general purposes of McCracken Memorial Church, i.e. to advance religion through the work of that particular church; (b) that in addition she had a particular intention to set up the bells trust in connection with that church; and (c) that the initial failure of the particular bells trust in no way invalidates the general trust for that church which remains perfectly good. In my view therefore an order for a cy-près scheme is the proper one in this case, and since the testatrix contemplated that, if necessary, the whole Residuary Bequest should be applied to the bells trust – which in the event has failed – I will direct the plaintiffs to bring in a scheme for the whole £18,000 or £20,000 or whatever the amount in the Residuary Bequest may be. I hope the Committee will co-operate in devising a scheme for the use of this substantial fund which will be linked in some appropriate way with the McCracken Church and which will command the support of the members in general of that church; but if there should be any difficulty about this I would if necessary widen the scope of the scheme to embrace a purpose or purposes of the Presbyterian Church as a whole. Since the testatrix expressly mentions her mother and sister in connection with the bells trust, I take it that her wish was to link her maiden name of "McCracken" with any trust which is set up. This point should therefore be borne in mind by the plaintiffs in bringing in their scheme.

Two final points: Mr. Paul Girvan for the plaintiffs raised an issue as to a possible lack of certainty in the property devoted to the bells trust and referred me to the following passage in *Tudor on Charities.*

> ". . . the general rule applicable to English trusts is considered to be well settled and to be that, where part of the fund is directed to be applied for charitable purposes but the actual amount or the proportion to be so applied is not stated in the relevant instrument and no guidance is given as to how its amount or proportion is to be ascertained, the attempted charitable trust is void for uncertainty" (6th ed., pp. 133-134).

In my view there is nothing in this point. The testatrix in the will made it clear that the Committee had power to use " all or any part" of the Residuary Bequest for the bells trust at their discretion, and accordingly there was no uncertainty.

The other point is this. In the course of argument I suggested that this case might come under section 22 (1) (e) (iii) of the Charities Act (Northern Ireland) 1964. On considering the matter further I have reached the conclusion that this is not the case. That section appears to deal with a situation in which, owing to a change in circumstances since the original gift was made, the intention underlying the gift would not be served by allowing it to take effect in its original form: *In re Lepton's Charity* [1972] 1 Ch 276. This is not the case as regards a bells trust.

In the result I answer the questions as follows:

(a) No.

(b) No.

(c) Yes.

I will direct the plaintiffs to bring in a scheme and I will also make the representation orders asked for at paragraphs 7 and 8 of the Summons."

Re Prescott: Purcell v. Pobjoy
[1990] 2 IR 342

The testatrix bequeathed her house to a Dublin parish of the 'Russian Orthodox Church abroad' and directed that if there were no parishioners or members of that church living in Ireland that it should be sold and the proceeds applied for the general purposes of the said church in England. At the time of the testatrix's death, the parish had ceased to exist and the executor applied to the court for directions as to the manner in which the proceeds of the sale of the house were to be distributed. MacKenzie J held that the gift of the house had lapsed as it was to a body which did not exist either at the time of making the will or at the death of the testatrix and the gift over being dependent on the validity of this gift also lapsed. He further held that there was no evidence of general charitable intention and that the doctrine of *cy-près* could not be applied.

MACKENZIE J stated at pp. 344–347: "The plaintiff in these proceedings is the executor of Mrs. Lydia Prescott who died on the 26th September, 1987. He asks the court to determine questions arising out of the administration of the estate of the said deceased and questions arising on the construction of her will. The said will was dated the 15th August, 1985. She resided in a house known as San Mario, Brookvale Road, Donnybrook, Dublin. The relevant part of the will is as follows:-

"I devise and bequeath my house San Mario aforesaid unto the Holy Protection Parish Dublin of the Russian Orthodox Church abroad under the jurisdiction of Metropolitan Vhilaret and the Sinod of Bishops of 73 93rd Street New York 10028 U.S.A.

I direct that my said house shall be used as a residence for clergy of the said Russian Orthodox Church abroad in Ireland excluding Constance Nicholas even if he become a priest and should only be sold if and when there are no parishioners or members of the said church living in Ireland. I also direct that in the event of any such sale the proceeds shall be applied for the general purpose of the said Russian Orthodox Church abroad in England."

The evidence disclosed that the Russian Orthodox Church in exile established a parish in Dublin to care pastorally for the Russian exiles settled in that city.

The resident priest died in 1977. The numbers of those faithful to the church dwindled and in 1983 the bishop of the diocese informed the community that they could no longer be regarded as a parish, rather they were to be an "obschima", the Russian word for a community where services are available for the faithful without full parochial status. The defendant, Fr. Alexis, said that there were now three members of the community, two very elderly Russians and the second defendant, Mr. MacEoghan. There would appear however to be a few others of which he was not cognisant but he said there was no other person in the community in Ireland. This information had been supplied by Fr. Alexis in a letter dated the 22nd February, 1988, to Mr. George Crawford, solicitor for the estate. Fr. Alexis however somewhat revised his opinion in giving evidence. In his view a parish centered around the priest and church building but in Dublin there is no priest or church, dues are not paid, no decrees are made nor instructions given nor do church records exist. Fr. Alexis produced the synod year book for 1989 and referred to an entry which gave Mr. MacEoghan's name and address and telephone number. The word community was used there. Fr. Alexis said he came to Dublin four times a year. The members of the church would collect money together to pay his expenses when he was required. I am sure he is convinced of this but I find it hard to believe that his visits are so frequent.

The evidence has been noted and it is unnecessary to review it in great detail. On the facts however I must hold that at the time the testator made her will in 1985 and at the time of her death and at present the Holy Protection Parish in Dublin of the Russian Orthodox Church abroad had ceased to exist. Obviously this presented a grave dilemma to the executor and most appropriately he applied to the court and with the consent of everyone concerned the house was sold and the proceeds retained. To answer the questions arising here one must assume that the house is still in existence. The testatrix decided it was to be used as a residence for clergy of the church in Ireland and it should be sold only if and when there were no parishoners or members of the said church in Ireland. In other words had all parties not sensibly agreed to the sale, the house would now be standing empty without a priest and would still be there and for who can say how long until there were no members of the church living in Ireland? The mind of God can only direct how long that would be. Counsel for the Attorney General informed me that there were present in court at least two other members of the church and they were identified; they were by no means elderly. I did not require their evidence, their presence confirms my opinion as to the uncertainty of the vesting of the gift (if it does vest) in the church. There is therefore no right in the executors to part with the proceeds of the sale. When they can do so is completely uncertain.

Mr. Geoghegan appearing for the residuary legatee submitted that as the parish had ceased to exist the gift therefore lapses and falls into residue.The gift he argues is either one to an institution or a purpose gift. He concedes that it is the former and he is right. The testator gave her house for a particular purpose which failed, continued Mr. Geoghegan. A new will therefore cannot be made for the testator. Knowing full well the situation she made a specific direction permitting the proceeds to go to England only if and when no members of the church were left. I think Mr. Geoghegan was right in a suggestion that this was her way of bringing a clergyman or priest back to Ireland, but in deciding the questions to be answered one should not be permitted to rely on this sort of speculation. The specified purpose however is not now practical. Mr. Geoghegan further submitted that no general charitable intent could be inferred from the will and he relied on the line of cases commencing with *In re Harwood; Coleman v. Innes* [1936] 1 Ch 285 and culminating in *In re Spence decd.; Ogden v. Shackleton* [1979] Ch 483.

Miss Laffoy for Fr. Alexis and the church said that the gift was for the parish for the particular purpose of providing a residence. If the parish had ceased to exist nevertheless it should be construed as synonymous with the community which was undoubtedly still their parish. She said it may have lost its status as a parish canonical but it was nevertheless a parish. She said that where the first gift had ceased to take effect thereafter the second gift of the proceeds of sale must then take effect. A misnomer she says does not affect the gift, citing *In re King; King v. Long* (1919) 53 ILTR 60. The evidence to my mind does not support this contention because the testatrix refused to face the reality of the situation when she made her will. Miss Laffoy also cited *In re Bonnet decd.; Johnston v. Langheld* [1983] ILRM 359. That case does not seem to help the problem here. It dealt with the question of general charitable intention of a gift to the Lutheran Church where the question was whether the gift was to the Lutheran Church or the Protestant Church in general. The testator in that case was a member of the Lutheran Church, the court deciding that that was the institution she desired to benefit. It was argued therefore that the court should go to lengths to implement the wishes of the testator. She relied also on *Duffy v. Doyle* (Unreported, High Court, McWilliam J., 9th May, 1979) where a gift to the parish of Bray that was uncertain as to the objects of the gift was held to be charitable and did not fail for uncertainty or pass on intestacy to the widow of the deceased.

In the present case there is uncertainty as to whether (a) there is a parish and (b) the gift to the church abroad can take effect when and if ever. Miss Laffoy submits that even if the testatrix' directions cannot be carried out and even if the gift to the parish lapses it should not fall into residue and she refers to s. 91 of the Succession Act, 1965.

It is my view that the parish certainly existed up to the death of Fr. Currias in 1966. At the date of the will and at the date of the death it is against reason to hold that the Russian Orthodox Church abroad were anything other than a community, priestless, without a church, without records, dues and very infrequent communications with clergy, no record of meetings, no meetings and most infrequent services. There was no parish if the house was not only for the benefit of the priest who would reside there but for the benefit of the congregation. The testatrix I believed hoped the community would regain the status of a parish sometime. I see no practical way within law of carrying out the intentions of Mrs. Prescott. In my opinion the gift lapses because it was a gift to a body which did not exist either at the date of the will or at the death of the testatrix.

The gift over being dependent on the validity of the bequest to the parish in my view also lapses and is also further void for uncertainty. Counsel for the Attorney General and Miss Laffoy urge that I should find a general charitable intent and apply the doctrine of cy-près. There may be cases of a single gift where the court can find in the mind of the testator a general charitable intention as in *Biscoe v. Jackson* (1887) 35 Ch D 460 where there was a general intention found in a bequest to the poor of a parish and as in *Duffy v. Doyle* (Unreported, High Court, McWilliam J., 9th May, 1979) where there was no indication that the testator had any other intention than to benefit the recipient but here however the recipient did not exist at the time of the will and death.

I answer the queries as follows as required in the special summons:
   (a) the proceeds vest in the residuary legatee;
   (b) the devise lapses;
   (c) the devise lapses;
   (d) void and of no effect;
   (e) see answers to (a), (b), (c), (d). The direction is void as uncertain and impossible and impracticable.
   (f) the proceeds cannot be applied for the general purposes of the Russian Orthodox Church abroad in England.
   (g) does not arise.
   Paragraph 2 need not therefore be uncertain."

Re Royal Kilmainham Hospital: Attorney General v. British Legion
[1966] IR 451

A hospital founded by Charles II in 1684 for the support and maintenance of old soldiers of his army and those of his successors gradually ceased to function after the setting up of the Irish Free State and the Irish government took over control of the lands and buildings. In 1961, the Royal Kilmainham Hospital Act was passed which provided, *inter alia*, for the settling of a scheme for some specified charitable purpose or purposes for the benefit of some classes of members of the defence forces. It was held by Budd J that the available funds should be applied *cy-près* and he directed that they should be used to benefit certain classes of former members of the Defence Forces and the British Army.

BUDD J stated at pp. 468–469 and 482–489: "A number of questions of no little difficulty arose on the contentions put forward by the parties, which I will only outline at the moment. The first was whether the foundation of the Hospital in the sense of the granting of lands to it by Charles II constituted a valid charitable trust in favour of a class of persons who may be briefly described as maimed and infirm officers and soldiers of the Army in Ireland of King Charles II and his successors. Mr. Matheson, for the respondents, submitted that it did. Consequently, he said, the funds in question remained impressed with a valid subsisting trust and that some members of the classes he represented answered the description of beneficiaries and should be held entitled as such to the benefit of the funds in that they are ex-members of the Army of Charles the Second's royal successor. If they were not entitled as *cestuis que trustent* owing to the failure of the charitable trust for any reason, then, he contended, they were the proper persons to designate as beneficiaries under a *cy-près* application of the funds. Counsel for the Attorney General submitted that the foundation of the Hospital was an executive act of the Crown in its executive capacity and that no valid charitable trust ensued. Such trust as was created had come to an end on the dissolution of the Corporation so that the trust funds had reverted to the State as successors of the Crown, and were now at the disposal of the Legislature, which had under the Act of 1962 designated objects for whose benefit the funds should be applied under a scheme to be settled by the Court. Alternatively, it was submitted, that even if a valid charitable trust was created by the endowment of the Hospital it was so created by virtue of a Crown grant and that by reason thereof the trust property would, on the dissolution of the Corporation, likewise revert to the State as the successor of the Crown and was again capable of disposal by the Legislature. In the further alternative, assuming a valid charitable trust to have been created and that there was no reverter, it was submitted that it had not failed as to objects since some classes of members or former members of the Defence Forces answered literally the description of the object class in the changed political circumstances as being soldiers of the Army of Ireland, and, if otherwise qualified as charitable objects, were entitled to benefit. If, on the other hand, the charitable trust had wholly failed then it was contended that the same classes ought to be the proper objects of any *cy-près* application of the funds. It is thus necessary to determine whether or not a valid charitable trust was constituted on the foundation of the Hospital by virtue of the gift of the lands to it and then, if so, whether the charitable trust has failed and, if it has, should the funds be applied *cy-près*.

The law requires that if a charity can be administered according to the directions of the founder it should be so administered. When it is established that a gift has been made with a general intention of charity and a failure of purposes ensues it is not allowed to fail but will be carried out *cy-près*. Likewise, where there is an absolute perpetual gift to a charity, even though the trusts be only for the accomplishment of a particular charitable purpose, the same results ensue. The principle is applied where the method indicated by the donor of carrying out his charitable intention becomes impracticable, or his intentions cannot be executed literally, most frequently owing to altered circumstances.

Trusts for charitable purposes in the legal sense include trusts for the relief of aged, impotent and poor persons and such objects as are analogous thereto, and there can be little doubt that a trust for the relief of poor, aged, maimed and infirm officers and soldiers would ordinarily be regarded as a valid charitable gift. The *cy-près* principle is confined, however, to cases where property is given with a general intention to charity with this exception, that where property is given absolutely and perpetually to charity for a particular purpose and has vested in the charity the fund can be applied *cy-près* irrespective of the donor's particular intention. As to what is to be regarded as a general charitable intention, no hard and fast rule can be laid down. Courts have differed much as to what is sufficient to indicate such an intention. The test suggested by Kay J. in *Re Taylor; Martin v. Freeman* (1888) 58 LT (NS) 538, at p. 543, is one that carries great weight: ".... if upon the whole scope and intent of the will you discern the paramount intention of the testator was to benefit not a particular institution, but to effect a particular form of charity independently of any special institution or mode, then . . . . . if the particular mode for any reason fails, the Court, if it sees a sufficient expression of a general intention of charity, will, to use the phrase familiar to us, execute that *cy-près* . . . ." The question as to whether the form of a gift indicates a general intention of charity depends upon the construction of the document by which the gift is given."

. . . .

"It is clear that administration *cy-près* of some sort is called for, in that at present there exists no means of administering the trust. The only matter requiring particular attention is the existence of this ever-decreasing class whose members appear to be in the position of establishing that they sufficiently answer the description of the object class, so that there has not been a complete failure of the original purposes of the charitable gift. Whatever difficulty there might have been in ordering the application of the funds *cy-près* owing to the existence of this pre-1922 class has however been removed by the provisions of s. 47 of the Charities Act, 1961. As pointed out, in Delany's "Law relating to Charities in Ireland," that section specified certain circumstances, short of an absolute failure of the trust, which are required to exist before the purposes of a charity can be altered and an order made directing a *cy-près* application. In as much as sub-s. 2 provides that the provisions of sub-s. 1 shall not affect the conditions which must be satisfied in order that property given for charitable purposes may be applied *cy-près* except in so far as those conditions require a failure of the original purposes, I have only to point out that I have already found that the conditions which must be satisfied exist, in that the gift was made in pursuance of a general charitable intention and was made out-and-out.

The relevant provisons of the section are contained in sub-s. 1, paras. (*a*) (ii) and (*e*) (iii):-

> "(1) Subject to sub-section (2), the circumstances in which the original purposes of a charitable gift may be altered to allow the property given or part of it to be applied *cy-près* shall be as follows:–
>
> (*a*) where the original purposes, in whole or in part . . . .
>
>> (ii) cannot be carried out, or cannot be carried out according to the directions given and to the spirit of the gift;"
>
> "(*e*) Where the original purposes, in whole or in part, have, since they were laid down . . . .
>
>> (iii) ceased in any other way to provide a suitable and effective method of using the property available by virtue of the gift, regard being had to the spirit of the gift."

The sub-section applies to the circumstances of this case. In the first place the original purposes of the gift cannot be carried out according to the directions given and the spirit of the gift in that the mode of carrying out the purposes through the Hospital and its corporate organisation is gone. Furthermore, the original purposes have in part at least ceased to provide a suitable and effective method of using the property now available by virtue of the fact that there is now no royal army pertaining to the whole of Ireland from whom the object class can derive now or in the future.

The fact that a vanishing remnant still survives of those that could be said to form the object class does not in my view lead to a conclusion that the original purposes provide in whole a suitable and effective method of using the property in that the continuous admission of qualified persons to the benefits of the Hospital was part of the original purposes according to the spirit of the gift. The whole matter is moreover thrown open when an application *cy-près* is directed and the position of this class can be adequately provided for in the scheme by according some particular and appropriate consideration to it. It would be quite possible to frame the scheme in favour of what I have termed the pre-1922 class alone and then to have a further scheme later when it had died out. But it would be quite illusory to have a scheme operating for so short a time and quite unnecessary to throw the expense of a further hearing and a resettlement of the scheme on a comparatively small fund.

Having regard to my findings, therefore, the application in so far as contained in para. 1(b) of the originating summary summons, must be refused and the proper course to follow in my view is to grant the alternative relief sought in para. 2 thereof, by ordering that the funds in question should be applied *cy-près* and for that purpose that a scheme for the management and application of the trust funds be prepared by the Examiner to be settled by the Court."

Legislative Reform of the Cy-près Doctrine

At common law this jurisdiction could only be exercised where it was impossible or impracticable to give effect to the wishes of a donor in the precise terms which he intended. However, s.47 of the Irish Charities Act 1961 now lays down much broader parameters for the exercise of this jurisdiction, allowing a *cy-près* order to be made in circumstances where there were difficulties in implementing the original terms or where more effective use might be made of the trust property by framing an alternative scheme, using the property available.

S.47 of the Charities Act 1961:

47.–(1) Subject to subsection (2), the circumstances in which the original purposes of a charitable gift may be altered to allow the property given or part of it to be applied *cy-près* shall be as follows:

    (a) where the original purposes, in whole or in part–
        (i) have been as far as may be fulfilled; or
        (ii) cannot be carried out, or cannot be carried out according to the directions given and to the spirit of the gift; or
    (b) where the original purposes provide a use for part only of the property available by virtue of the gift; or
    (c) where the property available by virtue of the gift and other property applicable for similar purposes can be more effectively used in conjunction, and to that end can suitably, regard being had to the spirit of the gift, be made applicable to common purposes; or
    (d) where the original purposes were laid down by reference to an area which then was but has since ceased to be a unit for some other purpose, or by reference to a class of persons or to an area which has for any reason since ceased, either to be suitable, regard being had to the spirit of the gift, or to be practical in administering the gift; or
    (e) where the original purposes, in whole or in part, have, since they were laid down–
        (i) been adequately provided for by other means; or
        (ii) ceased, as being useless or harmful to the community or for other reasons, to be in law charitable; or
        (iii) ceased in any other way to provide a suitable and effective method of using the property available by virtue of the gift, regard being had to the spirit of the gift.

(2) Subsection (1) shall not affect the conditions which must be satisfied in order that property given for charitable purposes may be applied *cy-près*, except. in so far as those conditions require a failure of the original purposes.

(3) References in the foregoing subsections to the original purposes of a gift shall be construed, where the application of the property given has been altered or regulated by a scheme or otherwise, as referring to the purposes for which the property is for the time being applicable.

(4) It is hereby declared that a trust for charitable purposes places a trustee

under a duty, where the case permits and requires the property or some part of it to be applied *cy-près*, to secure its effective use for charity by taking steps to enable it to be so applied.

(5) This section shall apply to property given for charitable purposes, notwithstanding that it was so given before the commencement of this Act.

Representative Church Body v. Attorney General
[1988] IR 19

The plaintiff sought a *cy-près* order under s.47 authorising the sale of a collection of books kept in the Old Library attached to St Canice's Cathedral, Kilkenny and the application of the proceeds to the maintenance and repair of the cathedral. It was held by O'Hanlon J that the original purposes of the charitable gifts had ceased to provide a suitable or effective method of using the property available, regard being had to the spirit of the gift and he made an order authorizing the sale of the collection by the plaintiff so that the proceeds might be applied to the repair and maintenance of the cathedral.

O'HANLON J stated at pp. 20–22: "A library attached to St. Canice's Cathedral, Kilkenny, is divided into two sections. One section, called "the Old Library", contains books which were printed in earlier centuries. The other section, called "the New Library", contains books collected over the last 150 years or thereabouts. The plaintiff, the Representative Church Body, claims ownership of the entire collection under the provisions of the Irish Church Act, 1869, and wishes to sell the entire collection comprised in "the Old Library" and to apply the proceeds towards the maintenance and upkeep of the Cathedral, including the carrying out of repair works which are now urgently necessary. In these proceedings, in which the Attorney General is named as defendant, the plaintiff seeks a cy-près order under the provisions of the Charities Act, 1961, s. 47, authorising the sale of the books and the application of the proceeds of sale in the desired manner, notwithstanding the terms of two wills - that of Bishop Otway, who died prior to 1693, and that of Bishop Maurice, who died, apparently, in the latter half of the 18th century. Most of the books contained in "the Old Library" are made up of bequests under these two wills, and are affected by the trusts of the wills.

In the case of the will of Bishop Otway, neither the original nor any exact copy of the will can be located, but an abstract of the terms of the will which exists in the Office of Arms in Dublin Castle reads as follows:

"Gives books and £200 for library at St. Canice's, Kilkenny. Makes provision for fitting up of this library, including desks and shelves and chains for every particular book, partly out of £97.10.0 Shillings of Spanish and other foreign gold and old English gold in the hands of George Thornton (of Arran Key, Dublin)."

The bequest in the will, dated the 6th January, 1756, of Bishop Maurice reads as follows:

"I Edward Maurice Bishop of Ossory while I am of sound mind and memory leave my printed books to the library founded by Bishop Otway at Kilkenny all that are now at Dunmore as well as those that are at Kilkenny together with ten double cases of one form made of Dunsick oak now in my lib-rary at Dunmore, provided a fair catalogue be made of the books and security given by the Librarian to exhibit them once every year or oftener if occasion to two persons appointed by the Bishop, in his own presence if convenient, provided likewise that an oath be taken by the Librarian not to embezzle or deface or lend any book out of the library but to give due attendance to such clergymen and gentlemen as may be disposed to study there from six o'clock in the morning to the tolling of the bell for morning prayer at the Cathedral of St. Canice Kilkenny.

For his attendance and care of these books I bequeath to the Librarian and his successors, appointed by the Bishop, Twenty Pounds a year to be paid out of my estate at Milltown in the County of Kilkenny and if it shall happen that this legacy shall be found not to answer the purposes intended I impower the Bishop of Ossory for the time being with the consent of the Dean and Chapter of St. Canice to sell the books and apply their price together with the said salary of the Librarian towards raising or adorning the imperfect steeple of their Cathedral."

As to the other books donated from time to time to the library, no record exists of such donations or any of them having been made subject to any particular trusts.

An affidavit by the present Dean of Ossory, in support of the application, deposes that the books in the old library are no longer used at all either by the clergy or by members of the laity. Tourists or visitors sometimes ask to see the old library as a matter of historical or antiquarian interest. For many years past no librarian has been employed for the old or the new library; the stipend of twenty pounds per annum referred to in the will of Bishop Maurice has long since ceased to be paid, and the Bishop's Vicar for the time being has been acting as honorary librarian.

A further affidavit by David Young, architect, confirms that the Cathedral had fallen into a serious state of disrepair, entailing expenditure in excess of £300,000 for essential and urgent repairs and restorations. It is stated that "considerably more money would have to be spent on the Cathedral to carry out a full restoration of the Building." As of the 25th May, 1987, it was estimated that a sum of £269,568 was required (exclusive of VAT and professional fees) to carry out further urgent work over and above what had been completed in the 1983-1986 period. An appeal launched by the Chapter of the Cathedral had brought in approximately £230,000, towards the end of 1986, obviously leaving a huge gap to be bridged as it now appears that the total expenditure involved will exceed £500,000. If it were permissible to sell the books in the old library and apply the proceeds towards the restoration fund, it is estimated that a sum in the region of £90,000 might be realised.

The application is, however, opposed by the Attorney General, and an affidavit sworn by Muriel McCarthy, who is the person having responsibility for Marsh's Library at St. Patrick's Close, and Librarian of the Worth Library of Dr. Steeven's Hospital, has been filed on his behalf. Ms. McCarthy regards the collection of books in the old library of St. Canice's Cathedral (with which she is familiar) as an important cultural asset for Kilkenny and for Ireland, and she is apprehensive that, if put up for sale, they will leave the country as there is no effective legal restriction on the export of old books.

It appears to me that Bishop Otway and Bishop Maurice in donating their collections of books to St. Canice's Cathedral intended that a library in the true sense of the word would be established as an adjunct to the Cathedral, and that clergymen and lay persons would be able to make use of the books on a regular basis for purposes of scholarship. While the new library may still be used in this way, it seems clear that no such use has been made of the old library on any regular basis for very many years past, and that the books have simply become collector's items for antiquaries.

I further conclude that the original purposes of the charitable gift of the collections of books have ceased to provide a suitable and effective method of using the property available by virtue of the gift, regard being had to the spirit of the gift, and that in the circumstances of the present case it is permissible to alter the original purposes of the charitable gift (both in the case of the Bishop Otway bequest and the Bishop Maurice bequest) to allow the property given to be applied cy-près. Bishop Maurice himself contemplated that such a situation might arise and provided by his will that in such event the books might be sold and the proceeds applied towards the repair of the steeple of the Cathedral. The steeple in question was removed completely in the mid-19th century and no longer exists.

I do not find it necessary to settle an elaborate scheme for the purpose of giving effect to the doctrine of cy-près in this case, and instead I will merely make an order in the terms sought by the plaintiff, authorising the sale of the collection of books comprised in the old library, as identified in these proceedings, in whatever manner the plaintiff may be advised to effect such sale, and to apply the proceeds thereof towards the repair and maintenace of St. Canice's Cathedral, Kilkenny."

CHAPTER 11
Void and Voidable Trusts

INTRODUCTION

Where a trust is illegal or contrary to public policy, it is void, in other words, it is regarded as being invalid *ab initio* and never comes into effect. Alternatively, a trust may be voidable in which case it will remain in operation unless or until its validity is successfully challenged.

VOID TRUSTS

A trust may be void for various reasons e.g. because it offends the rules against perpetuities or inalienability[1] or because it may be contrary to public policy. An example of trusts in the latter category would be those which tend to interfere with parental duties and the effect of the decision of Dixon J in *Re Blake*[2] would seem to be that a gift made subject to a condition precedent which has such an effect will be void. However, it should be noted that Kenny J appears to have held subsequently in *Re Doyle*[3] that when a condition precedent attaches to a gift is in violation of the donees's constitutional rights, the latter may take the benefit of the gift without complying with the condition.

Re Blake: Lynch v. Lombard
[1955] IR 89

A testator bequeathed a legacy to trustees to apply the income towards the maintenance and education of his daughter's children provided they were brought up as Roman Catholics. It was held by Dixon J that the condition was void as being against the policy of the law, being an attempt to fetter the constitutional right and duty of parents to provide for the education of their children and that the gift failed.

DIXON J stated at pp.93–108: "The first question arising in this case is whether the conditions attached to the trusts in favour of the infant defendants (the

---

[1] *O'Byrne v. Davoren* [1994] 3 IR 373. See further *supra* Chapter 4, p.133.
[2] [1955] IR 89.
[3] High Court, 1972 (Kenny J). See Wylie, *Irish Land Law* (3rd ed., 1997) p.555.

children of the deceased's daughter, Mary Rosamund) in respect of the income and capital of the "trust legacy" of £6,000 bequeated by the will are void for uncertainty or as being contrary to public policy or for any other reason. This legacy was given by the will in these terms:– "I bequeath a sum of £6,000 to my trustees upon the trusts and with and subject to the powers and provisions hereinafter expressed that is to say my trustees shall invest the said sum of £6,000 with power to vary the investment thereof and shall stand possessed thereof and of the investments representing the same (hereinafter called 'the trust legacy') in trust to apply the income thereof for or towards the maintenance and education of the children of my daughter Mary Rosamund provided they shall be brought up in the Roman Catholic faith and subject to the application of the said income in trust for all the children of my said daughter Mary Rosamund provided they shall have been brought up in the Roman Catholic faith who being sons attain the age of twenty-one years or being daughters attain that age or marry under that age in equal shares and if there shall be only one such child the whole to be for that one and if the said children shall not be brought up in the Roman Catholic faith and no one of them shall live to attain a vested interest in the trust legacy the same shall fall into my residuary estate."

At the date of the will, the testator's daughter had been already married to a member of the Church of Ireland and since her marriage has adhered to that Church. There are three infant children of the marriage, all of whom have been baptised as members of the Church of Ireland. All the children were born in the lifetime of the testator, two of them before the date of the will. The present position is that the daughter and her husband have brought up their children in the Church of Ireland and it is not their intention to make any change in that respect. The children are now aged ten, seven and three years respectively.

I do not think there is any uncertainty about the requirement that a child should be brought up or should have been brought up in the Roman Catholic faith. Analogous expressions have been considered in several cases and it was not held that there was insufficient certainty in ascertaining the meaning of such phrases as "be a Roman Catholic": *In re May; Eggar v. May* [1932] 1 Ch 99; "become a convert to the Roman Catholic religion": *In re Evans; Hewitt v. Edwards* [1940] 1 Ch 629; "marry a Roman Catholic": *In re McKenna; Higgins and Others v. Bank of Ireland and Others* [1947] IR 277; "become a Roman Catholic": *McCausland and Others v. Young and Others* [1949] NI 49. In the last-mentioned case, the Court of Appeal in Northern Ireland was considering the terms of a settlement but the words of Andrews L.C.J. (at p. 57) as to ascertaining the meaning of the expressions used by the settlor are fully as apt in the case of a will:– "Why should they not bear the meaning in which they would naturally be used by the settlor – the meaning assigned to them in ordinary every-day speech?"

The expressions used in the will in this case, and those used in the wills considered in the cases just cited, do not suffer from the ambiguity inherent in the use of phrases such as "be openly or avowedly Protestant": *In re Borwick; Borwick v. Borwick* [1933] 1 Ch 657; "at all times conform to and be members of the Established Church of England": *In re Tegg; Public Trustee v. Bryent* [1936] 2 All ER 878; "cease to practise the Roman Catholic religion": *Burke and O'Reilly v. Burke and Quail* [1951] IR 216. There is a subjective element latent in such conditions which is, I think, absent in the requirement in the present case. Nothing active is required of the children and they do not have to hold or profess any particular beliefs. What is required is that they should be brought up in the Roman Catholic faith – a matter for those responsible for their religious education while under age. If the children are baptised and received into the Roman Catholic Church, receive the appropriate instruction and fulfil, so far as it can be secured, their appropriate religious duties, I do not think there could be any doubt, in the mind of any reasonable person, that that is what the testator contemplated by the words he used. I feel I may echo, and apply to the present case, the very cogent observations of Gavan Duffy P. in considering the expression, "shall marry a Roman Catholic," in *In re McKenna; Higgins and Others v. Bank of Ireland and Others* [1947] IR 277, at p. 285:– "I have only to construe the plain words used by a plain man in a sense plain to all of us; and I shall not make the law justly ridiculous in the eyes of persons of common sense by declaring a current expression, which the People knows and understands, to be unintelligible in the High Court of Justice in Ireland."

It is true that it can be plausibly suggested that there might be uncertainty in particular circumstances, for example, while any child was too young to understand or profit by any form of religious instruction or where the instruction had only been intermittent or had not extended over the whole period of minority. Any such difficulties, however, seem to me to relate to the ascertainment of whether the intention of the testator had been fulfilled rather than to any uncertainty in that intention. It is significant that the parents of the children evidently felt that there was no difficulty or ambiguity in their stating to their solicitor that their children had been brought up in the Church of Ireland, although two of the children are now only aged seven and three respectively. A Court which had to consider the matter would probably take the view that, so far as the gift of the capital was concerned, the process of bringing up the children in the Roman Catholic faith was one which at least required to be in operation at the time of each child attaining his or her majority, but, subject to that, any difficulties in determining the question would be merely those created by some special or peculiar circumstances. Again, it has to be borne in mind that each requirement, so far as it is a condition, is in the nature of a condition precedent rather than a condition subsequent; and it was laid down in England by the Court of Appeal in *In re Allen, Deceased; Faith v. Allen* [1953] 1 Ch 810, that in the case of a condition precedent or a qualification it was not necessary that its scope should be capable of exact definition. All that a claimant had to show was that he, at least, was within the requirement. This is a view which I respectfully adopt. Accordingly, in my view, neither requirement in the present case is void for uncertainty.

The testator's intention is manifest. He wished to secure, so far as the promise or gift of his bounty could do so, that his grandchildren should be brought up in the Roman Catholic faith and that only those grandchildren who were so brought up should benefit either during their minority or on coming of age. To take the last event first, there is only a gift of the capital to those who shall have been brought up in that faith. I am not at the moment concerned with the ambiguity that the gift is to "all the children" provided they shall have been so brought up, and that questions might arise as to the proper interpretation if only one or some of the children qualified for the gift, although I hardly think a Court would find these questions insoluble. A more fundamental difficulty arises from the nature of the condition itself. No child can take a vested interest in the capital unless the prescribed condition is fulfilled and this indicates the nature of it as being a condition precedent or a qualification antecedent to taking any benefit. No question of a voluntary choice or election on the part of the children arises, since the condition must be fulfilled at latest at the attainment of twenty-one years of age, that is, before any child would be legally capable of making a binding choice or election. This circumstance distinguishes the case from those in which an election was required of a minor and the requirement was held either not to be binding during minority or to be capable of being postponed until majority. Examples are *In re May* [1917] 2 Ch 126; [1932] 1 Ch 99; *McCausland and Others v. Young and Others* [1949] NI 49. What is involved in the present case is that the parents or other persons responsible for the upbringing of the children should have brought up the children in the Roman Catholic faith, irrespective of any independent volition on the part of the children and irrespective of the degree of success achieved in such upbringing. The testator was evidently sufficiently confident of the result of such upbringing not to impose any penalty, by way of defeasance or forfeiture – as was attempted to be done in many cases – if any child, after attaining the age of choice, changed his religion or ceased to practise or profess the religion in which he was brought up. As already pointed out, the testator was fully aware of the circumstances of his daughter's marriage and of the birth and baptism of two of his grandchildren, at the date of his will; and he must be taken to have made his will in the light of those circumstances.

Given the natural desire of parents to secure the welfare and material prosperity of their children, a provision such as the present could only operate, and be intended to operate, as an inducement to the parents and a form of indirect pressure on them to change the religion of their children from that which they themselves professed or had adopted and in which they had baptised the children. Similar provisions have been considered in a number of cases and have been held void as being contrary to public policy in tending to interfere with the parental right and duty of providing for and prescribing the manner of education, including the religious instruction, of children. This view was taken by Bennett J. in *In re Borwick; Borwick v. Borwick* [1933] 1 Ch 657. An earlier case, which he followed, was *In re Sandbrook; Noel v. Sandbrook* [1912] 2 Ch 471, a decision of Parker J. There, the condition was directed against the children living with their father and it was held void because it was inserted with the object of deterring the father from performing his parental duties. Another example of an analogous provision was *In re Boulter; Capital and Counties Bank v. Boulter* [1922] 1 Ch 75, where Sargant J. held a condition against living abroad void as being against public policy in tending to the possible separation of the parents from their children. A more recent example was *Re Tegg; Public Trustee v. Bryant* [1936] 2 All ER 878, where Farwell J. held that a condition aimed at preventing the children being sent to any Roman Catholic school was void as being a fetter upon the right of the mother to do what she might think best for the welfare and education of her children. See also *Re Piper* [1946] 2 All ER 503, referred to later. While I accept and respectfully adopt the reasoning and conclusions in these cases, I have no need to have recourse to them, as the same result would follow from a recent decision of Gavan Duffy P. in our own Courts – the only case here to which I was referred – that seems to have touched on the point. This was *Burke and O'Reilly v. Burke and Quail* [1951] IR 216, where the learned President held that a direction in a will that the selection of a school should be in the absolute discretion of the trustees was inoperative and must be ignored since it tended to override the parental authority and right and duty of education declared by Article 42 of the Constitution.

This Article puts the matter on a different and higher plane in this country, as the parental right and duty is declared and guaranteed by our fundamental law. Under it, the State "guarantees to respect the inalienable right and duty of parents to provide, according to their means, for the religious and moral, intellectual, physical and social education of their children." It is clear that any attempt to restrict or fetter that right would be contrary to the solemnly declared policy and conceptions of the community as a whole and therefore such as the Courts established under that Constitution could not and would not lend their aid to. The provision in the will that the children to benefit should have been brought up in the Roman Catholic faith is, therefore, void as against public policy and cannot be given effect to. It is hardly necessary to add that this principle applies and must be applied irrespective of the particular religion involved.

It makes no difference, in my opinion, to this view whether the provision in the will as to the capital is called a condition precedent or a qualification. If it is regarded as a qualification, in the sense that the claimant to the capital must show at the prescribed age that he answers the particular description, this involves that, during all or some of the period when the matter was one for his parents and not for himself, he had been brought up in the Roman Catholic faith.

If the condition is void, is the gift void also or can it be allowed to take effect, whether the condition is fulfilled or not? Can the condition be simply disregarded, as could be done in the case of a void condition subsequent intended to operate by way of defeating or divesting, upon the happening of a given event, a previously vested interest? As pointed out by Gavan Duffy P. in *Burke's Case* [1951] IR 216, at p. 224, a condition precedent is one which must be fulfilled before the gift can take effect at all and a gift made subject to a condition precedent fails altogether, as a rule, if the condition is found to be void. The use of the words, "as a rule," in this passage may have been intended to leave open the possibility of there being an exception to the rule – the point did not arise for decision in *Burke's Case* [1951] IR 216 – and it has been argued in the present case that the gift in question here belongs to an exceptional class which the law allows to take effect notwithstanding the general rule. Before dealing with this question, I think it preferable to consider the provision in the will as to the application of the income of the property during the minority of the children.

The intention and effect of this provision seems to be that the income should be applied for the maintenance and education of the children so long as they are being brought up in the Roman Catholic faith and only so long as they are being so brought up. That seems to me to be the plain, ordinary meaning of the words used by the testator. It is implicit in them that before the income should be so applied it should be reasonably clear to the trustees that the children were being so brought up. It is, I think, also implicit that should it become equally clear to the trustees that there had been any fundamental or radical change in the religious upbringing of the children, the income should cease to be so applied. The provision would, thus, imply something in the nature of a series of intermittent or alternating conditions precedent and conditions subsequent, but such a series has never received legal recognition. The true view, I think, is that the provision constitutes a limitation of the income for the benefit of the children during a specified period or specified periods, that is, so long as the children are being brought up in the specified faith. Here, however, the element of an unlawful attempt to dictate the religious education of the children and to trammel the exclusive responsibility of the parents again obtrudes, and again it is an attempt which the Court will not aid. It was clearly not the intention of the testator that the income should be applied for the benefit of the children unless they were being brought up as he desired, and therefore they cannot have the income during the whole of their minority on the basis of disregarding his definition of the period of enjoyment except so far as it contemplated minority. This would not only disregard that definition and turn a limited gift into an unqualified one but would defeat his clear wishes. A similar question arose before and was decided by the Court of Appeal in England in *In re Moore; Trafford v. Maconochie* (1887) 39 Ch D 116. There the testator had made provision for a weekly payment to his sister during such time as she might live apart from her husband, and it was held that the payments were to be made during a period the commencement and duration of which were fixed in a way which the law does not allow and the gift was void. The principle and authority of this decision were not questioned by P.O. Lawrence J. in *In re Lovell; Sparks v. Southall* [1920] 1 Ch 122, but he distinguished it on the ground that, in the case before him, the husband and wife were already separated at the date of the will and the bequest by the testator was intended to provide for the wife while so separated rather than to induce her to live apart from her husband, which would have conflicted with public policy.

I am of opinion, therefore, that the gift of the income fails by reason of the manner in which it is limited being contrary to public policy.

It is necessary now to return to the question whether the gift of the capital also fails, the condition upon which it depends being void. If it does not, the curious result would ensue that, by some over-refinement of the law, the children would become entitled to the capital, but not to the income, in circumstances in which it appears reasonably plain the testator never intended them to have either. I have no hesitation in saying that I should require to feel coerced by the weight and logic of an argument to this effect, before I would subscribe to such an absurd result, involving, as it would, disregarding or paying the merest lip-service to the consideration that the object of these proceedings, and the Court's function, is to endeavour to ascertain, and, so far as legally possible, to carry out the intentions of the testator as to the disposal of his property after his death.

The argument, for which some judicial sanction can be shown, is that there is an exception to the general rule of a gift dependent on a void condition precedent being also void where the condition contemplates or requires something which is *malum prohibitum* as opposed to something which is *malum in se*. This is a curious and somewhat pedantic distinction to introduce in ascertaining the wishes of testators who, in the vast majority of cases, would be quite unaware of the existence of the distinction and, even if they were aware of it, might be unable to obtain from lawyers any very precise idea of the nature and limits of the distinction. I feel I am entitled to say this because I have the authority of an eminent, contemporary English judge in a recent case on the topic. This is *Re Piper* [1946] 2 All ER 503, where Romer J. said (at p. 505):– "The difference between *malum prohibitum* and *malum in se* has never been very precisely defined or considered." Notwithstanding this uncertainty, he felt satisfied that the condition in question in the case before him – directed against children residing with their father – was *malum prohibitum* and not *malum in se* with the result that the gift took effect freed and discharged from the void condition. For the principle involved, he relied on a passage in Jarman on Wills (7th ed., vol. 2, at p. 1443), which was also relied on in other recent cases on the matter and which states the proposition in these terms:– ". . . the civil law, which in this respect has been adopted by courts of equity, differs in some respects from the common law in its treatment of conditions precedent; the rule of the civil law being that where a condition precedent is originally impossible, or is illegal as involving *malum prohibitum*, the bequest is absolute, just as if the condition had been subsequent. But where the performance of the condition is the sole motive of the bequest, or its impossibility was unknown to the testator, or the condition which was possible in its creation has since become impossible by the act of God, or where it is illegal as involving *malum in se*, in these cases the civil agrees with the common law in holding both gift and condition void."

Romer J. also derived assistance from a passage in Sheppard's Touchstone (vol. 1, at p. 132) which he quoted and which may be quoted here, before returning to the passage from Jarman. It is as follows:– "All conditions annexed to estates, being compulsory, to compel a man to do any thing that is in its nature good or indifferent; or being restrictive, to restrain or forbid the doing of anything which, in its nature, is *malum in se*, as to kill a man, or the like; or *malum prohibitum*, being a thing prohibited by any statute, or the like; all such conditions are good, and may stand with the estates. But if the matter of the condition tend to provoke or further the doing of some unlawful act, or to restrain or forbid a man the doing of his duty; the condition for the most part is void."

I must confess I can derive no assistance whatever from this last passage on the question I am now concerned with, possibly because it does not seem to be concerned with that question. As I understand it, the author was distinguishing between conditions which were good from those which were "for the most part" void. In the former class he placed together those restraining or forbidding either *mala prohibita* or *mala in se*, thus treating the matter from the point of view of negative conditions. He was not considering at all the question of positive conditions directed to the procurement of either type of *malum*, nor was he considering the effect of a condition being void on the validity of the gift dependent on it. He says nothing as to this last matter and it is unlikely that he intended to convey any distinction in this respect, as the reference to "estates" suggests that he was dealing with devises of real property where the rule seems to be invariable that if the condition, being a condition precedent, is void, the devise is void. The passage is of some help as to the difference between the two types of *mala*, although, even here, the qualification imported in each case by the use of the words, "or the like," detracts from precision.

The passage from Jarman already quoted appears to depend in the main, as do some of the later cases, on the authority of *Reynish v. Martin* (1746) 3 Atk 330, a decision of Lord Chancellor Hardwicke in reference to a legacy given to a daughter on condition of her marrying with the consent of trustees and in which he held that the legacy held good although she had married without consent. He first considered the matter as a personal legacy to be paid out of the personal estate only and said (at p. 331):– "I apprehend that taking this as a mere personal legacy, the plaintiff by the rules of the civil and ecclesiastical law, and which have been constantly adhered to in this court, will be intitled [*sic*] to the legacy; for it is an established rule in the civil law, and has long been the doctrine of this court, that where a personal legacy is given to a child on condition of marrying with consent, that this is not looked on as a condition annexed to the legacy, but as a declaration of the testator *in terrorem*."

This passage shows a sufficient ground for the decision and, to that extent, renders the subsequent passage, on the question in issue, *obiter*. This later passage, after referring to the difference in effect of a condition precedent being void and of a condition subsequent being void, continues:- "but this difference only holds where the legacy is a charge on the real assets, and therefore, if this had been merely a personal legacy, I should have been of opinion that as the marriage without consent would not have precluded Mary of her right to this legacy in the ecclesiastical court, no more would it have done so here; and to this purpose several cases were cited, which are taken notice of in the case of *Harvey v. Aston* (1737) 1 Atk 361, and which I shall not repeat, but refer to that case for them."

This reference to *Harvey v. Aston* is significant as that case dealt only with conditions and limitations concerned with marriage with consent, and it shows, as the passage itself would suggest, that the Lord Chancellor was not dealing with any wider question. The remainder of his judgment dealt with the question whether, on the terms of the will, the legacy was a charge on the real estate, and having found that it was not, he concluded:– "this case must be considered as a mere personal legacy, and as such to be governed by the rules of the civil and ecclesiastical law."

Reynish v. Martin, therefore, appears to be no more than authority for the proposition that, in the case of a personal legacy subject to a condition precedent as to marriage with consent, the legacy is not avoided by breach of the condition where there is no gift over. There is no reference anywhere in the case to *malum prohibitum* or *malum in se*.

Neither is there any such reference in the case of *Brown v. Peck* (1758) 1 Eden 140, which is cited as an authority in Roper on Legacies for the proposition which is relied on in support of the present argument. This is as follows (4th ed., at p. 757):– "When, however, the illegality of the condition does not concern anything *malum in se*, but is merely against a rule or the policy of law, the condition only is void, and the bequest single and good; for the condition not being lawful, it is held in the phrase of the Civil law *pro non adjecta*."

As he had been speaking, in the preceding paragraph, of a condition precedent requiring the performance of an act *malum in se*, a cursory reading of the passage cited might suggest that he was there dealing with *mala prohibita*, as being the natural opposition to *mala in se*. Closer attention to it, however, makes it, I think, plain that this was not the meaning or intention of the passage. If this particular distinction had been intended, the learned author would probably have expressed it with his usual clarity. Instead he referred to things "merely against a rule or the policy of law." Such things are not necessarily *mala prohibita* (they are, in my view, entirely different) and it seems highly unlikely that the author intended to suggest that they were the same. By referring to the conditions as not being lawful, he may have meant no more than that they were unenforceable. This view of the passage is reinforced by turning to the case of *Brown v. Peck* itself, where it will be found that the decision was that a condition as to a married woman living apart from her husband was *contra bonos mores* and void but the gift dependent on it was good. There is, quite understandably, no reference in it to *mala* either *prohibita* or *in se*, the condition belonging to neither category.

If *Brown v. Peck* is an authority for anything, it is for the proposition that, if a condition precedent attached to a personal legacy is void as being against public policy, the gift may still be good. It is, however, a very doubtful authority. The report is short and not too easy to follow and it was subjected to some criticism by the Court of Appeal in *In re Moore; Trafford v. Maconochie* (1887) 39 Ch D 116, already referred to. Cotton L.J. (at p. 129) said that "the report is not clear either as regards the facts or the principle laid down"; and Bowen L.J. (at p. 132) said it "appears to have been compromised after an expression of opinion by the Court." In the Court of first instance in *In re Moore*, Kay J. had said (at p. 124) of it and of *Wren v. Bradley* (1848) 2 De G & Sm 49:– "I confess that I find it difficult to understand these two decisions"; and I respectfully echo his words. The latter case – *Wren v. Bradley* – was interpreted by the Court of Appeal as having being a decision on the basis of the condition being a condition subsequent and therefore inapplicable in the case before them as it is also, for the same reason, inapplicable in the present case. *Brown v. Peck* I regard as too obscure and doubtful a case to follow.

The proposition contended for has, as we have seen, been adopted in *Re Piper* [1946] 2 All ER 503, already referred to, and also in a later case of *In re Elliott, Deceased* [1952] 1 Ch 217, decided by Harman J. Neither of these cases is, of course, binding on me although entitled to the greatest respect as persuasive authorities. In *In re Elliott, Deceased*, Harman J. decided that a bequest of personalty subject to an illegal condition precedent is void if the condition be *malum in se*, but if the condition be only *malum prohibitum*, the bequest will be effective and unfettered by the condition; and this is a clear statement of the principle contended for in the present case. In that case, the condition offended against the rule against perpetuities and Harman J. held that this was *malum prohibitum*. He took the view that the principle he enunciated had been imported into equity from the civil law on the authority of *Reynish v. Martin*, quoted and accepted by Bowen L.J. in *In re Moore*. I have already suggested that *Reynish v. Martin* is not an authority for this proposition; and the Court of Appeal decided *In re Moore* on the ground that they were concerned with a limitation and that, if any such principle applied in the case of a condition, it did not apply to a limitation: see Cotton L.J., at p. 129. What Bowen L.J. said, as to the matter, was (at p. 131):– "Accepting that as law with respect to legacies of personal estate on a condition, the question remains whether this is a legacy on a condition"; and he found that it was, instead, a limitation. I do not think therefore that *In re Moore* could be rightly regarded as adopting or approving the supposed principle. It is difficult to see why, if a limitation which is contrary to public policy avoids a gift, a condition which is contrary to public policy should not do so also. It was, however, sufficient for the decision in *In re Moore* that the provision was found to be a limitation. Harman J. in *In re Elliott, Deceased,* may possibly have intended to convey some doubt on the matter in his own mind by saying (at p. 222):– ". . . if this doctrine of the civil law has been imported into the English law, the condition can be disregarded." He then went on to say:– "Mr. Roper is of the opinion that this rule was imported into equity . . ."; and he referred to *Reynish v. Martin* and *In re Moore*. As has been seen, the basis of Roper's assertion was *Brown v. Peck*.

I have devoted some time to this question because of the support to be apparently found for the proposition in textbooks and in high judicial decision; but there is a more fundamental consideration which would have disposed of the matter, in my view, more shortly, if it had not been for the decisions referred to. This is the question whether, assuming the proposition to be sound, the provision in question here is *malum in se* or *malum prohibitum* or neither. In my view it is neither. As already noted, the precise nature of the distinction is somewhat indefinite and elusive, but it seems reasonably certain that it is a distinction between different types of crime or offence according to the origin of their sanction. Thus, Holland, Jurisprudence (7th ed., p. 34), says:– "Acts prohibited by positive law, but not by the so-called natural law, are said to be '*mala prohibita,*' not '*mala in se.*' Thus a government may find it expedient to forbid certain acts, such as the planting of tobacco, which are not regarded as odious by the public sentiment." Byrne, Law Dictionary, says:– "*Mala in se* are acts which are wrong in themselves, such as murder, as opposed to *mala prohibita (mala quia prohibita)*, that is to say, those acts (such as smuggling) which are only wrong because they are prohibited by law." *Cf.* the passage already quoted from Sheppard's Touchstone, where *malum prohibitum* is referred to as "a thing forbidden by any statute, or the like." This limitation in scope of the distinction is borne out by recalling the matters in which the distinction was or might be of any importance. These appear to be chiefly the question of ambassadorial exemption from criminal process and the question of the degree of *mens rea* requisite in the case of some offences.

An attempt to influence or fetter parents in their discretion as to the choice of religion and religious instruction for their children is not, so far as I am aware, a crime or offence of any kind. It is simply opposed to the policy of the law – now written into the fundamental law of this country. What this means was pointed out by Kekewich J. in *Re Hope Johnstone; Hope Johnstone v. Hope Johnstone* [1904] 1 Ch 470, at p. 479 – and quoted by Romer J. in *Re Piper* [1946] 2 All ER 503 at p. 505 – in these words:– "The phrase means no more than that the provision is not enforceable by anyone or in any court."

So far, therefore, as the contention depends on the provision belonging to one branch rather than the other of this archaic distinction, I am of opinion that the contention fails for the reason that the provision belongs to neither branch. Could it, however, be said that the proposition has validity if it were put in a different way, namely, that, if a condition precedent is contrary to public policy, a gift of personalty dependent on the condition is nevertheless good? This might be the meaning of *Brown v. Peck*, in which the condition was stated to be *contra bonos mores*, and it seems to be the approach to the matter of Kay J. in *In re Moore*, where he quoted from Swinburne on Wills and, later, refers to "the doctrine that conditions precedent as well as conditions subsequent which are against the policy of the law are treated as void in cases of legacies of personal estate, and that the legacy 'stands pure and simple.'" He quotes the second of Swinburne's four classes of impossible conditions, being those "which be contrary to law or good manners" and the two examples, respectively, given by Swinburne, i.e., "if he murder such a man or deflower such a woman"; but he does not quote the next part of the sentence, which is: "this condition is unlawful and unhonest, and consequently to be deemed unpossible" (Part IV, sect. 5, para. 8). Swinburne then states his rule that, with certain exceptions, when a condition is impossible the legacy may still be recovered; and proceeds to consider the exceptions. Amongst these occurs one set out in the following words (also quoted by Kay J.):– "When the condition is both impossible and unhonest, for then the disposition is thereby void; and that in disfavour of the testator, who added such a condition. Whereas if the condition had been only impossible or unlawful, the disposition had been good, and that in favour of the testament."

This last sentence is the only one that could possibly lend any support to the proposition now under consideration and such support would depend solely on the meaning to be given to the words "or unlawful" as used by the author. The disjunctive cannot have been intended to suggest an alternative to an impossible condition, as the whole section is only dealing with such conditions, and I confess I find it very hard to know what meaning could or should be given to the word, "unlawful." The sense of the passage, taken as a whole, would have led one to expect an opposition between "impossible and unhonest" conditions on the one hand and "impossible but not unlawful" conditions on the other hand; but it would be rather late in the day now to suggest a typographical error in a work of such antiquity. Whatever the meaning of the words, there is a clear and unambiguous statement that the disposition is void when the condition is "impossible and unhonest"; and the earlier passage made it equally clear that Swinburne included in this category of condition one "contrary to good manners," which is equivalent to one *contra bonos mores* or opposed to the policy of the law. The second example he gives also makes this clear, as it contemplates something which is not necessarily any crime or offence but merely disapproved by public morality. I cannot find, therefore, that Swinburne's statement of what the ecclesiastical law was lends any support to the principle enunciated in *Brown v. Peck*, or the cases which have followed or applied its supposed principle. Swinburne seems to me to be authority for the directly contrary proposition.

To summarise:– the provisions in the will as to bringing up the children in the Roman Catholic faith are not too uncertain in their meaning not to be given effect to, if this were the only matter in issue. The phrase is one generally used and popularly understood, and an individual, or the Court if necessary, would not have too much difficulty in determining whether a particular child was being brought up or had been brought up in a particular faith. The provisions, however, constitute an attempt to interfere with or fetter the right and duty guaranteed to parents by the Constitution to provide for the education, including the religious education, of their children. As such, they are opposed to the policy of the law and cannot be enforced or given effect to in any Court in this country. Being, thus, void and unenforceable, the gifts, both of capital and income, dependent on their being carried out, are also void and unenforceable. The gifts to the children therefore fail and the legacy falls into the residue of the estate.

In my view, the principle stated to have been imported from ecclesiastical law, that even though the condition upon which a legacy is given is contrary to public policy the legacy may still take effect, is not borne out by the authorities cited for it nor was it a rule of ecclesiastical law. If it had been part of ecclesiastical law, as applied to wills in the Church Courts in England, it might have been necessary to enquire as to when the principle was adopted, as those Courts retained a large part of their jurisdiction even after the Reformation and were not finally deprived of their temporal jurisdiction in testamentary and other matters until 1857. Rules adopted or laid down during the last two centuries of the functioning of those Courts could not be accepted without question as part of the law of this country. No Irish case was cited, nor do I know of one, which decided the point at issue.

On another ground, if necessary, I should have been inclined to hold that, the condition being contrary to public policy, the bequest failed. This is that the performance of the condition was the sole motive of the bequest. This is an admitted exception to the supposed principle that the bequest may hold good. Reading the will as a whole, it is impossible to escape the conclusion that the paramount object of the testator, so far as his grandchildren were concerned, was that they should be brought up in his own faith and that only on that basis should they benefit. There is no indication that he intended them to benefit even if his wishes could not be carried out and, therefore, as the law will not enforce the condition, it would be defeating his real intention to uphold the gift while allowing the condition to be disregarded or rejected.

For these reasons, the gift fails."

VOIDABLE TRUSTS

Trusts falling within this category come into operation and will remain effective unless and until they are set aside in court proceedings. A trust may be voidable for a variety of reasons often because it comes into being as a result of mistake, misrepresentation, fraud, duress or undue influence. In addition a trust may be set aside where it amounts to an attempt to defraud a settlor's creditors or subsequent purchasers or where the settlor becomes bankrupt within a specified period of settling the property

Settlements Defrauding Creditors

S. 10 of the Conveyancing Act (Ireland) 1634 provides that any gift or conveyance of real or personal property, made for the purpose of delaying, hindering or defrauding creditors is 'void' as against such creditors, although this phrase has been interpreted as meaning 'voidable'. S.14 of the 1634 Act goes on to provide that this provision will not extend to conveyances *bona fide* made for good consideration without notice of any fraud. It has been established in this jurisdiction that a case may fall within the ambit of the statute where no fraudulent intention actually exists but where such intent is, as a matter of law, assumed from the necessary or probable consequences of the act done.[4] The onus of proving that the transaction was intended to defraud lies on the party making the allegation and this may be more difficult to prove where the transaction is one for valuable consideration.[5] However, as the *dicta* of Palles CB in *Re Moroney* makes clear, even where a conveyance is for valuable consideration, this fact alone will not suffice to prevent the application of s.10.

Re Moroney
(1887) 21 LR Ir 27

Moroney was served with a writ for one year's rent and subsequently sold his cattle and paid a sum of money to the local trustees of the 'Plan of Campaign', an organisation of agricultural tenants. It was held by the Irish Court of Appeal that the sale of the cattle and the payment to the trustees constituted acts of bankruptcy and further that it was a fraud within the meaning of the Conveyancing Act (Ireland) 1634 for a debtor to part with any portion of his property without consideration and with intent to defraud or delay a particular creditor.

PALLES CB stated at pp.58–64: "I also am of opinion that the payment by the appellant of £25 to the trustees of the "Plan of Campaign" and the sale by him of his cattle amounted to acts of bankruptcy. In expressing this opinion, I

---

[4] *Re Moroney* (1887) 21 LR Ir 27 and *McQuillan v. Maguire* [1996] 1 ILRM 395.
[5] See e.g. *Bryce v. Fleming* [1930] IR 376.

must entirely disclaim yielding to one of the arguments of the learned counsel for the respondents, in which he asked us to overrule the long line of authorities, commencing in the time of Lord Kenyon and continuing to the present time, of which *Wood v. Dixie* (1845) 7 QB 892, is a typical example. In arriving at the conclusion I have mentioned, I do not overrule any authority. I do no more than ascertain the well-known principles of bankruptcy law, and apply them to the admitted facts of the particular case before us.

The clause of the statute upon which the question arises is s. 21, sub-section 2, of the Bankruptcy Act (Ireland), 1872, which enacts that if a debtor has, in Ireland or elsewhere, made a fraudulent conveyance, gift, delivery, or transfer of his property, or of any part thereof, he shall be held to have committed an act of bankruptcy. This sub-section occurs in a code of bankruptcy law, which regulates the rights, in bankruptcy administration, of creditors against their debtors, and of creditors *inter se*. Its interpretation is well expounded by Mellish, L.J., in *Re Wood* (1872) LR 7 Ch App 302. Speaking there of the corresponding section in force in England, the Lord Justice says:– "Now, against whom must the conveyance be fraudulent? Why, clearly against creditors, because a man may make fraudulent conveyances of other kinds, as, for instance, with intent to defraud a purchaser, which it would be absurd to treat as acts of bankruptcy."

I therefore read the clause as if the description of the avoided conveyance was one "fraudulent against creditors." We have heard a vast amount of argument as to the words "intent to defraud creditors," and we are told that we are bound to read the section as if those words were contained in it. In one sense, I agree in this contention. I agree that the words "fraudulent conveyance" in the section must now receive the same interpretation as the words in the former statutes, "conveyance with intent to defeat or delay creditors," formerly bore. I agree that there is no difference between a conveyance fraudulent against creditors and a conveyance with intent to defeat or delay them. But in my view, and as held by the Court of Appeal in *Re Wood,* the reason the words were omitted was, not because they were to be implied by construction, but because they were "superfluous and misleading." The words "intent to defeat or delay creditors" in the former Bankruptcy Acts had, as pointed out by Lord Justice Mellish, a different interpretation according as they were applied to different acts of bankruptcy. "All were described as acts with intent to defeat or delay creditors; but as to some, it was necessary to prove, as matter of fact, that the act was done with an intent in the mind of the bankrupt to defeat or delay his creditors – as, for instance, departing from the realm, or absenting himself, or keeping house – all these were in themselves innocent actions, and to make them acts of bankruptcy it was necessary to prove an intent to delay or defeat creditors. If the case was tried at law, the Judge would leave to the jury . . . whether the debtor had done the act with intent to delay or defeat his creditors? But, as respects a *fraudulent* conveyance, the rule was quite different, for the mere act was necessarily an act of bankruptcy, and the law assumed the intent to defeat or delay creditors as a necessary consequence of the act."

Thus the expression "fraudulent conveyance," in section 21, sub-section 2, includes two distinct classes of conveyance – one, the class of conveyance fraudulent in fact; secondly, conveyances of such a character that their necessary or probable result was to defeat or delay creditors; and in such cases the inference that they were fraudulent was a conclusion of law, not a matter of fact.

Taking, then, the subject-matter of this sub-section to be conveyances and transfers fraudulent against creditors, we are asked to limit the operation of the sub-section, so far as relates to conveyances to strangers, as distinguished from conveyances to one or more particular creditors, to conveyances which are within the 10th Charles I, sess. 1, c. 3 (Irish), corresponding to the English Act, 13th Elizabeth, c. 5. I am far from saying that Mr. Carton is wrong in this contention; but if he be right in it, it is only because the latter statute comprises, as in my opinion it does, frauds against creditors of every kind. Lord Justice James, in *Ex parte Pearson* (1873) LR 8 Ch App 673, thus refers to the wide-reaching effect of the English sub-section corresponding to our second sub-section of section 21:– "I am of opinion that Lord Mansfield, and the other eminent judges who established the law as to fraudulent preference and fraudulent assignments by a debtor, would not have any difficulty in applying that law to a case like the present. I am of opinion that the power and the duty which have been exercised by our fathers have not been abdicated or repudiated by the Courts in later times, and that the Legislature, is adopting the old decisions, and crystallizing them into positive enactments, have in no way abrogated the duty of this Court to apply the same principles in proper cases."

That, in my view, is the true interpretation of this sub-section. I need not, however, discuss this matter further, for whether it does or does not comprise fraudulent conveyances or tranfers to strangers, not within the statute of Charles, there can be no doubt, and it was so expressly admitted by the learned counsel for the appellant, that any conveyance fraudulent within the former Act, is also within the latter, and is consequently an act of bankruptcy.

This brings me to the interpretation of the statute of Charles, and I confess that until the argument of this appeal, I thought it as well settled as the construction of any statute could be determined by judicial decision. But there has been, during the argument of this appeal, that which, in my opinion, is such a *misinterpretation* of the leading cases upon the subject, and one so likely, if not corrected, to lead to mischief, that I shall take the liberty of stating, what I should otherwise have deemed to be wholly unnecessary, my general view as to the interpretation of this statute, as uniformly adopted during the period of nearly three hundred years, which have elapsed since it became law.

The statute avoids "conveyances, &c., devised and contrived of fraud, covin, &c, to the intent to delay, hinder, or defraud creditors of their just and lawful actions, debts, &c." Therefore to bring a conveyance within the statute, first, it must be fraudulent; secondly, the class of fraud must be an intent to delay, hinder, or defraud creditors. Whether a particular conveyance be within this description may depend upon an infinite variety of circumstances and considerations. One conveyance, for instance, may be executed with the express intent and object in the mind of the party to defeat and delay his creditors, and from such an intent the law presumes the conveyance to be fraudulent, and does not require or allow such fraud to be deduced as an inference of fact. In other cases, no such intention actually exists in the mind of the grantor, but the necessary or probable result of his denuding himself of the property included in the conveyance, for the consideration, and under the circumstances actually existing, is to defeat or delay creditors, and in such a case, as stated by Mellish, L.J., in *Re Wood*, the intent is, as matter of law, assumed from the necessary or probable consequences of the act done; and in this case, also, the conveyance, in point of law, and without any inference of fact being drawn, is fraudulent within the statute. In every case, however, no matter what its nature, before the conveyance can be avoided, fraud, whether expressly proved as a fact, or as an inference of law from other facts proved, must exist. What, then, is the nature of this fraud which will avoid a conveyance? The object of the statute was to protect the rights of creditors as against the property of their debtor. It was no part of its object to regulate the rights of creditors *inter se*, or to entitle them to an equal distribution of that property. One right, however, of the creditors, taking them as a whole, was that all the property of the debtor should be applied in payment of the demands of them, or some of them, without any portion of it being parted with without consideration, or reserved or retained by the debtor to their prejudice. Now, it follows from this, that security given by a debtor to one creditor, upon a portion of or upon all his property (although the effect of it, or even the intent of the debtor in making it, may be to defeat an expected execution of another creditor), is not a fraud within the statute; because notwithstanding such an act, the entire of the property remains available for the creditors, or some or one of them, and as the statute gives no right to rateable distribution, the right of the creditors by such an act is not invaded or affected. This is the true ground of the decisions, so much relied on by the appellant, of *Holbird v. Anderson* (1793) 5 Term Rep 235; *Pickstock v. Lyster* (1815) 3 M & S 371; *Darvill v. Terry* (1861) 6 H & N 807; and *Alton v. Harrison* (1869) LR 4 Ch App 622.

Again, the right of the creditors is, not that the debtor shall not *part with* any of his property, but that no such parting shall be without consideration. "If," says Alderson, B., in *Siebert v. Spooner* (1836) 1 M & W 714, "an equivalent is given, there is only a change in the nature of the property which the party has, but not a conveying of it away." When, therefore, there is a *bona fide* sale for value of part of the property of the debtor really intended to have effect and operation between the parties to it, the right of the creditors is not invaded. No doubt the property sold has ceased to be available for their demands; but in lieu of it, there has been been substituted the consideration for the sale, which may be assumed to be a substantial equivalent. Such a sale, therefore, would not be a fraud within the statute, merely because it was made with the express intent to defeat or delay the execution of a creditor. Were there nothing more in the case, the consideration would remain capable of being made available, not under the intended execution, but by some one or other of the modes known to the law; and, therefore, in such a case, there would not be a fraud within the statute. This was the ground of the decisions in the only other cases cited by the appellant on this branch of the argument, viz. *Wood v. Dixie* and *Hale v. Saloon Omnibus Company* (1859) 4 Drew 492. It is to be observed, however, that the decision in *Wood v. Dixie*, goes no further than determining that an intent to defeat a particular creditor in the case of a *bona fide* sale for value, does not *per se*, and as a matter of law, render the conveyance fraudulent. If, however, in such a case, the intent were not only to sell the property, but forthwith to abscond with the proceeds, so as in effect to withdraw the property from the fund available for the creditors without providing an equivalent, I should entertain no doubt that in such a case there would be an intention to defraud creditors, which, if the purchaser had notice of, would avoid the sale, and which, whether he had notice or not, would be an act of bankruptcy by the vendor.

If I be right in this view of these decisions, not one of them is an authority for the proposition that a parting with, without consideration, of any substantial *part* of the debtor's property, with an intent to defeat or delay a particular creditor, is not a fraud within the statute. Mark here the distinction between such a case and those to which I have already referred. In such a case, the property is withdrawn from the fund available for payment of all the creditors. It passes, not to one of the creditors, but to a stranger. No equivalent is provided for it, and it is a direct invasion of the right of all the creditors, as against the property of their debtor. It must be borne in mind that every allocation of part of the debtor's property which is made to a stranger, without an equivalent being provided, may injuriously affect all of them, by diminishing the fund applicable for payment of all, although the particular intent, and more immediate effect, may be to defeat that creditor only who has been most pressing. Again, if the conveyance reserve, either expressly, or by some collateral or secret arrangement, any interest, no matter how small, to the grantor, under such circumstances as to make it impossible or difficult to resort to it if the deed be binding, the conveyance would be a fraud within the statute, because by it that interest in the debtor would be reserved for him in preference to his creditors, and so withdrawn from the fund to which they were entitled to resort.

The authorities upon the two classes of frauds I have last referred to have been always uniform. Since *Twyne's Case* (1601) 3 Co Rep 80b downward, no one has ever doubted that reserving an interest to the grantor was a badge of fraud; and in *Holbird v. Anderson* (1793) 5 TR 238 and *Alton v. Harrison* (1869) LR 4 Ch Ap 622, the circumstance that no benefit was reserved to the grantor is pointedly referred to in the judgments upholding the transactions.

It remains but to refer to the decisions upon voluntary deeds, made with intent to avoid one creditor only, but the effect of which, as I have already pointed out, must be to prejudice all creditors. The decisions upon these instruments have uniformly been that they are fraudulent within the statute. Of the many decisions which can be referred to, it is unnecessary to mention more than *Coulston v. Gardiner* 3 Swanst 279, *Blenkinsopp v. Blenkinsopp* (1850) 12 Beav 568; on appeal 1 De G M & G 496, *Bott v. Smith* (1856) 21 Beav 511, and *Barling v. Bishopp* (1860) 29 Beav 417.

Applying these principles to the £25 given under the "Plan of Campaign," it seems to me clear that this parting with a substantial part of the debtor's property without consideration, and with express intent to defeat and delay the plaintiff, was fraudulent under the statute of Charles, and therefore an act of bankruptcy."

Bryce v. Fleming
[1930] IR 376

The plaintiff obtained judgment against the first named defendant and three days later the latter assigned lands to the second named defendant who subsequently stated in evidence that she had paid the full value of the lands and that she had no knowledge of the judgment which had been obtained against the vendor. The plaintiff was granted a declaration in the Circuit Court that the assignment was void. On appeal the High Court (Meredith and Johnston JJ) dismissed the plaintiff's action on the basis that the assignment was for valuable consideration and the plaintiff's evidence had not established that there was any knowledge of fraud on the part of the second named defendant nor did it show that she had sought to acquire the land other than as a *bona fide* purchaser.

MEREDITH J stated at pp.378–384: "This is an appeal against the judgment of Circuit Court Judge Power, by which an assignment, dated the 9th March, 1928, whereby certain lands of Ballybroney and Balladallagh, in the County of Mayo, were assigned by the defendant, Thomas Fleming, to the defendant, Mary Gilvarry, was declared void as against the plaintiff and all other the creditors of the defendant, Thomas Fleming, and was ordered to be delivered up to be cancelled.

The declaration and order purported to be made under the Irish statute, 10 Chas. 1, Sess. 2, c. 3, against covinous or fraudulent conveyances, which corresponds to the English statute, 13 Eliz. c. 5. The assignment was an out-and-out assignment. There was no reservation of any kind, express or secret, in favour of the vendor, Thomas Fleming, and the price was determined as the result of genuine bargaining, and reflected simply the estimate which the parties placed on the value of the lands. The assignment was, therefore, unquestionably for good consideration, and *bona fide*. But at the time it was made Patrick Bryce, the plaintiff, had obtained judgment against the defendant, Thomas

Fleming, for necessaries supplied to his wife, and, as Fleming had unsuccessfully appealed against this judgment, the plaintiff was a creditor of Fleming to a considerable amount – apparently nearly half the value of the lands assigned. The learned Judge was satisfied that Fleming's intention in selling the lands was to divest himself of the only property on which the plaintiff, Bryce, could levy execution, and that, accordingly, the assignment came within sect. 10 of the statute. He further refused to believe the evidence of the defendant, Mary Gilvarry, that she had no notice of the fraudulent nature of the transaction. Accordingly, he held that the assignment to her was not protected by sect. 14, which contains a proviso in favour of *bona fide* conveyances for good consideration without notice, and so he declared the deed void as against the creditors of Thomas Fleming. The order further directed the assignment to be delivered up to be cancelled. That, of course, was a mistake; for it is quite clear that sect. 10 only makes an assignment which is fraudulent against creditors void as against them, and that in the present case Mary Gilvarry is in any event entitled to the benefit of her purchase, subject to the claim of the plaintiff. The proper form of order is set out in *Bott v. Smith* (1856) 21 Beav 511.

The circumstances under which a *bona fide* conveyance for valuable consideration might yet be fraudulent within sect. 10 are indicated in a passage in the judgment of Palles C.B. in *In re Moroney* (1887) 21 LR Ir 27, at p. 63. Dealing with the case of a *bona fide* sale for value, he says that if "the intent were not only to sell the property, but forthwith to abscond with the proceeds, so as in effect to withdraw the property from the fund available for the creditors without providing an equivalent, I should entertain no doubt that in such a case there would be an intention to defraud creditors, which, if the purchaser had notice of, would avoid the sale." As a matter of fact, the point that a conveyance might be within sect. 10, or, rather, the corresponding English section, though for valuable consideration, had been well settled as far back as the time of Lord Mansfield, who states the position with great clearness in his judgment in *Cadogan v. Kennett* (1776) 2 Cowp 432, at p. 434: "But if the transaction be not *bona fide*, the circumstance of its being done for a *valuable consideration*, will not *alone* take it out of the statute. I have known several cases where persons have given a fair and *full price* for goods, and where the *possession* was *actually changed*; yet being done for the purpose of defeating creditors, the transaction has been held fraudulent, and therefore void. One case was, where there had been a decree in the Court of Chancery, and a sequestration. A person with knowledge of the decree, bought the house and goods belonging to the defendant, and gave a full price for them. The Court said the purchase, being with a manifest view to defeat the creditor, was fraudulent; and therefore, notwithstanding a valuable consideration, void. So, if a man knows of a judgment and execution, and, with a view to defeat it, purchases the debtor's goods, it is void: because the *purpose* is iniquitous. It is assisting one man to cheat another, which the law will never allow." Later cases, where deeds for valuable consideration were held within the section, are referred to in *Bott v. Smith*; see also the more modern case of *In re Johnson; Golden v. Gillam* (1881) 20 Ch D 389, at p. 393. The difficulties, however, in the way of a creditor who seeks to impugn a deed for valuable consideration are emphasised in *Harman v. Richards* (1852) 10 Hare 81, at p. 89. There Turner L.J. said: "A deed, though made for valuable consideration, may be affected by *mala fides*. But those who undertake to impeach for *mala fides* a deed which has been executed for valuable consideration, have, I think, a task of great difficulty to discharge."

These authorities indicate under what circumstances a creditor's claim under the statute will be good even against an assignee for valuable consideration. No such circumstances exist in the present case. If a man has lands, and can only pay his debts by selling his lands, the honest thing for him to do is to sell them. It is also the prudent thing to do; for if he sells them himself he will probably get a better price, and avoid unnecessary costs. Consequently, the mere fact that a man in such a position is selling his lands is no evidence whatever that his intention is to defeat his creditors rather than to obtain the wherewithal to pay his debts. Still more is it obvious that mere knowledge of such a simple fact is not a sufficient ground for imputing to a purchaser knowledge of a fraudulent intention on the part of his vendor. Voluntary assignments by a debtor stand on one footing. But once valuable consideration is given a new element enters into the case. As Fry J. says in *In re Johnson; Golden v. Gillam*, at p. 393, it is always "a material ingredient in considering the case, and for very obvious reasons: the fact that there is valuable consideration shows at once that there may be purposes in the transaction other than defeating or delaying creditors, and renders the case, therefore, of those who contest the deed more difficult."

Now, unquestionably the only knowledge bearing on the question of Fleming's intention that was brought home to the mind of Mary Gilvarry was the simple fact that Fleming probably could not satisfy the plaintiff's claim without a sale of the lands. Further, Mary Gilvarry's testimony was that she had no knowledge of or notice of any fraudulent intention on Fleming's part. The learned Judge, however, took the view that the *onus* of proving absence of knowledge lay on Mary Gilvarry, and, as he did not regard her as a creditable witness, he rejected her testimony, and so he considered that she had failed to discharge the *onus*, with the result that he avoided the deed. In this way the task which Turner L.J. described as so difficult to discharge was performed with such ease that Mary Gilvarry most probably left the Court in a state of utter bewilderment at the extreme simplicity of the proceeding by which, despite her uncontradicted testimony, she was deprived of all benefit of her £200.

Now, on this appeal, we are pressed with the point that the defendant's *onus* of proving that she had no notice cannot be discharged by her testimony if it is not to be believed, and that the question of the creditability of a witness is for the Judge of first instance. But, even assuming that the *onus* was on

Mary Gilvarry of showing absence of notice, I am inclined to think that the *onus* was shifted once she swore that she had no notice, and that the learned Judge was not entitled to reject her testimony in the absence of any positive evidence whatever of anything from which knowledge should be imputed to her. This is not a case of conflict of testimony, and it is not like the case of the testimony of a claimant in support of a claim against the estate of a deceased. A number of authorities on the analogous case where absence of notice is averred to support the equitable plea of purchase for value without notice will be found collected in the note to *Jones v. Thomas* (1733) 3 P Wms 243; see also *Vane v. Vane* (1872) 8 Ch App 383, at p. 398, where Sir Wm. James L.J. (having stated that the plaintiff alleged in so many words that he never did know or suspect at the time anything of the alleged fraud) said: "That we must take to be true, unless we are enabled judicially to conclude from other statements of his in the bill that that allegation is false." In general, "the defence of a purchase without notice is one which ought to be specifically alleged as well as proved by those who rely upon it": *per* Thesiger L.J. in *Attorney-General v. Biphosphated Guano Co.* (1874) 11 Ch D 327, at p. 337. The question, however, is one of some difficulty, as the learned Judge gave as his reason for disbelieving Mary Gilvarry that she denied having heard of the result of the unsuccessful appeal, heard in Dublin, in the action already referred to, taken by Bryce against Fleming, in respect of necessaries supplied to Mrs. Fleming. The learned Judge held that that was in itself an incredible statement, and so he said he would reject her evidence entirely.

If, however, the *onus* was on the plaintiff to prove that the defendant was aware of the intention of Thomas Fleming, then that *onus* could not be discharged by rejecting the evidence of the defendant that she had no knowledge. Hence, instead of examining the authorities as to the position if the defendant was to prove absence of notice, I prefer to turn to the question of whether, in the case of a purchase for valuable consideration, the *onus* is not on the creditor to prove that the purchaser was aware of his vendor's fraudulent intent. The answer to that question must depend upon whether an innocent purchaser is saved by reason of his conveyance not originally coming within sect. 10 at all, or only by reason of his being protected by the proviso contained in sect. 14. It may be anticipated that it will not prove an altogether easy matter to clear up this question by reference to the authorities, as a certain amount of confusion in the older authorities is recognised in the observation of Parker J. in *Glegg v. Bromley* [1912] 3 KB 474, at p. 492, that "There is, however, a proviso for the protection of a purchaser for good consideration without notice of the illegal intention. In the authorities which deal with the statute it is not always clear whether the Judges are dealing with the operative part of the Act or with the proviso." An example of one of the many passages which Parker J. must have had in view is the following, in *French v. French* (1855) 6 De GM & G 95, at p. 101:– "Mr. Gibbons had no knowledge of the state of Mr. French's affairs, therefore the transaction, as far as he is concerned, ought not to be impeached." Does Lord Cranworth mean that the transaction, as far as he is concerned, is not avoided under the operative section, or that his estate or interest is protected under the proviso? There is a similar difficulty in respect of the observation, already cited, of Palles C.B. in *In re Moroney* (1887) 21 LR Ir 27, for it is implied that if the purchaser had no notice the sale would not be avoided. Are we entitled to press the implication, that it is the sale itself that would not be avoided, as against a suggestion that it is only the estate or interest of the purchaser that would be protected? Numerous other instances might be cited of passages in which an expectation of a clear statement on the point is disappointed. It must be admitted, however, that, from *Twyne's Case* (1601) 1 Smith's LC 1 down, there are several passages in the authorities which assume, but without considering any alternative view, that it is the proviso which protects a purchaser for value without notice. But these *obiter dicta* cannot have very much weight, since it was not until *Halifax Joint Stock Banking Co. v. Gledhill* [1891] 1 Ch 31 that it was clearly decided that the proviso covered the case of a subsequent transfer; and, of course, if the proviso was not dealing with subsequent transactions it must have been dealing with the original transaction. Hence the assumption to which I have referred.

Turning to the wording of the operative section, it is obvious that the question whether or not it hits a *bona fide* purchaser for valuable consideration without notice must depend on whether the "intent" referred to in the section is solely the intent of the vendor in such a case or is the intent of the transaction as a whole, so as to make the intent of the purchaser material. Certainly, on the plain reading of the section itself, it is the latter view that would commend itself. But the authorities on which one most readily lights seem in favour of the former – as far as *dicta* go. Thus, in *Nunn v. Wilsmore* (1800) 8 TR 521, at p. 530, Le Blanc J. says: "Whether or not a deed is to be considered as fraudulent with respect to creditors must depend on the motives of the party making the deed." But it does not seem that deeds for valuable consideration were here in contemplation. The same may be said of the observations of Kindersley V.C. in *Thompson v. Webster* (1859) 4 Drew 628, at p. 632: "The principle now established is this:– The language of the Act being, that any conveyance of property is void against creditors if it is made with intent to defeat, hinder, or delay creditors, the Court is to decide in each particular case whether, on all the circumstances, it can come to the conclusion that the *intention* of the settlor in making the settlement was to defeat, hinder, or delay his creditors." But I have not found any passage in which the case of a purchase for valuable consideration is expressly considered, and in which the intention of the purchaser is treated as immaterial. But there is authority to the contrary. In *Cadogan v. Kennett* (1776) 2 Cowp 432 Lord Mansfield, in the passage already cited, stresses throughout the intention of the purchase and of the purchaser. In the case where the creditor had obtained a decree, he says: "The Court said, the purchase" – not the sale – "being with a manifest view to defeat the creditor, was fraudulent; and, therefore, notwithstanding a valuable consideration, void."

He uses similar language in the second instance which he gives:– "So, if a man knows of a judgment and execution, and, with a view to defeat it, purchases the debtor's goods, it is void: because the *purpose is iniquitous.* It is assisting one man to cheat another, which the law will never allow." *Cadogan v. Kennett* does not appear to have been cited in *In re Johnson; Golden v. Gillam* (1881) 20 Ch D 389, but in that case Fry J. arrives independently at the same view as to the materiality of the purchaser's intention. He says (at p. 394): "I therefore proceed to inquire, looking to all the circumstances of the case and at the nature of the instrument itself, whether I can or ought to infer an intent to defraud creditors in the parties to the deed. I say in the parties to the deed, because it appears to me to be plain that whatever fraudulent intent there may have been in the mind of Judith Johnson, it would not avoid the deed unless it was shown to have been concurred in by Alice, who became the purchaser under the deed. It has not been contended, and it could not be contended, that the mere fraudulent intent of the vendor could avoid the deed, if the purchaser were free from that fraud." Accordingly, the action was dismissed, and it is clear that the learned Judge was relying on his interpretation of the operative section, not on the proviso. The case is, therefore, an authority for the proposition that where there is a *bona fide* purchase for valuable consideration the transaction cannot be impeached under the operative section unless the purchaser is shown to have been privy to the vendor's intention. Hence this appeal must be allowed, since the *onus* lay on the plaintiff, and he certainly made no attempt to discharge it himself, and it certainly was not discharged by the learned trial Judge not accepting the defendant's denial.

Although it would be sufficient for me to rely on the clear decision of Fry J. in the case to which I have referred, I should like to add that to my mind that decision is in accord with the plain reading of the sections. Once it is seen that at all events the primary object of sect. 14 was to protect a certain class of transferees under assignments subsequent to the original fraudulent conveyance, there is no incentive to construe sect. 10 in such a way that it will not already safeguard an original innocent purchaser. Similarly, if the purchase in such a case is not within sect. 10 there is no reason for not construing sect. 14 as dealing exclusively with subsequent transactions, and, in my opinion, sect. 14 does not deal with the original transaction at all, but only with subsequent transfers. First of all, it does not seem to me that sect. 14 is appropriately worded to meet the case of the original conveyance. For, if the original purchase is to be protected, then sect. 10 does not operate at all, and the provision should be that sect. 10 should not extend to, or be construed to, impeach the conveyance in such a case. The wording we should expect would be similar to that in sect. 4 of 27 Eliz. c. 4, viz.: "Provided also . . . that this Act . . . shall not extend or be construed to impeach, defeat, make void or frustrate any conveyance . . . made upon or for good consideration and *bona fide,*" &c. But sect. 14 does not exempt the fraudulent conveyance from the operation of sect. 10; in fact, it does not deal directly with any conveyance at all, but only with estates or interest conveyed in the manner stated. That is appropriate to a subsequent alienation, for what is alienated may only be a portion of the property originally conveyed or only a limited interest, and it is only such estate or interest that is protected in the case provided for, while, subject to the protection afforded to the estate or interest in question, sect. 10 operates on the original conveyance. Broadly, the effect of sect. 10 is only to charge the estate conveyed by the original conveyance, but the charge does not affect a subsequent *bona fide* purchaser for good consideration without notice. The case of *Halifax Joint Stock Banking Co. v. Gledhill* [1891] 1 Ch 3 shows how appropriate sect. 14 is to a subsequent transfer, and sect. 4 of 27 Eliz. c. 4 shows how inappropriate it would be in the case of the original conveyance. Further, it may be said that the nature and circumstances of the original transaction and of a subsequent transfer generally stand on such a different footing that it seems unlikely that they would have been grouped together. Now that it has been definitely decided that the original purchase is not hit by sect. 10, and that subsequent purchases are dealt with by sect. 14, the way is clear, despite observations in the older authorities, to hold that sect. 14 only deals with subsequent transfers.

The appeal must, therefore, be allowed, and the action dismissed with costs."

Voluntary Settlements to Defraud Purchasers

S.1 of the Conveyancing Act (Ireland) 1634 provides that any voluntary conveyance made with the intention of defrauding subsequent purchasers is void (interpreted as meaning voidable), as against subsequent purchasers for value, and s.3 of the Act goes on to exclude *bona fide* conveyances for good consideration from the ambit of the section. This legislation was interpreted in an unduly restrictive manner from the point of view of the person conveying the property[6] and as a result, the Voluntary Conveyances Act 1893 was passed which provided that no voluntary conveyance, if in fact made *bona fide* and without any fraudulent intent, should be deemed fraudulent by reason of any subsequent purchase for value. It was suggested by O'Connor MR in *National Bank Ltd v. Behan*[7] that despite this provision, the onus of proving the *bona fides* of a voluntary settlement still lay on the person seeking to uphold it. However, serious doubts were raised about the validity of such an interpretation by O'Brien LC in *Moore v. Kelly*[8] who suggested that the burden of proving fraud in such cases should lie on the person alleging it.

---

[6]   See e.g. *Gardiner v. Gardiner* (1861) 12 ICLR 565.
[7]   [1913] 1 IR 512.
[8]   [1918] 1 IR 169.

Moore v. Kelly
[1918] 1 IR 169

The defendants alleged that an indenture had been executed by an individual in difficult financial circumstances with the object of hindering and defeating a creditor. It was held by the Irish Court of Appeal that the onus of showing that the deed had been executed *mala fide* lay on the defendants and there was no evidence from which the court could infer any intention to defeat a creditor.

SIR IGNATIUS J. O'BRIEN C stated at pp.174–180: "By indenture, made on the 11th October, 1888, between John Moore, of the first part; Joseph Kelly and Christopher Moore, of the second part; and Christopher Moore, of the third part, Christopher Moore purported to convey to Joseph Kelly and Christopher Moore part of the lands of Finnea, to hold to them upon trust to pay the income to John Moore and his assigns during his life, and after his death for Christopher Moore absolutely; but, in the event of Christopher pre-deceasing John Moore without leaving issue him surviving at the decease of John Moore, it was provided that the lands should be held upon a series of trusts which it is not necessary to consider, as the events provided for did not happen. It was also provided that John Moore should grant to Rose Moore, his wife, if she survived him, a rent-charge of £40 per annum; and the lands were charged by him with the payment of the following sums of money: – £150 for his daughter Mary, £100 each for his daughters Kate and Anne, and £100 for each of his sons Peter, Thomas, John, Luke, and Owen – in all £750, to be payable on the death of John Moore. There was a provision for the maintenance, education, and advancement of his sons and daughters under the age of twenty-one, with power to pay to the daughters, on marriage, their portions.

Christopher Moore was married in September, 1901, to Julia White. She had a fortune of £300, and a settlement was made on the 14th September between John Moore, father, Rose Moore, his wife, Christopher Moore, son, and Julia White, the intended wife. It recited the indenture of the 11th October, 1888, and after the following recital:– "Whereas all the charges on the said lands of Finnea have been paid off and satisfied by the said John Moore," it was witnessed that in consideration of the marriage and of the sum of £300 to be secured to the said John Moore by the promissory note of Julia White and her brother, the lands were conveyed by John Moore to Christopher Moore and Julia White upon limitations which in effect conferred life estates upon them and the survivor of them with remainder to their children as appointed.

The recital that the charges created by the earlier deed had been paid off was not true in fact. Mary, a daughter of John Moore, appears to have been paid a portion of the fortune of Julia White; but the other members of the family had not in fact received their portions; it may, however, have been thought that, although not paid, they had been, in fairness, settled with. Now, however, the father having died, the plaintiffs have brought the present action for a declaration that the sum of £750 provided by the settlement of 1888 – in so far, of course, as any claims may not have been paid or discharged – may be raised out of the lands.

One cannot help having very great sympathy with the defendant Christopher Moore; and, certainly, it is very hard that the fortune of his wife should have been parted with, and that the provision which was intended to be made for her may, to a great extent, if not altogether, fail. But one cannot decide a case having regard merely to sympathy. If, therefore, the claims of some of these children are good in law, and if the voluntary settlement made by their father must be regarded as an honest dealing with the property, they also have got rights which in justice ought not to be disturbed. It is to be regretted that the honest efforts which were made to effect an adjustment of the rights of all the parties, irrespective of strictly legal considerations, did not succeed. This cannot affect the decision.

This defence in substance is this: It is not admitted that the deed of 1888 was a voluntary settlement; but it is contended that the 14th September, 1901, placed the defendants in the position of purchasers for value, so that if the first deed was voluntary (and as everything had taken place prior to the statute 56 & 57 Vict. c. 21), the first deed should be treated as fraudulent and void as against those claiming under the second deed. I assume in my judgment that the first deed was voluntary. I have so clear an opinion of the legal question involved that I prefer to treat the case on that footing although it may be otherwise in fact. The Voluntary Conveyances Act, 1893, has, however, made a vital alteration in the law; and the contention on behalf of the respondents is that it operates as a complete answer to the defence.

Several questions of law have been argued before us on behalf of the appellants, the defendants in the action; and one question of pure fact has also been discussed, It was urged by the appellants that at the date of the execution of the deed of 1888, John Moore, the settlor, was indebted in a large sum of money to a man named Carson; that he was in embarrassed circumstances and financial difficulties; and that the deed was executed with the object of hindering and defeating this particular creditor, along with other creditors; that it was never intended to be acted upon, and was never acted upon; and that this arrangement was made with the consent of all the parties, and to aid in the carrying out of the fraudulent object in view.

Assuming the true view of the facts to be as suggested, and that the object of the deed was to hinder and defeat the creditors of John Moore, it was then argued as a matter of law that the deed was avoided by the second deed, even though none of the parties could be regarded as a creditor of John Moore; that, in order to bring the deed within the statute of 1893, it was necessary for the plaintiffs to negative the existence of any mala fides; and that if the object of the deed was to hinder, defeat, and delay creditors, a fraudulent intent was established, which would make it void in favour of a subsequent purchaser, even though there was no attempt to commit a fraud on a purchaser, as distinguished from a creditor, and although no creditor had elected to treat the deed as fraudulent as against him.

The Master of the Rolls held, as a fact, that there was no evidence from which he could infer any intention to defeat Carson or any other creditors, and I agree with him in that view. This, of course, is a complete answer to the appellants' case in so far as it is based on the argument that an intent to defeat creditors under the 13 Eliz. will enable a deed to be avoided as against a purchaser under the 27 Eliz. I do not, however, assent to the legal contention put forward, which I will deal with later on. There remains the other view, namely, that under the Act of 1893, the plaintiffs were bound, affirmatively, to prove that the deed as executed by John Moore, had been executed bona fide. I may say at once that I do not see any evidence from which to infer that this deed was not intended to be an operative instrument, or that there was in fact, and as distinguished from legal presumption, any intent to hinder or defeat any future purchasers.

It is true that the deed was not delivered to one of the trustees, and it certainly appears to have remained in the house of the settlor; but when inquiries were made with regard to it, on the occasion of the marriage of Christopher Moore, it was treated as being a deed fully in operation, and the only question raised was whether the terms of it had been satisfied. Indeed the defendants are precluded, I think, from contending that the deed was a mere pocket instrument, inasmuch as it is treated in the deed under which they themselves take as having been a perfectly good instrument, although by an unhappy but innocent representation an error was made as to the beneficiaries under the first deed, in fact, having been satisfied. As for the contention which appears on the pleadings, that the beneficiaries had abandoned all claim under the deed, the evidence is all the other way. A case is sought to be made against one member of the family on the ground that she wrote letters which brought home to her mind the inaccuracy of the statement contained in the deed, but she was very young; moreover, she acted only as an amanuensis, and, in the circumstances, I can see no reason for binding her to any waiver of the trusts in her favour.

I do not think it is necessary to go into the details of the evidence which satisfies me as to the correctness of the inference which the Master of the Rolls has drawn, and which I also draw. I propose now to deal with the questions of law which were raised, and which I have already indicated. It was decided by the Master of the Rolls in *National Bank v. Behan* [1913] 1 IR 512 that on the true construction of the Voluntary Conveyances Act, 1893, the onus of proving that a voluntary deed was made bona fide and without fraudulent intent lay upon the party seeking the protection of the Act. I need hardly say that the opinion and judgment of so experienced a lawyer as the Master of the Rolls would never be overruled by me unless I considered that I was absolutely bound to come to a different conclusion. The fact that a similar view of the law is stated in May on Fraudulent and Voluntary Conveyances does not, of course, add any authoritative weight to the judgment of the Master of the Rolls; but it is, at the same time, a statement which I should not be disposed to treat in any other way than with respect.

Let us consider what was the position of affairs with regard to voluntary deeds under 27 Eliz. c. 4, apart from the Act of 1893. The purpose of that Act was to protect purchasers of lands against gifts and conveyances "meant and intended by the parties that so make the same to be fraudulent and covenous of purpose and intent to deceive such as have purchased or shall purchase the same" and then for remedy it was enacted that every such conveyance had or made or to be had or made "for the intent and of purpose to defraud and deceive" such persons as had purchased or should purchase, should, as against such purchasers, be deemed to be utterly void. What, to many lawyers appeared to be a singular and unreasonable construction was put on an Act which, on the face of it, might be regarded as fairly clear. Although voluntary conveyances were not mentioned in the Act, it was ultimately determined judicially, that the mere fact that a conveyance was voluntary and without consideration made it ipso facto void as against anyone who might afterwards become a purchaser of the lands dealt with by the voluntary conveyance. A fraudulent intent was presumed by the courts; and this presumption was conclusive and irrebuttable, so that, however honest, reasonable, fair, or just a voluntary conveyance was, it became mere waste paper on the production of a conveyance for value to a subsequent purchaser. A Statute which was framed to prevent injustice was so read as to do grave and serious injustice. Against this construction of the statute the feeling both of the profession and the public became in the end so strong that in 1893 the statute at present under consideration was passed.

The Act 27 Eliz. c. 4, of course, is not repealed, and it remains in operation to prevent fraud of the character described in the statute; but a presumption of fraudulent intent, wholly the outcome of judicial decision, has been got rid of by the Act of 1893. By sect. 2 of the Voluntary Conveyances Act, 1893, the rule of law, which defeated, irrespective of fairness, a voluntary conveyance, was abrogated, and the statute 27 Eliz. c. 4 was allowed to speak for itself and to avoid deeds, the real object of which was proved to be to defeat a future purchaser; but the onus of proving fraud is always on the person alleging it, though in many cases its existence may be an almost certain inference. And it seems to me that it would defeat the very object of sect. 2 of the Act of 1893, which was intended to destroy the former rule of law, to hold that it was only intended to modify it to the extent that a party, supporting an honest deed, might be at liberty to show as a substantive case that the deed was made bona fide. How such an onus could be discharged it is difficult to see. It seems to me that practically it could only take the form of swearing to a negative – a perfectly futile proceeding. The words "if in fact made bona fide and without any fraudulent intent" appear to me to have been inserted lest the latter part of the section might be construed to have gone too far, and to have amounted to a repeal of 27 Eliz. c. 4, or of 10 Chas. 1, s. 2, c. 3 (Ir.), dealing with this question. I think it could never have been intended that there was to be read into the statute of 27 Eliz. c. 4 what in substance would be this: "voluntary conveyances shall be deemed to be fraudulent unless the contrary is proved." The intention was, I think, to get rid of an inequitable rule with regard to voluntary conveyances, leaving them to be destroyed by evidence of fraudulent intent; and, ordinarily, I should have thought that the person on whom the onus of proof would lie under 27 Eliz. c. 4, once the irrebuttable presumption to which I have referred was swept away, was the person alleging fraud, just as under 13 Eliz, c. 5, where an actual intent to defraud the grantor's creditors is alleged, the burden of proving such intent falls on the person alleging it. The two classes of deeds appear to me to be placed on the same footing in this respect; and the Act of 1893 might, in many cases, wholly fail to get rid of the evil it was intended to remove if it was held to have set up a new role quite as artificial, if not more artificial, than that which it was designed to destroy.

The same method of reasoning induces me, without hesitation, to decide against the appellants' contention with regard to the second question argued by them, namely, that "without any fraudulent intent" did not mean a fraudulent intent to defeat purchasers. The expression "if in fact made bona fide and without any fraudulent intent" must, to my mind, be read as referring to 27 Eliz. c. 4. Of course, there may have been cases where a voluntary deed could have been avoided under 13 Eliz. c. 5 as well as under 27 Eliz. c. 4, where it was found simpler to apply the irrebuttable legal presumption which got rid of it under 27 Eliz. c. 4. But if the latter Act and that of 1893 are read together, as they must be, I cannot read into 27 Eliz. words which would extend the operation of that statute in a direction, to my mind, never contemplated. Gifts intended to defeat purchasers are the transactions that are avoided. The fraudulent intent in 27 Eliz. is a fraudulent intent to defeat purchasers. Why should I read fraudulent intent in the Act of 1893 in a different sense from what it bears in the statute 27 Eliz. c. 4?

If sect. 2 of the Act of 1893 was to be taken as a perfectly independent enactment affirmatively avoiding all voluntary conveyance unless any kind of fraudulent intent was negatived, then the contention of the appellants on both grounds might be right; but once I treat it as a statute to get rid of certain effects, of judge-made law, and to be read with the Act of 27 Eliz. c. 4, and not as an independent enactment, the construction put upon it by the appellants, to my mind, is not sustainable."

Settlements by Bankrupts

S.59 of the Bankruptcy Act 1988[9] provides that any settlement of property, not being a settlement before and in consideration of marriage, or made in

---

[9] This section replaced s.52 of the Bankruptcy (Ireland) Amendment Act 1872.

favour of a purchaser or incumbrancer in good faith and for valuable consideration, shall be void (interpreted as voidable) as against the official assignee if the settlor is adjudicated bankrupt within two years of the date of the settlement and, if the settlor is adjudicated bankrupt within five years of the date of the settlement, shall be void (interpreted as voidable) unless the parties claiming under the settlement prove that the settlor was, at the time of making the settlement, able to pay all his debts without the aid of the property comprised in it and that the interest of the settlor in such property passed to the trustee of the settlement on its execution.

There is no requirement to prove any fraudulent intent on the part of the settlor and it is the mere fact of him becoming bankrupt within the period of time laid down in the statute which brings the section into operation. In order to secure protection against its provisions it is necessary that the conveyance should be both for valuable consideration and *bona fide* or that the settlement should not be one in consideration of marriage.[10]

S.59 of the Bankruptcy Act 1988:

59.—(1) Any settlement of property, not being a settlement made before and in consideration of marriage, or made in favour of a purchaser or incumbrancer in good faith and for valuable consideration, shall—

(a) if the settlor is adjudicated bankrupt within two years after the date of the settlement, be void as against the Official Assignee, and

(b) if the settlor is adjudicated bankrupt at any subsequent time within five years after the date of the settlement, be void as against the Official Assignee unless the parties claiming under the settlement prove that the settlor was, at the time of making the settlement, able to pay all his debts without the aid of the property comprised in the settlement and that the interest of the settlor in such property passed to the trustee of such settlement on the execution thereof.

(2) A covenant or contract made by any person (in this section called the settlor) in consideration of his or her marriage, either for the future payment of money for the benefit of the settlor's spouse or children, or for the future settlement, on or for the settlor's spouse or children, of property wherein the settlor had not at the date of the marriage any estate or interest, whether vested or contingent, in possession or remainder, shall, if the settlor is adjudicated bankrupt and the covenant or contract has not been executed at the date of the adjudication, be void as against the Official Assignee, except so far as it enables the persons entitled under the covenant or contract to claim for dividend in the settlor's bankruptcy under or in respect of the covenant or contract, but any such claim to dividend shall be postponed until all the claims of the other creditors for valuable consideration in money or money's worth have been satisfied.

(3) Any payment of money (not being payment of premiums on a policy of

---

[10] *Re O'Neill* [1989] IR 544.

life assurance) or any transfer of property made by the settlor in pursuance of a covenant or contract to which *subsection (2)* applies shall be void as against the Official Assignee in the settlor's bankruptcy, unless the persons to whom the payment or transfer was made prove that:

(*a*) the payment or transfer was made more than two years before the date of the adjudication of the settlor, or

(*b*) at the date of the payment or transfer, the settlor was able to pay all his debts without the aid of the money so paid or the property so transferred, or

(*c*) the payment or transfer was made in pursuance of a covenant or contract to pay or transfer money or property expected to come to the settlor from or on the death of a particular person named in the covenant or contract, and was made within three months after the money or property came into the possession or under the control of the settlor;

but, in the event of any such payment or transfer being declared void, the persons to whom it was made shall be entitled to claim for dividend under or in respect of the covenant or contract in like manner as if it had not been executed at the date of the adjudication.

(4) In this section "settlement" includes any conveyance or transfer of property.

Re O'Neill
[1989] IR 544

The bankrupt conveyed his interest in premises to his daughter for slightly below the market value less than two years prior to being adjudicated bankrupt. The official assignee applied to have the conveyance set aside on the grounds that it had not been entered into *bona fide* and for valuable consideration. Hamilton P held, in granting the application, that while the daughter must be regarded as a purchaser for valuable consideration, she had not purchased the premises in good faith as she must have been aware of her father's financial position and of the fact that the object of the transaction was to hinder, delay and defraud his creditors.

HAMILTON P stated at pp.549–553: "In the absence of evidence to the contrary, I must accept Miss O'Neill's averment that she had, in May and June, 1985, paid to her father and mother the sums of £7,000 and £5,000 respectively and that she had guaranteed her father's liability of approximately £16,000 to Lombard and Ulster Banking Limited by way of letter of lien over her deposit account with that company and that she had suffered a loss of £3,738 upon the giving of that guarantee and that these payments were reflected in the purchase price, though these facts would appear to be at variance with the averment contained in paragraph 10 of her affidavit that:–

"It would never have occurred to me, prior to the sale aforesaid, and up to the time when I became aware of his bankruptcy, to question my father's solvency."

I am satisfied that at the time of the transaction sought to be set aside by the Official Assignee:

(1) The bankrupt was insolvent;

(2) Judgment against him in the sum of £63,000 had been obtained by the petitioning creditor;

(3) The terms upon which the stay of execution had been granted had not been honoured.

(4) The injunction granted on the 23rd July, 1984, and continued by the order made on the 17th October, 1985, remained in force;

(5) The said Susan O'Neill was at all times fully aware of the action by the petitioner against Central Financiers Ltd. and the bankrupt, her father; of the injunction granted by the High Court; of the terms of the order made on the 17th October, 1985; of the amounts payable in accordance with the consent executed by the parties, the dates of such payments and, at least in a general way, of her father's financial position.

In support of this application, the Official Assignee relies on the provisions of three Irish Statutes namely, the Fraudulent Conveyances Act, 1634 (10 Chas. 1, sess. 2, c. 3), s. 1, the Irish Bankrupt and Insolvent Act, 1857, and the Bankruptcy Ireland (Amendment) Act, 1872.

By the statute of 10 Chas. 1, sess. 2, c. 3, s. 1 it is enacted that every feoffment, gift, grant, alienation, bargain and conveyance of lands, tenements, hereditaments, goods and chattels, or of any lease, rent, common or other profit out of the same or any of them, by writing or otherwise; and every bond, suit, judgment and execution made for the purpose and intent to delay, hinder or defraud creditors and others of their just and lawful debts, rights and remedies shall be henceforth deemed and taken (only against that person or persons, his or their heirs, successors, executors, administrators and assigns whose debts, rights and remedies are, shall or might be in any way disturbed, hindered, delayed or defrauded) to be clearly and utterly void.

But it is further provided that this Act shall not extend to any estate or interest in any lands, tenements, hereditaments or chattels assured upon good consideration and *bona fide* to any person not having, at the time of such conveyances or assurances to them made, any manner of notice or knowledge of the intended fraud.

Section 314 of the Irish Bankrupt and Insolvent Act, 1857, provides:

"If any bankrupt or insolvent, being at the time in insolvent circumstances, shall (except upon the marriage of any of his children or for some valuable consideration) have conveyed, assigned, or transferred to any of his children or to any other person any hereditaments, offices, fees, annuities, leases, goods or chattels or have delivered or made over to any such persons any bills, bonds, notes, or other securities, or have transferred his debts to any other person or into any other person's name, the Court shall have power to order the same to be sold and disposed of for the benefit of the creditors; and every such sale shall be valid against the bankrupt or insolvent and such children and persons, and against all persons claiming under him."

Section 52 of the Bankruptcy (Ireland) Amendment Act, 1872, provides that:-

> "Any settlement of property made by a trader after the commencement of this Act, not being a settlement made before and in consideration of marriage, or made in favour of a purchaser or incumbrancer in good faith and for valuable consideration, or a settlement made on or for the wife or children of the settlor of property which has accrued to the settlor after marriage in right of his wife, shall, if the settlor becomes bankrupt within two years after the date of such settlement, be void as against the assignees or trustee of such bankrupt under the said Act or this Act, and shall, if the settlor becomes bankrupt at any subsequent time within ten years after the date of such settlement, unless the parties claiming under such settlement can prove that the settlor was at the time of making the settlement able to pay all his debts without the aid of the property comprised in such settlements, be void against such assignees or trustee. . . .
>
> 'Settlement' shall for the purposes of this section include any conveyance or transfer or property."

As I am satisfied that the conveyance sought to be set aside was made for some valuable consideration, the provisions of s. 314 of the Irish Bankrupt and Insolvent Act, 1857, do not apply or assist, in any way, the application of the Official Assignee in this case.

The provisions of s. 1 of 10 Chas. 1., sess. 2, c. 3, and s. 52 of the Bankruptcy (Ireland) Amendment Act, 1872, do not extend to conveyances made in good faith and upon good or valuable consideration. Both statutes protect conveyances if they have been made for valuable consideration and *bona fide* and to secure this protection it is necessary that the conveyance should be both for valuable consideration and *bona fide*.

I am not for the purposes of this application concerned with the adequacy or otherwise of the consideration, save and in so far as the adequacy or otherwise of the consideration is relevant to the question whether the transaction sought to be impugned was made in "good faith" as I am, as already stated, satisfied that the sum of £48,000 was paid by Susan O'Neill to the bankrupt and his wife in consideration of the assignment of the premises to her. Susan O'Neill must, in my opinion, be regarded as being a purchaser for valuable consideration and consequently the fundamental issue for determination by me in this case is whether in entering this impugned transaction Miss O'Neill acted in "good faith" because it is sufficient if Miss O'Neill acted in good faith and for valuable consideration.

In the course of his judgment in *Mackintosh v. Pogose* [1895] 1 Ch 505 at p. 509, Stirling J. stated:

> "But was the settlement made in good faith? Here I have not the same clear guidance. In *Hance v. Harding* (1888) 20 QBD 732 the Court were unanimously of opinion that all the parties had acted in good faith, and it is said that here one

of the parties at least (Mr. Pogose) did not so act, and that, consequently Mrs. Pogose is not a 'purchaser in good faith' within the meaning of the Act. Now, I am of opinion that a person is a 'purchaser in good faith' within the meaning of section 47 of the Bankruptcy Act of 1883, if he himself acts in good faith, and it is not necessary that both parties should act in good faith."

Though this statement dealt with the interpretation of "purchaser in good faith" within the meaning of s. 47 of the Bankruptcy Act, 1883, I am satisfied that it applies with equal validity to the terms of the two Irish statutes which I have quoted.

In the course of his said judgment, Mr. Justice Stirling further stated at p. 510 that:

"Lastly, in the case of *Butcher v. Stead* (1875) LR 7 HL 839, the House of Lords held that the words "in good faith" in sect. 2 of the Bankruptcy Act of 1869 must be taken to mean without notice that any fraud or fraudulent preference is intended."

With regard to the use of the term "*bona fide*" or "in good faith" in the statute of 10 Chas. 1, sess. 2, c. 3, s.1, I am satisfied that the use of the term must be taken to mean without notice of the intention to delay, hinder or defraud creditors of their lawful debts, rights and remedies.

As stated by Mr. Robb in his book "The Law and Practice of Bankruptcy and Arrangements in Ireland" at p. 19:

"It will be noticed that the element always necessary to avoid any conveyance under this statute is, that it should have been made 'with intent to delay, hinder or defraud creditors of their just debts'. Now where such intent can be established by direct proof the conveyance or settlement can always be set aside, notwithstanding that it has been made for valuable consideration for in this latter case it has not been made *bona fide*, although there is valuable consideration, for both are necessary. But in most cases it is not possible to give direct proof of the fraudulent intent, and those impeaching the deed, bill of sale, or other transaction have to ask the Court to presume the intent from the circumstances."

The onus is on the Official Assignee to establish as a matter of probability that the conveyance sought to be set aside was made by the bankrupt with intent to delay, hinder or defraud creditors of their lawful debts, rights and remedies. It is impossible to expect the Official Assignee to provide evidence by way of direct proof of such intent and it is open to the court to infer such intent from the circumstances.

Due to the failure of the bankrupt to disclose his whereabouts and to file a statement of affairs or otherwise co-operate with the Official Assignee, I am not in possession of all the circumstances relevant to this transaction. However, on the basis of the facts established by the Official Assignee, I have no doubt whatsoever that the intention of the bankrupt in executing the deed of conveyance sought to be impugned and set aside was to hinder, delay and defraud his creditors including the petitioning creditor herein. The circumstances upon which I rely in being satisfied as to this intent are as set out in the course of this judgment, and it is not necessary for me to repeat them.

I am, as I have said, satisfied that the intention of the bankrupt in entering into this transaction and the subsequent transaction entered into on the 15th January, 1986, whereby he conveyed to his daughter Jacqueline his interest in the other premises of which he was joint owner with his wife, namely, the apartment situate at No. 12 The Orchard, Grove House, Milltown in the City of Dublin, was to hinder, delay and defraud his creditors.

These transactions were entered into at a time when there was due and payable by him a sum of £63,000 to the petitioning creditor and when he was subject to the terms of an injunction granted by the High Court on the 23rd July, 1984, and continued by the terms of the order made by the High Court on the 17th October, 1985.

As the conveyance was made within two years of the adjudication of Thomas O'Neill as a bankrupt, the Official Assignee was entitled by virtue of the provisions of s. 52 of the Bankruptcy (Ireland) Amendment Act, 1872, to a declaration that the conveyance dated the 31st December, 1985, is void unless the conveyance was made in good faith and for valuable consideration.

The finding by me that the conveyance was made by the bankrupt with intent to hinder, delay and defraud his creditors does not decide the matter.

It must be established that the conveyance was not made in good faith and for valuable consideration.

It is submitted on behalf of the Official Assignee that the onus in this regard rests on Susan O'Neill and it is submitted on her behalf that the onus rests on the Official Assignee.

In *Halsbury's Laws of England* (4th ed.) Vol. 3, para. 901 it is stated that:-

> "A purchase for value, but not made in good faith, that is, where the purchaser is privy to an intention to defeat creditors, is voidable. The onus of proof that the transaction was not made in good faith and for valuable consideration lies on the trustee in bankruptcy."

Without deciding finally on whom the onus on this issue rests, I am prepared to deal with this particular case on the basis that the onus is on the Official Assignee to establish the lack of good faith on the part of Susan O'Neill in this transaction because I am satisfied from the evidence available to me that Susan O'Neill must have been aware of the financial position of her father, the terms of the order made by the High Court on the 17th October, 1985, the obligations of her father on foot thereof and that the object of the transaction was to hinder, delay and defraud his creditors particularly the petitioning creditor. She has failed to make herself available for examination by the court in connection with this transaction though a subpoena was served on her through her solicitor to attend such examination and she further failed to attend at the hearing of this application.

No affidavit was filed by her in reply to the grounding affidavit of the Official Assignee. In fairness to her, I have had regard to the affidavit sworn by her on the 30th September, 1987, grounding an application to set aside an injunction made by me restraining her from dealing with or disposing of the property, No. 1, Ardilea Downs.

Consequently, I am satisfied that:–

1. The conveyance was made by the bankrupt with intent to hinder, delay and defraud his creditors including the petitioning creditor.

2. Susan O'Neill had due notice of his intention in that regard.

3. The purchase of the premises was not made by her in good faith.

Being so satisfied, the Official Assignee is entitled to a declaration that as regards the interest of the bankrupt in the said premises, the conveyance of such interest is void and should be set aside."

CHAPTER 12

The Administration of Trusts

THE OFFICE OF TRUSTEE

The circumstances in which a trustee may be appointed, retire from office or be removed from his position will be governed in the first instance by the terms of the trust instrument. In addition, beneficiaries may act to facilitate retirement or to effect the removal of a trustee provided that they are *sui juris* and between them absolutely entitled to the entire beneficial interest. However, statutory provisions often play an important role in determining such issues and the relevant sections of the Trustee Act 1893 are set out below.

Appointment of Trustees

Section 10 of the Trustee Act 1893:

Powers of appointing new trustees

10.—(1) Where a trustee, either original or substituted, and whether appointed by a court or otherwise, is dead, or remains out of the United Kingdom for more than twelve months, or desires to be discharged from all or any of the trusts or powers reposed in or conferred on him, or refuses or is unfit to act therein, or is incapable of acting therein, then the person or persons nominated for the purpose of appointing new trustees by the instrument, if any, creating the trust, or if there is no such person, or no such person able and willing to act, then the surviving or continuing trustees or trustee for the time being, or the personal representatives of the last surviving or continuing trustee, may, by writing, appoint another person or other persons to be a trustee or trustees in the place of the trustee dead, remaining out of the United Kingdom, desiring to be discharged, refusing, or being unfit or being incapable, as aforesaid.

(2) On the appointment of a new trustee for the whole or any part of trust property—

   (a) the number of trustees may be increased; and

   (b) a separate set of trustees may be appointed for any part of the trust property held on trusts distinct from those relating to any other part or parts of the trust property, notwithstanding that no new trustees or trustee are or is to be appointed for other parts of the trust property, and any existing trustee may be appointed or remain one of such separate set of trustees; or, if only one trustee was originally appointed, then one separate trustee may be so appointed for the first-mentioned part; and

   (c) it shall not be obligatory to appoint more than one new trustee where only one trustee was originally appointed, or to fill up the original number of trustees where more than two trustees were originally appointed; but, except where only one trustee was originally appointed, a trustee shall not be discharged under this section from his trust unless there will be at least two trustees to perform the trust; and

(d) any assurance or thing requisite for vesting the trust property, or any part thereof, jointly in the persons who are the trustees, shall be executed or done.

(3) Every new trustee so appointed, as well before as after all the trust property becomes by law, or by assurance, or otherwise, vested in him, shall have the same powers, authorities, and discretions and may in all respects act, as if he had been originally appointed a trustee by the instrument, if any, creating the trust.

(4) The provisions of this section relative to a trustee who is dead include the case of a person nominated trustee in a will but dying before the testator, and those relative to a continuing trustee include a refusing or retiring trustee, if willing to act in the execution of the provisions of this section.

(5) This section applies only if and as far as a contrary intention is not expressed in the instrument, if any, creating the trust, and shall have effect subject to the terms of that instrument and to any provisions therein contained.

(6) This section applies to trusts created either before or after the commencement of this Act.

Section 25 of the Trustee Act 1893:

Power of the Court to appoint new trustees

25.—(1) The High Court may, whenever it is expedient to appoint a new trustee or new trustees and it is found inexpedient, difficult, or impracticable so to do without the assistance of the Court, make an order for the appointment of a new trustee or new trustees either in substitution or in addition to an existing trustee or trustees, or although there is no existing trustee. In particular and without prejudice to the generality of the foregoing provision, the Court may make an order for the appointment of a new trustee in substitution for a trustee who is convicted of felony, or is a bankrupt.

(2) An order under this section, and any consequential vesting order or conveyance, shall not operate further or otherwise as a discharge to any former or continuing trustee than an appointment of new trustees under any power for that purpose contained in any instrument would have operated.

(3) Nothing in this section shall give power to appoint an executor or administrator.

Retirement of Trustees

Section 11 of the Trustee Act 1893:

Retirement of trustees

11. —(1) Where there are more than two trustees, if one of them by deed declares that he is desirous of being discharged from the trust, and if his co-trustees and such other person, if any, as is empowered to appoint trustees, by deed consent to the discharge of the trustee and to the vesting in the co-trustees alone of the trust property, then the trustee desirous of being discharged shall be deemed to have retired from the trust and shall, by the deed, be discharged therefrom, under this Act, without any new trustee being appointed in his place.

(2) Any assurance or thing requisite for vesting the trust property in the continuing trustees alone shall be executed or done.

(3) This section applies only if and as far as a contrary intention is not expressed in the instrument, if any, creating the trust, and shall have effect subject to the terms of that instrument and to any provisions therein contained.

(4) This section applies to trusts created either before or after the commencement of this Act.

Removal of Trustees

Arnott v. Arnott
(1924) 58 ILTR 145

The plaintiffs sought to have the defendant trustee removed from her position on the grounds that her persistent non-co-operation rendered the trust virtually unworkable. Murnaghan J held that the jurisdiction of the court to remove a trustee should be exercised if the welfare of the beneficiaries demanded it and granted the relief sought.

MURNAGHAN J stated at pp. 145–147: "In this case, Sir John Alexander Arnott, a trustee and beneficiary under the will of his father Sir John Arnott, which will with four codicils was proved on April 13, 1898, and Mrs. Rosina Johnston, also a beneficiary under the said will, have invoked the aid of the Court, and seek an order removing Lady Emily Jane Fitzgerald Arnott, the widow of the deceased and stepmother of the plaintiffs, from the trusteeship of the said will and codicils. They also ask for the appointment of a new trustee in the place of Lady Fitzgerald Arnott, and for consequential relief. This action is based, not upon specific acts of personal default, but upon a course of conduct on the part of Lady Fitzgerald Arnott, said to be persistent and unjustifiable obstruction in the matter of the trust, amounting to misconduct. Lady Fitzgerald Arnott has denied these allegations and brought a number of counter-charges against Sir John Arnott, some of them dealing with matters as far back as the year 1898, which, she alleges, made it necessary for her to investigate closely the actions of her co-trustee. She, in addition, alleges that she had discovered errors in the accounts of the trust estate, which made it desirable to have these accounts investigated, and has by a counterclaim asked to have a complete account taken of all dealing with the trust estate and the income thereof from March 28, 1898, down to the present time. The action, I regret to say, is one of a family nature, which manifests the existence of difficulties too serious to be bridged over. Had it been otherwise I would at some stage of the proceedings have suggested to the parties the possibility of arriving at some method of composing their differences. As a consequence, the principal dealings with the trust estate during the period of twenty-five years have been investigated before me, and a great mass of evidence, documentary and oral, has been adduced. It is necessary, therefore, that I should state the findings of fact which I have arrived at in reference to the principal matters before I come to apply what I conceive to be the law to these findings. Under clause 18 of the will, Sir John Arnott was given full power and authority to make all necessary decisions and to act in all matters connected with the administration of the estate on his own responsibility, and Lady Fitzgerald Arnott's formal assent alone was necessary. It is quite easy to understand that a man engaged in carrying on several large and successful business concerns foresaw the desirability of having a single head and undivided control, and whilst he was anxious to nominate his wife as executrix and trustee as a mark of his affection he did so with a qualification which enabled his son, Sir John Arnott, to continue the management of affairs with undivided control. Lady Fitzgerald Arnott alleged that she signed certain documents without knowledge and in circumstances that would amount to fraud on the part of Sir John Arnott, but her evidence was quite at variance with her letter to Sir John Arnott, dated May 28, 1898. As regards the Bristol Navigation Steamship shares, I find that they were fairly valued at £3 10s. per share in the valuation submitted to Lady Fitzgerald Arnott, the form of appropriation of which she signed, and that in the whole transaction Sir John Arnott did nothing which fairly gave rise to criticism, much less to censure. Since 1914 the estate had greatly benefited by the enormous appreciation which the shares of this Company, in common with most Shipping Companies, had experienced. But it is as idle to make this unforeseen appreciation in value the basis of a charge of misconduct on the part of Sir John Arnott as it was to blame him, as Lady Fitzgerald Arnott did, for investing in consols in the year 1900 at 86. The flotation of the *Irish Times* into a limited company was in precisely the same position as the Bristol Steamship Navigation shares. Lady Fitzgerald Arnott, in May, 1898, wrote that her children would be perfectly satisfied and pleased to accept shares in the *Irish Times*. The defendant subsequently raised objection to the proposed amount of capital, and the formation of the company was postponed. In 1900, however, the company was formed with a capital of £450,000, divided into 55,000 preference shares of £5 each and 35,000 ordinary shares of £5 each. The ordinary shares were largely held as portions of the trust estate, and I find that the transaction was carried out with prudence and judgment by Sir John Arnott, and resulted in great benefit to the estate. It is to be remarked that in 1917 Lady Fitzgerald Arnott was pressing to have the trust moneys invested in preference shares in the *Irish Times* which she advocated in preference to 4 per cent tax free War Loan. [His lordship then referred to the previous litigation between the Parties to this action *(Arnott, deceased; Arnott v. Arnott* [1899] 1 IR 201; *Arnott v. Arnott* [1906] 1 IR 127.] About the beginning of 1920 an alteration was made in the Articles of Association of the *Irish Times,* Ltd., which was the subject-matter of complaint in paragraph 4 of the defence. This alteration of the Articles gave to the holder of preference shares, who had hitherto been excluded from voting, save in certain specified matters, voting rights after the death of Sir John Arnott, or earlier, at his option. The avowed object of this alteration was to counteract the power which Lady Fitzgerald Arnott would have as the registered owner of ordinary shares in the event of the death of Sir John Arnott. Sir John Arnott stated in his evidence that this alteration was made in the interests of the trust estate and of the shareholders of the company, and was done in the belief that it was necessary to avoid having Lady Fitzgerald Arnott in control of the paper. Lady Fitzgerald Arnott contended that such action on the part of Sir John Arnott was contrary to the terms of the will, but in my opinion Sir John Arnott was within his rights in bringing about this alteration. In the years 1920 and 1921 a series of very disagreeable incidents occurred. Lady Fitzgerald Arnott adopted the plan of sending numerous post cards, mostly unstamped, containing demands for money and payment of expenses in connection with the grave of the late Sir John Arnott. Some of them were directed to the Viceregal Lodge and other places, with a view, as Lady Fitzgerald Arnott said in the witness box, of causing hurt and annoyance. Lady Fitzgerald Arnott, I believe realizes how improper her actions were in this respect and suggests that she acted under great provocation. It is evident that all chance of harmonious working together was rendered impossible. In the years 1922 and 1923 there was considerable delay in the signing of cheques on the part of Lady Fitzgerald Arnott. She wished to have a voice in the selection of the charities to benefit under the trusts of the will and finally she wrote as if it were an accepted fact, that the will of the late Sir John Arnott was forged. Lady Fitzgerald Arnott refused to sign certain cheques, and on May 2, 1923, she wrote challenging the validity of the 18th clause, and stating most emphatically that the will of the late Sir John Arnott was forged and that she was prepared to prove the truth of her statement. That charge was made without any foundation, and it is difficult to know whether Lady Fitzgerald Arnott appreciated the meaning of the terms which she so often repeated, and she has now admitted that it was the language of anger and not of reason. Her feelings towards Sir John Arnott are, however, none the less bitter. In her cross-examination she stated that she was tricked by him and did not trust him and by means of misreading the judgments of Sir A. Porter in *Arnott v. Arnott* [1899] 1 IR 127, claimed the right to be consulted before any action was taken by Sir John Arnott and by that means to render nugatory the 18th clause in the will to which she so strongly objected. In the defendant's counter-claim her allegation is that the accounts of the trust estate which have been furnished to her have been wholly inadequate, misleading and illusory. It has, however, been proved that the accounts have since 1898 been investigated by Messrs. Stokes Bros. & Pim, an eminent firm of chartered accountants and that each year a capital account and an income account has been prepared and furnished to Lady Fitzgerald Arnott. It is difficult to see what greater care in the preparation of the accounts could have been taken by the most zealous and scrupulous trustee. Mr. Bailey, a chartered accountant has investigated these accounts on behalf of Lady Fitzgerald Arnott, and spent over six weeks in the examination. Mr. Bailey stated that he sought to obtain certain documents. These documents were refused on the ground that Mr. Bailey was conducting an audit and not an examination, but information was offered on any matter that required examination. In my opinion Sir John Arnott was justified in refusing to have the audit already made checked over a second time. As regards the item in connection with the life interest of Lady Fitzgerald Arnott in Woodlands, which was purchased by the estate for £1,500, which was paid out of income, this payment out of income was made on the advice of Messrs. Stokes Bros. & Pim, on the ground that no value was placed on the life interest and there was nothing to write off and they thought it prudent to write off against income. I cannot see that the purchase of a life interest, which must cease on Lady Fitzgerald Arnott's death, could properly have been paid out of capital, and, personally, Lady Fitzgerald Arnott has enjoyed her share of the profits which have come to the estate by reason of the purchase of her life interest. It appeared at the trial that the revenue of the estate in respect of sales of timber was treated as income, save in the case of extraordinary sales, when tracts – *e.g.*, of 10 to 12 acres – were sold by auctions. In this way about £6,400 was treated as income, while £6,987 6s. was placed to capital, and it is suggested that if an exact account was taken Lady Fitzgerald Arnott would be found to have received as income sums considerably in excess of that to which she was entitled. I see no reason to have an account of the dealings with the trust estate taken in court by reason of the matters above mentioned. They are relied upon as instances justifying an order for an account, but in my opinion they fall far short of the grounds which would justify the court in re-opening at great expense long and dreary accounts which have been carefully prepared by skilled accountants. Stress was laid upon the admission of Mr. Pim that he throughout believed Lady Fitzgerald Arnott was interested in the capital – it must, I think, be that he regarded her and her children, who succeed to one-third of her residue, as having identical interests. No application has been made for an enquiry as to any specific matter which is alleged to have been erroneously dealt with. In my opinion the defendant's counter-claim must be dismissed. I now come to the question – What is the proper decision in reference to the plaintiff's claim for an order removing Lady Fitzgerald Arnott from the trusteeship? Her counsel have pointed out that the jurisdiction of the court to remove a trustee is a delicate one, and should be exercised with caution. It is usually resorted to when the trustee has mismanaged the trust, or has been proved to be dishonest or incompetent. But the guiding principle to which all others must be subordinate, in these matters is that laid down in *Letterstedt v. Broen* (1884) 9 App Cas 391 – that the main guide to the court must be the welfare of the beneficiaries. Their lordships in that case pointed out that if it appeared clear that the continuance of the trustee would be detrimental to the execution of the trusts, if for no other reason than that human infirmity would prevent those beneficially interested from working in harmony with the trustee, and there was no reason to the contrary from the intentions of the framer of the trust to give their trustee a benefit or otherwise, the court might think it proper to remove him, if, without reasonable ground, he refused to resign the trust. In that case their Lordships were dealing with a sole surviving trustee, who had differences with the beneficiary. Story in his "Equity Jurisprudence," section 1288, suggests that the court might remove a joint trustee from a trust who wished to continue in it without any direct or positive proof of his personal default upon the mere ground that the other co-trustee would not act with him. I need not, however, go so far but found my opinion upon what I conceive to be the welfare of the beneficiaries. In my opinion the trust estate would be endangered if matters are allowed to continue in the present unsatisfactory state; in my opinion the difficulties have been brought about by the unreasonable conduct of Lady Fitzgerald Arnott. It appears to be impossible to make Lady Fitzgerald Arnott realise her position in the working of the trust as defined in the 18th clause in the will, and there is a danger to the trust in the future if she is allowed to continue as trustee. Apart from all questions of conduct, the 18th clause of the will places Sir John Arnott in an exceptional position, and he is entitled to the assistance of a trustee who will co-operate with him and who will not regard every action of his with distrust. For these reasons it is my duty to make an order removing Lady Fitzgerald Arnott from the further execution of the trusts created by the will. Lady Fitzgerald Arnott must pay the costs of the counter-claim, which has failed. As to the costs of the action, I believe that justice will be done by directing the plaintiff's costs to be paid out of the estate and that Lady Fitzgerald Arnott should bear her own costs. The question of the substitution of a trustee was referred to chambers."

Moore v. M'Glynn
[1894] 1 IR 74

The testator, who was a shopkeeper and postmaster, bequeathed all his property to his brother and son to be held on trust and managed by them for the benefit of his wife and children. The testator's brother was appointed postmaster and carried on this role in the same premises for a number of years but when he set up his own business in the town he opened the post office there. While Chatterton VC held that the new business should not be affected with a trust for the benefit of his brother's estate he was satisfied that it would be improper for the trustee to continue in a position where his personal interests and his duty to the trust might conflict.

CHATTERTON VC stated at pp.89–90: "Then as to the defendant Edward M'Glynn. He has been accused of gross breaches of trust on several grounds. The chief complaint is for setting up in business in the same town, which, to a considerable extent, was of the same nature as that carried on in the testator's house of business. I have not been referred to, nor am I aware of, any case deciding that an executor or trustee of a will carrying on the business of his testator is disabled from setting up a similar business in the same locality on his own account. If he in any way represents to the public that his own business is the same concern as that of which he is trustee, as by using the name of the testator's concern in connexion with his own business, or otherwise seeking to draw away the customers to his own shop, there might be some ground for an application to restrain him from so doing. But I am not prepared to hold that a trustee is guilty of a breach of trust in setting up for himself in a similar line of business in the neighbourhood, provided that he does not resort to deception, or solicitation of custom from persons dealing at the old shop. I have no sufficient proof here of any such malpractices by the defendant Edward M'Glynn. It is admitted that he did, on first opening his shop, send out circulars in the town, stating his having done so. No copy of the circulars has been proved, and I must take them to be such as described by the defendant in his uncontradicted evidence, and as not containing any such misleading statements. It is plain that the setting up a shop in a small town to a certain extent in rivalry with another must tend more or less to injure the business of any similar shop in the locality, and I think there would be an inconsistency between the duties of the defendant Edward, as trustee and manager of the testator's business, and the necessary personal interest which he must take in his own. I do not think I could, under such circumstances, grant an injunction to restrain him from carrying on his own business, or direct an inquiry whether any damages were occasioned by his doing so, but I am of opinion that his new position disqualifies him from remaining any longer a trustee, and it would have been better for him to have procured his removal from the trusteeship before setting up for himself. He should not be continued in a position where his duties and his self-interest may conflict. He has himself expressed by his counsel his willingness to retire from the trusts, and I shall remove him from being a trustee and manager, and appoint a new trustee in his place. I shall not appoint a receiver or manager of the business; the effect of my doing so would probably be ruinous to the business, and I have no reason to be dissatisfied with the management by the defendant Patrick J. M'Glynn."

Spencer v. Kinsella
[1996] 2 ILRM 401

Showgrounds in Gorey were vested in trustees on trust so that they might be used as a sports ground, park or pleasure ground subject to conditions as to payment or otherwise to be prescribed by the trustees. In recent years the grounds had been used by a local football club and coursing club and the land had also been used for the grazing of sheep. Complaints against the trustees were made by the football club which had spent money on the repair and maintenance of the grounds, and it was alleged that they were neglecting their duties and that the grounds were being allowed to fall into a state of disrepair. The plaintiffs sought the removal of the trustees on the basis that they had persistently refused to act when called on to do so and submitted that the welfare of the beneficiaries required this course of action. Barron J accepted that there was a conflict of interest and that the welfare of the beneficiaries was being affected and adjourned the matter for six months to enable the administration of the trust to be placed on a proper footing.

BARRON J stated at pp.408–410: "In all cases of trust, it is a truism to say that no trustee should allow his interests to conflict with his duty. Mr Byrne assumed that in making decisions he was there to protect the interests of the coursing club. Mr Kinsella has been cast in the same role on behalf of the football club.

It is difficult in a small town to find local people who would have no affiliation with any organisation seeking to use the grounds. Clearly, trustees should be persons without such affiliations. If such people cannot be found, then persons who are not too closely identified with any such organisation must act.

The deed provides for a management committee. Its function should be to ensure the smooth working of the use of the grounds having regard to the terms upon which the clubs and other organisations are entitled to use them. It is on this committee that those closely identified with any particular club or organisation have their proper place.

Part of the fault in the present situation lies with the officials of the department who became involved in 1976 and following the letter in 1993. It must have been clear to them that the fault lay as much with the absence of implementation of clause 11 of the trust deed as with the attitude of the trustees. These proceedings have been brought to have the trustees removed. The question for determination is whether having regard to the causes of the present situation which have been identified such a course is appropriate.

In *Arnott v. Arnott* (1924) 58 ILTR 145, Murnaghan J accepted the guiding principle for the removal of a trustee as being the welfare of the beneficiaries. In that case there was a long and irreconcilable dispute between two members of the Arnott family. As a result it was found that there would be a danger to the trust in the future if the trustee to be removed was allowed to continue in her office. In that case the trustee had engaged in a long drawn out course of conduct which opposed all and every action of her co-trustee and would have continued to do so to the detriment of the trust.

A trust is set up for the welfare of its beneficiaries. In my view therefore before determining whether or not any trustee should be removed from his or her office it is necessary to determine whether his or her continuation in that office will be detrimental to such welfare.

In the present case the main problem lies in the failure of the trustees to execute agreements with the users of the trust. There is also the further problem that some of the trustees are too closely identified with the interests of some of those users to be regarded as being capable of being truly impartial in any decision making process involving the trustees. None of these faults have resulted from any deliberate or conscious conduct or misconduct on the part of the trustees. Nevertheless where conflict of interest arises it is doubtful that a continuation by such persons in office could be remedied.

I accept the submission on behalf of the minister that it is the function of the court and not of the minister to dismiss trustees if that be the appropriate course and that the court has no function to direct the minister to exercise his powers in that regard. I do not accept however that the remedy for the present disputes lies in the operation of s. 69(3) of the Land Act 1923. The issues go beyond the reversal of the decisions of the trustees.

The welfare of the beneficiaries is being affected by the present situation. There is a conflict of interest which I have identified and it would be difficult to reorganise with such conflict on the part of some of the trustees continuing to exist. It is accordingly appropriate that such persons should step down. It will however serve no purpose if they step down, but at the same time no other reorganisation takes place.

What is needed is the appointment of trustees who are, so far as is possible, impartial as between the users of the grounds. The execution of agreements with such users and the appointment of a management committee to manage in accordance with such agreements is a further necessity.

I do not propose to exercise the powers of the court at present. It is essentially a matter for the people of Gorey and the department to reorganise the administration of the trust. Any order made by the court must, having regard to the matters in issue before it, deal only with part of what is required, which would not be satisfactory.

Accordingly the matter will be adjourned for six months to enable the administration of the trust to be placed upon a proper footing. Only if this cannot be done will the court consider how the exercise of its powers can be used to alleviate the then situation."

DUTIES OF TRUSTEES

Duty of Investment

A trustee's duty to invest trust property is governed in the first instance by the terms of the trust instrument although no matter how extensive the power conferred, he is under an obligation to observe certain minimum standards of care and not to act in a dishonest or negligent manner. In the absence of any express guidance in the trust instrument or subject to what it may provide, trustee investment powers may be delimited by what is defined as an authorised investment as set out in section 1 of the Trustee (Authorised Investments) Act 1958, as updated by statutory instrument (see SI No. 28 of 1998). As the case law considered below suggests, while there has been little change in the statement of the standard of care to be adhered to by trustees over the past 100 years, changing economic and financial practices have conferred a greater measure of discretion on trustees. However, it is important to stress that the law is still weighted in favour of a trustee who merely maintains trust assets and against one who is prepared to engage in a limited degree of risk taking in order to increase the value of these assets.[1] This must be questionable particularly where the trustee who pursues the latter course genuinely believes himself to be acting in the best interests of the beneficiaries and fears that inactivity on his part will lead to a diminution in real terms in the value of the trust.

From the point of view of the beneficiary, it is clear that where the default on the part of the trustees is due to lack of initiative rather than to speculative investment decisions, it would still seem to be extremely difficult for a beneficiary to succeed in establishing a breach of trust on the part of the trustee. Beneficiaries may legitimately have concerns that the law as it stands at present does not adequately protect them from the trustee who is guilty of inactivity or even neglect in relation to his investment duties. However, whether one views the law from the perspective of beneficiary or trustee, it is clear that any attempt to change existing principles will be problematic in view of the need to avoid encouraging trustees to engage in excessive speculation.

SI No. 28 of 1998:

TRUSTEE (AUTHORISED INVESTMENTS) ORDER, 1998

I, CHARLIE McCREEVY, Minister for Finance, in exercise of the powers conferred on me by subsection (1) of section 2 (inserted by section 80 of the Central Bank Act, 1997 (No. 8 of 1997)) of the Trustee (Authorised Investments) Act, 1958 (No. 8 of 1958), and having complied with subsection (3) of the said section 2, hereby order as follows:

1. (1) This Order may be cited as the Trustee (Authorised Investments) Order, 1998.

    (2) This Order shall come into operation on the 9th day of March, 1998.

---

[1] See *Nestle v. National Westminster Bank plc* [1993] 1 WLR 1260 and *Stacey v. Branch* [1995] 2 ILRM 136.

2.   (1) In this Order –
"authorised credit institution" means –

    (a) a person who is the holder of a licence under section 9 of the Central Bank Act, 1971 (No. 24 of 1971),

    (b) a person referred to in section 7 (4)(a)(ii) (inserted by section 30 of the Central Bank Act, 1989 (No. 16 of 1989)) of the Central Bank Act, 1971,

    (c) a building society within the meaning of the Building Societies Act, 1989 (No. 17 of 1989), or

    (d) a person who is the holder of an authorisation under the European Communities (Licensing and Supervision of Credit Institutions) Regulations, 1992 (S.I. No. 395 of 1992);

"authorised insurance undertaking" means the holder of an authorisation under the Insurance Acts and Regulations;

"the Bank" means the Central Bank of Ireland;

"the Life Assurance Regulations" means the European Communities (Life Assurance) Framework Regulations, 1994 (S.I. No. 360 of 1994);

"recognised credit-rating agency" means a credit-rating agency recognised by the Bank for the purposes of Council Directive 93/6/EEC of 15 March 1993 (O.J. No L 141/1 of 11.6.93);

"recognised exchange" means an exchange recognised by the Bank for the purposes of Council Directive 93/6/EEC of 15 March 1993;

"relevant collective investment scheme" means –

    (a) a unit trust scheme authorised by the Bank under the Unit Trusts Act, 1990 (No. 37 of 1990),

    (b) a designated investment company authorised by the Bank under Part XIII of the Companies Act, 1990 (No. 33 of 1990),

    (c) a collective investment scheme authorised by the Bank under the European Communities (Undertakings for Collective Investment in Transferable Securities) Regulations, 1989 (S.I. No. 78 of 1989),

    (d) a collective investment scheme established in another Member State of the European Communities that has been authorised in accordance with Council Directive 85/611/EEC of 20 December 1985 (O.J. No L 375/3 of 31.12.85), or

    (e) any other collective investment scheme established in another state and approved by the Bank for the purpose of its being marketed in the State,

but excluding a collective investment scheme that is marketed solely to professional or qualifying investors of such class or classes as may be determined by the Bank;

"relevant State body" means a public company (within the meaning of the Companies Act, 1963 (No. 33 of 1963)) the majority of whose shares are held by a Minister of the Government or a body established by or under an Act of the Oireachtas (other than the Companies Acts, 1963 to 1990).

(2) In this Order a reference to any Act of the Oireachtas or any instrument made under such an Act shall be construed as a reference to that Act or instrument as amended by or under any subsequent such Act or instrument.

3. The investments specified in section 1 (inserted by section 1 of the Trustee (Authorised Investments) Act, 1958 (No. 8 of 1958)) of the Trustee Act, 1893, are hereby varied by–
    (a) the deletion of the investments specified in that section, and
    (b) the insertion in that section of the investments specified in the First Schedule to this Order.

4. (1) Subject to section 2 (4) (inserted by section 80 of the Central Bank Act, 1997 (No. 8 of 1997)) and section 5 (inserted by the said section 80) of the Trustee (Authorised Investments) Act, 1958, a trustee shall comply with the conditions specified in the Second Schedule to this Order in respect of the investment of trust funds.
    (2) Nothing in that Schedule shall affect the powers of investment of a trustee of a scheme to which the Pensions Act, 1990 (No. 25 of 1990), applies.

FIRST SCHEDULE   Article 3

1. (1) securities issued by the State,
    (2) securities guaranteed as to capital and interest by the Minister for Finance or any other Minister of the Government,
    (3) securities (other than shares) of a relevant State body that either–
        (a) had net assets of not less than £100 million at the end of each of the three financial years immediately preceding the date of the investment, or
        (b) is referred to in section 7 (4)(a)(ii) (inserted by section 30 of the Central Bank Act, 1989) of the Central Bank Act, 1971,
    (4) securities (other than shares) of an authorised credit institution–
        (a) having maturity dates that are one year or less after the dates of their issue, or
        (b) that are listed on a recognised exchange if such securities have maturity dates that are more than one year after the dates of their issue,
    (5) securities of an issuer that have a rating–
        (a) in the case of long-term securities, that is not lower than AA or its equivalent, or
        (b) in the case of short-term securities, that is not lower than A1 or its equivalent,
    (6) an interest bearing deposit account with an authorised credit institution or, subject to section 137 (2) of the Central Bank Act, 1989, with the Bank,

(7) units or shares in a relevant collective investment scheme,

(8) annuity contracts specified at Class I of Annex I to the Life Assurance Regulations issued by an authorised insurance undertaking,

(9) life assurance contracts specified at Class I of Annex I to the Life Assurance Regulations issued by an authorised insurance undertaking and under which the capital sum repayable at maturity is not less than the capital sum invested,

(10) life assurance contracts specified at Class III of Annex I to the Life Assurance Regulations issued by an authorised insurance undertaking and linked to investment funds where an amount of those funds equal to not less than 90 per cent. of the net asset value thereof is held in cash deposits or in instruments that are listed on a recognised exchange,

(11) the equity of companies listed on the Irish Stock Exchange, being companies whose market capitalisation was not less than £100 million at the end of each of the three financial years immediately preceding the date of the investment,

(12) the equity of companies listed on a recognised exchange, being companies whose market capitalisation was not less than £500 million or its equivalent in the currency of another state at the end of each of the three financial years immediately preceding the date of the investment.

2. In paragraph 1 (5) of this Schedule "rating" means a rating given by not less than two recognised credit-rating agencies or a rating given by one recognised credit-rating agency in a case in which a rating lower than that rating is not given by any other such agency.

SECOND SCHEDULE   Article 4

1. A trustee shall not invest in instruments denominated in a currency other than the currency of the State if, immediately after the investment, the proportion of the trust funds invested in currencies other than the currency of the State would exceed 40 per cent of those funds.

2. A trustee shall not invest in a relevant collective investment scheme or in a life assurance contract of the class specified in paragraph 1(10) of the First Schedule to this Order if, immediately after the investment, the proportion of the trust funds invested in that particular scheme or, as may be appropriate, that particular contract would exceed one third of those funds.

3. (1) A trustee shall not invest in the equity of a company if, immediately after the investment, the proportion of the trust funds invested in that equity would exceed 10 per cent of those funds.

(2) Nothing in this paragraph shall prevent a trustee from taking up a bonus issue of shares, or a rights issue of shares, accruing to an investment of the trust funds in the equity of a company.

4. Where any part of the trust fund is invested in equities, the trustee shall review those investments at intervals of not more than six months.

GIVEN under my Official Seal, this 9th day of February, 1998.

CHARLIE McCREEVY
Minister for Finance.

EXPLANATORY NOTE

(This note is not part of the Instrument and does not purport to be a legal interpretation.)

This Order replaces the previous list of investments in which trust funds may be invested, as set out in section 1 of the Trustee (Authorised Investments) Act, 1958, with a new list. The Order also specifies conditions which, subject to the Trustee (Authorised Investments) Act, 1958, as amended by section 80 of the Central Bank Act, 1997, are to apply to the investment of trust funds. The Order comes into operation on 9 March, 1998.

Re O'Connor
[1913] 1 IR 69

A summons was taken out by the trustees of the testator's will for the determination of certain questions arising out of the administration of the property set aside by his trustees for his daughter and her children. The testator had left the residue of his property to trustees 'being at liberty to sell all my ships, houses and other property of mine, and invest same as they think most desirable but not in British funds...'

O'CONNOR MR stated at pp.75–77: "The principal question for determination is whether the trustees of the will had power to invest the testator's residuary estate in the purchase of freehold or leasehold property as well as on loan or in the purchase of such stocks, shares, or other property as they should think fit. One thing is certain, however unlimited the power of investment may be, the trustee remains subject to the jurisdiction of the Court. The trustee has no power to act dishonestly, negligently, or in breach of trust to invest on insufficient security, but, subject to the power of the Court to compel a dishonest, grossly negligent, or grossly incompetent trustee to account for money he has so invested, it is in the power of a testator or settlor to place in the hands of his trustee money to be invested in the fullest sense of the word, and I need no further or better authority for the proposition that a power to invest *simpliciter* enables a trustee to invest in the purchase of real estate, provided he does so honestly and as a reasonable man, than the Trustee Act, 1893, section 6 of which is a sufficient justification for the conclusion at which I have arrived on that point. The section runs as follows: – "A trustee having power to invest in the purchase of land or on mortgage of land may invest in the purchase or on mortgage of any land, notwithstanding the same is charged with a rent, under the powers of the Public Main Drainage Acts, 1846 to 1856, or the Landed Property Improvement (Ireland) Act, 1847, or by an absolute order made under the Improvement of Land Act, 1864, unless the terms of the trust expressly provide that the land to be purchased or taken in mortgage shall not be subject to any such prior charge." The word "invest" is there used as equivalent to purchase. A reference to Murray's New English Dictionary shows that the term "invest" is used in the sense of to purchase, as well as placing out money on loan or other security.

In my opinion, the dictionaries, lay and legal, support the view of Mr. Brown that the term "invest," unless cut down or minimized by the testator or settlor, embraces purchase of land with moneys, as well as placing money on loan. But Mr. Wilson's argument was a very cogent one, that the liberty given by the testator to the trustees to invest the proceeds of the sale of his property as they thought most desirable, except in British funds, did not authorize them to purchase land, and that a power to invest was not regarded as a power to purchase, and that all the provisions of the Trustee Act assumed or begged the question that there was on the face of the instrument a power to purchase land.

In my opinion there is the clearest and most express power in this will to invest in land, the only investment that is barred by the testator being that which is always regarded as most secure, the British funds. He empowers his trustees to sell all his property, and to invest the proceeds "as they think most desirable, but not in the British funds". There are no restrictions here except one, investment in British funds. If I may misuse the maxim *expressio unius est exclusio alterius*, it comes to this that the negation of the power to invest in British funds is an expression of a power and liberty to invest in any kind of investment known to the law, but the testator was well aware that the Court of Chancery would hold the trustees responsible for moneys that came to their hands, for the benefit of minors and others, if they did not act in the way in which a reasonable man acting with reasonable prudence and not grossly negligent would act, and that when trustees came to make up their accounts with their *cestui que trusts,* it could not be said that they had authority to purchase, *e.g.,* a number of houses in a street in such a state of disrepair that the local authority would order them to be pulled down."

Bartlett v. Barclays Bank Trust Co. Ltd
[1980] Ch 515

The defendant bank was trustee of a trust, the only assets of which were nearly all the shares in a family property company. It was thought that funds might be more readily raised to pay taxes due on the death of the life tenants if the company went public and that a public issue would be more successful if the company was also involved in property development. One speculative purchase resulted in large losses to the trust fund, and the plaintiff beneficiaries succeeded in their claim against the bank for breach of trust.

BRIGHTMAN J stated at pp 530–535: "What, then, was the duty of the bank and did the bank fail in its duty? It does not follow that because a trustee could have prevented a loss it is therefore liable for the loss. The questions which I must ask myself are (1) What was the duty of the bank as the holder of 99.8 per cent of the shares in BTL and BTH? (2) Was the bank in breach of duty in any and if so what respect? (3) If so, did that breach of duty cause the loss which was suffered by the trust estate? (4) If so, to what extent is the bank liable to make good that loss? In approaching these questions, I bear in mind that the attack on the bank is based, not on wrongful acts, but on wrongful omissions, that is to say, non-feasance not misfeasance.

The cases establish that it is the duty of a trustee to conduct the business of the trust with the same care as an ordinary prudent man of business would extend towards his own affairs: *In re Speight* (1883) 22 Ch D 727, *per* Sir George Jessel M.R. at p. 739 and Bowen L.J. at p. 762; affirmed on appeal, *Speight v. Gaunt* (1883) 9 App Cas 1, and see Lord Blackburn at p. 19. In applying this principle, Lindley L.J. (who was the third member of the court in the *Speight* case) added in *In re Whiteley* (1886) 33 Ch D 347, 355:

> ". . . care must be taken not to lose sight of the fact that the business of the trustee, and the business which the ordinary prudent man is supposed to be conducting for himself, is the business of investing money for the benefit of persons who are to enjoy it at some future time, and not for the sole benefit of the person entitled to the present income. The duty of a trustee is not to take such care only as a prudent man would take if he had only himself to consider; the duty rather is to take such care as an ordinary prudent man would take if he were minded to make an investment for the benefit of other people for whom he felt morally bound to provide. That is the kind of business the ordinary prudent man is supposed to be engaged in; and unless this is borne in mind the standard of a trustee's duty will be fixed too low; lower than it has ever yet been fixed, and lower certainly than the House of Lords or this Court endeavoured to fix it in *Speight v. Gaunt.*"

See on appeal *Learoyd v. Whiteley* (1887) 12 App Cas 727, where Lord Watson added, at p. 733:

> "Business men of ordinary prudence may, and frequently do, select investments

which are more or less of a speculative character; but it is the duty of a trustee to confine himself to the class of investments which are permitted by the trust, and likewise to avoid all investments of that class which are attended with hazard."

That does not mean that the trustee is bound to avoid all risk and in effect act as an insurer of the trust fund: see Bacon V.-C. in *In re Godfrey* (1883) 23 Ch D 483, 493:

> "No doubt it is the duty of a trustee, in administering the trusts of a will, to deal with property intrusted into his care exactly as any prudent man would deal with his own property. But the words in which the rule is expressed must not be strained beyond their meaning. Prudent businessmen in their dealings incur risk. That may and must happen in almost all human affairs."

The distinction is between a prudent degree of risk on the one hand, and hazard on the other. Nor must the court be astute to fix liability upon a trustee who has committed no more than an error of judgment, from which no business man, however prudent, can expect to be immune: see Lopes L.J. in *In re Chapman* [1896] 2 Ch 763, 778:

> "A trustee who is honest and reasonably competent is not to be held responsible for a mere error in judgment when the question which he has to consider is whether a security of a class authorized, but depreciated in value, should be retained or realized, provided he acts with reasonable care, prudence, and circumspection:"

If the trust had existed without the incorporation of BTL, so that the bank held the freehold and leasehold properties and other assets of BTL directly upon the trusts of the settlement, it would in my opinion have been a clear breach of trust for the bank to have hazarded trust money upon the Old Bailey development project in partnership with Stock Conversion. The Old Bailey project was a gamble, because it involved buying into the site at prices in excess of the investment values of the properties, with no certainty or probability, with no more than a chance, that planning permission could be obtained for a financially viable redevelopment, that the numerous proprietors would agree to sell out or join in the scheme, that finance would be available upon acceptable terms, and that the development would be completed, or at least become a marketable asset, before the time came to start winding up the trust. However one looks at it, the project was a hazardous speculation upon which no trustee could properly have ventured without explicit authority in the trust instrument. I therefore hold that the entire expenditure in the Old Bailey project would have been incurred in breach of trust, had the money been spent by the bank itself. The fact that it was a risk acceptable to the board of a wealthy company like Stock Conversion has little relevance.

I turn to the question, what was the duty of the bank as the holder of shares in BTL and BTH? I will first answer this question without regard to the position of the bank as a specialist trustee, to which I will advert later. The bank, as trustee, was bound to act in relation to the shares and to the controlling position which they conferred, in the same manner as a prudent man of business. The prudent man of business will act in such manner as is necessary to safeguard his investment. He will do this in two ways. If facts come to his knowledge which tell him that the company's affairs are not being conducted as they should be, or which put him on inquiry, he will take appropriate action. Appropriate action will no doubt consist in the first instance of inquiry of and consultation with the directors, and in the last but most unlikely resort, the convening of a general meeting to replace one or more directors. What the prudent man of business will *not* do is to content himself with the receipt of such information on the affairs of the company as a shareholder ordinarily receives at annual general meetings. Since he has the power to do so, he will go further and see that he has sufficient information to enable him to make a responsible decision from time to time either to let matters proceed as they are proceeding, or to intervene if he is dissatisfied. This topic was considered by Cross J. in *In re Lucking's Will Trusts* [1968] 1 WLR 866, more fully reported in [1967] 3 All ER 726. In that case nearly 70 per cent of the shares in the company were held by two trustees, L and B, as part of the estate of a deceased; about 29 per cent belonged to L in his own right, and 1 per cent belonged to L's wife. The directors in 1954 were Mr. and Mrs. L and D, who was the manager of the business. In 1956 B was appointed trustee to act jointly with L. The company was engaged in the manufacture and sale of shoe accessories. It had a small factory employing about 20 people, and one or two travellers. It also had an agency in France. D wrongfully drew some £15,000 from the company's bank account in excess of his remuneration, and later became bankrupt. The money was lost. Cross J. said, at p. 874:

> "The conduct of the defendant trustees is, I think, to be judged by the standard applied in *Speight v. Gaunt,* namely, that a trustee is only bound to conduct the business of the trust in such a way as an ordinary prudent man would conduct a business of his own. Now what steps, if any, does a reasonably prudent man who finds himself a majority shareholder in a private company take with regard to the management of the company's affairs? He does not, I think, content himself with such information as to the management of the company's affairs as he is entitled to as shareholder, but ensures that he is represented on the board. He may be prepared to run the business himself as managing director or, at least, to become a non-executive director while having the business managed by someone else. Alternatively, he may find someone who will act as his nominee on the board and report to him from time to time as to the company's affairs. In the same way, as it seems to me, trustees holding a controlling interest ought to ensure so far as they can that they have such information as to the progress of the company's affairs as directors would have. If they sit back and allow the company to be run by the minority shareholder and receive no more information than shareholders are entitled to, they do so at their risk if things go wrong."

I do not understand Cross J. to have been saying that in every case where trustees have a controlling interest in a company it is their duty to ensure that one of their number is a director or that they have a nominee on the board who will report from time to time on the affairs of the company. He was merely outlining convenient methods by which a prudent man of business (as also a trustee) with a controlling interest in a private company, can place himself in a position to make an informed decision whether any action is appropriate to be taken for the protection of his asset. Other methods may be equally satisfactory and convenient, depending upon the circumstances of the individual case. Alternatives which spring to mind are the receipt of copies of the agenda and minutes of board meetings if regularly held, the receipt of monthly management accounts in the case of a trading concern, or quarterly reports. Every case will depend on its own facts. The possibilities are endless. It would be useless, indeed misleading, to seek to lay down a general rule. The purpose to be achieved is not that of monitoring every move of the directors, but of making it reasonably probable, so far as circumstances permit, that the trustee or (as in the *Lucking* case) one of them will receive an adequate flow of information in time to enable the trustees to make use of their controlling interest should this be necessary for the protection of their trust asset, namely, the shareholding. The obtaining of information is not an end in itself, but merely a means of enabling the trustees to safeguard the interests of their beneficiaries.

The principle enunciated in the *Lucking* case appears to have been applied in *In re Miller's Deed Trusts* (unreported), March 21, 1978, a decision of Oliver J. No transcript of the judgment is available but the case is briefly noted in the Law Society's Gazette published on May 3, 1978. There is also a number of American decisions proceeding upon the same lines, to which counsel has helpfully referred me.

So far, I have applied the test of the ordinary prudent man of business. Although I am not aware that the point has previously been considered, except briefly in *In re Waterman's Will Trusts* [1952] 2 All ER 1054, I am of opinion that a higher duty of care is plainly due from someone like a trust corporation which carries on a specialised business of trust management. A trust corporation holds itself out in its advertising literature as being above ordinary mortals. With a specialist staff of trained trust officers and managers, with ready access to financial information and professional advice, dealing with and solving trust problems day after day, the trust corporation holds itself out, and rightly, as capable of providing an expertise which it would be unrealistic to expect and unjust to demand from the ordinary prudent man or woman who accepts, probably unpaid and sometimes reluctantly from a sense of family duty, the burdens of a trusteeship. Just as, under the law of contract, a professional person possessed of a particular skill is liable for breach of contract if he neglects to use the skill and experience which he professes, so I think that a professional corporate trustee is liable for breach of trust if loss is caused to the trust fund because it neglects to exercise the special care and skill which it professes to have. The advertising literature of the bank was not in evidence (other than the scale of fees) but counsel for the defendant did not dispute that trust corporations, including the bank, hold themselves out as possessing a superior ability for the conduct of trust business, and in any event I would take judicial notice of that fact. Having expressed my view of the higher duty required from a trust corporation, I should add that the bank's counsel did not dispute the proposition.

In my judgment the bank wrongfully and in breach of trust neglected to ensure that it received an adequate flow of information concerning the intentions and activities of the boards of BTL and BTH. It was not proper for the bank to confine itself to the receipt of the annual balance sheet and profit and loss account, detailed annual financial statements and the chairman's report and statement, and to attendance at the annual general meetings and the luncheons that followed, which were the limits of the bank's regular sources of information. Had the bank been in receipt of more frequent information it would have been able to step in and stop, and ought to have stopped, Mr. Roberts and the board embarking on the Old Bailey project. That project was imprudent and hazardous and wholly unsuitable for a trust whether undertaken by the bank direct or through the medium of its wholly owned company. Even without the regular flow of information which the bank ought to have had, it knew enough to put it upon inquiry. There were enough obvious points at which the bank should have intervened and asked questions. Assuming, as I do, that the questions would have been answered truthfully, the bank would have discovered the gamble upon which Mr. Roberts and his board were about to embark in relation to the Old Bailey site, and it could have, and should have, stopped the initial move towards disaster, and later on arrested further progress towards disaster. I have indicated in the course of this judgment a number of obvious points at which the bank should have intervened, and it would be repetitive to summarise them.

I hold that the bank failed in its duty, whether it is judged by the standard of the prudent man of business or of the skilled trust corporation. The bank's breach of duty caused the loss which was suffered by the trust estate. If the bank had intervened as it could and should have, that loss would not have been incurred. By "loss," I mean the depreciation which took place in the market value of the BT shares, by comparison with the value which the shares would have commanded if the loss on the Old Bailey project had not been incurred, and reduction of dividends through loss of income. The bank is liable for the loss so suffered by the trust estate, except to the extent that I shall hereafter indicate."

Nestle v. National Westminster Bank plc
[1993] 1 WLR 1260

By virtue of the terms of a settlement made in 1922 the defendant bank, the successor to the original trustee, was given wide powers to invest in equities.

However, the bank never obtained legal advice about the scope of its powers of investment and assumed that these were narrower than they in fact were. The plaintiff, the remainder beneficiary, contended that the trust fund which was worth approximately £269,000 when she became absolutely entitled in 1986 should have been worth well over £1 million by then if the fund had been properly invested. Hoffman J rejected the plaintiff's claim and concluded that the bank had acted conscientiously, fairly and carefully throughout its administration of the trust. The Court of Appeal (Staughton and Legatt JJ) dismissed the plaintiff's appeal and concluded that the plaintiff had not succeeded in establishing that she had suffered loss.

LEGATT LJ stated at pp.1281–1285: "When trusts came into their own in Victorian times they were no doubt intended to preserve capital while assuring beneficiaries of a steady, if conservative, income. Little was demanded of a trustee beyond the safeguarding of the trust fund by refraining from improvident investment. This process was no doubt also intended to save beneficiaries from trouble and anxiety, or what is now called "hassle."

But during the 64 years for which the trust set up by the plaintiff's grandfather endured, the contentment of his descendants declined. The plaintiff's uncle and father conducted with the respondent bank vigorous campaigns designed to improve their respective incomes, which, if the bank had not resisted them, would have worked to the ultimate detriment of the plaintiff, while the plaintiff herself is now locked in mortal financial combat with the bank.

George and John Nestle saw the bank, or said they saw the bank, as unfairly looking out for the plaintiff at their expense. In fact John turns out to have had a fortune of his own, which was invested in equities. So to the extent that he was successful in getting the bank to invest in gilts he was achieving a balance between his funds. The plaintiff, on the other hand, with whom her father was latterly at odds, has become obsessed with the idea that the bank over the years has failed to look after her interests. She claims that the sum of £269,203 which she inherited should have been larger than it was. It will not be of any consolation to her to reflect that, if since 1986 she had in that period done for the fund what she claims that the bank ought to have done for it previously, and it had grown at the same rate as the cost of living, it would probably now be worth over £400,000.

There is no dispute about the nature of the bank's duty. It was, as Lindley L.J. has expressed it, a duty "to take such care as an ordinary prudent man would take if he were minded to make an investment for the benefit of other people for whom he felt morally bound to provide:" *In re Whiteley; Whiteley v. Learoyd* (1886) 33 Ch D 347, 355. The trustee must have regard "not only to the interests of those who are entitled to the income, but to the interests of those who will take in future:" *per* Cotton L.J., at p.350. "A trustee must not choose investments other than those which the terms of his trust permit:" *Speight v. Gaunt* (1883) 9 App Cas 1, 19, *per* Lord Blackburn. So confined, the trustee must also "avoid all investments of that class which are attended with hazard:" *Learoyd v. Whiteley* (1887) 12 App Cas 727, 733, *per* Lord Watson. The power of investment

> "must be exercised so as to yield the best return for the beneficiaries, judged in relation to the risks of the investments in question; and the prospects of the yield of income and capital appreciation both have to be considered in judging the return from the investment:" *Cowan v. Scargill* [1985] Ch 270, 287.

Since the Trustee Investments Act 1961 came into force a trustee has been required by section 6(1) to have regard in the exercise of his powers of investment "to the need for diversification of investments of the trust, in so far as is appropriate to the circumstances of the trust." It is common ground that a trustee with a power of investment must undertake periodic reviews of the investments held by the trust. In relation to this trust, that would have meant a review carried out at least annually, and whenever else a reappraisal of the trust portfolio was requested or was otherwise requisite. It must also be borne in mind that, as expressed by the Report of the Scarman Committee on the Powers and Duties of Trustees (1982) ((Law Reform Committee: 23rd Report) Cmnd. 8733), at para. 2.15, "Professional trustees, such as banks, are under a special duty to display expertise in every aspect of their administration of the trust."

The plaintiff alleges that the bank is in breach of trust because over the years since her grandfather set up the trust the bank has supposed that its power of investment was more limited than it was; has failed to carry out periodic reviews of the portfolio, and to maintain a proper balance between equities and gilts, and to diversify the equity investments; and has unduly favoured the interests of her father and her uncle as life-tenants at the expense of her own interest as remainderman. She says that in consequence the trust fund was worth less in 1986 than it should have been.

The essence of the bank's duty was to take such steps as a prudent businessman would have taken to maintain and increase the value of the trust funds. Unless it failed to do so, it was not in breach of trust. A breach of duty will not be actionable, and therefore will be immaterial, if it does not cause loss. In this context I would endorse the concession of Mr. Nugee for the bank that "loss" will be incurred by a trust fund when it makes a gain less than would have been made by a prudent businessman. A claimant will therefore fail who cannot prove a loss in this sense caused by breach of duty. So here in order to make a case for an inquiry, the plaintiff must show that loss was caused by breach of duty on the part of the bank.

On the plaintiff's behalf Mr. Lyndon-Stanford seeks to rely on a presumption against a wrongdoing trustee. He invokes Brightman J.'s dictum in *Bartlett v. Barclays Bank Trust Co. Ltd. (Nos. 1 and 2)* [1980] Ch 515, 545, that "The trustee's obligation is to restore to the trust estate the assets of which he has deprived it." But that presupposes deprivation.

The plaintiff alleges, and I am content to assume, that the bank was at all material times under a misapprehension about the meaning of the investment clause in the will, with the result that the bank believed that the scope of its powers of investment was more confined than it was. I also regard it as unlikely that the bank conducted any reviews of the portfolio between 1922 and 1959. If any were conducted, they were unplanned, sporadic and indecisive. Mr. Lyndon-Stanford argues that it should be presumed that, had there been a better balance between gilts and equities and had the equity investment been more diversified, the fund would ultimately have been worth more than it was. The fallacy is that it does not follow from the fact that a wider power of investment was available to the bank than it realised either that it would have been exercised or that, if it had been, the exercise of it would have produced a result more beneficial to the bank than actually was produced. Loss cannot be presumed, if none would necessarily have resulted. Until it was proved that there was a loss, no attempt could be made to assess the amount of it.

In *Guerin v. The Queen* (1984) 13 DLR (4th) 321 the Crown leased to a golf club land belonging to an Indian band to which the Crown owed a fiduciary duty. Since the terms of the lease were unsatisfactory and the lease for 85 years was irrevocable, the court had to evaluate the loss to the band, and did so by presuming against the Crown that the band would have made the most profitable use of the land by letting it for residential development. That loss had been suffered by the letting to the golf club was obvious: the presumption applied in proving the extent of the loss by relieving the band from the need to prove that they would have let the land for development.

In my judgment either there was a loss in the present case or there was not. Unless there was a loss, there was no cause of action. It was for the plaintiff to prove on balance of probabilities that there was, or must have been, a loss. If proved, the court would then have had to assess the amount of it, and for the purpose of doing so might have had recourse to presumptions against the bank. In short, if it were shown that a loss was caused by breach of trust, such a presumption might avail the plaintiff in quantifying the loss. The plaintiff's difficulty is in reaching that stage.

The plaintiff therefore had to prove that a prudent trustee, knowing of the scope of the bank's investment power and conducting regular reviews, would so have invested the trust funds as to make it worth more than it was worth when the plaintiff inherited it. That was a matter for expert evidence. In the result there was evidence which the judge was entitled to accept and did accept that the bank did no less than expected of it up to the death of the testator's widow in 1960.

The proportion of the fund already invested in equities at the time when "Winterbourne" was sold makes it impossible in my judgment to impugn the decision to put the proceeds of sale into conversion stock.

After 1960 investment of the trust funds preponderantly in tax-exempt gilts for the benefit of life-tenants resident abroad is not shown to have produced a less satisfactory result for the remainderman than an investment in equities after taking into account savings in estate duty and capital transfer tax, because this policy had the effect of preserving the capital. By the time that John Nestle died the equities to replace the tax-exempt gilts would have had to be worth more than twice as much as the gilts in order to achieve the same benefit net of tax.

It is true that the calculations upon which the bank relied in making these comparisons were based on the assumptions that the whole fund was subject to estate duty, and that the bank did not contemplate that it might be able to take advantage of a late switch into gilts, especially in relation to Mrs. Elsie Nestle. But even if a less favourable assumption were made in relation to estate duty, the result would not have been so inferior as to demonstrate failure to look out for the remainderman amounting to a breach of trust. Similarly, although the fact that Mrs. Elsie Nestle returned to live in this country now indicates that it might have been advantageous if a switch into equities had been made after George's death, the bank cannot in my judgment be reproached for failing to anticipate that she would outlive her husband by 10 years, and that she would destroy the benefit of investment in tax-exempt gilts by resuming her domicile in England. Had she not done so, it would have been impossible for the bank to assess with any accuracy the timing of a switch back into gilts. In any event, without having pleaded any defect in the management of Mrs. Elsie Nestle's fund, the plaintiff cannot now rely on this argument.

No testator, in the light of this example, would choose this bank for the effective management of his investment. But the bank's engagement was as a trustee; and as such, it is to be judged not so much by success as by absence of proven default. The importance of preservation of a trust fund will always outweigh success in its advancement. Inevitably, a trustee in the bank's position wears a complacent air, because the virtue of safety will in practice put a premium on inactivity. Until the 1950s active management of the portfolio might have been seen as speculative, and even in these days such dealing would have to be notably successful before the expense would be justified. The very process of attempting to achieve a balance, or (if that be old-fashioned) fairness, as between the interests of life-tenants and those of a remainderman inevitably means that each can complain of being less well served than he or she ought to have been. But by the undemanding standard of prudence the bank is not shown to have committed any breach of trust resulting in loss.

I am therefore constrained to agree that the appeal must be dismissed."

Stacey v. Branch
[1995] 2 ILRM 136

The plaintiff beneficiary brought a claim against the defendant trustee alleging a breach of trust on the grounds that the latter had not managed a trust property with the necessary degree of care and claimed specifically that if this house had been let over a period of 14 years rather than maintained by a caretaker, it would have yielded a substantial rental income. The trust deed conferred on the defendant the power to deal with this property 'as he in his absolute discretion shall think fit' pending the attainment of 21 years by the plaintiff. Murphy J made it clear that words such as 'absolute discretion' would not necessarily relieve a trustee from his duty to exercise reasonable care and prudence. However, he was satisfied that the defendant's decision to place the caretaker in occupation of the premises was one made *bona fide* in the exercise of his discretion and he dismissed the plaintiff's claim.

MURPHY J stated at pp. 142–144: "What is the nature of the duty imposed upon a trustee? A trustee must, of course, invest trust funds in the securities authorised by the settlement or by statute. To invest in any other securities would be of itself a breach of trust; but, even with regard to those securities which are permissible, the trustee must take such care as a reasonably cautious man would take having regard not only to the interest of those who are entitled to the income but to the interest of those who will take in the future. In exercising his discretion a trustee must act honestly and must use as much diligence as a prudent man of business would exercise in dealing with his own private affairs; in selecting an investment he must take as much care as a prudent man would take in making an investment for the benefit of persons for whom he felt morally bound to provide. Businessmen of ordinary prudence may, and frequently do, select investments which are more or less of a speculative character; but it is the duty of a trustee to confine himself not only to the class of investments which are permitted by the settlement or by statute, but to avoid all such investments of that class as are attended with hazard.

Neither party dissented from the foregoing views taken from the leading textbooks and based on the decision of the House of Lords in *Learoyd v. Whiteley* (1887) 12 App Cas 727. Counsel on behalf of the plaintiffs emphasised the matter of fact that the beneficiary was at all material times an infant in need of financial support and asserted the proposition of law based on the decision in *Charles v. Jones* (1887) 35 Ch D 544 that a trustee is bound to set aside trust monies in such a way 'as to be fruitful for the benefit of the persons beneficially entitled to it'. However, without necessarily accepting either proposition, I am convinced that the course adopted by Mr Branch in relation to the property at Bettystown would not have amounted to an adequate discharge by a trustee of his duties as such in the absence of special authority or provision in that behalf.

Counsel on behalf of Mr Branch draws attention to the fact that the trustee was given, in certain respects at any rate, an 'absolute discretion' and it is asserted that provided that such discretion was exercised honestly it was not open to review by the court or capable of giving rise to an action for breach of trust. Reliance upon a discretion expressed to be absolute can be deceptive. In Snell's *Equity*, 29th ed. at p. 225 the authors comment as follows:

> However wide the language of such clauses, they give the trustee an absolute discretion in appearance only; as in the case of all discretionary powers, he must act honestly and with ordinary prudence. If, therefore, he selects an investment for the purpose of making a private gain, or if at the request of an importunate *cestui que trust* he invests the trust funds in notoriously doubtful security, even though it may be expressly authorised, he would be liable for any resulting loss.

That quotation is perhaps misleading. It is true to the extent that words such as 'absolute discretion' would not necessarily relieve a trustee from his duty to exercise reasonable care and prudence. On the other hand there is no doubt that an absolute owner of property can settle his affairs in such a way and on such terms as would relieve his trustees from the responsibility to exercise the degrees of care and prudence which would otherwise be inferred (see *Gisborne v. Gisborne* (1877) 2 App Cas 300 and *Tabor v. Brooks* (1878) 10 Ch D 273). At the end of the day the extent of the obligations imposed on a trustee or the degree to which he is relieved from responsibilities ordinarily assumed is a matter of the construction of the terms of the document under which the trustee is appointed.

The brief paragraph dealing with the trust of Windswept contains a number of clear provisions. First, the trustee was directed to hold the particular land in trust for John Stacey. The trustee was to hold Windswept and, subject to the exercise of any of the powers conferred on him, to transfer that property to the beneficiary as and when he attained the age of twenty one years. Secondly, no part of the trust property and in particular the trust of Windswept comprised or included liquid assets so that there was no fund available from the property as settled with which to make advances for maintenance or education or even to discharge such costs as might properly arise in the administration of the trust. Thirdly, it was expressly provided that 'in the meantime' – that is between the date of the trust deed and the attainment by the beneficiary of his majority – 'the trustee should have full power to deal with the aforesaid property as he in his absolute discretion shall think fit'. The powers of dealing with the property were expressed as including leasing the land on such conditions as the trustee should think fit and selling the land but in the latter case it is to be noted that the power to sell the land only arose if a sale was, or became, 'necessary'. Fourthly, the trusts declared of this property expressly provided that in the event of it being sold, the monies realised, to the extent that they were to be invested in funds, were required to be invested 'in investments for the time being authorised by or for the investment of trust funds'. Fifthly, it was expressly provided that in the event of any income being derived from the property known as Windswept, the trustees might at their discretion advance the same to Mrs Monahan for the maintenance and education of her son.

There is, therefore, an extraordinary emphasis placed on the discretion conferred upon the trustee to deal with the property as originally settled. It is in relation to that, and that alone, that 'full power to deal with' and 'absolute discretion' is conferred. Cash investments are limited expressly to trust securities and the sale of the property could only be permitted to the trustee or justified to a purchaser by establishing that such a sale was 'necessary'. The power of leasing which is included in the power 'to deal' is to be on conditions as the trustee 'thinks fit'.

Further assistance may be obtained by contrasting the trusts declared of Fairwinds with those declared in respect of Windswept. In relation to the former he expressly provided for the keeping of the property in a reasonable condition have regard to its age and condition where no such provision was made in explicit terms at any rate for Windswept.

It is clear that the settlor intended that Windswept should be kept by the trustee and ultimately transferred to his son. That would necessarily involve taking some steps to preserve the property between the creation of the trust and the property vesting in possession in the beneficiary. No funds were provided for that purpose. It was in those circumstances that the settlor purported to confer on the trustee 'full power to deal with the aforesaid property as he in his absolute discretion shall think fit'. In my view, the settlor meant what he said. He intended the trustee to have and to exercise his own honest but absolute discretion as to how this basic objective should be achieved. I am satisfied that the decision of Mr Branch to put the premises in the occupation of Mr Desmond Stacey was a decision made *bona fide* in pursuance of that discretion. It was not made with the dominant intention of benefiting Mr Desmond Stacey, though no doubt it did have that effect. Nor do I believe that the decision was made for the trustee's own convenience. Whilst I doubt that any competent valuer or other expert would have recommended or approved the course adopted by the trustee, I do have some sympathy with Mr Branch's viewpoint. He expressed his view that the sale of the property and the investment of the proceeds in shares would not necessarily have provided a good solution. He was sceptical of the wisdom of investing in shares. Likewise, he was critical of the solution which involved lettings to a succession of tenants. He is entitled to say that the property has, by and large, been well preserved over the past fourteen years and he states with confidence that it would be vested in the beneficiary on his majority in that good condition. Unusual though the trustee's attitude has been and unsupported by expert evidence as it is, I believe that his decision was honestly made and that it was made in exercise of the discretion which the settlor conferred on the trustee and reflected the trust and confidence reposed in him. In these circumstances it seems to me that an action for breach of trust must fail and I will dismiss the claim accordingly."

Cowan v. Scargill
[1985] Ch 270

A mineworkers pension fund was managed by ten trustees, five of whom were members of the National Union of Mineworkers. These five trustees refused to agree to a revised investment plan put forward on the basis, *inter alia*, that it contemplated increased overseas investment and investment in forms of energy such as oil and gas which were in competition with coal. It was held by Megarry VC that these trustees were in breach of duty in refusing to concur in the adoption of this investment plan.

MEGARRY VC stated at pp.286–289: "I turn to the law. The starting point is the duty of trustees to exercise their powers in the best interests of the present and future beneficiaries of the trust, holding the scales impartially between different classes of beneficiaries. This duty of the trustees towards their beneficiaries is paramount. They must, of course, obey the law; but subject to that, they must put the interests of their beneficiaries first. When the purpose of the trust is to provide financial benefits for the beneficiaries, as is usually the case, the best interests of the beneficiaries are normally their best financial interests. In the case of a power of investment, as in the present case, the power must be exercised so as to yield the best return for the beneficiaries, judged in relation to the risks of the investments in question; and the prospects of the yield of income and capital appreciation both have to be considered in judging the return from the investment.

The legal memorandum that the union obtained from their solicitors is generally in accord with these views. In considering the possibility of investment for "socially beneficial reasons which may result in lower returns to the fund," the memorandum states that "the trustees' only concern is to ensure that the return is the maximum possible consistent with security"; and then it refers to the need for diversification. However, it continues by saying:

> "Trustees cannot be criticised for failing to make a particular investment for social or political reasons, such as in South African stock for example, but may be held liable for investing in assets which yield a poor return or for disinvesting in stock at inappropriate times for non-financial criteria."

This last sentence must be considered in the light of subsequent passages in the memorandum which indicate that the sale of South African securities by trustees might be justified on the ground of doubts about political stability in South Africa and the long-term financial soundness of its economy, whereas trustees could not properly support motions at a company meeting dealing with pay levels in South Africa, work accidents, pollution control, employment conditions for minorities, military contracting and consumer protection. The assertion that trustees could not be criticised for failing to make a particular investment for social or political reasons is one that I would not accept in its full width. If the investment in fact made is equally beneficial to the beneficiaries, then criticism would be difficult to sustain in practice, whatever the position in theory. But if the investment in fact made is less beneficial, then both in theory and in practice the trustees would normally be open to criticism.

This leads me to the second point, which is a corollary of the first. In considering what investments to make trustees must put on one side their own personal interests and views. Trustees may have strongly held social or political views. They may be firmly opposed to any investment in South Africa or other countries, or they may object to any form of investment in companies concerned with alcohol, tobacco, armaments or many other things. In the conduct of their own affairs, of course, they are free to abstain from making any such investments. Yet under a trust, if investments of this type would be more beneficial to the beneficiaries than other investments, the trustees must not refrain from making the investments by reason of the views that they hold.

Trustees may even have to act dishonourably (though not illegally) if the interests of their beneficiaries require it. Thus where trustees for sale had struck a bargain for the sale of trust property but had not bound themselves by a legally enforceable contract, they were held to be under a duty to consider and explore a better offer that they received, and not to carry through the bargain to which they felt in honour bound: *Buttle v. Saunders* [1950] 2 All ER 193. In other words, the duty of trustees to their beneficiaries may include a duty to "gazump," however honourable the trustees. As Wynn-Parry J. said at p. 195, trustees "have an overriding duty to obtain the best price which they can for their beneficiaries." In applying this to an official receiver in *In re Wyvern Developments Ltd.* [1974] 1 WLR 1097, 1106, Templeman J. said that he "must do his best by his creditors and contributories. He is in a fiduciary capacity and cannot make moral gestures, nor can the court authorise him to do so." In the words of Sir James Wigram V.-C. in *Balls v. Strutt* (1841) 1 Hare 146, 149:

> "It is a principle in this court, that a trustee shall not be permitted to use the powers which the trust may confer upon him at law, except for the legitimate purposes of his trust; . . ."

Powers must be exercised fairly and honestly for the purposes for which they are given and not so as to accomplish any ulterior purpose, whether for the benefit of the trustees or otherwise: see *Duke of Portland v. Topham* (1864) 11 HLC 32, a case on a power of appointment that must apply a fortiori to a power given to trustees as such.

Third, by way of caveat I should say that I am not asserting that the benefit of the beneficiaries which a trustee must make his paramount concern inevitably and solely means their financial benefit, even if the only object of the trust is to provide financial benefits. Thus if the only actual or potential beneficiaries of a trust are all adults with very strict views on moral and social matters, condemning all forms of alcohol, tobacco and popular entertainment, as well as armaments, I can well understand that it might not be for the "benefit" of such beneficiaries to know that they are obtaining rather larger financial returns under the trust by reason of investments in those activities than they would have received if the trustees had invested the trust funds in other investments. The beneficiaries might well consider that it was far better to receive less than to receive more money from what they consider to be evil and tainted sources. "Benefit" is a word with a very wide meaning, and there are circumstances in which arrangements which work to the financial disadvantage of a beneficiary may yet be for his benefit: see, for example, *In re T.'s Settlement Trusts* [1964] Ch 158 and *In re C.L.* [1969] 1 Ch 587. But I would emphasise that such cases are likely to be very rare, and in any case I think that under a trust for the provision of financial benefits the burden would rest, and rest heavy, on him who asserts that it is for the benefit of the beneficiaries as a whole to receive less by reason of the exclusion of some of the possibly more profitable forms of investment. Plainly the present case is not one of this rare type of cases. Subject to such matters, under a trust for the provision of financial benefits, the paramount duty of the trustees is to provide the greatest financial benefits for the present and future beneficiaries.

Fourth, the standard required of a trustee in exercising his powers of investment is that he must

> "take such care as an ordinary prudent man would take if he were minded to make an investment for the benefit of other people for whom he felt morally bound to provide:"

per Lindley L.J. in *In re Whiteley* (1886) 33 Ch D 347, 355; see also at pp. 350, 358; and see *Learoyd v. Whiteley* (1887) 12 App Cas 727. That duty includes the duty to seek advice on matters which the trustee does not understand, such as the making of investments, and on receiving that advice to act with the same degree of prudence. This requirement is not discharged merely by showing that the trustee has acted in good faith and with sincerity. Honesty and sincerity are not the same as prudence and reasonableness. Some of the most sincere people are the most unreasonable; and Mr. Scargill told me that he had met quite a few of them. Accordingly, although a trustee who takes advice on investments is not bound to accept and act on that advice, he is not entitled to reject it merely because he sincerely disagrees with it, unless in addition to being sincere he is acting as an ordinary prudent man would act."

Duty to Convert

A duty to convert may arise under what is known as the rule in *Howe v. Earl of Dartmouth*.[2] The purpose of this rule is to achieve equality as between those currently beneficially entitled and those who may become so in the future. It

---

[2] (1802) 7 Ves 137.

aims to prevent a tenant for life enjoying assets of a wasting nature to the detriment of a remainderman and to prevent the latter benefiting from future or reversionary interests which a tenant for life cannot take advantage of.

Re Harris
[1907] 1 IR 32

The testatrix after making certain specific bequests left the residue of her property both real and personal to her trustees to pay her nephew an annuity and directed that the remainder of the income to be derived from the property should be paid to her husband for his life and after his death that half the income should be paid to a niece and the other half in equal shares to two other nieces. She then gave further directions in respect of what should be done in the event of her nephew's death. The testator's property consisted, *inter alia*, of two houses held on leases which had 30 and 40 years to run respectively and the court had to consider whether the conversion of these leaseholds should be ordered. It was held by the Irish Court of Appeal (Sir Samuel Walker C, Fitzgibbon and Holmes LJJ) that there had been no sufficient indication of intention on the part of the testatrix that the property should be enjoyed *in specie* to exclude the application of the rule in *Howe v. Earl of Dartmouth* and that the property should be converted for the benefit of those entitled in remainder.

SIR SAMUEL WALKER stated at pp.35–38: "The question in this case is whether the well-known rule established in *Howe v. Lord Dartmouth* (1802) 7 Ves 137 applies to the bequest in this will, or whether the case is taken out of the rule by an intention to enjoy the property in *specie* being shown by the language of the will. The general rule is, that where there is a general residuary bequest of personal estate, including chattels real, to be enjoyed by persons in succession, the Court puts upon the bequest the interpretation that the persons indicated are to enjoy the same thing in succession, and converts the property as the only means of giving effect to that intention.

It is said, in at least one case, that a slight indication of intention to the contrary will be sufficient, but I adopt the rule laid down by James, L.J., in *Macdonald v. Irvine* (1878) 8 Ch D 101, that the rule in *Howe v. Lord Dartmouth* must be applied unless, upon the fair construction of the will, you find a sufficient indication of intention that, it is not to be applied, and that the burden in every case is upon the person who says the rule of the Court ought not to be applied in the particular case.

There are numerous cases in which the burden was held to be discharged by the language of the particular will in question, and two especially were referred to by Mr. Matheson: *Collins v. Collins* (1838) 2 Myl & K 703 and *Pickering v. Pickering* (1839) 2 Beav 31, which he said were undistinguishable from the present.

The first consideration is the language of the will we have to construe:–[His Lordship referred to the terms of the will]. The leading subject dealt with all through is "the rest and remainder of my property of every kind." It is out of that the annuity is given, and what is given to the husband for life in the first instance is "the remainder of the income to be derived from my said property or the investments representing the same"; this clause is more consistent with the interpretation "investments for the time being," but the meaning is not very clear, and the same remaining income, after his decease, is given to the two nieces. It is out of the same property the £4,000 is to be raised if it becomes payable; and, subject to the annuity and the husband's life estate, the appellant gets "one-half of my said property absolutely, and the other two nieces the remaining half absolutely. Each of the devisees gets the same subject described in the same words, one getting it for life and the others in succession.

Prima facie, a clearer case for the application of the rule in *Howe v. Lord Dartmouth* (1802) 7 Ves 137 cannot be stated.

Let us see now what were the bequests in the two cases mainly relied on. In *Collins v. Collins* (1838) 2 Myl & K 703 the bequest was: "I give to my wife, Sarah Collins, all and every part of my property in every shape, and without any reserve, and in whatsoever manner it is situated, for her natural life ; and at her death the property is left to be divided in the following manner." The Master of the Rolls gives no reasons for his conclusions, but the argument shows that the points relied on were the words, in the wife's case, "without any reserve," and the language of the direction for the division as showing there was to be no conversion till after the decease of the wife.

In *Pickering v. Pickering* (1839) 2 Beav 31 the bequest was as follows: "I give and bequeath to my said wife all the interest, rents, dividends, annual produce and profits, use and enjoyment of all my estate and effects whatsoever, real and personal, for and during the term of her natural life." It appears the executors paid the income to the wife as if she was entitled in specie for thirty years, which influenced Lord Cottenham in his decision, but he relies on – (1) *Collins v. Collins* in the direction to divide after the death; (2) the gift of the rents, dividends, annual produce and profits, during her life; (3) the language of the specific gift of the chattels; and, lastly, the gift, after her life, of "the rest and residue of the estate," which was not the rest and residue at the testator's death. The judgment of Lord Langdale proceeded mainly upon the language of the gift to the wife herself.

On the other hand, the case of *Macdonald v. Irvine* (1878) 8 Ch D 101 seems a very strong authority in favour of the appellant:—[His Lordship referred to the terms of the will there in question, and continued]. Thesiger, L.J., there said: " I come to the consideration whether there can be gathered from the will and codicil in the present case any expression of intention that the property in question is to be enjoyed *in specie*. In almost all, if not all, the cases which have been cited in argument, where such an intention was found to exist, we find either words, in their natural and literal sense, importing use and enjoyment of the property in the state in which the testator left it at his death, or directions contained in the will as to the conversion of the property which were inconsistent with a conversion by the Court taking place upon the death of the testator." On those grounds he distinguished *Collins v. Collins* and *Pickering v. Pickering.* Baggallay, L.J., who dissented, rested his judgment upon the language of the codicil, upon which, no doubt, there was much to be said.

The case of *In re Game* [1897] 1 Ch 881 is very like the present. There the testator, after certain specific bequests, directed that the rents and profits of his residuary real and personal estate which he might be possessed of or entitled to at the time of his decease, should be paid to his wife for life, for her own use and benefit, and after her death, he gave his residuary estate to others in succession, subject to certain annuities, and conferred upon the annuitants a power of distress. Stirling, LJ., there held that neither the use of the word "rents," nor the power of distress conferred on the annuitants, was enough to exclude the rule in *Howe v. Lord Dartmouth.*

There may be a difficulty in reconciling all the cases cited, and an element of difference may be noted in some of them, as in *Morgan v. Morgan* (1851) 14 Beav 72 by the direction as to varying investments.

But the case before the Court appears to me a typical one for applying the rule in *Howe v. Lord Dartmouth.* What is dealt with, in the first instance, is "the rest and remainder of my property of every kind." It is all through, both as regards the tenant for life and those taking in remainder, spoken of as "my said property." There is no postponing of conversion beyond what is implied in every gift to a tenant for life and remaindermen. According to the argument, if three-fourths of the property consisted of wasting securities, there could be no conversion. Further, the £4,000 could clearly be raised out of the house property as well as the other.

Upon the whole, I see no sufficient indication of intention to prevent the application of the rule of law in *Howe v. Lord Dartmouth,* and the order of Mr. Justice Barton must be discharged."

Duty to Distribute

A trustee is under an obligation to ensure that the trust property is distributed in accordance with the terms of the trust instrument and where necessary may have to take steps to ascertain the identity of the beneficiaries. In addition doubt may arise about the whereabouts or continued existence of beneficiaries and in such circumstances it may be necessary to apply to the court for directions before proceeding to distribute the trust property.

Re Green's Will Trusts
[1985] 3 All ER 455

The testatrix's son went missing in 1943 while on a wartime bombing raid and was subsequently certified by the Air Ministry as presumed dead. She bequeathed the residue of her estate to trustees for her son's benefit and directed that if he had not come forward to claim the property by the year 2020 the trustees were to establish a charitable foundation for the benefit of cruelly treated animals. Counsel for the Attorney General submitted that the court should make a declaration that the son had predeceased his mother and counsel for the defendants contended that the evidence before the court did not conclusively establish this fact. The court gave the executors liberty to deal with the estate on the basis that the son had predeceased the testatrix and made a Benjamin order, the effect of which was to enable the charity to enjoy the testatrix's estate as from the date of her death.

NOURSE J stated at pp.461–463: "In order to assess the merits of these rival arguments, I must now give careful consideration to the facts and the decision in *Re Benjamin, Neville v Benjamin* [1902] 1 Ch 723. In that case the testator had 13 children. By his will made in 1891 he gave his net residuary estate to his children who should be living at his death in equal shares. One of the children, P D Benjamin, was last seen on 1 September 1892 at Aix-la-Chapelle, whence he started by train, apparently for London. Nothing more was ever heard of him. The testator died on 25 June 1893, some ten months after P D Benjamin had last been seen. In due course the trustees of the testator's will sought the directions of the court as to how P D Benjamin's share ought to be dealt with or disposed of by them. In answer to an inquiry the master stated that he was unable to certify whether P D Benjamin was living or dead or, if dead, when he died. The trustees then asked for an order giving them liberty to distribute the estate as if P D Benjamin had predeceased his father. The contest was between the trustees of the will, who argued for the interests of the testator's surviving children, and the administrator of P D Benjamin's estate. In giving judgment Joyce J said (at 725-726):

> "I think in this case that Philip David Benjamin must be presumed to be dead. There is no reason why he should hesitate to come home now, although there might have been at first. The question is as to when he died. If he is to be presumed to be dead, I think the case of *In re Walker* ((1871) LR 7 Ch App 120) distinctly applies, and the onus of proof is on his administrator. He has failed to adduce any evidence to shew that P. D. Benjamin survived the testator. I myself consider it highly probable that he died on September 1, 1892, or at all events shortly after. I am clearly of opinion that the onus is on those claiming under him to prove that he survived the testator. In my opinion, therefore, the trustees are at liberty to distribute. I am anxious, however, not to do anything which would prevent his representative from making any claim if evidence of his death

at any other time should be subsequently forthcoming. I shall not, therefore, declare that he is dead . . ."

The judge then went on to make a declaration in the form which is now well known.

As to the facts of that case, it is somewhat surprising on what can be gathered from the report that the judge should have considered it highly probable that P D Benjamin died on 1 September 1892 or at all events shortly after. There was evidence, to which I have not referred, to show that he might have had good reason for not returning to London, and a possible view would have been that he had taken his own life. However, the second sentence of the judgment would suggest that that was not the view of Joyce J. He must have thought that he had died from some other cause. But it would seem to me to have been equally possible that P D Benjamin had gone into hiding, perhaps in Paris, and was still alive at his father's death only some ten months later. Be that as it may, the important point for present purposes is that the judge did state his opinion that it was highly probable that P D Benjamin had died on 1 September 1892 or shortly after. I must assume that he would not have made the order which he did make if he had thought that the evidence fell short of that standard of proof.

Whatever may have been the processes of thought of Joyce J in that case, it seems to me on the evidence before the court that the present is a far, far stronger case. I consider it virtually certain that Barry Green died on the night of 17-18 January 1943, the conclusive factor being that nothing has ever been seen or heard of any of the seven members of the crew. The inference that the Halifax crashed or was shot down and that all its crew perished is irresistible. Had it not been for the marvellous and enduring faith of Mrs Green, nobody could ever have doubted it. I do not think that it would be right to incur the expense or additional delay of a formal inquiry by the court. I can only arrive at the conclusion that Barry Green must be presumed to have died on the night of 17-18 January 1943.

I now turn to the submission of counsel for the second to fifth defendants that Mrs Green deliberately kept open the possibility of her son's coming to light before 2020 and that she did not intend that charity should take before then merely on a presumption of his death. It will be clear from the views which I have already expressed that I accept that submission as truly representative of Mrs Green's intention. I do not, however, accept it as being determinative of what the court ought to do. I can see that there is emotional force in the submission, but I do not think that it withstands the test of rational analysis.

In deciding what the court ought to do, exactly the same could, as it seems to me, have been said of the testator in *Re Benjamin*. He did not intend that his other children should take P D Benjamin's share merely on a presumption that the latter had predeceased him. It is true, as counsel for the second to fifth defendants points out, that the testator there did not express himself in such clear and persuasive terms as did Mrs Green, but that, I think is not the point. The true view is that a *Re Benjamin* order does not vary or destroy beneficial interests. It merely enables trust property to be distributed in accordance with the practical probabilities, and it must be open to the court to take a view of those probabilities entirely different from that entertained by the testator. Once counsel for the second to fifth defendants accepts, as he is bound to, that the gift to charity is, as a matter of construction, accelerated if it is impossible for Barry Green to come forward and claim, and once the court has, on the evidence, thought it right to presume that he predeceased his mother, then her actual intentions, although remaining paramount in regard to construction, are no bar to a *Re Benjamin* order.

I also reject the subsidiary submission of counsel for the second to fifth defendants that a *Re Benjamin* order ought not to be made during the 21-year period. The position is that if Barry Green predeceased his mother, then charity is entitled to stop the accumulations and take as from her death. There is therefore an existing competition between charity and accumulation. If it is right to presume that Barry Green predeceased his mother, then that point is not, as I see it, an objection to making a *Re Benjamin* order now. I do not think that the question whether such an order should be made depends on whether or not there will be administrative inconveniences caused by the trustees retaining the fund. I think it depends on whether in all the circumstances the trustees ought to be allowed to distribute and the beneficiaries to enjoy their apparent interests now rather than later.

In the circumstances, I am in no doubt that the arguments of counsel for the Attorney General must prevail. There remains the question whether I ought to make a declaration that Barry died before his mother or an order in the *Re Benjamin* form. The reason which Joyce J gave for not making a declaration in *Re Benjamin* was his anxiety not to do anything which would prevent P D Benjamin's administrator from making any claim, if evidence of his death at any other time should be subsequently forthcoming. In that case, although the executors of Mrs Green's will are also the administrators de bonis non of the estate of Barry, they are not before the court in that capacity. Accordingly, the reason for not making the declaration in *Re Benjamin* does not exist here. However, I do not in this case propose to make a declaration. Counsel for the Attorney General, as I have said, accepts that the practical effect of a *Re Benjamin* order will be the same, and I agree with him.

I have not been able to give full consideration to the niceties which may be involved in taking one or other of the two courses. My impression is that in recent years the practice of the court has been to make a *Re Benjamin* order and not a declaration. It may not have been the practice before *Re Benjamin*. It is also possible that it may not be right to make a declaration in a case where there has been no formal inquiry by the court. In any event I leave this question open. It may be one, I do not know, which will have to be decided in some other case. It does not have to be decided in this.

Accordingly, subject to discussion of the terms with counsel, I propose to make an order in the *Re Benjamin* form, the effect of which will be to enable charity to enjoy Mrs Green's estate as from the date of her death."

Duty to Keep Accounts and Provide Information

A trustee is under an obligation to keep accounts of the trust property and a beneficiary is entitled to inspect such accounts. Some doubt remained about the entitlement of a beneficiary under a discretionary trust in this regard which was resolved by the High Court in *Chaine-Nickson v. Bank of Ireland*.

Chaine-Nickson v. Bank of Ireland
[1976] IR 393

The plaintiff was one of a number of potential beneficiaries under a settlement of property vested in the defendants as trustees on discretionary trusts. The plaintiff sought an order directing the defendants to give him particulars with regard to matters relating to the administration of the trust. The trustees contended that the plaintiff was not a person who was entitled to enforce any obligation under the settlement as the trustees had a complete discretion as to the persons to who they would make payments and that, unless there was an allegation of misconduct, the plaintiff had no right to any information or accounts. Kenny J held that a potential beneficiary under a discretionary trust is entitled to copies of the trust accounts and to details of the investments representing the trust fund. He granted an order directing that the plaintiff was entitled, at his expense, to be furnished with copies of the trust accounts and that the defendants give the plaintiff particulars of certain matters relating to the administration of the trust property.

KENNY J stated at pp.396–399: "When a beneficiary has a vested interest in a trust fund so that he has a right to payment of the income, the trustees must at all reasonable times at his request give him full and accurate information as to the amount and state of the trust property and permit him, or his solicitor, to inspect the accounts and vouchers and other documents relating to the trust: See Underhill on the Law relating to Trusts and Trustees – 11th ed. (1959) at p. 401. When a beneficiary asks for copies of accounts or trust documents, he is bound to pay the copying charges for these. However, in the case of a discretionary trust, none of the potential beneficiaries have any right to be paid capital or income. All the trust fund is held by the trustees in this case on discretionary trusts and, if the plaintiff is not entitled to the trust accounts and particulars of the investments, it follows that none of the potential beneficiaries have a valid claim to any information from the trustees. The result is that the trustees are not under an obligation to account to anyone in connection with their management of the trust fund. This logical conclusion from the defendants' argument leads to remarkable consequences.

The amount of remuneration to which the trustees are entitled is specified in the settlement and the potential beneficiaries have an interest in seeing that the amount is not exceeded, for they are the persons who will ultimately benefit by payments of capital and income The defendants' contention, however, has the result that they do not have to account for or disclose the amount of their remuneration. This seems to me to be contrary to the basic concept of a trustee being accountable for his management of the trust fund. In a case where the investment powers of trustees under a discretionary trust are limited, the beneficiaries have a clear interest in getting information as to how the trust fund has been invested but again, if the defendants' contention is correct, the potential beneficiaries can never get the details to ascertain whether the trust fund has been invested in accordance with the terms of the settlement. Indeed, the trustees might make loans out of the trust fund to themselves, and the potential beneficiaries would have no means of ascertaining this. These remarkable results of the defendants' argument convince me that the proposition advanced by their counsel is not the law and that a potential beneficiary under a discretionary trust is entitled to copies of the trust accounts and to information as to the investments which represent the trust fund. The obligation of the trustees is not satisfied by giving particulars of the payments made by them.

This conclusion in principle gets some support from one of the cases which were cited. In *Moore v. McGlynn* [1894] 1 IR 74 the testator left all his property to his brother and his son to be held by them in trust and to be managed by them for the benefit of his wife and children and he gave them power "to arrange for the settlement of my children as they may determine, and in case they disagree, I will that the parish priest, Reverend M. Gaffney, have full and absolute power to determine both as to amount payable and times of payment." The trustees managed the business owned by the testator for some years, then made a valuation of the property available for distribution and divided the sum at which it was valued in 10 equal shares. The testator had been survived by a widow and nine children. When they offered this sum to one of the children, she declined to accept it and brought proceedings for the administration of the estate. The trustees had refused to give any account of the property which was subject to the trust or of their administration of it.

Vice-Chancellor Chatterton said that while the division of the estate into equal shares was free from objection it was going too far to contend that the ascertainment of the assets to be divided was not subject to investigation by the Court. At p. 86 of the report he said:

> "The trustees may have had full and absolute authority to arrange and settle the shares to be given to each child of the sum to be divided; but it would be dangerous to hold that there is no control over their ascertainment of the total amount. They would in such case be judges in their own cause. They had from

the death of the testator the entire administration of the assets entrusted to them, including the management of the trading carried on by them. The amount distributable among the children of course depended on the due discharge of those duties, so that if their decision on that amount was to be conclusive, it would be in their power to protect themselves against liability for any default. It is not necessary for the *cestuis que trust* to prove any breach of duty by the trustees for the purpose of having accounts taken of the trust property, as their right to this results from the mere relation between them . . . There must, therefore, be the usual accounts of the real and personal estate."

Counsel for the plaintiff has argued that the trust in *Moore v. McGlynn* [1894] 1 IR 74 was a discretionary one only and that if one of the potential beneficiaries was entitled to an account of the estate subject to the trust, it must follow that each potential beneficiary under a discretionary trust is entitled to information as to the way in which the trust fund has been invested and of the dealings by the trustees with it. I think that this conclusion is correct and is in accordance with principle.

The other case, *Londonderry's Settlement; Peat v. Walsh* [1965] Ch 918, seems to me to have no relevance to the matters in issue in this case. The Seventh Marquess of Londonderry had made a settlement under which the trustees could divide the capital among the members of a specified class in such shares and proportions as they thought fit. Until the capital had been distributed, the trustees were to hold the income of the trust fund upon trust for such member or members of the specified class as the trustees might determine and, in default of any such determination, upon trust to pay an annuity to the wife of the Seventh Marquess and, subject thereto, to pay the income to his eldest son during his life and, after his death, to the child or children of the Seventh Marquess for the time being living and, if more than one, in equal shares until the death of the last survivor of them. The widow of the Seventh Marquess and the Eighth Marquess had died and a daughter of the Seventh Marquess sought details of the administration of the trust fund. Before the proceedings were brought, she had been given copies of the trust accounts and so her right to these was not discussed. The trustees had decided on a division of the capital, and the information sought by the daughter related to the reasons which the trustees had for their decision. The trustees then brought proceedings for a decision as to what information they were bound to disclose to the daughter. She had a vested interest in the income which had not been distributed under the discretionary trust and was, therefore, not a potential beneficiary but one who had an enforceable right against the trustees.

In *Peat's Case* the High Court (Plowman J.), misled by a grossly inaccurate report of an earlier decision, ordered the trustees to furnish information as to their meetings and as to the correspondence which they had received from the beneficiaries. The Court of Appeal decided that the trustees were not bound to disclose the agenda of the meetings of the trustees, correspondence passing between the individuals who were trustees and the persons whose consent to the exercise of the trustees' powers had to be obtained, correspondence between the trustees and beneficiaries, and minutes of meetings of the trustees. The case is not a decision that a potential beneficiary is entitled to copies of the trust accounts or as to the information to which he is entitled. It decides only what trustees under a discretionary trust are not obliged to disclose.

It seems to me that legal principle and the one relevant authority establish that a potential beneficiary under a discretionary trust is entitled to copies of the trust accounts and to details of the investments representing the trust fund. I do not propose to order any accounts to be taken by the Court, but I will declare that the plaintiff, as a potential beneficiary under the settlement of the 2nd March, 1956, is entitled at his expense to be furnished by the defendant with copies of the trust accounts relating to that settlement since 1956 and to the balance sheet and profit and loss accounts of Muckmore Investments since the incorporation of that company. I shall also declare that the plaintiff is entitled to be informed by the defendants of the names of the persons residing in any landed property purchased by the trustees and of the outgoings in connection with it paid out of the trust funds.

As there was no decision by the Courts on this matter, and as the trustees were acting on the advice of counsel, the plaintiff and the defendants will be awarded their costs of these proceedings to be paid out of the capital of the funds settled by the settlement of 1956."

POWERS OF TRUSTEES

The Trustee Act 1893 confers a number of powers on trustees in relation to the management of trust property. However, these statutory powers are not as comprehensive as they might be and it is still important to ensure that any necessary powers are conferred by the trust instrument if there is likely to be any room for doubt.

Powers of Purchase and Sale

Sections 13 –15 of the Trustee Act 1893:

> *Power of trustee for sale to sell by auction, &c.*
>
> **13.**—(1) Where a trust for sale or a power of sale of property is vested in a trustee, he may sell or concur with any other person in selling all or any part of the property, either subject to prior charges or not, and either together or in lots, by public auction or by private contract, subject to any such conditions respecting title or evidence of title or other matter as the trustee thinks fit, with power to vary any contract for sale, and to buy in at any auction, or to rescind any contract for sale and to re-sell, without being answerable for any loss.
>
> (2) This section applies only if and as far as a contrary intention is not expressed in the instrument creating the trust or power, and shall have effect

subject to the terms of that instrument and to the provisions therein contained.

(3) This section applies only to a trust or power created by an instrument coming into operation after the thirty-first of December one thousand eight hundred and eighty-one.

Power to sell subject to depreciatory conditions

14.—(1) No sale made by a trustee shall be impeached by any beneficiary upon the ground that any of the conditions subject to which the sale was made may have been unnecessarily depreciatory unless it also appears that the consideration for the sale was thereby rendered inadequate.

(2) No sale made by a trustee shall, after the execution of the conveyance, be impeached as against the purchaser upon the ground that any of the conditions subject to which the sale was made may have been unnecessarily depreciatory, unless it appears that the purchaser was acting in collusion with the trustee at the time when the contract for sale was made.

(3) No purchaser, upon any sale made by a trustee, shall be at liberty to make any objection against the title upon the ground aforesaid.

(4) This section, applies only to sales made after the twenty fourth day of December one thousand eight hundred and eighty-eight.

Power to sell under 37 & 38 Vict., c.78

15.— A trustee who is either a vendor or a purchaser may sell or buy without excluding the application of section two of the Vendor and Purchaser Act, 1874.

Power to Insure

Section 18 of the Trustee Act 1893:

Power to insure building

18.—(1) A trustee may insure against loss or damage by fire any building or other insurable property to any amount (including the amount of any insurance already on foot) not exceeding three equal fourth parts of the full value of such building or property, and pay the premiums for such insurance out of the income thereof or out of the income of any other property subject to the same trusts, without obtaining the consent of any person who may be entitled wholly or partly to such income.

(2) This section does not apply to any building or property which a trustee is bound forthwith to convey absolutely to any beneficiary upon being requested to do so.

(3) This section applies to trusts created either before or after the commencement of this Act, but nothing in this section shall authorise any trustee to do anything which he is in express terms forbidden to do, or to omit to do anything which he is in express terms directed to do, by the instrument creating the trust.

Power to Compound Liabilities

Section 21 of the Trustee Act 1893:

Power for executors and trustees to compound, &c

21.—(1) An executor or administrator may pay or allow any debt or claim on any evidence that he thinks sufficient.

(2) An executor or administrator, or two or more trustees, acting together, or a sole acting trustee where by the instrument, if any, creating the trust a sole trustee is authorised to execute the trusts and powers thereof, may, if and as he or they may think fit, accept any composition or any security, real or personal, for any debt or for any property, real or personal, claimed, and may allow any time for payment for any debt, and may compromise, compound, abandon, submit to arbitration, or otherwise settle any debt, account, claim, or thing whatever relating to the testator's or intestate's estate or to the trust, and for any of those purposes may enter into, give, execute, and do such agreements, instruments of composition or arrangement, releases, and other things as to him or them seem expedient, without being responsible for any loss occasioned by any act or thing so done by him or them in good faith.

(3) This section applies only if and as far as a contrary intention is not expressed in the instrument, if any, creating the trust, and shall have effect subject to the terms of that instrument, and to the provisions therein contained.

(4) This section applies to executorships, administratorships and trusts constituted or created either before or after the commencement of this Act.

Power of Maintenance

Section 43 of the Conveyancing Act 1881:

Application by trustees of income of property of infant for maintenance, &c.

43.—(1) Where any property is held by trustees in trust for an infant, either for life, or for any greater interest, and whether absolutely, or contingently on his attaining the age of twenty-one years, or on the occurrence of any event before his attaining that age, the trustees may, at their sole discretion, pay to the infant's parent or guardian, if any, or otherwise apply for or towards the infant's maintenance, education, or benefit, the income of that property, or any part thereof, whether there is any other fund applicable to the same purpose, or any person bound by law to provide for the infant's maintenance or education, or not.

(2) The trustees shall accumulate all the residue of that income in the way of compound interest, by investing the same and the resulting income thereof from time to time on securities on which they are by the settlement, if any, or by law, authorized to invest trust money, and shall hold those accumulations for the benefit of the person who ultimately becomes entitled to the property from which the same arise; but so that the trustees may at any time, if they think fit, apply those accumulations, or any part thereof, as if the same were income arising in the then current year.

(3) This section applies only if and as far as a contrary intention is not expressed in the instrument under which the interest of the infant arises, and shall have effect subject to the terms of that instrument and to the provisions therein contained.

(4) This section applies whether that instrument comes into operation before

or after the commencement of this Act.

In addition to this statutory power, the court has an inherent jurisdiction to sanction payment of maintenance even out of the trust capital in circumstances where it is deemed to be necessary.

Re O'Neill
[1943] IR 562

By his will the testator devised and bequeathed all his property to his executors and trustees upon trust to pay the income to his wife for her life or for so long as she should remain his widow and after her death or in the event of her remarriage, on trust for his four children. The children's guardians sought a court order for the payment of maintenance including a payment out of capital moneys and the executors and trustees did not oppose the application.

MAGUIRE P stated at pp.564–565: "I have previously granted at least two applications of this nature. In one case the facts were very similar to those now presented to me, and I allowed an advance out of the capital of a trust fund which was not sanctioned by the will of the settlor, but which was clearly for the benefit of the minors. In the other case I also allowed an advance out of capital but I required that an assurance policy upon the life of the minor concerned should be taken out to cover the extent of the advance.

Neither of these cases appears to have been reported. In both cases I took the view that in applications of this kind something more is required than evidence that an advance would be of benefit to the minors. I must be satisfied that such a course is not only beneficial but necessary to the welfare of the minors. As to this I accept the view expressed by Kekewich J. in *In re Tollemache* [1903] 1 Ch 457, at p. 459. He says:– "The most common application going beyond the administration of a trust according to the instrument creating it is one for advances for the benefit of an infant out of capital not sanctioned by the instrument creating the trust. I have never hesitated to do this where satisfied that the advancement is certainly beneficial, and where the infant is contingently interested, as, for instance, entitled only on attaining majority, I have included in the advance the sum necessary to effect a policy of insurance to cover the contingency. This is an illustration of the maxim that necessity has no law."

The jurisdiction to make an advance out of capital is not to be exercised lightly. Where a minor is actually destitute the way is clear, but where the minors, as here, are not destitute, the question of the existence of a sufficient element of necessity becomes a difficult problem.

In the present case there is a considerable capital fund subject to the trusts of the will of the minors' father. The terms of the will require that the trustees shall pay to the minors' mother the entire income of the estate during widowhood for her own support and maintenance, and the support, maintenance and education of the four minors, and that on her death the capital of the estate shall pass to the minors equally as tenants in common. The evidence before me shows that the minors have reached an age when, if they are to take the position in life for which their upbringing has been preparing them, the expenditure upon their education and maintenance must be increased to a sum greater than the income available. Their mother strongly supports the application. It clearly may be to the advantage of a child to expend capital moneys to which he is absolutely entitled upon his education. Where, however, as here, the interest of the child in the fund is merely an interest in remainder, I have to ask myself, not only would such an expenditure be to the child's advantage, but is it necessary.

Taking all the circumstances into consideration, I hold that the expenditure which I am asked to sanction is necessary. Accordingly I allow the application, and direct the payment out of capital of the sum of £301 8s. 4d., being the amount of the past expenses already incurred on foot of the maintenance and education of the minors, together with the sum of £146, being the amount certified by the Registrar to be required for their maintenance and education for the coming year."

LIABILITY OF TRUSTEES FOR BREACH OF TRUST

The principles relating to equitable compensation for breach of trust have been considered in detail by the House of Lords in *Target Holdings Ltd v. Redferns*.

Target Holdings Ltd v. Redferns
[1996] 1 AC 421

The plaintiff finance company instructed the defendant solicitors to act for it in relation to the provision of a loan as mortgagee on commercial property. The finance company paid over a sum of £1,525,000 to the solicitors to be transferred to the mortgagor once the property had been bought and charged to it. The solicitors paid out a sum of £1,490,000 before the prospective mortgagor had purchased the property and without having received any charge on it. The finance company brought proceedings against the solicitors alleging breach of trust and seeking restitution. Warner J refused the finance company's application for summary judgment, a decision which was reversed by the Court of Appeal. The House of Lords allowed the solicitors' appeal and held that they were entitled to defend the claim for breach of trust.

LORD BROWNE-WILKINSON stated at pp.435–441:

"Argument (A)

As I have said, the critical step in this argument is that Target is now entitled to an order for reconstitution of the trust fund by the repayment into client account of the moneys wrongly paid away, so that Target can now demand immediate repayment of the whole of such moneys without regard to the real loss it has suffered by reason of the breach.

Even if the equitable rules developed in relation to traditional trusts were directly applicable to such a case as this, as I have sought to show, a beneficiary becoming absolutely entitled to a trust fund has no automatic right to have the fund reconstituted in all circumstances. Thus, even applying the strict rules so developed in relation to traditional trusts, it seems to me very doubtful whether Target is now entitled to have the trust fund reconstituted. But in my judgment it is in any event wrong to lift wholesale the detailed rules developed in the context of traditional trusts and then seek to apply them to trusts of quite a different kind. In the modern world the trust has become a valuable device in commercial and financial dealings. The fundamental principles of equity apply as much to such trusts as they do to the traditional trusts in relation to which those principles were originally formulated. But in my judgment it is important, if the trust is not to be rendered commercially useless, to distinguish between the basic principles of trust law and those specialist rules developed in relation to traditional trusts which are applicable only to such trusts and the rationale of which has no application to trusts of quite a different kind.

This case is concerned with a trust which has at all times been a bare trust. Bare trusts arise in a number of different contexts: e.g. by the ultimate vesting of the property under a traditional trust, nominee shareholdings, and, as in the present case, as but one incident of a wider commercial transaction involving agency. In the case of moneys paid to a solicitor by a client as part of a conveyancing transaction, the purpose of that transaction is to achieve the commercial objective of the client, be it the acquisition of property or the lending of money on security. The depositing of money with the solicitor is but one aspect of the arrangements between the parties, such arrangements being for the most part contractual. Thus, the circumstances under which the solicitor can part with money from client account are regulated by the instructions given by the client: they are not part of the trusts on which the property is held. I do not intend to cast any doubt on the fact that moneys held by solicitors on client account are trust moneys or that the basic equitable principles apply to any breach of such trust by solicitors. But the basic equitable principle applicable to breach of trust is that the beneficiary is entitled to be compensated for any loss he would not have suffered but for the breach. I have no doubt that, until the underlying commercial transaction has been completed, the solicitor can be required to restore to client account moneys wrongly paid away. But to import into such trust an obligation to restore the trust fund once the transaction has been completed would be entirely artificial. The obligation to reconstitute the trust fund applicable in the case of traditional trusts reflects the fact that no one beneficiary is entitled to the trust property and the need to compensate all beneficiaries for the breach. That rationale has no application to a case such as the present. To impose such an obligation in order to enable the beneficiary solely entitled (i.e. the client) to recover from the solicitor more than the client has in fact lost flies in the face of common sense and is in direct conflict with the basic principles of equitable compensation. In my judgment, once a conveyancing transaction has been completed the client has no right to have the solicitor's client account reconstituted as a 'trust fund'.

Argument (B)

I have already summarised the reasons of the majority in the Court of Appeal for holding that Redferns were liable to pay to Target, by way of compensation, the whole sum paid away in breach of trust, less the sum recovered by Target. Mr Patten supported this argument before your Lordships.

The key point in the reasoning of the Court of Appeal is that where moneys are paid away to a stranger in breach of trust, an immediate loss is suffered by the trust estate: as a result, subsequent events reducing that loss are irrelevant. They drew a distinction between the case in which the breach of trust consisted of some failure in the administration of the trust and the case where a trustee has actually paid away trust moneys to a stranger. There is no doubt that in the former case, one waits to see what loss is in fact suffered by reason of the breach, i.e. the restitution or compensation payable is assessed at the date of trial, not of breach. However, the Court of Appeal considered that where the breach consisted of paying away the trust moneys to a stranger it made no sense to wait: it seemed to Peter Gibson LJ ([1994] 1 WLR 1089, 1103G-H) obvious that in such a case 'there is an immediate loss, placing the trustee under an immediate duty to restore the moneys to the trust fund'. The majority of the Court of Appeal therefore considered that subsequent events which diminished the loss in fact suffered were irrelevant, save for imposing on the compensated beneficiary an obligation to give credit for any benefit he subsequently received. In effect, in the view of the Court of Appeal one 'stops the clock' at the date the moneys are paid away: events which occur between the date of breach and the date of trial are irrelevant in assessing the loss suffered by reason of the breach.

A trustee who wrongly pays away trust money, like a trustee who makes an unauthorised investment, commits a breach of trust and comes under an immediate duty to remedy such breach. If immediate proceedings are brought, the court will make an immediate order requiring restoration to the trust fund of the assets wrongly distributed or, in the case of an unauthorised investment, will order the sale of the unauthorised investment and the payment of compensation for any loss suffered. But the fact that there is an accrued cause of action as soon as the breach is committed does not in my judgment mean that the quantum of the compensation payable is ultimately fixed as at the date when the breach occurred. The quantum is fixed at the date of judgment, at which date, according to the circumstances then pertaining, the compensation is assessed at the figure then necessary to put the trust estate or the beneficiary back into the position it would have been in had there been no breach. I can see no justification for 'stopping the clock' immediately in some cases but not in others: to do so may, as in this case, lead to compensating the trust estate or the beneficiary for a loss which, on the facts known at trial, it has never suffered.

Moreover, in my judgment the distinction is not consistent with the decision in *In re Dawson, decd.* [1966] 2 NSWR 211. In that case a testator had established separate executors for his New Zealand and his Australian estates. In 1939 the New Zealand estate was under the administration of attorneys for, amongst others, PSD. PSD arranged that N.Z. £4,700 should be withdrawn from the New Zealand estate and paid away to a stranger, X, who in turn was supposed to lend the moneys to an Australian company in which PSD was interested. X absconded with the money. In that case, therefore, the trust money had been paid away to a stranger. Street J had to decide whether the liability of PSD to compensate the estate was to be satisfied by paying sufficient Australian pounds to buy N.Z. £4,700 at the rate of exchange at the date of breach (when there was parity between the two currencies) or at the date of judgment (when the Australian pound had depreciated against the New Zealand pound). He held that the rate of exchange was to be taken as at the date of judgment. Although, contrary to the present case, this decision favoured the beneficiaries at the expense of the defaulting trustee, the principle is of general application whether operating to the benefit or the detriment of the beneficiaries. The equitable compensation for breach of trust has to be assessed as at the date of judgment and not at an earlier date.

In *Canson Enterprises Ltd v. Boughton & Co.* (1991) 85 DLR (4th) 129 the plaintiffs had bought some property in a transaction in which they were advised by the defendant, a solicitor. To the knowledge of the solicitor, but not of the plaintiffs, there was an improper profit being made by the vendors. If the plaintiffs had known that fact, they would not have completed the purchase. The defendant solicitor was in breach of his fiduciary duties to the plaintiffs. After completion the plaintiffs built a warehouse on the property, which due to the negligence of engineers and builders, was defective. The question was whether the defendant solicitor was liable to compensate the plaintiffs for the defective building, the plaintiffs contending that 'but for' the defendant's breach of fiduciary duty they would not have bought the property and therefore would not have built the warehouse. Although the Supreme Court of Canada were unanimous in dismissing the claim, they reached their conclusions by two differing routes. The majority considered that damages for breach of fiduciary duty fell to be measured by analogy with common law rules of remoteness, whereas the minority considered that the equitable principles of compensation applied. Your Lordships are not required to choose between those two views. But the judgment of McLachlin J (expressing the minority view) contains an illuminating exposition of the rules applicable to equitable compensation for breach of trust. Although the whole judgment deserves study, I extract the following statements:

> At p. 160: "While foreseeability of loss does not enter into the calculation of compensation for breach of fiduciary duty, liability is not unlimited. Just as restitution in specie is limited to the property under the trustee's control, so equitable compensation must be limited to loss flowing from the trustee's acts in relation to the interest he undertook to protect. Thus, Davidson states ['The Equitable Remedy of Compensation' (1982) 3 Melb UL Rev 349] 'It is imperative to ascertain the loss *resulting from breach of the relevant equitable duty*'" [at p. 354 emphasis added] . . .

> At p. 162: "A related question which must be addressed is the time of assessment of the loss. In this area tort and contract law are of little help . . . The basis of compensation at equity, by contrast, is the restoration of the actual value of the thing lost through the breach. The foreseeable value of the items is not in issue. As a result, the losses are to be assessed as at the time of trial, *using the full benefit of hindsight*." (Emphasis added)

> At p. 163: "In summary, compensation is an equitable monetary remedy which is available when the equitable remedies of restitution and account are not appropriate. By analogy with restitution, it attempts to restore to the plaintiff what has been lost as a result of the breach, i.e., the plaintiff's loss of opportunity. The plaintiff's actual loss as a consequence of the breach is to be assessed with the full benefit of hindsight. Foreseeability is not a concern in assessing compensation, but it is essential that the losses made good are only those which, *on a common sense view of causation*, were caused by the breach." (Emphasis added)

In my view this is good law. Equitable compensation for breach of trust is designed to achieve exactly what the word compensation suggests: to make good a loss in fact suffered by the beneficiaries and which, using hindsight and common sense, can be seen to have been caused by the breach.

The Court of Appeal relied on two authorities in support of the 'stop the clock' approach. *Alliance and Leicester Building Society v. Edgestop Ltd* unreported, 18 January 1991, a decision of Hoffmann J, was another case of mortgage fraud very similar to the present. The plaintiff building society had paid moneys to solicitors in circumstances similar to the present case and the solicitors had wrongly paid them away in breach of their instructions. The building society obtained orders for interim payment against the solicitors on the grounds that they were liable for breach of trust. The case however is distinguishable because of one crucial difference, viz. the judge found that if the building society had known the true facts it would not have made the advance, i.e. one of the facts that has to be assumed to the contrary in the present case. In that case therefore at the date of judgment a certain loss had been demonstrated in that the breach of trust had caused the building society to enter into a transaction in which they would not have participated had there been no breach of trust.

In *Bishopsgate Investment Management Ltd v. Maxwell (No. 2)* [1994] 1
All ER 261 the plaintiff company was a trustee of a pension fund. It brought
proceedings for breach of fiduciary duty against a director who had improperly
transferred to a stranger shares held by the plaintiff company as such trustee.
The Court of Appeal held that the judge had properly given summary judgment
for an assessment of damages for breach of fiduciary duty and ordered an
interim payment of £500,000. In that case, apart from one possibility, there
was no doubt the shares were irretrievably lost and that the value of the shares
so lost was in excess of £500,000. The only possibility of reducing that loss
was that the plaintiff might have a claim to recover the shares from the transferee
on the grounds that the transferee had notice of the impropriety. In the context
of the claim for an interim payment, Hoffmann LJ said, at 267:

> "Secondly, [counsel] says it does not follow that the company's loss would be
> the full value of the shares. It might be able to get something back from Crédit
> Suisse. But the company held the shares as trustee for the pension funds and its
> liability as trustee was to restore the fund. Prima facie, therefore, its loss was its
> liability to make good the value of the shares. Crédit Suisse appears to have
> taken the shares on the basis that they were registered in the name of Robert
> Maxwell Group plc and claim to be bona fide pledgees. I do not think that the
> judge was required to speculate on the possibility that the company might be
> able to defeat this plea. It has no duty to engage in doubtful litigation for the
> purpose of minimising the loss for which Mr Ian Maxwell is liable. In my
> judgment therefore the judge was acting within his discretion in deciding that
> £500,000 was a reasonable proportion of the damages which the company was
> likely to recover."

In my judgment these remarks provide no basis for holding that final judgment
can be given when on the facts known at the date of judgment the plaintiff has
eventually suffered no loss. First, Hoffmann LJ was only considering the amount
of the interim payment: the order for final judgment was for damages to be
assessed. Secondly, it is sound law that a plaintiff is not required to engage in
hazardous litigation in order to mitigate his loss. The only way in which the
plaintiff company's loss could be less than the value of the shares wrongly
transferred was if such hazardous litigation should be successfully pursued to
judgment. It did not lie in the mouth of the wrongdoing director to seek to
reduce the quantum of his liability by relying on the plaintiff company to take
steps it was under no legal duty to take. The position is wholly different in the
instant case where, on the facts to be assumed, it is demonstrated that no loss
has in fact been incurred by reason of the breach of trust.

Mr Patten for Target relied on *Nant-y-glo and Blaina Ironworks Co. v.
Grave* (1878) 12 Ch D 738 as showing that a trustee can be held liable to
recoup to the trust fund the value of shares at the highest value between the
date of breach and the date of judgment. In my view that case has no relevance.
The claim there was not for breach of trust but for account of profits made by
a fiduciary (a company director) from shares which he had improperly received

in breach of his duty. The amount recoverable in an action claiming an account of profits is dependent upon the profit made by the fiduciary, not the loss suffered by the beneficiary.

Mr Patten also relied on *Jaffray v. Marshall* [1993] 1 WLR 1285, where the principles applicable in an action for an account of profits were, to my mind wrongly, applied to a claim for compensation for breach of trust. In my judgment that case was wrongly decided not only because the wrong principle was applied but also because the judge awarded compensation by assessing the quantum on an assumption (viz. that the house in question would have been sold at a particular date) when he found as a fact that such sale would not have taken place even if there had been no breach of trust.

For these reasons I reach the conclusion that, on the facts which must currently be assumed, Target has not demonstrated that it is entitled to any compensation for breach of trust. Assuming that moneys would have been forthcoming from some other source to complete the purchase from Mirage if the moneys had not been wrongly provided by Redferns in breach of trust, Target obtained exactly what it would have obtained had no breach occurred, i.e. a valid security for the sum advanced. Therefore, on the assumption made, Target has suffered no compensatable loss. Redferns are entitled to leave to defend the breach of trust claim.

However, I find it very difficult to make that assumption of fact. There must be a high probability that, at trial, it will emerge that the use of Target's money to pay for the purchase from Mirage and the other intermediate transactions was a vital feature of the transaction. The circumstances of the present case are clouded by suspicion, which suspicion is not dissipated by Mr Bundy's untruthful letter dated 30 June informing Target that the purchase of the property and the charges to Target had been completed. If the moneys made available by Redferns' breach of trust were essential to enable the transaction to go through, but for Redferns' breach of trust Target would not have advanced any money. In that case the loss suffered by Target by reason of the breach of trust will be the total sum advanced to Crowngate less the proceeds of the security. It is not surprising that Mr Sumption QC was rather muted in his submission that Redferns should have had unconditional leave to defend and that the order for payment into court of £1m should be set aside. In my judgment such an order was fully justified.

I would therefore allow the appeal, set aside the order of the Court of Appeal and restore the order of Warner J."

Liability of Trustees Inter Se

It is important to bear in mind that a trustee may be held liable for a breach of trust where he has been guilty of no more than inaction even where another beneficiary has for example actually effected an unauthorised investment. So, while not all trustees may be equally blameworthy in a given situation, once it is found that they have acted in breach of trust, they are all equally liable and liability is joint and several. This rather harsh reality is well illustrated by the decision of the Court of Appeal in *Bahin v. Hughes*.

Bahin v. Hughes
(1886) 31 Ch D 390

A testator gave a legacy to his three daughters on trust to pay the income to the plaintiff for life and after her death to her children. One of the daughters and the husband of another effected an unauthorized investment in leasehold property and when this security proved insufficient, the plaintiff sought to impose liability on all the trustees. The Court of Appeal (Cotton, Bowen and Fry LJJ) held that the trustees were jointly and severally liable and all equally responsible for indemnifying the beneficiaries.

COTTON LJ stated at pp 393–396. "This is an appeal by Edward Edwards, who married one of the three daughters of the testator, Robert Hughes, who were the trustees under the will. The appeal raises two points. The first was this. The Appellant contends that the Plaintiffs, who were the beneficiaries under the will, and were entitled to the sum of £2000 on account of the loss of which this action was brought, have no claim against him under the circumstances of the case. All Mr. Edwards alleged he had done in the matter was to leave it in the hands of his wife, and he repudiated the allegation that either he or she were negligent as to the disposition of the trust. The counsel for the Appellant has used the term "*devastavit*," as applying to this case. But *devastavit* is a term which has no application to the law of trustees, but rather to that of executors. As regards this first question, namely, whether Mr. Edwards is answerable for the default of his wife in committing such a breach of trust as this, as much as if she had misspent the money, in my opinion he is altogether answerable. It was an action brought for the loss of the fund, occasioned by a breach of trust, being negligence, on the part of the trustees. We feel no doubt that the *cestui que trust* is entitled to redress as against the trustees, and therefore consider both that the wife of Mr. Edwards and himself, as well as Mr. and Mrs. Burden, were answerable. The facts are these. The money was invested on a Mersey Docks and Harbour bond, but in order to keep up the income it was decided, when the Mersey Docks Company reduced their interest, to withdraw the money, and place it on mortgage, and it was especially at the instance of Miss Hughes that this was done. Mr. Edwards alleges that both Mrs. Edwards and himself were unwilling for this to be done; but it was done. The money got into the hands of two of the trustees, and was ultimately mortgaged at the instance of Mr. Burden and Miss Hughes. Well, beyond question that was a breach of trust, and the *cestuis que trust* had a right to claim for any loss that might be occasioned in consequence of the trustees not having taken care that the money was properly invested, and in my opinion it would be wrong to raise a distinction as regards the liability of Mr. Edwards. He is answerable for the same breach of trust, and is not to be differently treated from the other trustees in the matter. The husband is acting and administering on the part and in the right of his wife the duty of trusteeship, who cannot act in the matter without him; therefore he is liable for the breaches of trust committed by her, without drawing any minute distinctions, as might have been done if the case had come within a recent Act, the Married Women's Property Act. But that Act does not apply to this case.

But then we come to another and more difficult question, namely, how far Mr. Edwards can, as against Miss Hughes, have indemnity for the loss, on the ground that she was the acting trustee, that she and Mrs. Burden took upon themselves to invest this money, and that although both she and Mr. Edwards are liable to the beneficiaries, she is liable to Mr. Edwards, who left the matter in her hands. On going into the authorities, there are very few cases in which one trustee, who has been guilty with a co-trustee of breach of trust and held answerable, has successfully sought indemnity as against his co-trustee. *Lockhart v. Reilly* (1856) 25 LJ Ch 697 and *Thompson v. Finch* (1856) 22 Beav 316; 8 De GM & G 560 are the only cases which appear to be reported. Now in *Lockhart v. Reilly*, it appears from the report of the case in the Law Journal that the trustee by whom the loss was sustained had been not only trustee, but had been and was a solicitor; and acting as solicitor for himself and his co-trustee, and it was on his advice that Lockhart had relied in making the investment which gave rise to the action of the *cestui que trust*. The Lord Chancellor (Lord Cranworth) 25 LJ Ch 702, refers to the fact that he was a solicitor, and makes the remark: "The whole thing was trusted to him. He was the solicitor, and, independently of the consideration that one cannot help seeing it was done with a view of favouring his own family, yet, if that had not been so, the co-trustee leaves it with the solicitor-trustee, by whose negligence (I use no harsher word) all this evil, in a great degree, has arisen." Therefore the Lord Chancellor, in giving his decision, relies upon the fact of the trustee being a solicitor. In *Thompson v. Finch* a right was conceded to prove against the estate of the deceased trustee for the full loss sustained; but it appears that in this case also he was a solicitor, and that he really took this money to himself, for he mixed it with his own money, and invested it on a mortgage; and therefore it was held that the trustee was entitled to indemnity from the estate of the co-trustee, who was a solicitor. This was affirmed in the Court of Appeal; and the Court of Appeal took so strong a view of the conduct of the solicitor that both of the Judges concurred in thinking that he ought to be called on to show cause why he should not be struck off the rolls. Of course where one trustee has got the money into his own hands, and made use of it, he will be liable to his co-trustee to give him an indemnity. Now I think it wrong to lay down any limitation of the circumstances under which one trustee would be held liable to the other for indemnity, both having been held liable to the *cestui que trust*;

but so far as cases have gone at present, relief has only been granted against a trustee who has himself got the benefit of the breach of trust, or between whom and his co-trustees there has existed a relation, which will justify the Court in treating him as solely liable for the breach of trust. Here, when Miss Hughes got the money, she handed it over to the mortgagor – as I understand, she handed over to them the actual cheque received from the Mersey Docks Company. The Appellant, Mr. Edwards, relies on the fact that she sent him a letter with the cheque for him and his wife to indorse, saying that nothing should be done with the money without consulting him; but I think Mr. Edwards' own conduct showed that that was not the view which he took. For she said in that letter that when a suitable mortgage was found and approved of, notice should be sent to the trustees; and undoubtedly on the 2nd of November, after the mortgage was completed, she wrote him with the information that the money had been invested upon leasehold houses. But nothing was done by him with reference to the matter till the 18th of May following, and I can hardly suppose that if he wished for information before the investment was taken that he would have made no inquiry as to what had been done with the money after he had notice that it had been invested. Miss Hughes was the active trustee and Mr. Edwards did nothing, and in my opinion it would be laying down a wrong rule to hold that where one trustee acts honestly, though erroneously, the other trustee is to be held entitled to indemnity who by doing nothing neglects his duty more than the acting trustee. That Miss Hughes made an improper investment is true; but she acted honestly, and intended to do the best she could, and believed that the property was sufficient security for the money, although she made no inquiries about their being leasehold houses. In my opinion the money was lost just as much by the default of Mr. Edwards as by the innocent though erroneous action of his co-trustee, Miss Hughes. All the trustees were in the wrong; and everyone is equally liable to indemnify the beneficiaries."

Protection of Trustees

The fact that a beneficiary has instigated or participated in a breach of trust may provide a trustee with a good defence to a claim for breach of trust.[3] In addition, even a beneficiary's consent to or acquiescence in a breach of trust may protect a trustee from personal liability.

French v. Graham
(1860) 10 Ir Ch R 522

Two trustees, one of whom was a solicitor, lent trust funds at the request of the

---

[3] *Re Pauling's Settlement Trusts* [1964] Ch 303, 335.

tenant for life of a settlement on a security which proved totally inadequate. The solicitor trustee had not made a sufficient investigation of title in relation to the transaction in question. Brady LC held that the non-professional trustee who had been induced to commit a breach of trust at the request of one of the beneficiaries was entitled to be indemnified by the tenant for life in respect of his liability. However, he was satisfied that the tenant for life had relied on the trustee solicitor advising him in the transaction in his professional capacity and as the latter had made no sufficient investigation of the title of the property involved, he was not entitled to be indemnified by the tenant for life.

BRADY LC stated at pp.525–527: "In this case there has been clearly a breach of trust committed, accompanied by much carelessness and negligence; but I must acquit the trustees of everything like *mala fides*. There was a sum of £700, included in Mr. French's settlement, which, in the inception of these transactions, was well secured by the mortgage of an estate sufficient for the purpose, and by an assignment of a charge for nearly £2000, payable out of the funds in the cause of *Beytagh v. Concannon*. The settlement authorised a loan, upon approved security; and so matters stood until the money was paid off by Mr. M'Nevin, and restored to the hands of the trustees, to whom it was properly payable. I must treat the lodgment to their credit as a payment to them; and the money remained quite safe, and at their disposal, until Mr. M'Nevin negotiated with them for a new loan, to which the trustees agreed. All through, this is spoken of as a new loan, and not as a rescission of the original payment, even if such a thing could be. In the meantime, however, Mr. M'Nevin had dealt with his property, had subjected the whole, or a considerable portion of it, to a strict settlement, for full and valuable consideration, and had made the residue of it a fund for indemnifying the settled portion against all charges then affecting it. The property in fact became so much entangled that, from being an ample security, it rested totally on the covenant of Daniel Charles M'Nevin. It is impossible to consider this a fitting security for the investment of trust funds. In point of fact, it was utterly valueless, and the money was lost by this transaction.

In that state of facts, it seems to me that the trustees are responsible. Mr. Graham having taken on himself to be his own adviser and the adviser of his co-trustee, they cannot be held less responsible than they would have been had they obtained the advice of Counsel, in the ordinary way, which never would have absolved them if they had fallen into such a manifest error. Mr. Graham contends that Mr. Digby French is bound to recoup him; and perhaps he might be, save for this, that Mr. French cast on him the onus of considering and advising in this transaction; so that it is not possible here to separate his position as trustee from that of professional adviser. He cannot say, I have given you advice which has misled you, but you are bound to indemnify me for the loss which that advice has occasioned to me as your trustee. On the contrary, it is a question whether an action for negligence might not have been maintained against Mr. Graham, and therefore it seems to me that he is not entitled to be in any way indemnified by Mr. Digby French.

There is, however, considerable difficulty, in my mind, respecting Mr. Edward Hyde French, the other trustee. He was not a professional man; he rested on the skill and character of Mr. Graham, and, at the same time, he stood in the ordinary position of a trustee who has been induced to commit a breach of trust, at the request of one of his *cestuis que trust*. I will assume that he knew everything which Mr. Graham or Mr. Digby French knew; but if he was induced by Mr. Digby French to concur in this loan, it then becomes precisely similar to the common case of money lent to a tenant for life. That is not an answer to a suit against the trustee, but it gives him a right to be recouped as against the tenant for life. Here, certainly, there are letters from Digby French, which lead to the inference that he did induce his brother to join in the new transaction; and there are paragraphs in Miss French's affidavit, which, not being answered, must be taken to be true, and would be *prima facie* conclusive that such was the real state of facts. If no further inquiry be pressed for, I must take them to be true. The primary consequence of this will be, that if Miss French admits assets, she must be ordered to bring in the amount. The order must be on both, to bring in the entire amount; and then, as to one moiety of the interest, Miss French will be entitled to it forthwith, and she will be entitled to be indemnified, even so far as the principal, out of any interest Mr. Digby French has in the fund to be brought in.

Then the question arises, what will be the result of that arrangement upon Mr. Graham and I cannot see that if Mr. Edward Hyde French's assets be absolved by the act of Digby French, any further or more stringent decree ought, on that account, to be made against Mr. Graham. As to the principal, that must be brought in by both; but as to one moiety of the interest, Miss French is entitled to retain it.

The case of *Raby v. Ridehalgh* (1855) 7 De G M & G 104 certainly seems to have gone a great length in relieving trustees, as against the *cestui que trust* who asks trustees to do what amounts to a breach of trust. It was a case in which executors, not having an express power to lend on real security, invested the fund on mortgage, by the wish of a tenant for life, who had requested them not to invest in stock, but on mortgage. Of course it was quite right to charge the tenant for life with the increased interest which had been received by him; but it was going very far to make his whole future life estate responsible to replace the trust fund which had been lost, the Court not deciding that the loan upon mortgage at all was a breach of trust. If it had decided that, I could have better understood the principle, as the tenant for life had actually interfered to prevent the trustees lending on Government security: but Lord Justice Turner says: "The first question which arises upon this appeal is, whether, under the trusts of this will, the trustees were justified in laying out the trust money upon mortgage at all ? That is a question which may admit of some difficulty, and is one upon which I desire to give no conclusive opinion;" and then he considers the course to be taken as against the tenant for life. Here the petitioner Digby French has, by his own conduct, become bound to indemnify one of the trustees; but I do not think that this gives any right to shift an increased responsibility upon the other."

VARIATION OF TRUSTS

As the law stands at present in this jurisdiction, there is no legislation providing for variation in the terms of a trust instrument. Under the Rule in *Saunders v. Vautier*[4] a variation may take place without court approval where the beneficiaries are all *sui juris* and entitled to the entire beneficial interest. In addition, the terms of a trust may be varied with court approval in limited circumstances, namely in order to effect 'emergency or salvage' jurisdiction, to bring about a compromise of a dispute[5] or to permit the payment of maintenance to a minor. Clearly the law in this area is unduly restrictive and the Law Reform Commission in its *Report on the Variation of Trusts*[6] recommended that legislation be introduced to provide the courts with more extensive jurisdiction to permit variations in the terms of a trust.

Re Johnson's Settlement
[1944] IR 529

The trustees of a settlement applied for an order directing that a specified sum be raised out of property subject to the trusts of the settlement by sale or mortgage for the purpose of carrying out repairs to the settled property. The tenant for life supported the application which was granted by the High Court.

GAVAN DUFFY J stated at pp.533–534: "This equitable tenant for life is in a peculiarly advantageous position, and the trustees in the present case appear to be bare trustees with no powers of management. In these circumstances the trustees themselves come into Court and rely on the principle of salvage to justify this application, outside the Settled Land Acts, having, as they say, no other means of saving the situation. Where trustees are not trustees for sale and have no power of sale or management, and where the limitations are equitable, I hold that the Court can, as a last resort if no other way is open, apply the principle of salvage in order to sanction the expenditure out of capital

---

[4] (1841) Cr & Ph 240.
[5] However, as the majority of the House of Lords made clear in *Chapman v. Chapman* [1954] AC 429 there must be a genuine dispute for this jurisdiction to be brought into effect.
[6] LRC 63 – 2000.

of the money necessary for doing such repairs, constituting permanent improvements, as are essential to the preservation of the settled property. I need refer only, in support of this view, to *In re Hotchkys* (1886) 32 Ch D 408, *In re Freman* [1898] 1 Ch 28 (decided by the same learned Judge who decided the case of *In re Lord de Tabley*; *Leighton v. Leighton* (1896) 75 LTR 328), and to *In re Smith's Settled Estates* [1901] 1 Ch 689, to which I may add *Neill v. Neill* [1904] 1 IR 513.

I am satisified that the items marked *a* (1) to *a* (10) (inclusive) and *a* (12) to *a* (15) (inclusive) in the estimate referred to in the architect's affidavit represent essential work within this principle and I shall sanction accordingly the raising of a sum of money not exceeding the estimated cost, according to Mr. Miller's affidavit, of those items, together with an addition of 15 per cent upon that sum, the addition being due to possible fluctuation of prices as a result of the present emergency conditions; to this sum may be added a reasonable sum not exceeding one hundred guineas for the architect's fees.

I authorise the trustees to mortgage or concur in a mortgage of the settled lands for the purpose of raising this money, and the income of the tenant for life will, of course, be reduced accordingly."

LAW REFORM COMMISSION REPORT NO. 63 – 2000

Variation of Trusts Bill 2001

AN ACT TO EXTEND THE JURISDICTION OF COURTS OF JUSTICE TO VARY TRUSTS IN THE INTERESTS OF BENEFICIARIES AND SANCTION DEALINGS WITH TRUST PROPERTY AND TO PROVIDE FOR RELATED MATTERS.

BE IT ENACTED BY THE OIREACHTAS AS FOLLOWS:

Jurisdiction of courts to vary trusts

   1.—(1) Where property, whether real or personal, is held on trusts arising, whether before or after the passing of this Act, under any will, settlement or other disposition, the court may, if it thinks fit, on application by any person specified in *section* 2 of this Act, by order approve,[1] on behalf of any person referred to in *subsection* (2) of this section, any arrangement[2]—
   (i)   varying, resettling or revoking all or any of the trusts, or
   (ii) enlarging, adding to or restricting the powers of the trustees to manage or administer any of the property subject to the trusts,

---

1. The term "approve" would appear to be more appropriate in this context than "consent to". The former connotes sanction by a higher authority, the latter agreement by an equal.
2. The phrase "any arrangement" is very broad and encompasses both permanent and once-off arrangements.

whether or not there is any other person beneficially interested who is capable of assenting thereto and:

provided that the court shall not approve an arrangement on behalf of any person unless the carrying out thereof would be for the benefit of that person.

(2) The court may by order approve an arrangement under *subsection* (1) of this section on behalf of the following persons:

(a) any person having an interest, whether vested or contingent, under the trusts who by reason of infancy or other incapacity is incapable of assenting,[3]

(b) any person unborn,

(c) any person whose identity, existence or whereabouts cannot be established by taking reasonable measures,

(d) any person having a contingent interest under the trusts, other than a person to whom *paragraph (a)* of this section applies.

Persons who may apply under section 1

2.—The following persons may apply for, or appear and be heard at an application for, an order under *section 1* of this Act:

(a) any trustee under the will, settlement or other disposition,

(b) any beneficiary thereunder,

(c) such other person as the court sees fit.

Hearing of applications otherwise than in public

3.—The court may hear an application for an order under *section 1* of this Act otherwise than in public.

Jurisdiction and venue of Circuit Court

4.—(1) The Circuit court shall, concurrently with the High Court, have all the jurisdiction of the High Court to hear and determine an application under *section* 1 of this Act.[4]

(2) The jurisdiction conferred on the Circuit Court by this Act may be exercised by the judge of the circuit in which any of the parties to the proceedings ordinarily resides or carries on any business, profession or occupation.

---

3. The term "assenting", rather than "consenting", has been used because it does not preclude approval of an existing arrangement. By contrast, the term "consent" would seem to suggest that no arrangement can be possible without such "consent". The chosen term has the added advantage of following the English precedent (Variation of Trusts Act, 1958) which, as stated in the Report has been widely tried and tested.

4. For alternative precedents, see: s. 22 of the *Courts (Supplemental Provisions) Act, 1961,* as amended, and s.38 of the *Family Law (Divorce) Act, 1996,* both of which are examples of the conferral of limited concurrent jurisdiction on the Circuit Court. In particular, note that s. 2 (1) (a) of the *Courts Act, 1981* amends column (3) at reference number 18 of the Third Schedule of the said *Courts (Supplemental Provisions) Act, 1961* with the apparent effect that it results in full concurrent jurisdiction in the Circuit Court in proceedings for the dissolution of a partnership or the taking of partnership or other accounts where the property of the partnership consists of personalty. It seems unlikely that the above provision could be thought unconstitutional under Article 34.3.4°. See Casey, *Constitutional Law in Ireland* (Round Hall, Sweet and Maxwell, 2000) p.281.

Saver for existing jurisdictions

5.—Nothing in this Act shall be taken to derogate from any power of varying, resettling or revoking a trust or enlarging, adding to or restricting the powers of the trustees to manage or administer any of the property subject to the trust which may, whether before or after the passing of this Act, be vested in any person or court,[5] by statute or otherwise, and the powers conferred by this Act shall be in addition to, and not in substitution for, such first-mentioned powers.

Non-application of Act

6.—This Act shall not apply to trusts affecting property settled by any enactment being

    (a) a British statute,

    (b) a Saorstát Éireann statute, or

    (c) an Act of the Oireachtas (whether passed before or after this Act).

Short title

7.—This Act may be cited as the Variation of Trusts Act, 2001.

---

5. "Person" by virtue of the *Interpretation Act, 1937,* includes both an unincorporated and an incorporated body. It has been included so as to leave unaffected powers vested in bodies other than the courts, for example those powers vested in the Commissioners of Charitable Donations and Bequests by virtue of the *Charities Act, 1961,* section 29.

CHAPTER 13

Injunctions

GENERAL DISCRETIONARY PRINCIPLES

It is a fundamental principle that injunctions like other equitable remedies are discretionary in nature. Therefore factors such as the inadequacy or inappropriateness of damages as a remedy, the conduct of the parties to the proceedings in relation to the subject matter of the dispute and the principles of laches and acquiescence must be borne in mind. The taking into account of further issues such as the potential effect on third parties of any order which the court may make is more controversial.

The Inadequacy of Damages as a Remedy and the Conduct of the Parties

The question of whether difficulty in the assessment of damages should be a ground for characterising the remedy as inadequate and the relevance of the conduct of the parties to the proceedings were considered by the Supreme Court in *Curust Financial Services Ltd v. Loewe Lack-Werk Otto Loewe Gmbh.*

Curust Financial Services Ltd v. Loewe-Lack-Werk Otto Loewe GmbH & Co. K.G.
[1994] 1 IR 450

The plaintiffs sought injunctions restraining the first named defendant from, *inter alia,* granting the right to the second named defendant to manufacture, sell or distribute its products within Ireland or the UK and restraining the second named defendant from manufacturing, selling or distributing any of the products of the first named defendant in these countries. The relief sought was granted by Barron J in the High Court but the defendants' appeal against the granting of an injunction was allowed by the Supreme Court.

FINLAY CJ stated at pp.467–472:

"(2) Does a breach by Curust of the agreement of 1986, consisting of their sub-contracting the manufacture of the product without the prior written consent of Loewe, disentitle them to an injunction?

On this issue I have come to the following conclusions. I accept that, the granting of an injunction being an equitable remedy, the court has a discretion, where it is satisfied that a person has come to the court, as it is so frequently expressed, otherwise than "with clean hands", by that fact alone to refuse the equitable relief of an injunction. It seems to me, however, that this phrase must of necessity involve an element of turpitude and cannot necessarily be equated with a mere breach of contract.

If Curust is correct in the contention which it is making, Loewe in March of 1992 was still bound by the agreement of November, 1986, and was prohibited by the terms of that agreement from entering into any agreement with any other supplier to manufacture or distribute these products in Ireland, and was furthermore obliged not unreasonably to withhold its consent to the sub-contracting by Curust of any part of its rights or obligations under that agreement. It must be on the basis that Curust may succeed in establishing such a case finally at the hearing that the question of an interlocutory injunction must be viewed. If it does, then obviously Loewe in March of 1992 was quite wrong in asserting that it had no obligation to Curust, and quite wrong in proceeding, as it obviously was proceeding, to enter into arrangements with another party to sell this product in Ireland. Having regard to those facts, it seems to me that it was entirely justifiable for the representative of Curust to seek an assurance from the representative of Loewe that he would not interfere with or, presumably, intimidate any person with whom Curust were negotiating in order to sub-contract the manufacturing of this product. Having regard to that view, I conclude that it would be unreasonable to say that what may be established as a breach by Curust of the agreement not to sub-contract without prior consent, which may also be established as having been provoked by a repudiation which was wrongful on the part of Loewe of the existing contractual obligations subsisting under the 1986 agreement, and a refusal, which would also have been wrongful, to undertake not to interfere with what would appear to be almost certainly a right on the part of Curust at least to negotiate in general terms with other parties, should disentitle it to an injunction if it was otherwise entitled to it. I would, therefore agree with the view of the learned trial judge that this did not constitute a ground for rejecting the claim for an injunction.

(3) Are damages an adequate remedy for Curust?

I am satisfied the following considerations apply to this issue which, in my view, is the most difficult issue arising on this appeal.

(a) No suggestion has been made that if Curust was to obtain a decree for damages arising out of Loewe's breach of contract, Loewe would not be in a position to pay the amount of such damages.

(b) Whilst the loss likely to be sustained by Curust in the event of an injunction not being granted is purely and simply a commercial loss arising from a diminution in trade and, therefore, ostensibly capable of quantification and assessment, it asserts that there would be considerable difficulty in such quantification and a real risk that damages assessed in accordance with the evidence would not be adequate. This assertion largely consists of an assertion that whilst it might be possible to calculate, between the time of the advent into the market of Sales Ltd. and the time of the successful conclusion by Curust of their action and the obtaining of a permanent injunction, the loss of trade and, therefore, the loss of profits sustained by Curust, it would be extremely difficult, if not impossible, to quantify into the future the loss of profits which would continue to be sustained until such time as Curust recovered its pre-1992 share of the market.

(c) It is asserted on behalf of Curust that if it loses the substantial market in these products, which it had up to the end of 1991, and continues to suffer that loss up to the date of the determination of the action, having regard to the proportion which the sales of this product constituted of both their turnover and gross profits, they might not survive as a solvent, trading unit.

To these issues the following general principles apply. The loss to be incurred by Curust if it succeeds in the action and no interlocutory injunction is granted to them, is clearly and exclusively a commercial loss, in what had been, apparently, a stable and well-established market. In those circumstances, *prima facie*, it is a loss which should be capable of being assessed in damages both under the heading of loss actually suffered up to the date when such damages would fall to be assessed and also under the heading of probable future loss. Difficulty, as distinct from complete impossibility, in the assessment of such damages should not, in my view, be a ground for characterising the awarding of damages as an inadequate remedy.

With regard to the particular question of the agreement of damages in respect of any period after the granting of a permanent injunction to Curust while its share of the market is being recovered, it does not seem to me that insuperable difficulties of quantification could arise. The extent of the market to which Curust was accustomed before an interruption in its exclusive rights of sale and distribution is ascertainable; the quantity sold by Sales Ltd. from April, 1992, until the conclusion of the action would also be ascertainable, as would its value. Evidence in such a situation could surely be adduced which would permit a judge to make a reasonable forecast of the period during which Curust may suffer a continued diminution of trade and the approximate extent of that. In those circumstances, I do not see, by reason of difficulties in quantification, any ground for holding that damages are not an adequate remedy. So much of the learned trial judge's judgment on this issue as refers to Lord Cairns' Act and the question of an injunction being in many ways preferable to the awarding of damages, except in cases where damages are very small, relates more correctly, in my view, to the final decision as to whether relief being claimed for a breach of contract which is continuing should be in the form of a permanent injunction or in the form of an assessment of damages, but is not strictly relevant to the issues which arise with regard to an interlocutory injunction.

There remains the question as to whether, on the evidence which was before the learned trial judge, it was open to him to conclude that damages would not constitute an adequate remedy by reason of a real risk that the postponement of their payment necessarily involved until after the determination of the action, would lead to the collapse, from a financial point of view, of Curust. Although this issue was submitted in the High Court and is the subject matter of certain averments in the affidavits, it was not decided by the learned trial judge because, for other reasons, he concluded that damages would not be an adequate remedy and proceeded on to consider the balance of convenience.

The factual information contained in the affidavits which is relevant to this issue is as follows. Mr. Brocklesby in his affidavit of the 15th June, 1992, stated as follows:

> "31. Further, although Curust sells a range of hardware products, including turpentine, brush cleaner, teak oil, penetrating oil and a range of branded locks and door catches, Curust's principal business is with Loewe Rust Primer and with white spirits. The rust primer not only gives the best margin but sales of rust primer also tend to lead to sales of all other products.
>
> 32. In the circumstances, I am extremely concerned that if R.S. Sales is allowed to continue sales of rust primer pending the hearing of the action, there will not only be very serious direct results as a result of loss of sales of Loewe Rust Primer, but there will be consequential reduction in turnover of other products. This would be likely to prejudice the viability of both Curust Industries and Curust Financial Services. Loewe Rust Primer has been a mainstay of Curust's business since the early 1960s and considerable advance planning would be required to build up other aspects of the business or introduce new products to replace it without doing very great longterm damage to the viability of both the plaintiff companies. Further, the paint market is seasonal, and the prime selling period is April to October."

In the same affidavit Mr. Brocklesby stated a turnover figure for the plaintiff companies of £650,000 per annum.

In paragraph 20 of Mr. Schoening's affidavit, dated the 25th June, 1992, he stated as follows:

> "I beg to refer to paragraph 32 of Mr. Brocklesby's said affidavit wherein he avers that the loss of sale of Loewe Rust Primer 'would be likely to prejudice the viability of both Curust Industries and Curust Financial Services'. Having regard to both the turnover figure of £650,000 per annum given at paragraph 4 of Mr. Brocklesby's said affidavit and the sales figures in relation to the supply of primer by the first defendant to the plaintiffs for the past three years I am at a loss to understand this averment."

The deponent then went on, in the form of Deutschmarks converted to Irish pounds, to give the figure for supply of primer for the three years as follows:

"1989   DM 104,828 =   IR£39,155.83
1990   DM 61,814 =   IR£23,089.04
1991   DM 157,920 =   IR£58,987.01."

He further explained that the figures were somewhat deceptive in that those
for 1991 included both an item which would ordinarily have been costed into
the 1990 year, and an item which would have been costed into 1992 year. The
average for the three years would appear to be slightly more than £40,000. In
the supplemental affidavit of Mr. Brocklesby, dated the 26th June, 1992, he
dealt with this issue at paragraph 12, in the following terms:

> "With regard to paragraph 20, I have not had time to check the figures which are
> given by Mr. Schoening in respect of the value to Loewe of sales for the years
> 1989 to 1991, but I am able to say that in 1988 Curust's turnover was £575,000
> of which £145,000 was attributable to Loewe Rust Primer. In 1989 the turnover
> was £632,000, of which £153,700 was attributable to Loewe Rust Primer. In the
> same year the total gross profit of Curust was £259,000 of which £88,000 (more
> than a quarter) is attributable to Loewe Rust Primer. In 1990 the proportion was
> even higher. The total gross profit was £200,606, of which £92,000 was
> attributable to Loewe. In 1991 the total gross profit was £220,000, of which
> £99,000 was attributable to Loewe."

Considering these facts, it is necessary to add in as a relevant factor that it is
anticipated that the substantive action, in which a statement of claim has been
filed and in which, we are informed, the defence is almost ready, is likely to be
heard, on the state of the High Court list, some time in the Spring of 1993. If
the injunction were now set aside, Curust would not be deprived of access to
the market in rust primer, but rather would be obliged to share it in competition
with Sales Ltd.

Since this issue on affidavit and the inferences to be drawn from it was not
decided in the High Court, by reason of the learned trial judge's view that
damages were for other reasons not an adequate remedy, and since I find myself
in disagreement with that view, it is necessary that I should reach a conclusion
on the affidavit evidence as to whether it has, as a matter of probability, been
established at this stage for the purpose of the interlocutory injunction that
damages would not be an adequate remedy, by reason of the real risk of the
financial collapse of the Curust companies. In my view, having regard to all
the factors which I have outlined, there has not been established such a case as
a matter of probability. No information is forthcoming about the general position
of the companies with regard to their indebtedness or net assets situation. No
attempt has been made to assess the probable result of competition between
Curust and Sales Ltd. in relation to this market for rust primer, except an
averment on affidavit that Sales Ltd. is underselling Curust with regard to the
cost of the rust primer being offered for sale. In these circumstances, where
damages can be quantified, the loss is quite clearly a commercial loss, there is
no doubt about the capacity of the defendants to pay any damages awarded

against them and there is no element of new or expanding business which may make quantification particularly difficult, as a matter of principle, I conclude that damages must be deemed to be an adequate remedy in this case, and I would therefore allow the appeal and set aside the order made in the High Court. In so doing, however, I have as a factor taken into consideration an estimate of the probable date on which this case will come on for hearing and, having regard to that fact, would request that all parties should inform the High Court of a request emanating from this Court that the proceedings should be given a speedy trial, and that both parties should expedite the completion of pleadings to facilitate such an event."

The Effect on Third Parties

The general consensus is that in considering whether to grant an injunction the court should confine itself to considering the interests of the parties to the case before it and should not have regard to the wider public interest. While this approach, which was adopted by the majority of the Supreme Court in *Bellew v. Cement Ltd,* has not really been called into question, it should be noted that it appears that the courts have in subsequent cases been influenced by the effect which a decision might have on third parties.[1]

Bellew v. Cement Ltd
[1948] IR 61

The plaintiffs sought an interlocutory injunction to restrain the defendants, who were the sole manufacturers of cement in the State, from carrying out blasting operations in a quarry which it was alleged constituted a nuisance. The defendants argued that in view of the importance of their products to the building industry and having regard to the fact that because of the impending long vacation, blasting operations would have to cease for several months, an injunction should not be granted. The majority of the Supreme Court (Maguire CJ, Murnaghan and Geoghegan JJ) held in granting the order sought that the plaintiff had made out a *prima facie* case of nuisance and that the court was not entitled to take the public convenience into consideration when dealing with the rights of private parties. O'Byrne and Black JJ dissented.

MAGUIRE CJ stated at pp.63–64: "In my opinion this appeal should be dismissed and the interlocutory injunction, granted in the Court below, should stand.

---

[1]   See *Howard v. Commissioners for Public Works* High Court (O'Hanlon J) 3 December 1992 and *Phonographic Performance (Ireland) Ltd v. Chariot Inns* High Court (Keane J) 7 October 1992.

It is unnecessary, and perhaps undesirable, to discuss in detail, the evidence contained in the affidavits. It appears, however, clear that, for a time at least, there was a nuisance to Mr. Bellew through the company's blasting operations. It is true that, in order to meet Mr. Bellew's complaints, an alteration was made in the company's methods. I am not satisfied, however, that the change made is sufficient to justify a refusal of Mr. Bellew's application for an interlocutory injunction. In my opinion, the affidavits show that there is a substantial question of fact to be tried. I take the view that, as there is a substantial question raised, the Court should interfere to preserve the *status quo* as far as possible. It was mainly with a view to preserving the *status quo* that the injunction was granted, and I am of opinion that, in all the circumstances, the proper course is to see that the *status quo* is preserved.

A large part of the argument in this Court was devoted to the question of public convenience. I am afraid that I cannot attach very much importance to the effect of this injunction upon the public convenience. It is suggested that, to restrain the company in the way in which the injunction would restrain them, would have a serious effect on building operations throughout the entire country. I am not altogether clear how far it was intended to press that argument, but I am of the opinion that the Court is not entitled to take the public convenience into consideration when dealing with the rights of private parties. This matter is a dispute between private parties, and I think that the Court should be concerned, only, to see that the rights of the parties are safeguarded. It is my view, on the affidavits, that blasting, with charges on the scale recently adopted, should not be carried on, pending the trial of this action. There is no doubt that it constitutes a grave inconvenience to Mr. Bellew, and I am not satisfied that it has been established that any greater inconvenience would be caused by granting this injunction, than by refusing it.

For these reasons I am of the opinion that this appeal must be dismissed and the injunction granted by the High Court allowed to stand."

BLACK J stated at pp.70–71: "In my opinion, it must be plain that the inconvenience to the company entailed by an injunction would transcend, perhaps a hundred-fold, the inconvenience that would result to the plaintiff from its refusal pending the trial. Nor, is it the defendants alone that would suffer. To stop their work, must have grave consequences for the public at a time when, as stated, more than four-fifths of the entire cement used in this country is produced by the defendants, and at a time when houses are badly wanted, and when the building trade is expected to be about to awake from its long torpor. No doubt, as has often been laid down, public convenience cannot justify refusal of a remedy for a nuisance. It is another matter to say that it cannot, or ought not to, affect the way in which a nuisance should be dealt with. In *Price's Patent Candle Co., Ltd. v. London County Council* [1908] 2 Ch 526, Cozens-Hardy M.R. said (at p. 544):– "Considerations of public welfare may justify the suspension of an injunction upon terms, but they do not justify the denial of relief to the private person whose rights have been affected." In both *Price's Case* and in *Colwell's Case* [1904] 1 Ch 707 which I previously quoted, the injunction was only granted at the trial of the action and not on an interlocutory motion. It is not suggested in the present case that the plaintiff should be denied relief, if he establishes that his rights have been affected. What I have suggested is, not that relief, but that the particular form of relief by injunction should be denied him, if it turns out, after investigation at a full trial, that an alternative form of relief by way of damages would be an adequate, and, in all the circumstances, a less objectionable remedy.

I have also suggested, for the reasons stated, and not, I think, without the support of high authority, that neither the question of whether an actionable nuisance exists nor the question of whether, in case it does, the remedy should be by injunction or by damages, should be determined in so doubtful a case upon an interlocutory application. I think it highly undesirable and dangerous to grant an injunction pending the proper trial and that the application therefor should have been refused, and that the order of the High Court should be discharged."

JURISDICTION TO AWARD DAMAGES UNDER LORD CAIRNS' ACT

The Chancery Amendment Act 1858 (Lord Cairns' Act) authorized the Court of Chancery in all cases where it had jurisdiction to grant an injunction or an order of specific performance to award damages either in addition to or in substitution for the other remedies. The discretion granted by Lord Cairns' Act is similar to that exercised since the enactment of the Judicature Act to make an award of damages in lieu of granting an injunction.

Shelfer v. City of London Electric Lighting Co.
[1895] 1 Ch 287

The defendant electric lighting company caused considerable discomfort and annoyance to the plaintiff lessee of premises by carrying out excavation work. At first instance Kekewich J held that while the defendant had created a continuing nuisance, damages should be the only remedy, although the Court of Appeal allowed the plaintiff's appeal against the refusal of an injunction.

A.L. SMITH LJ stated at pp.319–324: "The present case is not for a threatened injury, but for a continuing nuisance existing at the date of the writ whereby damages have been, and still are being, sustained.

That jurisdiction to award damages exists in the present case I cannot doubt; but whether it should be exercised in such a case is quite another question, and I will deal with that hereafter. It was argued on behalf of the Defendants that even if they were committing the nuisance to the Plaintiff and his family, as found by Mr. Justice Kekewich, no injunction could be granted against them, for that the combined effect of sects. 10 and 17 of the Electric Lighting Act, 1882 (45 & 46 Vict. c. 56) was to authorize their doing what they were upon making full compensation to the Plaintiff for all damage sustained by him thereby.

In my judgment, this is not the true reading of these sections. Sect. 10, read in conjunction with the interpretation section (32), is confined to construction of the works required to supply electricity, and does not apply to their subsequent user; and sect. 17 is confined to payment of damages caused by the execution of such works, and does not apply to damages caused by their user. And, further, whatever be the true construction of these sections, the Defendants were only authorized by the Act of 1882 to set up works and supply electricity subject to and in accordance with the provisions and restrictions of the order or special Act authorizing or affecting their undertaking; and by the Provisional Order, confirmed by Act of Parliament, under which the Defendants were authorized to erect works and supply electricity, it is expressly provided that nothing therein contained shall exonerate the Defendants from any indictment, action, or other proceedings for nuisance in the event of any nuisance being caused by them.

This point of the Defendants appears to me to be wholly untenable, and I agree in the conclusion Mr. Justice Kekewich arrived at thereon; and if authorities were wanted (though I think they are not) I refer to the cases cited at the Bar of *Attorney-General v. Gaslight and Coke Company* (1877) 7 Ch D 217 and *Attorney-General v. Leeds Corporation* (1870) LR 5 Ch App 583.

I now come to the question whether, in a case like the present, to award damages in substitution for an injunction is, or is not, an altogether erroneous exercise of the jurisdiction given by the section. Mr. Justice Kekewich has found, and these findings are unappealed against, that the Defendants were, at the date of action brought, creating a continuing nuisance by means of vibration, noise, and steam which were produced by the working of their plant and machinery, whereby not only annoyance, inconvenience, and personal discomfort were occasioned to the Plaintiff, his wife and daughter in the occupancy of their house, but the two latter had been, by the nuisance, made actually ill. There was also evidence that the Defendants, by the erection of their works, had let down the buildings of the Plaintiffs, which consequently cracked, and that the continuous vibration which subsequently arose from the user of their plant and machinery was constantly increasing and aggravating these cracks.

It was proved that the Defendants were producing electricity by means of engines of from 4000 to 5000 horse-power, and that unless stopped by injunction they were about to increase their engine power to not less than at least 20,000 horsepower.

It appears to me, to use the words in the judgment of the Court in *Martin v.*

Price [1894] 1 Ch 276, 285, to which I was a party, that "the plaintiff's legal right, and its infringement already, and threatened further infringement, to a material extent," has been established, and that "the plaintiff is entitled to an injunction according to the ordinary principles upon which the Court is in the habit of acting in these cases."

Then what is there in this case to take it out of the ordinary rule?

There is no suggestion of any conduct on the Plaintiff's part depriving him of his *prima facie* right to an injunction.

Then why is it that Mr. Justice Kekewich awarded damages in the place of an injunction?

The learned Judge appears to have thought that, because the Defendants at the trial had consented to abate the nuisance caused by steam, though not that caused by vibration and noise, damages were the proper remedy and adequate to compensate the Plaintiff. But I would point out that the learned Judge himself stated in his judgment that he was unable to allot to the different matters complained of the part each took in creating the undoubted nuisance proved to exist, and the reasons he gives for awarding damages are as follows: "Having regard to the occupation not having been as a matter of money interfered with, having regard also to this, that the inconvenience is felt very much more at one part of the house than the other, almost exclusively as regards a great part of the complaint in the upper floors, and having regard at any rate to the possibility of some inconvenience and probably some loss of accommodation, of making sleeping arrangements elsewhere, which I suppose is possible, having regard also to the large inconvenience to say no more of stopping a business such as carried on by the Defendants, I think this is a case in which damages are a very fair compensation."

It is here that I cannot agree with the learned Judge. Because the Plaintiff does not suffer a money loss, and is only driven out of his upper floors, and has only to make arrangements for sleeping elsewhere, he, according to the Judge, is not entitled to stop the continuance of the nuisance, but damages are a very fair compensation.

Many Judges have stated, and I emphatically agree with them, that a person by committing a wrongful act (whether it be a public company for public purposes or a private individual) is not thereby entitled to ask the Court to sanction his doing so by purchasing his neighbour's rights, by assessing damages in that behalf, leaving his neighbour with the nuisance, or his lights dimmed, as the case may be.

In such cases the well-known rule is not to accede to the application, but to grant the injunction sought, for the plaintiff's legal right has been invaded, and he is *prima facie* entitled to an injunction.

There are, however, cases in which this rule may be relaxed, and in which damages may be awarded in substitution for an injunction as authorized by this section.

In any instance in which a case for an injunction has been made out, if the plaintiff by his acts or laches has disentitled himself to an injunction the Court may award damages in its place. So again, whether the case be for a mandatory injunction or to restrain a continuing nuisance, the appropriate remedy may be damages in lieu of an injunction, assuming a case for an injunction to be made out.

In my opinion, it may be stated as a good working rule that–

(1.) If the injury to the plaintiff's legal rights is small,

(2.) And is one which is capable of being estimated in money,

(3.) And is one which can be adequately compensated by a small money payment,

(4.) And the case is one in which it would be oppressive to the defendant to grant an injunction:

then damages in substitution for an injunction may be given.

There may also be cases in which, though the four above-mentioned requirements exist, the defendant by his conduct, as, for instance, hurrying up his buildings so as if possible to avoid an injunction, or otherwise acting with a reckless disregard to the plaintiff's rights, has disentitled himself from asking that damages may be assessed in substitution for an injunction.

It is impossible to lay down any rule as to what, under the different circumstances of each case, constitutes either a small injury, or one that can be estimated in money, or what is a small money payment, or an adequate compensation, or what would be oppressive to the defendant. This must be left to the good sense of the tribunal which deals with each case as it comes up for adjudication. For instance, an injury to the plaintiff's legal right to light to a window in a cottage represented by £15 might well be held to be not small but considerable; whereas a similar injury to a warehouse or other large building represented by ten times that amount might be held to be inconsiderable. Each case must be decided upon its own facts; but to escape the rule it must be brought within the exception. In the present case it appears to me that the injury to the Plaintiff is certainly not small, nor is it in my judgment capable of being estimated in money, or of being adequately compensated by a small money payment.

For nineteen years the Plaintiff is saddled with his lease, and for that period, upon the hypothesis of the nuisance continuing, he is to suffer whatever annoyance, inconvenience, and personal discomfort other than by steam may be created by the user of the works of the Defendants, and the cracks in the walls of the house already made by the Defendants' works are to be increased, and it may be that his wife and daughter throughout that period are to continue to be made ill as heretofore. Can any one truly say that that is a small injury to the Plaintiff's legal rights?

Moreover, how are these injuries to be put into money, and upon what principle are these damages to be assessed so as to represent the continuing injury to the Plaintiff? To guess at them is not assessing them at all.

In order to constitute a real assessment it appears to me that the principle of purchasing the Plaintiff's interest in his lease for the unexpired term will have to be adopted as the basis upon which the assessment is to be made, and, as I have before stated, this is never sanctioned by the Court at the instance of a tortfeasor. The assessment upon the facts proved will manifestly not result in a small money payment.

In my judgment, for the reasons above, this is clearly not a case in which damages should be granted to the Plaintiff in substitution for the injunction which he asks for, which is an injunction to restrain the continuance of the existing nuisance.

If the remedies the Defendants are about to apply to the steam will abate the nuisance, well and good, and the injunction will not injure them; but if, on the other hand, a nuisance still continues, in my judgment this case is by no means brought within the exception to the ordinary rule, which I have endeavoured to express, and Mr. Justice Kekewich's judgment, wherein he awarded damages in substitution for an injunction, must be reversed, and an injunction as prayed for granted."

Patterson v. Murphy
[1978] ILRM 85

The plaintiffs sought damages and an injunction arising out of alleged acts of nuisance caused by blasting and quarrying activities carried on by the defendants in a field adjoining their house. Costello J found that these activities did constitute acts of nuisance and awarded them damages under a number of headings. Costello J then considered the plaintiffs' claim for an injunction and decided to grant the relief sought, setting out a number of useful general principles in the course of his judgment.

COSTELLO J stated at pp. 99–101: "The defendants have submitted that even if an infringement of the plaintiffs' rights has been established the court has the discretion to award damages in lieu of an injunction and that it should do so in this case. I agree that relief by way of injunction is a discretionary remedy. There are, however, well established principles on which the court exercises this discretion. The relevant ones for the purposes of this case can be summarised as follows:

1. When an infringement of the plaintiffs' right and a threatened further infringement to a material extent has been established the plaintiff is *prima facie* entitled to an injunction. There may be circumstances however, depriving the plaintiff of this *prima facie* right but generally speaking the plaintiff will only be deprived of an injunction in very exceptional circumstances.

2. If the injury to the plaintiffs' rights is small, and is one capable of being estimated in money, and is one which can be adequately compensated by a small money payment, and if the case is one in which it would be oppressive

to the defendant to grant an injunction, then these are circumstances in which damages in lieu of an injunction may be granted.

3. The conduct of the plaintiff may be such as to disentitle him to an injunction. The conduct of the defendant may be such as to disentitle him from seeking the substitution of damages for an injunction.

4. The mere fact that a wrong-doer is able and willing to pay for the injury he has inflicted is not a ground for substituting damages. (See *Shelfer v. City of London Electric Company* [1895] 1 Ch 287; and *Kerr on Injunctions* 6th Edition, pp. 656, 657).

I was referred to the judgment of Gannon J in *Halpin v. Tara Mines Ltd* (unreported, 16 February 1976). It is however clear that that was a case in which an injunction was refused because of the improved working standards employed subsequent to the plaintiffs' original complaint, and was not one of the substitution of damages for an injunction.

In the present case there are no circumstances which can deprive the plaintiffs of the relief to which they are *prima facie* entitled. The infringement of their rights is a most serious one; the injury which they have suffered and will suffer if the nuisance is permitted to continue has been and will be a considerable one; damages would not adquately compensate them. I should add that whilst I am conscious of the financial consequences for the defendants of the granting of an injunction I do not think bearing in mind that the sale to the plaintiffs took place at a time when Mr Murphy was aware of the possibility that quarrying operations in the adjoining field might take place, and bearing in mind that both defendants must have fully appreciated the great inconvenience to the plaintiffs which the quarrying operations would cause, that relief by way of an injunction could be termed oppressive.

In the course of counsel's submissions I was referred to *Miller v. Jackson* [1977] 1 QB 966, a case in which the plaintiff claimed an injunction to stop the playing of cricket. I do not think this is an authority which helps the defendants in the present case. The three Judges of the Court of Appeal took different views of the matter before them, Cumming-Bruce LJ took the view that the defendants were liable in negligence and nuisance to the plaintiffs but considered an injunction should not be granted, quoting with approval the following passage from *Spry on Equitable Remedies* (1971 Ed. p. 365).

> ... Where the plaintiff has prima facie a right to specific relief the Court of Equity will if occasion should arise weigh the disadvantage or hardship which he will suffer if relief were refused against any hardship or disadvantage which should be caused to third persons or to the public generally if relief were granted.

He held (as did the Master of the Rolls) that it was in the public interest on the facts which he was considering that damages rather than an injunction should be granted. In the present case no question of any hardship or disadvantage to the public arises if an injunction is granted.

I will now turn to the defendants' second line of defence on this part of the case; to their submission that an injunction should not issue because the nuisance can be and will be remedied. It was clear from the evidence that serious consideration to remedial action was only given during the course of the hearing. It was unsupported by any professional opinion. As to the nuisance from noise from the quarry field, Mr Daragh proposed moving the crusher and screening plant about seventy yards further away from the plaintiffs' house, lowering the hopper so that the distance which the material had to fall was reduced, putting rubber lining on the chute, and putting another silencer on the machine to reduce engine noise. I regret to say that I have no doubt that these measures would have at best only a marginal effect on the noise levels at the plaintiffs' house and I accept Mr Tennyson's opinion in this regard that they would not abate the nuisance. I also accept his evidence on the proposals made to suppress the dust from the quarry field. Mr Magee a director of a Northern Ireland firm specialising in this work, gave evidence about a dust control system marketed by his firm. The system was based on the use of water to which a chemical wetting agent is added. The water is sprayed on to the material by means of nozzles attached to the machines. Spraying on waste material can also be undertaken. Whilst the system he proposed might be of assistance in reducing the level of dust to which the operatives at the site are exposed, I do not think that it would adequately deal with the nuisance in this case. In Mr Tennyson's opinion (which I accept) the spraying techniques are not, in practice, satisfactory and in the present case would not be adequate to deal with the many sources from which dust escapes from the quarry field. As to the nuisance from the lane way, Mr Daragh said that access to the quarry could be obtained by another route. No evidence was given by the Murphys in this connection and I am not satisfied that such an alternative route is feasible or readily available. Even if it was, however, in the absence of any undertaking to discontinue the present use of the lane way a proposal of an alternative route does not disentitle the plaintiffs to an injunction in relation to the present user of the lane way. It follows that the plaintiffs are entitled to injunctions to stop the nuisance complained of."

MANDATORY INJUNCTIONS

A mandatory injunction is one which compels a defendant to carry out an obligation or to perform a specified act and it may be restorative and enforcing in nature. While the general view is that there should be no difference between the principles which apply to the granting of a mandatory and prohibitory injunction at the trial of an action, it must be recognised that in practical terms the making of a mandatory order will usually impose an additional degree of hardship or expense on a defendant and such factors may often influence a judge in deciding how to exercise his discretion. The decision of the House of Lords in *Redland Brick Ltd v. Morris* (*infra*) contains a useful summary of some of the considerations which may be relevant in such cases although it should be noted that these principles have been criticised and should not necessarily be accepted unquestioningly.

Redland Brick Ltd v. Morris
[1970] AC 652

Land owned by the respondents, who carried on the business of strawberry farming, was affected by subsidence caused by quarrying work undertaken by the appellant on adjoining property. It was estimated that the cost of remedying the subsidence would be wholly disproportionate to the value of the land affected. The respondents were awarded damages and both prohibitory and mandatory injunctions to restrain further excavation, but the House of Lords, placing emphasis on the disproportionate cost of remedial work, allowed the appellant's appeal against the grant of a mandatory injunction.

LORD UPJOHN stated at pp. 664–668: "But to prevent the jurisdiction of the courts being stultified equity has invented the quia timet action, that is an action for an injunction to prevent an apprehended legal wrong, though none has occurred at present, and the suppliant for such an injunction is without any remedy at law.

My Lords, before considering the principles applicable to such cases, I must refer to the judgments in the court below. Unfortunately, due possibly to some misunderstanding, much of the judgments were taken up with a consideration of the applicability of the principles laid down in *Shelfer v. City of London Electric Lighting Co.* [1895] 1 Ch 287, CA, in the well-known judgment of A.L. Smith L.J. That case was, however, concerned exclusively with the proper principles upon which in practice Lord Cairns' Act (which gave a discretion to the Court of Chancery to award damages in lieu of an injunction) should be applied. Before your Lordships, counsel on both sides said that in the Court of Appeal they had never relied on Lord Cairns' Act or on *Shelfer's* case; indeed in an action started in the county court with its limited jurisdiction as to damages it was obvious that this must be so; and they did not reply on these matters before your Lordships. So for my part, I do not find the observations of the Court of Appeal as helpful as usual, for neither Lord Cairns' Act nor *Shelfer's* case have anything whatever to do with the principles of law applicable to this case.

My Lords, quia timet actions are broadly applicable to two types of cases: first, where the defendant has as yet done no hurt to the plaintiff but is threatening and intending (so the plaintiff alleges) to do works which will render irreparable harm to him or his property if carried to completion. Your Lordships are not concerned with that and those cases are normally, though not exclusively, concerned with negative injunctions. Secondly, the type of case where the plaintiff has been fully recompensed both at law and in equity for the damage he has suffered but where he alleges that the earlier actions of the defendant may lead to future causes of action. In practice this means the case of which that which is before your Lordships' House is typical, where the defendant has withdrawn support from his neighbour's land or where he has so acted in depositing his soil from his mining operations as to constitute a menace to the plaintiff's land. It is in this field that the undoubted jurisdiction of equity to grant a mandatory injunction, that is an injunction ordering the defendant to carry out positive works, finds its main expression, though of course it is equally applicable to many other cases. Thus, to take the simplest example, if the defendant, the owner of land, including a metalled road over which the plaintiff has a right of way, ploughs up that land so that it is no longer usable, no doubt a mandatory injunction will go to restore it; damages are not a sufficient remedy, for the plaintiff has no right to go upon the defendant's land to remake his right of way.

The cases of *Isenberg v. East India House Estate Co. Ltd.* (1863) 3 De GJ & S 263 and *Durell v. Pritchard* (1865) 1 Ch App 244 have laid down some basic principles, and your Lordships have been referred to some other cases which have been helpful. The grant of a mandatory injunction is, of course, entirely discretionary and unlike a negative injunction can never be "as of course." Every case must depend essentially upon its own particular circumstances. Any general principles for its application can only be laid down in the most general terms:

1. A mandatory injunction can only be granted where the plaintiff shows a very strong probability upon the facts that grave damage will accrue to him in the future. As Lord Dunedin said in 1919 it is not sufficient to say "timeo." [*Attorney-General for the Dominion of Canada* v. *Ritchie Contracting and Supply Co.* [1919] AC 999, 1005, PC]. It is a jurisdiction to be exercised sparingly and with caution but in the proper case unhesitatingly.

2. Damages will not be a sufficient or adequate remedy if such damage does happen. This is only the application of a general principle of equity; it has nothing to do with Lord Cairns' Act or *Shelfer's* case [1895] 1 Ch 287.

3. Unlike the case where a negative injunction is granted to prevent the continuance or recurrence of a wrongful act the question of the cost to the defendant to do works to prevent or lessen the likelihood of a future apprehended wrong must be an element to be taken into account:

(*a*) where the defendant has acted without regard to his neighbour's rights, or has tried to steal a march on him or has tried to evade the jurisdiction of the court or to sum it up, has acted wantonly and quite unreasonably in relation to his neighbour he may be ordered to repair his wanton and unreasonable acts by doing positive work to restore the status quo even if the expense to him is out of all proportion to the advantage thereby accruing to the plaintiff. As illustrative of this see *Woodhouse v. Newry Navigation Co.* [1898] 1 IR 161;

(*b*) but where the defendant has acted reasonably, though in the event wrongly, the cost of remedying by positive action his earlier activities is most important for two reasons. First, because no legal wrong has yet occurred (for which he has not been recompensed at law and in equity) and, in spite of gloomy expert opinion, may never occur or possibly only upon a much smaller scale than anticipated. Secondly, because if ultimately heavy damage does occur the plaintiff is in no way prejudiced for he has his action at law and all his consequential remedies in equity.

So the amount to be expended under a mandatory order by the defendant must be balanced with these considerations in mind against the anticipated possible damage to the plaintiff and if, on such balance, it seems unreasonable to inflict such expenditure upon one who for this purpose is no more than a potential wrongdoer then the court must exercise its jurisdiction accordingly. Of course, the court does not have to order such works as upon the evidence before it will remedy the wrong but may think it proper to impose upon the defendant the obligation of doing certain works which may upon expert opinion merely lessen the likelihood of any further injury to the plaintiff's land. Sargant J. pointed this out in effect in the celebrated "Moving Mountain" case, *Kennard v. Cory Bros. & Co. Ltd* [1922] 1 Ch 265 at the foot of p. 274 (his judgment was affirmed in the Court of Appeal [1922] 2 Ch 1).

4. If in the exercise of its discretion the court decides that it is a proper case to grant a mandatory injunction, then the court must be careful to see that the defendant knows exactly in fact what he has to do and this means not as a matter of law but as a matter of fact, so that in carrying out an order he can give his contractors the proper instructions.

This has been well settled for a long time and I regret that I cannot agree with Danckwerts L.J. ([1967] 1 WLR 967, 974B), that the observations of Joyce J., in *Attorney-General v. Staffordshire County Council* [1905] 1 Ch 336, 342 have not been followed in practice. My experience has been quite the opposite. There may be some cases where, to revert to the simple illustration I gave earlier, the defendant can be ordered " to restore the right of way to its former condition." This is so simple as to require no further elucidation in the court order. But in anything more complicated the court must in fairness to the defendant tell him what he has to do, though it may well be by reference to plans prepared by some surveyor, as pointed out by Sargant J., in the passage in the "Moving Mountain" case to which I have already referred. The principle is summed up by Maugham L.J., in *Fishenden v. Higgs & Hill Ltd.* (1935) 153 LT 128, 142:

> "I should like to observe, in the first place, that I think a mandatory injunction, except in very exceptional circumstances, ought to be granted in such terms that the person against whom it is granted ought to know exactly what he has to do."

My Lords, I shall apply these principles or conditions to this case, and I can do so very shortly.

1. As a matter of expert evidence supported by the further slip of land during the hearing it is obvious that this condition, which must be one of fact in each case, is satisfied and, indeed, is not disputed.

2. Damages obviously are not a sufficient remedy, for no one knows whether any further damage will occur and, if so, upon what scale – upon the expert evidence it might be very substantial.

3. The appellants have not behaved unreasonably but only wrongly. Upon the facts of this case the judge in my opinion would have been fully justified in imposing upon the appellants an obligation to do some reasonable and not too expensive works which might have a reasonable chance of preventing further damage. He did not do so and it is not surprising that in the county court this was not further explored. Alternatively he might have given leave to apply for a mandatory injunction.

4. But in making his mandatory order in my opinion the judge totally disregarded this necessary and perfectly well settled condition. The terms of the order imposed upon the appellants an absolutely unqualified obligation upon them to restore support without giving them any indication of what was to be done. The judge might have ordered the appellants to carry out the remedial works described by the respondents' expert in his evidence though it would have to be set out in great detail. I could have understood that, but as it was thought to cost £30,000 that would have been most unreasonable and would have offended principle 3, but the order in fact imposed went much further; it imposed an unlimited and unqualified obligation upon the appellants, and I do not know how they could have attempted to comply with it. The expenditure of the sum of £30,000 which I have just mentioned would not necessarily have complied with it for though it would in all probability have prevented any further damage it was not guaranteed to do so and that is what in effect the mandatory order of the learned judge required. My Lords, in my opinion that part of the order of the county court judge cannot stand and the appeal must be allowed.

I have given anxious consideration to the question whether some order could not be made with a view to imposing upon the appellant some obligation to make a limited expenditure (by which I mean a few thousand pounds) to lessen the likelihood of further land slips to the respondents' land but, not without reluctance, I do not think this would be a helpful course. First, the matter would have to be tried de novo as a matter of expert evidence because the trial judge is not available and because two and a half years have elapsed since the trial, without, so far as their Lordships know, any further land slips and upon that expert evidence may have something to say. The costs of such a further enquiry would be very heavy and the enquiry possibly inconclusive. Secondly, the respondents are not unduly prejudiced, for in the event of a further land slip all their remedies at law and in equity will be open to them and they will no doubt begin in a more appropriate forum than the county court.

For these reasons I would allow the appeal. The appellants, however, must pay the respondents' costs here and below in accordance with their undertaking."

It has been suggested that, while the court has jurisdiction to grant a mandatory injunction on an interlocutory application, the principles which apply to the grant of mandatory as opposed to prohibitory injunctions of an interlocutory nature are different.[2] Uncertainty still surrounds the question of the test which should be applied in the case of mandatory interlocutory injunctions in this jurisdiction. Some decisions show evidence of a much more restrictive test than that which applies to the grant of interlocutory injunctions of a prohibitory nature[3] while others suggest that the granting or withholding of an mandatory interlocutory injunction should not be related to or dependent on the strength of the applicant's case.[4]

It appears to have been accepted in England that in 'a normal case' the court must feel 'a high degree of assurance' that at the trial it will appear that the mandatory interlocutory injunction was correctly granted.[5] However, it has also been accepted that in an exceptional case, where withholding a mandatory interlocutory injunction would carry a greater risk of injustice than granting it even though the court does not feel a 'high degree of assurance' about the plaintiff's chances of establishing his right, there cannot be any rational basis for withholding the injunction.[6]

Boyhan v. Tribunal of Inquiry into the Beef Industry
[1992] ILRM 545

The plaintiffs sought interlocutory relief in the form of a mandatory injunction directing the respondent tribunal to grant the United Farmers Association full legal representation for that part of the tribunal's proceedings encompassing allegations relevant to them. Denham J concluded that the limited representation afforded to the plaintiffs was sufficient to safeguard their rights and refused the application for interlocutory relief.

DENHAM J stated at p.556: "It is clear that the plaintiffs are in the position of a witness to the tribunal. There are no allegations made against them and

---

[2] *Irish Shell Ltd v. Elm Motors* [1984] IR 200, 217.

[3] *Boyhan v. Tribunal of Inquiry into the Beef Industry* [1992] ILRM 545 and *Boyle v. An Post* [1992] 2 IR 437.

[4] *Bula Ltd v. Tara Mines Ltd (No.2)* [1987] IR 95. See also the comments of O Caoimh J in *de Burca v. Wicklow County Council* High Court, 24 May 2000.

[5] *Shepherd Homes Ltd v. Sandham* [1971] Ch 340.

[6] *Films Rover International Ltd v. Cannon Films Sales Ltd* [1987] 1 WLR 670.

the tribunal is satisfied that the UFA will not be prejudicially affected in any way by the evidence which may be given at the hearings – or by any of the tribunal's findings. A tribunal is not a court of law – either civil or criminal. It is a body – unusual in our legal system – an inquisitorial tribunal. It does not have an adversary format. There is no evidence that the plaintiffs will be prejudiced by the tribunal. The tribunal has clearly stated that the rules of natural justice will apply.

It is manifestly clear that the tribunal was acting within its discretion and jurisdiction in making its decision. There is no evidence which even questions the decision on the ground of reasonableness or jurisdiction.

In these circumstances, I do not consider that the High Court has jurisdiction to interfere with the decision of the tribunal. The remedy which is sought by the plaintiff is that of a mandatory injunction. This is a powerful instrument of the High Court. On the facts in this case, it would effectively mean an order of *mandamus* to the tribunal. If this were an application for *mandamus* it could not succeed. In seeking this exceptional form of relief, a mandatory injunction, it is up to the plaintiffs to establish a strong and clear case – so that the court can feel a degree of assurance that at a trial of the action a similar injunction would be granted. I do not believe that such an injunction would be granted at a full trial herein. It appears to me that the plaintiffs have misconstrued the position of the tribunal and perceived it as a court with the adversarial system of procedure in which the plaintiff is in jeopardy. This is not the case. Nor indeed have the plaintiffs established that there is a fair question to be tried on the issues raised on the facts herein, for the same reasons as set out before. The plaintiffs have not presented an arguable case that the tribunal's decision is untenable or endangers constitutional rights. The plaintiff has not established a right to the mandatory injunction sought.

I refuse the application."

Bula Ltd v. Tara Mines Ltd (No.2)
[1987] IR 95

The plaintiffs sought various reliefs against the defendants including damages for inflicting economic loss on the plaintiffs by unlawful means arising out of a dispute in relation to the exploitation of mineral assets. Various injunctions were also claimed in the proceedings and in the motion before the court the plaintiffs claimed interlocutory relief of a mandatory nature directing a number of defendants, *inter alia*, to take steps to cause the first named defendants to meet the plaintiffs to discuss arrangements for the use of the first named defendant's facilities. Murphy J refused the plaintiffs' application for a mandatory interlocutory injunction.

MURPHY J stated at pp.102–106: "The plaintiffs assert that damages would be an inadequate remedy for them. First they say that the sums involved would be enormous. Secondly it is pointed out that there would be extraordinary difficulties in calculating the loss. Thirdly it is submitted that the recovery of damages would not compensate the individual plaintiffs for the embarrassment and ignominy of their bankrupcy which may result from the alleged breach of the contracts by the defendants in circumstances in which the plaintiffs have guaranteed very substantial sums of money which have now been called in.

In opposing the application the defendants relied on a number of propositions. First, it was said that a mandatory injunction would be granted at the interlocutory stage only in a very strong case. This proposition was supported by the decision in *Shepherd Homes Ltd v. Sandham* [1971] Ch 340. In his judgment Megarry J. at p. 349 commented as follows:

> "At the trial of the action, the court will, of course, grant such injunctions as the justice of the case requires; but at the interlocutory stage, when the final result of the case cannot be known and the court has to do the best it can, I think the case has to be unusually strong and clear before a mandatory injunction will be granted, even if it is sought in order to enforce a contractual obligation."

Whilst I would respectfully agree with much of what the learned judge said in the *Shepherd Homes Case* [1971] Ch 340 about the important differences between prohibitory and mandatory injunctions I would be reluctant to accept the proposition, if that is what it is, that the granting or withholding of a mandatory injunction on an interlocutory application should be related to or depend upon the strength of the applicant's case. As has been pointed out in a number of cases in recent years there are grave difficulties in evaluating the strength of an applicant's case on fact or even in law at any time before a full hearing has taken place.

The defendants also referred to the decision of the Supreme Court in *Campus Oil Ltd. v. Minister for Industry (No. 2)* [1983] IR 88 and in particular a passage from the decision of O'Higgins C.J. at p. 107 thereof in the following terms:

> "The plaintiffs also argue that, in so far as the relief which was granted was mandatory in nature, such should not have been given by way of interlocutory relief. It is correct to say that a mandatory injunction does not usually issue prior to the trial of an action. However, there are exceptions and, in my view, this case is one of them."

The then Chief Justice went on to consider the exceptional nature of the issue before the Court.

In the course of his judgment he had also commented upon the general nature of interlocutory relief (at p. 106) in the following terms:

> "As I have already mentioned, interlocutory relief is intended to keep matters in *status quo* until the trial, and to do no more. No rights are determined nor are issues decided."

The third matter of principle on which the defendants placed reliance was the need for certainty in a mandatory order. In this connection reference was made to *Redland Bricks Ltd. v. Morris* [1970] AC 652. In delivering the unanimous opinion of the House of Lords Lord Upjohn adopted at p. 667 of the report the principle enunciated by Maugham L.J. in *Fishenden v. Higgs & Hill Ltd.* (1935) 153 LT. 128 at p. 142 in the following terms:

> "I should like to observe, in the first place, that I think a mandatory injunction, except in very exceptional circumstances, ought to be granted in such terms that the person against whom it is granted ought to know exactly what he has to do."

It should be emphasised that the *Redland Brick Case* [1970] AC 652 concerned a mandatory order granted after a plenary hearing. It does seem to me, however, that the same principle is at least equally applicable to the granting of a mandatory order at the interlocutory stage.

If one then reverts to the notice of motion and examines the terms of the relief sought, not with a view to raising procedural or technical difficulties but for the purpose of understanding what is involved in the interlocutory relief sought, one finds that the plaintiffs require an order directing:

> "The first named defendant, its servants or agents, to meet with the plaintiffs, their servants or agents at such times and with such frequency as may be necessary for the purpose of discussing what arrangements may be made between the first-named plaintiff and the first-named defendant as regard the use of the first-named defendant's facilities in the exploitation of the mineral assets of the first-named plaintiff and for the purpose of discussing such other proposals as may be put forward by any party with a view to ensuring that the said mineral assets and the mineral assets the subject matter of the Lease dated the 19th of September, 1975, between the last-named defendant's predecessor in Title of the first part, the Minister for Finance of the second part and the first named defendant of the third part, are exploited in the most efficient and most economical manner with consequent benefit to all concerned."

What would the defendants have to do to comply with an order in those terms? Would attendance at one or two meetings suffice? Must they actively participate in discussions at such meetings? Would they be entitled to adopt negotiating positions in which they would not, in the first instance at any rate, put forward their best proposals? Above all could it happen that the Court would be required to test the sincerity of the defendants in their purported compliance with the order.

The plaintiffs of course were fully conscious of these problems. Counsel on their behalf was not prepared to accept that the mere physical presence of representatives of Tara at a meeting would be adequate to resolve the plaintiffs' immediate problems. On behalf of the plaintiffs it was clearly and fairly said that the meeting to be directed was a meeting under and for the purposes of clause f of the State mining lease and that being so, it was contended that the arbitration clause in the State mining lease could be invoked to test whether

Tara had complied with its undertaking "to act reasonably in all negotiations". It seems to me that this line of reasoning does not in fact provide a solution to the problem. Whether or not there has been compliance with an order of the Court is a matter which the Court itself must be in a position to determine and it seems to me that it would be wrong in principle and unhelpful in practice if the Court were to make an order in the very general terms of the notice of motion on the basis that any uncertainty would be corrected by the intervention of a third party whose decision was in no way dependent upon or related to the decision of the Court. The plaintiffs' argument involves a further problem. To direct that the meeting should be held for the purposes of clause f in my view involves prejudging one of the crucial issues in the action. So far from maintaining the *status quo* it would compel the parties not merely to take certain actions but also to decide, at least on some temporary or conditional basis, the legal framework within which those actions were to be taken. In my view it would be quite wrong for the Court to adopt that course at an interlocutory stage.

Finally, I think it is proper, particularly in the interests of the Minister for Energy, to recall the factual position with regard to the negotiations between the parties. On behalf of Bula it has been suggested that the appropriate method of exploiting the Bula orebody would be by means of a "tolling arrangement" between Tara and Bula and a proposal to the effect in general terms was made by Bula in the months of September and October of last year. It was in that background that the Chief State Solicitor wrote to the solicitors on behalf of the plaintiffs on the 18th November, 1986, in the following terms:

> "I act for the Minister for Energy.
>
> I wish to inform you
> (1). that the Minister is and always has been willing to see discussions between Tara and Bula about a tolling arrangement;
> (2). that the legal advice available to the Minister is that there are no further steps the Minister could take to require Tara to give any further consideration to the tolling arrangement than they have already done; and
> (3). that if your clients wish to make further or more detailed proposals concerning a tolling arrangement they will be communicated to Tara who will be requested to consider them in the light of their obligations under the agreement."

In these circumstances it seems clear that the Minister is not refusing his co-operation though there may well be a considerable difference between him and the plaintiffs as to the precise extent of his obligations or the nature of the intervention which he could make.

In all of the circumstances it seems to me that this is not a case in which it would be proper to grant a mandatory order in the terms sought or any other mandatory injunction to a like effect."

INTERLOCUTORY INJUNCTIONS

The Principles Governing the Grant of Interlocutory Injunctions

While traditionally, a plaintiff would be granted an interlocutory injunction only if he could establish a '*prima facie* case', this test was rejected by the House of Lords in *American Cyanamid Co. v. Ethicon Ltd*[7] and subsequently by the Supreme Court in *Campus Oil Ltd v. Minister for Industry and Energy (No.2)*[8] in favour of a less rigorous one. As a result in order to obtain an interlocutory injunction, a plaintiff must generally satisfy the court that there is a serious or fair question to be tried and that the balance of convenience between the parties favours the grant of the relief.

American Cyanamid Co. v. Ethicon Ltd
[1975] AC 396

The plaintiff sought an interlocutory injunction to restrain the defendant from marketing surgical sutures in infringement of the plaintiff's patent. The House of Lords held in granting the relief that the plaintiff had established that there was a serious question to be tried and that the balance of convenience favoured this course of action.

LORD DIPLOCK stated at pp.404–410: "My Lords, the question whether the use of XLG as an absorbable surgical suture is an infringement of Cyanamid's patent depends upon the meaning to be given to the three words "a polyhydroxyacetic ester" in the principal claim. Cyanamid's contention is that at the date of publication of the patent those words were used as a term of art in the chemistry of polymerisation not only in the narrower meaning of a homopolymer of which the units in the chain, apart from the end stabilisers, consisted solely of glycolide radicals but also in the broader meaning of a copolymer of which up to 15 per cent. of the units in the chain would be lactide radicals; and that what was said in the body of the patent made it clear that in the claim the words were used in this wider meaning.

Ethicon's first contention is that the words "a polyhydroxyacetic ester" in the principal claim bear the narrower meaning only, viz. that they are restricted to a homopolymer of which all the units in the chain except the end stabilisers consist of glycolide radicals. In the alternative, as commonly happens where the contest is between a narrower and a wider meaning in a patent specification, they attack the validity of the patent, if it bears the wider meaning, on the grounds of inutility, insufficiency, unfair basis and false suggestion. These

---

[7] [1975] AC 396.
[8] [1983] IR 88.

objections are really the obverse of their argument in favour of the narrower construction. They are all different ways of saying that if the claim is construed widely it includes copolymers which will not have as surgical sutures the characteristics described in the body of the patent. Ethicon also attack the validity of the the patent on the ground of obviousness.

Both Graham J. and the Court of Appeal felt constrained by authority to deal with Cyanamid's claim to an interlocutory injunction by considering first whether, upon the whole of the affidavit evidence before them, a prima facie case of infringement had been made out. As Russell L.J. put it in the concluding paragraph of his reasons for judgment with which the other members of the court agreed [1974] FSR 312, 333:

> ". . . if there be no prima facie case on the point essential to entitle the plaintiffs to complain of the defendants' proposed activities, that is the end of the claim to interlocutory relief."

"Prima facie case" may in some contexts be an elusive concept, but the sense in which it was being used by Russell L.J. is apparent from an earlier passage in his judgment. After a detailed analysis of the conflicting expert testimony he said, at p. 330:

> "I am not satisfied on the present evidence that on the proper construction of this specification, addressed as it is to persons skilled in the relevant art or science, the claim extends to sterile surgical sutures produced not only from a homopolymer of glycolide but also from a copolymer of glycolide and up to 15 per cent. of lactide. That is to say that I do not consider that a prima facie case of infringement is established."

In effect what the Court of Appeal was doing was trying the issue of infringement upon the conflicting affidavit evidence as it stood, without the benefit of oral testimony or cross-examination. They were saying:

> "If we had to give judgment in the action now without any further evidence we should hold that Cyanamid had not satisfied the onus of proving that their patent would be infringed by Ethicon's selling sutures made of XLG."

The Court of Appeal accordingly did not find it necessary to go into the questions raised by Ethicon as to the validity of the patent or to consider where the balance of convenience lay.

Graham J. had adopted the same approach as the Court of Appeal; but, upon the same evidence he had come to the contrary conclusion on the issue of infringement. He considered (at p. 321) that on the evidence as it stood Cyanamid had made out a "strong prima facie case" that their patent would be infringed by Ethicon's selling sutures made of XLG. He then went on to deal briefly with the attack upon the validity of the patent and came to the conclusion that upon the evidence before him none of the grounds of invalidity advanced by Ethicon was likely to succeed. He therefore felt entitled to consider the balance of convenience. In his opinion it lay in favour of maintaining the status quo until the trial of the action. So he granted Cyanamid an interlocutory injunction restraining Ethicon from infringing the patent until the trial or further order.

The grant of an interlocutory injunction is a remedy that is both temporary and discretionary. It would be most exceptional for your Lordships to give leave to appeal to this House in a case which turned upon where the balance of convenience lay. In the instant appeal, however, the question of the balance of convenience, although it had been considered by Graham J. and decided in Cyanamid's favour, was never reached by the Court of Appeal. They considered that there was a rule of practice so well established as to constitute a rule of law that precluded them from granting any interim injunction unless upon the evidence adduced by both the parties on the hearing of the application the applicant had satisfied the court that on the balance of probabilities the acts of the other party sought to be enjoyed would, if committed, violate the applicant's legal rights. In the view of the Court of Appeal the case which the applicant had to prove before any question of balance of convenience arose was "prima facie" only in the sense that the conclusion of law reached by the court upon that evidence might need to be modified at some later date in the light of further evidence either detracting from the probative value of the evidence on which the court had acted or proving additional facts. It was in order to enable the existence of any such rule of law to be considered by your Lordships' House that leave to appeal was granted.

The instant appeal arises in a patent case. Historically there was undoubtedly a time when in an action for infringement of a patent that was not already "well established," whatever that may have meant, an interlocutory injunction to restrain infringement would not be granted if counsel for the defendant stated that it was intended to attack the validity the patent.

Relics of this reluctance to enforce a monopoly that was challenged, even though the alleged grounds of invalidity were weak, are to be found in the judgment of Scrutton L.J. as late as 1924 in *Smith v. Grigg Ltd* [1924] 1 KB 655; but the elaborate procedure for the examination of patent specifications by expert examiners before a patent is granted, the opportunity for opposition at that stage and the provisions for appeal to the Patent Appeal Tribunal in the person of a patent judge of the High Court, make the grant of a patent nowadays a good prima facie reason, in the true sense of that term, for supposing the patent to be valid, and have rendered obsolete the former rule of practice as respects interlocutory injunctions in infringement actions. In my view the grant of interlocutory injunctions in actions for infringement of patents is governed by the same principles as in other actions. I turn to consider what those principles are.

My Lords, when an application for an interlocutory injunction to restrain a defendant from doing acts alleged to be in violation of the plaintiff's legal right is made upon contested facts, the decision whether or not to grant an interlocutory injunction has to be taken at a time when ex hypothesi the existence of the right or the violation of it, or both, is uncertain and will remain uncertain until final judgment is given in the action. It was to mitigate the risk of injustice to the plaintiff during the period before that uncertainty could be resolved that the practice arose of granting him relief by way of interlocutory injunction; but since the middle of the 19th century this has been made subject to his undertaking to pay damages to the defendant for any loss sustained by reason of the injunction if it should be held at the trial that the plaintiff had not been entitled to restrain the defendant from doing what he was threatening to do. The object of the interlocutory injunction is to protect the plaintiff against injury by violation of his right for which he could not be adequately compensated in damages recoverable in the action if the uncertainty were resolved in his favour at the trial; but the plaintiff's need for such protection must be weighed against the corresponding need of the defendant to be protected against injury resulting from his having been prevented from exercising his own legal rights for which he could not be adequately compensated under the plaintiff's undertaking in damages if the uncertainty were resolved in the defendant's favour at the trial. The court must weigh one need against another and determine where the balance of convenience lies.

In those cases where the legal rights of the parties depend upon facts that are in dispute between them, the evidence available to the court at the hearing of the application for an interlocutory injunction is incomplete. It is given on affidavit and has not been tested by oral cross-examination. The purpose sought to be achieved by giving to the court discretion to grant such injunctions would be stultified if the discretion were clogged by a technical rule forbidding its exercise if upon that incomplete untested evidence the court evaluated the chances of the plaintiff's ultimate success in the action at 50 per cent or less, but permitting its exercise if the court evaluated his chances at more than 50 per cent.

The notion that it is incumbent upon the court to undertake what is in effect a preliminary trial of the action upon evidential material different from that upon which the actual trial will be conducted, is, I think, of comparatively recent origin, though it can be supported by references in similar cases to the need to show "a probability that the plaintiffs are entitled to relief" (*Preston v. Luck* (1884) 27 Ch D 497, 506, *per* Cotton L.J.) or "a strong prima facie case that the right which he seeks to protect in fact exists" (*Smith v. Grigg Ltd.* [1924] 1 KB 655, 659, *per* Atkin J.). These are to be contrasted with expressions in other cases indicating a much less onerous criterion, such as the need to show than there is "certainly a case to be tried," (*Jones v. Pacaya Rubber and Produce Co. Ltd* [1911] 1 KB 455, 457, *per* Buckley L.J.) which corresponds more closely with what judges generally treated as sufficient to justify their considering the balance of convenience upon applications for interlocutory injunctions, at any rate up to the time when I became a member of your Lordships' House.

An attempt had been made to reconcile these apparently differing approaches to the exercise of the discretion by holding that the need to show a probability or a strong prima facie case applied only to the establishment by the plaintiff of his right, and that the lesser burden of showing an arguable case to be tried applied to the alleged violation of that right by the defendant (*Donmar Productions Ltd. v. Bart (Note)* [1967] 1 WLR 740, 742, *per* Ungoed-Thomas J., *Harman Pictures N.V. v. Osborne* [1967] 1 WLR 723, 738, *per* Goff J.). The suggested distinction between what the plaintiff must establish as respects his right and what he must show as respects its violation did not long survive. It was rejected by the Court of Appeal in *Hubbard v. Vosper* [1972] 2 QB 84 – a case in which the plaintiff's entitlement to copyright was undisputed but an injunction was refused despite the apparent weakness of the suggested defence. The court, however, expressly deprecated any attempt to fetter the discretion of the court by laying down any rules which would have the effect of limiting the flexibility of the remedy as a means of achieving the objects that I have indicated above. Nevertheless this authority was treated by Graham J. and the Court of Appeal in the instant appeal as leaving intact the supposed rule that the court is not entitled to take any account of the balance of convenience unless it has first been satisfied that if the case went to trial upon no other evidence than is before the court at the hearing of the application the plaintiff would be entitled to judgment for a permanent injunction in the same terms as the interlocutory injunction sought.

Your Lordships should in my view take this opportunity of declaring that there is no such rule. The use of such expressions as "a probability," "a prima facie case," or "a strong prima facie case" in the context of the exercise of a discretionary power to grant an interlocutory injunction leads to confusion as to the object sought to be achieved by this form of temporary relief. The court no doubt must be satisfied that the claim is not frivolous or vexatious; in other words, that there is a serious question to be tried.

It is no part of the court's function at this stage of the litigation to try to resolve conflicts of evidence on affidavit as to facts on which the claims of either party may ultimately depend nor to decide difficult questions of law which call for detailed argument and mature considerations. These are matters to be dealt with at the trial. One of the reasons for the introduction of the practice of requiring an undertaking as to damages upon the grant of an interlocutory injunction was that "it aided the court in doing that which was its great object, viz. abstaining from expressing any opinion upon the merits of the case until the hearing": *Wakefield v. Duke of Buccleugh* (1865) 12 LT 628, 629. So unless the material available to the court at the hearing of the application for an interlocutory injunction fails to disclose that the plaintiff has any real prospect of succeeding in his claim for a permanent injunction at the trial, the court should go on to consider whether the balance of convenience lies in favour of granting or refusing the interlocutory relief that is sought.

As to that, the governing principle is, that the court should first consider whether, if the plaintiff were to succeed at the trial in establishing his right to a permanent injunction, he would be adequately compensated by an award of damages for the the loss he would have sustained as a result of the defendant's continuing to do what was sought to be enjoined between the time of the application and the time of the trial. If damages in the measure recoverable at common law would be adequate remedy and the defendant would be in a financial position to pay them, no interlocutory injunction should normally be granted, however strong the plaintiff's claim appeared to be at that stage. If, on the other hand, damages would not provide an adequate remedy for the plaintiff in the event of his succeeding at the trial, the court should then consider whether, on the contrary hypothesis that the defendant were to succeed at the trial in establishing his right to do that which was sought to be enjoined, he would be adequately compensated under the plaintiff's undertaking as to damages for the loss he would have sustained by being prevented from doing so between the time of the application and the time of the trial. If damages in the measure recoverable under such an undertakaking would be an adequate remedy and the plaintiff would be in a financial position to pay them, there would be no reason upon this ground to refuse an interlocutory iniunction.

It is where there is doubt as to the adequacy of the respective remedies in damages available to either party or to both, that the question of balance of convenience arises. It would be unwise to attempt even to list all the various matters which may need to be taken into consideration in deciding where the balance lies, let alone to suggest the relative weight to be attached to them. These will vary from case to case.

Where other factors appear to be evenly balanced it is a counsel of prudence to take such measures as are calculated to preserve the status quo. If the defendant is enjoined temporarily from doing something that he has not done before, the only effect of the interlocutory injunction in the event of his succeeding at the trial is to postpone the date at which he is able to embark upon a course of action which he has not previously found it necessary to undertake; whereas to interrupt him in the conduct of an established enterprise would cause much greater inconvence to him since he would have to start again to establish it in the event of his succeeding at the trial.

Save in the simplest cases, the decision to grant or to refuse an interlocutory injunction will cause to whichever party is unsuccessful on the application some disadvantages which his ultimate success at the trial may show he ought to have been spared and the disadvantages may be such that the recovery of damages to which be would then be entitled either in the action or under the plaintiff's undertaking would not be sufficient to compensate him fully for all of them. The extent to which the disadvantages to each party would be incapable of being compensated in damages in the event of his succeeding at the trial is always a significant factor in asssessing where the balance of convenience lies; and if the extent of the uncompensatable disadvantage to each party would not differ widely, it may not be improper to take into account in tipping the balance the relative strength of each party's case as revealed by the affidavit evidence adduced on the hearing of the application. This, however, should be done only where it is apparent upon the facts disclosed by evidence as to which there is no credible dispute that the strength of one party's case is disproportionate to that of the other party. The court is not justified in embarking upon anything resembling a trial of the action upon conflicting affidavits in order to evaluate the strength of either party's case.

I would reiterate that, in addition to those to which I have referred, there may be many other special factors to be taken into consideration in the particular circumstances of individual cases. The instant appeal affords one example of this.

Returning, therefore, to the instant appeal, it cannot be doubted that the affidavit evidence shows that there are serious questions to be tried. Graham J. and the Court of Appeal have already tried the question of infringement on such affidavit evidence as was available and have come to contrary conclusions. Graham J. has already also tried the question of invalidity on these affidavits and has come to the conclusion that the defendant's grounds of objection to the patent are unlikely to succeed, so it was clearly incumbent upon him and on the Court of Appeal to consider the balance of convenience.

Graham J. did so and came to the conclusion that the balance of convenience lay in favour of his exercising his discretion by granting an interlocutory injunction. As patent judge he has unrivalled experience of pharmaceutical patents and the way in which the pharmaceutical industry is carried on. Lacking in this experience, an appellate court should be hesitant to overrule his exercise of his discretion, unless they are satisfied that he has gone wrong in law.

The factors which he took into consideration, and in my view properly, were that Ethicon's sutures XLG were not yet on the market; so they had no business which would be brought to a stop by the injunction; no factories would be closed and no work-people would be thrown out of work. They held a dominant position in the United Kingdom market for absorbent surgical sutures and adopted an aggressive sales policy. Cyanamid on the other hand were in the course of establishing a growing market in PHAE surgical sutures which competed with the natural catgut sutures marketed by Ethicon. If Ethicon were entitled also to establish themselves in the market for PHAE absorbable surgical sutures until the action is tried, which may not be for two or three years yet, and possibly thereafter until the case is finally disposed of on appeal, Cyanamid, even though ultimately successful in proving infringement, would have lost its chance of continuing to increase its share in the total market in absorbent surgical sutures which the continuation of an uninterrupted monopoly of PHAE sutures would have gained for it by the time of the expiry of the patent in 1980. It is notorious that new pharmaceutical products used exclusively by doctors or available only on prescription take a long time to become established in the market, that much of the benefit of the monopoly granted by the patent derives from the fact that the patented product is given the opportunity of becoming established and this benefit continues to be reaped after the patent has expired.

In addition there was a special factor to which Graham J. attached importance. This was that, once doctors and patients had got used to Ethicon's product XLG in the period prior to the trial, it might well be commercially impracticable for Cyanamid to deprive the public of it by insisting on a permanent injunction at the trial, owing to the damaging effect which this would have upon its goodwill in this specialised market and thus upon the sale of its other pharmaceutical products.

I can see no ground for interfering in the learned judge's assessment of the balance of convenience or for interfering with the discretion that he exercised by granting the injunction. In view of the fact that there are serious questions to be tried upon which the available evidence is incomplete, conflicting and untested to express an opinion now as to the prospects of success of either party would only be embarrassing to the judge who will have eventually to try the case. The likelihood of such embarrassment provides an additional reason for not adopting the course that both Graham J. and the Court of Appeal thought they were bound to follow, of dealing with the existing evidence in detail and giving reasoned assessments of their views as to the relative strengths of each party's cases.

I would allow the appeal and restore the order of Graham J."

Campus Oil Ltd v. Minister for Industry and Energy (No.2)
[1983] IR 88

The plaintiff claimed a declaration that the obligation imposed on it by statutory instrument to buy a specified portion of its petroleum oil supplies from a State owned refinery was contrary to Articles 30 and 31 of the EC Treaty. The issue was referred to the European Court of Justice and the defendants sought an interlocutory injunction compelling the plaintiff to comply with the terms of the order pending determination of the plaintiff's claim at the trial of the action. It was held by Keane J in granting an interlocutory injunction that the probability of success at the trial was not the proper test to be applied by the court in deciding whether to grant such an injunction. Instead an applicant must establish that there is a fair question to be determined and that the balance of convenience lay on the side of granting the injunction. This finding was upheld by the Supreme Court.

O'HIGGINS CJ stated at pp.105–107: "The basic contention of the plaintiffs has been that Mr. Justice Keane, in granting interlocutory relief on the application of the defendants, failed to have regard to the correct criteria to be applied in considering an application for an interlocutory injunction and, in particular, when considering an application for an injunction of a mandatory nature. They submit that he was in error in failing to require of the defendants that they should establish a substantial question to be tried and a probability that the plaintiffs would fail at the trial in relation to such a question. It seems to me that these contentions raise a question of some importance as to the manner in which a court should act in considering interlocutory relief.

Interlocutory relief is granted to an applicant where what he complains of is continuing and is causing him harm or injury which may be irreparable in the sense that it may not be possible to compensate him fairly or properly by an award of damages. Such relief is given because a period must necessarily elapse before the action can come for trial and for the purpose of keeping matters *in statu quo* until the hearing. The application is made on motion supported by affidavit. It frequently happens that neither the applicant's right nor the fact of its violation is disputed by the person whose acts are sought to be restrained. In such case an injunction may be given almost as of course. The application for an interlocutory injunction is often treated by the parties as the trial of the action. When that happens, the rights of the parties are finally determined on the interlocutory motion. In cases where rights are disputed and challenged and where a significant period must elapse before the trial, the court must exercise its discretion (to grant interlocutory relief) with due regard to certain well-established principles. Not only will the court have regard to what is complained of and whether damages would be an appropriate remedy but it will consider what inconvenience, loss and damage might be caused to the other party, and will enquire whether the applicant has shown that the balance of convenience is in his favour.

None of these matters, however, are directly in issue on this appeal. Here interlocutory relief was granted to the defendants in pursuance of their counter-claim seeking a permanent injunction at the trial. The plaintiffs against whom it was granted contend that the learned trial judge should have required the defendants to establish a probability that their counterclaim would succeed at the trial and that the plaintiffs' claim would be dismissed. Mr. Fitzsimons, on behalf of those plaintiffs, argued that the existence of such a probability test as a guide to the granting of interlocutory relief was recognised by the former Supreme Court in *Educational Company of Ireland Ltd. v. Fitzpatrick* [1961] IR 323. In particular, he relied on the judgment of Lavery J. in that case. I must say at once that I do not agree. In my opinion, the judgments in that case do not support this argument. It is true that there is one reference to "probability" contained in an extract from Kerr on Injunctions (6th ed.) which was quoted by Lavery J. at p. 336 of the report. That reference, in its context, is of doubtful significance. However, at p. 337 of the report, Lavery J. clearly laid down what he regarded as the proper test when he said:–

> "The plaintiffs have to establish that there is a fair question raised to be decided at the trial. The arguments, lasting three days in this Court, show I think that there is such a question to be determined."

In any event, I would regard the application of the suggested test as contrary to principle. As I have already mentioned, interlocutory relief is intended to keep matters *in statu quo* until the trial, and to do no more. No rights are determined nor are issues decided. I think that the principle is stated correctly in the following passage from Kerr on Injunctions (6th ed. p. 2), which was noted by Lavery J. in the *Educational Company Case*:–

> "In interfering by interlocutory injunction, the Court does not in general profess to anticipate the determination of the right, but merely gives it as its opinion that there is a substantial question to be tried, and that till the question is ripe for trial, a case has been made out for the preservation of the property in the meantime *in statu quo*."

The application of the plaintiffs' criterion on a motion for interlocutory relief would involve the Court in a determination of an issue which properly arises for determination at the trial of the action. In my view, the test to be applied is whether a fair *bona fide* question has been raised by the person seeking the relief. If such a question has been raised, it is not for the Court to determine that question on an interlocutory application: that remains to be decided at the trial. Once a fair question has been raised, in the manner in which I have indicated, then the Court should consider the other matters which are appropriate to the exercise of its discretion to grant interlocutory relief. In this regard, I note the views expressed by Lord Diplock, with the concurrence of the other members of the House of Lords, at p. 407 of the report of *American Cyanamid v. Ethicon Ltd*. I merely say that I entirely agree with what he said.

In my view, therefore, the learned trial judge, in considering whether the defendants had raised a fair question as to whether their rights had been violated, applied the correct test. I must add that, in my view, such a question had been raised and that the trial judge was correct in approaching the exercise of discretion on that basis.

The plaintiffs also argue that, in so far as the relief which was granted was mandatory in nature, such should not have been given by way of interlocutory relief. It is correct to say that a mandatory injunction does not usually issue prior to the trial of an action. However, there are exceptions and, in my view, this case is one of them. The order which is challenged was made under the provisions of an Act of the Oireachtas. It is, therefore, on its face, valid and is to be regarded as a part of the law of the land, unless and until its invalidity is established. It is, and has been, implemented amongst traders in fuel, but the appellant plaintiffs have stood aside and have openly defied its implementation. On the evidence, their action clearly threatens the continued operation of the regime established by the Order. This is so because the other oil companies, particularly the Majors, have threatened the continued operation of the regime established by the order. It seems to me that in such circumstances it was proper to direct, by way of mandatory injunction, compliance with the order of 1983. If this were not done the existing position, in so far as the operation of the order is concerned, could not be preserved and, on the evidence before the learned trial judge, there was a grave danger of very great and extensive damage being caused to the Whitegate refinery. Therefore, although one of the injunctions granted was mandatory in its nature, I think it was proper in the circumstances of this case that it should have been granted by way of interlocutory relief.

In my view, this appeal should be dismissed for these reasons."

Westman Holdings Ltd v. McCormack
[1992] 1 IR 151

The plaintiff sought an interlocutory injunction to prevent the defendants, who had been employed by a company from which the plaintiff had bought a business, from picketing their premises. The Supreme Court (Finlay CJ, O'Flaherty and Egan JJ) concluded that there was a fair question to be tried between the parties and that the balance of convenience favoured granting the relief sought and held that an interlocutory injunction granted to the plaintiffs should continue until the trial of the action.

FINLAY CJ stated at pp.157–159: "I am satisfied there is a fair question to be tried on the issues thus raised.

Having regard to the decision of this Court in *Campus Oil v. The Minister for Energy (No. 2)* [1983] IR 88, and in particular to the judgment of O'Higgins C.J. in that case, I am satisfied that once a conclusion is reached that the plaintiff seeking an interlocutory injunction has raised a fair question to be tried at the hearing of the action in which, if he succeeded, he would be entitled to a permanent injunction that the Court should not express any view on the strength of the contending submissions leading to the raising of such a fair and *bona fide* question, but should proceed to consider the other matters which then arise in regard to the granting of an interlocutory injunction. They are, firstly, as to whether the plaintiff could, in the event of being refused an injunction and succeeding in the action, be adequately compensated by damages. That question raises two separate issues, potentially, in every case. The first is the question as to whether damages would be an adequate remedy, and the second is as to whether there is a defendant liable to pay such damages who is able to do so, and thus the appropriate compensation could actually be realised.

The loss which will be suffered by the plaintiff if it is right in its claim in this case that the picketing is unlawful, were it to be refused an injunction, is exclusively pecuniary loss, being a diminution of trade in the premises. It is quite clear, therefore, that if compensation could be obtained by way of damages arising out of the picketing from a defendant able to pay the sums involved, that damages would be an adequate remedy.

I am satisfied, however, that the obvious conclusion in this case must be that a combination of an inability to pay on the part of some of the individual defendants and a potential immunity from liability to pay damages for the trade union, who could probably afford to compensate the plaintiff, which is contained in s. 13 of the Act of 1990, make it extremely improbable that the plaintiff would, if refused an injunction, be able to obtain adequate compensation in the event of their establishing that the picket was unlawful.

Having reached that conclusion, the next inquiry must be as to whether, in the event of the injunction being granted, the defendants who would be thereby restrained could if they proved correct in their contention be compensated adequately for any loss they suffered by a combination of the undertaking which must necessarily be given by the plaintiff in order to obtain an injunction and to the existence of any separate claim for damages to be entered by way of counterclaim or otherwise against the plaintiff.

With regard to this issue on the facts in this case, I have come to the conclusion that there are two quite separately identifiable forms of loss which the defendants may incur, if their contention that they are at present entitled to be in continued employment with the plaintiff is found to be correct. The first is that they will lose wages which they should have been receiving from April, 1991. With regard to that loss, I am satisfied that the undertaking which the plaintff must give, if they are to obtain the interlocutory injunction which was given in the High Court, would be an appropriate and adequate method of compensating the defendants in respect of that loss, and on the information with regard to the assets and financial affairs of the plaintiff it is reasonably probable that it would be able to meet the undertaking it gives. In addition, however, I am satisfied that the defendants, if prevented from striking at this stage, can be said to have suffered a less tangible loss than the mere loss of wages, namely, their opportunity to re-enter employment. If at the conclusion of the hearing of this action the defendants' assertion of rights pursuant to the Directive and statutory instrument is upheld, quite clearly they then will be in a position, if necessary and if appropriate, to force the plaintiff to re-employ them, and on its refusal so to do, could lawfully mount a picket at that stage and have the effective pressure for negotiations such a situation gives to them. There is, however, some substance, in my view, in the assertion made on behalf of the defendants that if they could mount that picket now that it would be an even greater pressure to aid them in the negotiations to re-enter employment in these premises.

In these circumstances, it seems to me, having regard to the authorities, that I must balance the convenience between the two parties. In my view, the balance of convenience, having carefully considered the factors which arise, is with the granting of an injunction. If no injunction is granted, it is clear that a very substantial loss indeed will be incurred by the plaintiff, even if a trial can be obtained in the High Court in the relatively short time of two or three months. I am satisfied that the high probability is that if that occurs and if the plaintiff succeeds eventually in the action that it will recover no part of its loss.

If, on the other hand, the injunction is continued and at the hearing of the action, after two or three months, the defendants' contention is upheld the greater part of the loss which the defendants have suffered will be recoverable against the plaintiff, and only a part of the disadvantage occurring to them by reason of the injunction restraining them from picketing will remain uncompensated.

In those circumstances, I conclude that the injunction should continue as an interlocutory injunction, and I would dismiss this appeal."

Circumstances in which a Departure from Cyanamid Guidelines Justified

It is important to stress that the *American Cyanamid/Campus Oil* principles set out above are merely guidelines and that it is not appropriate to apply them in every case. Some of the circumstances in which a departure from these guidelines may be justified will now be considered.

Where an Interlocutory Injunction is Sought in the Context of a Trade Dispute

The conclusion reached by the Supreme Court in *Westman Holdings Ltd v. McCormack*[9] made it clear that the *American Cyanamid/Campus Oil* principles clearly favoured the employer where proceedings were brought seeking to restrain picketing by means of an interlocutory injunction. Attempts have been made to redress this imbalance by means of legislation and s.19 of the Industrial Relations Act 1990[10] has qualified the effect of these principles in the context of trade disputes. The effect of s.19(2) would appear to be that once a plaintiff establishes an entitlement to an interlocutory injunction by showing that there is a fair question to be tried, the court must consider whether the defendants can establish a fair case that they were acting in furtherance or contemplation of a trade dispute. If they can, the injunction will not be granted; if they cannot, the court will go on to consider as it does at common law, whether the balance of convenience favours the grant of an injunction.

Section 19 of the Industrial Relations Act 1990:

> **Restriction of rights to injunction**
> **19.**—(1) Where a secret ballot has been held in accordance with the rules of a trade union as provided for in *section 14*, the outcome of which or, in the case of an aggregation of ballots, the outcome of the aggregated ballots, favours a strike or other industrial action and the trade union before engaging in the strike or other industrial action gives notice of not less than one week to the employer

---

[9] [1992] 1 IR 151. See also *Bayzana Ltd v. Galligan* [1987] IR 238.
[10] See Kerr (1990) ICLSA 90/19-33

concerned of its intention to do so, that employer shall not be entitled to apply to any court for an injunction restraining the strike or other industrial action unless notice of the application has been given to the trade union and its members who are party to the trade dispute.

(2) Where a secret ballot has been held in accordance with the rules of a trade union as provided for in *section 14,* the outcome of which or, in the case of an aggregation of ballots, the outcome of the aggregated ballots, favours a strike or other industrial action and the trade union before engaging in the strike or other industrial action gives notice of not less than one week to the employer concerned of its intention to do so, a court shall not grant an injunction restraining the strike or other industrial action where the respondent establishes a fair case that he was acting in contemplation or furtherance of a trade dispute.

(3) Notice as provided for in *subsection (1)* may be given to the members of a trade union by referring such members to a document containing the notice which the members have reasonable opportunity of reading during the course of their employment or which is reasonably accessible to them in some other way.

(4) *Subsections (1)* and *(2)* do not apply—

    (*a*) in respect of proceedings arising out of or relating to unlawfully entering into or remaining upon any property belonging to another, or unlawfully causing damage or causing or permitting damage to be caused to the property of another, or

    (*b*) in respect of proceedings arising out of or relating to any action resulting or likely to result in death or personal injury.

(5) Where two or more secret ballots have been held in relation to a dispute, the ballot referred to in *subsections (1)* and *(2)* shall be the last such ballot.

G.& T. Crampton Ltd v. Building and Allied Trades Union
[1998] 1 ILRM 430

The plaintiff sought an interlocutory injunction to restrain the defendants from picketing their premises. The plaintiff argued that a precondition to the operation of s.19(2) of the Industrial Relations Act 1990 had not been complied with as there has been no effective secret ballot held sufficient to comply with the requirements of s.14 of the Act. Laffoy J granted the interlocutory injunction sought and the defendants appealed. The Supreme Court (Hamilton CJ, O'Flaherty and Barrington JJ) was satisfied that the trial judge had been entitled to come to the conclusion that a condition precedent to the implementation of s.19 had not been established and upheld the conclusions which she had made in deciding the matter on the basis of the principles set out in the *Campus Oil* case.

HAMILTON CJ stated at pp.434–438:

"The findings of the trial judge

The issues before the learned trial judge related to the provisions of s. 11 of the Industrial Relations Act, the provisions of s. 14 of the same Act and the provisions of s. 19. The facts relevant to the issues which come before this Court are set out in detail in the judgment of the learned trial judge and it is not necessary for me at this stage to refer to them. I am very conscious of the fact that in her recital of the relevant facts, she did not have the benefit of the affidavits sworn by Mr Lamond dealing in detail with the circumstances in which the secret ballot was held, the voting thereon and of such like.

Now in the course of her judgment, the learned trial judge stated at p. 8:

> There is no evidence whatever before the court as to the outcome of the secret ballot conducted by the union and in particular there is no evidence that its outcome favoured picketing the site.

On this ground alone, she stated:

> I am satisfied that there is no evidence before the court that one of the preconditions stipulated in s. 19(2) has been complied with.

I have already stated the provisions of s. 19(2) and the portion thereof that she was referring to was the necessity to have a secret ballot in accordance with the provisions of s. 14 of the Act.

The appellants are, to say the least of it, aggrieved by this particular finding by the learned trial judge. It is submitted that this issue was not raised in the affidavit filed on behalf of the plaintiff and that they had not in view of the shortness of time and the manner in which the case was dealt with, the opportunity of satisfactorily dealing with this point. It is true that the affidavit upon which the plaintiff's application was grounded referred to a breach of the provisions of s. 19 of the Act; but the affidavit clearly referred to that on the basis that the persons likely to be affected by the decision were not notified of the ballot and were in effect deprived of the opportunity of voting thereon.

As I said, the learned trial judge in the course of her judgment stated in particular that there is no evidence that the outcome favoured picketing the site and I have already stated that picketing is a strong weapon in the armoury of a trade union and this raises the question of the interpretation of both s. 14 and s. 19 of the Act and requirements of what is necessary to have an effective secret ballot on the issues. The Act deals with a strike or other industrial action and the question arises as to the nature of the proposals that should go before the members to have an effective ballot on the issues be it secret or otherwise.

S. 8 of the Act deals with the definitions of strike and industrial action and it is not necessary for me to refer to them other than to say that industrial action encompasses many different activities: picketing is only one of them, and the question arises on a possible interpretation of the Act (and I go no further) as to whether there is an obligation on the union in conducting a ballot to phrase the proposals so as to give a clear indication of the nature of the action to be taken by the trade union. The notice given by the letter to which I have referred dated 7 November relates to 'strike or other industrial action' and does not purport to particularise the nature of the industrial action sought to be taken and a question arises on the interpretation of ss. 14 and 19 as to whether it is sufficient merely to have a proposal before members on the question of strike or other industrial action without specifying the nature of the action for which the members' approval is sought and necessary by virtue of the terms of ss. 14 and 19.

In my opinion, on this issue alone there is a fair question to be tried. There is also a fair question to be tried as to a need for the entire of the circumstances of the ballot to be investigated for the purpose of ascertaining whether or not the members whom it was reasonable to expect at the time would be called upon to engage in the strike or other industrial action were given a fair opportunity of voting. It is alleged on behalf of the appellants that all the members who were likely to be so affected were notified of the ballot, it is submitted on behalf of the employer by Mr Stewart SC that other members of the union who were likely to be affected were not balloted or given an opportunity of voting on the proposal. So there is another issue to be tried there as to the adequacy of the ballot.

It is quite clear from a consideration of the ballot papers that it is just described – 'official ballot paper, ballot on proposal to engage in strike or other industrial action'. Then you have the word 'proposal' with a blank space after it and below that the words 'in favour' and 'against'. But the ballot papers do not contain the proposal or indeed any proposal upon which the members were being called to ballot. Now whether the ballot paper is adequate to comply with the requirements of s. 14 of the Industrial Relations Act or the rules of the trade union is also a relevant issue which arises on the proceedings.

The learned trial judge also found that there is a fair issue to be tried between the plaintiff and the defendants on the question as to whether or not the members Messrs Leonard and Deacon are entitled to the protection of s. 2(1) of the Act. She had regard to what she described as the very comprehensive arguments advanced by Mr Kerr on behalf of the defendants and by Mr Horan on behalf of the plaintiff in this regard. She went on to say that the nub of Mr Horan's argument was that as regards union members picketers the plaintiff was not their employer in the context of which the expression is used in s. 11, whereas Mr Kerr contended that it was having regard to the definition of employer in s. 8 of the 1990 Act which defines that word as meaning, *inter alia*, a person for whom one or more workers seek to work having previously worked for that person. She said on the evidence before her that she had no doubt that the plaintiff's contention that the picketers are not entitled to the protection of s. 11 raises a fair issue to be tried between the parties.

When a court holds that there is an issue to be tried, the position is as set out in the judgment of the former Chief Justice, Finlay CJ in *Westman Holdings Ltd v. McCormack* [1992] 1 IR 151; [1991] ILRM 833 with which judgment my colleague, O' Flaherty J, concurred and I would like to refer to the portion thereof reported in [1992] 1 IR 151; [1991] ILRM 833. The passage to which I would refer is contained at pp. 157/838 of the report:

Having regard to the decision of this Court in *Campus Oil v. Minister for Industry and Energy* and in particular the judgment of O'Higgins CJ in that case, I am satisfied that once a conclusion is reached, that the plaintiff seeking an interlocutory injunction has raised a fair question to be tried at the hearing of the action in which if he succeeded he would be entitled to a permanent injunction, the court should not express any view on the strength of the contending submissions leading to the raising of such a fair or *bona fide* question but should proceed to consider the other matters which then arise in regard to the granting of an interlocutory injunction.

I am satisfied that the affidavits disclosed a fair question to be tried on the question as to whether or not the provisions of s. 11(1) apply to the defendants in the proceedings and also that a number of questions stand to be determined with regard to the interpretation of the provisions of s. 14 and s. 19 of the Industrial Relations Act and the questions to be raised there as to whether or not in the conduct of a ballot a union should be required to particularise the nature of the industrial action for which they seek support of their members and that the proposal being put before those members should particularise such action and (I am expressing no concluded view on it), whether it is not sufficient to comply with the requirements of such Act merely to have a ballot favouring a strike or other industrial action without particularising the nature of the industrial action to be taken by the union and for which they seek their members' approval. This is a serious issue to be tried in this case because undoubtedly from an examination of the ballot papers, first of all, no actual proposal was placed before the members and even if it were interpreted that the heading 'Ballot on proposal to engage in strike or other industrial action' was held to be a sufficient proposal, the question arises again as to whether it is in compliance with the provisions of s. 14 and s. 19 of the Act.

Conclusion

That being so I am satisfied that there are two issues to be tried in this case that have been raised by the plaintiff in these proceedings and I am satisfied that there is a fundamental issue with regard to the interpretation of ss. 14 and 19 of the Act and that the learned trial judge was entitled to come to the conclusion that the condition precedent to the implementation of s. 19 was not established.

She then proceeded to deal with the matter on the basis set forth in the decision in the *Campus Oil* case and she found that such a question had been raised, she found that damages would be an inadequate remedy and that the balance of convenience was in favour of the granting of the injunction.

In the circumstances which I have attempted to outline at short notice, I am satisfied that she was entitled to come to such a conclusion and that in the circumstances the appeal brought by the first and second named defendants should be dismissed."

Where an Interlocutory Injunction is Sought in Proceedings for Defamation

It is clear from the case law that it is more difficult for a plaintiff to obtain an interlocutory injunction where it is sought to restrain publication of alleged defamatory matter. The relevant principles are well set out in the judgment of Kelly J in *Reynolds v. Malocco*.

Reynolds v. Malocco
[1999] 2 IR 203

The plaintiff sought an interlocutory injunction to restrain the defendants from publishing an article about him which he alleged defamed him in two respects. He contended that the words in the article in their natural and ordinary meaning or by innuendo alleged, first, that he permitted the sale of drugs in his nightclub premises and was benefiting therefrom and, secondly, that he was a homosexual. The defendant contended in relation to the first complaint that the words did not bear the meaning ascribed to them and argued that if they did, he would plead justification at the trial and asserted in relation to the second complaint that the words did not bear the meaning contended for. Kelly J granted the interlocutory injunction sought.

KELLY J stated at pp.209–212 and 218–220: "The Judicature (Ireland) Act, 1877, confers jurisdiction on the High Court to grant injunctions in all cases where it appears just and convenient to do so, and on such terms as the court sees fit. Order 50, r. 6 of the Rules of the Superior Courts authorises the granting of interlocutory injunctions.

The exercise of this power by the court has been the subject of numerous court decisions and it is possible to divine from these the relevant principles which the court applies in deciding to grant or withhold interlocutory injunctive relief.

In an ordinary case the court considers whether the plaintiff has raised a fair or serious issue to be determined at the trial of the action. If it considers that such a question has been raised it goes on to decide whether damages would adequately compensate the plaintiff in respect of any loss or damage which may be suffered as a result of the activity which is sought to be enjoined. If it decides that damages would not be an adequate remedy it then proceeds to consider whether on the balance of convenience an injunction should be granted or not. (See *Campus Oil v. Minister for Industry (No 2)* [1983] IR 88 and *American Cyanamid v. Ethicon Ltd.* [1975] AC 396).

These principles have a wide, but not universal, application. In a small number of cases special rules which are not encompassed by these principles apply. One such type of case arises in the field of contracts of employment. Normally courts will not grant an injunction to restrain breaches of covenant in a contract of employment if that would amount to indirect specific performance of such a contract or would perpetuate a relationship based on mutual trust which no longer exists. Another exception to the general principles which I have already described arises in cases of the type in suit.

A plaintiff in an action such as this, in order to obtain an interlocutory injunction, must show not merely that he has raised a serious issue concerning the words complained of but that there is no doubt that they are defamatory. Furthermore, if the defendant intends to plead justification or any other recognised defence, normally an injunction of this type will be refused.

The jurisdiction to grant interlocutory injunctions to restrain publication of defamatory statements has been described as one "of a delicate nature" which "ought only to be exercised in the clearest cases". (See the judgment of Esher M.R. in *Coulson v. Coulson* (1887) 3 TLR 846).

That approach was expressly approved by the Supreme Court in *Sinclair v. Gogarty* [1937] IR 377. In the course of his judgment Sullivan C.J., with whom all four other members of the Court agreed, said at p. 384:–

> "The principle upon which the Court should act in considering such applications was stated by Lord Esher M.R. in *Coulson v. Coulson* (1887) 3 TLR 846, and his statement of the principle was approved of and adopted by the Court of Appeal in *Bonnard v. Perryman* [1891] 2 Ch 269. The principle is this, that an interlocutory injunction should only be granted in the clearest cases where any jury would say that the matter complained of was libelous, and where if the jury did not so find the Court would set aside the verdict as unreasonable."

The reason for the reluctance on the part of the courts to grant interlocutory injunctions in cases of this sort is grounded on the importance attached to the right to free speech. This has been the position from at least as far back as the decision in *Bonnard v. Perryman* [1891] 2 Ch 269 where Coleridge L.J. said at p. 284:–

> "... the importance of leaving free speech unfettered is a strong reason in cases of libel for dealing most cautiously and warily with the granting of interim injunctions."

The sentiments expressed by Coleridge L.J. have been heeded by the courts and nowadays are fortified by the provisions of Art. 10 of the European Convention for the Protection of Human Rights and Fundamental Freedoms.

Coleridge L.J. went on to say:–

> "The right of free speech is one which it is for the public interest that individuals should possess, and, indeed, that they should exercise without impediment, so long as no wrongful act is done; and, unless an alleged libel is untrue, there is no wrong committed; but, on the contrary, often a very wholesome act is performed in the publication and repetition of an alleged libel. Until it is clear that an alleged libel is untrue, it is not clear that any right at all has been infringed ..."

It is therefore clear that the first matter which I must inquire into is whether or not the plaintiff's complaints are made out with the degree of clarity required so as to enable me to conclude that the words complained of are undoubtedly defamatory.

If I so conclude in favour of the plaintiff, I then have to consider whether, in the light of the defendants' stated intention to plead justification concerning the drug dealing allegation, an injunction can be granted at all.

The reason why I have to consider this aspect of the matter arises because of the decision in *Bonnard v. Perryman* [1891] 2 Ch 269. As I have already pointed out, the decision in that case was approved by the Supreme Court in *Sinclair v. Gogarty* [1937] IR 377. The rule established by that decision is that where a defendant in a libel action intends to plead justification, a court will not grant an interlocutory injunction to restrain publication of the statement complained of.

The question then arises as to whether a bald statement of intention to plead justification is sufficient to debar a plaintiff, who might otherwise be entitled to an injunction, from such relief. If it is, then the plaintiff's application in respect to the drug dealing activities must be doomed to failure. Counsel on behalf of the plaintiff urges me not to adopt this approach but rather to conduct an examination of the defendant's evidence so as to establish whether the plea of justification has any substance or prospect of success.

There appear to be two conflicting decisions in this jurisdiction as to the proper approach to take on this topic.

On the one hand there is the decision in *Gallagher v. Tuohy* (1924) 58 ILTR 134, where the matter complained of consisted of a circular containing defamatory statements concerning the plaintiff in his business capacity. Murnaghan J. stated at p. 135:–

> "The question I have to decide is whether an order should be made restraining the defendants from repeating statements which they allege to be true and provable. Against the granting of even an order the authority of *Bonnard v. Perryman* has been cited to me, and that authority has not been controverted by the plaintiff. The effect of that decision seems to be reasonably clear. The Court should not readily restrain the publication of any matter which is not obviously a libel. I would have no difficulty at all in deciding that the statement was defamatory but for the plea of justification. That plea having been raised, it seems to me that I cannot prejudge the issue . . . and decide that the plea of justification is erroneous. That would be the effect of granting the injunction sought."

On the other hand, the decision of the Supreme Court in *Cullen v. Stanley* [1926] IR 73 demonstrates a different approach. There the plaintiff sought an interlocutory injunction to restrain the publication of statements by the defendants to the effect that he had acted as a "scab" on the occasion of a bakers' strike. The plaintiff deposed that the statements were absolutely false and that he believed the publication was for the purpose of prejudicing his position as a candidate in an election. One of the defendants submitted an affidavit stating that all the allegations were true, and that he would prove this at trial. The Supreme Court nonetheless granted an interlocutory injunction. O'Connor J. referred to the argument of the defendant to the effect that the rule in *Bonnard v. Perryman* [1891] 2 Ch 269, automatically precluded the grant of an interlocutory injunction once the defence of justification was raised. He said at p. 84:-

> "I do not think that the Court of Appeal intended to lay down a rule which should be rigidly applied to every case, because the judgment of Coleridge C.J. wound up with the observation that, on the whole, the Court thought that it was wiser *in that case*, as it generally, and in all but exceptional cases, must be, to abstain from interference until the trial of the plea of justification."

The judge then examined the detailed affidavit of the plaintiff, which he contrasted with the "baldest affidavit" of the defendant. He held that on the evidence before that Court that there was nothing to support the plea of justification.

> Of these two approaches I prefer the latter. I do not think that a rule which permits a defendant to, in effect, oust the ability of this Court to intervene by way of injunction in an appropriate case by the simple expedient of expressing an intention to plead justification at the trial of the action, is consistent with the obligations imposed on the court under the Constitution. Furthermore, the application of such a rigid rule, without an ability on the part of the court to ascertain whether the plea of justification had any substance or not, would provide a happy hunting ground for unscrupulous defamers.

> I am therefore satisfied that it is open to the court to examine the evidence adduced by the defendant in support of the justification plea so as to ascertain whether it has any substance or prospect of success. I turn now to consider the complaints made by the plaintiff."

. . . .

"The discretion
The grant of injunctive relief is always discretionary.

In the present case I now have to consider, having found in favour of the plaintiff in respect of the complaints concerning the libels alleged, whether or not an injunction ought to be granted.

This is "a jurisdiction of a delicate nature" and the court must be circumspect to ensure that it does not unnecessarily interfere with the right to freedom of expression.

I would not wish to set out in a hard and fast manner the factors which the court should or could take into account in the exercise of this discretion. It is sufficient if I identify one item of particular importance which affects me in the exercise of my discretion in this case.

If I refuse the plaintiff this injunction, it is clear that the article will be published and the plaintiff will be left to his remedy in damages at a trial to be held at some time in the future. Damages are the normal remedy for defamation and injunctions are not. Nothing in this judgment should be taken to dilute that approach. In the present case, however, the question arises as to what damages the plaintiff would be likely to recover against the defendants at trial.

The first defendant, has, on his own admission, recently completed a lengthy prison sentence imposed for offences of dishonesty. He formerly practised as a solicitor but that option is no longer open to him. There is uncontroverted evidence that he has unsatisfied judgments against him for a sum of money in excess of £40,000. It is also uncontroverted that he has other outstanding liabilities arising from the period when he practised as a solicitor. It seems to me, as a matter of probability, that the prospects of the plaintiff ever recovering other than a paper judgment against the first defendant are remote.

From the information that emerged at the hearing on Monday and Tuesday of this week, Messrs. Murray and White do not exist.

There remains the curious figure of the fourth defendant. He did not appear either personally or through counsel. Whilst in the magazine he gives his address as "London", the only address to which the proceedings could be directed was at Foxrock post office. He describes himself as being the magazine's publisher yet we now know that the publisher is the fifth defendant, the added defendant. It seems to me that the shadowy figure of the fourth defendant is unlikely to prove to be any better a prospect for the recovery of damages than the first defendant.

Finally, there is the fifth defendant. This two pound company, with both shares held by another limited liability company, seems unlikely to make any judgment which the plaintiff may obtain against it any less hollow than the judgment against the other defendants.

In these circumstances I am quite satisfied that my discretion must be exercised in favour of granting an injunction rather than refusing it. To refuse it would be to consign the plaintiff to a trial where damages would be an inadequate remedy because of the virtual impossibility of ever recovering any sum awarded.

Conclusion

It follows that the plaintiff is entitled to interlocutory relief and I therefore grant, until trial, an order restraining the defendants and each of them, their servants or agents or any person acting in concert with them or any person with notice of the making of this order, from in any manner or fashion howsoever publishing of or concerning the plaintiff an article entitled "Operation Night-cap causes John Reynolds sleepless nights as cops raid club" or any matter contained therein defamatory of the plaintiff's reputation."

Where an Interlocutory Injunction is Sought to Restrain the Presentation of a Petition for the Winding Up of a Company

This exception has been recognised in England for some time,[11] and the approach taken there has been followed by the High Court in this jurisdiction in *Truck and Machinery Sales Ltd v. Marubeni Komatsu Ltd.*

Truck and Machinery Sales Ltd v. Marubeni Komatsu Ltd
High Court (Keane J) 23 February 1996

The plaintiff sought an injunction to restrain the defendant from presenting a petition to wind a company up. Counsel for the plaintiff sought to rely on the *Campus Oil* principles and argued that the plaintiff had raised a serious question as to whether the sum claimed was due and owing by it and that the balance of convenience lay in favour of restraining the petition until the hearing of the action. Counsel for the defendant argued that in order to obtain such relief, the plaintiff would have to establish that the presentation of the petition was an abuse of process and that it was bound to fail or at least, that there was an alternative remedy available. Keane J stated that it would not be appropriate to apply the *Campus Oil* guidelines and held that the interlocutory injunction sought should be refused.

KEANE J stated at pp.17–21: "It is also clear that, even where the company appears to be insolvent, the Court may nonetheless, in the exercise of its equitable discretion, restrain the presentation of the petition where it is satisfied that the petition is being presented for an ulterior or collateral purpose and not in good faith by a creditor forming part of a class of creditors who seeks the administration of the assets of the company for the benefit of that class in an orderly manner under the supervision of the Court: see *Re A Company* [1983] BCLC 492.

I am also satisfied, however, that the jurisdiction to restrain the presentation of the petition is one to be exercised only with great caution. In *Bryanston Finance Limited v. De Vries (No. 2)*, Buckley L.J., with whom the other members of the Court agreed, observed that:

> "It has long been recognised that the jurisdiction of the Court to stay an action in limine as an abuse of process is a jurisdiction to be exercised with great circumspection and exactly the same considerations must apply to a quia timet injunction to restrain commencement of proceedings. These principles are, in my opinion, just as applicable to a winding-up petition as to an action. The right to petition the Court for a winding-up order in appropriate circumstances is a right conferred by statute. A would-be petitioner should not be restrained from

---

[11] *Bryanston Finance Ltd v. De Vries (No.2)* [1976] Ch 63.

exercising it except on clear and persuasive grounds. I recognise that the presentation of a petition may do great damage to a company's business and reputation, though I think that the potential damage in the present case may have been rather exaggerated. The restraint of a petition may also gravely affect the would-be petitioner and not only him but also others, whether creditors or contributories. If the presentation of the petition is prevented the commencement of the winding-up will be postponed until such time as the petition is presented or a winding-up resolution is passed. This is capable of far reaching effects."

It is also clear that, while the form of the relief sought in such cases is normally, as here interlocutory in nature, the principles laid down by the Supreme Court in *Campus Oil Limited v. Minister for Industry and Energy (No. 2)* as to the factors to which the Court must have regard in granting or withholding interlocutory injunctive relief are not necessarily applicable. Typically in an application for an interlocutory injunction, the Court is invited to restrain an action which is alleged to be a violation of the plaintiff's rights where there is a fair question to be tried, where damages will not be an adequate remedy and where the balance of convenience (including the desirability of preserving the *status quo* pending the determination of the action) points to the granting of such relief. Different considerations entirely apply where, as here, the object of the application is to prevent the respondent from exercising his right of access to the Courts, whether by way of ordinary process or a winding-up petition. In such a case, the factors which the Court should taken into account were also identified in *Bryanston Finance*. Thus, Buckley L.J. said that:

"The plaintiff company cannot assert such a right in respect of any particular anticipated litigation without demonstrating that, at least *prima facie*, that litigation would be an abuse."

In the same case, Stephenson L.J. expressly rejected the *American Cyanamid* criteria as being applicable and went on to say that it was for the plaintiff company

"to prove that the defendant's exercise of his right to bring legal proceedings is in fact an abuse of process."

The learned judge also commented that:

"(*Charles Forte Investments Limited v. Amanda* [1964] 1 Ch 240) still binds us to hold that unless the plaintiff company can prove that the petition is bound to fail – or perhaps that there is a suitable alternative remedy to the petition – the defendant cannot be restrained, even temporarily from presenting it."

The approach in that case was also adopted by the Court of Appeal in *Coulson Sanderson & Ward v. Ward*. In that case, Slade LJ said:

"This decision, therefore, is clear authority for the proposition that the Court should not, on the hearing of an interlocutory motion, interfere with what would otherwise appear to be the legitimate presentation of a winding-up petition by someone qualified to present it unless the evidence before it is sufficient to

> establish *prima facie* that the plaintiff company will succeed in establishing that the proceedings sought to be restrained would constitute an abuse."

I am satisfied that this is the approach which should also be adopted in this jurisdiction. The constitutional right of recourse to the courts should not be inhibited, save in exceptional circumstances, and this applies as much to the presentation of a petition for the winding-up of a company by a person with the appropriate *locus standi* as it does to any other form of proceedings. The undoubted power of the Courts to restrain proceedings which are an abuse of process is one which should not be lightly exercised. In the context of winding-up petitions, I have no doubt that it should be exercised only where the plaintiff company has established at least a *prima facie* case that its presentation would constitute an abuse of process. In many cases, a *prima facie* case will be established where the plaintiff company adduces evidence which satisfies the Court that the petition is bound to fail or, at the least, that there is a suitable alternative remedy. It would not be appropriate to apply the principles laid down by the Supreme Court in *Campus Oil Ltd. v. Minister for Industry and Energy (No. 2)* in cases of this nature where it is the creditors' right to have recourse to the Courts, rather than any right of the plaintiff company, which is under threat."

Where the Trial of the Action is Unlikely

Where the grant or refusal of an interlocutory injunction would in effect dispose of the action finally in favour of whichever party was successful, the degree of likelihood that the plaintiff would have succeeded in establishing his right to an injunction if the action had gone to trial is a factor to be brought into the balance by the court. This principle was laid down by Lord Diplock in *N.W.L. Ltd v. Woods*[12] as follows and is now well established:

> Where ... the grant or refusal of the interlocutory injunction will have the practical effect of putting an end to the action because the harm that will have been already caused to the losing party by its grant or refusal is complete and of a kind for which money cannot constitute any worthwhile recompense, the degree of likelihood that the plaintiff would have succeeded in establishing his right to an injunction if the action had gone to trial is a factor to be brought into the balance by the judge in weighing the risks that injustice may result from his deciding the application one way rather than the other.

Lansing Linde Ltd v. Kerr
[1991] 1 WLR 251

The plaintiff company sought an interlocutory injunction to enforce a clause

---

[12] [1979] 1 WLR 1294, 1307.

in the defendant's contract of employment which stipulated that he would not work for any of its competitors for a period of 12 months after termination of his employment with the company. The defendant, who occupied a senior position in the company, had given six months notice and a month later accepted the position of managing director of a competitor. It was held by the Court of Appeal (Butler-Sloss, Staughton and Beldam LJJ) in refusing the injunction that the trial judge had properly taken into account the plaintiff's prospects of success at the trial, having regard to the fact that it would not be possible to hold a trial before the period for which the plaintiff claimed to be entitled to an injunction had expired, or substantially expired, and that in those circumstances it was not enough to decide merely that there was a serious issue to be tried.

STAUGHTON LJ stated at pp.256–259: "In brief the conclusions of Knox J. were as follows. (1) Since a trial could not take place until the 12-month period of restraint had almost expired, it was necessary to assess and take into account the prospects of the plaintiff succeeding at trial, before granting an interlocutory injunction. (2) The defendant occupied a position in the plaintiff where he probably came to know trade secrets and confidential information. (3) This would support a covenant against competition in the United Kingdom. (4) However, a worldwide covenant against competition would probably prove too wide to be enforceable at trial. (5) Taking that into account with other aspects of the balance of convenience, the judge would not grant an injunction. (6) "The result could easily have been different" if he had only had to consider the balance of convenience on the basis that there was a serious question to be tried.

It is thus apparent that the first issue in this appeal is whether the judge, having regard to *American Cyanamid Co. v. Ethicon Ltd.* [1975] AC 396 and subsequent cases, was right to take into account the prospects of success at trial. Other issues raised were whether a covenant against competition could be justified to protect trade secrets only, or some wider class of confidential information; whether the defendant's position was such that he would be likely to know trade secrets and confidential information; if so, whether that would justify a worldwide restraint on competition; and whether the termination agreement in July 1990 affected the result. In addition there were points raised on behalf of the defendant as to the interpretation of clause 19(B), and as to a suggested estoppel.

In this court a further affidavit with a substantial exhibit was introduced on behalf of the plaintiff, without objection on behalf of the defendant. There was also a further affidavit by him in reply, with exhibits. All this evidence was concerned with the extent of the actual information acquired by the defendant while he was working for the plaintiff in the United Kingdom, and how secret or confidential it was.

(A) American Cyanamid and the prospects of success at trial

As is well known, the *American Cyanamid* case laid down the balance of convenience test for the grant or refusal of an interlocutory injunction. Once it is shown that there is at least a serious issue to be tried, the court should not embark further upon an examination of the plaintiff's prospects of success. The main question is then one of lesser evil: will it do less harm to grant an injunction which subsequently turns out to be unjustified, or to refuse one if it subsequently turns out that an injunction should have been granted? In either case the adequacy of a remedy in damages, and the likelihood of its being enforceable, is very important. I suspect that many short-term injunctions were granted on that principle long before the *American Cyanamid* case: if they were to last only for a few days or weeks, there would be little harm to the defendant, and what there was could be compensated in damages.

Subsequent cases show that a wider survey of the balance of convenience may sometimes be necessary, including an assessment of the plaintiff's prospects of success at trial. Thus in *N.W.L. Ltd. v. Woods* [1979] 1 WLR 1294, 1306, Lord Diplock said that a judge ought to "give full weight to all the practical realities of the situation to which the injunction will apply" and that the *American Cyanamid* decision

> "was not dealing with a case in which the grant or refusal of an injunction at that stage would, in effect, dispose of the action finally in favour of whichever party was successful in the application, because there would be nothing left on which it was in the unsuccessful party's interest to proceed to trial."

Lord Diplock continued:

> "Cases of this kind are exceptional, but when they do occur they bring into the balance of convenience an important additional element."

In *Cayne v. Global Natural Resources Plc.* [1984] 1 All ER 225 an interlocutory injunction was refused. In the view of Kerr L.J., at p. 236, the action was never likely to be taken to trial if the plaintiffs obtained an injunction. Hence

> "the overriding consideration for present purposes is that, if an injunction is granted, the effective contest between the parties is likely to have been finally decided summarily in favour of the plaintiffs."

The third case is *Lawrence David Ltd. v. Ashton* [1989] ICR 123. There an early trial was possible, and an injunction was granted. But Balcombe L.J. said, at p. 135:

> "It is only if the action cannot be tried before the period of the restraint has expired, or has run a large part of its course, that the grant of the interlocutory injunction will effectively dispose of the action, thus bringing the case within the exception to the rule in *American Cyanamid,* such as was considered by the House of Lords in *N.W.L. Ltd. v. Woods* [1979] ICR 867 (and I refer in particular

to Lord Diplock's speech at p. 880) and also by this court in *Cayne v. Global Natural Resources Plc.* [1984] 1 All ER 225. It is then that the judge may properly go on to consider the prospects of the employers' succeeding in the action. Another way of reaching the same conclusion is to say that the longer the period of the interlocutory injunction, the more likely it is that the employee may suffer damage (if the injunction is wrongly granted) which is uncompensatable by the employers on their cross-undertaking, and therefore it becomes necessary to consider the relative strength of each party's case as revealed by the affidavit evidence, under the last stage of the *American Cyanamid* process: see [1975] AC 396, 409, and *N.W.L. Ltd. v. Woods* [1979] ICR 867, 880."

Mr. Brodie submitted that these dicta were obiter and wrong; alternatively, that (i) delay caused by congestion in the courts should not be taken into account, (ii) the court should not speculate, and should only embark on a wider consideration of the merits if it is certain that the grant of an injunction will bring the dispute to an end, and (iii) in any event delay before a trial can take place is not decisive, and is at most a factor to be taken into account.

For my part I readily accept the last of Mr. Brodie's contentions; but I reject the others. If it will not be possible to hold a trial before the period for which the plaintiff claims to be entitled to an injunction has expired, or substantially expired, it seems to me that justice requires some consideration as to whether the plaintiff would be likely to succeed at a trial. In those circumstances it is not enough to decide merely that there is a serious issue to be tried. The assertion of such an issue should not operate as a lettre de cachet, by which the defendant is prevented from doing that which, as it later turns out, he has a perfect right to do, for the whole or substantially the whole of the period in question. On a wider view of the balance of convenience it may still be right to impose such a restraint, but not unless there has been some assessment of the plaintiff's prospects of success. I would emphasise "some assessment," because the courts constantly seek to discourage prolonged interlocutory battles on affidavit evidence. I do not doubt that Lord Diplock, in enunciating the *American Cyanamid* doctrine, had in mind what its effect would be in that respect. Where an assessment of the prospects of success is required, it is for the judge to control its extent.

I do not see that delay caused by congestion in the court's list should be left out of account. This is a practical reality as much as anything else. The very reason for granting interlocutory relief is that a trial cannot take place immediately. Delay for the parties' preparations is necessary; but there is very often also delay before the court can arrange a trial. It does not seem to me a matter for surprise or reproach that in early September the Chancery Division could not arrange a trial lasting five days before the following March or April. Nor do I see why, as part of the practical realities, the judge should not consider how likely it is that a trial will ever take place. On the contrary, this seems to have been considered at least to some extent in the *N.W.L.* case and in *Cayne's* case.

Turning to the present case, I do not consider it at all likely that the defendant will wish to bring the action to trial in or after April 1991, if an injunction is now granted. He has the support of his present employers in these proceedings for the purpose of resisting an injunction, and to enable a credible undertaking in damages to be given on his behalf. But we are not told that he would have that support for a five-day trial designed to secure damages for himself and freedom from restraint for the last two or three months of the 12-month period. In *American Cyanamid* both parties were chemical companies, no doubt with substantial resources and accustomed to litigation. Not so the defendant. Mr. Brodie asserts that, even on the hypothesis of an interlocutory injunction being granted, the plaintiff would wish to proceed to trial in order to recover damages for the period from 30 July to today, in which the defendant has broken his contract. I regard that too as unlikely.

So if an injunction had been granted by the judge, or is now granted, the likely effect would be to decide the dispute against the defendant for good and all. In those circumstances justice requires, in my opinion, some assessment of the merits and more than merely a serious issue to be tried. But the situation would have been different if, in early September, there had been a prospect of a trial in November. The plaintiff would have been obliged to proceed to trial if it wished to maintain its injunction for more than a small proportion of the 12-month period (and, incidentally, the defendant would still have had the support of his new employers).

The judge was therefore right, in my judgment, to take into account the strength of the plaintiff's claim. He would have been wrong to regard that as the sole consideration; but he did not do so. He also took into account the narrower aspects of the balance of convenience, such as the difficulty that the plaintiff would have in proving damage, and a similar difficulty (to my mind somewhat overstated by the judge) that the defendant would face in claiming damages for loss of employment and interruption of his career.

In the event, it would seem that the judge's view as to the strength of the claim did prove determinative, in the sense that he might well have granted an injunction if he had thought the claim likely to succeed at trial. But when a number of factors have to be taken into account, it is inevitable that one of them may tip the scale. That does not mean that the judge has treated the factor in question as the sole consideration, decisive in itself. As I have said, the judge did not do that in this case.

So I must turn to consider the other issues, in order to see whether the judge was right in his assessment of the strength of the claim. In doing so I must emphasise that the views expressed on these issues are for the purposes of this interlocutory appeal only, and should not affect the trial of the action (if there is one)."

QUIA TIMET INJUNCTIONS

The onus of proof which lies on a plaintiff seeking a *quia timet* injunction, which may be granted where injury to the plaintiff is merely threatened or apprehended, has been stated in terms varying from a 'strong probability',[13] a 'reasonable probability'[14] to a 'probability'[15] simplicter. The most recent decision in this area, *Szabo v. ESAT Digiphone Ltd*, while it appears to favour the test of a 'proven substantial risk of danger' does not entirely resolve this issue.

Szabo v. ESAT Digiphone Ltd
[1998] 2 ILRM 102

The plaintiffs, who were schoolchildren attending a national school, sought *quia timet* injunctions to restrain the erection and operation of a mobile phone base station in the grounds of a garda station located beside their school. Geoghegan J referred to the principle set out by Spry[16] and said that whichever test is applied, in practice it should remain more difficult to obtain an injunction of this nature, not least because if no wrongdoing has yet occurred, it will be more difficult to establish, as a matter of evidence, that there is a sufficient risk of a future injury to justify the grant of an injunction. He concluded that it was highly improbable at the very least that any injury would ensue to the children before the hearing of the action and in these circumstances he did not think that it would be just or reasonable to grant a *quia timet* injunction.

GEOGHEGAN J stated at pp.109–112: "It has long been established that at the stage of an application for an interlocutory injunction, the court is not normally entitled to consider the weight of the evidence on each side or to form even preliminary conclusions as to the probable outcome of the case. But I think that in a case such as this particular one, where I am being asked to consider the risk of danger to the plaintiffs and where the entitlement to the injunction is dependent on that risk, I am entitled to have some regard to the respective qualifications, expertise and background of the respective expert witnesses relied on. This base station has neither been constructed nor put into operation as yet and therefore even the permanent injunctions being sought are of a *quia timet* nature. A number of authorities have been cited to me in

---

[13] *Attorney General (Boswell) v. Rathmines and Pembroke Joint Hospital Board* [1904] 1 IR 161.

[14] *Independent Newspapers Ltd v. Irish Press Ltd* [1932] IR 615.

[15] *Whelan v. Madigan* [1978] ILRM 136.

[16] See Spry *Equitable Remedies* (5th ed., 1997) p. 469. See also *Ryanair Ltd v. Aer Rianta cpt* High Court (Kelly J) 25 January 2001 and Supreme Court, 26 October 2001.

relation to *quia timet* injunctions. In *Attorney General v. Manchester Corporation* [1893] 2 Ch 87 it was held that a person seeking an injunction to restrain an alleged future nuisance, be it public or private, must show a strong case of probability that the apprehended mischief will arise. In that particular case there was a proposal to establish a smallpox hospital close to a cemetery and an injunction was applied for to restrain the defendants from establishing the hospital so as to cause a nuisance to the inhabitants of the neighbourhood or to persons frequenting the cemetery. It was held on the evidence adduced by the plaintiffs that they had failed to show there was a probability, much less a high degree of probability, that the apprehended danger would ensue and therefore the injunction was refused. That decision has since been criticised in some quarters and I am inclined to think that it goes too far but for a *quia timet* injunction to be granted there would have to be a proven substantial risk of danger. I think that this view is supported by the decision of the Irish Court of Appeal in *Attorney General (Boswell) v. Rathmines and Pembroke Joint Hospital Board* [1904] IR 161. That case also referred to a smallpox hospital, this time in Vergemount, Clonskeagh, Co. Dublin. What was at issue was a permanent injunction rather than an interlocutory injunction. The Vice Chancellor who tried the action had this to say (at pp. 166-167):

> This is a case of much difficulty and public importance. The action is one of the class termed *quia timet* actions, and is brought not so much to obtain relief against wrongs already committed by which the plaintiffs have suffered actual damage, as to protect them from damage which they have reason to fear would be the result of the work which the defendants are carrying out, if it were allowed to proceed. In such cases it must be shown that the complainants entertain a reasonable, well-grounded apprehension that the work which the defendants are carrying out would, if allowed to proceed, result in substantial damage to the complainants. A mere fanciful objection to it will not be a sufficient ground for obtaining relief, but it must be shown that the work is, or would be, a substantial injury to the persons or property of the complainants.

The Vice Chancellor, applying those principles, granted the injunction but an appeal from his order was allowed by the Court of Appeal. In his judgment in the Court of Appeal, FitzGibbon LJ formulated the principle this way (at p. 171):

> It is a *quia timet* action: the projected hospital has not been built, but we are not altogether without experimental evidence of its probable effects, because a temporary iron hospital was erected in January 1903, and either in it or in an adjacent building, six or eight smallpox patients had been treated before the trial, of whom two were then still upon the premises. To sustain the injunction, the law requires proof by the plaintiff of a well-founded apprehension of injury – proof of actual and real danger – a strong probability, almost amounting to moral certainty, that if the hospital be established, it will be an actionable nuisance.

Later in the judgment, FitzGibbon LJ makes the point that local experience was against the inference of danger in that no one of the six or eight patients hitherto treated in the makeshift hospital at Clonskeagh had any infections spread even within the Vergemount area. It is not without relevance in this case that no known ill effects have arisen from radio and television etc. over the past 50 years in Ireland with particular reference to persons living in the vicinity of transmission areas. I think that this may be a particularly relevant consideration when all I have to consider on an application for an interlocutory injunction is whether there would be any danger of injury arising in the limited period between now and the hearing of the action. In the same Court of Appeal, Walker LJ expressed the view that where there was conflicting expert evidence, the judge could not himself form an opinion as an expert and if the result of the conflict was to leave him in doubt, he cannot in a *quia timet* action decide that the case for the plaintiff has been made out (see p. 192 of the report).

What are the correct principles to be applied in relation to applications for interlocutory *quia timet* injunctions? That is the next question which I must consider. I would adopt and accept the treatment of the subject in *Spry on Equitable Remedies*, 4th ed., p. 459. The author makes clear that there is no difference in the legal principles to be applied to a *quia timet* injunction as to any other injunction and that *ipso facto* there is no difference between the principles to be applied to an interlocutory *quia timet* injunction than to the granting of any other kind of interlocutory injunction. In each case what is being stopped is future conduct or misconduct and the fact that there may have been legal wrongs of the nature sought to be injuncted committed already is of evidentiary significance only. That is to say, it may aid in the consideration of whether such future wrong may in fact occur. Spry, in his treatment of *quia timet* injunctions in general at p. 370, says the following:

> It should not be thought, however, that it is never material that no breach of the rights of the applicant has taken place at the time of the hearing of the application of the plaintiff. On the contrary, the fact that no breach has yet taken place is a matter of relevance, the precise weight of which varies according to all the circumstances. So if no breach has taken place it may be more difficult to establish, as a matter of evidence, that there is a sufficient risk of a future injury to justify the immediate grant of an injunction; and in exercising its discretion the court is found here to be 'balancing the magnitude of the evil against the chances of its occurrence'. If in all the circumstances the likelihood that an injury will take place is not sufficiently high, *quia timet* relief will be refused, and the applicant will be left either to avail himself of such other remedies as may be open to him or else to renew his application should subsequently the likelihood of an injury increase sufficiently to render equitable intervention appropriate.

On the evidence before me, I have come to the conclusion that it is highly improbable at the very least that any injury will ensue to the children between now and the hearing of the action and I think that that is as far as I should go in terms of comment on the facts. In those circumstances, I do not think that it would be just or reasonable to grant a *quia timet* injunction which would have disastrous effects as far as the first named defendant is concerned, as not only would it be prevented from going ahead with the Easkey project but in reality the injunction would have very considerable repercussive effects likely to damage the first named defendant's highly competitive business throughout the country.

For the reasons which I indicated early on in this judgment, I am very reluctant to adopt the traditional language of 'serious issue to be tried, balance of convenience and damages as an adequate remedy' and I believe that this is a case in which those categories are neither appropriate nor helpful. But in case I am wrong about that, I would still have to come down in favour of refusing an injunction. Having regard to the stringent requirement of probability before a *quia timet* injunction would be granted on a permanent basis, I am very doubtful that there is a serious issue to be tried here, but even if there is, I have no doubt that for the reasons I have indicated, the balance of convenience requires that I should refuse any temporary injunction pending the hearing of the case.

I therefore refuse the interlocutory relief sought."

SPECIFIC CIRCUMSTANCES IN WHICH AN INJUNCTION WILL BE GRANTED

To Restrain a Breach of Contract

Enforcement of Negative Obligations

It was held in *Doherty v. Allman*[17] that where an injunction is sought to secure enforcement of a negative contractual obligation, it will issue almost as a matter of course. While this approach appears to have been accepted by the Supreme Court in *Dublin Port and Docks Board v. Britannia Dredging Co. Ltd*[18] this decision has since been distinguished on a number of occasions[19] and it must be open to question whether the principles set out therein can be considered to be of general application.

---

[17] (1878) 3 App Cas 709, 720.

[18] [1968] IR 136.

[19] *TMG Group Ltd v. Al Babtain Trading and Contracting Co.* [1982] ILRM 349; *Irish Shell Ltd v. Elm Motors Ltd* [1984] IR 200 and *Premier Dairies Ltd v. Doyle* [1996] 1 ILRM 363.

Dublin Port and Docks Board v. Britannia Dredging Co. Ltd
[1968] IR 136

The plaintiff sought an interlocutory injunction to restrain the defendant from removing dredging equipment from a site where it had undertaken to carry out work. The Supreme Court (Ó Dálaigh CJ, Haugh and Budd JJ) held that as the defendant had agreed to this negative term and as it was satisfied that a breach of the covenant was imminent, an interlocutory injunction should be granted. Ó Dálaigh CJ concluded that the principle in *Doherty v. Allman* was applicable and said that the court was not concerned to examine either the balance of convenience or the amount of damage.

Ó DÁLAIGH CJ stated at pp.144–148: "Mr. Justice Teevan came to the conclusion that the plaintiffs, on the terms of the contract, were entitled to an interlocutory injunction, but he declined to make the order sought because his view was that, in the circumstances of this case, the granting of the injunction would amount to an order for specific performance of a contract for personal service. [His Lordship referred to the passage in the judgment of Mr. Justice Teevan "It is clear that . . . effect or consequence."] He therefore refused the application, and reserved the costs until the termination of the action. Counsel for the plaintiffs on this appeal has submitted that the judge has misconceived the position, and that the enforcement of Clause 53(1) is not equivalent to specific performance. Counsel for the defendants have supported the judge's view. They submitted that the application is an attempt on the plaintiffs' part to keep the defendants working on the site.

An examination of the clause indicates that its purpose is to make the plant, temporary works and materials, provided by the contractor, available to the employer to proceed with the completion of the works in the absence and independent of the contractor. That is to say, it contemplates not the continuation of the work by the contractor but, on the contrary, his discontinuance of the work, arising either from voluntary withdrawal or compulsory exclusion from the site. Far from being designed to compel specific performance, the purpose of the clause is to assist the employer whose contractor, for whatever reason, has abandoned the work. It is appreciated that inability to remove plant and gear might deter a contractor from withdrawing from the work on a calculation of balance of monetary advantage or disadvantage. But this is an extraneous factor and, in any event, is wholly absent in this case. The Court is, therefore, of opinion that the judge was wrong in holding that to grant the injunction sought would amount to ordering specific performance of the work.

Counsel for the defendants have advanced other grounds in opposition to the granting of the injunction. First, they have said the application is premature. The Court's jurisdiction is not restricted to cases of actual breach of contract. The Court also has jurisdiction to restrain an apprehended or threatened breach. The passages from the affidavit of the managing director of the defendant company, cited earlier in this judgment, demonstrate that the defendants cannot continue work and that a breach is imminent. The Court cannot accept the submission that the plaintiffs' application is premature.

Secondly, counsel for the defendants submitted that, on the balance of convenience of the parties and in the absence of proof by the plaintiffs of irreparable loss, the Court should not make the order sought. The answer made on behalf of the plaintiffs is that it is not necessary in the circumstances of this case for the Court to consider either balance of convenience or the question of irreparable loss since here there is an express negative covenant, and that the observations of Lord Cairns, L.C. in *Doherty v. Allman* (1878) 3 App Cas 709 are in point. At p. 720 of the report the Lord Chancellor said:— "If parties, for valuable consideration, with their eyes open, contract that a particular thing shall not be done, all that a Court of Equity has to do is to say, by way of injunction, that which the parties have already said by way of covenant, that the thing shall not be done; and in such case the injunction does nothing more than give the sanction of the process of the Court to that which already is the contract between the parties. It is not then a question of the balance of convenience or inconvenience, or of the amount of damage or of injury—it is the specific performance, by the Court, of that negative bargain which the parties have made, with their eyes open, between themselves." The observations of Lord Cairns have been applied in a number of cases to which the Court has been referred: *Formby v. Barker* [1903] 2 Ch 539; *Elliston v. Reacher* [1908] 2 Ch 374 and *Marco Productions Ltd. v. Pagola* [1945] KB 111.

It is to be noted that the order made in *Doherty v. Allman* (1878) 3 App Cas 709 was made on the trial of the action, and the position was similar in each of the other cases cited. No case has been brought to the notice of the Court in which the principles stated by Lord Cairns have been applied on the granting of an interlocutory motion.

The defendants' contention is that they are not bound by the contract relied upon by the plaintiffs because of the alleged inaccuracy of the Orrje survey which, they say, goes to the root of the bargain. Counsel for the plaintiffs has called attention to a clause in the contract which, he submitted, precludes the defendants from complaining of the inaccuracy of the Orrje survey. The clause is Clause 20 of the special conditions, and it is in these terms:— "It is an essential feature of the Contract that the Contractor shall be deemed to have inspected the site, and to have made all necessary tests and enquiries to satisfy himself as to the conditions under which the work is to be carried out, the nature of the materials to be dealt with, the delays likely to be caused by bad weather, by obstructions in the area to be dredged, and local conditions as to labour and the supply of materials. The Employer gives no guarantee as to any of these matters, and shall not be held liable for any claim of any kind on account of misrepresentation or absence of information on all or any of them." It is hard to envisage a clause which could have more expressly put the defendants on notice that the plaintiffs could not take, and were not accepting, responsibility for the accuracy and reliability of the Orrje survey, and that the defendants must themselves take such steps as they considered proper to inform themselves of the nature of the harbour and river bed.

The reference in the clause to "misrepresentation" would undoubtedly cover innocent misrepresentation, but it would not extend to fraudulent misrepresentation: see *S. Pearson & Son Ltd. v. Dublin Corporation* [1907] AC 351. There the stipulation in the contract was that the contractor should satisfy himself as to the dimensions, levels and nature of all existing works and other things connected with the contract works, and that the corporation did not hold itself responsible for the accuracy of the information as to the sections or foundations of existing walls or works, and that no charges for extra work or otherwise would be allowed in consequence of incorrect information or inaccuracies in the drawings or specifications. Lord Loreburn, L.C., observed that the clauses before them contemplated honesty on both sides and protected only against honest mistakes. The Court has not heard it suggested on behalf of the defendants that the plaintiffs in furnishing the Orrje survey to the defendants did so other than honestly and in good faith; nor is the high reputation of Orrje in this particular field of work questioned.

In the result, as matters stand on the hearing of this motion, the position as the Court sees it is that the defendants have not shown that they are not bound by the contract relied upon by the plaintiffs; and the position is therefore not different from what it would be if at the trial the court should reach the same conclusion. The principle stated in *Doherty v. Allman* is accordingly applicable and the Court is not concerned to examine either the balance of convenience or the amount of damage. The parties entered into this negative covenant, and the Court's duty is to hold the defendants to their bargain pending the trial. It hardly needs to be said that the Court's ruling is made on the material now before the Court and in no way prejudices the case which the defendants may make at the trial.

Finally, the defendants object that the injunction should not go because, with the exception of the tug *Corunna*, the plant in question is not their property but is the property of the parent company from whom they have hired it. The plaintiffs are not privy to the arrangements between the defendants and Breejenbout and these arrangements are not a valid reason for modifying the order which the plaintiffs are entitled to as against the defendants. Breejenbout are not parties to these proceedings and the order which the Court proposes to make offers no opinion as to what rights Breejenbout may have to recover the property from the plaintiffs. The Court notes that the plaintiffs have said that they will seek to argue that Breejenbout participated in the negotiations for this contract to a degree that could warrant the Court in identifying the defendants and Breejenbout. This, however, is not a matter which is now before the Court for decision.

The Court will therefore allow this appeal and grant an injunction in the terms of Clause 53(1) of the contract. The Court wishes to state expressly that it offers no opinion as to what grounds would warrant the plaintiffs' engineer in withholding his consent to removal of the plant. The plaintiffs must give the usual undertaking as to damages."

Irish Shell Ltd v. Elm Motors Ltd
[1984] IR 200

The plaintiff sought interlocutory injunctions, *inter alia*, compelling the defendant to comply with covenants in a lease which required it to buy the petroleum products which it needed for sale or use in a petrol station exclusively from the plaintiff. Costello J applied the principles set out in *Doherty v. Allman* stating that he did not think it mattered that the covenant had been expressed in the form of a positive rather than a negative obligation. He said that it was clear that the defendant had agreed that it would not buy petroleum products from any supplier other than the plaintiff and that it was the court's duty to see that the contract, which was an enforceable one, was carried out. In the circumstances he was satisfied that no question arose concerning the balance of convenience or the nature of the damage which the plaintiff would suffer and concluded that the plaintiff was entitled to an injunction restraining the defendant from purchasing petroleum products in breach of their covenant. However, while the Supreme Court (O'Higgins CJ, McCarthy and Griffin JJ) affirmed in part the order of the High Court, it did so on the basis that the plaintiff had raised a fair question for determination at the trial and that the balance of convenience favoured the continuation of the injunction.

McCARTHY J stated at pp.228–229: "In my view, it is unnecessary to enter upon an examination of the conclusions to which the learned trial judge came on the hearing of the interlocutory application, and the reasons for them. I am satisfied that it was unnecessary and, in an interlocutory application, undesirable that he should have come to the firm conclusion set out in his judgment. It may well be that his conclusion was correct; I express no view upon it save to state that an examination of the judgment itself demonstrates the complexity of the legal issue that arose and the certain need that all the facts, including the exact nature and location of the development that took place, should be established before any view of the legal position is formed. The difficult legal issues raised by this undisputed fact, for instance, that the covenants are in form affirmatory rather than negative indicate the wide range of the problem; indeed the learned trial judge's own analysis of the alleged anomalies originally suggested as arising out of the *Esso Case* in an article in volume 85 of The Law Quarterly Review at p. 229 adds force to this view. If the covenants are, in fact, negative, it is contended that the balance of convenience need not be taken into consideration upon the principle allegedly founding the decision in *Doherty v. Allman*. That case was the subject of comment by Ó Dálaigh C.J. in *Dublin*

Port & Docks Board v. Brittania Dredging Co. Ltd., which decision was considered by Mr. Justice Keane in *TMG Group v. Al Babtain*. In referring to the *Brittania Case*, Mr. Justice Keane said at pp. 353-4 of the report:—

> "The defendants in that case were proposing to repudiate the contract in its entirety in circumstances where the court was satisfied that they were not entitled so to do. The circumstances of the present case are wholly different: the defendants strenuously contend that neither of the transactions which the company proposes to enter into will constitute a breach of their contractual obligations under the shareholders' agreement. I do not think that Ó Dálaigh, C.J. in the passages to which I have referred, was laying down any general principle that, in all cases where the plaintiff establishes a *prima facie* case of a breach of a negative stipulation in a contract, the court could disregard any question of the balance of convenience as between the parties. His observations were clearly confined to a case where one party to a contract was proposing to act in breach of a negative contract (and indeed to repudiate the whole contract) in circumstance where the court was not satisfied on the evidence that they were entitled so to do. I do not think that the passage lends any support to the proposition that even where the violation of the plaintiff's right is denied, as it unquestionably is in the present case, the court can disregard the balance of convenience to the parties."

It is right to point out that it does not appear that the learned judge in the High Court was referred to the decision of Mr. Justice Keane in the *TMG Case*; that case was appealed to this Court but this point was not canvassed. I would endorse the views expressed by Mr. Justice Keane, as cited above, and I repeat my firm view that, save in the most exceptional circumstances (which it would be invidious to attempt to detail or delimit), the determination of an application for an interlocutory injunction lies, and lies only, in the answers to the two material questions as to there being a fair case to be made and where the balance of convenience lies.

In the result, whilst, due to the passage of time and the events that have taken place in the interval, it is clear that the balance of convenience lies in the continuance of the injunction and that, save as already indicated, the order of the High Court should stand, in principle, I would allow this appeal."

Particular Considerations which Apply to Contracts for Personal Services

The courts have traditionally been reluctant to force individuals to work together particularly where the relationship of trust and confidence which should exist between them has broken down.[20] It is generally accepted that in the context

---

[20] However, note the recent decision of Macken J in *Martin v. Nationwide Building Society* High Court (Macken J) 19 May 1999 in which she granted interlocutory injunctions the effect of which was to reinstate the plaintiff as a branch manager in one of the defendant's offices.

of contracts for personal services, an injunction should not be granted by the court where this would indirectly provide for specific performance of the positive terms of the contract. However, on occasion, as in *Warner Brothers Pictures Incorporated v. Nelson*[21] the courts have permitted the issue of an injunction to restrain a negative undertaking in a contract for personal services which may indirectly cause the contract to be performed. More recently it has been recognised in decisions such as *Warren v. Mendy*[22] that this approach is tantamount to ordering specific performance of a contract for services and a more reasonable attitude has been adopted in relation to the effect which an injunction may have on an individual who possesses particular skills.

Warren v. Mendy
[1989] 1 WLR 853

A boxer agreed that he would not be managed by anyone except the plaintiff for a three year period but subsequently entered into a management agreement with the defendant. The plaintiff sought an injunction to restrain the defendant from inducing a breach of contract and from acting for the boxer. The effect of such an injunction would have been to restrain the boxer from performing services for the defendant and would arguably have compelled him to perform his agreement with the plaintiff. The Court of Appeal (Purchas, Nourse and Stuart-Smith LJJ) held that no injunction should be granted.

NOURSE LJ stated at pp.860–868: "Any consideration of the authorities must be made with two general thoughts in mind. First, in this as much as in any other area of the law an injunction is a discretionary remedy, whose grant or refusal, especially at an interlocutory stage, depends on the infinitely variable facts of the individual case. Although statements of the principles on which the discretion ought to be exercised in some particular area are often authoritative, they are principles of practice rather than of law, whose application may be rendered inappropriate by the finest of factual variations between one case and another. Secondly, the discretion belongs, as always, to the judge of first instance. His decision can only be interfered with by an appellate court if he has erred in principle, if he has not exercised his discretion at all or if he has exercised it in a manner which is plainly wrong.

We deal first with those cases where the injunction has been sought directly against the servant. In *Lumley v. Wagner* (1852) 1 De GM & G 604 the defendant bound herself to sing at the plaintiff's theatre, Her Majesty's, for three months from 1 April 1852. She also engaged herself not to use her talents at any other theatre, nor in any concert or reunion, public or private, without

---

[21] [1937] 1 KB 209. See also *Lumley v. Wagner* (1852) 1 De G M & G 604.
[22] [1989] 1 WLR 853. See also *Page One Records v. Britton* [1968] 1 WLR 157.

the written authorisation of the plaintiff. The defendant subsequently made another engagement with a third party, by which it was agreed that she should, for a larger sum, sing at Covent Garden and abandon the agreement with the plaintiff. On 9 May 1852 Parker V.-C. granted the plaintiff an injunction restraining the defendant from singing and performing or singing at Covent Garden or at any other theatre or place without the sanction or permission in writing of the plaintiff during the existence of her agreement with him. On 26 May 1852 the defendant's appeal from that decision was dismissed by Lord St. Leonards L.C. sitting as the Court of Appeal in Chancery. He described it as a mixed case, consisting not of two correlative acts to be done, one by the plaintiff and the other by the defendant, but of an act to be done by the defendant alone, to which was superadded a negative stipulation on her part to abstain from the commission of any act which would break in upon her affirmative covenant – the one being ancillary to, concurrent and operating together with the other. Having observed that beyond all doubt the court could not interfere to enforce the specific performance of the whole of the contract, the Lord Chancellor continued, at p. 619:

> "Wherever this court has not proper jurisdiction to enforce specific performance, it operates to bind men's consciences, as far as they can be bound, to a true and literal performance of their agreements; and it will not suffer them to depart from their contracts at their pleasure, leaving the party with whom they have contracted to the mere chance of any damages which a jury may give. The exercise of this jurisdiction has, I believe, had a wholesome tendency towards the maintenance of that good faith which exists in this country to a much greater degree perhaps than in any other; and although the jurisdiction is not to be extended, yet a judge would desert his duty who did not act up to what his predecessors have handed down as the rule for his guidance in the administration of such an equity. It was objected that the operation of the injunction in the present case was mischievous, excluding the defendant J. Wagner from performing at any other theatre while this court had no power to compel her to perform at Her Majesty's Theatre. It is true that I have not the means of compelling her to sing, but she has no cause of complaint if I compel her to abstain from the commission of an act which she has bound herself not to do, and thus possibly cause her to fulfil her engagement."

In *Whitwood Chemical Co. v. Hardman* [1891] 2 Ch 416 the defendant, a manufacturing chemist, was appointed to be the manager of the plaintiff company's works for a ten year term expiring in September 1895, the defendant agreeing, amongst other things, to give the whole of his time to the plaintiff's business. In 1891 the defendant threatened to join a proposed rival establishment nearby and the plaintiff obtained an interlocutory injunction restraining him from giving less than the whole of his time to the plaintiff's business. On the defendant's appeal to this court the injunction was discharged. We will quote two passages from the judgment of Lindley L.J., the first at p. 427:

> "What injunction can be granted in this particular case which will not be, in

substance and effect, a decree for specific performance of this agreement? It appears to me the difficulty of the plaintiffs is this, that they cannot suggest anything which, when examined, does not amount to this, that the man must either be idle, or specifically perform the agreement into which he has entered. Now there, it appears to me, the case goes beyond *Lumley v. Wagner*. . . . The principle is that the court does not decree specific performance of contracts for personal service, and the question is, whether there is anything in this case which takes it out of that principle. I cannot see that there is."

At p. 428:

"I agree with what the late Master of the Rolls, Sir G. Jessel, said about there being no very definite line. I agree, also, in what Fry L.J. has said more than once, that cases of this kind are not to be extended. I confess I look upon *Lumley v. Wagner* rather as an anomaly to be followed in cases like it, but an anomaly which it would be very dangerous to extend."

Kay L.J. said of *Lumley v. Wagner*, at p. 431:

"That case, certainly at the time it was decided, was understood to have carried the power of the Court of Chancery in granting injunctions to the extreme limit to which it could go. The contract there was one which the court could not specifically perform. It could not compel Miss Wagner to sing. Lord St. Leonards distinctly disclaims any power in the Court of Equity to do anything of the kind."

In *Warner Brothers Pictures Inc. v. Nelson* [1937] 1 KB 209, the defendant, a film actress better known by her professional name of Bette Davis, entered into a contract in the U.S.A. with the plaintiff, a company of film producers, for a one year period, renewable at the option of the plaintiff until 1942. The defendant agreed, first, to render her exclusive services as a motion picture and/or legitimate stage actress to the plaintiff and to perform solely and exclusively for it, and secondly, that she would not, during the term of the contract, render any services for or in any other phonographic, stage or motion picture production or productions or business of any other person. It was held by Branson J., at the trial of the action, that a final injunction ought to be granted to restrain the defendant's breach of her negative obligation, but he limited its operation to the continuance of the contract or for three years from the date of judgment, whichever period should be the shorter. Having referred to *Lumley v. Wagner* and a number of later authorities, including *Whitwood Chemical Co. v. Hardman,* the judge said, at p. 217, 219:

"The conclusion to be drawn from the authorities is that, where a contract of personal service contains negative covenants the enforcement of which will not amount either to a decree of specific performance of the positive covenants of the contract or to the giving of a decree under which the defendant must either remain idle or perform those positive covenants, the court will enforce those negative covenants . . . . The case before me, is, therefore, one in which it would be proper to grant an injunction unless to do so would in the circumstances be tantamount to ordering the defendant to perform her contract or remain idle or unless damages would be the more appropriate remedy. With regard to the first of these considerations . . . It was also urged that the difference between what the defendant can earn as a film artiste and what she might expect to earn by any other form of activity is so great that she will in effect be driven to perform her contract. That is not the criterion adopted in any of the decided cases. The defendant is stated to be a person of intelligence, capacity and means, and no evidence was adduced to show that, if enjoined from doing the specified acts otherwise than for the plaintiffs, she will not be able to employ herself both usefully and remuneratively in other spheres of activity, though not as remuneratively as in her special line. She will not be driven, although she may be tempted, to perform her contract, and the fact that she may be so tempted is no objection to the grant of an injunction. This appears from the judgment of Lord St. Leonards in *Lumley v. Wagner* . . ."

Having then held that damages was not the more appropriate remedy, the judge granted the injunction in the form already stated.

In *Page One Records Ltd. v. Britton* [1968] 1 WLR 157 the defendants, members of the Troggs pop group, entered into management and agency agreements with the first plaintiff for a period of five years, whereby the first plaintiff agreed to advance their professional careers and secure suitable work and engagements for them and so on, the defendants agreeing that the first plaintiff should be their sole and exclusive manager, agent and personal representative and that they would not during the period engage any third party to act as managers or agents for them nor act themselves in such capacity. The defendants claimed that the agreements had been repudiated by the first plaintiff and they purported to accept such repudiation. Having held that the plaintiffs had made out a prima facie case for the recovery of damages in the action, Stamp J. nevertheless refused to grant them an interlocutory injunction. He said, at p. 165:

> "The present case is clearly distinguished, in principle, from such cases as *Lumley v. Wagner* (1852) 1 De GM & G 604, for there the only obligation on the part of the plaintiffs seeking to enforce the negative stipulation was an obligation to pay remuneration and an obligation which could clearly be enforced by the defendants. But here the obligations of the first plaintiff, involving personal services, were obligations of trust and confidence and were obligations which, plainly, could not be enforced at the suit of the Troggs. Here, indeed, so it seems to me, the totality of the obligations between the parties are more a joint venture, almost approaching the relationship of partners than anything else, involving mutual confidence and reciprocal obligations on all sides."

The judge also held that, apart altogether from the want of mutuality, the claim for an injunction failed on the more general principle formulated by Branson J., although he preferred to state it in the converse form. In other words, he thought that the grant of an injunction would amount to a giving of a decree under which the defendants must either remain idle or perform the positive covenants of the agreements. Having read the second passage which we have quoted from the judgment of Branson J., Stamp J. continued, at p. 166:

> "So it was said in this case that if an injunction is granted the Troggs could, without employing any other manager or agent, continue as a group on their own or seek other employment of a different nature. So far as the former suggestion is concerned, in the first place I doubt whether consistently with the terms of the agreement which I have read, the Troggs could act as their own managers; and, in the second place, I think I can, and should, take judicial notice of the fact that these groups, if they are to have any great success, must have managers. Indeed, it is the plaintiffs' own case that the Troggs are simple persons, of no business experience, and could not survive without the services of a manager. As a practical matter on the evidence before me, I entertain no doubt that they would be compelled, if the injunction was granted, on the terms that the plaintiffs seek, to continue to employ the first plaintiff as their manager and agent and it is, I think, on this point that this case diverges from *Lumley v. Wagner* (1852) 1 De GM & G 604 and the cases which have followed it, including the *Warner Brothers'* case [1937] 1 KB 209 for it would be a bad thing to put pressure upon these four young men to continue to employ as a manager and agent in a fiduciary capacity one who, unlike the plaintiff in those cases (who had merely to pay the defendant money) has duties of a personal and fiduciary nature to perform and in whom the Troggs, for reasons good, bad or indifferent, have lost confidence and who may, for all I know, fail in its duty to them."

In *Nichols Advanced Vehicle Systems Inc. v. De Angelis* (unreported), 21 December 1979, the first defendant, an Italian Formula 1 racing driver aged 21, agreed to drive one of the plaintiffs' "Shadow" motor cars in Grand Prix events for part of 1979 and for the years 1980 and 1981 as well. He also agreed not to use or compete in any racing car other than a Shadow car in any of the Grand Prix events during the years in question. However, on 1 November 1980 he entered into a contract to drive for the second defendant, Team Lotus Ltd., in the 1980 season, subject to his obtaining before the 15 November a release from his contract with the plaintiffs. That not having been obtained, on 16 November the first defendant entered into an exclusive driver's contract with a foreign associated company of Lotus for the year 1980, renewable at the option of Lotus for 1981 and 1982. The plaintiffs thereupon commenced proceedings and applied for an interlocutory injunction to enforce the first defendant's negative obligation. Although he took an extremely unfavourable view of the first defendant's conduct, Oliver J. refused to grant an injunction against him. Having fully considered the more important of the earlier authorites, he recognised that there was a conflict between the approach of Branson J. in *Warner Brothers Pictures Inc. v. Nelson* [1937] 1 KB 209 and that of Stamp J. in *Page One Records Ltd. v. Britton* [1968] 1 WLR 157. He described the former decision as representing the high watermark of the application of *Lumley v. Wagner* and said that up to that point no such injunction had been granted, at any rate so far as the reported cases went, in relation to anything but short-term engagements. Later he said that the injunction in that case appeared to him to be coming extremely close to specific performance. He said:

> "I do not find *Warner Brothers Pictures Inc. v. Nelson* and *Page One Records Ltd. v. Britton* easy to reconcile, but I am bound to say that the approach of Stamp J. in his consideration of what in substance amounts to specific performance seems to me, if I may say so respectfully, to be the more realistic one. It simply does not, with respect, seem to me to be realistic to say that nothing short of idleness and starvation is compulsive, and therefore no injunction which involves anything less than that can be said to infringe the principle that the court will not specifically enforce a contract of personal services. The injunction in *Warner Brothers Pictures Inc. v. Nelson* did not in practice leave the defendant in that case much freedom of choice if she wanted to pursue her chosen profession. No doubt it might have been quite otherwise if, as in the other previous cases in which similar injunctions had been granted, the contract had been a very short-term one."

In that case the plaintiff company had evinced a clear intention to force the first defendant back to drive for it and the evidence on both sides assumed that that would be the effect of an injunction. Oliver J. concluded that an injunction would force the first defendant either to drive for the plaintiffs or to give up his career for so long as the injunction continued. He refused relief accordingly.

With the exception of Branson J., no significant inconsistency of approach is discoverable amongst the judges who decided these cases. On a first consideration, that judge's view that Miss Bette Davis might employ herself both usefully and remuneratively in other spheres of activity for a period of up to three years appears to have been extraordinarily unrealistic. It could hardly have been thought to be a real possibility that an actress of her then youth and soaring talent would be able to forego screen and stage for such a period. (Although the injunction operated only within the jurisdiction of the English court, it must, we think, have been assumed that the negative covenants could and would be enforced in California. The 1930s was the high period of the studio contract system in Hollywood. We believe that the Warner Brothers' studio was markedly forthright in enforcing its contracts.) But then it is to be observed that Miss Davis did not give evidence, a feature of the case which made a great impression on the judge: see [1937] 1 KB 209, 215-216. In the absence of evidence from her, the judge no doubt thought that it was not for the court to assume that she could not or would not employ herself both usefully and remuneratively in other spheres of activity. From what can be gathered from the report it cannot be said with confidence that the injunction was wrongly granted.

Special considerations apart, we are firmly with Oliver J. in preferring the approach of Stamp J. to that of Branson J., both on grounds of realism and practicality and because that approach is more consistent with the earlier authorities. Any of these cases can be explained by the particular considerations which there arose, but we agree with Oliver J. in thinking that the most significant feature of each of those in which an injunction was granted before *Warner Brothers Pictures Inc. v. Nelson* was that the term of the engagement was short, in none of them exceeding 20 weeks. In *Lumley v. Wagner* itself the contractual period was three months, of which there were less than two to run when the injunction was granted. That was the maximum period for which Miss Wagner would have had to remain idle in England. It might even not have been too late for her to return to Berlin and sing there during the summer season. Although it is impossible to state in general terms where the line between short and long term engagements ought to be drawn, it is obvious that an injunction lasting for two years or more (the period applicable in the present case) may practically compel performance of the contract.

Chief amongst the other considerations which have been decisive in those cases where an injunction has been refused are the absence of mutuality and, on the other hand, the presence of obligations involving mutual trust and confidence. By the absence or want of mutuality reference is meant to the old established rule that the court would not grant specific performance at the suit of one party to a contract where it could not do so at the suit of the other. We very much doubt whether a want of mutuality alone would now be decisive in a case of the kind with which we are here concerned. There is a valuable discussion of the present standing of the rule in *Snell: The Principles of Equity*, 28th ed. (1982), pp. 579-580. But the presence of obligations involving mutual trust and confidence may well be decisive, not merely because they are not mutually enforceable but because their enforcement, more especially where the servant's trust in the master may have been betrayed or his confidence in him has genuinely gone, will serve the better interests of neither party. That was a consideration which carried weight with Stamp J. in *Page One Records Ltd. v. Britton* [1968] 1 WLR 157 and with Oliver J. in *Nichols Advanced Vehicle Systems Inc. v. De Angelis*, in the latter case reliance being placed also on the fact that the contract involved a very high risk to life and limb on the part of the first defendant.

Having thus far considered only the more common case where the injunction is sought directly against the servant, we must now introduce the unusual feature of this case, which is that an injunction is not sought against the servant but only against a third party who must for present purposes be taken to have induced a breach of the contract between master and servant.

It appears that there is only one known case in which that point has been considered, a decision of Nourse J. in *Lotus Cars Ltd. v. Jaguar Cars Ltd.* (unreported), 1 July 1982. In that case the plaintiff claimed that the defendant had induced an employee of the plaintiff, its sales director, to act in breach of his current contract of employment. The plaintiff sought an interlocutory injunction against the defendant, but not against the employee. The reason for that appeared clearly to have been that the contract of employment contained an exclusive services provision to the same effect as that which was considered in *Whitwood Chemical Co. v. Hardman* [1891] 2 Ch 416. On behalf of the defendant it was submitted that in substance what the plaintiff was seeking to do was to enforce, albeit indirectly, specific performance of the employee's positive obligations under his contract of service with the plaintiff. A special feature of the case, which may in retrospect seem curious, was that the uncontroverted evidence of the employee established that his only two possible employers were the plaintiff and the defendant; so that if the injunction was granted he would, not by virtue of his contract of employment but as a matter of fact, be driven to continue to work for the plaintiff. Nourse J. said:

> "It may be that there has never been a case of this kind before, perhaps because in normal circumstances there are always other possible employers to whom the employee can go if he does not wish to continue to work for his present employer. In that kind of case an injunction restraining a tortious inducement by one prospective employer would not tie the employee to continued employment with his present employer because he could always go elsewhere. However, on the evidence as it stands in this case, it does appear clear to me, for the reasons which Mr. Irvine has advanced as I have stated them, that the effect of granting an injunction against Jaguar would be to tie Mr. Putnam to Lotus, to prevent him going elsewhere and therefore to decree specific performance of the positive covenants in Mr. Putnam's contract of employment with Lotus. In that state of affairs, it seems to me that this is a case where, although the court has no doubt power to grant an injunction, on well-established principles it ought not to do so."

Although the point has no doubt been more fully argued on this appeal than it was in that case, we are all of the opinion that the court ought usually to refuse the grant of an injunction against a third party who induces a breach of the contract if on the evidence its effect would be to compel performance of the contract. If that were not so, the master could, as Mr. Irvine submitted in *Lotus Cars Ltd. v. Jaguar Cars Ltd.,* obtain by the back door relief which he could not obtain through the front. The material considerations will not be exactly the same as in a case where the relief is sought directly against the servant. Most significantly, the court must take account not only of other third parties with whom the servant may be able to contract but also the likelihood or not that the plaintiff will take similar proceedings against them.

This consideration of the authorities has led us to believe that the following general principles are applicable to the grant or refusal of an injunction to enforce performance of the servant's negative obligations in a contract for personal services inseparable from the exercise of some special skill or talent. (We use the expressions "master" and "servant" for ease of reference and not out of any regard for the reality of the relationship in many of these cases.) In such a case the court ought not to enforce the performance of the negative obligations if their enforcement will effectively compel the servant to perform his positive obligations under the contract. Compulsion is a question to be decided on the facts of each case, with a realistic regard for the probable reaction of an injunction on the psychological and material, and sometimes the physical, need of the servant to maintain the skill or talent. The longer the term for which an injunction is sought, the more readily will compulsion be inferred. Compulsion may be inferred where the injunction is sought not against the servant but against a third party if either the third party is the only other available master or if it is likely that the master will seek relief against anyone who attempts to replace him. An injunction will less readily be granted where there are obligations of mutual trust and confidence, more especially where the servant's trust in the master may have been betrayed or his confidence in him has genuinely gone.

In stating the principles as we have, we are not to be taken as intending to pay anything less than a full and proper regard to the sanctity of contract. No judge would wish to detract from his duty to enforce the performance of contracts to the very limit which established principles allow him to go. Nowhere is that duty better vindicated than in the words of Lord St. Leonards L.C. in *Lumley v. Wagner* (1852) 1 De GM & G 604, 619. To that end the judge will scrutinise most carefully, even sceptically, any claim by the servant that he is under the human necessity of maintaining the skill or talent and thus will be compelled to perform the contract, or that his trust in the master has been betrayed or that his confidence in him has genuinely gone. But if, having done that, the judge is satisfied that the grant of an injunction will effectively compel performance of the contract, he ought to refuse it. To do otherwise would be to disregard the authoritative observations which were made in this court in *Whitwood Chemical Co. v. Hardman* [1891] 2 Ch 416. Again with Oliver J., we express our concurrence in the observations of Sir George Jessel M.R. in *Fothergill v. Rowland* (1873) LR 17 Eq 132, 140:

> "Then it is said, assuming this contract to be one which the court cannot specifically perform, it is yet a case in which the court will restrain the defendants from breaking the contract. But I have always felt, when at the Bar, a very considerable difficulty in understanding the court on the one hand professing to refuse specific performance because it is difficult to enforce it, and yet on the other hand attempting to do the same thing by a roundabout method."

This brings us to a final general observation in regard to damages. In most of the decided cases it is assumed that damages will not be an adequate alternative remedy to the grant of an injunction and the point is not much discussed. Thus in *Lumley v. Wagner* itself it was assumed that the mere chance of any damages which a jury might give was not worth very much. Now that these damages are invariably assessed by a judge or master we do not think that it can be assumed that they will always be an inadequate remedy. For example, in a case like the present it would be open to the court to refuse injunctive relief at the interlocutory stage on an undertaking by the defendant to keep full and proper accounts of his receipts from acting on behalf of the servant and to pay a specified proportion of them into court or into a joint account. An arrangement such as that would achieve the twin objectives of going some way to quantify the plaintiff's damages and preserving funds to meet any award which might later be made."

To Restrain a Breach of Constitutional Rights

The question of whether specific principles apply where an injunction is sought to restrain a breach of constitutional rights was considered by the Supreme Court in *Society for the Protection of Unborn Children (Ireland) Ltd v. Grogan.*

Society for the Protection of Unborn Children (Ireland) Ltd v. Grogan
[1989] IR 753

The plaintiffs sought an interlocutory injunction to restrain the defendants from distributing certain information in relation to abortion services available outside the State. The Supreme Court (Finlay CJ, Walsh, Griffin, Hederman and McCarthy JJ) allowed the plaintiff's appeal against the decision of Carroll J to refer questions of interpretation to the European Court of Justice without making any order in relation to the grant of the injunction.

FINLAY CJ stated at pp.763–766:

"The nature of the injunction sought
The nature of the plaintiff's asserted cause of action in aid of which the injunction is sought and the defendants' main defence to it is of fundamental importance for the determination of this appeal.

The plaintiff seeks to protect by injunction the right to life of the unborn which is acknowledged and guaranteed protection by Article 40, s. 3, sub-s. 3 of the Constitution.

The defendants assert that the acknowledgement and guarantee of protection to the life of the unborn contained in Article 40, s. 3, sub-s. 3 of the Constitution must, by virtue of the provisions of Article 29, s. 4, sub-s. 3 of the Constitution, be interpreted as being subject to and qualified by a right in the defendants, arising from European Community law, to the publication and distribution of material in Ireland to inform the mother of an unborn child of the location, identity and method of communication with abortion clinics in the United Kingdom in which she may, if she so wishes, obtain a service consisting of the intentional termination of the life of her unborn child. It is submitted on behalf of the defendants that since it appears from the affidavits that the information, publication and distribution of which was sought to be restrained, had already been published and distributed in various ways prior to the application the *status quo ante* was the availability of such information and accordingly no injunction could or should be granted.

This submission, in my view, completely ignores the nature of this action and the principles applicable to it. It was decided by this Court in *A.G. (S.P.U.C.) v. Open Door Counselling Ltd.* [1988] IR 593 at p. 627 "that the activities of the defendants, their servants or agents in assisting pregnant women within the jurisdiction to travel abroad to obtain abortions by referral to a clinic; by the making of their travel arrangements, or by informing them of the identity and location of and method of communication with a specified clinic or clinics are unlawful, having regard to the provisions of Article 40, s. 3, sub-s. 3 of the Constitution." This Court by the same order restrained the defendants in that action by permanent injunction from carrying on these activities. That decision clearly established that the actual activity which the defendants in this case are claiming and intending to pursue as of right is unlawful, having regard to the provisions of Article 40, s. 3, sub-s. 3 of the Constitution.

I reject as unsound the contention that the activity involved in this case of publishing in the students' manuals the name, address and telephone number, when telephoned from this State, of abortion clinics in the United Kingdom, and distributing such manuals in Ireland, can be distinguished from the activity condemned by this Court in *A.G. (S.P.U.C.) v. Open Door Counselling* [1988] IR 593 on the grounds that the facts of that case were that the information was conveyed during periods of one to one non-directive counselling. It is clearly the fact that such information is conveyed to pregnant women, and not the method of communication which creates the unconstitutional illegality, and the judgment of this Court in the *Open Door Counselling* case is not open to any other interpretation.

This application for an interlocutory injunction, therefore, consists of an application to restrain an activity which has been clearly declared by this Court to be unconstitutional and therefore unlawful and which could assist and is intended to assist in the destruction of the right to life of an unborn child, a right acknowledged and protected under the Constitution. That constitutionally guaranteed right must be fully and effectively protected by the courts.

If and when a decision of the Court of Justice of the Europeran Communities rules that some aspect of European Community law affects the activities of the defendants impugned in this case, the consequence of that decision on these constitutionally guaranteed rights and their protection by the courts will then fall to be considered by these courts.

Having regard to that duty of the Court, it is clearly quite inappropriate to approach the exercise of the discretion to grant or refuse an interlocutory injunction upon the basis of a supposed *status quo ante* consisting of activities which are constitutionally forbidden acts. The true principle which falls to be considered in this case in relation to the exercise of that discretion is the unqualified existence of the relevant provisions of the Constitution at the time of the application for an injunction which, in my view, having regard to the constitutional law applicable, replaces the ordinary concept of *status quo ante* arising in interlocutory injunction cases.

With regard to the issue of the balance of convenience, I am satisfied that where an injunction is sought to protect a constitutional right, the only matter which could properly be capable of being weighed in a balance against the granting of such protection would be another competing constitutional right.

I am quite satisfied that in the instant case where the right sought to be protected is that of a life, there can be no question of a possible or putative right which might exist in European law as a corollary to a right to travel so as to avail of services, counterbalancing as a matter of convenience the necessity for an interlocutory injunction.

One further submission remains to be considered. On behalf of the defendants it was submitted as a final alternative that if all the other contentions made on their behalf were to fail, this Court was obliged by the terms of Article 177 of the Treaty to refer to the Court of Justice of the European Communities for preliminary determination the question as to whether the granting of an interlocutory injunction was possible or appropriate according to European law. This submission was almost entirely based on the decision of the House of Lords in *Factortame Ltd. v. Secretary of State* [1989] 2 All ER 692. In that case what was being sought pending the determination by the Court of Justice of the European Communities of certain questions of Community law rights pursuant to Article 177, was an injunction restraining the implementation of an Act of the United Kingdom parliament. Having regard to the supremacy of parliament in the constitutional law of the United Kingdom, such a relief was absolutely prohibited by national law. The question, therefore, which was by the decision of the House of Lords referred under Article 177, was as to whether such an interim or interlocutory injunction was either obligatory or permissible under European Community law and if it were permissible only, by what standards the discretion as to whether to grant or refuse it should be exercised.

No such question arises in our national law where an injunction such as is here sought is not only consistent with but is in full accord with our constitutional law.

It is quite clear that where the courts of a member state decide to refer a question pursuant to Article 177 of the Treaty of Rome for a preliminary ruling by the Court of Justice of the European Communities, both the question as to the stage of the action in the member state at which that reference is made and what steps, if any, other than a final determination of the action the courts of the member state may take pending that determination are peculiarly matters for the national courts to be considered and decided in accordance with national law.

I would, therefore, allow this appeal and I would grant to the plaintiff an injunction in terms of the notice of motion of the 25th September, 1989. Such injunction should last until the trial and final determination of this action with liberty to either party to apply to the High Court for a variation of this order in the light of the preliminary ruling by the Court of Justice of the European Communities prior to that time of the questions referred to it by the High

Court under Article 177 of the Treaty.

Any application in respect of the enforcement of this injunction would, of course, be made in the High Court."

To Protect Public Rights

It is well established that an injunction may issue to restrain activities which are detrimental to the public generally but a question which has provoked considerable debate is whether an injunction may be granted to restrain the infringement of a public right even where a statutory remedy exists, in particular where the activity also constitutes a criminal offence. This question was answered in the affirmative by Costello J in *Attorney General v. Paperlink.*

Attorney General v. Paperlink
[1984] ILRM 373

An injunction was sought to restrain the defendants from operating a courier service in breach of the statutory power of the Minister for Posts and Telegraphs under the Post Office Act 1908. Costello J granted the injunction sought by the plaintiffs.

COSTELLO J stated at pp.389–393: "I come now, in conclusion, to explain why the Attorney General is entitled to the relief he claims.

It was made clear when counsel opened the plaintiffs' case that this was not a relator action in which the Attorney General was suing on the relation of the Minister as the person entitled to the exclusive privilege conferred by the 1908 Act. This, it was said, is an action which the Attorney General has brought *ex officio* as guardian of public rights. I heard arguments on the defendants' behalf at the close of the plaintiffs' case to the effect that these proceedings were misconceived. Having considered them I indicated that I could not accede to them and I will give my reasons for this conclusion now. Before doing so, however, I should record that at the end of the case during counsel's closing submissions it was submitted on the plaintiffs' behalf that apart from an independent right of the Attorney General to maintain these proceedings in the public interest the facts had established that a civil wrong had been committed and that the Minister in his own right had a right to protect the exclusive privilege given to him by the Act. I made no ruling on this point, save to indicate that I did not consider that the plaintiffs were estopped from making it. I should make clear, however, that the issue which I had been asked to determine (and did so in the plaintiffs' favour) was the Attorney General's right to the relief claimed and that had I decided this point against the plaintiffs I would have dismissed the case as the alternative argument had not then been advanced.

In opening the plaintiffs' case counsel referred to certain passages in *Halsbury's Laws of England* (4th Ed., Vol. 24. paras. 1030 and 1031) in which it was stated that when an illegal act which affects the public is committed or threatened the court has jurisdiction to grant an injunction at the suit of the Attorney General; that the public is concerned to see that Acts of parliament are observed; and that the court has jurisdiction to grant an injunction even though the right was conferred by a statute which prescribed criminal sanctions for its enforcement.

Mr Gleeson, on the defendants' behalf, submitted at the close of the plaintiffs' case that the remedy now being sought by the plaintiffs was unconstitutional and furthermore that the courts had no jurisdiction in equity to grant the relief claimed. The argument proceeded as follows. It was said that the proceedings amounted to an unprecedented attempt to make a finding of criminal guilt in civil proceedings and that such a course of action infringed Article 31.1 of the Constitution which provides that no person shall be tried on any criminal charges save in due course of law. The State, it was urged, had ignored the criminal remedies available to it and had opted instead for declaratory and injunctive relief. To obtain this relief the State was required to establish that criminal offences had taken place and the State thereby had deprived the defendants of a criminal trial. The State cannot abandon the criminal code and opt for a trial in a civil action in which the level of proof is different. Counsel referred to the three English cases relied on by the plaintiffs (*AG v. Sharp* [1931] 1 Ch 121 and *AG v. Premier Line Ltd* [1932] 1 Ch 303 and *AG v. Harris* [1961] 1 QB 74), and pointed out that in each of these cases criminal prosecutions had been instituted before the Attorney General had applied to the High Court for relief by way of injunction. It was conceded that in certain circumstances the Attorney General can apply for an injunction to restrain a breach of statute but it was urged that when a criminal sanction is contained in the statute the application can only be brought after it has been shown that the criminal proceedings have been ineffective.

I was also referred to the recent decision in the High Court in *Campus Oil Ltd v. AG* [1984] ILRM 45. This was a case in which the Attorney General applied for an interlocutory order to restrain the plaintiffs from failing to comply with the provisions of the Fuels (Petroleum Oils) Order 1983 which had been made under the provisions of s. 2 of the Fuels (Control of Supplies) Act, 1971. In that case an injunction was granted on the application of the Attorney General notwithstanding the fact that breaches of the statutory order involved criminal sanctions under the 1971 Act. Counsel, however, maintained that the plaintiffs in that case had not argued that the penalty provisions of the 1971 Act were a bar to the relief claimed by the Attorney General and so it is not authority to justify the court granting relief in the present case.

The role of the Attorney General as guardian of the public interest has, I think, been correctly stated by Professor Casey in 'The Office of the Attorney General in Ireland' at page 149 where he writes:

> It is possible (for the Attorney General) to obtain an injunction to restrain someone from acting in breach of a statutory provision even where his action constitutes an offence.

The authority quoted for this statement is the *Attorney General (O'Duffy) v. Mr Appleton, Surgeon Dentist Ltd* [1907] 1 IR 252. This was a relator action in which the Irish branch of the British Dental Association alleged that a company had been formed for fraudulent purposes contrary to the Dentists Act, 1878 and it was held that the Attorney General suing in the public interest was entitled to an injunction. In the course of his judgment the Master of Rolls said:

> The only real difficulty that has occurred to me in this case was that of jurisdiction. This is a new offence. There is a remedy provided under the Dentists Act – that is, by prosecution of the offender in a court of summary jurisdiction. Generally speaking, where there is a new offence the remedy given by the statute creating the offence is exclusive. But the existence of a power to sue for penalties does not of itself prevent the interference of the Attorney General seeking an injunction in the interests of the public by way of information. The public interests are committed to the care of the Attorney General, as representing the Crown, and in that way he represents the public (p. 257).

The more recent authorities in England do not, in my view, alter the legal situation I have just quoted. Whilst undoubtedly there are differences between the roles and functions of the Attorney General in this country and those of the Attorney General of England and Wales none the less assistance can be found in recent English authorities in determining (a) the jurisdiction of the courts to entertain an application for an injunction at the suit of the Attorney General when breaches of statute have been established and (b) the exercise of the court's jurisdiction in such circumstances – decisions which do not conflict with the earlier Irish authority I have quoted. Firstly, I accept as correct the following general principle:

> Whenever parliament has enacted a law and given a particular remedy for the breach of it, such remedy being in an inferior court, nevertheless, the High Court always has a reserve power to enforce the law so enacted by way of an injunction or other suitable remedy. The High Court has jurisdiction to ensure obedience to the law whenever it is just and convenient so to do.

Per Lord Denning MR *AG v. Chaudry* [1971] 1 WLR 1614, 1624.

Secondly, the Attorney General as part of his general power to enforce in the public interest public rights has the right *ex officio* to apply for an injunction to restrain breaches of statute, even when the statute prescribes other remedies, including criminal sanction.

Thirdly, whilst the High Court has jurisdiction to grant an injunction in the circumstances just outliend the jurisdiction should only be exercised in exceptional cases (see *Gouriet v. UPW* [1978] AC 435).

Fourthly, in deciding whether to exercise its jurisdiction the court will consider the adequacy of the alternative statutory remedy. If satisfied that these alternative remedies are inadequate then the court can properly grant relief by way of injunction. In deciding on the adequacy of the alternative remedies, however, the court must look at all the circumstances of the case and the fact that a criminal prosecution has not been brought does not in itself preclude the court from granting an injunction.

I have come to the conclusion that this is a case in which the Attorney General has established that there are exceptional circumstances and that it is one in which it would be just and convenient to grant the remedies sought. Counsel has informed me that the reason why these proceedings were instituted was that it was considered that the penalties imposed by the Act were totally inadequate and that criminal sanctions would be wholly ineffective to remedy the situation. I have no reason to disagree with the conclusions which the Attorney General had reached. A criminal offence is created by s. 34(4) of the 1908 Act which provides that if a person conveys any letter or makes a collection of excepted letters for the purpose of conveying them by post or otherwise he is liable to be fined a sum not exceeding £5 for every letter. This fine was established three-quarters of a century ago and it seems to me to be totally inadequate to meet the circumstances of the present case. It seems to me that it was unnecessary for the Attorney General to consider requesting the Director of Public Prosecutions to institute criminal proceedings and then to await to see whether if successful the defendant company would pay the fine and desist trading. It was reasonable for him to assume that in this case the deterrent effect of the sub-section was in fact negligible and so it seems to me reasonable for the court to exercise its discretion in the plaintiffs' favour.

There is, however, another reason peculiar to the particular provisions of the 1908 Act which clearly establishes the right of the Attorney General to apply for equitable relief and justifies the court in granting it. The 1908 Act contains two different sanctions, a criminal one and also a civil remedy. S. 34(5) provides that if any person is in the practice of doing any of the acts prohibited by sub-section (4) then he shall forfeit for every week during which the practice continues £100. S. 70 provides that the fine or forfeiture imposed by the Act may be recovered by an action in the High Court. Thus the statutory remedy for breach of the Minister's exclusive privilege is not one confined to the criminal courts and the defendants cannot complain that it is unjust that the issues in dispute between them and the Minister should be tried in a Civil Court where the onus of proof is different to that in a criminal court. Here the dispute could have been determined in a civil court if the Minister had chosen to institute proceedings in the High Court to recover the fine and/or the forfeiture to which I have referred. If the civil remedy is ineffective then there can be no objection to the Attorney General exercising in the public interest his right to apply to stop the statutory breaches by means of a High Court injunction and there is no reason why the court should not exercise its discretion and prohibit the continued breaches of the law which the evidence shows is taking place.

Once it is clear that the courts have jurisdiction to grant an injunction even in cases where criminal sanctions exist in respect of the acts complained of then no constitutional impropriety is involved if it exercises that jurisdiction as requested. The courts are not then trying a criminal charge within the meaning of Article 38 of the Constitution but are merely exercising a distinct and different jurisdiction in civil proceedings.

There will be a declaration and an injunction in the forms set out in paragraphs 12 (a) and (b) of the statement of claim except that the word 'packet' will not form part of the declaration or the injunction as the delivery of 'packets' has not been established."

MAREVA INJUNCTIONS

A Mareva injunction is a form of interim or interlocutory injunction which may be granted to restrain a defendant from disposing of his assets either within the jurisdiction or on a worldwide basis with the intention of evading his obligation to the plaintiff and may be granted either before a trial or after it in order to prevent a defendant from seeking to frustrate an order of the court.

Countyglen plc v. Carway
[1995] 1 ILRM 481

The applicant company brought proceedings against the respondents seeking various orders including a declaration that they had been guilty of fraud and/ or conspiracy to defraud, breach of trust and breach of duty and orders pursuant to s.12 of the Companies Act 1990 directing the respondents to repay sums which they had allegedly unlawfully and wrongfully removed from the company. The High Court granted an interim Mareva injunction restraining a number of the respondents from disposing of their assets within the jurisdiction so as to reduce their value below a specified sum and in particular from disposing of a named property. The applicant then sought an interlocutory Mareva injunction and ancillary relief. Murphy J granted the interlocutory Mareva injunction sought and ordered the respondents to swear an affidavit disclosing their assets within the jurisdiction.

MURPHY J stated at pp.486–489: "This application poses the question 'In what circumstances should a Mareva type injunction be granted'?

Counsel on behalf of the applicant contends that the tests to be met for obtaining a Mareva injunction are similar in substance to those identified by the Supreme Court in *Campus Oil Ltd v. Minister for Industry and Energy* [1983] IR 88; [1984] ILRM 45. In that case the Supreme Court concluded that it was the duty of a court exercising its jurisdiction in granting or refusing an interlocutory injunction to determine whether a fair *bona fide* or serious question had been raised to be decided at the trial by the party seeking relief. The Supreme Court pointed out that the court dealing with the matter ought not to weigh up the relative strengths of the parties' cases on the evidence available at the interlocutory stage as that evidence would be necessarily incomplete. Once a fair or serious question has been raised, the court must then go on to consider where the balance of convenience lies.

Counsel on behalf of the respondents in the present motion contends that something more is required where a Mareva injunction is sought. In the *Mareva* case itself *(Mareva Compania Naviera SA v. International Bulkcarriers SA* [1975] 2 Lloyd's Rep 509, the burden was stated as follows (at p. 510):

> If it appears that the debt is due and owing - and there is a danger that the debtor may dispose of his assets so as to defeat it before judgment - the court has jurisdiction in a proper case to grant an interlocutory judgment so as to prevent him disposing of those assets.

In *Rasu Maritima SA v. Perusahaan Pertambangin Minyak* [1978] QB 644, Lord Denning MR extended this – as he explained himself – to cases where the plaintiff could show that he had 'a good arguable case'. In *Z Ltd v. A-Z and AA-LL* [1982] QB 558, Kerr LJ in the course of his judgment expressed his view as to the circumstances in which a Mareva injunction should be granted in the following terms (at p. 585):

> It follows that in my view Mareva injunctions should be granted, but granted only, when it appears to the court that there is a combination of two circumstances. First, when it appears likely that the plaintiff will recover judgment against the defendant for a certain or approximate sum. Secondly, when there are also reasons to believe that the defendant has assets within the jurisdiction to meet the judgment, in whole or in part, but may well take steps designed to ensure that these are no longer available or traceable when judgment is given against him.

Indeed in *Fleming v. Ranks (Ireland) Ltd* [1983] ILRM 541 (the only reported Irish case on the circumstances in which a Mareva injunction will be granted) McWilliam J decided that the plaintiff must show that he has a 'good arguable case'.

I doubt that there is any significant difference between the expressions 'good arguable case' and a 'substantial question to be tried' but if such a distinction exists, I would prefer the latter criterion as the one approved by the Supreme Court in the *Campus Oil* case although not specifically related to the Mareva type injunction. What I reject emphatically is that a plaintiff seeking a Mareva injunction must establish as a probability that his claim would succeed. This 'probability' test was rejected by the Supreme Court in the *Campus Oil* case as a matter of precedent and of principle. O'Higgins CJ explained the position at p. 61 of the report in the following terms:

> The application of the criterion suggested by the appellants in this case would

> involve the court in a determination on an application for interlocutory relief of an issue which properly arises for determination at the trial of the action. In my view, the test to be applied is whether a fair *bona fide* question has been raised by the person seeking relief. If such a question has been raised, it is not for the court on an interlocutory application to determine that question; that remains to be decided at the trial.

In my view, it would be entirely inappropriate for the court on an interlocutory application to review such of the evidence as is available to it and attempt to forecast the outcome of the proceedings as a matter of probability or likelihood. What can and should be done is to determine that there is a fair, serious question to be tried.

In the present case there is evidence to support the serious allegations of fraud and breach of trust made against the defendants. At the same time I recognise that in the voluminous affidavits sworn by Mr John Carway the validity of this evidence and the weight to be attached to it has been challenged on numerous grounds and that those issues too are serious and *bona fide*. It is not my task, however, to assess which case is likely to prevail.

It is in relation to the risk of the defendants' assets being dissipated in advance of any judgment in the matter with a view to defeating the same and also with regard to the general balance of convenience that considerations different from those pertaining in relation to the conventional injunctions arise. In *Fleming v. Ranks (Ireland) Ltd* McWilliam J summarised the circumstances in which a Mareva injunction would be granted (at p. 546 of the judgment) in the following terms:

> I am satisfied that there is jurisdiction to grant such an injunction and that the cases in which it may be granted are not confined to cases in which a defendant is resident outside the State. From the cases cited I would accept that there must be a real risk of the removal or disposal of the defendants' assets, that there must be a danger of default by the defendant, that the plaintiff must show that he has a good arguable case, and, weighing the considerations for and against the grant of an injunction, the balance of convenience must be in favour of granting it.

There were two further points to which the late McWilliam J drew attention. In my view both are important and it is proper that I should refer to them as follows:

(1) It was accepted in the *Ranks* case that the defendants proposed to dispose of its assets. What the judge accepted however was that there was no intention of disposing of assets *with a view* to evading any obligation to the plaintiff. It was for that reason that he declined to make the order sought.

(2) He accepted as correct the statement of Sir Robert Megarry VC in *Barclay-Johnson v. Yuill* [1980] 1 WLR 1259 at p. 1266. That statement was as follows:

> I would regard the *Lister* principle as remaining the rule, and the Mareva doctrine

as constituting a limited exception to it.

That rule or principle was to the effect that the court will not grant an injunction to restrain a defendant from parting with his assets so that they may be preserved in case the plaintiff's claim succeeds. The basis of the Mareva injunction is to prevent an anticipated abuse by a defendant of his legal rights so as to frustrate unjustly the anticipated order of the court.

The actual evidence adduced by the applicant in the present case as to the nature or extent of the assets of the defendants within the jurisdiction of this Court and of the danger of the defendants dissipating those assets or transferring them outside the jurisdiction is extremely limited. The only asset identified was the family home in Killaloe and whatever inference might be drawn from the statement that Mr Carway 'lives a high lifestyle and is involved in substantial business transactions'. What emerges clearly from the affidavit of Mr Duggan and indeed the report of the inspector is that the nature of Mr Carway's business and his lifestyle is such as would facilitate the transfer of assets on an international basis. Indeed it is significant that Mr Carway now appears to be living in the Isle of Man whereas he was living in Co. Clare when the investigation by the inspector took place.

The position now is that the defendants have had the opportunity of adducing such evidence as they think fit in relation to the matters in issue on this motion. Mr Carway has sworn three lengthy affidavits on this motion incorporating, as exhibits or by reference, numerous other documents. The averments contained in those affidavits are material in so far as they indicate the basis of the defendants' challenge to the plaintiff's claim herein. However, what is striking is that in the lengthy and carefully prepared affidavits Mr Carway does not deal at all with the question of what assets he has within the jurisdiction of this Court or the allegation, suspicion or inference that the same may be dissipated so as to frustrate an order of this Court. Even more surprising is the fact that Mr Carway does not claim that the interim order or the interlocutory order claimed has caused or will cause any particular difficulty for him. Counsel on behalf of the defendants asserts that a Mareva injunction must of necessity impinge upon a defendant's constitutional rights in relation to private property and his or her right to earn his livelihood. However, that argument merely relates to the existence of the rights and the likelihood of some measure of inconvenience. Whether that inconvenience has any degree of significance cannot be assessed without the assistance of the defendants. It may be that the assets of the defendants in the State far exceed the amount which the plaintiff seeks to freeze. At the other end of the scale the defendants may have no assets available to them within the jurisdiction. In either case, the actual hardship or inconvenience would be little or none. If the defendants disclose the existence of some asset within the jurisdiction of this Court, then it might be anticipated in accordance with the guidelines indicated in the English cases and the practice adopted in this jurisdiction that the Mareva injunction, if granted, would be fine-tuned to ensure that the interest of the plaintiff would be protected without any unnecessary hardship to the defendants. However, on the basis of the evidence presently available to the court, it seems to me that the proper inference to draw is that the defendants do have assets in the jurisdiction; that there is a real risk that those assets will be dissipated and that the defendants are not apprehensive of any real inconvenience to them as a result of a Mareva injunction being granted.

In those circumstances I will make an order, a Mareva injunction, in the terms of paragraph (1) of the notice of motion herein. The order will be confined to assets within the jurisdiction of this Court. That a Mareva injunction should be so restricted appears to have been established by the decision in *Allied Arab Bank Ltd v. Hajjar* [1988] QB 787. It is in any event the form of the order sought herein."

O'Mahony v. Horgan
[1995] 2 IR 411

The applicant had been appointed liquidator of a company of which the respondents were directors. Murphy J granted an interlocutory injunction to restrain the second named respondent from disposing of or dissipating a sum of money payable under an insurance policy. The Supreme Court (Hamilton CJ, O'Flaherty and Blayney JJ) allowed the appeal of the second named respondent and held that this was not a situation in which a Mareva injunction should be granted.

HAMILTON CJ stated at pp.417–421: "The common law, traditionally, expressed the principle that the plaintiff is not entitled to require from the defendant, in advance of judgment, security to guarantee satisfaction of a judgment that the plaintiff may eventually obtain.

This position was altered in the United Kingdom by two decisions of the Court of Appeal in 1975, *viz. Nippon Yusen Kaisha v. Karagerogis* [1975] 1 WLR 1093 and *Mareva Compania Naviera SA v. International Bulkcarriers SA* [1980] 1 All ER 213.

These cases involved claims for damages arising from shipping contracts brought against foreign defendants. In both, the plaintiffs obtained orders (*ex-parte*) restraining the defendants from removing their funds out of the jurisdiction pending the adjudication of the actions.

Injunctions of this type became known as *Mareva* injunctions. A Mareva injunction is an *ad personam* order, restraining the defendant from dealing with assets in which the plaintiff claims no right whatsoever. A Mareva order does not give the plaintiff any precedence over other creditors with respect to the frozen assets.

Because of the draconian nature of such orders, Lord Denning in *Third*

Chandris Shipping Corporation v. Unimarine SA [1979] QB 645 at pp. 668-669, laid down the five criteria to be established before such injunctions are granted which are the criteria set forth in the learned trial judge's judgment.

In *Z. Ltd. v. A-Z and AA-LL* [1982] 1 QB 558, Kerr L.J., in the course of his judgment, stated his view as to the circumstances in which a *Mareva* injunction should be granted in the following terms at p. 585:—

> "It follows that in my view Mareva injunctions should be granted, but granted only, when it appears to the court that there is a combination of two circumstances. First, when it appears likely that the plaintiff will recover judgment against the defendant for a certain or approximate sum. Secondly, when there are also reasons to believe that the defendant has assets within the jurisdiction to meet the judgment, in whole or in part, but may well take steps designed to ensure that these are no longer available or traceable when judgment is given against him."

Consequently a *Mareva* injunction will only be granted if there is a combination of two circumstances established by the plaintiff i.e. (i) that he has an arguable case that he will succeed in the action, and (ii) the anticipated disposal of a defendant's assets is for the purpose of preventing a plaintiff from recovering damages and not merely for the purpose of carrying on a business or discharging lawful debts.

In the course of his judgment in *Fleming and ors. v. Ranks (Ireland) Ltd. and anor.* [1983] ILRM 541, the late Mr. Justice McWilliam stated at p. 546 of the report:—

> "I am satisfied that there is jurisdiction to grant such an injunction . . . From the cases cited I would accept that there must be a real risk of the removal or disposal of the defendant's assets, that there must be a danger of default by the defendant, that the plaintiff must show that he has a good arguable case, and, weighing the considerations for and against the grant of an injunction, the balance of convenience must be in favour of granting it. See *Barclay-Johnson v. Yuill* [1980] 1 WLR 1259 at page 1265."

With regard to the facts in the *Ranks* case, he stated:—

> "Although a special account has been opened by Ranks for the sums to which the plaintiffs are entitled under the Redundancy Acts, it appears to me that, if damages are awarded to the plaintiffs on the basis of their claims, there is a danger of default by Ranks through inability to pay the amounts of the awards. But I am of opinion that, to justify such an injunction, the anticipated disposal of a defendant's assets must be for the purpose of preventing a plaintiff from recovering damages and not merely for the purpose of carrying on a business or discharging lawful debts."

At the end of p. 546, he went on to say:—

> "I would accept as correct the statement of Sir Robert Megarry, V.C., at p. 1266 of the *Barclay-Johnson* case ([1980] 1 WLR 1259) where he said — 'I would regard the *Lister* principle as remaining the rule, and the Mareva doctrine as constituting a limited exception to it'. 'The Lister rule' refers to the case of

Lister and Co. v. Stubbs mentioned above, ((1890) 45 Ch D 1 C.A.) and is that the court will not grant an injunction to restrain a defendant from parting with his assets so that they may be preserved in case the plaintiff's claim succeeds."

In *Polly Peck International Plc. v. Nadir* [1992] 4 All ER 769 both the Master of the Rolls and Scott L.J., stressed that such relief is not intended to give security in advance of judgment but merely to prevent the defendant from defeating the plaintiff's chance of recovery by dissipation of assets.

Consequently, the cases establish that there must be an intention on the part of the defendant to dispose of his assets with a view to evading his obligation to the plaintiff and to frustrate the anticipated order of the court. It is not sufficient to establish that the assets are likely to be dissipated in the ordinary course of business or in the payment of lawful debts.

Has the liquidator in the instant case adduced evidence to show, or to entitle the learned trial judge to infer, that the appellant is likely to dissipate the asset referred to, *viz.* the proceeds of an insurance policy, with the intention of evading his obligation (if any) to the liquidator?

In his affidavit sworn on the 17th June, 1993, he states at para. 47 (a) thereof that:—

> "I am naturally concerned, having regard to the manner in which the affairs of the company were conducted to ensure that the said sum of £71,000 should be available to meet any decree which may be made in favour of the company in liquidation against the second respondent, and apprehensive that in the absence of such an order the said sum will not be available."

His apprehension may well be justified but he does not state or allege that the appellant would dissipate the asset with the intention of frustrating any order of the court that may be made.

The learned trial judge himself stated:—

> "All the plaintiff has said is that he is apprehensive in this regard. That is a far cry undoubtedly from evidence of conscious abuse"

and

> "No direct evidence is given that monies would be dissipated, but in the context of the sums involved and the parties' obligations to the banks, the concern of the official liquidator has not been shown to be misplaced."

As appears from his affidavit, the liquidator's concern was to ensure that the said sum of £71,000 should be available to meet any decree which might be made in favour of the company in liquidation.

The learned trial judge does not appear to have considered the question whether the apprehended dissipation of the asset was for the purpose of evading any decree that might be made in the proceedings.

Before being entitled to the relief sought by him, the liquidator must establish that there was a likelihood that the assets would be dissipated with the intention that they would not be available to meet any decree or part of a decree ultimately made against the appellant in the proceedings.

In my view, no such intention was established in this case. The entitlement of the appellant to the proceeds of the policy of insurance issued by the Norwich Union Fire Insurance Society arose because of a fire on the appellant's property which destroyed a shed thereon.

While the use of such proceeds to replace the shed, or in the ordinary course of his business as a farmer, or to pay his lawful debts, would mean that such asset would not be available to meet any decree which the liquidator might obtain against the appellant, that fact does not entitle the liquidator to the injunction sought. He must further establish that such utilisation of the asset was made with the intention of evading payment to the liquidator.

As no such intention was established in this case, the appellant's appeal must be allowed on this ground.

Being of this view, it is not necessary for me to consider whether or not the learned trial judge was entitled to place a limit of £25,000 on the undertaking required to be given by the liquidator and I will reserve for future consideration the powers of the court in this regard should it arise in the future. I incline however to the views in this regard expressed in the judgment about to be delivered by Mr. Justice O'Flaherty."

The decision in *Bennett Enterprises Ltd v. Lipton* clarified how the 'requisite intention', on the defendant's part to dispose of his assets with a view to evading his obligation to the plaintiff may be established, and also examined a number of issues relating to the granting of Mareva injunctions on a worldwide basis.

Bennett Enterprises Inc. v. Lipton
[1999] 1 ILRM 81

The plaintiffs instituted proceedings against the defendants for breach of contract and sought, *inter alia*, an interlocutory injunction restraining the defendants from reducing the monies in certain trust funds below a stated sum. O'Sullivan J granted an interlocutory Mareva injunction on a worldwide basis subject to a '*Babanaft* proviso'.

O'SULLIVAN J stated at pp.86–92: "An interim *Mareva* type injunction was granted by me on the *ex parte* application of the plaintiffs on 8 May 1998 and on the following day, which was a Saturday, similar orders were granted to the plaintiffs by the court in Hong Kong and these orders in both jurisdictions are continuing in effect. The defendants say that it is onerous on them that they should be obliged to meet the plaintiffs' cases in two jurisdictions but the plaintiffs respond that the curtailing of the initial and any subsequent orders (in line with the restriction adopted by the Court of Appeal in *Babanaft International Co. SA v. Bassatne* [1990] 1 Ch 13) implies that proceedings in one or more jurisdictions are likely if not inevitable. They also say that the Irish proceedings were instituted first in time and that the more appropriate jurisdiction is the one already chosen by the defendants themselves.

It is against this background that the plaintiffs now seek the orders referred to above. The defendants have raised a number of points in response to this application and I will deal with these one by one as follows.

In reliance on the tests set out by the Supreme Court in *O'Mahony v. Horgan* [1995] 2 IR 411; [1996] 1 ILRM 161 the defendants say, first, that the plaintiffs have failed to make full and frank disclosure of all relevant facts and that therefore they are not entitled to the relief claimed.

This point relates to two matters, namely, the fact that Mr Sprague, who has sworn the principal affidavit on behalf of the plaintiffs, is himself the subject of federal indictments in relation to alleged revenue offences committed in the early to mid-1980s in the United States.

This fact was, however, known to the defendants from the beginning of their relationship with the plaintiffs and with Mr Sprague but despite this, they were prepared to deal with him and Privacy Consultants up to approximately November 1997. In these circumstances I am not satisfied that this is a non-disclosure which is relevant to the instant application.

Secondly, the defendants say that Mr Sprague's affidavit failed to disclose either at all or with sufficient clarity the fact that the defendants' refusal to pay the admittedly owing money (namely, the sum of $300,000 referred to above) was upon the basis that the identity of the beneficiaries was not being revealed to the defendants and that therefore this constituted a failure to make full and frank disclosure in the affidavit grounding this application. This matter is dealt with at paragraph 60 of Mr Sprague's affidavit sworn on 5 May 1998 and, in my view, there is sufficient disclosure of this matter in what is a lengthy and complex affidavit accompanied by voluminous documentation. Accordingly, I cannot agree with the defendants that the application should be dismissed upon the basis that full and frank disclosure has not been made.

The second point taken by the defendants is that particulars of the plaintiffs' claim have not been adequately set out. This point was not strenuously pressed by the defendants at the hearing before me, possibly because the application has been accompanied by voluminous documentation. I do not think that the application should be refused on this ground.

Thirdly, the defendants assert that the plaintiffs have not set out any evidence to show that the defendants have assets within the jurisdiction. This is true: it is clear that there are no assets within this jurisdiction. The plaintiffs respond, however, that if there were sufficient assets or any assets within this jurisdiction, this would eliminate or reduce the need for a worldwide *Mareva* type injunction or an injunction having extra territorial effect. Counsel for the plaintiffs relies in particular on the judgment of the Master of the Rolls, Lord Donaldson in *Derby & Co. Ltd v. Weldon (Nos. 3 & 4)* [1990] 1 Ch 65 at p. 79 as follows:

The normal form of order should indeed be confined to assets within the jurisdiction, although the practice has changed since the decision in the MBPXL case and such an order could well extend to the disposition of a freehold interest in a house. The reason why at present the normal form of order should be so confined is that most defendants operate nationally rather than internationally. But, once the court is concerned with an international operator, the position may well be different.

In my judgment, the key requirement for any *Mareva* injunction, whether or not it extends to foreign assets, is that it shall accord with the rationale upon which the *Mareva* relief has been based in the past . . . namely, that no court should permit a defendant to take action designed to frustrate subsequent orders of the court. If for the achievement of this purpose it is necessary to make orders concerning foreign assets, such orders should be made, subject, of course, to ordinary principles of international law. . . .

Returning to Mr Bompas' submission, I can see neither rhyme nor reason in regarding the existence of some asset within the jurisdiction of however little value as a precondition for granting a *Mareva* injunction in respect of assets outside the jurisdiction. The existence of *sufficient* assets within the jurisdiction is an excellent reason for confining the jurisdiction to such assets, but, other considerations apart, the fewer the assets within the jurisdiction the greater the necessity for taking protective measures in relation to those outside it.

Earlier in the same judgment, the learned judge had said (at p. 77):

We live in a time of rapidly growing commercial and financial sophistication and it behoves the courts to adapt their practices to meet the current wiles of those defendants who are prepared to devote as much energy to making themselves immune to the courts' orders as to resisting the making of such orders on the merits of their case. Hence it comes about that, as was pointed out by Neill LJ in *Babanaft International Co. SA v. Bassante* [1990] 1 Ch 13, 37F and by May LJ in *Derby v. Weldon (No. 1)* [1990] 1 Ch 48, 54 C-D, this is a developing branch of the law. To that I would add that a failure or refusal to grant an injunction in any particular case is an exercise of discretion which cannot, as such, provide a precedent binding upon another court concerned with another case, save insofar as that refusal is based upon basic principles applicable in both such cases.

I would point out that in the *Babanaft* case [1990] 1 Ch 13 Kerr LJ at p. 33 had noted that:

But it should also be said, with equal emphasis, that some situations, which are nowadays by no means uncommon, cry out – as a matter of justice to plaintiffs – for disclosure orders and *Mareva* type injunctions covering foreign assets of defendants even before judgment.

I should also point out that in *O'Mahony v. Horgan* the Supreme Court was not dealing with a claim for an order affecting assets outside the jurisdiction. In these circumstances I do not consider that the alleged failure of the plaintiffs to establish that there are assets within the jurisdiction is necessarily fatal to their application. On the contrary, I can see force in the observation of the

Master of the Rolls, Lord Donaldson in *Derby (Nos. 3 & 4)* to the effect that the fewer the assets within the jurisdiction the greater the necessity for taking protective measures in relation to those outside it. Accordingly, I do not accept the defendants' submission that the application must fail on this ground.

A further ground advanced by the defendants is that there is no evidence to establish a risk of the assets being removed or dissipated by the defendants as contemplated by the Supreme Court in *O'Mahony v. Horgan*. The Chief Justice, Hamilton CJ at p. 418 said:

> Consequently a *Mareva* injunction will only be granted if there is a combination of two circumstances established by the plaintiff, *i.e.* (i) that he has an arguable case that he will succeed in the action, and (ii) the anticipated disposal of a defendant's assets is for the purpose of preventing a plaintiff from recovering damages and not merely for the purpose of carrying on a business or discharging lawful debts.

Later (at p. 419) the learned Chief Justice said:

> Consequently, the cases establish that there must be an intention on the part of the defendant to dispose of his assets with a view to evading his obligation to the plaintiff and to frustrate the anticipated order of the court. It is not sufficient to establish that the assets are likely to be dissipated in the ordinary course of business or in the payment of lawful debts.

I fully accept these quotations. It is clear, of course, that if any dissipation of assets were to occur in the ordinary course of business, this of itself would not justify the granting of a *Mareva* injunction. The anticipated dissipation must be for the purpose of the defendant evading his obligation to the plaintiff. Equally, however, I consider that direct evidence of an intention to evade will rarely be available at the interlocutory stage. I consider it is legitimate for me to consider all the circumstances in relation to the case and I do not consider that this approach is in any way prohibited by or at variance with the principles set out in the Supreme Court judgment in *O'Mahony v. Horgan*. The plaintiffs point to a number of specific matters which, they say, give rise to a reasonable apprehension that the assets will be dissipated (or removed from the jurisdiction of the courts) with a view to depriving the plaintiffs of their monies in the event that they succeed in their action. I will not refer to all of the specific matters which are set out *in extenso* in the plaintiffs' written legal submissions dated 11 June 1998. Some of these considerations are:

(a) the defendants have failed to repay five plaintiffs monies agreed to be owing since November 1997;

(b) they have sought to impose additional obstacles in the way of the plaintiffs withdrawing monies and in particular have insisted on an indication of the identity of the beneficiaries;

(c) they have refused to accept instructions from Privacy Consultants despite having done so up to 1997;

(d) they are ambivalent in their own description of the Genesis and Exodus Funds describing them as trust funds in the relevant prospectuses and correspondence but in other correspondence as an 'equity partnership';

(e) Mr Lipton, who swore the principal replying affidavit, has used and insisted on the use of aliases, namely 'Dominique' and 'Vincenzo'. This is averred to by Mr Sprague in his affidavit and although denied by Mr Lipton, the plaintiffs say that there is internal documentary evidence, arising from correspondence signed 'Dominique' or 'Vincenzo' which make it more probable that Mr Sprague's evidence on this point is correct;

(f) the defendants have failed to furnish the plaintiffs with monthly statements of account since December 1997 notwithstanding the fact that their own documentation indicates that monthly accounts are available;

(g) the reason given for the refusal of the defendants to conduct an audit of the two trust funds, to the effect that this would be impossible, is unbelievable;

(h) the failure of the defendants to lodge the admittedly due monies in court or to 'inter-plead' same even in the course of these proceedings;

(i) the absence of any address for Mr Lipton in his own affidavit, the absence of any identifiable or tangible presence for Genesis and Exodus in any country, including the failure to identify trading addresses or offices for these funds;

(j) the furnishing of documentation to the plaintiffs which show IBI as having an address at premises which turns out to be a handbag shop and the vague existence of IBI as a currency trader trading in a premises which shows no signs of currency trading;

(k) the fact that the defendants have not exhibited any documentation to substantiate their claimed valuation of the overall Genesis and Exodus Trust Funds at $70 million;

(l) the intimation by Mr Lipton that the Exodus Fund never operated as a separate trust fund and has been dissolved;

(m) the fact that the responding affidavit sworn by Ms Lam with almost one month's notice provides no information in relation to the value of these trust funds and exhibits no bank statements or anything which might allay the fears of the plaintiffs that these funds are in danger of being dissipated or removed from the jurisdiction of the courts;

(n) the claimed value of these trust funds at $70 million in Mr Lipton's affidavit contrasts with an earlier estimate of a year ago of $29 million without any apparent explanation.

In addition to the foregoing, a consideration of the documentation generated by the operators of the Genesis (and Exodus) Funds leaves one with the impression that the whole arrangement is disturbingly vague and free of identifiable structures. For example, in a document entitled 'Security with Genesis' which is exhibited to an affidavit sworn by Edmund Fry on 27 May 1998, the following appears under the heading 'Privacy and Asset Protection':

> Genesis is an Irish formation trust. All participants in Genesis are equity partners. Genesis has a contractual relationship with International Bright Investments Limited ('IBI'), who is a Macau-based currency dealer (operating similarly to, but not quite the same as a commodities broker in the United States). . .

> The board acts as the fund's fiduciary and directs the administrative responsibilities including the accounting which is performed by three accountants. Only one of these accountants, Centrix Management, a Vanuatu [in the South Pacific] based company, has the [confidential] detailed information about each participant in the fund. The other two US-based accountants have no participant detail available to them. The three accountants reconcile their records monthly with IBI which emulates a monthly audit.

> The details of each participating account cannot be disclosed by IBI or by Hong Kong Shanghai Bank to any regulatory agency or judicial system since they have no such detail. The release of confidential information by Centrix could only be done under a Vanuatu court order. There is no reciprocal relationship between the United States and Vanuatu or Ireland and the United States, or Vanuatu and Ireland for that matter. If you want more information on Vanuatu and Ireland, you can get this easily through the Internet.

> If some party wanted to seize your assets which included your holdings in Genesis, they would have no way of seizing those funds, since those funds belong to the Irish trust [Genesis], not you. The entity through which you participate [in Genesis] would be the only party under whose authority the release of your funds [held by Genesis] could be effected.

In my view the apprehensions of the plaintiffs that the assets will be either dissipated or removed from the jurisdiction of the courts with a view to depriving the plaintiffs of their money are reasonably founded and I consider that the plaintiffs have established sufficiently that there is a risk that the assets would be either removed from the jurisdiction of the courts or dissipated with a view to an evasion by the defendants of their obligations to the plaintiffs in the event that the plaintiffs succeed. Accordingly, I hold that the defendants have not established that the plaintiffs should fail to be granted relief on this ground.

The defendants further say that the plaintiffs have given no satisfactorily backed undertaking as to damages in the event that they fail at the hearing of the action.

It is true that the plaintiffs have no assets within this jurisdiction. On the other hand, they respond to this point by saying that the defendants admittedly are in possession of $5 million belonging to the plaintiffs. The defendants in return claim that a *Mareva* style injunction prohibiting the defendants world-wide from reducing their assets below $5 million could tie up the entire fund claimed to be valued at some $70 million with the result that losses in the order of $15 or $20 million could be sustained. They have given no detailed or specific account as to how this might happen and, in my view, the defendants cannot be heard to say that the plaintiffs have given no adequate undertaking or security in the circumstances that the defendants are in possession, as they admit, of $5 million worth of the plaintiffs' funds.

Apart from the foregoing defences, a general point is made by the defendants to the effect that it is only in very special circumstances that a worldwide *Mareva* type injunction should be granted by this Court.

The plaintiffs say that such special circumstances apply in this case. They say in the first instance that the very business of the defendants is to trade internationally, that the courts must adapt their practices to meet the current wiles of such defendants (to borrow the phrase of Lord Donaldson MR in *Derby (No. 3 & 4)*) and they point to the fact that the defendants have boasted that they can move funds internationally in nanoseconds. Accordingly, the plaintiffs say that in the particular circumstances of this case justice will be done and will only be done if a worldwide *Mareva* type injunction is granted.

The plaintiffs further offer the court undertakings that they will not issue proceedings in any other jurisdiction unless they first apply to this Court for permission so to do and they are also prepared to undertake to proceed against the defendants in the Irish proceedings (who are also defendants in proceedings in Hong Kong) in this jurisdiction and not to proceed against those defendants in the Hong Kong jurisdiction unless ordered or permitted so to do by the court in Hong Kong. They also accept that any order will be subject to the limitation which has come to be known as the *Babanaft* proviso.

Having considered the voluminous documentation and the lengthy and comprehensive submissions on behalf of both parties, my view is that I should give an interlocutory order in principle as sought by the plaintiffs and I will discuss with counsel the precise form of the order together with any limitations thereon and also the appropriate undertakings to be given to this Court on behalf of the plaintiffs."

ANTON PILLER ORDERS

An *Anton Piller* order is a form of injunction which aims to prevent a defendant from destroying or otherwise disposing of vital evidence pending a trial. Orders of this nature usually authorise a plaintiff accompanied by his solicitor to enter a defendant's premises to inspect and if necessary remove documents or articles specified in the order.

Anton Piller KG v. Manufacturing Processes Ltd
[1976] Ch 55

The plaintiffs claimed that the defendants were selling confidential information to their competitors which they had obtained in their capacity as selling agents for the plaintiff's electrical equipment and sought access to documents on the defendant's premises. The Court of Appeal made an *ex parte* order permitting the plaintiffs and their solicitors to enter the defendant's premises for the purpose of inspecting documents or other articles and removing those which belonged to the plaintiffs.

LORD DENNING MR stated at pp.58–61: "During the last 18 months the judges of the Chancery Division have been making orders of a kind not known before. They have some resemblance to search warrants. Under these orders, the plaintiff and his solicitors are authorised to enter the defendant's premises so as to inspect papers, provided the defendant gives permission.

Now this is the important point: The court orders the defendant to give them permission. The judges have been making these orders on ex parte applications without prior notice to the defendant. None of the cases have been reported except the one before Templeman J. on December 3, 1974, *E.M.I. Ltd. v. Pandit* [1975] 1 WLR 302. But in the present case Brightman J. refused to make such an order.

On appeal to us, Mr. Laddie appears for the plaintiffs. He has appeared in most of these cases, and can claim the credit – or the responsibility – for them. He represented to us that in this case it was in the interests of justice that the application should not be made public at the time it was made. So we heard it in camera. It was last Tuesday. After hearing his submissions, we made the order. We now come to give our reasons in public. But at the outset I must state the facts, for it is obvious that such an order can only be justified in the most exceptional circumstances.

Anton Piller KG ("Pillers"), the plaintiffs, are German manufacturers of high repute. They make electric motors and generators. They play an important part in the big new computer industry. They supply equipment for it. They have recently designed a frequency converter specially for supplying the computers of International Business Machines.

Since 1972 Pillers have had, as their agents in the United Kingdom, a company here called Manufacturing Processes Ltd. ("M.P.L."), which is run by Mr. A. H. S. Baker and Mr. B. P. Wallace, their two directors. These agents are dealers who get machines from Pillers in Germany and sell them to customers in England. Pillers supply M.P.L. with much confidential information about the machines, including a manual showing how they work, and drawings which are the subject of copyright.

Very recently Pillers have found out – so they say – that these English agents, M.P.L., have been in secret communication with other German

companies called Ferrostaal and Lechmotoren. The object of these communications is that M.P.L. should supply these other German companies with
drawings and materials and other confidential information so that they can
manufacture power units like Pillers. Pillers got to know of these communications through two "defectors," if I may call them so. One was the
commercial manager of M.P.L., Mr. Brian Firth; the other was the sales manager,
Mr. William Raymond Knight. These two were so upset by what was going on
in M.P.L. that on their own initiative, without any approach by Pillers whatever,
on October 2, 1975, one or both flew to Germany. They told Pillers what they
knew about the arrangements with Ferrostaal and Lechmotoren. They disclosed
also that M.P.L. was negotiating with Canadian and United States firms. In
making these disclosures, both Mr. Firth and Mr. Knight were putting
themselves in a perilous position, but Pillers assured them that they would
safeguard their future employment.

The disclosures – coming from defectors – might have been considered
untrustworthy. But they were supported by documents which emanated from
both Ferrostaal and Lechmotoren. They showed that M.P.L. was in regular
communication with those German companies. They were sending them
drawings and arranging for inspection of the Piller machine, for the express
purpose that the Lechmotoren company might manufacture a prototype machine
copied from Pillers. One of the most telling communications was a telex from
a representative of Ferrostaal to Mr. Wallace saying:

> "It is the opinion of Mr. S. (of Lechmotoren) that the best way to find a final
> solution for the . . . prototype is to send Mr. Beck (also of Lechmotoren) to you
> as soon as the . . . latest design of P. (Piller) has arrived in your factory. In this
> case it is guaranteed that the Lech prototype will have exactly the same features
> as the P-type. We hope you will agree to this proposal and we ask you to let us
> have your telex in order to arrange Mr. Beck's visit accordingly."

On getting this information, Pillers were extremely worried. They were about
to produce a fine new frequency converter called the "Silent Block." They
feared that M.P.L., in co-operation with the German manufacturers, would
make a copy of their "Silent Block" and ruin their market. They determined to
apply to the court for an injunction to restrain M.P.L. and their directors, the
defendants, from infringing their copyright or using confidential information
or making copies of their machines. But they were fearful that if the defendants
were given notice of this application, they would take steps to destroy
documents or send them to Germany or elsewhere, so that there would be
none in existence by the time that discovery was had in the action.

So, on Wednesday, November 26, 1975, Pillers' solicitors prepared a draft
writ of summons and, with an affidavit, they went before Brightman J. and
asked, first, for an interim injunction to restrain infringement, etc., and,
secondly, for an order that they might be permitted to enter the defendants'
premises so as to inspect the documents of the plaintiffs and remove them, or

copies of them. Brightman J. granted an interim injunction, but refused to order inspection or removal of the documents. He said:

> "There is strong prima facie evidence that the defendant company is now engaged in seeking to copy the plaintiffs' components for its own financial profit to the great detriment of the plaintiffs and in breach of the plaintiffs' rights."

He realised that the defendants might suppress evidence or misuse documentary material, but he thought that that was a risk which must be accepted in civil matters save in extreme cases.

> "Otherwise," he said, "it seems to me that an order on the lines sought might become an instrument of oppression, particularly in a case where a plaintiff of big standing and deep pocket is ranged against a small man who is alleged on the evidence of one side only to have infringed the plaintiffs' rights."

Let me say at once that no court in this land has any power to issue a search warrant to enter a man's house so as to see if there are papers or documents there which are of an incriminating nature, whether libels or infringements of copyright or anything else of the kind. No constable or bailiff can knock at the door and demand entry so as to inspect papers or documents. The householder can shut the door in his face and say "Get out." That was established in the leading case of *Entick v. Carrington* (1765) 2 Wils KB 275. None of us would wish to whittle down the principle in the slightest. But the order sought in this case is not a search warrant. It does not authorise the plaintiffs' solicitors or anyone else to enter the defendants' premises against their will. It does not authorise the breaking down of any doors, nor the slipping in by a back door, nor getting in by an open door or window. It only authorises entry and inspection by the permission of the defendants. The plaintiffs must get the defendants' permission. But it does do this: It brings pressure on the defendants to give permission. It does more. It actually orders them to give permission – with, I suppose, the result that if they do not give permission, they are guilty of contempt of court.

This may seem to be a search warrant in disguise. But it was fully considered in the House of Lords 150 years ago and held to be legitimate. The case is *United Company of Merchants of England, Trading to the East Indies v. Kynaston* (1821) 3 Bli (O.S.) 153. Lord Redesdale said, at pp.163-164:

> "The arguments urged for the appellants at the Bar are founded upon the supposition, that the court has directed a forcible inspection. This is an erroneous view of the case. The order is to permit; and if the East India Company should refuse to permit inspection, they will be guilty of a contempt of the court. . . . It is an order operating on the person requiring the defendants to permit inspection, not giving authority of force, or to break open the doors of their warehouse."

That case was not, however, concerned with papers or things. It was only as to the value of a warehouse; and that could not be obtained without an inspection. But the distinction drawn by Lord Redesdale affords ground for thinking that there is jurisdiction to make an order that the defendant "do permit" when it is necessary in the interests of justice.

Accepting such to be the case, the question is in what circumstances ought such an order be made. If the defendant is given notice beforehand and is able to argue the pros and cons, it is warranted by that case in the House of Lords and by R.S.C., Ord. 29, r. 2 (1) and (5). But it is a far stronger thing to make such an order ex parte without giving him notice. This is not covered by the Rules of the Supreme Court and must be based on the inherent jurisdiction of the court. There are one or two old precedents which give some colour for it, *Hennessy v. Rohmann, Osborne & Co.* [1877] WN 14, and *Morris v. Howell* (1888) 22 LR Ir 77, an Irish case. But they do not go very far. So it falls to us to consider it on principle. It seems to me that such an order can be made by a judge ex parte, but it should only be made where it is essential that the plaintiff should have inspection so that justice can be done between the parties: and when, if the defendant were forewarned, there is a grave danger that vital evidence will be destroyed, that papers will be burnt or lost or hidden, or taken beyond the jurisdiction, and so the ends of justice be defeated: and when the inspection would do no real harm to the defendant or his case.

Nevertheless, in the enforcement of this order, the plaintiffs must act with due circumspection. On the service of it, the plaintiffs should be attended by their solicitor: who is an officer of the court. They should give the defendants an opportunity of considering it and of consulting their own solicitor. If the defendants wish to apply to discharge the order as having been improperly obtained, they must be allowed to do so. If the defendants refuse permission to enter or to inspect, the plaintiffs must not force their way in. They must accept the refusal, and bring it to the notice of the court afterwards, if need be on an application to commit.

You might think that with all these safeguards against abuse, it would be of little use to make such an order. But it can be effective in this way: It serves to tell the defendants that, on the evidence put before it, the court is of opinion that they ought to permit inspection – nay, it orders them to permit – and that they refuse at their peril. It puts them in peril not only of proceedings for contempt, but also of adverse inferences being drawn against them; so much so that their own solicitor may often advise them to comply. We are told that in two at least of the cases such an order has been effective. We are prepared, therefore, to sanction its continuance, but only in an extreme case where there is grave danger of property being smuggled away or of vital evidence being destroyed.

On the evidence in this case, we decided last Tuesday that there was sufficient justification to make an order. We did it on the precedent framed by Templeman J. It contains an undertaking in damages which is to be supported (as the plaintiffs are overseas) by a bond for £10,000. It gives an interim injunction to restrain the infringement of copyright and breach of confidential information, etc. It orders that the defendants do permit one or two of the plaintiffs and one or two of their solicitors to enter the defendants' premises for the purpose of inspecting documents, files or things, and removing those which belong to the plaintiffs. This was, of course, only an interim order pending the return of the summons. It is to be heard, we believe, tomorrow by the judge."

ORMROD LJ stated at pp.61–62: "I agree with all that Lord Denning M.R. has said. The proposed order is at the extremity of this court's powers. Such orders, therefore, will rarely be made, and only when there is no alternative way of ensuring that justice is done to the applicant.

There are three essential pre-conditions for the making of such an order, in my judgment. First, there must be an extremely strong prima facie case. Secondly, the damage, potential or actual, must be very serious for the applicant. Thirdly, there must be clear evidence that the defendants have in their possession incriminating documents or things, and that there is a real possibility that they may destroy such material before any application inter partes can be made.

The form of the order makes it plain that the court is not ordering or granting anything equivalent to a search warrant. The order is an order on the defendant in personam to permit inspection. It is therefore open to him to refuse to comply with such an order, but at his peril either of further proceedings for contempt of court – in which case, of course, the court will have the widest discretion as to how to deal with it, and if it turns out that the order was made improperly in the first place, the contempt will be dealt with accordingly – but more important, of course, the refusal to comply may be the most damning evidence against the defendant at the subsequent trial. Great responsibility clearly rests on the solicitors for the applicant to ensure that the carrying out of such an order is meticulously carefully done with the fullest respect for the defendant's rights, as Lord Denning M.R. has said, of applying to the court, should he feel it necessary to do so, before permitting the inspection.

In the circumstances of the present case, all those conditions to my mind are satisfied, and this order is essential in the interests of justice.

I agree, therefore, that the appeal should be allowed."

Columbia Picture Industries Inc. v. Robinson
[1987] Ch 38

The plaintiffs obtained an *Anton Piller* order which was executed at both a business premises and at one of the defendant's homes. A number of documents and items were taken which had not been included in the order and subsequently the defendants ceased trading. The defendants then brought a motion seeking to have the order set aside and an award of damages. Scott J declined to set aside the order as it had already been executed and there was no practical advantage in doing so but awarded damages to the defendant.

SCOTT J stated at pp.68–77: "This is in many ways the most important part of this case. The damage done by the defendants to the plaintiffs' intellectual property rights are, of course, very important to the plaintiffs and I hope I have dealt with them accordingly. But the defendants' complaints regarding the manner in which the *Anton Piller* order was obtained and executed raise questions of general importance concerning the administration of justice.

Before I come to deal with the specific complaints made by the defendants in this case I should, I think, review the state of the law and practice relating to *Anton Piller* orders. The grant of *Anton Piller* orders dates from 1974. The first reported case was one in which an order was made by Templeman J. in *E.M.I. Ltd. v. Pandit* [1975] 1 WLR 302. The practice received the imprimatur of the Court of Appeal in the case which has given its name to the orders, *Anton Piller KG v. Manufacturing Processes Ltd.* [1976] Ch 55. In that case the rationale of *Anton Piller* orders was described by Lord Denning M.R. in these words, at p. 60:

> "Let me say at once that no court in this land has any power to issue a search warrant to enter a man's house so as to see if there are papers or documents there which are of an incriminating nature, whether libels or infringements of copyright or anything else of the kind. No constable or bailiff can knock at the door and demand entry so as to inspect papers or documents. The householder can shut the door in his face and say 'Get out.' That was established in the leading case of *Entick v. Carrington* (1765) 2 Wils KB 275. None of us would wish to whittle down that principle in the slightest. But the order sought in this case is not a search warrant. It does not authorise the plaintiffs' solicitors or anyone else to enter the defendants' premises against their will. It does not authorise the breaking down of any doors, nor the slipping in by a back door, nor getting in by an open door or window. It only authorises entry and inspection by permission of the defendants. The plaintiffs must get the defendants' permission. But it does do this: it brings pressure on the defendants to give permission. It does more. It actually orders them to give permission with, I suppose, the result that if they do not give permission they are guilty of contempt of court. This may seem to be a search warrant in disguise. But it was fully considered in the House of Lords 150 years ago and held to be legitimate."

Lord Denning M.R. then went on to consider the circumstances in which an *Anton Piller* order could properly be made. He said, at p. 61:

> "It seems to me that such an order can be made by a judge ex parte, but it should only be made where it is essential that the plaintiff should have inspection so that justice can be done between the parties: and when, if the defendant were forewarned, there is a grave danger that vital evidence will be destroyed, that papers will be burnt or lost or hidden, or taken beyond the jurisdiction, and so the ends of justice be defeated: and when the inspection would do no real harm to the defendant or his case."

A little later on Lord Denning M.R. said of the practice, at p. 61:

"We are prepared, therefore, to sanction its continuance, but only in an extreme case where there is grave danger of property being smuggled away or of vital evidence being destroyed."

Ormrod L.J. said, at p. 62:

"There are three essential pre-conditions for the making of such an order, in my judgment. First, there must be an extremely strong prima facie case. Secondly, the damage, potential or actual, must be very serious for the applicant. Thirdly, there must be clear evidence that the defendants have in their possession incriminating documents or things, and that there is a real possibility that they may destroy such material before any application inter partes can be made."

Finally, Shaw L.J. said, at p. 62:

"The overriding consideration in the exercise of this salutary jurisdiction is that it is to be resorted to only in circumstances where the normal processes of the law would be rendered nugatory if some immediate and effective measure was not available. When such an order is made, the party who has procured the court to make it must act with prudence and caution in pursuance of it."

The practice of granting *Anton Piller* orders was considered obliquely by the House of Lords in *Rank Film Distributors Ltd. v. Video Information Centre* [1982] AC 380. It was approved in principle. Lord Fraser of Tullybelton said, at p. 444:

"The first four respondents are alleged to be dealers in pirated copies of many of these films, and the fifth and sixth respondents are alleged to be makers of pirate copies. The appellants are naturally concerned to protect their valuable copyright in these films. Ordinary actions against dealers in illicit films are of little avail to the copyright owners because the dealers are unlikely to be able to pay substantial damages and injunctions against them merely close down one outlet for the films and do not prevent the manufacture of more unauthorised copies which can then be sold through other outlets. The main concern of the appellants is, therefore, to trace the whereabouts of the master tapes in order to take action against those who control them. For this purpose a form of order has been devised which is generally referred to as an *Anton Piller* order, from the case of *Anton Piller KG v. Manufacturing Processes Ltd.* [1976] Ch 55. These orders are only made when the plaintiff produces strong prima facie evidence of infringement of his copyright. They are made on the ex parte application of the plaintiff, are served on the defendants without previous notice and order the defendants to make immediate discovery of documents and to give immediate answers to interrogatories designed to find out particularly the names and addresses of their suppliers."

There is, accordingly, no doubt at all but that *Anton Piller* orders have become established as part of the tools of the administration of justice in civil cases. It may be thought, as, I think, Lord Denning M.R. thought, that they play a part not unlike that played by search warrants in the area of crime and suspected crime. But the legitimate purposes of Anton Piller orders are clearly identified by the leading cases which have established the legitimacy of their use. One, and perhaps the most usual purpose, is to preserve evidence necessary for the plaintiff's case. *Anton Piller* orders are used to prevent a defendant, when warned of impending litigation, from destroying all documentary evidence in his possession which might, were it available, support the plaintiff's cause of action. Secondly, *Anton Piller* orders are often used in order to track to its source and obtain the possession of the master tape or master plate or blueprint by means of which reproductions in breach of copyright are being made. This purpose is, perhaps, no more than a sub-division of the first.

It is implicit in the nature of *Anton Piller* orders that they should be applied for ex parte and dealt with by the courts in secrecy. In the Queen's Bench Division applications for *Anton Piller* orders are heard in chambers. Secrecy is ensured. In this division applications are heard in court but it is customary for the court to sit in camera. Otherwise there is a risk that the defendant may become aware of the litigation and the whole purpose of the *Anton Piller* procedure will be frustrated.

Anton Piller orders and procedure have, therefore, these characteristics: no notice to the defendant of what is afoot, and secrecy. A third and, perhaps, the most significant feature of *Anton Piller* orders is that they are mandatory in form and are designed for immediate execution. The respondent to the order is required by the order to permit his premises to be entered and searched and, under most if not all orders, to permit the plaintiff's solicitors to remove into the solicitors' custody articles covered by the order.

Further, *Anton Piller* orders are almost invariably accompanied by *Mareva* injunctions freezing the bank accounts of the respondent and restraining him from making any disposition of his assets. *Anton Piller* orders and *Mareva* injunctions granted ex parte always reserve liberty for the respondent to apply on short notice for them to be discharged. This provides a reasonable safeguard in the case of *Mareva* injunctions. They can be lifted on very short notice. Harm may already have been done but can be expected to be of a limited nature. But in relation to any *Anton Piller* order, the liberty to apply to have it discharged is of little, if any, value to the respondent. He does not know the order has been made until it has been served upon him. At the same time as the order is served, the respondent comes under an immediate obligation to consent to the entry onto and search of his premises and the removal of material from his premises specified by the order. If he does not consent, he is at risk of committal to prison for contempt of court. This is so even if the reason for his refusal to consent is his intention to apply to have the order discharged.

The peril in which respondents to *Anton Piller* orders are placed is exemplified by *Wardle Fabrics Ltd. v. G. Myristis Ltd.* [1984] FSR 263. There the plaintiffs had obtained an *Anton Piller* order. The defendant company by its managing director refused consent to the entry on to its premises that the order required, and applied for the order to be discharged on the ground that all material facts had not been disclosed to the court by the plaintiffs when applying for the order. The plaintiffs applied to punish the defendant and its managing director for contempt in failing to obey the *Anton Piller* order. Goulding J., on the defendant's application, found the allegations of inadequate disclosure made out and discharged the *Anton Piller* order. On the plaintiffs' application for contempt, Goulding J. found the contempt proved and, after contemplating fining the defendant and its managing director, dealt with the contempt by requiring them to pay the plaintiffs' costs of the contempt application on an indemnity basis. Goulding J. said, at p. 271:

> "What is the position in those circumstances? In the absence of authority, and if I were free to look at the matter from first principles, I would have thought that if the court makes an order within its jurisdiction, by which I mean in such circumstances that the purported order is not a nullity in law, then a party is bound to obey it at his risk of contempt proceedings if he does not, and that the subsequent discharge of the order as having been irregularly obtained would not in logic and principle affect the disobedient party's liability to penalties for contempt. It seems to me the system of administering justice would break down if the subjects were entitled to apply their own or their advisers' ideas to the possibilities of subsequently setting aside an order and to disobey on the strength of such private judgment and then, if the judgment turned out not to have been right, be free from all penalty."

Goulding J.'s reasoning is, if I may respectfully say so, difficult to fault. Moreover, if respondents to *Anton Piller* orders were to be allowed to delay their execution while applications to apply to discharge were being made, the purpose of *Anton Piller* orders and procedure would be largely lost. Ample time would then be available to those disposed to destroy evidence or to secrete away master tapes to do so.

But notice the position that *Anton Piller* procedure, and its logical consequences, produces: a mandatory order is made in the absence of the respondent and in secret; it is served upon and executed against the respondent without his having any chance to challenge the correctness of its grant or to challenge the evidence on which it was granted.

Now let the possible and, perhaps, probable effects of an *Anton Piller* order be considered. The order is served and executed. If the order is in the terms of the order in the present case and is executed as it was in the present case, there will be a wholesale removal of all business material, whether stock-in-trade, bank statements, cheque books or correspondence. The continuance of the business by the respondent to the order is thereby made impossible. How can a business be continued without records? How can it be continued without stock-in-trade? It will be recalled that, in the present case, the order authorised the removal of, inter alia, the video recorders at 8, Frederick Street. They were not, in the event, removed but, if they had been, the whole of Mr. Robinson's copying business would for that reason alone have been closed down. It is customary, on account of the *Mareva* injunction accompanying *Anton Piller* orders, for a copy of the order to be served on the respondent's bankers. That was done in the present case. The almost certain effect of that being done will be that the bankers will decline to allow any further credit to the respondent. The order will throw such a question mark over the business of the respondent as to make any other course commercially imprudent and, therefore, unlikely. In the present case, Barclays Bank, upon service of the order, refused to allow the defendants any further credit.

The service and execution of an *Anton Piller* order is likely to have on a respondent a personal as well as a commercial effect. *Anton Piller* orders are often granted not simply in respect of business premises but in respect of the respondent's home. He is required, on pain of committal, to open the doors of his house to the plaintiffs' representatives and to permit a search of the contents thereof. The plaintiffs and their representatives are at liberty to search and rummage through the personal belongings of any occupant of the house and to remove the material they consider to be covered by the terms of the order. The traumatic effect and the sense of outrage likely to be produced by an invasion of home territory in the execution of an *Anton Piller* order is obvious.

When, in 1974 and shortly thereafter, *Anton Piller* orders became established weapons to combat, inter alia, copyright piracy, it was supposed that they would be relatively infrequently granted. They lay, it was said, at the very limit of the in personam jurisdiction proper to be exercised by the courts. But, since 1974, Hamlins have obtained and executed, I was told, some 300 *Anton Piller* orders, 200 in audio piracy cases and about 100 in video piracy cases. Other firms of solicitors may perhaps be able to match those figures. *Anton Piller* orders are not rarities at all. They are regularly applied for and granted in all the divisions of the High Court. In no case previously, I was told, had the propriety of the obtaining and execution of an *Anton Piller* order been examined otherwise than in interlocutory proceedings. I was told by one or other of the Hamlins witnesses – it matters not which – that this is the first case in the experience of that firm which has come to a full trial after the grant and execution of an *Anton Piller* order. This case provides, therefore, an opportunity, after a full hearing and after oral evidence from all the relevant participants, for a long, careful look at *Anton Piller* procedure and at the manner in which it is operating. It justifies, in my judgment, very grave disquiet.

It has to be accepted that a common, perhaps the usual, effect of the service and execution of an *Anton Piller* order is to close down the business which, on the applicants' evidence, is being carried on in violation of their rights. Mr. Cumberland, Hamlins' experienced legal executive, accepted this. In the transcript of 12 July there is the exchange between him and Mr. Beveridge to which I have already referred. But the question whether a business, alleged by applicants for an *Anton Piller* order to be illicit, is in fact illicit or is genuine cannot ordinarily be answered until final judgment. Given that none of the many *Anton Piller* cases with which Mr. Cumberland had been concerned has ever come to trial, his answers must be read as meaning that an *Anton Piller* order and its execution have the effect of closing down the business, which the plaintiffs have, on the ex parte application, satisfied the judge is, prima facie, an illicit business.

It is a fundamental principle of civil jurisprudence in this country that citizens are not to be deprived of their property by judicial or quasi-judicial order without a fair hearing. Audi alterem partem is one of the principles of natural justice and contemplates a hearing at which the defendant can, if so advised, be represented and heard. As was said by Isaacs J. in *Thomas A. Edison Ltd. v. Bullock* (1912) 15 CLR 679, 681, in a passage cited by Slade L.J. in *Bank Mellat v. Nikpour* [1985] FSR 87, 92, and by Whitford J. in *Jeffrey Rogers Knitwear Productions Ltd. v. Vinola (Knitwear) Manufacturing Co.* [1985] FSR 184, 187:

> "There is a primary precept governing the administration of justice, that no man is to be condemned unheard; and, therefore, as a general rule, no order should be made to the prejudice of a party unless he has the opportunity of being heard in defence."

What is to be said of the *Anton Piller* procedure which, on a regular and institutionalised basis, is depriving citizens of their property and closing down their businesses by orders made ex parte, on applications of which they know nothing and at which they cannot be heard, by orders which they are forced, on pain of committal, to obey, even if wrongly made?

There are some possible answers to this criticism of *Anton Piller* orders and their effect. One is that every *Anton Piller* order records an undertaking by the applicants who have obtained it to compensate the respondent for any damage caused to him by the order and for which the court thinks the plaintiff ought to pay. This is theoretically a valuable safeguard. In the present case the defendants are seeking compensation under just such an undertaking. But, in my judgment, it does not meet the main objection to *Anton Piller* procedure. The main objection to the procedure is that the orders made produce for the respondents damaging and irreversible consequences without any hearing at which they can be heard. The respondents may lack the means or the strength of purpose to pursue the applicants for relief under the undertaking in damages. And even villains ought not to be deprived of their property by proceedings at which they cannot be heard.

The second comment is that which Mr. Cumberland gave in the course of his cross-examination. *Anton Piller* orders, he said, are not sought by his firm against innocent persons. Mr. Hoffman, too, emphasised in his evidence the care with which Hamlins satisfy themselves, before applying for *Anton Piller* orders, that the proposed objects of *Anton Piller* procedure have been engaged in piratical activities. This comment serves, in my opinion, not to mitigate but to underline the dangers inherent in ex parte procedure and, a fortiori, ex parte procedure where the object is to obtain a mandatory order intended for immediate execution.

It is the experience of Hamlins that, when they apply for *Anton Piller* orders, they almost invariably succeed in getting them. Mr. Beveridge asked Mr. Cumberland how many applications for *Anton Piller* orders had, in his experience with the firm, resulted in failure. Mr. Cumberland's answer was, "None." This answer did not surprise me. Hamlins are a very experienced firm in this field and they employ experienced and competent counsel. Once they have satisfied themselves that an application for an *Anton Piller* order ought to be made, it is to be expected that the application will be prepared and presented to the court in a form and manner that is likely to be successful. I do not imply in that remark any impropriety on the part of solicitors or counsel concerned. There is nothing inconsistent with, on the one hand, the discharge of the duty of full disclosure and, on the other hand, the presentation of the material in a manner likely to satisfy a judge that the application ought to be granted.

But the effect of this state of affairs is that it is the solicitors and counsel acting for the plaintiffs who take perhaps the critical decision. I have myself on many occasions read the material in support of a plaintiff's application for an interlocutory injunction and have formed the view that the application ought to succeed; but then, on reading the material put forward by the defendant in opposition to the grant of an injunction, have changed my mind. This is not because the plaintiff's affidavits have omitted relevant material. It is rather an indication of how the same material may be differently presented depending on the interest of the presenter. It underlines the need, if justice is to be done, for a defendant to have an opportunity to be heard.

The criticism that *Anton Piller* orders produce damaging and irreversible consequences for respondents without their having an opportunity to be heard is not, in my judgment, answered by pointing to the care that the plaintiffs' legal advisers take to ensure that the innocent are not pursued.

The third comment is that respondents are safeguarded by the duties of full disclosure that the solicitors and counsel acting for the applicant owe to the court and that execution of *Anton Piller* orders is customarily required to be supervised by solicitors. This comment underlines, in my view, the unsatisfactory position in which the *Anton Piller* procedure places solicitors and, to a lesser extent, since they depend on solicitors for their instructions, counsel. The solicitors are retained by and owe a duty to their clients, the applicants. They satisfy themselves that their clients' interests require the protection of an *Anton Piller* order and are instructed by their clients to obtain one. They have a duty to see that full disclosure is made to the court of any relevant evidence. But relevance and irrelevance are not matters of white and black. There is usually a grey area of arguable relevance and arguable irrelevance. What is a solicitor's duty in respect of evidence falling into the grey area? It is to be borne in mind that the solicitor, when taking his decision as to what is relevant to be included in the affidavits in support of the *Anton Piller* application, will be likely already to have satisfied himself, as his clients will have been satisfied, that the respondent is a rogue against whom an *Anton*

Piller order ought to be granted. The solicitor does not, and cannot be expected to present the available evidence from the respondent's point of view.

Finally, it may be pointed out that an *Anton Piller* order always contains a liberty for the respondent to apply on short notice for the order to be set aside. But this cannot in practice be done until after the order has been executed. In order to obtain back his business records and place his business once more in a viable position, the respondent to the order has to make a successful application to the court. There are often very real financial difficulties which stand in his way. As happened in the present case, the respondent's bankers may, on learning of the order, have cut off his funds. The obtaining of legal aid may not be possible and, even if possible, may involve lengthy delays. And the will of a respondent to take on a powerful and determined opponent in expensive litigation may waver. The respondent, often with very good reason, may lack confidence in the successful outcome of the litigation.

These answers to the criticism of *Anton Piller* procedure do not, in my opinion, match the force of the criticism. There is and can be no adequate substitute for the right of a person against whom immediate mandatory judicial relief is sought to appear and be heard at the judicial hearing which deals with the matter. But this is not possible where *Anton Piller* procedure is concerned.

I have made these general comments about *Anton Piller* orders not for the purpose of casting doubts on the jurisdiction of the court to make them nor for the purpose of casting doubt on the propriety, in appropriate cases, of *Anton Piller* orders being granted. But a decision whether or not an *Anton Piller* order should be granted requires a balance to be struck between the plaintiff's need that the remedies allowed by the civil law for the breach of his rights should be attainable and the requirement of justice that a defendant should not be deprived of his property without being heard. What I have heard in the present case has disposed me to think that the practice of the court has allowed the balance to swing much too far in favour of plaintiffs and that *Anton Piller* orders have been too readily granted and with insufficient safeguards for respondents.

The Draconian and essentially unfair nature of *Anton Piller* orders from the point of view of respondents against whom they are made requires, in my view, that they be so drawn as to extend no further than the minimum extent necessary to achieve the purpose for which they are granted, namely, the preservation of documents or articles which might otherwise be destroyed or concealed. Anything beyond that is, in my judgment, impossible to justify. For example, I do not understand how an order can be justified that allows the plaintiffs' solicitors to take and retain all relevant documentary material and correspondence. Once the plaintiffs' solicitors have satisfied themselves what material exists and have had an opportunity to take copies thereof, the material ought, in my opinion, to be returned to its owner. The material need be retained no more than a relatively short period of time for that purpose.

Secondly, I would think it essential that a detailed record of the material taken should always be required to be made by the solicitors who execute the order before the material is removed from the respondent's premises. So far as possible, disputes as to what material was taken, the resolution of which depends on the oral testimony and credibility of the solicitors on the one hand and the respondent on the other hand, ought to be avoided. In the absence of any corroboration of a respondent's allegation that particular material, for instance, divorce papers, was taken, a solicitor's sworn and apparently credible denial is likely always to be preferred. This state of affairs is unfair to respondents. It ought to be avoided so far as it can be.

Thirdly, no material should, in my judgment, be taken from the respondent's premises by the executing solicitors unless it is clearly covered by the terms of the order. In particular, I find it wholly unacceptable that a practice should have grown up whereby the respondent to the order is procured by the executing solicitors to give consent to additional material being removed. In view of the circumstances in which *Anton Piller* orders are customarily executed (the execution is often aptly called "a raid"), I would not, for my part, be prepared to accept that an apparent consent by a respondent had been freely and effectively given unless the respondent's solicitor had been present to confirm and ensure that the consent was a free and informed one.

Fourthly, I find it inappropriate that seized material the ownership of which is in dispute, such as allegedly pirate tapes, should be retained by the plaintiffs' solicitors pending the trial. Although officers of the court, the main role of solicitors for plaintiffs is to act for the plaintiffs. If the proper administration of justice requires that material taken under an *Anton Piller* order from defendants should, pending trial, be kept from the defendants, then those responsible for the administration of justice might reasonably be expected to provide a neutral officer of the court charged with the custody of the material. In lieu of any such officer, and there is none at present, the plaintiffs' solicitors ought, in my view, as soon as solicitors for the defendants are on the record, to be required to deliver the material to the defendants' solicitors on their undertaking for its safe custody and production, if required, in court.

Finally, the nature of *Anton Piller* orders requires that the affidavits in support of applications for them ought to err on the side of excessive disclosure. In the case of material falling into the grey area of possible relevance, the judge, not the plaintiffs' solicitors, should be the judge of relevance. Whitford J., whose experience in these matters probably exceeds that of any other first instance judge, has recently drawn attention to the particular importance of full disclosure on *Anton Piller* applications. In the *Jeffrey Rogers Knitwear* case [1985] FSR 184 Whitford J. said, at p. 189:

> "I wholly reject the suggestion . . . that when seeking an *Anton Piller* order there is no need to investigate the question whether or not in the absence of an order there is a real possibility that infringing material or evidence will be done away with. Any plaintiff seeking an *Anton Piller* order must place before the court all the information they have relating to the circumstances of the defendant which

they can suggest points to the probability that in the absence of an *Anton Piller* order material which should be available will disappear."

Microsoft Corporation v. Brightpoint Ireland Ltd
[2001] 1 ILRM 540

The plaintiff companies which carried on the business of software development and production instituted proceedings against the defendant company alleging copyright infringement, trade mark infringement and passing off. The plaintiffs sought and obtained an *Anton Piller* order requiring the defendant to deliver up infringing copies of the plaintiff's computer programmes and allowing representatives of the plaintiffs to enter the defendant's premises for the purpose of inspecting and preserving copies of software and documents. Following execution of the order the parties applied for various reliefs. Smyth J granted the relief sought by the plaintiffs and refused the relief sought by the defendant save for an order restraining the parties from communicating in the media any matter relating to the action pending its final determination.

SMYTH J stated at pp.545–552:

"(C) The Anton Piller order, obtained ex parte
The essence of this order is surprise. In the instant case it was granted in the following terms:

And IT IS ORDERED that the defendant its servants or agents do forthwith:

(a) deliver up all infringing copies of the plaintiffs' computer programs and any other copies of works which are or appear to be infringing copies whether they be on the hard disk of computers, central processing units or held in any form whether on floppy disk, compact disk, tape or any form whatsoever which are in the possession, custody or control of the defendant its servants or agents to the plaintiffs or their authorised agent.

(b) allow representatives of the plaintiffs to enter onto the defendant's premises for the purposes of the inspection, detention and preservation of all copies of Microsoft Office 95, Microsoft Office 97, Microsoft Exchange 5.5, Microsoft Outlook, Windows N.T., Norton Anti-Virus and P.C. Anywhere which are or appear to be infringing copies and also all documents in relation thereto which are in the control, possession or procurement of the defendant, its servants or agents together with books, records, agreements, letters, correspondence, accounts, cheques, receipts and credit notes.

On the matter coming on before Quirke J it is recorded that there was apparently no one from the press or media in court. Mr Nesbitt SC for the defendant submits that it is of the essence that the *ex parte* application is conducted *in camera.* I reject this submission for the following reasons:

(a) There is a constitutional obligation (Article 34.1) that:

> Justice shall be administered in courts established by law by judges appointed in the manner provided by the Constitution, and, save in such special and limited cases as may be prescribed by law, shall be administered in public.

(b) Certain exceptions to this general requirement (e.g. s. 205(7) of the Companies Act 1963 considered and determined by the Supreme Court in *In re R. Ltd* [1989] IR 126 and statutes touching upon family law matters) have from time to time been prescribed by statute.

(c) Subject to the constitutional requirement and settled case law, there may be occasions (necessarily rare) where in the interests of justice and for good and proper reason a judge may direct a hearing *in camera.*

(d) In exercising its inherent jurisdiction a judge sitting in open court may direct or limit or inhibit publication of the order made in open court.

The publication of the existence (not to mind the exact contents) of an *Anton Piller* order in advance of its execution could weaken or deprive it of the element of surprise. The defendant submits and the case law (*Columbia Picture Industries Inc. v. Robinson* [1987] Ch 38) sustains the view that an affidavit in support of the application for the order ought to err on the side of excessive disclosure, because in the case of material which falls into the area of possible relevance, the judge, and not the plaintiffs or their advisors should be the judge of relevance. In this regard it is contended that there were three important elements of non-disclosure:

(a) The status or size of the defendant and its operation.

Notwithstanding the legal biographical details of the defendant at paragraphs 5 and 6 of Mr Doak's affidavit of 15 June 2000 and his assertion in paragraph 7 that the defendant is part of an established and reputable group of companies, I am satisfied that Mr Woodley's affidavit of 2 June when read with its exhibits indicates that the defendant is an operation of substance and significance. Furthermore the question of licences was a live issue in December 1999 and April 2000.

(b) The full to true status of Mr Woodley is not disclosed.

Assuming the relevance of this matter, I am satisfied from the tenor of Mr Woodley's affidavit and his ceasing to be employed by the defendant as of 12 April 2000 (paragraph (ii) of his affidavit) and Mr O'Connor's averments in paragraphs 22 and 23 of his affidavit (of 2 June 2000) that a judge would have no difficulty in drawing the clear inference that Mr Woodley was a disaffected former employee. The provision of relevant information does not impose an obligation to be exhaustive. This case is clearly distinguishable from the *Columbia Pictures* case where the affidavit failed to disclose Mr Robinson's role as an informant [1987] Ch 38 (at p. 54(d)).

(c) No grounds of fear of destruction are advanced to warrant the intervention of the court.

In my judgment Mr O'Connor's affidavit at paragraphs 23, 24, 25, 26, 28 and 29 seem reasoned deductions from opinions formed on the actual facts averred to. In the nature of the expression of an apprehension there is an element of speculation: that is not to say that the court should be moved on a hunch of the plaintiff. In the instant case there were problems for months prior to 2 June 2000 – there are still problems with the licences. In my judgment a court could come to the view on the affidavits that the fact that the defendant was operating without licences would not be something it would wish to be discovered and understandably (if it valued its reputation and business, as it did) might well seek to dispose of any unfavourable records of such operations. Generally commercial enterprises do not maintain for inspection by third parties, especially potential adversaries, confessional records of wrongs done by themselves.

In my judgment there was such full and proper disclosure as the circumstances of the case warranted to seek and obtain an *Anton Piller* order, which was to the purpose and not unduly wide in its terms. I am satisfied that there was strong *prima facie* evidence of dishonest conduct by the defendant which indicated a strong probability that it would be likely to destroy the records (e.g *Tate Access Floors Inc. v. Boswell* [1991] Ch 512 (at p. 532)).

(D) The execution of the Anton Piller order
The complaint of the defendant is that the order was oppressively and excessively executed.

The application was sought and obtained in the time scale set out in Mr O'Connor's affidavit of 22 June 2000, paragraph 4. I am unconvinced that the plaintiffs and their solicitor sought deliberately to disadvantage the defendant to the greatest degree possible in the whole timescale of the application and the implementation of the order.

In my judgment the period between 14 April 2000 when it came to Mr O'Connor's attention 'that the defendants . . . were using unauthorised illegal copies . . .', and 2 June 2000 when the application to court was made is not a delay such as would disentitle injunctive relief. A reasonable time to gather the facts, perhaps assess Mr Woodley as a witness, the engagement of counsel, allowing for the Easter Holidays, indicate a timescale similar to that in the *Columbia Pictures* case. There is no good time for a defendant to receive an *Anton Piller* order. The conflict of evidence on the occasion of the execution of the order can only be resolved by an oral hearing and I am not disposed to setting aside an order of the court in the circumstances of this conflict. The *Columbia Pictures* case was determined after a full and oral hearing of several weeks. It would be improper of me to express any view on the conflict of evidence given its extent.

I am unable to accept that the servicing of the order was irregular and as to the time of its execution it is clear that immediate effect was given to it. The question of obtaining legal advice was raised before any inspection took place and while a defendant to an *Anton Piller* order has no real choice but to comply with it, Mr Doak's attitude (as conveyed in paragraph 31 of his affidavit of 15 June 2000) was:

> I advised Mr O'Connor that the defendant had nothing to hide from Microsoft, and that the defendant was prepared to fully co-operate.

That attitude accords with Mr O'Connor's record of paragraph (31) of his affidavit of 22 June 2000: 'Mr Doak confirmed to me that he understood the reason why I was there and the terms of the order and declined the opportunity to seek legal advice.'

Submissions were made on behalf of the defendant, that the plaintiffs, through their agent(s) failed to advise the defendant (through its officers and/ or employees) as to its right against self-incrimination. As the pleadings stand at the moment there is no plea of fraud or conspiracy. Amongst the cases cited in support of this contention is *Access Floors Inc. v. Boswell* [1991] Ch 512 (at pp. 527-532)) which in the judgment of Sir Nicholas Browne-Wilkinson VC (as he then was), considered the question 'Was there a risk of self-incrimination?' and in the 'conclusion' of his judgment he declined to set aside the *Anton Piller* order as against the company defendants since no one had shown any risk of the company defendants being incriminated. Mr Doak insists that the company is compliant with the law; if he is correct and so found to be on a full hearing then self-incrimination simply cannot arise. Accordingly this is not a basis for setting aside the *Anton Piller* order.

In the matter of records, the following brief extracts from the papers seem appropriate:

1. Mr Doak's affidavit of 23 June 2000 states at paragraph 8:

> The main concern of the defendant is to have this matter litigated in court, and its rights and the liabilities of the plaintiffs determined at the soonest possible opportunity.

2. At paragraph 11 of the same affidavit, he avers:

> At present a very small percentage of the programs the subject of this claim are programs for which a licence is not yet physically available or in respect of which no evidence exists to show the program does in fact enjoy a licence. The time and effort now being spent searching out documents from storage to complete the licence trail is now becoming uneconomic. The cost is greatly disproportionate to the cost of buying the latest version of the software. Rather than continue this disproportionately expensive (in terms of time and cost) search I am minded to simply buy new programs. I do not make this statement as an admission that licences do not exist, but rather to underscore the fact that the

allegation of international copyright infringements is quite misplaced. The defendant is a compliant company when it comes to its licence obligations. Any inability to produce licences now is for an innocent reason and does not mean the program is unlicensed. If it proves impossible to establish the whereabouts of the few outstanding program licences within the next four weeks, the defendant intends to purchase new programs or delete its old programs.

3. Mr O'Leary in his affidavit of 25 June 2000 at paragraph 12(1) under the title 'office' noted that he has 'not yet been able to locate the licences'.

4. Mr Delaney in his affidavit of 23 June, avers (at paragraph 5):

> I say that even allowing for the documentation furnished by the defendant on 16 June 2000 and comparing same to the results of my inspection of the disks containing the results of the search on 2 June 2000 the defendant has significant shortfalls in respect of licences in particular in relation to Microsoft Office and is substantially not in compliance with his licensing obligations. . . .

Mr Delaney's supplemental affidavit contains a reply to Mr Doak's second affidavit and Mr O'Leary's affidavit clearly raises very serious issues of new compliance.

5. While it might have been a sensible thing at the time of inspection for an agreed list or inventory of the copy documents taken to have been made and signed, there was no obligation on the plaintiffs to provide a list as requested in the defendant's solicitor's letter of 9 June 2000. However, the tone of the plaintiffs' solicitor's letter of 12 June 2000 was an unhelpful response. As there is already an obligation to preserve all copies taken (under the *Anton Piller* order), the furnishing of a list was a courtesy that should have been accorded between officers of the court.

In my opinion the law on this issue is very properly put by Scott J in *Columbia Picture Industries v. Robinson* [1987] Ch 38 (at p.76):

> . . . it [is] essential that a detailed record of the material taken should always be required to be made by the solicitors who execute [an *Anton Piller* order] before the material is removed from the respondent's premises. So far as possible, disputes as to what material was taken, the resolution of which depends on the oral testimony and credibility of the solicitors on the one hand and the respondent on the other hand, ought to be avoided. In the absence of any corroboration of a respondent's allegation that particular material . . . was taken, a solicitor's sworn and apparently credible denial is likely always to be preferred. This state of affairs is unfair to respondents. It ought to be avoided so far as it can be.

(E) Conduct Post 2 June 2000

1. Mr Molly on behalf of BSA was a proper person to have attended the inspection. His interview with 'Good Morning Ireland' did not identify the defendant, and accordingly the defendant's submission of impropriety is rejected.

2.   If the report in 'Ireland on Sunday' is correct, and its content is not put in issue, it concludes: 'Representatives of Brightpoint were contacted by Ireland on Sunday to comment on the raid, but they did not return any calls.'

On the basis that an opportunity was given to the defendant to comment and none was forthcoming, I find no basis in law as at present advised for criticising the article.

3.   Subsequent to the order and search, a press release and item on the website of the plaintiffs informed those who might contact the website of the fact of the order, its date, the identity in effect of BSA and the defendant and that the purpose of the exercise was 'to seize and preserve evidence or *suspected* end-user piracy at Brightpoint and is the first *Anton Piller* raid conducted by the BSA in Ireland. End-user piracy involves the use of software in greater numbers than is permitted by the licences the relevant organisation has.'

The defendant's response was also of a public relations character suffused with a tone of moral outrage.

Both parties to the litigation would be much better served in devoting their energies and resources to either trying to resolve their differences by agreement or on foot of the 'liberty to apply' in the order of 2 June 2000 to both return to court and move the legal process forward.

I reject the defendant's submissions on implied undertakings; in effect this is to seek to import into this jurisdiction the legal rights, duties and responsibilities in England and Wales where legislative and rule provisions deal with the type of undertakings spoken of.

On the basis of the documentary evidence and information placed before me I am satisfied that the *Anton Piller* order was justified in its making and that the subsequent conduct in this case was not such as should or could be regarded as contemptuous (the standard of proof in which is 'beyond a reasonable doubt' *per* Keane J (as he then was) in *National Irish Bank Ltd v. Graham* [1994] 1 IR 215 at p.220) or scandalising the court or warrant the relief sought by the defendant. Notwithstanding the defendant's perception that the disclosure of the existence of the High Court order – a public document, being the written record of the decision made in open court, the manner of its publication was perhaps subjectively inappropriate, but it was not illegal or prohibited expressly or by implication nor in my opinion was it improper. The *Anton Piller* order and its extent is a matter of true fact, whether the evidence that supported the application at the e*x parte* stage will be sustained when tested at a hearing is another matter. It is unfortunate that the differences between the parties have been exacerbated by the engagement of press officers, public relations consultants or spin doctors. Having entrusted the dispute to the legal process both parties might make more progress in giving it their attention than engaging in charge and countercharge in 'the media'.

(F) The defendant's ex parte application

Notwithstanding the liberty to apply in the order of Quirke J the defendant after entering an appearance and having had correspondence with the plaintiffs' solicitor, applied *ex parte* to Herbert J. The explanation given to me was that the defendant was not entitled to go before the court under the order of Quirke J until the return day, and the defendant had to apply *ex parte* to seek the relief it wished to have. I regard this as spurious science. I say this notwithstanding the decision in *Columbia Picture Industries Inc. v. Robinson* [1987] Ch 38 at p. 71 *per* Scott J (as he then was):

> . . . in relation to any *Anton Piller* order, the liberty to apply to have it discharged is of little, if any, value to the respondent. He does not know the order has been made until it has been served on him. At the same time as the order is served, the respondent comes under an immediate obligation to consent to the entry onto and search of his premises and the removal of material from his premises specified by the order. If he does not consent, he is at risk of committal to prison for contempt of court. This is so even if the reason for his refusal to consent is his intention to apply to have the order discharged.

To the extent that a view can be formed on affidavit evidence and argument advanced at this stage (and it cannot be a concluded view given the controversies and conflicts to which I have alluded) I am of the opinion that it was the publication of the making of the order that fuelled the fires of discontent, more than that an order was sought and made, the search made and maybe the manner of the search and the tone of the letter of Mr O'Connor of 12 June 2000. However, proceedings were in being, an appearance entered, a known solicitor on record and there was nothing to prevent the type of application made *ex parte* before Herbert J from being on notice, with the defendant's entitlement to seek on the date of that application an abridgement of the time prescribed by the rules (if at all necessary), given the 'liberty to apply' in the order of Quirke J. The defendant did not have to await the return date in the order of Quirke J. In *Columbia Picture Industries Inc. v. Robinson* [1987] Ch 38 (at p. 86):

> The significance of the return date is that it provides a fixed date on which the respondent, if so advised, can apply to *vary* or *set aside* [the order first made]. It does not, in my judgment, preclude a respondent who does not take advantage of the return date from applying subsequently (emphasis added).

With or without an expressed 'liberty to apply' provision in the order of June 2000, in my judgment a court should be most responsive to a defendant/respondent in an appropriate case without waiting for the return date because of the nature of an *Anton Piller* order. I am left with the clearest impression that the second *ex parte* order was sought to try and off-set the first *ex parte* order. Court orders are not designed by the courts to be used as instruments of commercial warfare.

For the avoidance of further unnecessary doubt or controversy I order and direct that until the final determination of this action neither party 'directly or indirectly' through any other person or persons or body corporate or unincorporated make any communication in the print or broadcast media of the matters in issue in this suit and that if either has on its website any information whatsoever concerning this suit that same be erased and removed not later than 12 noon on Wednesday, 12 July 2000.

I dismiss the defendant's motion. I grant the interlocutory relief sought by the plaintiffs.

Costs – Plaintiffs' *ex parte* and two-thirds of this interlocutory application against defendant – defendant's motion – bear its own costs of the *ex parte* and this motion.

       – but no execution until final determination."

CHAPTER 14

Specific Performance

GENERAL DISCRETIONARY PRINCIPLES

Conlan v. Murray
[1958] NI 17

The plaintiff brought an action for specific performance of a contract for the sale of a farm against the vendor which was continued against her executors after her death. The vendor was an elderly lady who had agreed to the sale in a distressed state without taking any time for reflection and without the benefit of independent advice. While Black LJ acknowledged that specific performance of a contract will not be refused on the sole ground that one of the parties had not received legal advice, he expressed the opinion that in view of the 'extraordinary and unexplained haste' with which the transaction had been rushed through, the court should hesitate to decree specific performance. The Northern Irish Court of Appeal (Lord McDermott LCJ, Black LJ and Sheil J) affirmed the order of Curran J refusing the plaintiff's claim for specific performance.

BLACK LJ stated (at pp.25–27): "The remedy of specific performance still retains the character of an equitable remedy. It is not granted as of right but is a discretionary remedy which may be withheld in cases of a type where the court, having regard to the conduct of the parties and all the circumstances of the case, considers in its discretion that the remedy ought not to be granted. This discretion is not, of course, the arbitrary discretion of the individual judge but is a discretion to be exercised on the principles which have been worked out in a multitude of decided cases. And it is well established that there is a class of cases in which a contract may be such and entered into in such conditions that the court will not order it to be rescinded but, at the same time, looking to the substantial justice of the case, will not order it to be specifically performed. It follows naturally, as observed in Kerr on Fraud and Mistake, 7th ed. (1952) p. 568 that when the aid of a court is sought by way of specific performance of a contract the principles of ethics have a more extensive sway than when a contract is sought to be rescinded.

In the present case Mrs. Sheridan was 69 years of age and, although admitted to be mentally alert and vigorous, was suffering from two painful and weakening ailments. It is not surprising that after the trouble with her brother she should have an impulse to get rid of the responsibility of the house and the farm and express a readiness to sell it. This might prove a mere transitory mood or it might not. But the idea of selling the farm raised questions requiring deliberation and reflection. If the treatment which she might have to undergo was successful (and for all that she then knew it might have been) where was she to go to live when she came out of hospital? And what was to happen to her brother? Where was he to go to live if the farm was sold? Both of these were matters which required thoughtful and anxious consideration. But neither seems to have been mentioned or considered when the bargain was made in Mrs. Sheridan's bedroom on the night of May 25 and, whether one accepts Carahar's evidence or Conlon's, the question of what was to happen to the brother was not even raised until the agreement was actually being drafted by Carahar on the morning of May 26. The truth of the matter seems to be that in her plight on the night of May 24 the plaintiff impulsively accepted Collins' suggestion that she should sell her farm and that Collins and Conlon both recognised that this mood might well prove to be a transitory one and that if Conlon was to get the farm it behoved them to obtain Mrs. Sheridan's signature to a document without delay. Conlon seems to have first heard of the opportunity from Collins about 7 o'clock on the evening of May 25, and at 11 p.m. on the same evening – a peculiar hour for legitimate business – they visit Mrs. Sheridan in her bedroom and the bargain is made for the sale of the farm to Conlon at £2,000 – the figure mentioned by Collins the previous night – without any higgling or negotiation and without any mention of when possession would be given or that it would be necessary to put Toner out. Then on the next morning Mr. Carahar is brought out in a taxi paid for by Mr. Conlon to draft the necessary agreement. The reason why Mr. Carahar is brought is because Mrs. Sheridan regards Mr. O'Connor as her solicitor. But conceiving himself as being there as much in the interests of Mr. Conlon as of Mrs. Sheridan he inserts on his own volition (if his evidence on this point is to be accepted) a special clause in the agreement for the benefit of Conlon. I quite appreciate that specific performance of a contract will not be refused on the sole ground that one of the parties had not legal advice. A man can enter into a binding contract without having his solicitor at his elbow. But as Mr. O'Connor observed in his evidence, Mrs. Sheridan should have had independent legal advice in a transaction of this kind. And quite apart from any other consideration the way in which Mrs. Sheridan's expression of her willingness to sell the farm was jumped at by Collins and Conlon and the extraordinary and unexplained haste with which the transaction was rushed through raise of themselves such a degree of suspicion as would lead a court of Equity to be hesitant about granting specific performance of a contract concluded in such circumstances.

It was argued on behalf of the plaintiff that cases in which equity refuses the remedy of specific performance fall within one or other of certain defined categories. I cannot accept this view. Certainly equity acts on certain broad and ascertained principles but it has always refused to be forced into rigid categories. This is, I think, well stated in Story's Equity Jurisprudence 10th ed. (1870), vol. 1, p. 739: "In truth the exercise of this whole branch of equity jurisprudence respecting the rescission and specific performance of contracts is not a matter of right in either party; but it is a matter in the discretion of the Court, not indeed of arbitrary or capricious discretion, dependent upon the mere pleasure of the judge, but of that sound and reasonable discretion which governs itself so far as it may by general principles; but at the same time which witholds or grants relief according to the circumstances of each particular case, when these rules and principles will not furnish any exact measure of justice between the parties. On this account it is not possible to lay down any rules and principles which are of absolute obligation and authority in all cases; and, therefore, it would be a waste of time to attempt to limit the principles, or the exceptions, which the complicated transactions of the parties and the everchanging habits of society may at different times and under different circumstances require the Court to recognise or consider." A good instance of a case which it would be found difficult to fit into any of the suggested categories in which specific performance will be refused is the case *Twirling v. Morrice* (1788) 2 Bro CC 326 referred to in the course of the hearing.

I am accordingly of opinion that Curran J's judgment refusing the plaintiff's claim for specific performance should be affirmed."

SPECIFIC PERFORMANCE OF PARTICULAR TYPES OF CONTRACTS

Contracts for the Sale of Land

In order to successfully obtain specific performance of a contract for the sale of land where it is not in writing, certain requirements must be satisfied. First, it must be established that there is a concluded oral contract. Secondly, there must be a sufficient note or memorandum in writing to satisfy the Statute of Frauds (Ireland) 1695 or there must be a good reason why non-compliance with the Statute will be overlooked *viz.*, where to insist on strict compliance would facilitate a fraud or where there are sufficient acts of part performance.

Boyle v. Lee
[1992] 1 IR 555

In May 1988, an estate agent received instructions to put on the market for sale by private treaty the dwelling house and premises situated at No. 32 Elgin Road in the City of Dublin which were owned by the defendants. Negotiations took place between the estate agent and the first named plaintiff and the latter made an offer of £90,000 for the property which the defendants agreed to accept. The evidence showed that the plaintiff was aware that the premises had been converted into flats in a manner which contravened the planning code and that he had indicated to the estate agent that he was willing to waive this matter and was prepared to buy the property subject to the existing tenancies. It appeared that the question of a deposit had been discussed but that no sum had been agreed upon and that the estate agent had told the plaintiff that this question would be dealt with by the parties' solicitors. On 8 July 1988, the estate agent wrote to the vendors' solicitors confirming that his company had received instructions to accept the offer of £90,000 made by the plaintiff 'subject to contract' and setting out that the letter itself was for information purposes only and 'did not by itself constitute part of a binding contract'. The plaintiffs instituted proceedings on 11 November 1988 by plenary summons seeking specific performance of the agreement which it claimed had been concluded between the parties for the sale of the premises. Barrington J held in an *ex tempore* judgment delivered on 30 June 1989 that there had been a concluded oral agreement between the parties for the sale of the premises in question at a price of £90,000 prior to 8 July 1988 and set out the terms of the agreement as found by him. In addition, he held that there was a sufficient note or memorandum of the said oral agreement to satisfy the requirements of s. 2 of the Statute of Frauds (Ireland) 1695 contained in the letter from the estate agent to the vendors' solicitors dated 8 July 1988. The defendants appealed to the Supreme Court on the grounds that the learned trial judge had misdirected himself in law and on the facts in holding that the evidence supported or was capable of supporting a finding that prior to 8 July 1988 there was a concluded oral agreement between the parties and that the latter had erred in law in holding that the letter of that date constituted a sufficient note or memorandum of an oral agreement to satisfy the statutory requirements. The majority of the Supreme Court (Finlay CJ, Hederman and O'Flaherty JJ) allowed the defendant's appeal.

FINLAY CJ stated at pp.567–574: "The defendants appeal to this Court on two grounds:

(a) That the learned trial judge misdirected himself in law and on the facts in holding that the evidence supported or was capable of supporting a finding that prior to the 8th July, 1988, there was a concluded oral agreement for the sale of the premises at £90,000.

(b) That the learned trial judge erred in law in holding that the letter dated the 8th July, 1988, from Mr. McManus to Messrs. P.J. Walsh & Company constituted a sufficient note or memorandum of an oral agreement to satisfy the Statute of Frauds, 1695.

Defendants' submissions on this appeal
With regard to the first ground it is contended on behalf of the defendants that the following matters, separately or together, made it impossible to conclude, even accepting in full the first plaintiff's evidence, that there was a concluded and complete agreement between the parties for the sale of the premises. They

are (i) the absence of any agreement as to the amount of deposit to be paid by the purchaser, the time at which it was to be paid, or the terms under which it was to be held, (ii) the absence of any agreement with regard to the closing date to be provided in the contract for sale, (iii) the absence of any identification by schedule or otherwise of what were the contents of the house, (iv) the absence of any information of a detailed nature as to the precise terms of each of the tenancies in the flats contained in the premises, so as to identify the burden and benefit of tenancies which were being undertaken by the plaintiffs.

With regard to the issue of whether the letter of the 8th July, 1988, written to Mr. P.J. Walsh, solicitor, could constitute in law a sufficient note or memorandum for the purposes of the Statute of Frauds, 1695, the defendants' submissions were: (i) that the true legal test applicable to the sufficiency of the letter of the 8th July as a note or memorandum under the Statute of Frauds is to be found in a summary of the legal position appearing in the judgment of Keane J. in *Mulhall v. Haren* [1981] IR 364, at p. 386, where he stated as follows:

> "It appears to me that the wording of s. 2 of the Statute of 1695 plainly envisages a writing which is evidence of a contract entered into by the party sought to be charged, and that this is not met by writing which uses language inconsistent with the existence of a concluded contract. It also appears to me that a long line of authorities has clearly established that the use of the words 'subject to contract' is inconsistent with the existence of a concluded agreement, save in the most exceptional cases."

(ii) that this conclusion is not inconsistent with the decision of this Court in *Kelly v. Park Hall School* [1979] IR 340 and *Casey v. Irish Intercontinental Bank* [1979] IR 364 both of which should be considered as "exceptional cases" within this statement of principle, (iii) that this fact is confirmed in the course of the judgment of Henchy J. in *Carthy v. O'Neill* [1981] ILRM 443 and (iv) in the alternative, it was submitted on behalf of the defendants that if this Court should conclude that the decisions in either *Kelly v. Park Hall School* [1979] IR 340 or *Casey v. Irish Intercontinental Bank* [1979] IR 364 were inconsistent with the principle above set out, and taken from the judgment of Keane J. in *Mulhall v. Haren* [1981] I.R. 364 that this Court should review those two decisions and should not now follow them.

Submissions on behalf of the plaintiffs
On behalf of the plaintiffs it was submitted:

(1) With regard to the conclusion of an oral contract
  (a) that the learned trial judge found as a primary fact that a completed oral contract had been made, that there was evidence to support such a finding and that this Court cannot interfere with that finding,
  (b) that for a concluded contract for sale to have been made orally, as was alleged in this case, it was not necessary that every term of it should

have been spelt out, but only that the important or major terms, as viewed by the parties, should be concluded.

Having regard to that it was submitted that the failure to reach agreement on the amount of a deposit, in a case where it was agreed that the concluding of the sale should be as soon as possible and where the purchaser was aware of the usual provision for a deposit and in a position to pay it, was unimportant and irrelevant. It was further submitted that the evidence supported the finding of the learned trial judge that there was an agreement that the closing date should be as soon as possible after the completion of legal formalities which was a sufficiently precise closing date for a validly concluded contract.

With regard to issues such as the tenancies and the contents of the house it was submitted that, as far as the first plaintiff was concerned, he was clearly, on his evidence, prepared to take them as they were, whether they should be particularly advantageous or not, and that if he was prepared so to do, it could not lie in the vendors to assert that there was not a concluded contract because the purchaser had not pursued some matter which would have been peculiarly to his own advantage. With regard to the closing date, an alternative submission was also made that, in particular, in a case where an investment property was being sold that the necessity for a very specific closing date was nothing like as great or plausible as would occur in the sale of a residential property which a purchaser was going to occupy or with the sale of a shop or public house as a going concern.

(2) With regard to the question of the note or memorandum, it was submitted as follows:

(a) that once the learned High Court judge had concluded that a completed oral contract had been reached between the parties that the letter of the 8th July, 1988, was incapable of being distinguished on any point of principle from the letter found by this Court to be a sufficient note or memorandum in *Kelly v. Park Hall School* [1979] IR 340 and that that was a decision which this Court should follow. In the course of this submission it was pointed out that in considering the two letters the following was evident:

(i) each was written by an authorised agent who confirmed that he had agreed terms with the contracting party,

(ii) each set out the agreed terms,

(iii) each referred to "a proposed purchaser",

(iv) each stated the agreement was subject to contract, a phrase unilaterally introduced in each case by the author of the letter and not part of the oral agreement which had been concluded,

(v) each recorded all the essential terms which had been agreed.

Furthermore, in this context it is submitted that the decision in *Mulhall v. Haren* [1981] IR 364, though it purports to be applied to a case where the learned trial judge was satisfied that a concluded oral agreement was in existence which was complete, in fact, fails to distinguish two wholly separate methods of establishing an enforceable contract for the sale of land, having regard to the provisions of the Statute of Frauds, 1695.

Such an enforceable contract can arise from an agreement in writing, all the terms of which are contained in the writing and which is signed by the party to be charged therewith, or a person lawfully authorised by him to do so. In such an instance, it is submitted, of course the document must directly recognise or acknowledge the existence of an agreement, because the submission being made is that it constitutes the agreement. On the other hand an enforceable agreement, it is submitted, for the sale of land under the Act of 1695 can consist either of a wholly oral, concluded agreement, or an agreement partly oral and partly in writing, concluded and complete, in which instance all that is necessary is that the person to be charged therewith, or his agent, shall have written down in a document the essential terms of the concluded oral, or partly oral, agreement. In that instance, it is submitted, no express or implied recognition of the existence of a contract is necessary, the purpose of s. 2 of the Act of 1695 being evidential only.

In support of these contentions, in effect, the plaintiffs submitted that *Mulhall v. Haren* [1981] IR 364 must be interpreted as being a decision on the failure of proof of a concluded oral agreement, and not a decision as to the inadequacy of the note or memorandum under s. 2 of the Act of 1695, and if it is otherwise to be interpreted it is incorrectly decided.

In short, the contention between the parties with regard to s. 2 of the Act of 1695, apart from a consideration of the Irish cases to which I have referred, is to a large extent dependent on whether the views expressed by the Court of Appeal in *Law v. Jones* [1974] Ch 112 or the diametrically contradictory views expressed by the same court in *Tiverton Estates v. Wearwell Ltd.* [1975] Ch 146 are correct.

The decision

Completed oral contract
In the course of his judgment the learned trial judge stated that he believed both of the witnesses to be honest and candid in their evidence. His findings on the question as to whether an oral contract for sale had been made, and completely made, between the first plaintiff and Mr. McManus is based not, therefore, on the acceptance of the truth of one witness and the rejection of the truth or accuracy of another, but rather on inferences which he drew from the evidence. In particular, his finding that the failure of the parties to reach any agreement on the question of a deposit was irrelevant since it was of no importance in the contract, is a mixed finding of law and fact.

In my view, this finding was in error. The amount of a deposit to be made, even if a purchaser is willing to make a deposit of the appropriate amount, or the usual amount then experienced in transactions in Dublin, is too important a part of a contract for the sale of land in the large sum of £90,000 to be omitted from a concluded and complete oral agreement unless the parties in such an agreement had agreed that no deposit would be paid. In this case the evidence irresistibly leads to the conclusion that both the first plaintiff and Mr. McManus agreed that there had to be a deposit, but left it over to be agreed between the solicitors when the formal contract was being settled as to its amount and form. In my view, that evidence, which was not in contest, must lead to a conclusion that there was not a complete contract made orally between the first plaintiff and Mr. McManus before the 8th July, 1988.

That conclusion would determine this appeal, but since both parties have made the most careful and detailed submissions to this Court on the legal question arising with regard to the sufficiency of the note or memorandum, consisting of the letter written by Mr. McManus to Mr. Walsh, and since the submissions so made raise in question the meaning and effect of previous decisions of this Court, I am satisfied that I should express a view on the questions thus raised.

Adequacy of the note or memorandum
Section 2 of the Irish Statute of Frauds, 1695, in so far as its provisions are relevant to the issues in this action, is as follows:

> ". . . no action shall be brought whereby to charge . . . any person . . . upon any contract of sale of lands, tenements or hereditaments, or any interest in or concerning them . . . unless the agreement upon which such action shall be brought, or some memorandum or note thereof, shall be in writing, and signed by the party to be charged therewith, or some other person thereunto by him lawfully authorised."

I have carefully considered this section, and leaving aside for the moment the strength or weakness of contending decisions, it appears clear that the section required that the *agreement* with which the person concerned was to be charged had either to be in writing and signed by the party to be charged, or to be evidenced by some memorandum or note in writing, signed by the party to be charged. This must, it seems to me, inevitably lead to the conclusion that such of the decisions as speak of the necessity for the terms of be evidenced by a note or memorandum, or for the important terms, or necessary terms, to be so evidenced are, strictly speaking, incorrect.

It is obvious that in certain instances a total recital of all the necessary ingredients of a contract for the sale of land, that is to say, the names of the purchaser and the vendor, the exact description of the property and such other terms as would be considered essential, namely, the price, deposit, closing date, resumé of the title, etc., could without any other expression indicating an acknowledgement of a binding or completed contract, necessarily imply the existence of such a contract.

Where, however, on the other hand, a document which contains a recital of certain terms, obviously relevant to a purchase and sale of land, purports to deny the existence of a completed or concluded contract, or makes use of expressions specially adapted to exclude the existence of a completed or concluded contract, it does not seem to me that as a matter of first principle the terms of s. 2 of the Act of 1695 could be complied with.

The argument largely put against this strict interpretation, which is, of course, an acceptance of the broad statement of principle to which I have already referred, and which is contained in the judgment of Keane J. in *Mulhall v. Haren* [1981] IR 364, is that a party to an orally concluded agreement which is complete and intended to be complete, should not be permitted by the unilateral insertion into a note or memorandum in writing which he makes of the terms of that agreement, of a denial of it, or of a provision such as the phrase "subject to contract" which is inconsistent with it, to escape on his own behalf or on behalf of his principal, from the enforcement of the contract.

To advance that argument is, of course, attractive but, in my view, it necessarily involves the precise mischief which the Statute of Frauds, 1695, was intended to avoid, and that is that it invites the Court to amend by deletion, or by ignoring one of its terms, the note or memorandum relied upon by the plaintiff and signed by the defendant, such amendment or deletion depending on the finding by the court on oral evidence as to what was the agreement between the parties.

Such a principle clearly puts the oral evidence as superseding the only written evidence that is available. In broad terms, it is the clearest possible purpose of the Statute of Frauds, 1695, to put the written evidence as dominant and superseding any oral evidence.

It is possible, without much difficulty, to see on consideration of the cases to which we have been referred, that the many instances which occurred of the making of contracts orally for the sale of land the existence of which and the complete nature of which is not even denied in subsequent litigation, has led courts to view with considerable disfavour the defence of non-enforceability due to a want of sufficient note or memorandum under the Statute of Frauds. It does not seem to me, however, that it can be justified, having regard to the obligation of the courts in the implementation of a plain statutory provision, to introduce into the interpretation of s. 2 of the Act of 1695 clauses or provisos which are not consistent with its plain meaning. Furthermore, all one's experience of the massive losses and inconvenience which can be suffered by prospective purchasers or vendors of land from non-completion of what they believe to be a contract and the subsequent delays and difficulties arising from complicated litigation concerning it indicates that the requirements of justice are that the law applicable to the formation of contracts for the purchase of land should be as certain as it is possible to make it. In modern times, probably the most important legal transaction a great number of people make in their lifetimes is the purchase or sale of their home. The avoidance of doubt and, therefore, the avoidance of litigation concerning such a transaction must be a well worthwhile social objective, as far as the law is concerned. To that end certainty in the question of what is or is not a sufficient note or memorandum is a desirable aim. In my view, the very definite statement that a note or memorandum of a contract made orally is not sufficient to satisfy the Statute of Frauds unless it directly or by very necessary implication recognises, not only the terms to be enforced, but also the existence of a concluded contract between the parties, and the corresponding principle that no such note or memorandum which contains any term or expression such as "subject to contract" can be sufficient, even if it can be established by oral evidence that such a term or expression did not form part of the originally orally concluded agreement, achieves that certainty. The existence of such a rule or provision would not, in my view, allow for the "exceptional cases" mentioned by Keane J. in the decision in *Mulhall v. Haren* [1981] IR 364.

The decision in *Kelly v. Park Hall School* [1979] IR 340, in so far as it appears to amend by deletion the note or memorandum in writing signed on behalf of the vendor by reference to the evidence of the oral agreements which had previously been arrived at between the parties, with great reluctance, is not a decision which I think this Court can and should follow.

Similar considerations may, it seems to me, apply to the decision of this Court in *Casey v. Irish Intercontinental Bank* [1979] IR 364, though a decision on the validity of the concept of oral waiver of a suspensory condition in the writings which were part of the formation of the contract is not a question at issue in this case. I would, therefore, allow this appeal and answer the questions raised in the issue: *no* to question (a) and *no* to question (c); question (b) does not therefore arise. The action must therefore be dismissed."

Supermac's Ireland Ltd v. Katesan (Naas) Ltd
[2001] 1 ILRM 401

The plaintiffs brought an action for specific performance of an agreement for the sale of property. The defendants alleged that there had been no concluded agreement reached between the parties and that even if there had been, that there was no note or memorandum to satisfy the requirements of the Statute of Frauds (Ireland) 1695, and they further contended that the plaintiff could not claim that there had been part performance. The defendants' application to dismiss the plaintiffs' action on the grounds that it was unsustainable and an abuse of process was dismissed by the Supreme Court (Denham, Hardiman and Geoghegan JJ).

HARDIMAN J (Denham J concurring) stated at pp. 405–410:

"*Deposit*
It is convenient to deal first with the question of deposit because this is the core and height of the defendants' case.

In *Boyle v. Lee* [1992] 1 IR 555, Finlay CJ held that the parties had agreed that there would be a deposit but left it to their respective solicitors to agree the amount and form of it. In those circumstances, the learned Chief Justice said (at p. 571):

> The amount of a deposit to be made, even if a purchaser is willing to make a deposit of the appropriate amount, or to the usual amount then experienced in transactions in Dublin, is too important a part of a contract for the sale of land in the large sum of £90,000 to be omitted from a concluded and complete oral agreement unless the parties in such an agreement had agreed that no deposit would be paid.

It seems clear that this passage, if and in so far as it suggests that one can never have a concluded agreement for the sale of land without agreement as to the payment of a deposit, represented a considerable development of what the position had previously been. Both *Barrett v. Costelloe* High Court 1973 No. 703P, 13 July 1973 and *Black v. Kavanagh* (1973) 108 ILTR 91 had stated that it is not essential for a concluded agreement that there should be a stipulation in relation to a deposit. In the latter case Gannon J having held that neither party attached any importance to the matter of the payment of a deposit or its amount, said:

> The question of whether or not a deposit should be paid was not considered by the parties to be a material matter, and in my opinion is not an essential term of such a contract.

The plaintiffs' answer to the submission based on *Boyle v. Lee* is first to distinguish that case on its facts and to contend that the evidence here is open to the interpretation that there was to be no deposit. This, Mr MacCann said, could be decided as a matter of interpretation of the words and conduct of the parties: there is no necessity for an express agreement that there would be no deposit. Secondly, the defendants contend that it is not obvious (and they need go no further for the purpose of this motion) that the passage quoted above from Finlay CJ represented the view of the majority. If it did, it would represent a substantial change in the pre-existing law: there is ample scope for argument, it was contended, that the judgment of O'Flaherty J which is pivotal on the point having regard to the views expressed by McCarthy and Egan JJ, did not go as far as the Chief Justice on the question of deposit.

There is no doubt that an agreement in relation to a deposit is usual in concluded agreements for the sale of land. But the cases prior to *Boyle v. Lee* demonstrate that it is not invariable. The evidence on affidavit falls well short of certainty in relation to what if anything was agreed on this point and it must not be forgotten that the agreement was between franchisor and franchisee and involved the sale of assets other than real property in addition to the premises themselves. In such an agreement, I believe there is at least scope for contention that a deposit may not have been considered essential. It seems to me that the factual position will be a good deal clearer after discovery and, more importantly, oral evidence, and I could not say that I am confident that, no matter what transpired at the trial, the defendants would necessarily win.

Furthermore, since there is scope for the view that the parties agreed nothing whatever about a deposit, it seems to me at least arguable that *Boyle v. Lee* is distinguishable in the present circumstances. The circumstances of that case were that there had been an express agreement that there would be a deposit. It is not manifestly clear that the judgment of the Chief Justice in that case was intended to apply to other circumstances. It is also in my view arguable that the judgment of Finlay CJ did not represent the view of a majority. On a motion such as this it is neither necessary nor desirable to go further than saying that I am not convinced that the defendants must win no matter what happens at the trial. It is noteworthy that *Boyle v. Lee* was itself a decision of this Court after a full hearing in the High Court and Finlay CJ was careful, at p. 563 of the report, to set out precisely what the oral evidence on this topic had been. In my view it would be necessary to hear the evidence in this case before a final decision can be made as to what if anything was agreed between the parties on this topic, what may be implied from what they did and from other facts and to hear legal argument based on that evidence.

Completion date

Mr Cush also contends that the absence of agreement as to completion date is a fatal defect in the proposition that there was a concluded agreement. In relation to the Naas premises there was a statement on affidavit that completion was to be after vacant possession had been obtained; there was no reference to a completion date at all in relation to the other five properties. He further submitted that there was no evidence on the basis on which a completion date could be implied.

In *Boyle v. Lee*, Egan J at p. 593 of his judgment stated that:

> It has long been established that where no time for performance is agreed the law implies an undertaking by each party to perform his part of the contract within a time which is reasonable having regard to the circumstances of the case: *Simpson v. Hughes* (1896) 66 LJ Ch 143.

This is a long standing and, to my knowledge, unchallenged statement of the law.

Accordingly, it cannot be said with certainty that, if the other essentials of a concluded agreement are present, the plaintiffs' case is bound to fail by reason of the non-specification of a completion date.

Vacant possession

Mr Cush contended that, in order to construe the November agreements as constituting a completed agreement for the sale of land, one has to construe the evidence as committing the defendants to getting vacant possession. This is nowhere stated. He further points out that the evidence is silent on the question of what was to happen if vacant possession was not obtained.

In paragraph 5 of his affidavit the mediator, Mr Chambers, says that the second named defendant pointed out during discussions that the Naas property had a sitting tenant and that there was a court case pending in relation to that person's entitlements. He goes on:

> As a result of this difficulty and because of the fact that vacant possession was not available, a sum of money was agreed to accommodate the eventuality of allowing this property out of a deal. In other words figures were agreed for either five properties or alternatively six properties.

This is at variance with the defendants' contention that no provision was made about the eventuality that vacant possession was not obtained. It is unnecessary to go further than holding that there is clearly an evidential issue on this matter. There is also a legal issue which may arise as to the significance of the fact that vacant possession was, in fact, subsequently obtained. Furthermore, there is a distinction between the elements necessary to constitute a completed agreement on the one hand and the consequences of failure to honour such agreement in relation to vacant possession on the other. It is at least arguable that the parties' failure to reach any agreement (if that is found to have occurred) on the question of vacant possession would merely have exposed the defendants to a claim for damages, if vacant possession had not been obtained.

Subject to contract
Mr Cush submitted that all discussions between Mr McDonagh, Mr Sweeney and Mr Chambers should be interpreted 'against the background' of the correspondence between solicitors all of which was 'subject to contract'. This, he says, colours all dealings between the second named plaintiff and the second named defendant.

In my view it is plainly arguable that the use of this rubric by the solicitors does not preclude the existence of a 'done deal' between the parties themselves, which the plaintiffs contend for. In so far as it is contended that the plaintiffs are estopped by the use of the rubric from asserting a completed and enforceable agreement, this seems to me to be plainly a matter for evidence at the trial. I did not understand this point to be vigorously pressed on the hearing of the appeal.

No note or memorandum
The learned trial judge held that she had to approach this question on the assumption that the plaintiffs will prove that Mr Chambers was acting as the defendants' agent. I agree with that finding.

The defendants' submissions as to deposit, completion and vacant possession have already been summarised. The contention that the purported memorandum fails to record one or more of these matters must await a finding, after evidence has been heard, as to what was in fact agreed on these topics.

Mr Cush says, however, that of the two documents produced by Mr

Chambers, only the first in time is signed: he says that if two documents are to be read together, and only one is signed, it is imperative that the signed document must be the last in point of time 'for it would be absurd to hold that a person who signed a document could be regarded as having signed another document which was not in existence when he signed the first' (*McQuaid v. Lynam* [1965] IR 564 at p. 570).

The same case, however, is also authority for the proposition that where an oral agreement is intended to be the contract 'evidence may be given of an agreed variation even if there is a memorandum or note of the contract but not of the variation'. In my view it is at least arguable that this is the case here and certainly oral evidence will be necessary in order further to explore the contention. The nub of the plaintiffs' case is that there was a 'done deal', as it is expressed, orally arrived at. There is a considerable similarity between the two documents and the variations apparently came about as a result of discussions or correspondence between the parties' accountants as to the best way to effect the transaction. In my view it is not possible to be confident that discovery will not reveal further or other documents on the topic of the variation and this too is a matter suggesting that the case go to trial.

Part performance
On the topic of part performance, the issue as it can be discerned at present comes down to whether, as the plaintiffs contend, there was an overall contract to sell the six premises, the goodwill and other items for £4,000,000. The alternative for which the defendants contend is that there were six individual transactions so that the completion of five of them has nothing to say to the sixth.

It seems to me obvious that it is at least possible that the evidence as a whole will disclose an overall transaction with the individual considerations, the subdivision thereof into various headings and the individual modes of completion tailored by the parties' professional advisers so as to be mutually beneficial from a tax point of view and otherwise. Indeed, this proposition seems compatible with the background set out in Mr McDonagh's affidavit of a decision to end the dispute which had arisen about the defendants' involvement with 'Mother Hubbards' by the severance of their entire business connection. In all these circumstances I cannot say that I am confident that the plaintiffs' contention must necessarily fail.

Conclusion
For these reasons I would dismiss the appeal and affirm the order of the learned trial judge.

GEOGHEGAN J (Denham J concurring) stated at pp.411–417 and 422–423: "At the hearing of the appeal before this Court, counsel for the appellant Mr Cush SC argued that the plaintiffs could not succeed in the action in that in relation to the sixth property, the subject of the action, there was allegedly never a concluded agreement or alternatively that if there was, there was no note or memorandum thereof sufficient to satisfy the Statute of Frauds. He further argued that the plaintiffs could not succeed on the basis of part performance both because there was no concluded agreement in the first instance and because such agreement as there was in relation to the particular property in question had not been partly performed.

Although Mr Cush opened the case on the basis that there was no concluded agreement because there had been no agreement on the deposit and the amount thereof, no agreement on a completion date and no agreement concerning the possession of the Naas property, there being at the time potential problems about possession, he more or less conceded ultimately that for the purposes of this motion at least, the absence of agreement on the deposit was the only factor, but a very important factor, on which he could rely. Obviously at the hearing of the action there could be argument as to whether there might have been an implied term that the sale would be completed within a reasonable time or some other kind of implied term relating to completion date. In relation to the question of possession it might be argued at the full hearing, that in the absence of any mention of this, there would be an obligation to give up clear vacant possession. The deposit however was quite a different matter. Mr Cush argues that if on any view of the facts as they are before the court at this stage it must have been intended that there would be a deposit, the absence of any agreement as to the amount of it must necessarily mean that there was no concluded agreement. If there was no concluded agreement then the question of the sufficiency of a note or memorandum does not arise and *ipso facto* the question of part performance does not arise either. In his submissions regarding the deposit counsel for the appellants principally relies on the decision of this Court in *Boyle v. Lee* [1992] 1 IR 555; [1992] ILRM 65. That case related to a sale of a house and the issue which fell to be determined was whether there was a concluded oral agreement and if so whether there was a sufficient note or memorandum of it to satisfy the Statute of Frauds. It was common case that there had been no specific agreement in relation to tenancies to which the property was subject or as to a closing date or as to the deposit. Separate judgments were delivered by Finlay CJ, McCarthy, O'Flaherty and Egan JJ. The fifth member of the court Hederman J agreed with the judgment of Finlay CJ. Effectively Finlay CJ, Hederman and O'Flaherty JJ held that there was no concluded agreement but McCarthy and Egan JJ dissented. It would appear that McCarthy and Egan JJ took the view that it would be wrong to assume that the parties considered it essential to agree on a deposit and if they had agreed on the other main terms as they had there was no reason to hold that a final agreement had not been reached. This however was the minority view. As to what exactly the majority view was has never been entirely clear. The judgments of Finlay CJ and O'Flaherty J have been open to different interpretations and the problems arising out of them have been discussed by the learned author of Farrell on *The Irish Law of Specific Performance*. The different arguments of interpretation were recently presented before me as a High Court judge in *Shirley Engineering Ltd v. Irish Telecommunications Investments plc* High Court 1997 No. 8063P. I had considerable difficulties with them as is clear from my unreported judgment delivered on 2 December 1999. It is in relation to the question of the deposit that the problems mainly arise. The learned High Court judge in that case, Barrington J, had held that the failure of the parties to reach any agreement on the question of a deposit was irrelevant since it was of no importance in the contract. The former Chief Justice, when commenting on that finding, described it as a mixed finding of law and fact, and he then went on to say the following (at pp. 571/75):

> In my view, this finding was in error. The amount of a deposit to be made, even if a purchaser is willing to make a deposit of the appropriate amount, or the usual amount then experienced in transactions in Dublin, is too important a part of a contract for the sale of land in the large sum of £90, 000 to be omitted from a concluded and complete oral agreement unless the parties in such an agreement had agreed that no deposit would be paid. In this case the evidence irresistibly leads to the conclusion that both the first named plaintiff and Mr McManus agreed that there had to be a deposit, but left it over to be agreed between the solicitors when the formal contract was being settled as to its amount and form. In my view, that evidence, which was not in contest, must lead to a conclusion that there was not a complete contract made orally between the first named plaintiff and Mr McManus before 8 July 1988.

It is important to subject that passage to some analysis. First of all in holding that there had to be agreement on the deposit the former Chief Justice was dealing only with the question whether there was a concluded agreement and not in any way with the question of whether there was a sufficient note or memorandum to satisfy the Statute of Frauds. The passage therefore has no bearing on any question as to whether if a deposit is agreed the amount of it should be set out in the note or memorandum. Secondly, it is quite clear from the passage that Finlay CJ was holding beyond doubt on the evidence that the amount of the deposit was still to be negotiated. If that was so that was clearly the end of the matter because if a term of an agreement has still to be negotiated how can it be said that there is a concluded agreement? When read in that light the passage in the judgment is crystal clear. Confusion has arisen because of references both in the case law and in the text books to expressions such as 'material terms' or similar words in relation to the issue of whether there is a concluded agreement. That type of wording should have no place in that consideration. It is a wholly different matter when one comes to consider the sufficiency of a note or memorandum. Only the 'material terms' need be included in a note or memorandum for it to be sufficient but all the terms, whether they be important or unimportant, must be agreed before there can be said to be a concluded agreement. It follows therefore that if the evidence is that there is going to be a deposit but that the amount of it is still to be negotiated, there cannot be a concluded agreement. The third point which arises from the passage cited relates to the words 'even if a purchaser is willing to make a deposit of the appropriate amount, or the usual amount then experienced in transactions in Dublin.' Some interpret these words as meaning that there can never be an implied agreement as to the deposit. I cannot agree with that view. What the former Chief Justice is saying is that the mere fact that the purchaser was willing to make an appropriate deposit could not render the agreement a concluded agreement if the understanding was that the deposit was to be negotiated. If the evidence establishes that two proposed parties to an agreement intended that their agreement should contain an express term relating to a deposit there cannot then be an implied term. Finlay CJ is merely pointing out that a unilateral willingness on the part of the purchaser to pay a reasonable deposit is irrelevant in the absence of an agreement by the other party to accept that amount.

It is now necessary to consider what O'Flaherty J had to say on this matter. Unlike this case there had been a 'subject to contract' issue in *Boyle v. Lee* and *a propos* of that phrase O'Flaherty J said the following (at pp. 581-582/83):

> Before examining this phrase at all, it is necessary to go to back to the rudiments of the law of contract and find out whether there was an offer and acceptance and an intention to create legal relations. That there was an agreement on price, offer and acceptance, there is no doubt. But beyond that, in my judgment, there was much to be sorted out. For a start, the matter of the tenancies was not resolved. It was easy for the first named plaintiff to say at the trial that he was prepared to take the property subject to the tenancies whatever kind they were – but one of his answers suggested that he might have had to engage in litigation because of what he felt was a misrepresentation in relation to a tenant who had, in effect, a six year tenancy. It is common case that Mr McManus left him under the impression that they were all short tenancies, meaning thereby not more than one year. Then, there was no closing date agreed. Mr McManus expressly declined to take a deposit believing that that was a matter proper to be put into the formal contract. So it appears to me, that there was no *consensus ad idem*. There was, at the most, an agreement to agree.

It is clear from this passage that the evidence in the case must have been that Mr McManus as agent for the vendor had expressly declined to take a deposit on the basis that the deposit question was to be left to be put into the formal contract. There might be situations where that would not necessarily mean that there was not a concluded agreement as, for instance, where each side simply trusted the other to submit to reasonable arrangements which the solicitors might include in the contract relating to deposit and other matters etc. But it is obvious that on the transcript of evidence in *Boyle v. Lee* both Finlay CJ and O'Flaherty J accepted that the question of the deposit was still to be negotiated and that it was intended to be a term of the agreement. In my view Finlay's CJ reference to the importance of a deposit in such a transaction was simply a comment on credibility. He was taking the view that once the deposit was still to be negotiated that meant there was an actual term of the contract still to be negotiated and therefore there was no concluded contract. The views of O'Flaherty J, although expressed differently, are not dissimilar.

Before considering the application of those principles to this case I think it appropriate briefly to review some other relevant authorities. In an unreported judgment of this Court delivered on 8 May 1975 in *Lynch v. O'Meara*, Supreme Court 1974 No. 12 Henchy J (with whom O'Higgins CJ and Walsh J concurred) had this to say:

> In this Court, counsel for the plaintiff contended that the first document and the second document should be read together and as such should be held to constitute the note or memorandum required by the Statute of Frauds. However, before one comes to the question of a note or memorandum it is necessary to see if an entire contract was concluded on Sunday, 24 October, for it is only in that event that the statutory note or memorandum would be required. If the negotiations between the parties had not ripened into the fullness of an entire contract the plaintiffs' claim for specific performance would fail, not for want of the statutory evidence necessary for the enforcement of a contract for the sale of lands, but simply in default of the existence of any such contract. There would be no contract to be specifically enforced.

I merely quote that passage because of its clarity as to the correct approach. There cannot be a concluded agreement unless everything intended to be covered by the agreement has been either expressly or impliedly agreed.

Black v. Kavanagh (1974) 108 ILTR 91 would seem to be an example of a case where on the evidence the judge (Gannon J) took the view that the parties intended to reach a concluded agreement without dealing with the question of a deposit. It seems clear from the following passage in the judgment:

> I am satisfied on the evidence that the plaintiff and the defendant entered into a firm agreement for the sale and purchase of the defendant's house at Number 1 Dodder Park Grove, Rathfarnham, and the specific contents identified by them before they went to their respective solicitors about the matter. At that stage each of them believed that he had entered into a binding agreement which he expected and intended would be legally enforceable by or against him subject only to an obligation to facilitate the other reasonably as to when possession would be given and received. I find that neither of them attached any importance to the matter of the payment of a deposit or as to its amount. On the evidence before me I am satisfied that neither of them gave any authority to his solicitor to enter into or negotiate the terms of a contract in any way at variance with the agreement they had already reached, and that on the unconcluded matter of the date of possession their final agreement would be communicated – but not decided – by their solicitors. Both of them recognised and accepted that legal formalities, which to them were no more than formalities, were necessary and that the procedures of such nature would be followed on their behalf by the named solicitors, and no further authority was given to either solicitor. They relied on their solicitors to prepare any documents necessary to give legal force and effect to their agreement, and each was willing and expected to put his hand

> to whatever documents his solicitor required for that purpose whether it be called
> the contract, or a draft contract, or a memorandum of agreement.

In this respect it is clear that the evidence in *Black v. Kavanagh* as to the status
of the deposit was quite different from the evidence in *Boyle v. Lee*.

In *Barrett v. Costello* High Court 1973 No. 703P (Kenny J) 13 July 1973
(but noted in (1973) 107 ILT 239) the plaintiff told his agent that he was
prepared to pay £40,000 and auctioneer's fees in relation to a particular property
but had stipulated that there was a deposit of 10%. The agent spoke to the
vendor and told him of the offer but omitted to mention the stipulation about
the deposit of 10%. The defendant approved the sale and although it had not
been mentioned to him he would have agreed to the 10% deposit had it been
mentioned. On the particular facts of the case and the evidence as to how the
negotiations ran Kenny J held that there was an oral concluded agreement
without any express term relating to the deposit. But he went on to observe as
follows:

> In former times a deposit of 25% was usual but the evidence satisfies me that a
> deposit of 10% has become a common practice in property sales in Dublin. I do
> not accept the submission of the defendant's counsel that there was never a
> concluded contract between the parties.

While it is not entirely clear, I think that Kenny J was effectively holding that
there was an implied term as to a deposit of 10% rather than that there was no
agreement of any kind relating to deposit. But it does not much matter because
if Kenny J was holding that there was neither an express nor an implied term
as to the deposit then effectively he was holding that there was a concluded
agreement with both parties ignoring the question of a deposit and leaving it
as something to be dealt with ultimately when the formal contracts were drawn
up. In such a situation however if for some reason or other the solicitors drawing
up the contract were unable to agree on a deposit, the original oral agreement
would remain binding and there would be no contractual deposit. The
underlying legal principle was referred to by Kingsmill Moore J in his majority
judgment in *Godley v. Power* (1957) 95 ILTR 135 at p.147 where he quotes
with approval what he described as 'the oft quoted and oft approved' passage
from the judgment of Parker J in *Von Hatzfeldt-Wildenberg v. Alexander* [1912]
1 Ch 284 at pp.288-289. The passage reads as follows:

> It appears to be well settled by the authorities that if the documents or letters
> relied on as constituting a contract contemplate the execution of a further contract
> between the parties, it is a question of construction whether the execution of the
> further contract is a condition or term of the bargain, or whether it is a mere
> expression of the desire of the parties as to the manner in which the transaction
> already agreed to will go through. In the former case there is no enforceable
> contract either because the condition is unfulfilled or because the law does not
> recognise a contract to enter into a contract. In the latter case there is a binding
> contract and the reference to the more formal document may be ignored.

Applying the above principles as enunciated in the case law to this particular case, it would seem that if this action goes to trial there may be a number of alternative arguments relating to the question of the deposit. I would list these as follows:

(1) That it was always intended that the parties would be contractually bound by a particular deposit yet to be negotiated.

(2) That having regard to the nature of the transaction in this case and in particular the fact that there was a franchisor – franchisee relationship between the parties, it was not intended that there be a deposit.

(3) That in all the circumstances of the case there would have been an implied term that a reasonable deposit would be paid.

(4) That in all the circumstances there was an implied term that the standard deposit normally payable in transactions of this kind would be paid.

(5) That it would never have occurred to any of the parties that there would be a problem about the deposit and that a concluded agreement was reached ignoring it with the assumption that the solicitors when drawing up formal contracts would agree a deposit.

If the trial judge held in favour of the first of those arguments the action would undoubtedly have to be dismissed because there would then have been no concluded agreement. But the action would not have to be dismissed if any of the remaining four arguments held good. At this stage of the proceedings it would be wrong and indeed it would not be possible for this Court to hold that only the first argument was open. There can be no question therefore in my view of the proceedings being struck out at this stage on the basis that there was no concluded agreement as to deposits.

Still less could this Court hold at this stage that there was no concluded agreement because of there being no reference to a completion date. In many sets of circumstances the court implies a term that the agreement will be completed within a reasonable time. The evidence in this case suggests that a speedy completion date was desired but it was known to both parties that there were problems of vacant possession in relation to the actual property the subject matter of this action and at this stage it could not be said with certainty that there was not an implied term as to completion.

Nor is the absence of any stipulation about vacant possession in relation to the property the subject matter of the action fatal to the plaintiffs' claim. On the contrary the general rule would be that in the absence of any such stipulation an obligation to give vacant possession must be presumed.

I now turn to the next of the defendants' arguments. The defendants maintain that if contrary to what they submit, there may arguably have been a concluded agreement, there is no note or memorandum of such agreement which could arguably satisfy the Statute of Frauds. To explain this part of the argument it is necessary to go into the facts of the case in more detail."

. . . .

"It would be immediately apparent to any lawyer that all kinds of problems could arise from any attempt to set up either or both of these documents as a memorandum for the purposes of the Statute of Frauds. There is first of all the point that Mr Chambers signed the first document but not the second and that nobody signed the second. If the action goes to trial the defendants will be strongly arguing that Mr Chambers was never an agent of the defendants for the purposes of signing any memorandum. However their counsel Mr Cush fairly concedes that there is an issue to be tried on that point and he could not succeed in having the action struck out on that basis at this stage. He does however strongly rely on the absence of any signature on the second document. In my view, it would not be correct for this Court to strike out the proceedings at this stage on that account. There has been a good deal of development of the case law relating to memoranda to satisfy the Statute of Frauds and as to when and where signatures have to be appended and as to the connection to be made between one document and another. These various cases have been considered by the learned author of Farrell on the *Irish Law of Specific Performance*. It would not seem to me that beyond doubt the plaintiffs could not rely on the first document or the first document combined with the second as a sufficient memorandum. It is a matter which should be argued out and tried at the action. Nor do I consider that either because of the reference to 'Sale contracts' in each of the documents or the apportionment of price between the different properties as set out in the second document that the plaintiffs could never succeed in establishing the first document or the first document combined with the second as a sufficient memorandum of the contract alleged in the statement of claim that is to say the composite contract for £4m.

If, notwithstanding the absence of any express reference to a deposit, the court should ultimately hold that there was a concluded agreement the absence of any reference to the deposit in the alleged note or memorandum would not necessarily be fatal. If there was an implied term as to the deposit it is well established that there is no need for such implied term to be expressed in the note or memorandum. If on the other hand the question of the deposit was to be left to the solicitors but that there was nevertheless a concluded agreement reached beforehand then the absence of any mention of the deposit in the memorandum is irrelevant. Even if there had been, which there was not, an express agreement as to the amount of the deposit there would still be plenty of room for argument that it does not have to be referred to in the note or memorandum as it might not in all the circumstances of the case be regarded as 'a material term'.

The denials of contract in the solicitors' correspondence may or may not be helpful to the defendants at the ultimate hearing but at this stage it could not possibly be said that the heads of agreement arrived at were definitely not intended to be a concluded contract.

The part performance argument can be dealt with very briefly. If there was a concluded agreement of the kind alleged in the statement of claim, that is to say, a composite contract and involving the sale of all the properties for a composite sum of £4m the completion, which has in fact taken place of all the other sales, must arguably constitute the relevant part performance.

For all these reasons therefore I would affirm the order of the learned High Court judge and dismiss the appeal."

Mackie v. Wilde
[1998] 2 IR 578

The plaintiff and the first named defendant were the owners of a joint fishery on rivers in Co. Donegal. The original rules for the operation of the fishery had been laid down in an indenture but the plaintiff was dissatisfied with the arrangements relating to the number of people who could fish on the rivers and the parties met with a view to reaching agreement about the number of annual licences and daily tickets which would be issued. Subsequently correspondence took place between the parties in which the plaintiff sought to obtain the defendant's written agreement to the limiting of the number of licences for the fishery. The plaintiff then instituted proceedings claiming that there was a binding agreement that each party would be limited to the granting of 25 annual licences and submitted that there had been part performance on foot of the agreement. Costello P held that a concluded agreement to this effect had been reached and that an additional term relating to the number of day tickets which could be granted had also been agreed upon. He therefore ordered that the first named defendant be restrained from issuing more than 25 annual licences and ten day tickets and this finding was reversed by the Supreme Court. Barron J concluded that there had not been a concluded agreement reached and held that even if there had been a concluded oral agreement as claimed, there were no acts on the part of the plaintiff which showed an intention to perform the alleged contract.

BARRON J stated at pp.583–588: "The essential question is whether the parties have left over some matter to be determined which can only be determined by themselves. So an agreement to enter into an agreement is not a concluded contract.

In the instant case, the agreement was not capable of being saved by any of the means available to the Court to which I have referred. The parties did not intend to be limited to 25 annual licences without any day tickets. Nor could the number be determined by what is reasonable. Reasonableness in law is an expression capable of certainty. But there can be no certainty here. The learned trial judge has held that the ten day tickets would be reasonable. But equally any other number between two and ten would have been said also to have been reasonable. When an apparently uncertain term is saved on the basis of what is reasonable, it is because this is imparting certainty, something which cannot be done by choosing which of several reasonable answers is the correct one. In other words, the court cannot make the agreement for the parties by saying this is reasonable. In the instant case what the parties have left over, what is meant by the word "few", is something which only they can settle. It follows that there was no concluded agreement.

Turning to the question of part performance, it is submitted that the plaintiff permitted the first defendant to make greater use of the two beats, the use of which was restricted by the 1920 deed. If the first defendant's records were correct, and the evidence suggested that they may not have been, then he did issue 50% more day tickets in 1986, than in 1985, but as against that the number of season tickets was reduced to 25% of those issued in the previous year.

The nature of the doctrine is comprehensively stated in the judgment of Simon L.J. in *Steadman v. Steadman* [1976] AC 536 at p. 558, as follows:

> ". . . almost from the moment of passing of the Statute of Frauds, it was appreciated that it was being used for a variant of unconscionable dealing, which the statute itself was designed to remedy. A party to an oral contract for the disposition of an interest in land could, despite performance of the reciprocal terms by the other party, by virtue of the statute disclaim liability for his own performance on the ground that the contract had not been in writing. Common law was helpless. But equity, with its purpose of vindicating good faith and with its remedies of injunction and specific performance, could deal with the situation. The Statute of Frauds did not make such contracts void but merely unenforceable; and, if the statute was to be relied on as a defence, it had to be specifically pleaded. Where, therefore, a party to a contract unenforceable under the Statute of Frauds stood by while the other party acted to his detriment in performance of his own contractual obligations, the first party would be precluded by the Court of Chancery from claiming exoneration, on the ground that the contract was unenforceable, from performance of his reciprocal obligations; and the court would, if required, decree specific performance of the contract. Equity would not, as it was put, allow the Statute of Frauds "to be used as an engine of fraud." This became known as the doctrine of part performance - the "part" performance being that of the party who had, to the knowledge of the other party, acted to his detriment in carrying out irremediably his own obligations (or some significant part of them) under the otherwise unenforceable contract."

The basis of this principle was that the contract by reason of its part performance passed from being a purely executory contract and might create equities which would justify the court enforcing it specifically, something it would not have done while it remained purely executory because of the absence of writing to satisfy the statute.

It is not surprising therefore that the older authorities require evidence of part performance before considering the terms of the agreement. In *Maddison v. Alderson* (1883) 8 App Cas 467, O'Hagan L.J. said at p. 483:

> "The alleged agreement regarded an interest in lands and the statute nullified it for the purpose of the action. *Per se*, it was of no account and could have no value given to it unless, in the first instance, it was evidenced by acts to be accounted for only on the supposition of its existence. The allegation of it could

not be made the subject of judicial consideration as founding any right of suit, in the absence of such acts, satisfactorily ascertained."

Later on p. 484 he said:

"The previous question as to the sufficiency of the part performance must be settled before the construction and operation of the unwritten contract can be legitimately approached. 'The principle of the case is, says Sir William Grant, that the act must be of such a nature that, if stated, it would of itself infer the existence of some agreement; and then parol evidence is admitted to show what the agreement is.' Then, but not till then."

As regards the nature of the acts which could be relied upon as part performance, the Earl of Selbourne L.C., with whom O'Hagan L.J. and Fitzgerald L.J. concurred, said at p. 479:

"All the authorities show that the acts relied upon as part performance must be unequivocally, and in their own nature, referable to some such agreement as that alleged . . ."

At p. 485 O'Hagan L.J. said:

"But there is no conflict of judicial opinion, and in my mind no ground for reasonable controversy as to the essential character of the act which shall amount to a part performance, in one particular. It must be unequivocal. It must have relation to the one agreement relied upon, and to no other. It must be such, in Lord Hardwicke's words, 'as could be done with no other view or design than to perform that agreement'. It must be sufficient of itself, and without any other information or evidence, to satisfy a court, from the circumstances it has created and the relations it has formed, that they are only consistent with the assumption of the existence of a contract the terms of which equity requires, if possible, to be ascertained and enforced."

While these passages appear to indicate that the terms of the contract could be investigated by the court, it seems that it was generally taken that the acts of part performance had to relate unequivocally to the actual contract. This was disapproved by Andrews L.J. in *Lowry v. Reid* [1927] NI 142, who after analysing various passages from the judgments in *Maddison v. Alderson* (1883) 8 App Cas 467, and having indicated that he was not prepared to follow such strict rules said at p. 159:

"I make no apology for citing, in conclusion, as a correct summary of the law a passage from Fry on Specific Performance, 5th Edit. 292, where the editor states that the true principle of the operation of acts of part performance seems only to require that the acts in question be such as must be referred to some contract, and may be referred to the alleged one; that they prove the existence of some contract, and are consistent with the contract alleged."

The learned judge then pointed out that the paragraph from *Fry* on Specific Performance of which he approved was in the same form as that in the edition published in 1881 which was before the decision in *Maddison v. Alderson*

(1883) 8 App Cas 467 and that that decision necessitated no alteration in the text.

It is still necessary to show that the other party was aware of what was being done whether by standing by and not doing anything or by more active participation. An example of the latter is to be seen in *Lowry v. Reid* [1927] NI 142, where Moore L.C.J. at p. 152 referred to the facts of that case as follows:

> "In my judgment there is relief for him, because on the facts of the case, having given up his own property to his own detriment, on the faith of his mother's representations, this is a parol contract for the specific performance of which he is entitled in equity to a decree to carry those representations into execution, and if he is entitled to such a decree, he is equally entitled to rely on the doctrine of part performance to take the case out of the statute . . ."

It must not be forgotten that ultimately the court is seeking to ensure that a defendant is not, in relying upon the Statute, breaking faith with the plaintiff, not solely by refusing to perform the oral contract, but in the manner contemplated from the passage from the judgment of Simon L.J. to which I have referred.

The doctrine is based upon principles of equity. There are three things to be considered:

(1) The acts on the part of the plaintiff said to have been in part performance or of concluded agreement;

(2) the involvement of the defendant with respect to such acts;

(3) the oral agreement itself.

It is obvious that these considerations only relate to a contract of a type which the courts will decree ought to be specifically performed. Each of the three elements is essential. In my view, it does not matter in which order they are considered. Ultimately what is essential is that:–

(1) there was a concluded oral contract;

(2) that the plaintiff acted in such a way that showed an intention to perform that contract;

(3) that the defendant induced such acts or stood by while they were being performed; and

(4) it would be unconscionable and a breach of good faith to allow the defendant to rely upon the terms of the Statute of Frauds to prevent performance of the contract.

If the terms of the contract cannot be considered until the acts of the plaintiff have been found capable of being acts of part performance, there is the possibility, admittedly not a very strong one, that the acts might well have been inconsistent with the terms of the contract and in fact not carried out in pursuance of it, but for a different reason. I do not suggest that in such circumstances, the court would still accept that there had been part performance. But it does show that it is more logical to find out what the parties agreed since, in the absence of a concluded agreement, there is no point in seeking to find acts of part performance. The court can only then begin its determination whether the behaviour of the parties justifies the application of the equitable doctrine to modify the legal rule.

In the result it seems to me that while the passage from *Fry* on Specific Performance cited by Andrews L.J. in *Lowry v. Reid* [1927] NI 142, expresses the law, the different approach requires the statement of principle to be altered. It would then read: What is required is that the acts relied upon as being acts of part performance be such that on examination of the contract which has been found to have been concluded and to which they are alleged to refer show an intention to perform that contract.

In all the earlier cases, it was assumed that the acts of part performance must necessarily relate to and affect land: see the judgment of Fitzgerald L.J. in *Maddison v. Alderson* (1883) 8 App Cas 467 at p. 491. Nothing which I have said should be taken to suggest a modification of that position.

There is no evidence in the instant case that the plaintiff issued any more or any less licences than he had the previous year nor that the defendant was aware of how many he was issuing. The plaintiff had never complained during the season that too many tickets were being issued by the first defendant and in that regard there was nothing different in his behaviour as between 1985 and 1986. The detriment to the plaintiff which is alleged is presumably the lessening in value of the fishery by over-fishing. But the detriment to the plaintiff must be the result of what the plaintiff does with the defendant standing by and not detriment to the plaintiff as a result of what the defendant does with the plaintiff standing by. There was nothing in what was alleged which would in any way be a breaking of faith by the first defendant with the plaintiff for the first defendant to plead the Statute. Even, if there had been a concluded oral agreement as claimed, there were no acts on the part of the plaintiff which show an intention to perform that contract.

I would allow the appeal and refuse the relief sought."

Contracts Requiring Supervision

Traditionally the courts were unwilling to order specific performance of contracts which would require constant supervision by the court.[1] More recent authorities suggest that the difficulty of supervising the enforcement of contracts of this nature should merely be a discretionary factor and importance has also been placed on whether there is a sufficient definition of what has to be done in order to comply with the order of the court.[2] The decision of the House of Lords in *Co-Operative Insurance Society Ltd v. Argyll Stores (Holdings) Ltd*[3] illustrates that a distinction may be drawn between orders which require a

---

[1] *Ryan v. Mutual Tontine Westminster Chambers Association* [1893] 1 Ch 116.
[2] *Posner v. Scott-Lewis* [1987] Ch 25. See also *Tito v. Wadell (No.2)* [1977] Ch 106, 322.
[3] [1998] AC 1.

defendant to carry on an activity such as running a business and orders which require him to achieve a result. The judgment of Costello P in *Wanze Properties (Ireland) Ltd v. Five Star Supermarket*,[4] which concerned a similar issue of whether an anchor tenant in a shopping centre could be required to comply with a covenant obliging it to continue trading, resulted in a different outcome. However, it should be pointed out that the *Wanze* case concerned an application for an interlocutory injunction rather than an order of specific performance and other features of the case, such as the fact that the supermarket had been trading at a profit, distinguished it from *Co-Operative*.

Posner v. Scott-Lewis
[1987] Ch 25

The terms of the lease between the defendants, who owned a block of flats, and the plaintiff tenants contained a covenant that they would employ a resident porter. The person employed as a porter ceased to be resident in the building and the plaintiffs brought an action for specific performance of the covenant. Mervyn Davies J agreed that the arrangements which had been made were insufficient to ensure compliance with the clause in the lease and held that there had been a breach of covenant. He held that an order of specific performance should be granted in the circumstances.

MERVYN DAVIES J stated at pp.33–36: "Since I am of the view that the defendants are in breach of clause 3(11), the question arises whether or not clause 3(11) is a provision susceptible of specific performance. I was referred to *Ryan v. Mutual Tontine Westminster Chambers Association* [1893] 1 Ch 116. That is a case where the Court of Appeal considered a contract between a landlord and his tenant by which the landlord undertook to employ a porter to perform certain services for the benefit of the tenant. The contract was held to be not specifically enforceable. One ground of the decision was that the execution of the contract would require "constant superintendence by the court."

A close examination of the facts in the *Ryan* case [1893] 1 Ch 116, 117-120 shows the situation in that case differs in some respects from the situation before me. For example, in the *Ryan* case the porter was to "be and act as the servant of the tenants." That is not so at Danes Court. Again the Danes Court lease has, but the *Ryan* lease has not, covenants by the lessor whereby the porter's duties are, at any rate as to clause 3(11)(a) and (b), elsewhere in the lease seen as direct obligations of the lessor to the lessee: see clause 3(2), (7), (10) and (13). There is also the fact that the scheme of apportioning service charges between the Danes Court tenants involves taking account of the costs of maintaining and repairing the porter's flat: see clause 3(12).

---

[4]   High Court (Costello P) 24 October 1997.

Drawing attention to these differences between *Ryan v. Mutual Tontine Westminster Chambers Association* [1893] 1 Ch 116 and the present case, Mr. Tager for the plaintiffs submitted that the *Ryan* case should be distinguished. In short, he said that since the resident porter's functions at Danes Court were already obligations of the lessor to the lessees, there were no duties on the part of the porter towards the tenants that the tenants were seeking to enforce. All that was required was the appointment of a resident porter, whereas in the *Ryan* case the plaintiff was in effect seeking to enforce performance of duties said to be owed by the porter to the plaintiff. I do not accept or reject Mr. Tager's able argument. I suspect that it is difficult to distinguish the *Ryan* case. However that may be, the *Ryan* case has been remarked upon in many later authorities.

In *C.H. Giles & Co. Ltd. v. Morris* [1972] 1 WLR 307 Megarry J., after referring to *Ryan's* case, said, at p. 318:

> "One day, perhaps, the courts will look again at the so-called rule that contracts for personal services or involving the continuous performance of services will not be specifically enforced. Such a rule is plainly not absolute and without exception, nor do I think that it can be based on any narrow consideration such as difficulties of constant superintendence by the court. Mandatory injunctions are by no means unknown, and there is normally no question of the court having to send its officers to supervise the performance of the order of the court. Prohibitory injunctions are common, and again there is no direct supervision by the court. Performance of each type of injunction is normally secured by the realisation of the person enjoined that he is liable to be punished for contempt if evidence of his disobedience to the order is put before the court; and if the injunction is prohibitory, actual committal will usually, so long as it continues, make disobedience impossible. If instead the order is for specific performance of a contract for personal services, a similar machinery of enforcement could be employed, again without there being any question of supervision by any officer of the court. The reasons why the court is reluctant to decree specific performance of a contract for personal services (and I would regard it as a strong reluctance rather than a rule) are, I think, more complex and more firmly bottomed on human nature. If a singer contracts to sing, there could no doubt be proceedings for committal if, ordered to sing, the singer remained obstinately dumb. But if instead the singer sang flat, or sharp, or too fast, or too slowly, or too loudly, or too quietly, or resorted to a dozen of the manifestations of temperament traditionally associated with some singers, the threat of committal would reveal itself as a most unsatisfactory weapon: for who could say whether the imperfections of performance were natural or self-induced? To make an order with such possibilities of evasion would be vain; and so the order will not be made. However, not all contracts of personal service or for the continuous performance of services are as dependent as this on matters of opinion and judgment, nor do all such contracts involve the same degree of the daily impact of person upon person. In general, no doubt, the inconvenience and mischief of decreeing specific performance of most of such contracts will greatly outweigh the advantages, and specific performance will be refused. But I do not think that

it should be assumed that as soon as any element of personal service or continuous services can be discerned in a contract the court will, without more, refuse specific performance. Of course, a requirement for the continuous performance of services has the disadvantage that repeated breaches may engender repeated applications to the court for enforcement. But so may many injunctions; and the prospects of repetition, although an important consideration, ought not to be allowed to negative a right. As is so often the case in equity, the matter is one of the balance of advantage and disadvantage in relation to the particular obligations in question; and the fact that the balance will usually lie on one side does not turn this probability into a rule. The present case, of course, is a fortiori, since the contract of which specific performance has been decreed requires not the performance of personal services or any continuous series of acts, but merely procuring the execution of an agreement which contains a provision for such services or acts."

Those observations do not of themselves enable me to disregard *Ryan v. Mutual Tontine Westminster Chambers Association* [1893] 1 Ch 116. But then one comes to *Shiloh Spinners Ltd. v. Harding* [1973] AC 691. At p. 724c-d Lord Wilberforce seems to say that "the impossibility for the courts to supervise the doing of work" may be rejected as a reason against granting relief. Finally there is *Tito v. Waddell (No. 2)* [1977] Ch 106. Sir Robert Megarry V.-C. said, at p. 321:

"In cases of this kind it was at one time said that an order for the specific performance of the contract would not be made if there would be difficulty in the court supervising its execution: see, e.g., *Ryan v. Mutual Tontine Westminster Chambers Association* [1893] 1 Ch 116, especially at pp. 123, 125, 128. Sir Archibald Smith M.R. subsequently found himself unable to see the force of this objection (see *Wolverhampton Corporation v. Emmons* [1901] 1 QB 515, 523); and after it had been discussed and questioned in *C.H. Giles & Co. Ltd. v. Morris* [1972] 1 WLR 307, 318, the House of Lords disposed of it (I hope finally) in *Shiloh Spinners Ltd. v. Harding* [1973] AC 691, 724. The real question is whether there is a sufficient definition of what has to be done in order to comply with the order of the court. That definition may be provided by the contract itself, or it may be supplied by the terms of the order, in which case there is the further question whether the court considers that the terms of the contract sufficiently support, by implication or otherwise, the terms of the proposed order."

In the light of those authorities it is, I think, open to me to consider the making of an order for specific performance in this case; particularly since the order contemplated is in the a fortiori class referred to by Megarry J. in the last sentence of the extract from *C.H. Giles & Co. Ltd. v. Morris* [1972] 1 WLR 307 quoted above. Damages here could hardly be regarded as an adequate remedy.

Whether or not a specific performance order should be made seems to me to depend on the following considerations: (a) is there a sufficient definition of what has to be done in order to comply with the order of the court? (b) Will enforcing compliance involve superintendence by the court to an unacceptable degree? (c) What are the respective prejudices or hardships that will be suffered by the parties if the order is made or not made?

As to (a), one may in this case sufficiently define what has to be done by the defendants by ordering the defendants, within say two months, to employ a porter to be resident at Danes Court for the purpose of carrying out the clause 3(11) duties. It is to be borne in mind that there is still a vacant flat available for a resident porter. As to (b), I do not see that such an order will occasion any protracted superintendence by the court. If the defendants without good cause fail to comply with the order in due time, then the plaintiffs can take appropriate enforcement proceedings against the defendants. As to (c), I see no hardship or prejudice resulting to the defendants from the order. They will simply be performing what they have promised to do and what has been carried out by the lessors over the past 20 years. On the other hand I see considerable inconvenience, if not exactly hardship, for the plaintiffs if, having bargained for a resident porter and paid a premium and having enjoyed his presence for 20 years, they are to be expected for the future to be content with a porter who simply walks up and down the stairs for two hours only during the day doing his cleaning and refuse collection. It follows that there should be an order for specific performance."

Co-Operative Insurance Society Ltd v. Argyll Stores (Holdings) Ltd
[1998] AC 1

The plaintiff landlord sought specific performance of a covenant in a lease requiring the defendant, which was the anchor tenant in a shopping centre, to keep its supermarket premises open for retail trade during usual business hours for the duration of the lease. The trial judge refused to order specific performance on the basis that there was a settled practice that an order which would require a defendant to run a business would not be made but the majority of the Court of Appeal ordered that the covenant be specifically performed. The House of Lords allowed the defendant's appeal and held that specific performance would not be granted.

LORD HOFFMANN stated at pp.9–19:

"*1. The Issue*
In 1955 Lord Goddard C.J. said:

> "No authority has been quoted to show that an injunction will be granted enjoining a person to carry on a business, nor can I think that one ever would be, certainly not where the business is a losing concern." *(Attorney-General v. Colchester Corporation* [1955] 2 QB 207, 217).

In this case his prediction has been falsified. The appellants Argyll Stores

(Holdings) Ltd ("Argyll") decided in May 1995 to close their Safeway supermarket in the Hillsborough Shopping Centre in Sheffield because it was losing money. This was a breach of a covenant in their lease, which contained in clause 4(19) a positive obligation to keep the premises open for retail trade during the usual hours of business. Argyll admitted the breach and, in an action by the landlord, the Co-operative Insurance Society ("CIS") consented to an order for damages to be assessed. But the Court of Appeal, reversing the trial judge, ordered that the covenant be specifically performed. It made a final injunction ordering Argyll to trade on the premises during the remainder of the term (which will expire on 3 August 2014) or until an earlier sub-letting or assignment. The Court of Appeal suspended its order for three months to allow time for Argyll to complete an assignment which by that time had been agreed. After a short agreed extension, the lease was assigned with the landlord's consent. In fact, therefore, the injunction never took effect. The appeal to your Lordships is substantially about costs. But the issue remains of great importance to landlords and tenants under other commercial leases.

2. The facts
A decree of specific performance is of course a discretionary remedy and the question for your Lordships is whether the Court of Appeal was entitled to set aside the exercise of the judge's discretion. There are well established principles which govern the exercise of the discretion but these, like all equitable principles, are flexible and adaptable to achieve the ends of equity, which is, as Lord Selborne L.C. once remarked, to "do more perfect and complete justice" than would be the result of leaving the parties to their remedies at common law. (*Wilson v. Northampton and Banbury Junction Railway Co.* (1874) LR 9 Ch App 279, 284). Much therefore depends upon the facts of the particular case and I shall begin by describing these in more detail.

The Hillsborough Shopping Centre consists of about 25 shops. Safeway was by far the largest shop and the greatest attraction. Its presence was a commercial benefit to the smaller shops nearby. The lease was for a term of 35 years from 4 August 1979 with five-yearly rent reviews. Clause 4(12)(a) contained a negative covenant as to the user of the premises:

> "Not to use or suffer to be used the demised premises other than as a retail store for the sale of food groceries provisions and goods normally sold from time to time by a retail grocer food supermarkets and food superstores. . . ."

Clause 4(19) was the positive covenant enforced in this case:

> "To keep the demised premises open for retail trade during the usual hours of business in the locality and the display windows properly dressed in a suitable manner in keeping with a good class parade of shops."

Competition in the supermarket business is fierce and in 1994 Argyll undertook a major review of its business and decided to reduce the scale of its operations.

The management was to be reorganised, 27 loss-making or less profitable supermarkets closed and thousands of employees made redundant. Hillsborough, which according to Argyll's management accounts had made a loss of about £70,000 in the previous year, was on the list for closure. For administrative reasons as well as to avoid the demoralising effect of successive closure announcements, it was decided to close all the supermarkets at once and try to negotiate the disposal of their sites as a package. In early April 1995 Argyll announced that Hillsborough and the other supermarkets would close on 6 May 1995.

As soon as CIS heard of the impending closure, it protested. On 12 April 1995 Mr. Wightman, the Regional Surveyor of the Investment Department, wrote to Mr. Jefferies of Safeway:

> "Whilst obviously there is little point in trying to influence your corporate decision with regard to the closure of this unit I am dismayed at the short period of notice given which will undoubtedly have immediate impact on the Centre and all the other tenants trading therein."

He drew attention to the covenant to keep open, invited Safeway to agree to continue trading until a suitable assignee had been found, offered to negotiate a temporary rent concession and asked for a reply by return of post.

Unfortunately he received no answer. Mr. Jefferies had himself fallen victim to the reorganisation; he had been made redundant. No one else dealt with the letter. On Saturday 6 May 1995 the supermarket closed and over the next two weeks its fittings were stripped out. On 22 May 1995 CIS issued a writ claiming specific performance of the covenant to keep open and damages.

3. The trial
CIS issued a summons for judgment under RSC Ord 14 but when the matter came before His Honour Judge Maddocks, sitting as a judge of the High Court on 1 August 1995 it was agreed that, since the material facts were not in dispute, the hearing should be treated as the trial of the action. The learned judge was therefore invited by CIS to make a final order that the covenant be performed for the remainder of the lease or until an earlier assignment or subletting. By this time Argyll were already in serious negotiation with another supermarket chain for an assignment but no contract had yet been signed.

The judge refused to order specific performance. He said that there was on the authorities a settled practice that orders which would require a defendant to run a business would not be made. He was not content, however, merely to follow authority. He gave reasons why he thought that specific performance would be inappropriate. Two such reasons were by way of justification for the general practice. An order to carry on a business, as opposed to an order to perform a "single and well defined act," was difficult to enforce by the sanction of committal. And where a business was being run at a loss, specific relief would be "too far reaching and beyond the scope of control which the court should seek to impose." The other two related to the particular case. A resumption of business would be expensive (refitting the shop was estimated to cost over £1 million) and although Argyll had knowingly acted in breach of covenant, it had done so "in the light of the settled practice of the court to award damages." Finally, while the assessment of damages might be difficult, it was the kind of exercise which the courts had done in the past.

4. The settled practice

There is no dispute about the existence of the settled practice to which the judge referred. It is sufficient for this purpose to refer to *Braddon Towers Ltd. v. International Stores Ltd.* [1987] 1 EGLR 209, 213, where Slade J. said:

> "Whether or not this may be properly described as a rule of law, I do not doubt that for many years practitioners have advised their clients that it is the settled and invariable practice of this court never to grant mandatory injunctions requiring persons to carry on business."

But the practice has never, so far as I know, been examined by this House and it is open to the respondents to say that it rests upon inadequate grounds or that it has been too inflexibly applied.

Specific performance is traditionally regarded in English law as an exceptional remedy, as opposed to the common law damages to which a successful plaintiff is entitled as of right. There may have been some element of later rationalisation of an untidier history, but by the nineteenth century it was orthodox doctrine that the power to decree specific performance was part of the discretionary jurisdiction of the Court of Chancery to do justice in cases in which the remedies available at common law were inadequate. This is the basis of the general principle that specific performance will not be ordered when damages are an adequate remedy. By contrast, in countries with legal systems based on civil law, such as France, Germany and Scotland, the plaintiff is prima facie entitled to specific performance. The cases in which he is confined to a claim for damages are regarded as the exceptions. In practice, however, there is less difference between common law and civilian systems than these general statements might lead one to suppose. The principles upon which English judges exercise the discretion to grant specific performance are reasonably well settled and depend upon a number of considerations, mostly of a practical nature, which are of very general application. I have made no investigation of civilian systems, but a priori I would expect that judges take much the same matters into account in deciding whether specific performance would be inappropriate in a particular case.

The practice of not ordering a defendant to carry on a business is not entirely dependent upon damages being an adequate remedy. In *Dowty Boulton Paul Ltd. v. Wolverhampton Corporation* [1971] 1 WLR 204, Sir John Pennycuick V.-C. refused to order the corporation to maintain an airfield as a going concern because: "It is very well established that the court will not order specific performance of an obligation to carry on a business": see p. 211. He added: "It is unnecessary in the circumstances to discuss whether damages would be an adequate remedy to the company": see p. 212. Thus the reasons which underlie the established practice may justify a refusal of specific performance even when damages are not an adequate remedy.

The most frequent reason given in the cases for declining to order someone to carry on a business is that it would require constant supervision by the court. In *J. C. Williamson Ltd. v. Lukey and Mulholland* (1931) 45 CLR 282, 297-298, Dixon J. said flatly "Specific performance is inapplicable when the continued supervision of the Court is necessary in order to ensure the fulfilment of the contract."

There has, I think, been some misunderstanding about what is meant by continued superintendence. It may at first sight suggest that the judge (or some other officer of the court) would literally have to supervise the execution of the order. In *C.H. Giles & Co. v. Morris* [1972] 1 WLR 307, 318 Megarry J. said that "difficulties of constant superintendence" were a "narrow consideration" because:

> "there is normally no question of the court having to send its officers to supervise the performance of the order . . . . Performance . . . is normally secured by the realisation of the person enjoined that he is liable to be punished for contempt if evidence of his disobedience to the order is put before the court; . . ."

This is, of course, true but does not really meet the point. The judges who have said that the need for constant supervision was an objection to such orders were no doubt well aware that supervision would in practice take the form of rulings by the court, on application made by the parties, as to whether there had been a breach of the order. It is the possibility of the court having to give an indefinite series of such rulings in order to ensure the execution of the order which has been regarded as undesirable.

Why should this be so? A principal reason is that, as Megarry J. pointed out in the passage to which I have referred, the only means available to the court to enforce its order is the quasi-criminal procedure of punishment for contempt. This is a powerful weapon; so powerful, in fact, as often to be unsuitable as an instrument for adjudicating upon the disputes which may arise over whether a business is being run in accordance with the terms of the court's order. The heavy-handed nature of the enforcement mechanism is a consideration which may go to the exercise of the court's discretion in other cases as well, but its use to compel the running of a business is perhaps the paradigm case of its disadvantages and it is in this context that I shall discuss them.

The prospect of committal or even a fine, with the damage to commercial reputation which will be caused by a finding of contempt of court, is likely to have at least two undesirable consequences. First, the defendant, who ex hypothesi did not think that it was in his economic interest to run the business at all, now has to make decisions under a sword of Damocles which may descend if the way the business is run does not conform to the terms of the order. This is, as one might say, no way to run a business. In this case the Court of Appeal made light of the point because it assumed that, once the defendant had been ordered to run the business, self-interest and compliance with the order would thereafter go hand in hand. But, as I shall explain, this is not necessarily true.

Secondly, the seriousness of a finding of contempt for the defendant means that any application to enforce the order is likely to be a heavy and expensive piece of litigation. The possibility of repeated applications over a period of time means that, in comparison with a once-and-for-all inquiry as to damages, the enforcement of the remedy is likely to be expensive in terms of cost to the parties and the resources of the judicial system.

This is a convenient point at which to distinguish between orders which require a defendant to carry on an activity, such as running a business over or more or less extended period of time, and orders which require him to achieve a result. The possibility of repeated applications for rulings on compliance with the order which arises in the former case does not exist to anything like the same extent in the latter. Even if the achievement of the result is a complicated matter which will take some time, the court, if called upon to rule, only has to examine the finished work and say whether it complies with the order. This point was made in the context of relief against forfeiture in *Shiloh Spinners Ltd. v. Harding* [1973] AC 691. If it is a condition of relief that the tenant should have complied with a repairing covenant, difficulty of supervision need not be an objection. As Lord Wilberforce said, at p. 724:

> "[W]hat the court has to do is to satisfy itself, ex post facto, that the covenanted work has been done, and it has ample machinery, through certificates, or by inquiry, to do precisely this."

This distinction between orders to carry on activities and to achieve results explains why the courts have in appropriate circumstances ordered specific performance of building contracts and repairing covenants: see *Wolverhampton Corporation v. Emmons* [1901] 1 QB 515 (building contract) and *Jeune v. Queens Cross Properties Ltd.* [1974] Ch 97 (repairing covenant). It by no means follows, however, that even obligations to achieve a result will always be enforced by specific performance. There may be other objections, to some of which I now turn.

One such objection, which applies to orders to achieve a result and a fortiori to orders to carry on an activity, is imprecision in the terms of the order. If the terms of the court's order, reflecting the terms of the obligation, cannot be precisely drawn, the possibility of wasteful litigation over compliance is increased. So is the oppression caused by the defendant having to do things under threat of proceedings for contempt. The less precise the order, the fewer the signposts to the forensic minefield which he has to traverse. The fact that the terms of a contractual obligation are sufficiently definite to escape being void for uncertainty, or to found a claim for damages, or to permit compliance to be made a condition of relief against forfeiture, does not necessarily mean that they will be sufficiently precise to be capable of being specifically performed. So in *Wolverhampton Corporation v. Emmons* [1901] 1 QB 515, Romer L.J. said that the first condition for specific enforcement of a building contract was that, at p. 525:

> "the particulars of the work are so far definitely ascertained that the court can sufficiently see what is the exact nature of the work of which it is asked to order the performance".

Similarly in *Redland Bricks Ltd. v. Morris* [1970] AC 652, 666 Lord Upjohn stated the following general principle for the grant of mandatory injunctions to carry out building works:

> "[T]he court must be careful to see that the defendant knows exactly in fact what he has to do and this means not as a matter of law but as a matter of fact, so that in carrying out an order he can give his contractors the proper instructions."

Precision is of course a question of degree and the courts have shown themselves willing to cope with a certain degree of imprecision in cases of orders requiring the achievement of a result in which the plaintiff's merits appeared strong; like all the reasons which I have been discussing, it is, taken alone, merely a discretionary matter to be taken into account: see Spry, *Equitable Remedies* (4th ed., 1990) at p. 112. It is, however, a very important one.

I should at this point draw attention to what seems to me to have been a misreading of certain remarks of Lord Wilberforce in *Shiloh Spinners Ltd. v. Harding* [1973] AC 691, 724. He pointed out, as I have said, that to grant relief against forfeiture subject to compliance with a repairing covenant involves the court in no more than the possibility of a retrospective assessment of whether the covenanted work has been done. For this reason, he said:

> "Where it is necessary, and, in my opinion, right, to move away from some 19th century authorities, is to reject as a reason against granting relief, the impossibility for the courts to supervise the doing of work."

This is plainly a remark about cases involving the achievement of a result, such as doing repairs, and, within that class, about making compliance a condition of relief against forfeiture. But in *Tito v. Waddell (No. 2)* [1977] Ch 106, 322 Sir Robert Megarry V.-C. took it to be a generalisation about specific performance and, in particular, a rejection of difficulty of supervision as an objection, even in cases of orders to carry on an activity. The Vice-Chancellor regarded it as an adoption of his own views (based, as I have said, on incomplete analysis of what was meant by difficulty of supervision) in *C.H. Giles & Co. Ltd. v. Morris* [1972] 1 WLR 307, 318. In the present case [1996] Ch 286, 292-293, Legatt LJ took this claim at face value. In fact, Lord Wilberforce went on to say that impossibility of supervision "is a reality, no doubt, and explains why specific performance cannot be granted of agreements to this effect." Lord Wilberforce was in my view drawing attention to the fact that the collection of reasons which the courts have in mind when they speak of difficulty of supervision apply with much greater force to orders for specific performance, giving rise to the possibility of committal for contempt, than they do to conditions for relief against forfeiture. While the paradigm case to which such objections apply is the order to carry on an activity, they can also apply to an order requiring the achievement of a result.

There is a further objection to an order requiring the defendant to carry on a business, which was emphasised by Millett L.J. in the Court of Appeal. This is that it may cause injustice by allowing the plaintiff to enrich himself at the defendant's expense. The loss which the plaintiff may suffer through having to comply with the order (for example, by running a business at a loss for an indefinite period) may be far greater than the plaintiff would suffer from the contract being broken. As Professor R. J. Sharpe explains in *Specific Remedies for Contract Breach*, Ch. 5 of *Studies in Contract Law* (1980) (ed. Reiter and Swan), p. 129:

> "In such circumstances, a specific decree in favour of the plaintiff will put him in a bargaining position *vis-à-vis* the defendant whereby the measure of what he will receive will be the value to the defendant of being released from performance. If the plaintiff bargains effectively, the amount he will set will exceed the value to him of performance and will approach the cost to the defendant to complete."

This was the reason given by Lord Westbury L.C. in *Isenberg v. East India House Estate Co. Ltd.* (1863) 3 De GJ & S 263, 273 for refusing a mandatory injunction to compel the defendant to pull down part of a new building which interfered with the plaintiff's light and exercising instead the Court of Chancery's recently-acquired jurisdiction under Lord Cairns's Act 1858 (21 & 22 Vict. c. 27) to order payment of damages:

> "... I hold it ... to be the duty of the court in such a case as the present not, by granting a mandatory injunction, to deliver over the defendants to the plaintiff bound hand and foot, in order to be made subject to any extortionate demand that he may by possibility make, but to substitute for such mandatory injunction an inquiry before itself, in order to ascertain the measure of damage that has been actually sustained."

It is true that the defendant has, by his own breach of contract, put himself in such an unfortunate position. But the purpose of the law of contract is not to punish wrongdoing but to satisfy the expectations of the party entitled to performance. A remedy which enables him to secure, in money terms, more than the performance due to him is unjust. From a wider perspective, it cannot be in the public interest for the courts to require someone to carry on business at a loss if there is any plausible alternative by which the other party can be given compensation. It is not only a waste of resources but yokes the parties together in a continuing hostile relationship. The order for specific performance prolongs the battle. If the defendant is ordered to run a business, its conduct becomes the subject of a flow of complaints, solicitors' letters and affidavits. This is wasteful for both parties and the legal system. An award of damages, on the other hand, brings the litigation to an end. The defendant pays damages, the forensic link between them is severed, they go their separate ways and the wounds of conflict can heal.

The cumulative effect of these various reasons, none of which would necessarily be sufficient on its own, seems to me to show that the settled practice is based upon sound sense. Of course the grant or refusal of specific performance remains a matter for the judge's discretion. There are no binding rules, but this does not mean that there cannot be settled principles, founded upon practical considerations of the kind which I have discussed, which do not have to be re-examined in every case, but which the courts will apply in all but exceptional circumstances. As Slade J. said in the passage which I have quoted from *Braddon Towers Ltd. v. International Stores Ltd.* [1987] 1 EGLR 209, 213 lawyers have no doubt for many years advised their clients on this basis. In the present case, Leggatt L.J. remarked that there was no evidence that such advice had been given. In my view, if the law or practice on a point is settled, it should be assumed that persons entering into legal transactions will have been advised accordingly. I am sure that the learned Lord Justice would not wish to encourage litigants to adduce evidence of the particular advice which they received. Indeed, I doubt whether such evidence would be admissible.

5. The decision of the Court of Appeal

I must now examine the grounds upon which the majority of the Court of Appeal thought it right to reverse the judge. In the first place, they regarded the practice which he followed as outmoded and treated Lord Wilberforce's remarks about relief against forfeiture in *Shiloh Spinners Ltd. v. Harding* [1973] AC 691, 724 as justifying a rejection of the arguments based on the need for constant supervision. Even Millett L.J., who dissented on other grounds, said that such objections had little force today. I do not agree. As I have already said, I think that Lord Wilberforce's remarks do not support this proposition in relation to specific performance of an obligation to carry on an activity and that the arguments based on difficulty of supervision remain powerful.

The Court of Appeal said that it was enough if the contract defined the tenant's obligation with sufficient precision to enable him to know what was necessary to comply with the order. Even assuming that this to be right, I do not think that the obligation in clause 4(19) can possibly be regarded as sufficiently precise to be capable of specific performance. It is to "keep the demised premises open for retail trade." It says nothing about the level of trade, the area of the premises within which trade is to be conducted, or even the kind of trade, although no doubt the tenant's choice would be restricted by the need to comply with the negative covenant in clause 4(12)(a) not to use the premises "other than as a retail store for the sale of food groceries provisions and goods normally sold from time to time by a retail grocer food supermarkets and food superstores." This language seems to me to provide ample room for argument over whether the tenant is doing enough to comply with the covenant.

The Court of Appeal thought that once Argyll had been ordered to comply with the covenant, it was, as Roch L.J. said, at p. 298, "inconceivable that they would not operate the business efficiently." Leggatt L.J. said that the requirement

> "was quite intelligible to the defendants, while they were carrying on business there.... If the premises are to be run as a business, it cannot be in the defendants' interest to run it half-heartedly or inefficiently. . ."

This treats the way the tenant previously conducted business as measuring the extent of his obligation to do so. In my view this is a non sequitur: the obligation depends upon the language of the covenant and not upon what the tenant has previously chosen to do. No doubt it is true that it would not be in the interests of the tenant to run the business inefficiently. But running the business efficiently does not necessarily mean running in the way it was run before. Argyll had decided that, from its point of view, the most efficient thing to do was to close the business altogether and concentrate its resources on achieving better returns elsewhere. If ordered to keep the business open, it might well decide that the next best strategy was to reduce its costs as far as was consistent with compliance with its obligations, in the expectation that a lower level of return would be more than compensated by higher returns from additional expenditure on more profitable shops. It is in my view wrong for the courts to speculate about whether Argyll might voluntarily carry on business in a way which would relieve the court from having to construe its order. The question of certainty must be decided on the assumption that the court might have to enforce the order according to its terms.

The respondent argued that the court should not be concerned about future difficulties which might arise in connection with the enforcement of the order. It should simply make the order and see what happened. In practice Argyll would be likely to find a suitable assignee (as it in fact did) or conduct the business so as to keep well clear of any possible enforcement proceedings or otherwise come to terms with the CIS. This may well be true, but the likelihood of Argyll having to perform beyond the requirements of its covenant or buy its way out of its obligation to incur losses seems to me to be in principle an objection to such an order rather than to recommend it. I think that it is normally undesirable for judges to make orders in terrorem, carrying a threat of imprisonment, which work only if no one inquires too closely into what they mean.

The likelihood that the order would be effective only for a short time until an assignment is an equivocal argument. It would be burdensome to make Argyll resume business only to stop again after a short while if a short stoppage would not cause any substantial damage to the business of the shopping centre. On the other hand, what would happen if a suitable assignee could not be found? Would Argyll then have to carry on business until 2014? Mr. Smith Q.C. who appeared for the CIS, said that if the order became oppressive (for example, because Argyll were being driven into bankruptcy) or difficult to enforce, they could apply for it to be varied or discharged. But the order would be a final order and there is no case in this jurisdiction in which such an order has been varied or discharged, except when the injuncted activity has been legalised by statute. Even assuming that there was such a jurisdiction if circumstances were radically changed, I find it difficult to see how this could be made to apply. Difficulties of enforcement would not be a change of circumstances. They would have been entirely predictable when the order was made. And so would the fact that Argyll would suffer unquantifiable loss if it was obliged to continue trading. I do not think that such expedients are an answer to the difficulties on which the objections to such orders are based.

Finally, all three judges in the Court of Appeal took a very poor view of Argyll's conduct. Leggatt L.J. said that they had acted "with gross commercial cynicism"; Roch L.J. began his judgment by saying that they had "behaved very badly" and Millett L.J. said that they had no merits. The principles of equity have always had a strong ethical content and nothing which I say is intended to diminish the influence of moral values in their application. I can envisage cases of gross breach of personal faith, or attempts to use the threat of non-performance as blackmail, in which the needs of justice will override all the considerations which support the settled practice. But although any breach of covenant is regrettable, the exercise of the discretion as to whether or not to grant specific performance starts from the fact that the covenant has been broken. Both landlord and tenant in this case are large sophisticated commercial organisations and I have no doubt that both were perfectly aware that the remedy for breach of the covenant was likely to be limited to an award of damages. The interests of both were purely financial: there was no element of personal breach of faith, as in the Victorian cases of railway companies which refused to honour obligations to build stations for landowners whose property they had taken: compare *Greene v. West Cheshire Railway Co.* (1871) LR 13 Eq 44. No doubt there was an effect on the businesses of other traders in the Centre, but Argyll had made no promises to them and it is not suggested that CIS warranted to other tenants that Argyll would remain. Their departure, with or without the consent of CIS, was a commercial risk which the tenants were able to deploy in negotiations for the next rent review. On the scale of broken promises, I can think of worse cases, but the language of the Court of Appeal left them with few adjectives to spare.

It was no doubt discourteous not to have answered Mr. Wightman's letter. But to say, as Roch L.J. did, that they had acted "wantonly and quite unreasonably" by removing their fixtures seems to me an exaggeration. There was no question of stealing a march, or attempting to present CIS with a fait accompli, because Argyll had no reason to believe that CIS would have been able to obtain a mandatory injunction whether the fixtures had been removed or not. They had made it perfectly clear that they were closing the shop and given CIS ample time to apply for such an injunction if so advised.

6. Conclusion

I think that no criticism can be made of the way in which His Honour Judge Maddocks Q.C. exercised his discretion. All the reasons which he gave were proper matters for him to take into account. In my view the Court of Appeal should not have interfered and I would allow the appeal and restore the order which he made."

Wanze Properties (Ireland) Ltd v. Five Star Supermarket
High Court (Costello P) 24 October 1997

The defendant company held a lease on a premises in a shopping centre which contained a covenant that it would be used as a supermarket and that it would trade during usual business hours. Costello P granted an interlocutory injunction to the plaintiff lessor requiring the defendant to comply with the covenants in the lease.

COSTELLO P stated at pp.1–5: "In this case the Defendant company holds the premises, the subject matter of these proceedings, under a lease which contains a covenant on the part of the lessee to use the demised premises for the purpose of the business of a supermarket and all business ancillary thereto only and without the landlord's consent in writing, it shall not be held reasonable to permit such property to be used for any other purpose. It also contains a covenant 11 of the tenant's covenant as follows: To keep the demised premises, or such portion thereof as is normally open to the public, open for the purpose of the said trade during the usual hours of business appropriate to the tenant's business, at least unless required to close by law or trade union regulation.

There has been quite clearly a flagrant breach and a deliberate breach of this covenant. The Defendant accepts that it breached the covenant and did so with his eyes open on the basis that it was prepared to pay damages. The Defendants submit that the only remedy available to the Plaintiffs for the loss which the Plaintiffs sustained as a result of the breach is that the loss should be quantified and damages awarded and further submit that it is settled law that the remedy which is also sought in these proceedings by the Plaintiff – namely an order of injunction or specific performance – is not available to the Plaintiff.

Now, as stated by Mr. O'Neill, and as indeed expressly agreed by Mr. Farrell on behalf of the Defendant, I am not deciding today whether or not I should grant an order for specific performance or a mandatory injunction. This is only the interlocutory stage of the action. What I have to decide is whether or not there is a reasonable probability that such an order shall be made and indeed this case really turns on this legal point because, the Defendants are prepared to pay damages but claim that the Court has no jurisdiction to grant the relief sought.

I am aware that the Courts have in the recent past been developing the law both in the area of specific performance and in the area of injunctions and I have been referred by Mr. O'Neill to the decisions of the High Court in this country in which orders for specific performance have been granted where on previous occasions it seems to me it is unlikely that they would have been granted. The Lift Manufacturers case was an order for the specific performance of a business contract. The Pharmacy Limited case was another case in which the Defendant was forced to do business with the Plaintiff company and I think some years ago such an order would not have been made. Similarly, in a more recent case, a decision of Mr. Justice McCracken, the Court in that case directed the Defendant to carry on certain business arrangements with the Plaintiff. So that it does seem to me that there has been a development of the law in this area in this country which has not yet gone as far as that urged by Mr. O'Neill on behalf of the Plaintiff. What has happened in England has been that in a case very analogous to the present case, the Court of Appeal in England reached a decision which was favourable to the Plaintiff's case in the instant case. That is to say it was a case in which a shopping centre was owned by the Plaintiffs and the Court ordered the Defendant supermarket to continue business in the premises. The House of Lords unanimously overruled the majority decision of the Court of Appeal and the House of Lords decision is one on which the Defendants in this case strongly rely and what I have to decide is whether or not the Plaintiffs in this case have made out a case that there is a reasonable probability that in the particular facts of this case, the Irish Courts would follow the decision of the House of Lords.

Now, it is clear from the headnote – and I think it is agreed that the headnote correctly summarises the judgment of the House of Lords – that the decision of the House of Lords indicated a rule of law which should be applied other than in exceptional circumstances. What the Plaintiffs say in this case is that the facts of this case are different to the facts in the House of Lords case to which I have referred in one significant way. In the House of Lords case the Defendant supermarket was running a business at a loss. The Court decided that it would not grant an order which would require the Defendant company to continue carrying on that business even though it had agreed to do so in the terms of its lease and it is of interest to note that in the case, to which Mr. Farrell referred me of Mr. Justice Slade, the Defendant company in that case was also suffering a loss and desired to cease business in the premises because of that fact.

This case, the Plaintiffs argue, is different. In this case the Defendant company took a deliberate decision, a deliberate commercial decision that it would expand its business in a different area close by, 400 yards away, in a different shopping centre which was then being developed. This was, I am sure, taken after very careful consideration of the economic benefits to the Defendant company in the move but there was a factor which had to be taken into account, namely that it had this lease under which for a further period of 12 years it had covenanted to remain in possession and carry on business in the Athlone Shopping Centre.

In my view it is open to the Plaintiffs to argue, and it is certainly a strong arguable case, that the financial loss which the Defendants would suffer as a result of being required to carry on business in the supermarket in the Athlone centre was brought on their own head by the Defendants own action and this factor is a different factor to that contained in the House of Lords case and in the decision of Mr. Justice Slade to which I have been referring.

In those circumstances it does seem to me that the Plaintiffs have been able to satisfy me that they have a strong arguable case that at the hearing they will obtain the relief they seek. Now, I am not deciding today that I should so make the order but I am deciding that in the case at the trial of the action. I am merely deciding that they have made out a strong case that there is a reasonable probability that they would get the order that they seek.

So at the interlocutory stage, applying the well established principles on which the Court grants interlocutory relief, the Plaintiffs have cleared the first hurdle. As to whether or not if the Plaintiffs succeed in this action, damages would be an adequate remedy again I will decide in favour of the Plaintiffs. I am quite satisfied that if the Court decides that it has power to grant an injunction or an order for specific performance, it would so do. It would not give damages in lieu because damages would be an entirely inadequate remedy.

The Plaintiff company has made out a prima facie case that it is facing very serious financial loss, perhaps catastrophic loss, as a result of the Defendants action and I do not think that if the Court came to a conclusion that it had a jurisdiction to grant the equitable relief, that it would not give damages instead of it.

As to the balance of convenience, again I think the Plaintiffs have made out a case that on the balance of convenience the Court should grant the relief sought once it decides that the Plaintiffs have made out a reasonable case on the law. Should it transpire that I wrongly refused today to grant the relief sought at the trial of the action it was quite clear that very, very serious injury would have been caused to the Plaintiff by this wrongful decision and in some amount of time when this hearing is being held, it would be very difficult if not impossible for the Court to compensate the Plaintiff for that loss."

Contracts to Build or Repair

While the degree of supervision which an order for specific performance would require will be a factor for a court in deciding whether to grant such orders in respect of contracts to build or repair, a crucial issue will be whether the contractual obligations are defined with sufficient precision. A further issue is whether the defendant is in possession of the lands in question as, if he is, it may not be possible for the plaintiff to employ a third party to carry out the works.

Wolverhampton Corporation v. Emmons
[1901] 1 KB 515

The plaintiff corporation sold land, which was part of a scheme for street improvement, to the defendant who agreed to build houses on the land. The Court of Appeal (AL Smith MR, Romer and Collins LJJ) held that the plaintiff could not be sufficiently compensated by an award of damages and ordered specific performance of the covenant to build.

ROMER LJ stated at pp.524–527: "I am also of opinion that the judgment of Wills J. should be affirmed. The question, which is not free from difficulty, is whether, under the circumstances of this case, an order for specific performance should be made in favour of the plaintiffs. There is no doubt that as a general rule the Court will not enforce specific performance of a building contract, but an exception from the rule has been recognised. It has, I think, for some time been held that, in order to bring himself within that exception, a plaintiff must establish three things. The first is that the building work, of which he seeks to enforce the performance, is defined by the contract; that is to say, that the particulars of the work are so far definitely ascertained that the Court can sufficiently see what is the exact nature of the work of which it is asked to order the performance. The second is that the plaintiff has a substantial interest in having the contract performed, which is of such a nature that he cannot adequately be compensated for breach of the contract by damages. The third is that the defendant has by the contract obtained possession of land on which the work is contracted to be done. The rule on this subject is stated by Fry L.J. in his work on Specific Performance, 3rd ed. pp. 44, 45, in substantially the same terms as those in which I have just stated it. The question is whether the plaintiffs in this case have brought themselves within the exception so stated. In my opinion they have. The first question is whether the work, of which specific performance is claimed, is sufficiently defined. I think that it is. No doubt, by the original covenant contained in the conveyance of July 31, 1897, the defendant, although he covenanted to erect buildings, did not covenant to erect buildings which were defined in the sense in which I have used the term; and I think that; if the case had rested upon that covenant, the plaintiffs would have failed to obtain a decree for specific performance. But subsequently to July 31, 1897, under circumstances which may be gathered from the correspondence between the parties, it appears that a supplemental agreement was ultimately entered into, with reference to the defendant's obligation under the original covenant, whereby the defendant did for valuable consideration undertake to erect houses in accordance with certain plans. When those plans are looked at, it seems to me that the work which the defendant undertook to carry out was perfectly defined by them, or at any rate sufficiently defined for the purposes of the doctrine which I am considering. They shew the elevations and sections of the houses, and the form of them in every respect, and I think, though I do not say that would necessarily be essential, they sufficiently shew the materials of which the houses were to be constructed. This supplemental agreement was made, as I have said, for valuable consideration: it is in writing, being contained in the correspondence between the parties: and it is an agreement which sufficiently defines the works to be done to be capable of being enforced by a decree for specific performance. That being so, the first feature to which I have alluded, as essential to bring a case within the exception to the rule I have mentioned, exists in the present case. The next question is whether in this case the plaintiffs were interested in the performance of the contract in such a manner that damages would be no adequate compensation to them for the breach of it. To my mind they clearly were so interested. I do not see how it is possible adequately to estimate in money the loss which would be suffered by the plaintiffs, if the defendant's agreement to build these houses were not performed. The object of the plaintiffs, in requiring the defendant to enter into the contract to build on the land, obviously was to benefit the town, and to increase the rateable value of the property therein. That the improvement of this part of the town was a matter which they had in view, and which they deemed important, is shewn by the original deed of July 31, 1897, which, although it does not specify the exact character of the buildings to be erected, contains a covenant by the defendant that he will not build any building of which the elevation has not been previously approved by the public works committee of the corporation. It appears to me that under the circumstances the plaintiffs have such an interest in having the defendant's contract specifically performed that the breach of it is not capable of being compensated for by pecuniary compensation. The only question that remains is as to the existence of the third feature which I have mentioned as an essential in these cases – namely, whether the defendant obtained possession of the land on which the buildings were to be erected by means of the contract for their erection. Clearly he did. I therefore find that all the three matters which I have mentioned as essential to the plaintiffs' title to specific performance exist in this case. No case has been cited, and I do not know of any, where, upon those three matters being shewn to the Court to exist, a decree for specific performance has been refused. On the other hand we have the case of *Cubitt v. Smith* (1864) 11 LT 298, which, so far as I know, has never been dissented from by any Court. Prima facie, therefore, at any rate the plaintiffs are in my opinion entitled to specific performance of the defendant's contract. Then, are there any good reasons why the Court should not grant the plaintiffs that remedy? I cannot see that any reason has been put forward for the defendant which affects the plaintiffs' right, or which ought to induce the Court to refuse to make an order for specific performance. It is urged that the defendant will have to make a large expenditure in performing his contract, which may not prove remunerative. What have the plaintiffs to do with that? The defendant knew, or ought to have known, what he was binding himself to do when he entered into the original covenant of July 31, 1897. I must say that, if ever there was a case in which the conduct of the defendant was such that the Court ought not to shew any indulgence in the matter of ordering specific performance, it is the present case, the defendant having again and again obtained indulgence from the plaintiffs on representations that he was about to perform his contract, whereas in the result it appears that he cannot be made to perform it at all without the intervention of the Court. For these reasons I think that the appeal should be dismissed."

Rushbrooke v. O'Sullivan
[1908] 1 IR 232

The defendant agreed to take a lease of premises from the plaintiff and to carry out specified repairs and improvements to it. The plaintiff's action for specific performance of the agreement to repair failed on the basis that the nature of the work had not been so specifically defined to justify a decree and Porter MR held that the plaintiff's remedy lay in damages.

PORTER MR stated at pp. 234–237: "I do not see my way to make an order for specific performance in this case. The views of Courts of Equity as to enforcing covenants to build and covenants to repair have not always been consistent. In earlier days the Courts of Equity appear to have specifically enforced such covenants. Sir Edward Fry, in his book on Specific Performance, section 98 (4th ed.), p. 41, states that "in some old cases, the Court of Chancery entertained suits in respect of building contracts: and what has been considered one of the earliest traces of the jurisdiction in specific performance is a dictum of Genney, J., in the 8 Edward 4, that a promise to build a house would be specifically enforced. Lord Hardwicke also maintained this view of the jurisdiction of the Court. But it is now clearly settled that, subject to certain exceptions, the Court will not specifically enforce contracts to build or repair, both because specific performance is 'decreed only where the party wants the thing in specie, and cannot have it any other way,' and because such contracts are for the most part so uncertain that the Court would be unable to enforce its own judgment" The case of *Wolverhampton Corporation v. Emmons* [1901] 1 KB 515 gives judicial sanction to the statement of the eminent text writer, and, while recognizing the general rule, affords a notable illustration and example of the class of cases in which the Courts have recognized exceptions from the general rule.

What were the facts of that case? [The Master of the Rolls referred to the report and continued.] It is plain that the determining factor in the decision of that case was the "subsequent agreement," the "supplemental agreement," by which, as Cotton, L.J., says (at page 524), "the buildings to be erected were specifically defined in all particulars." This is plain from the judgments of the Master of the Rolls and the Lords Justices.

The Master of the Rolls says (at page 522):

> "The authorities to which reference has been made appear to me to show that, where there is a definite contract, by which a person, who has acquired land in consideration thereof, has agreed to erect on the land so acquired a building, of which the particulars are clearly specified, and the erection of which is of an importance to the other party which cannot adequately be measured by pecuniary damages, that is a case in which, according to the doctrine acted upon by Courts of Equity in relation to such matters, specific performance ought to be ordered."

Collins, L.J., says (at page 524):

> "Whatever the exact principle of equity on the subject may be, I think it is clear on the authorities that the elements exist in this case which in previous cases of the kind have been held to justify the Court in making a decree for specific performance. In this case land was conveyed to the defendant by the plaintiffs, part of the consideration being the covenant by him to erect buildings on it; by the subsequent agreement the buildings to be erected were specifically defined in all particulars; and, having regard to the circumstances and the position of the plaintiffs, it appears to me that damages would not be an adequate compensation to the plaintiffs for the breach by the defendant of his contract. I think, therefore, that this is a case in which the Court has power to make an order for specific performance, and in which such an order ought to be made."

Romer, L.J., says (at page 824):

> "There is no doubt as a general rule the Court will not enforce specific performance of a building contract, but an exception from the rule has been recognized. It has, I think, for some time been held that, in order to bring himself within that exception, a plaintiff must establish three things. The first is that the building work, of which he seeks to enforce the performance, is defined by the contract; that is to say, that the particulars of the work are so far definitely ascertained that the Court can sufficiently see what is the exact nature of the work of which it is asked to order the performance. The second is that the plaintiff has a substantial interest in having the contract performed, which is of such a nature that he cannot be adequately compensated for the breach of contract by damages."

The present case does not fall within the class of exceptional cases. It fails because there are no plans, particulars, or specifications. The contract is "within twelve months from the date of the agreement to expend the sum of £600 at the least in such substantial repairs and improvements as are mentioned in the second schedule hereto of and in the said messuage, hereditaments, and premises described in the first schedule, hereto, and in such manner as the landlord or his architect or surveyor shall approve or direct, and shall prove such expenditure as aforesaid to the satisfaction of the landlord or his architect or surveyor." The repairs and improvements mentioned in the second schedule are these: "To take down, rebuild, and repair such portion or portions of said premises as said architect shall direct under his directions and to his satisfaction." Where is there anything definite in that? Where is there any plan showing the particulars of the work to be done, such as was held to have been arranged and agreed upon in *Wolverhampton Corporation v. Emmons* [1901] 1 KB 515? Could anything be less definite than this schedule? If the plaintiff's architect had before the action was brought made out his plans and specifications, and had said: "There is what you must do; you must take down here; you must rebuild and repair there," then *Wolverhampton Corporation v. Emmons* would apply; but personally I am not disposed to extend the class of exceptions further than it has been extended. I agree that the question is a most difficult one; it must often be a matter of the utmost delicacy for the Court to determine how far it will go in granting specific performance of a covenant to build or repair; but in the present case I am clear that the exact nature of the work to be done has not been so specifically defined or ascertained as to justify a decree for specific performance.

The plaintiff is entitled to judgment on the pleadings for the breach by the defendant of his covenant; but the remedy lies in damages and in damages only. There will be judgment for the plaintiff with costs, and an inquiry as to damages. I hope that the judgment of the Court will not be misinterpreted by the defendant; he is mistaken if he thinks he will escape his liability."

DEFENCES TO AN ACTION FOR SPECIFIC PERFORMANCE

Lack of Mutuality

Traditionally it was accepted that it was not fair to order specific performance at the suit of one party when a court could not do so at the suit of the other party[5] and lack of mutuality is well recognised as a discretionary bar to relief. While it has been suggested that the appropriate date for assessing lack of mutuality is the date the contract was entered into,[6] the better view is that it should be tested at the date of the hearing.[7] A number of issues relating to the defence of lack of mutuality were examined by O'Connor LJ in the course of his judgment in *O'Regan v. White*.

---

[5] Although it has also long been recognised that this principle is subject to exceptions e.g. *Fennelly v. Anderson* (1851) 1 Ir Ch R 706.

[6] *Murphy v. Harrington* [1927] IR 339, 344.

[7] *Price v. Strange* [1978] Ch 337 and *O'Regan v. White* [1919] 2 IR 339.

O'Regan v. White
[1919] 2 IR 339

O'CONNOR LJ stated at pp.392–395: "A further point has been raised by the plaintiff, that inasmuch as the contract found by the jury included an obligation on the part of Robert White to manage the creamery – an obligation in its nature incapable of specific performance – the obligation on the other side to make over the land was equally incapable of specific performance, and that, therefore, the defendants, having no equitable right to have the lands conveyed to them, the ejectment must issue against them.

The general principle as to the necessity for mutuality in a suit for specific performance is laid down in a text-book of great authority, thus:– "A contract to be specifically enforced by the Court must, as a general rule, be mutual – that is to say, such that it might, at the time it was entered into, have been enforced by either of the parties against the other of them" (Fry on Specific Performance, 5th ed., p. 231). If the words "as a general rule" be taken as equivalent to "subject to the exceptions hereinafter set forth," and which exceptions I need not further refer to, as they throw no light upon this case, I think this statement requires some modification.

The foundation of the doctrine of specific performance is thus stated by Farwell J., in *Hexter v. Pearce* [1900] 1 Ch 341:– "To my mind the whole doctrine of specific performance rests on the ground that a man is entitled in equity to have in specie the specific article for which he has contracted, and is not bound to take damages instead." One of the limitations to the doctrine is that equity will not aid one party to an agreement to have in specie that for which he bargained unless it can likewise aid (if necessary) the other party to have in specie that for which he bargained. A good example of that is the case of *Blackett v. Bates* (1865) LR 1 Ch App 117. In that case an arbitrator made an award that the defendant should execute to the plaintiff a lease of the right to use such part of a certain railway made by the plaintiff as was upon the land of the defendant, and that the defendant should have a right of running carriages over the whole line on certain terms, and might require the plaintiff to supply engine power, and that the plaintiff should during the term keep the whole railway in good repair. It was held that specific performance of the award could not be decreed, inasmuch as the provisions in favour of the defendant could not be enforced at once, but gave the defendant a right to have certain duties continuously performed by the plaintiff for a number of years, and the Court could not undertake to see to such performance. Lord Cranworth said (at p. 124):– "The rights of the parties in respect of specific performance are the same as if the award had been simply an agreement between them. Had it been an agreement, would there have been a case for specific performance? I think not, and for this short and simple reason that the Court does not grant specific performance unless it can give full relief to both parties. Here the plaintiff gets at once what he seeks – the lease; but the defendant cannot get what he is entitled to, for his right is not a right to something which can be performed at once, but a right to enforce the performance by the plaintiff of daily duties during the whole term of the lease. The Court has no means of enforcing the performance of these duties."

Now, it will be observed that in that case, and, I think, in all the other cases in which relief has been refused on the ground of want of mutuality, the obligation on the plaintiff under the contract, as well as the obligation of the defendant under the contract, not having been performed, the mutual obligations were, wholly or partially, in fieri.

Generally speaking, at any rate, it would not be even-handed justice to compel specific performance against the one party, where the same remedy would not be available against the other party in respect of matters to be by him performed under the contract. But has the reason for this limitation on the powers of the Court any application where the party seeking specific performance has done everything by him to be done under the contract? Take a very simple case: A says to B, "If you agree to go to India and transact such and such a business there, I will, on your completing your agreement, convey to you my lands of Blackacre." B, who would not have undertaken the business at all but for the tempting offer of Blackacre, accepts, goes to India, transacts the business he engages for, and on his return demands Blackacre from A. Shall he not have it? If not, why not? Is it on the ground of want of mutuality? What mutuality? The contract itself provided that the obligation on A should never arise until B had entirely performed his obligation; in other words, the contract negatived all idea of mutuality at the time A's obligation to convey arose. In such a case, in my opinion, the defence as to the want of mutuality fails. I am confirmed in this view by the circumstance that in *Maddison v. Alderson* (1883) 8 App Cas 467, which to all intents and purposes was a suit for specific performance, and the contract in which did not in essentials vary from the illustration I have given, the elaborate discussion and judgments as to part performance would have been wholly unnecessary if the point as to mutuality were a good point in a case of the kind.

The illustration I have put is one in which the obligation sought to be enforced arises only and is dependant upon the other party's completion of his obligation. There are other cases in which the obligations on both sides are concurrent – that is to say, they arise immediately on the execution of the contract. In such cases it may in future be argued that the complete performance by the plaintiff of an obligation in its nature not capable of being specifically enforced gives him the right to specific performance as against the defendant of an obligation in its nature capable of being specifically enforced. I express no final opinion as to that; but I can imagine cases where, the plaintiff having, at the time of action brought, performed all his obligations under the contract, it would be a hardship to refuse him specific performance merely on the ground that at the date of the contract the plaintiff's oblgation could not have been specifically enforced against him. I should also like to point out that a case, relevant on this point, and cited in Fry (at p. 285) of *Hope v. Hope* (1857) 8 De GM & G 731, 748, does not seem to me an authority for the proposition in the text. That proposition is – "From the time of the execution of the contract, being the time to judge of its mutuality, it further follows that the subsequent performance by one party of terms which could not have been enforced by the other will not prevent the objection which would arise from the presence of such terms." In my opinion, the passage from Turner L.J.'s judgment does not bear out that proposition. This is the passage:– "Lastly, it was urged on the plaintiff's behalf that whatever objection there might have been to this agreement in its inception, what remains to be performed is legal and unobjectionable; but to hold that an agreement so objectionable as that this Court would not perform it can be rendered capable of performance by the objectionable parts of it having been carried into execution, is a doctrine to which I cannot assent." That seems to me tantamount to saying that equity will not aid an agreement which, in part at any rate, is *contra bonos mores*. I have said enough to show that the doctrine of mutuality as generally stated needs some modification. On the extent of that modification I give no opinion save so far as is necessary for this case; but it seems to me that there is a great deal of forge in the observations of the learned writer in 19 Law Quarterly Review, July, 1903, at p. 341 (cited in Fry, p. 235, n. 2), that the exceptions to the doctrine of mutuality "are all referable to one and the same general principle, viz., that the defence of want of mutuality will not avail to prevent the Court from exercising its beneficial jurisdiction where the contract can be properly enforced without any possible injustice to the defendant, provided a corresponding equitable remedy" (he might have said "if necessary") "becomes available against the plaintiff on or before his institution of the action"."

Misrepresentation

Where a misrepresentation is serious enough to justify rescission of a contract it will also suffice to provide a defence to an action for specific performance and an order of specific performance may also be refused where there is no right to rescind.[8] While an innocent misrepresentation may even suffice to provide a defence,[9] in such cases it may be necessary to establish that this led to fundamental unfairness in the transaction. These issues are considered in the decision of the Supreme Court in *Smelter Corporation of Ireland Ltd v. O'Driscoll*.

---

[8] *Re Banister* (1879) 12 Ch D 131, 142 *per* Jessel MR.
[9] *Ibid.* at 147 *per* James LJ.

Smelter Corporation of Ireland Ltd v. O'Driscoll
[1977] IR 305

The plaintiff claimed an order of specific performance in relation to a contract for the sale of lands. The plaintiff's agent had told the defendant in the course of negotiations that if she did not agree to sell, the local authority would acquire the lands compulsorily and although the agent believed this statement to be true, it was actually without foundation. The Supreme Court (O'Higgins CJ, Kenny and Parke JJ) held that while the plaintiff's agent had acted in a *bona fide* manner, by reason of the misrepresentation of the facts by the agent, the defendant had been under a 'fundamental misapprehension' as to the true position. O'Higgins CJ concluded that in these circumstances there was a fundamental unfairness in the transaction and that it would be unjust to grant a decree of specific performance.

O'HIGGINS CJ stated at pp.306–312: "This is an appeal brought by the plaintiffs from the decision and judgment of Mr. Justice Butler refusing their claim for specific performance of an agreement entered into by the defendant for the sale to them of 55 acres 0 roods and 36 perches of land situate at Carrigrenan in the county of Cork.

The plaintiffs are a limited liability company formed for the purpose of establishing in Ireland a smelter or base-metal reduction plant. At the time of the agreement sought to be enforced, the plaintiffs were engaged in the acquisition of land as a suitable site for such a plant in the Little Island area of Cork. The defendant is the owner of the land which is the subject of the agreement, but the negotiations in relation to the agreement were conducted on her behalf by her husband, Michael O'Driscoll, and later by her solicitor who has since died. The agreement necessarily took the form of an option to purchase, and was dated the 25th November, 1969.

Under the agreement the plaintiffs, in consideration of the payment of £7,000, were given for 12 months an option to purchase at a price to be determined by Mr. Owen MacCarthy (the well-known arbitrator to the Land Values Reference Committee) on an arbitration specially held for that purpose. Provision was made for the extension of the option for a further period of six months on the payment of a further sum of £3,250 and there were other clauses which are not relevant to the issues raised in this appeal. In the event of the option being exercised, it was provided that the option payments should be credited against the purchase money and, if the option was not exercised for any of the three grounds set out in clause 9, it was provided that one-half of such sums should be returned to the plaintiffs and that, in the meantime, such one-half should be secured on deposit. On the 10th January, 1970, Mr. Owen MacCarthy determined in his arbitration award that the purchase price of the land should be at the rate of £1,500 per acre, which resulted in a purchase price of £82,837.50.

By letter dated the 23rd November, 1970, the plaintiffs took a second option for six months for the sum of £3,250 which was thereupon paid to the defendant's solicitor. A third option for six months was then purchased by the plaintiffs as a result of negotiations between the auctioneer acting for the plaintiffs, Mr. Ahern, and the defendant's solicitor. The consideration for this option was also £3,250, but this sum was not to be credited against the purchase money should the plaintiffs exercise the option. At the expiration of the third option, a fourth was negotiated as is evidenced by a letter dated the 24th November, 1971, from the defendant's solicitor to the plaintiffs. This option was for a further six months for a nominal consideration but on the terms that the option monies paid under the original option should now be freed to the defendant and should not be credited against the purchase money in the event of the option being exercised. In effect, this arrangement constituted the ground of a fresh option to purchase for a fixed price of £93,087.50 being £82,837.50 as fixed by Mr. MacCarthy, plus the £10,250 paid in respect of the options under the agreement of 25th November, 1969. By letter dated 15th May, 1972, the plaintiffs purported to exercise this final option. The defendant was unwilling and refused to complete and these proceedings were commenced by the plaintiffs seeking specific performance of the agreement to sell, and associated relief.

The defence to the plaintiffs' claim is based on two main grounds. In the first place it is contended at paragraph 3 of the defence that the option or options to purchase were given by the defendant "subject to a condition precedent that a smelter plant otherwise a base metal reduction plant would be built on the said lands and that the said lands would be used for no other purpose but the plaintiffs do not propose to build or utilise a smelter plant or base metal reduction plant on the said lands and the said condition precedent to the exercise of the said option has not been fulfilled and will not be fulfilled and the plaintiff is thereby debarred from exercising the said or any option."

At paragraph 4 of the defence it is also contended with regard to the option that "the same was obtained from the defendant under duress and coercion whereby the plaintiffs caused or permitted a local authority to clearly give her to understand that if she did not sell the said lands or give an option over the same to the plaintiffs for the purpose of a smelter plant or base metal reduction plant, then the said lands would be acquired by compulsory acquisition by the said local authority and given to the plaintiffs for the stated purpose, and the defendant believed that this threat would be carried out to her damage and it was further represented to the defendant that she had a national and patriotic duty to permit employment on a large scale to be afforded by the plaintiffs at the said smelter plant or base metal reduction plant and it was in those circumstances and only on the understanding and pre-condition, express or implied, as hereinbefore indicated, that the defendant afforded such option to the plaintiffs."

To assess the validity of these two grounds of defence or of either of them, regard must be had to the evidence adduced at the trial before the learned High Court judge. Apart from the documents already referred to which relate to evidence of the option arrangements entered into between the parties, it appears that much happened before these arrangements became possible. The plaintiffs had engaged Mr. Ahern (the principal of Marsh & Co., auctioneers) to conduct negotiations on their behalf with local land owners including the defendant.

On behalf of the plaintiffs Mr. Ahern interviewed the defendant's husband and offered £800 per acre for the land which was subsequently the subject of the options. Believing that the Cork County Council as the planning authority had power under s. 77 of the Local Government (Planning & Development) Act, 1963, to acquire these lands compulsorily for the development contemplated by the plaintiffs, and further believing that, as a matter of probability, this power would be exercised, Mr. Ahern so informed the defendant's husband. He did this in good faith, as the learned trial judge has found, believing his statement to represent the reality of the situation facing the defendant. Mr. Ahern followed up this verbal statement with a letter dated the 11th August, 1969, which was written to the solicitor acting for the defendant. In this letter he again made an offer of £800 per acre but added:-
"We are suggesting that, since the probability of a compulsory purchase order being made is admitted, the necessity of having the order made be dispensed with and that the value of the land be submitted to an independent arbitrator acceptable to both parties, and that both parties be bound by his decision."
This letter was a clear indication of Mr. Ahern's view, as the negotiator on behalf of the plaintiffs, that if the £800 per acre was not acceptable the defendant ought to agree to the price being determined by an independent arbitrator in order to avoid a compulsory purchase order.

It seems clear that the defendant's solicitor did not doubt for a moment the soundness of the view expressed by Mr. Ahern, and that subsequent negotiations were conducted on the basis that, if agreement was not possible, compulsory purchase would be the next step.

It appears that Mr. Filer, the managing director of the plaintiffs, was made aware of the manner in which Mr. Ahern was negotiating with the defendant, and of the arguments and representations he used and made. This appears from the fact that at the end of August, 1969, Mr. Filer was given Mr. Ahern's complete file of correspondence which included the letter of the 11th August.

Despite the efforts of Mr. Ahern, the defendant, through her husband, could not be persuaded to sell although the offer made on behalf of the plaintiffs was substantially increased.

By the 9th October, 1969, all negotiations had come to an end and the possibility of the plaintiffs securing the defendant's lands by agreement seemed remote in the extreme. On that date a number of people, representing the plaintiffs, called to the County Hall in Cork which is the headquarters of the Cork County Council. These included Mr. Filer, the managing director and

Mr. Ahern, the auctioneer. They there met the county manager, Mr. Conlon, the chairman of the County Council, Mr. Michael Pat Murphy, the vice-chairman, Mr. Denis O'Sullivan, and the development officer, Mr. David Murphy. There appears to have been some slight conflict in the evidence at the trial as to the immediate purpose of this meeting. However, it is clear that following this meeting the county manager, the chairman, the vice-chairman, Mr. Ahern and the development officer went in a body to see the defendant's husband for the purpose of urging him to resume negotiations with the plaintiffs for the sale of the land. There was again a conflict in the evidence at the trial as to what was said at this interview with the defendant's husband. The defendant's husband maintained that it was made clear to him by the gentlemen who called to see him that, if he was not willing to sell, the lands would be acquired compulsorily by the County Council. This was disputed by the County Council witnesses. However, the learned trial judge was satisfied that at this interview there had been a reference to the compulsory purchase of the lands and that this, coupled with what had previously been said and written by Mr. Ahern, operated on the mind of the defendant's husband. This, of course, is a finding of fact by the learned trial judge which is binding on this Court.

On the following day the defendant's husband telephoned the development officer to say that he was prepared to negotiate with the plaintiffs, and the agreement was executed on the 25th November, 1969.

At the trial it was made clear by the county manager when he gave evidence that the belief held and expressed by Mr. Ahern was incorrect. The county manager made it perfectly clear in his evidence that there was no question of the County Council acquiring these lands for the plaintiffs. Whatever views he may have had as to the Council's powers in this respect, he said that such an exercise of compulsory acquisition had never been attempted and certainly was neither planned nor contemplated in this case. From this it follows that all suggestions made to the defendant's husband, to the effect that if the lands were not sold voluntarily they would be acquired compulsorily, were ill-founded.

I now turn to the grounds relied on by the defendant for resisting the order for specific performance claimed in this case. I wish to say at once that I find no substance in the first ground of objection. In my view, the purpose for which the plaintiffs sought to purchase lands or the use to which they intended to put them in no way affected the transaction. I can see no basis for suggesting that the proposed acquisition of the defendant's lands depended on the smelter project proceeding.

However, the second objection must be viewed in a different light. Specific performance is a discretionary remedy. The discretion to grant or refuse the relief must be exercised in a manner which is neither arbitrary nor capricious but which has regard to the essential fairness of the transaction involved. In effect, it is here suggested that the defendant was coerced or forced into granting the option or options to the plaintiffs by the threat of compulsory purchase. It does not seem to me on the evidence that a threat, as such, was ever used. At the same time it seems perfectly clear that the defendant was at a serious disadvantage.

The defendant's husband, who acted for her throughout the negotiations, believed that if there was not a voluntary sale there would be a compulsory acquisition of the lands. He so believed because he was told this by the plaintiffs' agent, Mr. Ahern. It is quite clear that this view was repeated to him by the defendant's solicitor, and on the 9th October, 1969, further corroboration was provided by those who came to see him and who represented Cork County Council. Believing this to be the situation, there was no real purpose in refusing to sell or to give an option once, as was suggested, the price was to be determined by an agreed arbitrator. To refuse in these circumstances meant acquisition anyway, and the determination of the price by an arbitrator in whose appointment the defendant might have no say. It now transpires that the situation was not as was intimated to the defendant's husband. It is now clear that, at the time that these negotiations were proceeding, the County Council had no plans whatsoever to interfere by way of the compulsory acquisition of the defendant's lands.

It is well established that the discretion to grant specific performance should not be exercised if the contract is not equal and fair. In this instance the defendant was under a fundamental misapprehension as to the true facts. This misapprehension was brought about by the plaintiffs' agent, Mr. Ahern. While Mr. Ahern acted bona fide, this does not alter the situation which he created. He led the defendant's husband and her solicitor to believe that, if the defendant did not agree to sell, the lands would be acquired. It appears clear also that the plaintiffs' managing director was aware of the true position so far as compulsory acquisition was concerned. It is to be noted that he had Mr. Ahern's file of correspondence and, therefore, should have been aware of the incorrect picture which Mr. Ahern had painted. Nevertheless, the plaintiffs' managing director allowed the negotiations to proceed.

In these circumstances it appears to me that there was a fundamental unfairness in the transaction. The defendant agreed to sell believing that she had no real option, and the plaintiffs accepted her agreement to sell knowing that this was not so. In my view it would create a hardship and would be unjust to decree specific performance in this case. I agree with the decision of the learned trial judge. I would refuse specific performance but would order that all monies paid to the defendant by the plaintiffs be returned to the plaintiffs by the defendant."

Mistake

Where a plaintiff is aware of a mistake and seeks to take advantage of it, a court will allow a defendant to rely on mistake as a defence.[10] However, where

---

[10] *Webster v. Cecil* (1861) 30 Beav 62.

a plaintiff has in no way contributed to a mistake, a defendant is unlikely to be able to resist the making of an order of specific performance, although as James LJ pointed out in *Tamplin v. James*,[11] he may be able to rely on mistake as a defence where 'a hardship amounting to an injustice' would otherwise be inflicted upon him.

Tamplin v. James
(1880) 15 Ch D 215

Property was offered for sale by reference to plans which correctly described the area of the site. The defendant did not look at the plans and mistakenly assumed that a piece of land behind the premises was included in the sale and agreed to buy on this basis. The plaintiff was granted a decree of specific performance when the defendant failed to complete the purchase.

JAMES LJ stated at pp.220–221: "In my opinion, the order and appeal is right. The vendors did nothing tending to mislead. In the particulars of sale they described the property as consisting of Nos. 454 and 455 on the tithe map, and this was quite correct. The purchaser says that the tithe map is on so small a scale as not to give sufficient information, but he never looked at it. He must be presumed to have looked at it, and at the particulars of sale. He says he knew the property, and was aware that the gardens were held with the other property in the occupation of the tenants, and he came to the conclusion that what was offered for sale was the whole of what was in the occupation of the tenants, but he asked no question about it. If a man will not take reasonable care to ascertain what he is buying, he must take the consequences. The defence on the ground of mistake cannot be sustained. It is not enough for a purchaser to swear, "I thought the farm sold contained twelve fields which I knew, and I find it does not include them all," or, "I thought it contained 100 acres and it only contains eighty." It would open the door to fraud if such a defence was to be allowed. Perhaps some of the cases on this subject go too far but for the most part the cases where a Defendant has escaped on the ground of a mistake not contributed to by the Plaintiff, have been cases where a hardship amounting to injustice would have been inflicted upon him by holding him to his bargain, and it was unreasonable to hold him to it. *Webster v. Cecil* (1861) 30 Beav 62 is a good instance of that, being a case where a person snapped at an offer which he must have perfectly well-known to be made by mistake, and the only fault I find with the case is that, in my opinion, the bill ought to have been dismissed with costs. It is said that it is hard to hold a man to a bargain entered into under a mistake, but we must consider the hardship on the other side. Here are trustees realizing their testator's estate, and the reckless conduct of

---

[11] (1880) 15 Ch D 215.

the Defendant may have prevented their selling to somebody else. If a man makes a mistake of this kind without any reasonable excuse he ought to be held to his bargain."

O'Neill v. Ryan (No.3)
[1992] 1 IR 166

The plaintiff had instituted various proceedings against a number of defendants including an action under s.205 of the Companies Act 1963, claiming oppression and seeking damages for wrongful dismissal, fraud, mis–representation and conspiracy. He claimed that the respondents in the s.205 proceedings had offered to buy his shares in the company at a stipulated price and to pay his costs and sought specific performance of this agreement. The defendants resisted the claim contending that the agreement relied on had been entered into by mistake and that they had intended this offer to settle to apply to more than just the s.205 action and submitted that as the parties had not been *ad idem* there was no contract in existence which could be specifically enforced. Costello J held that a valid enforceable agreement had come into existence, that the plaintiff had in no way contributed to the situation which had arisen and concluded that the plaintiff was entitled to an order of specific performance. The Supreme Court dismissed the defendants' appeal and held that Costello J had properly exercised his discretion in granting relief by way of specific performance.

COSTELLO J stated at pp.183–192: "The legal effect of, and remedies available arising from, a mistake which affects contractual relations depends on the nature of the mistake which is shown to have occurred. A preliminary problem that arises in analysing the nature of a mistake is a terminological one, for whilst the courts and text-book writers have used such descriptive terms as "common", or "mutual" or "unilateral" to categorise the mistake which has affected the parties' contract, unfortunately these adjectives have not been used consistently with the same meaning. So, at the risk of some circumlocution, I will endeavour to explain exactly the sense in which these terms will be used in the course of this judgment, and avoid their use when possible.

There is a category of cases in which it is accepted that there was an offer and acceptance and agreement reached between the parties but in which it is claimed that the parties shared a common mistake which has resulted in the agreement being void. For example where both parties agree on the purchase and sale of a painting believing it to be a Gainsborough and it is subsequently established that this is not so, or where both parties agree on the sale of tenanted property and both believe that the tenant is protected by the Rent Restriction Acts and subsequently ascertain that this is not so, the existence of a valid offer and acceptance is not in doubt and what is in issue is the effect on the parties' contract of what I will call a shared common mistake. There is another category of cases (in which the present case falls) in which it is alleged that the effect of the mistake was that there was no concluded agreement. Before referring to this category it will help if I first briefly refer to the principles applicable to that of the first category.

There were a number of earlier cases in which a shared common mistake as to the *existence* of the subject matter of the contract, enabled the court to declare the contract to be void. Thus an assignment of a life assurance policy was held to be void where it was shown that at its date the person whose life was assured was wrongly assumed by both parties to have been alive (*Scott v. Coulson* [1903] 2 Ch 249), and a separation deed was declared a nullity because it was made by the common and shared mistake that the parties were married to each other (*Galloway v. Galloway* (1914) 30 TLR 531). But later cases have shown that the circumstances in which a shared common mistake will nullify a contract are extremely limited. *Solle v. Butcher* [1950] 1 KB 671 was a case of a shared common mistake, both parties believing that a flat had been so extensively reconstructed that it was no longer controlled by the Rent Restrictions Acts as a result of which a rent was agreed that was higher than that which would have been payable had the true position been known. But the tenant failed in his claim to recover the rent he had overpaid on the grounds of the common mistake. The law on the subject was stated by Denning L.J. at p. 691, in terms which were approved in a later case as follows:–

> ". . . once a contract has been made, that is to say, once the parties, whatever their inmost states of mind, have to all outward appearances agreed with sufficient certainty in the same terms on the same subject matter, then the contract is good unless and until it is set aside for failure of some condition on which the existence of the contract depends, or for fraud, or on some equitable ground. Neither party can rely on his own mistake to say it was a nullity from the beginning, no matter that it was a mistake which to his mind was fundamental, and no matter that the other party knew that he was under a mistake. A fortiori, if the other party did not know of the mistake, but shared it."

In most cases, then, a shared common mistake will not result in a void contract. This does not mean however that an injured party is without a remedy. As *Solle v. Butcher* [1950] 1 KB 671 showed the court may in the exercise of equitable jurisdiction *set aside* an agreement even though it is not avoided by common shared mistake. Denning L.J. expressed the courts' equitable jurisdiction as follows at p. 693 of the report:-

> "A contract is also liable in equity to be set aside if the parties were under a common misapprehension either as to facts or as to their relative and respective rights, provided that the misapprehension was fundamental and that the party seeking to set it aside was not himself at fault."

And in that case the Court of Appeal set aside the lease on terms, the tenant being allowed to surrender the lease entirely or of remaining in possession at the rent payable under the Rent Restriction Act. The court will also grant relief by way of *rectification* where the parties have reached an agreement but where an error is made in giving effect to the parties' common intention in a written agreement. The general rule is that where there is a common shared mistake in that the written agreement fails to record the intention of both parties the court will order its rectification. *Rectification* may also be ordered when a party who has entered into a written agreement by mistake, if he establishes that the other party with knowledge of the mistake concluded that agreement (see judgment of the Supreme Court in *Irish Life Assurance Co. Ltd. v. Dublin Land Securities Ltd.* [1989] IR 253, 260 and *Monaghan County Council v. Vaughan* [1948] IR 306, 312). And in the exercise of its discretion the court may refuse to make an order for *specific performance* in cases of common shared mistakes. *Grist v. Bailey* [1967] Ch 532 was a case in which both the vendor and purchaser of a tenanted house contracted in the same mistaken belief that the tenancy was protected. When the mistake was ascertained the vendor tried to avoid the contract. The court held that the contract was a valid one but that in the exercise of its discretion it would refuse the purchaser's claim for specific performance and allow the defendant's counterclaim for rescission.

I come now to the category of mistake which it is said operated in this case, that is one in which each party is mistaken as to the other's intention, although neither appreciates that he is misunderstood. This can arise, and has here arisen as the defendants submit, where one party makes an offer which the other party accepts in a fundamentally different sense from that intended by the offeror. The legal principles to be applied in such cases have been long established and I adopt the following passages of Chitty on Contracts, 26th ed., vol. 1, paragraphs 351 and 352, as a correct statement of the law:-

> "The intention of the parties is, as a general rule, to be construed objectively. The language used by one party, whatever his real intention may be, is to be construed in the sense in which it would be reasonably understood by the other, or at least in the sense in which a reasonable person would construe it. Nevertheless cases may occur in which the terms of the offer and acceptance suffer from such latent ambiguity that it is impossible reasonably to impute any agreement between them; or it may happen that one party knowingly accepts a promise in different terms from those intended by the other. In such circumstances, the mistake may render the contract void.

> In most cases the application of the objective test will preclude a party who has entered into a contract under a mistake from setting up his mistake as a defence to an action against him for breach of contract. If a reasonable man would have understood the contract in a certain sense, then, despite his mistake, the court will hold that the mistaken party is bound. But where parties are genuinely at cross-purposes as to the subject-matter of the contract and the terms of the offer and acceptance are so ambiguous that it is not possible to point to one or other of the interpretations as the more probable, the court must necessarily hold that no contract exists."

It is the principle of law thus formulated that I applied earlier in this judgment. It required me to consider the words used by the defendants' solicitors in their letter of the 24th May, 1990, and to construe them objectively in the sense in which they would reasonably be understood. In doing so I concluded that they would be reasonably understood as an offer to settle the s. 205 proceedings only and not as an offer to settle those proceedings and the plenary action. It was in this sense that the offer was accepted by the letter of the 30th May, 1990. The defence of mistake therefore fails as I cannot take into account that the authors of the letter may have intended to make an offer of settlement different to that which a reasonable construction of the words they used disclosed.

There are a number of reasons why the court should adopt this rule. As explained by the Supreme Court in *Mespil Ltd. v. Capaldi* [1986] ILRM 373 at p. 376 of the report:-

> ". . . when a person enters into an agreement, giving the other person the impression that he understands the nature and effect of the agreement, the general rule is that he will not be allowed to say later that he should not be bound by the agreement because he did not at the time understand its import or effect. That is undoubtedly correct law. Business relations would be thrown into undesirable uncertainty if a party to an agreement, who at the time gave no indication that he did not understand what he was doing, could later renounce the agreement on subjective considerations. If he freely and competently entered into the agreement, he will not normally escape being bound by saying that he misunderstood its effect."

In addition to the reason there given the rule is required for the proper administration of justice. As explained, a considerable time ago, in Fry on Specific Performance, 5th ed., p. 765 and quoted with approval in *Eastes v. Russ* [1914] 1 Ch 468, 480:

> "It seems on general principles clear that one party to a contract can never defend himself against it by setting up a misunderstanding on his part as to the real meaning and effect of the contract, or any of the terms in which it is expressed. To permit such a defence would be to open the door to perjury and to destroy the security of contracts."

Furthermore it seems to me that an estoppel arises which precludes an offeror adducing evidence of intention. If an offeror intends his offer in one sense but fails to convey that sense in the words he uses (as objectively determined) and the offeree accepts it in the sense in which the words could reasonably be construed it seems to me that the offeror is estopped from relying on his own error if detriment would thereby be suffered by the offeree. As quite clearly detriment would be suffered by the plaintiff if the defendants for the purpose of showing the parties were not *ad idem* were at liberty to adduce evidence to contradict the sense in which the words in the letter of the 24th May, 1990, can reasonably be construed, the law should not permit such evidence to be adduced.

As my conclusions imply a rejection of the submissions advanced on the defendants' behalf on the issue as to whether or not a concluded contract existed, I should explain my view on those submissions.

1. In their defence and counterclaim the defendants submitted that the letter of 24th May, 1990, could reasonably be understood only as an offer to settle the two actions, that the *plaintiff accepted it on that basis* but later resiled from the agreement and the plaintiff should be ordered to perform the agreement to settle both actions. At the commencement of the hearing I was informed that the defendants were not pursuing their claim for an order for specific performance and an amendment deleting this claim was made.

2. At the hearing the plaintiff's solicitor gave evidence to the effect that he understood the letter of the 26th May, 1990, as an offer to settle the s. 205 proceedings only. He was not cross-examined as to the reasonableness of this belief and the defendants accepted that he *bona fide* held it. What was urged was that

    (a) the words employed in the offer could only reasonably be construed as meaning that it was an offer to settle the two actions,

    (b) that the *plaintiff's solicitor erroneously understood* them as an offer to settle only the s. 205 proceedings, and

    (c) that the parties were not *ad idem* and so no contractual nexus arose. For reasons given earlier I have concluded that, construing the words objectively, the offer was an offer only to settle the s. 205 proceedings and that the plaintiff's solicitor was not in error in accepting it in the sense he did.

3. By way of alternative it was urged that the rules of evidence relating to the construction of written documents permit the court to consider the evidence of the intention of the authors of the letter of 24th May, 1990, as part of the surrounding circumstances in which the letter was written and that in the light of this evidence the offer which was made was an offer to settle the two sets of proceedings, and that as the plaintiff's solicitor intended to settle only the s. 205 proceedings the parties were not *ad idem*. In support of this submission I was referred to the passages in Chitty on Contracts dealing with the admissibility of extrinsic evidence to interpret and explain written agreements (para. 867 *et seq.* of the 26th ed.) and Phipson on Evidence (para. 196 *et seq.* of the 12th ed.) to *Prenn v. Simmonds* [1971] 1 WLR 1381, 1383-4. The passage of *Prenn* (approved by O'Hanlon J. in *British Leyland Exports v. Brittain Manufacturing Ltd.* [1981] IR 335 at 346) to which I was referred is as follows:-

> "The time has long passed when agreements, even those under seal, were isolated from the matrix of facts in which they were set and interpreted purely on internal linguistic considerations. There is no need to appeal here to any

> modern, anti-literal, tendencies, for Lord Blackburn's well-known judgment in *River Wear Commissioners v. Adamson* (1877) 2 App Cas 743, 763 provides ample warrant for a liberal approach. We must, as he said, inquire beyond the language and see what the circumstances were with reference to which the words were used, and the object, appearing from those circumstances, which the person using them had in view."

This judgment affords justification for hearing extrinsic evidence of the general circumstances in which the offer of settlement was made and accepted, including the pleadings in the two sets of proceedings, the motion to consolidate, what transpired at its hearing and the judgment on it, as an aid to construe the written contract contained in the two letters. It is not however an authority for the proposition that the parties can adduce evidence as to their intention in entering the written agreement. In *Prenn v. Simmonds* [1971] 1 WLR 1381 the court was concerned with the construction of a written contract. Counsel for the defendant, Dr. Simmonds, had argued that in considering it prior negotiations could be looked at as an aid to construction. Rejecting this submission Lord Wilberforce said at p. 1385 of the report:-

> "In my opinion, then, evidence of negotiations, or of the parties' intentions, and a fortiori of Dr. Simmonds' intentions, ought not to be received, and evidence should be restricted to evidence of the factual background known to the parties at or before the date of the contract, including evidence of the 'genesis' and objectively the 'aim' of the transaction." (emphasis added)

And I do not think that the passages in Chitty on Contracts relating to the admissibility of extrinsic evidence to which I was referred must be taken as in some way modifying the earlier passages on the law of mistake which I have already quoted, nor do those general principles on the same subject in Phipson on Evidence allow the defendant to adduce evidence which in effect contradicts the reasonable construction of the words used in the written agreement.

4. Finally it was submitted that the objective test as set out in Chitty on Contracts must be read in the light of the Supreme Court decision in *Mespil Ltd. v. Capaldi* [1986] ILRM 373 and that *Mespil* is authority for the proposition that in considering whether parties are *ad idem* the court is not bound by the construction of the words used in the written document but may take into account the subjective intent of the offeror when writing them.

I do not think that *Mespil Ltd. v. Capaldi* [1986] ILRM 373 supports this view. That was a case in which a settlement of an action had been negotiated by counsel for the plaintiff and counsel for the defendant. The result of their negotiations was reduced into writing and was headed "Full and final settlement of all matters and acts in dispute between the parties in these proceedings". A dispute arose as to the terms of the settlement and proceedings were instituted.

Evidence was given at the trial by the plaintiff's counsel to the effect that the words did not mean that an existing dispute unrelated to the proceedings between the parties about the user of the premises was settled, whilst counsel for the defendants gave evidence that the words meant that all matters in dispute (including the user dispute) between the parties and not just those referred to in the two actions were settled. The Supreme Court held, at p. 376, that it was clear that the form of the written consent, viewed in terms of its wording and of the negotiations leading up to it, was capable of justifying the opinion of counsel for the defendant, but that it could also be said that on an objective consideration of the relevant circumstances that the plaintiff's counsel's construction was justified. There was therefore a latent ambiguity and a mutual mis-understanding which meant that in fact there was no agreement.

Mespil Ltd. v. Capaldi [1986] ILRM 373 is an example of a case where, looking at the words used by the parties, the court could come to the conclusion that, objectively speaking, they suffered from such ambiguity that it was impossible to conclude that the parties had reached an agreement. That is not, in my judgment, the situation which pertains in this case. In my view the words used by the defendant's solicitors could only be construed as an offer to settle the s. 205 proceedings only. This was the sense in which they were understood by the plaintiff's solicitor, and accepted by him.

There is another aspect of the principles enunciated in the quotation from Chitty on Contracts to which I should refer. If one party knows that a mistake is made by the offeror in the offer and accepts it with this knowledge the mistaken party may give evidence of what his intention was and the fact that the parties were at cross-purposes will mean that the contract was void. The principle is illustrated by *Hartog v. Colin & Shields* [1939] 3 All ER 566. That was a case dealing with the sale of hare skins by the defendant to the plaintiff. In pre-contract negotiations the parties bargained on the basis of the skins being sold at a price per piece. By mistake the defendant eventually offered them at a price based on their *weight*, an offer which the plaintiff accepted. When the defendant ascertained his mistake and refused to deliver the skins he was sued by the purchaser for damages for non-delivery. It was held that the objective test did not apply because the plaintiff must have known that the offer did not reflect the defendant's true intention and that the contract was void.

I draw attention to this principle because it was relevant to know whether the plaintiff's solicitor knew that the defendants had made an error in their letter of 24th May, 1990. Had he known that they intended to make an offer to settle both sets of proceedings then the objective test would not apply and the apparent agreement would be declared void. His evidence was therefore relevant to the issues I had to consider and I do not think that by tendering it the plaintiff thereby is precluded from objecting to the relevance of the evidence of the intention of the defendant's solicitors. As he clearly did not know of their intention and could not reasonably have known it the objective test applies.

Having concluded that a valid enforceable contract came into existence I must then consider the plaintiff's remedies. Clearly the plaintiff would be entitled to damages for its breach. He has, however, claimed equitable relief - an order for specific performance. And a question arises as to whether, in the exercise of my discretion, the plaintiff should be afforded this relief. I should make clear however what the issue is. Once it is decided that an enforceable agreement exists by the application of the principles I have noted then equitable principles determine, not the validity of the contract, but the exercise of the court's discretion to grant equitable relief.

There may be circumstances in which the courts may refuse to order the specific performance of a valid contact. The manner in which the court should exercise its discretion has been stated in *Burrow v. Scammell* (1881) 19 Ch D 175 in general terms as follows at p. 182 of the report:

> "It cannot be disputed that Courts of Equity have at all times relieved against honest mistakes in contracts, where the literal effect and the specific performance of them would be to impose a burden not contemplated, and which it would be against all reason and justice to fix, upon the person who, without the imputation of fraud, has inadvertently committed an accidental mistake; and also where not to correct the mistake would be to give an unconscionable advantage to either party."

And in another case, decided at about the same time, *Tamplin v. James* (1880) 15 Ch D 215, James L.J. pointed out at p. 221 of the report that:

> "for the most part the cases where a Defendant has escaped on the ground of a mistake not contributed to by the Plaintiff, have been cases where a hardship amounting to injustice would have been inflicted upon him by holding him to his bargain, and it was unreasonable to hold him to it."

In the instant case the defendant's solicitors had intended that the offer was to settle the two sets of proceedings, and so the defendants would suffer a hardship by a decision which holds them bound to a different contract. But in deciding whether the plaintiff should be left to a claim for damages rather than obtain an order that the contract be specifically enforced I have against the defendant's hardship to balance the hardship which the plaintiff would suffer if the contract was not specifically enforced. An award for damages would be based on the difference between the actual value of the shares and the price offered and the plaintiff would be left holding shares in a company engaged in business in a highly volatile industry whose value would be liable to fluctuate, and in a company from the employment of which he had been dismissed (wrongly he claims) and over which he had no control. The plaintiff in no way contributed to the situation which arose. I conclude that it would not be unjust and unreasonable to require the defendants to carry out their contract and that a refusal of such an order would, on the other hand, result in considerable injustice to the plaintiff.

There will therefore be an order in accordance with the prayer of paragraph

11 (a) of the statement of claim. I will discuss with counsel the exact terms in which the order should be drawn."

Hardship

Specific performance of a contract may be refused where it would inflict unnecessary hardship on a defendant. Generally the courts have insisted that only hardship existing at the date the contract is entered into may be taken into account[12] and supervening hardship will provide a defence only in exceptional circumstances.[13] It seems that hardship suffered by third parties may also be taken into account.[14]

Roberts v. O'Neill
[1983] IR 47

The plaintiff claimed specific performance of a contract for the sale of a licensed premises. The defendants claimed that to grant specific performance of the contract with the plaintiff would be to impose unreasonable hardship on them because of the large increase in the value of the property since the date of the contract. McCarthy J stated that subsequent hardship should operate as a defence only in exceptional cases and the Supreme Court (O'Higgins CJ, Hederman and McCarthy JJ) held that a decree of specific performance should be granted.

MCCARTHY J stated at pp.51–57: "This is an action for specific performance of a contract dated the 17th January, 1978, and made between the plaintiff (in trust) and the defendants for the sale by the defendants to the plaintiff of the Silver Tassie, being licensed premises at Loughlinstown in the county Dublin. In the High Court Mr. Justice McWilliam granted the order sought by the plaintiff and also awarded damages which were measured at bank interest on the sum of £30,000 (paid as a deposit on the signing of the contract) up to the date of judgment. The first defendant, who is the husband of the second defendant, appeals against the order for specific performance and seeks, in effect, an order that the plaintiff be compensated in damages only, so that the first defendant and his wife may retain the licensed premises. For the reasons that I shall state, in my judgment, the appeal fails.

The facts
It is desirable to set out the sequence of events in some detail. In the year

---

[12] *Lavan v. Walsh* [1964] IR 87 and *Roberts v. O'Neill* [1983] IR 47.

[13] E.g. *Patel v. Ali* [1984] Ch 283.

[14] *Conlon v. Murray* [1958] NI 17. See *supra* p. 786.

1973, the defendants bought the Silver Tassie, for an undisclosed sum and, thereafter, remained joint owners. In November, 1977, their daughter was "coshed" in a burglary at their home, which is a bungalow adjoining the Silver Tassie. Because of that incident, the first defendant became increasingly worried and thought it might be better to sell the premises – a view which was not shared by his wife, who wanted their son, then aged 13, to continue in the business. What one might call the defendants' experience in the public-house business only began in the year 1973.

During the weekend before the 16th January, 1978, discussions took place between Corry Buckley (acting on behalf of Mr. Gerard Carthy), the defendants, and Gerard Black, who was their solicitor. It was subsequently maintained by Mr. Carthy that, arising from those discussions, there was an enforceable contract for the purchase by him of the premises for £190,000.

The plaintiff is a nominee for the Madigan Group, owners of a chain of public houses. On the 16th January the plaintiff learnt of the possibility that the premises might be on the market and he called there on that night. The plaintiff's son-in-law, Mr. Madigan, contacted Mr. Moore who is the agent for the defendants. On the next day a formal contract, in the printed form authorised and issued by the Incorporated Law Society of Ireland, suitably completed as to amount, closing date, deposit and details of title, was executed by the plaintiff personally and by Mr. Black, solicitor, as agent for the defendants. The closing date was fixed for the 17th February, upon which date the plaintiff's solicitors sent a draft conveyance to the defendants' solicitors.

On the 21st February, in a letter to the plaintiff's solicitors, Mr. Black stated:– "6. Since formally replying to your requisitions on title herein we have been notified by another firm of solicitors that a client of theirs may institute proceedings against the vendor. Such proceedings were in fact issued against the wrong party (not our client) about three weeks ago but we returned same to the said solicitors indicating that the proceedings were not in order. To-date neither we nor our clients have received any amended or new summonses." On the 28th February, Mr. Black wrote to the plaintiff's solicitors enclosing "herewith memorandum and index relating this matter." On the 6th March, the plaintiff's solicitors wrote to Mr. Black in these terms:– "In order to protect our client's interests, we have registered the contract for sale dated the 17th January 1978 and in order to protect our clients' interests further, we feel that a lis pendens must be registered. This means that proceedings must be commenced and we will be issuing plenary summons in this regard tomorrow. Please let us know what steps your clients intend to take to have the lis pendens in the Carthy action removed as obviously while this is still on the record we cannot advise our client to complete."

On the 7th March, 1978, a plenary summons was issued by the plaintiff but no reply to the observation about the lis pendens appears to have been received at any time. On the 7th June a statement of claim was delivered claiming an order for specific performance of the agreement and damages. On the 19th

July a joint defence and counter-claim was delivered on behalf of the defendants in which they pleaded, essentially, that because of the Carthy action, they were unable to complete the sale. In particular, they pleaded at paragraph 4:- "If, contrary to the defendant's contention, the contract for sale was not conditional upon the said Gerard Carthy not succeeding in claiming that he had entered into a binding contract for the sale of the said premises to him, the contract is in any event impossible of performance until the determination of the said proceedings, *and, in the event of the said proceedings being determined in favour of the defendants, they are ready and willing to complete the sale to the plaintiff.*" (I have added the emphasis.)

The action by Mr. Carthy against Mr. O'Neill was heard on the 4th and 5th July, 1979, by Mr. Justice Gannon, who delivered judgment in October. The learned judge held that the Carthy contract was legally enforceable and he joined Mrs. O'Neill as a defendant to that action. The O'Neills appealed and the Supreme Court, in its judgment of the 30th January, 1981, allowed that appeal and dismissed Mr. Carthy's action.

On the 2nd March, 1981, the plaintiff's solicitors called upon the defendants, through their solicitors, to complete the sale forthwith and indicated a claim for damages for delay. On the 19th March, Mr. Black informed the plaintiff's solicitors that "we will be applying on behalf of the first named defendant to amend the defence as it is the first named defendant's contention that this is not a proper case for specific performance." Mr. Black had ceased to act on behalf of the second defendant. The terms of the amended defence of the first defendant were sent sometime towards the end of March, 1981, to the plaintiff's solicitors, and the amended defence of the second defendant, in which she denied Mr. Black's authority, was filed on the 5th May, 1981. This contention of the second defendant was rejected by the trial judge, and no appeal has been brought against that finding.

On the 6th May, 1981, an amended defence and counter-claim was filed on behalf of the first defendant, and the material portion of this was to strike out the words (to which I have added emphasis) in the original defence and counter-claim at paragraph 4 and to add a plea to this effect:– "In the period between the making of the contract for sale to the plaintiff in these proceedings and the delivery of the judgment [*of the Supreme Court in Carthy v. O'Neill*] the value of the said premises had greatly increased as has the value of licensed premises generally. The first named defendant is a publican and it would be grossly unjust if the defendants were obliged to sell said premises to the plaintiff at the contract price, which would now be a gross undervalue and whereby the plaintiff would be unjustly enriched. Accordingly, the Court in its discretion should refuse to grant an order of specific performance." Up to that date, from the delivery of the original joint defence and counter-claim on the 19th July, 1978, the attitude expressly maintained on behalf of both defendants insofar as an examination of the court record would disclose was that the sole bar to the closing of the sale to the plaintiff was the existence of the Carthy action.

The adjourned hearing of this action took place before Mr. Justice McWilliam on the 4th and 5th June, 1981. On the 3rd July, 1981, he delivered judgment in which he rejected the defendants' contention that specific performance should not be granted and that damages in lieu thereof was the appropriate remedy.

The appeal
The first defendant has appealed, by a notice of appeal dated the 5th August, 1981, against the order for specific performance but without stating in the notice of appeal what he suggests is the alternative order. On the hearing of this appeal, counsel for the first defendant has limited the appeal to seeking a finding that the order of specific performance would cause excessive hardship to the defendants and should, therefore, be refused; and that, in lieu thereof, damages (to be assessed in the High Court) should be awarded to the plaintiff in accordance with Lord Cairns' Act. It is fair to say that the sixth ground of appeal contains this essential matter and that no argument was advanced on any other of the grounds of appeal.

During the course of the argument, Mr. Justice Hederman drew attention to the absence of any appeal by the second defendant and postulated the question as to what the situation would be if the Court were to allow the first defendant's appeal whilst an order for specific performance remained in existence against the second defendant. It was indicated that the second defendant was prepared to join in the appeal, if necessary. Having regard, however, to my view on the substantial matter raised in the appeal, it is unnecessary to consider this aspect of the case further. There would appear to be adequate powers under order 58, r. 8, to deal with such a situation.

The argument
As I understand the argument advanced on behalf of the first defendant, and which I accept as being appropriate to be considered as if advanced on behalf of the second defendant, his case may be stated as follows:-

1. An order of specific performance is an equitable remedy and, accordingly, discretionary in all cases.

2. There may be cases of real hardship caused by the grant of an order for specific performance.

3. The time to test or measure the degree of hardship is not at the date of the contract which is sought to be specifically performed, but rather at the date of trial.

4. In the instant case, there exists a circumstance over which neither plaintiff nor defendant had control and it prevented the closing of the sale until after the judgment of this Court in the Carthy case was delivered on the 30th January, 1981, by which time the original purchase price was but half of the then current value of the property because of the huge nationwide increase in the value of licensed premises due to the high inflationary trends at the time.

5. That is a circumstance over which none of the parties had any control; it effects a great hardship on the defendants because they cannot now afford to buy an alternative public-house such as would cater for their plans to have their son continue in that business. The only hardship on the plaintiff (and it, perhaps, a nominal one only, since he appears to have been buying in trust) is the very fact of not obtaining specific performance and having to settle for damages.

The plaintiff's answer is a short one. He says that any hardship that exists has arisen after the date of the contract and after the date for its completion; and that he has not caused or added to that hardship. In addition, it might be added that the defendants have been in receipt of all the profits of the business since the original intended date for closing. A further comment is made that the first defendant wanted initially, at least, to get out of the public-house business because of the unhappy burglary incident. Neither the High Court nor this Court was given any information about the purchase price paid by the defendants in 1973 and, consequently, the degree of hardship necessitated by them having to pay capital gains tax cannot be assessed.

The law

Mr. Fennelly has argued that the correct approach is to measure the hardship existing at the date of the hearing. That argument is unsupported by authority and is, indeed, contradicted by *Lavan v. Walsh* [1964] IR 87 in which Budd J. said at pp. 102-3 of the report:– "The defendant in this case also relies on the plea that enforcement of the contract in this case would cause great hardship on her. It is pointed out that the order is a discretionary one and it is strongly urged that the Court in the exercise of a proper judicial discretion should not grant the relief of specific performance because of the special facts of the case which I will deal with later. Again, however, I must first refer to a matter of law. The Court, it is well established, will not enforce the specific performance of a contract the result of which would be to impose great hardship on either of the parties to it. It is conceded, however, that the question of the hardship of a contract is generally to be judged at the time it is entered into. Change of circumstances taking place later, making the contract less beneficial to one party, are immaterial as a rule unless brought about by the action of the other party. It is stated, however, in Fry on Specific Performance (6th ed., at p. 200):– 'It cannot, however, be denied that there are cases in which the Court has refused its interference by reason of events subsequent to the contract.' From an examination of the cases of *The City of London v. Nash* (1747) 1 Ves Sen 12 and *Costigan v. Hastler* (1804) 2 Sch & Lef 160 it appears that this is so, but exceptions to the general rule appear very rare. . . . I must, however, approach the consideration of these matters dispassionately and exercise what I conceive to be the proper judicial discretion. In the first place, as I have pointed out, it is undoubtedly the position in law that save in exceptional cases only a matter of hardship existing at the time of the contract can be taken into consideration.

Hardship existing at the time of the contract is out of the case. It thus requires a strong case to be made out before one should accede to a plea for the exercise of judicial discretion in a quite unusual way, that is, by reason of hardship arising subsequently to the contract, and, the onus being on the defendant to satisfy me of the existence and genuineness of the alleged hardship on her, the proof of it should be strong and above suspicion."

Whilst, as Budd J. said, the relevant-time issue appears to have been conceded, I do not overlook the quite exceptional standing as a lawyer in which the late Mr. Roger O'Hanrahan S.C. (the counsel who made the concession) was held by Bench and Bar alike. Further, although Budd J. referred to the matter as being conceded, he expressed his own view in the most positive terms without reference to such concession. Mr. Fennelly has suggested that there is an illogicality in taking the date of the contract as the relevant one, since it is unlikely that there would have been any contract if the hardship had been known then. This very argument perhaps answers the problem. Hardship is permitted to defeat specific performance where an existing hardship was not known at the relevant time, being the date of the contract. While recognising that there may be cases in which hardship arising after the date of the contract is such that to decree specific performance would result in great injury, there must be few such cases and, in my view, they should not include ordinarily cases of hardship resulting from inflation alone. To permit, as an ordinary rule, a defence of subsequent hardship, would be to add a further hazard to the already trouble-strewn area of the law of contracts for the sale of land.

The application of the law
An examination of the evidence, including the summary at the commencement of this judgment, throws doubt upon the reality of the alleged claim of hardship. At all material times the defendants knew that they would have to complete a sale of the premises either to Mr. Carthy or to the plaintiff. The plaintiff's advisers took meticulous care to make the plaintiff's position clear and, indeed, readily accepted that they could not press for completion until the Carthy case was resolved. The original motivation to leave the particular type of business was because of personal hazards; at no time from February, 1978, to March, 1981, was it ever suggested to the plaintiff or his advisers that there was any doubt about the eventual completion, assuming a satisfactory result to the first action. At no time did the defendants embark on any inquiry about a substitute public-house in order that their son might pursue what was alleged to be their wish for his career.

The second defendant, having dispensed with the services of her original solicitor, embarked upon a spurious defence based on an alleged absence of authority; she now seeks to join her husband in criticising the plaintiff (who is a vehicle builder aged 76 years, without any other connection with the licensed trade save that his daughter is married to one of the Madigans) because he assented in evidence to an extract from a letter dated 29th July, 1979, written by his solicitors to Mr. Black, specifying four items of alleged damages of which the fourth was "the difference in value between the premises as they are valued at the date of the hearing and their value at which we purchased them." It is to be noted that this letter, to which there appears to have been no reply, was written after the hearing of the Carthy case before Mr. Justice Gannon and before judgment was delivered in that case. I know little of what transpired at that hearing save for some extracts from the transcript of it which were used in evidence in the trial of this case, but it does appear that the second defendant did not give evidence at that hearing, apparently because she would have supported Mr. Carthy's claim.

The result

It may be that there are other circumstances surrounding the alleged hardship but I think that I have cited the salient ones. In my judgment, they fall far short of establishing the type of case in which the Court should intervene to deny the ordinary remedy to one of the contracting parties in what was, at the time, a perfectly fair and proper transaction. There may be cases in which the Court should intervene or, to put it more crudely, interfere with the express wording of a contract, and in which the duty to do justice may override strictly legal principles and the well-recognised procedures of the courts of equity. Such is not the case here; indeed, justice here demands that the contract be specifically performed.

I have not overlooked the observations of the learned trial judge in respect of the balancing of the hardship to the defendants themselves whether or not an order of specific performance is granted. I do not dissent from his views as so expressed, but I prefer ro rest my judgment as I have endeavoured to explain."

Delay

Where a plaintiff has delayed for an unreasonable period of time before bringing proceedings, he may disentitle himself to relief where this delay is coupled with circumstances which would make it inequitable to grant relief.

Guerin v. Heffernan
[1925] 1 IR 57

The defendant sought to repudiate a contract for the purchase of a farm and the plaintiff, after threatening to institute proceedings against him, did nothing for a period of over a year. The Supreme Court (Kennedy CJ, O'Connor and Fitzgibbon JJ) held that the plaintiff was not entitled to relief in the form of specific performance. O'Connor J concluded that during the intervening time the defendant might well have assumed that the plaintiff had abandoned his rights under the contract and had accepted the defendant's repudiation.

O'CONNOR J stated at pp.67–69: "On the pleadings in this action, apart from formal traverses, the only issue raised is that the contract for sale of the lands was induced by a misrepresentation made by the plaintiff to the defendant that the latter would be allowed to enter peaceably upon the lands without claims, molestations, or threats by the plaintiff's family or other persons.

The trial of the action lasted three days, and the transcript of the very voluminous evidence shows that every conceivable topic was dealt with – so much so, that it is difficult to gather from the evidence what were the issues to which it was directed. It certainly was not confined to the only issue which was raised by the pleadings. An explanation is to be found in the way in which the trial, with the assent of both parties, was conducted. The pleadings were disregarded, and plaintiff and defendant were left at large without being called upon to formulate the issues by amended pleadings. The result seems to have been that no one at the trial seems to have had a clear conception of the material issues, and much time was wasted and the whole case obscured by evidence of the most rambling and confusing character. I consider this case to be a glaring example of the inconvenience resulting from the absence of proper pleadings raising the real issues to be tried. I do not wish to be taken as an advocate of rigid adherence to pleadings on which an action is brought to trial. Very frequently it appears at the trial that material issues have not been raised by the pleadings, and that it would be unjust to shut out the parties from raising them, but I do maintain that, when the proper issues become manifest, the parties should be called upon to formulate them by proper amendments. This is by no means a matter of merely formal compliance with rules. I know nothing which is more conducive to clear thinking, whether on the Bench or at the Bar, than the proper formulation of a legal claim or a legal defence, while there is nothing more calculated to lead to confusion and waste of time with consequent expense than to allow a case to drag along without exact knowledge of the issues which are raised.

Reading the evidence I am able to extract from it three grounds of defence which may easily be brought under well-defined heads:– 1, Delay and laches on the plaintiff's part in bringing his action; 2, repudiation by the defendant and acquiesence by the plaintiff in such repudiation; 3, a change of position to the prejudice of the defendant caused by the plaintiff's conduct – a defence closely associated with defence No. 1. These do not exhaust the issues to be extracted from the evidence, but I will confine myself to them, as sufficient for the purpose of my judgment.

A contract for the sale of a farm is one which ought to be expeditiously carried out. A farm is a property which requires immediate attention and treatment. The times for doing things on a farm wait not for the farmer. He must always be up and doing. When he buys his farm he ought to get immediate possession. If he is delayed he may miss a sowing, or a reaping, or a market. Consequently, if there is a dispute between a vendor and purchaser of a farm, the purchaser should know at once whether he is to be on or off with his contract. He ought not to be kept in suspense.

In this case the contract was made on the 18th March, 1922. The date fixed for completion was the 8th April, 1922. Everyone knows that this is the time of year at which it is important for a farmer to get immediate possession. Immediately after the making of the contract the defendant had reasons for regretting it. It is not necessary to go into particulars. He repudiated it. He may at one time have withdrawn his repudiation, but it is certain that he finally, and in the clearest manner, repudiated it on the 19th April, 1922. This repudiation was met by a notice from the plaintiff that he would at once institute legal proceedings. I will assume that the plaintiff had then a good cause of action for damages for breach of contract or for specific performance. He might have rested on his claim for damages until it was barred by the Statute of Limitations; but, if he intended to seek the equitable relief of specific performance he was bound to proceed without delay. A man who sleeps on his rights does not find favour in a Court of equity.

The plaintiff, instead of proceeding as he had threatened the defendant that he would, did nothing to assert his rights until the 13th June, 1923, when he issued his writ. During the intervening period the defendant might very well have assumed that the plaintiff had abandoned his rights under the contract and had accepted the defendant's repudiation. It would certainly be a hardship on the defendant to have his fear of liability lulled, while in the meantime the plaintiff would have the option of selling the farm to advantage and, that failing, of enforcing the contract. On the ground of delay alone I think that the plaintiff is not entitled to equitable relief. There is ample authority to support this view: see Fry on Specific Performance, 6th edit., pars. 1071, 1072, and 1073. The length of the delay depends on the circumstances of each case, and, having regard to the nature of the property now in question, I am of opinion that the delay was altogether unreasonable. But the plaintiff's delay was accompanied by acts which are only consistent with his acquiescence in the repudiation and his election to treat the contract as at an end. A considerable time after the day fixed for completion of the contract the plaintiff advertised the meadows on the lands. That was wholly inconsistent with the defendant's rights under the contract if it were to be enforced against him. The letting of the meadows would have incapacitated the plaintiff from giving up clear possession.

Further, I am satisfied on the evidence that the defendant, acting under the belief that the contract was abandoned by the plaintiff, released a purchaser of one of his own farms, which he had agreed to sell, in consequence of the purchase of the plaintiff's farm – whether the defendant has suffered actual loss from this I do not know – but it was a change in position, which, with the other elements in the case, should be taken into consideration.

On these grounds alone I am of opinion that the plaintiff lost the right which may have been vested in him originally of getting a decree for specific performance, and I do not consider it necessary to give any decision on the defence of misrepresentation.

In my judgment the appeal should be dismissed with costs."

Impossibility

Specific performance of a contract will not be ordered where it would not be possible for a defendant to comply with the order and supervening events may render it impossible to perform contractual obligations or lead to frustration of a contract.

Neville and Sons Ltd v. Guardian Builders Ltd
[1995] 1 ILRM 1

The plaintiff and defendant entered into an agreement whereby the plaintiff contracted to build houses on a site owned by the defendant. It was accepted that the only effective means of access to the site would be by the construction of a new roadway which involved the acquisition of a strip of land owned by the county council and difficulties arose in the course of negotiations about acquiring this land. The plaintiff sought specific performance of the agreement and the defendant contended that by reason of the difficulties which had arisen in relation to access to the site, performance of the contract had been rendered impossible or possible only in circumstances so different from those contemplated that both parties were relieved from further performance. The Supreme Court (Finlay CJ, Blayney and Denham JJ) ordered specific performance of the contract.

BLAYNEY J stated at pp. 7–12: "It is necessary first, therefore, to determine what are the principles which should be applied in relation to the doctrine of the frustration of contracts.

I am satisfied that this issue in effect falls into two separate sub-questions. The first being the necessity to define the circumstances in which frustration takes place and the second being to determine the basis on which, if those circumstances do occur, the court has power to declare that the contract is at an end.

The circumstances in which frustration takes place were defined as follows by Lord Simon in his speech in *National Carriers Ltd v. Panalpina (Northern) Ltd* [1981] AC 675 at p. 700F:

> Frustration of a contract takes place when there supervenes an event (without default of either party and for which the contract makes no sufficient provision) which so significantly changes the nature (not merely the expense or onerousness) of the outstanding contractual rights and/or obligations from what the parties could reasonably have contemplated at the time of its execution that it would be unjust to hold them to the literal sense of its stipulations in the new circumstances; in such case the law declares both parties to be discharged from further performance.

In the same case Lord Roskill in his speech analysed the circumstances in which frustration occurs in terms which I am satisfied are virtually identical in their effect where at p. 717D he stated as follows:

> There must have been by reason of some supervening event some such fundamental change of circumstances as to enable the court to say; 'this was not the bargain which these parties made and their bargain must be treated as at an end' – a view which Lord Radcliffe himself tersely summarised in a quotation of five words from the *Aeneid: non haec an foedera veni.*

I am satisfied that these two quotations from the decision of the House of Lords represent a correct statement of the principles of law applicable to frustration in our law and I am prepared to adopt them as being a correct statement of principle.

With regard to the basis on which in the circumstances in which frustration occurs the court has power to declare that the contract is at an end I find again in the case of *National Carriers Ltd v. Panalpina (Northern) Ltd* and this time in the speech of Lord Wilberforce, what I am satisfied is a correct statement of the principles on this issue where at p. 693-694G he states as follows:

> Various theories have been expressed as to its justification in law [i.e. the doctrine of frustration]: as a device by which the rules as to absolute contracts are reconciled with a special exception which justice demands, as an implied term, as a matter of construction of the contract, as related to removal of the foundation of the contract, as a total failure of consideration. It is not necessary to attempt selection of any one of these as the true basis: my own view would be that they shade into one another and that a choice between them is a choice of what is most appropriate to the particular contract under consideration. One could see, in relation to the present contract, that it could provisionally be said to be appropriate to refer to an implied term, in view of the grant of the right of way, or to removal of the foundation of the contract – viz. use as a warehouse. In any event, the doctrine can now be stated generally as part of the law of contract; as all judicially evolved doctrines it is, and ought to be, flexible and capable of new applications.

What has to be determined is whether there were in the present case circumstances such as those outlined in the speeches of Lord Simon and Lord Roskill in the case of *National Carriers Ltd v. Panalpina (Northern) Ltd.* Did an event supervene which so significantly changed the nature of the outstanding obligations of Guardian from what the parties could reasonably have contemplated at the time the licence agreement was entered into? Or was there by some supervening event some such fundamental change of circumstances that the court could say, 'this is not the bargain that these parties made and their bargain must be treated as at an end'? In my opinion the answer to both these questions is no.

As far back as 1984 Guardian had reached agreement with the county council for the acquisition of the 150 sq. metre strip. The terms of the agreement are set out in a letter of 12 March 1984 from Dublin County Council to

Guardian. One of the terms in the agreement was as follows:

3. That in part consideration for the disposal to Guardian Builders Ltd of the plot referred to in (1) above it will give the council a formal undertaking to permit the owners and patrons of the adjoining property now known as Parkes Hotel to have a permanent free vehicular access from the car park at the rear of that property over the new access road to be constructed by Guardian Builders Ltd, on its site, linking its development to the realigned Stillorgan Road. The access road will be constructed by Guardian Builders within twelve months from the date planning permission is granted for that portion of its site which is located in the Dun Laoghaire Borough area.

Clause 6 of the terms provided that they were subject to the following conditions:

(a) To the necessary statutory approvals and consents being obtained.
(b) To Guardian Builders Ltd obtaining a grant of planning permission from Dun Laoghaire Borough, which permits commercial development on the portion of its site located within Dun Laoghaire Borough boundary.
(c) To formal contract being entered by both parties.

Condition (b) was complied with on 16 September 1986 when Guardian, on appeal to the planning board obtained planning permission from Dun Laoghaire Borough for the erection of two three-storey office developments. One of the conditions to which this planning permission was subject was as follows:

1. The proposed access road and its junction with Stillorgan Road shall be designed and constructed to standards which will render it acceptable for taking in charge by the planning authority (Dun Laoghaire Corporation). The access road shall be capable of accommodating the traffic (pedestrian and vehicular) which will be generated by the development, the subject of this application, and by possible future development of the lands to the east of the site which are located in the functional area of Dublin County Council and are zoned for residential use.

On 25 August 1987 Guardian's solicitor wrote to the county council with a view to having the terms set out in the county council's letter of 12 March 1984 put into effect. After some further correspondence and discussions between Guardian's solicitor and the county council, the county council wrote on 4 December 1987 saying that they were not prepared to proceed in accordance with the terms set out in their letter of 12 March 1984 as Guardian 'did not construct the road referred to at item 3', i.e. the access road.

Further meetings and correspondence then took place between Guardian and its solicitor on the one hand and the county council on the other with a view to coming to a new agreement. A problem had emerged in regard to the position of the exit from the Parkes Hotel car park on to the access road. In a planning permission XA 1181 which the hotel had obtained from the county council on 5 December 1983, the exit was shown in the middle of the car park.

Its position there interfered with the planning permission in respect of the licence plot and Guardian wished to have it moved closer to the Stillorgan Road. Parkes Hotel was not agreeable to this and the county council were not prepared to permit any change in the position without the hotel's consent in case it could result in their having to pay additional compensation to the hotel. Under an interim award by an arbitrator the county council had paid compensation to the hotel for the compulsory acquisition of the car park formerly in front of the hotel which had been acquired for the widening of the road.

New terms which are set out in a letter from the county council dated 8 September 1988 were then agreed upon. They provided for the acquisition of the 150 sq. metre strip by Guardian in consideration of the payment of £37,500. In addition Guardian had to 'construct, at its own expense, a new junction and access road leading from the carriageway of the Stillorgan Road to the development site via the proposed car park entrance as per planning permission Reg. Ref. XA 1181'.

The terms also included the following:

(8) The entrance from the access road to the car park is to be located in accordance with the details outlined in planning permission Reg. Ref. XA1181, or, in the event that it is located elsewhere the provision of clause (9) hereunder will apply.

(9) In the event that a mutual agreement is reached between Guardian Builders Ltd and the owners of Parkes Hotel to locate the car park entry/exit at a location other than that provided for by planning permission Reg. Ref. XA1181, then Guardian Builders Ltd must submit to the council a formal legal agreement signed by the owners of Parkes Hotel, acknowledging that the access as proposed is acceptable to it as fully discharging Dublin County Council's commitment to it to provide an access to the car park, and confirming that it will make no further claims for compensation against the council in relation to this access or any matter arising from the change of its location from that proposed in planning permission Reg. Ref. XA1181.

These terms were accepted by Guardian in a letter of 13 September 1988 and on 26 October 1988 Mr Loftus the law agent for the county council wrote to Guardian's solicitor stating that he was preparing a draft contract. In the meantime these proceedings had been commenced by Neville by a plenary summons which was served on 11 October 1988, and Guardian did not go ahead with the agreement. If it had done so, it would have been in a position to construct the access road and so comply with its obligation to give Neville access to the licence plot.

Before completing this narrative of the relevant facts, there is one further letter I should refer to as it pinpoints the cause of the problem in regard to the access road. It is a letter of 26 July 1988 from Guardian's solicitor, Mr Owens, to Mr Loftus and is as follows:

26 July 1988 to Mr Dermot Loftus, Dublin County Council, 2/3 Parnell Square,

Dublin 1
Re: Our client: Guardian Builders Ltd
Your client: Dublin County Council
Re: Access to the Gables Site, Stillorgan Road.

Dear Mr Loftus

I refer to our telephone conversation today and to the agreement reached between our respective clients in 1984 in respect of the above. As you are aware, your client pointed out that the one outstanding matter in the 1984 agreement was the location of the access to Parkes Hotel which we discussed with both yourself and Mr Fallon at our last meeting in your office. I now set out hereunder the wording to get over this difficulty which we agreed this morning:

> The owners of Parkes Hotel acknowledge that the access as proposed in paragraph 1 above will not give rise to a claim by it against the county council as a result of the change in its location from that proposed in planning permission reference XA1181 already obtained.

We will now endeavour to get its agreement to the inclusion of such a paragraph as the above in an agreement with our client. Failing reaching such an agreement with it, our client may have to revert back to the old access as proposed by Parkes Hotel in planning permission reference XA 1181 as a result of the views you expressed at our last meeting in your office.

As agreed on the telephone such an agreement (if reached) will be signed on behalf of Parkes Hotel by its manager and on behalf of Guardian Builders Ltd by its principal.

I trust the above is in order.

Yours sincerely
Michael Owens.

When one looks at these facts it is in my opinion impossible to say that the performance of this contract was frustrated. No event supervened which significantly changed the nature of Guardian's obligation to provide access to the licence plot which involved constructing the access road. When Guardian entered into the licence agreement, it had the informal agreement of 10 March 1984 with the county council which, if implemented, would have enabled it to construct the road. And in fact, under the terms of the agreement, it had an obligation to do so since it was a condition of the agreement that it would construct the road within twelve months of obtaining planning permission for its office development from the Dun Laoghaire Borough, and this had been obtained on 16 September 1986. And when this agreement went off, the county council showed its willingness to enter into a new agreement in September 1988. Furthermore, it is quite clear from the evidence of the county council's witnesses that the county council wanted this access road built. The only unexpected problem that Guardian had was the county council insisting that the position of the exit from the Parkes Hotel car park to the access road should not be altered, but this could not by any means be termed a supervening event which significantly changed the nature of Guardian's obligation under the licence agreement. It made it more onerous, but that was all.

I am satisfied, therefore, that the defence of frustration fails, and that having been the only defence which was raised against Neville's claim for specific performance, I would allow this appeal and direct specific performance of the licence agreement. And the court will hear counsel on the question of damages, if any."

CHAPTER 15

Rectification

MUTUAL AND UNILATERAL MISTAKE

Rectification is concerned with defects in the recording, not in the making of an agreement.[1] It is now accepted that there is no need to establish the existence of an antecedent agreement capable of being enforced prior to the drawing up of the instrument sought to be rectified provided that there is a common intention between the parties which continues until the contract is executed.[2] However, it will be necessary to establish precisely what the common intention of the parties was before a court will grant an order of rectification.[3]

As a general principle, a court will only rectify an agreement where it fails to record the intention of both parties.[4] However, where the plaintiff can establish that the defendant was aware of his error and sought to take advantage of it, rectification may be granted even in cases of unilateral mistake.[5]

Monaghan County Council v. Vaughan
[1948] IR 306

The plaintiff county council invited tenders for demolition work and the removal of valuable materials from a derelict site. Dixon J found that it was the clear intention of both parties that the defendant would pay for the right to carry out the works. However, when the county council executed a contract it provided that the defendant should be paid for the demolition work. Dixon J granted rectification of the agreement.

---

[1] *Mackenzie v. Coulson* (1869) LR 8 Eq 368, 375 *per* James VC and *Irish Life Assurance Co. Ltd v. Dublin Land Securities Ltd* [1989] IR 253, 260 *per* Griffin J.

[2] *Monaghan County Council v. Vaughan* [1948] IR 306 and *Irish Life Assurance Co. Ltd v. Dublin Land Securities Ltd* [1989] IR 253.

[3] *McD. v. McD.* [1993] ILRM 717 and *Irish Life Assurance Co. Ltd v. Dublin Land Securities Ltd* [1989] IR 253. See also *Ferguson v. Merchant Banking Ltd* [1993] ILRM 136 although as Murphy J commented this case was far weaker from the defendant's point of view than that presented to the court by the plaintiff in the *Irish Life Assurance* case and there was an 'absence of a pre-existing concluded agreement establishing the common intention of the parties with a sufficient degree of particularity'.

[4] *Irish Life Assurance Co. Ltd v. Dublin Land Securities Ltd* [1989] IR 253, 260 *per* Griffin J.

[5] *Irish Life Assurance Co. Ltd v. Dublin Land Securities Ltd* [1986] IR 332, 349-354 *per* Keane J and *Thomas Bates & Son Ltd v. Wyndam's (Lingerie) Ltd* [1981] 1 WLR 505.

DIXON J stated as follows at pp.309–317: "I have had an opportunity of considering fully the facts in this case and of considering the numerous authorities opened to me by counsel. The case has been so well presented to the Court by counsel for each party, that I feel that I can give judgment now while the facts are fresh in my mind.

My view of the facts in the case is this. At the close of the plaintiffs' case, I had no doubt (and still have none), that a mistake was made by them in the written form of the contract. The terms of the advertisement and of the form of tender, together with the prior offers made by Messrs. McEntee and Roche Brothers, show that the contract was regarded by the plaintiffs as a valuable concession. In addition, the circumstances themselves indicated that valuable material would be obtained from the demolition work – material for which there was a rising market price, as a result of which, no doubt, the offers already received had been refused as insufficient. These factors, of course, do not all necessarily affect the defendant.

The clear intention of the County Council was that they should be paid for granting the right to carry out the work of demolition, and, while the defendant's offer was ambiguous in form, leaving it doubtful as to whether it contemplated that he was to pay or to be paid the sum of £1,200, I have no doubt that the County Council construed it as meaning that they were to be paid that sum by the defendant, particularly as they had already received and refused an offer by Messrs. Roche Brothers to do the work and to pay a sum of £1,125 for the concession.

As to what the defendant's intention really was, I regard his evidence as being very unconvincing and, having regard to his demeanour in the witness box, I am unable to accept very much of what he said. Furthermore, most of his evidence conflicts sharply with the probabilities in the matter.

The plaintiffs have made a *prima facie* case on the language of the advertisement, that their offer was for a payment to them of whatever sum should be agreed upon in return for the right to carry out the demolition work. Clause 13 of the specification was called to the attention of the defendant, and both its terms and the fact that the material to be obtained by way of salvage on the demolition would have a substantial value, are consistent only with the intention of both parties having been that the County Council should be paid and not that they should have to pay. This conclusion appears to me to be strengthened rather than rebutted by the evidence of the defendant himself.

Accordingly, I must hold that the intention of the defendant as well as that of the plaintiffs was that the defendant should pay to the plaintiffs a sum of £1,200 for the right to carry out the demolition work.

I am prepared to accept the evidence of the defendant that he saw his solicitor with respect to the matter, but here a difficulty arises as to the date of the interview. He says that it was after he had submitted the tender, although on re-examination he admitted that he did not definitely know when it was. Mr. O'Malley, his solicitor, states that the interview was some time before tender was made, and I accept that evidence, but it does not strengthen the defendant's case.

On the 26th or 28th September, the specification was sent by the County Council to the defendant, after which the defendant went and saw his solicitor. I feel that the probability is that he went and saw his solicitor before travelling to Clones on the 3rd October, and therefore that he did not then know exactly the nature of the work to be done, and probably consulted his solicitor mainly with a view to ascertaining the precise meaning of the contract and particularly of clause 13. Mr. O'Malley very properly advised him that clause 13 was more consistent with the defendant paying the County Council, but if payment were to be the other way, it might be construed consistently with that by modifying the meaning of the word "credit" in it. Having made the inspection on October the 3rd, the defendant submitted his offer to the County Council on October the 5th, and he must then have known that the position was that he would have to pay, rather than be paid. He had then also an approximate idea of the value of the materials and had also the advantage of fifteen years' experience of demolition work, including several contracts in which he had paid for the right to carry out the work.

The only meaning which I can give to his offer, is that he intended to pay this sum of £1,200. He produced two pages of notes of calculations said to have been made by him on October the 3rd, but I view them with the gravest suspicion and feel that they were probably made after the event and with a view to this litigation. They were produced by him when asked by his solicitor how he had arrived at the contract price, and were probably prepared at that stage. Even on their face value, however, they do not give much help. They show an estimated profit of £3 and an arbitrary figure of £1,200 as the amount to be asked for, representing an 80% profit on outlay. I find nothing helpful to the defendant's case in such calculations and figures.

Digressing for a moment, I view with equal suspicion the defendant's evidence as to the actual outlay and receipts. The figures show a great lack of particularity and many items are open to doubt or suspicion. I may instance the payment of £10 per week to his nephew, the complete mystery as to the item of £72 10s, the absence of particulars of private sales, and the obscurity as to approximately 2,200 slates taken to Limerick. Even, however, accepting what the defendant said, if he were to be paid £1,200, his profit would have been £2,400, while if he were to pay £1,200 the transaction would work out about evenly.

I therefore hold that the offer meant, and that the defendant intended it to mean, that he would pay the sum of £1,200 to the County Council. As to the evidence of Mr. Griffin, it does not establish a state of mind of the defendant which would displace the conclusion at which I have arrived. Here again there is a difficulty about a date, namely, that upon which the amount of the bond was fixed. The proposal form is dated 23rd of November, and in my opinion the earliest date on which the defendant could have known of the amount of the bond would have been a date on which he also must have known the contents of the draft contract. Mr. Griffin's evidence does not satisfy me that the defendant genuinely thought he was to be paid a sum of £1,200. This constitutes no reflection whatever on Mr. Griffin's evidence, as it is quite natural that he is unable, after the lapse of time, to recollect with sufficient accuracy for my purposes what took place at the interview except so far as the documents disclose it.

For these reasons I am satisfied that it was the intention of both parties that the defendant should pay the sum of £1,200 to the County Council, and I am of opinion that the defendant saw the error into which the County Council had fallen when the contract was read over to him and decided to take advantage of it. I regard this as a case of mutual mistake. I think that it is immaterial that one party knows the document to be inaccurate for the purposes of the application of the principles of law applicable to mutual mistake. What is material is that both parties were agreed upon certain matters and that the completed contract did not correctly represent the substance of their agreement. A unilateral mistake arises where one of two or more parties is not *ad idem* with the other party or parties, and there is therefore, no real agreement between them. In such a case, rescission may be appropriate, but the present is a different case. It is not a case of unilateral mistake in that sense, but to speak of it as a case of mutual mistake may obscure its true character of a common or mutual intention misrepresented by the record of that intention.

If the defendant had really intended that he should be paid the sum of £1,200 the position would be entirely different, but on the evidence I reject that view and hold that he attempted to take advantage of the error made by the County Council and that his conduct was dishonest and approximated to fraud.

The cases which were opened to me, turning on the law of conveyancing, are somewhat different from the present, for they are instances of mistake arising from the failure of the conveyance to conform with the prior written agreement (i.e. the contract of sale). Such mistake might be mutual or unilateral, these terms being used in the sense of the parties' knowledge of the conformance or otherwise of the conveyance in question with the prior contract, and the conveyance being a sequel to, rather than a record of, such contract. Here, however, when the document alleged to be erroneously framed does not record the agreed intention, it represents a case for rectification if the plaintiffs are in a position to overcome the legal difficulties they have to face.

I have been referred to some relevant passages in the sixth edition of Fry on Specific Performance. The first of these (par. 791), reads as follows:– "It follows from the nature of the jurisdiction that there can be no rectification where there is not a prior actual contract by which to rectify the written document: so that, for instance, a policy cannot be rectified by the slip, because the slip constituted no contract, and there was no contract till the policy was signed and the premium paid."

I think this only means that there must be some agreement between the parties. In the instance given, the "slip" was only a proposal and, until the policy had been signed and the first premium paid, there was no agreed intention. The paragraph is consistent with the statement that the Court will not rectify contracts in themselves, but merely the instruments in which the contracts are set out.

The next paragraph illustrates this:– "It equally follows that the mistake of one party to a contract can never be a ground for compulsory rectification, so as to impose on the second party the erroneous conception of the first. The error of the plaintiff alone may, however, where (but, it is conceived, only where) there has been fraud or conduct equivalent to fraud on the part of the defendant, be a ground for putting the defendant to elect between having the transaction annulled altogether or submitting to the rectification of the deed in accordance with the plaintiff's intention."

In other words, an erroneous conception of the intended agreement by one of the parties is sufficient to prevent there being a mutual agreement.

Paragraph 793 of the same work is also of importance:– "Parol evidence is admitted to show the common mistake of both parties in reducing the contract into writing, and as the ground for rectifying it. 'I think it impossible,' said Lord Thurlow, 'to refuse, as incompetent, parol evidence which goes to prove that the words taken down in writing were contrary to the concurrent intention of all parties.'"

The "concurrent intention" referred to here by the author is shown in the present case by the documents and by the circumstances existing before the formal document was executed.

The essence of the present case is that this written document is inconsistent with the mutual agreement between the parties, and for that reason the decision at which I have arrived does not, in my opinion, conflict with the result of cases such as *Garrard v. Frankel* (1862) 30 Beav 445. In that case an intended lessee signed an agreement to take a lease of premises at a yearly rent of £230 and on the terms of a lease on which the said agreement was written but which erroneously stated the yearly rent to be £130. A lease was subsequently executed in which the rent was erroneously stated to be £130 per annum. The error on the part of the lessor was proved, and the Court considered that the lessee must have perceived the discrepancy between the amount of rent previously stated by the lessor and specified in the agreement and that reserved by the lease, but held that the lessor was not entitled to have the lease reformed and that the proper relief was to give the lessee an option of agreeing to having the lease reformed or of rejecting it and paying a rental for past occupation and a mortgage on the lease created by the lessee.

It is clear that that was a case of unilateral mistake because of the possibility that the lessor had changed his mind as to the amount of the rent. I find it impossible, however, in the present case to hold that the County Council had changed its mind in the manner suggested by the defendant or that the defendant honestly believed such a change of mind to have taken place.

The case of *Paget v. Marshall* (1884) 28 Ch D 255 is also distinguishable from the present for the reason that in that case the Judge felt that he had insufficient evidence before him of the existence of a mutual mistake.

In *Hartog v. Colin and Shields* [1939] 3 All ER 566 the claim of the plaintiffs was somewhat different from that in the present case and the mistake there may, upon my reading of the report, have been unilateral mistake.

Similarly, in *Nolan v. Graves and Hamilton* [1946] IR 376, Haugh J. held that the mistake was unilateral. Furthermore, the circumstances there were different from those in the present case and I think it is very questionable that his Lordship intended to lay down, as has been suggested, that the knowledge of one party of the true facts will always prevent a mistake from being treated as a mutual mistake.

I think that the principle which is applicable here is most clearly set out in the decision in *Fowler v. Fowler* (1859) 4 De G & J 250 where, at page 265, the Lord Chancellor said:– "It is clear that a person who seeks to rectify a deed upon the ground of mistake must be required to establish, in the clearest and most satisfactory manner, that the alleged intention to which he desires it to be made conformable continued concurrently in the minds of all parties down to the time of its execution, and also must be able to show exactly and precisely the form to which the deed ought to be brought. For there is a material difference between setting aside an instrument and rectifying it on the ground of mistake. In the latter case you can only act upon the mutual and concurrent intention of all parties for whom the Court is virtually making a new written agreement." I am satisfied that in the present case the two requirements mentioned in this passage have been fulfilled by the plaintiffs.

Gun v. M'Carthy (1883) 13 LR Ir 304 was also a case of mutual mistake and there Flanagan J. said (at p. 309) that he had always understood the law to be that when you seek to reform a conveyance you must first establish that there was a definite concluded agreement between the parties, but which, by mistake common to both parties, had not been carried out in the conveyance executed pursuant to the real agreement. But when the mistake is not common, he asks, by what can it be reformed? "To reform," he continues, "implies a previous *agreement*; but when the evidence shows that there was no agreement to which both parties assented, but only a mistake on one side, and not a common mistake, in my opinion it is impossible to support a suit to *reform*, whatever equity the party who has made the mistake may have in certain cases to rescind, the conveyance." His Lordship here seems to be drawing a contrast between cases where the parties are *ad idem* in intention and cases where they are not.

As to the question of negligence, there may have been a degree of negligence on the part of the County Council and their officials and possibly also, although to a much lesser extent, on the part of their solicitor, but I am not satisfied (and there is authority to the contrary), that in the case of a claim for rectification of a contract on the ground of mutual mistake, negligence on the part of the plaintiffs can be raised as a defence.

Again as to estoppel, the contention of the defendant upon this plea is also inapplicable to the circumstances before me. I am satisfied that the County Council did not change its mind between the date of receiving the tender and the date of the making of the contract, nor did it intend to make a fresh offer. I am satisfied that the defendant could not honestly have believed such a complete reversal of intention on the part of the plaintiffs to have been intended. He was not misled, he did not act on the basis of any misrepresentation and he is not entitled now, in my opinion, to rely upon estoppel.

Lastly, it has been argued on behalf of the defendant that s. 100 of the Local Government (Ir.) Act, 1898, has had the effect of removing an essential condition necessary to confer upon the Court, in a case such as the present, any jurisdiction to rectify a contract. This section deals mainly with a question of procedure rather than with matters of *ultra vires*, that is, with form rather than substance, and does not render the local authority incapable of making the particular contract. If construed in the manner suggested, the section would lead to absurd and harsh results, and I would be slow to accept such a construction as being correct, unless supported by well-settled or coercive authorities. So far from this being the case, an answer to the contention is to be found in the judgment of Lord Birkenhead in the case of *United States v. Motor Trucks, Ltd.* [1924] AC 196, where, at pages 200 and 201, he said:– "And indeed the power of the Court to rectify mutual mistake implies that this power may be exercised notwithstanding that the true agreement of the parties has not been expressed in writing. Nor does the rule make any inroad upon another principle, that the plaintiff must shew first that there was an actually concluded agreement antecedent to the instrument which is sought to be rectified; and secondly, that such agreement has been inaccurately represented in the instrument. When this is proved, either party may claim, in spite of the Statute of Frauds, that the instrument on which the other insists does not represent the real agreement. The statute, in fact, only provides that no agreement not in writing and not duly signed shall be sued on; but when the written instrument is rectified there is a writing which satisfies the statute, the jurisdiction of the Court to rectify being outside the prohibition of the statute." I find it impossible to see any difference in principle between the case of a contract which cannot be enforced because of the Statute of Frauds and one which is alleged to be unenforceable by reason of s. 100 of the Act of 1898.

Again, the precise point is dealt with in the case of *Shipley U.D.C. v. Bradford Corporation* [1936] Ch 375 and I adopt the reasoning and conclusions of Mr. Justice Clauson at page 398 where he says:– "If the matter had rested there, it may be that the defendants' argument would never have been put forward, but there are two cases in which the exact point arose which is in issue here – namely, whether a document sealed by a corporation which can bind itself only by seal, can be rectified. In each case an actual decision was unnecessary, but in each case the learned judge (Younger J. in the one case and Romer J. in the other), expressed by way of *dictum* a provisional view which certainly supports the defendants' argument, but in neither case were the early authorities discussed. Those cases are *Faraday v. Tamworth Union* 86 LJ Ch 436 and *Higgins (W.) Ltd. v. Mayor of Northampton* [1927] 1 Ch 128. In each case the Court found that there was no mutual mistake, but in each case the judge intimated that he would have felt a difficulty in rectifying the document, because that would amount to binding the corporate body to a document which requires a seal, but which the body have in fact never sealed. Not only were the earlier cases not cited, but attention was not in either case drawn to the decision of the Court of Appeal in *Hall-Dare v. Hall-Dare* (1885) 31 Ch D 251, which seems to show that a deed rectified by the Court so as to conform to the true intention of the executing party at the moment of execution must be taken to be his deed and to have been (at all events, for any purpose relevant to this case) his deed in the rectified form as from the date of execution: see also *Meeking v. Meeking* [1917] 1 Ch 77.

"Had it been necessary for me to decide the point, I should have felt some difficulty in following the *dicta* in these two cases, and I should have felt bound to hold that the proof in the present case that the concurrent intention of the parties was, at the moment of execution, to contract on the footing of the £540 being a sum per annum and the 450,000 gallons a yield per diem would have made it necessary (but for my construing the instrument as I have construed it) to rectify the instrument so as to accord with that concurrent intention, notwithstanding that the parties can be bound only by their respective seals."

This is the latest of three cases (the earlier two of which are cited in the passage just read), in which the point is dealt with by way of *obiter dictum*, and I prefer the view expressed in it.

For all these reasons, I consider that the plaintiffs' case for rectification has been fully established and I grant the relief as claimed. The plaintiffs are entitled to their costs."

Irish Life Assurance Co. Ltd v. Dublin Land Securities Ltd
[1989] IR 253

The plaintiff company owned a large portfolio of ground rents and also valuable lands which had been made the subject of compulsory purchase orders. A contract of sale between the plaintiff and the defendant was drawn up and while it was the intention of the plaintiff to exclude the lands subject to the C.P.O.s from the sale, due to a mix up in its legal department, they were included in the contract. The plaintiff's intention to exclude these lands was communicated to an agent of the defendant in a rather imprecise way but was not passed on to the defendant. The plaintiff sought rectification of the contract, while the defendant sought specific performance of the agreement in its original form. Keane J found that the defendant did not know of the plaintiff's intention to exclude the properties in question and dismissed the plaintiff's claim on the grounds that there was no common intention between the parties to this effect. On appeal, the Supreme Court (Finlay CJ, Griffin and McCarthy JJ) upheld the order of the High Court.

GRIFFIN J stated at pp. 259–265: "After a full and complete hearing in the High Court, the learned trial judge reserved judgment, and, in his judgment, he fully reviewed all the facts and the considerable body of law to which he was referred. His conclusions may, I think, broadly be summarised as follows:-

1. In the circumstances of the case, although the principal (Mr. Frederick) may be deemed to have notice of what was communicated by Mr. Nowlan to his agent, Mr. White, he was not deemed to have assented to the inclusion of a term to that effect in the proposed contract and to be bound by it where it was omitted from the contract because of the mistake by the appellant who was the party seeking to rely on it;

2. That it was a principle of fundamental importance that the courts will not reform a contract in writing in the absence of convincing proof that the contract, as the result of a mistake, has failed to give effect to the common intention of the parties previously manifested in outward accord;

3. The appellant had not discharged the heavy burden of proof which lay on it to establish that there was a common continuing intention on the part of Mr. Frederick and the appellant to exclude the vacant lands at Palmerstown from the sale, which was, through mistake, not embodied in the contract and was outwardly expressed and communicated between the parties;

4. The mistake in question was a unilateral mistake rather than common or mutual mistake, and there was no element of fraud, dishonesty or sharp practice on the part of Mr. Frederick or his agents, Mr. White or Mr. Miley;

5. Even if the knowledge of Mr. White could be treated as an adequate basis for the notional consent of the respondent to the inclusion of the disputed term in the contract, the uncertainty in the description of what was to be excluded was fatal to the appellant's claim, and the appellant had failed to discharge the onus of proof on it of establishing that the exclusion of the lands in Palmerstown was the result of a common or mutual mistake.

He dismissed the appellant's claim for rectification of the agreement, and on the respondent's counterclaim made a declaration that the respondent was the owner of and lawfully entitled to the lands in Folio 5245, and that the same were comprised in and part of the subject matter of the contract of sale of the 23rd December, 1981, and he made an order for the specific performance of the contract for sale. From that decision and the conclusions of the learned trial judge the appellant has appealed to this court.

It should be emphasised that the claim of the appellant in this case is solely for rectification of the contract for sale. There is no claim for rescission although it is quite clear, and the learned judge so held, that it was at all times the intention of the appellant to exclude the lands in question. In *Monaghan County Council v. Vaughan* [1948] IR 306 at p. 312, Dixon J., in contrasting rescission and rectification, stated that where the parties contract under a mutual mistake of fact the agreement is liable to be rescinded at the instance of either party, since in such a case no contract came into being; likewise, where there is a unilateral mistake, and one of two or more parties is not *ad idem* with the other party or parties, there is no real agreement between them and rescission may also be appropriate. During the course of the hearing of this appeal the Court indicated to counsel for the appellant that, even at this late stage, it would consider an application to amend the pleadings to include a claim for rescission of the agreement if the appellant wished to apply for such amendment, in case it should transpire that this was a more appropriate remedy when all the matters in issue were being considered. The appellant however steadfastly refused to apply for any such amendment, as it did not seek nor did it want rescission of the agreement. The appellant's attitude is readily understandable having regard to its reasons for selling the rent roll in the first instance. The appellant was supported in this attitude by the respondent, so that neither party wished to contemplate rescission of the agreement. In these circumstances, this Court is solely concerned with the issue of rectification, upon which the claim of the appellant must stand or fall, and I would express no view on the question as to whether the remedy of rescission is appropriate or otherwise.

Rectification is concerned with defects in the recording, not in the making, of an agreement.

"Courts of Equity do not rectify contracts; they may and do rectify instruments purporting to have been made in pursuance of terms of contracts" – *per* James V.C. in *Mackenzie v. Coulson* (1869) LR 8 Eq 368 at p. 375.

As a general rule, the courts only rectify an agreement in writing where there has been mutual mistake – *i.e.* where it fails to record the intention of *both* parties. Although that was the original conception of reformation of an instrument by rectification, nowadays a party who has entered into a written agreement by mistake will also be entitled to rectification if he establishes by convincing evidence that the other party, with knowledge of such intention and mistake, nevertheless concluded the agreement – see Kenny J. in *Lucey v. Laurel Construction Co. Ltd.* (Unreported, High Court, 18th December, 1970); *Roberts and Co. Ltd. v. Leicestershire County Council* [1961] Ch 555; *Riverlate Properties Ltd. v. Paul* [1975] 1 Ch 133. In the last case it was considered by the Court of Appeal that the knowledge of such other party must be such as to involve him in a degree of sharp practice. On the hearing of this appeal the appellant's counsel conceded that there was no suggestion or allegation on the appellant's part of *mala fides* or improper conduct or sharp practice on the part of Mr. Frederick or Mr. Miley or Mr. White, a very proper concession in view of the holding of the learned trial judge that neither Mr. Frederick nor Mr. Miley was aware of the appellant's mistake either before or at the time of entering into the agreement in writing.

It was formerly considered that the court could not rectify a document in writing unless it was preceded by a concluded oral contract. In taking this view, Kenny J. in *Lucey v. Laurel Construction Co. Ltd.* (Unreported, High Court, 18th December, 1970) cited with approval what was said by Denning L.J. (as he then was) in *Rose v. Pim* [1953] 2 QB 450 at p. 461:

> "Rectification is concerned with contracts and documents, not with intentions. In order to get rectification it is necessary to show that the parties were in complete agreement on the terms of their contract, but by an error wrote them down wrongly; and in this regard, in order to ascertain the terms of their contract, you do not look into the inner minds of the parties – into their intentions – any more than you do in the formation of any other contract. You look at their outward acts, that is, at what they said or wrote to one another in coming to their agreement, and then compare it with the document which they have signed. If you can predicate with certainty what their contract was, and that it is, by a common mistake, wrongly expressed in the document, then you rectify the document; but nothing less will suffice. [It is not necessary that all the formalities of the contract should have been executed so as to make it enforceable at law (see *Shipley Urban District Council v. Bradford Corporation* [1936] Ch 375) but, formalities apart, there must have been a concluded contract]. There is a passage in *Crane v. Hegeman-Harris Co. Inc.* [1939] 1 All ER 662, 664 which suggests that a continuing common intention alone will suffice; but I am clearly of opinion that a continuing common intention is not sufficient unless it has found expression in outward agreement. There could be no certainty at all in business transactions if a party who had entered into a firm contract could afterwards turn around and claim to have it rectified on the ground that the parties intended something different. He is allowed to prove, if he can, that they *agreed something different*: see *Lovell & Christmas v. Wall*, per Lord Cozens-Hardy M.R., and per Buckley L.J. (1911) 104 LT 85, 88, 93, but not that they *intended* something different."

Two things need to be noted – the emphasis was Denning L.J.'s; and the sentence inside square brackets was inadvertently omitted from the quotation by Kenny J., presumably in transcription.

Kenny J. does not appear to have been referred to *Joscelyne v. Nissen* [1970] 2 QB 86, a decision of the Court of Appeal reported some months before *Lucey v. Laurel Construction Ltd.* (Unreported, High Court, 18th December, 1970). In *Joscelyne v. Nissen* [1970] 2 QB 86 the judgment was delivered by Russell L.J. and was the judgment of the court. In giving judgment he reviewed what he himself described as "the train of this undoubtedly formidable array of judicial opinion" from the decision of *Mackenzie v. Coulson* (1869) LR 8 Eq 368 (one hundred years earlier) onwards. Amongst the cases considered was *Crane v. Hegeman-Harris Co. Inc.* [1939] 1 All ER 662 decided by Simonds J. Buckley L.J. at p. 95 (*inter alia*) cited the following passage from the judgment of Simonds J. at p. 664 of [1939] 1 All ER:

> "I am clear that I must follow the decision of Clauson J., as he then was, in *Shipley Urban District Council v. Bradford Corpn.* [1936] 1 Ch 375, the point of which is that, in order that this court may exercise its jurisdiction to rectify a

written instrument, it is not necessary to find a concluded and binding contract between the parties antecedent to the agreement which it is sought to rectify. The judge held, and I respectfully concur with his reasoning and his conclusion, that it is sufficient to find a common continuing intention in regard to a particular provision or aspect of the agreement. If one finds that, in regard to a particular point, the parties were in agreement up to the moment when they executed their formal instrument, and the formal instrument does not conform with that common agreement, then this court has jurisdiction to rectify, although it may be that there was, until the formal instrument was executed, no concluded and binding contract between the parties . . .

Secondly, I want to say this upon the principle of the jurisdiction. It is a jurisdiction which is to be exercised only upon convincing proof that the concluded instrument does not represent the common intention of the parties. That is particularly the case where one finds prolonged negotiations between the parties eventually assuming the shape of a formal instrument in which they have been advised by their respective skilled legal advisers. The assumption is very strong in such a case that the instrument does represent their real intention, and it must be only upon proof which Lord Eldon, I think, in a somewhat picturesque phrase described as 'irrefragable' that the court can act, I would rather, I think, say that the court can only act if it is satisfied beyond all reasonable doubt that the instrument does not represent their common intention, and is further satisfied as to what their common intention was. For let it be clear that it is not sufficient to show that the written instrument does not represent their common intention unless positively also one can show what their common intention was."

In *Joscelyne v. Nissen* [1970] 2 QB 86 Russell L.J. in considering what was said in *Rose v. Pim* [1953] 2 QB 450 said at p.97:

"The decision in our judgment does not assert or reinstate the view that an antecedent complete concluded contract is required for rectification: it only shows that prior accord on a term or the meaning of a phrase to be used must have been outwardly expressed or communicated between the parties."

He then referred to the passage from the judgment of Denning L.J. already cited, and said:

"In so far as this passage might be taken to suggest that an antecedent complete concluded contract is necessary it would be in conflict with the views of both courts in *Crane v. Hegeman-Harris* [1939] 1 All ER 662 and is not supported by the other judgments" (those of Singleton L.J. and Morris L.J. who were the other members of the Court in *Rose v. Pim* [1953] 2 QB 450). And at p. 98 he said:

"In our judgment the law is as expounded by Simonds J. in *Crane's* case with the qualification that some outward expression of accord is required. We do not wish to attempt to state in any different phrases that with which we entirely agree, except to say that it is in our view better to use only the phrase "convincing proof" without echoing an old fashioned word such as "irrefragable" and without importing from the criminal law the phrase "beyond all reasonable doubt"."

In *Rooney and McParland Ltd. v. Carlin* [1981] NI 138 at p. 146 Lord Lowry L.C.J. summarised the principles clarified by Russell L.J. in the following terms:

> "1. There must be a concluded agreement antecedent to the instrument which is sought to be rectified; but
>
> 2. The antecedent agreement need not be binding in law (for example, it need not be under seal if made by a public authority or in writing and signed by the party if relating to a sale of land) nor need it be in writing: such incidents merely help to discharge the heavy burden of proof; and
>
> 3. A complete antecedent concluded contract is not required, so long as there was prior accord on a term of a proposed agreement, outwardly expressed and communicated between the parties, as in *Joscelyne v. Nissen*."

Like the learned trial judge, I would adopt what was said by Russell L.J. and Lord Lowry L.C.J. as representing the law on the subject in question in this jurisdiction.

Applying those principles to the facts of this case, and bearing in mind the heavy burden of proof that lies on those seeking rectification, the question to be addressed is whether there was convincing proof, reflected in some outward expression of accord, that the contract in writing did not represent the common continuing intention of the parties on which the court can act, and whether the plaintiff can positively show what that common intention was in relation to the provisions which the appellant says were intended to exclude the vacant lands at Palmerstown.

None of the lands was inspected by or on behalf of the respondent - with upwards of 10,000 properties included in the sale it would be wholly unrealistic and virtually impossible to 'walk the lands' as is usually done in a normal sale. Daily meetings took place between and discussions were held by the legal representatives of the parties. Mr. Devlin put his board room at the disposal of Mr. Miley and his assistants for a period of six months prior to the completion of the agreement. It is somewhat extraordinary, but nevertheless was accepted by the learned trial judge, that there was no reference whatever to the significant vacant land in Palmerstown between March, 1981, and the completion of the contract on the 23rd December, 1981. In these circumstances, in my opinion, Mr. Frederick was entitled to assume, when the time for completion of the contract came, that any problems as to what lands the appellant intended to be included in the sale would have been ironed out, and that having regard to the note on the last page of the blue booklet that the appellant *would* be bound by exchange of contracts under its seal.

Having regard to the conclusion at which I have arrived on the question of common intention, I do not consider it necessary to consider the extent to which the knowledge obtained by Mr. White from Mr. Nowlan should be imputed to Mr. Frederick. Like the learned trial judge, I am quite satisfied that the instant case is one of unilateral mistake and not of common or mutual mistake. Assuming, though not deciding, that the knowledge obtained by Mr. White could be treated as an adequate basis for what the learned trial judge described as Mr. Frederick's notional assent to the inclusion of the disputed term, what was said by Mr. Nowlan to Mr. White falls very far short of establishing that there was a common intention of the parties that the vacant lands at Palmerstown, or any part of them, should be excluded from the sale. What Mr. Nowlan referred to in evidence as "a significant area of land the subject of a c.p.o. at Palmerstown", and "significant vacant lands in Palmerstown" completely lacked the precision necessary to enable a court to conclude what was the common intention of the parties. The lands could very readily have been described by reference to the Folio or their precise area. Although reference was made to "a significant holding of land the subject of a c.p.o. at Palmerstown", and to "significant vacant land at Palmerstown", there were in fact two c.p.o.s, not one, but combined they did not exhaust the area of the vacant land. The learned trial judge, in my view correctly, posed the question as to whether Mr. Nowlan was referring to the County Council's c.p.o., or Dublin Corporation's c.p.o.'s, or to both combined, or to both combined together with the portion of land not included in either c.p.o. but which was ultimately sold to the local authority by agreement. In common with the trial judge, I am quite satisfied that the appellant has failed to discharge the onus of proof which is on it of establishing that the exclusion of the lands at Palmerstown was the result of a common or mutual mistake which would entitle it to rectification.

What occurred on the completion of the contract is also of considerable importance. Mr. Miley was not satisfied that all the properties to which his client would become entitled were in fact included in the schedules. He was given what amounts to an ultimatum that his client either completed the contract on that date in the form presented to him by the appellant, and including such properties only as were included in the draft contract, or the deal was off. Mr. Frederick was thus required to accept the contract and to complete it on the basis that all the properties to which he became entitled were included in it. This he agreed to do, and if there had been omissions he would in the circumstances have found it extremely difficult to obtain rectification of the document. What the appellant in effect is now claiming is that although Mr. Frederick had to take the contract in its then form, and with such properties as were included in it, nevertheless, without any contribution to the mistake on his part, the appellant was not to be bound by the contract in writing even though the mistake was a unilateral one on its part. If that claim was to prevail, it would in my view be unjust to the respondent.

In my judgment the learned trial judge was correct in refusing to rectify the contract for sale and I would affirm his order both in respect of rectification and the counterclaim, and would accordingly dismiss this appeal."

While it is not essential that the parties to the litigation should be privy to the same contract in order to obtain rectification, they must be privy to or affected by the same mistake in such a way that it would be unconscionable for the defendant in such proceedings to seek to rely on the decision which erroneously recorded the true agreement. This point was made clear by Murphy J in *Lac Minerals Ltd v. Chevron Mineral Corporation of Ireland.*

Lac Minerals Ltd v. Chevron Mineral Corporation of Ireland
[1995] 1 ILRM 161

The first and second named defendants entered into a joint venture agreement to exploit mineral rights. The plaintiff entered into an agreement for the indirect acquisition of the first named defendant's interest. The joint venture agreement gave a right to either party to transfer its interest to a third party provided the other was given a right of pre-emption in respect of that interest. The plaintiff claimed that the time within which the right of pre-emption could be exercised was limited to 45 days and that as this period had expired, the second named defendant could no longer exercise that right. The plaintiff contended that if the agreement did prescribe a period of 60 days this was due to a mistake and that it should be rectified to provide for a period of 45 days instead. Murphy J dismissed the plaintiff's claim.

MURPHY J stated at pp.172–180: "In my view, it is impossible for Lac, whose claim derives solely from the Lac agreement, the August side letter and the alleged variations thereof, to maintain a claim for the rectification of the JVA to which they are not parties and under which they derive no estate.

The burden falling on a party claiming rectification – as opposed to rescission – of a document on the basis of mutual mistake is a heavy one. The Supreme Court – in upholding the order of the High Court – in *Irish Life Assurance Co. Ltd v. Dublin Land Securities Ltd* [1989] IR 253 reiterated that such was the case in the following terms at p. 263:

> Applying those principles to the facts of this case, and bearing in mind the heavy burden of proof that lies on those seeking rectification, the question to be addressed is whether there was convincing proof, reflected in some outward expression of accord, that the contract in writing did not represent the common continuing intention of the parties on which the court can act, and whether the plaintiff can positively show what that common intention was in relation to the provisions which the appellant says were intended to exclude the vacant lands at Palmerstown.

However, it is not the extent of the evidence, but the nature and availability of the remedy, which is of decisive importance in the present case.

Spry on Equitable Remedies (3rd ed. at p. 572) explains the remedy in the following terms:

The rectification of documents is a remedy that has been granted by courts of equity for many centuries. It is not ancillary to other remedies such as specific performance, but is independent, and its basis is the relief of an applicant so that he is not put at risk or prejudiced by the existence of a document reliance on which would, *without rectification, be unconscionable.* Rectification is, like other equitable remedies, discretionary.

In another passage (also quoted by Lac) from *Chitty* 26th ed. at para. 375 the matter is put in the following terms:

It has long been an established rule of equity that where a contract has by reason of a mistake common to the contracting parties been drawn up so as to militate against the intentions of both as revealed in their previous oral understanding, the court will rectify the contract so as to carry out such intentions so long as there is an issue between the parties as to their legal rights *inter se.* If there is no such issue or if no substantive relief is sought and no practicable purpose will be achieved rectification may be refused.

The claim for rectification was based largely on the evidence of Mr James D. Mancuso, a highly qualified geologist, who joined the Chevron group in 1984 as manager in charge of business development and subsequently as vice-president in charge of exploration. Apparently, Chevron had inherited the mineral interests at Lisheen in Co. Tipperary from Gulf Oil and in 1989 sought to dispose of all or part of their interest therein. It was that general intention which led to the execution of the JVA on 15 November 1989. Negotiations leading to the execution of that document were conducted between Mr Mancuso and originally a Mr Schaffalitzky but subsequently Mr Hough on behalf of Ivernia. Certainly, it was the evidence of Mr Mancuso that all of the material negotiations were conducted with Mr Hough who was the managing director of Ivernia. These negotiations were conducted by means of transatlantic telephone call and by fax. There were no face to face meetings between the negotiators. Three drafts of the agreement were produced but only the first and third were transmitted by Mr Mancuso to Mr Hough. It was the evidence of Mr Mancuso that the first draft included the figure of 60 days in both clauses of ss. 15.3.1 and 15.3.2. Mr Mancuso gave evidence that Mr Hough, having perused the first draft of the contract, suggested that the period of 60 days was too long and that a proposal was made that, instead, a period of 30 days should be substituted. Mr Mancuso says he proposed a compromise of 45 days and that this was accepted by Mr Hough. It was Mr Mancuso's evidence that he forwarded the notes of his telephone conversation with Mr Hough and the correspondence or fax from Ivernia's solicitors to Mr James H. Harris, Chevron's in-house solicitor, and that it was Mr Harris who purported to implement the particular changes agreed between Mr Hough and Mr Mancuso. Whilst Mr Harris did not give evidence before the court his memorandum to Mr Mancuso dated 25 September 1989 expressly records in s. 20 thereof that amendments had been made by the legal advisers by reference to notes on Mr

Mancuso's draft of the agreement. These amendments included the following: s. 15.3.1.4 is changed to 45 days.

Perhaps even more dramatic evidence in support of Mr Mancuso's account is to be found in the draft agreement which apparently was before Mr Hough at the time when he was discussing its contents with Mr Mancuso. That draft shows the figure of 45 days inserted opposite s. 15.3.1.4. Moreover, it would appear that the figure of 45 in blue ink was superimposed on a figure of 30 in black ink. As this document only came to the attention of Mr Mancuso following discovery thereof by Ivernia it does corroborate to an extraordinary extent the evidence given by Mr Mancuso.

Mr Hough rejected the account given by Mr Mancuso as to the circumstances in which the 60 day time limit in s. 15.3.1.4 came to be altered to 45 days. He says emphatically that it was never his intention that the 60 day time limit should be altered to 45 days. In particular, he denies that he ever had a discussion with Mr Mancuso prior to the execution of the JVA agreement with regard to the time limits for the exercise of the pre-emptive right. That version of the evidence leaves Mr Hough with the burden of explaining how it was that the figures, originally 30 and subsequently 45, came to be written – admittedly in his writing – opposite s. 15.3.1.4 on his draft. He says that sometime after receiving the first draft and perhaps in the month of September 1989 he had a telephone conversation with his adviser Mr Schaffalitsky in which they discussed how the Amax Preussag JVA pre-emption clause (the A-P clause) could or should be reconciled with the Chevron/Ivernia pre-emption clause in the JVA. He explained that Mr Schaffalitsky drew his attention to the fact in the first instance that the A-P clause involved a 30 day period and that subsequently Mr Schaffalitsky contacted him again to point out that in fact the A-P clause involved a further 15 day period and accordingly the original estimate of 30 days was altered to 45. It was, explained Mr Hough, in those circumstances that the figures of 30 and subsequently 45 were written in on the margin to the draft JVA. I find this explanation extraordinarily unsatisfactory and indeed the coincidence between the figures discussed between Mr Schaffalitsky and Mr Hough with those discussed between Mr Mancuso and Mr Harris improbable in the extreme. Whilst it would be explicable that Mr Hough and his advisers would be concerned to ensure that the A-P clause would fit within the terms of the JVA, it is stunning that he should have recorded the outcome of the debate in that context immediately opposite s. 15.3.1.4 and that it was that section which was subsequently amended by a direction or comment communicated by Mr Mancuso to Mr Harris, with the result that the figure which originally had appeared there was varied to 45. Apart from finding Mr Hough's explanation unconvincing the fact is that Mr Mancuso is the only witness who offered any explanation as to how the regrettable blunder occurred. Mr Hough simply dismisses it as a 'mystery'. I accept that some misgivings arise with regard to the evidence of Mr Mancuso as to the date or dates in which his discussions with Mr Hough took place and, more particularly, I recognise that, in cross-examination by counsel on behalf of Ivernia, questions were raised which impugned seriously Mr Mancuso's credibility. Having regard to the concessions made by Mr Mancuso under cross-examination as to discussions which he had with officials of Ivernia as to the evidence which he could or would give and the terms on which he was prepared to do so in relation to the matters in issue, I think that the evidence of Mr Mancuso must be approached not merely with care but with suspicion. However, even making that allowance it seems to me that I am forced to conclude on the balance of probabilities that an agreement was reached between Mr Hough and Mr Mancuso that the period for the exercise of the pre-emptive right contained in s. 15.3 of the JVA should be 45 days from receipt of the offer and not 60 days as included in the original draft.

If this evidence had been presented on behalf of CMCI in, say, 1991 in support of an application for rectification I am by no means certain that the court would have granted such relief. If neither party was at the time engaged in negotiations for the sale of its interest under the JVA the time limit as between 45 days and 60 days would surely be a matter of very limited importance. A court in its discretion might well prefer to leave it to the parties to resolve the patent ambiguity in whatever way they thought fit. If, on the other hand, some third party had acquired rights under the JVA the court would not permit rectification in such a way as to prejudice the rights of such a party. In any event the court in the exercise of its jurisdiction would be bound to take into account the conduct of both parties and to consider, in particular, whether the party seeking relief had moved with reasonable expedition to rectify the mistake after it had been adverted to. On balance, I think it unlikely that the courts exercising what is conventionally described as their 'equitable jurisdiction' would have ordered the rectification of the JVA to substitute the figure of 45 days for 60 days throughout s. 15.3, even accepting – as I have done – the evidence of Mr Mancuso as against that of Mr Hough.

If the parties adverted to the inconsistency between the time limits specified in s. 15.3 of the JVA and neglected or declined themselves to rectify the error, their conduct might well be described as imprudent but I do not see it as being unconscionable having regard to the absence of any particular benefit or detriment to one party as against the other.

In the present action the claim for rectification is not made by either party involved in the original error but by Lac who are undoubtedly affected by the JVA but are and were in no sense privy to the manner in which that agreement was negotiated or the circumstances in which the error occurred.

Counsel on behalf of Lac argue that rectification is not restricted to the original parties to a contract. In support of that argument they rely in particular on two cases, namely, *Majestic Homes Property Ltd v. Wise* [1978] Qd R 225 and *Shepheard v. Graham* (1947) 66 NZLR 654. It is true to say that in each of those cases the plaintiff was not a party to the first document which mistakenly recorded the bargain between the parties thereto. Indeed both cases expressly support the proposition that privity of contract is not an essential precondition to a claim for the rectification thereof. On the other hand, it is obvious that there must be some nexus between a plaintiff claiming rectification and the document in respect of which the reformation is sought. The two cases cited are very helpful in that regard.

In the *Majestic Homes* case, the Gartons leased certain property to David and Peter Wise for a period of three years from 1 February 1971 and gave to the lessees an option to renew the lease for a further three years. The Gartons sold the property to a Mr Hamilton subject to and with the benefit of the lease and this gave rise to a threat of litigation by the lessees against Mr Hamilton. Before those proceedings were commenced Mr Hamilton sold on the lessor's interest to a Mr Mitchell who was the nominee for Majestic Homes Property Ltd. The claim by the lessees against Mr Hamilton was compromised on the basis that the lessees would be given 'a lease in registrable form' which would have certain priorities but the undoubted and admitted bargain between Mr Hamilton and the Wises was that the lease would be for the same term as that granted in 1971. However, it was accepted that instead of granting a lease for three years with an option to renew for a further three years that the new lease in registrable form would be for the full period of six years from February 1971. By what was admitted to be a mistake, the solicitors on behalf of the lessors drafted the registrable lease for the full term of six years but by error retained the option to renew for an additional three years. The error was not adverted to by Mr Hamilton but it was recognised by Mr Peter Wise when he signed the document. Indeed, he discussed the 'bonus' of three years with his solicitor and both of them agreed, in the words of the evidence given by the solicitor, 'to let sleeping dogs lie'. Not only was Mr Hamilton and his solicitor unaware of the error that had occurred, but the purchasers from him, Majestic Homes and its solicitors, had entered into the agreement to purchase the property subject to the 1971 lease and on investigation of the matter by their solicitors it was not appreciated that the new form of lease had altered significantly the term of years granted by the 1971 document.

In the circumstances, it is not surprising that the trial judge found that the position of the Wises was unmeritorious and that what they did amounted to sharp practice.

There could be no doubt but that Mr Hamilton was entitled to rectification of the lease granted in registrable form. The issue was whether a similar right was enjoyed by the purchaser from him. The trial judge held that Hamilton had in fact assigned his interest in the right of rectification to Majestic Homes. It is significant, however, that the Court of Appeal held in addition that the Wises had become trustees of their alleged interest for Hamilton. They referred to the decision in *Craddock Brothers v. Hunt* [1923] 2 Ch 136 as authority for the proposition that title acquired by mistake is held on trust. They quoted the words of Lord Stemdale MR at p. 155 as follows:

I can see no conscience or honesty in the defendant's claim, and I think he should be declared a trustee for the plaintiff's land to which he has by mistake got a title which he knew had been knocked down to them and which he never thought was intended to be sold to him or had been bought by him.

On the particular issue of privity of contract the Court of Appeal in the *Majestic Homes* case relied upon the decision in *Shepheard v. Graham* (1947) 66 NZLR 654. In that case a Mrs Graham agreed in 1938 to sell property known as number 70 Idris Road to one Lady Clifford. The property was inspected and readily identifiable as a single residence which was surrounded by an appropriate fence. Undoubtedly an error was made as to the area involved in the take and that led the advisers on behalf of the purchaser to believe that the entire of 70 Idris Road was comprised in what was known as Lot 5 (which I presume represents a particular division for the purpose of the New Zealand registration of title legislation). Accordingly, the property was conveyed or transferred by reference to that lot number. In fact the property agreed and intended to be sold comprised two lots those numbered 2 and 5. Lady Clifford went into occupation of the entire of the premises without any objection by the vendor. About a year later Lady Clifford sold on the property to the plaintiff in the action. On that sale the same mistake was repeated. (Perhaps not surprisingly as the solicitor who had acted for Lady Clifford also acted for the purchaser). In any event both Lady Clifford and the purchaser from her - the plaintiff in the action – clearly understood that the property for sale was that known as 70 ldris Road fenced as a single unit. The transfer to Lady Clifford in the first instance and to the plaintiff in the second instance in describing the property as Lot 5 did not give effect to that understanding. It was eight years later before it was discovered that the property intended to be transferred to the successive purchasers comprised more than Lot 5. In those circumstances the second purchaser instituted proceedings against the second named defendant as legal personal representative of Lady Clifford for rectification of the transfer to him and against the first named defendant, who was the legal personal representative of Mrs Graham for the rectification of the transfer by Mrs Graham to Lady Clifford.

The Supreme Court in New Zealand held – following the decision in *Craddock v. Hunt* (above) – that the absence of privity between the plaintiff and the first named defendant was no bar to the claim for rectification. It was held that a mutual mistake occurred in the first sale and was repeated on the second sale with the result that Mrs Graham retained the legal title thereto but as it had been sold to Lady Clifford and the vendor had received the consideration under the contract that she, Mrs Graham, held that the land in question 'merely as trustee for Lady Clifford or her assignee'.

It seems to me that whilst those cases demonstrate that the action for rectification does not require that the parties to the litigation should be privy to the same contract, they must be privy to or affected by the same mistake in such a way that it would be unconscionable for the defendant in such proceedings to seek to rely on the document which erroneously recorded or mistakenly implemented the true agreement. In the *Shepheard v. Graham* case there was that specific finding that the original mutual mistake was repeated in and carried forward to the transaction involving the plaintiff with the result that property erroneously omitted from the first transfer was held in trust by the original vendor (or her successor in title) for the plaintiff. In the *Majestic Homes* case it was clear that the mistaken addition of an option to increase the term from six years to nine years misled the particular lessor and the purchaser from him. Both were under the impression – as was the lessee – that the maximum term intended to be granted was the term of six years. Again, therefore, the third party was affected by the error with the result that such interest as the lessee acquired under the mistaken document was held by him on trust for the plaintiff in the case. It is clear that in those cases that if relief had not been granted the defendants would have retained a wholly unconscionable benefit to the detriment of the plaintiff in the action rather than his predecessor in title.

So far from drawing a parallel between those actions and the present case, it seems to me that crucial distinctions must be made. In the first place Lac and their representatives were wholly unaware at any material time of the agreement which I accept was reached between Mr Mancuso and Mr Hough. Whilst a lawyer reading the JVA on behalf of Lac would have recognised that there was an inconsistency between certain provisions in the document, there was nothing which would have indicated how this came about. The 60 day time limit for acceptance may have been a mistake which should have been corrected but it was not a mistake which conferred a property right which could be the subject matter of a trust by one party in favour of another. It was an erroneous statement as to a procedural matter which, if uncorrected, might operate for the benefit or detriment of either party. It seems to me that the crucial distinction between the cases which have been analysed and the present matter is the fact that the mistake between Chevron and Ivernia was in no sense repeated or extended to Lac. Lac were presented with the JVA in the form in which it had been executed and it was that document and in that form which was incorporated into their transaction with Chevron. The transaction between Lac and Chevron (and in particular the August side letter) focused on the right of pre-emption conferred on the participating parties. The material clauses must have been considered by the legal advisers to both Lac and Chevron with some care as both parties felt in a position to reach the conclusion that the bargain between them involving as it did a transfer of shares rather than underlying assets – did not trigger off a right of pre-emption in favour of Ivernia. It seems to me, in those circumstances that, as between Lac and Chevron (and indeed Ivernia in so far as it concerned them) the JVA fell to be considered in accordance with the terms contained therein and that none of the parties could procure the rectification of the JVA no matter how strong the evidence might have been of a mutual mistake having been made by the original parties to the JVA. The very basis on which the plaintiffs present their case for construction of the JVA is that it was the document in those terms upon which they had relied.

I can see no basis on which it could be inferred that Lac were bound by or entitled to the benefit of any agreed term not contained in the documents presented to them. Clearly a claim for rectification, if permitted, could result in far-reaching alterations of the written record which could be wholly unfair to a third party in the position of Lac. This problem was discussed by Mr Robert Mullen, an attorney at law, called on behalf of Lac to give evidence of the law of the state of New York. In the course of his cross-examination he was asked to express a view as to whether, under New York law, Lac would be entitled to apply for rectification (or reformation as it is described in New York) of the JVA. After some research, Mr Mullen expressed the view that Lac would have that right but he accepted that the matter did not appear to be covered by legal authority in New York. However, it was significant that when he was faced with the problem that reformation in accordance with the intention of the parties might throw up terms wholly unfavourable to Lac, such as, a time limit for acceptance of 200 days, he expressed the view that reformation would arise from the obvious inconsistency between the time limits of 45 days and 60 days and that rectification would be confined within those parameters. In my view rectification as understood and granted in this country cannot be limited in that way. Effectively this would be doing no more than allowing in parol evidence to explain a patent error. If one admits the concept of rectification, I think the plaintiff must accept that the true bargain – whatever it may be – is to be substituted for the mistaken version. I can see no basis on which a plaintiff should be entitled to pick and choose as to what alterations he would accept. Perhaps this dilemma is another consequence of the fact that the plaintiffs were never privy to or misled by any mistake so that they had no prospect of asserting that an error had been made until they became aware of Mr Mancuso's evidence and no interest in making that case until they were aware that his version of the bargain coincided with the case which they were anxious to make. In my view, the defendants are correct in their contention that Lac has no *locus standi* to maintain a case for rectification of the JVA or any term thereof."

CHAPTER 16

Rescission

MISTAKE

There is an equitable jurisdiction to rescind a contract where the parties are under a common misapprehension as to the facts or their rights provided the misapprehension is fundamental and the party seeking to set it aside is not himself at fault. This equitable jurisdiction also allows a court to set aside a contract on such terms which to it appear just.[1]

Solle v. Butcher
[1950] 1 KB 671

The defendant lessee leased a flat from the plaintiff for a term of years on the basis of an erroneous assumption made by both parties, that as a result of substantial alterations it was no longer subject to the provisions of the Rent Restriction Acts. The plaintiff brought proceedings against the defendant alleging that the standard rent was substantially less than the sum agreed and sought to recover the overpaid rent. The Court of Appeal (Bucknill, Denning and Jenkins LJJ) held that the lease should be set aside on the grounds of common mistake.

DENNING LJ stated at pp.689–698: "The first question is, what is the rent which may lawfully be charged for this flat and garage? The judge has, I think, misdirected himself in several respects, so it is open to this court to review his findings: *British Launderers Research Association v. Borough of Hendon Rating Authority* [1949] 1 KB 462. On this review I think that the structural alterations and improvements were not such as to destroy the identity of the original flat. The landlord was entitled, therefore, to increase the rent by 8 per cent. of their cost, but was not able on this account to charge a new rent unrestricted by the Acts.

The inclusion in the lease of a garage, which had previously not formed part of the demise, gives rise to difficult questions. Even when taken together with the structural alterations, the addition of the garage does not change the identity of the flat. The standard rent, therefore, remains at 140*l*.: *Hemns v. Wheeler* [1948] 2 KB 61 and *Langford Property Co. Ld. v. Batten* (1949) 65

---

[1] *Cooper v. Phibbs* (1867) LR 2 HL 149 and *Solle v. Butcher* [1950] 1 KB 671.

TLR 577. It does not follow, however, that the tenant gets the benefit of the garage for nothing. The landlord is probably entitled to increase the rent on account of it. Such an increase is justified by s. 2, sub-s. 3 of the Act of 1920 as interpreted by this court in *Seaford Court Estates Ld. v. Asher* [1949] 2 KB 481. Just as the landlord was entitled in that case to increase the rent because the tenant was relieved of the contingent burden of providing himself with hot water, if he wanted it, so here the tenant is relieved of the contingent burden of providing himself with a garage, if he wants one. I do not, however, pursue the point, because it was not argued before us. It is said that, even allowing nothing for the garage, the permitted increase for structural alterations and improvements and increase of rates bring up the rent lawfully payable from 140*l*. to 250*l*. If, therefore, the landlord had served the prospective tenant with a proper notice of increase, the lease at 250*l*. a year would have been valid. But he did not serve any notice at all, because he thought that, owing to the improvements, the new rent was not restricted by the Acts. The tenant says that, there having been no notice, the landlord can only recover 140*l*. a year for the seven years of the lease.

So long as the lease stands the tenant's argument is unanswerable. The Rent Restriction Acts prevent the landlord from recovering any more than the standard rent unless a notice of intention to increase the rent is given either to the sitting tenant or to a prospective tenant; and, although errors or omissions in a notice are not necessarily fatal, nevertheless there must be a notice, however informal. In this case the landlord conceded that no notice was served before the new lease was granted. It follows that the raising of the rent from 140*l*. to 250*l*. was invalid, and the landlord can do nothing now to repair the omission because no fresh notice of increase can be effective so long as the lease continues. The landlord tried to overcome this difficulty by saying that the tenant was estopped from saying that the rent of 250*l*. was invalid; but, just as parties cannot contract out of the Acts, so they cannot defeat them by any estoppel.

In this plight the landlord seeks to set aside the lease. He says, with truth, that it is unfair that the tenant should have the benefit of the lease for the outstanding five years of the term at 140*l*. a year, when the proper rent is 250*l*. a year. If he cannot give a notice of increase now, can he not avoid the lease? The only ground on which he can avoid it is on the ground of mistake. It is quite plain that the parties were under a mistake. They thought that the flat was not tied down to a controlled rent, whereas in fact it was. In order to see whether the lease can be avoided for this mistake it is necessary to remember that mistake is of two kinds: first, mistake which renders the contract void, that is, a nullity from the beginning, which is the kind of mistake which was dealt with by the courts of common law; and, secondly, mistake which renders the contract not void, but voidable, that is, liable to be set aside on such terms as the court thinks fit, which is the kind of mistake which was dealt with by the courts of equity. Much of the difficulty which has attended this subject has arisen because, before the fusion of law and equity, the courts of common law, in order to do justice in the case in hand, extended this doctrine of mistake beyond its proper limits and held contracts to be void which were really only voidable, a process which was capable of being attended with much injustice to third persons who had bought goods or otherwise committed themselves on the faith that there was a contract. In the well-known case of *Cundy v. Lindsay* (1876) 1 QBD 348; (1878) 3 App Cas 459, Cundy suffered such an injustice. He bought the handkerchiefs from the rogue, Blenkarn, before the Judicature Acts came into operation. Since the fusion of law and equity, there is no reason to continue this process, and it will be found that only those contracts are now held void in which the mistake was such as to prevent the formation of any contract at all.

Let me first consider mistakes which render a contract a nullity. All previous decisions on this subject must now be read in the light of *Bell v. Lever Bros. Ld.* [1932] AC 161, 222, 224, 225-7, 236. The correct interpretation of that case, to my mind, is that, once a contract has been made, that is to say, once the parties, whatever their inmost states of mind, have to all outward appearances agreed with sufficient certainty in the same terms on the same subject matter, then the contract is good unless and until it is set aside for failure of some condition on which the existence of the contract depends, or for fraud, or on some equitable ground. Neither party can rely on his own mistake to say it was a nullity from the beginning, no matter that it was a mistake which to his mind was fundamental, and no matter that the other party knew that he was under a mistake. A fortiori, if the other party did not know of the mistake, but shared it. The cases where goods have perished at the time of sale, or belong to the buyer, are really contracts which are not void for mistake but are void by reason of an implied condition precedent, because the contract proceeded on the basic assumption that it was possible of performance. So far as cases later than *Bell v. Lever Bros., Ld.* are concerned, I do not think that *Sowler v. Potter* [1940] 1 KB 271 can stand with *King's Norton Metal Co. Ld. v. Edridge* (1897) 14 TLR 98, which shows that the doctrine of French law as enunciated by Pothier is no part of English law. Nor do I think that the contract in *Nicholson and Venn v. Smith-Marriott* (1947) 177 LT 189 was void from the beginning.

Applying these principles, it is clear that here there was a contract. The parties agreed in the same terms on the same subject-matter. It is true that the landlord was under a mistake which was to him fundamental: he would not for one moment have considered letting the flat for seven years if it meant that he could only charge 140*l.* a year for it. He made the fundamental mistake of believing that the rent he could charge was not tied down to a controlled rent; but, whether it was his own mistake or a mistake common to both him and the tenant, it is not a ground for saying that the lease was from the beginning a nullity. Any other view would lead to remarkable results, for it would mean that, in the many cases where the parties mistakenly think a house is outside the Rent Restriction Acts when it is really within them, the tenancy would be a nullity, and the tenant would have to go; with the result that the tenants would not dare to seek to have their rents reduced to the permitted amounts lest they should be turned out.

Let me next consider mistakes which render a contract voidable, that is, liable to be set aside on some equitable ground. Whilst presupposing that a contract was good at law, or at any rate not void, the court of equity would often relieve a party from the consequences of his own mistake, so long as it could do so without injustice to third parties. The court, it was said, had power to set aside the contract whenever it was of opinion that it was unconscientious for the other party to avail himself of the legal advantage which he had obtained: *Torrance v. Bolton* (1872) LR 8 Ch 118, 124 per James L.J.

The court had, of course, to define what it considered to be unconscientious, but in this respect equity has shown a progressive development. It is now clear that a contract will be set aside if the mistake of the one party has been induced by a material misrepresentation of the other, even though it was not fraudulent or fundamental; or if one party, knowing that the other is mistaken about the terms of an offer, or the identity of the person by whom it is made, lets him remain under his delusion and concludes a contract on the mistaken terms instead of pointing out the mistake. That is, I venture to think, the ground on which the defendant in *Smith v. Hughes* (1871) LR 6 QB 597 would be exempted nowadays, and on which, according to the view by Blackburn J. of the facts, the contract in *Lindsay v. Cundy* (1876) 1 QBD 348, 355; (1878) 3 App Cas 459, was voidable and not void; and on which the lease in *Sowler v. Potter* [1940] 1 KB 271, was, in my opinion, voidable and not void.

A contract is also liable in equity to be set aside if the parties were under a common misapprehension either as to facts or as to their relative and respective rights, provided that the misapprehension was fundamental and that the party seeking to set it aside was not himself at fault. That principle was first applied to private rights as long ago as 1730 in *Lansdown v. Lansdown* (1730) Mos 364; 2 Jac & W 205. There were four brothers, and the second and third of them died. The eldest brother entered on the lands of the deceased brothers, but the youngest brother claimed them. So the two rival brothers consulted a friend who was a local schoolmaster. The friend looked up a book which he then had with him called the Clerk's Remembrancer and gave it as his opinion that the lands belonged to the youngest brother. He recommended the two of them to take further advice, which at first they intended to do, but they did not do so; and, acting on the friend's opinion, the elder brother agreed to divide the estate with the younger brother, and executed deeds and bonds giving effect to the agreement. Lord Chancellor King declared that the documents were obtained by a mistake and by a misrepresentation of the law by the friend, and ordered them to be given up to be cancelled. He pointed out that the maxim ignorantia juris non excusat only means that ignorance cannot be pleaded in excuse of crimes. Eighteen years later, in the time of Lord Hardwicke, the same principle was applied in *Bingham v. Bingham* (1748) 1 Ves Sen 126; Belt's Supplement 79.

If and in so far as those cases were compromises of disputed rights, they have been subjected to justifiable criticism, but, in cases where there is no element of compromise, but only of mistaken rights, the House of Lords in 1867 in the great case of *Cooper v. Phibbs* (1867) LR 2 HL 149, 170, affirmed the doctrine there acted on as correct. In that case an uncle had told his nephew, not intending to misrepresent anything, but being in fact in error, that he (the uncle) was entitled to a fishery; and the nephew, after the uncle's death, acting in the belief of the truth of what the uncle had told him, entered into an agreement to rent the fishery from the uncle's daughters, whereas it actually belonged to the nephew himself. The mistake there as to the title to the fishery did not render the tenancy agreement a nullity. If it had done, the contract would have been void at law from the beginning and equity would have had to follow the law. There would have been no contract to set aside and no terms to impose. The House of Lords, however, held that the mistake was only such as to make it voidable, or, in Lord Westbury's words, "liable to be set aside" on such terms as the court thought fit to impose; and it was so set aside.

The principle so established by *Cooper v. Phibbs* (1867) LR 2 HL 149 has been repeatedly acted on: see, for instance, *Earl Beauchamp v. Winn* (1873) LR 6 HL 223, 234, and *Huddersfield Banking Co. Ld. v. Lister* [1895] 2 Ch 273. It is in no way impaired by *Bell v. Lever Bros. Ld.* [1932] AC 161, which was treated in the House of Lords as a case at law depending on whether the contract was a nullity or not. If it had been considered on equitable grounds, the result might have been different. In any case, the principle of *Cooper v. Phibbs* has been fully restored by *Norwich Union Fire Insurance Society Ld. v. William H. Price, Ld.* [1934] AC 455, 462-3.

Applying that principle to this case, the facts are that the plaintiff, the tenant, was a surveyor who was employed by the defendant, the landlord, not only to arrange finance for the purchase of the building and to negotiate with the rating authorities as to the new rateable values, but also to let the flats. He was the agent for letting, and he clearly formed the view that the building was not controlled. He told the valuation officer so. He advised the defendant what were the rents which could be charged. He read to the defendant an opinion of counsel relating to the matter, and told him that in his opinion he could charge 250*l.* and that there was no previous control. He said that the flats came outside the Act and that the defendant was "clear." The defendant relied on what the plaintiff told him, and authorized the plaintiff to let at the rentals which he had suggested. The plaintiff not only let the four other flats to other people for a long period of years at the new rentals, but also took one himself for seven years at 250*l.* a year. Now he turns round and says, quite unashamedly, that he wants to take advantage of the mistake to get the flat at 140*l.* a year for seven years instead of the 250*l.* a year, which is not only the rent he agreed to pay but also the fair and economic rent; and it is also the rent permitted by the Acts on compliance with the necessary formalities. If the rules of equity have become so rigid that they cannot remedy such an injustice, it is time we had a new equity, to make good the omissions of the old. But, in my view, the established rules are amply sufficient for this case.

On the defendant's evidence, which the judge preferred, I should have thought there was a good deal to be said for the view that the lease was induced by an innocent material misrepresentation by the plaintiff. It seems to me that the plaintiff was not merely expressing an opinion on the law: he was making an unambiguous statement as to private rights; and a misrepresentation as to private rights; equivalent to a misrepresentation of fact for this purpose: *MacKenzie v. Royal Bank of Canada* [1934] AC 468. But it is unnecessary to come to a firm conclusion on this point, because, as Bucknill L.J. has said, there was clearly a common mistake, or, as I would prefer to describe it, a common misapprehension, which was fundamental and in no way due to any fault of the defendant; and *Cooper v. Phibbs* (1867) LR 2 HL 149 affords ample authority for saying that, by reason of the common misapprehension, this lease can be set aside on such terms as the court thinks fit.

The fact that the lease has been executed is no bar to this relief. No distinction can, in this respect, be taken between rescission for innocent misrepresentation and rescission for common misapprehension, for many of the common misapprehensions are due to innocent misrepresentation; and *Cooper v. Phibbs* shows that rescission is available even after an agreement of tenancy has been executed and partly performed. The observations in *Seddon v. North Eastern Salt Co. Ld.* [1905] 1 Ch 326, have lost all authority since Scrutton L. J., threw doubt on them in *Lever Bros, Ld. v. Bell* [1931] 1 KB 557, 588, and the Privy Council actually set aside an executed agreement in *MacKenzie v. Royal Bank of Canada*. If and in so far as *Angel v. Jay* [1911] 1 KB 666 decided that an executed lease could not be rescinded for an innocent misrepresentation, it was in my opinion, a wrong decision. It would mean that innocent people would be deprived of their right of rescission before they had any opportunity of knowing they had it. I am aware that in *Wilde v. Gibson* (1848) 1 HLC 605, Lord Campbell said that an executed conveyance could be set aside only on the ground of actual fraud; but this must be taken to be confined to misrepresentations as to defects of title on the conveyance of land.

In the ordinary way, of course, rescission is only granted when the parties can be restored to substantially the same position as that in which they were before the contract was made; but, as Lord Blackburn said in *Erlanger v. New Sombrero Phosphate Co.* (1878) 3 App Cas 1218, 1278-9: "The practice has always been for a court of equity to give this relief whenever, by the exercise of its powers, it can do what is practically just, though it cannot restore the parties precisely to the state they were in before the contract." That indeed was what was done in *Cooper v. Phibbs* (1867) LR 2 HL 149. Terms were imposed so as to do what was practically just. What terms then, should be imposed here? If the lease were set aside without any terms being imposed, it would mean that the plaintiff, the tenant, would have to go out and would have to pay a reasonable sum for his use and occupation. That would, however, not be just to the tenant.

The situation is similar to that of a case where a long lease is made at the full permitted rent in the common belief that notices of increase have previously been served, whereas in fact they have not. In that case, as in this, when the lease is set aside, terms must be imposed so as to see that the tenant is not unjustly evicted. When Sir John Romilly M.R., was faced with a somewhat similar problem, he gave the tenant the option either to agree to pay the proper rent or to go out: see *Garrard v. Frankel* (1862) 30 Beav 445; and when Bacon V.-C. had a like problem before him he did the same, saying that "the object of the court is, as far as it can, to put the parties into the position in which they would have been in if the mistake had not happened": see *Paget v. Marshall* (1884) 28 Ch D 255, 267. If the mistake here had not happened, a proper notice of increase would have been given and the lease would have been executed at the full permitted rent. I think that this court should follow these examples and should impose terms which will enable the tenant to choose either to stay on at the proper rent or to go out.

The terms will be complicated by reason of the Rent Restriction Acts, but it is not beyond the wit of man to devise them. Subject to any observations which the parties may desire to make, the terms which I suggest are these: the lease should only be set aside if the defendant is prepared to give an undertaking that he will permit the plaintiff to be a licensee of the premises pending the grant of a new lease. Then, whilst the plaintiff is a licensee, the defendant will in law be in possession of the premises, and will be able to serve on the plaintiff, as prospective tenant, a notice under s. 7, sub-s. 4, of the Act of 1938 increasing the rent to the full permitted amount. The defendant must further be prepared to give an undertaking that he will serve such a notice within three weeks from the drawing up of the order, and that he will, if written request is made by the plaintiff, within one month of the service of the notice, grant him a new lease at the full permitted amount of rent, not, however, exceeding 250*l.* a year, for a term expiring on September 29, 1954, subject in all other respects to the same covenants and conditions as in the rescinded lease. If there is any difference of opinion about the figures stated in the notice, that can, of course, be adjusted during the currency of the lease. If the plaintiff does not choose to accept the licence or the new lease, he must go out. He will not be entitled to the protection of the Rent Restriction Acts because, the lease being set aside, there will be no initial contractual tenancy from which a statutory tenancy can spring.

In my opinion, therefore, the appeal should be allowed. The declaration that the standard rent of the flat is 140*l.* a year should stand. An order should be made on the counterclaim that, on the defendant's giving the undertakings which I have mentioned, the lease be set aside. An account should be had to determine the sum payable for use and occupation. The plaintiff's claim for repayment of rent and for breach of covenant should be dismissed. In respect of his occupation after rescission and during the subsequent licence, the plaintiff will be liable to pay a reasonable sum for use and occupation. That sum should, prima facie, be assessed at the full amount permitted by the Acts, not, however, exceeding 250*l* a year. Mesne profits as against a trespasser are assessed at the full amount permitted by the Acts, even though notices of increase have not been served, because that is the amount lost by the landlord. The same assessment should be made here, because the sums payable for use and occupation are not rent, and the statutory provisions about notices of increase do not apply to them. All necessary credits must, of course, be given in respect of past payments, and so forth."

Where one party is aware of the other's mistake in relation to a material term of a contract and seeks to take advantage of it, equity will allow the contract to be rescinded particularly where enforcement would cause hardship to the mistaken party.[2]

Gun v. McCarthy
(1883) 13 LR Ir 304

A lessor's agent offered a lease at a rent of £33.10s instead of £53.10s as intended. It was accepted by the court that the sum of £33.10s had been inserted by mistake in the lease and that the lessee had taken it with knowledge of this mistake. On the defendant's appeal from the decision of the County Court Judge that the lease should be rectified, Flanagan J. held that it should instead be delivered up to be cancelled.

FLANAGAN J stated at pp.308–312: "It was strongly argued by Mr. Jellett and Sergeant Hemphill that parol evidence is not admissible. Their argument comes to this, that where there is an agreement for a lease, and that lease is afterwards executed – in other words where an executory agreement becomes an executed one – parol evidence cannot be received to explain it, or to prove that the terms expressed in it are different from the real terms between the parties; that under the provisions of the Statute of Frauds the terms of the agreement are to be discovered from the agreement itself, where that agreement is in writing, and that you cannot resort to any parol evidence to explain it. In my opinion the determination of that question depends upon the character of the suit which is instituted, and of the relief which is sought. If the relief sought is to reform an instrument, it may, on the authorities as they exist, be doubtful whether, if there be a written agreement and subsequently an executed conveyance, parol evidence is admissible *dehors* the agreement; though where

---

[2] *Gun v. McCarthy* (1883) 13 LR Ir 304.

there is no written agreement, but simply an executed conveyance, parol evidence is clearly admissible to prove what the real agreement was. In *Davies v. Fitton* (1842) 2 Dr & W 225, Lord St. Leonards held that parol evidence was not admissible to prove that a lease executed in the expressed terms of a written agreement for the lease was contrary to the real agreement, and that there was something *dehors* the terms of the written contract omitted from the written agreement and the lease: *see* Lord St. Leonards' judgment, p. 232. The other case relied upon in support of this view is *The Attorney-General v. Sitwell* (1835) 1 Y & C Ex 559, before Baron Alderson, in which he expressed a strong opinion that where the mistake is not admitted by *both sides* the Court would not on parol evidence reform an executory agreement and then enforce the agreement as reformed. On the other hand, these cases have not been received with universal or perhaps general assent. In Mr. Justice Fry's book he discusses these cases and expresses a strong opinion [Fry on Specific Performance (2nd ed.) §§ 789-790, p. 349] as to the absurd anomaly that if there is a written agreement for a lease, and afterwards a lease executed, parol evidence cannot be given; but if there is no written agreement, but only an executed conveyance or lease, you can give parol evidence. And he refers to numerous cases which would appear to show, as a universal proposition, that if there be an agreement, whether in writing or not, and you can prove there was a mistake in the conveyance as executed, common to both parties, parol evidence is admissible.

I have always understood the law to be that when you seek to reform a conveyance you must first establish – whether by parol evidence or otherwise – that there was a definite concluded agreement between the parties, but which, by mistake common to both parties to the agreement, had not been carried out in the conveyance executed pursuant to the real agreement. But when the mistake is not common, what can you reform by? To reform implies a previous *agreement;* but when the evidence shows that there was no agreement to which both parties assented, but only a mistake on one aide, and not a common mistake, in my opinion it is impossible to support a suit to *reform,* whatever equity the party who has made the mistake may have in certain cases to rescind, the conveyance.

The only cases referred to which seem not to bear out that proposition are *Garrard v. Frankel* (1862) 30 Beav 445 and *Harris v. Pepperell* (1867) LR 5 Eq 1, in which Lord Romilly held that the Court could reform an agreement where there was a mistake on one side only.

It will be observed, however, that he gave the other party the option of having the contract rescinded if he did not wish to have it reformed; and it appears to me that is the true ground on which those cases can be supported. Mr. Justice Fry, in his book on Specific Performance (2nd ed.), p. 340, § 759, says:– "The mistake of one party can never be a ground for compulsory rectification. It may be a reason for setting the whole thing aside, but never for imposing on one party the erroneous conception of the other." So, in *Mortimer v. Shortall* (1842) 2 Dr & W 363, Lord St. Leonards lays it down that a mistake on one side may be a ground for rescinding a contract; but that, unless there was evidence of a mistake on both sides, the contract could not be rectified. And I find the same proposition laid down in *Fowler v. Fowler* (1859) 4 De G & J 250.

Whether, however, parol evidence be admissible or not where a written agreement exists, I am clearly of opinion that so far as the relief sought is to reform the lease, a mutual mistake must be proved; and this, in my opinion, the facts show did not exist. But, further, I am of opinion that so far as the relief sought is to rescind the contract, parol evidence is admissible, whether there was or was not a written agreement prior to the executed conveyance; and that, on such facts, it becomes a question whether they raise a sufficient equity to justify the Court in making a decree for the rescission of the contract as executed.

[His Lordship, having reviewed the evidence as to the alleged mistake, stated that he had clearly come to the conclusion that the Defendant, on the 1st October, 1881, when he accepted the offer of Rahilly, knew perfectly well that Rahilly had inserted £33 10s. by mistake; and that the evidence clearly showed that £53 10s. was the rent which the Plaintiff intended to reserve; and proceeded:–]

In my opinion, where there being a clear undoubted mistake by one party in reference to a material term of the contract which he entered into with another, and the other party knowingly seeks to avail himself of that, and seeks to bind the other to the mistake, the law of this Court is, that it will not allow such a contract to be binding on the parties, but will give relief against it. I do not think the contract could be reformed; there is nothing to reform it by. If the Court comes to the conclusion that the parties have never entered into an agreement, it would be a contradiction in terms for it to say that it could reform the agreement. I say that with the greatest respect for the decisions in *Garrard v. Frankel* (1862) 30 Beav 445, and *Harris v. Pepperell* (1867) LR 5 Eq 1. I confess I think these decisions can only be supported in the way suggested by Mr. Justice Fry: that the contracts were reformed on the ground that the party, against whom the decision was, elected to take the contracts reformed. But where the party insists generally on his right to retain the contract in the terms of the conveyance as executed, my opinion is, that the contract ought to be rescinded: and the decision I have come to is, I shall reverse the decision of the County Court Judge, so far as he directs this lease and agreement to be reformed, but I shall direct the lease and agreement to be delivered up to be cancelled, as I think the contract cannot be retained by the Defendant, as I think his seeking to do so is uncandid and dishonest, and that if he had come in here to enforce the contract his action would have been dismissed; and on the authority of the case of *Tamplin v. James* (1880) 15 Ch D 215, I have no hesitation in saying it would be dismissed with costs, on the ground that it was a dishonest attempt on his part to take advantage of a mistake. Lord Justice

James, in his judgment in that case, says that the only fault he has to find with the case of *Webster v. Cecil* (1861) 30 Beav 62 was that in his opinion the bill in that case ought to have been dismissed with costs. *Webster v. Cecil* was a case where the defendant proposed to sell to the plaintiff his premises for £1250, and the plaintiff by letter accepted the offer. As a matter of fact, his so fixing the sum for which the premises were offered was proved to be a mistake; the sum intended was £2250, and the error arose from a mistake in the tot of a calculation made by the defendant. Then the plaintiff filed a bill for specific performance. The mistake of the defendant was clearly proved, and that before bill filed it was communicated to the plaintiff, and the bill was dismissed without costs. James, L.J., says, as I have observed, that it ought to have been dismissed with costs.

In the present case, having regard to all the facts, I shall direct the lease and agreement to be delivered up to be cancelled. I shall direct that the Plaintiff shall pay to the Defendant all moneys *bona fide* expended by him in improvement of the premises, and shall direct an account of those moneys. I shall direct that the National Bank, they so consenting, shall be paid the sum due to them on foot of their equitable mortgage by deposit. I shall direct that the Defendant be charged with an occupation rent with regard to these premises; and I shall let both parties abide their own costs of the appeal, and shall give the Plaintiff the costs of the hearing below. I rule the costs in this way for this reason – I quite accede to the argument of Mr. Jellett, that there was no fraud on the part of the Defendant in the inception of this agreement, but in my opinion he dishonestly availed himself of the Plaintiff's mistake, and his doing so was what led to this suit. He acted unconscientiously in reference to the original agreement, having been aware all through of the Plaintiff's mistake, and never called his attention to it."

MISREPRESENTATION

Fraudulent Misrepresentation

The circumstances in which a contract may be rescinded in equity on grounds of fraudulent misrepresentation were examined by the Supreme Court in *Northern Bank Finance Corporation Ltd v. Charlton,* as was the extent to which *restitutio in integrum* must be possible before such a remedy will be granted.

Northern Bank Finance Corporation Ltd v. Charlton
[1979] IR 149

The plaintiff bank loaned the defendants a sum of money to facilitate their objective of acquiring control of a public company. When the defendants defaulted on the loan repayments, the plaintiff claimed the balance and interest and the defendant counter-claimed that it had entered into the original transaction because of the fraudulent misrepresentations of the plaintiff. In the High Court, Finlay P made an order dismissing the plaintiff's claim and allowing the defendants' counter-claim on the basis that the defendant had been induced by a fraudulent misrepresentation to enter into the transactions. The Supreme Court agreed that the plaintiffs' claim should be dismissed but the majority of the court[3] held that the order of rescission granted by the High Court should be set aside because the principle of *restitutio in integrum* could not apply.

HENCHY J stated at pp.195–199: "Having found that the defendants were induced to proceed with the take-over and with the purchase of Patrick Quinn's shares in Pat Quinn Holdings, the judge dealt with the resultant legal position as follows:–

"On these findings of fraudulent misrepresentation inducing the defendants to enter into both the original transaction and the purchase of Patrick Quinn's shares, the general legal principle applicable is that the defendants are entitled to have all the consequent transactions between them and the bank declared invalid and set aside. Insofar as it does not prejudice rights or interests acquired by innocent third parties, they are entitled to the return of any property or rights purporting to have been transferred to or vested in the bank. In addition, they are entitled to a sum of damages which, reasonably and fairly assessed between the parties, will restore them, having regard to the other relief obtained, to the position in which they would have been if the fraud had not been committed and they had not engaged in the transactions induced by it."

That is the only passage in the judgment under review which deals with the law governing the relief that should be granted when a person has been induced by a fraudulent inducement to enter into a detrimental transaction of this kind. In the passage I have quoted, the judge deduced that there was a general legal principle entitling the defendants to rescission and *restitutio in integrum*. He thus rejected the submission, which was forcefully made both at the trial and in this Court, that the only relief that could be granted was an award of damages and that no damages resulting from fraudulent inducement had been proved. For the purpose of deciding whether rescission or damages is the relief to which the defendants are entitled, it is necessary to consider both the relevant factual situation and the applicable legal principles.

First, as to the role played by the bank, it is a merchant bank and a wholly-owned subsidiary of the Northern Bank Ltd; in regard to the venture in which the three defendants (in conjunction with Patrick Quinn and Vincent Duignan) proposed to purchase the Mooney share capital, the bank acted as the defendants' agent. This is a function which is nowadays regularly committed

---

[3] Henchy, Griffin and Parke JJ.

to a merchant bank by the company or group who propose to effect the take-over of a public company which has a stock exchange quotation for its shares. The financial, corporate and stock-exchange complexities of that situation are such that it is usually necessary to call on the services of a merchant bank, which will assist in arranging the financing of the offer, advise on the size and form of the offer, prepare and circulate the offer documents, ensure that stock-exchange requirements are complied with, and generally make its expertise available to its principals to the end that not only will the take-over be successful but that it will result in the principals having acquired ownership or control at an economic cost. The services of the bank for those purposes were particularly required by these defendants and their two associates, for they were five individuals who were not incorporated as a company. It was necessary to arrange for the formation of a company (Pat Quinn Holdings) to act as the take-over vehicle. The promoters of the take-over were dependent on the bank for part of the finance required for the operation, for the preparation and issue of the offer documents, for technical advice as to the various steps to be taken and, finally, for the purchase on their behalf of the Mooney shares.

However, important as it was in its various activities in connection with the take-over, the bank at all times continued to act as the agent of the promoters in its dealings with third parties. At no stage in the course of the take-over did the bank shed that agency and became a principal. The importance of that relationship in this case is that, when two of the bank's officials made fraudulent inducements to the defendants in the course of the take-over and when, by the operation of *respondeat superior*, it became liable for those inducements, the bank's liability was the liability of an agent to a principal for whom it was advising and acting.

When an agent-adviser (such as a solicitor, banker, stockbroker, architect, auctioneer or estate agent) induces a client or customer, by means of a fraudulent misrepresentation, to purchase property from a third party, and when the purchaser, having completed the purchase and acquired ownership of the property, discovers the fraud, then I understand the law to be that the remedy of the purchaser lies in damages and not in rescission. The reason is that, in such circumstances, as between the agent-adviser and the purchaser there is no form of rescission and restitution which could restore, even substantially, the *status quo ante* – being the respective positions of the parties before the fraudulent misrepresentation was acted on to the purchaser's detriment. An order such as was made in this case (binding the misrepresentor to acquire the property which was bought on foot of the misrepresentation and to pay the purchase price to the misrepresentee) so far from restoring the *status quo ante* results in a situation which never before existed. In this case the return of the purchase money might be said to restore the purchasers' former position, but the compulsory subrogation whereby the misrepresentor would be required to step into the purchaser's shoes and take over the ownership of the property bought, which the misrepresentor had never owned, would have the effect of thrusting on the misrepresentor a wholly new factual and legal situation which would be incompatible with the mutuality and fairness inherent in the concept of restoring the *status quo ante*. Counsel for the defendants are unable to point to any judicial precedent for such an order.

Where a person has been induced by a fraudulent misrepresentation made collaterally by the other party to a contract to alter his position to his disadvantage, there are two alternative courses open to him: he may claim damages in tort for the deceit or he may sue for rescission of the contract which was induced by the misrepresentation. The latter relief, which is an equitable one, will be granted when the court considers that it would be just and equitable to do so in order to restore the parties, at least substantially, to their respective positions before the fraudulent misrepresentation was acted on. That is the relief which the defendants have chosen primarily in their counterclaim, and it is the relief which the order of the High Court purported to give them. But, be it noted, the *restitutio in integrum* by restoring the *status quo ante* (which is the object of this form of relief) can be granted only as an adjunct to the rescission of the contract between the parties. In this case the defendants sought and were granted rescission of the contract between the defendants and the bank but, in an effort to restore the *status quo ante*, the court went further. By requiring the bank to take the place of the defendants in each of the many instances of the purchase of shares, the court purported to rescind and amend executed contracts which had been made between the defendants and third-party vendors of shares who were not before the court. In my opinion, that is something which the court had no jurisdiction to do.

Since the purpose of the rescission of a contract on the ground of misrepresentation is the restoration of the *status quo ante* on the ground that the voidable contract is to be deemed wholly void *ab initio*, each side must divest itself in favour of the other of what it has received under the contract. As Bowen L. J. put it in *Newbigging v. Adam* (1886) 34 Ch D 582 at p. 595 of the report, there ought to be "a giving back and a taking back on both sides." Now, in the present case, the order of rescission made in the High Court cannot operate in that way. The moneys which it requires the bank to repay to the defendants are not moneys which it received, in any permanent or beneficial sense, under the contract with the defendants. Those moneys only passed through the bank's hands on their way to the vendors of the shares in question. It was those vendors who really received those moneys under the contract. So the bank cannot, by way of rescission, be compelled to repay them to the defendants. But, even more radically, the order of rescission, in requiring the bank to take up all the shares purchased by them for the defendants, runs counter to the object of the restoration of the *status quo ante*. The compulsory acquisition by the bank of those shares could not be said to be a "taking back" since the bank had never owned those shares. If effect were to be given to the order of rescission made in the High Court, the bank (which, as far as one can gather from the evidence, was never the beneficial owner of a single Mooney share) would become the unwilling owners of over 900,000 shares in that company. Clearly an order of rescission with that result could not be said to restore the *status quo ante*.

Counsel for the defendants, in arguing in support of the order of rescission made in the High Court, have been unable to refer to any case in which such a result was produced. The authority they rely on most is *Armstrong v. Jackson* [1917] 2 KB 822 but, in my view, that decision defeats the argument for the defendants. In that case, the plaintiff had engaged the defendant stockbroker to buy 600 shares in a company. In purported execution of that order, the defendant sent to the plaintiff a contract note showing that the shares had been purchased for him at a specified price. The plaintiff allowed some time to elapse before taking up the shares and, during that time, the value of the shares dropped. Nevertheless, the defendants advised the plaintiff to complete the purchase and he did so. Some four years later, the plaintiff obtained information which caused him to issue proceedings seeking rescission of the transaction or, in the alternative, damages. In the course of the hearing it was shown that, at the time of the purchase, the defendant was the *owner* of the shares – a fact which he had fraudulently concealed from the plaintiff. In granting an order of rescission, under which the defendant was required to repay all sums received by him from the plaintiff (less a credit for the amount of a dividend paid to the plaintiff) and the plaintiff to transfer the 600 shares to the defendant, McCardie J. said at p. 823 of the report:- "From first to last the defendant made no disclosure whatever to the plaintiff as to the true facts. He purported to act as a broker, whereas he was really acting as a principal." Therein lies the basis of the rescission granted in that case: the fact that the stockbroker, being the owner of the shares, was really acting as principal. It is inherent in the decision that, if the defendant had not been the owner of the shares and had been merely an agent (which was the position of the bank in the present case), rescission would not have been granted since the mutual repayment of money and re-transfer of shares would not have accorded with the *status quo ante*. Instead, there would have been a decree for damages.

In my opinion, the order of rescission made in the High Court, and the orders consequential and ancillary thereto, should be set aside."

GRIFFIN J stated at pp. 206–210: "The next question argued in the appeal was the form of the relief to which the defendants are entitled. Although in their defence and counterclaim the defendants did not expressly claim rescission, the order of the President effectively granted rescission and this was in line with the run of the case and the arguments advanced on behalf of the defendants. Although we have no copy of the transcript of the hearing when the matter came back to the President on the 17th September, 1977, pursuant to his order of the 8th August, 1977, we were informed by counsel that the President held that the defendants sought rescission; and this appeal proceeded on that basis.

An action or counterclaim for rescission is the usual form of proceeding for obtaining a judicial annulment of a contract induced by misrepresentation. As stated in Spencer Bower and Turner's Law of Actionable Misrepresentation (3rd ed., para 249) the primary purpose of all proceedings for rescission, as contrasted with that of actions for damages, is to restore the "status quo" and bring back the original position by undoing all that has intervened between it and the present. "The purpose of the relief is not punishment, but compensation" – *per* Lord Wright in *Spence v. Crawford* [1939] 3 All ER 271 at p. 289 of the report. Therefore, the rule is that rescission cannot be enforced if events, which have occurred since the contract and in which the representee has participated, make it impossible to restore the parties substantially to their original position. If a contract cannot be rescinded *in toto* it cannot be rescinded at all – see Cheshire and Fifoot's Law of Contract (9th ed. p. 269).

The object to be achieved by rescission is the restoration of both parties as nearly as may be to the position which each occupied before the transaction. The representee must be not only willing but also able to make *restitutio in integrum*. A large number of cases were cited both in the High Court and on this appeal, and what is recognised as the classical statement on this topic is that of Lord Blackburn in *Erlanger v. New Sombrero Phosphate Co.* (1878) 3 App Cas 1218 where he says at pp. 1278-9 of the report:– "It is, I think, clear on principles of general justice, that as a condition to a rescission there must be a *restitutio in integrum*. The parties must be put *in statu quo* . . . It is a doctrine which has often been acted upon both at law and in equity. But there is a considerable difference in the mode in which it is applied in Courts of Law and Equity, owing, as I think, to the difference of the machinery which the Courts have at command." Having dealt with the common-law remedy of damages, he went on to say:- "But a Court of Equity could not give damages, and, unless it can rescind the contract, can give no relief. And, on the other hand, it can take accounts of profits, and make allowance for deterioration. And I think the practice has always been for a Court of Equity to give this relief whenever, by the exercise of its powers, it can do what is practically just, though it cannot restore the parties precisely to the state they were in before the contract."

At law, if precise restitution was impossible, the defrauded party had to fall back on his action for damages for deceit. The distinction between the remedies at law and equity to which Lord Blackburn referred is no longer of importance as the High Court has full original jurisdiction and power to determine all matters and questions. As stated by the High Court of Australia (Dixon C.J., Webb, Kitto and Taylor JJ.) in *Alati v. Kruger* (1955) 94 CLR 216 at p. 223-4 of the report, even though precise *restitutio in integrum* is not possible it is now sufficient "if the situation is such that, by the exercise of its powers, including the power to take accounts of profits and to direct inquiries as to allowances proper to be made for deterioration, it can do what is practically just between the parties, and by so doing restore them substantially to the *status quo.*"

Although these principles are quite clear and there was no real dispute in argument concerning them, they are not easy to apply in practice. The type of contract in respect of which rescission is claimed is commonly that in which there is what might be called a vendor and purchaser relationship – for example, contracts relating to sales of land, goods, or of shares; the sale of a business or of an interest in a professional practice; and such like, where property has passed *from* the representor *to* the representee, or vice versa, under the contract. Many cases are to be found in the law reports in which an order for rescission was made on the application of the defrauded representee, whether he be vendor or purchaser. In such cases, there will be a decree for rescission because mutual restoration *in specie* of all benefits received by either party under the contract can take place and, even though precise *restitutio in integrum* is not possible, the parties can be restored substantially to the status quo.

Both parties to a transaction can "as nearly as may be" be put back to the position they occupied before the transaction was entered into, even though the property which was the subject matter of the contract may have deteriorated in value in the meantime. For example, in *Armstrong v. Jackson* a contract for the sale of shares by the defendant, a stockbroker, to the plaintiff was induced by the fraudulent misrepresentation of the defendant, who represented that he was purchasing shares for the plaintiff on the market whereas he was selling his own shares. The contract was rescinded although the shares had fallen considerably on the stock exchange in the meantime. The shares were the same shares and the defendant was getting back the shares he would have had if he had not sold them fraudulently to the plaintiff.

However, counsel for the plaintiff bank submitted that, in the circumstances of this case, there cannot be *restitutio in integrum* because the parties to the transactions cannot be restored to their original positions, either substantially or at all. The defendants claimed that they were induced, by the fraudulent misrepresentations of the bank's servants, to embark on and continue in their attempt to take over Mooney and, in 1972, to enter into the commitments referred to in the judgment of the President, which included the payment by them of £350,000 and the raising of a loan from the bank of approximately £1.6 million. The defendants also claimed that subsequently they were induced, by a continuance of those fraudulent representations and by further fraudulent representations made by the servants of the bank, to purchase the shares of Patrick Quinn in Pat Quinn Holdings for a total sum of £225,000. When the take-over was successful, approximately 83% of the issued shares in Mooney were acquired by Pat Quinn Holdings in which the defendants had a controlling interest. These shares were acquired by Pat Quinn Holdings as purchasers from the several shareholders who owned the shares and who sold their shares on the terms offered in the take-over. The principals in each transaction were the acquiring company, as purchasers, and the several shareholders, as vendors. The price of the shares was paid from (inter alia) the £350,000 contributed by the defendants and the loan raised from the bank. Shortly after the take-over, the board of Mooney acquired 32 premises formerly owned by Tara Electric Co. and so counsel on behalf of the bank say that Mooney (the sole asset of Pat Quinn Holdings) has been altered radically in nature since it was acquired and that it is now essentially a property company rather than a company carrying on the business of licensed premises. Again, in respect of the sale to the defendants of the shares of Patrick Quinn in Pat Quinn Holdings, counsel for the bank submit that this sale, although induced by the fraud of the bank, was a sale by Patrick Quinn, as vendor, to the defendants, as purchasers; they contend that there cannot be an order for rescission of that transaction, especially when Patrick Quinn is not a party to the proceedings.

At the trial, and again on this appeal, the defendants sought rescission of the entire of the transactions entered into between them and the bank; they submitted to the High Court and to this Court that, in the words of Lord Wright in *Spence v. Crawford*, the Court should do its best to unravel the complexities of the case and that, to do this, it would be necessary to rescind the transactions between the bank and them. Accepting the submissions of counsel for the defendants, the President made orders (inter alia) for the repayment to the defendants of the sum of £350,000 deposited by them in the bank for the purposes of the take-over, and of the £300,000 paid by the defendants Hugh Charlton and Gerard Sheehy in respect of the issue and allotment to them and their nominees of shares in Pat Quinn Holdings. He also ordered the payment by the bank to the defendants of the sums paid by them in part to Patrick Quinn and in part to the bank in respect of the purported purchase of the shares of Patrick Quinn in Pat Quinn Holdings in January, 1974.

Even if the order made in the High Court were capable of restoring the defendants substantially to the position they occupied before entering into these transactions – and this would be doubtful having regard to the events that have occurred since I.T.G. was backed into Mooney – in my view it is not possible to restore the bank substantially to its pre-contractual situation. As stated earlier, there cannot be partial rescission; it has to be *in toto* or not at all.

The order of the President, inter alia, requires Hugh Charlton to transfer 19,440 stock units of 50p each to the plaintiff bank; it requires each of the defendants to transfer to the bank all the shares in Pat Quinn Holdings issued and allotted to them and to Charlton Holdings; and it requires each of the defendants to transfer to the bank all the shares in Pat Quinn Holdings purchased by them from Patrick Quinn. This order purports to rescind the contract between the defendants and Patrick Quinn in respect of the sale of his shares to the defendants, but I find it difficult to understand the basis on which the transfer to the bank of the shares held by Patrick Quinn in Pat Quinn Holdings could be *restitutio in integrum*, or could be regarded as restoring the bank to the status quo, since the bank never had any interest in these shares which passed between Patrick Quinn as vendor and the defendants as purchasers. In the same way, it seems to me that the order requiring Hugh Charlton to transfer the 19,440 Mooney shares to the bank, or the order requiring the defendants to transfer to the bank the shares issued and allotted to them or to Charlton Holdings in Pat Quinn Holdings, cannot be regarded as substantially restoring the status quo since, again, the bank never had any interest whatever in these shares.

Therefore, in my view there cannot be *restitutio in integrum* in this case, particularly and additionally where the nature of Mooney (the sole asset of Pat Quinn Holdings) has altered radically in the meantime from being a company carrying on the business of licensed premises to that substantially of a property company; the reason for the change may be in dispute but is not relevant on this topic. In my opinion, counsel for the bank are correct in their submission that, on the facts of this case, an order effectively rescinding the transactions between the bank and the defendant should not have been made."

Innocent Misrepresentation

It would appear that an innocent misrepresentation may suffice to justify rescission where the contract has not yet been completed and where the representation was a material one which induced the plaintiff to enter into the contract.[4]

Gahan v. Boland
Supreme Court, 20 January 1984

The plaintiff sought rescission of a contract for the purchase of a property from the defendants. Prior to signing the contract he had been assured by the first named defendant that a proposed motorway would not affect the property. The plaintiff discovered after he had signed the contract that the motorway was in fact routed to pass through the property and sought rescission on the basis of misrepresentation.

HENCHY J stated at pp.1–4: "The defendants Maurice and Wendy Boland are husband and wife. In February 1981 they had on offer for sale the property known as Glencarrig, situate at Bride's Glen, Loughlinstown, Co. Dublin. That property consists of a dwellinghouse and some 3¼ acres of land.

The plaintiff, who is a solicitor, entered into a written contract on Monday the 16 February 1981 for the purchase of the property for £135,000. In the present proceedings he has sought an order for the rescission of that contract. When his case came for hearing before Murphy J. in the High Court he succeeded in getting that order. The defendants now appeal.

---

4 *Gahan v. Boland* High Court (Murphy J) 21 January 1983 and Supreme Court, 20 January 1984.

The order for rescission was made as a result of certain events which are said to have taken place on Friday the 13 February 1981. On that day the plaintiff visited the defendants at Glencarrig. The purpose of the visit was to inspect the property and to make certain inquiries about it. The plaintiff says that amongst the inquiries he made was one as to whether a projected motorway connecting Dublin and Wicklow would affect the Glencarrig property. His evidence was that Mr. Boland assured him that the property would not be affected by the proposed motorway and that this assurance led him to enter into a written contract on the following Monday for the purchase of the property. It seems to be common case that the proposed motorway is in fact routed to pass through the Glencarrig property. That is something the plaintiff did not discover until after he had signed the contract.

There was a conflict of evidence as to what representation, if any, was made as to the motorway. The judge, however, having reviewed the evidence was of the clear opinion that an innocent but false representation was made by Mr. Boland to the effect that the property would not be affected by the motorway, if and when it came to be constructed; that this representation was a material one made with the intention of inducing the plaintiff to act on it; and that it was one of the factors that induced the plaintiff to enter into the written contract on the following Monday to purchase the property.

Having perused the transcript of the evidence, I am satisfied that there was ample evidence to support those findings as to the misrepresentation relied on by the plaintiff for rescission of the contract. Once there was evidence to support the judge's findings in that respect, the defendants' main ground of appeal, namely that the findings as to misrepresentation are unsustainable, must be held to fail. This Court cannot set aside primary facts of that nature found by the judge and supported by evidence.

The alternative or secondary ground of appeal argued was that, even if the defendants' argument as to the misrepresentation fails, the claim for rescission should have been rejected because the plaintiff should be held to have had constructive notice of the true position as to the route of the proposed motorway. It was suggested that the plaintiff, a solicitor and an intending purchaser, having made inquiries of the vendors as to whether the property would be affected by the motorway, was required, by the application of the doctrine of constructive notice, to pursue those inquiries in quarters where he would have been reliably informed as to the true position. For that reason, it is submitted, he should be held disentitled, for the purposes of rescission, to rely on the misrepresentation made and should be deemed to have constructive notice of the true position as to the route of the motorway.

I was unable to accept this argument. I consider it to be well-settled law that the only knowledge that will debar a purchaser from repudiating a contract he has been induced into by the vendor's misrepresentation is actual and complete knowledge of the true situation. It does not lie with a vendor, who has by his misrepresentation induced the purchaser to enter into a contract to purchase, to have his misrepresentation excused or overlooked and to have the purchaser deprived of a right to rescind because he did not ignore the misrepresentation and pursue matters further so as to establish the truth of what was misrepresented. That would be unconscionable and unfair. The doctrine of constructive notice, as it arises under s. 3 of the Conveyancing Act, 1882 and as it was applied by this Court in *Somers v. W.* [1979] IR 94, has no application to the facts of this case.

I would dismiss this appeal."

However, it would appear that where a contract has been completed that an innocent as opposed to a fraudulent misrepresentation will not justify rescission.[5]

Lecky v. Walter
[1914] 1 IR 378

The plaintiff sought to have the sale to him by the defendant of bonds in a company set aside on the grounds that he was induced to enter into the contract by misrepresentations made innocently by the defendant. O'Connor MR stated that he was satisfied from the plaintiff's evidence that the representation that the bonds were charged on property, which they were not, was a material inducement to purchase them. However, he held that inasmuch as the contract was completed and there was no fraud, he would not set the sale aside.

O'CONNOR MR stated at pp.384–389: "I do not consider that the failure of the plaintiff to prove the second misrepresentation is a material element in the case, because the first representation was one of a most important character, and such as would necessarily influence any person invited to purchase the bonds, and I am satisfied from the plaintiff's evidence that the statement that the bonds were charged on the oil-fields was, if not the only inducement, a material inducement to purchase them.

I need not pause to establish the proposition that it is not necessary to prove that a particular representation was the sole cause of the transaction, and that it is enough that it constituted a material inducement. I have now come to the point when I consider it established that the plaintiff purchased the bonds from the defendant, and that he was induced to make the purchase by misrepresentation by the defendant's agent, which is equivalent to misrepresentation by the defendant himself. The purely legal question then arises, does this state of affairs give the plaintiff the right to set aside a transaction which has been in fact completed, and is not merely in the process of completion? It must be borne in mind that there is no allegation of fraudulent

---

[5] *Lecky v. Walter* [1914] 1 IR 378.

misrepresentation, and therefore the case is to be treated as one in which a *bona fide* mistake was made by the defendant.

Mr. Healy, counsel for the defendant, contended that in such circumstances the plaintiff had no cause of action, and he relied upon the judgment of Lord Campbell in the House of Lords in *Wilde v. Gibson* (1848) 1 HLC 605, at pp. 632–3, where he says:– "My Lords, after the very attentive and anxious consideration which this case has received, I have come to the clear conclusion that the decree appealed against ought to be reversed; and I must say that in the Court below the distinction between a bill for carrying into execution an executory contract, and a bill to set aside a conveyance that has been executed, has not been very distinctly borne in mind. With regard to the first: if there be, in any way whatever, misrepresentation or concealment, which is material to the purchaser, a court of equity will not compel him to complete the purchase; but where the conveyance has been executed, I apprehend, my Lords, that a court of equity will set aside the conveyance only on the ground of actual fraud. And there would be no safety for the transactions of mankind, if, upon a discovery being made at any distance of time of a material fact not disclosed to the purchaser, of which the vendor had merely constructive notice, a conveyance which had been executed could be set aside."

In *Brownlie v. Campbell* (1880) 5 App Cas 925, at p. 937, Lord Selborne affirms the same principle. He says there: "Passing from the stage of correspondence and negotiation to the stage of written agreement, the purchaser takes upon himself the risk of errors. I assume them to be errors unconnected with fraud in the particulars, and when the conveyance takes place it is not, so far as I know, in either country the principle of equity that relief should afterwards be given against that conveyance, unless there be a case of fraud, or a case of misrepresentation amounting to fraud, by which the purchaser may have been deceived."

There appears to be no doubt that the law established by these cases is just as applicable to the sale of a chattel or a chose in action as to the sale of real property which is carried out by conveyance: *Seddon v. The North Eastern Salt Co., Limited* [1905] 1 Ch 326.

How are these authorities met by the plaintiff's counsel? Mr. Wilson in reply admitted, as of course he was obliged to admit, that the authorities referred to were binding on this Court; but argued that they only apply to cases in which the purchaser has got in substance what he contracted to buy, and have no application when he got something substantially different; and he relies upon the judgment of Blackburn, J., in *Kennedy v. Panama, New Zealand, and Australian Mail Co.* (1867) LR 2 QB 580, and particularly on the passage quoted by Joyce, J., in *Seddon v. The North Eastern Salt Co., Limited*. Lord Blackburn, then Blackburn, J., says at p. 587– "There is, however, a very important difference between cases where a contract may be rescinded on account of fraud, and those in which it may be rescinded on the ground that there is a difference in substance between the thing bargained for and that obtained. It is enough to show that there was fraudulent representation as to *any part* of that which induced the party to enter into the contract which he seeks to rescind; but where there has been an innocent misrepresentation or misapprehension, it does not authorize a rescission unless it is such as to show that there is a complete difference in substance between what was supposed to be and what was taken, so as to constitute á failure of consideration. For example, where a horse is bought under the belief that it is sound, if the purchaser was induced to buy by a fraudulent representation as to the horse's soundness, the contract may be rescinded. If he was induced by an honest misrepresentation as to its soundness, though it may be clear that both vendor and purchaser thought they were dealing about a sound horse and were in error, yet the purchaser must pay the whole price, unless there was a warranty; and even if there was a warranty, he cannot return the horse and claim back the whole price, unless there was a condition to that effect in the contract."

Now, if I may so speak of such an eminent judge as Lord Blackburn, the proposition which he there lays down must commend itself, not only to all lawyers, but to all persons of sound judgment. If there is a complete difference in substance between the thing contracted for and the thing delivered, there is a complete failure of consideration, and the price may be recovered. But if the thing delivered is in substance what was contracted for, and the price is paid, the transaction stands, and the purchaser has no remedy unless there has been a warranty. I am speaking of course of cases in which there has been no fraud, and where any misrepresentation which has induced the contract was a wholly innocent misrepresentation. Lord Blackburn gives as an example the common case of a horse bought on the representation that it was sound. The purchaser has no remedy unless he has got a warranty; and why? Because he has got in substance what he contracted for, viz., a horse. The horse may be in fact unsound, but still it is a horse, even though a very inferior one; and there is not a complete failure of consideration.

There would, of course, be a complete difference in substance if some animal other than a horse had been delivered, if such a thing can be imagined. I will try to give an example nearer akin to the present case. If a man contracts to purchase mortgage debentures of a public company, and takes delivery of what he believes to be such, but what he afterwards discovers to be ordinary shares, he has not got in substance what he bargained for, but something quite different, one being a specifically secured liability of the company, the other being a share in the company's undertaking on which the liability is imposed. Here again there is a complete failure of consideration. In *Kennedy v. Panama, New Zealand, and Australian Mail Co.*, the plaintiff sought to set aside the contract for taking shares in the company on the ground that it was induced by an untrue statement in the company's prospectus that the company had a contract with the Government of New Zealand for an important monthly mail service. The statement was made quite innocently, and as the result of mistake. It was held that the plaintiff was not entitled to any relief, there having been no fraud, and he having got what he contracted for, viz., shares, although not so valuable as they would have been if the company had had the mail contract mentioned. Lord Blackburn, in his judgment, referred to two reported cases: *Gompertz v. Bartlett* (1853) 2 E & B 849 and *Gurney* v. *Wormersley* (1854) 4 E & B 133, in which the plaintiffs got relief on the ground that they did not get what they bargained for. In each ease there was a sale of a bill of exchange: in one case the bill was a forgery; in the other the bill was void under the stamp laws. In neither case did the plaintiff get what he contracted for – a valid bill of exchange.

I think that these decisions make it easy to determine whether in the present case the plaintiff got in substance what he agreed to buy.

Let me refer to the statement of claim. In the second paragraph the contract is stated thus – "2. By a contract, made in the month of May, 1910, the plaintiff agreed to purchase from the defendant, and the defendant agreed to sell to the plaintiff, eight 6 per cent. bonds of the face value of 1000 florins (Dutch), equivalent to £83 6s. 8d. of the Petroleum Maatschappij 'Henderson,' a limited liability company established in the Hague in Holland, at the price of £72 18s., 4d. per bond." Well, the plaintiff has got what he bought. He agreed to buy bonds and he has got bonds. They may be of little or no value, but they are bonds. It is not alleged that they are forgeries. Their validity is not in any way impeached. In substance, then, the plaintiff has got what he bargained for. Mr. Wilson's answer to this is that the bonds were represented to the plaintiff, to be charged upon and fully secured on the oil-fields. But this is not alleged as a matter of contract. It is alleged as a matter of inducement leading up to the contract, which is wholly different. This is the way the case was presented both by the statement of claim, by the opening statement of counsel, and by the evidence. It was not until the defence was opened up by Mr. Healy that any attempt was made to represent the contract as anything other than that alleged in the second paragraph of the statement of claim. If the contract was as contended for by Mr. Wilson, that is, if the representation was part of the contract, there might have been a warranty which would give the plaintiff the right to relief. But a representation is not necessarily a warranty. It may be only an inducement, and such it appears to me to have been in the present case. I am, therefore, bound to hold that inasmuch as the contract was completed, and there was no fraud, the sale cannot be set aside, and the action must be dismissed with costs to be paid by the plaintiff to the defendant."

UNDUE INFLUENCE

General Principles

Undue influence has been described as gaining an unfair advantage 'by an

---

[6]   *R. (Proctor) v. Hutton* [1978] NI 139, 146.

unconscientious use of power in the form of some unfair and improper conduct'[6] and where it is established, may justify the setting aside of a transaction. A distinction should be drawn between cases of actual and presumed undue influence.[7] In the former case it is necessary for a claimant to prove that the wrongdoer actually exerted undue influence on him to enter into the particular transaction. In the latter case the complainant has to establish that there was a relationship of trust and confidence between the parties of such a nature that it is fair to assume the wrongdoer abused the relationship. Once such a relationship is proved by the complainant, the burden shifts to the wrongdoer to prove that the complainant entered into the transaction of his own free will. This may be done by establishing that the donor received independent legal advice[8] or that the gift was 'a spontaneous and independent act'.[9] So, in cases of presumed undue influence there is no need to adduce evidence that undue influence was actually exerted in relation to the particular transaction impugned.[10] Cases of presumed undue influence fall into two categories; first those where the relationship raises the presumption as a matter of law[11] and secondly those where the complainant proves the existence of circumstances which establish that he generally reposed trust and confidence in the wrongdoer.

Gregg v. Kidd
[1956] IR 183

The plaintiff executor succeeded in having a voluntary settlement made by the deceased, *inter alia*, in favour of his nephew, the defendant, set aside on the grounds that the relationship between the testator on the one hand, and the nephew and his mother on the other hand, was such as to raise a presumption of influence which had not been rebutted.

BUDD J stated at pp.193–207: "Voluntary gifts, made *inter vivos*, obtained by persons standing in a confidential, fiduciary, or other relation to the donor in which dominion may be exercised over him may, upon principles of general public policy, be set aside where there has been some improper conduct, overreaching or coercion exercised against the donor. The general principles are well stated in White and Tudor's Leading Cases in Equity in the notes appended to the case of *Huguenin v. Baseley* (1807) 14 Ves 273. As Lord

---

[7] See *Bank of Credit and Commerce International SA v. Aboody* [1990] 1 QB 923, 953 and *Barclay's Bank plc v. O'Brien* [1994] 1 AC 180. See also *O'Flanagan v. Ray-Ger Ltd* High Court (Costello J) 28 April 1983.

[8] Or possibly as Shanley J suggested in *Carroll v. Carroll* [1998] 2 ILRM 218, 229 'competent and honest lay advice'.

[9] *Re Brocklehurst's Estate* [1978] Ch 14.

[10] *Barclay's Bank plc v. O'Brien* [1994] 1 AC 180 and *Carroll v. Carroll* [1999] 4 IR 241.

[11] E.g. Solicitor and client, doctor and patient.

Cottenham states in *Dent v. Bennett* (1839) 4 My & Cr 269:– "The relief . . . stands upon a general principle, applying to all variety of relations in which dominion may be exercised by one person over another." It applies of course where the gift is the result of influence expressly used by the donee and also "where the relations between the donor and donee have at or shortly before the execution of the gift been such as to raise a presumption that the donee had influence over the donor. In such a case the Court sets aside a voluntary gift, unless it is proved that in fact the gift was the spontaneous act of the donor acting under circumstances which enabled him to exercise an independent will and which justifies the Court in holding that the gift was the result of a free exercise of the donor's will": per Cotton L. J. in *Allcard v. Skinner* (1887) 36 Ch D 145, at p. 171.

The courts have never confined the application of the principle to any stated forms of relationship. To do so would fetter that wide jurisdiction to relieve against all manner of constructive fraud which courts administering equitable principles have always exercised. The principle has been exercised in the case of an improvident voluntary settlement by a younger sister in favour of an elder sister, who had obtained great ascendancy and influence over the younger sister, the younger sister not having the benefit of independent advice: *Harvey v. Mount* (1845) 8 Beav 439. In *Sharp v. Leach* (1862) 31 Beav 491 a voluntary deed, under which a brother obtained an advantage from a sister who lived with him and consulted him about her affairs, was set aside. The improvidence of the transaction was held to cast the onus on the defendant to show that the deed emanated from the free will of the sister after it had been explained to her. Similarly in *Griffiths v. Robins* (1818) 3 Madd 191, an old lady, nearly blind, who reserving only a life estate to herself, made a deed of gift of all her property to her niece and her husband, on whose kindness and assistance she depended, was held entitled to have the deed set aside. The onus was held to be upon the recipients to establish that the deed was made of her own free will and effected through the intervention of some indifferent person.

The authorities cited leave no doubt that the principle can be extended to the relationship of brother and sister, where a sister has for one reason or another acquired an influence or dominion over a brother and uses that influence improperly for her own ends. Likewise it can be extended in similar circumstances to the relationship between uncle and nephew. The influence may arise or be acquired in many ways, such as through disparity of age or the mental or physical incapacity of the donor or, indeed, out of a mere dependence upon the kindness and assistance of another. To bring the principle into play it must be shown that the opportunity for the exercise of the influence or ascendancy on the donor existed, as where the parties reside together or meet frequently. While close family relationship creates a situation where influence is readily acquired, mere blood relationship is not sufficient of itself to call the principle into play; it must be shown that the actual relations between the parties give rise to a presumption of influence.

Although the exercise of undue influence is pleaded against the donee of the deed impugned, as well as against others, it is true to say that the evidence was mainly directed to establishing that influence had been obtained and exercised over the donor by Mrs. Hannah Kidd, mother of the donee. There is in my mind no doubt that if it be shown that this deed was obtained by the undue influence of Mrs. Hannah Kidd or as a result of her dominion of mind over her brother, improperly exercised to benefit a member of her family, this deed cannot stand. Indeed, it is only right to say that a contention to the contrary was never made by the advisers of the defendants. Although authority is scarcely required on the point, I recall the words of Lord Eldon in the first paragraph of his judgment in *Huguenin v. Baseley* (1807) 14 Ves 273 where he says:– "I should regret that any doubt could be entertained, whether it is not competent to a Court of equity to take away from third persons the benefits which they have derived from the fraud, imposition, or undue influence of others." If the proper deductions from the evidence adduced are that Jack Kidd knew perfectly well that his mother had acquired influence over the donor and that they acted together in order to obtain some advantage from the donor, the grounds for interfering are all the stronger.

Some debate took place during the hearing as to where the onus of proof lay. In the case of a voluntary gift where the relations between the donor and donee are such as to raise a presumption that the donee had influence over the donor, the onus lies, in my view, on the donee to establish that the gift was the spontaneous act of the donor acting in circumstances which enabled him to exercise an independent will and that the gift was the result of a free exercise of the donor's will. This proposition I believe to be one well established. Authority will be found for it in the cases of *Allcard v. Skinner* (1887) 36 Ch D 145, *Sharp v. Leach* (1862) 31 Beav 491, and *Griffiths v. Robins* (1818) 3 Madd 191, already referred to, and also in the observations of Lord Romilly in *Cooke v. Lamotte* (1851) 15 Beav 234. If more modern authority is required it will be found in the judgment of Lord Hailsham in the comparatively recent case of *Inche Noriah v. Shaik Allie Bin Omar* [1929] AC 127. Where the relations between the donor and another person raise a presumption that that other person had influence over the donor and the evidence shows that that third party is both closely related to the donee and was closely associated in action and interest with the donee at the time of the events leading to the transaction, it would seem to me on principle that the onus in such circumstances must be likewise thrown on the donee to establish that the gift resulted from the free exercise of the donor's will.

The presumption may, of course, be rebutted either by showing that the donor has had competent independent advice and acted of his own free will or in some other way. As Lord Hailsham says, in *Inche Noriah v. Shaik Allie Bin Omar* (at p. 135):– "The most obvious way to prove" that the gift was the result of the free exercise of independent will is to establish "that the gift was made after the nature and effect of the transaction had been fully explained to the donor by some independent and qualified person so completely as to satisfy the Court that the donor was acting independently of any influence from the donee and with full appreciation of what he was doing." If that method of rebutting the presumption is adopted, and it is not the only method open, the advice relied on must, in the words of Lord Hailsham, "be given with a knowledge of all relevant circumstances and must be such as a competent and honest adviser would give if acting solely in the interests of the donor." The nature of that advice naturally must vary with the circumstances of each particular case.

Although there is considerable difference of medical opinion as to George Gregg's mental and physical condition at the time when the deed was executed and during the period immediately preceding that event, I have formed these conclusions as to his health during the relevant period: he had had at least one stroke and two serious relapses; he was partially paralysed and virtually bedridden; he suffered from a condition the usual progress of which is one of deterioration; during the summer and autumn his reasoning faculties became impaired; at times his memory was intermittent and faulty and I believe that he could not concentrate for any appreciable length of time; he had periods of confusion of mind. In character he had formerly been voluble and cheerful but had changed to saying little and had become difficult to get answers from. I believe that his capacity to make rational decisions was by the autumn, definitely impaired and that his capacity to resist influence and suggestions was very slight and easily overcome. At times, I think, he might have been fit to make a simple officious will or simple disposition of his property if uninfluenced and properly advised, but it would, in my view, have been difficult to discover just when he was in that condition and equally difficult to bring him to a full understanding of the transaction. Someone well acquainted with him would obviously be the best person to make the attempt, but even such a person would require to exercise care and patience in examining him before coming to a conclusion as to his capacity. Even if he could be shown to have had the capacity to bring a reasoning mind to bear on such a disposition there would still remain the formidable difficulty of ascertaining and ensuring that his mind was emancipated from the influence and dominion of others alleged to have existed.

The last above-mentioned matter brings me to a consideration of the relations between the donor, on the one hand, and the donee and his mother, Mrs. Hannah Kidd, on the other hand, at and immediately before the execution of the deed. As far back as the end of May, 1953, George Gregg had been moved to the Kidds' house and he had remained with them until his death. During most of that time he was a very sick man, only a wreck of his former self. He was during that period entirely dependent on the Kidd family for all the attention his helpless condition required. If and when he was fit for company and conversation it would naturally be members of that family whom he would generally see and he does not seem to have seen much of other members of his family from June onwards. I believe that he knew with more or less clarity, according to the varying state of his health, that he was then dependent on the Kidd family and that he was at times at least most apprehensive as to what would bcome of him were they to refuse to look after him any longer. In short, his circumstances and condition laid him open in a high degree to the influence of that family, more particularly to that of Mrs. Hannah Kidd, having regard to her relationship to him and her position in the household. Mrs. Kidd's character as revealed by her evidence and demeanour is not, in this connection, by any means irrelevant to what I am dealing with, and I should say that she struck me as a woman of forceful and determined character, who believed in having her own way without much regard to the views or advice of others.

Apart from these circumstances which I have mentioned, there is a considerable body of evidence as to the actual relations existing between George Gregg and his relatives, the Kidds, and of their attitude to him, to which I must briefly refer. Before doing so I should say that it must, in all fairness, be recognised that the Kidds acted with kindness in taking George Gregg into their house, having regard to his condition, and I see no reason to doubt that they treated him kindly and looked after him to the best of their ability. No one would suggest that it would have been unreasonable for Mrs. Kidd to seek reasonable recompense for the onerous services she performed. Unfortunately, I regret to say that the evidence does not lead me to believe that the Kidds' motives were by any means solely altruistic and moreover I was forced to take an unfavourable view of the veracity of such members of the family as gave evidence before me in respect of a good deal of what they told me.

The evidence leads me to believe that from an early stage Mrs. Kidd formed the view, shared by her son, Jack Kidd, that George Gregg's farm at Tinryland should go to the Kidds in return for looking after him. It does not matter, to my mind, whether the idea originated with Dawson Miller or Mrs. Kidd herself or her son. The attempts to get George Gregg to make some further settlement of his affairs, other than that provided for in his existing will, indicated by the approaches of Mrs. Kidd and Jack Kidd to Mr. Jeffers and of Mrs. Kidd to Mr. Cody, all indicate their frame of mind. Likewise, the fact that they kept stressing that doctors other than Dr. Seale thought George Gregg fit to transact business betrayed their anxiety to have something done and I am satisfied that what was aimed at was the making of some disposition of George Gregg's property in favour of Mrs. Kidd or some of her family and not merely obtaining some reasonable recompense for her services.

That Mrs. Kidd realised that she was in a position to influence her brother and was prepared to put pressure upon him is revealed strikingly on several occasions. Dr. Seale's view was that George Gregg should go to Dublin for further examination and treatment by Dr. Mayne towards the end of June. He did not go and the real reason is to be found in Mrs. Kidd's attitude. Having regard to all the circumstances, especially the burden he must have been to her, it is difficult to avoid drawing the inference that she wished to keep him in her house for purposes of her own not difficult to seek. She showed her hand clearly on the 27th July when she insisted that George Gregg should make a will, although he was unwilling to do so, and brought what must be regarded as strong pressure to bear on him to do so, having regard to his condition, by threatening to put him out if he did not do so. At the same time she rejected the suggestion that a money payment might be arranged for and insisted on a will being made, and there can be little doubt that it was one benefitting the Kidds that she had in view. That she was of the same mind in August and still prepared to exercise pressure is shown by the terms of her letter of the 15th August indicating that George would have to go to Tinryland or the County Hospital. She must have known that her attitude as revealed in this letter would be made known to George Gregg and would profoundly affect him. In September she made several visits to Mr. Cody, who was not George Gregg's solicitor, and I believe that her object again was to see if she could get something done, through the intervention of Mr. Cody, which would achieve her objects. Mr. Miller in the beginning, I believe, supported her, but he only plays a secondary role.

Although he plays a lesser part than his mother the evidence establishes also that the defendant, John George Kidd, was a party to his mother's activities and took an active part in the endeavours made to get George Gregg to make a fresh disposition of his property in a fashion favourable to the Kidd family. He was party, along with Mr. Dawson Miller, to the original suggestion made in Mr. Jeffers' office on the 15th June that arrangements should be made to have the farm at Tinryland transferred to Mrs. Kidd or one of the family, an idea that originated with them and not with George Gregg, who had at that stage not even mentioned settling his affairs. It was Jack Kidd again who went to Mr. Jeffers on the 25th July to get him to go out to make a will for George Gregg. He did not scruple on that occasion to make what I regard as an untrue statement as to George Gregg's health with the object, I am satisfied, of allaying Mr. Jeffers' anxieties as to George Gregg's capacity. Indeed, that was not the only occasion on which he saw fit to suggest that George Gregg's health was better than it was so as to induce Mr. Jeffers to go out and make a will for him. He knew all about his mother's efforts to get the clergy to intervene to get George Gregg to make a will, but saw fit to deny that he had told Mr. Jeffers of these approaches by his mother. His testimony was so uncandid as to lead me to the belief that he was involved even more than the direct evidence indicates. The evidence satisfies me that Jack Kidd was of one mind with his mother. He was, I believe, perfectly aware of his mother's influence over his uncle and perfectly willing to accept the benefit of its exercise on his behalf.

The facts as proved are such as to lead me to the conclusion not only that the relations between George Gregg and his sister were such as to raise a presumption that she had influence over him, but that she was exercising that influence towards securing his farm for some one or other of her family. She was certainly using active pressure on the 27th July, 1953, and her subsequent activities lead me to believe that that pressure was not relaxed to the date on which the deed was executed; that influence was such, having regard to George Gregg's incapacity and circumstances, as to preclude the exercise by him of a free and independent judgment. The facts are sufficient to support a finding of the actual exercise of undue influence, but it is sufficient to say that the relations between the donor, on the one hand, and his sister and nephew, on the other, were such as to raise a presumption that the donee's mother had influence over the donor. I am satisfied that the donee was aware of this influence and acted in combination with his mother; the onus consequently lies on the defendants to establish that the gift resulted from the free exercise of the donor's will acting in circumstances which enabled him to exercise an independent will.

Before passing to a consideration of the evidence of Mr. Cody, relied upon by the defendants to show that the deed was the free act of the settlor acting in circumstances which enabled him to exercise an independent will, I wish to say something about the deed itself, since its form and contents may, apart from the other circumstances of the case, afford some evidence that the donor did not understand the transaction and so of undue influence. After reserving a life estate to the donor, the effect of the deed is to transfer an estate in remainder to the donee of practically all the donor's property, since apart from the farm he only possessed chattel property of small value. It contains no covenants or other safeguards to ensure that George Gregg would be looked after for the rest of his life by the Kidds or to secure that his farm would be worked during his lifetime. The medical evidence satisfies me that George Gregg might well have lingered on for a matter of years and, while I do not suggest that they would have done so, there was nothing to prevent the Kidds from putting him out of their house after he had executed the deed, in which event he would only have the value of his life estate as a bargaining factor to secure his future comfort. This deed was therefore on the face of it improvident, a fact affording at least some indication militating against the contention that it was the spontaneous product of an independent mind.

Another factor of weight in connection with the form of the deed is that it contains no power of revocation, a fact not brought to the attention of the donor. I accept the view contended for by the defendants that the absence of a power of revocation in a voluntary deed is not of itself a sufficient ground for the cancelling of the deed. It is, as Turner L.J. states in *Toker v. Toker* (1863) 3 De J & S 487, at p. 491, approved by James L.J. in *Hall v. Hall* (1873) 8 Ch App 430, a circumstance to be taken into consideration and it is a circumstance of more or less weight according to the facts of each particular case. It is, I apprehend, a material factor where the deed is improvident unless the donor is protected by such a power. FitzGibbon L.J. in *Horan v. MacMahon* (1886) 17 LR Ir 641 stated at p. 654 his view, frequently quoted, that to get over the absence of the clause in a voluntary deed the "other circumstances must show . . . that it is the free act of a settlor who knows what he is doing; and, 2, either that it is a deed provident and just in itself, or that any apparent improvidence and injustice is in accordance with the actual intention of the settlor." I shall have to revert to these considerations after considering the effect of Mr. Cody's evidence.

The duty of a solicitor advising a donor suffering from a degree of mental or physical infirmity about to make a voluntary settlement of the greater portion of his property is not an easy one. The judgment of Farwell J. in *Powell v. Powell* [1900] 1 Ch 243 has been relied on as stating the duty. Having stated that in his view a solicitor who acts for both parties cannot be independent of the donee in fact and that it is not sufficient that the donor should have an independent adviser unless he acts on the advice, Farwell J. points out that it is the duty of the solicitor to protect the donor against himself and not merely against the personal influence of the donee. He was dealing with a case of child and step-parent but the same considerations apply, in my view, to a case such as the present. He goes on to say that the solicitor does not discharge his duty by satisfying himself simply that the donor understands and wishes to carry out the particular transaction, and adds (at p. 247):- "He must also satisfy himself that the gift is one that it is right and proper for the donor to make under all the circumstances; and if he is not so satisfied, his duty is to advise his client not to go on with the transaction, and to refuse to act further for him if he persists." He found that the solicitor in question had not, *inter alia*, advised the donor in that case of the proper course to adopt or recommended the insertion in the settlement of a power of revocation. The Privy Council in *Inche Noriah v. Shaik Allie Bin Omar* [1929] AC 127 were not prepared to affirm that independent legal advice, when given, does not rebut the presumption unless it be shown that the advice was taken. What is necessary, Lord Hailsham said, is that the donee should prove that the gift was the result of the free exercise of independent will. He adds that the most obvious way to prove this is by establishing that the gift was made after the nature and effect of the transaction had been fully explained to the donor by some independent and qualified person so completely as to satisfy the Court that the donor was acting independently of any influence from the donee and with the full appreciation of what he was doing. Finally, he says, the advice must be given with a knowledge of all relevant circumstances and must be such as a competent adviser would give if acting solely in the interests of the donor. With great respect to that learned Judge there are two statements in his judgment on which I venture to differ from the views of Farwell J. In accordance with the view of the Privy Council it seems to me that independent legal advice may in certain circumstances rebut the presumption even though that advice is not taken. Moreover, I do not think that a solicitor is bound to refuse to act further for his client in all cases of the nature I am dealing with where his advice to his client not to proceed with the transaction is not taken, though in some extreme cases that may be the proper course. Apart from these two matters I adopt the views of Farwell J. and Lord Hailsham as to the duties of a solicitor in similar cases, observing, however, that they are not necessarily exhaustive. The nature of the advice to be given must in all instances depend upon the facts and circumstances of each case.

These views of a general nature as to the duties of a solicitor in cases of this kind have now to be applied in a practical fashion to the particular circumstances of this case and, without purporting to deal with every detail, I conceive that a solicitor advising one in the circumstances of George Gregg is at least under the following obligations to his client. To begin with, he should apprise himself of the surrounding circumstances in so far as he reasonably can; if he does not do this he can never put himself in a position to advise his client fully and effectively. He would need to discover the nature of the donor's illness so as to be able to estimate in some reasonable degree the nature of his incapacity. He would need to know how far his reasoning capacity was affected and how far he was capable of comprehending the manner in which the proposed transaction would affect his own interests and his future and to what extent he was competent to come to a rational decision. Without knowing all that, he could not be said to have sufficient knowledge of his client to enable him to judge the nature of the advice he should give him and the degree of protection he would require. With the knowledge that he would have gained upon inquiry that the donor was incapacitated to some degree both mentally and physically and had been living for some time with the family of the proposed transferee, by one of whom the solicitor in this case had originally been consulted with a view to having something done about the donor's affairs, he ought then to have been put on his guard and he should, in my view, then endeavour to discover whether his client was subject to the influence of the donee or any member of his family and, if so, the extent of that influence. Having discovered the extent of the donor's incapacity he should make sure that he was capable of fully understanding the nature and results of a transaction such as that proposed. Without that capacity the transaction could not be proceeded with, but, assuming that the solicitor satisfies himself that it exists, he should then make sure that his client did thoroughly understand what he was doing and how it would affect him. He would need in this connection to consider very carefully whether the transaction was one for this benefit and, as I see it, this was a case that called for positive and definite advice, not mere explanation. The suggested transfer was, on the face of it, an improvident transaction. The plight of the donor demanded that he should be protected against himself. He should have been told clearly that the transaction was improvident, that it secured nothing for him in return for what he was giving, and that he was not only depriving himself of most of what he possessed, but also the means of securing his future comfort. He should have been advised against entering into the proposed transaction unless he was adequately and properly safeguarded. In particular, he should have been told that he might safeguard himself to a great degree by having a power of revocation inserted in the instrument. Before he could conscientiously advise his client to proceed with the transaction the solicitor would also need to satisfy himself that his intervention and advice had emancipated the donor from any adverse influence he lay under and that he was acting of his own free will.

Mr. Cody was faced with an unenviable task of difficulty and delicacy when he was called upon to attend George Gregg in September, 1953. It is easy to be wise after the event and I feel sure that Mr. Cody would have acted differently had he appreciated what the real circumstances were. It may well be that he was to some extent misled and it is right to say that he was quite candid about the advice he gave. I must, however, consider whether such advice as he did give could have the results contended for by the defendants. While I am alive to the fact that it was Mrs. Kidd, and not the donee, who had previously consulted him I have the gravest doubts whether Mr. Cody could be properly described as an independent solicitor; but even assuming for the moment that he was, Mr. Cody did not, I fear, appreciate the full extent of George Gregg's physical and mental incapacity. He had not known his client previously and was not in a position to judge how much he had deteriorated and I believe he did not appreciate the extent to which his reasoning power and ability to make rational decisions was affected. He did not sufficiently consider what effect the transaction would have on George Gregg's future nor what would happen should he fall out with the Kidds, nor did he consider in what way George Gregg might be safeguarded, nor did he, I believe, appreciate the entire improvidence of the transaction. It follows that he did not feel called upon to give, nor did he give, George Gregg any positive advice in the way of dissuading him from entering into the transaction as proposed nor did he advise George Gregg as to the various ways in which he might be safeguarded from the improvidence he contemplated nor urge him to adopt any suggestions calculated to safeguard him. In particular, he never brought to his notice the possibility of inserting a power of revocation in the deed nor did he urge on him the desirability of such a course, which I believe the circumstances called for. Furthermore, Mr. Cody did not appreciate the true nature of the relations existing between the donor and Mrs. Kidd and the donor and the donee, to a lesser degree. Deprived of that knowledge, he was never in a position to consider what advice and warning he should properly give to the donor and what steps he should take to make sure that the settlor was acting with a free and independent mind and was emancipated from the influence of his sister. As a result, no steps were taken to ensure that George Gregg acted independently and freed from the effects of his sister's influence. The advice received by the donor was not therefore sufficient to enable the donor to understand fully and properly the nature of the entire transaction nor such as to protect the donor against himself; nor was it sufficient to rebut the presumption, nor does it satisfy me that the gift was the spontaneous act of a donor who knew what he was doing.

The findings I have so far made are sufficient to determine the action, but the plaintiff does not rest his case solely on the contentions I have dealt with. He also relies on the decision in *Grealish v. Murphy* [1946] IR 35, a decision of Gavan Duffy J., as he then was, and says that the circumstances of this case cause it to fall within the principle of that decision.

The plaintiff in that proceeding, who was mentally deficient, executed a deed transferring his farm to a much younger man. The deed reserved a life estate to the plaintiff but the lands were charged with the defendant's right of residence and maintenance during the plaintiff's life. The defendant covenanted to reside on, and to work and manage, the farm without reward during the plaintiff's lifetime, to account for moneys received and expended and to pay the plaintiff £1 for every week in which he failed to reside on the farm and to indemnify the plaintiff for any loss or expense incurred or the maintenance or wages of any person employed to do work which the defendant failed to do. I have only taken the salient factors of the deed. They show that the plaintiff was more adequately protected than was George Gregg. Gavan Duffy J. took the view that the circumstances of the case brought into operation the principle stated by Lord Hatherley, in *O'Rorke v. Bolingbroke* (1877) 2 App Cas 814, at p. 832 (in which he dissented on facts), that equity comes to the rescue whenever the parties to a contract have not met upon equal terms, the corollary being, he said, that the Court must inquire whether a grantor, shown to be unequal to protecting himself, has had the protection which was his due by reason of his infirmity. Having stated that the principle applies to improvident grants and that in several instances the inadequacy of the explanations given to the grantor has been a decisive factor in the Court's action against an improvident deed, the learned Judge set aside the improvident deed by reason of the plaintiff's weakness of mind coupled with the deficiencies of the legal advice under which he acted and his unawareness.

The late President expressly stated that the deed could not be avoided by reason of any undue influence and that the case was not one where any presumption of undue influence arose from the relationship of the parties. The degree of the plaintiff's incapacity coupled with deficiencies of advice and the improvidence of the transaction was held sufficient in the circumstances of that case to entitle the donor to relief. That degree of incapacity was that the donor had not attained the normal power of an adult. I have already expressed the view that the deed made by George Gregg was improvident. He was suffering from such incapacity as would prevent him from understanding anything but the simplest transaction. His solicitor had not got the facts as to the nature of his illness or his incapacity. Apart from any question of the donor being subject to influence, he did not consider what safeguards might be necessary to protect George Gregg for the future nor warn him as to the improvidence of what he contemplated and against entering into the transaction as proposed. He did not advise him as to what steps he ought to take to protect himself, such as the insertion of a power of revocation. Since he was not warned of the improvidence of the transaction nor told what steps could be taken to safeguard himself, George Gregg was never fully aware of what he was doing or its consequences and could not, in my view, be said to have fully understood the transaction. The case therefore in some of its essential features falls within the principle of the decision of Gavan Duffy J. in *Grealish v. Murphy*, but as, in my view, the case falls more properly within the principles laid down in the other cases I have dealt with, I prefer to rest my judgment on the basis that the relations existing between the donor, on the one hand, and the donee and his mother, on the other, were such as to raise a presumption that the donee's mother and the donee acting through and with her had influence over the donor and that that presumption has not been rebutted by showing that in fact the gift was the spontaneous act of the donor acting under circumstances which enabled him to exercise an independent will and that the gift resulted from a free exercise of the donor's will.

The indenture of the 28th September, 1953, must, therefore, be set aside and the deed must be delivered up to be cancelled."

Carroll v. Carroll
[1998] 2 ILRM 218 (HC) [1999] 4 IR 241 (SC)

The plaintiffs, who were the daughters and personal representatives of an elderly donor, sought to have the transfer of a pub and residential accommodation set aside on the grounds that it had been procured by undue influence and was an improvident transaction. After his wife's death, the donor had transferred the property to his son without disclosing this fact to his daughters. The donor and his son both subsequently died and tensions arose between the plaintiffs and the son's widow, the defendant, which led to the bringing of proceedings to have the original transfer set aside. The donor had discussed making the transfer to his son on two occasions with the solicitor who effected it, although the latter was in reality acting for both parties. While the donor was mentally alert at that time, he was subject to a number of physical infirmities which made him increasingly dependent on others. The plaintiffs submitted that the relationship between the donor and donee was such as to raise a presumption of undue influence, which they argued had not been rebutted. The defendant conceded that the relationship between the parties did give rise to a presumption of undue influence but submitted that it has been rebutted in the circumstances. Shanley J granted an order setting aside the transaction on the grounds that the presumption of undue influence had not been rebutted and the defendant's appeal was dismissed by the Supreme Court (Denham, Lynch and Barron JJ).

SHANLEY J stated at pp.228–232:
"(i) One of the grounds on which the courts are prepared to set aside transactions for value, or gifts, is where there has been undue influence exercised upon the donor or transferor of the property. It has long been accepted that cases of undue influence fall into two categories: the first being those where the relationship between the parties to the transaction (or parties involved

in the transaction) is such as to raise a presumption of undue influence. The second category arises where no relationship gives rise to any presumption of undue influence, but the parties so alleging undue influence adduce evidence which satisfies the court, on the balance of probabilities, that the transaction was not the result of the free exercise of the will of the donor. As to the first category, it is suggested, correctly in my view, that the law will not concern itself with insignificant transactions and that the presumption will only arise where one party to a transaction has derived a substantial benefit from it. The relevant principles are well summarised by Costello J. in *O'Flanagan v. Ray-Ger Ltd* High Court 1980 No. 2858P where he stated (adopting the principles formulated by Cotton L.J. in *Allcard v. Skinner* (1887) 36 Ch D 145 at p. 171):

> The cases where a plaintiff seeks to set aside a gift or other transaction on the ground that it was procured by undue influence have been divided into two classes; firstly, those in which it can be expressly proved that undue influence was exercised, in which circumstances the court intervenes on the principle that no one should be allowed to retain any benefit arising from his own fraud or wrongful act; secondly, those in which the relations between the donor and donee have at or shortly before the execution of a gift been such as to raise a presumption that the donee had influence over the donor. Then, the court intervenes . . . on the ground of public policy and to protect the relations which existed between the parties and the influence arising therefrom being abused.

The categories of relationship which will give rise to the presumption are never 'closed', as Budd J. observed in *Gregg v. Kidd* [1956] IR 183, and the categories recognised in decided cases as capable of raising the presumption include those of parent and child, lawyer and client, an individual and a spiritual advisor, a patient and his doctor, an uncle and his nephew. Where the presumption exists, it may be rebutted by evidence which establishes on the balance of probability that the transaction was the consequence of the exercise of the donor of his own free will and not the result of undue influence. Such evidence may be evidence that the donor had independent legal advice – or competent and honest lay advice. As Lord Hailsham LC, said in *Inche Noriah v. Shaik Allie Bin Omar* [1929] AC 126 at p. 135:

> It is necessary for the donee to prove that the gift was the result of the free exercise of independent will. The most obvious way to prove this is by establishing that the gift was made after the nature and effect of the transaction had been fully explained to the donor by some independent and qualified person so completely as to satisfy the court that the donor was acting independently of any influence from the donee and with the full appreciation of what he was doing; and in cases where there are no other circumstances this may be the only means by which the donee can rebut the presumption.

It is to be noted from the advices of Lord Hailsham that he did not regard independent legal advice, of itself, as being an essential element in rebutting the presumption: independent advice by a suitably qualified person could suffice.

(ii) Where the relationship between the parties to the transaction does not give rise to the presumption of undue influence, but nonetheless a plaintiff seeks to set aside a transaction on such grounds, then the burden of proof is on the plaintiff to establish that the transaction in question was not the result of a free exercise of the donor's will, but rather resulted from pressure of one kind or another described as 'undue influence' upon the donor.

(iii) Apart from the courts' jurisdiction to set aside a transaction on the grounds of undue influence, there is also a jurisdiction to set aside as 'unconscionable' other transactions where the parties to the transaction have unequal bargaining positions and the weaker party has not been adequately protected. Hanbury & Martin, *Modern Equity* (4th ed., 1991) at p. 821 states that the jurisdiction will only be exercised where:

> First, that one party was at a serious disadvantage to the other by reason of poverty, ignorance or otherwise, so that circumstances existed of which unfair advantage could be taken; secondly, that the transaction was at an undervalue; and thirdly, that there was a lack of independent legal advice.

In *Grealish v. Murphy* [1946] IR 35 Gavan Duffy J. expressly recognised that the court had jurisdiction to set aside a deed on the ground that it was an improvident transaction. He referred with approval to the principle that (at p. 49):

> Equity comes to the rescue whenever the parties to a contract have not met upon equal terms . . . the corollary is that the court must inquire whether a grantor, shown to be unequal to protecting himself, has had the protection which was due by reason of his infirmity, and the infirmity may take various forms.

(iii) Delay will not always disentitle a plaintiff to relief: the delay must be such as to have given rise to an inference that the plaintiff had acquiesced in the infringements of the rights he now asserts, and the delay must also be of such a nature as to have caused some detriment to the defendant: see generally Keane, *Equity and the Law of Trusts in the Republic of Ireland* at paragraph 17.16.

Conclusions
(i) The transfer in issue in this case related to property which had an open market value in 1990 of between £100,000 and £125,000. The property represented the only real asset of the deceased, Thomas Carroll Snr. The transfer was one from father to son. I am satisfied that the significant benefit obtained by the donee from the transaction and the relationship between donor and donee are such as to raise a presumption of undue influence.

(ii) I am not satisfied that the defendant has established as a matter of probability that the transaction was the result of the free exercise of the donor's will such as to rebut the presumption of undue influence. Mr Joyce allowed that in substance and fact he was acting as the 'family solicitor' in the transaction for both parties. He saw the donor on two occasions for a total of about 35-40 minutes, not all of which was devoted to the business of the transfer. It is clear that the donor never read the transfer deed nor had it read to him by anyone else. While its contents were apparently discussed between him and Mr Joyce, I am not satisfied that any real consideration was given to the fact that the donor (a frail man, in dependant circumstances) was disposing of all his real assets without reserving to himself (by way of a revocation clause or by way of charging the property with his maintenance and support), any protection for his own future particularly in the event of a falling out with his son, or in the event of his son predeceasing him. It is, I think, clear that Philip Joyce was not aware of the family's circumstances either in the context of the position of the other members of the family, the totality of the assets held by the family members or the assurances given by the donor to other members of the family including the plaintiffs as to their user of the Burke Street premises during their lifetimes. Thus, while I accept the evidence (which was not really disputed) that the donor was a man who was mentally alert at the date of the transfer, I am not at all happy that at the date of the transfer he had the necessary independent advice (whether it was that of a legal advisor or a competent and qualified lay person) such as would persuade me that the transaction was made of his own free will. For completeness I feel I should express my conclusions as to other aspects of the evidence which I have heard and which have assisted me in further deciding that the deed should be set aside. I should first of all say that all of the persons who gave evidence gave it truthfully: that is not to say that the witnesses had the same recollections or were of the same opinions: they were not; but neither were any of them attempting to overstate or exaggerate their evidence.

I was satisfied that the nuclear family to which the plaintiffs belonged was indeed a close knit and caring family; I was satisfied that the plaintiffs were extremely close to their father and he to them: I have little doubt that he did indeed constantly reassure them that there would always be a home for them in Burke Street. His failure (between 1990 and 1992) to disclose to Winifred Carroll and Mary Jane Carroll the actual transfer of the property to their brother (as opposed to the running of the business) was not, in my view, likely to have been an act of concealment; it is more likely that Mr Carroll Snr did not truly understand or appreciate the nature and effect of the 1990 deed which he had executed in favour of his son. Equally, I am satisfied that the plaintiffs themselves did not become aware of the transfer of ownership until they were told the position by Philip Joyce in early 1994 at his offices. It is somewhat surprising that they, the plaintiffs, appear never to have been told of the true position by their brother in his lifetime or by their sister-in-law who says that she herself was aware of the true position prior to her marriage to Thomas Carroll Jnr. The plaintiffs' ignorance of the true nature of the 1990 transaction was shared by the relatives of the plaintiffs who gave evidence on their behalf. It was ignorance apparently shared by the community in Fethard as there was no one save the defendant, who claimed to know the true nature of the 1990 deal during the lifetime of the donor. All of the foregoing matters strengthen me in my view that the presumption of undue influence has not been rebutted by evidence which establishes as a matter of probability that the transfer was the result of the exercise of the free will of Thomas Carroll Snr.

While I have concluded that the 1990 transaction should be set aside on the grounds of undue influence, I should also state that I am also satisfied that the transaction would be set aside and should be set aside on the grounds that it was an improvident transaction. It is worth recalling that the donor disposing of the Burke Street premises was disposing of the only real asset he possessed. He was disposing of it at a time when he was dependant on his son for his maintenance and support. He was physically frail; he was in pain with arthritis; he was hard of hearing and he had bad eyesight and he was somewhat depressed. Notwithstanding his physical infirmities, he transferred the premises without reserving to himself any right of maintenance and support: and he did all this without the benefit of any independent advice whether legal or otherwise. There are few donors who more deserve the protection of equity than Thomas Carroll Snr did in 1990 in that few parties would have come to a transaction on more unequal terms than Mr Carroll Snr did in relation to his son. This in my view is a clear case where the equitable jurisdiction can and should be invoked with a view to setting aside the transaction on the grounds of its improvidence.

(iii) As to the issue of laches, I do not believe that there is any real substance to this allegation; the plaintiffs became aware of the real nature of the transaction in early 1994: at the end of July 1994 they obtained a copy of the deed from Philip Joyce for the first time; by November 1994 proceedings which were ultimately issued were then threatened. While the correspondence between the solicitors prior to November 1994 concentrated on claims to the furniture in the premises, it was not such as to lead the defendant in my view to believe that the plaintiffs had abandoned any claim to the premises and any works executed on the premises at Burke Street by the defendant in this narrow period of time (from the delivery of the deed in July 1994 to the threat of proceedings in November 1994) cannot be said to have been induced by any acquiescence of the plaintiffs in respect of their rights relating to the premises. Accordingly this plea in the defence fails.

Having regard to my view that the deed of 3 May 1990 should be set aside, I shall hear counsel as to the form of order to be made."

DENHAM J stated at pp.253–260:

"Undue influence – decision
There are two classes of transactions which may be set aside on the grounds of undue influence. They were described by the House of Lords (in the judgment of Cotton L.J) in *Allcard v. Skinner* (1887) 36 Ch D 145 at p. 171 as:

"The question is – Does the case fall within the principles laid down by the decisions of the Court of Chancery in setting aside voluntary gifts executed by parties who at the time were under such influence as, in the opinion of the Court, enabled the donor afterwards to set the gift aside? These decisions may be divided into two classes - First, where the Court has been satisfied that the gift was the result of influence expressly used by the donee for the purpose; second, where the relations between the donor and donee have at or shortly before the execution of the gift been such as to raise a presumption that the donee had influence over the donor. In such a case the Court sets aside the voluntary gift, unless it is proved that in fact the gift was the spontaneous act of the donor acting under circumstances which enabled him to exercise an independent will and which justifies the Court in holding that the gift was the result of a free exercise of the donor's will ... In the second class of cases the Court interferes, not on the ground that any wrongful act has in fact been committed by the donee, but on the ground of public policy, and to prevent the relations which existed between the parties and the influence arising therefrom being abused."

This case arises under the second class of case. Counsel for the defendant quite rightly accepted that this case falls into the latter category. He acknowledged that the relationship between Thomas Carroll senior and Thomas Carroll junior and the surrounding circumstances gave rise to the presumption of undue influence.

The legal situation arising on such relationship being established was described in *"Equity and the Law of Trusts in Ireland"* by Hilary Delany at p. 482 as:

"Once a relationship giving rise to a presumption of undue influence is established, and it is shown that a 'substantial benefit' has been obtained, the onus lies on the donee to establish that the gift or transaction resulted from the 'free exercise of the donor's will'. As Dixon J. put it in *Johnson v. Butress*, the evidence must establish that the gift was 'the independent and well-understood act of a man in a position to exercise a free judgment based on information as full as that of the donee'. The manner in which this presumption may be rebutted relates to two main issues; first, the question of whether independent legal advice has been received and secondly, whether it can be shown that the decision to make the gift or transfer was 'a spontaneous and independent act' or that the donor 'acted of his own free will'."

I adopt this analysis of the law and apply it. In this case the presumption is established and a substantial benefit was obtained thus the onus lies on the donee, the defendant, to establish that the transfer was the free exercise of the will of the donor, Thomas Carroll senior. Thus, it was for the defendant to provide the evidence that the transfer was the independent and free gift of Thomas Carroll senior. The issue then arising is whether there was evidence upon which the learned trial judge could be satisfied that the presumption was not rebutted. In analysing this the first matter is that of independent legal advice. Although it was submitted that Mr. Joyce was the family solicitor on the evidence he appears to have been predominantly that of Thomas Carroll junior.

The legal advice relied upon was given by Mr. Joyce. Mr. Joyce was engaged and paid by Thomas Carroll junior. It was Thomas Carroll junior's name which was on the file. In his evidence Mr. Joyce referred to "his instructions". He appeared to misconceive his duty. Further, Mr. Joyce did not know that the asset being transferred was practically the sole asset of Thomas Carroll senior and so could not advise him fully or explain the consequences of his action. Nor did he know of the family, the relationships with the daughters, and so could not advise on this matter either. In light of the absence of this information he could not advise Thomas Carroll senior appropriately.

In considering whether Thomas Carroll senior acted of his own free will an important matter was whether or not the transfer was read over to Thomas Carroll senior. There was no evidence of this even though the defendant was given an opportunity in the High Court to address the matter.

This case is not about the presence or absence of mental capacity. The onus is on the defendant to produce evidence to dislodge the presumption of undue influence.

The learned trial judge concluded, on this aspect of the case, at p. 230 that:

> "I am not satisfied that the [defendant] has established as a matter of probability that the transaction was the result of the free exercise of the donor's will such as to rebut the presumption of undue influence. Mr Joyce allowed that in substance and fact he was acting as the 'family solicitor' in the transaction for both parties. He saw the donor on two occasions for a total of about 35-40 minutes, not all of which was devoted to the business of the transfer. It is clear that the donor never read the transfer deed nor had it read to him by anyone else. While its contents were apparently discussed between him and Mr Joyce, I am not satisfied that any real consideration was given to the fact that the donor (a frail man, in dependant circumstances) was disposing of all his real assets without reserving to himself (by way of a revocation clause or by way of charging the property with his maintenance and support), any protection for his own future particularly in the event of a falling out with his son, or in the event of his son predeceasing him. It is, I think, clear that Philip Joyce was not aware of the family's circumstances either in the context of the position of the other members of the family, the totality of the assets held by the family members or the assurances given by the donor to other members of the family including the plaintiffs as to their user of the Burke Street premises during their lifetimes. Thus, while I accept the evidence (which was not really disputed) that the donor was a man who was mentally alert at the date of the transfer, I am not at all happy that at the date of the transfer he had the necessary independent advice (whether it was that of a legal advisor or a competent and qualified lay person) such as would persuade me that the transaction was made of his own free will."

There was evidence before the learned trial judge upon which he could reach these conclusions of fact. Thus, I would affirm his determination.

Counsel for the defendant submitted that for the plaintiffs to succeed there should be evidence that Thomas Carroll junior exercised undue influence on Thomas Carroll senior. This submission was at the core of the appeal. Counsel argued strongly that as Thomas Carroll junior himself had not unduly influenced his father that was sufficient to rebut the presumption. He argued that in this case Thomas Carroll junior did not exercise undue influence, or in counsel's word, "wiles" on Thomas Carroll senior. That being the case, it being accepted that Thomas Carroll senior was mentally capable, it was submitted that he could give away his assets as he wished. Counsel for the defendant relied on the lack of undue influence exercised by Thomas Carroll junior and referred to *Reg. (Proctor) v. Hutton* [1978] NI 139.

However, this is not a case of actual undue influence being expressly exercised but is rather a case in which the relationship between the donor and donee has raised the presumption of undue influence. It is then for the defendant to rebut the presumption. The burden was described in *Inche Noriah v. Shaik Allie Bin Omar* [1929] AC 127 at p. 135 by Hailsham L.C.:

> "It is necessary for the donee to prove that the gift was the result of the free exercise of independent will. The most obvious way to prove this is by establishing that the gift was made after the nature and effect of the transaction had been fully explained to the donor by some independent and qualified person so completely as to satisfy the Court that the donor was acting independently of any influence from the donee and with the full appreciation of what he was doing; and in cases where there are no other circumstances this may be the only means which the donee can rebut the presumption. But the fact to be established is that stated in the judgment already cited of Cotton L.J., and if evidence is given of circumstances sufficient to establish this fact, their Lordships see no reason for disregarding them merely because they do not include independent advice from a lawyer. Nor are their Lordships prepared to lay down what advice must be received in order to satisfy the rule in cases where independent legal advice is relied upon, further than to say that it must be given with a knowledge of all relevant circumstances and must be such as a competent and honest adviser would give if acting solely in the interests of the donor."

In *Reg. (Proctor) v. Hutton* [1978] NI 139 at p. 146, Lowry L.J. described the different approaches to the different classes of undue influence. He stated:

> "When relying on 'express undue influence' the plaintiff must prove that an unfair advantage has been gained by an unconscientious use of power in the form of some unfair and improper conduct, some coercion from outside, some overreaching, some form of cheating. The undue influence which is *presumed* in the second class of case is influence of the same kind: the difference lies in not being able to prove its exercise but, by virtue of the presumption, undue influence is deemed to have been exercised until its exercise is negatived on a balance of probabilities by evidence."

It is clear that what is at issue is whether the donee has taken advantage of his position or "... been assiduous not to do so. The question can only be answered in each case by a meticulous consideration of the facts": Hanbury, *"Modern Equity"* (9th ed.) p. 652.

I am satisfied that this is the correct approach. In this case, the presumption existing, it was then necessary to conduct a careful analysis of the facts. On the facts it was a matter of determining if the donee, Thomas Carroll junior, had taken advantage of his position or had been assiduous not to do so. This was not a case where the issue was whether Thomas Carroll junior had taken advantage of his position expressly. Rather it was a case where in the circumstances assiduous care should have been taken not to take advantage of the position of Thomas Carroll senior.

The learned trial judge conducted a painstaking analysis of the facts as has been set out fully in this judgment. I am satisfied that the appeal was argued on a mistaken approach to the law. The reason for the equitable law to protect Thomas Carroll senior is one of public policy – to protect a frail person. As Cotton L.J. said in *Allcard v. Skinner* (1887) 36 Ch D 145 at p. 171:

> "In the second class of cases the Court interferes, not on the ground that any wrongful act has in fact been committed by the donee, but on the ground of public policy, and to prevent the relations which existed between the parties and the influence arising therefrom being abused."

Thus, the issue is whether on the facts and circumstances of the case the donee has rebutted the presumption of undue influence. The facts and circumstances of this case were fully considered and determined by the learned High Court Judge. In this case the donor was giving away practically his sole asset and the learned trial judge made careful findings of fact about the transaction.

The conclusions reached in *Inche Noriah v. Shaik Allie Bin Omar* [1929] AC 127, are analogous on the law and facts to those found by the learned trial judge. In that case Hailsham L.C., describing amongst other matters the conduct of the lawyer, Mr. James Aitken, stated at p. 136:

> "In the present case their Lordships do not doubt that Mr. Aitken acted in good faith; but he seems to have received a good deal of his information from the respondent; he was not made aware of the material fact that the property which was being given away constituted practically the whole estate of the donor, and he certainly does not seem to have brought home to her mind the consequences to herself of what she was doing, or the fact that she could more prudently, and equally effectively, have benefited the donee without undue risk to herself by retaining the property in her own possession during her life, and bestowing it upon him by her will. In their Lordships' view the facts proved by the respondent are not sufficient to rebut the presumption of undue influence which is raised by the relationship proved to have been in existence between the parties; and they regard it as most important from the point of view of public policy to maintain the rule of law which has been laid down and to insist that a gift made under circumstances which give rise to the presumption must be set aside unless the donee is able to satisfy the Court of facts sufficient to rebut the presumption."

The learned trial judge reached a similar conclusion on the law in this case. I am satisfied that he was correct, it was not necessary to prove specific acts of undue influence by Thomas Carroll junior. The evidence as a whole must be considered to see whether the presumption of undue influence has been rebutted. This was done most carefully by the learned trial judge. I would affirm his decision on this aspect of the appeal.

Improvidence of the transaction – decision
Thomas Carroll senior was disposing of practically his only asset. At the time he was frail. He did not retain any right of maintenance or support. I have already analysed the nature of the legal advice he received and affirmed the decision that it was inadequate. In all the circumstances, as described above, it is clear that Thomas Carroll senior was an unequal party. In *Grealish v. Murphy* [1946] IR 35 at p. 49-50, the High Court (Gavan-Duffy J.) stated:

> "The issue thus raised brings into play Lord Hatherley's cardinal principle (from which the exceptions are rare) that Equity comes to the rescue whenever the parties to a contract have not met upon equal terms, see Lord Hatherley's judgment (dissenting on facts) in *O'Rorke v. Bolingbroke;* the corollary is that the Court must inquire whether a grantor, shown to be unequal to protecting himself, has had the protection which was his due by reason of his infirmity, and the infirmity may take various forms. The deed here was in law a transaction for value: *Colreavy v. Colreavy* ; however tenuous the value may have proved to be in fact, and, of course, a Court must be very much slower to undo a transaction for value; but the fundamental principle to justify radical interference by the Court is the identical principle, whether value be shown or not, and the recorded examples run from gifts and voluntary settlements (including an abortive marriage settlement) to assignments for a money consideration. The principle has been applied to improvident grants, whether the particular disadvantage entailing the need for protection to the grantor were merely low station and surprise (though the grantor's rights were fully explained): *Evans v. Llewellin,* or youth and inexperience: *Prideaux v. Lonsdale; Everitt v. Everitt*; or age and weak intellect, short of total incapacity, with no fiduciary relation and no 'arts of inducement' to condemn the grantee: *Longmate v. Ledger; Anderson v. Elsworth.* Even the exuberant or ill-considered dispositions of feckless middle-aged women have had to yield to the same principle: *Phillipson v. Kerry; Wollaston v. Tribe.*"

He also concluded at p. 51:

> "In my judgment, without any regard to any question of undue influence, upon Lord Hatherley's principle and the concurrent authorities the plaintiff by reason of his own weakness of mind, coupled with the deficiencies in the legal advice under which he acted and his unawareness, is entitled to have the improvident indenture of settlement, dated October 24th, 1942, set aside and the Register of Freeholders rectified."

Whilst one might not agree with all of the classifications recognised by Gavan-Duffy J. the legal principle is stated clearly and is applicable to this case.

In light of the evidence, of the omissions in relation to the legal advice given, the fact that there was no evidence that the transfer was read over to Thomas Carroll senior, his frail health, his lack of practically any other assets, his relationship with his daughters and all the circumstances, there was clear evidence upon which the learned trial judge could come to the determination, which he did, at p. 232, that:

> "This in my view is a clear case where the equitable jurisdiction can and should be invoked with a view to setting aside the transaction on the grounds of its improvidence."

I would affirm his conclusion.

Acquiescence laches – decision
I am satisfied there are no grounds raised upon which the appeal on this point could succeed. On the evidence the plaintiffs learnt of the transfer, obtained a copy thereof and issued proceedings all well within one year. I am satisfied that the learned trial judge was correct in his conclusion that there was no acquiescence by the plaintiffs. Consequently, I would dismiss the appeal on this ground also.

Conclusion
I affirm the judgment and order of the High Court that the deed of the 3rd May, 1990, should be set aside."

Undue Influence and Third Parties

The principles considered above also extend to cases where the person who has been subjected to undue influence enters into obligations to a third party, often a financial institution. While it is accepted that the relationship between husband and wife does not of itself give rise to a presumption of undue influence,[12] in a particular case where a wife relies on her husband in all financial matters a presumption may arise.[13]

As a general principle where a wife has been induced to stand as a surety for her husband's debt as a result of some wrongdoing on his part, she has an equity against him to set aside the transaction which will be enforceable against third parties if the husband was acting as the third party's agent or the third party had actual or constructive knowledge of the facts giving rise to the equity.[14] A financial institution will be fixed with constructive notice if it is put on inquiry for example by the fact a wife has offered to stand surety for her husband's debts[15] and fails to take reasonable steps to ensure that the borrower

---

[12] Note the 'special equity' theory referred to by Lord Browne-Wilkinson in *Barclays Bank plc v. O'Brien* [1994] 1 AC 180, 187-188.

[13] *Barclays Bank plc v. O'Brien* [1994] 1 AC 180, 190. See also *Barclays Bank plc v. Coleman* [2001] QB 20.

[14] *Barclays Bank plc v. O'Brien* [1994] 1 AC 180, 195. See also *Bank of Nova Scotia v. Hogan* [1996] 3 IR 239, 248.

[15] *Barclays Bank plc v. O'Brien* [1994] 1 AC 180, 196 and *Royal Bank of Scotland v. Etridge (No. 2)* [2001] 3 WLR 1021, 1037.

understands the nature of the transaction. The 'reasonable steps' suggested by Lord Browne-Wilkinson in *Barclays Bank plc v. O'Brien*[16] consisted of insisting that the wife attend a private meeting in the absence of her husband with a representative of the creditor at which the extent of her liability is explained to her, she is warned of the risk she is running and is urged to take legal advice. However, as Steyn L.J. subsequently made clear in *Massey v. Midland Bank plc*[17] these guidelines should not be mechanically applied and alternative precautions may suffice to avoid a financial institution being fixed with constructive notice. It has recently been acknowledged by Lord Nicholls in *Royal Bank of Scotland v. Etridge (No. 2)*[18] that the practice of banks generally is not to have a private meeting with the wife in such cases and that the furthest that a bank can be expected to go is to take reasonable steps to satisfy itself that the wife has had brought home to her, in a meaningful way, the practical implications of the proposed transaction.[19]

The predominant view in England is that a financial institution is entitled to rely on the fact that a solicitor advising the wife has undertaken this task in a sufficiently independent manner, even if he has previously acted for the husband or the financial institution.[20] The view expressed by Lord Nicholls in *Royal Bank of Scotland v. Etridg (No. 2)*[21] is that a solicitor may also act for the husband or the bank provided that he is satisfied that it is in the wife's best interests to do so and that it will not give rise to any conflict of duty or interest. This approach would seem to be in line with the *obiter* comments of Murphy J. in *Bank of Nova Scotia v. Hogan*[22] where he characterised advice given by a solicitor in a firm which had previously acted for the husband and the bank as 'appropriate legal advice' which would have provided the bank with a defence against any equity to set aside the transaction.

A final point to which reference should be made is that it has been held in England that the need to establish manifest disadvantage in cases of actual undue influence may be dispensed with,[23] although in practice questions of undue influence are only likely to occur when a transaction is disadvantageous either from the outset or as matters turn out.[24] Despite some questioning of the

---

[16] [1994] 1 AC 180.

[17] [1995] 1 All ER 929. In this case the Court of Appeal was satisfied that the bank had taken 'reasonable steps' where it had ensured that the mortgagee received independent legal advice although there had been no separate meeting between her and a representative of the bank unattended by her partner.

[18] [2001] 3 WLR 1021, 1039.

[19] *Ibid.* at 1040.

[20] *Banco Exterior Internacional v. Mann* [1995] 1 All ER 936, *Bank of Baroda v. Rayarel* [1995] 2 FLR 376 and *Barclays Bank plc v. Thomson* [1997] 4 All ER 816.

[21] [2001] 3 WLR 1021, 1044.

[22] [1996] 3 IR 239.

[23] *CIBC Mortgages plc v. Pitt* [1994] 1 AC 200.

[24] *Royal Bank of Scotland v. Etridge (No. 2)* [2001] 3 WLR 1021, 1030, *per* Lord Nicholls.

need to retain the requirement of proving manifest disadvantage in cases of presumed undue influence[25] it would appear that it is this ingredient is still necessary.[26]

Barclays Bank plc v. O'Brien
[1994] 1 AC 180

The second named defendant joined in a charge over the family home jointly owned by her and the first named defendant, her husband, as security for overdraft facilities extended by the plaintiff bank to a company in which her husband had an interest. In the circumstances, it was held that the bank was fixed with constructive notice of the husband's wrongful misrepresentation and the wife was entitled as against the bank to set aside the legal charge on the matrimonial home securing the husband's liability to the bank.

LORD BROWNE-WILKINSON stated at pp.185–199: "My Lords, in this appeal your Lordships for the first time have to consider a problem which has given rise to reported decisions of the Court of Appeal on no less than 11 occasions in the last eight years and which has led to a difference of judicial view. Shortly stated the question is whether a bank is entitled to enforce against a wife an obligation to secure a debt owed by her husband to the bank where the wife has been induced to stand as surety for her husband's debt by the undue influence or misrepresentation of the husband.

The facts
The facts of the present case are very fully set out in the judgment of Scott L.J. in the Court of Appeal [1993] QB 109. I will only state them in summary form. Mr. and Mrs. O'Brien were husband and wife. The matrimonial home, 151, Farnham Lane, Slough, was in their joint names subject to a mortgage of approximately £25,000 to a building society. Mr. O'Brien was a chartered accountant and had an interest in a company, Heathrow Fabrications Ltd. The company's bank account was at the Woolwich branch of Barclays Bank. In the first three months of 1987 the company frequently exceeded its overdraft facility of £40,000 and a number of its cheques were dishonoured on presentation. In discussions in April 1981 between Mr. O'Brien and the manager of the Woolwich branch, Mr. Tucker, Mr. O'Brien told Mr. Tucker that he was

---

[25] *Barclays Bank plc v. Coleman* [2001] QB 20.
[26] As Lord Nicholls commented in *Royal Bank of Scotland v. Etridge (No. 2)* [2001] 3 WLR 1021, 1033, 'something more' is needed before the law reverses the burden of proof in cases of presumed undue influence and in such cases the greater the disadvantage to the vulnerable person, the more cogent must be the explanation before the presumption will be regarded as rebutted.

remortgaging the matrimonial home: Mr. Tucker made a note that Mrs. O'Brien might be a problem. The overdraft limit was raised at that stage to £60,000 for one month. Even though no additional security was provided, by 15 June 1987, the company's overdraft had risen to £98,000 and its cheques were again being dishonoured.

On 22 June 1987, Mr. O'Brien and Mr. Tucker agreed (1) that the company's overdraft limit would be raised to £135,000 reducing to £120,000 after three weeks (2) that Mr. O'Brien would guarantee the company's indebtedness and (3) that Mr. O'Brien's liability would be secured by a second charge on the matrimonial home.

The necessary security documents were prepared by the bank. They consisted of an unlimited guarantee by Mr. O'Brien of the company's liability and a legal charge by both Mr. and Mrs. O'Brien of the matrimonial home to secure any liability of Mr. O'Brien to the bank. Mr. Tucker arranged for the documents, together with a side letter, to be sent to the Burnham branch of the bank for execution by Mr. and Mrs. O'Brien. In a covering memorandum, Mr. Tucker requested the Burnham branch to advise the O'Briens as to the current level of the facilities afforded to the bank (£107,000) and the projected increase to £135,000. The Burnham branch was also asked to ensure that the O'Briens were "fully aware of the nature of the documentation to be signed and advised that if they are in any doubt they should contact their solicitors before signing."

Unfortunately the Burnham branch did not follow Mr. Tucker's instructions. On 1 July, Mr. O'Brien alone signed the guarantee and legal charge at the Burnham branch, the document simply being produced for signature and witnessed by a clerk. On the following day Mrs. O'Brien went to the branch with her husband. There were produced for signature by Mrs. O'Brien, the legal charge on the matrimonial home together with a side letter which reads:

> "We hereby agree acknowledge and confirm as follows: (1) That we have each received from you a copy of the guarantee dated 3 July 1987 (a copy of which is attached hereto) under which Nicholas Edward O'Brien guarantees the payment and discharge of all moneys and liabilities now or hereafter due owing or incurred by Heathrow Fabrications Ltd. to you. (2) That the liability of the said Nicholas Edward O'Brien to you pursuant to the said guarantee is and will be secured by the legal charge dated 3 July 1987 over the property described above made between (1) Nicholas Edward O'Brien (2) Nicholas Edward O'Brien and Bridget Mary O'Brien and (3) Barclays Bank Plc. (3) That you recommended that we should obtain independent legal advice before signing this letter."

In fact the Burnham branch gave Mrs. O'Brien no explanation of the effect of the documents. No one suggested that she should take independent legal advice. She did not read the documents or the side letter. She simply signed the legal charge and side letter and her signature was witnessed by the clerk. She was not given a copy of the guarantee.

The company did not prosper and by October 1987 its indebtedness to the bank was over £154,000. In November 1987 demand was made against Mr.

O'Brien under his guarantee. When the demand was not met, possession proceedings under the legal charge were brought by the bank against Mr. and Mrs. O'Brien. Mrs. O'Brien seeks to defend these proceedings by alleging that she was induced to execute the legal charge on the matrimonial home by the undue influence of Mr. O'Brien and by his misrepresentation. The trial judge, Judge Marder Q.C., and the Court of Appeal rejected the claim based on undue influence: on the appeal to this House the claim based on undue influence is not pursued. However the judge did find that Mr. O'Brien had falsely represented to Mrs. O'Brien that the charge was to secure only £60,000 and that even this liability would be released in a short time when the house was remortgaged. On those findings of fact, the trial judge granted an order for possession against Mrs. O'Brien holding that the bank could not be held responsible for the misrepresentation made by Mr. O'Brien.

The decision of the Court of Appeal

The Court of Appeal (Purchas, Butler-Sloss and Scott L.JJ.) reversed his decision. The leading judgment in the Court of Appeal was given by Scott L.J. who found that there were two lines of authority. One line would afford no special protection to married women: the rights of the creditor bank could only be adversely affected by the wrongful acts of the principal debtor, the husband, in procuring the surety's liability if the principal debtor was acting as the agent of the creditor in procuring the surety to join or the creditor had knowledge of the relevant facts. I will call this theory "the agency theory." The other line of authority detected by Scott L.J. (which I will call "the special equity theory") considers that equity affords special protection to a protected class of surety viz. those where the relationship between the debtor and the surety is such that influence by the debtor over the surety and reliance by the surety on the debtor are natural features of the relationship. In cases where a surety is one of this protected class, the surety obligation is unenforceable by the creditor bank if (1) the relationship between the debtor and the surety was known to the creditor (2) the surety's consent was obtained by undue influence or by misrepresentation or without "an adequate understanding of the nature and effect of the transaction" and (3) the creditor had failed to take reasonable steps to ensure that the surety had given a true and informed consent to the transaction. The Court of Appeal preferred the special equity principle. They held that the legal charge on the O'Brien's matrimonial home was not enforceable by the bank against Mrs. O'Brien save to the extent of the £60,000 which she had thought she was agreeing to secure.

Policy considerations

The large number of cases of this type coming before the courts in recent years reflects the rapid changes in social attitudes and the distribution of wealth which have recently occurred. Wealth is now more widely spread. Moreover a high proportion of privately owned wealth is invested in the matrimonial home.

Because of the recognition by society of the equality of the sexes, the majority of matrimonial homes are now in the joint names of both spouses. Therefore in order to raise finance for the business enterprises of one or other of the spouses, the jointly owned home has become a main source of security. The provision of such security requires the consent of both spouses.

In parallel with these financial developments, society's recognition of the equality of the sexes has led to a rejection of the concept that the wife is subservient to the husband in the management of the family's finances. A number of the authorities reflect an unwillingness in the court to perpetuate law based on this outmoded concept. Yet, as Scott L.J. in the Court of Appeal rightly points out [1993] QB 109, 139, although the concept of the ignorant wife leaving all financial decisions to the husband is outmoded, the practice does not yet coincide with the ideal. In a substantial proportion of marriages it is still the husband who has the business experience and the wife is willing to follow his advice without bringing a truly independent mind and will to bear on financial decisions. The number of recent cases in this field shows that in practice many wives are still subjected to, and yield to, undue influence by their husbands. Such wives can reasonably look to the law for some protection when their husbands have abused the trust and confidence reposed in them.

On the other hand, it is important to keep a sense of balance in approaching these cases. It is easy to allow sympathy for the wife who is threatened with the loss of her home at the suit of a rich bank to obscure an important public interest viz., the need to ensure that the wealth currently tied up in the matrimonial home does not become economically sterile. If the rights secured to wives by the law renders vulnerable loans granted on the security of matrimonial homes, institutions will be unwilling to accept such security, thereby reducing the flow of loan capital to business enterprises. It is therefore essential that a law designed to protect the vulnerable does not render the matrimonial home unacceptable as security to financial institutions.

With these policy considerations in mind I turn to consider the existing state of the law. The whole of modern law is derived from the decision of the Privy Council in *Turnbull & Co. v. Duval* [1902] AC 429 which, as I will seek to demonstrate, provides an uncertain foundation. Before considering that case however, I must consider the law of undue influence which (though not directly applicable in the present case) underlies both *Duval's* case and most of the later authorities.

Undue influence

A person who has been induced to enter into a transaction by the undue influence of another ("the wrongdoer") is entitled to set that transaction aside as against the wrongdoer. Such undue influence is either actual or presumed. In *Bank of Credit and Commerce International S.A. v. Aboody* [1990] 1 QB 923, 953, the Court of Appeal helpfully adopted the following classification.

Class 1: Actual undue influence
In these cases it is necessary for the claimant to prove affirmatively that the wrongdoer exerted undue influence on the complainant to enter into the particular transaction which is impugned.

Class 2: Presumed undue influence
In these cases the complainant only has to show, in the first instance, that there was a relationship of trust and confidence between the complainant and the wrongdoer of such a nature that it is fair to presume that the wrongdoer abused that relationship in procuring the complainant to enter into the impugned transaction. In Class 2 cases therefore there is no need to produce evidence that actual undue influence was exerted in relation to the particular transaction impugned: once a confidential relationship has been proved, the burden then shifts to the wrongdoer to prove that the complainant entered into the impugned transaction freely, for example by showing that the complainant had independent advice. Such a confidential relationship can be established in two ways, viz.

Class 2 (A)
Certain relationships (for example solicitor and client, medical advisor and patient) as a matter of law raise the presumption that undue influence has been exercised.

Class 2 (B)
Even if there is no relationship falling within Class 2(A), if the complainant proves the de facto existence of a relationship under which the complainant generally reposed trust and confidence in the wrongdoer, the existence of such relationship raises the presumption of undue influence. In a Class 2(B) case therefore, in the absence of evidence disproving undue influence, the complainant will succeed in setting aside the impugned transaction merely by proof that the complainant reposed trust and confidence in the wrongdoer without having to prove that the wrongdoer exerted actual undue influence or otherwise abused such trust and confidence in relation to the particular transaction impugned.

As to dispositions by a wife in favour of her husband, the law for long remained in an unsettled state. In the 19th century some judges took the view that the relationship was such that it fell into Class 2(A) i.e. as a matter of law undue influence by the husband over the wife was presumed. It was not until the decisions in *Howes v. Bishop* [1909] 2 KB 390 and *Bank of Montreal v. Stuart* [1911] AC 120 that it was finally determined that the relationship of husband and wife did not as a matter of law raise a presumption of undue influence within Class 2(A). It is to be noted therefore that when the *Duval* case was decided in 1902 the question whether there was a Class 2(A) presumption of undue influence as between husband and wife was still unresolved.

An invalidating tendency?

Although there is no Class 2(A) presumption of undue influence as between husband and wife, it should be emphasised that in any particular case a wife may well be able to demonstrate that de facto she did leave decisions on financial affairs to her husband thereby bringing herself within Class 2(B) i.e. that the relationship between husband and wife in the particular case was such that the wife reposed confidence and trust in her husband in relation to their financial affairs and therefore undue influence is to be presumed. Thus, in those cases which still occur where the wife relies in all financial matters on her husband and simply does what he suggests, a presumption of undue influence within Class 2(B) can be established solely from the proof of such trust and confidence without proof of actual undue influence.

In the appeal in *C.I.B.C. Mortgages Plc. v. Pitt* (judgment in which is to be given immediately after that in the present appeal), post, p. 200, Mr. Price for the wife argued that in the case of transactions between husband and wife, there was an "invalidating tendency" i.e. although there was no Class 2(A) presumption of undue influence, the courts were more ready to find that a husband had exercised undue influence over his wife than in other cases. Scott L.J. in the present case also referred to the law treating married women "more tenderly" than others. This approach is based on dicta in early authorities. In *Grigby v. Cox* (1750) 1 Ves Sen 517 Lord Hardwicke, whilst rejecting any presumption of undue influence, said that a court of equity "will have more jealousy" over dispositions by a wife to a husband. In *Yerkey v. Jones* (1939) 63 CLR 649, 675, Dixon J. refers to this "invalidating tendency." He also refers to the court recognising "the opportunities which a wife's confidence in her husband gives him of unfairly or improperly procuring her to become surety." see p. 677.

In my judgment this special tenderness of treatment afforded to wives by the courts is properly attributable to two factors. First, many cases may well fall into the Class 2(B) category of undue influence because the wife demonstrates that she placed trust and confidence in her husband in relation to her financial affairs and therefore raises a presumption of undue influence. Second, the sexual and emotional ties between the parties provide a ready weapon for undue influence: a wife's true wishes can easily be overborne because of her fear of destroying or damaging the wider relationship between her and her husband if she opposes his wishes.

For myself, I accept that the risk of undue influence affecting a voluntary disposition by a wife in favour of a husband is greater than in the ordinary run of cases where no sexual or emotional ties affect the free exercise of the individual's will.

Undue influence, misrepresentation and third parties

Up to this point I have been considering the right of a claimant wife to set aside a transaction as against the wrongdoing husband when the transaction has been procured by his undue influence. But in surety cases the decisive question is whether the claimant wife can set aside the transaction, not against the wrongdoing husband, but against the creditor bank. Of course, if the wrongdoing husband is acting as agent for the creditor bank in obtaining the surety from the wife, the creditor will be fixed with the wrongdoing of its own agent and the surety contract can be set aside as against the creditor. Apart from this, if the creditor bank has notice, actual or constructive, of the undue influence exercised by the husband (and consequentially of the wife's equity to set aside the transaction) the creditor will take subject to that equity and the wife can set aside the transaction against the creditor (albeit a purchaser for value) as well as against the husband: see *Bainbrigge v. Browne* (1881) 18 Ch D 188 and *Bank of Credit and Commerce International S.A. v. Aboody* [1990] 1 QB 923, 973. Similarly, in cases such as the present where the wife has been induced to enter into the transaction by the husband's misrepresentation, her equity to set aside the transaction will be enforceable against the creditor if either the husband was acting as the creditor's agent or the creditor had actual or constructive notice.

Turnbull & Co. v. Duval [1902] AC 429

This case provides the foundation of the modern law: the basis on which it was decided is, to say the least, obscure. Mr. Duval owed three separate sums to a firm, Turnbull & Co., including £1,000 owed to the Jamaican branch for beer. Turnbulls' manager and agent in Jamaica was a Mr. Campbell. Mr. Campbell was also an executor and trustee of a will under which Mrs. Duval had a beneficial interest. Mr. Campbell threatened to stop supplying beer to Mr. Duval unless security was given for the debts owed and, with Mr. Campbell's knowledge, a document was prepared under which Mrs. Duval charged her beneficial interest under the will to secure the payment of all debts owed by Mr. Duval to Turnbull, i.e., not only the money owed for beer but all the debts. Mr. Duval put pressure on Mrs. Duval to sign the document. She was under the impression that the document was to secure the beer debt only.

The trial judge in the Court of Appeal in Jamaica held that the security document should be set aside as against Turnbulls on the sole ground that Mr. Campbell, as executor of the will, was in a fiduciary capacity *vis-à-vis* his beneficiary, Mrs. Duval, and his employers could not uphold the security document unless they could show that Mrs. Duval was fully aware of what she was doing when she entered into it and did it freely. The Privy Council dismissed Turnbulls' appeal, Lord Lindley expressing the ratio in these terms, at pp. 434-435:

> "In the face of such evidence, their Lordships are of opinion that it is quite impossible to uphold the security given by Mrs. Duval. It is open to the double objection of having been obtained by a trustee from his cestui que trust by pressure through her husband and without independent advice, and of having been

obtained by a husband from his wife by pressure and concealment of material facts. Whether the security could be upheld if the only ground for impeaching it was that Mrs. Duval had no independent advice has not really to be determined. Their Lordships are not prepared to say it could not. But there is an additional and even stronger ground for impeaching it. It is, in their Lordships' opinion, quite clear that Mrs. Duval was pressed by her husband to sign, and did sign, the document, which was very different from what she supposed it to be, and a document of the true nature of which she had no conception. It is impossible to hold that Campbell or Turnbull & Co. are unaffected by such pressure and ignorance. They left everything to Duval, and must abide the consequences."

The first ground mentioned by Lord Lindley (i.e. Campbell's breach of fiduciary duties) raises no problems. It is the second ground which has spawned the whole line of cases with which your Lordships are concerned. It raises two problems. The passage appears to suggest that Mr. Duval had acted in some way wrongfully *vis-à-vis* his wife, and that Turnbulls who "had left everything to Duval" were held liable for Duval's wrong. What was the wrongful act of Duval *vis-à-vis* his wife? Second, why did the fact that Turnbulls "left everything to Duval" render them unable to enforce their security?

Duval's case: was the husband in breach of duty to his wife?
Thanks to the industry of counsel, we have seen the case lodged on the appeal to the Privy Council. The pleadings contain no allegation of undue influence or misrepresentation by Mr. Duval. Mrs. Duval did not in evidence allege actual or presumptive undue influence. The sole ground of decision in the courts below was Campbell's fiduciary position. There is no finding of undue influence against Mr. Duval. No one appeared for Mrs. Duval before the Privy Council. Therefore the second ground of decision sprung wholly from the Board and Lord Lindley's speech gives little insight into their reasoning.

For myself I can only assume that, if the Board considered that Mr. Duval had committed a wrongful act *vis-à-vis* his wife, it proceeded on a mistaken basis. It will be remembered that in 1902 it had not been finally established that a presumption of undue influence within Class 2(A) did not apply as between husband and wife. The Board may therefore have been proceeding on the basis that the presumption of undue influence applied as between Mr. and Mrs. Duval. This was certainly one contemporary understanding of the ratio decidendi: see *Bischoff's Trustee v. Frank* (1903) 89 LT 188. Alternatively, the Board may have been mistakenly applying the heresy propounded by Lord Romilly to the effect that when a person has made a large voluntary disposition the burden is thrown on the party benefiting to show that the disposition was made fairly and honestly and in full understanding of the nature and consequences of the transaction: see *Hoghton v. Hoghton* (1852) 15 Beav 278. Although this heresy has never been formally overruled, it has rightly been regarded as bad law for a very long time: see the account given by Dixon J. in *Yerkey v. Jones* (1930) 63 CLR 649, 678 *et seq*. It is impossible to find a sound basis for holding that Mrs. Duval was entitled to set aside the transaction as against her husband. How then could she set it aside as against Turnbulls?

Duval's case: Was the creditor under a direct duty to the wife?
It is the lack of any sound basis for holding that Mr. Duval was guilty of a legal wrong for which Turnbulls were indirectly held liable which has led to the theory that the creditor, Turnbulls, were themselves in breach of some duty owed by them as creditors directly to the surety, Mrs. Duval. No one has ever suggested that in the ordinary case of principal and surety the creditor owes any duty of care to the surety: in the normal case it is for the surety to satisfy himself as to the nature and extent of the obligations he is assuming. Therefore, it is said, there must be some special feature of the case where a wife stands surety for her husband's debt which gives rise to some special duty. This is the explanation of the decision of Duval's case given by Dixon J. in *Yerkey v. Jones* (1939) 63 CLR 649, 675, which, in turn, is the basis on which the Court of Appeal in the present case adopted the view that the law imposed on the creditor itself a duty to take steps to ensure not only that the husband had not used undue influence or made a misrepresentation but also that the wife had "an adequate understanding of the nature and effect" of what she was doing. If this interpretation of *Duval's* case is correct, the law not only imposes on the creditor a duty *vis-à-vis* a particular class of surety (where ordinarily there would be none) but the extent of that duty is greater than that which, under the ordinary law, a husband would owe to his wife: a transaction between husband and wife cannot, in the absence of undue influence or misrepresentation, be set aside simply on the ground that the wife did not fully understand the transaction.

Duval's case: "They left everything to Duval and must abide the consequences"
These words provide the only guidance as to the circumstances which led the Board to set aside the surety agreement as against Turnbulls. In later cases the words have often been treated as indicating that Mr. Duval (but not Turnbulls themselves) acted in breach of duty to Mrs. Duval, that Mr. Duval was Turnbulls' agent and that Turnbulls could not be in a better position than its agent. Quite apart from the difficulty of identifying what was the breach of duty committed by Mr. Duval, the concept of Mr. Duval having acted as agent for Turnbulls to procure his wife to become surety for the debt was artificial in *Duval's* case itself and in some of the later cases becomes even more artificial. As the Court of Appeal in this case point out, in the majority of cases the reality of the relationship is that, the creditor having required of the principal debtor that there must be a surety, the principal debtor on his own account in order to raise the necessary finance seeks to procure the support of the surety. In so doing he is acting for himself not for the creditor.

The subsequent authorities

The authorities in which the principle derived from the *Duval* case has been applied are fully analysed in the judgment of Scott L.J. and it is unnecessary to review them fully again.

Scott L.J. analyses the cases as indicating that down to 1985 there was no decision which indicated that the agency theory, rather than the special equity theory, was the basis of the decision in *Duval*. I agree. But that is attributable more to the application of the *Duval* principle than to any analysis of its jurisprudential basis. The only attempts to analyse the basis of the decision in *Duval's* case were the Australian decisions in *Bank of Victoria Ltd. v. Mueller* [1925] VLR 642 and the judgment of Dixon J. in *Yerkey v. Jones* (1939) 63 CLR 649. The former decision was reached by applying the Romilly heresy which, as I have already said, is bad law. The judgment of Dixon J. undoubtedly supports the special equity theory.

From 1985 down to the decision of the Court of Appeal in the present case the decisions have all been based on the agency theory i.e. that the principal debtor has acted in breach of duty to his wife, the surety, and that, if the principal debtor was acting as the creditor's agent but not otherwise, the creditor cannot be in any better position than its agent, the husband. In all the cases since 1985 the principal debtor has procured the agreement of the surety by a legal wrong (undue influence or misrepresentation). In all the cases emphasis was placed on the question whether the creditor was infected by the debtor's wrongdoing because the debtor was acting as the agent of the creditor in procuring the wife's agreement to stand as surety. I am unable to agree with Scott L.J. that the decision in *Kings North Trust Ltd. v. Bell* [1986] 1 WLR 119 was not based on the agency theory: Dillon L.J., at p. 123F-G, expressly makes it a necessary condition that the creditor has entrusted to the husband the task of obtaining his wife's signature.

However, in four of the cases since 1985 attention has been drawn to the fact that, even in the absence of agency, if the debtor has been guilty of undue influence or misrepresentation the creditor may not be able to enforce the surety contract if the creditor had notice, actual or constructive, of the debtor's conduct: see *Avon Finance Co. Ltd. v. Bridger* [1985] 2 All ER 281, *per* Brandon L.J., at p. 287E; *Coldunell Ltd. v. Gallon* [1986] QB 1184, 1201; *Midland Bank Plc. v. Shephard* [1988] 3 All ER 17, 23; *Bank of Credit and Commerce International S.A. v. Aboody* [1990] 1 QB 923, 973. As will appear, in my view it is the proper application of the doctrine of notice which provides the key to finding a principled basis for the law.

Accordingly, the present law is built on the unsure foundations of the *Duval* case. Like most law founded on obscure and possibly mistaken foundations it has developed in an artificial way, giving rise to artificial distinctions and conflicting decisions. In my judgment your Lordships should seek to restate the law in a form which is principled, reflects the current requirements of society and provides as much certainty as possible.

Conclusions
(a) Wives

My starting point is to clarify the basis of the law. Should wives (and perhaps others) be accorded special rights in relation to surety transactions by the recognition of a special equity applicable only to such persons engaged in such transactions? Or should they enjoy only the same protection as they would enjoy in relation to their other dealings? In my judgment, the special equity theory should be rejected. First, I can find no basis in principle for affording special protection to a limited class in relation to one type of transaction only. Second, to require the creditor to prove knowledge and understanding by the wife in all cases is to reintroduce by the back door either a presumption of undue influence of Class 2(A) (which has been decisively rejected) or the Romilly heresy (which has long been treated as bad law). Third, although Scott L.J. found that there were two lines of cases one of which supported the special equity theory, on analysis although many decisions are not inconsistent with that theory the only two cases which support it are *Yerkey v. Jones* (1939) 63 CLR 649, and the decision of the Court of Appeal in the present case. Finally, it is not necessary to have recourse to a special equity theory for the proper protection of the legitimate interests of wives as I will seek to show.

In my judgment, if the doctrine of notice is properly applied, there is no need for the introduction of a special equity in these types of cases.

A wife who has been induced to stand as a surety for her husband's debts by his undue influence, misrepresentation or some other legal wrong has an equity as against him to set aside that transaction. Under the ordinary principles of equity, her right to set aside that transaction will be enforceable against third parties (e.g. against a creditor) if either the husband was acting as the third party's agent or the third party had actual or constructive notice of the facts giving rise to her equity. Although there may be cases where, without artificiality, it can properly be held that the husband was acting as the agent of the creditor in procuring the wife to stand as surety, such cases will be of very rare occurrence. The key to the problem is to identify the circumstances in which the creditor will be taken to have had notice of the wife's equity to set aside the transaction.

The doctrine of notice lies at the heart of equity. Given that there are two innocent parties, each enjoying rights, the earlier right prevails against the later right if the acquirer of the later right knows of the earlier right (actual notice) or would have discovered it had he taken proper steps (constructive notice). In particular, if the party asserting that he takes free of the earlier rights of another knows of certain facts which put him on inquiry as to the possible existence of the rights of that other and he fails to make such inquiry or take such other steps as are reasonable to verify whether such earlier right does or does not exist, he will have constructive notice of the earlier right and take subject to it. Therefore where a wife has agreed to stand surety for her husband's debts as a result of undue influence or misrepresentation, the creditor will take subject to the wife's equity to set aside the transaction if the circumstances are such as to put the creditor on inquiry as to the circumstances in which she agreed to stand surety.

It is at this stage that, in my view, the "invalidating tendency" or the law's "tender treatment" of married women, becomes relevant. As I have said above in dealing with undue influence, this tenderness of the law towards married women is due to the fact that, even today, many wives repose confidence and trust in their husbands in relation to their financial affairs. This tenderness of the law is reflected by the fact that voluntary dispositions by the wife in favour of her husband are more likely to be set aside than other dispositions by her: a wife is more likely to establish presumed undue influence of Class 2(B) by her husband than by others because, in practice, many wives do repose in their husbands trust and confidence in relation to their financial affairs. Moreover the informality of business dealings between spouses raises a substantial risk that the husband has not accurately stated to the wife the nature of the liability she is undertaking, i.e., he has misrepresented the position, albeit negligently.

Therefore in my judgment a creditor is put on inquiry when a wife offers to stand surety for her husband's debts by the combination of two factors: (a) the transaction is on its face not to the financial advantage of the wife; and (b) there is a substantial risk in transactions of that kind that, in procuring the wife to act as surety, the husband has committed a legal or equitable wrong that entitles the wife to set aside the transaction.

It follows that unless the creditor who is put on inquiry takes reasonable steps to satisfy himself that the wife's agreement to stand surety has been properly obtained, the creditor will have constructive notice of the wife's rights.

What, then are the reasonable steps which the creditor should take to ensure that it does not have constructive notice of the wife's rights, if any? Normally the reasonable steps necessary to avoid being fixed with constructive notice consist of making inquiry of the person who may have the earlier right (i.e. the wife) to see whether such right is asserted. It is plainly impossible to require of banks and other financial institutions that they should inquire of one spouse whether he or she has been unduly influenced or misled by the other. But in my judgment the creditor, in order to avoid being fixed with constructive notice, can reasonably be expected to take steps to bring home to the wife the risk she is running by standing as surety and to advise her to take independent advice. As to past transactions, it will depend on the facts of each case whether the steps taken by the creditor satisfy this test. However for the future in my judgment a creditor will have satisfied these requirements if it insists that the wife attend a private meeting (in the absence of the husband) with a representative of the creditor at which she is told of the extent of her liability as surety, warned of the risk she is running and urged to take independent legal advice. If these steps are taken in my judgment the creditor will have taken such reasonable steps as are necessary to preclude a subsequent claim that it had constructive notice of the wife's rights. I should make it clear that I have been considering the ordinary case where the creditor knows only that the wife is to stand surety for her husband's debts. I would not exclude exceptional cases where a creditor has knowledge of further facts which render the presence of undue influence not only possible but probable. In such cases, the creditor to be safe will have to insist that the wife is separately advised. I am conscious that in treating the creditor as having constructive notice because of the risk of Class 2(B) undue influence or misrepresentation by the husband I may be extending the law as stated by Fry J. in *Bainbrigge v. Browne* (1881) 18 Ch D 188, 197, and the Court of Appeal in the *Aboody* case [1990] 1 QB 923, 973. Those cases suggest that for a third party to be affected by constructive notice of presumed undue influence the third party must actually know of the circumstances which give rise to a presumption of undue influence. In contrast, my view is that the risk of Class 2(B) undue influence or misrepresentation is sufficient to put the creditor on inquiry. But my statement accords with the principles of notice: if the known facts are such as to indicate the possibility of an adverse claim that is sufficient to put a third party on inquiry.

If the law is established as I have suggested, it will hold the balance fairly between on the one hand the vulnerability of the wife who relies implicitly on her husband and, on the other hand, the practical problems of financial institutions asked to accept a secured or unsecured surety obligation from the wife for her husband's debts. In the context of suretyship, the wife will not have any right to disown her obligations just because subsequently she proves that she did not fully understand the transaction: she will, as in all other areas of her affairs, be bound by her obligations unless her husband has, by misrepresentation, undue influence or other wrong, committed an actionable wrong against her. In the normal case, a financial institution will be able to lend with confidence in reliance on the wife's surety obligation provided that it warns her (in the absence of the husband) of the amount of her potential liability and of the risk of standing surety and advises her to take independent advice.

Mr. Jarvis, for the bank, urged that this is to impose too heavy a burden on financial institutions. I am not impressed by this submission. The Report by Professor Jack's Review Committee on Banking Services: Law and Practice (1989) (Cmnd. 622), recommended that prospective guarantors should be adequately warned of the legal effects and possible consequences of their guarantee and of the importance of receiving independent advice. Pursuant to this recommendation, the Code of Banking Practice (adopted by banks and building societies in March 1992) provides in paragraph 12.1 as follows:

> "Banks and building societies will advise private individuals proposing to give them a guarantee or other security for another person's liabilities that: (i) by giving the guarantee or third party security he or she might become liable instead of or as well as that other person; (ii) he or she should seek independent legal advice before entering into the guarantee or third party security. Guarantees and other third party security forms will contain a clear and prominent notice to the above effect."

Thus good banking practice (which applies to all guarantees, not only those given by a wife) largely accords with what I consider the law should require when a wife is offered as surety. The only further substantial step required by law beyond that good practice is that the position should be explained by the bank to the wife in a personal interview. I regard this as being essential because a number of the decided cases show that written warnings are often not read and are sometimes intercepted by the husband. It does not seem to me that the requirement of a personal interview imposes such an additional administrative burden as to render the bank's position unworkable.

(b) Other persons
I have hitherto dealt only with the position where a wife stands surety for her husband's debts. But in my judgment the same principles are applicable to all other cases where there is an emotional relationship between cohabitees. The "tenderness" shown by the law to married women is not based on the marriage ceremony but reflects the underlying risk of one cohabitee exploiting the emotional involvement and trust of the other. Now that unmarried cohabitation, whether heterosexual or homosexual, is widespread in our society, the law should recognise this. Legal wives are not the only group which are now exposed to the emotional pressure of cohabitation. Therefore if, but only if, the creditor is aware that the surety is cohabiting with the principal debtor, in my judgment the same principles should apply to them as apply to husband and wife.

In addition to the cases of cohabitees, the decision of the Court of Appeal in *Avon Finance Co. Ltd. v. Bridger* [1985] 2 All ER 281 shows (rightly in my view) that other relationships can give rise to a similar result. In that case a son, by means of misrepresentation, persuaded his elderly parents to stand surety for his debts. The surety obligation was held to be unenforceable by the creditor inter alia because to the bank's knowledge the parents trusted the son in their financial dealings. In my judgment that case was rightly decided: in a case where the creditor is aware that the surety reposes trust and confidence in the principal debtor in relation to his financial affairs, the creditor is put on inquiry in just the same way as it is in relation to husband and wife.

Summary
I can therefore summarise my views as follows. Where one cohabitee has entered into an obligation to stand as surety for the debts of the other cohabitee and the creditor is aware that they are cohabitees: (1) the surety obligation will be valid and enforceable by the creditor unless the suretyship was procured by the undue influence, misrepresentation or other legal wrong of the principal debtor; (2) if there has been undue influence, misrepresentation or other legal wrong by the principal debtor, unless the creditor has taken reasonable steps to satisfy himself that the surety entered into the obligation freely and in knowledge of the true facts, the creditor will be unable to enforce the surety

obligation because he will be fixed with constructive notice of the surety's right to set aside the transaction; (3) unless there are special exceptional circumstances, a creditor will have taken such reasonable steps to avoid being fixed with constructive notice if the creditor warns the surety (at a meeting not attended by the principal debtor) of the amount of her potential liability and of the risks involved and advises the surety to take independent legal advice.

I should make it clear that in referring to the husband's debts I include the debts of a company in which the husband (but not the wife) has a direct financial interest.

The decision of this case

Applying those principles to this case, to the knowledge of the bank Mr. and Mrs. O'Brien were man and wife. The bank took a surety obligation from Mrs. O'Brien, secured on the matrimonial home, to secure the debts of a company in which Mr. O'Brien was interested but in which Mrs. O'Brien had no direct pecuniary interest. The bank should therefore have been put on inquiry as to the circumstances in which Mrs. O'Brien had agreed to stand as surety for the debt of her husband. If the Burnham branch had properly carried out the instructions from Mr. Tucker of the Woolwich branch, Mrs. O'Brien would have been informed that she and the matrimonial home were potentially liable for the debts of a company which had an existing liability of £107,000 and which was to be afforded an overdraft facility of £135,000. If she had been told this, it would have counteracted Mr. O'Brien's misrepresentation that the liability was limited to £60,000 and would last for only three weeks. In addition according to the side letter she would have been recommended to take independent legal advice.

Unfortunately Mr. Tucker's instructions were not followed and to the knowledge of the bank (through the clerk at the Burnham branch) Mrs. O'Brien signed the documents without any warning of the risks or any recommendation to take legal advice. In the circumstances the bank (having failed to take reasonable steps) is fixed with constructive notice of the wrongful misrepresentation made by Mr. O'Brien to Mrs. O'Brien. Mrs. O'Brien is therefore entitled as against the bank to set aside the legal charge on the matrimonial home securing her husband's liability to the bank.

For these reasons I would dismiss the appeal with costs."

Bank of Nova Scotia v. Hogan
[1996] 3 IR 239

The first named defendant borrowed money from the plaintiff on the security of equitable mortgages created over properties which he owned. Subsequently in return for releasing the security over two of these properties, the plaintiff took an equitable mortgage over a further property owned by the second named defendant, the first named defendant's wife. Prior to depositing the title deeds, a solicitor from a firm which had acted for the second named defendant and her husband in the past, and also for the bank from time to time, explained to her that the plaintiff would be entitled to sell the property in the event of her husband's default. The plaintiff sought and obtained a declaration, *inter alia*, that certain sums were secured by the equitable mortgage created by the deposit of the title deeds by the second named defendant. The defendants' appeal was dismissed by the Supreme Court.

MURPHY J stated at pp.242–249: "This is an appeal against the order and judgment of Keane J. made and given herein on the 21st December, 1992.

The order made by Keane J. declared that the sum of £263,992.77 was secured, first, by the equitable mortgage created by the deposit made on the 2nd February, 1987, by the first defendant, Ben Hogan, of the deeds to the lands specified at numbers 1 and 2 in the schedule to the order (the premises known as 77 Roebuck Downs, Dublin 14, and 32 Brookevale Downs, Rathfarnham, Dublin 14) on Mr. Hogan's interest in the said lands and premises and, secondly, by the equitable mortgage created by the deposit made on the 26th May, 1987, by the second defendant, Margaret Hogan, of the title deeds to the lands described as number 3 in the said schedule (being the lands and premises known as St. Rita's, Kilternan, Co. Dublin) on Mrs. Hogan's interest in those premises. The order of Keane J. went on to set out the directions and provisions ordinarily contained in a primary order in mortgage proceedings.

The particular issue which Keane J. tried on oral evidence evolved from a pleading contained in para. 7 of the defence filed by the defendants herein on the 25th October, 1991. Having averred that Mrs. Hogan did not give any security to the plaintiff, the pleadings went on to allege as follows:

> "If the second defendant did give any such security (which is denied) which was valid (which is denied) same was obtained from her improperly or unconscionably and by reason of the inequality of bargaining power which existed between herself and the plaintiff and by reason of its undue influence over her and ought to be declared void on that account and by reason of the fact that the plaintiff by its servants or agents represented and agreed that as a condition of and in return for a deposit of title deeds by her they would advance the sum of £75,000 to the first defendant or to Drefflane Associates Ltd. if he so directed, which advance the plaintiff failed or refused to make."

The background against which that issue fell to be considered may be summarised by reference to the judgment of the learned trial judge in the following terms. On the 23rd January, 1987, the plaintiff (the Bank) agreed to advance the sum of £150,000 to the first defendant (Mr. Hogan). As security for that advance Mr. Hogan made an equitable deposit with the Bank of the title deeds to three residential properties which he owned, i.e., numbers 69 and 77 Roebuck Downs, Goatstown Road, Dublin 14, and 32 Brookevale Downs, Rathfarnham, Dublin 14. The sum was duly advanced and on the 28th

January, 1988, the amount due by Mr. Hogan on foot of the advance to the Bank including interest, was £189,285.79. On that date, by agreement between the Bank and Mr. Hogan, the then existing facility was converted into a term loan from the Bank to Mr. Hogan in the sum of £190,000 which was to be repaid with interest in five equal annual instalments, the first instalment to be paid one year from the date of the agreement.

The title deeds to St. Rita's, Kilternan, were deposited with the Bank on the 26th May, 1989, by Mrs. Hogan and controversy existed as to the purpose for which such deposit was made or perhaps, more particularly, the extent of the security which it was intended thereby to create.

It is common case that the advance in January, 1987, was made to Mr. Hogan to enable him to purchase as an investment the two properties, namely 77 Roebuck Downs and 32 Brookevale Downs. Mr. Hogan was also a controlling shareholder of a company called Drefflane Associates Ltd. ("the company"). The company was advanced substantial sums from time to time by the Bank. Ultimately the Bank called in its loans to the company and, payment not being forthcoming, appointed a receiver under the powers in that behalf contained in the mortgage debenture which they held over the assets and undertaking of the company. It was part of the defence of Mr. and Mrs. Hogan that the Bank was at all times in a fiduciary position in relation to them and also exercised a position of dominance over them. Mr. and Mrs. Hogan contended that the sum claimed by the Bank was not a loan to Mr. Hogan but was part of, and related to, the finances made available to the company and that the Bank negligently and in breach of its fiduciary duty so acted in relation to the company as to render it incapable of carrying on business.

In 1989, Mr. Hogan wished to sell two of the properties the title deeds to which had been lodged by him with the Bank by way of security, namely, number 69 and 77 Roebuck Downs. The Bank contended that they had agreed to release the two properties from the equitable mortgage provided that the title deeds of St. Rita's were lodged with them in substitution for the deeds of the properties being sold. In the event only number 69 was sold and the title deeds of St. Rita's were undoubtedly deposited with the Bank. Mr. and Mrs. Hogan put forward a different explanation of the arrangement. They said that the Bank had agreed to advance the sum of £75,000 on the security of the deeds of St. Rita's and further that this loan would be repaid out of the profits of the company. The borrowers maintained that they had been assured that this was a temporary arrangement and that the deeds would be returned to Mrs. Hogan within a few months. More particularly the defendants contend that Mrs. Hogan made the deposit when she was acting under the influence of the Bank and without independent legal advice.

It was not disputed that Mrs. Hogan purchased St. Rita's for a sum in the order of £79,000 of which approximately £71,000 was made available to her by the company. The amount so paid by the company to Mrs. Hogan – with the knowledge of the Bank – represented the repayment of monies advanced by her to the company to pay staff wages from time to time. Messrs. Orpen Franks & Co., solicitors, acted for Mr. and Mrs. Hogan in relation to the purchase of the various properties with which these proceedings are concerned. In addition they acted for the Bank from time to time. Arrangements were made for Mrs. Hogan to deposit with the Bank the title deeds to St. Rita's. The deposit was to be made on the 26th May, 1989. A few days before that Mr. Jackson of Orpen Franks & Co. told Mrs. Hogan that the title deeds were required by the Bank to secure the advances made to Mr. Hogan. Some discussion took place between Mr. Jackson and Mrs. Hogan in the course of that conversation in relation to the transaction.

On the occasion of the deposit on the 26th May, 1989, there was present Mr. John Farrell a manager of the Bank, Mr. Brian Perry, the area manager of the Bank of Ireland, Mr. Hogan, Mrs. Hogan and Mr. Edward Hickey, then a solicitor in the firm of Orpen Franks & Co.

There is a significant dispute between the parties as to what took place on that occasion. Mrs. Hogan gave positive evidence as to her understanding as to the bargain between the parties and the extent of the security which she had agreed to provide. It was her evidence that the security was limited to the sum of £75,000 which was to be advanced by the Bank to Mr. Hogan or the company. It was the evidence of the officers of the Bank and of Mr. Hickey that the security was to extend without limitation to any indebtedness on the part of either Mr. Hogan or Mrs. Hogan. On that fundamental issue of primary fact the trial judge found in favour of the Bank and rejected the version put forward on behalf of the defendants.

In addition Mr. Hickey gave evidence of the fact that he had explained to Mrs. Hogan at the meeting in the Bank that she was under no obligation to make the deposit which she did in fact make on that date but that, if she did so, the Bank would be entitled to sell the property in the event of a default by her husband. Mr. Hickey's evidence in that respect was confirmed by Mr. Farrell and it was supported by a detailed memorandum prepared and signed by Mr. Hickey some five days afterwards, which memorandum was admitted in evidence. Again the learned trial judge accepted the evidence of Mr. Hickey to the effect that he had given advice in the terms set out in the memorandum.

Whilst the greater part of the argument before this Court (and much of the judgment of the learned trial judge) related to the sufficiency of the advice given by Mr. Hickey, or indeed Mr. Jackson, to Mrs. Hogan it must be recognised that once Mrs. Hogan's version of the events was rejected there was no evidential basis to ground an argument that she had been misled or overborne or would or might have acted differently in the event of her obtaining more comprehensive legal advice.

The independence of the advice was challenged on the basis that Messrs. Orpen Franks & Co. had undoubtedly and admittedly acted for the Bank in relation to other matters. Apart from any potential conflict of interest, it was contended on behalf of the defendants that the circumstances in which the advices – if that is what they were – were given were so unsatisfactory as to render the advice worthless. The complaint was made that the consultation between Mr. Hickey and Mrs. Hogan took place in the Bank and in the presence of its officials and more particularly it took place at a time when Mrs. Hogan was effectively committed to the transaction. It was argued that independent legal advice should be given privately and in good time so that a client could, without undue embarrassment, withdraw from a transaction if that was to be the outcome of the advice given to her or to him.

Objections were also made to the content of the advices or information provided for Mrs. Hogan. It is clear that what Mr. Hickey did was to explain to Mrs. Hogan the legal consequences of making the deposit of title deeds. It was not suggested by him that he offered any advice as to the prudence of engaging in such a transaction and, indeed, he very fairly conceded that he knew nothing whatever of the financial affairs of Mr. and Mrs. Hogan or how the relationship between Mr. Hogan and the company might impinge upon the transaction.

The learned trial judge concluded that the Bank had ensured that advice available to Mrs. Hogan was adequate in all the circumstances. The learned judge also pointed out that the transaction could be viewed, *quoad* Mrs. Hogan, as a normal banking transaction, as that expression was explained by Lord Scarman speaking in the House of Lords in *National Westminster Bank plc v. Morgan* [1985] AC 686, and in that event no special relationship or position of dominance on the part of the Bank would arise which would require the giving of independent legal advice.

In this Court, the onus on the Bank to prove the validity of the equitable mortgage or, alternatively, the obligation on it to provide advice, was explored by reference to two cases, one Irish and the other English which were decided and reported subsequent to the judgment of the learned trial judge, namely *Bank of Ireland v. Smyth* [1995] 2 IR 459 and *Barclays Bank plc v. O'Brien* in which the decision of the Court of Appeal was reported at [1993] QB 109 and that of the House of Lords at [1994] 1 AC 180.

Whilst there is a similarity between the facts in *Bank of Ireland v. Smyth* [1995] 2 IR 459, and certain of the facts in the present case, there is also a fundamental difference which renders the Irish case of little assistance in resolving the problems which arise here.

Bank of Ireland v. Smyth [1995] 2 IR 459 did concern a dealing by a spouse with a matrimonial home in circumstances which were likely to be – as the events proved – to her detriment and that of the family. Those facts indicate the resemblance with the situation in which Mrs. Hogan found herself. On the other hand the crucial distinction is that Mrs. Hogan was dealing with property of which she was the owner whereas Mrs. Smyth was being asked to give, and purported to give, her consent under s. 3 of the Family Home Protection Act, 1976, to a mortgage of the family home by her husband. Whilst it might appear that a person dealing with his or her own property is entitled to as much protection as a person called upon to give a consent in relation to a dealing with the property by another, that is not the case. The analysis made by Blayney J. of the Act of 1976 and in particular s. 3 thereof shows why this is not the case. As a result of s. 3, sub-s. 1 of the Act of 1976 certain dispositions of an interest in a family home are void unless the purported conveyance by one spouse is made with the consent of the other. From that statutory provision two consequences flow, first, that a grantee or purchaser must, in his own interest, ensure that the necessary statutory consent is forthcoming and, secondly, that the consent, if given, is a true consent, that is to say, constitutes a decision which represents a fully free exercise of the independent will of the spouse concerned. Thus, cases turning on the adequacy of a consent required and alleged to have been given under the Family Home Protection Act, 1976, are distinguishable from those in which it is alleged that a spouse in the dealing with his or her own property did, or may have, acted under undue influence.

The decision in *Barclays Bank plc v. O'Brien* [1994] 1 AC 180 is, however, both relevant and helpful.

In that case, the first and second defendants therein, a husband and wife, agreed to execute a second mortgage of their matrimonial home as security for overdraft facilities extended by the plaintiff to a company in which the husband, but not the wife, had an interest. The wife signed the deed of mortgage without reading it, in reliance on her husband's false representation that it was limited to £60,000 and would last only three weeks. When the company's overdraft exceeded £154,000 the bank sought to enforce the mortgage and obtained an order for possession thereof. The judge of the High Court dismissed the wife's appeal, holding that since there was no evidence that in deceiving his wife the husband was acting on behalf of the bank, the bank could not be held responsible for his misrepresentation and therefore the charge was enforceable against her. That decision was reversed on appeal to the Court of Appeal and their decision was upheld by the House of Lords. The lengthy judgments delivered in the Court of Appeal, and in particular that of Scott L.J., reviewing the numerous, and sometimes conflicting, authorities in relation to the presumption or possible presumption of undue influence by a husband over his wife demonstrate the difficult problems which exist in this area of the law.

In the single speech delivered in the House of Lords by Lord Browne-Wilkinson, an effort was made to resolve conflicting principles which had been identified in the Court of Appeal. No difficulty arises in relation to the well established propositions identified by him, namely that:

(i)   As between the innocent party and the alleged wrongdoer, the burden of proving the exercise of undue influence falls on the innocent party.

(ii)   There are, however, recognised categories of relationships within which there is a presumption that the alleged wrongdoer has abused his position so that the onus is on him to prove that such was not the case.

(iii) The decision in *Bank of Montreal v. Stuart* [1911] AC 120 determined that the relationship between husband and wife did not as a matter of law raise a presumption of undue influence by a husband over his wife.

Notwithstanding the fact that the relationship of husband and wife has been held not to raise a presumption of undue influence, some special status does appear to have been accorded to wives in a variety of decided cases. Scott L.J. referred to married women being treated by the law "more tenderly" than others and in the Australian case of *Yerkey v. Jones* (1939) 63 CLR 649, Dixon J. referred to "the invalidating tendency" applied by the courts in relation to transactions between a husband and wife. The consequence appears to be that whilst the matrimonial relationship as such does not give rise to a presumption of undue influence it may be possible to identify circumstances in a particular case which would more readily raise that presumption in favour of a wife than any outside party. I confess that I do not find the conclusions of the House of Lords in this regard satisfying as a matter of legal logic or fully acceptable as an analysis of the rights or capabilities of women generally and married women in particular.

However, the issue in the present case does not immediately concern the rights as between husband and wife but as between a creditor or other third party and the wife. These rights were analysed by Lord Browne-Wilkinson at p. 195 of the report in the following terms:

> "A wife who has been induced to stand as a surety for her husband's debts by his undue influence, misrepresentation or some other legal wrong has an equity against him to set aside that transaction. Under the ordinary principles of equity, her right to set aside that transaction will be enforceable against third parties (e.g. against a creditor) if either the husband was acting as the third party's agent or the third party had actual or constructive notice of the facts giving rise to her equity . . . The doctrine of notice lies at the heart of equity. Given that there are two innocent parties, each enjoying rights, the earlier right prevails against the later right if the acquirer of the later right knows of the earlier right (actual notice) or would have discovered it had he taken proper steps (constructive notice). In particular, if the party asserting that he takes free of the earlier rights of another knows of certain facts which put him on inquiry as to the possible existence of the rights of that other and he fails to make such inquiry or take such other steps as are reasonable to verify whether such earlier right does or does not exist, he will have constructive notice of the earlier right and take subject to it."

I would adopt and apply that reasoning to the facts of the present case. The House of Lords went on to apply the "invalidating tendency" and "tender treatment" principles to the facts of that case and concluded that, having regard to the nature of the transaction guaranteed by the wife and the absence of any financial advantage to her, there was a presumption of undue influence so that the creditor was put on enquiry to satisfy himself that the wife's agreement to stand surety had been properly obtained. By failing to make those enquiries, Barclays Bank had constructive notice of the rights of the wife. The conclusion was expressed by Lord Browne-Wilkinson in the following terms (page 196):

> "Therefore where a wife has agreed to stand surety for her husband's debts as a

result of undue influence or misrepresentation, the creditor will take subject to the wife's equity to set aside the transaction if the circumstances are such as to put the creditor on enquiry as to the circumstances in which she agreed to stand surety."

Assuming, without deciding, that married women in this jurisdiction may in certain circumstances enjoy as against their husbands a presumption that undue influence was exercised and allowing that those circumstances existed in the present case, the fatal flaw in Mrs. Hogan's case is that no undue influence was exercised by her husband and that she has no equity against him to have the transaction set aside and, that being so, she has no prior equity on which she can rely in order to defeat the Bank's claim. The availability of appropriate independent legal advice to Mrs. Hogan would afford the Bank a defence on a claim by her in respect of an equity to set aside the transaction if such equity had existed. But Mrs. Hogan had no equity. She did not allege that her husband misrepresented the situation or exercised undue influence over her. This is confirmed by the fact that she and her husband instructed the same solicitors and counsel to represent them.

With regard to the allegation that the Bank itself exercised undue influence over Mrs. Hogan this was completely unsupported by any evidence. There was no evidence that any officer of the Bank advised Mrs. Hogan that the borrowing would be limited to £75,000 or that the security would be released after a limited period. Moreover, Mrs. Hogan's evidence to the effect that this was her belief was rejected by the learned trial judge. The relationship between the Bank and Mrs. Hogan did not of itself give rise to a presumption of undue influence and no evidence was given as to the dealings between them which would raise an inference of any such wrongdoing. So far from it, it appears that Mrs. Hogan was contacted in relation to the deposit through her solicitor, Mr. Jackson, and she was attended in the Bank on the occasion when the deposit was made by Mr. Jackson's deputy, Mr. Hickey. There does not appear to have been any opportunity for the exercise of undue influence less still any evidence that it was so exercised.

In these circumstances it seems to me that the appeal must be dismissed."

Royal Bank of Scotland v. Etridge (No. 2)
[2001] 3 WLR 1021

In a number of cases wives charged their interests in their homes in favour of financial institutions as security for their husbands' indebtedness or the indebtedness of a company through which he carried on business. When the banks sought to enforce the charges, the wives raised the defence that they had signed them as a result of the undue influence of their husbands. The House of Lords heard a number of appeals together and set out the principles which should apply in such cases.

LORD NICHOLLS stated at pp. 1028–1044:

"My Lords, Before your Lordships' House are appeals in eight cases. Each case arises out of a transaction in which a wife charged her interest in her home in favour of a bank as security for her husband's indebtedness or the indebtedness of a company through which he carried on business. The wife later asserted she signed the charge under the undue influence of her husband. In *Barclays Bank plc v. O'Brien* [1994] 1 AC 180 your Lordships enunciated the principles applicable in this type of case. Since then, many cases have come before the courts, testing the implications of the *O'Brien* decision in a variety of different factual situations. Seven of the present appeals are of this character. In each case the bank sought to enforce the charge signed by the wife. The bank claimed an order for possession of the matrimonial home. The wife raised a defence that the bank was on notice that her concurrence in the transaction had been procured by her husband's undue influence. The eighth appeal concerns a claim by a wife for damages from a solicitor who advised her before she entered into a guarantee obligation of this character.

Undue influence
The issues raised by these appeals make it necessary to go back to first principles. Undue influence is one of the grounds of relief developed by the courts of equity as a court of conscience. The objective is to ensure that the influence of one person over another is not abused. In everyday life people constantly seek to influence the decisions of others. They seek to persuade those with whom they are dealing to enter into transactions, whether great or small. The law has set limits to the means properly employable for this purpose. To this end the common law developed a principle of duress. Originally this was narrow in its scope, restricted to the more blatant forms of physical coercion, such as personal violence.

Here, as elsewhere in the law, equity supplemented the common law. Equity extended the reach of the law to other unacceptable forms of persuasion. The law will investigate the manner in which the intention to enter into the transaction was secured: 'how the intention was produced', in the oft repeated words of Lord Eldon LC, from as long ago as 1807 (*Huguenin v. Baseley* (1807) 14 Ves 273, 300). If the intention was produced by an unacceptable means, the law will not permit the transaction to stand. The means used is regarded as an exercise of improper or 'undue' influence, and hence unacceptable, whenever the consent thus procured ought not fairly to be treated as the expression of a person's free will. It is impossible to be more precise or definitive. The circumstances in which one person acquires influence over another, and the manner in which influence may be exercised, vary too widely to permit of any more specific criterion.

Equity identified broadly two forms of unacceptable conduct. The first comprises overt acts of improper pressure or coercion such as unlawful threats. Today there is much overlap with the principle of duress as this principle has subsequently developed. The second form arises out of a relationship between two persons where one has acquired over another a measure of influence, or ascendancy, of which the ascendant person then takes unfair advantage. An example from the 19th century, when much of this law developed, is a case where an impoverished father prevailed upon his inexperienced children to charge their reversionary interests under their parents' marriage settlement with payment of his mortgage debts: see *Bainbrigge v. Browne* (1881) 18 Ch D 188.

In cases of this latter nature the influence one person has over another provides scope for misuse without any specific overt acts of persuasion. The relationship between two individuals may be such that, without more, one of them is disposed to agree a course of action proposed by the other. Typically this occurs when one person places trust in another to look after his affairs and interests, and the latter betrays this trust by preferring his own interests. He abuses the influence he has acquired. In *Allcard v. Skinner* (1887) 36 Ch D 145, a case well known to every law student, Lindley LJ, at p 181, described this class of cases as those in which it was the duty of one party to advise the other or to manage his property for him. In *Zamet v. Hyman* [1961] 1 WLR 1442, 1444-1445 Lord Evershed MR referred to relationships where one party owed the other an obligation of candour and protection.

The law has long recognised the need to prevent abuse of influence in these 'relationship' cases despite the absence of evidence of overt acts of persuasive conduct. The types of relationship, such as parent and child, in which this principle falls to be applied cannot be listed exhaustively. Relationships are infinitely various. Sir Guenter Treitel QC has rightly noted that the question is whether one party has reposed sufficient trust and confidence in the other, rather than whether the relationship between the parties belongs to a particular type: see *Treitel, The Law of Contract*, 10th ed (1999), pp 380-381. For example, the relation of banker and customer will not normally meet this criterion, but exceptionally it may: see *National Westminster Bank Plc v. Morgan* [1985] AC 686, 707-709.

Even this test is not comprehensive. The principle is not confined to cases of abuse of trust and confidence. It also includes, for instance, cases where a vulnerable person has been exploited. Indeed, there is no single touchstone for determining whether the principle is applicable. Several expressions have been used in an endeavour to encapsulate the essence: trust and confidence, reliance, dependence or vulnerability on the one hand and ascendancy, domination or control on the other. None of these descriptions is perfect. None is all embracing. Each has its proper place.

In *CIBC Mortgages Plc v. Pitt* [1994] 1 AC 200 your Lordships' House decided that in cases of undue influence disadvantage is not a necessary ingredient of the cause of action. It is not essential that the transaction should be disadvantageous to the pressurised or influenced person, either in financial terms or in any other way. However, in the nature of things, questions of undue influence will not usually arise, and the exercise of undue influence is unlikely to occur, where the transaction is innocuous. The issue is likely to arise only when, in some respect, the transaction was disadvantageous either from the outset or as matters turned out.

Burden of proof and presumptions

Whether a transaction was brought about by the exercise of undue influence is a question of fact. Here, as elsewhere, the general principle is that he who asserts a wrong has been committed must prove it. The burden of proving an allegation of undue influence rests upon the person who claims to have been wronged. This is the general rule. The evidence required to discharge the burden of proof depends on the nature of the alleged undue influence, the personality of the parties, their relationship, the extent to which the transaction cannot readily be accounted for by the ordinary motives of ordinary persons in that relationship, and all the circumstances of the case.

Proof that the complainant placed trust and confidence in the other party in relation to the management of the complainant's financial affairs, coupled with a transaction which calls for explanation, will normally be sufficient, failing satisfactory evidence to the contrary, to discharge the burden of proof. On proof of these two matters the stage is set for the court to infer that, in the absence of a satisfactory explanation, the transaction can only have been procured by undue influence. In other words, proof of these two facts is prima facie evidence that the defendant abused the influence he acquired in the parties' relationship. He preferred his own interests. He did not behave fairly to the other. So the evidential burden then shifts to him. It is for him to produce evidence to counter the inference which otherwise should be drawn.

The case of *Bainbrigge v. Browne* (1881) 18 Ch D 188, already mentioned, provides a good illustration of this commonplace type of forensic exercise. Fry J. held, at p 196, that there was no direct evidence upon which he could rely as proving undue pressure by the father. But there existed circumstances 'from which the court will infer pressure and undue influence.' None of the children were entirely emancipated from their father's control. None seemed conversant with business. These circumstances were such as to cast the burden of proof upon the father. He had made no attempt to discharge that burden. He did not appear in court at all. So the children's claim succeeded. Again, more recently, in *National Westminster Bank Plc v. Morgan* [1985] AC 686, 707, Lord Scarman noted that a relationship of banker and customer may become one in which a banker acquires a dominating influence. If he does, and a manifestly disadvantageous transaction is proved, 'there would then be room' for a court to presume that it resulted from the exercise of undue influence.

Generations of equity lawyers have conventionally described this situation as one in which a presumption of undue influence arises. This use of the term 'presumption' is descriptive of a shift in the evidential onus on a question of fact. When a plaintiff succeeds by this route he does so because he has succeeded in establishing a case of undue influence. The court has drawn appropriate inferences of fact upon a balanced consideration of the whole of the evidence at the end of a trial in which the burden of proof rested upon the plaintiff. The use, in the course of the trial, of the forensic tool of a shift in the evidential burden of proof should not be permitted to obscure the overall position. These cases are the equitable counterpart of common law cases where the principle of res ipsa loquitur is invoked. There is a rebuttable evidential presumption of undue influence.

The availability of this forensic tool in cases founded on abuse of influence arising from the parties' relationship has led to this type of case sometimes being labelled 'presumed undue influence'. This is by way of contrast with cases involving actual pressure or the like, which are labelled 'actual undue influence': see *Bank of Credit and Commerce International SA v. Aboody* [1990] 1 QB 923, 953, and *Royal Bank of Scotland Plc v. Etridge (No. 2)* [1998] 4 All ER 705, 711-712, paras 5-7. This usage can be a little confusing. In many cases where a plaintiff has claimed that the defendant abused the influence he acquired in a relationship of trust and confidence the plaintiff has succeeded by recourse to the rebuttable evidential presumption. But this need not be so. Such a plaintiff may succeed even where this presumption is not available to him; for instance, where the impugned transaction was not one which called for an explanation.

The evidential presumption discussed above is to be distinguished sharply from a different form of presumption which arises in some cases. The law has adopted a sternly protective attitude towards certain types of relationship in which one party acquires influence over another who is vulnerable and dependent and where, moreover, substantial gifts by the influenced or vulnerable person are not normally to be expected. Examples of relationships within this special class are parent and child, guardian and ward, trustee and beneficiary, solicitor and client, and medical adviser and patient. In these cases the law presumes, irrebuttably, that one party had influence over the other. The complainant need not prove he actually reposed trust and confidence in the other party. It is sufficient for him to prove the existence of the type of relationship.

It is now well established that husband and wife is not one of the relationships to which this latter principle applies. In *Yerkey v. Jones* (1939) 63 CLR 649, 675 Dixon J. explained the reason. The Court of Chancery was not blind to the opportunities of obtaining and unfairly using influence over a wife which a husband often possesses. But there is nothing unusual or strange in a wife, from motives of affection or for other reasons, conferring substantial financial benefits on her husband. Although there is no presumption, the court will nevertheless note, as a matter of fact, the opportunities for abuse which flow from a wife's confidence in her husband. The court will take this into account with all the other evidence in the case. Where there is evidence that a husband has taken unfair advantage of his influence over his wife, or her confidence in him, 'it is not difficult for the wife to establish her title to relief': see *In re Lloyds Bank Ltd, Bomze v. Bomze* [1931] 1 Ch 289, at p 302, per Maugham J.

Independent advice

Proof that the complainant received advice from a third party before entering into the impugned transaction is one of the matters a court takes into account when weighing all the evidence. The weight, or importance, to be attached to such advice depends on all the circumstances. In the normal course, advice from a solicitor or other outside adviser can be expected to bring home to a complainant a proper understanding of what he or she is about to do. But a person may understand fully the implications of a proposed transaction, for instance, a substantial gift, and yet still be acting under the undue influence of another. Proof of outside advice does not, of itself, necessarily show that the subsequent completion of the transaction was free from the exercise of undue influence. Whether it will be proper to infer that outside advice had an emancipating effect, so that the transaction was not brought about by the exercise of undue influence, is a question of fact to be decided having regard to all the evidence in the case.

Manifest disadvantage

As already noted, there are two prerequisites to the evidential shift in the burden of proof from the complainant to the other party. First, that the complainant reposed trust and confidence in the other party, or the other party acquired ascendancy over the complainant. Second, that the transaction is not readily explicable by the relationship of the parties.

Lindley L.J. summarised this second prerequisite in the leading authority of *Allcard v. Skinner* (1887) 36 Ch D 145, where the donor parted with almost all her property. Lindley L.J. pointed out that where a gift of a small amount is made to a person standing in a confidential relationship to the donor, some proof of the exercise of the influence of the donee must be given. The mere existence of the influence is not enough. He continued, at p 185:

> 'But if the gift is so large as not to be reasonably accounted for on the ground of friendship, relationship, charity, or other ordinary motives on which ordinary men act, the burden is upon the donee to support the gift.'

In *Bank of Montreal v. Stuart* [1911] AC 120, 137 Lord Macnaghten used the phrase 'immoderate and irrational' to describe this concept.

The need for this second prerequisite has recently been questioned: see Nourse L.J. in *Barclays Bank Plc v. Coleman* [2001] QB, 20, 30-32, one of the cases under appeal before your Lordships' House. Mr Sher QC invited your Lordships to depart from the decision of the House on this point in *National Westminster Bank Plc v. Morgan* [1985] AC 686.

My Lords, this is not an invitation I would accept. The second prerequisite, as expressed by Lindley L.J., is good sense. It is a necessary limitation upon the width of the first prerequisite. It would be absurd for the law to presume that every gift by a child to a parent, or every transaction between a client and his solicitor or between a patient and his doctor, was brought about by undue influence unless the contrary is affirmatively proved. Such a presumption would be too far-reaching. The law would be out of touch with everyday life if the presumption were to apply to every Christmas or birthday gift by a child to a parent, or to an agreement whereby a client or patient agrees to be responsible for the reasonable fees of his legal or medical adviser. The law would be rightly open to ridicule, for transactions such as these are unexceptionable. They do not suggest that something may be amiss. So something more is needed before the law reverses the burden of proof, something which calls for an explanation. When that something more is present, the greater the disadvantage to the vulnerable person, the more cogent must be the explanation before the presumption will be regarded as rebutted.

This was the approach adopted by Lord Scarman in *National Westminster Bank Plc v. Morgan* [1985] AC 686, 703–707. He cited Lindley L.J.'s observations in *Allcard v. Skinner* (1887) 36 Ch D 145, 185, which I have set out above. He noted that whatever the legal character of the transaction, it must constitute a disadvantage sufficiently serious to require evidence to rebut the presumption that in the circumstances of the parties' relationship, it was procured by the exercise of undue influence. Lord Scarman concluded, at p 704:

> 'The Court of Appeal erred in law in holding that the presumption of undue influence can arise from the evidence of the relationship of the parties without also evidence that the transaction itself was wrongful in that it constituted *an advantage taken of the person subjected to the influence which, failing proof to the contrary, was explicable only on the basis that undue influence had been exercised to procure it.*' (Emphasis added)

Lord Scarman attached the label 'manifest disadvantage' to this second ingredient necessary to raise the presumption. This label has been causing difficulty. It may be apt enough when applied to straightforward transactions such as a substantial gift or a sale at an undervalue. But experience has now shown that this expression can give rise to misunderstanding. The label is being understood and applied in a way which does not accord with the meaning intended by Lord Scarman, its originator.

The problem has arisen in the context of wives guaranteeing payment of their husband's business debts. In recent years judge after judge has grappled with the baffling question whether a wife's guarantee of her husband's bank overdraft, together with a charge on her share of the matrimonial home, was a transaction manifestly to her disadvantage.

In a narrow sense, such a transaction plainly ('manifestly') is disadvantageous to the wife. She undertakes a serious financial obligation, and in return she personally receives nothing. But that would be to take an unrealistically blinkered view of such a transaction. Unlike the relationship of solicitor and client or medical adviser and patient, in the case of husband and wife there are inherent reasons why such a transaction may well be for her benefit. Ordinarily, the fortunes of husband and wife are bound up together. If the husband's business is the source of the family income, the wife has a lively interest in doing what she can to support the business. A wife's affection and self-interest run hand-in-hand in inclining her to join with her husband in charging the matrimonial home, usually a jointly-owned asset, to obtain the financial facilities needed by the business. The finance may be needed to start a new business, or expand a promising business, or rescue an ailing business.

Which, then, is the correct approach to adopt in deciding whether a transaction is disadvantageous to the wife: the narrow approach, or the wider approach? The answer is neither. The answer lies in discarding a label which gives rise to this sort of ambiguity. The better approach is to adhere more directly to the test outlined by Lindley L.J. in *Allcard v. Skinner* (1887) 36 Ch D 145, and adopted by Lord Scarman in *National Westminster Bank Plc v. Morgan* [1985] AC 686, in the passages I have cited.

I return to husband and wife cases. I do not think that, *in the ordinary course*, a guarantee of the character I have mentioned is to be regarded as a transaction which, failing proof to the contrary, is explicable only on the basis that it has been procured by the exercise of undue influence by the husband. Wives frequently enter into such transactions. There are good and sufficient reasons why they are willing to do so, despite the risks involved for them and their families. They may be enthusiastic. They may not. They may be less optimistic than their husbands about the prospects of the husbands' businesses. They may be anxious, perhaps exceedingly so. But this is a far cry from saying that such transactions as a class are to be regarded as prima facie evidence of the exercise of undue influence by husbands.

I have emphasised the phrase 'in the ordinary course'. There will be cases where a wife's signature of a guarantee or a charge of her share in the matrimonial home does call for explanation. Nothing I have said above is directed at such a case.

A cautionary note

I add a cautionary note, prompted by some of the first instance judgments in the cases currently being considered by the House. It concerns the general approach to be adopted by a court when considering whether a wife's guarantee of her husband's bank overdraft was procured by her husband's undue influence. Undue influence has a connotation of impropriety. In the eye of the law, undue influence means that influence has been misused. Statements or conduct by a husband which do not pass beyond the bounds of what may be expected of a reasonable husband in the circumstances should not, without more, be castigated as undue influence. Similarly, when a husband is forecasting the future of his business, and expressing his hopes or fears, a degree of hyperbole may be only natural. Courts should not too readily treat such exaggerations as misstatements.

Inaccurate explanations of a proposed transaction are a different matter. So are cases where a husband, in whom a wife has reposed trust and confidence for the management of their financial affairs, prefers his interests to hers and makes a choice for both of them on that footing. Such a husband abuses the influence he has. He fails to discharge the obligation of candour and fairness he owes a wife who is looking to him to make the major financial decisions.

The complainant and third parties: suretyship transactions
The problem considered in *O'Brien's* case and raised by the present appeals is of comparatively recent origin. It arises out of the substantial growth in home ownership over the last 30 or 40 years and, as part of that development, the great increase in the number of homes owned jointly by husbands and wives. More than two-thirds of householders in the United Kingdom now own their own homes. For most home-owning couples, their homes are their most valuable asset. They must surely be free, if they so wish, to use this asset as a means of raising money, whether for the purpose of the husband's business or for any other purpose. Their home is their property. The law should not restrict them in the use they may make of it. Bank finance is in fact by far the most important source of external capital for small businesses with fewer than ten employees. These businesses comprise about 95 percent of all businesses in the country, responsible for nearly one-third of all employment. Finance raised by second mortgages on the principal's home is a significant source of capital for the start-up of small businesses.

If the freedom of home-owners to make economic use of their homes is not to be frustrated, a bank must be able to have confidence that a wife's signature of the necessary guarantee and charge will be as binding upon her as is the signature of anyone else on documents which he or she may sign. Otherwise banks will not be willing to lend money on the security of a jointly owned house or flat.

At the same time, the high degree of trust and confidence and emotional interdependence which normally characterises a marriage relationship provides scope for abuse. One party may take advantage of the other's vulnerability. Unhappily, such abuse does occur. Further, it is all too easy for a husband, anxious or even desperate for bank finance, to misstate the position in some particular or to mislead the wife, wittingly or unwittingly, in some other way. The law would be seriously defective if it did not recognise these realities.

In *O'Brien's* case this House decided where the balance should be held between these competing interests. On the one side, there is the need to protect a wife against a husband's undue influence. On the other side, there is the need for the bank to be able to have reasonable confidence in the strength of its security. Otherwise it would not provide the required money. The problem lies in finding the course best designed to protect wives in a minority of cases without unreasonably hampering the giving and taking of security. The House produced a practical solution. The House decided what are the steps a bank should take to ensure it is not affected by any claim the wife may have that her signature of the documents was procured by the undue influence or other wrong of her husband. Like every compromise, the outcome falls short of achieving in full the objectives of either of the two competing interests. In particular, the steps required of banks will not guarantee that, in future, wives will not be subjected to undue influence or misled when standing as sureties. Short of prohibiting this type of suretyship transaction altogether, there is no way of achieving that result, desirable although it is. What passes between a husband and wife in this regard in the privacy of their own home is not capable of regulation or investigation as a prelude to the wife entering into a suretyship transaction.

The jurisprudential route by which the House reached its conclusion in *O'Brien's* case has attracted criticism from some commentators. It has been said to involve artificiality and thereby create uncertainty in the law. I must first consider this criticism. In the ordinary course a bank which takes a guarantee security from the wife of its customer will be altogether ignorant of any undue influence the customer may have exercised in order to secure the wife's concurrence. In *O'Brien* Lord Browne-Wilkinson prayed in aid the doctrine of constructive notice. In circumstances he identified, a creditor is put on inquiry. When that is so, the creditor 'will have constructive notice of the wife's rights' unless the creditor takes reasonable steps to satisfy himself that the wife's agreement to stand surety has been properly obtained: see [1994] 1 AC 180, 196.

Lord Browne-Wilkinson would be the first to recognise this is not a conventional use of the equitable concept of constructive notice. The traditional use of this concept concerns the circumstances in which a transferee of property who acquires a legal estate from a transferor with a defective title may nonetheless obtain a good title, that is, a better title than the transferor had. That is not the present case. The bank acquires its charge from the wife, and there is nothing wrong with her title to her share of the matrimonial home. The transferor wife is seeking to resile from the very transaction she entered into with the bank, on the ground that her apparent consent was procured by the undue influence or other misconduct, such as misrepresentation, of a third party (her husband). She is seeking to set aside her contract of guarantee and, with it, the charge she gave to the bank.

The traditional view of equity in this tripartite situation seems to be that a person in the position of the wife will only be relieved of her bargain if the other party to the transaction (the bank, in the present instance) was privy to the conduct which led to the wife's entry into the transaction. Knowledge is required: see *Cobbett v. Brock* (1855) 20 Beav 524, 528, 531, per Sir John Romilly MR, *Kempson v. Ashbee* (1874) LR 10 Ch App 15, 21, per James LJ, and *Bainbrigge v. Browne* (1881) 18 Ch D 188, 197, per Fry J. The law imposes no obligation on one party to a transaction to check whether the other party's concurrence was obtained by undue influence. But *O'Brien* has introduced into the law the concept that, in certain circumstances, a party to a contract may lose the benefit of his contract, entered into in good faith, if he *ought* to have known that the other's concurrence had been procured by the misconduct of a third party.

There is a further respect in which *O'Brien* departed from conventional concepts. Traditionally, a person is *deemed* to have notice (that is, he has 'constructive' notice) of a prior right when he does not actually know of it but would have learned of it had he made the requisite inquiries. A purchaser will be treated as having constructive notice of all that a reasonably prudent purchaser would have discovered. In the present type of case, the steps a bank is required to take, lest it have constructive notice that the wife's concurrence was procured improperly by her husband, do not consist of making inquiries. Rather, *O'Brien* envisages that the steps taken by the bank will reduce, or even eliminate, the risk of the wife entering into the transaction under any misapprehension or as a result of undue influence by her husband. The steps are not concerned to discover whether the wife has been wronged by her husband in this way. The steps are concerned to minimise the risk that such a wrong may be committed.

These novelties do not point to the conclusion that the decision of this House in *O'Brien* is leading the law astray. Lord Browne-Wilkinson acknowledged he might be extending the law: see [1994] 1 AC 180, 197. Some development was sorely needed. The law had to find a way of giving wives a reasonable measure of protection, without adding unreasonably to the expense involved in entering into guarantee transactions of the type under consideration. The protection had to extend also to any misrepresentations made by a husband to his wife. In a situation where there is a substantial risk the husband may exercise his influence improperly regarding the provision of security for his business debts, there is an increased risk that explanations of the transaction given by him to his wife may be misleadingly incomplete or even inaccurate.

The route selected in *O'Brien* ought not to have an unsettling effect on established principles of contract. *O'Brien* concerned suretyship transactions. These are tripartite transactions. They involve the debtor as well as the creditor and the guarantor. The guarantor enters into the transaction at the request of the debtor. The guarantor assumes obligations. On the face of the transaction the guarantor usually receives no benefit in return, unless the guarantee is being given on a commercial basis. Leaving aside cases where the relationship between the surety and the debtor is commercial, a guarantee transaction is one-sided so far as the guarantor is concerned. The creditor knows this. Thus the decision in *O'Brien* is directed at a class of contracts which has special features of its own. That said, I must at a later stage in this speech return to the question of the wider implications of the *O'Brien* decision.

The threshold: when the bank is put on inquiry

In *O'Brien* the House considered the circumstances in which a bank, or other creditor, is 'put on inquiry.' Strictly this is a misnomer. As already noted, a bank is not required to make inquiries. But it will be convenient to use the terminology which has now become accepted in this context. The House set a low level for the threshold which must be crossed before a bank is put on inquiry. For practical reasons the level is set much lower than is required to satisfy a court that, failing contrary evidence, the court may infer that the transaction was procured by undue influence. Lord Browne-Wilkinson said ([1994] 1 AC 180, 196):

> 'Therefore in my judgment a creditor is put on inquiry when a wife offers to stand surety for her husband's debts by the combination of two factors: (a) the transaction is on its face not to the financial advantage of the wife; and (b) there is a substantial risk in transactions of that kind that, in procuring the wife to act as surety, the husband has committed a legal or equitable wrong that entitles the wife to set aside the transaction.'

In my view, this passage, read in context, is to be taken to mean, quite simply, that a bank is put on inquiry whenever a wife offers to stand surety for her husband's debts.

The Court of Appeal, comprising Stuart-Smith, Millett and Morritt LJJ, interpreted this passage more restrictively. The threshold, the court said, is somewhat higher. Where condition (a) is satisfied, the bank is put on inquiry if, but only if, the bank is aware that the parties are cohabiting or that the particular surety places implicit trust and confidence in the principal debtor in relation to her financial affairs: see *Royal Bank of Scotland Plc v. Etridge (No. 2)* [1998] 4 All ER 705, 719.

I respectfully disagree. I do not read (a) and (b) as factual conditions which must be proved in each case before a bank is put on inquiry. I do not understand Lord Browne-Wilkinson to have been saying that, in husband and wife cases, whether the bank is put on inquiry depends on its state of knowledge of the parties' marriage, or of the degree of trust and confidence the particular wife places in her husband in relation to her financial affairs. That would leave banks in a state of considerable uncertainty in a situation where it is important they should know clearly where they stand. The test should be simple and clear and easy to apply in a wide range of circumstances. I read (a) and (b) as Lord Browne-Wilkinson's broad explanation of the reason why a creditor is put on inquiry when a wife offers to stand surety for her husband's debts. These are the two factors which, taken together, constitute the underlying rationale.

The position is likewise if the husband stands surety for his wife's debts. Similarly, in the case of unmarried couples, whether heterosexual or homosexual, where the bank is aware of the relationship: see Lord Browne-Wilkinson in *O'Brien's* case, at p 198. Cohabitation is not essential. The Court of Appeal rightly so decided in *Massey v. Midland Bank Plc* [1995] 1 All ER

929: see Steyn LJ, at p 933.

As to the type of transactions where a bank is put on inquiry, the case where a wife becomes surety for her husband's debts is, in this context, a straightforward case. The bank is put on inquiry. On the other side of the line is the case where money is being advanced, or has been advanced, to husband and wife jointly. In such a case the bank is not put on inquiry, unless the bank is aware the loan is being made for the husband's purposes, as distinct from their joint purposes. That was decided in *CIBC Mortgages Plc v. Pitt* [1994] 1 AC 200.

Less clear cut is the case where the wife becomes surety for the debts of a company whose shares are held by her and her husband. Her shareholding may be nominal, or she may have a minority shareholding or an equal shareholding with her husband. In my view the bank is put on inquiry in such cases, even when the wife is a director or secretary of the company. Such cases cannot be equated with joint loans. The shareholding interests, and the identity of the directors, are not a reliable guide to the identity of the persons who actually have the conduct of the company's business.

The steps a bank should take
The principal area of controversy on these appeals concerns the steps a bank should take when it has been put on inquiry. In *O'Brien* Lord Browne-Wilkinson, at [1994] 1 AC 180, 196-197, said that a bank can reasonably be expected to take steps to bring home to the wife the risk she is running by standing as surety and to advise her to take independent advice. That test is applicable to *past* transactions. All the cases now before your Lordships' House fall into this category. For the *future* a bank satisfies these requirements if it insists that the wife attend a private meeting with a representative of the bank at which she is told of the extent of her liability as surety, warned of the risk she is running and urged to take independent legal advice. In exceptional cases the bank, to be safe, has to insist that the wife is separately advised.

The practice of the banks involved in the present cases, and it seems reasonable to assume this is the practice of banks generally, is not to have a private meeting with the wife. Nor do the banks themselves take any other steps to bring home to the wife the risk she is running. This has continued to be the practice since the decision in *O'Brien's* case. Banks consider they would stand to lose more than they would gain by holding a private meeting with the wife. They are, apparently, unwilling to assume the responsibility of advising the wife at such a meeting. Instead, the banking practice remains, as before, that in general the bank requires a wife to seek legal advice. The bank seeks written confirmation from a solicitor that he has explained the nature and effect of the documents to the wife.

Many of the difficulties which have arisen in the present cases stem from serious deficiencies, or alleged deficiencies, in the quality of the legal advice given to the wives. I say 'alleged', because three of the appeals before your

Lordships' House have not proceeded beyond the interlocutory stage. The banks successfully applied for summary judgment. In these cases the wife's allegations, made in affidavit form, have not been tested by cross-examination. On behalf of the wives it has been submitted that under the current practice the legal advice is often perfunctory in the extreme and, further, that everyone, including the banks, knows this. Independent legal advice is a fiction. The system is a charade. In practice it provides little or no protection for a wife who is under a misapprehension about the risks involved or who is being coerced into signing. She may not even know the present state of her husband's indebtedness.

My Lords, it is plainly neither desirable nor practicable that banks should be required to attempt to discover for themselves whether a wife's consent is being procured by the exercise of undue influence of her husband. This is not a step the banks should be expected to take. Nor, further, is it desirable or practicable that banks should be expected to insist on confirmation from a solicitor that the solicitor has satisfied himself that the wife's consent has not been procured by undue influence. As already noted, the circumstances in which banks are put on inquiry are extremely wide. They embrace every case where a wife is entering into a suretyship transaction in respect of her husband's debts. Many, if not most, wives would be understandably outraged by having to respond to the sort of questioning which would be appropriate before a responsible solicitor could give such a confirmation. In any event, solicitors are not equipped to carry out such an exercise in any really worthwhile way, and they will usually lack the necessary materials. Moreover, the legal costs involved, which would inevitably fall on the husband who is seeking financial assistance from the bank, would be substantial. To require such an intrusive, inconclusive and expensive exercise in every case would be an altogether disproportionate response to the need to protect those cases, presumably a small minority, where a wife is being wronged.

The furthest a bank can be expected to go is to take reasonable steps to satisfy itself that the wife has had brought home to her, in a meaningful way, the practical implications of the proposed transaction. This does not wholly eliminate the risk of undue influence or misrepresentation. But it does mean that a wife enters into a transaction with her eyes open so far as the basic elements of the transaction are concerned.

This is the point at which, in the *O'Brien* case, the House decided that the balance between the competing interests should be held. A bank may itself provide the necessary information directly to the wife. Indeed, it is best equipped to do so. But banks are not following that course. Ought they to be obliged to do so in every case? I do not think Lord Browne-Wilkinson so stated in *O'Brien*. I do not understand him to have said that a personal meeting was the only way a bank could discharge its obligation to bring home to the wife the risks she is running. It seems to me that, provided a suitable alternative is available, banks ought not to be compelled to take this course. Their reasons for not wishing to hold a personal meeting are understandable. Commonly, when a bank seeks to enforce a security provided by a customer, it is met with a defence based on assurances alleged to have been given orally by a branch manager at an earlier stage: that the bank would continue to support the business, that the bank would not call in its loan, and so forth. Lengthy litigation ensues. Sometimes the allegations prove to be well founded, sometimes not. Banks are concerned to avoid the prospect of similar litigation which would arise in guarantee cases if they were to adopt a practice of holding a meeting with a wife at which the bank's representative would explain the proposed guarantee transaction. It is not unreasonable for the banks to prefer that this task should be undertaken by an independent legal adviser.

I shall return later to the steps a bank should take when it follows this course. Suffice to say, these steps, together with advice from a solicitor acting for the wife, ought to provide the substance of the protection which *O'Brien* intended a wife should have. Ordinarily it will be reasonable that a bank should be able to rely upon confirmation from a solicitor, acting for the wife, that he has advised the wife appropriately.

The position will be otherwise if the bank knows that the solicitor has not duly advised the wife or, I would add, if the bank knows facts from which it ought to have realised that the wife has not received the appropriate advice. In such circumstances the bank will proceed at its own risk.

The content of the legal advice

In *Royal Bank of Scotland Plc v. Etridge (No. 2)* [1998] 4 All ER 705, 715, para 19, the Court of Appeal set out its views of the duties of a solicitor in this context:

> 'A solicitor who is instructed to advise a person who may be subject to the undue influence of another must bear in mind that it is not sufficient that she understands the nature and effect of the transaction if she is so affected by the influence of the other that she cannot make an independent decision of her own. It is not sufficient to explain the documentation and ensure she understands the nature of the transaction and wishes to carry it out: see *Powell v. Powell* [1900] 1 Ch 243, 247, approved in *Wright v. Carter* [1903] 1 Ch 27. His duty is to satisfy himself that his client is free from improper influence, and the first step must be to ascertain whether it is one into which she could sensibly be advised to enter if free from such influence. If he is not so satisfied, it is his duty to advise her not to enter into it, and to refuse to act further for her in the implementation of the transaction if she persists. In this event, while the contents of his advice must remain confidential, he should inform the other parties (including the bank) that he has seen his client and given her certain advice, and that as a result he has declined to act for her any further. He must in any event advise her that she is under no obligation to enter into the transaction at all and, if she still wishes to do so, that she is not bound to accept the terms of any document which has been put before her: see *Credit Lyonnais Bank Nederland NV v. Burch* [1997] 1 All ER 144.'

I am unable to accept this as an accurate formulation of a solicitor's duties in cases such as those now under consideration. In some respects it goes much too far. The observations of Farwell J. in *Powell v. Powell* [1900] 1 Ch 243, 247, should not be pressed unduly widely. *Powell v. Powell* was a case where strong moral pressure was applied by a stepmother to a girl who was only just twenty one. She was regarded as not really capable of dealing irrevocably with her parent or guardian in the matter of a substantial settlement. Farwell J's observations cannot be regarded as of general application in all cases where a solicitor is giving advice to a person who may have been subject to undue influence.

More pertinently, in *In re Coomber, Coomber v. Coomber* [1911] 1 Ch 723, 730, Fletcher Moulton L.J. summarised the general rules applicable to cases of persons who are competent to form an opinion of their own:

> 'All that is necessary is that some independent person, free from any taint of the relationship, or of the consideration of interest which would affect the act, should put clearly before the person what are the nature and the consequences of the act. It is for adult persons of competent mind to decide whether they will do an act, and I do not think that independent and competent advice means independent and competent approval. It simply means that the advice shall be removed entirely from the suspected atmosphere; and that from the clear language of an independent mind, they should know precisely what they are doing.'

Thus, in the present type of case it is not for the solicitor to veto the transaction by declining to confirm to the bank that he has explained the documents to the wife and the risks she is taking upon herself. If the solicitor considers the transaction is not in the wife's best interests, he will give reasoned advice to the wife to that effect. But at the end of the day the decision on whether to proceed is the decision of the client, not the solicitor. A wife is not to be precluded from entering into a financially unwise transaction if, for her own reasons, she wishes to do so.

That is the general rule. There may, of course, be exceptional circumstances where it is glaringly obvious that the wife is being grievously wronged. In such a case the solicitor should decline to act further. In *Wright v. Carter* [1903] 1 Ch 27, 57-58, Stirling L.J. approved Farwell J's observations in *Powell v. Powell* [1900] 1 Ch 243, 247. But he did so by reference to the extreme example of a poor man divesting himself of all his property in favour of his solicitor.

In *Royal Bank of Scotland Plc v. Etridge (No. 2)* [1998] 4 All ER 705, 722, para 49, the Court of Appeal said that if the transaction is 'one into which no competent solicitor could properly advise the wife to enter', the availability of legal advice is insufficient to avoid the bank being fixed with constructive notice. It follows from the views expressed above that I am unable to agree with the Court of Appeal on this point.

I turn to consider the scope of the responsibilities of a solicitor who is advising the wife. In identifying what are the solicitor's responsibilities the starting point must always be the solicitor's retainer. What has he been retained to do? As a general proposition, the scope of a solicitor's duties is dictated by the terms, whether express or implied, of his retainer. In the type of case now under consideration the relevant retainer stems from the bank's concern to receive confirmation from the solicitor that, in short, the solicitor has brought home to the wife the risks involved in the proposed transaction. As a first step the solicitor will need to explain to the wife the purpose for which he has become involved at all. He should explain that, should it ever become necessary, the bank will rely upon his involvement to counter any suggestion that the wife was overborne by her husband or that she did not properly understand the implications of the transaction. The solicitor will need to obtain confirmation from the wife that she wishes him to act for her in the matter and to advise her on the legal and practical implications of the proposed transaction.

When an instruction to this effect is forthcoming, the content of the advice required from a solicitor before giving the confirmation sought by the bank will, inevitably, depend upon the circumstances of the case. Typically, the advice a solicitor can be expected to give should cover the following matters as the core minimum. (1) He will need to explain the nature of the documents and the practical consequences these will have for the wife if she signs them. She could lose her home if her husband's business does not prosper. Her home may be her only substantial asset, as well as the family's home. She could be made bankrupt. (2) He will need to point out the seriousness of the risks involved. The wife should be told the purpose of the proposed new facility, the amount and principal terms of the new facility, and that the bank might increase the amount of the facility, or change its terms, or grant a new facility, without reference to her. She should be told the amount of her liability under her guarantee. The solicitor should discuss the wife's financial means, including her understanding of the value of the property being charged. The solicitor should discuss whether the wife or her husband has any other assets out of which repayment could be made if the husband's business should fail. These matters are relevant to the seriousness of the risks involved. (3) The solicitor will need to state clearly that the wife has a choice. The decision is hers and hers alone. Explanation of the choice facing the wife will call for some discussion of the present financial position, including the amount of the husband's present indebtedness, and the amount of his current overdraft facility. (4) The solicitor should check whether the wife wishes to proceed. She should be asked whether she is content that the solicitor should write to the bank confirming he has explained to her the nature of the documents and the practical implications they may have for her, or whether, for instance, she would prefer him to negotiate with the bank on the terms of the transaction. Matters for negotiation could include the sequence in which the various securities will be called upon or a specific or lower limit to her liabilities. The solicitor should not give any confirmation to the bank without the wife's authority.

The solicitor's discussion with the wife should take place at a face-to-face meeting, in the absence of the husband. It goes without saying that the solicitor's explanations should be couched in suitably non-technical language. It also goes without saying that the solicitor's task is an important one. It is not a formality.

The solicitor should obtain from the bank any information he needs. If the bank fails for any reason to provide information requested by the solicitor, the solicitor should decline to provide the confirmation sought by the bank.

As already noted, the advice which a solicitor can be expected to give must depend on the particular facts of the case. But I have set out this 'core minimum' in some detail, because the quality of the legal advice is the most disturbing feature of some of the present appeals. The perfunctory nature of the advice may well be largely due to a failure by some solicitors to understand what is required in these cases.

Independent advice
I turn next to the much-vexed question whether the solicitor advising the wife must act for the wife alone. Or, at the very least, the solicitor must not act for the husband or the bank in the current transaction save in a wholly ministerial capacity, such as carrying out conveyancing formalities or supervising the execution of documents and witnessing signatures. Commonly, in practice, the solicitor advising the wife will be the solicitor acting also for her husband either in the particular transaction or generally.

The first point to note is that this question cannot be answered by reference to reported decisions. The steps a bank must take once it is put on inquiry, if it is to avoid having constructive notice of the wife's rights, are not the subject of exposition in earlier authority. This is a novel situation, created by the *O'Brien* decision.

Next, a simple and clear rule is needed, preferably of well nigh universal application. In some cases a bank deals directly with a husband and wife and has to take the initiative in requiring the wife to obtain legal advice. In other cases, a bank may deal throughout with solicitors already acting for the husband and wife. The case of *Bank of Baroda v. Rayarel* [1995] 2 FLR 376 is an example of the latter type of case. It would not be satisfactory to attempt to draw a distinction along these lines. Any such distinction would lack a principled base. Inevitably, in practice, the distinction would disintegrate in confusion.

Thirdly, here again, a balancing exercise is called for. Some features point in one direction, others in the opposite direction. Factors favouring the need for the solicitor to act for the wife alone include the following. Sometimes a wife may be inhibited in discussion with a solicitor who is also acting for the husband or whose main client is the husband. This occurred in *Banco Exterior Internacional v. Mann* [1995] 1 All ER 936: see the finding of the judge, at p 941F-G. Sometimes a solicitor whose main client is the husband may not, in practice, give the same single-minded attention to the wife's position as would a solicitor acting solely for the wife. Her interests may rank lower in the solicitor's scale of priorities, perhaps unconsciously, than the interests of the husband. Instances of incompetent advice, or worse, which have come before the court might perhaps be less likely to recur if a solicitor were instructed to act for the wife alone and gave advice solely to her. As a matter of general understanding, independent advice would suggest that the solicitor should not be acting in the same transaction for the person who, if there is any undue influence, is the source of that influence.

The contrary view is that the solicitor may also act for the husband or the bank, provided the solicitor is satisfied that this is in the wife's best interests and satisfied also that this will not give rise to any conflicts of duty or interest. The principal factors favouring this approach are as follows. A requirement that a wife should receive advice from a solicitor acting solely for her will frequently add significantly to the legal costs. Sometimes a wife will be happier to be advised by a family solicitor known to her than by a complete stranger. Sometimes a solicitor who knows both husband and wife and their histories will be better placed to advise than a solicitor who is a complete stranger.

In my view, overall the latter factors are more weighty than the former. The advantages attendant upon the employment of a solicitor acting solely for the wife do not justify the additional expense this would involve for the husband. When accepting instructions to advise the wife the solicitor assumes responsibilities directly to her, both at law and professionally. These duties, and this is central to the reasoning on this point, are owed to the wife alone. In advising the wife the solicitor is acting for the wife alone. He is concerned only with her interests. I emphasise, therefore, that in every case the solicitor must consider carefully whether there is any conflict of duty or interest and, more widely, whether it would be in the best interests of the wife for him to accept instructions from her. If he decides to accept instructions, his assumption of legal and professional responsibilities to her ought, in the ordinary course of things, to provide sufficient assurance that he will give the requisite advice fully, carefully and conscientiously. Especially so, now that the nature of the advice called for has been clarified. If at any stage the solicitor becomes concerned that there is a real risk that other interests or duties may inhibit his advice to the wife he must cease to act for her."

CHAPTER 17

Equitable Estoppel

INTRODUCTION

Two main aspects of equitable estoppel have traditionally been recognised, promissory and proprietary estoppel. Promissory estoppel may arise where a promise has been made to a party to the effect that the promisor will not seek to assert his strict legal rights which causes the latter to act to his detriment. The basis of the doctrine of proprietary estoppel is to prevent a person from insisting on his legal rights where another has acted to his detriment on the basis of an expectation or belief that he has or will be given rights over property.

The elements which it is generally accepted are required in order to establish a claim based on proprietary estoppel are assurance, reliance and detriment. The assurance need not necessarily be express but it must have been made with the intention that it should be relied upon. Reliance will be relatively easy to establish once it is shown that a representation 'was calculated to influence the judgment of a reasonable man'[1] but there must be a sufficient link between the promises relied upon and the conduct which constitutes the detriment.[2] Detriment will be suffered where the assurance on which reliance is placed is withdrawn and it has been stated that 'detriment need not consist of the expenditure of money or other quantifiable financial detriment, so long as it is something substantial'.[3] As Robert Walker LJ suggested in *Gillett v. Holt*[4] '[t]he requirement must be approached as part of a broad inquiry as to whether repudiation of an assurance is or is not unconscionable in all the circumstances'.

The cases in which proprietary estoppel may arise have tended to be based on the concepts of common expectation and unilateral mistake, although more recently there has been evidence, particularly in England, of a movement towards utilizing the notion of unconscionability as a basis for the doctrine.

COMMON EXPECTATION

Proprietary estoppel may arise where a party acts to his detriment under an expectation, created or encouraged by the owner of land, that he shall have an

---

[1] *Brikom Investments Ltd v. Carr* [1979] QB 467, 483 *per* Denning MR.
[2] *Wayling v. Jones* (1993) 69 P & CR 170, 173 *per* Balcombe LJ.
[3] *Gillett v. Holt* [2000] 3 WLR 815, 835.
[4] [2000] 3 WLR 815, 835.

interest in the property. In addition, it should be noted that while equity will not complete an imperfect gift in favour of a volunteer,[5] in certain circumstances the subsequent acts of the donor may give rise to a claim which he did not acquire from the original gift.[6]

The basis for the common expectation formulation of proprietary estoppel was laid down by Lord Kingsdown in *Ramsden v. Dyson*[7] in the following terms and has been approved and recently applied in this jurisdiction in *Haughan v. Rutledge*[8]:

> If a man, under a verbal agreement with a landlord for a certain interest in land, or, what amounts to the same thing, under an expectation, created or encouraged by the landlord, that he shall have a certain interest, takes possession of such land, with the consent of the landlord, and upon the faith of such promise or expectation, with the knowledge of the landlord, and without objection by him, lays out money upon the land, a Court of equity will compel the landlord to give effect to such a promise or expectation.
>
> If, on the other hand, a tenant being in possession of land, and knowing the nature and extent of his interest, lays out money upon it in the hope and expectation of an extended term or an allowance for expenditure, then, if such expenditure has not been created or encouraged by the landlord, the tenant has no claim which any Court of law or equity can enforce.

Haughan v. Rutledge
[1988] IR 295

The plaintiffs, who were trustees of an association which promoted harness racing sought to lease the defendant's land for the purpose of holding races. The parties agreed that the defendant would let a field for a trial period and the plaintiffs would construct a racetrack on it. It was further agreed that if at the end of this period the plaintiffs left the property, they would pay no rent and the defendant would retain the benefit of the works carried out. A dispute arose and the defendant re-possessed the lands and the plaintiffs sought specific performance of the alleged agreement to grant a lease of the lands or alternatively an order requiring the defendant to let them into possession. Blayney J dismissed the plaintiffs' claim.

BLAYNEY J stated at pp.300–303: "I now come to deal with the law. On behalf of the plaintiffs it was submitted that they were entitled to a right or

---

[5]   *Milroy v. Lord* (1862) 4 De GF & J 264.
[6]   *Dillwyn v. Llewelyn* (1862) 4 De GF & J 517. See also *Cullen v. Cullen* [1962] IR 268, 282.
[7]   (1866) 1 LR 1 HL 129, 170-171.
[8]   [1988] IR 295.

interest in the race track on the ground of proprietary estoppel. I was referred to Snell's Equity (28th edition 1982) at p. 559 where the four conditions which need to be satisfied for such an estoppel to arise are set out, and it was submitted that on the facts these were satisfied in the present case.

These four conditions are as follows:

1. Detriment.

> "There is no doubt that for proprietary estoppel to arise the person claiming must have incurred expenditure or otherwise have prejudiced himself or acted to his detriment."

2. Expectation or Belief.

> "A must have acted in the belief either that he already owned a sufficient interest in the property to justify the expenditure or that he would obtain such an interest."

3. Encouragement.

> "A's belief must have been encouraged by O or his agent or predecessor in title."

4. No bar to the equity.

> "No equity will arise if to enforce the right claimed would contravene some statute, or prevent the exercise of a statutory discretion or prevent or excuse the performance of a statutory duty."

In my opinion, it is a correct statement of the law that if these four conditions are satisfied then an equity will arise which can be enforced against the owner of the land, and this was not disputed by counsel for the defendant. His submissions were directed to demonstrating that, on the evidence, the conditions had not been satisfied. I have had great difficulty in forming a clear view on this, which is the essential issue in the case, but after lengthy consideration I have come to the conclusion that some of the conditions have not been satisfied and accordingly that the plaintiffs have not established that they are entitled to the equity they are now claiming.

Where the claim falls down, in my opinion, is in satisfying the second and third conditions. The second condition requires that the plaintiffs should have built the race track in the belief either that they owned a sufficient interest in the land to justify the expenditure or that they would obtain such an interest. Since I have found that the defendant did not agree to lease the land to the plaintiffs for 20 years, it follows that the plaintiffs could not have believed that they had an agreement for such a lease and so could not have believed that they had a sufficient interest in the land to justify the expenditure. As a result, the question to be considered is whether they built the track in the belief that they would obtain such an interest. The onus of proof is on the plaintiffs to establish this. In my opinion that onus has not been discharged. There has been no evidence that I accept of what the plaintiffs' belief was when the work was being done. The only material evidence on the point was the evidence of Messrs. Hudson, Haughan and Loughran that the defendant had agreed to give them a lease for 20 years, but as I rejected that evidence it follows that I must hold they did not believe that the defendant had agreed to give them such a lease. No inference can be drawn from this as to what belief they did in fact have. It was submitted on their behalf that they believed they would obtain an interest because the position as to the future was left vague; they were to pay £2,000 for the first year if they wanted to stay on but nothing was agreed as to what the position would be thereafter. There was no evidence to support the submission that such was their belief. None of the three plaintiffs who gave evidence indicated any belief other than that the defendant had agreed to give them a lease for 20 years which, as I have already said, I do not accept. In these circumstances the plaintiffs have not satisfied me that they believed either that they had a sufficient interest in the land to justify the expenditure on the track or that they would obtain such an interest.

Even if I had been satisfied that they had the required belief, I would still not have been satisfied that that belief had been encouraged by the defendant. I have already held that the agreement between the parties was that the defendant would permit the plaintiffs to construct a trotting track on a ten acre field and to use it for a trial period; that if they did not wish to continue to use the track after the trial period, they would not have to pay the defendant anything – he would be compensated by the work they had done; if they wished to continue to use the track, there was no agreement as to what the position was to be except that the plaintiffs would pay £2,000 for the first year. I do not think that such an agreement could have encouraged a belief in the plaintiffs that they would obtain an interest in the land sufficient to justify the expenditure which they subsequently incurred in making the track. It must be borne in mind that the original arrangement was to have a lime dust track laid on grass, which clearly would have been a temporary arrangement, so the plaintiffs would not have needed any long term interest and for that reason could not have believed they would obtain one, so it seems to me no question arose at that stage of the defendant encouraging such a belief. When the situation changed, and the plaintiffs began to lay a permanent track, I do not think that the defendant's agreement to this, which was simply a variation of the original arrangement, could have encouraged a belief in the plaintiffs that they would obtain any greater interest than they would otherwise be entitled to. The defendant did not give any indication that any other term of the agreement was altered. All that happened was that the defendant agreed that a different type of track could be made and this could not be construed as being a representation by the defendant that he would give the plaintiffs a greater interest in the land. Furthermore, the defendant's attitude subsequently, when the work was going on, could not in my opinion be described as acquiescence. Because of the agreement he had made, the defendant was obliged to permit the plaintiffs make the track, even though the extent of the work considerably exceeded everyone's expectations. So it seems to me that there was no encouragement by acquiescence either.

In view of the conclusions I have reached that the plaintiffs are unable to satisfy the second and third conditions enumerated by Snell, it is not necessary to consider the fourth condition and I express no view on it.

This effectively disposes of the case but I think I should refer also to some of the passages in the judgments in the leading case of *Ramsden v. Dyson* (1866) LR 1 HL 129 as, in my opinion, they support the conclusion at which I have arrived. Lord Cranworth L.C. said in his judgment at p. 141:

> "It follows as a corollary from these rules, or, perhaps, it would be more accurate to say it forms part of them, that if my tenant builds on land which he holds under me, he does not thereby, in the absence of special circumstances, acquire any right to prevent me taking possession of the land and buildings when the tenancy has determined. He knew the extent of his interest, and it was his folly to expend money upon a title which he knew would or might soon come to an end."

In my opinion, this statement of the law applies to the present case. While the facts are unusual, there are no special circumstances sufficient to take the case out of the rule. And, I should add, I consider the rule would still apply even if the letting were void as being contrary to s. 12 of the Land Act, 1965, as was submitted by counsel for the defendant in the course of the argument. I see no reason why a party who has expended money on land believing he had a tenancy should be in a stronger position *vis-à-vis* his landlord if it turns out that his tenancy was void. If the landlord is entitled to possession on the termination of the tenancy, he must equally be entitled to possession when it is discovered that there never was a tenancy at all.

Lord Kingsdown in his judgment in the same case at pp. 170-171, postulated two classes of circumstances, and it seems to me that the present case comes within the second.

> "If a man, under a verbal agreement with a landlord for a certain interest in land, or, what amounts to the same thing, under an expectation, created or encouraged by the landlord, that he shall have a certain interest, takes possession of such land, with the consent of the landlord, and upon the faith of such promise or expectation, with the knowledge of the landlord, and without objection by him, lays out money upon the land, a court of equity will compel the landlord to give effect to such promise or expectation ...
>
> If, on the other hand, a tenant being in possession of land, and knowing the nature and extent of his interest, lays out money upon it in the hope and expectation of an extended term or an allowance for expenditure, then, if such hope or expectation has not been created or encouraged by the landlord, the tenant has no claim which any court of law or equity can enforce."

I consider that the plaintiffs laid out money on the construction of the track in the hope and expectation that the defendant would continue to make lettings of the track to them, but as that hope and expectation was not created or encouraged by the defendant, the plaintiffs have no claim which can be enforced at law or in equity.

Three recent cases in England were cited to me, *Inwards v. Baker* [1965] 2 QB 29, *Pascoe v. Turner* [1979] 1 WLR 431 and *Greasley v. Cooke* [1980] 1 WLR 1306, but while they dealt with the general principle of proprietary estoppel none was directly in point, as in each of them the party claiming the equity was a licensee in possession whereas, in the present case, the plaintiffs were not licensees but tenants at the time of the relevant expenditure, and at the date of the institution of the proceedings were not in possession. For these reasons no great assistance can be derived from these cases and so it would be of no advantage to discuss them in detail.

Evidence was given by the defendant of monies owing by the plaintiffs but it seems to me having regard to the form in which the matter came before me – the plaintiffs' motion being treated as the trial of the action, so that there have been no pleadings and in particular no counterclaim – that I cannot deal with this and accordingly I do not propose to make any order on this aspect of the case.

The only order accordingly will be an order dismissing the plaintiffs' claim."

Smyth v. Halpin
[1997] 2 ILRM 38

The plaintiff asked his father to provide him with a site on the latter's land so that he could build a house for himself. The father's reply was to the effect that the family house would be his after his mother's death and why would he want two houses and suggested that the plaintiff instead build an extension onto the family home. The father made a number of wills during his lifetime but in the last of these he left the house to his wife for her life and thereafter to the second named defendant, one of his daughters. After the father's death the plaintiff instituted proceedings seeking, *inter alia,* a declaration that he was entitled to the reversionary interest in the property following the life interest in favour of his mother. Geoghegan J ordered that a deed or instrument should be executed vesting the fee simple remainder interest in the house in the plaintiff.

GEOGHEGAN J stated at pp.40–45: "The plaintiff was brought up in a house and farm situated at Mill Road, Knock, Castletown, Co. Meath. In 1987, the plaintiff decided to marry one Patricia Fox. The plaintiff intended, if he could obtain a suitable site that he could afford, to build a dwelling house for himself and his new wife. He requested his father to provide him with a site on the father's land. According to the plaintiff's own account (which I accept) his father's response was in words to the following effect:

> This place is yours after your mother's day – what would you be doing with two places?

The father suggested that the plaintiff build an extension to the family home. The reference to the plaintiff being left the place after his mother's day did not take the plaintiff by surprise because in 1983 he had had an earlier discussion with his father in the kitchen of the house during which the father asked him did he want the place and he said he did. I accept that this conversation took place also.

For the purpose of constructing the extension to the house, the services of an architect, Mr O'Daly were retained and his designs were done in the context that the entire house would ultimately become the plaintiff's. In order to build the extension, the plaintiff had to apply for a loan from the First National Building Society but that society needed security. Accordingly, the site had to be transferred to the plaintiff and this was done. What emerged was in no real sense a separate house but rather a self-contained section of a house. Even if nobody knew of any conversations between father and son, I think that any reasonable person with knowledge of the family such as a friend or relation would have assumed that the intention at all material times was that the entire house would become the property of the plaintiff upon the deaths of his parents. I find it difficult to conceive that the plaintiff would ever have adopted his father's suggestion in relation to the extension to the house if it was not understood that he was to become the ultimate owner of the entire house.

The plaintiff's father who is now deceased made a number of wills. The earliest will that can be traced was one dated as far back as 20 April 1966. That will contained the following bequest:

> I give, devise and bequeath my cottage with plot of land attached at Knock aforesaid and also my farm of land in the townland of Knock to my wife, Mary Anne Smyth for her life or until she remarries and on her death or remarriage to my son, Ian Smyth absolutely subject at all times to the rights of my children to reside in the cottage until they shall respectively attain the age of 25 years or marry.

The Ian Smyth referred to in that devise and bequest is a brother of the plaintiff. Under the father's next will, however, dated 13 February 1976 which again predated the relevant conversations, he made the following devise and bequest:

> I give, devise and bequeath my cottage with plot of land attached at Knock aforesaid and also my farm of land in the townland of Knock to my wife, Mary Anne Smyth for her life or until she remarries and on her death or remarriage to my son, Felix Gerard Smyth absolutely subject at all times to the rights of my children to reside in the cottage until they shall respectively attain the age of 25 years or marry.

It is to be noted therefore that as early as 1976 it was the testator's intention that the plaintiff should ultimately receive both the house and the farm.

The next will was dated 21 October 1986. This will post-dated the original conversation but predated the discussions at the time of the engagement. The relevant devise and bequest under this will is slightly altered and reads as follows:

> I give, devise and bequeath my lands together with my dwelling house at Knock, Castletown, to my wife, Mary Anne for her life and thereafter to my son, Felix Gerard but subject to the right of my daughters, Ann and Regina to have the option to choose a half-acre site each off my lands for the purpose of erecting a dwelling house thereon. Ann and Regina are to have the option for a period of four years from the date of my death.

The 'Regina' referred to is the second named defendant in this action. It is to be noted that under the 1986 will also subject to the option in relation to the sites, the plaintiff was to get the house and lands after his mother's death. The next will which was the second last will of the deceased is dated 25 June 1991 and is of considerable interest. Under that will, the lands at Knock were devised and bequeathed to the plaintiff's mother for her life and thereafter to the plaintiff absolutely. The dwelling house at Knock was bequeathed to the plaintiff's mother for her life and thereafter to the second named defendant absolutely. It is clear that at that stage the deceased changed his mind in relation to the dwelling house. Finally, under the last will dated 23 July 1992, the plaintiff appointed the first named defendant and one Thomas Smyth (now deceased) to be executors of the will and he devised and bequeathed the lands at Knock to his wife Mary Anne for her life and thereafter to the plaintiff absolutely. But he also devised and bequeathed the dwelling house at Knock to his wife for life and thereafter to the second named defendant, that is his daughter Regina absolutely. Various pecuniary legacies were given to other children and the will then contained the following devise and bequest which is also of some controversy in these proceedings:

> I give, devise and bequeath to my son, Felix Gerard the right of way currently used by him for the benefit of his property over the lands surrounding my dwelling house at Knock, Castletown absolutely.

The plaintiff of course knew nothing of the father's change of mind in relation to the house and only learnt that when the will was read out after the death. These proceedings have now been instituted by him seeking a declaration that he is entitled to the reversionary interest in the dwelling house expectant after the lifetime of Mary Anne Smyth. He is also seeking an order by the court directing that the first named defendant do transfer to the plaintiff the interest to which the plaintiff is entitled to. Alternatively, the plaintiff is seeking to recover the monies expended on the house and he is also seeking to establish that the right of way given to him under the last will is a right of way across the garden attached to the deceased's dwelling house to the rear of the dwelling and not the alternative right of way as apparently suggested by his mother and the second named defendant.

The plaintiff does not and indeed cannot ground his action upon contract.

He does not suggest that there was any agreement on his part to confer any benefit on his father in return for making over the dwelling house. The fact that the plaintiff has not tried to make that very convenient case is to his overall credit in my view when assessing the credibility of his evidence. It might have been easy for him to have suggested that the father indicated that it would suit him if the plaintiff could look after him and his wife in their old age and that in return for that he would allow him build an extension to the house for immediate living in and give him the entire house in due course along with the land. Although such an agreement would not have been in writing or indeed evidenced by writing, it might have been quite a simple matter to establish it through acts of part performance. However, none of that arises. The plaintiff does not suggest that there was a contract. His claim to have the reversionary interest transferred to him is an equitable claim based on the principle of proprietary estoppel. The question I have had to consider therefore is whether in the light of the authorities on proprietary estoppel the facts of this case give rise to a proper recourse to that principle and if so, whether the application of the principle of proprietary estoppel in this case actually requires that this Court make an order directing a transfer of the reversionary interest. The granting of the latter remedy would effectively involve permitting the estoppel to be used as a sword and not merely a shield and would also be an exceptional inroad into the well established principle that equity will not complete an uncompleted gift.

The kind of proprietary estoppel invoked in this case has its origins in *Dillwyn v. Llewelyn* (1862) 4 De GF & J 517. In that case a father had placed a son in possession of land and at the same time signed a document which was intended to be a conveyance of the land to him but proved not to be sufficient for the purpose. The son, with the full approval of the father, built a house on the land and occupied it as his own residence. After the father's death, he claimed and obtained a court declaration that he was beneficially entitled to the land and an order requiring the trustee to whom the father had devised the land under his will to convey it to him. Two important principles emerged from that case. First of all the extent of the estate to be handed over was determined not by what was in the document but by the nature of the transaction and the entitlement then to that estate arose by reason of the expenditure acquiescence. The same principle has been applied in a number of other English cases. In *Inwards v. Baker* [1965] 1 All ER 446, for instance, the Court of Appeal held that in a case where a father had suggested to his son that he build on his land which the son then did largely at his own expense, the son had an equity to remain in the house for the rest of his life notwithstanding that the father in fact left all his property to a lady with whom he had lived for some years and the two children he had by her. The son who lived in the house in that case was unmarried and the court took the view that a life interest was sufficient. The following passage from the judgment of Lord Denning MR at p. 449 illustrates the position:

In this case, it is quite plain that the father allowed an expectation to be created in the defendant's mind that this bungalow was to be his home. It was to be his home for his life or, at all events, his home as long as he wished it to remain his home. It seems to me that, in the light of that equity, the father could not in 1932 have turned to the defendant, and said 'you're to go, it is my land and my house'. Nor could he at any time thereafter so long as the defendant wanted it as his home.

Counsel for the plaintiffs put the case of a purchaser. He suggested that the father could sell the land to a purchaser who would get the defendant out but I think that any purchaser who took with notice would clearly be bound by the equity. So here, too, the plaintiffs, the successors in title of the father, are clearly themselves bound by this equity. It is an equity well recognised in law. It arises from the expenditure of money by a person in actual occupation of land when he is led to believe that, as a result of that expenditure he will be allowed to remain there. It is for the court to say in what way the equity can be satisfied. I am quite clear in this case that it can be satisfied by holding that the defendant can remain there as long as he desires to use it as his home.

The important sentence in that passage is:

It is for the court to say in what way the equity can be satisfied.

As I understand the authorities, the court is at large as to how best it will protect the equity and of course it has to consider what the equity is. In this case the clear expectation on the part of Mr Smyth was that he would have a fee simple in the entire house. The protection of the equity arising from the expenditure therefore requires in this case that an order be made by this Court directing a conveyance of that interest to him. The same principle is well enunciated in the judgment of Cumming-Bruce LJ in *Pascoe v. Turner* [1979] 2 All ER 945 at p. 950 where the following passage appears:

So the principle to be applied is that the court should consider all the circumstances and the counter-claimant having at law no perfected gift or licence other than a licence revocable at will, the court must decide what is the minimum equity to do justice to her, having regard to the way in which she changed her position for the worse, by reason of the acquiescence and encouragement of the legal owner. The defendant submits that the only appropriate way in which the equity can here be satisfied is by perfecting the imperfect gift as was done in *Dillwyn v. Llewelyn*.

Later on in the judgment at p. 951, Cumming-Bruce LJ had this to say:

We are satisfied that the problem of remedy on the facts resolves itself into a choice between two alternatives; should the equity be satisfied by a licence to the defendant to occupy the house for her lifetime or should there be a transfer to her of the fee simple?

The main consideration pointing to a licence for her lifetime is that she did not, by her case at the hearing, seek to establish that she had spent more money or done more work in the house than she would have done had she believed that she had only a licence to live there for her lifetime. But the court must be cautious about drawing any inference from what she did not give in evidence as the hypothesis put is one that manifestly never occurred to her. Then it may be reasonably held that her expenditure and effort can hardly be regarded as comparable to the change of position of those who have constructed buildings on land over which they had no legal rights.

The court went on to take the view that the equity established in that case could only be satisfied by granting a remedy which ensured to the defendants security of tenure and quiet enjoyment. The court therefore ordered that the gift be perfected by the execution of the appropriate conveyance.

In my view, the plaintiff has clearly established that he falls within these principles. The only remaining question to be considered is the right of way. I am entirely satisfied that having regard to all the surrounding circumstances of the case, the right of way being referred to in the will is the way which has been used by the plaintiff close to the house. It is unfortunate that there is now bad feeling between the plaintiff on the one hand and his mother and sister on the other hand who are occupying the original part of the house. I would hope therefore that the plaintiff would be as considerate and tactful as he can in the use of the right of way but I will declare his entitlement to it as I do not find it credible that the way referred to in the will is the other right of way for the benefit of the farm.

I will direct that an appropriate deed or instrument be executed to effect the vesting of the remainder interest in the house in the plaintiff and I will discuss further with counsel as to the nature of that document and as to who are to be the parties to it."

UNILATERAL MISTAKE

Proprietary estoppel may also arise where a claimant has made a mistake about the nature of his legal rights and has suffered detriment as a result of this mistaken belief in circumstances where the true owner knows of this mistake and refrains from asserting his rights. This formulation was set out by Lord Cranworth in *Ramsden v. Dyson*[9] in the following terms:

> If a stranger begins to build on my land supposing it to be his own, and I, perceiving his mistake, abstain from setting him right, and leave him to persevere in his error, a Court of equity will not allow me afterwards to assert my title to the land on which he had expended money on the supposition that the land was his own. It considers that, when I saw the mistake into which he had fallen, it was my duty to be active and to state my adverse title, and that it would be dishonest in me to remain wilfully passive on such an occasion, in order afterwards to profit by the mistake which I might have prevented.

---

[9] (1866) LR 1 HL 129, 140-141.

But it will be observed that to raise such an equity two things are required, first, that the person expending the money supposes himself to be building on his own land; and secondly, that the real owner at the time of the expenditure knows that the land belongs to him and not to the person expending the money in the belief that he is the owner. For if a stranger builds on my land knowing it to be mine, there is no principle of equity which would prevent my claiming the land with the benefit of all the expenditure made on it. There would be nothing in my conduct, active or passive, making it inequitable in me to assert my legal rights.

Therefore it is necessary that the person spending the money thought that he was building on his own land and that the real owner knew at the time that the land did in fact belong to him. This point is well illustrated by the decision of Blayney J in *O'Callaghan v. Ballincollig Holdings Ltd.*[10]

O'Callaghan v. Ballincollig Holdings Ltd
High Court (Blayney J) 31 March 1993

The plaintiffs claimed that they had acquired title to a house by adverse possession and this claim was rejected by the defendant and a notice to quit served. The plaintiffs sought a declaration of their title or alternatively a declaration that they had a lien on the house for monies spent on reinstating it while the defendant counter-claimed for possession. The plaintiffs' claim to a lien was based on the grounds of proprietary estoppel and unjust enrichment. They argued that the defendant had stood idly by while they had spent substantial sums of money reinstating the house and that this precluded it from recovering the property without compensating the plaintiffs for their expenditure. Blayney J was satisfied that this submission was not well founded; as long as the plaintiffs' tenancy continued to subsist, the defendant was not entitled to interfere and it was not a case of the defendant standing idly by. He concluded that the plaintiffs could not prevent the defendant from claiming the house with the benefit of their expenditure on it.

BLAYNEY J stated at pp.1–9: "In 1959 the plaintiffs became tenants of a house in Chapel Lane, Ballincollig, Co. Cork at the weekly rent of £1.50. The landlord was James Walsh. His interest was acquired by the defendants in 1974.

By a letter dated the 23rd April 1987, written on behalf of the plaintiffs by their solicitor, the plaintiffs claimed that they had acquired title to the house by adverse possession. This claim was rejected by the defendants and a notice to quit was served. The plaintiffs then issued the present proceedings seeking a declaration of their title, and by a subsequent amendment, claiming in the

---

[10] High Court (Blayney J) 31 March 1993.

alternative a declaration that they had a lien on the house for monies they had expended on reinstating it after it had been damaged by two fires, one in 1981 and the other in 1983. In their defence the defendants denied the plaintiffs' claim and counterclaimed for possession.

The plaintiffs' claim was dismissed by His Honour Judge Murphy and an order for possession was made on the counterclaim. The entire of that order was appealed by the plaintiffs and the appeal came before me in Cork on the 22nd February 1992. With the agreement of both parties, I dealt solely with the issue of whether the plaintiffs had acquired a statutory title, and I held against the plaintiffs on that and confirmed the order for possession on the counterclaim but put a stay on that order pending the decision on the plaintiffs' alternative claim to a lien for the monies spent on reinstating the house.

That issue was argued before me on the 5th March, 1993 and was confined to the question of whether, accepting the facts as pleaded by the plaintiffs, they had a valid claim for a lien. This claim was pleaded as follows in the civil bill:

> "5(b) Further and in the alternative and without prejudice to the foregoing in or about the year 1981 the premises the subject matter of these proceedings was substantially damaged by fire without fault to the plaintiffs or one of them herein. Subsequently the plaintiffs expended the sum of £27,000 on the reinstatement of the said premises without covenants, contract or obligation to do so.
>
> (c) Further in or about the year 1983 the premises the subject matter of these proceedings were further damaged by fire without fault to the plaintiffs or one of them herein. Subsequently the plaintiffs expended the sum of £16,000 on the reinstatement of the said premises without covenants, contract or obligation to do so.
>
> (d) The plaintiffs rely on the matter set out in the next preceding paragraph in order to establish a lien on the premises to the extent of £43,000 together with interest thereon running from the date of expenditure."

Mr. Hayden, on behalf of the plaintiffs, put their case on two separate grounds:
1. Proprietary estoppel, and
2. unjust enrichment.

As regards the first ground, he submitted that estoppel may give rise to a cause of action and that this was a case of estoppel by acquiescence. The defendants stood idly by while the plaintiffs spent substantial monies reinstating the house, and this precluded them from recovering the house now without compensating the plaintiffs for their expenditure.

When regard is had to the particular facts of this case, I am satisfied that this submission is not well-founded. The relationship of landlord and tenant existed at all times between the parties. The plaintiffs had, accordingly, exclusive possession of the house. They were entitled to carry out whatever repairs they liked. The defendants had no right to stop them. So it was not a case of the defendants standing idly by. As long as the plaintiffs' tenancy continued to subsist, the defendants were not entitled to interfere.

It seems to me that the case comes within the following quotation from the judgment in *Ramsden v. Dyson* (1866) LR 1 HL 129 at p. 140:

> "For if a stranger builds on my land knowing it to be mine, there is no principle of equity which would prevent my claiming the land with the benefit of all the expenditure made on it. There would be nothing in my conduct, active or passive, making it inequitable in me to assert my legal rights."

The plaintiffs knew that they held the house as tenants from the defendants, so they knew they were reinstating a house to which the defendants were entitled subject to their tenancy. They cannot, accordingly, prevent the defendants from claiming the house with the benefit of their expenditure on it.

The plaintiffs' position was somewhat similar to that of a purchaser of property who goes into possession before completion and then rejects the title. "He may be ejected by the vendor; and cannot at law claim any allowance for improvements or repairs: nor will equity afford him any relief unless there has been fraud on the part of the vendor" (Dart on Vendor and Purchaser 7th edition at p. 516/517).

In my opinion this is not a case in which the facts give rise to a proprietary estoppel and so the plaintiffs' first ground fails.

In support of his second ground, unjust enrichment, Mr. Hayden cited *Rogers v. Louth County Council* [1981] ILRM 144 and *O'Connor v. Listowel UDC* [1957] Ir Jur Rep 43. In my opinion both of these cases are clearly distinguishable on their facts from the instant case. In *Rogers v. Louth County Council* the issue was whether the plaintiff could recover monies which had been paid under a mistake of law, and in *O'Connor v. Listowel UDC* the question was whether an engineer, whose appointment by the UDC was void, was entitled, by way of an action on a quantum meruit, to recover reasonable remuneration for services actually rendered to the UDC. There is clearly no question of the plaintiffs being able to recover on a quantum meruit in the instant case, and in so far as monies paid under a mistake of law are concerned, no monies were paid by the plaintiffs to the defendants so the claim is not a claim to recover monies alleged to have been paid but monies alleged to have been expended on reinstating the house.

There are two things that the plaintiffs would have to establish in order to succeed in their claim for a lien: firstly, that they are entitled to recover from the defendants the amount they expended in reinstating the house, and secondly, that in law the amount of the expenditure is a charge on the house and so gives the plaintiffs a lien on it. For the reasons I have given I am satisfied that the plaintiffs cannot establish the first of these matters and it follows that they cannot be entitled to any lien.

It would appear that from the time the plaintiffs stopped paying rent for the house, which was in the early 1970s, they may have been under a misapprehension that they owned the house, or at least that they would become the owners, and this may have influenced them in deciding to reinstate it after the two fires. Unfortunately for them they were still tenants and the fact that they may have acted under a misapprehension gives them no rights against the defendants as the latter were in no way responsible for the plaintiffs being under a misapprehension. In the circumstances I have to decide this issue also against the plaintiffs with the result that their entire appeal must be dismissed."

The principles set out by Lord Cranworth in *Ramsden v. Dyson* were considered by Fry J in *Wilmott v. Barber*[11] and he formulated the following five probanda which he suggested must be complied with in order to found a claim based on proprietary estoppel.

1. The claimant must have made a mistake as to his legal rights.
2. The claimant must have expended some money or done some act on the faith of his mistaken belief.
3. The owner of the land must know of his own right which is inconsistent with the right claimed by the plaintiff.
4. The owner must know of the claimant's mistaken belief as to his rights.
5. The owner must have encouraged the claimant in relation to the expenditure incurred or other acts done, either directly or by refraining from asserting his legal rights.

A Move Towards a Test of Unconscionability

Following the decision in *Wilmott v. Barber*, the courts in England tended to insist on compliance with these five elements in order to establish grounds for proprietary estoppel irrespective of whether it was a claim based on common expectation or unilateral mistake.[12] More recently the courts in that jurisdiction have begun to move away from this restrictive formulation and in *Taylor's Fashions Ltd v. Liverpool Victoria Trustee Co. Ltd*[13] Oliver J suggested a broader approach 'directed rather at ascertaining whether, in particular circumstances, it would be unconscionable for a party to be permitted to deny that which, knowingly or unknowingly, he has allowed or encouraged another to assume to his detriment rather than inquiring whether the circumstances can be fitted within the confines of some preconceived formula serving as a universal yardstick for every form of unconscionable behaviour'.

The concept of unconscionability also appeared to underlie the decision of Finlay P in *McMahon v. Kerry County Council.*[14]

---

[11] (1880) 15 Ch D 96.
[12] There was also evidence of this tendency in this jurisdiction, see e.g. *Cullen v. Cullen* [1962] IR 268.
[13] [1982] QB 133, 151-152.
[14] [1981] ILRM 419. However, note the criticisms of this decision by Mee (1998) 33 Ir Jur 187.

McMahon v. Kerry County Council
[1981] ILRM 419

The plaintiffs bought a plot of land for the purpose of building a school, however shortly afterwards they abandoned their plan and did not visit the site again for a further three years. They then discovered that the defendant council which had originally known of their purchase, was preparing to build on the land and, upon a complaint being made, the work ceased. Four years later the defendant built two houses on the site and the following year the plaintiffs discovered this and instituted proceedings to recover possession of the site. Counsel for the defendant relied on *Ramsden v. Dyson* but Finlay P concluded that the facts of the case did not fall within the principle laid down by Lord Cranworth LC in that case and said that there was no question of the plaintiffs remaining wilfully passive when the defendant commenced to build on their land. However, Finlay P held that in the circumstances, it would be unjust and unconscionable that the plaintiffs should recover possession and he held that that they were only entitled to the market value of the site without the houses and to damages.

FINLAY P stated at pp.419–424: "I am satisfied on the evidence that whilst the plaintiffs took no or practically no steps either to supervise, protect or guard their property they had not got actual knowledge of the building of these houses until December of 1973 when they were practically completed.

From these facts Mr Sutton on behalf of the plaintiffs urges upon me the simple proposition that they are the owners of this plot of land; that they have not with the knowledge of the construction by the defendants of a building on it stood by and permitted that to happen, and that in the absence of that sort of acquiescence on their part their right as registered owners to the recovery of the possession of the lands is absolute and cannot be interfered with. In the alternative he submits that some servant or agent of the Kerry County Council knew at the time of the commencement of the construction of these houses that the land on which they were being built was the property of the plaintiffs and that even if the engineers and other persons concerned with the design and building of the houses did not have that knowledge that the County Council must have imputed to it the knowledge of all its servants and that accordingly the defendant's position in law is that they are people who with knowledge of the ownership of this land as being in the McMahons built houses upon it and that therefore an order for possession of the houses must be granted against them.

Mr O'Flaherty on behalf of the defendants contends that there is a general equitable principle which restrains the court in granting a decree for possessson where with knowledge of the building of premises on it an owner stands by acting thus mala fide whilst the person who has gone into occupation and has built the premises acts by way of a bona fide mistake. He concedes that that is not the position on my finding of facts in this case but urges upon me that it is a principle which should be extended in equity to the facts of the present case and that it would be unconscionable for equity to permit what would in effect be an unjust enrichment of the plaintiffs on the facts as I find them.

Counsel in support of their arguments referred me to the following cases. *Ramsden v. Dyson* (1866) LR 1 HL 129, *Cullen v. Cullen* [1966] IR 268, *Ward v. Kirkland* [1966] 1 All ER 609, and I have also considered the case of *Fung Kai Sun v. Chan Fui Hing* [1951] AC 489 in which *Ramsden v. Dyson* was discussed.

The locus classicus of the principles for which Mr O'Flaherty is contending is of course the case of *Ramsden v. Dyson* still cited with approval where it applies. In particular the statement to be found at p. 140 of the report requires to be considered and quoted in full.

> If a stranger begins to build on my land supposing it to be his own, and I, perceiving his mistake, abstain from setting him right, and leave him to persevere in his error, a Court of Equity will not allow me afterwards to assert my title to the land on which he had expended money on the supposition that the land was his own. It considers that, when I saw the mistake into which he had fallen, it was my duty to be active and to state my adverse title, and that it would be dishonest in me to remain wilfully passive on such an occasion, in order afterwards to profit by the mistake which I might have prevented.
>
> But it will be observed that to raise such an equity two things are required first, that the person expending the money supposes himself to be building on his own land; and secondly, that the real owner at the time of the expenditure knows that the land belongs to him and not to the person expending the money in the belief that he is the owner. For if a stranger builds on my land knowing it to be mine, there is no principle of equity which would prevent my claiming the land with the benefit of all the expenditure made on it. There would be nothing in my conduct, active or passive, making it inequitable in me to assert my legal rights.

I am satisfied that this case falls into neither of the categories or propositions contained in the passage which I have just quoted. There is no question of the plaintiffs in this case remaining wilfully passive when the defendants commenced to build on their land for I am satisfied on the evidence that they did not know of such building until December when they immediately made a complaint to the County Council.

I have carefully considered Mr Sutton's submission that some servant of the County Council must have known that the land had been transferred to the plaintiffs in 1964 because some servant or servants of the County Council had dealt with that transaction and that therefore the County Council must be categorised as a person building on land and knowing it to be the property of another. I reject that submission because it seems clear to me that the second proposition contained in the passage which I have quoted must be applicable to real knowledge which would involve a wilful act on the part of the party who has done the building and that it cannot truly be said that the County Council in this case wilfully built on the land of the plaintiffs Mr and Mrs McMahon. The question therefore arises what is the real underlying principle of the statement which I have read from *Ramsden v. Dyson*. It is an enunciation of a principle of equity solely referable to the conduct of the plaintiff. If it were then it could not apply to this case and unless some other principle prevented the assertion by the plaintiff of his right to possession of these lands together with the value of these two houses on them he must succeed. Undoubtedly the first proposition dealing with the person who remains wilfully passive whilst another builds on his land is referable to the conduct of the plaintiff equity preventing him in effect from profiting by a conscious wrong. The very last sentence in the passage which I have quoted, would seem to suggest that the second category falls also into a consideration of the conduct of the plaintiff where the judgment states: 'There would be nothing in my conduct active or passive making it inequitable in me to assert my legal rights'. The example, however, of the case where the person may recover his land with the value of the building made by a stranger on it clearly provides 'if the stranger builds on my land *knowing* it to be mine'.

It seems to me that the principles of equity stated in this passage depend not exclusively on the action or inaction of the plaintiff or on the state of his knowledge but have regard also to the action of the defendant. In the first case where the defendant is protected it is of course essential that he was innocent and in the second case where he is deprived of the buildings he has made it seems to be an essential constituent that he put them on the land of another knowing that it was the land of another and therefore either acting fraudulently or at least with knowledge of the risk he was running.

If a court applying equitable principles is truly to act as a court of conscience then it seems to me unavoidable that it should consider not only conduct on the part of the plaintiff with particular regard to whether it is wrong or wilful but also conduct on the part of the defendant and furthermore the consequences and the justice of the consequences both from the point of view of the plaintiff and of the defendant.

On the findings of fact which I have made in this case certain factors would appear to be clearly material to any such consideration of the application of an equitable principle. The first is that the plaintiffs purchased these lands in the first instance on a bona fide representation of their intention to provide something which would have been of general public benefit namely a new secondary school building in the village of Causeway. It is a reasonable assumption from the evidence before me and from the correspondence which was proved in the case that had the plaintiffs in the year 1960 applied to purchase this particular plot of land from the County Council solely for the purpose of providing themselves with a building site for a private residence that their request would not have been granted and it is equally probable on the evidence that even if the County Council felt obliged or wanted at that time to dispose of this particular plot as being a piece of surplus land (which I consider unlikely had it not been for the purpose of a school) that it would have been given by them as it was in fact eventually given back to the O'Driscoll family who probably would not have sold it to the plaintiffs unless the plaintiffs were going to build a school something which in the correspondence it is clear Mrs McMahon properly represented that Mrs O'Driscoll was enthusiastic or keen on.

The second factor is that from the time of the purchase of these lands they were enclosed within the curtilage of a wall which contained the existing housing estate of 15 houses and the dispensary and were in no way identifiable as a separate unit. The plaintiffs took no steps whatever by fencing or any form of demarcation to identify them nor did they in the succeeding years with the exception of the one instance in 1968 when they complained about the workman clearing up the land on behalf of the County Council even keep a surveyance over this plot of land to see if any wrongful trespass or wrongful user of it had been made. The third material factor in my view is that it is quite clear that there is no intrinsic value in this land as far as the plaintiffs are concerned, it does not have any sentimental or family connotation, it was not chosen by them at the time of its purchase as a plot of land on which they might in the future desire to build a house for themselves or for any member of their family but it became available to them for that purpose solely as the result of an adventitious occurrence namely the change in the State education system which decided Mrs McMahon to abandon the project of building a school in Causeway. There was no evidence before me that would suggest that the plaintiffs would not be equally well served and rewarded by having a plot of building land on any other equivalent site in quite a significant area around Tralee in Kerry. Fourthly I am satisfied that whilst the officials of the County Council clearly made a mistake which could by careful examination of the records available to them in one or other of their own offices have been avoided, that existence of the surrounding wall and the total inactivity of the plaintiffs concerning the land for so many years and their failure to mark it out made for a mistake which is entirely understandable and to that extent entirely excusable. If the plaintiffs were now to recover possession of these lands with the two houses built upon them then they would be obtaining for an expenditure of £40 in 1960 and without any effort or expenditure on their part in between property probably worth in the region of £18,000. Furthermore these houses are at present available as houses rented by the County Council pursuant to their housing scheme to persons requiring housing which is a matter, on the evidence before me, of considerable urgency in Kerry at present and a decree for possession in favour of the plaintiffs will make two less local authority houses available for persons in genuine need of them.

All these factors and considerations drive me to the conclusion that it would truly be unconscionable and unjust that the plaintiffs should recover possession of this land with these two houses built upon it. To avoid, however, the classic fault of creating bad law by the consideration of a hard case I would emphasise that it is only the combination of factors which I have outlined which are many and possibly in their combination unique which forces me to the conclusion that equity should restrain the full operation of the plaintiffs' legal right to recover possession of these lands. It is clear however that the plaintiffs are by no means in the same position as the person who has wilfully stood by and allowed a stranger to improve or enrich his land and that therefore there can be no question of their being deprived of their legal right without ample and adequate compensation.

I accept the contention made by Mr O'Flaherty on behalf of the defendants that ample and adequate compensation should consist of the full market value of these lands as a building site plus a sum for damages in addition. A written valuation of the lands prepared by Messrs Giles and Company, Auctioneers of Tralee was by agreement between the parties submitted to me without oral evidence but the agreement did not of course extend to the correctness of the valuation so produced on behalf of the defendants. It indicates that this is a site with a frontage of 80 feet, with a width of 75 feet and a depth on one side of 148 feet and on the other of 165 feet. It is close to all ordinary services and close, of course, to the village of Causeway and the market value of it is assessed upon the basis that it would be suitable for one private residence or for a residential business premises to serve the adjoining housing development and is fixed at £1,000. Whilst there was no opportunity for counsel on behalf of the plaintiffs to cross-examine the auctioneer concerning this valuation Mr Sutton made to me the point that the valuation should be higher because it would be possible to provide more than one house upon the site. I accept this as a valid criticism and contention and having regard to the ample nature of the compensation to which I believe the plaintiffs are entitled I am assessing the market value of these premises at £1,500. The plaintiffs are clearly entitled in addition to that to damages and they should be such sum as will permit the plaintiffs not only to purchase an equivalent site which should be possible for £1,500 but to have in addition such sum that would cover the expenses which might be involved in such a purchase and would leave them with an extra amount which might permit them to purchase against a contending buyer. Damages therefore in addition to the £1,500 should in my view be measured at £500.

The form of order which I will accordingly make is that I will grant to the plaintiffs a decree for possession of these lands but I will put a stay on that decree for a period of three months from this date providing that if within that period of three months the defendants pay to the plaintiffs the sum of £2,000 the stay will be permanent. I wish to make it clear as Kenny J did under similar though by no means identical circumstances in the case of *Cullen v. Cullen* that if at the period of 12 years from 1973 the defendant County Council apply to have themselves registered as owners of this folio by reason of their adverse title to it, it appears to me that is an order to which they should be entitled and that they should therefore at that time become the owners in law as well as they are now the owners in fact as a result of my judgment.

Having regard to the fact that the plaintiffs were in this action asserting a clear and well established right and have been defeated in the enjoyment of that by what I conceive to be a novel application of a general equitable principle it seems to me just that the costs to which they are clearly entitled against the defendants should be taxed on a solicitor and client basis."

A useful recent example of how estoppel may arise is the decision of the Court of Appeal in *Gillett v. Holt*[15] in which Robert Walker LJ stated that the fundamental principle that equity is concerned to prevent unconscionable conduct permeates all elements of the doctrine of proprietary estoppel.

Gillett v. Holt
[2000] 3 WLR 815

The plaintiff spent his working life as a farm manager for the first defendant who repeatedly promised him that he would succeed to the farming business and the house in which the plaintiff and his family had lived for over 25 years. After relations between the parties deteriorated and the plaintiff was dismissed from his job, the first defendant made dispositions of the property to the second named defendant in whose favour he also altered his will. Carnwath J dismissed the plaintiff's claim based on proprietary estoppel finding that the representations made could not be construed as an irrevocable promise and that the claim would in any event have failed because the plaintiff had not proved himself to have suffered sufficient detriment in reliance on the first named defendant's assurances to give rise to proprietary estoppel. Carnwath J agreed that the overriding principle was that a defendant should be held to his representation 'only if it would be unconscionable to go back on it' but stressed that estoppel must be founded on an expectation, created or encouraged by the party alleged to be bound, in reliance on which the other party has acted to his detriment. The plaintiff's appeal was allowed by the Court of Appeal (Robert Walker, Waller and Beldam LJJ).

ROBERT WALKER LJ stated at pp. 828–842:

"*Proprietary estoppel*
This judgment considers the relevant principles of law, and the judge's application of them to the facts which he found, in much the same order as the appellant's notice of appeal and skeleton argument. But although the judgment is, for convenience, divided into several sections with headings which give a

---

[15] [2000] 3 WLR 815.

rough indication of the subject matter, it is important to note at the outset that the doctrine of proprietary estoppel cannot be treated as subdivided into three or four watertight compartments. Both sides are agreed on that, and in the course of the oral argument in this court it repeatedly became apparent that the quality of the relevant assurances may influence the issue of reliance, that reliance and detriment are often intertwined, and that whether there is a distinct need for a "mutual understanding" may depend on how the other elements are formulated and understood. Moreover the fundamental principle that equity is concerned to prevent unconscionable conduct permeates all the elements of the doctrine. In the end the court must look at the matter in the round.

In his discussion of the law the judge took as his starting point the decision of Mr. Edward Nugee Q.C. in *In re Basham decd.* [1986] 1 WLR 1498. In that case the claimant and her husband had helped her mother and her stepfather in all sorts of ways throughout the claimant's adult life. She received no remuneration but understood that she would inherit her stepfather's property when he died. After her mother's death in 1976, and until her stepfather's death in 1982, she and her husband lived near the cottage to which her stepfather had moved (but never lived in the cottage). The claimant was told by her stepfather that "she would lose nothing" by her help and (a few days before his death) that she was to have the cottage. The deputy judge held that she was entitled, by proprietary estoppel, to the whole of the estate of her stepfather (who died intestate). He rejected the submission that the principle could not extend beyond cases where the claimant already had enjoyment of an identified item of property: see pp. 1509–1510. In that context he referred to the well known judgment of Oliver J. in *Taylors Fashions Ltd. v. Liverpool Victoria Trustees Co. Ltd. (Note) (1979)* [1982] QB 133. That judgment has been described as "a watershed in the development of proprietary estoppel" – see Gray, *Elements of Land Law,* 2nd ed. (1993), p. 324. In it Oliver J. stated that in the light of the more recent cases the principle, at pp. 151–152:

> "requires a very much broader approach which is directed rather at ascertaining whether, in particular individual circumstances, it would be unconscionable for a party to be permitted to deny that which, knowingly, or unknowingly, he has allowed or encouraged another to assume to his detriment than to inquiring whether the circumstances can be fitted within the confines of some preconceived formula serving as a universal yardstick for every form of unconscionable behaviour."

In re Basham may be difficult to reconcile with the decision of Scott J. in *Layton v. Martin* [1986] 2 FLR 227, which was not cited in *In re Basham* and may not have been reported at the time when Mr. Nugee heard the case. Nevertheless *In re Basham* has been referred to at least twice in this court without its correctness being challenged. In *Jones v. Watkins* (unreported), 26 November 1987; Court of Appeal (Civil Divison) Transcript No. 1200 of 1987, Slade L.J. referred to it as containing a helpful statement of the principle. Slade L.J.'s judgment also contains some important observations about the possibility of proprietary estoppel (unlike promissory estoppel) arising even from an equivocal representation:

> "At first sight, it may be surprising that a promise to confer an interest in property which is so equivocal in its terms that it would be incapable of giving rise to a binding contract may be capable of conferring on the promisee a right in equity to a transfer of the whole property. However, I think that [counsel] must be right in describing this as simply one instance of equity supplementing the law. The equivocal nature of the promises found by the judge is clearly one relevant factor when considering whether or not it would be unconscionable to permit the administrators to rely on their strict legal title, having regard to any detriment suffered by the plaintiff in reliance on them."

The other case in which *In re Basham* has been referred to in this court is *Wayling v. Jones* (1993) 69 P & CR 170. It concerned an assurance ("It'll all be yours one day") given by the elder partner in a male homosexual relationship to his younger partner. Balcombe L.J. cited Mr. Nugee's statement of principle in *In re Basham decd.* [1986] 1 WLR 1498, 1503 as having been accepted by the parties:

> "The plaintiff relies on proprietary estoppel, the principle of which, in its broadest form, may be stated as follows: where one person, A, has acted to his detriment on the faith of a belief, which was known to and encouraged by another person, B, that he either has or is going to be given a right in or over B's property, B cannot insist on his strict legal rights if to do so would be inconsistent with A's belief."

Balcombe L.J. went on to state the relevant principles as to reliance and detriment, at p. 173:

> "(1) There must be a sufficient link between the promises relied upon and the conduct which constitutes the detriment – see *Eves v. Eves* [1975] 1 W.L.R. 1338, 1345C-F, in particular *per* Brightman J. *Grant v. Edwards* [1986] Ch 638, 648-649, 655-657, 656-H, *per* Nourse L.J. and per Browne-Wilkinson V.-C. and in particular the passage where he equates the principles applicable in cases of constructive trust to those of proprietary estoppel. (2) The promises relied upon do not have to be the sole inducement for the conduct: it is sufficient if they are an inducement – *Amalgamated Property Co. v. Texas Bank* [1982] QB 84, 104-105. (3) Once it has been established that promises were made, and that there has been conduct by the plaintiff of such a nature that inducement may be inferred then the burden of proof shifts to the defendants to establish that he did not rely on the promises – *Greasley v. Cooke* [1980] 1 WLR 1306; *Grant v. Edwards* [1986] Ch 638, 657."

Irrevocability of assurances

The judge referred to these authorities and then to the decision of Judge Weeks Q.C. in *Taylor v. Dickens* [1998] 1 FLR 806 (which has since been compromised on appeal). That was the case of the elderly lady who said that she would leave her estate to the gardener and did so, but then changed her mind (without telling him) after he had stopped charging her for his help with gardening and odd jobs. Judge Weeks rejected the claim and, at p. 821, criticised *In re Basham* in two respects. The first criticism was that Mr. Nugee's judgment omitted the requirement of unconscionability. That criticism seems misplaced: see [1986] 1 WLR 1498, 1504A-B and 1509A-C. The second criticism was [1998] 1 FLR 806, 821:

> "it is not sufficient for A to believe that he is going to be given a right over B's property if he knows that B has reserved the right to change his mind. In that case, A must show that B created or encouraged a belief on A's part that B would not exercise that right."

For that proposition Judge Weeks referred to the decision of the Privy Council in *Attorney-General of Hong Kong v. Humphreys Estate (Queen's Gardens) Ltd.* [1987] AC 114.

Taylor v. Dickens has itself attracted a good deal of criticism: see, for instance, Professor M. P. Thompson, "Emasculating Estoppel" [1998] Conv. 210, and William Swadling [1998] RLR 220; but compare the contrary view in M. Dixon, "Estoppel: A panacea for all wills?" [1999] Conv 39, 46. Mr. Swadling's comment is short and pithy:

> "This decision is clearly wrong, for the judge seems to have forgotten that the whole point of estoppel claims is that they concern promises which, since they are unsupported by consideration, are initially revocable. What later makes them binding, and therefore irrevocable, is the promisee's detrimental reliance on them. Once that occurs, there is simply no question of the promisor changing his or her mind."

Mr. McDonnell has added his voice to the criticism. In his skeleton argument he has submitted that *Taylor v. Dickens* is "simply wrong." Mr. Martin, while reminding the court that it is not hearing an appeal in *Taylor v. Dickens,* has not given the case whole-hearted support. He has been inclined to concede that Judge Weeks should have focused on the promise which was made and whether it was of an irrevocable character, instead of looking for a second promise not to revoke a testamentary disposition.

In my judgment these criticisms of *Taylor v. Dickens* are well founded. The actual result in the case may be justified on the other ground on which it was put (no unconscionability on the facts); or (as Mr. Swadling suggests later in his note) the gardener's unremunerated services might have merited some modest restitutionary relief. But the inherent revocability of testamentary dispositions (even if well understood by the parties, as Mr. Gillett candidly accepted that it was by him) is irrelevant to a promise or assurance that "all this will be yours" (the sort of language used on the occasion of The Beeches incident in 1975). Even when the promise or assurance is in terms linked to the making of a will (as at the 1974 Golf Hotel dinner) the circumstances may make clear that the assurance is more than a mere statement of present (revocable) intention, and is tantamount to a promise. *Attorney-General of*

Hong Kong v. Humphreys Estate (Queen's Gardens) Ltd. [1987] AC 114, on which Judge Weeks relied, is essentially an example of a purchaser taking the risk, with his eyes open, of going into possession and spending money while his purchase remains expressly subject to contract. Carnwath J. observed that the advice to the claimant in *Taylor v. Dickens* "not to count his chickens before they were hatched" is [1998] 3 All ER 917, 929:

> "an apt statement of how, in normal circumstances, and in the absence of a specific promise, any reasonable person would regard – and should be expected by the law to regard – a representation by a living person as to his intentions for his will."

In the generality of cases that is no doubt correct, and it is notorious that some elderly persons of means derive enjoyment from the possession of testamentary power, and from dropping hints as to their intentions, without any question of an estoppel arising. But in this case Mr. Holt's assurances were repeated over a long period, usually before the assembled company on special family occasions, and some of them (such as "it was all going to be ours anyway" on the occasion of The Beeches incident) were completely unambiguous. With all respect to the judge, I cannot accept the conclusion which he reached on this point (at p. 932, a passage which I have already quoted). The judge attached weight to The Beeches incident in reaching his conclusion. To my mind it is highly significant, but its significance goes the other way. I find it wholly understandable that Mr. and Mrs. Gillett, then 10 years married and with two young sons, may have been worried about their home and their future depending on no more than oral assurances, however emphatic, from Mr. Holt. The bitterly fought and ruinously expensive litigation which has ensued shows how right they would have been to be worried. But Mr. Gillett, after discussing the matter with his wife and his parents, decided to rely on Mr. Holt's assurances because "Ken was a man of his word." Plainly the assurances given on this occasion were intended to be relied on, and were in fact relied on. In any event reliance would be presumed: see *Greasley v. Cooke* [1980] 1 WLR 1306; Mr. Martin accepted that, while challenging the suggestion that that case also supported any presumption of detriment.

It may be that the judge, having gone deeply and correctly into the law of mutual wills in *In re Goodchild decd.* [1996] 1 WLR 694 (affirmed by this court [1997] 1 WLR 1216) went too far in seeking a parallel between those principles and those of proprietary estoppel. Mr. Nugee also discerned a parallel in *In re Basham decd.* [1986] 1 WLR 1498, 1504. But although both doctrines show equity intervening to prevent unconscionable conduct, the special feature of the mutual wills and secret trust cases is that they involve not two parties but three. In mutual wills cases they are (typically) a testator (A), a testatrix (B) and an intended beneficiary or class of beneficiaries (C). In secret trust cases they are the testator (A), the secret trustee (B) and the beneficiary (C). There must be an agreement between A and B as to conferring a benefit on C because it is the agreement (and not C's moral claims) which would make it unconscionable for B to resile from his agreement. The judge did make clear [1998] 3 All ER 917, 929, and again at p. 930, that he was well aware of the differences between mutual wills and proprietary estoppel as regards the need for a binding contract. But whether or not he was influenced in that way, I differ from his conclusion that Mr. Holt's assurances were incapable of forming the foundation for an enforceable claim based on proprietary estoppel. In my judgment they were well capable of doing so.

Mr. Martin has in two spirited passages of his oral submissions supported the judge's paragraph headed "Conclusion," at p.932, as containing findings of fact which the judge reached after seeing and hearing the witnesses (in particular, Mr. Gillett, who was cross-examined for the best part of three days). Mr. Martin forthrightly submitted that it was not open to this court to disregard or disturb these findings of fact made by the judge. That submission calls for serious consideration and it has led to some close textual analysis of the paragraph in question. When the judge stated, at p. 932:

> "What I am unable to find in the representations reviewed above is anything which could reasonably be construed as an irrevocable promise that the Gilletts would inherit, regardless of any change in circumstances,"

he must, it seems to me, have been exaggerating the degree to which a promise of this sort must be expressly made irrevocable if it is to found an estoppel. As already noted, it is the other party's detrimental reliance on the promise which makes it irrevocable. To that extent the judge seems to have misdirected himself as to what he was looking for in the facts.

Mr. Gillett was cross-examined at length about some increasingly improbable eventualities: that Mr. Holt would marry his housekeeper, that he would have children, that his elderly sister would suddenly lose all her investments and turn to him for help. Mr. Gillett naturally enough conceded that in those circumstances Mr. Holt could or would have made some provision for these moral obligations. But, in giving evidence, he stuck resolutely to the promises made to him:

> "I am aware that promises were made by Mr. Holt to me and I continued through 40 years of my life on the basis of those promises . . ." and: "This was a partnership arrangement effectively between Ken and [me] over many, many years and hypothetical situations like that are inappropriate I would have thought."

The last two sentences of the "Conclusion" paragraph begin [1998] 3 All ER 917, 932: "No doubt it was because of this insecurity . . ." and "He must have been well aware . . ." Neither of these sentences can readily be described as a simple finding of primary fact. Moreover the second sentence does, with great respect to the judge, beg the whole question, because Mr. Gillett was not in the witness box to take part in a seminar on the elements of proprietary estoppel (although parts of his cross-examination suggest otherwise). He was there to give evidence, which was largely unchallenged and which the judge accepted, about the assurances made to him and his detrimental reliance on them. Whether those assurances put his expectations on a legally enforceable foundation was not a question for him. But unfortunately he was right in his instinct that his lack of success in getting Mr. Holt to give him anything more formal might lead to tears.

I would if necessary take the view that these alleged findings of fact in the "Conclusion" paragraph were against the weight of the evidence. But it is not necessary to go that far. They are not simple findings of fact, and they take their colour from the judge having misdirected himself as to what he was looking for.

Mutual understandings and reliance

The judge's approach seems also to have been influenced by the need to find what he called, at p. 929:

> "a mutual understanding – which may be express or inferred from conduct – between promisor and promisee, both as to the content of the promise and as to what the promisee is doing, or may be expected to do, in reliance on it."

Similarly he set out his view that at p. 932, "the *In re Basham* principle requires some mutual 'understanding' as to the quid pro quo" – i.e. the consideration – "for the promise . . ."

Here again I think that the judge may have been too influenced by the cases on mutual wills in which a definite agreement is an essential part of the doctrine. There is of course a kernel of truth, indeed a considerable nugget of truth in this approach, because (as Balcombe L.J. said in *Wayling v. Jones* (1993) 69 P & CR 170, and other distinguished judges said in the earlier cases which he cited) there must be a sufficient link between the promises relied on and the conduct which constitutes the detriment. In cases where the detriment involves the claimant moving house (as in *Watts v. Story* (unreported), 14 July 1983; Court of Appeal (Civil Division) Transcript No. 319 of 1983), or otherwise taking some particular course of action at the other party's request, the link is, in the nature of things, going to have some resemblance to the process of offer and acceptance leading to a mutual understanding. But in other cases well within the mainstream of proprietary estoppel, such as *Inwards v. Baker* [1965] 2 QB 29 and the 19th century decisions which this court applied in that case, there is nothing like a bargain as to what particular interest is to be granted, or when it is to be granted, or by what type of disposition it is to be granted. The link is provided by the bare fact of A encouraging B to incur expenditure on A's land.

The judge seems to have recognised this point when he said, at p. 930:

> "It may be easier to infer a fixed intent when the subject matter is a particular property, which the plaintiff has been allowed to enjoy in return for services, than in relation to a whole estate."

But when he got to his conclusion he was taking too restricted a view of the first essential element of this very flexible doctrine. If it had been necessary to find a mutual understanding in this case, the judge might readily have found it in Mr. Holt promising to reward Mr. Gillett for his past, present and future loyalty and hard work which (backed up by that of Mrs. Gillett) made Mr. Holt's life more pleasant and prosperous. That seems to have been the general theme of the speech which Mr. Holt made on the occasion of his 70th birthday party in 1984. It also seems to be reflected in an exchange in Mr. Martin's cross-examination of Mr. Gillett:

> "Question: Let us take an example, you say, as I understand it, that Ken's promises were not a one-way street. You had obligations too. You were obliged to provide companionship and keep on working for him? Answer: Yes, that's fair."

But particular findings of that sort were not necessary because Mr. Gillett had abandoned his claim in contract.

Detriment

It is therefore necessary to go on to consider detriment. The judge would have decided the case against Mr. Gillett on this point also, as he indicated at the end of his judgment in the main action [1998] 3 All ER 917, 932-936. The judge devoted almost all of this part of his judgment to an analysis of whether Mr. Gillett was substantially underpaid between 1965 and 1995. He dealt with the other matters relied on as detriment in a manner which Mr. McDonnell has described as perfunctory.

It is understandable that the judge devoted most attention to the issue of Mr. Gillett being underpaid because that was the issue (affecting detriment) on which most time was spent in cross-examination, and on which Mr. Martin seems to have made most progress. It was therefore particularly expedient for the judge to record his findings about it. Mr. McDonnell called a distinguished expert witness, Professor A. K. Giles O.B.E., emeritus professor of farm management in the University of Reading. Professor Giles had prepared a report the general effect of which was to compare Mr. Gillett's salary, bonuses and other benefits during his working life (as reported by Mr. Gillett) with those reported by farm managers who participated in surveys conducted (at intervals of four or five years) by the farm management unit of the University of Reading. The results of the comparison are summarised in appendix 6 and appendix 7 to Professor Giles's report (but those appendices must of course be read subject to all the explanations and qualifications in the body of the report).

Professor Giles concluded that over the whole period from 1964 to 1995 Mr. Gillett had received earnings and benefits amounting to about 80 per cent. of the average disclosed by the survey, whereas his above average level of responsibility would have justified earnings and benefits 5 to 10 per cent. above the average. The judge noted and accepted two main criticisms of this conclusion, in addition to the small size of the sample on which the average was based: first, that some of Mrs. Gillett's earnings from K.A.H.L, were in effect a redistribution of those of her husband; and second, that no account was taken of the time which Mr. Gillett was, after 1988, devoting to the business of Countryside Companions. The judge said that he was not persuaded, on the evidence, that Mr. Gillett did in fact receive less than a reasonable wage for his services as a manager, or that he did so as part of an understanding related to his expectations, and that conclusion has not been seriously challenged in this court. The judge then said, at p. 936:

"Various other matters were relied on by Mr. Gillett in support of his case of 'detriment:' for example his refusal of inquiries from other employers, the limited provision made for his pension, the domestic tasks undertaken by him and Sally for Mr. Holt, and the money spent by him on improving The Beeches. Against that, he acknowledges that Mr. Holt was generous with gifts to the family, in paying Robert's school fees, and in other ways. It is impossible and inappropriate to attempt to weigh the balance of advantage and disadvantage. The Gilletts decided at an early stage that their future lay with Mr. Holt, and as with most human relationships that involved obligations and compensations. I cannot find in them such a balance of 'detriment' as to support the case for a legally enforceable obligation."

Both sides agree that the element of detriment is an essential ingredient of proprietary estoppel. There is one passage in the judgment of Lord Denning M.R. in *Greasley v. Cooke* [1980] 1 WLR 1306, 1311 which suggests that any action in reliance on an assurance is sufficient, whether or not the action is detrimental. In *Watts v. Story*, 14 July 1983, Dunn L.J. (who was a party to the decision in *Greasley v. Cooke*) explained Lord Denning M.R.'s observations as follows:

"Nor, if that passage from Lord Denning M.R.'s judgment is read as a whole, was he stating any new proposition of law. As the judge said, it matters not whether one talks in terms of detriment or whether one talks in terms of it being unjust or inequitable for the party giving the assurance to go back on it. It is difficult to envisage circumstances in which it would be inequitable for the party giving an assurance alleged to give rise to a proprietary estoppel, i.e. an estoppel concerned with the positive acquisition of rights and interests in the land of another, unless the person to whom the assurance was given had suffered some prejudice or detriment."

The overwhelming weight of authority shows that detriment is required. But the authorities also show that it is not a narrow or technical concept. The detriment need not consist of the expenditure of money or other quantifiable financial detriment, so long as it is something substantial. The requirement must be approached as part of a broad inquiry as to whether repudiation of an assurance is or is not unconscionable in all the circumstances.

There are some helpful observations about the requirement for detriment in the judgment of Slade L.J. in *Jones v. Watkins*, 26 November 1987. There must be sufficient causal link between the assurance relied on and the detriment asserted. The issue of detriment must be judged at the moment when the person who has given the assurance seeks to go back on it. Whether the detriment is sufficiently substantial is to be tested by whether it would be unjust or inequitable to allow the assurance to be disregarded – that is, again, the essential test of unconscionability. The detriment alleged must be pleaded and proved.

As authority for the second of these observations Slade L.J. referred to *Spencer Bower & Turner on Estoppel by Representation,* 3rd ed. (1977), p. 110, which in turn cites the judgment of Dixon J. in *Grundt v. Great Boulder Pty. Gold Mines Ltd* (1938) 59 CLR 641, 674-675 (High Court of Australia):

> "One condition appears always to be indispensable. That other must have so acted or abstained from acting upon the footing of the state of affairs assumed that he would suffer a detriment if the opposite party were afterwards allowed to set up rights against him inconsistent with the assumption. In stating this essential condition, particularly where the estoppel flows from representation it is often said simply that the party asserting the estoppel must have been induced to act to his detriment. Although substantially such a statement is correct and leads to no misunderstanding, it does not bring out clearly the basal purpose of the doctrine. That purpose is to avoid or prevent a detriment to the party asserting the estoppel by compelling the opposite party to adhere to the assumption upon which the former acted or abstained from acting. This means that the real detriment or harm from which the law seeks to give protection is that which would flow from the change of position if the assumption were deserted that led to it. So long as the assumption is adhered to, the party who altered his situation upon the faith of it cannot complain. His complaint is that when afterwards the other party makes a different state of affairs the basis of an assertion of right against him then, if it is allowed, his own original change of position will operate as a detriment. His action or inaction must be such that, if the assumption upon which he proceeded were shown to be wrong and an inconsistent state of affairs were accepted as the foundation of the rights and duties of himself and the opposite party, the consequence would be to make his original act or failure to act a source of prejudice."

This passage was not directed specifically to proprietary estoppel, but Slade L.J. was right, in my respectful view, to treat it as applicable to proprietary estoppel as well as to other forms of estoppel.

The point made in the passage may be thought obvious, but sometimes it is useful to spell out even basic points. If in a situation like that in *Inwards v. Baker* [1965] 2 QB 29, a man is encouraged to build a bungalow on his father's land and does so, the question of detriment is, so long as no dispute arises, equivocal. Viewed from one angle (which ignores the assurance implicit in the encouragement) the son suffers the detriment of spending his own money in improving land which he does not own. But viewed from another angle (which takes account of the assurance) he is getting the benefit of a free building plot. If and when the father (or his personal representative) decides to go back on the assurance and assert an adverse claim then, as Dixon J. put it in the passage just quoted from *Grundt v. Great Boulder Pty. Gold Mines Ltd.,* "if [the assertion] is allowed, his own original change of position will operate as a detriment."

The matters which Mr. Gillett pleaded as detriment, and on which he adduced evidence of detriment, included, apart from the level of his remuneration, (i) his continuing in Mr. Holt's employment (through K.A.H.L.) and not seeking or accepting offers of employment elsewhere, or going into business on his own account; (ii) carrying out tasks and spending time beyond the normal scope of an employee's duty; (iii) taking no substantial steps to secure his future wealth, either by larger pension contributions or otherwise; and (iv) expenditure on improving The Beeches farmhouse which was, Mr. Gillett said, barely habitable when it was first acquired by K.A.H.L. in 1971. That company paid for some structural work, with a local authority improvement grant, but Mr. Gillett paid for new fittings and materials and carried out a good deal of the work himself. The details are set out in part 3 and appendix 1 of Mr. Gillett's witness statement.

I have to say that I see some force in Mr. McDonnell's criticism of the judge's approach to this part of the evidence (although the judge, having decided the main action on the issue of assurances, was not obliged to cover the issue of detriment in great detail). After listening to lengthy submissions about the judgment, and after reading much of Mr. Gillett's evidence both in his witness statement and under cross-examination, I am left with the feeling that the judge, despite his very clear and careful judgment, did not stand back and look at the matter in the round. Had he done so I think he would have recognised that Mr. Gillett's case on detriment (on the facts found by the judge, and on Mr. Gillett's uncontradicted evidence) was an unusually compelling one.

In my judgment the cumulative effect of the judge's findings and of the undisputed evidence is that by 1975 (the year of The Beeches incident) Mr. Gillett had an exceptionally strong claim on Mr. Holt's conscience. Mr. Gillett was then 35. He had left school before he was 16, without taking any of the examinations which might otherwise have given him academic qualifications, against the advice of his headmaster and in the face of his parents' doubts, in order to work for and live with a 42 year old bachelor who was socially superior to, and very much wealthier than, his own parents. Mr. Holt seriously raised the possibility of adopting him. Mr. Holt's influence extended to Mr. Gillett's social and private life and it seems to have been only through the diplomacy of Miss Sally Wingate (as she then was) that Mr. Holt came to tolerate, and then accept, the notion of Mr. Gillett having a girlfriend. Mr. Holt had said that he would arrange for Mr. Gillett to go to agricultural college but then did not arrange it, and it was only through Mr. Gillett's own hard work and determination that he learned additional skills at evening classes. He proved himself by getting in the harvest in 1964 when Mr. Holt was away fishing. All these matters preceded the first of the seven assurances on which Mr. Gillett relied, so they are in a sense no more than background. But they are very important background because they refute Mr. Martin's suggestion (placed in the forefront of his skeleton argument) that Mr. Gillett's claim should be regarded as a "startling" claim by someone who was no more than an employee. On the contrary, Mr. McDonnell was not putting it too high when he said that for 30 years Mr. and Mrs. Gillett and their sons provided Mr. Holt with a sort of surrogate family.

However, a surrogate family of that sort is not the same as a birth family, and it is clear that Mr. Gillett and his wife must often have been aware of the ambivalence of their position. Mr. Holt was generous but it was the generosity of the patron; his will prevailed; Mr. and Mrs. Gillett were expected to, and did, subordinate their wishes to his: compare *In re Basham, decd.* [1986] 1 WLR 1498, 1505. One telling example of this was over the education of their sons. Mr. Holt decided that he would like to pay for the Gilletts' elder son, Robert, to go to Mr. Holt's old school (Greshams in Norfolk). The offer did not extend to their younger son, Andrew, and the Gilletts not unnaturally felt that if one boy was to go to boarding school then both should go. In the end Robert went to Greshams and Andrew to a less well known boarding school at Grimsby, and Mr. and Mrs. Gillett used some maturing short-term endowment policies and increased their overdraft in order to bear half the combined cost of the school fees and extras.

Mr. Gillett also incurred substantial expenditure on the farmhouse at The Beeches, most of it after the clear assurance which Mr. Holt gave him when, in 1975, he ventured to ask for something in writing: "that was not necessary as it was all going to be ours anyway." This was after the Gilletts had sold their own small house at Thimbleby and so had stepped off the property-owning ladder which they had got on to in 1964.

It is entirely a matter of conjecture what the future might have held for the Gilletts if in 1975 Mr. Holt had (instead of what he actually said) told the Gilletts frankly that his present intention was to make a will in their favour, but that he was not bound by that and that they should not count their chickens before they were hatched. Had they decided to move on, they might have done no better. They might, as Mr. Martin urged on us, have found themselves working for a less generous employer. The fact is that they relied on Mr. Holt's assurance, because they thought he was a man of his word, and so they deprived themselves of the opportunity of trying to better themselves in other ways. Although the judge's view, after seeing and hearing Mr. and Mrs. Gillett, was that detriment was not established, I find myself driven to the conclusion that it was amply established. I think that the judge must have taken too narrowly financial a view of the requirement for detriment, as his reference [1998] 3 All ER 917, 936 to "the balance of advantage and disadvantage" suggests. Mr. Gillett and his wife devoted the best years of their lives to working for Mr. Holt and his company, showing loyalty and devotion to his business interests, his social life and his personal wishes, on the strength of clear and repeated assurances of testamentary benefits. They received (in 1983) 20 per cent. of the shares in K.A.H.L., which must be regarded as received in anticipation of, and on account of, such benefits. Then in 1995 they had the bitter humiliation of summary dismissal and a police investigation of alleged dishonesty which the defendants called no evidence to justify at trial. I do not find Mr. Gillett's claim startling. Like Hoffmann L.J. in *Walton v. Walton* (unreported), 14 April 1994; Court of Appeal (Civil Division) Transcript No. 479 of 1994, I would find it startling if the law did not give a remedy in such circumstances.

Satisfying the equity

Since Mr. Gillett has established his claim to equitable relief, this court must decide what is the most appropriate form for the relief to take. The aim is, as Sir Arthur Hobhouse said in *Plimmer v. Wellington Corporation* (1884) 9 App Cas 699, 714, to "look at the circumstances in each case to decide in what way the equity can be satisfied." The court approaches this task in a cautious way, in order to achieve what Scarman L.J., in *Crabb v. Arun District Council* [1976] Ch 179, 198, called "the minimum equity to do justice to the plaintiff." The wide range of possible relief appears from *Snell's Equity,* 30th ed. (2000), pp. 641-643.

In this case the satisfaction of the equity presents unusually difficult problems. Often (as in *Inwards v. Baker* [1965] 2 QB 29 or *In re Basham, decd.* [1986] 1 WLR 1498) the property in dispute is a small house or a small house and some modest savings and the litigants are not wealthy enough to be much troubled by inheritance tax, capital gains tax or Schedule E tax on "golden handshakes." In this case, by contrast, it is necessary to take account of taxes and the constraints of company law. Since the litigation began Mr. Holt has made some very substantial gifts in favour of Mr. Wood. These have involved some complex manoeuvres (although these seem to have been inspired by legitimate tax-planning considerations, and not by a desire to put assets beyond Mr. Gillett's reach). It is therefore necessary to summarise the present position (as it was explained to this court on instructions).

In April 1997 the freehold in The Limes was acquired from Merton College for £1,251,000. The purchase price originated from Mr. Holt, but the transactions were structured with the use of a nominee company so as to keep Mr. Holt's tenancy in existence until Mr. Holt had completed other dispositions which he wished to make in favour of Mr. Wood. The position on the ground is now as follows.

The Limes farmhouse (with about 19 acres and two cottages in Baumber): Mr. Wood is now legal and beneficial owner with vacant possession. A minor complication (but an important one from the Gilletts' point of view) is that on part of the 19 acres there are polytunnels (prefabricated polythene greenhouses) in which Mr. Gillett has started off trees and shrubs for the business of Countryside Companions. It has recently been decided that Countryside Companions does not have an agricultural tenancy of these structures and the land which they occupy.

White House Farm (235 acres): Mr. Wood has been legal and beneficial owner since April 1996. The land is in hand and farmed under a contract farming agreement by Aubourn Farming Ltd. ("Aubourn").

The Limes farmland (520 acres): The freehold is held by K.A.H.L. as legal and beneficial owner, but K.A.H.L. owes £ 1m. to Edgescan Ltd. ("Edgescan"), its controlling shareholder (see below). This borrowing is unsecured. The tenancy has come to an end. The land is in hand and farmed by Aubourn.

The Beeches (105 acres): This land has the most complicated pattern of ownership and occupation. The freehold belongs to K.A.H.L., as it has since 1971, subject to a bank mortgage. The farmhouse is occupied by Mr. and Mrs. Gillett under a tenancy to Mr. Gillett which has limited protection under the Rent (Agriculture) Act 1976. The rent is £70 a week. The central area of the land and a small area at the east end (in all about 39 acres) are occupied by Countryside Companions under a tenancy protected by the Agricultural Holdings Act 1986. The rest of the land is in hand and farmed by Aubourn; this year's crop is wheat.

K.A.H.L.: This company has an issued capital of 2,500 £1 shares, of which 1,999 (80 per cent.) are held by Edgescan, 251 (10 per cent.) by Mr. Gillett and 250 (10 per cent.) by Mrs. Gillett. It has an unsecured liability of £1m. to Edgescan and a further liability (secured on The Beeches) of an unknown amount to the bank. The court was not told about any other assets which it owns, or of the precise terms of its contract farming arrangement with Aubourn.

Edgescan: This company is owned as to 70 per cent. by Mr. Holt and as to 30 per cent. by Mr. Wood. Mr. Holt and Mr. Wood do therefore have complete control of Edgescan and (through Edgescan) they have voting control of K.A.H.L., including control on questions which require a 75 per cent. majority.

In my judgment the extent of Mr. Holt's property in respect of which the equity is established is Mr. Holt's farming business as the parties would have contemplated it during the period when the assurances were given and down to the time when those assurances were repudiated. That is a long period and a broad approach is necessary. The property extended to the tenancy of The Limes, to the freehold of The Beeches and to the freehold of White House Farm. It did not extend to the tenancy of Greenfield Farm (which had come and gone in the ordinary course of events) or to the freehold of The Limes (acquired only in 1997). Nor did it extend to the rest of Mr. Holt's assets, even though he did between 1976 and 1991 plan to leave almost his entire estate to the Gilletts. During the late 1970's there were prolonged discussions about tax planning (in which Mr. Gillett had some involvement) and it was at that time contemplated that most of Mr. Holt's other assets might be required in order to pay capital transfer tax on the farming assets. Since then the relevant agricultural and business reliefs have become more extensive (although how long they will remain in their present form is of course unpredictable).

That is in my view the maximum extent of the equity. The court's aim is, having identified the maximum, to form a view as to what is the minimum required to satisfy it and do justice between the parties. The court must look at all the circumstances, including the need to achieve a "clean break" so far as possible and avoid or minimise future friction: see *Pascoe v. Turner* [1979] 1 WLR 431, 438-439.

In satisfying the equity it is not necessary to resort to the court's special jurisdiction under sections 459 and 461 of the Companies Act 1985, since Mr. Holt and Mr. Wood are before the court and they have complete control (subject to the constraints of company law and tax law) of Edgescan and its 80 per cent. subsidiary, K.A.H.L. Nor would it be appropriate to exercise that statutory jurisdiction unless the case for its exercise is made out, on the principles explained by the House of Lords in *In re A Company (No. 00709 of 1992)* [1999] 1 WLR 1092. The judge did not have the benefit of that decision but it confirms his view that the case was not made out in relation to K.A.H.L., in which Mr. Gillett did not have any significant holding until 1983 (he was given a single share much earlier, in 1964, when he became company secretary). The judge said [1998] 3 All ER 917, 940:

> "Any hopes Mr. Gillett may have had of becoming the owner of the company were in his personal capacity as a potential heir to Mr. Holt. They were not expectations on which he was entitled to rely in his capacity as a shareholder of K.A.H.L. Indeed, they predated his becoming a shareholder."

Apart from the formality of the single share, I agree with that; and I agree with the judge's conclusion that Mr. Gillett's section 459 petition should be dismissed.

Nevertheless it is most desirable that the Gilletts should be disentangled from K.A.H.L., just as Mr. Holt has (as part of the terms of settlement of another part of the litigation) been disentangled from G. & H. I think that the court should therefore take on itself the responsibility for directing the general machinery to be adopted in order to satisfy the equity, while leaving the parties and their advisers some room for discussion and manoeuvre (which they will, I hope, use constructively in the knowledge that they may still be neighbours for some years to come). One decision (for Mr. Gillett and his advisers alone) will be whether he and his wife, as (virtually) equal shareholders in K.A.H.L., should participate equally in the satisfaction of the equity, or whether Mr. Gillett as sole claimant should take the whole benefit of his success in the appeal.

I would dispose of the appeal in the main action by allowing it and substituting for the judge's order directions on the following lines.

The substance of *the result to be achieved*
Mr. and Mrs. Gillett are to be entitled to the freehold of the whole of The Beeches (that is the farmhouse, the land occupied by Countryside Companions and the land farmed under contract by Aubourn) together with the sum of £100,000 to compensate for the exclusion of Mr. Gillett from all the rest of the

farming business. That figure represents an overall assessment of what the justice of the case requires, taking account of numerous matters large and small, including Mr. Gillett's exceptionally long and devoted service on the one hand and the element of acceleration on the other hand. Liability for rent in respect of The Beeches will cease at once but Aubourn will be entitled to get in this year's harvest unless the parties agree otherwise. The bank mortgage must be discharged or shifted to other assets of K.A.H.L. The £100,000 will carry interest at 5 per cent. per annum from today. I do not exclude the possibility of some or all of that sum being satisfied (by agreement between the parties) by the transfer of other assets in specie, but I recognise that the layout of the properties, and the need for a clean break, may make such an agreement unlikely. It seems clear that the freehold of The Beeches plus £100,000 must exceed the net assets value of the Gilletts' 20 per cent. shareholdings in K.A.H.L.; but to the extent that it does not exceed that value, the distribution must be made either in satisfaction of (or otherwise in consideration of) their shareholdings.

The general machinery to achieve that result
Since there will also be liabilities for costs, it seems almost inevitable that K.A.H.L. will have to be put into liquidation to enable some or all of its assets to be sold or distributed in specie to its shareholders (Edgescan also being a substantial unsecured creditor). It may be that the requisite distribution in specie will require some preliminary action by Mr. Holt and Mr. Wood, as controllers of Edgescan, so as to bring the Gilletts' combined shareholdings in K.A.H.L. up to a level proportionate to what they are to receive (a deeply discounted rights issue of new K.A.H.L. shares, not taken up by Edgescan, might be one possibility). Alternatively Mr. Holt and Mr. Wood might prefer to make up some or all of the disparity by transfers of assets not held within the Edgescan group. They and their advisers must have the opportunity to consider the possibilities. The aim is not to inflict penal consequences on them, but to satisfy Mr. Gillett's equity, end Mr. and Mrs. Gillett's minority shareholdings in K.A.H.L., and give both sides the freedom to lead their own lives for the future.

I would therefore allow the appeal in the main action but dismiss the appeal in the section 459 petition relating to K.A.H.L."

SHOULD THERE BE A UNIFIED DOCTRINE OF ESTOPPEL?

In Australia as a result of decisions such as *Waltons Stores (Interstate) Ltd v. Maher*[16] and *Commonwealth v. Verwayen*[17] it would appear that there is 'but

---

[16] (1988) 164 CLR 387.
[17] (1990) 170 CLR 394.

one doctrine of estoppel'[18] based on the principle of unconscionability. However, in England despite suggestions to the effect that there should be 'one general principle shorn of limitation'[19] there have been no signs of a unified doctrine of estoppel emerging in recent years. Similarly, in this jurisdiction, despite the use of promissory estoppel in circumstances in which proprietary estoppel might have seemed more appropriate in *Re J.R.*[20], there is no real evidence of a concerted movement towards such a unified doctrine.

Re J.R.
[1993] ILRM 657

The committee of an elderly ward of court, who was living in a psychiatric hospital and was unable to manage his own affairs, sought to effect the sale of his house which had fallen into a dilapidated state. He had been living there with the respondent for many years and she maintained that when she went to live with him he had represented to her that he would look after her and that she would be sure of a home for the rest of her life. In his will the ward left everything to the respondent and at the time of its execution said to her that it was no longer his house but their house and that it would eventually be her house. Costello J found that the respondent had acted to her detriment on the representation made to her at the time she went to live with the ward that thereafter she could be sure of a home in his house for the rest of her life. He said that accordingly she had made out a case of promissory estoppel as she had acted on the representation made to her. He concluded that the equity which the respondent had been able to establish was a right to reside in the house for her life. However, in the special circumstances of the case as the house was in a serious state of dilapidation, the respondent's equity could be satisfied by selling the house and buying another one suitable for her needs.

COSTELLO J stated at pp.658–664: "Since 1990 the ward has been living in a psychiatric hospital, unable to manage his own affairs. The ward's committee now wants to sell the dwellinghouse in which he formerly lived because it has fallen into a dilapidated state. The ward is unmarried but his committee has ascertained that since 1978 he had been living in the dwellinghouse with a lady who still resides in it and who now claims rights in relation to it. This lady has been named as the respondent to this motion, a motion seeking an order for sale. As will appear later, it is obviously in the interests of the proper management of the ward's estate that this be done, but the court is of course

---

[18] *Commonwealth v. Verwayen* (1990) 170 CLR 394, 412.
[19] *Amalgamated Investement and Property Co. Ltd v. Texas Commerce International Bank Ltd* [1982] QB 84, 122.
[20] [1993] ILRM 657.

bound by any rights affecting the property and the court's power of sale may be restricted by rights which may have been created by the ward. The issues now for determination are the nature of the rights, if any, to which the respondent is entitled in the property, and the proper order to be made in the circumstances.

The ward is now aged 73 years. He was admitted to a psychiatric hospital in Dublin on 19 July 1990 for investigation of a depressed mood, weight loss and inability to take care of himself. He was then depressed and disorientated, with decreased concentration and some short term and some long term loss of memory. It was established on assessment that he could not live on his own and that he required help with dressing, bathing, toileting and even with sorting out his own possessions. A diagnosis of multiple infarct dementia having been made he was transferred to a psycho-geriatric unit. Since then his mood has fluctuated and at times he is regarded as a suicide risk. In February of this year he became very agitated but a change in medication seemed to bring about an improvement for a limited time. His cognitive functions cannot improve but there is a possibility, but it is only a possibility, that his depression may improve. His life expectation is quite good, but he will need full-time institutional care for the rest of his life. I am quite satisfied that he will never be able to return to live in his former dwellinghouse. He made a will in 1988 and I think it is extremely unlikely that he will ever be capable of making another will.

When taken into wardship on 8 October 1990 the General Solicitor was appointed committee of his person and his estate. There is presently standing to the credit of his account the sum of £39,205.61. In addition he is the owner of a dwelling house the subject of these proceedings.

The respondent to this motion was born on 2 November 1944 so that she is now nearly 48 years of age. She married in 1965 but her husband left her in September 1971 and she has not heard from him since. There were two children of the marriage, a son born in July 1968 and a daughter born in February 1970 but as the respondent was unable to look after them they were brought up by her mother. In 1968 she suffered a brain tumour. The operation to remove it was successful and thereafter for some years she was able to work as a tailoress. But in 1977 a second brain tumour developed and although it was successfully removed she has since been disabled; her leg is permanently weakened so that she has to use a stick, and one of her arms is almost powerless. She has been unable to work and has had only a small disability pension on which to live. She has suffered from depression. This was so severe that in 1978 she required hospitalisation in a Dublin hospital. There she met the ward. He too was undergoing psychiatric treatment. They struck up a friendship which developed into a deeper relationship and resulted in his asking her to go to live with him in the dwelling which is the subject of these proceedings. They lived together as man and wife until 1990 when the ward had to be taken into hospital because of the illnesses to which I have referred. When they lived together the ward maintained the respondent out of his resources, and in addition gave her a small allowance to augment her disability pension.

The respondent's claim to a legal interest in the ward's dwelling is based on the following facts. She says that when she went to live with him that he represented to her that he would look after her, and that she would be sure of a home for the rest of her life. She says that he continued to make these representations to her and she acted on them. Furthermore, on 2 November 1988 the ward made a will. By it he bequeathed

> all my property of every nature and kind whatsoever both real and personal including my residence at . . . to my great friend . . . [the respondent] for her own use and benefit absolutely. . . .

and he appointed the respondent executrix of his will. The evidence establishes that the will was validly executed, and that the ward was of sound mind, memory and understanding when he executed it. 2 November was the respondent's birthday. On that day he handed her a folder which contained his will and said to her, 'it's not my house now, it's our house and eventually it will be your house'. It will be recalled that the ward was then 69 years of age, and that the respondent was 44.

The ward's dwelling is now in a very dilapidated state, as appears from an architect's report of 31 July 1991. Urgent repairs are needed to the roof and the rear wall, the house timbers need to be checked and because of damp penetration their replacement may be necessary. The cost of making the house structurally sound is estimated at £34,000. The ward's only money is a sum of £39,205 and out of this, liabilities will have to be discharged including (a) such sums that may be due to the hospital, (b) the cost of future maintenance, (c) costs of the committee (past and future), (d) the possibility of future specialist nursing for the ward and (e) eventually his funeral expenses. The respondent agrees that the dwelling is in need of repairs but has obtained a contractor's estimate that urgent repairs could be carried out at a cost of £3,000.

The claims advanced on behalf of the respondent are based (a) on the representations made to her at the time she went to live with the ward and subsequently and (b) the representations made on 2 November 1988. She relies on the principles of the law of estoppel. For present purposes I will use the classification which is now generally accepted (see Snell's *Principles of Equity,* 28th ed., p. 554 and Halsbury's *Laws of England* (4th ed.), vol. 16, 1071, 1072) and refer to (i) promissory estoppel and (ii) proprietary estoppel. A promissory estoppel will arise where by words or conduct a person makes an unambiguous representation as to his future conduct, intending that the representation will be relied on, and to affect the legal relations between the parties, and the representee acts on it or alters his or her position to his or her detriment, the representor will not be permitted to act inconsistently with it (see Snell's *Principles of Equity*, 28th ed., 556). If the subject matter of the representation is land, no right or interest in the land results from this estoppel – a personal right is vested in the representee which will preclude the representor from enforcing a title to the land. A proprietary estoppel is different in a number of ways. When it relates to land it may result in the creation of rights in or over the land. It has been explained as follows.

> Where one person (A) has acted to his detriment on the faith of a belief, which was known to and encouraged by another person (B), that he either has or is going to be given a right in or over B's property, B cannot insist on his strict legal rights if to do so would be inconsistent with A's belief. (See *In re Basham* [1987] 1 All ER 405 at 410).

Maharaj v. Chand [1986] AC 898 illustrates the operation of the law relating to promissory estoppel. This was a case which originated in Fiji and was eventually decided by the Privy Council. The plaintiff and the defendant were living as man and wife (but unmarried) when the plaintiff applied to the housing authority for a lease to enable him to build a house. With the approval of the Native Land Trust Board he obtained a sub-lease and erected a house on the land demised to him. In reliance on a representation made by the plaintiff to her that it would be a permanent home for her and her children the defendant left her flat and went to live with the plaintiff. Their relationship later broke down. The plaintiff left the house, giving the defendant permission to remain in it. Later he revoked the permission and instituted ejectment proceedings against her. The trial judge dismissed the claim on the ground that the plaintiff was estopped from evicting her. On appeal the plaintiff succeeded on the ground that the licence he gave the defendant was an unlawful 'dealing' within the meaning of s. 12 of the Native Land Trust Act. The Privy Council allowed the defendant's appeal and restored the order of the trial judge.

In reaching its conclusions the Privy Council firstly held that s. 12 did not apply as the right on which the defendant relied was a purely personal right and no 'dealing' with the land in breach of the section had occurred. Its opinion was that it might have been possible, but for the provisions of that section, to have made out an entitlement to an equitable interest in the land but this had not been claimed. The claim advanced was a more modest one, namely that the requirements of a promissory estoppel existed. It was pointed out that the plaintiff had represented to the defendant that the house would be a permanent home for herself and her children, that in reasonable reliance on this representation she acted to her detriment by giving up her flat, that it was not possible to restore her to her former position. In these circumstances it would be 'plainly inequitable' the court concluded for the plaintiff to evict her and held that she had permission to reside permanently in the house, that this was a personal right which did not amount to a property interest diminishing the right of the plaintiff's lessor or mortgagee.

Greasley v. Cooke [1980] 1 WLR 1306 is an example of proprietary estoppel. It was a case in which the owners by inheritance of a dwelling house took ejectment proceedings against an occupier whose defence was that she had reasonably believed and was encouraged by members of the family of the deceased owner so to believe that she could regard the property as her home for the rest of her life and that she was entitled to a declaration to that effect. The evidence established that in 1938 at the age of 16 she went to the house as a maid servant of the deceased, that from 1946 she had co-habited in it with one of the deceased's sons, that after the owner's death she remained in the house and looked after it and also cared for the deceased's mentally ill daughter, that she received no payment, that she had been assured by members of the family that she could regard the house as her home for the rest of her life. It was held by the Court of Appeal that once it was shown that the defendant had relied on the assurances given to her then the burden of proving that she had acted to her detriment in staying on to look after the house without payment did not rest on her and that in the absence of proof to the contrary the court could infer that her conduct was induced by the assurances given to her, that expenditure of money was not a necessary element to establish proprietary estoppel, and that it was for the courts to decide in what way the equity established by the evidence should be satisfied.

Another example of the operation of the doctrine of proprietary estoppel is to be found in *In re Basham* [1987] 1 All ER 405. The plaintiff's mother married a second time when the plaintiff was aged 15. The plaintiff worked for her stepfather without payment for many years, helping him to run various public houses and a service station. After she had herself married she considered moving elsewhere but she was dissuaded by her stepfather from doing so. After the death of her mother she looked after her stepfather. He owned a cottage and on many occasions he indicated to her that she would get the cottage on his death in return for what she had been doing for him and also his estate. But he died intestate and two nieces were his next of kin. The plaintiff instituted these proceedings claiming a declaration that she was entitled to the deceased's entire estate because the deceased had induced and encouraged in her the expectation or belief that she would receive the estate on his death and because she had acted to her detriment in reliance on that expectation a proprietary estoppel arose in her favour. She succeeded in her claim.

Having stated the principle of proprietary estoppel already quoted, the court pointed out that although the principle is commonly known as proprietary estoppel where the belief is that A is going to be given a right in the future it may properly be regarded as giving rise to a species of constructive trust, the concept employed by a court of equity to prevent a person from relying on his legal rights when it would be unconscionable for him to do so. The court held that a proprietary estoppel could be raised when an expectation exists that future rights would be given over a person's residuary estate. As the plaintiff's belief that she would inherit the estate had been encouraged by the deceased and as the plaintiff had acted to her detriment in subordinating her own interests to the wishes of the deceased in reliance on her belief that she would inherit, she had established a proprietary estoppel and was entitled to the estate. The court considered how effect should be given to the equity which had arisen in the plaintiff's favour. It held that the extent of the equity was to have made good, as far as could fairly be done between the parties, the expectations which the deceased had encouraged. It followed from this that the plaintiff was entitled to a declaration that the personal representatives held the whole of the net estate in trust for the plaintiff.

Conclusions
In the light of the facts and the applicable legal principles, I have come to the following conclusions:

(1) The uncontradicted evidence is that at the time that the respondent went to live with the ward and thereafter he represented to her that he would look after her and that she could be sure of a home in his dwellinghouse for the rest of her life. I think the respondent acted on this representation and that she did so to her detriment. The law relating to the nature of detriment suffered by a representee has been clarified by a number of recent cases. As was shown in *Maharaj v. Chand* detriment may exist when a representee leaves a permanent home on the faith of a representation that another will be offered in its place. Whilst I have no evidence of where the respondent was living in 1978 I think I am entitled to assume that she had a house or a flat which she gave up to go live with the respondent and that accordingly she has made out a case of promissory estoppel as she acted on the representation made to her. It would be plainly inequitable for the ward now to deny that she has a right to live in his house and it seems to me that she has an equity which entitles her to stay in the house rent free for as long as she wishes to which the court must give effect.

(2) I do not think that any further or additional rights were conferred by the events of 2 November 1988. When on 2 November 1988 the ward handed the respondent a folder and said 'it's not my house now, it's our house and eventually will be yours' I think he was intending by those words to give a gift of an interest in the house to the respondent. But the respondent cannot claim any enforceable rights from this fact, because the gift was an imperfect one which the courts cannot enforce. I do not think that by using those words and handing her the executed will the ward thereby conferred on the respondent an immediate beneficial interest under a constructive trust – the ward intended that she would have (a) a right to reside in the house during his life and (b) ownership of it after his death, but he did not intend that she would have an immediate beneficial interest in it - if he had so intended he would have arranged to transfer the property either to her alone or jointly with him. And the respondent cannot rely on the doctrine of estoppel because she cannot show that she acted in any way to her detriment arising from the representation which was made to her on 2 November.

In cases such as this the court must (a) ascertain the nature of the equity to which a representee is entitled and (b) decide in what way the equity may be satisfied (see Denning MR in *Greasley v. Cooke, op. cit.,* p.1312). The equity which the respondent has been able to establish is a right to reside in the ward's dwellinghouse for her life and normally such a right would be satisfied by an order refusing to evict the representee or where the representor is a ward of court refusing to sell the dwellinghouse. But there are special circumstances in this case. The house is in a very serious state of dilapidation. Major work needs to be done on it. There has been severe damp penetration which has caused the timbers to rot. There is rising damp in the basement walls, the plumbing and electrical wiring needs to be replaced. The cost of doing the work was estimated last year as being £34,000 approximately. It is quite a large three storey house and the respondent no longer uses the basement. It is not reasonable to spend the ward's limited resources in attempting to repair it and the respondent herself has no money to do so and no doubt it is declining in value all the time. The respondent's equity can be satisfied by selling the house and buying another smaller one suitable for the respondent's needs. It should be bought in the ward's name but I will declare that the respondent has a right to reside in it for as long as she wishes. This will not of course prejudice in any way the rights she will have should the ward predecease her (as would normally be expected) and should he not revoke his will (a most remote eventuality).

In order to satisfy the equity the new house should meet the respondent's reasonable needs for accommodation as a single person. It should be purchased in consultation with the respondent and should any difference arise this motion can be re-entered. The committee should take expert advice as to when to sell and when to purchase the new property.

I will therefore order that the premises be sold provided that there is made available to the respondent suitable alternative accommodation in a dwelling to be purchased in the ward's name, and I will declare that the respondent has a right to live in the newly acquired dwelling for as long as she may wish."

CHAPTER 18

Tracing

TRACING IN EQUITY

General Principles

Tracing in equity is usually sought where property has come into the hands of trustees and other persons in a fiduciary relationship. It is a remedy *in rem*, 'a claim to follow and recover property with which, in equity at all events, [a person] had never really parted'.[1] The right to trace in equity also exists against an innocent volunteer who comes into possession of the trust property although it does not extend to purchasers for value of the property without notice of the right to trace.

Where a trustee has mixed trust funds with other monies the beneficiaries will have a charge over this mixed fund.[2] However, where a trustee has mixed the funds of more than one trust or has transferred funds to an innocent volunteer, the beneficiaries of these funds and the volunteer must share the mixed fund rateably.[3] As Lord Millett commented in *Foskett v. McKeown*[4] '[i]nnocent contributors, however, must be treated equally *inter se*. Where the beneficiary's claim is in competition with the claims of other innocent contributors, there is no basis upon which any of the claims can be subordinated to any of the others.'

Shanahan's Stamp Auctions Ltd v. Farrelly
[1962] IR 386

A company which grouped investors into syndicates and used their funds to buy stamps went into liquidation. Some of these investors had been allocated to syndicates at the time and the liquidator sought directions from the court about priority of payments as between the general creditors and the syndicated and unsyndicated investors. Budd J held that at all material times a fiduciary relationship existed between the company and the investors and that both classes of investors were entitled to trace their money. The stamps allocated to the syndicates were held to be subject to a charge in favour of the syndicated

---

[1] *Sinclair v. Brougham* [1914] AC 398, 418.
[2] *Re Hallett's Estate* (1880) 13 Ch D 696.
[3] *Re Diplock* [1948] Ch 465.
[4] [2000] 2 WLR 1299, 1327.

investors for the amount of the investment and the remaining stamps were held by the company subject to a charge in favour of the unsyndicated investors on a rateable basis.

BUDD J stated at pp.425–449: "Several leading cases were cited to me in connection with the rights of persons in the position of the investors in this case and these I now propose to examine in order to see what are the general principles applicable in cases of this kind and what resultant rights, if any, accrue to the investors, either at law or in equity.

I come first to the well-known case of *In re Hallett's Estate* (1880) 13 Ch D 696 which I may describe as the mainstay of the defendants' contentions. Several persons brought claims in the administration of the estate of Hallett against monies in his bankers' hands. Hallett was a solicitor. There was a claim by the trustees of his marriage settlement. A sum was settled for the benefit of Hallett, his wife and children. The trustees had allowed the fund to come into Hallett's hands. Several changes were made in the investment of the fund by Hallett. He held a considerable number of Russian bonds and the Court took the view that he had in 1877 allotted these bonds to the nominal amounts of £1554 and £1036 as representing the trust funds under the settlement. The bonds for £1554 were delivered to the trustees after his death. The bonds for £1036 were deposited by Hallett with his bankers. He had also acted for a Mrs. Cottrill, as her solicitor. It was proved that he had bought or appropriated, and in 1877 held for her, Russian bonds of £450 and £2242, nominal amount. In 1877, without authority from the trustees or Mrs. Cottrill, he directed his bankers to sell one of the sets of the bonds representing the trust funds mentioned above and both sets of Mrs. Cottrill's bonds. The amounts received were lodged to his bank account. Before his death he drew out different sums for his own purposes, so that the balance to his credit at the time of his death (if nothing more had been paid in) would have been £1708 16*s.* He had, however, paid in other sums, so that at the time of his death in 1878 he had a balance of £3029 15*s.* 1*d.* Of this, £2600 had been paid into Court in the administration action. The trustees of the settlement applied for the payment of £770 10*s.* 5*d.* out of the £2600 and for a declaration that the produce of the sale of the bonds for £1554 belonged to them. Mrs. Cottrill applied for the payment of the £1708 16*s.*, balance.

I need not dwell on the exact manner in which the Court determined the various conflicting claims but I wish to refer to certain statements as to the principles of equity applicable to such a case made in the Court of Appeal in the course of deciding the matter. Jessel M.R. found that Hallett stood in a fiduciary capacity to Mrs. Cotterill. He stated that the modern doctrine of equity with regard to property disposed of by persons standing in a fiduciary capacity was well settled. At page 708 he said:– "You can, if the sale was rightful, take the proceeds of the sale, if you can identify them. If the sale was wrongful, you can still take the proceeds of sale, in a sense adopting the sale for the purpose of taking the proceeds, if you can identify them. There is no distinction, therefore, between a rightful and a wrongful disposition of the property, so far as regards the right of the beneficial owner to follow the proceeds." He then goes on to deal with the case where the proceeds may have been invested, or have been invested along with money belonging to the person in a fiduciary capacity, in a purchase. In a case where the purchase has been made with trust money, he says, at p. 709:– ". . . the beneficial owner has a right to elect either to take the property purchased, or to hold it as a security for the amount of the trust money laid out in the purchase; or," in other words, "to have a charge on the property for the amount of the trust money." In the case, however, where the trustee has mixed the money with his own the *cestui que trust* or beneficial owner cannot elect to take the property, but, he says, "He is, however, still entitled to a charge on the property purchased, for the amount of the trust money laid out in the purchase and that charge is quite independent of the fact of the amount laid out by the trustee." He then makes it clear that what he has said applies to all persons in a fiduciary relationship. At page 710, he says:– "Therefore, the moment you establish the fiduciary relation, the modern rules of equity, as regards following trust money, apply." Later he refers to what Lord Ellenborough said in his reference to the case where money is mixed, and points out that "he was not aware of the rule of equity which gave you a charge." He points out that as regards following the money there is no difference in the position of the factor and the trustee.

He dealt then in another portion of the case on appeal with the point as to whether beneficiaries were entitled to say that the payments drawn out of the account by Hallett after November, 1877, and applied to his own use should be treated as appropriated to the repayment of his own monies or whether the executors were right in their contention that the payments out should be applied to the first item on the credit side in order of date, which would have meant that the trust funds were diminished. Approaching the point on principle, he said, at p. 727:– "Now, first upon principle, nothing can be better settled, either in our own law, or, I suppose, the law of all civilised countries, than this, that where a man does an act which may be rightly performed, he cannot say that that act was intentionally and in fact done wrongly." On that principle counsel for the investors strongly rely. Further on, he says:– "When we come to apply that principle to the case of a trustee who has blended trust monies with his own, it seems to me perfectly plain that he cannot be heard to say that he took away the trust money when he had a right to take away his own money."

Jessel M.R. then proceeds to deal with the rule in *Clayton's Case* (1816) 1 Mer 572 to the broad effect that the first sum drawn out is attributable to the first sum paid in. That is, he says, a very convenient rule which he has nothing to say against unless, inter alia, there be evidence of circumstances from which a contrary intention must be presumed when the presumption gives way to other considerations. Dealing with *Pennell v. Deffell* (1853) 4 De GM & G 372, he states his disagreement with portion of the application of the principle

in that case with regard to the rights of the *cestui que trust*. He says, at p. 730:–
"No human being ever gave credit to a man on the theory that he would
misappropriate trust money, and thereby increase his assets. No human being
ever gave credit, even beyond that theory, that he should not only misappropriate
trust monies to increase his assets, but that he should pay the trust monies so
misappropriated to his own banking account with his own monies, and draw
out after that a larger sum than the first sums paid in for the trust monies."

Baggallay L.J. construed the judgments in *Pennell v. Deffell* as enunciating
as a general principle that the rule in *Clayton's Case* must be applied to the
banking accounts of trustees for the purpose of determining the proportions in
which the *cestui que trust* and general creditors, or the several classes of *cestui
que trust*, are entitled to the debt due from the bankers on closing the account.
"But," he asks (at p. 738), "was it more than the enunciation of a general
principle; that is to say, a principle to be applied in the absence of special
circumstances, but liable to be modified in its application by reason of the
necessity or propriety of applying some other general principle of equal or
paramount importance?" He says that he can find no reason assigned why the
rule of attributing honest motives to a trustee was treated as having no
application. His view was that, in a case such as that which was the subject of
the appeal, full effect should be given to the principle of attributing the honest
intention where the circumstances of the case permit of such a presumption.
He thus agreed with the Master of the Rolls, so far. He said, however, that in
the case where the ultimate balance is not sufficient to meet the claims in
respect of distinct trusts the strict application of the rule of appropriating in
order of date the drawings out to the payments in probably would be correct.
In other words, *Clayton's Case* would in such instance apply as between various
cestuis que trustent. Fry J. in the Court below held the same view. He then
went on to say that where the dealings of the trustee have never reduced the
balances below the amount of the trust monies paid in, it was to his mind
difficult to attribute to the trustee any other intention than that of appropriating
his drawings to his own private monies, so as to leave the trust monies intact.

It would appear therefore that *Hallett's Case* (1880) 13 Ch D 696 establishes
certain principles.

If money held by a person in a fiduciary capacity, though not a trustee, has
been paid into his bank account, it can be followed by the beneficiary. Secondly,
the beneficiary has a charge for it on the balance in the banker's hands. Thirdly,
if the person holding the money in a fiduciary capacity mixed it with his own
the rule in *Clayton's Case* does not apply; such person must be taken to have
drawn out his own monies in preference to the trust monies but it would appear
to apply between beneficiaries. Fourthly, if the person in a fiduciary capacity
makes a purchase with mixed funds of his own and of the beneficiary, the
beneficiary is entitled to a charge to the extent of the amount of the trust money
laid out in the purchase. Finally, where a man does an act which may be rightly
performed he cannot say that the act was intentionally, and in fact, done wrongly.

There is, however, another point to which I must refer which is relevant to the facts of this case. Jessel M.R. refers (13 Ch D 696, at p. 718) to part of the judgment of Knight Bruce L.J. in *Pennell v. Deffell* (1853) 4 De GM & G 372. Lord Justice Knight Bruce had referred to the cases both of the trust fund being kept separate and mixed; and Jessel M.R. quotes with apparent approval what was next said, which is as follows:- "But not in either case, as I conceive, would the blending together of the trust monies, however confusedly, be of any moment as between various *cestuis que trustent* on the one hand and the executors, as representing the general creditors, on the other." As I construe the quotation as approved by Jessel M.R., that amounts to saying that the claim of the beneficiaries ranks before the claim of general creditors. The comments of Baggallay L.J., at p. 745, on *Pennell v. Deffell* also seem to me to support that view in so many words.

In re Hallett's Estate was applied in *Sinclair v. Brougham* [1914] AC 398. The case concerned conflicting claims in the winding up in 1911 of the Birkbeck Permanent Benefit Building Society, formed in 1851. It was empowered by its rules to borrow to an unlimited extent and developed a banking business. Questions of priority arose between the creditors, the unadvanced shareholders and the bank customers, called the depositors. The assets were insufficient to pay all the claimants in full. The creditors were paid by arrangement. The carrying on of the banking business was held *ultra vires* and it was also held that the depositors were not entitled to recover the monies paid by them on an *ultra vires* contract of loan on the footing of monies lent and received to their use. But applying the principle in *In re Hallett's Estate* it was held that the assets remaining after paying off the creditors must be taken to represent in part monies which the depositors could follow, as invalidly borrowed, and in part monies which the society could follow as having been wrongfully employed by its agents in the banking business and which ought to be distributed *pari passu* between the depositors and unadvanced shareholders according to the amounts respectively credited to them in the books of the society at the commencement of the winding up. That was, however, subject to any application by any individual depositor or shareholder with a view to tracing his money into any particular asset and to the costs of the liquidation.

It was, as I understood it, urged on behalf of the plaintiffs that the judgments in *Sinclair v. Brougham* showed that a proprietary interest must be shown to exist in the investors in specific stamps before they could claim the stamps or have a tracing order made. Certain portions of the judgment of Viscount Haldane L.C., at pp. 420 and 421, were relied on for this contention. Haldane L.C., stated that it is impossible to confine the right at law to follow where there was a fiduciary relationship. "The principle," he said – and this is what is relied on – "appears to me to cover all cases where the property in the money has not passed, and the money itself can be earmarked in the hands of the person who has wrongly obtained it." He goes on to say, in so many words, that he is dealing with the common law position and, as I read his judgment, goes on to show the limitations of the common law remedy, in that it gave no remedy where the money had been paid into the wrongdoer's account with his banker who simply owed him a debt so that no money could in the contemplation of a court of law be earmarked. But having considered these observations, it seems to me that they were as to the first part only directed merely to a consideration of the position at common law, and he later indicated that equity gave a further remedy. Dealing with the case of money paid into a wrongdoer's bank account he says, at p. 420:– "The Court of Chancery could and would declare, even as against the general creditors of the wrongdoer, that there was what it called a charge on the banker's debt to the person whose money had been paid into the latter's bank account in favour of the person whose money it really was." He goes on to point out with apparent approval to what Jessel M.R. said in *Hallett's Case*, that this equity was not confined to cases of trusts in the strict sense but applied to every case where there was a fiduciary relationship. He thought it merely an additional right which could be enforced whenever money was held in equity to belong to the plaintiff. He further indicates, in my view, by the way he proceeded that in a case where money was held in equity to belong to a plaintiff, he regarded the principle of declaring a charge on any mass of money or securities with which the plaintiff's money had been mixed to be applicable. I cannot read his judgment as in any way cutting down the equitable principle enunciated in *In re Hallett's Estate*. Indeed, his judgment may be said to carry the principle of following property outside the range of fiduciary relationships. It will be noted particularly that in that part of his judgment to which I have referred he seems to have regarded the right of the person to whom the money belonged in equity to come before the right of creditors, but it is right to say that he later points out that as the creditors had been paid by consent the House had not to consider their position. At pages 422 and 423 he indicates a distinction from *Hallett's Case* in that the investment of the depositors' money was not made in breach of fiduciary duty, but he states that the depositors had the right to follow their money invalidly borrowed into the assets of the society. It is argued that the investors have a similar right where the Company's purchase of stamps was not in breach of fiduciary duty.

On another aspect of the case relevant to the present case Haldane L.C., at p. 423, expresses the view that it makes no difference that the value of the assets has shrunk so that the two sets of claimants cannot be paid in full. The depositors have no right to disaffirm the transaction to the extent of claiming that their money has been applied in breach of trust, but they can adopt the dealings with the money they have handed over, under circumstances in which it never really ceased to be theirs, and he says that the depositors can claim the part of the mass of assets which represents their money as belonging to them in equity. Depreciation and loss, he says, must be borne *pro rata*. Assuming that specific tracing is not possible, he expresses the view that the proper direction to the liquidator is that he should apportion the remaining assets between depositors and shareholders in proportion to the amounts credited to them respectively in the books of the society at the commencement of the winding up. He later makes it clear that the distribution is to be subject to the payment of all proper costs, charges and expenses and to any application that might be made by any individual depositor or shareholder with a view to tracing his own money into any particular asset.

Lord Dunedin, at p. 438, also takes the view that in the absence of direct evidence the only equitable means is to let each party bear the shrinkage proportionately to the amount originally contributed even though not in a fiduciary relationship to one another.

Lord Parker of Waddington, at p. 440, dealt with the position of lenders in an *ultra vires* transaction. Although dealing with the particular facts, he dealt, I think it may be said, with principles of general application, at the end of page 441. Treating of cases where a fiduciary relationship existed, and having dealt with common law remedies, he stated that equity treated the matter from a different standpoint. "Starting," he said, "from a personal equity, based on the consideration that it would be unconscionable for anyone who could not plead purchase for value without notice to retain an advantage derived from the misapplication of trust money, it ended, as was so often the case, in creating what were in effect rights of property, though not recognised as such by the common law." He then referred with approval to what Jessel M.R. had said with regard to following trust money and particularly to the case where a purchase had been made partly with trust money and partly with money of the trustee. He takes an illustration relevant, I think, to the matter for decision in this case. "Suppose," he says, at p. 442, "the property is acquired by means of money, part of which belongs to one owner and part to another, the purchaser being in a fiduciary relationship to both. Clearly each owner has an equal equity. Each is entitled to a charge on the property for his own money, and neither can claim priority over the other. It follows that their charges must rank *pari passu* according to their respective amounts." He adds, however, I should say, that he thinks that as against the fiduciary agent they could by agreement claim to take the property itself, in which case they would become tenants in common in shares proportioned to amounts for which either could claim a charge. This latter *dictum* Mr. Matheson would, no doubt, seek to avail of.

Lord Sumner also thought that the principle of rateable division was sound on the facts of the case, i.e., where there are classes of claimants with equal claims, and he approved the application of the principles of *Hallett's Case*. I quote the words which he used, at p. 459, on this aspect of the case: he said:–
"My Lords, I agree, without recapitulating reasons, that the principle on which *Hallett's Case* is founded justifies an order allowing the appellants to follow the assets, not merely to the verge of actual identification, but even somewhat further in a case like the present, where after a process of exclusion only two classes or groups of persons, having equal claims, are left in and all superior

claims have been eliminated. Tracing in a sense it is not, for we know that the money coming from A. went into one security and that coming from B. went into another, and that the two securities did not probably depreciate exactly in the same percentage, and we know further that no one will ever know any more. Still I think this well within the 'tracing' equity, and that among persons making up these two groups the principle of rateable division of the assets is sound."

Whether the decision in *Sinclair v. Brougham* extends the principles laid down in *Hallett's Case* or illustrates how these principles can be applied it is not necessary to determine. It does, however, seem evident that the decision does not cut down in any way the principles of *Hallett's Case*. The decision seems relevant to the facts of this case in that it shows that where money belonging to a person in equity has been first mixed with the monies of another and then used in a further fashion, so that it is traceable to assets in the other's hands, a remedy of recovery by way of charge is open in equity. Furthermore, where the money thus used belongs to a number of people and the ultimate assets into which the money has found its way have shrunk or become depleted the proper remedy is to declare a charge and order a *pro rata* distribution amongst the parties entitled. Actual identification with any particular asset is apparently not essential to the application of the principle so long as by some process it can be shown that the monies of the claimants can be shown to have found their way into the property or assets held by another. Justice is done by allowing them to claim by way of charge in accordance with the amounts contributed by each.

In addition to the portions of the judgments I have referred to, the matter of the position of general creditors was touched on. Unfortunately the question of their rights did not come in issue directly because – possibly because since their claims were small – they were paid by agreement. Lord Haldane, it will have been noted, said that a person whose money had been paid by a wrongdoer into his bank could in equity obtain a charge, even as against the creditors of the wrongdoer, but with the qualification I have noted. However, dealing with the rights of depositors, at p. 424, he pointed out that there had been no breach of fiduciary duty on the part of the society and he says that that circumstance is material in distinguishing the consequences from those followed in *Hallett's Case*, on the footing that there the agent could not gain, at the expense of the principal, an advantage for himself or his general creditors by, in effect, setting up a breach of duty. The depositors could in his opinion only claim the depreciated assets which represented their money. I have some uncertainty as to whether this means merely that their claim is only to such depreciated assets as represent their money in the sense that they have no claim to come in before the shareholders or whether it means that they must take what is left after the creditors have been paid. I incline to the view that it means the former since it is not expressly said that the creditors were rightly paid first and having regard to what he had said immediately before which indicates that he is dealing with the state of affairs where both the society and depositors have rival claims.

Lord Dunedin also dealt with the creditors, at page 437. He started by saying their claims were paid because they were inconsiderable. But, although the point was not in issue, he went on to say that they were in his judgment rightly paid under the circumstances of the actual case as they would rank, after the expenses of liquidation, first in the ranking. He gave his reasons. In a question with the shareholders they were debts of a character which the directors had power to make. In a question with the depositors they were incurred in a business, illegal, no doubt, as for the society, but one which the depositors were willing that the directors should carry on. He seems then to equate them to the position of shareholders. I shall have to return later to what he said in dealing with the position of the creditors.

Lord Parker of Waddington, also, dealt with the position of creditors at pages 443 to 445. He was dealing with the case of *In re Guardian Permanent Benefit Building Society (Crace-Calvert's Case)* (1882) 23 Ch D 440. The Court of Appeal had decided in effect that the society had no power to borrow at all, a decision subsequently reversed by the House of Lords. Jessel M. R. had held as fully established that the assets of the society, which was in liquidation, had been increased by borrowed monies and had held that after the payment of the costs and all debts and everything to which the members were entitled by way of return of capital and bonus the surplus ought to be returned to the people who advanced the monies on the plainest of principles of equity. Lord Parker said he thought that what was meant was that it would be inequitable for the society to take advantage of the misapplication by its agents of money belonging to others and held in a fiduciary capacity. But he criticised the directions given by the Court with the object of working out this equity. He thought that if the monies were advanced when the assets of the society were insufficient to pay the creditors in full or anything to the contributories, but that by means of the *ultra vires* loans the assets at the date of the winding up had been so increased that both creditors and contributories could be paid in full, it would not be in accordance with equity and good conscience that these creditors and contributories should claim to be paid in full. It rather seemed to him that the increase in assets due to the *ultra vires* borrowing ought to be restored to the lenders. The basis of this reasoning was that the monies were in the position of trust monies. He said that neither creditors nor contributories ought, in equity, to be allowed to retain an advantage derived by reason of the misapplication by the society's agents of monies which were in the position of trust monies. Having criticised the manner in which counsel sought to explain the decision he did, however, say that if an inquiry had been directed it might have been shown that the debts due to the ordinary creditors had really been incurred in preserving the bulk of assets in which the shareholders and *ultra vires* lenders alike were interested, in which case it might be equitable that these debts should be paid first out of the fund. If the debts were shown, however, to have been incurred before *ultra vires* borrowings he said he could not at present see how the creditors could claim to be in a better position because of the *ultra vires* borrowing.

I have dwelt upon the reasoning of Lord Parker of Waddington as above stated because it was relied upon to support the case of the creditors in this case. But I do not think that anything which Lord Parker said is really relevant to the facts of the present case in that he was dealing with the claims of contributories and *ultra vires* lenders as against creditors. In the case now before me there is no question of the claim of contributories or *ultra vires* lenders. The claim is made by investors against the Company, who claim that the Company stands in a fiduciary position to them. They are not in the position of *ultra vires* lenders. Their investments were made in proper legal fashion. They are therefore entitled to follow or trace their money into the stamps purchased with it and on the principle of *Hallett's Case* they urge that their right to the proceeds of sale of the property purchased with trust monies takes priority to the claims of creditors.

The principles laid down in *Hallett's Case* were further considered *In re Diplock; Diplock v. Wintle* [1948] 1 Ch 465. Each side relied on various parts of the judgments in the case as supporting its contentions.

Caleb Diplock, by his will, directed his executors to apply his residuary estate "for such charitable institution or institutions or other charitable or benevolent object or objects in England as my acting executors or executor may in their or his absolute discretion select." The executors distributed a large portion of the residue amongst a large number of charities. The next-of-kin then challenged the validity of the bequest, which was held invalid. The claims of the next-of-kin against the executors were compromised. They then brought actions against institutions which had participated in the distribution. In most cases the cheques sent by the executors had been paid into the institution's general account. Some of these accounts were in credit, some overdrawn. In some cases payment was made to a special account; in a few instances it had been earmarked for a special purpose. In some instances the money was expended in altering or enlarging buildings on lands owned by the charity.

These claims of the next-of-kin were on two main grounds. Claims "*in personam*," based on an alleged equity of a creditor or next-of-kin to recover from an overpaid stranger, and also claims "*in rem*," based on the doctrine of tracing assets which are identifiable either unmixed or as a part of a mixed fund in the hands of a volunteer who has received them. It is with the parts of the judgments that relates to the latter type of claim that I am concerned in that the principles in *Hallett's Case* and *Sinclair v. Brougham* were considered. It was the view of the Court that one whose money has been mixed with another's may trace his money into the mixed fund or assets acquired therewith though such fund or assets be held, and the mixing done, by an innocent volunteer, provided that there was originally a fiduciary relationship between claimant and recipient of his money to give rise to an equitable proprietary interest in the claimant and the claimant's money is fairly identifiable. The equitable remedy by way of charge on the mixed fund or assets is not available, however, if it works an injustice.

There are some general observations on the nature of equitable remedies in cases of mixed funds to which it will be useful to refer as having some bearing on the present case.

Having referred to the limited nature of the remedies open at common law, the Court stated, at p. 520:– "Equity adopted a more metaphysical approach. It found no difficulty in regarding a composite fund as an amalgam constituted by the mixture of two or more funds each of which could be regarded as having, for certain purposes, a continued separate existence. Putting it in another way, equity regarded the amalgam as capable, in proper circumstances, of being resolved into its component parts." Later, at p. 521, it is stated:– "The equitable remedies pre-suppose the continued existence of the money either as a separate fund or as part of a mixed fund or as latent in property acquired by means of such a fund." Further on it is said:– "It is, therefore, a necessary matter for consideration in each case where it is sought to trace money in equity, whether it has such a continued existence, actual or notional, as will enable equity to grant specific relief." The equitable forms of relief which the Court was considering therefore extend to cases where the money is latent in property acquired by a mixed fund and may be followed where it has a notional existence. These observations seem very relevant to the claims of the investors in this case if their money be held latent in the stamps in the liquidator's hands which were purchased by the Company.

The next relevant point is that in the reference to the judgment of Wynn-Parry J., starting at p. 523, the Court accepts by implication the principle that equity can operate to enable money in a mixed fund to be recovered, not only where the mixing takes place in breach of some fiduciary relationship and in proceedings against a fiduciary agent, but also where the mixing has been done by an innocent volunteer. The extension of the doctrine is implicit in the decision of *Sinclair v. Brougham*. It also accedes, at p. 525, to the proposition that a person in a fiduciary position being a party to the action is precluded from setting up a case inconsistent with the obligations of his fiduciary position.

A further relevant observation is to be found at p. 527, where the Court points out that the submission that *Hallett's Case* was based "not upon trusteeship in the narrow sense, but upon ownership" was not accepted by the House in *Sinclair v. Brougham*. It also pointed out, at p. 528, that the House had rejected the suggestion that there could not be a tracing order in favour of a class. At page 540 it is made clear that the Court accepts the principle that the remedies in equity which I am at present concerned with are brought into existence in the case of fiduciary relationships, such as that of principals and agents. Thus, these observations as cited follow and accept the principles of *Hallett's Case* as explained in *Sinclair v. Brougham* and tend to support the contentions of the defendants. Indeed, the decision in the case extending the right to a charge to beneficiaries to the case where the monies sought to be traced are found in a mixed fund in the hands of an innocent volunteer goes beyond what it is necessary for the defendants to establish in this case.

Mr. O'Neill, however, sought to rely on certain other passages in the judgment to show that equity would not apply the principle of following or tracing where it was unjust. He said that, at p. 532, the Court had indicated approval of the view that equity intervenes, not to do what might be thought to be absolute justice to a claimant but to prevent a defendant from acting in an unconscionable manner. A defendant will not be restrained from asserting a claim save to the extent that it would be unconscionable for him to do so. Again, it is pointed out at p. 547 that the equitable owner of the trust money must submit to equality of treatment with the innocent volunteer, followed by the statement on p. 548 to the effect that where a declaration of charge does not produce an equitable result it is inapplicable as a remedy.

The effect of the decision in *In re Diplock* can, I think, be summarised in this way: the principles of *Halletts' Case* are extended in this way – that where money mixed with that of another can be traced into a mixed fund or assets acquired therewith it can be followed, even though mixed, by an innocent volunteer, provided the equitable remedy does not work an injustice. As to whether the application of the principles in *Hallett's Case* work such an injustice on creditors in this case as should prevent their application is a matter which I will deal with later.

The principles laid down in *Hallett's Case* which it is said are applicable to the facts of this case are first, that when a person in a fiduciary capacity makes a purchase with mixed funds of his own and the beneficiary, the beneficiary is entitled to a charge to the extent of the trust money laid out in the purchase; secondly, that where a person does an act which may be rightly performed he cannot say that the act was intentionally, and in fact, done wrongly; and, finally, that where a person holding money in a fiduciary capacity mixes them with his own, the rule in *Clayton's Case* (1816) 1 Mer 572 does not apply and such person must be taken to have drawn out his own monies in preference to the trust monies.

The practical application of these principles, has, then to be considered. This involves a consideration in the first instance of what was done by the Company with the investors' money and the actual financial position. The total claims against the Company amount to approximately £1,840,000. This sum includes a claim on behalf of the ordinary creditors to the extent of £34,300 13s. 3d.; the balance is to be attributed to the claims of the investors. The total monies received by the official liquidator amounts to £139,760 17s. 1d., from which must be deducted certain sums allowed on account of expenses and liquidation costs. The monies collected include cash to the credit of the Company's bank account, £5,930 13s. 9d., and monies collected from foreign banks, £86,364 7s. 3d. In addition, the liquidator holds stamps which have been valued at approximately £282,787. Roughly one-third in value of these had been allocated to various syndicates in the sales which were cancelled. These stamps are said to have since appreciated in value by about 10 per cent. There is thus a large deficit, so that the unfortunate investors can only hope to recover a small proportion of their capital invested. Whatever conclusions he came to, the claim of the investors that their money can properly be traced into the stamps in the liquidator's hands, formerly the possession of the Company, can be substantiated in the following fashion.

Now, the Company kept only one bank account in this country and so far as is known carried on its business through the medium of this account. The sums sent abroad came from it. It is accepted, as I understand it, in the absence of contrary evidence, that the proper inference is that the Company must have mixed its own funds, such as commissions deducted, along with the investors' money and money received from purchasers in this account. It would also appear to be the position that purchases of stamps were made by monies withdrawn from this account which included the investors' money entrusted to the Company. The Company is precluded in a case such as the present from alleging that the rule in *Clayton's Case* applies in so far as it is concerned. It must be presumed to have drawn its own monies first. Therefore, having regard to the deficit, no suggestion can be made that any of the Company's money is represented by the stamps in hands.

The plaintiff's own evidence is that the withdrawals sent to foreign banks were, presumably, in whole or in part, used in the purchase of stamps. We know that the value of the stamps found in the Company's possession, even if grossly undervalued, and the other monies recovered by the liquidator are far below the amount of the investors' investments. The claims, less those of general creditors, amounts in round figures to something like one and a half million pounds, while the monies collected and the value of the stamps, at the date of valuation, does not exceed half a million. Even allowing for a 100 per cent under-valuation of the stamps, which seems outside the bounds of practical possibility, it is clearly proved, and the only proper inference is, that the overwhelming portion of the investors' monies was withdrawn from the bank account. Now, the only proper purpose for which the Company could withdraw the investors' money from the the bank accounts was for the purchase of stamps. Applying the principle of *Hallett's Case* the Company as a fiduciary agent is precluded from setting up a case inconsistent with the obligations of its fiduciary position; it follows that the investors' money, having been drawn on to a far greater extent than the value of the stamps found by the liquidator in the Company's possession and those later recovered by him, which were formerly in the Company's possession, must be presumed to have been used in the purchase of these stamps. It follows from this that the investors can trace their money into the stamps purchased and held by the Company, including those recovered which were originally in the Company's possession, and are *prima facie* entitled to a tracing order or charge, subject to certain matters which I will deal with later. But I do not wish it to be thought that I have overlooked a submission of Mr. O'Neill's with regard to the unsyndicated investors and I will deal with this before coming to these other matters.

Assuming that it was held that a fiduciary relationship was created, then Mr. O'Neill contended that in that case it was a term of the contract that no ownership in the stamps passed until appropriated to a syndicate of which the investor was a member. They were only entitled to trace ownership to the stamps because they had been appropriated under the contract. That results, he claimed, in the unsyndicated investors being unable to claim any right of property, equitable or otherwise, in the stamps, since in their case no property was ever appropriated.

He relied on the analogy of the case of *Sealy v. Stawell* (1868) IR 2 Eq 326. We are only concerned here with so much of the case as concerned the fourth question dealt with by the Master of the Rolls, at p. 343 of the report. The relevant facts are that a sum of bank stock was transferred to a trustee to sell and invest the produce on lands which were to be held on certain trusts. After his death his administrator paid out £38,650 of his own money in the purchase of lands which were conveyed to him absolutely. The value of the stock at the time was £23,630. By deed reciting the purchase of the lands thereby conveyed and other lands and that a portion of the purchase money of the lands consisted of the bank stock and that the lands were conveyed to the administrator in part performance of the trusts declared of the stock and that he was desirous of fully performing the trusts by conveying the lands to the trusts, the administrator conveyed part of the purchased lands accordingly. It was claimed that the remaining lands purchased and not conveyed were appropriated to the trust on the basis that the lands were purchased with the intention of performing the trust as recited in the deed. No proof, however, was forthcoming that any part of the trust fund exceeding the value of the lands conveyed could be traced into the purchase. On the contrary, the evidence established that the amount which Francis Stawell, the purchaser, contributed out of his own money was more than the value of the unappropriated lands. The mere fact that he had trust monies on hands when he made the purchase was held not sufficient to attach the trusts to lands bought with his own money. As no part of the trust funds was traced as invested in the remaining lands no lien existed over them. The claims of the persons entitled to the trust estate were simply those of creditors on foot of a breach of trust.

The case was decided in 1867 and it may be doubted whether the same decision would have been arrived at to-day having regard to the principles stated in some of the cases cited. However, it seems to me that the case would only support Mr. O'Neill's argument if he could show that the Company had monies of its own on hands which were used for the purchase of stamps. Unless that can be done, any analogy fails. If the facts show, as Mr. Finlay contends, that only the investors' money went into the purchase of the stamps now in the official liquidator's hands or that they must be deemed in equity to have been purchased with the investors' money, then the case has no application.

Since the facts coupled with the application of the equitable principles indicate that the investors' money is properly traceable into the stamps in hands, the decision does not support plaintiffs' contentions based on *Sealy v. Stawell*.

But there are certain other matters which I stated I would deal with. The investors' funds have been mixed and depleted. There is a large deficit in the shape of the difference between the funds originally invested by the investors and the monies and stamps now to hand. The possibility of the application of the rule in *Clayton's Case* between the investors *inter se* must be considered. There is also the peculiar position of the syndicated shareholders and the question arises whether they have any special rights, even though they may have no claim to the syndicated stamp *in specie*. There is the matter of the guarantee and what rights that gives to investors and the matter of the plaintiffs' possible right to commission. There is also the position of the general creditors to be considered. Have they any right to be paid in priority to the investors or any equity to rank equally with them?

Having regard to the fact that the stamps represent the depleted money of the investors coming from a mixed fund, and if it be the fact that it is impossible to say whose money purchased any particular lot of stamps or in what order the purchases were made, it would appear that the principle of a *pro rata* distribution of the property amongst the beneficiaries, as was done in *Sinclair v. Brougham* would be the proper one to apply at least between the unsyndicated investors. The words of Lord Parker of Waddington, where he said in that case that where owners had an equal equity and neither could claim priority over the other it follows that their charges must rank *pari passu*, seem applicable *prima facie*. Therefore the unsyndicated investors would *prima facie* be entitled at least to a charge over the property in the shape of the unsyndicated stamps unless it can be shown that such relief is inequitable or should not for some particular reason on the facts of the case be applied. That relief would normally be implemented by way of ordering a sale and *pro rata* division of the proceeds of the property amongst the unsyndicated investors and that would seem the proper order to make as far as the unsyndicated stamps are concerned, unless the rule in *Clayton's Case* is applicable between the unsyndicated investors.

In general the rule in *Clayton's Case* is applicable as between *cestuis que trustent*; that is, that first drawings out are to be attributed to the first payments in. In other words, the trustee is deemed to draw out first the money of the *cestuis que trustent* that he paid first into the blended account. A difficult question arises as to whether this rule is applicable in the complex circumstances of the present case. It may be that the rule in *Clayton's Case* does not apply beyond tracing in a bank account and the principle may have no application to property acquired by means of a mixed fund. But I prefer to deal with the situation, for safety's sake, as if the principle can properly be applied to the case of property acquired with such a mixed fund. The practical position is that, in fact, the investors' money has been mixed twice; first, in the original banking account, and secondly, in the property in the shape of stamps in which the investors' money lies latent, again in a mixed fashion. It is, I gather, possible to trace to some extent through the Company's books the order in which investors' money was lodged to the bank account. The position is that after this stage it is impossible to say what monies were used for the purchase of any particular lot of stamps or to whom the monies were paid. I have sought further information on this point and in the result it would seem that while the order in which monies were shifted to foreign banks or made payable to Dr. Singer could be discovered, it is not possible to say in what order any particular sets of stamps in the possession of the official liquidator were purchased, so that it would not be possible from the practical point of view to discover the order in which the investors' money was used in purchasing the stamps now held. In other words, there having been a second mixing of the investors' funds into a second mixed amalgam of property, it would not be possible for any particular investor to say that this particular money was used before others in the purchase of the property in the shape of stamps. Tracing, in the exact sense of the term, is therefore not possible or practicable. A somewhat similar state of affairs arose in *Sinclair v. Brougham* and in that case, as I have indicated, the House of Lords took the view that a *pro rata* distribution was the practical and equitable solution, leaving it to any particular depositor or shareholder to apply with a view to tracing his own money into any particular asset. Therefore, the rule in *Clayton's Case* does not apply as between the unsyndicated investors and a *pro rata* distribution is the proper form of relief so far as they are concerned. In order to guard against a remote possibility of an investor being able to trace his money into any particular lot of stamps it may be that the final order should preserve the right of any investor who can do so to make his claim.

But then the peculiar position of the syndicated investors has to be dealt with. I have already stated that in my view, on the true construction of the contract, it was not the intention of the parties that the investors should be entitled to the stamps *in specie*. There is this also to be said with regard to their claim to have the syndicated stamps *in specie*: the Court should not make an order which is totally impracticable and virtually impossible to carry out in practice. No one has been able to suggest to me any practical and workable method whereby the official liquidator could carry out an order to deliver the syndicated stamps *in specie*. The insuperable difficulties of obtaining agreement amongst the very many investors in most syndicates as to what the official liquidator is to do physically with the stamps are obvious.

The question still remains as to whether or not the syndicated investors have any special rights in regard to the proceeds of sale of syndicated stamps. I must not lose sight of the fact that the investors' rights are governed by a contract, and, although certain equitable principles may have become applicable, that does not mean that if particular parties have rights under the contract different to other parties, these rights should not be given effect to.

It was part of the contract, as I have found it, that the stamps when purchased should be allotted to syndicates and then "treated" as their property. As regards the syndicated investors the contract with them at the time of liquidation had reached a certain stage. As Mr. Matheson says, they had been informed that their money had been used in the purchase of particular stamps, and again applying the principle in *Hallett's Case* that a person who does an act which may be rightly performed cannot say that it was done wrongly, it would seem that at least as between the syndicated investors and the Company it should be assumed that the act of purchase and allotment was done rightly and that the syndicated owners therefore have a particular equity as regards the syndicated stamps. If so, they would be entitled again *prima facie* to a charge over these stamps to which their money has been traced in equity and which have been appropriated to them and to a consequent right to have them sold for their benefit. Such *prima facie* right should not, however, be operated in their favour if it works an injustice. I will deal with the claims of creditors later, but for the moment I must pause to consider whether the declaration of a right to a charge and sale in favour of the syndicated investors as regards the syndicated stamps would operate to work an injustice on the general body of unsyndicated investors. This is undoubtedly a very debatable point, but having regard to the nature of the contract which all investors entered into it must have been clear to all that the stamps purchased with their money would in due course be allotted to syndicates and then "treated" as their property, the proceeds of the sale of stamps allotted being divided amongst the members of the syndicates to which they were respectively allotted. It so happened that in the case of some of the syndicated investors the stage of allotment had been reached. That was their good fortune and it does not seem to me that the unsyndicated investors can properly complain that any injustice is done to them if the syndicated investors are allowed to take advantage of the actual state of affairs that existed at the time of liquidation, because all investors knew the procedure that was to be operated under the contract and if it had reached a stage more favourable to some than others that was something that they must all be deemed to know would occur. Therefore it would seem to me that making a declaration of charge in favour of the syndicated investors over the syndicated stamps does not work an injustice on unsyndicated investors. Therefore sale of the syndicated stamps and rateable distribution amongst the syndicated investors would seem the proper relief to grant, subject again, however, to any rights the general body of creditors may have.

Ordinary creditors of a company who are not paid in full, of course, suffer an injustice in the abstract, but that is not the particular type of injustice I have to consider here where the question is as between them and the investors, whom I have found to have *prima facie* certain rights in equity by way of charge and *pro rata* distribution. In some cases, such as in the circumstances arising in respect of certain of the claims in *In re Diplock*, the equitable remedy of a charge on a mixed fund will not be granted where it will work an injustice. The question then arises as to whether the making of a tracing or charging order in favour of the investors would result in that particular type of injustice to the ordinary creditors that would make it inequitable to make the order to which I have held that the investors are *prima facie* entitled.

I must start, it seems to me, by having regard to what I may call the general principles applicable. Should a person, having trust property in his possession, die or go bankrupt, the beneficiaries under the trust take their property in full in priority to the general body of creditors. The same thing applies in the case of a company in liquidation. The blending of trust funds with the monies of the deceased trustee would not – it would appear from what was said in *Hallett's Case* – make any difference to the priority of the beneficiaries, and so it would be in the case of a company in liquidation. The creditor cannot claim to stand as against a *cestui que trust* in any better position than the deceased trustee would. Likewise, the creditors of a company are in general in no better position as against beneficiaries of trust monies in a company's hands at the time of liquidation than the company before liquidation. The distinction, as I understand, is based on the fact that the beneficiary seeks his own property, or the proceeds thereof, being aided in equity to obtain restitution. The ordinary creditor, however, can only seek payment of his debt to the extent that there are assets, the property of the deceased debtor, bankrupt or company in liquidation which are available to meet his claim.

Mr. O'Neill, however, suggested that the investors should not be given any priority over the ordinary creditors. His first ground was, of course, that the money of the investors was lent or given to the Company in such fashion as to create merely the relationship of creditor and debtor. That view I have rejected. But he also went further in order to meet the possible situation of it being held that a fiduciary relationship existed between investors and the Company and that they were entitled to the benefit of a tracing order or charge. The application of such equitable relief would, he said, work an injustice to creditors and it would be inequitable not to allow those whose goods or services had been used or availed of to enable the Company to carry on its business for the benefit of the investors by providing such things as stationery or doing printing, and so on, to stand in priority to the investors. The equitable relief by way of tracing order and charge were, he said, adopted to prevent a person holding the property of another from acting in an unconscionable manner and there was nothing unconscionable in the action of the official liquidator in seeking to see the ordinary creditors paid in full.

He relied on certain passages in *In re Diplock* to support his contentions, which I have already cited and need not repeat. But all these statements of principle must be viewed in the light of the circumstances of the case in which they were made. I have to point out that these observations were directed to the state of affairs where the Diplock money had been used by certain of the charities to alter property of their own. In such cases it does not follow that the trust money can be said to be present in the adapted property. For example, the alterations may have lowered the value of the property. In such cases the machinery of a charge would not place the innocent volunteer in a position comparable to the owner of the trust fund and the Court took the view that in such cases the Diplock money could not be traced in the true sense and that is why it was held that the remedy of charge was inapplicable. The contest in that case was, moreover, between the next-of-kin and institutions that had received the money in the capacity of innocent volunteers, who had done nothing wrong, the equitable doctrines in question thus being extended beyond the wrongdoer. The institutions stood in no fiduciary relationship to the next-of-kin. It was, I think, for these reasons that the limitations were placed on the equitable extension of the doctrine. That is not the state of affairs existing in the present case, where the claim of the investors is made against the Company which I have held to have stood in a fiduciary relationship to the investors. The reasons for narrowing the application of the equitable remedies given to a beneficiary of a charge and tracing order following their own money which existed in *Diplock's Case* do not exist in the present case where the fiduciary relationship exists. There are no analogous reasons in the present case.

I do not wish to depart from what was said by the Court in *In re Diplock* without this further comment: while I have treated the defendants as asserting claims against the Company for a tracing order or charge as against the Company, I am now dealing with another and different aspect of the matter. The official liquidator, seeking to collect and secure the assets of the Company is *inter alia* in effect asserting the rights of the creditors to come before the investors. Looked at in this fashion, the defendants may properly say in reply that they are in substance in the position of the innocent volunteer in *Diplock's Case*. They have done nothing wrong. They have not in fact, like the volunteers in *Diplock's Case*, received anybody's money. They can properly say:— "We are only seeking to obtain as much as we can of our own property and if we can show that it is traceable in the hands of the Company there is nothing unconscionable in our claiming our own property and resisting the claim of anyone else, such as the ordinary creditors, to share in it."

Reliance was further placed on what Lord Dunedin said in *Sinclair v. Brougham* about the payment of the creditors before the claims of shareholders and depositors were met. First, it is right to point out that what was said was *obiter*, as the question of the creditors' priority was not in question. Further, Lord Dunedin says they were paid because their claims were inconsiderable, which may well have been the reason. As far as the shareholders were concerned, having been properly incurred by the directors the debts of creditors would in any winding up of a company come before shareholders' claims.

What Lord Dunedin said about their priority to *ultra vires* depositors calls, however, for more thought. The debts were incurred, he pointed out, in a business, illegal no doubt, but one which the depositors were willing that the directors should carry on. He seems thus to have equated them with the position of the shareholders and that may be the true explanation as to why he approved of the payment of creditors first. He cannot, I think, have intended to say that where a person gives his money to an agent to use in a certain fashion, which creates a fiduciary relationship, and the purpose incidentally happens to be something which it is in the course of the agent's business to do, the principal is to be subordinated to the creditors of the agent in the business, because that would be contrary to the well established principles of equity to which I have referred. To take a concrete example: suppose that a stockbroker goes bankrupt having in his hands in cash the proceeds of sale of a customer's shares, handed to him for the specific purpose of sale. Could it be contended that the stockbroker's creditors for, say, stationery or office furniture supplied for use in his business, would rank before the customer with whom he stood in a fiduciary relationship and whose monies could be clearly traced? I would say not. That Lord Dunedin did not mean anything of the kind is, I think, made clear in the next page of his speech, where he says that this is not a case where one sharing party has the right to say to another:– "It is not in your mouth to say that the assets are not all mine, to the extent of my full claim." That would be just what a principal in a fiduciary relationship with his agent to whom he has given money for a specific purpose could say to an ordinary creditor of the agent. The true explanation of what was said may also be that the *ultra vires* depositors had no valid contract and the business their money was used in was illegal, therefore they should not rank with those whose money was used in the illegal business to their benefit.

Whatever the true explanation of Lord Dunedin's attitude was, it seems to me that there is no true analogy between the rights *inter se* of *ultra vires* depositors and creditors of an illegal business and the position of the investors in this case who handed their monies in a perfectly legal contract to an agent carrying on a business not in itself illegal. I have already dealt with the observations of Lord Parker of Waddington in the same case and I do not think that they assist Mr. O'Neill's argument on the facts of the present case.

The comments of Jessel M.R. in *Hallett's Case* in referring to what Knight Bruce L.J. had said in *Pennell v. Deffell* seem to me also opposed to Mr. O'Neill's contentions. Some of the other cases cited also indicate that the rights of a person in a position similar to that of a *cestui que trust* and able to trace his money or property in the hands of a trustee or other person in a fiduciary capacity come before the rights of general creditors. In *Taylor v. Plumer* (1815) 3 M & S 562 the principal was held entitled as against the assignees who would, in effect, have been asserting the creditors' claims. Likewise, the trustees in bankruptcy in the case of *Harris v. Truman* (1882) 9 QBD 264 would be in a like position, but the principals in both cases were in effect held entitled to their property in preference to the claims of the general creditors.

I was not referred to – nor have I been able to discover – any case in which it was expressly laid down that the ordinary creditors of a fiduciary agent, whose goods or money was used for the purposes of the agent's business, were entitled to rank before those whose money or property was held by the agent in a fiduciary capacity. Such a proposition would seem contrary to the view that equity aims in such cases at restitution. Further, it would seem contrary to the principle that as against a *cestui que trust* the creditors of a deceased or bankrupt trustee cannot claim to be in any better position than the trustee himself could be and, as I understand it, a fiduciary agent stands in the same position as a trustee in a case where he holds the property of his principal for a specific purpose. In *Hanbury on Equity* (7th ed., 1957, at p. 33) I find the general proposition that equities bind *inter alia* creditors, which supports this view. The alleged right of the creditors to take priority over the investors has not therefore been sustained.

I have therefore come to the conclusion that certain of the contentions made on behalf of the syndicated and unsyndicated investors are in principle correct and that the syndicated investors are entitled to a declaration of charge over the stamps allotted to their respective syndicates to be implemented by a sale thereof and the unsyndicated investors are in a like position as regards the unsyndicated stamps. They too, are entitled to a declaration of charge to be implemented by a sale. The proceeds in both cases should be divided *pro rata* between the members of the two respective classes according to the amounts of their investments, subject possibly to the right I have mentioned of any unsyndicated investor to assert a claim to be able to trace his money into any specific lot of stamps.

With regard to the guarantee, again it seems to me that the fact that the parties' rights are governed by the terms of the contract must be given effect to, and therefore both syndicated and unsyndicated investors are entitled to claim against the plaintiffs any deficit that may arise between what they receive in respect of the proceeds of the sale of the stamps and the amount of their respective investments. In that respect they would rank as ordinary creditors."

Foskett v. McKeown
[2000] 2 WLR 1299

A trustee fraudulently used money entrusted to him for a property development scheme to pay premiums on a life insurance policy. When the trustee died, a dispute arose as to entitlement to the death benefit on the policy. The House of Lords held that the investors were entitled to follow their money into the policy and from there into the hands of the trustees who were paid the death benefit so as to obtain reimbursement of the amount of the premiums paid with their money from the proceeds of the policy.

LORD MILLETT stated at pp.1322–1328: "My Lords, this is a textbook example of tracing through mixed substitutions. At the beginning of the story the plaintiffs were beneficially entitled under an express trust to a sum standing in the name of Mr. Murphy in a bank account. From there the money moved into and out of various bank accounts where in breach of trust it was inextricably mixed by Mr. Murphy with his own money. After each transaction was completed the plaintiffs' money formed an indistinguishable part of the balance standing to Mr. Murphy's credit in his bank account. The amount of that balance represented a debt due from the bank to Mr. Murphy, that is to say a chose in action. At the penultimate stage the plaintiffs' money was represented by an indistinguishable part of a different chose in action, viz., the debt prospectively and contingently due from an insurance company to its policyholders, being the trustees of a settlement made by Mr. Murphy for the benefit of his children. At the present and final stage it forms an indistinguishable part of the balance standing to the credit of the respondent trustees in their bank account.

Tracing and following

The process of ascertaining what happened to the plaintiffs' money involves both tracing and following. These are both exercises in locating assets which are or may be taken to represent an asset belonging to the plaintiffs and to which they assert ownership. The processes of following and tracing are, however, distinct. Following is the process of following the same asset as it moves from hand to hand. Tracing is the process of identifying a new asset as the substitute for the old. Where one asset is exchanged for another, a claimant can elect whether to follow the original asset into the hands of the new owner or to trace its value into the new asset in the hands of the same owner. In practice his choice is often dictated by the circumstances. In the present case the plaintiffs do not seek to follow the money any further once it reached the bank or insurance company, since its identity was lost in the hands of the recipient (which in any case obtained an unassailable title as a bona fide purchaser for value without notice of the plaintiffs' beneficial interest). Instead the plaintiffs have chosen at each stage to trace the money into its proceeds, viz., the debt presently due from the bank to the account holder or the debt prospectively and contingently due from the insurance company to the policy holders.

Having completed this exercise, the plaintiffs claim a continuing beneficial interest in the insurance money. Since this represents the product of Mr. Murphy's own money as well as theirs, which Mr. Murphy mingled indistinguishably in a single chose in action, they claim a beneficial interest in a proportionate part of the money only. The transmission of a claimant's property rights from one asset to its traceable proceeds is part of our law of property, not of the law of unjust enrichment. There is no "unjust factor" to justify restitution (unless "want of title" be one, which makes the point). The claimant succeeds if at all by virtue of his own title, not to reverse unjust enrichment. Property rights are determined by fixed rules and settled principles. They are not discretionary. They do not depend upon ideas of what is "fair, just and reasonable." Such concepts, which in reality mask decisions of legal policy, have no place in the law of property.

A beneficiary of a trust is entitled to a continuing beneficial interest not merely in the trust property but in its traceable proceeds also, and his interest binds every one who takes the property or its traceable proceeds except a bona fide purchaser for value without notice. In the present case the plaintiffs' beneficial interest plainly bound Mr. Murphy, a trustee who wrongfully mixed the trust money with his own and whose every dealing with the money (including the payment of the premiums) was in breach of trust. It similarly binds his successors, the trustees of the children's settlement, who claim no beneficial interest of their own, and Mr. Murphy's children, who are volunteers. They gave no value for what they received and derive their interest from Mr. Murphy by way of gift.

Tracing

We speak of money at the bank, and of money passing into and out of a bank account. But of course the account holder has no money at the bank. Money paid into a bank account belongs legally and beneficially to the bank and not to the account holder. The bank gives value for it, and it is accordingly not usually possible to make the money itself the subject of an adverse claim. Instead a claimant normally sues the account holder rather than the bank and lays claim to the proceeds of the money in his hands. These consist of the debt or part of the debt due to him from the bank. We speak of tracing money into and out of the account, but there is no money in the account. There is merely a single debt of an amount equal to the final balance standing to the credit of the account holder. No money passes from paying bank to receiving bank or through the clearing system (where the money flows may be in the opposite direction). There is simply a series of debits and credits which are causally and transactionally linked. We also speak of tracing one asset into another, but this too is inaccurate. The original asset still exists in the hands of the new owner, or it may have become untraceable. The claimant claims the new asset because it was acquired in whole or in part with the original asset. What he traces, therefore, is not the physical asset itself but the value inherent in it.

Tracing is thus neither a claim nor a remedy. It is merely the process by which a claimant demonstrates what has happened to his property, identifies its proceeds and the persons who have handled or received them, and justifies his claim that the proceeds can properly be regarded as representing his property. Tracing is also distinct from claiming. It identifies the traceable proceeds of the claimant's property. It enables the claimant to substitute the traceable proceeds for the original asset as the subject matter of his claim. But it does not affect or establish his claim. That will depend on a number of factors including the nature of his interest in the original asset. He will normally be able to maintain the same claim to the substituted asset as he could have maintained to the original asset. If he held only a security interest in the original asset, he cannot claim more than a security interest in its proceeds. But his claim may also be exposed to potential defences as a result of intervening transactions. Even if the plaintiffs could demonstrate what the bank had done with their money, for example, and could thus identify its traceable proceeds in the hands of the bank, any claim by them to assert ownership of those proceeds would be defeated by the bona fide purchaser defence. The successful completion of a tracing exercise may be preliminary to a personal claim (as in *El Ajou v. Dollar Land Holdings* [1993] 3 All ER 717) or a proprietary one, to the enforcement of a legal right (as in *Trustees of the Property of F.C. Jones & Sons v. Jones* [1997] Ch 159) or an equitable one.

Given its nature, there is nothing inherently legal or equitable about the tracing exercise. There is thus no sense in maintaining different rules for tracing at law and in equity. One set of tracing rules is enough, The existence of two has never formed part of the law in the United States: see *Scott on Trusts,* 4th ed. (1989), section 515, at pp. 605-609. There is certainly no logical justification for allowing any distinction between them to produce capricious results in cases of mixed substitutions by insisting on the existence of a fiduciary relationship as a precondition for applying equity's tracing rules. The existence of such a relationship may be relevant to the nature of the claim which the plaintiff can maintain, whether personal or proprietary, but that is a different matter. I agree with the passages which my noble and learned friend, Lord Steyn, has cited from Professor Birks's essay "The Necessity of a Unitary Law of Tracing," and with Dr. Lionel Smith's exposition in his comprehensive monograph *The Law of Tracing* (1997): see particularly pp. 120–130, 277–279 and 342-347.

This is not, however, the occasion to explore these matters further, for the present is a straightforward case of a trustee who wrongfully misappropriated trust money, mixed it with his own, and used it to pay for an asset for the benefit of his children. Even on the traditional approach, the equitable tracing rules are available to the plaintiffs. There are only two complicating factors. The first is that the wrongdoer used their money to pay premiums on an equity-linked policy of life assurance on his own life. The nature of the policy should make no difference in principle, though it may complicate the accounting. The second is that he had previously settled the policy for the benefit of his children. This should also make no difference. The claimant's rights cannot depend on whether the wrongdoer gave the policy to his children during his lifetime or left the proceeds to them by his will; or if during his lifetime whether he did so before or after he had recourse to the claimant's money to pay the premiums. The order of events does not affect the fact that the children are not contributors but volunteers who have received the gift of an asset paid for in part with misappropriated trust moneys.

The cause of action
As I have already pointed out, the plaintiffs seek to vindicate their property rights, not to reverse unjust enrichment. The correct classification of the plaintiffs' cause of action may appear to be academic, but it has important

consequences. The two causes of action have different requirements and may attract different defences.

A plaintiff who brings an action in unjust enrichment must show that the defendant has been enriched at the plaintiff's expense, for he cannot have been unjustly enriched if he has not been enriched at all. But the plaintiff is not concerned to show that the defendant is in receipt of property belonging beneficially to the plaintiff or its traceable proceeds. The fact that the beneficial ownership of the property has passed to the defendant provides no defence; indeed, it is usually the very fact which founds the claim. Conversely, a plaintiff who brings an action like the present must show that the defendant is in receipt of property which belongs beneficially to him or its traceable proceeds, but he need not show that the defendant has been enriched by its receipt. He may, for example, have paid full value for the property, but he is still required to disgorge it if he received it with notice of the plaintiff's interest.

Furthermore, a claim in unjust enrichment is subject to a change of position defence, which usually operates by reducing or extinguishing the element of enrichment. An action like the present is subject to the bona fide purchaser for value defence, which operates to clear the defendant's title.

The tracing rules

The insurance policy in the present case is a very sophisticated financial instrument. Tracing into the rights conferred by such an instrument raises a number of important issues. It is therefore desirable to set out the basic principles before turning to deal with the particular problems to which policies of life assurance give rise.

The simplest case is where a trustee wrongfully misappropriates trust property and uses it exclusively to acquire other property for his own benefit. In such a case the beneficiary is entitled at his option either to assert his beneficial ownership of the proceeds or to bring a personal claim against the trustee for breach of trust and enforce an equitable lien or charge on the proceeds to secure restoration of the trust fund. He will normally exercise the option in the way most advantageous to himself. If the traceable proceeds have increased in value and are worth more than the original asset, he will assert his beneficial ownership and obtain the profit for himself. There is nothing unfair in this. The trustee cannot be permitted to keep any profit resulting from his misappropriation for himself, and his donees cannot obtain a better title than their donor. If the traceable proceeds are worth less than the original asset, it does not usually matter how the beneficiary exercises his option. He will take the whole of the proceeds on either basis. This is why it is not possible to identify the basis on which the claim succeeded in some of the cases.

Both remedies are proprietary and depend on successfully tracing the trust property into its proceeds. A beneficiary's claim against a trustee for breach of trust is a personal claim. It does not entitle him to priority over the trustee's general creditors unless he can trace the trust property into its product and establish a proprietary interest in the proceeds. If the beneficiary is unable to trace the trust property into its proceeds, he still has a personal claim against the trustee, but his claim will be unsecured. The beneficiary's proprietary claims to the trust property or its traceable proceeds can be maintained against the wrongdoer and anyone who derives title from him except a bona fide purchaser for value without notice of the breach of trust. The same rules apply even where there have been numerous successive transactions, so long as the tracing exercise is successful and no bona fide purchaser for value without notice has intervened.

A more complicated case is where there is a mixed substitution. This occurs where the trust money represents only part of the cost of acquiring the new asset. As James Barr Ames pointed out in "Following Misappropriated Property into its Product" (1906) 19 Harv L Rev 511, consistency requires that, if a trustee buys property partly with his own money and partly with trust money, the beneficiary should have the option of taking a proportionate part of the new property or a lien upon it, as may be most for his advantage. In principle it should not matter (and it has never previously been suggested that it does) whether the trustee mixes the trust money with his own and buys the new asset with the mixed fund or makes separate payments of the purchase price (whether simultaneously or sequentially) out of the different funds. In every case the value formerly inherent in the trust property has become located within the value inherent in the new asset.

The rule, and its rationale, were stated by Samuel Williston in "The Right to Follow Trust Property when Confused with other Property" (1888) 2 Harv L Rev 28, 29:

> "If the trust fund is traceable as having furnished in part the money with which a certain investment was made, and the proportion it formed of the whole money so invested is known or ascertainable, the cestui que trust should be allowed to regard the acts of the trustee as done for his benefit, in the same way that he would be allowed to if all the money so invested had been his; that is, he should be entitled in equity to an undivided share of the property which the trust money contributed to purchase – such a proportion of the whole as the trust money bore to the whole money invested. The reason in the one case as in the other is that the trustee cannot be allowed to make a profit from the use of the trust money, and if the property which he wrongfully purchased were held subject only to a lien for the amount invested, any appreciation in value would go to the trustee."

If this correctly states the underlying basis of the rule (as I believe it does), then it is impossible to distinguish between the case where mixing precedes the investment and the case where it arises on and in consequence of the investment. It is also impossible to distinguish between the case where the investment is retained by the trustee and the case where it is given away to a gratuitous donee. The donee cannot obtain a better title than his donor, and a donor who is a trustee cannot be allowed to profit from his trust.

In *In re Hallett's Estate; Knatchbull v. Hallett* (1880) 13 Ch D 696, 709 Sir George Jessel M.R. acknowledged that where an asset was acquired exclusively with trust money, the beneficiary could either assert equitable ownership of the asset or enforce a lien or charge over it to recover the trust money. But he appeared to suggest that in the case of a mixed substitution the beneficiary is confined to a lien. Any authority that this dictum might otherwise have is weakened by the fact that Sir George Jessel M.R. gave no reason for the existence of any such rule, and none is readily apparent. The dictum was plainly obiter, for the fund was deficient and the plaintiff was only claiming a lien. It has usually been cited only to be explained away: see for example *In re Tilley's Will Trusts* [1967] Ch 1179, 1186, *per* Ungoed-Thomas J.; Burrows, *The Law of Restitution* (1993), p. 368. It was rejected by the High Court of Australia in *Scott v. Scott* (1963) 109 CLR 649: see the passage at pp. 661-662 cited by Morritt L.J. below [1998] Ch 265, 300-301. It has not been adopted in the United States: see the *American Law Institute, Restatement of the Law, Trusts, 2d* (1959) at section 202(h). In *Primeau v. Granfield* (1911) 184 F 480, 482 Learned Hand J. expressed himself in forthright terms: "On principle there can be no excuse for such a rule."

In my view the time has come to state unequivocally that English law has no such rule. It conflicts with the rule that a trustee must not benefit from his trust. I agree with Burrows that the beneficiary's right to elect to have a proportionate share of a mixed substitution necessarily follows once one accepts, as English law does, (i) that a claimant can trace in equity into a mixed fund and (ii) that he can trace unmixed money into its proceeds and assert ownership of the proceeds.

Accordingly, I would state the basic rule as follows. Where a trustee wrongfully uses trust money to provide part of the cost of acquiring an asset, the beneficiary is entitled *at his option* either to claim a proportionate share of the asset or to enforce a lien upon it to secure his personal claim against the trustee for the amount of the misapplied money. It does not matter whether the trustee mixed the trust money with his own in a single fund before using it to acquire the asset, or made separate payments (whether simultaneously or sequentially) out of the differently owned funds to acquire a single asset.

Two observations are necessary at this point. First, there is a mixed substitution (with the results already described) whenever the claimant's property has contributed in part only towards the acquisition of the new asset. It is not necessary for the claimant to show in addition that his property has contributed to any increase in the value of the new asset. This is because, as I have already pointed out, this branch of the law is concerned with vindicating rights of property and not with reversing unjust enrichment. Secondly, the beneficiary's right to claim a lien is available only against a wrongdoer and those deriving title under him otherwise than for value. It is not available against competing contributors who are innocent of any wrongdoing. The tracing rules are not the result of any presumption or principle peculiar to equity. They correspond to the common law rules for following into physical mixtures (though the consequences may not be identical). Common to both is the principle that the interests of the wrongdoer who was responsible for the mixing and those who derive title under him otherwise than for value are subordinated to those of innocent contributors. As against the wrongdoer and his successors, the beneficiary is entitled to locate his contribution in any part of the mixture and to subordinate their claims to share in the mixture until his own contribution has been satisfied. This has the effect of giving the beneficiary a lien for his contribution if the mixture is deficient.

Innocent contributors, however, must be treated equally inter se. Where the beneficiary's claim is in competition with the claims of other innocent contributors, there is no basis upon which any of the claims can be subordinated to any of the others. Where the fund is deficient, the beneficiary is not entitled to enforce a lien for his contributions; all must share rateably in the fund.

The primary rule in regard to a mixed fund, therefore, is that gains and losses are borne by the contributors rateably. The beneficiary's right to elect instead to enforce a lien to obtain repayment is an exception to the primary rule, exercisable where the fund is deficient and the claim is made against the wrongdoer and those claiming through him. It is not necessary to consider whether there are any circumstances in which the beneficiary is confined to a lien in cases where the fund is more than sufficient to repay the contributions of all parties. It is sufficient to say that he is not so confined in a case like the present. It is not enough that those defending the claim are innocent of any wrongdoing if they are not themselves contributors but, like the trustees and Mr. Murphy's children in the present case, are volunteers who derive title under the wrongdoer otherwise than for value. On ordinary principles such persons are in no better position than the wrongdoer, and are liable to suffer the same subordination of their interests to those of the claimant as the wrongdoer would have been. They certainly cannot do better than the claimant by confining him to a lien and keeping any profit for themselves.

Similar principles apply to following into physical mixtures: see *Lupton v. White* (1808) 15 Ves 432; and *Sandeman & Sons v. Tyzack and Branfoot Steamship Co. Ltd.* [1913] AC 680, 695 where Lord Moulton said: "If the mixing has arisen from the fault of 'B,' 'A' can claim the goods." There are relatively few cases which deal with the position of the innocent recipient from the wrongdoer, but *Jones v. De Marchant* (1916) 28 DLR 561 may be cited as an example. A husband wrongfully used 18 beaver skins belonging to his wife and used them, together with four skins of his own, to have a fur coat made up which he then gave to his mistress. Unsurprisingly the wife was held entitled to recover the coat. The mistress knew nothing of the true ownership of the skins, but her innocence was held to be immaterial. She was a gratuitous donee and could stand in no better position than the husband. The coat was a new asset manufactured from the skins and not merely the product of intermingling them. The problem could not be solved by a sale of the coat in order to reduce the disputed property to a divisible fund, since (as we shall see) the realisation of an asset does not affect its ownership. It would hardly have been appropriate to require the two ladies to share the coat between them. Accordingly it was an all or nothing case in which the ownership of the coat must be assigned to one or other of the parties. The determinative factor was that the mixing was the act of the wrongdoer through whom the mistress acquired the coat otherwise than for value.

The rule in equity is to the same effect, as Sir William Page Wood V.-C. observed in *Frith v. Cartland* (1865) 2 H & M 417, 420: "if a man mixes trust funds with his own, the whole will be treated as the trust property, except so far as he may be able to distinguish what is his own." This does not, in my opinion, exclude a pro rata division where this is appropriate, as in the case of money and other fungibles like grain, oil or wine. But it is to be observed that a pro rata division is the best that the wrongdoer and his donees can hope for. If a pro rata division is excluded, the beneficiary takes the whole; there is no question of confining him to a lien. *Jones v. De Marchant* (1916) 28 DLR 561 is a useful illustration of the principles shared by the common law and equity alike that an innocent recipient who receives misappropriated property by way of gift obtains no better title than his donor, and that if a proportionate sharing is inappropriate the wrongdoer and those who derive title under him take nothing."

Tracing into a Bank Account

Where trust monies are mixed in a fund which is an active bank account, in certain circumstances a principle known as the rule in *Clayton's case*[5] may apply. In theory it applies to competing claims of beneficiaries of different trusts and of beneficiaries and innocent volunteers and the effect of the rule is 'first in, first out'. However, the rule in *Clayton's case* does not apply to competing claims of a trustee and beneficiary, as arose in *Re Hallett's Estate*,[6] as the trustee is presumed to be acting honestly and to draw on his own money in the account first. The view has been expressed by Woolf LJ in *Barlow Clowes International Ltd v. Vaughan*[7] that 'the rule need only be applied when it is convenient to do so and when its application can be said to do broad justice having regard to the nature of the competing claims' and it will not be applied where its application would be impractical or unjust. This would seem to accord with the attitude adopted by Laffoy J, albeit in an *obiter* context, in the recent decision of *Re Money Markets International Stockbrokers Ltd*[8] in

---

[5]　(1816) 1 Mer 572.
[6]　(1880) 13 Ch D 696.
[7]　[1992] 4 All ER 22, 39.
[8]　[1999] 4 IR 267.

which she stated that while as a general proposition the rule is applicable, its application may be displaced in the particular circumstances of the case.

Re Money Markets International Stockbrokers Ltd
[1999] 4 IR 267

The applicant instructed the company, a stock broking firm, to buy shares on the Irish Stock Exchange on his behalf and the sum due was transferred and credited to the company's bank account several days before the settlement date. The following day the Irish Stock Exchange suspended the right of the company to transact business on the exchange and the company was subsequently wound up and an official liquidator appointed. The liquidator acknowledged that the applicant's situation was different to that of other clients of the company as he had transferred monies to the company before the settlement date and these were identifiable in the client account of the company. It was agreed that the company stood in a fiduciary relationship to the applicant and that the funds transferred by the applicant to the company's account were held by the company as trust funds. These funds had been mixed with other funds and the dispute between the parties was in broad terms whether the rule in *Clayton's case* should be applied to determine who is entitled to the monies represented by the credit balance in the company's account. Laffoy J stated that on the application, she did not propose to determine whether as between all the parties who might have a claim to the balance in the current account, the rule in *Clayton's case* is applicable to determine entitlement. Laffoy J then said that having regard to the uniqueness of the applicant's position, she did not think that applying equitable principles, the applicant should be bound by a *pari passu* distribution. She concluded that the applicant was entitled to the return of the monies in the account transferred to the company.

LAFFOY J stated at pp.271–272 and pp.274–278: "It is agreed that the company stood in a fiduciary relationship to the applicant and that the funds transferred by the applicant to the company's account were held by the company as trust funds. When these funds were transferred into the company's account they were intermingled with trust funds of other client creditors and, the official liquidator contends, probably also with company monies because the company had regularly injected its own funds into client accounts to cover deficits. In broad terms, the dispute between the parties is whether the rule in *Clayton's case* should be applied to determine who is now entitled to the monies represented by the credit balance on the company's account in Ulster Bank Limited.

Counsel submitted on behalf of the applicant that it is settled law that where funds belonging to various beneficiaries have been mixed in a single bank account, priority as between the beneficiaries is generally determined by the rule in *Devaynes v. Noble, Clayton's case* (1816) 1 Mer 572, that is to say on a "first in, first out" principle. While the rule is not invariably applicable, the instant case is not one of the situations in which it should not be applied, it was submitted. For instance, the situation in the instant case is not analogous to the situation which arose in *Barlow Clowes International Limited (In Liquidation) v. Vaughan* [1992] BCLC 910, where the Court of Appeal refused to apply the rule because the investors were found to have a common purpose as participants in a common investment plan and decided that the distribution should be on a *pari passu* basis. The instant case, it was submitted, is distinguishable from *Barlow Clowes* because in the instant case there was no common purpose among the investors. The applicant and, it would appear, each other client creditor of the company was investing on his own behalf in specified stocks. Moreover, it was submitted that the position of the applicant was one that was recognised in the judgment of Woolf L.J. in *Barlow Clowes* as requiring special consideration. In his judgment Woolf L.J. stated as follows at p. 931:

> "Mr. Hart [counsel arguing for the application of the rule in *Clayton's* case] emphasised the theoretical position of an investor who advanced a sum of money just prior to the account of BCI being frozen. In that situation he contended correctly that in the normal way an investor must be able to trace the whole of his investment into the balance of the account; unless the investor intends his investment to be treated in the way that funds invested in a unit trust are treated (which he argues is not the position here). Mr. Hart submitted that it followed that the investor must be entitled to the whole of the sum in the account which can be identified if, since the investment, there has been no movement in the account. However, as Mr. Hart accepts, there is in this case no investor who is precisely in that position. If there was, I accept that the investors' situation would require special consideration."

On behalf of the official liquidator, counsel submitted that the rule in *Clayton's* case should not be followed, it being merely a rule of convenience, and not an invariable rule of law. It was submitted that it is open to the court to exclude the application of the rule where it would be impracticable or where it would result in an injustice as between client creditors. As regards the liquidation of the company, it was submitted that the general application of the rule in *Clayton's* case would be difficult if not impossible. Although the applicant's lodgment can be identified, it was submitted that subsequent movement in and out of the account makes it impossible to say that all of his monies are included in the final credit balance. Moreover, it was submitted that the application of the rule would produce an arbitrary result. It was submitted that the equities are equal as far as all of the client creditors are concerned and therefore, in the event of a deficit, they should be all treated equally. *Pari passu* distribution is the fairest and most equitable mode of distribution of client funds. In support of this submission counsel for the liquidator relied on the decision of the Court of Appeal in *Barlow Clowes International Limited (in liquidation) v. Vaughan* [1992] BCLC 910, and the decision of the New Zealand Court of Appeal in

Re Registered Securities Limited [1991] 1 NZLR 545. He also referred to Goff & Jones on *Restitution*, (5th ed., 1998 at p. 109) and Keane on *Equity and the Law of Trusts in the Republic of Ireland* at para. 20.13. Finally, he submitted that although part of the *ratio* of the Court of Appeal's decision in *Barlow Clowes* was that the investors were paying into a common fund, the fact that it might have been presumed by individual clients that their monies were being kept in segregated accounts or in a segregated manner did not trigger the automatic application of the rule in *Clayton's* case."

. . . .

"*The legal principles applicable*
In identifying the legal principles applicable to the issues which arise on this application, I consider that the starting point can be the decision of Budd J. in *Shanahans Stamp Auctions Limited v. Farrelly* [1962] IR 386. In that case, Budd J. held, on the facts, that investors' money was entrusted to the company for a specific purpose, namely, purchase of stamps and their resale, the proceeds and profits to be then remitted to the investor and on that basis he held that a fiduciary relationship was created between the investor and the company. He then went on to consider the authorities which had been cited in argument before him to determine what were the general principles applicable in cases of the type before him and what resultant rights, if any, accrued to the investors either at law or in equity. On the basis of his analysis of the authorities, Budd J. stated as follows at p. 442:

> "In general the rule in *Clayton's case* is applicable as between *cestuis que trustent*; that is, that first drawings out are to be attributed to the first payments in. In other words, the trustee is deemed to draw out first the money of the *cestuis que trustent* that he paid first into the blended account. A difficult question arises as to whether this rule is applicable in the complex circumstances of the present case. It may be that the rule in *Clayton's case* does not apply beyond tracing in a bank account and the principle may have no application to property acquired by means of a mixed fund."

In *Shanahans Stamp Auctions Limited v. Farrelly* [1962] IR 386, the investors' money had been mixed twice: first, in the original banking account, and, secondly, in the property in the shape of stamps in which the investors' money lay latent at the time of the proceedings, again in a mixed fashion. On the facts Budd J. concluded that, there having been a second mixing of the investors' funds into a second mixed amalgam of property, it would not be possible for any particular investor to say that his particular money was used before others in the purchase of the property in the shape of stamps. Accordingly, tracing, in the exact sense of the term, was not possible nor practicable. Therefore, Budd J. held that the rule in *Clayton's* case did not apply as between the unsyndicated investors and that a *pro-rata* distribution was the proper form of relief so far as they were concerned.

Even in its application to trust funds sourced from various beneficiaries blended in a single bank account, the application of the rule in *Clayton's* case has been criticised. In *Equity and the Law of Trusts in the Republic of Ireland*, at para. 20.13, Keane J. has described the application of the rule in such circumstances as "rough justice" and has further commented as follows:

> "It would appear, however, that the rule in *Clayton's case* should not apply where the money is no longer in the bank account; and it may even be doubtful whether the courts would now continue to apply *Clayton's case* (which has always been regarded as based on rather crude if convenient assumptions) to the case of competing claims of beneficiaries to money in a bank account."

In *Barlow Clowes International Limited (in liquidation) v. Vaughan* [1992] BCLC 910 the issue which was before the Court of Appeal was as to the method which should be adopted to apportion the assets salvaged after the collapse of Barlow Clowes International Limited among the investors who had a claim to those assets. The assets were represented by monies paid by investors seeking to invest in investment plans, monies to the credit of bank accounts and the net proceeds of other assets including a yacht and certain gilt edged investments. Two methods of apportionment were in contention; first, the "first in, first out" basis under the rule in *Clayton's* case; secondly, what Woolf L.J. called "the *pari passu ex post facto* solution", that is to say, establishing the total *quantum* of the assets available and sharing them on a proportionate basis among all the investors who could be said to have contributed to the acquisition of those assets, ignoring the dates on which they made their investment. Woolf L.J., having stated that in the circumstances of that case he had no doubt that, if, as matter of principle, the Court of Appeal was in a position to adopt the latter solution, it was the solution which was most appropriate, went on to consider the relevant authorities, which largely coincided with the authorities considered by Budd J. in *Shanahans Stamp Auctions Limited v. Farrelly* [1962] IR 386. On the basis of his analysis of the authorities, Woolf L.J. concluded at p. 928:

> "The decision in *Re Diplock's Estate* must be considered together with the other judgments to which I have referred. When this is done, short of the House of Lords, it is settled law that the rule in *Clayton's case* can be applied to determine the extent to which, as between each other, equally innocent claimants are entitled in equity to moneys which have been paid into a bank account and then subject to the movements within that account. However, it does not, having regard to the passages from the judgments in the other authorities cited, follow that the rule has always to be applied for this purpose. In a number of different circumstances the rule has not been applied. The rule need only be applied when it is convenient to do so and when its application can be said to do broad justice having regard to the nature of the competing claims. *Re Hallett's Estate* shows that the rule is displaced where its application would unjustly assist the trustee to the disadvantage of the beneficiaries. In *Re Diplock's Estate* the rule would have been displaced by the trustee subsequently earmarking the beneficiary's funds. It is not applied if this is the intention or presumed intention of the

beneficiaries. The rule is sensibly not applied when the cost of applying it is likely to exhaust the fund available for the beneficiaries."

Woolf L.J. referred to two other cases in which the rule in *Clayton's case* had not been applied which, although quite different from the facts under consideration by the Court of Appeal, he regarded as relevant because they helped to illustrate "the range of situations where the courts have already concluded they were not required to apply the rule". The rationale of favouring a rateable distribution over the application of the "first in, first out" rule where investors' funds are mixed in a pool discernible from the judgment of Woolf L.J. is the principle that equality is equity. In his judgment at p. 932 he stated as follows:

> "In order to obtain preference over the ordinary creditors, the investor has to rely on equity to trace his moneys into the account. Where the circumstances, convenience and justice so dictate, once the moneys are in the pool equity can require them to be treated as being subject to the other investors' equitable claims on the fund. There is nothing wrong in principle in treating the quantum of the latest investor's claim as either being reduced *pro-rata* by the earlier investors' claims or enhanced by the value of other assets, purchased earlier from the moneys in the pool, into which it is possible to trace."

The conclusions I draw from the authorities are that, as far as this Court is concerned, in the case of a current account such as the account in issue here where trust funds sourced from various beneficiaries are mixed or pooled in the account, it is settled law that as a general proposition the rule in *Clayton's* case is applicable in determining to whom the balance on the account belongs. However, the application of the rule may be displaced in the particular circumstance of a case, for instance, if it is shown or to be inferred that it does not accord with the intention or the presumed intention of the beneficiaries of the trust funds.

Application of the legal principles to the facts
On this application, I do not propose to determine, and I am not to be taken as expressing any view as to whether, as between all of the parties who may have a claim to the balance in the current account in issue, the rule in *Clayton's* case is applicable to determine entitlement, because I am not satisfied that all relevant interests were represented on this application and, in any event, I consider that it is not necessary to do so. What I propose to consider is whether, as between the applicant, on the one hand, and all other claimants to the funds represented by the balance on the current account, on the other hand, in accordance with equitable principles the applicant should be bound by a *pari passu* distribution, if the rule in *Clayton's* case is not applicable. It is not to be inferred, however, that I am of the view that a *pari passu* distribution is the appropriate method of distribution as between all other claimants to the monies represented by the credit balance on the account: on the evidence before the court the principles

to be deduced from the decision in *Re Hallett's Estate, Knatchbull v. Hallett* (1880) 13 Ch D 696 may come into play.

Having regard to the uniqueness of the applicant's position, I do not think that, applying equitable principles, the applicant should be bound by a *pari passu* distribution. The applicant transferred the monies in issue to the current account for a specific purpose, to discharge the sums due in respect of the share purchase transaction confirmed on the 15th February, 1999, to enable that purchase to be completed. The applicant transferred the monies into the company's current account prior to the settlement day and all the company did was to receive them. However, after the transfer and receipt of the monies and before the settlement day the suspension of the company as a member of the stock exchange supervened, so that the company was not in a position to use the monies transferred and received for the purpose for which they were intended because the company was not in a position to complete the purchase transaction. It seems to me that, given this combination of circumstances, the applicant must have a better equity than the other client creditors who have a claim against the monies represented by the balance on the current account. The equities are not equal and equitable principles do not require that the applicant be subjected to a *pari passu* distribution under which he would be treated in the same way as other clients who have equitable claims against the funds.

In reaching this conclusion I am not overlooking the fact that, while the affidavit sworn by the official liquidator on the 9th July, 1999, discloses that the vast bulk of the lodgments from clients within the last few days of trading of the company relate to transactions which settled, that is to say, the client received delivery of the stocks, in the case of at least two clients who made lodgments the transactions remain unsettled or partially unsettled. However, what distinguishes those transactions, in my view, from the instant case is that they were for settlement before the company was suspended.

If it is the case that the rule in *Clayton's* case is applicable in determining entitlement to the monies represented by the balance on the current account, it is clear from the details of the account which I have summarised above that, on the application of that rule, the applicant would be entitled to repayment of the entirety of the monies transferred by him to the company's account. On the other hand, if the rule in *Clayton's* case is not applicable, in my view, the equity of the applicant is superior to the equity of any other client creditor with an equitable claim against the monies in the account, so that the applicant cannot be bound by a rateable distribution, assuming such distribution would do justice among the other client creditors *inter se*, because such a rateable distribution would not do justice as between the applicant and the other client creditors."

The Requirement of a Fiduciary Relationship

The fact that a fiduciary relationship is required in order to establish a right to trace has been a well accepted principle in this jurisdiction[9] and in England.[10] However, it would appear to have been accepted in both jurisdictions that there need not be an initial fiduciary relationship and that it will suffice if it arises as a result of a payment being made.[11] Doubts have been expressed about the continuing need to establish such a relationship,[12] and there is growing uncertainty over this issue in England. However, the fact that the payment itself can give rise to a fiduciary relationship undoubtedly allows for greater flexibility, as the decision of Carroll J in *Re Irish Shipping Ltd* illustrates.

Re Irish Shipping Ltd
[1986] ILRM 518

A bank made a duplicate payment in error to the bank account in Citibank of Irish Shipping Ltd which subsequently went into liquidation. Citibank, the former bankers of Irish Shipping, claimed to be entitled to set off debts due by the company to them against the mistaken payment. It was held by Carroll J that where monies are paid by mistake into the account of a company such monies do not form part of the assets of the company at the date of the liquidation and she concluded that the bank which had made the duplicate payment was entitled to trace the money into the account.

CARROLL J stated at pp.519–523: "These two motions were heard consecutively and both concerned the right of Citibank NA (referred to as 'Citibank') the former bankers of Irish Shipping Ltd (in liquidation) (referred to as 'Irish Shipping') to claim a right of set-off under s. 251 of the Irish Bankrupt and Insolvent Act 1857 which was imported into the law on winding-up of insolvent companies by s. 284 of the Companies Act 1963 (cf. *Freaney v Bank of Ireland* [1975] IR 376).

The liquidator did not dispute the general right of Citibank to set off the accounts which were in credit against the accounts which were in debit as of the date of winding up (14 November 1984). However, the question of whether certain accounts or particular sums of money in certain accounts were captured by this general right of set-off were brought before the court for determination. These were:

---

9   *Re Shannon Travel Ltd* High Court (Kenny J) 8 May 1972.
10 *Sinclair v. Brougham* [1914] Ch 398; *Re Diplock* [1948] Ch 465 and *Boscawen v. Bajwa* [1996] 1 WLR 328.
11 *Chase Manhattan Bank NA v. Israel British Bank (London) Ltd* [1981] Ch 105 and *Re Irish Shipping Ltd* [1986] ILRM 518.
12 *Agip (Africa) Ltd v. Jackson* [1990] Ch 265, 290 *per* Millett J.

(1) Whether moneys standing to credit in an account in the name of Irish
     Shipping Ltd Agency Division:
     (a) were held in trust by Irish Shipping;
     (b) if so, whether Citibank could set off those moneys against moneys owing
        to them;
(2) Whether the sum of £31,486.87 received by Citibank through Barclays Bank,
     Dublin, on 15 November 1984, Barclays having been notified on 13
     November by their client that they should transfer the moneys on 15
     November, are subject to set-off by Citibank;
(3) Whether the sum of US$2,853.88 being a draft received by Citibank after
     14 September 1984 which was drawn by the payer prior to the liquidation,
     is subject to set-off by Citibank; and
(4) Whether the sum of US$65,777.86 being a duplicate payment made by a
     mistake by the paying bank, Korean Exchange Bank, into an account of
     Irish Shipping in credit, is subject to set-off by Citibank.

(1) No evidence was presented to the court that the account in question
operated by Irish Shipping as an Irish Shipping Ltd Agency Division Account
was an account into which moneys received or held on trust were paid. There
was no evidence that any claims (other than certain claims which have already
been dealt with) have been made to the liquidator or to Citibank or that Irish
Shipping held any money in trust. Mr O'Sullivan for the liquidator addressed
no arguments to the court that any of the funds in the Agency Division Account
were trust moneys. That being so, I consider that any argument directed to the
question of notice to the bank is unnecessary. If none of the funds in the account
are in fact trust funds, the argument does not arise and Citibank is entitled to
set-off in relation to the Agency Division Account.

(2) The evidence in relation to the sum of £31,486.87 was that Barclays
Bank, Dublin received instructions on 13 November 1984 to pay value on 15
November 1984.

Mr James Galvin, Vice-President of Citibank, gave evidence that the
explanation of the phrase 'to pay value 15 November 1984' was that it meant
it was the date on which Citibank received the moneys and gave credit to Irish
Shipping. He was clear that Citibank would not have received the moneys on
either 13 or 14 November.

Therefore, while the debtor had made arrangements with his bank on 13
November to pay Irish Shipping on 15 November, the money was not received
in Citibank until 15 November which was after the liquidation. Citibank argues
that they are entitled to include these moneys as part of the funds available for
set-off because instructions to pay were given before the liquidation.

The case cited as supporting that proposition was *Palmer v Day & Son*
[1895] 2 QB 618. In this case a debtor instructed a firm of auctioneers to sell
his house and furniture, and a sum of money became due from him to them in
respect of their charges. Subsequently he instructed the auctioneers to remove
to their own premises certain pictures which remained unsold and to sell them
subject to his approval of the price. The debtor became bankrupt while the

pictures were unsold. The pictures were subsequently sold by the auctioneers on the instructions of the trustee in bankruptcy and they then claimed to be entitled to deduct from the proceeds of sale, moneys due to them for the earlier sale.

It was held they were entitled to do so as there was mutual credit or mutual dealing between them:

> a credit on the one hand by them to him in respect of sums due to them on the furniture sale account and in respect of their charges for the attempted sale of the house, and a credit on the other hand by the bankrupt to them in respect of the pictures and the money to be released by the sale (see p. 613).

The court held that s. 38 of the Bankruptcy Act 1883 (similar to s. 251 of the Irish Bankrupt and Insolvent Act 1857) applied as there was a debt on one side and a delivery of property with directions to turn it into money on the other.

In my opinion the case has no application. There the right of set-off was claimed by one party to a contract which remained to be performed at the date of bankruptcy, not by a third party. In this case, Citibank had no function in respect of this payment other than to receive the payment on 15 November which they did.

(3) The same considerations apply to the bank draft for US$2,853.88. Even if the draft were received before the liquidation, that did not mean that value was received on that date. The draft had to be presented by Citibank in order to receive moneys on foot thereof. Mr Gavin said that a period of time elapses between receipt and presentation and the moneys being credited to the payee's account. But no point arises on this lapse of time as Mr Gavin said the actual draft was not received until after the date of liquidation. In my opinion the same considerations apply to this sum of money as to the payment made through Barclays on 15 November. The fact that a debtor obtained a bank draft prior to the date of liquidation which arrived in Citibank after that date, has no bearing on Citibank's right to set-off, which concerns money actually in the accounts of Irish Shipping on the date of liquidation.

(4) The last question concerns the entitlement of Citibank to claim set off against the sum of US$65,777.86 which was paid by mistake as a duplicate payment.

The facts in this case are that on 12 July 1984 Korean Exchange Bank gave instructions for the payment of US$65,777.86 to the credit of Irish Shipping at Citibank for its client Sam Mi Shipping Lines which was duly received on 13 July 1984. On 13 July 1984, due to a clerical error in Korean Exchange Bank, the bank gave a similar instruction for a duplicate payment to be made. This payment was received on 16 July 1984. The account into which the money was paid remained in credit to an amount in excess of the surplus payment to the date of liquidation. The error was not discovered by Korean Exchange Bank until 5 December 1984, by which time the liquidator had been appointed.

The Korean Exchange Bank claims the return of the money on the grounds that the money is held in trust because it was paid by mistake and that the bank is entitled in equity to trace the mistaken payment (see *Chase Manhattan Bank NA v Israel-British Bank (London) Ltd* [1979] 3 All ER 1025). Mr Fitzsimons SC submitted that the rule in *Hallett's Estate, In re* (1880) 13 Ch D 698 applies. This rule is that if a person who holds money as a trustee or in a fiduciary character pays it to his account at his bankers and mixes it with his own money and afterwards draws out sums by cheques in the ordinary manner, the rule in *Clayton's Case* (1816) 1 Mer 572 does not apply (i.e. that the first money drawn out is attributable to the first money paid in) and instead that the drawer must be taken to have drawn out his own money in preference to the trust money.

Mr Fitzsimons SC conceded that if the account was overdrawn after the mistake in payment, he could not claim. But in this case while there was movement in the account, the account was always in credit to an amount in excess of the payment made in error and therefore the money can be traced.

Citibank put their claim to the money on the basis that if the moneys are trust moneys, they had no notice of the existence of the trust and therefore they are entitled to treat the moneys as belonging to Irish Shipping and to set them off against moneys owing to them at the date of liquidation. In support of this Mr Fennelly SC cited *Clarke v Ulster Bank Ltd* [1950] NI 132, *Thompson v Clydesdale Bank* [1893] AC 282, *Union Bank of Australia Ltd v Murray-Aynsley* [1898] AC 693.

In *Union Bank of Australia Ltd v Murray-Aynsley* where a company received trust moneys and paid them into a bank, the company then went into liquidation and the beneficiary sued the bank, it was held that the bank was not shown to have received the moneys as trust funds or to have received notice of their trust character, during the currency of the account, and the bank was entitled to set them off against its own claim against the company in liquidation.

In the Northern Ireland case, *Clarke v Ulster Bank Ltd* [1950] NI 132, a solicitor who had an account opened a second account for the purpose of banking clients' money but did not state this purpose to the bank at the time the second account was opened. The bank claimed that it was entitled to set-off the amount which the first account was in debit against the amount which the second account was in credit and it was held the bank was entitled to do so.

Thompson v Clydesdale Bank Limited [1893] AC 282 is a decision to the same effect. It concerned moneys received by a stockbroker which he paid into his account at the bank without authority. The bank had no notice.

The principle behind those cases is summed up in the *Clydesdale Bank* case in Lord Watson's judgment:

> When a broker or other agent entrusted with the possession and apparent ownership of money, pays it away in the ordinary course of his business, for onerous consideration, I regard it as settled law that a transaction which is fraudulent as between the agent and his employer will bind the latter, unless he

can shew that the recipient of the money did not transact in good faith with his agent (at p. 289).

Mr Fitzsimons SC relied on the case of *Chase Manhattan Bank NA v Israel British Bank (London) Ltd* [1979] 3 All ER 1025. That case was very similar to the facts of this case in that a sum of money was mistakenly paid a second time to the account of a company which subsequently went into liquidation. It was held that the bank was entitled in equity to trace the mistaken payment and that the assets in the hands of the company in liquidation at the commencement of the winding-up did not belong to the company beneficially and never formed part of its property.

Goulding J said:

> It is common ground that if (as I have decided) there is a right in English law to trace money paid by mistake, it rests on a persistent equitable proprietary interest. . . .
>
> If I am right therefore . . . the assets (if any) in the defendant's hands properly representing the plaintiff's money at the commencement of the winding-up, did not belong to the defendant beneficially and never formed part of its property subject to the statutory trust. . . .
>
> There may, of course, be special cases where the conduct or inaction of a party who has paid money by mistake similarly makes it inequitable for him to recover it to the prejudice of third parties, but nothing in the facts pleaded and proved in the present case discloses any such situation (at p. 1033).

I am satisfied that that case correctly states the law as between the liquidator and the person who made a payment by mistake. However, the question of set-off was not raised in that case and it remains to be decided if the claim for set-off alters the right of the payer to the return of the money.

In the *Chase Manhattan Bank* case, Goulding J quotes (at p. 1037) from the judgment of Vinson CJ in an American Supreme Court decision (*Healy v Commissioner of Internal Revenue* (1953) 345 US 278) which seems to me to be very relevant:

> A constructive trust is a fiction imposed as an equitable device for achieving justice. It lacks the attributes of a true trust and is not based on any intention of the parties.

If the concept of a constructive trust is an equitable device for achieving justice, it should not work an injustice. If these funds are treated as ordinary trust moneys as in the cases cited by Mr Fennelly SC, Citibank would succeed. But this is a case of money coming into Irish Shipping's bank account in error. It is not on a par with cases involving stockbrokers or solicitors or fiduciary agents. In those cases the owners of the money consciously invested the broker or agent with apparent ownership of the trust moneys so that a bank dealing with them would not necessarily know that the moneys were trust moneys. Therefore, if the agent acted so that the trust funds were not identified as such in the hands of the banker, the beneficiary had to take the consequences of employing an agent who conducted his business in such a manner.

There is nothing akin to that here. Irish Shipping did not know of the duplicate payment. They were not 'entrusted' by Korean Exchange Bank with the custody and care of its money. Since Irish Shipping did not know, it could not give notice of the error to Citibank.

Citibank's claim is based on equating the constructive trust which arose through the mistake with an express trust where a beneficiary consciously places money at the disposal of a trustee who fails to notify the bank. In my opinion the same considerations do not apply. These funds cannot be regarded as trust funds in the ordinary sense which are deliberately entrusted to an agent, but rather as funds belonging at all times to the Korean Exchange Bank which were credited by mistake to Irish Shipping. They can be compared to lost property rather than trust property and the only function which Irish Shipping could ever have had, would be to return them to their rightful owner.

That being so, the only remaining question is whether due to the conduct or inactivity of Korean Exchange Bank it would be inequitable for them to recover the moneys to the detriment of Citibank, i.e. Citibank would have to set up some kind of equitable estoppel to prevent Korean Exchange Bank claiming back what was always their own money. There is no evidence that Citibank acted to their detriment as a result of the lodgment by mistake.

In my opinion Korean Exchange Bank is entitled to trace the money. If the rule in *Hallett's* case applies, the money which was paid in error remained in the account until the account was frozen at the date of the liquidation. I am satisfied that the rule is the appropriate rule to apply even though it is based on the assumption that the trustee knows he has trust moneys co-mingled with his own moneys. In this case the account holder did not know of the lodgment made in error but equally did not utilise the moneys by reducing the balance of the account below the amount of the mistaken lodgment. In my opinion the principle is basically the same.

Therefore, Korean Exchange Bank is entitled to the return of their money."

CHAPTER 19

Equitable Doctrines

THE DOCTRINE OF CONVERSION

The doctrine of conversion is based on the maxim that equity looks on that as done which ought to be done. It operates by regarding one form of property as being another because an obligation to convert it exists. The effect of the doctrine is that in certain circumstances the nature of property is notionally changed so that realty may be treated as personalty with the legal incidents of personalty and vice versa. Traditionally, the doctrine had an important effect on the passing of property where an individual died intestate, because real estate devolved to the heir-at-law and personalty to the next of kin. However, the practical significance of the doctrine has greatly diminished since the enactment of the Administration of Estates Act 1959 and the Succession Act 1965 which abolished these principles, although it remains relevant where a testator makes separate residuary dispositions of his real and personal property.

There are a number of situations in which the doctrine will operate and the following cases provide examples.

Trusts for Sale

Where trustees are directed to sell or purchase realty and there is some person who can insist on their doing so, the property is treated as being converted from the moment when the instrument comes into force.[1] So, in the case of a will, conversion takes place from the date of the testator's death and, in the case of a deed, from the date of its execution. However, as Chatterton VC stated in *McGwire v. McGwire*[2] there must be an imperative direction to convert the property or the doctrine will not operate.

McGwire v. McGwire
[1900] 1 IR 200

By a marriage settlement lands were vested in trustees on trust that they should

---

[1] It should be noted that in England the Trusts of Land and Appointment of Trustees Act 1996 abolishes the doctrine of conversion in relation to trusts for sale which are now replaced by a 'trust of land', in relation to which trustees have a power of sale, which may be exercised.

[2] [1900] 1 IR 200.

'upon such application, or with such consent, or at such discretion' sell the lands. The lands were not sold but it was held by Chatterton VC that no immediate conversion had been intended and that the lands should pass as realty.

CHATTERTON VC stated at pp.203–204: "Nothing was ever done by the trustees to convert these lands of Rathbrack, and they still remain unsold. The question then arises, whether there is to be found in the settlement an express and imperative direction to convert them, or a trust for their conversion? It is to be observed, as I have already mentioned, that these lands had been only recently purchased by Mr. McGwire, and that there remained a part of the purchase money unpaid, and provision is made for the payment of it out of the wife's money and for the repayment of such sum in case there should be no issue of conversion of those lands into personal estate. No purpose is disclosed which would have rendered a conversion of them necessary or convenient. It could not have been, because they were real estate, as the settlement provides for the purchase of real estate out of the trust funds. These, however, are mere speculations, and the question is what does the settlement in terms direct? The trustees were not required or empowered to sell of their own motion during the lives of the husband and wife or of the survivor of them, for they were directed to permit the lands on the one hand, and the money funds on the other, to remain in their then present state of investment, *or* to sell them, but this latter they were empowered to do only on the application or with the consent in writing of the husband and wife during their joint lives or of the survivor of them during his or her life. It was only after the death of the survivor that the trustees were empowered to sell at their own discretion. It is not alleged that any such application was made or consent given in the life time of the husband and wife, or the survivor of them, and the lands have remained vested in fee in the trustees to the present day. The trusts of the settlement are framed carefully on this basis; nowhere can I find in any of them any expression of an intention to convert out and out, or to deal with them in any other mode than that which I have pointed out. The expression as to "Rathbrack or the proceeds thereof *if sold*" in itself, shows that there was no imperative trust or direction for conversion; the trusts are expressly framed to suit either state of facts, viz. the lands remaining unconverted as fee-simple estate, or as converted if on the application or with the consent of the husband and wife or the survivor, they should have been sold, the proceeds becoming in their place the subject of the trusts. The lands are throughout the deed treated as possibly subsisting in *specie,* and even in the event of the death of the wife in his lifetime the husband is empowered to charge a jointure and portions on these lands as still remaining unconverted. All these considerations appear to me to show conclusively that there was no immediate conversion effected or intended."

Contracts or Conditional Contracts for the Sale or Purchase of Land

Where there is a valid contract to sell realty, the realty is treated as part of the vendor's personality from the time the contract is concluded. Where a vendor dies before completion of the contract, his representatives must convey the realty or will be entitled to enforce specific performance against the purchaser, and the proceeds of the sale will form part of the vendor's estate as personalty. If a purchaser dies before completion, his interest passes to those entitled to his realty, but subject to the obligation to pay the balance of the purchase price. This principle has been extended to conditional contracts and the most common example of these is where an option to purchase is created. The effect of the so called rule in *Lawes v. Bennett*[3] is that the exercise of an option to purchase after a testator's death will retrospectively convert the property into personalty. However, this principle is based on the presumed intention of the testator and will not apply where a contrary intention can be shown.[4] In addition, it should be noted that the application of the principle is limited to cases where there was no specific disposition of the property made after the date of the contract which gave the option to purchase.[5]

By Order of the Court

Conversion may occur by reason of a court order directing that property should be bought or sold and such conversion takes effect from the date of the order and not from the date of the sale.

Re Beamish's Estate
(1891) 27 LR Ir 326

Tenants in common of an unencumbered estate filed a petition for the sale of lands and an absolute order for sale was made. Before any sale was effected, one of the tenants in common died intestate. After her death part of the lands were sold and part remained unsold and the question arose whether there had been a conversion to personalty. It was held by Monroe J that the order for sale operated as a conversion into personalty.

MONROE J stated at pp.326–330: "The controversy in this case arises on an objection to the final schedule of incumbrances, and the facts, giving rise to the controversy are few and simple. A Mrs. Drinan was in her life-time, entitled for her separate use to one-sixth undivided share of certain unincumbered

---

[3]   (1785) 1 Cox 167.
[4]   *Miley v. Carty* [1927] IR 541.
[5]   *Duffield v. McMaster* [1896] 1 IR 370. See also *Steele v. Steele* [1913] 1 IR 292.

freehold property, part of the lands for sale in this manner. She and the owners of the other five-sixths filed their petition for sale of the entire lands in the Landed Estates Court, and the order for sale was duly made absolute. Before any sale was effected, she died intestate on the 28th September, 1882. She left her surviving, her husband, and an only child, a daughter named Dora. The husband took out letters of administration to his deceased wife. Since the death of Mrs. Drinan part of the lands have been sold, and part still remains unsold. In the final schedule of incumbrances, at 9 c., the name of Dora Drinan has been inserted as entitled to the proceeds of the sale, being her mother's heiress-at-law. The father of Dora objects, and claims to be entitled as his wife's administrator. The question is, has there been such a conversion of the real estate, sold and unsold, into personalty, as to justify the claim of the administrator to the entire of the proceeds?

Land held under freehold tenure, and directed by its owner to be sold, is, as a rule, to be considered as personal estate in whatever manner the direction is given, whether by will, by contract, marriage articles, settlement, or otherwise: *Fletcher v. Ashburner* (1779) 1 Bro CC 497. Where a Court of competent jurisdiction directs real estate to be sold, in the course, for example, of an administration suit, the land is converted into money, although more land may have been sold than was required for the purposes of the administration: *Flanagan v. Flanagan,* reported in White and Tudor's L. C., in the notes to *Fletcher v. Ashburner*. The principle of this case was followed in *Steed v. Preece* (1874) LR 18 Eq 102. There two persons, one an infant and the other an adult, were entitled in equity to real estate as tenants in common in tail, with cross-remainders between them. A suit was instituted by trustees for administration of the trusts of the instrument under which these persons were entitled; and, it having been considered for the infant's benefit that there should be a sale, and the adult so consenting, a sale was directed and took place. The infant having died before attaining his majority, his personal representatives were declared entitled to the fund. The same principle was subsequently extended to the case where a person interested in real estate died before the sale took place. *Arnold v. Dixon* (1874) LR 19 Eq 113 was a suit for the administration of real and personal estate, in which there was a claim for the partition of the real estate. A sale was directed, and one of the parties interested therein died. Although no sale had taken place in his lifetime, it was held that the estate had been sufficiently converted by the order for sale, and the proceeds of the estate, when sold, passed to the personal representative. *Hyett v. Makin* (1884) 25 Ch D 735 and *Wallace v. Greenwood* (1880) 16 Ch D 362 are to the same effect.

Mr. M'Carthy Mahony, who appeared for the heiress-at-law, did not seek to quarrel with these authorities. He admitted that an order for sale, duly made by the Court of Chancery in an administration suit, operated as a conversion of real estate. But he contended that an order for sale in the Landed Estates Court was entirely different; that, having regard to the 64th section of the

Landed Estates Court Act, a sale in that Court was analogous to a sale made under the Partition Act of 1868, which, by its 8th section incorporates the 23rd, 24th, and 25th sections of the Settled Estates Act, 1877. It is provided by the 8th section of the Partition Act of 1865, that the above sections of the Settled Estates Act, 1877, shall extend and apply to money to be received on any sale effected under the authority of the Partition Act. The 23rd section of the Settled Estates Act, 1877, provides that all money to be received on sales effected under the authority of that Act shall be applied – 1, to the purchase or reduction of the land-tax; or, 2, to the discharge or redemption of any incumbrance affecting the hereditments in respect of which such money was paid, or affecting any other hereditaments subject to the same uses or trusts; or, 3, in the purchase of other hereditaments to be settled in the same manner as the hereditaments in respect of which this money was paid; or, 4, in the payment to any person becoming absolutely entitled.

It will be observed that sales of land made under the authority of the Partition Acts are sales of the entire lands made at the instance of persons who are interested only in certain undivided shares, and these may be carried out against the will of the persons entitled to the other shares. It is therefore quite right and reasonable that the character of the interests of one person in his estate should not be altered at the mere instances of another person who possess by statute a right, under certain circumstances, to sell the entire lands against the will of the entire co-owners. If the person entitled to the proceeds of undivided shares of realty, sold without their consent, be not *sui juris*, so as to enable him to elect whether he will take the proceeds as real or personal estate, then the proceeds must be applied or reinvested as the Act directs, and pending such application or reinvestment will be regarded as real estate. Such was the decision in *Foster v. Foster* (1875) 1 Ch D 588. There the share of real estate to which infants were entitled was sold in a partition suit under the authority of the Partition Acts. Sir George Jessel held that the infants had an equity for reconversion, and that their share of the proceeds of the sale must be treated as realty. The same principle was applied in *In re Barker* (1881) 17 Ch D 241, where the property of a lunatic was sold under the Partition Acts, pursuant to a decree of the Court of Chancery in a suit for partition or sale. The lunatic having died intestate while the proceeds of the sale were in Court, it was held that they passed to his heir-at-law.

The 61th section of the Landed Estates Court Act, on which reliance was placed by Mr. Mahony, merely provides that, when lands are sold in that Court, the proceeds, after satisfying costs, charges, and incumbrances, are to be paid to the owner where he is absolutely entitled thereto, and if not so entitled, that they shall be paid out in the purchase of land to be settled in the same trusts as that which has been sold. There are no incumbrances on this estate; and had Mrs. Drinan lived till after the sale she would have been entitled to the procceeds absolutely, and in her hands the proceeds would have been personal estate. This is not the case of land sold under the Partition Acts, or taken under the

Lands Clauses Act. We are here dealing with real estate which the absolute owner has asked the Court to sell, and the Court has complied with her petition by directing a sale. Mrs. Drinan had a right to convert her real estate into money for the purpose of distribution among herself and her co-owners. She, with them, applied to the Court to sell for her, and the Court has said let it be so and has proceeded with the sale. If the land which she has directed to be sold, was not sold at the time of her death, what equity has her heir-at-law to stay the directions which she has given that her real is to be changed into personal estate? In *Wallace v. Greenwood*, where in a suit for partition or sale under the Partition Acts, a married woman consented to the order for sale, it was held that the conversion, so far as she was concerned, was complete from the date of the order. The sanction of the Vice-Chancellor of Ireland is given to this view in the case of *Ferguson v. Benyon* (1886) 17 LR Ir 212.

I am therefore of opinion that the order for sale of this unincumbered estate made at the request of the absolute owners of all the undivided shares operated as a conversion; and that the husband of Mrs. Drinan as her administrator must be placed on the schedule of incumbrances in respect of the proceeds both of the sold and the unsold lands, and I allow his objection with costs, his costs and the costs of Dora Drinan to be paid out of the proceeds of the sale coming to the administrator."

THE DOCTRINE OF RECONVERSION

In certain circumstances, property which has notionally been converted may be reconverted or theoretically returned to its actual physical form. Reconversion may either occur by act of the party or by operation of law.

Where a party is absolutely entitled to property and expresses the desire to take this property in its original unconverted form, on the basis that 'Equity, like nature, will do nothing in vain', the doctrine of reconversion intervenes. So, where beneficiaries who are of full age and capacity and between them absolutely entitled to trust property choose to take property in its actual form, notional reconversion occurs. The decision to reconvert may be expressly stated or it may be inferred from 'evidence of acts and circumstances'.[6]

Reconversion may also be effected by operation of law where property which has been notionally converted in equity becomes reconverted without any declaration or act of the party entitled. This will occur where, e.g. property which was subject to an obligation to convert comes into the possession of some person who is absolutely entitled, without having been converted, and he dies without making any declaration of intention in relation to it.

---

[6] *Hart v. McDougal* [1912] 1 IR 62, 75.

THE DOCTRINE OF ELECTION

Introduction

The doctrine of election is based on the principle that one cannot take a benefit and reject an associated burden. Where a testator or donor purports to confer a benefit on a donee and in the same instrument purports to transfer some of this donee's property to a third party, the donee must make an election between taking in accordance with the terms of the will or deed or against it. The donee is effectively faced with a choice; he may either take under the instrument, in which case he may take the benefit of the gift to himself but must also consent to the transfer of his own property to a third party. Alternatively, he may take against the instrument, in which case he will retain his own property but will lose the benefit of the gift which the donor directed that he should have to the extent to which it is required to compensate the third party for failing to receive the donee's own property.

It is necessary to establish an intention on the part of the testator or donor to dispose of the property in question, although it is irrelevant that he did not realise that the property was not in fact his.[7] The essentials for election were set out as follows by Jenkins LJ in *Re Edwards*:[8] 'there should be an intention on the part of the testator or testatrix to dispose of certain property; secondly, that the property should not in fact be the testator's or testatrix's own property; and, thirdly, that a benefit should be given by the will to the true owner of the property.' So in order for election to be necessary, it is essential that the donor has conferred a benefit on the donee with which he can compensate the third party if he elects to take against the instrument

Re Sullivan
[1917] 1 IR 38

A testator gave his wife a legacy of £3,000 to be paid in cash or out of his own or their joint shares as she should select. The Irish Court of Appeal (O'Brien LC, Ronan and Molony LJJ) held that the widow was bound to elect between the benefits conferred by the will and any claim to the stocks and shares invested in the joint names of herself and the testator.

RONAN LJ stated at pp. 42–45: " "Evidence of the circumstances surrounding the testator at the date of the will, the state of his family, and his property, is admissible in aid of construction. But evidence to show what were the *actual testamentary intentions* of the testator (as the instructions for a will . . .) is

---

[7] *Re Sullivan* [1917] 1 IR 38, 43 and *Minchin v. Gabbett* [1896] 1 IR 1, 12.
[8] [1958] Ch 168, 175.

admissible only" for purposes not applicable in this case: Hawkins, p. 14, 2nd edition.

At the date of the will in this case, apart from the two sets of shares standing jointly in his name and that of his wife, the testator's property amounted to about £2000, consisting mainly of shares standing in his own name. At the date of his death this was reduced to in or about £1200 or £1300, mainly owing to reduction in value of these shares.

As to the shares valued at £1748 there was a presumption of law that the testator put them in the joint names with the intention that the wife should take them if she survived him. As to those valued at £4891 the presumption was that he put them in the joint names upon trust for himself. The Act 7 Edw. 7, c. 47, does not affect this presumption: sect. 52 of the Act and *Re Whitfield* [1911] 1 Ch 310. In the present case it was affirmatively decided that the deceased had transferred these shares into the joint names with the actual intention that they should be her property if she survived him.

By the judgment in the case both sets of shares were declared to be the property of the wife.

The general principle applicable to election is thus stated by Lord Hatherley in *Cooper v. Cooper* (1874) LR 7 HL 53, at p. 70): "There is an obligation on him who takes a benefit under a will or other instrument to give full effect to that instrument under which he takes a benefit; and if it be found that that instrument purports to deal with something which it was beyond the power of the donor or settlor to dispose of, but to which effect can be given by the concurrence of him who receives a benefit under the same instrument, the law will impose on him who takes the benefit the obligation of carrying the instrument into full and complete force and effect." That is, of course, if he asserts his right to take the benefit under the instrument. It is for him to elect whether he will take it or not.

In the same case, at p. 67, Lord Cairns says: "The rule does not proceed either upon an expressed intention or upon a conjecture of a presumed intention, but it proceeds on a rule of equity, founded upon the highest principles of equity, and as to which the Court does not occupy itself in finding out whether the rule was present or was not present to the mind of the party making the will."

At pp. 70, 71 Lord Hatherley says: "The law inquires, on the death of the testator, when the will comes into operation, what is his intention, as expressed in the whole will, with reference to the disposition of that which he considers to be his property; and it being found clearly and distinctly (for it must be clearly and distinctly found) that he has expressed his intention of disposing of what belongs to another – when once that is ascertained completely, there is nothing else which the law implies with regard to his intention, beyond the ordinary intent implied in every man who affects by a legal instrument to dispose of property, that he intends all that he has expressed, and, among other things, that he intends to dispose of property as to which he has so expressed an intention, though it really does not belong to him."

Lord Hatherley, of course, does not mean to exclude from consideration the matters referred to in the rule I have cited from Hawkins.

Lord Parker (then Parker J.) says in *Re Harris* [1909] 2 Ch 206, at p. 209: "To raise a case of election under a will it must be, I think, reasonably clear from the will itself; having regard only to the circumstances under which it was made, and excluding evidence of intention, that the testator intended to dispose of property which in fact was not his own. Whether or not he knew it was not his own is, it seems to me, immaterial."

In the present case the testator, neither at the date of his will nor at any time afterwards, had any shares of his own standing in the names of himself and his wife.

It follows, therefore, that when he mentions "shares standing in her name jointly with mine," he must have meant either (a) these shares, or (b) shares which might afterwards be placed in their joint names upon trust for himself.

The strongest way the case can be put for the appellant is this: – Assume that after the date of the will the testator had done this, and that at the date of his death he had shares of his own in the joint names, then it is argued these shares alone would answer the entire description – "my shares standing in the joint names," and there would be no election; that the fact that this did not happen cannot affect the construction of the will.

This is, I think, a fallacy; in construing the will, we are bound to have regard to the state of the testator's property at the *date of the will*.

Having regard to the facts I have stated, I really have no doubt, reading the will by the light of these facts, as to the state of the testator's property and the position of these shares, that there is a clear and distinct expression of intention to treat these shares as part of his property, and to dispose of them as such under his will.

No case has been cited to us which goes quite to the point. But this is really a specific, not a general, description, as in *Dummer v. Pitcher* (1833) 2 M & K 262 where the words were "all my funded property or estate."

On the other hand, in *Coates v. Stevens* (1834) 1 Y & C Ex 66 and *Grosvenor v. Durston* (1858) 25 B 97, there were words confining the bequests to the state of things at the date of the will, though the descriptions were very general. In the latter case the words used were "my present funded stock."

It seems to me that the fallacy in the argument for the appellant lies in this. It assumes that no matter how specific the description may be, if it is *possible* for the testator, after the date of the will, to acquire property which will answer the description, there can be no claim of election.

For instance, if a testator gave to his son "my house in Merrion Square," and he was then living in a house in that square, the property of his wife, and had no other house there, could it be contended that because it was *possible* that he might afterwards purchase another house in the square, the wife would not be put to her election if she claimed benefits under the will? The question really is, as put in substance by Lord Parker in *Harris's Case* [1909] 2 Ch 209, is it reasonably clear that the testator intended to dispose of property not his own, or is it fairly open to the view that he meant property which he might afterwards acquire which would answer the description? He considered the case of the gold plate (see p. 212 of Report) "perhaps a more difficult one than the other." Comparing the description of the property in that instance with that in the present case, I think he certainly would have held the description in the present case sufficient to raise a case of election.

In my opinion, the notion that this testator in this will when speaking of the "shares in the joint names," ever thought of shares to be thereafter put in the joint names, is fanciful and extravagant, and ought not to be entertained by the Court.

I form this opinion on the will itself read in connexion with the facts already referred to. If this is so, it follows that he meant these shares by the will.

If so, there can be no doubt that he intended to dispose of them by his will in precisely the same way as his own shares standing in his own name.

I agree that the Appeal ought to be dismissed."

Making an Election

The requirements which must be satisfied in order for a valid election to be made under a will were considered by Chatterton VC in *Sweetman v. Sweetman*.[9]

Sweetman v. Sweetman
(1868) IR 2 Eq 141

The Vice Chancellor was required to decide whether the testator's son had elected to take under or against the will of his father. He held that the acts set forward in evidence did not amount to an election as there was no evidence to show that the parties were aware of their rights or obligations in relation to election at the time.

CHATTERTON VC stated at pp. 152–158: "I shall now consider the rules of equity applicable to the case, and then deal with the evidence at each side.

The requisites for holding a party bound by an election as concluded are, I think, these:– first, he must have a knowledge of his rights, that is to say, he must know that the property, which the testator attempted to give to another person, was not the testator's property, and that it would, upon the testator's decease, become, independently of the testator's will, the property of the party called upon to elect. It must be known by him, as a matter of fact, that the

---

[9]   (1868) IR 2 Eq 141, 152-153.

testator had not the power to give the property which he purported to devise, and that it belongs, not by the will, but by an earlier title, to the person who is called upon to elect. Next, he must know the relative values of the properties between which he is called upon to elect; and further, he must know, as a matter of fact, and not as a presumption of law, that the rule of equity exists, that he cannot, under such circumstances, take both estates, but must make an election between the two. And, further, the Court must be satisfied that he made a deliberate choice with the intention of making it. That is perfectly ascertained law; and I need not go beyond the case of *Spread v. Morgan* (1865) 11 HLC 588 for authority, as every one of these propositions was there laid down by the House of Lords.

But when I say that these propositions must be established to the satisfaction of the Court, I do not mean to say that there must be in every case actual, direct evidence of the existence of them. From a long course of dealing, from a series of acts, the Court is at liberty, as an inference of fact, to conclude that the party called upon to elect knew his rights, knew the value of both estates, and knew the rule of equity, that he was bound to elect, and had, with that full knowledge made his choice, with the intention of making it, and of electing between the two estates. To justify the Court, however, in arriving at that conclusion, there must be a series of acts or dealings, consistent only with the knowledge which I have already mentioned, and with the deliberate intention to elect; or, at least, a series of acts or dealings that preponderates so strongly in the mind of the Court, that no person could come reasonably to any other conclusion; and the onus of proof must rest always upon the party who alleges that the knowledge existed, and that the deliberate choice was made.

I shall next weigh the evidence relied on at each side. In the first place, as to the making of a deliberate choice, I can have no doubt whatever that, if the knowledge, necessary for the purpose of having an intention to elect, could have been shown to have existed in the present case, there were such acts done by both the brothers as would warrant the Court in concluding that the election and choice had been made by William Sweetman, for he, from the time of his father's death, permitted the widow of the testator to receive, not merely the £400 a year, but to receive an additional sum out of that which was his own estate as heir-at-law of the testator, and which sum must otherwise have been provided out of the general estate of the testator, which passed under his will; and, therefore, if it was shown that he had so permitted the receipt of those moneys, with full knowledge of his rights and obligations, that permission and receipt would, in itself, amount to an evidence of an election made. Besides, there are some other dealings having a tendency in this direction, and perhaps the most clear of them is the deed of renewal in 1834, reciting that the property was vested in both brothers as tenants in common, when, independently of the will, the entire of it was vested in the eldest son as heir-at-law. There are two suppositions, upon either of which the parties may be deemed to have proceeded: one, that the property did, as a matter of fact, pass by the will. This is relied upon by the counsel for William Andrew Sweetman; and the other, which is relied upon by the counsel for John Sweetman, that this property, though it did not pass actually by the will, was, however, operated upon virtually by it, by reason of the doctrine of election. With which of these two suppositions are the facts of this case most consistent? With sincere respect for the opinion of the Master, to whose report these exceptions have been taken, I, early in this case, formed the opinion that these dealings proceeded upon the mistaken assumption that this property did actually pass by the will; and that, therefore, there was an absence of that knowledge of rights, and of the rule of the Court, that is necessary to form an election. The will itself is quite enough to mislead parties not familiar with legal matters and documents, for it, on its face, deals with the property as if it was ground rents of premises to be conveyed by the Wide Street Commissioners, and dedicates the surplus rents to this lady. The settlement of 1805 recited the contract with the Commissioners, and gave powers of distress and entry for the recovery of the jointure. But, further, in 1827 I find that every other property, that had belonged to the testator, was dealt with by the two brothers, and divided between them, and that this property was omitted altogether from that arrangement. Why was it omitted? Was it because the parties knew that a case of election arose, and that William Sweetman was bound to elect or was it because they really believed that the property passed by the will, but that it effectually dedicated the entire of the rents to the widow, and that until her death nothing could come to them? If the matter rested there I should be strongly of opinion that they believed that the property actually, in point of fact, passed by the will, a belief which might have been strengthened by the fact that the testator had become the legal owner of it between the making of his will and his death. But I find next that a conveyance was executed in 1852 by John Andrew Sweetman to the Petitioner, which contains a recital that "under and by virtue of the settlement of 1805, and under and by virtue of the will of the said William Sweetman, bearing date the 11th of September, 1818, or under some other good and sufficient title; he, the said John Andrew Sweetman, was entitled to an estate in fee-simple in one undivided moiety of the premises, expectant upon the death of the said Charlotte Maria Dalton, otherwise Sweetman, the widow of the said William Sweetman, deceased, and which said several premises were granted and conveyed by the Commissioners of Wide Streets of the City of Dublin unto the said William Sweetman, deceased, by indenture bearing date the 17th of October, 1823." That recital shows that what was passing through the mind of that side of the family then was that, under the settlement of 1805, and under the will, a property in one moiety of the fee had been acquired by John Andrew Sweetman. The same supposition would readily account for the renewal of 1834; for if the two brothers believed that the property had, in point of fact, passed by the will, they would have framed the recital in that deed just as it is.

Then come the deeds relied upon by counsel for the Petitioner as showing an election. One of those deeds was a deed of mortgage, of the 24th of November, 1854, by William Andrew Sweetman to some parties who were lending him money. The description of the lands conveyed by that mortgage is contained, not in the parcels, but in a schedule showing what he thought he was dealing with; and the words of the fifth schedule are remarkable. They run thus: "Fifthly, all that and those the undivided moiety or half part, and other the part or share, parts or shares of the said William Andrew Sweetman, whether in possession, reversion, remainder, or expectancy, or whether legal or equitable or otherwise, of and in all and every the messuages, tenements, ground, and hereditaments whatsoever, situate and being in the city of Dublin aforesaid, which the Commissioners of Wide Streets in the said city, in or about or subsequently to the year 1804, granted or assigned, or are reputed to have granted or assured, or to have agreed to grant or assure, with certain ground rents incident thereto, amounting in the whole to the annual sum of £528 19s. sterling, unto William Sweetman, &c., and which the said William Sweetman, by his will, dated on or about the 11th day of September, 1818, devised, subject as therein mentioned, or incident thereto, unto his, the testator's, two sons, namely, William Sweetman and John Andrew Sweetman, their heirs and assigns, as tenants in common, &c., and particularly subject to certain annual charges of £400 and £200, to or in favour of his then wife, and now widow," and to the trusts and provisions for securing the same.

In my opinion this language tends strongly to show that the impression on the mind of William Andrew Sweetman at that time was that the property had actually passed by the will. It certainly shows nothing to the contrary. I therefore think that on both sides there existed this mistaken belief, and this would account for the dealings with the rents of the estate. I therefore am of opinion that there is no proof of that knowledge and deliberate choice on the part of the Respondent and his father necessary to establish a concluded election.

But I was also pressed very strongly with the argument that this case was to be dealt with as one of a family arrangement, which, therefore, cannot be disturbed, it being in the nature of a family settlement. Without considering the grounds upon which an arrangement of that kind will be supported in many cases, it must be remembered that in order to make a family arrangement binding upon this Court, the Court must be satisfied that such an arrangement was actually come to. Such an arrangement may be presumed from a long course of dealings, but the course of dealings must be consistent reasonably only with the fact of such an arrangement having been come to. Here the supposition is based upon the fact that, in 1827, the two brothers executed a deed selling, the one to the other, his moiety of the property. But I think that that furnishes a very strong argument against the hypothesis that such an arrangement was intended with respect to these premises, for if it existed, why should they alone be excluded from these deeds? If it was matter of family arrangement, surely some one of these six deeds of 1827 would have contained some reference to this particular property, which really was the only one requiring anything in the nature of a family arrangement to be made.

It was said with some appearance of reason that the possession of John Andrew Sweetman and the Petitioner was adverse to the rights of William Andrew Sweetman, the Respondent, since the death of his grandfather in 1826 and Mr. Palles very ingeniously sought to bring in aid the Statute of Limitations as affording an argument in the Petitioner's favour in this case. But that is met at once by the frame of this suit, which is based solely on the doctrine of election. If such a case were to be made the parties should have brought their ejectment to recover this moiety. But this long possession affords neither a substantive case nor an argument to the Petitioner, founded on that Statute, as the possession was in fact that of Mrs. Sweetman, the widow; and it is really begging the first question, that of election, to convert this into a constructive possession by John Sweetman. If there was an election, this argument is unnecessary; if there was not, then it was not a possession by John, and the argument fails. No possession on which the respondent could rely began till 1865, upon the death of Mrs. Sweetman, during whose life the two brothers had not any reason to complain of the application of the rents; and, therefore, I do not find any element here of a long possession which I should disturb, and which would influence my mind in coming to the conclusion that an arrangement in the nature of a family settlement would be interfered with.

These are all the topics with which I have to deal; and, with great respect for any decision arrived at by the very able Equity lawyer who made this report, I am clearly of opinion that there is not any evidence in this case, upon which I can act, showing that the parties made a concluded election. I shall, therefore, allow these three exceptions, and declare that the Respondent is to make his election. I shall permit the case to stand over for a few days, to give him time to do so. I shall reserve all question as to the costs until then."

THE DOCTRINES OF SATISFACTION AND ADEMPTION

This equitable doctrine is an illustration of the maxim that 'Equity imputes an intention to fulfil an obligation' and depends on a party's presumed intention to carry out an obligation. In certain circumstances set out below, performance of an act of a different nature to that which it has been agreed should be carried out may be construed in equity as being intended to satisfy the original obligation.

Cases in which the doctrine may operate are usually grouped into the following classifications.
1. Satisfaction of debts by legacies.
2. Satisfaction of portion debts by legacies.
3. Satisfaction of legacies by legacies.
4. Satisfaction or ademption of legacies by portions or lifetime gifts.

Satisfaction of Debts by Legacies

Where a testator leaves a legacy to a creditor, equity may presume that the legacy should be treated as being in satisfaction of the debt. However, the presumption may be fairly easily rebutted and where the will contains a direction to pay the testator's debts, the doctrine will not apply. The application of the doctrine may also be excluded by the nature of the debt, so for example, it will not apply to a continuous running account where the debt would have been uncertain at the time the will was drawn up.[10] In addition, the presumption may not operate as a result of the nature of the legacy and where it is of uncertain amount, for example a residuary interest, satisfaction will not be possible.[11] It should also be noted that the presumption will not operate where the amount of the legacy is less than the debt or if the legacy is different in character to the debt.[12]

Coates v. Coates
[1898] 1 IR 258

By virtue of a deed of separation, the testator covenanted that he, his executors and administrators, would pay his wife an annuity for life in the sum of 15s a week. In his will the testator bequeathed to his wife a weekly sum of 12s and the use of a house for life. It was held by Chatterton VC that the legacy of 12s could not operate as a satisfaction of the testator's liability under the deed of separation of a greater amount, and that the bequest of the use of the house for life could not be treated as satisfaction as it was not a gift of the same nature as the debt.

CHATTERTON VC stated at pp.260–262: "The first question is whether the provision made for the plaintiff by the deed of separation of the 8th of September, 1884, terminated on the death of her husband? I am of opinion that on the true construction of the deed it did not. The deed states the occasion for its execution, namely, the separation of the husband and wife in consequence of unhappy variances existing between them, and, in consideration of the regular payment by the husband to the wife *during the term of her natural life* of the weekly sum of 15*s.*, by way of separate allowance and maintenance, the wife bound herself not to cohabit thenceforth with her husband, or to annoy or molest him, and it was agreed that the weekly allowance should commence, accrue, and be payable to her from the 30th of August, 1884. And the husband thereby for himself, his executors, administrators, and assigns covenanted with

---

[10] *Buckley v. Buckley* (1888) 19 LR Ir 544.
[11] *Re Keogh's Estate* (1889) 23 LR Ir 257.
[12] *Coates v. Coates* [1898] 1 IR 258.

the wife, her executors, administrators, and assigns that he, *his executors, administrators,* and assigns should punctually pay to the wife, her executors, administrators, and assigns *the said* weekly separate maintenance as thereby provided. The allowance is therefore expressly payable to the wife for her life, and is payable not only by the husband but by his executors and administrators. No doubt this latter clause might be construed as applying only to any arrears due at the husband's death, but it is certainly wide enough to cover payments accruing after his death. As a matter of construction, I hold that the provision was made for the wife for her life, even in case she should survive her husband.

But it was contended that this, being a deed of separation, is to be dealt with in a different way from deeds for other purposes, and must be held to be incapable of subsisting after the death of the husband. There is no authority that I am aware of for this contention, and assuming the construction of the deed to be such as I hold it, I cannot so deal with it. That a deed of separation may be good after the death of the husband I find decided by the Vice-Chancellor of England in *Clough v. Lambert* (1839) 10 Sim 174. The question is whether it is to be construed as restricted to the joint lives of the husband and wife, and this must depend on the language of the instrument. An analogy was contended for between the case of the death of the husband and the return to cohabitation; but the latter case depends entirely on considerations which have no application to the former.

The second question then arises, whether the bequests to the wife in the will of the husband are to be deemed a satisfaction of the liability of the husband's assets to the payment of the allowance secured by his covenant. The rule of this Court as to the satisfaction of a debt by a legacy is simple in its terms, but it has been so restricted by fine distinctions that it is often hard to know what cases are or are not within it. The debt or obligation here is the personal covenant of the husband and nothing more; the amount is the weekly sum of 15s. The gifts by the will are, first, a weekly sum of 12s. and the life use of a house and its furniture. The objection that a legacy cannot operate in satisfaction of a debt of greater amount, even *pro tanto*, is sought to be got over by proof that the use of the house and furniture exceeded the deficiency of 3s. a-week, But this introduces another objection, namely, that the nature of the gift must correspond with the nature of the obligation which was held in *Bartlett v. Gillard* (1827) 3 Russ 149, following earlier cases, to be conclusive against satisfaction. If, then, recourse must be had to the house and furniture to get over the prior objection, it must be admitted that the whole of the obligation is not met by a gift of the same nature of the full amount; and, as satisfaction cannot operate *pro tanto,* this latter objection would seem to be equally conclusive. It was sought also to object on the ground that the allowance given by the will was not to arise till a week after the death of the testator. But even if such a trivial matter as the delay of one week were to be deemed sufficient evidence of an intention of the testator to take the case out of the general rule, it is conclusively met by the consideration that here there was no interval in the provision for the wife, as it ran from the death of the testator, although the first payment of it was not to be made till the end of a week from the death.

I am of opinion that on the other grounds I have mentioned I am precluded by the authorities referred to in argument from holding that the provision by the will was in satisfaction of the provision by the deed of separation, and I decide that the widow is entitled to both these provisions."

Satisfaction of Portion Debts by Legacies

Where a father, or another person *in loco parentis* to a child undertakes to make a gift of a substantial nature in the form of an advancement or portion and subsequently makes provision in his will for this child, the portion debt may be deemed to be satisfied. The question of whether a portion debt may be satisfied by a legacy is one of intention to be determined from the terms of the instrument in the absence of evidence to the contrary.[13] As a general principle the property left by will must be of the same general nature as the property to which the beneficiary is entitled by virtue of the existing obligation and the presumption of satisfaction may be rebutted by the difference in certainty and value between the two benefits.[14]

Re Battersby's Estate
(1887) 19 LR Ir 359

By virtue of a marriage settlement, the deceased granted land to trustees to raise the sum of £3,000 for the children of the marriage in such shares as he should appoint and in default of appointment equally amongst his children. In his will he bequeathed his residuary estate which exceeded what his daughters would have been entitled to under the settlement in default of appointment, on trust after his wife's death to pay each of his six daughters one sixth of the interest subject to a condition relating to their marrying with consent. It was held by Monroe J that the provision of the will operated as satisfaction of the portions given to the daughters in the marriage settlement.

MONROE J stated at pp.362–365: "The question arising in this case is, whether the provisions made by settlement for the children of an intended marriage are satisfied by the bequests to those children made by the settlor's will.

By a deed of settlement, made on the 23rd August, 1807, in contemplation of a marriage between John Battersby and Frances R. Wade, the lands of

---

[13] *Re Batterby's Estate* (1887) 19 LR Ir 359.
[14] *Smyth v. Gleeson* [1911] 1 IR 113.

Lakefield, the property of John Battersby, were granted to trustees, in trust to raise the sum of £3000 for the children of the marriage, in such shares as the settlor should appoint, and, in default of appointment, equally among them. There were three sons and six daughters issue of the marriage. The power of appointment was never exercised. Two of the sons and all the six daughters were alive when John Battersby made his will, bearing date the 24th April, 1839. By this will he devised to trustees the lands of Lakefield and several other denominations, in trust to raise the sum of £500 out of Herbertstown, and subject to this and some other charges, to hold these lands for his son Thomas Edward Battersby; and on further trust to raise the sum of £2000 out of the other lands, and, subject thereto, and to some other charges, to hold these other lands in trust for his son Robert Henry Battersby. These two sums of £500 and £2000 were to form part of his residuary estate. The residue of his real and personal estate he directed to be sold and invested. Portion of his wife's jointure was to be paid out of the interest. The residue of the interest he directed to be paid to his wife, during her life, for the maintenance of his six daughters. After his wife's death, the interest of this fund was to be paid to such of his daughters as should remain unmarried; on marriage, with the consent provided by the will, each daughter was to receive her share of one-sixth of the funds, and in the event of the death of any of the daughters, the others were to be entitled by survivorship. The residue of the testator's property, as directed to be realized, together with the sum of £2500, directed to be raised out of the real estates devised to his son, amounted to £6000. The widow of the testator is dead; Robert Henry Battersby, the owner, is the only surviving son. The daughters are still alive, except one.

By deed of the 18th December, 1880, the surviving daughters of John Battersby assigned to Joseph Kilbee whatever interest they had under the deed of settlement, if any, or under the will of their father, to secure advances made to the owner. The owner now contends that the provisions made by the will operated as a satisfaction of the portions given by the settlement. The assignees of Joseph Kilbee, who is a bankrupt, contend that they are entitled to both.

The question whether a portion given by a settlement is satisfied by a legacy in a subsequent will is entirely one of intention to be gathered in the absence of other evidence, from the terms of the two instruments, subject to this consideration, that the presumption of law is against double portions. If the provision made by the later instrument is equal to or greater than that made by the earlier one, and the limitations are substantially the same, double portions will not be allowed; the parties entitled will be put to their election. If the limitations are widely different, the presumption is that the provisions were to be cumulative.

It will be observed in this case that, under the terms of the settlement, John Battersby had the power of appointing the sum of £3000 among his children as he thought proper. Up to the date of making his will he had never done so, and by its terms he purports to dispose of all that he was possessed of. The sum set apart by the will for his daughters was more than twice as large as that given by the settlement, though there are some differences as regards the limitations. Under the settlement, in default of appointment, the daughters took their shares on their father's death; under the will, they do not become entitled to anything till after the mother's death: but the mother is entitled to the interest of the fund for her life, to be applied in the maintenance of her daughters. I consider this provision substantially the same.

Again, by the settlement in default of appointment, the daughters become absolutely entitled to equal shares in the fund. By the will each is entitled to her share of the interest in the fund, so long as she continues unmarried. If she dies unmarried she has no power of disposition; her share goes to the survivors. If she marries with consent, she is absolutely entitled to her share. Is this difference in the limitations sufficient to rebut the presumption that the testator did not intend to make a double provision for his daughters; or are the provisions substantially of the same nature? If the provisions are substantially the same, small differences will not operate to rebut the presumption of law: *Thynne v. Lord Glengall* (1848) 2 HLC 155; *Weall v. Rice* (1831) 2 Russ & M 251; *Chichester v. Coventry* (1867) LR 2 HL 71. The testator, purporting to make a just and fair distribution of all his property, and knowing that he had a power of appointment, sets apart a fund greater than that to which his daughters were entitled under the settlement. He enables each daughter, so long as she continues unmarried, to get her share of the interest, and when she marries to get her share absolutely. The only difference between the provisions of the two instruments is this – that in the event of her dying unmarried, she is precluded from making a disposition of her share, which, if she did make it, would, in ninety-nine cases out of a hundred, be the same as that contained in the father's will, viz. an equal distribution among the surviving members of the family.

In my opinion, there is not enough in this case to rebut the presumption against double portions, and I will allow the owner's objection; but I give the assignees their costs."

Smyth v. Gleeson
[1911] 1 IR 113

In a voluntary deed executed during his lifetime, the deceased purported to confer benefits on his older unmarried sister. In his will he subsequently gave her the income on a named sum. It was held by Barton J that assuming the testator had placed himself *in loco parentis* to his sister, the presumption of satisfaction had been rebutted by the difference in certainty and value between the obligations in the trust deed and the gift in the will.

BARTON J stated at pp.118–120: "The first question is, whether the testator stood at the date of the will *in loco parentis* to his sister. It is said, on the one hand, that the instructions to Mr. Drummond show that, in making a settlement on his sister, Gerald Gleeson was doing what he considered his father should have done, and, therefore, that he was taking his father's place. On the other hand, it is pointed out that Evelyn was an elder sister, considerably older than the testator; that she was under her father's will provided for by a fortune of £5000 and other property; and that the deed of 1896 more resembles a generous gift by an affectionate brother than the assumption of a parent's responsibility. I do not find it necessary to say more than that it is at least doubtful whether the testator ever placed himself *in loco parentis* towards his sister.

The next question is, whether this is a case to which the doctrine of satisfaction is applicable. By the voluntary deed of 1896 the testator severed in equity this O'Donoghue mortgage security from his estate. The trustees and executors of his will, who are also trustees of the deed of 1896, have treated it on that basis, and not as part of the estate of their testator. The doctrine of satisfaction has no application to cases where the prior portion has actually been transferred or paid. In the present case the mortgage debt had been transferred in equity, and the interest was regularly paid to Evelyn Gleeson during the testator's life. On the other hand, it might be contended that the obligations of the deed of 1896 being equitable, a Court of Equity would not enforce them without regard to the doctrine of satisfaction. It is by no means clear that this is a case to which the doctrine of satisfaction is applicable.

Assuming, however, that the testator did stand *in loco parentis* towards his sister, and that there was a presumtion of satisfaction, I think that the presumption is rebutted by the difference between the provision made by the voluntary deed and by the will. I do not refer to the differences as regards the subsequent limitations. I refer to the difference in point of value and certainty of the gifts. The provision by the voluntary deed is a sum of about £6900, well secured by a first mortgage upon an estate which shows, after providing for the mortgage debt and the interest thereon, an ample margin of income and of capital value. This appears both by the valuation made at the date of the deed and by the result of the sale of the O'Donoghue estates to the tenants through the Irish Land Commission. The powers of investment are very wide, and Miss Evelyn Gleeson has under the deed a well-secured income of from £250 to £300 a year for her life. The gift in the will is the interest on a sum of £6500, which he contemplates may fall below £180 a year, and if so is reducible to £100. There was a further gift of £400 in the codicil. Can a life interest in the income of a fund so variable and reducible to a sum relatively so small, be held to have been intended to be a satisfaction for the life interest in a well-secured first-mortgage debt, the interest on which is not reducible, or variable save by the exercise of a wide power of investment?

I am not aware of any case in which a bequest was held to be a satisfaction of a previous obligation when it was so different in point of certainty and value. In spite of the similarity of the amount settled by the deed and by the will respectively, I am of opinion that there was no satisfaction."

Satisfaction of Legacies by Legacies

This process of satisfaction of a legacy by another legacy is probably better described as an instance of construing a will so as to avoid duplication of legacies which a testator is not likely to have intended. Where two or more legacies are given to the same person either in the same will or more usually in a will and a codicil, the question arises whether these should be regarded as cumulative or substitutional. Generally, if the two legacies which are given to the same person are of the same value and are given in the same instrument, equity presumes that they are substitutional and the legatee can take only one. However, where the two legacies are given in the same instrument for different amounts,[15] or if they are given by different instruments irrespective of their value,[16] it is presumed that they are cumulative.

However, it is important to stress that these are merely presumptions which may be rebutted if on an overall reading of the instruments, the testator's intentions appear to give rise to an alternative construction.[17]

Quin v. Armstrong
(1876) IR 11 Eq 161

The plaintiff, a legatee of an annuity of £60, bequeathed to him by the will of the testator sought a declaration that he was also entitled to an annuity of £40 which the latter had previously agreed by a deed executed during his lifetime should be paid to him. It was held by O'Sullivan MR, in refusing the declaration, that the will operated as a revocation of the deed and that the plaintiff was entitled only to the annuity of £60 given to him by the will.

O'SULLIVAN MR stated at pp.168–172: "The principles of law affecting this case are clear, and no controversy has been raised on either side in respect of them. It is not necessary for a man who has executed a voluntary deed with a general power of revocation to make an express revocation of it. It is a sufficient revocation within the power if he makes a disposition of the estate inconsistent and which cannot stand with the voluntary deed. A revocation may be implied from the manner in which he has given the estate and the extent to which he has given it. There is also a rule of law which has been established by the many cases which were relied on at the Bar, that where a testator by his will gives a benefit to a person, and by a codicil to his will gives a benefit to the same person, the presumption of law is that he means to give twice; and it lies on the party who disputes it, to show why that construction of them should not be adopted. That is a very sensible and a very wise rule of

---

[15] *Brennan v. Moran* (1857) 6 Ir Ch R 126, 130.
[16] *Ibid.* and *Quin v. Armstrong* (1876) IR 11 Eq 161, 168.
[17] *Bell v. Park* [1914] 1 IR 158 and *Re Armstrong* (1893) 31 LR Ir 154.

law. I doubt very much whether that rule of law, which is so clearly applicable to a will and codicil, applies precisely to the case of a voluntary deed capable of being revoked by will, and to a will subsequently executed. However that may be in the abstract, in the case before me the question seems to me one of pure construction – namely, whether the disposition made by the will is of such a character as to compel the Court to hold that by it the voluntary deed is entirely revoked, or is left standing wholly or in part.

When the testator Joseph Jeffares came to devise these lands of Tinneranny, he had at the determination of his own life, when of course the will became operative, that shadowy reversion which I have described. It is plain that he was not merely dealing with that reversion; he plainly meant that his devise should have operation at the moment of his death. The Plaintiff's counsel are compelled to concede this. The testator was therefore to some extent exercising his power of revocation. No doubt this extent is not to be carried further than the dispositions in the will enforce it. If the new dispositions can to any extent fairly stand with the old ones, the rule is to preserve the old dispositions so far as the new dispositions do not interfere with them, and merely to hold the rest revoked.

Relying upon the rule of law as to cumulative gifts by will and codicil as applicable here, it was argued with great ability on the part of the Plaintiff, and rightly argued, that the Court ought not, from the similarity of the gifts being all annuities and from their being made to the same persons and apparently for the same reasons, to come to the conclusion that the testator meant to revoke the annuities given by the deed. So far I go entirely with the Plaintiff's argument before me. But there is a rule of law which is, in my opinion, of equal weight and importance as those which I have already mentioned – and that is, that you are to construe the language of a testator's will according to its plain well understood meaning, and if he tells you that he is disposing of his whole estate you are not to take upon yourself to say that he is disposing of part only. Well, but the Plaintiff's counsel say if you give the wide interpretation to the language of the devise, you must hold that the additional annuity of £100 granted by the deed of the 16th of July, 1866, to his daughter was revoked thereby. Now I may as well say that I think it clear he did not revoke that annuity, and that, without invading that annuity, the will may well operate to revoke all those granted by the deed of the 17th of July. *Pomfret v. Perring* (1854) 18 Beav 618 goes a long way to support the view that the annuity given by the deed of the 16th of July, 1866, was not revoked. It has been argued strongly that if the will did not revoke that additional annuity which was granted by the deed of the 16th of July, 1866, it could not have revoked the annuities granted by the deed of the 17th of July, 1866. I have not been able to appreciate the force of that argument. The two matters are essentially distinct, and stand on entirely different grounds.

Indeed I think that no two matters could be more distinct than the effect in law of the will on the state of things as it existed anterior to the deed of the

17th of July, 1866, and its effect after that deed, when he had nothing to dispose of but a shadowy reversion. If the testator was not by this will disposing of the estate under his power of revocation, what was the estate in Tinneranny which he was disposing of? The Plaintiff says that he was disposing of the estate subject to the annuities given by the deed of the 17th of July, 1866. In my opinion, the testator does not say anything of the sort; he tells me that he is disposing of all his estate and interest in the town and lands of Tinneranny. Now he had an estate and a present one under the deed of the 16th of July, 1866; he had none such under the deed of the 17th of July, 1866; and in my opinion the true construction of the words of devise is that they include all that he could dispose of under the power of revocation in the deed of the 17th of July, 1866. If that construction is put on those words, the whole is at once intelligible. But if any other construction is put upon them, inextricable difficulties arise as to how much of the limitations of the deed of the 17th of July, 1866, is cut away, and how much is left unaffected by the will. The better construction, and the more reasonable and consistent one, is to give the words "estate and interest" their ordinary and full meaning. In coming to that conclusion, I do not bring in aid the limitations in the will itself, which would go a long way to sustain that meaning; for the whole estate and interest in the lands is given, and trusts are fastened on it which are commensurate with the entire estate, showing an intention to revoke the deed of the 17th of July, 1866, by giving estates inconsistent with its preservation.

The case of *Beckett v. Harden* (1815) 4 M & S 1, relied on by Mr. O'Hagan, was a very clear case. But cases on the construction of the words of one will are seldom of use when applied to the construction of another will. In my opinion, *Beckett v. Harden* is not an authority for the Plaintiff in this case. That was a case sent to the Court of law by the Court of Chancery, and was disposed of according to the then existing practice by the certificate of the Judges, and the reasons for the decision are not given. But from the arguments in the report I am satisfied in my own mind what the reasons were; they are very readily to be gathered from the statement of the case.

It was suggested that in the clause "and subject to the annuity already charged upon said town and lands, and to the several and respective annuities newly charged," the word "annuity" should be read "annuities." I must leave the word "annuity" as I find it. I cannot change it into "annuities" for the purpose of controlling a very clear devise. It seems to me there is a clause in the will which much strengthens the view I have taken, namely, the testator's declaration "but as the annual rents and profits of said town and lands of Tinneranny may not be sufficient to pay the annual charges affecting the said lands and said several annuities hereinbefore devised, now in the event of there being a deficiency in any year after paying the charges affecting said lands of Tinneranny to pay each and every of said annuities, I hereby will and direct that in each and every year there shall be any such deficiency, said deficiency shall be made up and paid to said annuitants by my daughter-in-law

Isabella Jeffares out of the rents and profits of the other estates and properties given and bequeathed to her for the term of her natural life." That clause has been relied on by both sides – by the Plaintiff as showing that no revocation was intended – by the Defendant as showing that it was not intended that the annuities should be cumulative. If the testator did not mean to revoke the deed of the 17th of July, 1866, the annuities charged on the property would amount to £510, and the rental which was to meet those annuities was only £460. If, on the other hand, the will operated as a revocation of the deed of the 17th of July, 1866, the charges amounted to £390 a year, and they stood against a rental of £460. In my opinion, it appears to be a more reasonable construction to hold that the testator contemplated a charge of £390 against a rental of £460, than a charge of £510 against £460, which was £50 short of meeting it. The only answer which Mr. O'Hagan gave to that was that the testator may have contemplated the deaths of the annuitants, or of some of them. He does not say that; £390 is close on £460, and it might happen that in some years the rental of £460 might not be sufficient to meet it – and so the testator puts it. He treats the deficiency as an event which may happen, not as a thing which must happen, which it would be if there was a charge of £510 against a rental of £460.

Various other passages of the will have been relied upon, on the part of the Plaintiff, as inconsistent with the idea of revocation. I must say that, looking at the whole will – nay more, criticising its language as you may – I see nothing to take from the effect of the first devise of all his "estate and interest" in the lands of Tinneranny, but much to sustain it. The ground of my decision is that, by the devise of all his estate and interest in the lands of Tinneranny, the whole estate which he had power, by reason of the clause of revocation in the deed of the 17th of July, 1866, to devise, passed by the will, and that the annuities thereby given, and the limitations thereby made, entirely supersede those given and made by the deed of the 17th July, 1866.

I shall therefore declare that the Plaintiff is entitled to the annuity of £60 given by the will, but that he is not entitled to the annuity of £40 given by the deed."

Satisfaction or Ademption of Legacies by Portions or Lifetime Gifts

In certain circumstances, a legacy may be written off or 'adeemed' by an advance made during the intended legatee's lifetime. This may happen where a legacy is adeemed by a subsequent portion where the parties are father and child or where the donor is *in loco parentis*. This principle is only a presumption and may be rebutted by evidence of intention to the contrary and the burden of proving the intention necessary to rebut the presumption rests on the person claiming the double portion.[18] In addition, the doctrine of ademption can operate

---

[18] *Curtin v. Evans* (1872) IR 9 Eq 553.

in a more general context, and a legacy given for a specific purpose may be adeemed by a subsequent gift made during the donee's lifetime for the same purpose.[19]

Curtin v. Evans
(1872) IR 9 Eq 553

In his will the testator bequeathed the sum of £5,000 to his step daughter which was expressed to be in addition to a present of shares which he had previously made to her. He subsequently advanced the sum of £5,000 as a marriage portion on the basis that she transferred the shares he had given her to her brother. It was held by Sullivan MR that the presumption of ademption was rebutted by evidence showing that the testator's intention was that the legacy should not be adeemed by the marriage portion.

SULLIVAN MR stated at pp.557–558: "Owing to some arguments addressed to me on behalf of those who resist this claim, I think it is right that I should state my view as to the principles of law applicable to this case. They are, I conceive, very well settled, and they rest on a long line of decisions, many of them in the House of Lords. Those principles are as follows – viz., that there is a presumption raised by the law against double portions; and accordingly, when a parent, or one standing *in loco parentis*, gives by will a sum of money to a child, and afterwards a like or greater sum is secured by a settlement on the marriage of that child, the law presumes the legacy to be adeemed. But this is only a presumption, and therefore it may be rebutted by evidence of intention to the contrary. The burden of proof of intention to countervail the presumption rests on the person claiming the double portion. Parol evidence is admissible, even though the advancement is made under a marriage settlement as here, not (as explained by Vice-Chancellor Wigram, in *Kirk v. Eddowes* (1844) 3 Hare, 509) to show with what intent the written instrument was made, for the law has actually determined that intent; but for the purpose of ascertaining whether the presumption which the law has raised be well or ill founded. If the evidence rest in parol, the Court ought to view and examine it with scrupulous care and great discrimination, and ought not, I think, to act on it so as to rebut the legal presumption, unless it is free from suspicion, and it is clear to show the real intention of the party in reference to the very advancement he is making, which *prima facie* has adeemed the legacy,

In *Lord Chichester v. Coventry* (1867) LR 2 HL 71, Lord Cranworth makes the following pointed observations; at p. 87 he says:– "When, after the date of the will, he makes a settlement for the benefit of the person provided for by

---

[19] *Griffith v. Bourke* (1887) 21 LR Ir 92.

the will, the only question is, whether he intends the latter to supersede the former provision:" and at p. 88, "It has been truly said that no positive rule has been or can be laid down as to what is sufficient to rebut the *prima facie* presumption against double portions. That is a matter which, from the nature of things, must be left, in each particular case, to the judgment of the tribunal which has to decide it."

Accordingly particular cases which have been ruled, no matter what be their number, do not afford much assistance in determining on the special circumstances of future cases that arise, further than as elucidating or confirming the general principles which I have stated. In cases of this description the circumstances are constantly varying, from the shadowy line of demarcation which runs between two plainly distinguishable colours to that making the most decided contrast. The present seems to me a very peculiar case, having features quite its own."

Subject Index